MW00785070

Understanding Traumatic Brain Injury

Understanding Traumatic Brain Injury: Current Research and Future Directions

Edited by

Harvey S. Levin, David H. K. Shum, and Raymond C. K. Chan

OXFORD
UNIVERSITY PRESS

OXFORD
UNIVERSITY PRESS

Oxford University Press is a department of the University of Oxford.
It furthers the University's objective of excellence in research, scholarship,
and education by publishing worldwide.

Oxford   New York
Auckland   Cape Town   Dar es Salaam   Hong Kong   Karachi
Kuala Lumpur   Madrid   Melbourne   Mexico City   Nairobi
New Delhi   Shanghai   Taipei   Toronto

With offices in
Argentina   Austria   Brazil   Chile   Czech Republic   France   Greece
Guatemala   Hungary   Italy   Japan   Poland   Portugal   Singapore
South Korea   Switzerland   Thailand   Turkey   Ukraine   Vietnam

Oxford is a registered trademark of Oxford University Press
in the UK and certain other countries.

Published in the United States of America by
Oxford University Press
198 Madison Avenue, New York, NY 10016

© Oxford University Press 2014

All rights reserved. No part of this publication may be reproduced, stored in a
retrieval system, or transmitted, in any form or by any means, without the prior
permission in writing of Oxford University Press, or as expressly permitted by law,
by license, or under terms agreed with the appropriate reproduction rights organization.
Inquiries concerning reproduction outside the scope of the above should be sent to the
Rights Department, Oxford University Press, at the address above.

You must not circulate this work in any other form
and you must impose this same condition on any acquirer.

Library of Congress Cataloging-in-Publication Data
Understanding traumatic brain injury : current research and future
directions / edited by Harvey S. Levin, David H.K. Shum & Raymond C.K. Chan.
p. ; cm.
Includes bibliographical references and index.
ISBN 978–0–19–973752–9 (alk. paper)
I. Levin, Harvey S., editor of compilation.   II. Shum, David, editor of
compilation.   III. Chan, Raymond C. K., editor of compilation.
[DNLM: 1. Brain Injuries. WL 354]
RC387.5
617.4′81044—dc23
2013034628

1 2 3 4 5 6 7 8 9
Printed in the United States of America
on acid-free paper

Contents

Preface

Traumatic brain injury (TBI) research has proliferated during the past decade reflecting trends in rehabilitation, technological advances in brain imaging, translational research, and the application of models from cognitive neuroscience and social cognition. Major epidemiological studies have highlighted the public health impact of TBI and the relation of age, gender, and socioeconomic variables to incidence and outcome. The recent wars in Iraq and Afghanistan along with global terrorism have challenged emergency and military medicine with acute care and rehabilitation of victims of blast-related TBI and its comorbidities. In civilian life, sports concussion has been increasingly recognized during the past decade as a less benign injury than previously thought, especially in the case of repetitive concussion associated with subconcussive blows to the head. Early brain injury, once thought to have a better prognosis than TBI in adults and adolescents, has been shown to have poor long-term outcomes, especially severe diffuse injury. The chronic effects of TBI have also become more apparent as investigators have initiated multisite studies of long-term outcomes. Harmonization of acute TBI descriptors and outcome measures through the consensus development of Common Data Elements stands to facilitate comparison of results across studies. Although the morbidity of TBI remains considerable despite advances in acute management and rehabilitation, the emergence of translational research portends breakthroughs in diagnosis and treatment of TBI.

The international representation of the editors and chapter authors of this volume also points toward the global impact of TBI and the growing collaboration across disciplines and countries facilitated by electronic communications. This edited volume is intended to be a reference for current research and clinical applications that is informative for investigators, other academicians, clinicians, graduate students, and healthcare policy planners.

Acknowledgments

Development and administration of this book project was supported by National Institute of Health Grants NS-21889 and NS05622 and the Department of Veterans Affairs grants B4596R and B6812C to Harvey S. Levin; an Australian Academy of Science, Scientific Visits to China Grant and a Queensland International Fellowship to David Shum; the Project-Oriented Hundred Talents Programme (O7CX031003) and the Knowledge Innovation Project of the Chinese Academy of Sciences (KSCX2-EW-J-8), the Griffith University Allan Sewell Visiting Fellowship to Raymond Chan; and a grant from the initiation fund of the CAS/SAFEA International Partnership Programme for Creative Research Teams (Y2CX131003) to Raymond Chan and David Shum. The authors would also like to acknowledge Allana Canty, Lauren Spriggens, Sarah Walsh, and Yuling Zhang at Griffith University for their assistance in the preparation of this book. Finally, the three editors would like to acknowledge all the contributing authors for making this book project possible.

Contributors

VICKI ANDERSON
Department of Psychology
Royal Children's Hospital
Clinical Science
Murdoch Childrens Research Institute
Psychological Science and Pediatrics
University of Melbourne
Melbourne, Australia

KAREEM W. AYOUB
Physical Medicine and Rehabilitation Alliance
Baylor College of Medicine
University of Texas-Houston Medical School
Michael E. Debakey Veterans' Affairs
Medical Center
Houston, Texas

ANDREW BATEMAN
Oliver Zangwill Centre for Neuropsychological
Rehabilitation
Cambridge, United Kingdom

ERIN D. BIGLER
Departments of Psychology and Neuroscience
Brigham Young University
Provo, Utah
Department of Psychiatry
Utah Brain Institute
University of Utah
Salt Lake City, Utah

CLIFFORD J. BUCKLEY
VHA Central Texas Health Care System
Temple, Texas

ALLANA L. CANTY
Griffith Health Institute
Griffith University
Brisbane, Australia

RAYMOND C. K. CHAN
Institute of Psychology
Chinese Academy of Sciences
Beijing, China

SANDRA B. CHAPMAN
Center for BrainHealth
University of Texas at Dallas
Dallas, Texas

LORI G. COOK
Center for BrainHealth
University of Texas at Dallas
Dallas, Texas

GERALD M. CROSS
Department of Veterans Affairs
VA Central Office
Washington, DC

RALPH G. DE PALMA
Department of Veteran Affairs
VA Central Office
Washington, DC

DOUGLAS S. DEWITT
Department of Anesthesiology
University of Texas Medical Branch
The Moody Center of Traumatic Brain &
Spinal Cord Injury Research/Mission Connect
Galveston, Texas

JAMES M. ECKLUND
Department of Surgery Uniformed Services
University of the Health Sciences
Bethesda, Maryland

JONATHAN J. EVANS
Institute of Health and Wellbeing
University of Glasgow
Glasgow, United Kingdom

JESSICA E. FISH
Institute of Psychiatry
Kings College
London, United Kingdom

JENNIFER FLEMING
University of Queensland
Brisbane, Australia

WILLIAM GUNNAR
Department of Veterans Affairs
VA Central Office
Washington DC

FERGUS GRACEY
Cambridge Centre for Paediatric
Neuropsychological Rehabilitation
Cambridge, United Kingdom

ELEANOR HAMMERSLEY
Psychological Science
La Trobe University
Melbourne, Australia

RASHED HARUN
Department of Physical Medicine and
Rehabilitation
Safar Center for Resuscitation Research
University of Pittsburgh
Pittsburgh, Pennsylvania

JIA HUANG
Institute of Psychology
Chinese Academy of Sciences
Beijing, China

JILL V. HUNTER
Department of Radiology and
Physical Medicine and Rehabilitation Alliance
Baylor College of Medicine and
University of Texas-Houston Medical School
Department of Pediatric Radiology
Texas Children's Hospital
Houston, Texas

MICHELLE KELLY
School of Psychology
University of New South Wales
Sydney, Australia

GLYNDA J. KINSELLA
Psychological Science
La Trobe University & Psychology Department
Caulfield Hospital
Melbourne, Australia

HARVEY S. LEVIN
Departments of Physical Medicine &
Rehabilitation, Neurology, Neurosurgery,
Pediatrics, and Psychiatry
Baylor College of Medicine
Michael E. Debakey Veterans Affairs
Medical Center
Houston, Texas

DAVID W. LOVEJOY
Department of Neurosurgery and Department
of Psychiatry
Hartford Hospital/Institute of Living
Hartford, Connecticut
Department of Emergency Medicine and
Traumatology
University of Connecticut School of Medicine
Farmington, Connecticut

TOM MANLY
Medical Research Council
Cognition and Brain Sciences Unit
Cambridge, United Kingdom

BRENT E. MASEL
Transitional Learning Centre
Department of Neurology
University of Texas Medical Branch
The Moody Center of Traumatic Brain and
Spinal Cord Injury Research/Mission Connect
Galveston, Texas

DAVID L. MCARTHUR
Department of Neurosurgery
David Geffen School of Medicine
University of California
Los Angeles, California

SKYE MCDONALD
School of Psychology
University of New South Wales
Sydney, Australia

HOWARD J. OAKES
Department of Neurosurgery and Department
of Psychiatry
Hartford Hospital/Institute of Living
Hartford, Connecticut
Department of Emergency Medicine &
Traumatology
University of Connecticut School of Medicine
Farmington, Connecticut

JOHN OLVER
Clinical Institute of Rehabilitation
Epworth Healthcare & Rehabilitation Medicine
Monash University
Melbourne, Australia

BEN ONG
Psychological Science
La Trobe University
Melbourne, Australia

TAMARA OWNSWORTH
Griffith University
Brisbane, Australia

BETHAN PLOWRIGHT
Psychological Science
La Trobe University
Melbourne, Australia

JENNIE PONSFORD
School of Psychology and Psychiatry
Monash University
Melbourne, Australia

SARAH A. RASKIN
Department of Psychology and Neuroscience
Program
Trinity College
Hartfort, Connecticut

JACQUELINE RUSHBY
School of Psychology
University of New South Wales
Sydney, Australia

DAVID H. K. SHUM
Griffith Health Institute
Griffith University
Brisbane, Australia

ARIELLE DE SOUSA
School of Psychology
University of New South Wales
Sydney, Australia

MICHAEL C. STEVENS
Olin Neuropsychiatry Research Center
Hartford Hospital/Institute of Living
Hartford, Connecticut
Department of Psychiatry
Yale University School of Medicine
New Haven, Connecticut

ROBYN L. TATE
Rehabilitation Studies Unit
University of Sydney
Sydney, Australia

AMY K. WAGNER
Department of Physical Medicine and
Rehabilitation
Safar Center for Resuscitation Research
University of Pittsburgh
Pittsburgh, Pennsylvania

YA WANG
Institute of Psychology
Chinese Academy of Sciences
Beijing, China

ELISABETH A. WILDE
Physical Medicine and Rehabilitation Alliance
Departments of Radiology and Neurology
Baylor College of Medicine
University of Texas-Houston Medical School
Michael E. Debakey Veterans' Affairs
Medical Center
Houston, Texas

KEITH OWEN YEATES
Department of Pediatrics
The Ohio State University
Department of Psychology
Nationwide Children's Hospital
Centre for Biobehavioural Health
The Research Institute at Nationwide
Children's Hospital
Columbus, Ohio

MARTA ZAMROZIEWICZ
Neuroscience Program
Trinity College
Hartford, Connecticut

Understanding Traumatic Brain Injury

Part I

Introduction

1

Recent Advances in Traumatic Brain Injury Research: Introduction

Harvey S. Levin, David H. K. Shum, and Raymond C. K. Chan

The most common mechanism of traumatic brain injury (TBI) in civilians is closed head trauma due to sudden acceleration and deceleration of the head and blunt impact by an external mechanical force (Povlishock & Katz, 2005). Closed head trauma often results in focal and diffuse injuries to the brain arising from rotational acceleration imparted to the brain and more localized impacts from blunt trauma. Motor vehicle crashes, falls, assaults, and injuries sustained at work or in recreational activities are the most common causes of TBI in industrialized nations (Zaloshnja, Miller, Langlois, & Selassi, 2008). Infants, adolescents, and the elderly (75+ years) are the most frequent victims of TBI (Helps, Henley, & Harrison, 2008) and the incidence of TBI and rate of hospitalization for males per 100,000 population is over one and a half times that of females (Faul, Xu, Wald, & Coronado, 2010). Furthermore, blast-related TBI has been identified as one of the most frequent injuries sustained by U.S. and Allied service members during the recent wars in Iraq and Afghanistan (Desmoulin & Dionne, 2009; Elder & Cristian, 2009).

It is estimated that TBI accounts for approximately 50% of all trauma-related deaths worldwide, and is now considered the leading cause of death and disability in young adults (Basso, Previgliano, & Servadei, 2006). Although prevalence data vary across different countries, the World Health Organization (WHO) estimates that 150–300 people per 100,000 are affected globally by TBI (Basso et al., 2006). Moreover, it is estimated that 10 million people worldwide are either hospitalized or killed due to these injuries each year (Langlois, Rutland-Brown, & Wald, 2006). In the United States, TBI, as a proportion of all injuries, constitutes a mere 1.4% of all emergency department visits but 15.1% of all hospitalizations and 30.5% of all deaths due to injury (Faul et al., 2010). It must be acknowledged that there is a high proportion of cases with such injuries who fail to make contact with medical treatment facilities. As such, the rates published here may underestimate the true incidence of TBI. A more comprehensive synopsis of the epidemiology of TBI both in the United States and globally is provided in chapter 2.

The residual cognitive and behavioral effects of TBI on individuals and their families are often significant and long lasting (Khan, Baguley, & Cameron, 2003). Although individuals with moderate to severe TBI often have difficulty reintegrating into the community and returning to study or to work due to long-term, debilitating deficits, psychosocial deficits can also persist in a subgroup of persons sustaining mild TBI. Additionally, a substantial number of individuals sustaining TBI require long-term care and financial support, which in turn places substantial burden on significant others and health and welfare services. Despite evidence that many, if not most, cases of blast-related injury also involve mechanisms common to non-blast closed head trauma, the effects of blast appear to have some distinctive pathological features and sequelae. For a more detailed account of community adjustment post-TBI, and of blast injury specifically, please consult chapters 12 and 18, respectively.

Despite the socioeconomic, physical, and psychological burdens generated by the high incidence of TBI, the media has only recently recognized brain injury as a major cause of death and disability within Western societies. Increased dissemination of information about TBI in the media has been related to the high incidence of TBI in soldiers during the recent wars in Iraq and Afghanistan and the proliferation of studies on the acute and long-term effects of concussion (i.e., another term for mild TBI) sustained by athletes while engaged in contact sports. Findings from scientific research are essential to increase our understanding of the neurobehavioral effects of TBI and to improve management and treatment of TBI-related impairments. Since the 1960s, there has been an increase in the number of journal papers published in the TBI area. A quick search using Scopus indicated that 4,548 articles with either "closed head injury" or "traumatic brain injury" in their titles, abstracts, or keywords were published between 1960 and 1999. Research findings from many of these articles have been reviewed and summarized in a number of excellent books (e.g., Levin, Benton, & Grossman, 1982; Levin, Grafman, & Eisenberg, 1987; Richardson, 2000). Since the 2000s, however, many more articles have been published in this area. A similar Scopus search indicates that 19,308 articles have been published between 2000 and August 5th, 2012. More importantly, a lot of these articles presented exciting new findings reflecting technological and methodological advances in neuroimaing, cognitive neuroscience, neuropsychology, and neuropharmacology. Thus, it is timely to publish this edited book that encompasses many aspects of TBI research and their implications for management and rehabilitation.

This book brings together leaders and experts in their respective topic areas to write state-of-the-art reviews and to identify needs and challenges for future research. The authors bring a wealth of academic and clinical expertise in brain injury and are active practitioners and researchers. Accordingly, the material in this book comes out of direct experience with TBI patients at every level.

Given that TBI is a global health issue, we believe that this book will appeal to an international audience of researchers, physicians, and allied health professionals involved in investigating and treating people with TBI. It will also be suitable for graduate students and senior undergraduate students who are writing assignments or undertaking projects in the area. This book has been developed to serve as a user-friendly bedside or office tool for clinicians and researchers to gain innovative, comprehensive, and current knowledge about the epidemiology and outcome of TBI, including specific, real-world recommendations that will enhance care for the individual with TBI. Sufficient background information is also provided to allow the reader to appreciate the information reported by the chapter authors in the larger context of TBI management and rehabilitation.

This book is divided into five parts. Part one focuses on the history, epidemiology, and the neurological and physical sequelae of TBI. Part two features a synopsis of recent research covering those neurocognitive deficits and sequelae commonly studied by investigators and observed by clinicians (viz., attention, memory, executive function, language, emotion, and social cognition). Part three addresses the rehabilitation and expected neurological and functional outcomes of TBI. Part four summarizes recent advances in the field, noting advances in pharmacological treatment and neuroimaging. Part five of this book provides helpful insights into the unique subsets of the TBI population. These include children and adolescence, older individuals, mild TBI, and blast injury. The last chapter of this book discusses future directions and challenges in the field of TBI.

Turning to each chapter, chapter 2 by McArthur details the convoluted and confronting evolution of our understanding of brain injury from the ancient world through to the medieval world, and into the technological age. The chapter then discusses and integrates the most recent epidemiological analyses of head injury in the United States, China, and New Zealand. Finally, it addresses the challenges of performing quality epidemiological research in the field.

In chapter 3, Masel and DeWitt review the neurological consequences of a TBI. They argue that TBI is the beginning of a chronic disease process rather than a one-off event or the final outcome. Therefore, it may be disease causative and accelerative and should be managed and treated as a chronic disease.

Huang, Shum, Chan, and Canty provide a systematic review of attentional problems following TBI in chapter 4. This chapter extracts and discusses the interrelationships between attention and other cognitive functions, discusses the functional significance of attentional deficits, and contrasts techniques adopted to remediate these problems post-TBI.

Chapter 5 focuses on memory impairments resulting from TBI. Canty, Shum, Levin, and Chan begin by introducing neuropsychological models of memory, graduating through the spectrum of simple theoretical accounts to discussion of the intricacies of sensory, short-term, and long-term storage systems. The chapter then provides a synopsis of the literature on the effects of moderate-to-severe TBI on short- and long-term memory, and their respective subcomponents. The chapter concludes with a review of recent research on working memory, prospective memory and contextual/autobiographical memory.

Wang, Chan, and Shum explore deficits in executive functioning after TBI in chapter 6. It starts by dissecting the theoretical architecture of executive functioning and leads on to discuss effective and ecologically valid assessment paradigms that operationalize the defined constructs. The chapter proceeds to discuss the independent and intertwined nature of cool and hot executive function (EF) impairments, their correlates (e.g., injury severity, age and time since injury), and their association with functional outcomes. The chapter briefly touches on rehabilitation of EF impairments prior to concluding with directions for future research.

In chapter 7 Chapman and Cook review research that addresses deficits in high-level language skills after TBI. The chapter summarizes empirical evidence that demonstrates the extent to which high-level language/discourse skills (e.g., cohesion, coherence, and gist reasoning) are vulnerable to the long-term impact of TBI. The chapter progresses to discuss pivotal theories related to discourse-brain linkages, synthesizes findings, and offers implications for treatment to advance brain recovery in TBI. The chapter is enriched by its concluding segment which offers promising directions for future research and clinical management based on the current state-of-the-art understanding of high-level language abilities in TBI populations.

In chapter 8 McDonald, Rushby, Kelly, and de Sousa examine disorders of emotion, specifically emotion regulation, and also social cognition (i.e., the capacity to attend to, identify, and interpret social information including the emotional expressions and social behavior of others). The chapter has a unique focus on relating such deficits to neural structures that have been identified as mediating social and emotional processes in focal lesion and neuroimaging research. The chapter approaches the conclusion through an account of new developments (e.g., moral reasoning) in the area of social cognition in TBI.

Chapter 9, a chapter by Tate, reviews pertinent research on outcome measures used in TBI, within the framework of the International Classification of Functioning, Disability and Health (ICF; WHO, 2001). The chapter highlights gaps in measurement, particularly in the ICF components of participation and environmental factors. In turn, the author proposes a framework for conceptualizing outcome measurement after TBI and delivers an in-depth appraisal of a selection of established and newly developed instruments addressing these factors. The author concludes with a brief discussion of future directions for outcome measurement post-TBI.

Expanding upon the preceding two chapters, Ponsford discusses the functional consequences of TBI in the domains of impairment, activity limitations and restrictions on participation in community life, and "psychosocial adjustment" in chapter 10. Factors associated with or predictive of these outcomes are also explored. The author encourages a comprehensive understanding of community integration, including home integration (operation of the home), social integration (participation in activities outside the home and interpersonal relationships), and productive activities, including employment, study or voluntary activities. The chapter systematically navigates a broad range of factors that influence outcome post-TBI (e.g., PTA, intelligence, genetic factors, pre-injury coping style). In parallel, the authors offer much-needed insight into the vast array of difficulties faced by individuals with TBI and their families as a basis for allocation of resources, and planning of services to meet their needs.

The topic of chapter 11 is cognitive rehabilitation. In it, Manly, Evans, Fish, Gracey, & Bateman isolate the main cognitive difficulties highlighted by patients with TBI: memory, attention, and executive function. The authors also consider the importance of remediation aimed at mood management in contributing to cognitive outcome. The final section of the chapter discusses goal setting as a powerful tool that can be applied across many domains of rehabilitation and outlines the unique and innovative work of the Oliver Zangwill Center, a specialist rehabilitation unit for adults with acquired brain injury. The authors emphasize that cognitive remediation is not simply about improvement in cognitive capacity, or treating deficits in isolation, but rather a integrative range of techniques that can help clients and families to adapt to, compensate for, and reduce the functional impact of their multifaceted range of impairments.

In chapter 12 Ownsworth and Fleming review the key findings and methodological issues in community adjustment and re-engagement processes, particularly the significance of awareness of deficits and emotional reactions, resuming activities and social roles, and the impact of environmental factors (including the type of post-acute rehabilitation) during early community reintegration. The authors examine the period of community adjustment and re-engagement which occurs in the first year after discharge from hospitalization for individuals with TBI, arguing that it is this phase of the rehabilitation continuum that is typically associated with rapid functional gains and the return of independence in the home and community, as well as being a time in which individuals often become more aware of their post-injury impairments through feedback, task difficulty, and failure. The final segment of the chapter identifies a number of unanswered questions and the need for empirical evidence to guide the development of post-discharge services for people with TBI.

Complementing the earlier discussions, chapter 13 draws together research concerning pharmacological approaches to treating cognitive sequalae post-TBI. Harun and Wagner introduce readers via unfolding the neurobiological basis of cognitive changes often observed following TBI: problems with attention, arousal, memory, and executive control. The chapter graduates into a critique of the pharmacological strategies commonly used to treat cognitive dysfunction (e.g., cholinergic dysfunction) and behavioral sequelae (fatigue, sleep disturbance) resulting from TBI. The chapter concludes with a brief review of the literature on psychopharmacological approaches to treating post-traumatic depression and anxiety.

In chapter 14, Wilde, Ayoub, Bigler, Hunter, and Levin present the principles of structural imaging techniques used in TBI research, including volumetric magnetic resonance imaging (MRI) and diffusion tensor imaging (DTI). The authors present studies and images of patients to illustrate the capabilities and limitations of well established and evolving imaging techniques. The chapter also includes sections on functional magnetic resonance imaging (fMRI), including resting state and task-related fMRI. The functional imaging section includes caveats about applying this technique to studies of children and adults with TBI.

The goals of chapter 15 are to provide an overview of the current state of knowledge regarding pediatric TBI, to critique the existing research, and to suggest potentially fruitful directions for future investigation. Anderson and Yeates progress through epidemiology, pathophysiology, neurochemical and neurometabolic mechanisms, neurobehavioral consequences (e.g., motor skills and later academic achievements), outcome predictors, and interventions. As such, the natural history of pediatric TBI is studied extensively, presenting readers with a working understanding of the acute and long-term effects of injury for children and adolescents. The authors' perspective is unique in that the literature is tailored to demonstrate the heightened vulnerability of the developing brain, relative to adult TBI, due to the potential to disrupt critical stages of neural and cognitive maturation.

In chapter 16 Kinsella, Olver, Ong, Hammersley, and Plowwright provide a preliminary step to addressing the paucity of research concerning TBI outcome in older adults. The chapter entertains discussion of the characteristics and predictors of outcome following TBI in older adults. In parallel, the authors bring a unique perspective in that they explore the relationship between TBI and dementia. An underlying theme of the chapter is the emphasis on treating and conceptualizing TBI in the elderly as distinct from those in a younger population.

Raskin, Lovejoy, Stevens, Zamroziewicz, and Oakes summarize in chapter 17 current findings in the diagnosis of mild traumatic brain injury, including recent evidence from DTI. Variables that influence recovery are discussed, including both pre-existing and secondary emotional and psychiatric factors. Management of both cognitive and emotional difficulties is also reviewed.

Chapter 18 introduces readers to the challenging and heterogeneous nature of blast-related TBI. De Palma, Eckland, and Gunnar offer a detailed account of the pathophysiology of closed blast-related brain injury (cBTBI), its associated comorbidities, and challenges in assessing neurobehavioral outcomes as these evolve over time. The authors conclude with an insightful exploration of the relationship between PTSD and mild traumatic brain injury (mTBI), and the difficulties in distinguishing these disabilities.

This book concludes with chapter 19 by the three of us, which provides a final synopsis of the future of TBI research. This includes an account of the assessment techniques that have the potential to lead to a reduction in TBI-related morbidity and improved outcomes. Subsequently, the chapter zooms in on advances in cognitive rehabilitation, particularly the innovative use of electronic technologies including assistive devices and virtual reality. The chapter highlights important questions for consideration and explores the various challenges hindering potential developments in TBI research and practice.

In closing, conscious survivors living with residual effects of TBI can range from those who are severely disabled from profound injury to the "walking wounded" with potentially life altering sequelae after single or repeated concussions. All of these individuals deserve and will benefit from expert care and services, especially if these interventions occur in a timely and consistent manner. With this book, we hope to assist in raising the understanding of impairments and disability post-TBI and facilitate the return to productivity and health by anyone who has suffered a TBI.

References

Basso, A., Previgliano, I., & Servadei, F. (2006). Traumatic brain injuries. In J. A. Aarli, T. Dua, A. Janca & A. Muscetta (Eds.), *Neurological Disorders: Public Health Challenges*. Geneva: World Health Organization.

Desmoulin, G. T., & Dionne, J. P. (2009). Blast-Induced Neurotrauma: Surrogate Use, Loading Mechanisms, and Cellular Responses. *Journal of Trauma-Injury Infection and Critical Care, 67*(5), 1113–1122.

Elder, G. A., & Cristian, A. (2009). Blast-Related Mild Traumatic Brain Injury: Mechanisms of Injury and Impact on Clinical Care. *Mount Sinai Journal of Medicine, 76*(2), 111–118.

Faul, M., Xu, L., Wald, M. M., & Coronado, V. G. (2010). *Traumatic Brain Injury in the United States: Emergency Department Visits, Hospitalizations and Deaths 2002–2006*. Atlanta: Centers for Disease Control and Prevention, National Center for Injury Prevention and Control.

Helps, Y., Henley, G., & Harrison, J. (2008). *Hospital separations due to traumatic brain injury, Australia 2004–2005*. Adelaide: Australian Institute of Health and Welfare.

Khan, F., Baguley, I. J., & Cameron, I. D. (2003). Rehabilitation after traumatic brain injury. *Medical Journal of Australia, 178*, 290–295.

Langlois, J. A., Rutland-Brown, W., & Wald, M. M. (2006). The epidemiology and impact of traumatic brain injury: A brief overview. *Journal of Head Trauma Rehabilitation, 21*(5), 375–378.

Levin, H. S., Benton, A. L., & Grossman, R. G. (1982). *Neurobehavioral consequences of closed head injury*. New York: Oxford University Press.

Levin, H. S., Grafman, J., & Eisenberg, H. M. (1987). *Neurobehavioural recovery from head injury*. New York: Oxford University Press.

Povlishock, J. T., & Katz, D. I. (2005). Update of neuropathology and neurological recovery after traumatic brain injury. *Journal of Head Trauma Rehabilitation, 20*(1), 76–94.

Richardson, J. T. E. (2000). *Clinical and neuropsychological aspects of closed head injury* (2nd ed.). Hove, UK: Psychology Press.

Zaloshnja, E., Miller, T., Langlois, J. A., & Selassi, A. W. (2008). Prevalence of long-term disability from traumatic brain injury in the civilian population of the United States. *Journal of Head Trauma Rehabilitation, 23*(6), 394–400.

World Health Organization. (2001). *International classification of functioning, disability and health*. Geneva: World Health Organization.

2

Traumatic Brain Injury: Some History and Some Epidemiology

David L. McArthur

Introduction

The history of traumatic injury to the brain can be considered as a complex interweaving of individual tales about patients, pioneering physicians and their experiences, about the reasons people sustained injuries, and about the methods of protecting against injuries to the head. While a historical synthesis of these cross-linked components is by no means linear, and while this chapter makes no claim to have arrived satisfactorily at such a synthesis, their entwining contributes to an exceedingly diverse set of stories.[1]

Araminta Ross (1822(1820?)–1913) spent her first twenty-five years as a slave on the Eastern shore of Maryland. At age 13 (also reported as age 12 and age 15 by various sources), she was shielding a fellow slave from the wrath of an overseer when he hurled a two pound (900 gm) iron scale weight. The object, likely about 3" (7.6 cm) in diameter, caught her across the forehead, knocking her immediately unconscious and causing a depressed skull fracture. The injury was recognized as quite serious, though no record exists of any acute treatment. While numerous medical advances for treatment of brain injury had been made by this time, her care most likely would have been limited by

both her status and her rural location to two mutually competing simplistic bits of folk wisdom: administer something alcoholic by mouth for sedation and keep the patient from appearing to fall asleep.

She was returned to her owner physically disabled. Put up for sale, not surprisingly buyers were thoroughly disinterested, and she is quoted later as saying "They said they wouldn't give six-pence for me" (Bradford, 1869, p. 13). While she eventually recovered, the event resulted in a permanent indentation in her forehead along with life-long headaches, narcolepsy, recurring epileptic seizures that would render her unconsciousness without warning, plus visual and auditory hallucinations. In adulthood, at work as an abolitionist leader and social reformer and by now having taken the name Harriet Tubman, she was often reported to be asleep by the side of the road, then awakening with clear instructions from her inner voices as to how next to proceed.

Contemporaneous documentation survives, in a fiery abolitionist tract provocatively titled "Woman-whipping, ethically and esthetically considered," that at least one Southern newspaper had published a statement supporting slavery based on the thickness of the slave's skulls, sufficient to "....bear without injury the blows inflicted in sudden rage by their masters....with whatever weapon came to hand!" (Hopkins, 1869, p. 129).

In a different time and place a member of a different race of humans, homo neanderthalensis, also incurred a head injury from violence. Paleo-forensic evidence from France shows that an adult Neanderthal was interred with a

---

[1] For more complete appraisals of the history of head injury and neurosurgery, kindly see book-length treatments by Walker (1951); Horrax (1952); Sachs (1952); Gurdjian (1973a, 1973b); and chapters by Dagi, Flamm, Goodrich and others in Greenblatt et al. (1997).

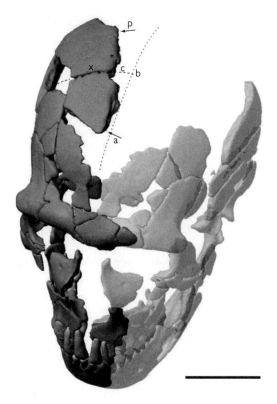

Figure 2-1. Computerized reconstruction of a Neanderthal skull with serious cranial injury, 36,000 BCE, viewed from the direction in which the blow was likely struck. Scale bar = 5 cm. Zollikofer et al. (2002), Figure 1. Reproduced with permission.

substantial cranial fracture (Figure 2-1). It was almost certainly the result of a forceful blow by a blade-shaped instrument wielded by someone in close proximity, perhaps in combat, perhaps in domestic violence, likely intent on causing harm. It is unknown whether this assailant was another Neanderthal, a homo sapiens, or a member of a recently discovered branch of the human family, a Denisova hominin, who may have lived in parallel with both Neanderthals and modern humans. While the victim's fractured skull did not result in immediate death, with high probability blood flowed, consciousness was altered, and intracranial contents were disrupted. The cranial bone provides evidence, however, that healing proceeded through resorption and deposition, a phenomenon occurring within two to three weeks after injury. While infection would have also been a significant risk, this individual did not show such signs and lived at least

some months after the event, circa 36,000 BCE. (Zollikofer, Ponce de Leon, Vandermeersch, & Leveque, 2002).

TBI in the Ancient World

As would be true for the vast proportion of those many centuries between the unnamed Neanderthal's demise and the iron scale weight striking young Harriet Tubman, human life, especially in the out-of-doors, was fraught with opportunity for severe injury. People grew up in a world that rarely offered even the most minimal of head protection or the simplest of barriers in place to guard against falls, for example. Anthropological study of remains in a rural British cemetery dating from the 10th through 12th centuries has shown that long-bone fractures occurred in one out of every five individuals, four times the rate of those dwelling in urban sites (Judd, 1999). Many such injuries, from whatever cause, would have effectively spelled an unpleasant end to independent living as they would have rendered the individual partially or entirely dependent on the kindness of kin. If a blow or a fall resulted in a brain injury, survival was chancy at best. With the literal horizon of life experience for many individuals just a short radius around the place they were born, exposure to opportunity for injury of any kind and head injury in particular would have been notably different from our own, principally in terms of contact with animals, transportation, industrial activity, and war.

Until the advent of railroads, the bulk of humanity had rarely exceeded the speed at which they themselves could run. Galloping freely on a horse would have been the joy, and falling off a galloping horse the pain, of only the upper echelons of civil and military society. Most domesticated horses until modern times were small sturdy dray animals whose capacity for a controlled gallop was nil. On the other hand, direct contact with animals in other ways would have occupied a much larger fraction of the population than in the present era and would have taken place from early childhood through old age. Even life in the town or village would have led most residents to some degree of frequent interaction with horses, bulls, and cows, and to a lesser degree wild animals, and some fraction of these encounters would have exposed the individual to flying hooves (Towner & Towner, 2008). A modern study of injuries involving large animals in rural settings found that falls, tramplings, and kicks are frequent in encounters with all of these animals. Head injuries have been identified most commonly in horse-related encounters, whereas bull and cow encounters usually result in torso injuries, and injuries to multiple body regions occurred in a third of the patients studied (Norwood et al., 2000). One analysis found that 280 of the Prussian army's finest horse cavalrymen died from horse kicks between 1875 and 1894 (Preece, Ross, & Kirby, 1988). The amount of force in a single kick by a horse can be as much as 60 joules or more (Abu-Zidan & Rao, 2003) (one joule is the energy released when a small apple falls one meter to the ground). Sixty joules represents a striking force sufficient to pierce medieval armor.

Until the industrial age, however, aside from injuries from animals only two other injury exposures of the same physical magnitude would have been present: falls and war. Falls would have been an underlying constant in the lives of those employed in construction, for example. Yet as the vast majority of buildings were only one story tall, many work-related falls would not have necessarily been grievous. A notable exception, however, would have been during construction of government or religious edifices: many ancient monuments and temples exceeded 65 feet (20 m) in height and medieval cathedrals frequently included open interiors of up to five stories tall. Nearly all of the workforce on those structures would have had no opportunities across their entire lives to have worked at such heights in any other circumstances, so it is probable that at least a few tumbled to their deaths from precarious, minimally protected work positions. Carved into the choir stalls and ceilings of many cathedrals are small pagan symbols (Ragland, 1939) perhaps placed by superstitious workers seeking maximal insurance against unforeseen troubles.

Even without employment in construction and in addition to regular exposure to wild and domesticated animals, members of pre-modern communities were at constant risk for injury throughout their lives from hostile enemies. Warfare was a major organizing force in the shaping of societies. With warfare came recognition that warriors needed to be properly equipped to avoid being victims of head injuries, which long beforehand were understood to be the most debilitating injuries that could be inflicted in hand-to-hand combat. Some of the earliest pictorial records in which humans are included show that substantial investment had been made in protective armor, especially for the head. A limestone stele from the land of Sumer in Mesopotamia, dating from about 2450 BCE, contains an image showing a collective force of soldiers, each identically helmeted (though whether in metal or perhaps turban fabric cannot be firmly determined) (Figure 2-2). It is quite improbable that an enterprising smithy, for no special reason, would have invented a wearable covering with a compound (rather than simply conical) shape to fit the head and feasible to make in multiple copies, and then would have convinced both whoever commanded the force and whoever held the purse strings that this item should be acquired for appearance sake alone. Much more probable is a scenario where it dawned

Figure 2-2. Helmeted soldiers, 2,450 BCE, "Stele of the Vultures," Sumerian, found at Ngirsu (modern Telloh), Iraq in 1881, now at Louvre, Dpt. des Antiquites Orientales, Paris, France. Photographer: Eric Gaba, Brasília, Brazil, reproduced under the terms of the GNU Free Documentation License.

on societal leaders, under many different conditions, to invest in technological advances for defending and preserving their military cadres' well-being, since, after all, they were a nontrivial expense to have organized and trained and a continuing expense to maintain as a cohesive military force. Metal smiths would have been pressed to improve on items dating back to the Neolithic era (Sawyer, 2011) assembled from cloth, hide, or rattan—materials of limited protection in actual battle.

Even at the most basic level, military reliance on technology was a scenario ripe for escalation, as the leaders of the opposing forces by necessity would have exerted some effort across time to bolster their offensive weaponry with sharper, heavier implements capable of inflicting damage right through the opponent's defensive wear. Then, in turn, those same metal smiths and their descendants would have been urged to improve on the quality of their products, upgrading the strength of the metal itself, the joinery holding the component parts together, and the wearability of each item. Indeed, it was not long before those soldiers who consciously elected to forgo protective armaments altogether when engaging in battle bare-headed came to be deemed by their opponents to be so remarkable as to earn their own description: "berserk" (Speidel, 2002). Either way, blood would be spilled.

Enough experience with injuries to the brain had been accumulated long before the first historical records for some unknown person to have invented the trepan, a non-intuitive device for the relief of signs and symptoms of head injury among that fraction of patients who are not killed outright by the initial trauma. It was in wide use even in the Stone Age (Piek, Lidke, Terberger, von Smekal, & Gaab, 1999), and may go back as many as 350,000 years. By the time of Hippocrates, use of the trepan differed depending on whether the case involved contusion, fissure fracture, skull indentation, or depressed fracture. Amazingly, the trepan appears to have been invented independently, possibly several times, in many parts of the world. A trepanned skull from Peru obtained in the 19th century by Paul Broca gave "....the most notable proof of surgical knowledge among the natives....as trepanation is one of the most difficult of surgical procedures...." (Horsley, 1887).

Around the time of the epic poems *Odyssey* and *Iliad*, first composed in roughly the 7th and 8th centuries BCE and codified several centuries later by Homer, the concepts of brain and brain injury had taken root. The word for brain occurs on seven occasions in the *Iliad* and three in the *Odyssey*, each time in the context of traumatic injury from a weapon or blow struck in combat. There were numerous additional descriptions of fatal head injuries without mention of the brain. Walshe (1997) credits the poet with "....keen powers of observation which describes the distinct ways in which the nervous system responds to injury" (p. 81).

The first written evidence of medical attention to brain injuries is found in Egyptian papyri dated 5,000 years from the present. The Edwin Smith Surgical Papyrus (3000–2500 BCE) provides descriptions of 13 separate cases of skull fractures with neurological features, plus 14 additional cases with soft tissue injuries only (Breasted, 1930). Each of these cases is described in detail along with specific treatment plans. Treatment frequently involved application of a piece of meat on the first day followed, if the patient survived, by a linen cloth soaked in honey or fat. Skull fracture patients would be kept sitting, which, by good fortune, would have appropriately reduced intracranial pressure and intracranial bleeding. On a wall of the Temple of Luxor, a wall painting, possibly the earliest of its kind, shows a neurosurgical procedure in progress on a seated patient in about 1600 BCE (Figure 2-3). However, papyri that have survived to the present day do not appear to contain much additional detail on the topic; the narrative record of medical progress may have languished through lengthy periods characterized by strongly religious concentrations of power and influence with little truck with interference from physicians.

One step forward in understanding injuries to the head was a major treatise on the subject by Hippocrates, a priest-physician who likely traveled widely performing cures in the 5th century BCE and who may have lived to over 100 years of age in a time when average lifespan was a mere three decades. Just who this person was continues to be subject to debate, and attribution of all his writings to a single man is probably not correct. Instead, they were likely composed over a

Figure 2-3. Neurosurgical procedure, 1,600 BCE, depicted in a wall painting at Luxor Temple, Old Thebes. Reproduced by kind permission of Dr. Abdel Wahab M. Ibrahem, Mansoura University School of Medicine, Mansoura, Egypt.

period of several hundred years, then collected and attributed to Hippocrates as part of efforts made by the scholars of the Alexandrian library to house all of the world's written information in a single location. That entire collection may have been accidently destroyed.[2] But copies and translations of varying degrees of fidelity to the originals had already been made and carried outward to other scholarly libraries, where more copies and translations, each introducing yet more inaccuracies, were executed and in turn carried even further afield. How faithfully the extant materials reflect the lost originals cannot be determined.

Medical knowledge at the time of Hippocrates had been characteristically handed down generation by generation among members of the guild of Asclepiads, followers of the god of medicine, Asclepius. Even as the guild's popular activities focused principally on ritual purifications and offerings at a series of special-purpose temples, the medical writings of the time were beginning to move toward objective descriptions of illness. With respect to head injuries, what survives as Hippocrates' essay titled "Of Injuries to

the Head" is a 6,000-word treatise that begins by describing the bones of the skull, selected areas of weakness, how injuries to the skull from sharp weapons differ depending on location and depth, and how injuries may occur in a different part of the head from the wound itself. Trepanning is described in detail and thought useful when the injury involves depressed fracture and contusion. Incisions of the patient's temporal bone may lead to contralateral convulsions but are allowable in other parts of the head. The document recognizes that a wound from a powerful blow, from a fall from a high place upon a hard object, or from a directly perpendicular strike to the head are more likely to be of greater severity. Instructions are given regarding the curing of wounds: bandages, poultices, plasters, and applications of liquids are to be avoided except for the forehead. Children's skull bones are recognized as different from those of adults, and so, too, their vulnerability to injury by weapons and the special care needed in trepanning of such cases. The document also addresses post-injury fever and convulsions and the resulting urgency in applying treatment (Adams, 1939; Dimopoulos, Machinis, Fountas, & Robinson, 2005; Dimopoulos, Robinson, & Fountas, 2008). Hippocrates included methodical examination and diagnosis of injuries in all his medical works, an approach to medical practice that would guide practice over the next fifteen centuries. Yet there were important controversies during that time. Celsus, only two centuries following Hippocrates, differed significantly in matters like diagnosis and treatment of extradural hematomas in the absence of skull fracture. He taught that the most severe brain injury was a brain stem injury. At least one case of cranial surgery with possible use of an herbal anesthetic is noted in the Talmud, specifically in the Gemara, which expands on the nature of Oral Law and whose origins date to as early as 300 BCE (Tubbs et al., 2008; Weinberg, 2006). Three separate deaths due to brain injury feature in the Bible: Sisera, Abilmelech, and Goliath (Feinsod, 1997).

TBI in the Medieval World

Through the long decline in Western civilization around the fall of the Roman Empire, Arabic medical specialists continued to produce

---

[2] Destruction may have occurred in 48 BCE in a firestorm ignited during war between Caesar and Ptolemy XIII. Alternatively, the originals may have survived at least another three centuries until their destruction during a suppression by the Romans of a revolt in Palmyra.

important and influential books. Rhazes (852–932) was the first to use the term *concussion*, and perhaps the first to recognize that concussion could occur without skull injury. He also noted that brain compression was more important than the depressed fracture that might be its cause, and counseled that operations not be delayed (Amr & Tbakhi, 2007; Tubbs, Shoja, Lukas, & Oakes, 2007). One of the many medical texts by Albucasis (936–1013) concerned skull fractures and their prognostic features (Spink & Lewis, 1973). Abu 'Ali al-Husayn ibn 'Abd Allah ibn Sina (980–1037), a Persian philosopher and physician known in the West as Avicenna, managed to combine materials from Graeco-Roman, Persian and Indian antecedents, and his prolific works bore heavily on the advances in medical thinking about head injury that followed (Sarrafzadeh & Sarafian, 2001).

The question of how such disparate early sources on brain injuries and their treatment came to have a wide intellectual and practical impact on later practice is worth considering. Translations were laborious and rarely completely accurate. However, medical professionals and the books themselves traveled extensively during the Middle Ages, regularly going from one country to another in exchanges of knowledge at the best universities as part of secular pilgrimages across cultures and languages. A fair amount of credit must be given as well both to involuntary displacements during times of war and to the penchant among kings across the ages for taking medical texts for their personal libraries as spoils of war (Régnier, 2007).

Four medieval physicians will serve here to characterize their era: Frugard, Lanfranco, Berengario da Carpi, and Leonard of Bertapaglia. Roger Frugard of Parma, who may have lived until the end of the 12th century, represented a break in a long-standing Western tradition at that time of simply honoring the old ways of doing medicine to the exclusion of all other information, and his work on surgery, the *Chirurgia*, became the standard text of the era across multiple translations. The work in question was not actually written by Roger but by a group of his pupils in Salerno, the center of medieval medical education. Those like Roger who were able to read Arabic and the ancients drew from a wide spectrum of available knowledge as they

sought a rebirth of the art and science of surgery (Frugardo, trans. 2002). Seventeen chapters in Book I of Roger's *Chirurgia* are devoted to wounds of the head and face, with attention to diagnostically relevant signs and symptoms, methods of surgical intervention, a variety of ointments and dressings, and instructions for dealing with complicated wounds such as those caused by barbed arrows.

Guido Lanfranco (d. ca 1310) contributed to further understanding of concussion. When symptoms following a head injury rapidly disappeared, he proclaimed, this was because the brain had simply been shaken. He urged that trepanation should only be done when dural irritation was caused by depressed bone fragments. He also claimed that if the patient showed both fever and convulsions prognosis was poor, but, if only one without the other, then survival was possible. He reported that loss of brain substance was compatible with survival though this would leave patients dull-witted (Lanfranco, trans. 2001).

In 1518 Giacomo Berengario da Carpi (ca 1462–1527) published one of the first books devoted exclusively to head injuries: *Tractates de fracture calve side crane*—"Treatise about fractures of the skull or cranium" (Berengario da Carpi, trans. 1990). In it he set out specific surgical techniques and presented at least one case of careful surgical cure:

I saw in my practice at Florence a boy.... who had been kicked by a mule. His cranium was fractured over a large area of bone and depressed inward about the width of a knife blade and separated throughout..... When we saw the depressed bone we decided to lift it up completely with the appropriate instruments. But in the process we saw a notable vein had been ruptured from which a considerable amount of blood was flowing and we recognized the great danger involved. We released the bone into its place again because it was holding back the blood, thinking we could remove it when the time was right. As we did so we saw the bone was in a healthy condition, nor were there any bad symptoms. [Later] I proceeded alone with the cure of the patient, and I saw the bone was consolidated from the sides by means of a callus. I released the bone to its position and the patient was perfectly cured (p. 37).

But in a time when style was important, his Latin was poor, so he may not have been as widely read as some of his contemporaries

(Prioreschi, 2007). His claim of success at this early date is notable, however, as brain injuries had been believed for generations to be nearly always fatal. One historian notes that in a review (not otherwise identified) conducted sometime in the late 17th century of the entire extant medical literature to that date, only about 100 individuals who had survived a brain injury had been reported in print (Rose, 1997).

Leonard of Bertapaglia (1380–1463), who lived in Italy at the beginning of the 16th century, was one of many medieval physicians interested in head injuries. He made note of thirty different local treatments for skull fracture. Following in large measure the recommendations of Avicenna, he created such curatives as a mixture of whipped egg white, powdered Armenian pills, and dragon blood—the latter two evidently well-known to other physicians of the time, and both used well into the 19th century (Bertapaglia, trans. 1989). The former was a resin from a South American leguminous tree, the latter a resin from fruit of a palm native to Sumatra and Borneo, doubtlessly imported at considerable expense. Another mixture advocated by Bertapaglia consisted of syrups of sage, marjory, honeysuckle, and wild thyme, and yet another of honey, sulphur, salt, cinnamon, and wormwood. All these potions and liniments point to the strong possibility that folk wisdom and ethnobotanical pharmacies may have been incorporated or indeed appropriated wholesale by the medical authorities of the time without reference to any objective information on the brain. At this juncture, however, credit must also be given to the monumental anatomic work of Vesalius (1514–1564), whose *De corporis humani fabrica, Libri septem* was first issued in 1543 and included highly detailed post-mortem illustrations of the skull and brain within, along with explicit recognition that a key task would be to find ways to "…. perceive by what the [living] brain is affected as is thoroughly put to a test daily in wounds of the head" (Lambert, 1936, p. 373).

By the early medieval period, the sophistication of armor had grown so great that combatants could be entirely encased in metal, albeit at substantial expense. The great helms of the era, both in Europe and Asia, were not only protective but explicitly declarative of the owner's prowess and sociopolitical stature (Blackburn, Edge, Williams, & Adams, 2000, Hamada & Hashimoto, 2002; Simpson, 1996). Their design and ornamentation meant that as their wearers struggled into fighting position they were assured, at the very least, of ample magnificence. However, physical safety was not assured. Even the best headgear had to leave some openings for sight, sound, and ventilation, but the larger those openings the greater the risk for getting struck through by an opponent's sharp implement. The opponent could also resort to brute force, using a club or mace to bash the headgear inward, or a lance to upend him entirely. The restricted sensation of the real world due to the helmet's design, and the sheer weight of the gear, up to 60+ pounds (27+ kgs), meant that men going to battle were prone to heat exhaustion and heart failure, not to mention significant disorientation. And, for all that, the helmet's strength simply may not have been sufficient at the instant when it was most needed (Figure 2-4).

TBI in the Technological World

Gunpowder profoundly changed the nature of injury. The configurations of wounds from gunpowder, balls, and bullets were vastly different than those inflicted by swords, arrows and other sharp implements of war, which as a rule had proved either to be immediately fatal or to lead to injuries that healed well. Gunshots, on the other hand, characteristically resulted in a mess: wounds simultaneously included lacerations, contusions, and foreign matter from skin and clothing carried deep below the wound surface. Infections, widely interpreted as forms of poisoning, were frequent. Physicians desperately attempted to find ways to destroy the venom until Paré and Brunschig succeeded in the 16th century in making dressings with antiseptic qualities (Billroth, 1931).

Brain injuries continued to be frequently fatal and how best to treat them the subject of great variation. Indeed, James Yonge (1646–1721), writing at the close of the 17th century, was unusual in declaring that wounds of the brain were curable (Yonge, 1682). One notes with interest that the close of his book's lengthy title

Figure 2-4. Helmet failure in combat, 1305–1340, from the Codex Manesse, or Große Heidelberger Liederhandschrift, Codex Palatinus Germanicus 848, folio 321v: Herr Dietmar der Setzer. Reproduced by kind permission of Universitätsbibliothek Heidelberg, Germany.

reads "…. for the vindication of the author," suggesting that few believed him. Henry-Francois le Dran (1685–1770), writing in France in the early 18th century, attributed symptoms following head injury to concussion of the brain, recommending that if it was only slight, the patient would be well-served by phlebotomy and "other convenient remedies." If considerable symptoms, however, a large incision of the cranium was appropriate in his view to further evaluate the extent of injury: "it is far more preferable to make a useless incision than to neglect it in a dubious case" (le Dran, 1740, p. 81). The trepan cannot be applied too often, he remarked.

Percival Pott (1713–1788) was one of a relatively small number of physicians who influenced 18th century thinking about brain injuries. In his book dated 1760, he recognized explicitly that the physicians' knowledge had

"little power of art in many cases to resist or to remove [the patient's symptoms], mak[ing] this a very melancholy part of practice" (Pott, 1760, p. xxv). He wrote about the frequent development of post-injury inflammation and fevers even in those who had appeared to be recovering well following their injuries, urging a rational basis for prognostication.

Among the earliest American medical writers was John Jones (1729–1791), one of the founders of, and the first professor of surgery at, the medical school that in time came to be the College of Physicians and Surgeons at Columbia. Publishing in 1776 on wounds and fractures, he considered injuries to the head to be separable into symptoms arising from concussion, fractures of the skull, and scalp injuries not involving the cranial contents. He described the trepanning operation for fracture repair as one in which "there is neither pain, difficulty, nor danger in it," but cautioned about the dangers of increased pressure on the brain, inflammation, and, in the instance of temporal trepanning, the danger of convulsions (Jones, 1776).

In the same year, 1776, another analysis of head wounds was published by the Irish physician William Dease (c.1750–1798), first professor of surgery at the Royal College of Surgeons in Ireland, and a man with broad medical interests (he published an essay on venereal warts that same year, for example). Dease effused over the progress of surgery in general over the preceding 50 years and commented that "…. the method of treating wounds of the head…. [has] long since arrived at a superior degree of perfection" (p. 5). But in subsequent pages he went on to note that the absence of knowledge about cerebral anatomy had led to many errors in treatment, and to decry the "extremely defective and ill-calculated" instruments of surgery used by some of his predecessors.

By the turn of the 19th century an increasing number of physicians and surgeons had turned to the problem of head injury. But there continued to be "much difference of opinion [and] dispute" according to Abernathy (1811, p. 4), who went on in his monograph on the subject to claim that concussion "produces a state of inflammation in the brain" treatable by "powerful stimulants such as wine, brandy, and volatile alkali" (p. 54). He did acknowledge, however, that such medicinals were likely to aggravate the patient's condition, but condoned it in that very little else was available by way of treatment.

George James Guthrie (1788–1856) wrote an extensive monograph on treatment of cranial injury. He elaborated on operations for extradural hemorrhage and epidural abscess, but recognized that brain injuries presented singular problems for the physician. "Injuries of the head affecting the brain are difficult of distinction, doubtful in their character, treacherous in their course, and for the most part fatal....," he wrote (Guthrie 1842, p. 1).

> There are no cases of convalescence after disease or injury which require more care than those which follow injuries of the head. Relapses, from apparently trifling causes, are extremely frequent, and gradually but certainly undermine the health; they are in fact connected with chronic derangement of the brain or its membranes, and unless successfully met, generally end, after the lapse of a few weeks or months, in irritative fever and death. (Guthrie, 1842, p. 33).

During the American Civil War, the Union lost 360,000 men, more than two in every three of whom succumbed not to injury but disease; the South lost 258,000 men in similar proportions. Death was visited upon both sides of the conflict to such a degree that nearly every citizen across the country was personally aware of a war fatality (Faust, 2008). This was the first war in which detailed medical records were kept, and from these can be determined that about 10% of injuries were to the head and neck. Between the American Revolution and the American Civil War there had been many dozens of wars involving gunshot wounds of the head. By the Civil War, a roster of specific pathophysiologies of head injuries was relatively well understood, though the principal deterrent to neurosurgical progress continued to be infection (Zellem, 1985), thought to be untreatable at that time. A variety of improved surgical kits had been designed (see for example Figure 2-5), and pocket surgical manuals were available to medical practitioners that included modest detail about pathology, bullet trajectories, clinical findings, and indications for surgical intervention for removal of bone fragments and trephination (Kaufman, 1993). During the Civil War, the challenge of treating

Figure 2-5. Surgical kit for neurosurgery, 17th c. Reproduced by kind permission of Douglas Arbittier M.D., York, PA.

head injuries and other injuries involving the nervous system was found very difficult to solve. In the field, practitioners labored under arduous conditions and were often well out of their depth of medical training. In the large hospitals where there might be persons with adequate medical preparation, brain injured soldiers arrived only after long delays, so those expiring soon after their injuries were simply not encountered. Those who made it to the large hospitals tended to be "....strange case[s] of wounds of nerves. Most of these presented phenomena which are rarely seen....Nowhere were these cases described at length in the textbooks and, except in a single untranslated French book [unfortunately not identified], their treatment was passed over in silence" (Mitchell et al., 1864, p. 3). But, in contrast, one well-regarded American physician declaimed just a few years later that "the principles on which to conduct the treatment of injuries of the head are so generally recognized as to need no allusion to them here" (MacCormac, 1870, p. 576). Much use was made of hypodermic injections for pain, along with repeated blistering, iron tonics, cod-liver oil, and moderate use of malt and spirituous liquors, quinine, and less frequently, mercury.

Historians have noted that during the Civil War, penetrating wounds made up 74% of the total injuries, yet less than 6% of these were due to artillery fire, torpedoes and grenades, and less than 0.4% to saber or bayonet. In contrast, more than three out of every four gun shot wounds during World War I were caused by shellfire (Adams, 1952), and penetrating wounds declined to only 35% of all head wounds in World War I, then to 14% in World War II, and to 10% in the Korean War (Rose, 1997).

The musket balls of the [Civil War] made for more wounds than modern steel-jacketed cartridges. The old lead bullet, traveling at low velocity, readily lost shape on impact, frequently lodged in the tissues, often carried with it particles of clothing and skin, and almost invariably left an infected wound.... The modern bullet is sterilized by heat, and does not lose its shape (Adams, 1952, p. 114.)

With the invention of gunpowder, the world had been turned on end, some said. But for an extended period the weaponry that made use of this invention had been crude, slow, and unwieldy. Gun bearers were at a disadvantage in military conflict, for their armaments were only capable of inflicting modest injury at any extended distance, yet at close range the owner was himself at great personal risk from opponents whose swords or battleaxes had no need to be reloaded. By the Civil War, however, the development of internal rifling that forced bullets into a stabilizing spin as they traveled the length of a gun barrel, and a reshaping of bullets from round to conoidal, increasing the effective range of these armaments by five times, so a well-trained rifleman could pick off at 500 yards an artilleryman whose cannon was only effective up to about 300 yards (Weiss, 2001). An estimate made by an unnamed correspondent for the *British Medical Journal* in 1915 was that, in wars before The Great War, some 60% of head wounds were instantly fatal, and that another quarter of those remaining would expire within 24 hours (Anon, 1915).

Yet the story was constantly changing. During the First World War, for example, the "close contact of well constructed and protected opposing trenches [which were located a mere 50 meters apart], the development of the hand grenade, bomb, high-explosive shell, shrapnel, machine gun, and asphyxiating gas.... all combined to greatly limit the usefulness of the rifle...." (Fauntleroy, 1915, p. 10). Bullets, however, still inflicted serious injury in no small part due to their relatively high remaining velocity at extreme range, plus deformation and fragmentation upon impact. As the war began, British and Australian soldiers wore cloth caps, the French wore soft képis, the Germans wore caps or helmets made out of pressed leather (Simpson, 1996). In recognition of the terrible death tolls in early battles of the Great War, steel helmets were brought back into use after having been completely abandoned over the preceding two centuries. In marked contrast to present military gear, these provided very little coverage of the head below the level of the tops of the earlobes (Figure 2-6).

In World War I, wounds seen at the base hospitals best equipped to handle serious medical conditions were generally those involving long bone fractures and mutilating wounds of the face. This was in part due to their need for complex surgical intervention, but also their characteristically involving soldiers who could safely bear transportation, generally three to five days in length, to the rear of military activity. Serious wounds such as head injuries were less likely to be transportable and were recognized as needing immediate care, so did not reach base hospitals until they were convalescent, that is, they had successfully survived the post-acute phase of injury (Fauntleroy, 1915). At base hospitals, it was recognized that large proportions of these cases would succumb, often to infection. Two investigations about this time found that cranial wounds with dura intact experienced only 8% mortality, while those with the dura torn showed up to 43% mortality. Within that group, if the wound was a penetrating wound affecting the ventricles, mortality rose to 100% in one series, 86% in the other (Neuhof, 1920). Harvey Cushing (1869–1939), serving as

Figure 2-6. American military helmets, World War I, from the Goodhue Flagpole, also known as the Pasadena Memorial Flagpole, 1927, Pasadena, CA. Photo by the author.

director of the U.S. Army Base Hospital of the British Expeditionary Force, published perhaps the largest single article to that date on wounds involving the brain, showing that progress in cutting mortality from penetrating brain injuries by half was being made through improved operative procedures (Cushing, 1918). Showing a fresh focus on war-time head trauma by the medical profession, the same journal issue also contained additional scientific articles on radiography of gunshot wounds to the head, and repair of skull injuries using thin plates of silver and by grafts of cartilage.

Like the Civil War, the balance of battle injuries would return to bullets as the principal cause during the Vietnam War. However, in the First Iraq War of 1991, one estimate was that the ratio of fragment injuries to bullet injuries was 95: 5. Injuries to the head and neck during Vietnam constituted 43% of all injuries, while by Iraq 2003 these had reduced to under 16% (Wade, Dye, Mohrle, & Galarneau, 2007). A major contributor to this change was the deployment of the Kevlar helmet, weighing about 2.9 to 3.9 pounds (1.3 to 1.8 kg) depending on size and made from polyaromatic amide chains that possess a strong crystalline regularity that renders the surface far more resistant to penetration than ordinary steel (Rustemeyer, Kranz, & Bremerich, 2007). Testing of helmets to certify adequate ballistic protection involves bullets moving at up to 2,860 mph (4,600 km/h), more than four times the speed of sound. But more head protection is frequently needed. The next line of helmet defense for the combat soldier has been inaugurated with the appearance of a helmet that includes a massive face-shield (Figure 2-7) to protect against bullets and fragments arriving frontally. Anecdotal reports indicate that the new design saves soldiers from what would be otherwise expected to be substantial injuries to the head as the result of improvised explosive devices. Epidemiologic data are currently lacking.

In closing this history of head injuries, the role of automobiles should not go unremarked. From the earliest days of steam-powered wagons through a large portion of the 20th century, vehicular injuries and fatalities were commonplace. Automobiles were considered by many, including President Woodrow Wilson writing

Figure 2-7. American military helmet, 2010: Predator Facial Armor System. Reproduced by kind permission of MTek Weapon Systems, Martinsville, IN.

in 1906, to be menacingly dangerous; "Horrible and gruesome incidents are of almost daily occurrence," said one congressman in 1910. In Michigan, at the opening of the century, two out of the three autos registered in the entire state were involved in a collision. In 1921, the first year for which U.S. records can be calculated with confidence, the estimated fatality rate was 24.085 per 100 million miles of travel, a figure that is sixteen times greater than the modern rate.[3] The first automotive safety improvement aimed directly at reducing head and facial trauma was use of Triplex safety glass in windshields, invented two decades earlier but not available until 1927 and then only as an option at slight extra charge on Chrysler models (Anon, 1927). At least another four decades would elapse before the next safety modifications explicitly addressing head injuries were regularly available: padded dashboards, seatbelts (for which the first patent had been issued in France in 1903),

---

[3] Recent estimates, though with somewhat reduced confidence, are that the number of fatalities from horse-related events in England in 1901, when horses were the predominant mode of ground propulsion, was 23.38 deaths per 100 million annual horse miles (Roots, 2007).

and airbags. How many head injuries could have been prevented with earlier adoption of those features is almost incalculable.

TBI Epidemiology in the United States

We turn to the most recent epidemiological analyses of head injury provided by the Centers for Disease Control and Prevention (CDC; Faul, Xu, Wald, & Coronado, 2010). This study examined three different national databases: the National Hospital Discharge Survey (NHDS), conducted annually as a national probability survey of about 500 non-Federal short-stay hospitals in the United States and including approximately 270,000 inpatient records; the National Hospital Ambulatory Medical Care Survey (NHAMCS), which annually collected about 75,000 individual records as samples from hospital emergency and outpatient departments and in ambulatory surgery centers; and the National Vital Statistics System (NVSS) which collects birth and death statistics nationwide. All three are products of the National Center for Health Statistics. TBI-related cases were selected for inclusion in the CDC report as long as any one diagnosis included the following: fracture of the vault or base of the skull; intracranial injury, including concussion, contusion, laceration, and hemorrhage; shaken baby syndrome; other and unqualified multiple fractures

of the skull; injury to optic nerve and pathways; or head injury, unspecified. Those emergency department patients who died in the emergency department, or who were later hospitalized or transferred to another facility were excluded from analyses of emergency department visits. During the study period from 2002 to 2006, the annual volume of cases considered ranged from 33,605 to 40,253, originating in between 352 and 406 participating hospitals.

As a proportion of all injuries, the CDC report estimates that TBI constitutes a mere 1.4% of all emergency department visits but 15.1% of all hospitalizations and 30.5% of all deaths due to injury. A brain-injured person is 3.25 times more likely to expire in the course of hospitalization than those persons hospitalized for any other reason. In contrast to many prior studies over time, the CDC report indicates increases, in absolute numbers over the five-year study period, in TBI-related emergency department (ED) visits (up 14.5%); hospitalizations (up 19.6%); and deaths (up 3.6%) in absolute numbers. Adjusted for population growth, the data show an increase of 10.3% in emergency department visits and an increase of 15.2% in hospitalizations, but a decrease of 0.2% in deaths.

The estimated average annual rates of TBI-related ED visits by age group (Figure 2-8) show a major peak in the youngest ages (0–4,

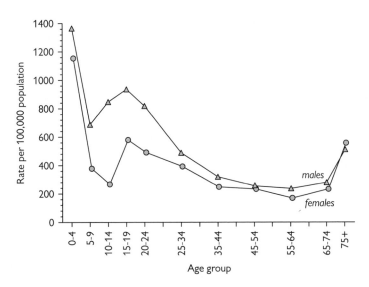

Figure 2-8. Annual rates per 100,000 population of TBI-related ED visits by age group. Faul et al. (2010), Table 3.

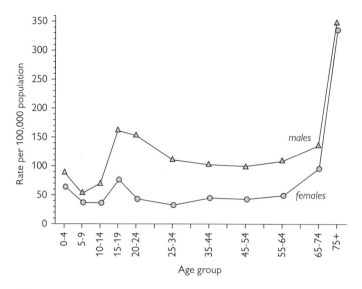

Figure 2-9. Annual rates per 100,000 population of TBI-related hospitalizations by age group, U.S. 2002– 2006. Faul et al. (2010), Table 9.

with 1,256 per 100,000 population); another smaller peak in older adolescents (15–19 years, with 757 per 100,000 population); and a third peak in the elderly (75+ years, 339 per 100,000 population). The structure of the age curve is not the same, however, for average annual rates of either TBI-related hospitalizations (Figure 2-9) or TBI-related deaths (Figure 2-10), both of which trend strongly upwards with age. The CDC data show that males are 1.62 times as likely to be hospitalized with TBI and 2.80 times as likely to expire compared with females. The leading cause of TBI is seen to be falls (2.39 times more ED visits and 1.10 times more hospitalizations than the next most frequent cause, motor-vehicle and traffic-related events). However, falls are the cause of 41.8% fewer deaths than motor-vehicle and traffic-related events.

Comparing the CDC's 2010 findings for the United States with one of several earlier studies of TBI also conducted by the CDC is instructive. Langlois et al. (2003) reported the results of a study that appraised 62,771 live TBI-related hospital discharges from 14 states that had been funded in 1997 to conduct surveillance of TBI: Alaska, Arizona, California, Colorado, Louisiana, Maryland, Minnesota, Missouri, Nebraska, New York, Oklahoma, Rhode Island, South Carolina, and Utah. After removing deaths from the tables of hospital discharges

in the 2010 report and combining the resulting rates into the same age-groups as used in the earlier report, the two sets of rates can be compared by age-group and by cause.[4] The ratios of the 2010 report's rates to the 2003 report's rates by age-group are shown in Table 2-1. In this comparison, female elderly show a 34% increase and male elderly show a 69% increase in rates of live discharge from hospital following TBI, while females in their early adulthood show a 13% decrease and males in their early adulthood show a 28% decrease.

Similarly, a comparison can be made between the two CDC reports in terms of selected causes by appropriately combining the more recent report's rates by age group and expressing them as ratios to the corresponding rates in the earlier report (Table 2-2). In this comparison,

---

[4] The comparisons are admittedly rough in that determination of live discharges is based in part on knowing the number of deaths occurring in hospital. The source of death reports in the 2010 study was not limited exclusively to hospitalized cases but were collected by states within the United States from death certificates completed by funeral directors, attending physicians, medical examiners, and coroners regardless of the setting in which the death occurred. These would have included persons who died at the scene, during transportation, or during resuscitation in the emergency department.

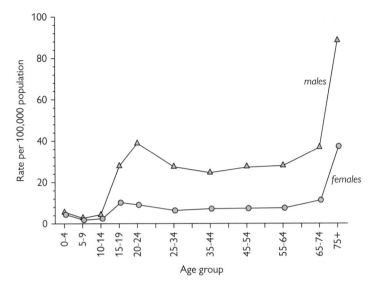

Figure 2-10. Annual rates per 100,000 population of TBI-related deaths by age group, U.S 2002–2006. Faul et al. (2010), Table 14.

Table 2-1. Ratio of Estimated Average Annual Rates per 100,000 Population of TBI-Related Hospitalizations Excluding Deaths, by Age Group and Sex, United States, 2002–2006, from Faul et al. (2010), Table 9, to Rates of TBI-Related Live Hospital Discharges—14 States, 1997, from Langlois et al. (2003), Table 1.

Age Group (years)	Males	Females
0–4	1.13	1.09
5–14	0.89	1.10
15–19	0.95	1.01
20–24	0.87	0.72
25–34	0.89	0.76
35–44	0.95	1.13
45–64	1.07	1.19
65+	1.34	1.69

rates for live discharge from hospital for motor vehicle-related TBI appear to have fallen in every age group, notably by more than half in all ages above the teens. The rate of live hospital discharge for the elderly who sustained an assault appears to be 88% smaller in the newer report compared with the older one. A portion of the reduction may stem from a trend across the United States, possibly driven as much or more by hospital economics as by medical advances, to reduce the number of hospital admissions for mildly injured cases. Aside from speculation about such trends and about the relative dimensions of hospitalized and nonhospitalized TBI-related deaths by age-group or cause, why the two reports differ so dramatically is, at present, not clear.

TBI Epidemiology Compared

For a variety of reasons, the current U.S. experience likely does not appear to apply uniformly across the rest of the world. One interesting contrast with the CDC Report findings is available in data collected by Wu et al.(2008), covering every hospital admission for brain injury for a period of one year collected from every one of the 77 hospitals servicing a densely urban region of eastern China with an estimated population of 373,310,000 persons. On an age-adjusted population basis the largest incidence of TBI occurred in the elderly (Figure 2-11), but this was at a rate of only 7.1 per 100,000 population, forty times smaller than the comparable U.S. experience.[5] Traffic accidents were the identified cause of injury in 60.9% of the cases, with falls accounting for only 13.1%, a pattern of cause quite unlike that seen in the United States. Of the traffic-related incidents, the authors identified

---

[5] Note that the authors mentioned rates but presented only tallies; rate data shown in Figure 11 are computed based on available population estimates from the Population Division, Department of Economic and Social Affairs, United Nations, 2006.

Table 2-2. Ratio of Estimated Annual Average Rates per 100,000 Population of TBI-Related Hospitalizations Excluding Deaths, by Age-Group and Cause, United States, 2002–2006, Computed from Faul et al. (2010), Tables 11 and 16, to Rates of TBI-Related Live Hospital Discharges—14 States, 1997, from Langlois et al. (2003), Tables 4 and 5.

Age Group (years)	Motor Vehicle	Fall	Assault	Struck by
0–4	0.70	0.88	0.53	1.27
5–14	0.51	0.68	0.83	1.05
15–19	0.56	1.03	0.39	0.94
20–24	0.46	0.61	0.33	0.36
25–34	0.49	0.93	0.46	0.95
35–44	0.46	0.93	0.52	1.10
45–64	0.43	0.84	0.47	0.74
65+	0.48	0.76	0.12	1.36

one third as motorcyclists, another third as pedestrians, a fifth as cyclists, and a mere 14% as occupants of motor vehicles.

Another comparison of the U.S. experience can be made with recent information on TBI in New Zealand, in which electronic data from the National Health Information Service covering all 85 publicly funded hospitals in the country were assessed from mid 1997 through mid 2004 (Barker-Collo, Wilde, & Feigin, 2009b). Using hospitalization information for cases involving conventional codes signifying brain injury, Figure 2-12 depicts standardized head injury incidence rates for 2003/2004 for males and

females by age-group for all of New Zealand. Like the U.S. data, this figure shows relatively high incidence rates among infants and teenagers (especially male teenagers) but compared with the United States it shows a far lower incidence rate for the elderly.

The New Zealand experience points out two key concerns in conducting epidemiologic studies of brain injury. The first concern is that the nature of the coding upon which the case finding is predicated itself can have dramatic effects on the ensuing findings. In that study the authors noted that the recent upgrade in the International Classification of Diseases

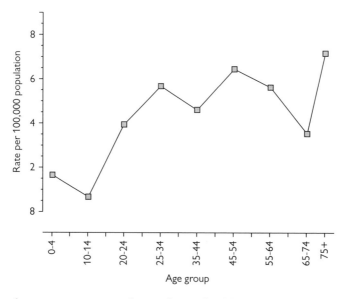

Figure 2-11. Annual rates per 100,000 population of TBI-related hospitalization by age group, China, 2004. Computed based on data from Wu et al. (2007), Table 1, with age-group populations adjusted to U.N. estimates for all of China (Population Department, 2006).

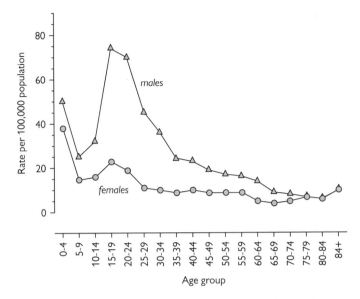

Figure 2-12. Annual rates per 100,000 population of TBI-related hospitalization by age group, New Zealand, 2004–2005, redrawn from Barker-Collo et al. (2009), Figure 2.

(from ICD-9 to ICD-10) resulted in a marked increase in apparent overall incidence, as the more recent codes include injuries to the head that may be less reflective of brain injury than the older codes, including open wounds, nerve injuries, and dislocations, for example.

The second concern is that across countries, different cultural manifestations of exposure to injury are likely. The lead author of the New Zealand study surmises that motor vehicle-related events may be less common in the New Zealand elderly relative to their counterparts in the United States, as many tend to live in rural communities where driving is often less necessary for daily life. Alternatively, the reduced number of elderly with TBI may result from the likelihood that New Zealand's substantial population of older immigrants from the Pacific Islands, Asia, and India are less likely to be driving than others (Personal communication, June 29, 2010). There are also strong indications that implementing aggressive state policies regarding driving behaviors can result in dramatic changes in motor-vehicle-related TBI: Spain experienced a remarkable 60.2% decline in such incidents over the decade 2000–2009 (Pérez et al., 2012).

We also note that comparing epidemiological findings about brain injury across different reports is fraught with difficulties such as unstandardized definitions, case finding procedures, data reporting, and other methodological differences (Tagliaferri, Compagnone, Korsic, Servadei, & Kraus, 2006). Thus the comparisons presented here, despite respectably large sample sizes, are subject to substantial and sometimes unresolvable variability. The interested reader is strongly urged to review other work by the CDC on this topic (see, for example, Guerrero et al., 2000; Jager et al., 2000; Rutland-Brown et al., 2006) as well as other recent epidemiological studies such as Engberg & Teasdale (2001), Rosso et al., (2007), and Myburgh et al. (2008).

In closing, we note an additional concern for understanding the epidemiology of TBI: the proportion of cases with such injuries who never make contact with medical treatment facilities and thus are never entered into any systematic roster, and from there never become a component of a published research effort concerning TBI incidence. Over a two-year period, a survey on the patient-oriented website of the University of Rochester Medical Center found that, out of 1,381 respondents who claimed to have met the investigators' definition of TBI, 584 (42%) reported they had not sought any medical care. This was particularly true for those who were older, those who had suffered a mild TBI, or those injured at home (Setnik & Bazarian, 2007).

Good epidemiologic studies of TBI are exceptionally difficult to perform. Efforts are currently underway, despite the expense, to achieve the fullest possible understanding of the distribution of TBI by age group, by causes and risk factors, by severity, by type and intensity of available treatment services, and by outcomes. Regrettably, many studies have been undertaken in the absence of agreed standards for even the simple task of grouping by age, not to mention more complex topics like determining diagnoses and severities, fully identifying the nature of treatments, and precisely describing the complete range of outcomes (one detailed unifying proposal is presented by Barker-Collo & Feigin, 2009a, discussed further by Theadom et al., 2012). Additionally, researchers continue to be hampered in settings in which reporting is incomplete (e.g., systematic mechanisms are missing that would uniformly preserve data from a TBI event outside the immediate clinical setting in which treatment was delivered); in settings in which the case catchment areas are porous (e.g., the geographic areas within which data are captured represent arbitrary jurisdictions or fail to coincide with natural or societal boundaries); and in settings in which cultural and political considerations give rise to differential access to care.

Acknowledgments

Support for this chapter from NINDS NS058489. Thanks to the staff of the History and Special Collections for the Sciences, Louise M. Darling Biomedical Library, UCLA.

References

Abernathy, J. (1811). *Surgical observations on injuries of the head and on miscellaneous subjects*. Philadelpha: Thomas Dobson.

Abu-Zidan, F. M., & Rao, S. (2003). Factors affecting the severity of horse-related injuries. *Injury, 34*, 897–900.

Adams, F.(1939). *The genuine works of Hippocrates, translated from the Greek*. Baltimore: Williams and Wilkins.

Adams, G. W. (1952). *Doctors in blue: The medical history of the Union army in the Civil War*. New York: Henry Schuman.

Amr, S. S., & Tbakhi, A. (2007). Abu Bakr Muhammad Ibn Zakariya Al Razi (Rhazes): Philosopher, physician and alchemist. *Arab and Muslim Physicians and Scholars, 27*, 305–307.

Barker-Collo, S. L., & Feigin, V. L. (2009a). Capturing the spectrum: suggested standards for conducting population-based traumatic brain injury incidence studies. *Neuroepidemiology, 32*, 1–3.

Barker-Collo, S. L., Wilde, N. J., & Feigin, V. L. (2009b). Trends in head injury incidence in New Zealand: A hospital-based study from 1997/1998 to 2003/2004. *Neuroepidemiology, 32*, 32–39.

Berengario, da Carpi. (1990). Tractatus de fractura calve sive cranei, II, x. *Berengario da Carpi On Fractures of the Skull or Cranium* (L. R. Lind, Trans.). Philadelphia, The American Philosophical Society.

Bertapaglia, L. (1989). *On nerve injuries and skull fractures* (J. C. Ladenheim, Trans.). NY: Futura.

Billroth, T. (1931). Historical studies on the nature and treatment of gunshot wounds from the fifteenth century to the present time. *Yale Journal of Biology and Medicine, 4*, 2–36.

Blackburn, T. P. D., Edge, D. A., Williams, A. R., & Adams, C. B. T. (2000). Head protection in England before the First World War. *Neurosurgery, 47*, 1261–1286.

Bradford, S. H. (1869). Scenes in the life of Harriet Tubman. Auburn NY: W.J. Moses.

Breasted, J. H. (1930 reissued 2006). *The Edwin Smith surgical papyrus: Hieroglyphic transliteration, translation, and commentary*. Chicago: University of Chicago Press.

Cushing, H. (1918). A study of a series of wounds involving the brain and its enveloping structures. *British Journal of Surgery, 5*, 558–684.

Dagi, T. F. (1997). The management of head trauma. In S. H. Greenblatt, T. F. Dagi, & M. H.Epstein (Eds.), *A history of neurosurgery in its scientific and professional contexts* (pp. 289-343). Park Ridge, IL: American Association of Neurological Surgeons.

Dease, W. (1776). *Observations on wounds of the head, with a particular enquiry into the parts principally affected, in those who die in consequence of such injuries*. London: G Robinson.

Dimopoulos, V. G., Machinis, T. G., Fountas, K. N., & Robinson, J. S. (2005). Head injury management algorithm as described in Hippocrates' "peri ton en cephali traumaton." *Neurosurgery. 57*, 1303–1305.

Dimopoulos, V. G., Robinson, J. S., & Fountas, K. N. (2008). The pearls and pitfalls of skull trephination as described in the Hippocratic Treatise "On Head Wounds." *Journal of the History of the Neurosciences, 17*, 131–140.

Engberg, A. W., & Teasdale, T. W. (2001). Traumatic brain injury in Denmark 1979–1996. A national study of incidence and mortality. *European Journal of Epidemiology, 17*, 437–442.

Faul, M., Xu, L., Wald, M. M., & Coronado, V. G. (2010). *Traumatic brain injury in the United States: Emergency department visits, hospitalizations and deaths 2002–2006.* Atlanta, GA: Centers for Disease Control and Prevention, National Center for Injury Prevention and Control.

Fauntleroy, A. M. (1915). *Report on the medico-military aspects of the European War.* Washington D.C. Government Printing Office.

Faust, D. G. (2008). *This republic of suffering: Death and the American civil war.* New York: Knopf.

Feinsod, M.(1997). Three head injuries: The Biblical account of the deaths of Sisera, Abilmelech and Goliath. *Journal of the History of the Neurosciences, 6*, 320–324.

Flamm, E. S.(1997). From signs to symptoms: The neurosurgical management of head trauma from 1517 to 1867. In S. H. Greenblatt, T. F. Dagi, & M. H. Epstein (Ed.), *A history of neurosurgery in its scientific and professional contexts* (pp. 65-81). Park Ridge IL: American Association of Neurological Surgeons.

Frugardo, R. (2002). *The Chirurgia of Roger Frugard* (L. D. Rosenman, Trans.). Philadelphia: Xlibris. (Original work published in 1546).

Goodrich, J. T. (1997). Neurosurgery in the ancient and medieval worlds. In S. H. Greenblatt, T. F. Dagi, & M. H. Epstein (Ed.), *A history of neurosurgery in its scientific and professional contexts* (pp. 37-64). Park Ridge IL: American Association of Neurological Surgeons.

Guerrero, J. T, Thurman, D. J., & Sniezek, J. E. (2000). Emergency department visits associated with traumatic brain injury: United States, 1995-1996. *Brain Injury, 14*, 181–186.

Gurdjian, E. S. (1973a). *Head injury from antiquity to the present with special reference to penetrating head wounds.* Springfield IL: Charles C Thomas.

Gurdjian, E. S. (1973b). Prevention and mitigation of head injury from antiquity to the present. *Journal of Trauma, 13*, 931–945.

Guthrie, G. J. (1842). *On injuries of the head affecting the brain.* London: John Churchill.

Hamada, J., & Hashimoto, N. (2002). The kabuto, or the Japanese helmet: Evolution from war implement to status symbol. *Neurosurgery, 51*, 871–879.

Hopkins, S. M. (1869). *Woman-whipping, ethically and esthetically considered.* Auburn NY: W J Moses, 1869.

Horrax, G. (1952). *Neurosurgery, an historical sketch.* Springfield IL: Charles C Thomas.

Horsley, V. (1887). Brain surgery in the stone age. *British Medical Journal, 1(1367)*, 582.

Jager, T. E., Weiss, H. B., Coben, J. H., & Pepe, P. E. (2000). Traumatic brain injuries evaluated in U.S. emergency departments, 1992–1994. *Academic Emergency Medicine, 7*, 134–140.

Jones, J. (1776). *Plain concise practical remarks on the treatment of wounds and fractures.* Philadelphia: Robert Bell.

Judd, M. A., & Roberts, C. A. (1999). Fracture trauma in a medieval British farming village. *American Journal of Physical Anthropology, 109*, 229–243.

Kaufman, H. H. (1993). Treatment of head injuries in the American Civil War. *Journal of Neurosurgery, 78*, 838–845.

Lambert, S. W. (1936). A reading from Andreae Vesalii, *De Corporis Humani Fabrica Liber Vii De Vivorum Sectione Nonnulla Caput XIX. Bulletin of the New York Academy of Medicine, 12*, 346–386.

Lanfranco of Milan. (2003). *The surgery of Lanfranchi of Milan: a modern English translation* (L. D. Rosenman, Trans.). Philadelphia: Xlibris (original work published in 1295).

Langlois, J. A., Kegler, S. R., Butler, J. A., Gotsch, K. E., Johnson, R. L., Reichard, A. A. et al. (2003). Traumatic brain injury-related hospital discharges: Results from a 14-state surveillance System, 1997. *Mortality and Morbidity Weekly Report Surveillance Summaries, 52*, 1–18.

le Dran, H.F. (1740) *Observations in surgery: containing one hundred and fifteen different cases with particular remarks on each, for the improvement of young students* (J. S. Surgeon, Trans.). London: James Hodges.

MacCormac, W. (1870). Recollections of work in an ambulance. *British Medical Journal, 2*, 575–577.

Medical arrangement of the British Expeditionary Force: Brain surgery in war (1915). *British Medical Journal, 1(2830)*, 567–571.

Mitchell, S. W., Morehouse, G. R., & Keen, W. W. (1864). *Gunshot wounds and other injuries of nerves.* Philadelphia: JB Lippincott.

Myburgh, J. A., Cooper, D. J., Finfer, S. R., Venkatesh, B., Jones, D., Higgins, A. et al. (2008). The Australasian Traumatic Brain Injury Study (ATBIS) Investigators for the Australian and New Zealand Intensive Care Society Clinical Trials Group. Epidemiology and 12 month outcomes from traumatic brain injury in Australia and New Zealand. *Journal of Trauma, 64*, 854–862.

Neuhof, H. (1920). The treatment of craniocerebral wounds and its results. *Annals of Surgery, 72*, 556–588.

Norwood, S., McAuley, C., Vallina, V. L., Fernandez, L. G., McLarty, J. W., Goodfried, G. (2000).

Mechanisms and patterns of injuries related to large animals. *Journal of Trauma, 48,* 740–744.

Pérez, K., Novoa, A. M., Santamariña, E., Narvaez, Y., Arrufat, V., Borrell, C. et al. (2012). Incidence trends of traumatic spinal cord injury and traumatic brain injury in Spain, 2000–2009. *Accident Analysis and Prevention, 46,* 37–44.

Piek, J., Lidke, G., Terberger, T., von Smekal, U., & Gaab, M. R. (1999). Stone Age skull surgery in Mecklenburg-Vorpommern: A systematic study. *Neurosurgery, 45,* 147.

Population Division, Department of Economic and Social Affairs, United Nations. (2006). *World Population Prospects 2006.*Retrieved June 23, 2010, from http://www.un.org/esa/population/publications/wpp2006/wpp2006.htm

Pott, P. (1760). *Observations on the nature and consequences of wounds and contusions of the head, fractures of the skull, concussions of the brain.* London: C. Hitch & L. Hawes.

Preece, D. A., Ross, G. J. S., & Kirby, P. J.(1988). Bortkewitsch's horse-kicks and the generalised linear model. *Statistician, 37,* 313–318.

Prioreschi, P. (2007). *A history of medicine: Renaissance medicine.* Omaha: Horatius Press.

Ragland, L. (1939). The "green man" in church architecture. *Folklore, 50,* 45–57.

Régnier, C. (2007). French medicine and Italy: A family affair. *Medicographia, 29,* 185–192.

Roots, R. (2007). The dangers of automobile travel, a reconsideration. *American Journal of Economics and Sociology, 66,* 959–975.

Rose, F. C. (1997). The history of head injuries: An overview. *Journal of the History of the Neurosciences, 6,* 154–180.

Rosso, A., Brazinova, A., Janciak, I., Wilbacher, I., Rusnak, M., & Mauritz, W. (2007). Severe traumatic brain injury in Austria II: Epidemiology of hospital admissions. *Wiener Klinische Wochenschrift, 119,* 29–34.

Rustemeyer, J., Kranz, V., & Bremerich, A. (2007). Injuries in combat from 1982–2005 with particular reference to those to the head and neck: a review. *British Journal of Oral and Maxillofacial Surgery, 45,* 556–560.

Rutland-Brown, W., Langlois, J. A., Thomas, K. E., & Xi, Y. L. (2006). Incidence of traumatic brain injury in the United States, 2003. *Journal of Head Trauma Rehabilitation, 21,* 544–548.

Sachs, E. (1952). *The History and Development of Neurological Surgery.* New York: Paul B. Hoefer.

Sarrafzadeh, A. S., Sarafian, N., Von Gladiss A., Unterberg A. W., & Lanksch WR. (2001). Ibn Sina (Avicenna): Historical vignette. *Neurosurgical Focus, 11,* 1–4.

Sawyer, R. D. (2011). *Ancient Chinese Warfare.* New York: Basic Books.

Setnik, L., & Bazarian, J. J. (2007). The characteristics of patients who do not seek medical treatment for traumatic brain injury. *Brain Injury, 21,* 1–9.

Simpson, D. (1996). Helmets in surgical history. *Australia New Zealand Journal of Surgery, 66,* 314–324.

Speidel, M. P. (2002). Berserks: A history of Indo-European "mad warriors." *Journal of World History, 13,* 253–290.

Spink, M. S., & Lewis, G. L. (1973). *Albucasis on surgery and instruments: A definitive edition of the Arabic text with English translation and commentary.* Berkeley: University of California Press.

Tagliaferri, F., Compagnone, C., Korsic, M., Servadei, F., & Kraus, J. (2006). A systematic review of brain injury epidemiology in Europe. *Acta Neurochirurgica, 148,* 255–268.

Theadom, A., Barker-Collo, S., Feigin, V. L., Starkey, N. J., Jones, K., Amertunga, S. et al. (2012). The spectrum captured: A methodological approach to studying incidence and outcomes of traumatic brain injury on a population level. *Neuroepidemiology, 38,* 18–29.

Towner, E., & Towner, J. (2008). The hazards of daily life: an historical perspective on adult unintentional injuries. *Journal of Epidemiology and Community Health, 62,* 952–956.

Triplex glass now a Chrysler option (1927). *Automobile Topics, 87,* 698.

Tubbs, R. S., Koukas, M., Shoja, M. M., Cohen-Gadol, A. A., Wellons, J. C. III, & Oakes, W. J. (2008). Roots of neuroanatomy, neurology, and neurosurgery as found in the Bible and Talmud. *Neurosurgery, 63,* 156–163.

Tubbs, R. S., Shoja, M. M., Loukas, M., & Oakes, W. J. (2007). Abubakr Muhammad Ibn Zakaria Razi, Rhazes (865–925 AD). *Child's Nervous System, 23,* 1225–1226.

Wade, A. L., Dye, J. L., Mohrle, C. R., & Galarneau, M. R. (2007). Head, face, and neck injuries during Operation Iraqi Freedom II: Results from the U.S. Navy-Marine Corps Combat Trauma Registry. *Journal of Trauma, 63,* 836–840.

Walker, A. E. (1951). *A history of neurological surgery.* Baltimore: Williams & Wilkins.

Walshe, T. M. (1997). Neurological concepts in archaic Greece: What did Homer know? *Journal of the History of the Neurosciences, 6,* 72–81.

Weinberg, A. (2006). A case of cranial surgery in the Talmud. *Journal of the History of the Neurosciences, 15,* 102–110.

Weiss, E. D. (2001). The second sacrifice: Costly advances in medicine and surgery during the Civil War. *Yale Journal of Biology and Medicine, 74,* 169–177.

Wu, X., Hu, J., Zhuo, L., Fu, C., Hui, G.Y., Yang, W., Teng, L. et al. (2008). Epidemiology of traumatic brain injury in eastern China, 2004: A prospective large case study. *Journal of Trauma, 64*, 1313–1319.

Yonge, J. (1682). *Wounds of the Brain Proved Curable, not only by the opinion and experience of many (the best) authors, but the remarkable history of a child four years old cured of two very large depressions, with the loss of a great part of the skull, a portion of the brain also issuing through a penetrating wound of the dura and pia mater*, published for encouragement of young chirurgeons, and vindication of the author. London: Printed by J.M. for Henry Faithorn & John Kersey.

Zellem, R. T. (1985). Wounded by bayonet, ball, and bacteria: Medicine and neurosurgery in the American Civil War. *Neurosurgery, 17*, 850–860.

Zollikofer, C. P. E., Ponce, de León. M. S., Vandermeersch, B., & Lévêque, F. (2002). Evidence for interpersonal violence in the St. Cesaire Neanderthal. *PNAS Proceedings of the National Academy of Sciences, 99*, 6444–6448.

3

Traumatic Brain Injury Disease: Long-term Consequences of Traumatic Brain Injury

Brent E. Masel and Douglas S. DeWitt

Introduction

The Funk and Wagnall's Standard Dictionary (Funk, 1980) defines an *event* as: "the final result; the outcome." Traumatic damage to the brain is seen by the insurance industry as well as many health care providers as an "event." Thus, a broken brain is the equivalent of a broken bone—the final outcome from an insult in an isolated body system. Once "fixed," the brain requires no further treatment beyond a relatively brief period of rehabilitation, and certainly there will be no lasting effects on other organ systems. In contrast, the World Health Organization (WHO) defines a chronic disease as having one or more of the following characteristics: it is permanent, caused by non-reversible pathological alterations, requires special training of the patient for rehabilitation and/or may require a long period of observation, supervision, or care (WHO, 2002). This clearly defines a TBI as well.

The prevalence of head injury among service personnel retuning from Operations Iraqi Freedom (OIF) and Enduring Freedom (OEF) has increased concern over the long-term effects of TBI. TBI accounts for a larger proportion of casualties among soldiers surviving wounds sustained in combat in Iraq and Afghanistan than in previous conflicts (Okie, 2005). Additionally, attention has focused on the chronic effects of TBI because of the association between repeated, usually mild TBIs and the early onset of Alzheimer's and other types of dementias in retired athletes, particularly professional football players (Schwarz, 2007a). Sports-related concussions in the United States annually have been estimated to be as high as 300,000 (Thurman, Branche, & Sniezek, 1998). Despite estimates that concussions involving loss of consciousness represented only 8% (Schultz et al., 2004) and 19.2% (Collins, Lovell, Iverson, Cantu, Maroon, & Field, 2002) of sports-related TBIs, Langlois, Rutland-Brown and Wald (2006) suggest that the true numbers of sports-related TBIs may range from 1.6 to 3.8 million annually. If only a fraction of those with combat- or sports-related TBIs exhibit long-term consequences, tens to hundreds of thousands of patients could be affected.

The purpose of this chapter is to review the neurologic consequences of a TBI and to encourage the classification of a TBI as the beginning of a chronic disease process, rather than an event or final outcome. Head trauma is the beginning of an on-going, perhaps life-long process that impacts multiple organ systems and may be disease causative and accelerative. A TBI should be managed as a chronic disease and defined as such by health care and insurance providers. Furthermore, if the chronic nature of TBI is recognized by government and private funding agencies, research can be directed at discovering therapies that may interrupt the disease processes months or even years after the initiating event.

Posttraumatic Mortality

TBI reduces life expectancy and increases long-term mortality. In a 2004 study of mortality one year post-injury among 2,178 moderate-severe TBI patients, Harrison-Felix,

Whiteneck, DeVivo, Hammond, and Jha (2004), found that individuals with a TBI were twice as likely to die as a similar non-brain injured cohort, with a life expectancy reduction of seven years. A follow-up study on causes of death revealed that individuals surviving more than one year post-injury were 37 times more likely to die from seizures, 12 times more likely to die from septicemia, four times more likely to die from pneumonia, and three times more likely to die from other respiratory conditions than a matched cohort of the general population (Harrison-Felix, Whiteneck, DeVivo, Hammond, & Jha, 2006). The largest proportion of deaths (29%) was from circulatory problems. Although this number was not significantly greater than that of the general population, there was still a 34% increase over the expected number of circulatory related deaths. In a retrospective analysis of charts from 1,678 TBI patients admitted between 1961 and 2002, Harrison-Felix, Whiteneck, Jha, DeVivo, Hammond, and Hart (2009), found that TBI patients were 49 times more likely to die of aspiration pneumonia, 22 times more likely to die of seizures, three times more likely to die of suicide, and 2.5 times more likely to die of digestive disorders than the general population matched for age, race, and gender. This same group, Ventura et al. (2010), characterized mortality in 18,998 Colorado residents discharged alive from acute hospitalizations between 1998 and 2003. Individuals with a TBI carried a 2.5 times risk of death when compared to the general population with an average life expectancy reduction of approximately six years.

McMillan, Teasdale, Weir, and Stewart (2011) followed a cohort of 767 individuals for 13 years following injury. Overall, the death rate was almost 2.5 times higher for the TBI group than for the community population. In young adults, the differences were more striking: (17.36 vs. 2.36 per 1,000 per year). The death rate for even mild TBIs was increased (14.82 vs. 2.21 per 1,000 per year). The main causes of death were quite similar to that found in the general population: circulatory, neoplasms, respiratory, and digestive.

Shavelle and colleagues (2001) reported that individuals with a TBI were three times more likely to die of circulatory conditions. Although it is somewhat intuitive that individuals with moderate-severe TBIs would have a higher mortality rate than the normal population, even individuals with mild TBIs exhibited a small but statistically significant reduction in long-term survival (Brown, Leibson, Malec, Perkins, Diehl, & Larson, 2004).

Based on an examination of mortality among 3,679 TBI patients within one year of discharge from acute care hospitals in South Carolina, Selassie McCarthy, Ferguson, Tian, and Langlois (2005) found a seven-fold excess risk of death overall (standardized mortality ratio (SMR) = 7.1; 95% CI, 6.3–7.9) within 15 months of discharge compared with the general U.S. population. Patients treated at Level 1 trauma centers were 44% (95% CI, 0.4–0.8) less likely to die during the follow-up period than those treated at hospitals without a trauma center. Interestingly, patients with a TBI who were insured by Medicare were 1.6 times (95% CI, 1.1–2.5) more likely to die than patients covered by commercial insurance.

In a retrospective study of 642 patients with TBI discharged from a large rehabilitation hospital in the years 1974–1984, 1988, and 1989, Ratcliff and colleagues (2005) estimated the ratio of the observed number of deaths to the expected number of deaths. The resulting SMR was 2.78, indicating a more than two and a half-fold increase in mortality rates in patients with TBIs. Brown et al. (2004) conducted a population-based, retrospective study of 1,448 (164 moderate-severe, 1,284 mild) patients with TBI from Olmsted County, MN during the years 1985 to 2000. The mortality risk ratio (95% CI) was 5.29 (4.11–6.71) in moderate-severe and 1.33 (1.05–1.65) in mild TBI patients. This indicated that patients with mild TBI exhibited a small but statistically significant reduction in long-term survival compared to the general population. Considering the far greater numbers of mild versus moderate-severe TBI patients, the increased mortality among patients with mild TBI would result in considerable numbers of TBI-related deaths.

Posttraumatic Morbidity

Although many patients survive the initial insult, TBI initiates a chronic disease process that may ultimately contribute to their deaths months to years later.

Neurological Disorders

Epilepsy. TBI is a major cause of epilepsy, accounting for 5% of all epilepsy in the general population (Hauser, Annegers, & Kurland, 1991). Individuals with a TBI are 1.5–17 times (depending on the severity of the TBI) more likely than the general population to develop seizures (Annegers, Hauser, Coan, & Rocca, 1998). Brain injury is the leading cause of epilepsy in the young adult population. Seizures were observed over a week after a penetrating TBI in 35–65% of individuals. In a study of 309 individuals with moderate-severe TBI followed as long as 24 years post-injury, 9% were being treated for epilepsy (Yasseen, Colantonio, & Ratcliff, 2008). In general, the risk of developing post-traumatic epilepsy (PTE) after a penetrating TBI is higher than after the most severe closed head injury. Englander and colleagues (2003) studied risk factors for the development of PTE in 647 patients with moderate-severe TBI. The highest probabilities of PTE were seen in individuals with dural penetration with bone and metal, bi-parietal contusions, multiple intracranial operations, multiple subdural contusions, subdural hematoma requiring evacuation and/or midline shift of greater than five mm. As the time from injury to the time of the first post-TBI seizure may be as long as 12 years (Aarabi, Taghipour, Haghnegahdar, Farokhi, & Mobley, 2000), there is a need for heightened awareness of the development of epilepsy on the part of the patient, family, and treating medical personnel.

Sudden death in epilepsy patients (SUDEP) also relates to the mortality issues surrounding the long-term consequences of a TBI. The risk of sudden death in patients with epilepsy is more that 20 times that of the general population (Shorvon & Tomson, 2011). This risk was strongly related to the frequency of the seizures. Individuals with one or two generalized convulsions per year had an odds ratio of sudden death of 2.94. This increased to 14.51 in patients with more than 50 seizures per year. The risk was elevated in males, patients with a long history of seizures, and those on polytherapy for their seizures.

Sleep Disorders

Sleep complaints are common following TBI. Subjective complaints of sleep disturbances have been reported in 70% of TBI outpatients (McLean, Dikmen, Temkin, Wyler, & Gale, 1984). Disturbed sleep as measured by polysomnogram was reported in 45% of a group of 71 individuals averaging three years post-injury (Masel, Scheibel, Kimbark, & Kuna 2001).

There is an increased incidence of obstructive sleep apnea (OSA) in TBI patients (Castriotta, Wilde, Lai, Atanasov, Masel, & Kuna, 2007). Obstructive sleep apnea not only is associated with decreased cognitive functioning (Wilde, Castriotta, Lai, Atanasov, Masel, & Kuna, 2007), but also with hemodynamic changes and severe cardiac arrhythmias during sleep. Such changes may be profound, with normotensive individuals developing systolic pressures approaching 300 mm Hg after apnea termination (Weiss, Launois, Anand, & Garpestad, 1999). Even individuals with mild OSA have significant mortality risks (Partinen, 1988).

Neurodegenerative Diseases

It is generally assumed that the cognitive gains made during the acute and post-acute period following TBI are maintained or may increase over the long term. There is a growing body of evidence, however, that suggests a subset of individuals exhibit gradual declines in cognitive function after their injury. Till and colleagues (2008) performed serial neuropsychological assessments on 33 individuals with moderate-severe TBI over the first five years post-injury. Statistically significant cognitive decline on at least two neuropsychological measures was observed in 27.3% of subjects. Interestingly, the best predictor of decline was the amount of therapy received at five months post-injury. Those who received more therapy in the early post-injury months, irrespective of severity of injury and level of neuropsychological impairment, were less likely to show decline over the long term. In their report on the Gulf War and Health, the Institute of Medicine (IOM) concluded: "There is sufficient evidence of a relationship between sustaining a penetrating TBI and decline in neurocognitive function

Table 3-1. Long-Term Central Nervous System Degeneration after Traumatic Brain Injury in Rats

Model	Survival	Results	References
Moderate psFPI (2.0–2.4 atm)	**2** mths	Significant loss of tissue volume in ipsilateral cortex, thalamus, & hippocampus 2 months post-TBI	(Bramlett, 1997b)
Severe psFPI (2.5–2.9 atm)	**1** hr–1 yr	Progressive atrophy & astrocytosis in cortex, hippocampus, thalamus, & septum; hippocampal neuronal death bilaterally	(Smith, 1997)
Severe psFPI (2.5–2.9 atm)	**1** hr–1 yr	Significant impairment of spatial learning (MWM) 2, 6, 12 months post-TBI. No impairment in spatial memory. Abnormal neuroscore 1 day, 1 & 2 weeks, and 2 months, but not 6 or 12 months post-TBI. Neuronal degeneration (APP IR) up to 1 yr in striatum, corpus callosum, and injured cortex.	(Pierce et al., 1998)
Moderate CCI	**2** wks–1 yr	Significant impairment of spatial memory (MWM) 3 & 12 months, but not 2 or 4 weeks or 6 months post-TBI. Hemispheric tissue loss (compared to sham) of 30.4±5.5 mm^3 & 51.5±8.5 mm^3 at 3 weeks & 12 months, respectively. VAChT IR increased in hippocampus & cortex & M$_2$ IR decreased in the ipsilateral hippocampus 1 year post-TBI	(Dixon, 1999)
Moderate psFPI (2.0–2.1 atm)	**3** days–1 yr	Significant reductions in ipsilateral cerebral cortex posterior to trauma site & cerebral peduncle & external capsule compared to sham animals. No significant reduction in volume of thalamus, hippocampus, internal capsule, corpus callosum, or dentate gyrus.	(Bramlett, 2002)
Moderate psFPI (1.8-2.2 atm)	**3** days–1 yr	Significant, time-dependent reduction in myelinated axons in injured hemisphere for 1 yr post-TBI; swollen axons & microglial/macrophage infiltration for 6 months post-TBI.	(Rodriguez-Paez, Brunschwig, & Bramlett, 2005)

APP—amyloid precursor protein; CBF—cerebral blood flow; CCI—controlled cortical impact; IR—immunoreactivity; M$_2$—muscarinic receptor subtype 2; MRI—magnetic resonance imaging; MWM—Morris water maze; NF-κB—neurofilament kappa B; psFPI—parasagittal fluid percussion injury; VAChT—vesicular acetylcholine transporter

associated with the affected region of the brain and the volume of brain tissue lost." (Institute of Medicine, 2009). In addition, age is clearly a factor in long-term cognitive outcome after TBI. Older patients show a greater decline over the first five years following a TBI than younger patients (Marquez de la Plata et al., 2008).

Dementia of the Alzheimer's Type. Although the cause of Alzheimer's dementia (AD) is unknown, numerous studies have shown that TBI may be a risk factor for the development of AD (Jellinger, Paulus, Wrocklage, & Litvan, 2001). In a large study of WW II veterans, Plassman and colleagues (2000) found that any history of brain injury more than doubled the risk of developing AD, as well as the chances of developing non-Alzheimer's dementia. They also observed that the worse the brain injury, the higher the risk for AD. Moderate brain

injury was associated with a 2.3 fold increase in the risk, while severe head injury more than quadrupled the risk of the subsequent development of AD. Even individuals with no known cognitive impairment after TBI exhibited increased risk of an earlier onset of AD (Schofield et al., 1997).

Barnes and colleagues (2011) looked at the risk of dementia in a cohort of 281,540 U.S. veterans age 55 and older. The risk of dementia was 15.3% in veterans who had a history of a TBI (many injuries were of a "civilian-type") as compared to 6.8% in those without a TBI. The severity of the injury made no difference in the chances of developing dementia.

In their excellent review on this subject, Lye and Shores (2000) suggested many possible etiologies for this connection: damage to the blood brain barrier causing leakage of plasma proteins into the brain, liberation of free oxygen radicals, loss of brain reserve capacity, as well as the deposition of amyloid-β (Aβ) plaques.

Neurofilament proteins (NF), amyloid precursor protein (APP), beta-site APP cleaving enzyme (BACE), presenilin-1 (PS-1), α-synuclein protein (α-syn), and Aβ were detected in human brain tissue samples harvested four weeks after TBI (Uryu et al., 2007). Amyloid-β plaques and neurofibrillary tangles comprised of tau protein are pathological characteristics of AD (Braak & Braak, 1991; Forman, Trojanowski, & Lee, 2004). BACE and PS1 are critical components of the anabolic pathway that cleaves APP into Aβ (DeStrooper et al., 1998; Selkoe, 2001).

Iwata and colleagues (2002) reported increased expression of the APP gene, APP751/770, two to seven days after fluid percussion TBI in rats. Interestingly, Aβ immunoreactivity and protein expression increased for as long as a year post-injury, indicating that Aβ accumulation may continue long after APP gene expression returned to normal. Apolipoprotein D (ApoD) mRNA and protein expression increased in cortex and hippocampus of adult rats 2–14 days after concussion. ApoD may contribute to neurodegeneration in AD since elevated ApoD levels have been observed in the CSF and hippocampus of AD patients (Terrisse et al., 1998).

Acute and chronic systemic inflammation/infections are associated with increases in serum tumor necrosis factor alpha (TNFα) resulting in a two-fold increase in the rate of cognitive decline over a six-month period in individuals with AD. Those with high baseline TNFα levels had a four-fold increase in the rate of cognitive decline (Holmes, et al., 2009).

Mild TBI

Long-Term Consequences of Mild TBI

Considering estimates that approximately 75% of the 1.4 million reported TBIs are classified as mild (Bruns & Jagoda, 2009); there are one million new mTBIs annually in the United States. The Centers for Disease Control and Prevention estimated that the economic costs of mTBI in 2003 approached 17 billion dollars (Bay & McLean, 2007). The Centers for Disease Control and Prevention defined mTBI as the occurrence of injury to the head resulting from blunt trauma or acceleration or deceleration forces with one or more of the following conditions attributable to the head injury during the surveillance time period (CDC, 2003):

1. Any period of observed or self-reported transient confusion, disorientation, or impaired consciousness.
2. Any period of observed or self-reported dysfunction of memory (amnesia) around the time of injury.
3. Observed signs of other neurological or neuropsychological dysfunction.
4. Any period of observed or self-reported loss of consciousness lasting 30 minutes or less.

In the absence of post-traumatic amnesia and CT abnormalities (Niogi et al., 2008), most mTBI patients recover completely, with the incidence of persistent neurological and neuropsychological deficits after mTBI controversial, although there are studies that indicate a significant number have some cognitive dysfunction one year after injury (Alves, Macciocchi, & Barth, 1993; van der Naalt, Hew, van Zomeren, Sluiter, & Minderhoud, 1999). On the basis of a careful review of 120 of what they considered the most valid outcome studies of TBI, the World Health Organization (WHO) Collaborating Centre Task Force on Mild Traumatic Brain Injury concluded that few (< 3%) of mTBI patients reported symptoms persisting beyond one month after TBI (Carroll et al., 2004). Carroll et al. (2004) examined 428 studies related to prognosis and outcome after mTBI and selected 120 articles that were judged to be the most relevant to mTBI in terms of diagnosis, risk factors, prognosis, treatment, rehabilitation, and prevention. Only five of those studies used injured controls (patients with non-TBI injuries) and tracked long-term (>1 month) outcome (Bazarian, Wong, Harris, Leahey, Mookerjee, & Dombovy, 1999; Dikmen, Machamer, Winn, & Temkin, 1995; Friedland & Dawson, 2001; Hanks, Temkin, Machamer, & Dikmen, 1999; Masson et al., 1996; Ponsford et al., 2000). Carroll et al. (2004) concluded that symptoms of cognitive dysfunction in most mTBI patients immediately after injury resolved within three to twelve months. In a meta-analysis of based on 39 studies (1,463 MTBI patients, 1,191 controls), Belanger and colleagues (2005a) concluded that mTBI had little effect on neuropsychological functioning by three months or greater post-injury. In contrast, abnormalities in cerebral blood flow (Ge et al., 2009; Jacobs, Put, Ingels, Put, & Bossuyt, 1996), symptoms of post-concussive syndrome (Bazarian et al., 1999; Deb et al., 1998; Masson et al., 1996) and deficits in cognitive and executive function (Bemstein, 2002; Kraus, Susmaras, Caughlin, Walker, Sweeney, & Little, 2007) may persist for months to years after mTBI. Although the incidence of chronic neurological, psychological, or psychiatric deficits after mTBI may be low, mild TBI is the most common type of brain injury, and the total numbers of patients with long-term consequences may have a significant impact on health care resources.

Chronic Traumatic Encephalopathy—Long-Term Effects of Repeated Mild TBI

The correlation between repeated, usually mild TBIs and chronic or late-developing cognitive dysfunction has been recognized for decades. "Punch drunk" and "dementia pugilistica" were described in the 1920 and 1930s (Martland, 1928; Millspaugh, 1937). The recent reports of impaired cognition, depression, and suicide in retired professional athletes have focused attention on long-term consequences of TBI (Epstein, 2010; King, 2010; Schwarz, 2007a; Schwarz, 2007b). Chronic traumatic encephalopathy begins insidiously with deterioration in concentration, attention, memory, judgment, and insight, occasionally accompanied by dizziness and headaches. Other symptoms include apathy, impulsiveness, and suicidal thoughts and actions (Gavett, Stern, & McKee, 2011). Severe cases eventually affect the pyramidal tract, resulting in progressive symptoms of Parkinsonism, including disturbed coordination, gait, slurred speech masked facies, dysphagia, and tremors (McCrory, Zazryn, & Cameron, 2007; DeKosky, Ikonomovic, & Gandy, 2010; McKee et al., 2010).

McKee et al. (2009) reported the results of histopathological analyses of the brains of professional athletes with symptoms of chronic traumatic encephalopathy (CTE). The sample included five professional football players with symptoms of CTE at the time of death. In all five cases, the ages of symptom onset and death were 35–40 and 45–50 years, respectively (McKee et al., 2009; Omalu et al., 2006; Omalu, DeKosky, Minster, Kamboh, Hamilton, & Wecht, 2005; Schwarz, 2007a; Schwarz, 2007b). All five were suffering from depression, four of five exhibited paranoia and memory deficits, and three of five had problems with anger and/or aggression. Neurofibrillary tangles and tau immunoreactivity were observed in four patients and two exhibited amyloid β immunoreactivity. A subsequent study of athletes with CTE after professional careers in football (7), boxing (4) or hockey (1) revealed that all 12 exhibited tau immunoreactivity of the brain stem, diencephalon, basal ganglia, and frontal, insular, and temporal cortices (McKee et al., 2010). Six patients showed evidence of amyloid β immunoreactivity and ten exhibited widespread TAR DNA-binding protein of approximately 43 kd (TDP-43) immunoreactivity of the frontal and temporal cortices, medial temporal lobe, basal ganglia, diencephalon, and brainstem. In a study of 3,439 retired NFL football players with at least five years of playing seasons, Lehman, Hein, Baron, and Gersic (2012) found that the neurodegenerative mortality was three times higher than that of the general U.S. population, and that for Alzheimer's Disease and Amyotrophic Lateral Sclerosis, the risk was four times higher. They also found a higher degenerative mortality for players in speed positions, e.g., backs and ends, as opposed to non-speed positions.

In addition to boxing and American football, repeated TBIs occur in soccer (Matser, Kessels, Jordan, Lezak, & Troost, 1998; Tysvaer, Storli, & Bachen, 1989); horse racing (McCrory, Turner, & Murray, 2004); hockey, rugby, skiing, lacrosse, and karate (McKee et al., 2010). There is preliminary but intriguing evidence that mTBI may result in cognitive deficits associated with specific neuroanatomical or functional lesions. In a small study of nine "concussed" athletes, Chen and colleagues (2008) observed abnormal fMRI activation in the dorsolateral prefrontal cortex (compared to six age-matched healthy athletes)

Table 3-2. Long-Term Effects of mTBI in Patients

GCS	n*	Effects	References
GCS ≥ 13	136	3, 6, & 12 months post-TBI, respectively, 45/136 (33%), 29/136 (21%) & 12/136 (9%) of pts had CBF abnormalities (^{99m}TC-HMPAO SPECT)	(Jacobs et al., 1996)
GCS ≥ 13	119	5 years post-TBI, 2.5% had unfavorable GOS; 39.5% reported ≥ 3 PCS symptoms (headache 44%, memory impairment 32%, fatigue 35%)	(Masson et al., 1996)
self reported[a]	32	Significant association between development of AD & a history of mTBI in preceding 30 years (RR 5.4). History of LOC > 5 min increased RR to 11.2	(Schofield et al., 1997)
GCS ≥ 13[b]	148	1 year post-TBI, 26% had moderate disability (GOS); 55% reported one or more PCS symptoms	(Deb et al., 1998)
GCS 15	71	6 months post-TBI, 25% reported symptoms of PCS	(Bazarian et al., 1999)
GCS ≥ 13	11	3–4 years post-TBI, deficits in executive function	(Mangels, Craik, Levine, Schwartz, & Stuss, 2002)
self-reported	13	8 years post-mTBI pts reported more sleep problems & cognitive failures than control age-matched controls (n=10). mTBI pts. performed significantly worse on dual auditory discrimination task.	(Bemstein, 2002)
not stated[c]	1,284	1.33 MRR during 7.4 year follow-up	(Brown et al., 2004)
GCS ≥ 13	20	7.7 years post-TBI, mTBI pts performed significantly worse on CPT test of pre-frontal function; mTBI associated with reduced white matter integrity (DTI)	(Kraus et al., 2007)
GCS ≥ 13	4411	Mortality rate for mTBI patient ≥ 15 yo = 0.9%	(Luerssen, Klauber, & Marshall, 1988)
GCS ≥ 13	21	↓ thalamic blood flow (arterial spin labeled MRI) vs. aged matched controls 2 years post-injury	(Ge et al., 2009)

^{99m}TC-HMPAO—hexamethylpropylene amine oxime; AD—Alzheimer's dementia; CBF—cerebral blood flow; CNS—central nervous system; CPT—Conners' continuous performance test; CSF—cerebral spinal fluid; GOS—Glasgow outcome scale; LOC—loss of consciousness; MRI—magnetic resonance imaging; MRR—mortality risk ratio; PCS—post-concussive syndrome (see below); RR—risk ration; SAH—subarachnoid hemorrhage; SPECT—single-photon emission computed tomography; ↓ lower levels or numbers/impaired performance, ↑ higher levels or numbers/improved performance
* number of mTBI patients (excluding normal or non-CNS injury controls);
a—history of mTBI from interviews with physician and/or risk factor analyzer
b—GCS 13–15 plus LOC or radiological or neurological evidence of focal brain injury
c—mTBI = one or more of the following: loss of consciousness, amnesia, post-concussive symptoms or focal neurological signs of brain injury w/o: skull fracture, intracranial hematoma, brain contusion, penetrating skull injury, brain stem injury, neurological surgery, CNS infection, SAH, hydrocephaly, CSF leakage
PCS = one or more of the following: headaches, fatigability, sleep disturbance, dizziness, irritability/aggressiveness, anxiousness/depression, missed work, relationship troubles, personality change, short-term memory impairment, difficulty with simple math

during a working memory task. All nine athletes reported symptoms of post-concussive syndrome (PCS) at the time of the initial testing (mean three months post-TBI). At the time of the follow-up testing, PCS symptoms resolved in four but remained essentially the same in five athletes. The athletes without PCS symptoms at follow-up showed significant improvement in fMRI activation while those with PCS symptoms continued to exhibit abnormal fMRI activation during a working memory task. This small but provocative study, consistent with

a previous study by the same group (Chen, Johnston, Frey, Petrides, Worsley, & Ptito, 2004) suggests an underlying pathophysiological correlate to persistent cognitive dysfunction after mTBI.

In contrast to reports of an association between sports concussions and chronic cognitive dysfunction, Belanger and Vanderploeg (2005b) concluded that sport-related concussions resulted in no significant neuropsychological impairments that persist beyond 7–10 days post-injury based on a meta-analysis of 21

Table 3-3. Comparison of Professional Football Players with Chronic Traumatic Encephalopathy

Identifier	Play (yrs)	Dysphor./depress.	Memory/attention	Anger/aggress.	Poor Judge.	Parano.	Dement.	Aβ	NFT/tau
Omalu 1	22	X	X		X			X	X
Omalu 2	14	X		X		X			X
Strzelczyk	23	X	X			X		X	X
Waters	17	X	X	X		X			
Case A	16	X	X	X		X	X		X

Aβ—amyloid β; Anger/aggress—anger/aggression; Dement.—dementia; Dysphor/depress—dysphoria/depression; NFT—neurofibrillary tangles; Parano.—paranoia; Play—Span of football, including high school, college & professional play; Poor judge.—poor judgment;
Omalu 1—from (Omalu, et al., 2005); Omalu 2—from (Omalu, et al., 2006); Strzelczyk—from (Schwarz, 2007b); Waters—from (Schwarz, 2007a); Case A—from (McKee, et al., 2009).

studies of athletes who sustained concussions in contact sports (790 concussed athletes, 2,014 control athletes). Despite this rather reassuring report, evidence indicates that high school (Collins et al., 2002) and collegiate (Guskiewicz et al., 2003) athletes are at risk for long-term neurocognitive deficits resulting from repeated TBIs. Considering the large number of high-school and college athletes involved in contact sports, there is a clear and urgent need for future research on the lasting consequences of sports-related TBI.

Neuropathologically, CTE is characterized by atrophy of the brainstem, cerebral hemispheres, thalamus, medial temporal lobe, and mammillary bodies, with ventricular dilatation and a fenestrated cavum septum pellucidum. Microscopically, there are extensive tau-immunoreactive neurofibrillary tangles, spindle-shaped and threadlike neurites, and astrocytic tangles throughout the brain. As opposed to other tauopathies, the neurofibrillary degeneration of CTE is distinguished by its irregular patchy distribution in the frontal and temporal cortices, preferential involvement of the superficial cortical layers, propensity for sulcal depths, prominent periventricular, perivascular, and subpial distribution, and the marked accumulation of tau-immunoreactive astrocytes (McKee et al., 2009).

In contrast to the absence of neurofibrillary tangles and the presence of diffuse amyloid beta protein seen following a single TBI, most individuals with CTE show essentially no amyloid beta protein deposition (DeKosky et al., 2010). Other tauopathies include: Parkinson's disease, frontotemporal dementia (Wunsch,

1998), corticobasilar degeneration (Feany, Ksiezak-Reding, Liu, Vincent, Yen, & Dickson, 1995), and Alzheimer's disease and progressive supranuclear palsy (Flament, Delacourte, Verny, Hauw, & Javoy-Agid, 1991). CTE is a neuropathologically distinct, slowly progressive tauopathy characterized by a clear environmental etiology.

There has been interest in the connection of some of the signs and symptoms from multiple blast injuries to that of CTE. Goldstein et al. (2012), compared the brains of four military veterans with a history of multiple blast exposures to the brains of four young athletes with histories of multiple concussions, and also compared them to the brains of four normal control subjects with no history of concussions or blast exposures. The brains of all four veterans revealed pathologic changes compatible with what is found in CTE. It should be noted, however, that the study was weakened by the fact that three of the four veterans also had a history of civilian-type concussions,

What makes CTE so different from an acute injury is that there are no symptoms initially, and then the clinical symptoms begin insidiously and continue to progress for decades after the activity that produced traumatic injury has stopped. This most likely represents the result of cascades of multiple pathological processes, with the more severe the original injury and the longer the individual's survival after the initial events, the greater the severity of the neurodegeneration (McKee et al., 2010). The incidence and prevalence of CTE are unknown. At present, there are no known biomarkers for this disease. Imaging studies will show cerebral atrophy and ventricular enlargement, but these changes are seen in many other disease states as well. Short of a brain biopsy, CTE remains a clinical diagnosis. Due to the large number of young men and women, as well as children participating in contact sports throughout the world, there is clearly the need for further study of this disease process.

Other Disease States

Brain Tumors. Chen, Keller, Kang and Lin (2012), published a population-based study looking at the incidence of malignant brain tumors within the three years following a TBI in a cohort of 5,007 subjects with a TBI in Taiwan. The comparison cohort was 25,035 randomly selected enrollees in the National Health Insurance Research Database. During the three-year tracking period, nine subjects in each group developed cerebral malignancies. Therefore, the incidence rate of malignant brain tumors was 6.28 per 10,000 person years in the TBI group compared to 1.25 in the non-TBI group.

Multiple Sclerosis. Kang and Lin (2012) used the same Taiwanese database to study the incidence of multiple sclerosis following a TBI. Using a six-year follow-up period, they found that the incidence of MD was 0.055% for the TBI (72,765 subjects) group versus 0.037% for a control group of 218,295 subjects.

Post-traumatic Hypopituitarism. A traumatic brain injury is associated with a host of neuroendocrine disorders, perhaps due to the induction of complex hormonal responses in the hypothalamic-pituitary-end organ axes ultimately leading to acute and/or chronic post-traumatic hypopituitarism (PTH). Hypopituitarism has been reported in approximately 30% of moderate-severe TBI patients over the first year after injury (Schneider, Kreitschmann-Andermahr, Ghigo, Stalla, & Agha, 2007a). Presently, studies on the relationship of PTH to mTBI are lacking. In contrast to patients with TBI who develop PTH that resolves over time, Aimaretti and colleagues (2005), reported that 5% of TBI patients studied had normal pituitary functioning at three

months, but later developed deficits a year post-injury, perhaps due to the loss of pituitary neuronal reserve.

Although the underlying causes of PTH are unclear, vascular and structural changes to the hypothalamus, pituitary stalk, and the pituitary itself have been theorized (Edwards & Clark, 1986; Kelly, Gonzalo, Cohan, Berman, Swerdloff, & Wang, 2000). Present routine clinical imaging techniques may be inadequate for clearly visualizing the structural pathology in the pituitary gland and tiny (2–3mm in diameter) pituitary stalk. Normal imaging does not rule out the possibility of PTH (Agha et al., 2004; Schneider et al., 2007b).

Chronic PTH results in several related neuroendocrine conditions including growth hormone (GH) and gonadotropin deficiencies and hypothyroidism. Growth hormone deficiency/insufficiency was found in approximately 20% of moderate-severe TBI patients (Agha & Thompson, 2006). Growth hormone deficiency (regardless of cause) was associated with an increased risk of fatigue, depression, decreased exercise tolerance, osteoporosis, hypercholesterolemia, and atherosclerosis, as well as a significant increase in mortality from vascular disease (Rosen & Bengtsson, 1990). Insulin-like growth factor-1 (IGF-1) is the major mediator of the actions of GH, and a low IGF-1 level is a hallmark of GH deficiency (Carro, Trejo, Gomez-Isla, LeRoth, & Torres-Aleman, 2002). In addition to enhancing neurogenesis and increasing neuronal excitability, IGF-1 enhances the clearance of Aβ from the brain (Carro et al., 2002).

Gonadotropin deficiency was found in approximately 10–15% of individuals post-TBI (Agha & Thompson, 2006). Symptoms in adult males include decreased libido, strength and muscle mass. A correlation has been found between low free testosterone levels and cognitive function, although there is no clear consensus on whether testosterone supplementation therapy will have an effect on cognition (Papaliagkas, Anogianakis, & Tsolaki, 2008).

Hypothyroidism has been found in approximately 5% of individuals post-TBI (Agha & Thompson, 2006). Associated signs and symptoms were dyspnea, weight gain, bradycardia, intellectual impairment (Agha & Thompson, 2006), depression, hyperlipidemia, hypothermia, cold intolerance, as well as irregular menses and infertility (Garber & Bergmann Khoury, 2009). A recent study revealed a connection between hypothyroidism in females and the subsequent development of Alzheimer's Disease (Tan et al., 2008).

The need for monitoring for the development of PTH was emphatically stated in the 2009 Institute of Medicine report on the Gulf War: "That hormonal alterations substantially modify the posttraumatic clinical course and the success of therapy and rehabilitation underscores the need for the identification and appropriate timely management of hormone deficiencies to optimize patient recovery from head trauma, to improve quality of life, and to avoid the long-term adverse consequences of untreated hypopituitarism." (Institute of Medicine, 2009).

Parkinson's Disease. Parkinson's disease (PD) has been classically characterized pathologically by the loss of neurons in the substantia nigra which lead to a selective loss of dopamine and its metabolites. Symptoms of PD include rigidity, dementia, tremor, postural instability, and slowness of movement (Dunnett & Bjorklund, 1999). Lewy bodies (concentric inclusion bodies in the neurons) are considered to be the histopathological signature of the disease (Zhang, Dawson, & Dawson, 2000). Noradrenergic and dopaminergic neuronal loss has been observed in the locus coeruleus, as have Lewy bodies and neuronal loss in the cerebral cortex, anterior thalamus, hypothalamus, amygdala, and basal forebrain (Zhang et al., 2000).

Although the pathology of PD is well recognized, the mechanisms of neuronal death are uncertain. Experimental studies have implicated oxygen free radicals and oxidative stress (Zhang et al., 2000). Alpha synuclein protein, implicated in other neurodegenerative diseases such as AD, may play a role in the development of PD after TBI (Bramlett & Dietrich, 2003). Alpha synuclein immunoreactivity is a hallmark pathological finding in PD, Lewy body dementia and multi-system atrophy (Norris, Giasson, & Lee, 2004; Smith, Uryu, Saatman, Trojanowski, & McIntosh, 2003). Increased

brain tissue synuclein levels have been observed in brain tissue samples from TBI patients (Uryu et al., 2007). Other putative pathophysiological mechanisms of PD include endogenous and exogenous toxins, mitochondrial abnormalities (Rango, Bonifati, & Bresolin, 2006), perturbations in the neuronal cytoskeleton and axonal transport, calcium induced injury, as well as apoptotic cell death (Dunnett & Bjorklund, 1999; Jenner & Olanow, 1998). Many of these mechanisms are thought to contribute to the pathophysiology of TBI (Bramlett & Dietrich, 2004).

Goldman and colleagues (2006) studied 93 pairs of twins from a database of World War II veterans. They observed that if both twins had PD, the one with a TBI was more likely to have an earlier onset of the disease. If only one twin had PD, that individual was more likely to have sustained a TBI. In a review of records of 196 PD patients from Olmstead County, MN, Bower and colleagues (2003) found an increased risk of PD in individuals who had sustained a TBI, a risk that increased with injury severity.

Psychiatric Disease

In terms of impact on patients, their families, and the cost to society, psychiatric disorders are among the most important of the nation's health care issues. Current estimates in the United States suggest that the collective cost of psychiatric diseases could be as high as one-third of the total health care budget (Voshol, Glucksman, & Van, 2003). Therefore it is critical to note that psychiatric and psychological deficits are among the most disabling consequences of TBI. Many individuals with a mild TBI, and the majority of those who survive moderate-to-severe TBI, are left with profound long-term neurobehavioral sequelae.

In addition to the aggression, agitation, and confusion, seen in the acute stages, TBI is associated with an increased risk of developing numerous psychiatric diseases including anxiety disorders, obsessive-compulsive disorders, psychotic disorders, mood disorders, and major depression (Fleminger, 2008; Zasler, Katz, & Zafonte, 2007), as well as substance abuse or dependence (Hibbard, Uysal, Kepler, Bogdany, & Silver, 1998; Holsinger et al., 2002; Koponen et al., 2002; Silver, Kramer, Greenwald, & Weissman, 2001). Traumatic brain injury is associated with high rates of suicidal ideation (Kishi, Robinson, & Kosier, 2001, Leon-Carrion et al., 2001); attempted suicide (Silver et al., 2001); and completed suicide (Teasdale & Engberg, 2001). In chronic TBI, the incidence of psychosis is 20%. The prevalence in TBI patients was 1–22% for mania, 18–61% for depression, 3–59% for posttraumatic stress disorder, and 20–40% for post-traumatic aggression (Kim et al., 2007).

In a study of 60 patients with a TBI followed for up to 30 years post-injury, Koponen et al. (2002) found that 50% percent developed a major mental disorder that began after their TBI. In a long-term follow-up study of 254 individuals at two and five years post-TBI, it was discovered that there was a higher incidence of cognitive, behavioral, and emotional changes at five years than at two years post-TBI (Olver, Ponsford, & Curran, 1996). Thirty-two percent of those working at two years were unemployed at five years. Therefore, in many patients, a TBI results in long-term or perhaps permanent vulnerability to psychiatric illness.

This lasting vulnerability to psychiatric disorders may be especially prominent in children, perhaps due to frequent damage to pre-frontal brain structures (Anderson, Catroppa, Morse, & Haritou, 1999). Many functions subserved by an individual's frontal lobes are more severely affected if the injury occurs in the early childhood years (Anderson et al., 1999). Moreover, as opposed to the anticipated improvement in behavior and cognitive functioning that normally occurs as a child matures, the young children who have sustained a TBI tend to worsen over time. Even mild TBI in childhood may lead to psychiatric issues in adolescence and early adulthood. McKinlay and colleagues (2002), who followed 1,000 infants in New Zealand from birth, reported that children who required merely overnight hospitalization due to mild TBI showed no academic or cognitive differences from the uninjured cohort before age 10. However, by ages 10–13, this group showed an increase in conduct disorder, oppositional-defiant disorder and attention-deficit hyperactivity disorder.

Non-Neurologic Disorders

Incontinence

One of the most frequent and psychologically devastating consequences of TBI is bladder and bowel incontinence. A TBI frequently affects the cerebral structures that control bladder storage and emptying functions, resulting in a neurogenic bladder. Based on a review of the records of over 1,000 TBI patients, Foxx-Orenstein and colleagues (2003) found that one third were incontinent of bowel at admission, 12% at discharge, and 5% at one year post-TBI. In their review of medical complications in 116 individuals with moderate-severe TBI, Safaz and colleagues (2008) found that 14% had fecal incontinence over one year post-injury. Fecal incontinence is obviously not only socially devastating, but it may contribute to skin breakdown, decubitus ulcers, and skin infections (Foxx-Orenstein et al., 2003).

Urinary incontinence is an enormous social and medical problem. Chua, Chuo, & Kong (2003) reviewed the records on 84 patients admitted to a rehabilitation unit within six weeks of injury. They observed that 62% reported urinary incontinence. This improved to 36% at discharge; however, 18% remained incontinent at six months. Safaz and colleagues (2008) found urinary incontinence in 14% of their cohort over a year post-injury. Urinary incontinence is associated with the development of frequent urinary tract infections and the development of decubitus ulcers.

Sexual Dysfunction

Sexuality, both functional and physiological, plays an enormous role in our lives. Sexual dysfunction is a large issue in the general population and is a major ongoing problem in the TBI population. Between 40 and 60% of TBI patients will complain of sexual dysfunction (Zasler et al., 2007). As noted previously, transient hypogonadism is common acutely following TBI; however, it persists in 10–17% of long-term survivors (Agha & Thompson, 2005). Beyond just the fertility and psychosocial issues presented by hypogonadism, muscle weakness and osteoporosis may have a significant impact on long-term function and health with the consequences exacerbated by long duration immobility following a TBI (Agha & Thompson, 2005).

Musculoskeletal Dysfunction. Spasticity, a common problem after moderate-severe TBI, is characterized by increased muscle tone that results in abnormal motor patterns and may well interfere with general functioning and limit mobility, self care, and independence in the activities of daily living (Elovic, Simone, & Zafonte, 2004). Untreated, it will eventually lead to muscle contractures, tissue breakdown, and skin ulceration (Zafonte, Elovic, & Lombard, 2004).

The incidence of fractures associated with a TBI is approximately 30%. Traumatic brain injury patients with fractures, especially fractures of the long bones, are at risk for heterotopic ossification (HO), which may develop as long as three months post-injury. Heterotopic ossification is defined as "the development of new bone formation in soft tissue planes surrounding neurologically affected joints," and has an incidence of 10–20% following a TBI (State of Colorado Department of Labor, 2006). This ectopic bone formation may eventually lead to limited joint mobility, increased spasticity, pain, neurovascular entrapment, and pressure ulcers. Safaz and colleagues (2008) found HO in 17% of their cohort over a year post-injury. Brain injury severity and autonomic dysregulation accurately predict HO in patients with a TBI (Hendricks, Geurts, van Ginneken, Heeren, & Vos, 2007).

One explanation for the development of HO is that osteoblasts (the pluripotent mesenchymal cells responsible for bone formation) experience inappropriate differentiation within muscles. Prostaglandins normally help regulate osteoclast (the cells that remove bone tissue by removing the matrix) and osteoblast function. It has been suggested that prostaglandin dysregulation after TBI may be a factor in the development of HO (Vanden Bossche & Vanderstraeten, 2005). The mechanism of increased post-traumatic osteogenesis is not fully understood; however, it is clear that there

are unknown centrally released osteogenic factors that that enter into the systemic circulation following a brain injury (Toffoli, Gautschi, Frey, Filgueira, & Zellweger, 2008).

Metabolic Dysfunction. A TBI appears to impact the way the body absorbs, utilizes and converts amino acids. Amino acids play a critical role in brain function because they are incorporated into functional and structural proteins and are the precursors of neurotransmitters involved in cognitive, motor, neuroendocrine, and behavioral functions. Aquiliani et al. (2000) found significant plasma amino acid abnormalities in individuals with an acute (30–75 days) TBI. All the essential amino acids (EAA, those that can not be synthesized by the body) and 50% of the non-essential amino acids (NEAA, those that can be synthesized by the body) were significantly lower in the individuals with brain injuries versus controls. The same group also found significant abnormalities at admission that were essentially unchanged upon discharge. Most notable was a reduction in tyrosine, a NEAA precursor to serotonin (Aquilani, Iadarola, Boschi, Pistarini, Arcidiaco, & Contardi, 2003).

Although the amino acid abnormalities in the acute and subacute phase of a TBI could be in part due to muscle tissue depletion, hypercatabolic states, and inadequate nutritional supply, Borsheim, Bui and Wolfe (2007) found significant abnormalities in plasma EAA and NEAA concentrations in chronic moderate-severe TBI patients. Compared to controls, TBI patients (17 ± 4 months post-injury) consuming a 2,000 cal/day, dietician-approved diet were found to have significantly lower plasma levels of the EAA, valine. Valine competes with tryptophan for the same transporter system into the brain, and low valine levels will increase tryptophan concentration in the brain (Borsheim et al., 2007). As tryptophan is a precursor to serotonin, an increase in tryptophan may increase serotonin production and consequently increase central fatigue.

When administered a drink containing of seven grams of EAA, subjects with TBI had significantly lower plasma levels of NEAA and valine than control subjects. The NEAAs with the smallest increases in the TBI group were alanine and glutamine, a precursor to the excitatory neurotransmitter, glutamate. Remarkably,

TBI patients who were eating a normal diet and were partially back in society and independently performing activities of daily living, still exhibited abnormalities in plasma amino acids more than 1.5 years post-injury (Borsheim et al., 2007). Glutamine concentrations were reduced by 14% in temporal lobe biopsies in patients with AD, suggesting a glutaminergic hypothesis to the decline in memory and learning seen in that disease (Francis, Sims, Procter, & Bowen, 1993). Moreover, abnormalities in amino acid metabolism may contribute to some of the symptoms (fatigue, decreased memory, poor learning) seen in patients with TBI.

Etiology

Long-Term Effects of TBI in Experimental Animals

Experimental TBI initiates processes that result in injury and degeneration in neurons and white matter tracts that continue for up to a year after injury in rodents (for review, see Bramlett & Dietrich, 2007). Smith et al. (1997) reported reduced tissue volumes and reactive astrocytosis in the ipsilateral cortex, thalamus, and hippocampus in rats one year after severe parasagittal fluid percussion TBI. Bramlett, Dietrich, Green, & Busto (1997a) observed significant reductions in tissue volume in the ipsilateral cortex, thalamus, and hippocampus of rats two months after moderate parasagittal FPI (Bramlett et al, 1997a), and significant atrophy in white matter tracts (external capsule, cerebral peduncles) one year after moderate parasagittal FPI in rats (Bramlett & Dietrich, 2002). Dixon et al. (1999) reported significant reductions in hemispheric tissue volume and impairment in spatial memory (Morris water maze) one year after moderate controlled cortical impact TBI. In contrast, severe parasagittal FPI was associated with significant impairment in spatial learning but not spatial memory one year post-TBI (Pierce, Smith, Trojanowski, & McIntosh, 1998). While it is clear that experimental TBI is associated with chronic, progressive gray and white matter degeneration, the contributing pathophysiological processes are unknown. Potential mechanisms include apoptosis, inflammation, ischemia related to prolonged hypoperfusion, and degeneration secondary to deafferentation (Bramlett & Dietrich, 2007).

Table 3-4. Long-Term Effects of TBI on Cerebral Blood Flow in Humans and Rats

Injury	Survival	Results	References
		Humans	
sTBI	6.8 yrs	↓ CBF in frontal & temporal cortical gray matter, but not in caudate, putamen or thalamus	(Terayama et al., 1991)
sTBI GCS 7–10	4.8 yrs	↓ CBF in cortical gray & white matter at 1st measurement; ↓ CBF in cortical gray matter, normal white matter CBF at 2nd measurement (2.7 ± 0.7 yrs later)	(Terayama, 1993)
mTBI; GCS > 13	< 1 yr	CBF abnormalities (^{99m}TC-HMPAO SPECT) in 73/136 (54%) pts. within 4 weeks post-TBI (83% within 1 week);12/136 (9%) of pts had CBF abnormalities at 12 months post-TBI	(Jacobs, 1996)
mTBI; GCS > 13	2 yrs	↓ thalamic blood flow (arterial spin labeled MRI) vs. aged matched controls 2 years post-injury	(Ge, 2009)
		Rats	
Mod CCI	1 yr	↓ CBF (MRI) in injured cortex (80% below sham), 52% & 67% reductions in CBF in ipsilateral cortical & hippocampal CBF. No other significant differences in CBF.	(Kochanek, Hendrich, Dixon, Schiding, Williams, & Ho, 2002)
Mod lFPI	8 mths	↓ CBF in cortex ipsilaterally & hippocampus bilaterally	(Hayward, Immonen, Tuunanen, Ndode-Ekane, Grohn, & Pitkanen, 2010)

CBF—cerebral blood flow; CCI—controlled cortical impact; lFPI—lateral fluid percussion injury; mTBI—mild traumatic brain injury; sTBI—severe traumatic brain injury; ↓—significantly reduced vs age-matched controls or sham animals

Traumatic central nervous system injury often results in chronic disability with lasting cognitive and motor disorders (Levin et al., 1987). However, what remains uncertain is whether chronic damage is due to long-term consequences of the initial traumatic insult, i.e., Wallerian degeneration (Adams, Graham, & Jennett, 2000; Graham, Adams, Nicoll, Maxwell, & Gennarelli, 1995), or progressive secondary injury (Bramlett and Dietrich, 2002; Bramlett, Kraydieh, Green, & Dietrich, 1997b; Dixon et al., 1999; Smith et al., 1997). Ng et al. (2008) used MRI to evaluate 14 patients 4.5 months and 29 months post-moderate to severe TBI. In 10 individuals, the MRIs showed progression of encephalomalacia. Greenberg, Mikulis, Ng, DeSouza and Green (2008) also used diffusion tensor imaging to study a similar cohort of 13 patients 4.5 months and 29 months following their moderate-severe TBI. The studies showed the progression of white matter injury in the frontal and temporal lobes bilaterally. Clinical (Anderson & Bigler, 1995) and experimental (Bramlett & Dietrich, 2002; Dixon et al., 1999, Smith et al., 1997) research has demonstrated progressive CNS atrophy after TBI. Anderson and Bigler (1995) reported on widespread white and gray matter atrophy in TBI patients, and observed that the extent of ventricular expansion positively correlated with severe memory deficits. Furthermore, the dilation of the anterior horn of the lateral ventricle was associated with atrophy of the corpus callosum (Anderson & Bigler, 1995). MRI images recorded as long as 603 days after TBI revealed significant atrophy of the head of the hippocampus. Interestingly, the atrophy involved both hippocampal heads regardless of the location of the primary injury (Ariza et al., 2006). A positive correlation between cognitive outcome and extent of brain atrophy has been observed in other studies of the chronic effects of TBI (Cullum & Bigler, 1986, Reider-Groswasser, Cohen, Costeff, & Groswasser, 1993).

Johnson, Stewart & Smith (2012), studied post mortem brains of 39 long term survivors of a single TBI and matched them to similar uninjured controls. Amyloid-beta plaques were also much more common in the TBI group. Neurofibrillary tangles were very rare in the uninjured controls, especially the young individuals; whereas interestingly, they were abundant in one-third of the TBIs. This suggests that the deposition of tau protein may also occur in a subset of individuals with a single TBI.

Mechanisms of Traumatic Chronic Neurodegeneration

Apoptosis. Although apoptosis and necrosis describe morphological characteristics of dying cells rather than mechanisms of cell death, in general, the terms are used to describe pathophysiological mechanisms as well. Apoptosis can be triggered by at least two pathways: usually termed caspase-independent and caspase-dependent, and caspase-dependent apoptosis can be subdivided into intrinsic and extrinsic pathways (Kunz, Dirnagl, & Mergenthaler, 2010; Zhang, Chen, Jenkins, Kochanek, & Clark, 2005; Lo, Moskowitz, & Jacobs, 2005). It has been estimated that, after TBI, caspase-dependent, caspase independent and necrotic mechanisms each contribute to a third of the cell death (Zhang et al., 2005).

Extrinsic, caspase-dependent apoptosis occurs when extracellular tumor necrosis factor (TNF), Fas ligand (FasL) or TNF-related apoptosis inducing ligand (TRAIL) bind with the cell surface "death receptors" TNF receptor, CD/Fas or DR4/5, respectively (Zhang et al., 2005; Kunz et al., 2010). Surface receptor binding by their respective ligands is followed by the assembly of a cytoplasmic death-inducing signaling complex (DISC).

Intrinsic, caspase-dependent apoptosis is a consequence of mitochondrial membrane damage and depolarization due to trauma-induced stressor such as increases in glutamate and intracellular Ca^{2+}, reactive oxygen species and/or DNA damage. Mitochondrial membrane depolarization and the formation of the mitochondrial permeability transition pore release cytochrome c into the cytoplasm. Cytoplasmic cytochrome c interacts with apoptotic protease activating factor-1 (Apaf-1), ATP and pro-caspase-9 to form an "apoptosome" (Kunz et al., 2010; Lo et al., 2005; Zhang et al., 2005).

The intrinsic and extrinsic pathways both result in the activation of initiator caspases (e.g., caspases 8, 9, 10) that activate the "executioner" caspases 7, 9 and 3 (Kunz et al., 2010; Zhang et al., 2005). Proteolysis by the executioner caspases leads to DNA fragmentation, inhibition of DNA repair enzymes (e.g., poly(ADP-ribose) polymerase, PARP), and degradation of cytoskeletal proteins.

In addition to the release of cytochrome c, mitochondrial membrane depolarization contributes to caspase-independent apoptosis through the release of apoptosis-inducing factor (AIF). Once released and activated, AIF translocates to the nucleus where it causes DNA fragmentation (Zhang et al., 2005).

Apoptosis can be identified by the presence of terminal deoxynucleotidyl transferase-mediated dUTP-biotin nick-end labeled (TUNEL) cells or with Annexin V, which stains phosphatidyl serine that has translocated to the outside of cell membranes (Galluzzi et al., 2009; Kunz et al., 2010). Evidence of acute, trauma-induced apoptosis has been observed in the brains or

brain specimens of humans (Clark et al., 1999; Clark et al., 2000a; Zhang et al., 2003; Zhang et al., 2005; Smith et al., 2000) and experimental animals (Zhang et al., 2005; Clark et al., 2000b; Zhang et al., 2002). Although, in most cases, evidence of apoptosis was detected in samples examined within days of TBI, there are reports of apoptosis years after TBI in humans. Williams, Raghupathi, MacKinnon, McIntosh, Saatman, and Graham (2001) observed TUNEL staining in cortical white matter in patients up to 12 months post-TBI. Wilson, Raghupathi, Saatman, MacKinnon, McIntosh, and Graham (2004) reported DNA fragmentation in brain specimens studied more than two years after injury. These studies, viewed in conjunction with evidence of long-term apoptosis after TBI or SCI in experimental animals (Beattie, Hermann, Rogers, & Bresnahan, 2002), suggest that apoptotic cell death may continue from months to years after TBI.

Table 3-5. Long-Term Effects of Traumatic Brain Injury (TBI) or Spinal Cord Injury (SCI) in Humans: Apoptosis and Inflammation

N	Survival (post-TBI)	Results	Reference
18 TBI 15 con.	< 12 mths	↑TUNEL positive cells in white & gray matter, including hippocampus; in gray matter, most resembled neurons morphologically; ↑CD68 & GFAP IR in white & gray matter	(Williams et al., 2001)
24 SCI 26 con.	> 12 mths	↑ serum levels of IL-2 & TNFα	(Hayes et al., 2002)
25 TBI 5 con.	1 hr–6 mths	↑ CD14 IR positive perivascular & parenchymal microglia/ macrophages at injury site & surrounding brain	(Beschorner, 2002)
15 TBI 15 con.	Grp 1: 4–8 wks Grp 2: 3–6 mths Grp 3: 1.5–2.4 yrs	↑TUNEL positive cells in cortico-spinal tracts & medial lemniscus in TBI pts.; ↑CD68 positive cells in TBI pts, Grps 1&2 > Grp 3; significant correlation between TUNEL & CD68 positive cells	(Wilson et al., 2004)
31 TBI 9 con.	4 wks → 22 yrs	↑ GFAP, CR3/45 & CD68 in thalamus of TBI pts.	(Maxwell et al., 2006)
17 SCI 4 con.	< 12 mths	Macrophages, reactive astrocytes & B-APP positive axons surrounding lesions	(Fleming et al., 2006)
10 TBI 22 con.	11 mths → 17 yrs	↑ microglial activation (PK PET) in thalami, putamen, occipital cortices & internal capsules	(Ramlackhansingh et al., 2011)

Con.—control; GFAP—glial fibrillary acidic protein; Grp—group; IR—immunoreactivity; mths—months; PK PET—[^{11}C] (R)PK11195 positron emission tomography; TUNEL—TdT-mediated UTP nick end labeling; wks—weeks; ⊠—increased vs. control

CD14 IR—macrophages/activated microglia
CD68 IR—macrophages/activated microglia
CR3/43 IR—macrophages/activated microglia
GFAP IR—astrocytes
PK binding—activated microglia
TUNEL—DNA fragmentation

Genetic changes affecting cellular demise by apoptosis has also been proposed as a mechanism in delayed radiation vasculopathy syndrome (O'Connor & Mayberg, 2000).

Inflammation

After TBI, inflammation begins with opening of the blood-brain barrier, activation of microglia and astrocytes, and the release of pro-inflammatory cytokines (e.g., IL-1α, IL-1β, TNFα, Interferon γ, IL-6) (Cederberg & Siesjo, 2010; Helmy, Simoni, Guilfoyle, Carpenter, & Hutchinson, 2011). Activated microglia and astrocytes and neurons release endothelial adhesion molecules (e.g., intracellular adhesion molecule-1, vascular cell adhesion molecule), chemotactic chemokines, and reactive oxygen and nitrogen species (Cederberg & Siesjo, 2010). The actions of the endothelial adhesion molecules and chemokines result in an influx of blood-borne macrophages and lymphocytes. This is followed by the release of cytokines, nitric oxide and vascular endothelial growth factor, and extracellular edema and complement activation (Cederberg & Siesjo, 2010; Helmy et al., 2011). Details of inflammation after traumatic brain and spinal cord injury can be found in several excellent reviews (Amor, Puentes, Baker, & van der Valk, 2010; Ankeny & Popovich, 2009; Cederberg & Siesjo, 2010; Griffiths, Gasque, & Neal, 2009; Helmy et al., 2011; Pajoohesh-Ganji & Byrnes, 2011; Ziebell & Morganti-Kossman, 2010).

Inflammation occurs within hours and persists for months to years after TBI (Helmy et al., 2011; Gentleman et al., 2004; Engel, Plesnila, Prehn, & Henshall, 2011). Although there are few studies of inflammation after TBI that included both acute and long-term sampling times, Beschorner et al. (2004) reported increases in the numbers of parenchymal activated microglia (CD14 immunoreactivity) in patients one to two days or six months post-injury. Williams et al. (2001) observed activated microglia and astrocytes (CD68 & GFAP immunoreactivity, respectively) in patients surviving for two to four weeks or three to six months post-injury. Activated microglia (CD68) were present in white matter tracts (cortico-spinal & external capsule) in patients surviving four to eight

weeks or 1.5 to 2.4 years after TBI (Wilson et al., 2004). Active inflammation 17 years after TBI was identified using positron emission tomography and ^{11}C-(R)-PK11195, a ligand that binds to binds to a protein expressed by mitochondria of activated microglia (Ramlackhansingh et al., 2011). Maxwell, MacKinnon, Smith, McIntosh, and Smith (2006) observed immunoreactivity to glial fibrillary acidic protein (GFAP, reactive astrocytes), CD68 antibody (macrophages and microglia), and CR3/43 antibody (B cells, macrophages and activated microglia) in the thalamus of patients surviving up to 22 years after TBI. Together, these reports indicate that inflammation begins soon after and continues for decades after TBI.

Chronic Cerebral Hypoperfusion

Cerebral blood flow is reduced acutely after fluid percussion (DeWitt, Jenkins, Wei, Lutz, Becker and Kontos, 1986; Yamakami & McIntosh, 1989 &1991), controlled cortical impact (Bryan, Cherian, & Robertson, 1995; Cherian, Robertson, Contant, & Bryan, 1994), and impact acceleration (Prat, Markiv, Dujovny, & Misra, 1997) TBI in experimental animals. Although in most head-injured patients, CBF is near normal while the cerebral metabolic rate for oxygen ($CMRO_2$) is reduced (Obrist, Langfitt, Jaggi, Cruz, & Gennarelli, 1984), there appears to be a sub-population of patients who experience significant cerebral hypoperfusion in the first few days after TBI (Bouma, Muizelaar, Choi, Newlon, & Young, 1991; Bouma, Muizelaar, Stringer, Choi, Fatouros, & Young, 1992). Severe TBI in humans is associated with long-term reductions in CBF. John Stirling Meyer's group reported significant reductions in CBF (stable xenon CT-CBF) in frontal and parietal gray matter, but not in sub-cortical gray matter (e.g., caudate, putamen, thalamus) in patients 6.8 years after severe TBI (Terayama, Meyer, Kawamura, & Weathers, 1991). In a later study from the same investigators, Terayama, Meyer, Kawamura, and Weathers (1993) observed significant reductions in CBF in cortical gray and white matter 4.8 years after severe TBI. Subsequent CBF measurements in the same patients 2.7 ± 0.7 years later revealed significantly reduced gray matter perfusion but CBF in white matter returned to nearly baseline levels. The restoration of white matter perfusion correlated with improvements in cognitive performance (cognitive capacity screening exam scores) (Terayama et al., 1993). Mild TBI also is associated with long-term reductions in CBF in some patients. Jacobs et al. (1996) reported significantly reduced CBF one year after mTBI in 9/136 (9%) of patients in whom perfusion was measured using ^{99m}TC- hexamethylpropylene amine oxime single photon emission tomography (^{99m}TC-HMPAO SPECT). Ge et al. (2009) reported significant reductions in thalamic CBF (arterial spin labeled MRI) in patients two years after mTBI. These observations indicate mTBI results in cerebral hypoperfusion for at least one to two years post-injury while severe TBI may lead to hypoperfusion lasting seven years or more.

The nature by which a brain injury can impact other organs is not known; however, there clearly is an indirect effect. Mirzayan and colleagues (2008) subjected mice to a controlled cortical impact brain injury and sacrificed them at 96 hours. Histopathologic changes were found in the liver and lung, suggesting that an isolated TBI can lead to the migration of immune incompetent cells to the peripheral organs, potentially leading to their dysfunction. The immune response is significantly impaired acutely following a TBI ("post-traumatic immune paralysis") and may be associated with the high prevalence of infections in patients who sustain a TBI (Kox, Pompe, Pickkers, Hoedemaekers, van Vugt, & van der Hoeven, 2008).

Polio and subsequent post-polio syndrome (PPS) may well serve as a model for chronic post-traumatic disease (CPD). A 1987 National Health Interview Survey estimated that after a period of neurologic and functional stability, of the 640,000 survivors of polio, approximately half had new late manifestations of the disease, with an average latency of 35 years. Fatigue and weakness were the most common symptoms (Jubelt, Drucker, & Younger, 1999).

In the PPS patient, the terminal axons of the surviving motor neurons sprouted in an attempt to reinnervate muscle fibers that had lost innervation from non-surviving motor neurons (Dalakas, 1995). The phenomenon was captured by single fiber EMG measuring increased jitter in these patients (Jubelt & Agre, 2000). Jitter measures the time difference of the depolarization of two muscle fiber potentials within the same motor unit upon in successive firings. Jitter increases after an attack of polio and can persist indefinitely, suggesting an ongoing process of denervation and reinnervation (Jubelt et al., 1999). Although the jitter in the axons of the peripheral nervous system cannot be measured within the axons of the brain, the concept of ongoing denervation and reinnervation within those axons certainly remains a possible explanation for the varying symptomatology displayed over time by individuals with a TBI. This "impaired transmission model" may partly explain why some individuals with a TBI have benefited from anticholinesterase medications (Silver et al., 2006). This ongoing process of denervation and reinnervation can be stressing to the neuronal cell bodies that may not be able to keep up with the required metabolic demands, thus causing them to fail. It is certainly possible that "injured" neurons may have a shorter than normal lifespan, and may succumb earlier to the normal aging process (Dalakas, 1995).

Summary

Historically, a TBI has been considered an injury that is either fatal, or after a period of recovery, becomes static. It is clear that a brain injury results in a chronic condition that is disease-causative and disease-accelerative. Patients, their families, and their caregivers must be educated and vigilant for neurologic changes over their lifetime. A TBI must be viewed by clinicians and researchers as an ongoing chronic process in order to develop and affect the best possible treatments for this disease.

Acknowledgments

The authors are grateful for support from the Moody Center for Traumatic Brain & Spinal Cord Injury Research/*Mission Connect* and for editorial assistance from Andrew Hall and Patrick Enos in the Office of Grants & Manuscript Preparation in the Department of Anesthesiology of The University of Texas Medical Branch.

References

Aarabi, B., Taghipour, M., Haghnegahdar, A., Farokhi, M. & Mobley, L. (2000). Prognostic factors in the occurrence of posttraumatic epilepsy after penetrating head injury suffered during military service. *Neurosurgical Focus, 8*, e1.

Adams, J. H., Graham, D. I., & Jennett, B. (2000). The neuropathology of the vegetative state after an acute brain insult. *Brain, 123*(7), 1327–1338.

Agha, A., Rogers, B., Sherlock, M., O'Kelly, P., Tormey, W., Phillips, J., et al. (2004). Anterior pituitary dysfunction in survivors of traumatic brain injury. *The Journal of Clinical Endocrinology & Metabolism, 89*, 4929–4936.

Agha, A., & Thompson, C. J. (2005). High risk of hypogonadism after traumatic brain injury: clinical implications. *Pituitary, 8*, 245–249.

Agha, A., & Thompson, C. J. (2006). Anterior pituitary dysfunction following traumatic brain injury (TBI). *Clinical Endocrinology, 64*, 481–488.

Aimaretti, G., Ambrosio, M. R., Di, S. C., Gasperi, M., Cannavo, S., Scaroni, C., et al. (2005). Residual pituitary function after brain injury-induced hypopituitarism: a prospective 12-month study. *The Journal of Clinical Endocrinology & Metabolism, 90*, 6085–6092.

Alves, W., Macciocchi, S., & Barth, J. (1993). Postconcussive symptoms after uncomplicated mild head injury. *Journal of Head Trauma & Rehabilitation, 8*, 48–59.

Amor, S., Puentes, F., Baker, D., & van der Valk, P. (2010). Inflammation in neurodegenerative diseases. *Immunology, 129*, 154–169.

Anderson, C. V., & Bigler, E. D. (1995). Ventricular dilation, cortical atrophy, and neuropsychological outcome following traumatic brain injury. *Journal of Neuropsychiatry & Clinical Neurosciences, 7*, 42–48.

Anderson, V. A., Catroppa, C., Morse, S. A., & Haritou, F.(1999). Functional memory skills following traumatic brain injury in young children. *Pediatric Rehabilitation, 3*, 159–166.

Ankeny, D. P., & Popovich, P. G. (2009). Mechanisms and implications of adaptive immune responses after traumatic spinal cord injury. *Neuroscience, 158*, 1112–1121.

Annegers, J. F., Hauser, W. A., Coan, S. P. & Rocca, W. A. (1998). A population-based study of seizures after traumatic brain injuries. *The New England Journal of Medicine, 338*, 20–24.

Aquilani, R., Iadarola, P., Boschi, F., Pistarini, C., Arcidiaco, P., & Contardi, A. (2003). Reduced plasma levels of tyrosine, precursor of brain catecholamines, and of essential amino acids in patients with severe traumatic brain injury after rehabilitation. *Archives of Physical Medicine and Rehabilitation, 84*, 1258–1265.

Aquilani, R., Viglio, S., Iadarola, P., Guarnaschelli, C., Arrigoni, N., Fugazza, G., et al. (2000). Peripheral plasma amino acid abnormalities in rehabilitation patients with severe brain injury. *Archives of Physical Medicine and Rehabilitation, 81*, 176–181.

Ariza, M., Serra-Grabulosa, J. M., Junque, C., Ramirez, B., Mataro, M., Poca, A., et al. (2006). Hippocampal head atrophy after traumatic brain injury. *Neuropsychologia, 44*, 1956–1961.

Barnes, D., Krueger, K., Byers, A., Diaz-Arrastia, R., &Yaffe, K. (2011). Traumatic brain injury and risk of dementia in older veterans. *Poster presented at the Alzheimer's Association International Conference.* France: Paris.

Bay, B., & McLean, S. A. (2007). Mild traumatic brain injury: An update for advanced practice nurses. *Journal of Neuroscience Nursing, 39*, 43–51.

Bazarian, J. J., Wong, T., Harris, M., Leahey, N., Mookerjee, S., & Dombovy, M. (1999). Epidemiology and predictors of post-concussive syndrome after minor head injury in an emergency population. *Brain Injury, 13*, 173–189.

Beattie, M. S., Hermann, G. E., Rogers, R. C., & Bresnahan, J. C. (2002). Cell death in models of spinal cord injury. In L. McKerracher, G. Doucet, S. Rossignol (Ed.), *Progress in Brain Research* (pp. 37–47). Amsterdam Netherlands: Elsevier.

Belanger, H. G., Curtiss, G., Demery, J. A., Lebowitz, B. K. & Vanderploeg, R. D. (2005a). Factors moderating neuropsychological outcomes following mild traumatic brain injury: A meta-analysis. *Journal of the International Neuropsychlogical Society, 11*, 215–227.

Belanger, H. G., &Vanderploeg, R. D. (2005b). The neuropsychological impact of sport related concussion: A meta-analysis. *Journal of the International Neuropsychological Society, 11*, 345–357.

Bemstein, D. M. (2002). Information processing difficulty long after self-reported concussion. *Journal of the International Neuropsychological Society, 8*, 673–682.

Beschorner, R., Nguyen, T. D., Gozalan, F., Pedal, I., Mattern, R., Schluesener, H. J., et al. (2002). CD14 expression by activated parenchymal microglia/macrophages and infiltrating monocytes following human traumatic brain injury. *Acta Neuropathologica, 103*, 541–549.

Borsheim, E., Bui, Q. U., & Wolfe, R. R. (2007). Plasma amino acid concentrations during late rehabilitation in patients with traumatic brain injury. *Archives of Physical Medicine and Rehabilitation, 88*, 234–238.

Bouma, G. J., Muizelaar, J. P., Choi, S. C., Newlon, P. G., & Young, H. F. (1991). Cerebral circulation and metabolism after severe traumatic brain injury: the elusive role of ischemia. *Journal of Neurosurgery, 75*, 685–693.

Bouma, G. J., Muizelaar, J. P., Stringer, W. A., Choi, S. C., Fatouros, P., & Young, H. F. (1992). Ultra-early evaluation of regional cerebral blood flow in severely head-injured patients using xenon-enhanced computerized tomography. *Journal of Neurosurgery, 77*, 360–368.

Bower, J. H., Maraganore, D. M., Peterson, B. J., McDonnell, S. K., Ahlskog, J. E., & Rocca, W. A. (2003). Head trauma preceding PD: A case-control study. *Neurology, 60*, 1610–1615.

Bramlett, H. M., & Dietrich, W. D. (2002). Quantitative structural changes in white and gray matter 1 year following traumatic brain injury in rats. *Acta Neuropatholigica, 103*, 607–614.

Bramlett, H. M., & Dietrich, W. D. (2003). Synuclein aggregation: possible role in traumatic brain injury. *Experimental Neurology, 184*, 27–30.

Bramlett, H. M., & Dietrich, W. D. (2004). Pathophysiology of cerebral ischemia and brain trauma: Similarities and differences. *Journal of Cerebral Blood Flow and Metabolism, 24*, 133–150.

Bramlett, H. M., & Dietrich, W. D. (2007). Progressive damage after brain and spinal cord injury: pathomechanisms and treatment strategies. *Progress in Brain Research, 161*, 125–141.

Bramlett, H. M., Dietrich, W. D., Green, E. J., & Busto, R. (1997a). Chronic histopathological consequences of fluid percussion brain injury in rats: effects of post-traumatic hypothermia. *Acta Neuropathologica. 93*, 190–199.

Bramlett, H. M., Kraydieh, S., Green, E. J., & Dietrich, W. D. (1997b). Temporal and regional patterns of axonal damage following traumatic brain injury: a beta-amyloid precursor protein immunocytochemical study in rats. *Journal of Neuropathology & Experimental Neurology, 56*, 1132–1141.

Braak, H., & Braak, E. (1991). Neuropathological stageing of Alzheimer-related changes. *Acta Neuropathologica, 82*, 239–259.

Brown, A. W., Leibson, C. L., Malec, J. F., Perkins, P. K., Diehl, N. N. & Larson, D. R. (2004). Long-term survival after traumatic brain injury: a population-based analysis. *NeuroRehabilitation, 19*, 37–43.

Bruns, J. J., &Jagoda, A. S. (2009). Mild traumatic brain injury. *Mount Sinai Journal of Medcine, 76*, 129–137.

Bryan, R. M., Cherian, L., & Robertson, C. S. (1995). Regional cerebral blood flow after controlled cortical impact injury in rats. *Anesthesia & Analgesia, 80*, 687–695.

Carro, E., Trejo, J. L., Gomez-Isla, T., LeRoth, D., & Torres-Aleman, I. (2002). Serum insulin-like growth factor I regulates brain amyloid-β levels. *Natural Medicine, 8*, 1390–1397.

Carroll, L. J., Cassidy, J. D., Peloso, P. M., Borg, J., von Holst, H., Holm, L., et al. (2004). Prognosis for mild traumatic brain injury: Results of the WHO Collaborating Centre Task Force on mild traumatic brain injury. *Journal of Rehabilitation Medicine, 43*, 84–105.

Castriotta, R. J., Wilde, M. C., Lai, J. M., Atanasov, S., Masel, B. E., & Kuna, S. T. (2007). Prevalence and consequences of sleep disorders in traumatic brain injury. *Journal of Clinical Sleep Medicine, 3*, 349–356.

CDC. (2003). *Report to Congress on Mild Traumatic Brain Injury in the United States: Steps To Prevent a Serious Public Health Problem. Prevention CfDCa (Ed.).* Atlanta: Centers for Disease Control and Prevention.,

Cederberg, D., & Siesjo, P. (2010). What has inflammation to do with traumatic brain injury? *Child's Nervous System, 26*, 221–226.

Chen, J. K., Johnston, K. M., Frey, S., Petrides, M., Worsley, K., & Ptito, A. (2004). Functional abnormalities in symptomatic concussed athletes: An fMRI study. *Neuroimage, 22*, 68–82.

Chen, J. K., Johnston, K. M., Petrides, M., Worsley, K., & Ptito, A. (2008). Recovery from mild head injury in sports: Evidence from serial functional magnetic resonance imaging studies in male athletes. *Clinical Journal of Sport Medicine, 18*, 241–247.

Chen, Y.-H., Keller, J. J., Kang, J. H., & Lin, H. C. (2012). Association between traumatic brain injury and the subsequent risk of brain cancer. *Journal of Neurotrauma, 29*, 1328–1333.

Cherian, L., Robertson, C. S., Contant, C. F., & Bryan, R. M. (1994). Lateral cortical impact injury in rats: Cerebrovascular effects of varying depth of cortical deformation and impact velocity. *Journal of Neurotrauma 11*, 573–585.

Chua, K., Chuo, A., & Kong, K. H. (2003). Urinary incontinence after traumatic brain injury: incidence, outcomes and correlates. *Brain Injury. 17*, 469–478.

Clark, R. S., Kochanek, P. M., Chen, M., Watkins, S. C., Marion, D. W., Chen, J., et al. (1999). Increases in Bcl-2 and cleavage of Caspase-1 and Caspase-3 in human brain after head injury. *The FASEB Journal, 13*, 813–821.

Clark, R. S. B., Kochanek, P. M., Adelson, P. D., Bell, M. J., Carcillo, J. A., Chen, M., et al. (2000a). Increases in bcl-2 protein in cerebrospinal fluid and evidence for programmed cell death in infants and children after severe traumatic brain injury. *Journal of Pediatrics, 137*, 197–204.

Clark, R. S. B., Kochanek, P. M., Watkins, S. C., Chen, M., Dixon, C. E., Seidberg, N. A., et al. (2000b). Caspase-3 mediated neuronal death after traumatic brain injury in rats. Journal of Neurochemistry, 74, 740–753.

Collins, M. W., Lovell, M. R., Iverson, G. L., Cantu, R. C., Maroon, J. C. & Field, M. (2002). Cumulative effects of concussion in high school athletes. Neurosurgery, 51, 1175–1181.

Cullum, C. M., & Bigler, E. D. (1986). Ventricle size, cortical atrophy and the relationship with neuropsychological status in closed head injury: a quantitative analysis. Journal of Clinical and Experimental, 8, 437–452.

Dalakas, M. C. (1995). Pathogenetic mechanisms of post-polio syndrome: morphological, electrophysiological, virological, and immunological correlations. Annals of the New York Academy of Sciences, 753, 167–185.

Deb, S., Lyons, I., & Koutzoukis, C. (1998). Neuropsychiatric sequelae one year after a minor head injury. Journal of Neurology, Neurosurgery & Psychiatry, 65, 899–902.

DeKosky, S. T., Ikonomovic, M. D., & Gandy, S. (2010). Traumatic brain injury—football, warfare, and long-term effects. The New England Journal of Medicine, 363, 1293–1296.

DeStrooper, B., Saftig, P., Craessaerts, K., Vanderstichele, H., Guhde, G., Annaert, W., et al. (1998). Deficiency of presenilin-1 inhibits the normal cleavage of amyloid precursor protein. Nature, 391, 387–390.

DeWitt, D. S., Jenkins, L. W., Wei, E. P., Lutz, H., Becker, D. P., & Kontos, H. A. (1986). Effects of fluid-percussion brain injury on regional cerebral blood flow and pial arteriolar diameter. Journal of Neurosurgery, 64, 787–794.

Dikmen, S. S., Machamer, J. E., Winn, H. R., & Temkin, N. R. (1995). Neuropsychological outcome at 1-year post head injury. Neuropsychology. 9, 80–90.

Dixon, C. E., Kochanek, P. M., Yan, H. Q., Schiding, J. K., Griffith, R. G., Baum, E., et al. (1999). One-year study of spatial memory performance, brain morphology, and cholinergic markers after moderate controlled cortical impact in rats. Journal of Neurotrauma, 16, 109–122.

Dunnett, S. B., & Bjorklund, A. (1999). Prospects for new restorative and neuroprotective treatments in Parkinson's disease. Nature, 399, A32–A39.

Edwards, O. M., & Clark, J. D. A. (1986). Post-traumatic hypopituitarism. Medicine, 65, 281–290.

Elovic, E. P., Simone, L. K., & Zafonte, R. (2004). Outcome assessment for spasticity management in the patient with traumatic brain injury: the state of the art. Journal of Head Trauma Rehabilitation, 19, 155–177.

Engel, T., Plesnila, N., Prehn, J. H., & Henshall, D. C. (2011). In vivo contributions of BH3-only proteins to neuronal death following seizures, ischemia, and traumatic brain injury. Journal of Cerebral Blood Flow & Metabolism, 31, 1196–1210.

Englander, J., Bushnik, T., Duong, T. T., Cifu, D. X., Zafonte, R., Wright, J., et al. (2003). Analyzing risk factors for late posttraumatic seizures: a prospective, multicenter investigation. Archives of Physical Medicine & Rehabilitation, 84, 365–373.

Epstein, D. (2010). The Damage Done. Sports Illustrated, 113, 42–47.

Feany, M. B., Ksiezak-Reding, H., Liu, W-K., Vincent, I., Yen, S-H. C. & Dickson, D. W. (1995). Epitope expression and hyperphosphorylation of tau protein in corticobasal degeneration: differentiation from progressive supranuclear palsy. Acta Neuropathologica, 90, 37–43.

Flament, S., Delacourte, A., Verny, M., Hauw, J. J., & Javoy-Agid, F. (1991). Abnormal Tau proteins in progressive supranuclear palsy. Similarities and differences with the neurofibrillary degeneration of the Alzheimer type. Acta Neuropathologica, 81, 591–596.

Fleming, J. C., Norenberg, M. D., Ramsay, D. A., Dekaban, G. A., Marcillo, A. E., Saenz, A. D., et al. (2006). The cellular inflammatory response in human spinal cords after injury. Brain, 129, 3249–3269.

Fleminger, S. (2008). Long-term psychiatric disorders after traumatic brain injury. European Journal of Anaesthesiology—Supplement, 42, 123–130.

Forman, M. S., Trojanowski, J. Q. & Lee, V. M. (2004). Neurodegenerative diseases: a decade of discoveries paves the way for therapeutic breakthroughs. Natural Medicine, 10, 1055–1063.

Foxx-Orenstein, A., Kolakowsky-Hayner, S., Marwitz, J. H., Cifu, D. X., Dunbar, A., Englander, J., et al. (2003). Incidence, risk factors, and outcomes of fecal incontinence after acute brain injury: findings from the Traumatic Brain Injury Model Systems national database. Archives of Physical Medicine and Rehabilitation, 84, 231–237.

Francis, P. T., Sims, N. R., Procter, A. W., & Bowen, D. M. (1993). Cortical pyramidal neurone loss may cause glutamatergic hypoactivity and cognitive impairment in Alzheimer's disease: investigative and therapeutic perspectives. Journal of Neurochemistry, 60, 1589–1604.

Friedland, J. F., & Dawson, D. R. (2001). Function after motor vehicle accidents: a prospective study of mild head injury and posttraumatic stress. Journal of Nervous and Mental Disease, 189, 426–434.

Funk, P. (1980). *Funk and Wagnalls Standard Dictionary*. New York: Lippincott and Crowell.

Galluzzi, L., Aaronson, S. A., Abrams, J., Alnemri, E. S., Andrews, D. W., Baehrecke, E. H., et al. (2009). Guidelines for the use and interpretation of assays for monitoring cell death in higher eukaryotes. *Cell Death & Differentiation*, 16, 1093–1107.

Garber, J. R., & Bergmann Khoury, C. (2009). Treatment of Hyper- and Hypothyroidism. *Review of Endocrinology*, 3, 20–23.

Gavett, B. E., Stern, R. A., & McKee, A. C. (2011). Chronic traumatic encephalopathy: A potential late effect of sport-related concussive and subconcussive head trauma. *Clinical Journal of Sports Medicine*, 30, 1799–188.

Ge, Y., Pate, L. M. B., Chen, Q., Grossman, E. J., Zhang, K., Miles, L., et al. (2009). Assessment of thalamic perfusion in patients with mild traumatic brain injury by true FISP arterial spin labelling MR imaging at 3T. *Brain Injury*, 23, 666–674.

Gentleman, S. M., Leclercq, P. D., Moyes, L., Graham, D. I., Smith, C., Griffin, W. S. T., et al. (2004). Long-term intracerebral inflammatory response after traumatic brain injury *Forensic Science International*, 146, 97–104.

Goldman, S. M., Tanner, C. M., Oakes, D., Bhudhikanok, G. S., Gupta, A., & Langston, J. W. (2006). Head Injury and Parkinson's Disease Risk in Twins. *Annals of Neurology*, 60, 65–72.

Goldstein, L. E., Fisher, A. M., Tagge, C. A,, Zhang, X.-L., Velisek, L., Sullivan, J. A., et al. (2012). Chronic traumatic encephalopathy in blast-exposed military veterans and a blast neurotrauma mouse model. *Science Translational Medicine*, 4, 134ra60.

Graham, D. I., Adams, J. H., Nicoll, J. A., Maxwell, W. L., & Gennarelli, T. A. (1995). The nature, distribution, and causes of traumatic brain injury. *Brain Pathology*, 5, 397–406.

Greenberg, G., Mikulis, D. J., Ng, K., DeSouza, D., & Green, R. E. (2008). Use of Diffusion Tensor Imaging to Examine Subacute White Matter Injury Progression in Moderate to Severe Traumatic Brain Injury. *Archives of Physical Medicine and Rehabilitation*, 89, S45–S50.

Griffiths, M. R., Gasque, P., & Neal, J. W. (2009). The multiple roles of the innate immune system in the regulation of apoptosis and inflammation in the brain. *Journal of Neuropathology & Experimental Neurology*, 68, 217–226.

Guskiewicz, K. M., McCrea, M., Marshall, S. W., Cantu, R. C., Randolph, C., Barr, W., et al. (2003). Cumulative effects associated with recurrent concussion in collegiate football players: The NCAA Concussion Study. *JAMA*, 290, 2549–2555.

Hanks, R. A., Temkin, N., Machamer, J, &. Dikmen, S. S. (1999). Emotional and behavioral adjustment after traumatic brain injury. *Achives of Physical Medicine and Rehabilitation*, 80, 991–997.

Harrison-Felix, C., Whiteneck, G., DeVivo, M., Hammond, F. M. & Jha, A. (2004). Mortality following rehabilitation in the Traumatic Brain Injury Model Systems of Care. *Neurorehabilitation*, 19, 45–54.

Harrison-Felix, C., Whiteneck, G., DeVivo, M. J., Hammond, F. M. & Jha, A. (2006). Causes of death following 1 year postinjury among individuals with traumatic brain injury. *The Journal of Head Trauma Rehabilitation*, 21, 22–33.

Harrison-Felix, C. L., Whiteneck, G. G., Jha, A., DeVivo, M. J., Hammond, F. M., & Hart, D. M. (2009). Mortality over four decades after traumatic brain injury rehabilitation: A retrospective cohort study. *Archives of Physical Medicine and Rehabilitation*, 90, 1506–1513.

Hauser, W. A., Annegers, J. F. & Kurland, L. T. (1991). Prevalence of epilepsy in Rochester, Minnesota: 1940–1980. *Epilepsia*, 32, 429–445.

Hayes, K. C., Hull, T. C., Delaney, G. A., Potter, P. J., Sequeira, K. A., Campbell, K., et al. (2002). Elevated serum titers of proinflammatory cytokines and CNS autoantibodies in patients with chronic spinal cord injury. *Journal of Neurotrauma*, 19, 753–761.

Hayward, N. M. E. A., Immonen, R., Tuunanen, P. I., Ndode-Ekane, X. E., Grohn, O., & Pitkanen, A. (2010). Association of chronic vascular changes with functional outcome after traumatic brain injury in rats. *Journal of Neurotrauma*, 27, 2203–2219.

Helmy, A., De Simoni, M. G., Guilfoyle, M. R., Carpenter, K. L. H., & Hutchinson, P. J. (2011). Cytokines and innate inflammation in the pathogenesis of human traumatic brain injury. *Progress in Neurobiology*, 95, 352–372.

Hendricks, H. T., Geurts, A. C., van Ginneken, B. C., Heeren, A. J., & Vos, P. E. (2007). Brain injury severity and autonomic dysregulation accurately predict heterotopic ossification in patients with traumatic brain injury. *Clinical Rehabilitation*. 21, 545–553.

Hibbard, M. R., Uysal, S., Kepler, K., Bogdany, J., & Silver, J. (1998). Axis I psychopathology in individuals with traumatic brain injury. *The Journal of Head Trauma Rehabilitation*, 13, 24–39.

Holmes, C., Cunningham, C., Zotova, E., Woolford, J., Dean, C., Kerr, S., et al. (2009). Systemic inflammation and disease progression in Alzheimer disease. *Neurology*, 73, 768–774.

Holsinger, T., Steffens, D. C., Phillips, C., Helms, M. J., Havlik, R. J., Breitner, J. C., et al. (2002). Head injury in early adulthood and the lifetime risk of depression. *Archives of General Psychiatry*, 59, 17–22.

Ikonomovic, M. D., Uryu, K., Abrahamson, E. E., Ciallella, J. R., Trojanowski, J. Q., Lee,VM-Y., et al. (2004). Alzheimer's pathology in human temporal cortex surgically excised after severe brain injury. *Experimental Neurology, 190*, 192–203.

Institute of Medicine. (2009). *Long-term consequences of traumatic brain injury.* Washington D.C.: The National Academies Press.

Iwata, A., Chen, X. H., McIntosh, T. K., Browne, K. D. & Smith, D. H. (2002). Long-term accumulation of amyloid-beta in axons following brain trauma without persistent upregulation of amyloid precursor protein genes. *Journal of Neuropathology & Experimental Neurology, 61*, 1056–1068.

Jacobs, A., Put, E., Ingels, M., Put, T., & Bossuyt, A. (1996). One-year follow-up of technetium-99m-HMPAO SPECT in mild head injury. *Journal of Nuclear Medicine, 37*, 1605–1609.

Jellinger, K. A., Paulus, W., Wrocklage, C. & Litvan, I. (2001). Traumatic brain injury as a risk factor for Alzheimer disease. Comparison of two retrospective autopsy cohorts with evaluation of ApoE genotype. *BMC Neurology, 1*, 3

Jenner, P., & Olanow, C. W. (1998). Understanding cell death in Parkinson's disease. *Annals of Neurology, 44*, S72–S84.

Johnson, V. E., Stewart, W., & Smith, D. H. (2012). Widespread tau and amyloid-Beta pathology many years after a single traumatic brain injury in humans. *Brain Pathology. 22*, 142–149.

Jubelt, B., & Agre, J. C. (2000). Characteristics and Management of Postpolio Syndrome. *JAMA, 284*, 412–414.

Jubelt, B., Drucker, J., & Younger, D. S. (1999). Poliomyelitis and the Post Polio Syndrome. In D. S. Younger (Ed.), *Motor Disorders* (pp. 381–395). Philadelphia: Lippincott Williams & Wilkins.

Kang, J. H. & Lin, H. C. (2012). Increased risk of multiple sclerosis after traumatic brain injury: a nationwide population-based study. *Journal of Neurotrauma, 29*, 90–95.

Kelly, D. F., Gonzalo, T. W., Cohan, P., Berman, N., Swerdloff, R., & Wang, C. (2000). Hypopituitarism following traumatic brain injury and aneurysmal subarachnoid hemorrhage: a preliminary report. *Journal of Neurosurgery, 93*, 743–752.

Kim, E., Lauterbach, E. C., Reeve, A., Arciniegas, D. B., Coburn, K. L., Mendez, M. F., et al. (2007). Neuropsychiatric complications of traumatic brain injury: a critical review of the literature (a report by the ANPA Committee on Research). *The Journal of Neuropsychiatry & Clinical Neurosciences, 19*, 106–127.

King, P. (2010). Concussions: The hits that are changing football. *Sports Illustrated, 1*, 34–40.

Kishi, Y., Robinson, R. G., & Kosier, J. T. (2001). Suicidal ideation among patients with acute life-threatening physical illness: patients with stroke, traumatic brain injury, myocardial infarction, and spinal cord injury. *Psychosomatics, 42*, 382–390.

Kochanek, P. M., Hendrich, K. S., Dixon, C. E., Schiding, J. K., Williams, D. S., & Ho, C. (2002). Cerebral blood flow at one year after controlled cortical impact in rats: Assessment by magnetic resonance imaging. *Journal of Neurotrauma, 19*, 1029–1037.

Koponen, S., Taiminen, T., Portin, R., Himanen, L., Isoniemi, H., Heinonen, H., et al. (2002). Axis I and II psychiatric disorders after traumatic brain injury: a 30-year follow-up study. *American Journal of Psychiatry, 159*, 1315–1321.

Kox, M., Pompe, J. C., Pickkers, P., Hoedemaekers, C. W., van Vugt, A. B., & van der Hoeven, J. G. (2008). Increased vagal tone accounts for the observed immune paralysis in patients with traumatic brain injury. *Neurology, 70*, 480–485.

Kraus, M. F., Susmaras, T., Caughlin, B. P., Walker, C. J., Sweeney, J. A., & Little, D. M. (2007). White matter integrity and cognition in chronic traumatic brain injury: A diffusion tensor imaging study. *Brain, 130*, 2508–2519.

Kunz, A., Dirnagl, U., & Mergenthaler, P. (2010). Acute pathophysiological processes after ischaemic and traumatic brain injury. *Best Practice & Research Clinical Anaesthesiology, 24*, 495–509.

Langlois, J. A., Rutland-Brown, W. & Wald, M. M. (2006). The epidemiology and impact of traumatic brain injury: A brief overview. *The Journal of Head Trauma Rehabilitation, 21*, 375–378.

Lehman, E. J., Hein, M. J., Baron, S. L. & Gersic, C. M. (2012). Neurodegenerative causes of death among retired National Football League players. *Neurology, 79* (19). 1970–1974.

Leon-Carrion, J., De Serdio-Arias, M. L., Cabezas, F. M., Roldan, J. M., Dominguez-Morales, R., Martin, J. M., et al. (2001). Neurobehavioural and cognitive profile of traumatic brain injury patients at risk for depression and suicide. *Brain Injury, 15*, 175–181.

Levin, H. S., Amparo, E., Eisenberg, H. M., Williams, D. H., High, W. M. Jr., McArdle, C. B., et al. (1987). Magnetic resonance imaging and computerized tomography in relation to the neurobehavioral sequelae of mild and moderate head injuries. *Journal of Neurosurgery, 66*, 706–713.

Lo, E. H., Moskowitz, M. A., & Jacobs, T. P. (2005). Exciting, radical, suicidal: how brain cells die after stroke. *Stroke 36*, 189–192.

Luerssen, T. G., Klauber, M. R., & Marshall, L. F. (1988). Outcome from head injury related to patient's age. A longitudinal prospective study of adult and pediatric head injury. *Journal of Neurosurgery. 68*, 409–416.

Lye, T. C., & Shores, E. A. (2000). Traumatic brain injury as a risk factor for Alzheimer's disease: a review. *Neuropsychology Review, 10*, 115–129.

Mangels, J. A., Craik, F. M., Levine, B., Schwartz, M. L., & Stuss, D. T. (2002). Effects of divided attention on episodic memory in chronic traumatic brain injury: A function of severity and strategy. *Neuropsychologia, 40*, 2369–2385.

Marquez de la Plata, C. D., Hart, T., Hammond, F. M., Frol, A. B., Hudak, A., Harper, C. R., et al. (2008). Impact of age on long-term recovery from traumatic brain injury. *Archives of Physical Medicine and Rehabilitation, 89*, 896–903.

Martland, H. S. (1928). Punch drunk. *JAMA, 91*, 1103–1107.

Masel, B. E., Scheibel, R. S., Kimbark, T. & Kuna, S. T. (2001). Excessive daytime sleepiness in adults with brain injuries. *Archives of Physical Medicine and Rehabilitation, 82*, 1526–1532.

Masson, F., Maurette, P., Salmi, L. R., Dartigues, J. F., Vecsey, J., Destaillats, J. M., et al. (1996). Prevalence of impairments 5 years after a head injury, and their relationship with disabilities and outcome. *Brain Injury. 10*, 487–498.

Matser, J. T., Kessels, A. G., Jordan, B. D., Lezak, M. D., & Troost, J. (1998). Chronic traumatic brain injury in professional soccer players. *Neurology, 51*, 791–796.

Maxwell, W. L., MacKinnon, M. A., Smith, D. H., McIntosh, T. K., & Smith, D. H. (2006). Thalamic nuclei after human blunt head injury. *Journal of Neuropathology & Experimental Neurology, 65*, 478–488.

McCrory, P., Turner, M., & Murray, J. (2004). A punch drunk jockey? *British Journal of Sports Medicine, 38*, E3.

McCrory, P., Zazryn, T., & Cameron, P. (2007). The evidence for chronic traumatic encephalopathy in boxing. *Sports Medicine, 37*, 467–476.

McKee, A. C., Cantu, R. C., Nowinski, C. J., Hedley-Whyte, E. T., Gavett, B. E., Budson, A. E., et al. (2009). Chronic traumatic encephalopathy in athletes: progressive tauopathy after repetitive head injury. *Journal of Neuropathology & Experimental Neurology, 68*, 709–735.

McKee, A. C, Gavett, B. E., Stern, R. A., Nowinski, C. J., Cantu, R. C., Kowall, N. W., et al. (2010). TDP-43 proteinopathy and motor neuron disease in chronic traumatic encephalopathy. *Journal of Neuropathology & Experimental Neurology, 69*, 918–929.

McKinlay, A., Dalrymple-Alford, J. C., Horwood, L. J., & Fergusson, D. M. (2002). Long term psychosocial outcomes after mild head injury in early childhood. *Journal of Neurology, Neurosurgery & Psychiatry, 73*, 281–288.

McLean, A. Jr., Dikmen, S., Temkin, N., Wyler, A. R. & Gale, J. L. (1984). Psychosocial functioning at 1 month after head injury. *Neurosurgery, 14*, 393–399.

McMillan, T. M., Teasdale, G. M., Weir, C. J. & Stewart, E. (2011). Death after head injury: the 13 year outcome of a case control study. *Journal of Neurology, Neurosurgery & Psychiatry, 82*, 931–935.

Millspaugh, J. A. (1937) Dementia pugilistica. *U.S. Naval Medicine Bulletin, 35*, 297–303.

Mirzayan, M. J., Probst, C., Krettek, C., Samii, M., Pape, H. C., van Griensven, M., et al. (2008). Systemic effects of isolated brain injury: an experimental animal study. *Journal of Neurology Research, 30*, 457–460.

Ng, K., Mikulis, D. J., Glazer, J., Kabani, N., Till, C., Greenberg, G., et al. (2008). Magnetic resonance imaging evidence of progression of subacute brain atrophy in moderate to severe traumatic brain injury. *Archives of Physical Medicine and Rehabilitation, 89*, S35–S44.

Niogi, S. N., Mukherjee, P., Ghajar, J., Johnson, C., Kolster, R. A., Sarkar, R., et al.(2008). Extent of microstructural white matter injury in postconcussive syndrome correlates with impaired cognitive reaction time: A 3T diffusion tensor imaging study of mild traumatic brain injury. *American Journal of Neuroradiology, 29*, 967–973.

Norris, E. H., Giasson, B. I., & Lee, V. M. (2004). Alpha-synuclein: normal function and role in neurodegenerative diseases. *Current Topics in Developmental Biology, 60*, 17–54.

Obrist, W. D., Langfitt, T. W., Jaggi, J. L., Cruz, J., & Gennarelli, T. A. (1984). Cerebral blood flow and metabolism in comatose patients with acute head injury. Relationship to intracranial hypertension. *Journal of Neurosurgery, 61*, 241–253.

O'Connor, M. M., & Mayberg, M. R. (2000). Effects of radiation on cerebral vasculature: A review. *Neurosurgery, 46*, 138–149.

Okie, S. (2005). Traumatic brain injury in the war zone. *The New England Journal of Medicine, 352*, 2043–2047.

Olver, J. H., Ponsford, J. L., & Curran, C. A. (1996). Outcome following traumatic brain injury: a comparison between 2 and 5 years after injury. *Brain Injury, 10*, 841–848.

Omalu, B. I., DeKosky, S. T., Hamilton, R. L., Minster, R. L., Kamboh, M. I., Shakir, A. M., et al. (2006). Chronic traumatic encephalopathy in a national football league player: part II. *Neurosurgery, 59*, 1086–1092.

Omalu, B. I., DeKosky, S. T., Minster, R. L., Kamboh, M. I., Hamilton, R. L. & Wecht, C. H. (2005). Chronic traumatic encephalopathy in a National Football League player. *Neurosurgery, 57,* 128–134.

Pajoohesh-Ganji, A., & Byrnes, K. R. (2011). Novel neuroinflammatory targets in the chronically injured spinal cord. *Neurotherapeutics, 8,* 195–205.

Papaliagkas, V. T., Anogianakis, G. A., & Tsolaki, M. N. (2008). Role of testosterone in patients with Alzheimer's disease. *Journal of Neurodegeneration and Regeneration, 1,* 35–42.

Partinen, M. (1988). Long-term outcome for obstructive sleep apnea syndrome patients. Mortality. *Chest, 94,* 1200–1204.

Pierce, J. E. S., Smith, D. H., Trojanowski, J. Q., & McIntosh, T. K. (1998). Enduring cognitive, neurobehavioral and histopathological changes persist for up to one year following severe experimental brain injury in rats. *Neuroscience, 87,* 359–369.

Plassman, B. L., Havlik, R. J., Steffens, D. C., Helms, M. J., Newman, T. N., Drosdick, D., et al.(2000). Documented head injury in early adulthood and risk of Alzheimer's disease and other dementias. *Neurology, 55,* 1158–1166.

Ponsford, J., Willmott, C., Rothwell, A., Cameron, P., Kelly, A. M., Nelms, R., et al. (2000). Factors influencing outcome following mild traumatic brain injury in adults. *Journal of the International Neuropsychological Society, 6,* 568–579.

Prat, R., Markiv, V., Dujovny, M., & Misra, M. (1997). Evaluation of cerebral autoregulation following diffuse brain injury in rats. *Journal of Neurology Research, 19,* 393–402.

Ramlackhansingh, A. F., Brooks, D. J., Greenwood, R. J., Bose, S. K., Turkheimer, F. E., Kinnunen, K. M., et al. (2011). Inflammation after trauma: microglial activation and traumatic brain injury. *Annals of Neurology, 70,* 374–383.

Rango, M., Bonifati, C., & Bresolin, N. (2006). Parkinson's disease and brain mitochondrial dysfunction: a functional phosphorus magnetic resonance spectroscopy study. *Journal of Cerebral Blood Flow & Metabolism, 26,* 283–290.

Ratcliff, G., Colantonio, A., Escobar, M., Chase, S. & Vernich, L. (2005). Longterm survival following traumatic brain injury. *Disability and Rehabilitation, 27,* 305–314.

Reider-Groswasser, I., Cohen, M., Costeff, H., & Groswasser, Z. (1993). Late CT findings in brain trauma: Relationship to cognitive and behavioral sequelae and to vocational outcome. *American Journal of Roentgenology, 160,* 147–152.

Rodriguez-Paez, A. C., Brunschwig, J. P., & Bramlett, H. M. (2005). Light and electron microscopic assessment of progressive atrophy following moderate traumatic brain injury in the rat. *Acta Neuropathologica, 109,* 603–616.

Rosen, T., & Bengtsson, B. A. (1990). Premature mortality due to cardiovascular disease in hypopituitarism. *Lancet, 336,* 285–288.

Safaz, I., Alaca, R., Yasar, E., Tok, F., & Yilmaz, B. (2008). Medical complications, physical function and communication skills in patients with traumatic brain injury: a single centre 5-year experience. *Brain Injury, 22,* 733–739.

Schneider, H. J., Kreitschmann-Andermahr, I., Ghigo, E., Stalla, G. K. & Agha, A. (2007a). Hypothalamopituitary dysfunction following traumatic brain injury and aneurysmal subarachnoid hemorrhage: a systematic review. *JAMA, 298,* 1429–1438.

Schneider, H. J., Samann, P. G., Schneider, M., Croce, C. G., Corneli, G., Sievers, C., et al. (2007b). Pituitary imaging abnormalities in patients with and without hypopituitarism after traumatic brain injury. *Journal of Endocrinological Investigation, 30,* RC9–RC12.

Schofield, P. W., Tang, M., Marder, K., Bell, K., Dooneief, G., Chun, M., et al. (1997). Alzheimer's disease after remote head injury: an incidence study. *Journal of Neurology, Neurosurgery & Psychiatry, 62,* 119–124.

Schultz, M. R., Marshall, S. W., Mueller, F. O., Yang, J., Weaver, N. L., Kalsbeek, W. D., et al. (2004). *Incidence and risk factors for concussion in high school athletes, North Carolina, 1996-1999.* American Journal of Epidemiology, 160, 937–944.

Schwarz, A. (2007a). *Expert ties ex-player's suicide to brain damage.* Retrieved month day, year of retrieval, from web address http://www.nytimes.com/2007/01/18/sports/football/18waters.html?pagewanted=all.

Schwarz, A. (2007b). *Lineman, dead at 36, exposes brain injuries.* Retrieved month day, year of retrieval, from web address http://www.nytimes.com/2007/06/15/sports/football/15brain.html?ref=alanschwarz&_r=0.

Selassie, A. W., McCarthy, M. L., Ferguson, P. L., Tian, J. & Langlois, J. A. (2005). Risk of posthospitalization mortality among persons with traumatic brain injury, South Carolina 1999 -2001. *Journal of Head Trauma Rehabilitation, 20,* 257–269.

Selkoe, D. J. (2001). Alzheimer's disease: genes, proteins, and therapy. *Physiological Review, 81,* 741–766.

Shavelle, R. M., Strauss, D., Whyte, J., Day, S. M. & Yu, Y. L. (2001). Long-term causes of death after traumatic brain injury. *American Journal of Physical Medicine & Rehabilitation, 80,* 510–516.

Shorvon, S. & Tomson, T. (2011). Sudden unexpected death in epilepsy. *Lancet, 378*(9808), 2028–2038.

Silver, J. M., Koumaras, B., Chen, M., Mirski, D., Potkin, S. G., Reyes, P., et al. (2006). Effects of rivastigmine on cognitive function in patients with traumatic brain injury. *Neurology, 67*, 748–755.

Silver, J. M., Kramer, R., Greenwald, S., & Weissman, M. (2001). The association between head injuries and psychiatric disorders: findings from the New Haven NIMH Epidemiologic Catchment Area Study. *Brain Injury, 15*, 935–945.

Smith, D. H., Chen, X. H., Pierce, J. E., Wolf, J. A., Trojanowski, J. Q., Graham, D. I., et al. (1997). Progressive atrophy and neuron death for one year following brain trauma in the rat. *Journal of Neurotrauma, 14*, 715–727.

Smith, D. H., Uryu, K., Saatman, K. E., Trojanowski, J. Q., & McIntosh, T. K. (2003). Protein accumulation in traumatic brain injury. *Neuromolecular Medicine, 4*, 59–72.

Smith, F. M., Raghupathi, R., MacKinnon, M. A., McIntosh, T. K., Saatman, K. E., Meaney, D. F., et al. (2000). TUNEL-positive staining of surface contusions after fatal head injury in man. *Acta Neuropathologica, 100*, 537–545.

State of Colorado Department of Labor, (2006). *Traumatic Brain Injury Medical Treatment Guidelines.* Denver: Colorado Government.

Tan, Z. S., Beiser, A., Vasan, R. S., Au, R., Auerbach, S., Kiel, D. P., et al. (2008). Thyroid function and the risk of Alzheimer disease: the Framingham Study. *Archives of Internal Medicine, 168*, 1514–1520.

Teasdale, T. W., & Engberg, A. W. (2001). Suicide after traumatic brain injury: a population study. *Journal of Neurology, Neurosurgery & Psychiatry, 71*, 436–440.

Terayama, Y., Meyer, J. S., Kawamura, J., & Weathers, S. (1991). Role of thalamus and white matter in cognitive outcome after head injury. *Journal of Cerebral Blood Flow & Metabolism, 11*, 852–860.

Terayama, Y., Meyer, J. S., Kawamura, J., & Weathers, S. (1993). Cognitive recovery correlates with white-matter restitution after head injury. *Surgical Neurology, 39*, 177–186.

Terrisse, L., Poirier, J., Bertrand, P., Merched, A., Visvikis, S., & Siest, G., et al. (1998). Increased levels of apolipoprotein D in cerebrospinal fluid and hippocampus of Alzheimer's patients. *Journal of Neurochemistry, 71*, 1643–1650.

Thurman, D. J., Branche, C. M. & Sniezek, J. E. (1998). The epidemiology of sports-related traumatic brain injuries in the United States: Recent developments. *The Journal of Head Trauma Rehabilitation, 13*, 1–18.

Till, C., Colella, B., Verwegen, J., & Green, R. E. (2008). Postrecovery cognitive decline in adults with traumatic brain injury. *Archives of Physical Medicine and Rehabilitation,, 89*, S25–S34.

Toffoli, A. M., Gautschi, O. P., Frey, S. P., Filgueira, L., & Zellweger, R. (2008). From brain to bone: evidence for the release of osteogenic humoral factors after traumatic brain injury. *Brain Injury, 22*, 511–518.

Tysvaer, A. T., Storli, O. V., & Bachen, N. I. (1989). Soccer injuries to the brain. A neurologic and electroencephalographic study of former players. *Acta Neurology Scandinavica, 80*, 151–156.

Uryu, K., Chen, X. H., Martinez, D., Browne, K. D., Johnson, V. E., Graham, D. I., et al. (2007). Multiple proteins implicated in neurodegenerative diseases accumulate in axons after brain trauma in humans. *Experimental Neurology, 208*, 185–192.

Vanden Bossche, L., & Vanderstraeten, G. (2005). Heterotopic ossification: a review. *Journal of Rehabilitation Medicine, 37*, 129–136.

van der Naalt, J., Hew, J. M., van Zomeren, A. H., Sluiter, W. J., & Minderhoud, J. M. (1999). Computed tomography and magnetic resonance imaging in mild to moderate head injury: early and late imaging related to outcome. *Annals of Neurology, 46*, 70–78.

Ventura, T., Harrison-Felix, C., Carlson, N., DiGuiseppi, C., Gabella, B., Brown, A., et al. (2010). Mortality after discharge from acute care hospitalization with traumatic brain injury: A population-based study. *Archives of Physical Medicine and Rehabilitation, 91*, 20–29.

Voshol, H., Glucksman, M. J., & Van, O. J. (2003). Proteomics in the discovery of new therapeutic targets for psychiatric disease. *Current Molecular Medicine, 3*, 447–458.

Weiss, J. W., Launois, S. H., Anand, A., & Garpesta, E. (1999). Cardiovascular morbidity in obstructive sleep apnea. *Progess in Cardiovascular Diseases, 41*, 367–376.

Wilde, M. C., Castriotta, R. J., Lai, J. M., Atanasov, S., Masel, B. E., & Kuna, S. T. (2007). Cognitive impairment in patients with traumatic brain injury and obstructive sleep apnea. *Archives of Physical Medicine and Rehabilitation, 88*, 1284–1288.

Williams, S., Raghupathi, R., MacKinnon, M. A., McIntosh, T. K., Saatman, K. E., & Graham, D. I. (2001). In situ DNA fragmentation occurs in white matter up to 12 months after head injury in man. *Acta Neuropathologica, 102*, 581–590.

Wilson, S., Raghupathi, R., Saatman, K. E., MacKinnon, M. A., McIntosh, T. K. and Graham, D. I. (2004). Continued in situ DNA fragmentation of microglia/macrophages in white matter weeks and months after traumatic brain injury. *Journal of Neurotrauma, 21*, 239–250.

World Health Organization. (2002). *Innovative care for chronic conditions: Building blocks for action: Global Report.* World Health Organization.

Wunsch, H. (1998). Mounting evidence implicates *tau* mutations in dementia disorder. *Lancet, 351*, 1790.

Yamakami, I., & McIntosh, T. K. (1989). Effects of traumatic brain injury on regional cerebral blood flow in rats as measured with radiolabeled microspheres. *Journal of Cerebral Blood Flow & Metabolism, 9*, 117–124.

Yamakami, I., & McIntosh, T. K. (1991). Alterations in regional cerebral blood flow following brain injury in the rat. *Journal of Cerebral Blood Flow & Metabolism, 11*, 655–660.

Yasseen, B., Colantonio, A. & Ratcliff, G. (2008). Prescription medication use in persons many years following traumatic brain injury. *Brain Injury, 22*, 752–757.

Zafonte, R., Elovic, E. P., & Lombard, L. (2004). Acute Care Management of Post-TBI Spasticity. *Journal of Head Trauma Rehabilitation, 19*, 89–100.

Zasler, N. D., Katz, D. I., & Zafonte, R. D. (2007). *Brain Injury Medicine: Principles and Practice.* New York, NY: Demos Medical Publishing, LLC.

Zhang, X., Chen, J., Graham, S. H., Du, L., Kochanek, P. M., Draviam, R., et al. (2002). Intranuclear localization of apoptosis-inducing factor (AIF) and large scale DNA fragmentation after traumatic brain injury in rats and in neuronal cultures exposed to peroxynitrite. *Journal of Neurochemistry, 82*, 181–191.

Zhang, X., Chen, Y., Jenkins, L. W., Kochanek, P. M., & Clark, R. S. (2005). Bench-to-bedside review: Apoptosis/programmed cell death triggered by traumatic brain injury. *Critical Care, 9*, 66–75.

Zhang, X., Graham, S. H., Kochanek, P. M., Marion, D. W., Nathaniel, P. D., Watkins, S. C., et al. (2003). Caspase-8 expression and proteolysis in human brain after severe head injury. *The FASEB Journal, 17*, 1367–1369.

Zhang, Y., Dawson, V. L., & Dawson, T. M. (2000). Oxidative stress and genetics in the pathogenesis of Parkinson's Disease. *Neurobiology of Disease, 7*, 240–250.

Ziebell, J. M., & Morganti-Kossman, M. C. (2010). Involvement of pro- and anti-inflammatory cytokines and chemokines in the pathophysiology of traumatic brain injury. *Neurotherapeutics, 7*, 22–30.

Part II

Neuropsychological Functions

4

Attentional Problems after Traumatic Brain Injury

Jia Huang, David H. K. Shum, Raymond C. K. Chan, and Allana L. Canty

Introduction

The residual cognitive effects of traumatic brain injury (TBI) are often significant and long-lasting (Ciaramelli, Serino, Di Santantonio, & Ladavas, 2006). Manifestations often include impairments of attention, decision making, language, memory, and executive function (Ciaramelli et al., 2006; Draper & Ponsford, 2008; Kim et al., 2009; Mathias & Wheaton, 2007). Deficits in these processes involve large scale neural interactions and arise, in part, due to the diffuse underlying neuropathology present after TBI. While focal lesions, particularly to prefrontal cortical regions, significantly affect functional outcomes, the presence of diffuse axonal injury (DAI) is more ubiquitous after TBI (Fujinaka, Kohmura, Yuguchi, & Yoshimine, 2003). The severity of these focal and diffuse pathological processes among patients with TBI is heterogeneous, resulting in marked inter-individual variation in the effects of TBI on cognitive processes. Persistent cognitive deficits can be categorized into three general domains: attention and information processing speed, memory, and executive function (Bales, Wagner, Kline, & Dixon, 2009). Of these clinical features, difficulties in attention are the most frequently reported and are considered by patients and caregivers as the most difficult to which to adapt (Hooper et al., 2004).

In this chapter we focus on the mechanism of attention—those cognitive processes that enable us to processes relevant inputs, thoughts, or actions while ignoring irrelevant or distracting stimuli (Posner, 2012). Difficulties in attention can be quantified by intensity and qualified by selectivity. Common examples of these problems include difficulty focusing attention on a task or thought over an extended time (i.e., intensity), difficulty returning to a task or thought after doing or thinking about something else, or inability to conduct multiple activities simultaneously (i.e., selectivity). These problems can have a pervasive impact on capacity for independent living, relationships, leisure activities, study, and employment. For example, many everyday activities rely on the integrity of attention capacity (e.g., driving a motor vehicle) (Cyr et al., 2009). Moreover, evidence indicates that patients with limited attention show poor functional outcomes and higher levels of anxiety up to a decade post-injury (Ponsford, Draper, & Schonberger, 2008). Therefore, providing a synopsis of the nature of attention deficits post-TBI has the potential to better inform assessment, assist in rehabilitation planning, and improve long-term outcomes.

This chapter aims to review the nature, breadth and treatment of attentional problems following TBI. The content is unique in its heightened emphasis on recent advances in understanding the cognitive correlates and remediation of attentional deficits post-TBI. The first section introduces the different theoretical conceptualizations of attention and the array of behavioral studies elucidating these. The second section navigates the cerebral representation and pathophysiology of attention in TBI. Discussion expands into the intricate relationships attention shares with other hot and cool components of cognitive functioning, pausing to reflect on profitable areas of future research. The last section overviews the current climate of interventional literature and summarizes therapeutic developments in attentional problems after TBI. The chapter concludes by pointing to the future of attention studies within the general framework created by cognitive neuroscience.

Theoretical Conceptualizations of Attention and Behavioral Studies

A major theoretical stride in the conceptualization of attentional processes came from the work of Mirsky and associates and their empirically derived model of attention (Mirsky, Anthony, Duncan, Ahearn, & Kellam, 1991). Based on factor analytic studies of tests considered to measure aspects of attention, Mirsky et al. conceptualized attention in terms of four components: (1) focus-execute; (2) sustain; (3) encode; and (4) shift. Each of these has been found to be supported by dissociable brain regions that if damaged, will result in specific deficits in the corresponding attentional process. This is a heuristically useful model that permits a refined conceptualization of the various types of attention described below.

There are a number of different types of attention that can be affected by TBI. One of the most basic of these is the ability to orient attention, which involves spatially directing or allocating attention to sensory information (Hills & Geldmacher, 1998). Another aspect of attention is attention span, which refers to the amount of information that can be processed at one time (Lezak, Howieson, & Loring, 2004). Selective or focused attention, on the other hand, involves an ability to selectively attend to information that is relevant to a task while ignoring irrelevant and distracting information (van Zomeren & Brouwer, 1992). Divided attention refers to the ability to simultaneously process more than one source of information at a time (Williamson, Scott, & Adams, 1996), and sustained attention refers to an ability to continuously maintain attentional focus under conditions of low stimulation and over a prolonged period of time (Williamson et al., 1996). Finally, supervisory

attentional control facilitates the strategic allocation of attentional resources in demanding situations in order to optimize performance (van Zomeren & Brouwer, 1994). In addition, reductions in information-processing speed can have pervasive effects on cognitive functioning, including attention.

Although deficits in attention are frequently reported following severe TBI, evidence-based conclusions concerning the nature and extent of these disturbances are lost amongst the high number of subprocesses (as detailed above) and methodological differences (e.g., different tasks) described within the literature. For example, evidence for a general reduction in speed of information processing following TBI has consistently been found (Felmingham, Baguley, & Green, 2004), as has specific deficits in the orienting of attention (Cremona-Meteyard, Clark, Wright, & Geffen, 1992), focused/selective attention (Chan, 2000; Mangels, Craik, Levine, Schwartz, & Stuss, 2002), divided attention (Leclercq et al., 2000), sustained attention (Chan, 2000), and supervisory attentional control (Rios, Perianez, & Munoz-Cespedes, 2004). Notwithstanding, other studies have failed to find evidence for the existence of these specific deficits (e.g., Bate, Mathias, & Crawford, 2001; Felmingham et al., 2004). This causes problems for clinicians when they are trying to determine which aspects of attention to assess and what measures to use when assessing the attention of a patient who has sustained a TBI.

An attempt to consolidate the literature concerning the types of attention affected post-TBI was made in a recent meta-analysis by Mathias and Wheaton (2007). Overall, large and significant deficits were found in specific measures of speed of information-processing, attention span, focused/selective attention, sustained attention, and supervisory attentional control following severe TBI. Moreover, performance deficits of one standard deviation or more below scores of their healthy peers are apparent on a range of commonly used measures, including visual search tasks, cancellation tasks (e.g. the Ruff 2 and 7 Test, letter and word cancellation tests), the Stroop Test (Word Reading, Color Naming, and Interference subtests), the Symbol Digit Modalities Test (oral and written versions), the Digit Symbol Test, and the Trail Making Test (Part A). However, the fact that many of these tests yield scores that reflect the time taken to complete a task or the number of correct responses within a fixed time interval suggests that the contribution of reduced processing speed to performance on tests of attention must be given careful consideration. Finally, although there is some suggestion that differences in patient variables (e.g., age, education, postinjury interval) do not significantly contribute to the extent of these deficits, this finding should be viewed with caution, as the authors were unable to analyze the moderating influence of these variables on specific measures.

Another limitation of research evaluating attention processes post-TBI is the predominant reliance on generic neuropsychological measures that have poorly established ecological validity. Addressing this, Park, Allen, Barney, Ringdahl, and Mayfield (2009) sought to evaluate the predictive value of neuropsychological tests of attention that purportedly tap Mirsky et al.'s four-component model in a child and adolescent sample of individuals with TBI. Participants (n = 151 TBI and n = 50 healthy controls) completed the Arithmetic, Digit Span, Digit Symbol Coding, and Symbol Search subtests from the WISC-III, the Trail Making Test A and B, and the Continuous Performance Test. Results from confirmatory factor analysis supported the four-component model and additional regression analyses suggested that scores on tasks assessing the Shift and Focus components of attention predicted TBI severity (Park et al., 2009).

Expanding Park's results, a recent study by Barney et al. (2011) examined the relationship between neuropsychological measures of attention (e.g., Wisconsin Card Sorting Test & Trial Making Test) that purportedly assess Mirsky et al.'s attentional components and parent-report behavioral ratings of attention problems and hyperactivity. A total of 65 children and adolescents who had sustained a TBI were included in the study. Principal components analysis identified the four aforementioned components in this sample, which accounted for 80.9% of the variance. However, correlations between the neuropsychological measures of attention and behavioral ratings of attention and hyperactivity were low and not significant. Such results suggest that neuropsychological and behavioral measures assess different aspects of attentional disturbances in children with TBI and highlight the demand for studies exploring the utility and validity of newly developed theoretically derived measures of attention.

Summary

Overall, it has become increasingly apparent that attention is composed of a number of dissociable components. Using factor analysis, a number of stable components of attention have been identified in patients with TBI. Specifically, attention can be divided into focus, encoding, sustain, and shift components. Research has consistently demonstrated that individuals with TBI show significant impairment in these attentional processes. Notwithstanding, methodological differences among studies with respect to the aspects of attention that are examined and the tests that are used have made it difficult for researchers to draw conclusions concerning which aspects of attention are most affected by TBI. Furthermore, a subtle paradigm shift is being witnessed in the literature whereby clinicians and researchers are less interested in models that can be used to solely explain attentional deficits, in favor of tasks that predict TBI status and functional outcomes.

Neural Anatomy and Physiology of Attention in TBI

This section begins by briefly describing the computational processes and mechanisms that enable attention. It will also review how attentional mechanisms are implemented in the brain's neuronal circuitry. Subsequently, the pathophysiology of attention deficits in TBI is discussed with emphasis on underlying neural anatomy and physiology. Enquiry into these areas has helped generate new ideas about brain attention systems that are, in many cases, highly complementary, but, in other cases, novel, generating new hypotheses to be explored in future research.

The Neural Network for Attention

According to Posner (2012), attention involves three interrelated subsystems: (1) orientation to sensory events; (2) detecting signals for focal processing and; (3) the maintenance of a vigilant or alert state to process high priority signals. Neuroimaging research has confirmed the relative independence among these networks (Fan et al., 2005). The "orienting" system has been associated with the posterior parietal lobe which first disengages attention from its present focus, the superior colliculus which relocates the index of attention to the area of the target, and the lateral pulvinar nucleus of the posteriorlateral thalamus which is involved in processing data from the indexed location (Fan et al., 2005; Posner, 2012). For the "detecting" system, studies have shown involvement of midline frontal areas, particularly the anterior cingulate gyrus and supplementary motor area (Dehaene, Posner, & Tucker, 1994). Interestingly, in cognitive studies where people are required to select a modality of input, the cingulate shows functional connectivity to the selected sensory system (e.g., visual, auditory; Crottaz-Herbette & Mennon, 2006). Similarly, when involved with emotional processing the cingulate shows a functional connection to limbic areas (Etkin et al., 2006). Lastly, imaging research has consistently identified that frontoparietal regions of the right cerebral hemisphere are responsible for modulating and maintaining the intensity of alert responding to incoming stimuli (i.e., the third system). This system is essential for maintaining an intrinsic goal-directed focus in otherwise unarousing contexts where exogenous stimuli are not present to increase alertness through novelty, demand, or perceived difficulty (Fan et al., 2005; Posner, 2012). Figure 4-1 presents a simplified illustration of Posner's model.

Pathophysiology of Attention in TBI

The pathophysiology of attention in TBI has attracted considerable attention within the experimental and imaging literature. Recent research has sought to unpack early holistic conclusions concerning abnormal neural circuitry of attention in TBI (e.g., cortical and medial fronto-tempo-parietal regions) by isolating specific patterns of activation. One such study was conducted by Rasmussen and colleagues (2008) who aimed to investigate the neuronal correlates of divided attention in severe TBI patients ($n = 10$) compared to healthy controls ($n = 11$). Results indicated similar and significant dual task interference in both TBI patients and controls. However, TBI patients and controls could be distinguished based on the TBI group's significantly reduced activation in occipital and posterior cingulate cortices during the single- compared to the dual-task condition. This pattern was reversed in the dual task condition with significantly increased activation of the predominantly left lateralized prefrontal-parietal network in the TBI group compared to the controls. Notwithstanding, this increase in activation occurred within regions described to be engaged in healthy volunteers as dual task cost increases. This finding suggests more effortful processing, substitution, and functional reorganization within the primary network subserving attentional processes following TBI.

In a similar study with children, Kramer et al. (2008) examined brain activation patterns during a continuous performance task (CPT) in a pediatric samples of TBI ($n = 5$; mean age = 9.4 years) and age-matched controls with orthopedic injuries (OI; $n = 8$). Interestingly, results indicated that performance on the CPT did not differ between groups and similar neural networks, relevant to sustained attention processing (e.g., right fronto-parietal regions), were active for both groups. Notwithstanding, the TBI group demonstrated significantly greater activation in a number of cortical regions including the superior frontal gyrus, precentral

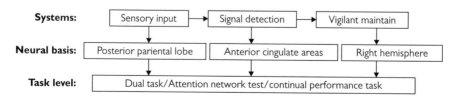

Figure 4-1. Illustration of neural model for attention.

gyrus, superior parietal lobe, middle occipital gyrus, fusiform gyrus, and right cerebellum.

This observed over-activation in the TBI group is consistent with the findings of Rasmussen et al. (2008) and can be explained by two possible neural mechanisms: (1) differences in attentional capacity whereby individuals with TBI have to allocate more effort to maintain the same behavioral performance in an attention task or, (2) individuals with TBI may have difficulties in effectively allocating neural resources. Furthermore, increases in the extent of neural activity after TBI is similar to patterns that have been observed during aging, where older participants show increased bilateral activity across a range of memory and attentional tasks in prefrontal cortex (Cabeza et al., 2004; de Chastelaine et al., 2011) as well as posterior parietal cortices (Huang et al., 2011; Vallesi et al., 2011). Greater recruitment of regions homologous to areas used for cognitive processes in controls has also been found (Maruishi et al., 2007, for exception see Perlstein et al., 2004).

Unique from the previous two studies, Scheibel and colleagues (2009) explored how the neural substrates of attention changed with TBI severity (*n* = 30 patients with moderate to severe TBI and 10 neurologically healthy controls with OI). Results indicated that lower total Glasgow Coma Scale (GCS) and GCS verbal component scores were associated with higher levels of brain activation during a sustained attention task. Patients with a total GCS score of eight or less demonstrated increased, diffuse activation that included structures (e.g., cingulate gyrus and thalamus) purportedly involved in visual attention and cognitive control. Taken together, these results suggest that the patterns of neural activation during tasks assessing attention are, in part, associated with TBI severity.

In another novel study, Raja et al. (2011) sought to explore how neural activity associated with attentional processing varied according to task complexity in patients with TBI (*n* = 8) and healthy controls (*n* = 10). Results indicated that during base-line and simple tasks, individuals with TBI and healthy controls engaged a similar neural network involving the limbic, prefrontal, and medial temporal structures. Interestingly, during more complex presentations, only

patients with TBI showed activations in additional frontal, parietal, and occipital regions. The authors concluded that such outcomes could be attributable, at least in part, to DAI, which affects integrated processing in distributed systems.

The experimental and clinical imaging studies of attention in TBI described thus far have focused on cortical (viz., posterior parietal and anterior midline brain) and thalamic regions, likely because these are common sites of focal injury. Although there is strong evidence to suggest a supportive role of these regions in attentional processes, recent findings suggest that deficits in attention could be due to the degeneration of nerve fibers (i.e., other medial white matter regions). Exploring this perspective, Spanos and colleagues (2007) measured cerebellar white and gray matter and lesion volumes 1–10 years following TBI in 16 children aged 9–16 and matched controls (*n* = 16). A significant group difference was found in cerebellar white and gray matter volume, with children in the TBI group consistently exhibiting smaller volumes. They also found that the cerebellum and its related projection areas, including the dorsolateral prefrontal cortex, thalamus, and pons, are highly vulnerable to fiber degeneration following traumatic insult.

Summary

In summary, attention is a complex and distributed neural activity (Pavlovskaya et al., 2007). This section presents consistent evidence of more widespread activation during attentional tasks in TBI patients as compared to healthy subjects, particularly in frontal and temporal–parietal areas (Levine et al., 2002; McAllister et al., 2006; Kim et al., 2008; Turner & Levine, 2008). Interesting and novel studies point to injury severity, DAI and task complexity as potential explanations of these activation patterns. Despite some promising advances, the research described in this section also highlights a common problem in assessing attention in TBI populations, whereby patients show relatively normal performance on traditional neuropsychological tests, despite complaints of having difficulty coping with activities of daily life. This insensitivity of traditional neuropsychological tests to the deficits reported by TBI patients poses a problem in terms of diagnosis and treatment. From this perspective, detection of altered patterns of neural activity may provide a more fine-tuned measure of decreased organization and efficiency of cognitive processes and may be a beneficial addition to clinician's standard diagnostic arsenal.

Attention and Cool/Hot Components of Cognitive Function

Individuals with TBI rarely experience attention deficits in isolation. Rather, attention impairments are often partnered by an array of complex secondary cognitive, behavioral and emotional difficulties (Zupan, Neumann, Babbage, & Willer, 2009). For example, individuals with TBI often report experiencing attention deficits in conjunction with a slowing of intellectual processes, difficulty recalling new material, and personality changes. It is the relationship between attentional deficits and impairments in other cognitive functions that captures the focus of this section. Cognitive functions are traditionally understood in terms of "cool" and "hot" components, and the section will be divided accordingly. "Cool" components involve information processing or an executive component (e.g., perception and memory). "Hot" components are infused with aspects of emotion, personality, or social attitude.

Relationship between Attention and Cool Components of Cognitive Functioning in TBI

Given the theoretical similarity, as well as the proximal location of the neural structures underpinning attention and other cool components of cognitive functioning, recent research has been interested in exploring the link between these processes. For example, Mangels et al. (2002) sought to test the hypothesis that deficits in episodic memory are a result of impaired attentional resources and/or strategic control. This was achieved by manipulating attentional load at encoding (focused versus divided attention) and environmental support at retrieval (free recall and recalled cued by

scene versus recognition of object and scene). Participants ($n = 11$ mild TBI (mTBI), $n = 13$ moderate-to-severe TBI, and $n = 10$ healthy controls) completed tests standardized neuropsychological tests of memory and frontal-lobe functions (e.g., Wechsler Memory Scale, Trial Making Test, WCST). Results indicated that individuals with TBI were disproportionately affected by the divided attention manipulation, but this effect was modulated by injury severity and encoding strategy. More specifically, episodic memory in individuals with mTBI was impaired only when items were encoded under divided attention—conditions that may more realistically simulate the multi-tasking demands associated with the activities that these patients find most challenging in everyday life. Furthermore, this result suggests that memory deficits are secondary to attention deficits in mTBI. Results concerning the demands of dual-task performance also revealed functional heterogeneity within the severe TBI group, whereby patients could be differentiated into two distinct subgroups based on whether they favored a strategy of attending to the encoding or digit-monitoring task. The subgroup favoring the digit-monitoring task demonstrated deficits in the focused attention condition, and disproportionate memory deficits in the divided attention condition. In contrast, the subgroup favoring the encoding task demonstrated intact performance across all memory measures, regardless of attentional load, and despite remarkable similarity to the other severe TBI subgroup on demographic, neuropsychological, and acute injury severity measures. These results highlight the importance of sensitive neuropsychological measurement of cognitive processes at acute and chronic stages of injury. By combining direct manipulation of task emphasis with more precise neurobehavioral and neurophysiological assessment at the time of acute injury, it may be possible to determine what combination of organic and behavioral factors predict the identified strategy differences.

In a similar study, Asloun and colleagues (2008) assessed the relationships between divided-attention deficits and working-memory limitations after severe TBI. Such a link is intuitive given the ability to deal with two tasks simultaneously is closely related to the functioning of the central executive system of working memory (Baddeley, 1992). Severe TBI patients (n = 43) and healthy controls (n = 43) were given an n-back task of three different load levels, which was performed as a single and a dual task. Results indicated that patients demonstrated significant difficulty in dual-task processing and an increased susceptibility to high working-memory load. Contrary to expectation however, significant interactions were not observed between dual-task performance and working-memory load. Notwithstanding, these findings are consistent with previous literature that suggested dual-task performance and working memory represent dissociable although interrelated abilities.

Expanding the work of Asloun et al. (2008), a recent study by Slovarp and colleagues (2012) evaluated the intricacies of working memory and sustained attention following severe TBI. Individuals with severe TBI (n = 9) and healthy controls (n = 9) completed two visual memory tasks, a two-back working memory task, and a measure of sustained attention. Results indicated that patients with TBI had lower hit rates and higher false alarm rates than healthy controls on the working memory task. Contrary to expectation, the TBI group did not perform significantly poorer on the measure of sustained attention albeit considerable variability within individual data. Consistent with previous studies (e.g., Asloun et al., 2008) however, the hit rates for both working memory and sustained attention tasks were positively correlated, suggesting these processes are interrelated. Taken together, this research supports previous findings suggesting that patients with severe TBI suffer from a constellation of attention deficits and from limitations in different aspects of memory and that impairments in these processes rely, at least in part, on distinct mechanisms. Future research which considers more precise manipulation of task emphasis may be able to reveal strategy differences on an individual basis which in turn could provide important information regarding the direction and success of an individual's rehabilitation program.

Diverging away from memory constructs, a recent study by Willmott et al. (2009) sought to explore the extent to which slowed information processing and reduced strategic control affects performance on selective attentional tasks after TBI. Participants (n = 40 moderate to severely TBI and n = 40 healthy controls) completed a battery of attentional tasks. Results indicated that group difference in reaction time on a measure of selective attention was a product of slowed processing speed, but not working memory. These results suggest that reduced processing speed accounts, in part, for the attentional deficits experienced by individuals with TBI. Notwithstanding, the potential additional contribution of other aspects of strategic control apart from working memory to the production of errors on complex attentional tasks requires further investigation. Future research in the realm of fMRI and other functional imaging technology may also assist in elucidating the underlying neuropathological and neurochemical alterations responsible for the complex interactions between these attentional processes.

Relationship between Attention and Hot Components of Cognitive Functioning in TBI

Research has invested considerable resources into exploring how emotion, motivation, self-esteem, empathy, and other "hot" cognitive components come together with attention processes to influence functional outcomes in TBI populations. For example, recent research explored how raising attention levels can improve social perception (i.e., facial expressions) post-TBI (McDonald, Bornhofen, & Hunt, 2009). These strategies included (1) focusing attention on relevant aspects of facial expression, and (2) mimicking facial expression. Individuals with severe TBI (n = 22) and healthy controls (n = 32) were asked to label six basic emotions spontaneously following direction in using either a "focus" or "mimic" strategy. Results indicated that the "focus" instruction assisted healthy participants to correctly identify facial expression but led to poorer performance in individuals with TBI. The "mimic" strategy resulted in little improvement for either group. Overall, these results suggest that people with TBI, who lack proficiency with emotion perception, do not benefit from mimicry or having their attention directed towards the relevant features of the facial expression, but rather, show a decrement in performance under these conditions. A possible avenue for future research is to explore the role of competing demands on limited attentional resources, the possibility of inaccurate mimicry, and the effects of self-consciousness as potential reasons underpinning these findings.

McDonald et al.'s (2009) conclusions are supported by research exploring the relationship between social cognition and attention in patients with TBI (Spikman, Timmerman, Milders, Veenstra, & van der Naalt, 2012). Participants (n = 28 moderate to severe TBI) completed measures of emotion recognition, theory of mind and empathy, and non-social cognitive processes (e.g., memory, processing speed, attention, and executive function). Patients performed significantly worse than healthy controls on all measures. However, correlation analyses yielded no significant (partial) correlations between social and non-social cognition tests. This suggests that poor performance on measures of social cognition was not due to general cognitive impairments. Notwithstanding, the work of Spikman et al. (2012) represents the first attempt to systematically investigate the relation between general and social cognition in TBI patients.

Whereas the research considered thus far has sought to identify how attention effects hot cognitive processes, a complementary stream of research has explored the extent to which emotion affects attention. One such study, conducted by Himanen et al. (2009), compared the extent and nature of attention deficits in TBI patients with (n = 32) and without (n = 29) depressive symptoms. Results suggested that problems in complex attention processing are more specific to TBI, while slowness in simple psychomotor speed and impaired sustained attention may be mostly related to depressive symptoms in patients with chronic TBI sequelae. These results suggest that the relationship between attention and emotion may be unique to specific attention processes. This study suggests that remediation programs may need to be tailored to take into account co-existing cognitive impairments. As such, a possible avenue for future research is to explore the benefit of remediation targeting processing speed and sustained attention for improving depressive symptoms in TBI.

Summary

Evidently, substantial research has been devoted to examining the factors contributing to impaired performance on attentional tasks of increasing complexity in individuals with TBI. There is considerable evidence to suggest attention deficits are associated with working memory deficits and reduced processing speed. However, further research exploring the functional relations of these processes is needed. Similarly, additional research is needed within the area of hot cognitive functions and their association with attentional processes. Although research has consistently suggested that social-cognitive and attention constructs (e.g., affect recognition, theory of mind) are theoretically and functionally distinct (e.g., McDonald et al., 2009; Spikman et al., 2012), other research has found that emotion affects attentional processes (Himanen et al., 2009). Research further exploring and dissecting the dynamics of these relationships provides a profitable area of future research.

Remediation of Attention Problems after TBI

As discussed in earlier sections, attention deficits are pervasive, long-lasting, and linked with a broad spectrum of social and cognitive impairments. Accordingly, there is a strong emphasis within the clinical and experimental literature to develop remediation programs targeted at improving attention processes post-TBI. This section will discuss novel research that has explored interventional and pharmaceutical treatment approaches to attention deficits in the TBI population.

Pharmaceutical Treatment of Attention Deficits in TBI

Traditional remediation protocols aimed at enhancing attention post-TBI have focused on increasing arousal. For example, a recent single case study assessed how aspects of cognition and communication improved in response to the pharmacological management of post-traumatic hypersomnia and mood disturbance (Wiseman-Hakes, Victor, Brandys,

& Murray, 2011). The participant was a male with severe TBI and cognitive-communication impairments, who subsequently developed sleep and mood disturbance and excessive daytime sleepiness. His sleep, wake, and mood difficulties were pharmacologically managed using lorazepam (1 mg) and citalopram (20 mg). There was a clear positive relationship between quality of sleep, language processing, attention, and memory seen across the phases of the medication intervention. These results suggest that comprehensive pharmacological management programs aimed at enhancing physiological states (e.g., mood, sleep, and arousal) can be successful in improving attention post-TBI. These findings suggest that pharmacological management of sleep/wake disturbances and mood post-TBI can potentially facilitate improvements in attention.

Adopting a slightly alternate approach, Whyte et al. (2004) evaluated the effects of methylphenidate (i.e., a psychostimulant) on a variety of aspects of attention, ranging from laboratory-based impairment measures to caregiver ratings and work productivity, in individuals with TBI. A total of 34 adults with moderate to severe traumatic brain injury and attention complaints in the postacute phase of recovery were enrolled in a six-week, double-blind, placebo-controlled, repeated crossover study of methylphenidate, administered in a dose of 0.3 mg/kg/dose, twice a day. Speed of information processing ($p <. 001$, $\eta^2 =. 48$), attentiveness during individual work tasks ($p =. 01$, $\eta^2 =. 62$), and caregiver ratings of attention ($p =. 01$, $\eta^2 =. 52$) showed significant treatment effects. However, no treatment-related improvement was seen in divided attention, sustained attention, or susceptibility to distraction. Although these results suggest that regular doses of methylphenidate can improve some aspects of attention deficits post-TBI, further research is needed to identify optimal dosages and to extend these findings to mTBI.

Expanding on these results, Kim et al. (2012) used perfusion fMRI as a biomarker of regional neural activity to examine the neural correlates of single-dose (0.3 mg/kg) methylphenidate administration in a randomized double-blind placebo-controlled crossover study design. Twenty-three individuals with

moderate to severe TBI were tested on two occasions approximately one week apart. Perfusion fMRI scanning was carried out at rest and while participants performed cognitive tasks requiring sustained attention and working memory. Behaviourally, methylphenidate significantly improved both accuracy and reaction time in the sustained attention task but only reaction time in the working memory task. A trend of global reduction of cerebral blood flow by methylphenidate was observed in all task conditions including resting. Voxel-wise whole-brain analysis revealed an interaction effect of drug by condition for the sustained attention task in the left posterior superior parietal cortex and parietooccipital junction. Furthermore, the magnitude of drug-related deactivation of this area during task performance was correlated with improvement in reaction time. These results suggest that suppression of activity in this area during task performance may reflect a compensatory mechanism by which methylphenidate ameliorates attention impairments in TBI.

Pharmacotherapies that target specific neurotransmitter systems offer a promising avenue for attenuating functional deficits and/ or enhancing rehabilitation following TBI (Whiting & Hamm, 2004; Warden et al., 2006). Several studies using different injury paradigms have yielded positive results using drugs that alter catecholaminergic neurotransmission. For example, recent studies have begun to define the role of dopamine (DA) in the recovery process following TBI. Several DA agonists have been used to treat cognitive and behavioral dysfunction following trauma. These studies demonstrate enhanced performance following post-injury treatment with the DA agonist amantidine (Dixon et al., 1999; Leone and Polsonetti, 2005), DA-associated methylphenidate (Kline et al., 2000), the MAO-B inhibitor L-Deprenyl (Zhu et al., 2000), which affects the breakdown of catecholamines, and the D2 agonist bromocriptine (Kline et al., 2002). Taken together, this research offers preliminary but promising evidence that drugs that positively influence DA can enhance many aspects of cognition including attention, concentration, and memory (Meythaler, Brunner, Johnson, & Nova, 2002; Whyte et al., 2004). Notwithstanding, the precise mode of impairment on the dopamine system is not fully understood, and further research is needed to establish a clear relationship between catecholamine levels and long-term behavioural outcomes.

Neurocognitive Therapy for Attention Deficits Post-TBI

Knowledge of the neurocognitive rehabilitation of attention deficits largely stems from clinical research on adults with acquired attention disorders and from the literature that focuses on children with neurodevelopmental disorders of attention, particularly attention deficit-hyperactivity disorder (Mateer, Kerns, & Eso, 1996; Shalev, Tsal, & Mevorach, 2007). Rehabilitation strategies in this area fall into one of four categories: attention process training, self-management strategies and environmental modifications, external aids to help track and organize information, and psychosocial supports for the emotional and social factors that result from or exacerbate attention difficulties (Michel & Mateer, 2006).

In one study of attention process training, Pero, Incoccia, Caracciolo, Zoccolotti, and Formisano (2006) evaluated the effectiveness of the Solhberg and Mateer's Attention Process Training (APT) using a comprehensive evaluation of various attentional processes. APT is a program created for the rehabilitation of attention deficits in patients with an acquired brain damage. The programme is directed toward four levels or components of attention: sustained attention, selective attention, alternated attention, and divided attention. For each of these four components a hierarchy of specific tasks was developed. Within each section the exercises are ordered by difficulty. In the administration of the APT, the manual does not establish a fixed number of sessions, but suggests two operational criteria for structuring the work. The first criterion regards execution time, which should be reduced by 35% before a specific task can be left. The second criterion sets that the patient must reach 85% accuracy on all tasks carried out. Two patients with severe TBI were administered APT. Training was started two years after injury and 85 sessions were required to complete the program. Attentional processes were evaluated at various stages

before, during, and after treatment, using the Testbatterie zur Aufmerksamkeitsprufung and the Test of Everyday Attention. Both patients showed some degree of recovery, particularly in attentional tasks with a selective component. Lesser improvement was present in the case of tasks mapping on the intensity dimension of attention (alertness, vigilance). Training achievements were confirmed by the use of a functional scale evaluating attention, pointing to the generality of improvements. These results provide preliminary evidence that APT can lead to improvements in the attentional disturbances of TBI patients.

In a more recent study, Galbiati et al. (2009) assessed the efficacy of a process-specific approach and metacognitive strategies (i.e., attention process training and self-management strategies) in improving attention post-TBI. Participants included sixty-five TBI patients (aged 6–18 years) with attention deficits. Participants were assessed at baseline and at one-year follow-up on the Wechsler Intelligence Scale and the Continuous Performance Test II (CPT II). The Vineland Adaptive Behavior Scales (VABS) was administered to assess the treatment's ecological validity. Each experimental patient ($n = 40$) received attention-specific neuropsychological training. Training included tabletop tasks and computerized tasks such as the Rehacom program and the Attenzione e Concentrazione program. The training took place four times a week and lasted six months, with individual sessions lasting 45 min. At baseline, all patients presented with a mild intellectual disability and pathological scores on the CPT II. At follow-up, significant differences were found between the two groups on the CPT II and VABS, indicating that specific remediation training for attention can improve attention performance.

An innovative study by Larson et al. (2011) evaluated the feasibility of applying virtual reality and robotics technology to improve attention in patients with severe TBI in the early stages of recovery. A sample of adult TBI patients ($n = 18$) who were receiving acute inpatient rehabilitation completed three-dimensional cancellation exercises over two consecutive days in an interactive virtual environment that minimized distractions and that integrated both visual and haptic (tactile) stimuli. Fifteen of the 18 patients demonstrated tolerance of the virtual environment, as indicated by completing the entire treatment protocol. Within-subjects comparisons of target acquisition time during treatment showed that a treatment condition that included haptic cues produced improved performance compared to a condition in which such cues were not provided. These results suggest that attention exercises using virtual environments are well-tolerated and engaging and that they could be beneficial for patients with severe TBI. Research such as this encourages researchers to consider and empirically evaluate the utility of virtual technology for the rehabilitation of attention deficits post-TBI.

Summary

Attempts to improve acquired attentional problems have included both cognitive-behavioral remediation efforts and psychopharmacological interventions. Although there is early evidence to suggest that these approaches can be of some therapeutic benefit in attenuating attention deficits post-TBI, there is a critical need for carefully controlled evaluations of treatment efficacy to support evidence-based approaches to intervention, for both cognitive-remediation and drug-based clinical-trial research. Another profitable area of future research is to evaluate the efficacy of combined neurocognitive-psychopharmacological programs in improving performance on measures of attention in patients with TBI. Furthermore, the availability of imaging as a means of examining brain networks prior to and following rehabilitation should provide opportunities for research that could fine-tune both behavioral and pharmacological intervention methods.

Chapter Summary

This chapter has sought to systematically review theoretical developments in understanding the nature, neural substrates, and physiology of attention in TBI, the relationship between attention and other cold and hot cognitive functions, and the remediation of attention processes post-TBI. Consistent evidence suggests that attention is composed of a number of stable processes including focus, encoding, sustain and shift components (Mirsky et al., 1991). Notwithstanding, methodological differences among studies with respect to the aspects of attention that are examined and the tests that are used, have made it difficult for researchers to draw conclusions concerning which aspects of attention are most affected by TBI. Despite these inconsistent findings, researchers have been successful in mapping the neural circuitry of attention processes, with distinct structures identified within frontal and temporal–parietal areas (Levine et al., 2002; McAllister et al., 2006; Kim et al., 2008; Turner & Levine, 2008). Regarding the correlates of attention, although consistent links have been identified between attention deficits and limitations of working memory and reduced processing speed, there is substantial evidence to suggest that social-cognitive and attention constructs (e.g., affect recognition, theory of mind) are theoretically and functionally distinct (e.g., McDonald et al., 2009; Spikman et al., 2012). Research further exploring and dissecting the dynamics of these relationships exists as a profitable area of future research. Lastly, this chapter reviewed recent advances in neurocognitive and psychopharmacological interventions targeting attention deficits in TBI. Research in this area has provided preliminary but promising evidence that these approaches can be of some therapeutic benefit in improving attention processes post-TBI. In conclusion, attention deficits have a considerable impact on the recovery and adjustment of patients with TBI. Thus it is hoped that by summarizing advances in understanding the nature, breadth and remediation of these deficits, this chapter has made some progress towards improving the outcomes of patients with TBI.

Acknowledgments

Preparation of this book chapter was supported by the grant of the National Science Fund China (31100747) to Jia Huang, the Project-Oriented Hundred Talents Programme (O7CX031003) and the Knowledge Innovation Project of the Chinese Academy of Sciences (KSCX2-EW-J-8), the Griffith University Allan Sewell Visiting Fellowship to Raymond Chan; an Australian

Academy of Science, Scientific Visits to China Grant to David Shum, and a grant from the initiation fund of the CAS/SAFEA International Partnership Programme for Creative Research Teams (Y2CX131003) to Raymond Chan and David Shum.

References

Asloun, S., Soury, S., Couillet, J., Giroire, J. M., Joseph, P. A., Mazaux, J. M., et al. (2008). Interactions between divided attention and working-memory load in patients with severe traumatic brain injury. *Journal of Clinical and Experimental Neuropsychology*, 30, 481–490.

Baddeley, A. (1992). Working Memory. *Science*, 255, 556–559.

Bales, J. W., Wagner, A. K., Kline, A. E., Dixon, C. E. (2009). Persistent cognitive dysfunction after traumatic brain injury: A dopamine hypothesis. *Neuroscience and Biobehavioral Reviews*, 33, 981–1003.

Barney, S. J., Allen, D. N., Thaler, N. S., Park, B. S., Strauss, G. P., Mayfield, J. (2011). Neuropsychological and behavioral measures of attention assess different constructs in children with traumatic brain injury. *The Clinical Neuropsychologist*, 25, 1145–1157.

Bate, A. J., Mathias, J. L., & Crawford, J. R. (2001a). The covert orienting of visual attention following severe traumatic brain injury. *Journal of Clinical and Experimental Neuropsychology*, 23, 386–398.

Cabeza, R., Daselaar, S. M., Dolcos, F., Prince, S. E., Budde, M., & Nyberg, L. (2004). Task-independent and task-specific age effects on brain activity during working memory, visual attention, and episodic retrieval. *Cerebral Cortex*, 14, 364–375.

Chan, R. C. K. (2000). Attentional deficits in patients with closed head injury: A further study to the discriminative validity of the Test of Everyday Attention. *Brain Injury*, 14, 227–236.

Ciaramelli, E., Serino, A., Di Santantonio, A., & Ladavas, E. (2006). Central executive system impairment in traumatic brain injury. *Brain and Cognition*, 60, 198–199.

Crottaz-Herbette, S., & Menon, V. (2006). Where and when the anterior cingulate cortex modulates attentional response: Combined fMRI and ERP evidence. *Journal of Cognitive Neuroscience*, 18(5), 766–780.

Cremona-Meteyard, S. L., Clark, C. R., Wright, M. J., & Geffen, G. M. (1992). Covert orientation of visual attention after closed head injury. *Neuropsychologia*, 30, 123–132.

Cyr, A. A., Stinchcombe, A., Gagnon, S., Marshall, S., Hing, M. M., & Finestone, H. (2009). Driving difficulties of brain-injured drivers in reaction to high-crash-risk simulated road events: a question of impaired divided attention? *Journal of Clinical and Experimental Neuropsychology*, 31, 472–482.

de Chastelaine, M., Wang, T. H., Minton, B., Muftuler, L. T., & Ruff, M. D. (2011). The effects of age and memory performance on the neural correlates of successful associative encoding. *Cerebral Cortex*, 21, 2166–2176.

Dehaene, S., Posner, M. I., Tucker, D. M. (1994). Localization of a neural system for error detection and compensation. *Psychological Science*, 5, 303–305.

Dixon, C. E., Kraus, M. F., & Kline, A. E. (1999). Amantadine improves water maze performance without affecting motor behavior following traumatic brain injury in rats. *Restorative Neurology and Neuroscience*, 14, 285–294.

Draper, K., & Ponsford, J. (2008). Cognitive functioning ten years following traumatic brain injury and rehabilitation. *Neuropsychology*, 22, 618–625.

Etkin, A., Egner, T., Peraza, D. M., Kandel, E. R., & Hirsch, J. (2006). Resolving emotional conflict: a role for the rostral anterior cingulate cortex in modulating activity in the amygdala. *Neuron*, 51, 871–882.

Fan, J., McCandliss, B. D., Fossella, J., Flombaum, J. I., & Posner, M. I. (2005). The activation of attentional networks. *NeuroImage*, 26, 471–479.

Felmingham, K. L., Baguley, I. J., & Green, A. M. (2004). Effects of diffuse axonal injury on speed of information processing following severe traumatic brain injury. *Neuropsychology*, 18, 564–571.

Fujinaka, T., Kohmura, E., Yuguchi, T., & Yoshimine, T. (2003). The morphological and neurochemical effects of diffuse brain injury on rat central noradrenergic system. *Neurological Research*, 25, 35–41.

Galbiati, S., Recla, M., Pastore, V., Liscio, M., Bardoni, A., Castelli, E., et al. (2009). Attention remediation following traumatic brain injury in childhood and adolescence. *Neuropsychology*, 23, 40–49.

Huang, C. M., Polk, T. A., Goh, J. O., & Park, D. C. (2011). Both left and right posterior parietal activations contribute to compensatory processes in normal aging. *Neuropsychologia*, 50(1), 55–66.

Hills, E. C., & Geldmacher, D. S. (1998). The effect of character and array type on visual spatial search quality following traumatic brain injury. *Brain Injury*, 12, 69–76.

Himanen, L., Portin, R., Tenovuo, O., Taiminen, T., Koponen, S., Hiekkanen, H., et al. (2009). Attention and depressive symptoms in chronic phase after traumatic brain injury. *Brain Injury*, 23, 220–227.

Hooper, S. R., Alexander, J., Moore, D., Sasser, H. C., Laurent, S., King, J., et al. (2004). Caregiver reports of common symptoms in children following a traumatic brain injury. *NeuroRehabilitation, 19*, 175–189.

Kim, J., Whyte, J., Patel, S., Europa, E., Wang, J et al. (2012). Methylphenidate modulates sustained attention and cortical activation in survivors of traumatic brain injury: A perfusion fMRI study. *Psychopharmacology, 222*, 47–57.

Kim, Y. H., Yoo, W. K., Ko, M. H., Park, C. H., Kim, S. T., & Na, D. L. (2009). Plasticity of the attentional network after brain injury and cognitive rehabilitation. *Neurorehabilitation and Neural Repair, 23*, 468–477.

Kline, A. E., Yan, H. Q., Bao, J., Marion, D. W., & Dixon, C. E. (2000). Chronic methylphenidate treatment enhances water maze performance following traumatic brain injury in rats. *Neuroscience Letters, 280*, 163–166.

Kline, A. E., Massucci, J. L., Marion, D. W., & Dixon, C. E. (2002). Attenuation of working memory and spatial acquisition deficits after a delayed and chronic bromocriptine treatment regimen in rats subjected to traumatic brain injury by controlled cortical impact. *Journal of Neurotrauma, 19*, 415–425.

Kramer, M. E., Chiu, C. Y., Walz, N. C., Holland, S. K., Yuan, W., Karunanayaka, P., et al. (2008). Long-term neural processing of attention following early childhood traumatic brain injury: fMRI and neurobehavioral outcomes. *Journal of the International Neuropsychological Society, 14*, 424–435.

Larson, E. B., Ramaiya, M., Zollman, F. S., Pacini, S., Hsu, N., et al. (2011). Tolerance of a virtual reality intervention for attention remediation in persons with severe TBI. *Brain Injury, 25*(3), 274–281.

Leclercq, M., Couillet, J., Azouvi, P., Marlier, N., Martin, Y., Strypstein, E., et al. (2000). Dual task performance after severe diffuse traumatic brain injury or vascular prefrontal damage. *Journal of Clinical and Experimental Neuropsychology, 22*, 339–350.

Leone, H. & Polsonetti, B.W. (2005). Amantadine for traumatic brain injury: does it improve cognition and reduce agitation? *Journal of Clinical Pharmacology & Therapeutics, 30*, 101–104.

Lezak, M. D., Howieson, D. B., & Loring, D. W. (2004). *Neuropsychological assessment* (4th ed.). New York: Oxford University Press.

Mangels, J. A., Craik, F. I., Levine, B., Schwartz, M. L., & Stuss, D. T. (2002). Effects of divided attention on episodic memory in chronic traumatic brain injury: a function of severity and strategy. *Neuropsychologia, 40*, 2369–2385.

Maruishi, M., Miyatani, M., Nakao, T., & Muranaka, H. (2007). Compensatory cortical activation during performance of an attention task by patients with diffuse axonal injury: A functional magnetic resonance imaging study. *Journal of Neurology, Neurosurgery and Psychiatry, 78*, 168–173.

Mateer, C. A., Kerns, K. A., & Eso, K. L. (1996). Management of attention and memory disorders following traumatic brain injury. *Journal of Learning Disabilities, 29*, 618–632.

Mathias, J. L., & Wheaton, P. (2007). Changes in attention and information-processing speed following severe traumatic brain injury: a meta-analytic review. *Neuropsychology, 21*, 212–223.

McDonald, S., Bornhofen, C., & Hunt, C. (2009). Addressing deficits in emotion recognition after severe traumatic brain injury: The role of focused attention and mimicry. *Neuropsychological Rehabilitation, 19*, 321–339.

Meythaler, J. M., Brunner, R. C., Johnson, A., & Novack, T. A. (2002). Amantadine to improve neuro-recovery in traumatic brain injury-associated diffuse axonal injury: A pilot double blind randomized trial. *Journal of Head Trauma Rehabilitation, 17*, 300–313.

Michel, J. A. & Mateer, C. A. (2006). Attention rehabilitation following stroke and traumatic brain injury. A review. *European Journal of Physical and Rehabilitation Medicine, 42*(1), 59–67.

Mirsky, A. F., Anthony, B. J., Duncan, C. C., Ahearn, M. B., & Kellam, S. G. (1991). Analysis of the elements of attention: A neuropsychological approach. *Neuropsychology Review, 2*, 109–145.

Park, B. S., Allen, D. N., Barney, S. J., Ringdahl, E. N., & Mayfield, J. (2009). Structure of attention in children with traumatic brain injury. *Applied Neuropsychology, 16*, 1–10.

Pavlovskaya, M., Groswasser, Z., Keren, O., Mordvinov, E., & Hochstein, S. (2007). Hemispheric visual attentional imbalance in patients with traumatic brain injury. [TBI]. *Brain and Cognition, 64*, 21–29.

Perlstein, W. M., Cole, M. A., Demery, J. A., Seignourel, P. J., Dixit, N. K., Larson, M. J., & Briggs, R. W. (2004). Parametric manipulation of working memory load in traumatic brain injury: Behavioural and neural correlates. *Journal of the International Neuropsychological Society, 10*, 724–741.

Pero, S., Incoccia, C., Caracciolo, B., Zoccolotti, P., & Formisano, R. (2006). Rehabilitation of attention in two patients with traumatic brain injury by means of attention process training. *Brain Injury, 20*, 1207–1219.

Ponsford, J., Draper, K., & Schonberger, M. (2008). Functional outcome 10 years after traumatic brain injury: its relationship with demographic, injury severity, and cognitive and emotional status.

Journal of the International Neuropsychological Society, 14, 233–242.

Posner, M. I. (2012). Imaging attention networks. *NeuroImage, 61*(2), 450–456.

Raja Beharelle, A., Tisserand, D., Stuss, D. T., McIntosh, A. R., & Levine, B. (2011). Brain activity patterns uniquely supporting visual feature integration after traumatic brain injury. *Frontiers in Human Neuroscience, 5,* 164.

Rasmussen, I. A., Xu, J., Antonsen, I. K., Brunner, J., Skandsen, T., Axelson, D. E., et al. (2008). Simple dual tasking recruits prefrontal cortices in chronic severe traumatic brain injury patients, but not in controls. *Journal of Neurotrauma, 25,* 1057–1070.

Rios, M., Perianez, J. A., & Munoz-Cespedes, J. M. (2004). Attentional control and slowness of information processing after severe traumatic brain injury. *Brain Injury, 18,* 257–272.

Scheibel, R. S., Newsome, M. R., Troyanskaya, M., Steinberg, J. L., Goldstein, F. C., Mao, H., et al. (2009). Effects of severity of traumatic brain injury and brain reserve on cognitive-control related brain activation. *Journal of Neurotrauma, 26,* 1447–1461.

Shalev, L., Tsal, Y., Mevorach, C. (2007). Computerized progressive attentional training (CPAT) program: Effective direct intervention for children with ADHD. *Child Neuropsychology, 13*(4), 382–388.

Slovarp, L., Azuma, T., & Lapointe, L. (2012). The effect of traumatic brain injury on sustained attention and working memory. *Brain Injury, 26,* 48–57.

Spanos, G. K., Wilde, E. A., Bigler, E. D., Cleavinger, H. B., Fearing, M. A., Levin, H. S., et al. (2007). Cerebellar atrophy after moderate-to-severe pediatric traumatic brain injury. *American Journal of Neuroradiology, 28,* 537–542.

Spikman, J. M., Timmerman, M. E., Milders, M. V., Veenstra, W. S., & van der Naalt, J. (2012). Social cognition impairments in relation to general cognitive deficits, injury severity, and prefrontal lesions in traumatic brain injury patients. *Journal of Neurotrauma, 29,* 101–111.

Turner, G. R., & Levine, B. (2008). Augmented neural activity during executive control processing following diffuse axonal injury. *Neurology, 71,* 812–818.

Vallesi, A., McIntosh, A. R., & Stuss, D. T. (2011). Over recruitment in the aging brain as a function of task demands: Evidence for a compensatory view. *Journal of Cognitive Neuroscience, 23,* 801–815.

van Zomeren, A. H. & Brouwer, W. H. (1992). Assessment of attention. In J. R. Crawford, D. M. Parker, & W. W. McKinlay (Eds.), *A handbook of neuropsychological assessment* (pp. 241–266). Hove, England: Erlbaum.

Warden, D. L., Gordon, B., & McAllister, T. W., et al. (2006). Guidelines for the pharmacologic treatment of neurobehavioral sequelae of traumatic brain injury. *Journal of Neurotrauma, 23,* 1468–1501.

Whiting, M. D. & Hamm, R. J. (2004). Treating chronic cognitive impairment after traumatic brain injury: A review of post-traumatic neurotransmitter-based interventions. *Physical & Rehabilitation Medicine, 16,* 273–290.

Whyte, J., Hart, T., Vaccaro, M., Grieb-Neff, P., Risser, A., et al. (2004). Effects of methylphenidate on attention deficits after traumatic brain injury: A multidimensional, randomized, controlled trial. *American Journal of Physical Medicine & Rehabilitation, 83,* 401–420.

Williamson, D. J. G., Scott, J. G., & Adams, R. I. (1996). Traumatic brain injury. In R. L. Adams, O. A. Parsons, J. L. Culbertson, & S. J. Nixon (Eds.), *Neuropsychology for clinical practice: Etiology, assessment and treatment of common neurological disorders* (pp. 9–64). Washington, DC: American Psychological Association.

Willmott, C., Ponsford, J., Hocking, C., & Schonberger, M. (2009). Factors contributing to attentional impairments after traumatic brain injury. *Neuropsychology, 23,* 424–432.

Wiseman-Hakes, C., Victor, J. C., Brandys, C., & Murray, B. J. (2011). Impact of post-traumatic hypersomnia on functional recovery of cognition and communication. *Brain Injury, 25,* 1256–1265.

Zupan, B., Neumann, D., Babbage, D. R., & Willer, B. (2009). The importance of vocal affect to bimodal processing of emotion: implications for individuals with traumatic brain injury. *Journal of Communication Disorders, 42,* 1–17.

Zhu, J., Hamm, R. J., Reeves, T. M., Povlishock, J. T., & Phillips, L. L. (2000). Post injury administration of L-deprenyl improves cognitive function and enhances neuroplasticity after traumatic brain injury. *Experimental Neurology, 166,* 136–152.

5

Memory Impairments after Traumatic Brain Injury

Allana L. Canty, David H. K. Shum, Harvey S. Levin, and Raymond C. K. Chan

Memory is the means by which we retain and draw on our past experiences to use that information in the present (Tulving, 2000). As a process, it refers to the dynamic mechanisms associated with the encoding, retention, and retrieval of information. Through linking the past, present, and future, our memories form the basis for our sense of self, guide our thoughts and decisions, influence our emotional reactions, and allow us to learn. As such, memory is pertinent to social, vocational, and cognitive functioning throughout all stages of human development (Tulving & Craik, 2005). The intrinsic value of this function is further illustrated by the pervasive impairments experienced by individuals who acquire damage to the brain (Baddeley, Kopelman, & Wilson, 2002).

One type of brain injury commonly associated with memory impairment is traumatic brain injury (TBI). Disturbances in memory functioning are frequently reported and commonly identified sequelae of TBI, often persisting beyond the period of immediate recovery. Disruptions of memory can include rapidly forgetting information over the course of hours, forgetting an item's location, or forgetting to do something in the future. New learning, such as retaining, recalling, or recognizing recent visual and auditory information may also be affected after TBI. Another common memory deficit post-TBI is the failure to recall or recognize past events. Memory for past events may be in the form of autobiographical information (e.g., one's date of birth) or general knowledge (e.g., what the capital of

Australia is). Persistent memory deficits can have a disabling impact on an individual's ability to live independently or return to work, and interfere with their capacity to form and maintain meaningful relationships (Ponsford, Olver, & Curren, 1995; Ryan, Sautter, Capps, Meneese, & Bath, 1992). As such, memory is often a key focus of long-term rehabilitation and adjustment after TBI. Paradoxically, the integrity of one's memory largely determines the extent to which one can actively participate and benefit from treatment (Williamson, Scott, & Adams, 1996).

Several review papers and textbook chapters have been dedicated to the effect of TBI on memory (e.g., Baddeley, Harris, Sunderland, Watts, & Wilson, 1987; Goldstein & Levin, 1995; Levin, 1990; Levin, Benton, & Grossman, 1982; Levin & Hanten, 2002; Richardson, 2000; Schacter & Crovitz, 1977; Vakil, 2005). In light of the considerable increase in general neuropsychological knowledge of memory, previous findings about TBI may be reinterpreted. Together with the findings reported by studies published since these papers and chapters, there is a need for an updated review of the literature in an attempt to organize and systematically compare the results of various studies on the effect of TBI on a large range of theoretically defined memory aspects. A better understanding of the nature of memory impairment following TBI could contribute primarily to the assessment and rehabilitation of this patient population.

This chapter has three aims. First, we briefly introduce neuropsychological models of memory.

As such, this section graduates from a review of the spectrum of simple theoretical accounts to more sophisticated discussion of the intricacies of sensory, short-term, and long-term storage systems. The second section of this chapter provides a synopsis of studies that have examined the effects of moderate-to-severe TBI on short- and long-term memory, and their respective subcomponents. The final section of this chapter provides a review of recent research that has focused on three memory constructs commonly impaired after TBI: working memory, prospective memory, and contextual/autobiographical memory.

Neuropsychological Models of Human Memory

There are several traditional models of memory. One of the earliest multidimensional models emerged in the mid 1960s and was based on the two structures of memory first proposed by William James (1890); *primary memory* which holds temporary information currently in use, and *secondary memory* which holds information indefinitely. Subsequently, Richard Atkinson and Richard Shiffin proposed the multi-store model which conceptualized memory in terms of three stores; (1) a *sensory store*, an initial repository for limited amounts of information for very brief periods; (2) a *short-term* store, capable of storing information for somewhat longer periods but also of relatively limited capacity; and (3) a *long-term* store, of very large capacity, capable of retaining information indefinitely (Atkinson & Shiffin, 1968). Figure 5-1 provides an illustration of the Atkinson and Shiffin model from an information-processing perspective.

Patterns of memory deficit observed in individuals with focal neuropsychological ailments provided sound evidence in support of the Atkinson-Shiffin model (1968) of memory. Observations of patients with profound amnesia following bilateral damage to the temporal lobes and hippocampi were particularly informative as they provided evidence of double dissociations (Squire, 1986). One particularly famous dissociation was that identified between patients K.F. and H.M. As a result of damage to the perisylvian region of the left hemisphere, patient K.F.'s immediate memory (i.e., short-term memory, STM) was impaired. However, this patient maintained a long-term memory (LTM) capacity within the normal range. The opposite pattern of impairment was demonstrated by patient H.M. who, after undergoing a bilateral excision of his hippocampi, was unable to retain new visual or verbal information (e.g., LTM). His immediate memory however, remained intact. This dissociation demonstrates that while long-term consolidation of new information can be impaired, STM ability can be preserved, and vice versa.

Although influential, these traditional models have been criticized as overly simplistic representations of memory and learning. Accordingly, more sophisticated models, which detail multiple interconnected systems, have gained popularity. One such model is the *level-of-processing framework*, which postulates that memory does not contain a specific number of separate stores; rather, it varies along a continuous dimension in

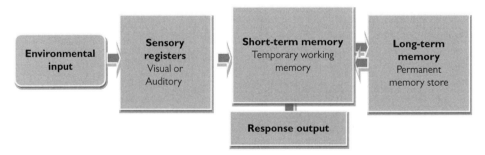

Figure 5-1. Atkinson and Shiffin (1968) Theoretical model for the flow of information through the human information processor. (Illustration by Allana Canty, adapted from "The Control of Short-Term Memory," by Richard C. Atkinson and Richard M. Shiffin. Copyright © 1971 by Scientific American, Inc. All rights reserved. Reprinted with permission).

terms of depth of encoding (Craik & Lockhart, 1972). According to this model, there are an infinite number of levels of processing (LOP) at which items can be encoded. In contrast to the Atkinson and Shiffin model (1968), the LOP model suggests that there are no distinct boundaries between one level and the next. Rather the emphasis in this model is on processing as the key to storage. The level at which information is stored will largely depend on how it is encoded. Moreover, the model suggests a strong relationship between LOP and retrieval whereby the deeper the LOP, the higher the probability that an item will be retrieved.

Like models of STM, simple theoretical representations of LTM have graduated into accounts of multifaceted systems mediated by intricate sub-processes. One useful division of LTM is between *explicit* memory (i.e., declarative; knowledge of facts) and *implicit* memory (i.e., non-declarative or procedural knowledge; e.g., knowing the steps involved in making spaghetti bolognese) (Roediger, 1990). Tulving (1972) suggested that explicit memory should be further divided into *episodic* and *semantic* memory. Episodic memory represents memory for events and experiences (e.g., memories of a time in childhood) whereas semantic memory involves generic knowledge of the world not bound to a particular context (e.g., knowing the meaning of "telephone" or knowledge of its function).

Just as the understanding of STM was strengthened by observations of neuropsychological patients, observation has been instrumental in isolating the subtypes of LTM. For example, Swiss psychiatrist Claparède (1911) described a memory deficit in an amnesic patient whom he pin-pricked when they first shook hands. Claparède observed that the patient refused to shake hands the following day, though when questioned as to why, the patient was unable to remember the reason substantiating his decline. This case suggests that memory does not require conscious recollection of the episode in which learning occurred (i.e., *source memory*). Another interesting case was the case of C.W. who contracted Herpes simplex encephalitis (Wilson, Baddeley, & Kapur, 1995). Consequently, C.W. developed both anterograde and retrograde amnesia. C.W. has little memory prior to contracting the virus in 1985 and

cannot learn new declarative knowledge (C.W.'s memory resets in thirty second intervals). That is, although the anterograde amnesia prevented C.W. from learning new information (i.e. semantic memory) and also prevented him from storing new memories of events or episodes (i.e., episodic memory), he retained his ability to play the piano and conduct choirs (i.e., procedural memory) despite having no conscious recollection of having learned music.

Another model of memory is that proposed by Baddeley and Hitch (1974), who elaborated the simple three store model by incorporating the role of *working memory*. Baddeley originally suggested that working memory comprises three components: the *central executive*, which coordinates attentional activities, governs responses, and essentially acts as a supervisory system which controls the flow of information to and from its two slave systems: the *phonological loop* and the *visuospatial sketchpad*. The slave systems are short-term storage systems dedicated to a content domain (i.e., verbal and visual, respectively). In 2000, a third slave system was added to this model, the *episodic buffer* that interfaces with LTM (Baddeley, 2000). Although Baddeley and Hitch's model frames working memory as an extension of STM, these two constructs have been typically emphasized as distinct processes. In brief, STM and WM are similar in that they both involve brief preliminary storage of information necessary for the long-term, and in turn both offer the functional role of information storage (i.e., new learning). Unlike STM, however, working memory involves the active manipulation of information. In parallel with this distinction, some researchers (e.g., Fisher, Ledbetter, Cohen, Marmor, & Tulsky, 2000) argue that adequate STM (e.g., recall) must exist before successful working memory (e.g., manipulation of the recalled information) can be achieved. The various components of memory described above are illustrated in the model adapted from Squire (1986; see Figure 5-2).

Summary of Research Assessing Short- and Long-Term Memory after TBI

Short-Term Memory

Studies investigating the extent to which STM is impaired after TBI, has shown evidence that

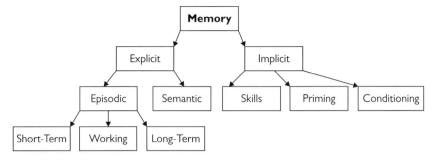

Figure 5-2. A neuropsychological model of human memory (adapted from Squire, 1992).

individuals, relative to healthy controls, perform significantly poorer on various indices derived from measures of STM including total recall, learning, cued-recall, and intrusion (Fisher et al., 2000; Vanderploeg, Crowell, & Curtiss, 2001; Langeluddecke & Lucas, 2005). More interesting, research has shown that individuals with TBI demonstrate problems in encoding as well as retrieval, are more prone to intrusion, and fail to spontaneously employ strategies to aid their memory. Despite these findings, there is also evidence to indicate STM is seldom impaired after moderate-to-severe TBI. Recent research substantiating each of these polarities is described in the following paragraphs.

To clarify the extent to which short-term, long-term, and working memory are impaired post-TBI, Fisher et al. (2000) compared the performance of 22 individuals with moderate-to-severe TBI on the Wechsler Memory Scale-III (WMS-III) with that of 23 individuals with mild TBI and 45 healthy control participants. The WMS-III produces six index scores including immediate auditory memory, immediate visual memory, delayed auditory memory, delayed visual memory, delayed auditory recognition, and working memory. Fisher et al. (2000) found that individuals with moderate-to-severe TBI performed significantly worse than healthy controls on all WMS-III index scores except Auditory Recognition Delayed. Furthermore, individuals with moderate-to-severe TBI performed significantly worse than individuals with mild TBI on the visual memory indices. Interestingly, relative to healthy controls, mild TBI patients were impaired on measures of Immediate and Delayed auditory memory, Visual Delayed

memory, Immediate Memory, and General Memory.

In another study, Vanderploeg et al. (2001) examined the nature of STM deficits in individuals with moderate-to-severe TBI. Three groups of participants were recruited for the study: (1) a sample of 55 individuals with moderate-to-severe TBI; (2) a control sample matched on age and initial performance on the California Verbal Learning Test (CVLT) Trial 5 and Sum of Trials 1 to 5 (*n* = 55); and (3) a control sample matched on age, education, and race, but not on initial CVLT learning performance (*n* = 55). The study produced several interesting findings. First, the rate of learning was comparable across groups, suggesting the groups did not vary in the extent to which they encoded new information. Second, that rate with which TBI patients forgot new information suggested that STM deficits identified in this group may result from problems in consolidation. Third, individuals with TBI and healthy controls did not differ in the extent to which they benefited from semantic or recognition retrieval cues. This finding suggests that the integrity of retrieval processes is relatively unaffected as a result of TBI. Vanderploeg et al.'s results support an impaired consolidation hypothesis, rather than encoding or retrieval deficits, as the primary deficit underlying memory impairment in TBI.

In a similar study, West, Curtis, Greve and Bianchini (2011) also examined the effects of TBI on WMS-III performance while addressing the effect of effort during testing. Low levels of effort were identified by suboptimal performance on either the Portland Digit Recognition Test and Reliable Digit Span. Participants were 44 mild TBI patients with good effort, 48 mild TBI patients with poor effort, and 40 moderate-to-severe TBI patients with good effort. Consistent with previous findings, a dose–response relationship between injury severity and WMS-III performance was demonstrated. Results indicated that although the WMS-III performance of mild TBI participants with good effort did not significantly diverge from the norms of healthy individuals, moderate-to-severe TBI had a moderate effect on all WMS-III scores. Consistent with Fisher et al., (2000) the moderate-to-severe TBI group scored the lowest on WMS-III Visual indices. Another interesting finding was that effort had a larger effect than injury severity on WMS-III scores.

In contrast to the above findings, Donders, Tulsky, and Zhu (2001) and Shum, McFarland and Bain (1990) found that individuals with moderate-to-severe TBI do not perform significantly poorer than healthy controls on the Digit Span subtests of the WAIS. In a similar study, Curtiss, Vanderploeg, Spencer, and Salazar (2001) used scores on the CVLT and the Digit Span subtest of the Wechsler Memory Scale-III to calculate indexes of seven specific short- and long-term memory processes: working memory span and central executive functions, and long-term memory encoding, consolidation, retention, retrieval, and control abilities. Scores on these indexes were then cluster-analysed to determine whether subtypes of memory performance exist that correspond to deficits in these theoretical memory constructs. Results indicated that individuals with moderate-to-severe TBI ($n = 301$) can be sub-grouped according to specific deficits in consolidation, retention, and retrieval processes. Interestingly, problems with control (e.g., keeping track of target versus distracter items) only appeared in conjunction with retrieval deficits. Working memory span and central executive functioning (i.e., the ability to manipulate information in working memory) do not appear to be deficits characteristic of TBI as no such clusters emerged in the analyses. These results suggest that STM dysfunction, regardless of visual or verbal modality, is not a characteristic cognitive sequela of TBI. One explanation for these findings is that the cortical areas subserving STM (viz., parietal lobes) are seldom damaged as a result of TBI. Taken together, there is mixed evidence concerning the extent to which STM is impaired as a result of moderate-to-severe TBI.

Long-Term Memory

Researchers have also been interested in whether individuals with TBI show impairment in areas of LTM, namely implicit and explicit memory. For example, Shum, Sweeper, and Murray (1996) aimed to assess whether implicit memory was preserved after TBI. Two explicit memory tasks (graphemic-cued recall and semantic-cued recall) and two implicit memory tasks (word fragment completion and general knowledge) were administered to 16 individuals with severe TBI and 16 healthy controls. Results indicated that although individuals with TBI performed significantly poorer than healthy controls on the explicit memory tasks, the performance of the two groups was relatively equivalent on the implicit memory tasks. Such results indicate that explicit memory may require the availability of additional attentional resources that are rarely preserved after severe TBI. Furthermore, by demonstrating that implicit memory is often preserved in this group of individuals, the results of Shum et al.'s (1996) study provide justification for using this intact process to enable TBI patients to acquire skills or information which in turn can be used to enhance their everyday functioning.

Supplementing these findings, Watt, Shores, and Kinoshita (1999) examined the implicit and explicit memory of individuals with severe TBI under conditions of full and divided attention. Participants included 12 individuals with severe TBI and 12 healthy controls. In Experiment 1, participants carried out an implicit test of word-stem completion and an explicit test of cued recall. Results demonstrated that TBI participants exhibited impaired explicit memory but preserved implicit memory. Experiment 2 demonstrated that by reducing attentional resources at the time of encoding, the explicit memory performance of both TBI and control participants was significantly reduced. This pattern of results may be attributable to the relative preservation of brain regions (e.g., parietal and occipital lobes) which mediate implicit memory and are infrequently compromised by TBI relative to prefrontal and temporal areas.

Further exploring the effects of TBI on explicit memory, Anderson and Schmitter-Edgecombe (2009) examined the extent to which episodic memory was preserved after moderate-to-severe TBI. Twenty-nine participants with TBI and 29 healthy controls completed a battery of memory tests and tasks assessing memory self-awareness and memory self-monitoring ability. To assess memory self-awareness, participants predicted the amount of information they would remember before completing list-learning tasks and visual-spatial memory tasks. Memory self-monitoring was assessed by participants' ability to increase their predictive accuracy in parallel with experience. Although individuals with TBI performed poorer than controls on both episodic memory tasks, no significant group differences emerged in self-awareness or self-monitoring ability. These results indicate that during the early stages of recovery, individuals with moderate-to-severe TBI can competently assess the demands of externally driven meta-memorial situations and utilize experience to accurately update their knowledge of memory abilities.

Other research in the field of LTM has focused on the integrity of semantic memory post-TBI. McWilliams and Schmitter-Edgecombe (2008) used an object definitions test to examine the extent to which individuals with severe TBI demonstrate impaired semantic memory and deficits in the organization of semantic knowledge. Twenty-four participants with moderate-to-severe TBI and 24 healthy controls were asked to describe three living and three non-living objects. Participants' verbal definitions were examined at a feature level and evaluated according to the extent to which they communicated core concepts. Results indicated that relative to healthy controls, individuals with TBI rarely provided object definitions that communicated core concepts and were more likely to include superordinate category information. The TBI group also detailed a smaller proportion of physical specific features. The findings were interpreted as suggesting a decreased efficiency in ability to access semantic information following moderate-to-severe TBI, which influenced core concept production, despite intact organization of semantic knowledge.

The effect of TBI on semantic memory was also assessed by Donders et al. (2001). In this study, the WAIS-III was administered to 59 individuals with moderate-to-severe TBI, 54 individuals with mild TBI, and 100 healthy controls. The result most relevant to this chapter was that the performances of the three groups on the Information subtest (i.e., ability to recall well-learned facts) were relatively comparable. This result is unusual in light of the formerly identified findings (e.g., McWilliams & Schmitter-Edgecombe, 2008). One possible explanation for this result is that the TBI sample used in this study contained few individuals with diffuse axonal injury (DAI). As the neural correlates of semantic memory are distributed throughout the cortex rather than concentrated to the temporal and frontal lobes commonly damaged as a result of TBI, a small number of individuals with DAI would account for the relatively high semantic memory scores recorded in this study.

Drawing the above studies together, this review strongly demonstrates that individuals with TBI are often impaired on those LTM processes (e.g., explicit memory) mediated by the temporal and frontal lobes, and diffuse neurological processes, but perform relatively equivalent to controls on tasks that assess those subcomponents of memory thought to be mediated by the parietal and/or occipital areas of the brain (e.g., implicit memory).

Effects of TBI on Working Memory, Prospective Memory, and Contextual/Autobiographical Memory

Working Memory

Individuals who have sustained a TBI often make subjective complaints of "slowed thinking" and frequently comment that they "can only focus on one thing at a time" or "lose concentration easily." Attentional and memory difficulties such as these are characteristics of *working memory*: the ability to hold information in storage while performing cognitive manipulations (Baddeley, 1987). Working memory is instrumental for complex cognitive abilities such as problem solving, planning, and language. As such, deficits in this type of memory can have a debilitating impact on everyday functioning. Results from functional neuroimaging studies in healthy populations indicate that working memory processes are associated with activation of the prefrontal lobes (in particular the middle frontal gyrus and inferior gyrus), the parietal lobes, and to a lesser extent, the temporal lobe (Cabeza & Nyberg, 2000; D'Esposito, Postle, & Rypma, 2000). Working memory, therefore, relies on neural networks which are particularly susceptible to damage after head trauma (Graham, Gennarelli, McIntosh, & Luntus, 2002). Thus, it is not surprising that working memory deficits are a frequently identified sequela of TBI.

Behavioral Studies. Utilizing a standard dual-task paradigm, McDowell, Whyte, and D'Esposito (1997) assessed working memory performance in 25 individuals with severe TBI and 25 healthy controls. Participants were administered a simple visual reaction time task in isolation and again during concurrent tasks of articulation or digit span. Results indicated that participants with TBI, relative to healthy controls, had slower reaction times and response accuracy on the primary task when performed alone and even greater decrements in performance during dual task conditions. This pattern of results remained when the baseline performances of the two groups were matched, thus eliminating lower arousal and slower response speed as explanations for differences in the groups' performance profiles. McDowell et al. (1997) deduced that the greater performance decrement demonstrated by TBI patients during the dual task condition indicates that working memory impairments are more likely to manifest when the integrity of the central executive system (CES) is threatened. Other researchers (e.g., Leclercq et al., 2000; Perlstein et al., 2004) have also found greater impairments in individuals with severe TBI using dual task paradigms similar to that adopted by McDowell et al. (1997).

Elaborating McDowell et al.'s (1997) research design, Serino, Ciaramelli, Santantonio, Malagu, Servadei, and La'Davas (2006) investigated whether cognitive impairment after TBI can be considered a consequence of either processing speed deficits or an impairment of the CES of working memory. Thirty-seven TBI patients underwent a standardized battery of neuropsychological tests evaluating processing speed, sustained attention, STM, working memory, divided attention, executive functions, and LTM. Results indicated that these individuals showed severe deficits in working memory, divided attention, executive functions, and LTM. Furthermore, divided attention, LTM, and executive functions performance significantly correlated with working memory, but not with speed processing. Another unique finding was that CES impairment, but not processing speed deficit, predicted level of deficit in divided attention, executive function, and LTM. The researchers concluded that cognitive impairments following TBI may be a consequence of CES impairment, rather than a deficit in processing speed.

In a more theoretically driven study, Vallat-Azouvi, Weber, Legrand, and Azouvi (2007) systematically evaluated the integrity of each subcomponent of working memory after TBI. Thirty patients with severe TBI and 28 healthy controls received a comprehensive assessment of working memory designed to differentially tap each component of Baddeley and Hitch's (1974) model. Analyses indicated that the performance of the two slave systems was only marginally poorer amongst the TBI group relative to the control group. Central executive functioning, however, was found to be significantly impaired in individuals with TBI relative to healthy participants. The three main functions of the central executive explored included the ability to simultaneously store and process information, dual-task processing, and updating. The researchers deduced that individuals with TBI perform poorer than healthy individuals on tasks requiring a high level of controlled processing and executive demands (e.g., tasks involving interference, or those requiring simultaneous storage and processing of information). A unifying feature of the aforementioned studies is the strong notion that working memory deficits manifesting after TBI can be explained by residual impairment of the CES (Serino et al., 2006; Vallat-Azouvi et al., 2007).

Neuroimaging Studies. Neuroimaging studies have become ubiquitous in the exploration of anatomic substrates underlying working memory. Imaging techniques such as PET and fMRI detect regional increases in brain activity as a participant performs a memory task. Accordingly, these measures go beyond identifying regional brain abnormalities responsible for working memory deficits to permitting researchers to discern the intricate communication pathways necessary for successful working memory processes (i.e., functional connectivity).

The first fMRI examination of working memory in individuals with moderate-to-severe TBI was performed by Christodoulou et al. (2001). In this study, a modified version of the Paced Auditory Serial Addition Task was administered to nine individuals with TBI and seven healthy controls. Results showed that patients with TBI, relative to healthy controls, made significantly more working memory errors and showed more dispersed frontal and temporal activation lateralized to the right hemisphere. This finding may represent an attempt by the brain to engage additional regional cerebral resources to complete the task similar to the increased cerebral representation seen using motor tasks. The researchers concluded that impaired working memory within the TBI population is associated with alterations in functional cerebral activity. Evidence of dispersed cerebral activation in patients with TBI suggests that fMRI can play an important part in characterizing the neurofunctional correlates of cognitive impairment in this patient population.

In a similar study, Perlstein et al. (2004) utilized fMRI to examine the effect of working memory task load on a visual n-back task and prefrontal cortex (PFC) activation after mild ($n = 16$), moderate ($n = 8$) and severe ($n = 18$) TBI. Individuals with TBI showed severity-dependent and load-related WM deficits in performance accuracy. That is, the working memory performance of individuals with mild TBI did not significantly differ from that of healthy controls, and the performance of patients with moderate and severe TBI during conditions with increased processing load was found to be significantly impaired relative to healthy controls and individuals with mild TBI. Furthermore, fMRI results indicated that the TBI patients exhibited load-related patterns

of activation in a number of brain regions associated with working memory, including the dorsolateral prefrontal cortex and Broca's area. Notably, the study showed that increased recruitment of the PFC was attributable to increases in processing load, and that reduced PFC activation was associated with performance decrements in patients with TBI relative to controls. Corroborating evidence from behavioral studies (e.g., McDowell et al., 1997), the pattern of behavioral responding, and the temporal course of activation suggests that working memory deficits in moderate-to-severe TBI are due to associative or strategic aspects of working memory (e.g., CES) rather than impairments in active maintenance of stimulus representations (i.e., phonological loop and visuospatial sketchpad).

Substantial effort has been devoted to replicating Perlstein et al.'s (2004) findings. One such study was that conducted by Scheibel et al. (2007), who sought to control for pre-injury behavioral factors (e.g., impulsivity or risk taking) and psychological effects of injury (e.g., post-traumatic stress), thus eliminating alternate explanations for identified patterns of brain activation. The researchers found that while undertaking n-back tasks during the low load condition, TBI patients displayed less activation in the PFC and greater activation in more posterior regions compared to the control group. In contrast to the findings presented by Perlstein et al. (2004), between group differences within the high memory load condition were less clear. Although future studies are required to specify how the recovery of working memory and other cognitive processes occurs following TBI, these results provide a sound indication of how severe TBI affects general working memory processing.

The key theme emerging from the research detailed above is that working memory deficits in the TBI population are associated with the disruption of the typical increase in PFC activation associated with increased processing load (Scheibel et al., 2007). Whether or not this relationship is a function of working memory load and how this relationship is mediated by injury severity is still unclear. Variation between studies in their reporting of load-dependent PFC activation during working memory tasks may result from differences in sampling and study design. It is possible that cerebral reorganization may differ between focal and diffuse injuries and between mild and moderate-to-severe injuries. Accordingly, studies which include individuals in heterogeneous samples are susceptible to artificially inflating or deflating results. Furthermore, TBI is commonly associated with depression and anxiety disorders, or with chronic pain, all of which may be responsible for observed reductions in neural processing during working memory tasks. As such, it is important that researchers rule out alternative pathologies as explanations for observed effects.

Correlates of Working Memory Performance after TBI. Although there is a wealth of research which has identified differences between individuals with TBI and healthy controls on working memory tasks, few researchers have sought to explore the correlates of working memory performance in this population. One area which has attracted attention is the relationship between working memory deficits and time since injury. One particularly influential study was that conducted by Sanchez-Carrion et al. (2008). These researchers longitudinally investigated changes in working memory performance and brain activation in a group of 12 severe TBI patients and 10 healthy controls over six months. Results indicated that progressive normalization of PFC activation corresponded with improvements in working memory performance and that marked group differences identified prior to the study were negligible at follow up. These results are congruent with the hypothesis of compensation. That is, in the early stages of recovery, individuals with moderate to severe TBI recruit neural resources from brain regions proximal to the prefrontal cortex to perform working memory tasks. In turn, Sanchez-Carrion and colleagues (2008) demonstrated that compensation decreases over the course of recovery in parallel with the improvement of working memory performance. Findings of dispersed neural activation during working memory tasks have also been observed in other neurological disorders (e.g., multiple sclerosis, HIV, and alcohol abuse).

Another area of interest is the relationship between working memory and sustained attention. Slovarp, Azuma, and LaPointe (2012) aimed to assess the relationship between working memory and sustained attention in the TBI population. Nine individuals with severe TBI and nine healthy controls participated in the study. Results indicated that although participants with TBI had lower hit rates and higher false alarm rates than healthy controls during the working memory task, sustained attention scores were relatively similar between groups. Notwithstanding, considerable variability in the sustained attention data of four participants with TBI was identified, suggesting that impaired attention processes can manifest in select individuals. Furthermore, task performance was strongly correlated, supporting the notion that working memory and sustained attention are related.

A collection of researchers have been particularly attracted to the neurochemical and neurogenetic correlates of working memory performance in the TBI population. For example, recent research suggests subtle alterations in central catecholaminergic sensitivity may underlie working memory deficits (Arnsten, 1998; Gualtieri, 1988). In a novel fMRI study, McAllister et al. (2011) investigated the effects of catecholaminergic agonists on the working memory performance of individuals with TBI. Results indicated that participants with mild TBI displayed a performance decrement on verbal working memory tasks following a low dose of a dopamine agonist (i.e., bromocriptine). In contrast, the performance of healthy control participants improved when administered bromocriptine. These results suggest that subjects with mild TBI and controls show differential responses to dopamine agonists and that group differences in performance are associated with localized increases in activation of the dorsolateral prefrontal cortex during working memory tasks (McAllister et al., 2011). Despite these initial findings, there is a paucity of studies exploring the extent to which neurotransmitter systems affect working memory following moderate-to-severe TBI.

A new line of research has investigated the influence of genetics in modulating recovery after TBI. For example, neurogenetics studies have investigated the influence of genotype on working memory impairment after TBI.

Specifically, Crawford et al. (2002) explored the influence of the Є4 allele of the APOE gene on working memory performance in the TBI population. The Є4 allele was found to be related to poorer performance on verbal working memory, but not other measures of executive function. Two mechanisms have been proposed to explain these findings. Either the APOE Є4 protein impedes neuronal repair processes in the medial temporal lobe after TBI, or the presence of APOE Є4 results in further damage to memory-related structures (Crawford et al., 2002). Identifying the role of genetics and neurotransmitters in memory processes has the potential to inform psychopharmacological interventions tailored to cognitive recovery after brain injury.

Rehabilitation. The different studies summarized above all suggest that moderate-to-severe TBI is associated with an impairment of executive aspects of working memory. However, there has been little research on rehabilitation of working memory after TBI. Training of working memory has been found useful in other conditions, such as children with ADHD (Klingberg, Forssberg, & Westerberg, 2002), stroke (Vallat et al., 2005), or patients with brain tumor (Duval, Coyette, & Seron, 2008). The aim of this subsection is to provide a brief overview of recent studies that have explored the efficacy of rehabilitation programs targeting working memory deficits in the TBI population.

Vallat-Azouvi, Pradat-Diehl, and Azouvi (2009) sought to assess the effectiveness of a comprehensive program of rehabilitation addressing the different components of working memory, according to Baddeley and Hitch's model, in two patients with severe TBI suffering from central executive deficits. An experimental single-case design was used whereby outcome was assessed using specific working memory tests (e.g., working memory span, Brown Peterson, n-back), nonspecific cognitive tasks requiring working memory (e.g., dual-task, arithmetic solving problem), an ecological questionnaire to assess generalization to everyday life, and tests designed to assess the specificity of the therapy. The intervention involved cognitive training modules, divisible by the 12 tasks designed to train the

central executive, the phonological loop, and the visuo-spatial sketchpad. Training was given twice a week for one hour over eight (Patient 1) or six (Patient 2) months. The difficulty level (e.g., capacity and level of processing) was progressively adapted to the patients' performance, starting at n-1 backward digit span level. Each level was trained until the patient succeeded in 90% of the trials. Both patients improved on all target measures, particularly for central executive tasks and for the questionnaire on attention failures in everyday life. In contrast, no change was found for non-target measures. In conclusion, this pattern of results for these two patients confirmed the effectiveness of a specific therapy focusing on central executive aspects of working memory and its generalization to daily-life activities in patients with severe TBI.

In an earlier study, Serino et al. (2006) demonstrated that a complex pattern of cognitive deficits (viz., divided attention, executive functions, and LTM deficits) are explained by impairment of the CES. Subsequently, this same group of researchers (Serino et al., 2007) evaluated the extent to which a CES rehabilitative program improved WM and other cognitive functions dependent on this system. Nine TBI patients with severe working memory deficits underwent two successive modules of experimental training: general stimulation training (GST, which consisted of four sessions a week, over a period of 4 weeks) and working memory training (WMT, which consisted of four sessions a week, over a period of 4 weeks). The WMT was based on the repeated administration of the Paced Auditory Serial Addition Test (PASAT) which has been demonstrated to tap CES processes (Vanderploeg, Curtiss, & Belanger, 2005) and on two experimental tasks we derived from the PASAT (i.e., the "Months task" and the "Words task"). In order to vary the difficulty of the tasks, the inter-stimulus interval was altered (i.e., 4,000 msec; 3,000 msec; 2,600 msec; 2,200 msec; 1,800 msec). Patients initially performed the slowest version of the tasks and when they achieved a predetermined level of performance the inter-stimulus interval was reduced. The initial GST sessions were directed towards providing the patients with a description and an interpretation of their cognitive impairments with the aim to increase patients' awareness of their cognitive deficits and disabilities. In addition, three simple decision tasks were repeatedly administered to patients during the GST. These tasks involved the same material used for the WMT tasks, but with a crucial difference: Whereas the three training tasks used during the WMT required the continuous manipulation and updating of information in working and therefore tapped CES processes, the tasks used during the GST only required basic-level attention demands, like the ability to maintain vigilance on a task over a long period of time. Patients' cognitive performance was evaluated at admission, after the GST, and at the end of the WMT. Results indicated that although the GST had no effect on patients' cognitive performance, significant improvements were made in all the cognitive processes dependent on the CES after WMT. Furthermore, results showed that TBI participants rated significantly higher on two measures of psychosocial functioning after WMT (i.e., RHFUQ and PCRS), suggesting that everyday functioning and perceived self-efficacy was enhanced in patients after receiving CES-targeted treatment. The researchers concluded that these results provide sound evidence to confirm that treatment acting on CES functioning is effective in ameliorating WM, improving the functioning of other cognitive processes thought to depend on this system (i.e., divided attention, long-term memory, and executive functions) and enhancing functional outcome.

The studies described above provide sound preliminary evidence suggesting that interventions tailored to treat working memory impairments are successful in the TBI population. However, there is a need for further research in the area of working memory impairments following TBI to enlighten practitioners to the benefits and limitations of past, current, and future treatment procedures, thus enabling them to provide further benefit to their patients. These preliminary findings also encourage development of randomized clinical trials of interventions for working memory deficit and associated impairments of everyday memory. Further understanding the neural correlates and functional outcomes of working memory deficits and designing interventions that will

transition individuals out of rehabilitative settings and make the most meaningful impact on their daily functioning should be the ultimate goal of future research.

Prospective Memory

Investigations of memory deficits within the TBI population have largely focused on impairments of *retrospective memory* (RM), that is, an individual's ability to recall or recognize past events or stimuli. This comprises both declarative and non-declarative memory as illustrated in Figure 5-1. However, in recent years, there is an increased interest in what is referred to as *prospective memory* (PM), or the ability to remember to carry out an intention in the future (Kliegel, McDaniel, & Einstein, 2008). Although RM impairments can impact on the daily functioning of those with TBI, many everyday activities also involve remembering to carry out an intended action in the future (e.g., remembering to pay a bill before its due date, turning up to an appointment at the right date and time, or taking medications; Shum, Fleming, & Neulinger, 2002). Forgetting to perform an intended action in the future is a common complaint of those who have sustained a TBI and is an enormous impediment to independent everyday functioning, recovery, and rehabilitation (Shum et al., 2002).

According to Ellis (1996), there are five stages of PM: (1) formation and encoding of intention; (2) retention interval; (3) performance interval; (4) initiation and execution of intention action; and (5) evaluation of outcome. In addition, it is generally agreed that a PM task has five characteristics (Shum & Fleming, 2011). They include: (1) a conscious intention needs to be formed about the content and context of realization of the intention; (2) a filled delay between encoding and execution of the intention; (3) an absence of an external prompt for the execution of the intention; (4) a need to interrupt other ongoing activities to execute the encoded intention; (5) a constraint time for successful execution of intention.

Three subtypes of PM have been identified in the literature according to task characteristics and reliance on self-initiated versus external cues (Kvavilashvili & Ellis, 1996). *Time-based* tasks involve performing a task or action at a certain time or after a certain time period has elapsed (e.g., taking medication at 4 p.m.), as compared to *event-based* tasks, which involve execution of a task or action when an external cue is present (e.g., posting a letter after seeing a letterbox), and *activity-based* tasks, where the cue is the preceding behavior or action (e.g., turn off the oven after baking). While RM is a function predominantly mediated by the medial temporal and hippocampal regions of the brain, PM is thought to be dependent on the prefrontal (Burgess, Scott, & Frith, 2003) and parietal lobes (Reynolds, West, & Braver, 2009). Considering that the prefrontal area is commonly damaged as a result of TBI, it is unsurprising that patients experience prospective memory difficulties after injury.

The history of PM research can be chaptered according to different waves of methodology. Measures include self- and other-report questionnaires and rating scales, behavioral tasks, psychometric tests, and virtual reality (VR) tasks. In a recent review of the PM literature, Shum, Levin, & Chan (2011) undertook a meta-analysis of results from studies that used either behavioral tasks, psychometric tests, or VR tasks to examine the extent to which PM is disrupted after TBI. Strong and consistent effects surfaced across methodologies for impairments in both time- and event-based PM. Contrary to expectation, individuals with TBI were not found to be significantly more impaired on time- than event-based PM tasks. Such a finding was surprising in lieu of the theoretical difficulty of time-based PM tasks (Einstein & McDaniel, 1990). The following subsections provide a review of the studies that have trialed the different methodologies identified above.

Self- and Other-Report of PM in Individuals with TBI. Several studies employing self-report questionnaires have found that individuals with TBI report significantly more PM problems than healthy controls. Mateer, Sohlberg, and Crinean (1987) conducted the first study that used a questionnaire to scale the occurrence of memory failures in individuals with severe closed head injury (CHI) (i.e., 121 CHI with coma, 57 without coma) and healthy controls ($n = 157$). The 30-item questionnaire covered six memory domains including anterograde episodic, anterograde semantic, retrograde episodic, retrograde semantic, working memory and PM. Mateer et al. (1987) found that PM failures ranked as the most commonly reported memory error amongst individuals with CHI.

In another study, Hannon, Adams, Harrington, Fries-Dias, and Gipson (1995) administered the Prospective Memory Questionnaire (i.e., developed for the purpose of their study) to 15 individuals with severe TBI and 114 controls. The questionnaire comprised 52 items which formed 4 scales: (1) long-term episodic (e.g., I forgot to return books to the library by the due date); (2) short-term habitual (e.g., I forgot to lock the door when leaving my apartment or house); (3) techniques to assist memory (e.g., I rehearse things in my mind so I will not forget to do them); and (4) internally cued (e.g., I was driving and temporarily forgot where I was going). The key finding emerging from this research was that individuals with TBI were found to rate differently than healthy controls on the short-term habitual subscale. This result indicates that TBI patients experience more problems, relative to their performance in other memory domains, with routine tasks that are to be completed within a few minutes of their respective cue.

Subsequently, Roche, Fleming, and Shum (2002) developed the Comprehensive Assessment of Prospective Memory (CAPM) to scale the occurrence of prospective forgetting over the last month. The questionnaire consists of 39 items which compose two subscales: common PM failures that are related to instrumental activities of daily living (IADL) or uncommon PM failures that are related to basic activities of daily living (BADL; see Table 5-1). Part A of the CAPM was administered to 33 individuals with severe TBI and 29 healthy controls. Unlike the study conducted by Hannon et al. (1995), the researchers also asked the significant others of the two groups of participants to rate their relative's or close friend's PM problems. Although Roche et al. (2002) did not find significant differences between the two groups of participants for either the IDAL or BADL scales, significant differences were found between the ratings by the significant others for the two CAPM scales. Specifically, the

Table 5-1. Examples from the Comprehensive Assessment of Prospective Memory

CAPM Subscales	Example Items
IDAL	Forgetting to buy an item at the grocery store
	Leaving the iron on
	Forgetting to put the garbage bin out
BDAL	Forgetting to eat a meal
	Not locking the door when leaving home
	Forgetting to get money from the bank/ATM

significant others of the TBI group were found to report more PM forgetting than the significant others of the controls (see Figure 5-3). The difference in results between Roche et al.'s (2002) study and the study reviewed prior (i.e., Hannon et al. 1995) is likely to be because TBI participants in the former study were in a later stage of recovery (i.e., mean time since injury was 3 years) than those recruited in the latter (i.e., mean time since injury was 58 weeks). As such, participants in Roche et al.'s (2002) study may have maintained a lower level of insight into their deficits and in turn, underreported the frequency of their PM problems.

In a more recent study, Roche, Moody, Szabo, Fleming, and Shum (2007) sought to clarify the reasons underlying PM impairment in individuals with TBI. Thirty-eight participants with severe TBI, 34 controls, and the significant others of these two groups were asked to rate their perceived reasons for their prospective remembering and forgetting using section C of the CAPM. This section of the questionnaire has 15 items which were selected to cover the five stages of prospective memory suggested by Ellis (1996; see Table 5-2). Findings of this study show that individuals with TBI are reported primarily to experience PM difficulties in the encoding phase relating to the source, motivation, and formation of prospective memory tasks, according to Ellis' model (1996). This study also indicates that difficulties in the retaining of PM information in the performance interval appear not to be unique to the brain-injured population. In conclusion, the researchers recommended that the use of external memory aids be encouraged and aimed towards the area of difficulty (encoding, performance interval, or the execution of intended action). Although Roche et al.'s (2007) study and other research which has used self-report measures provide sound preliminary data which can be used to inform diagnostic and treatment decisions, several critiques (e.g., Rabin, Burton, & Barr, 2007; Ruff, 2003; Uttl & Kibreab, 2011) posit that these

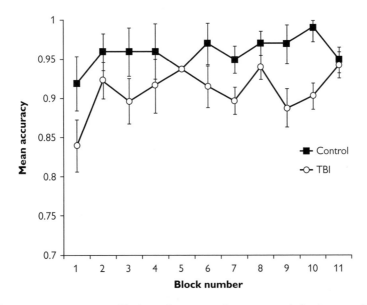

Figure 5-3. The mean accuracy across blocks in the sustained attention task for the control and TBI groups.

Table 5-2. Examples from Section C of the CAPM

Five Stages of Ellis' Model (1996)	Description of Problem	Example of Corresponding Item
Formation and encoding of intention	Patients may have problems with listening to instructions due to attentional problems.	Forgetting a change in your daily routine
Retention interval	Even if information was sufficiently encoded, it may extinguish from memory during the delay.	Forgetting to mention a point you intended to make during a conversation.
Performance interval	Retrieval cues may not be salient enough for initiating retrieval, or self-initiated retrieval may not be possible in time-based tasks.	Forgetting to take tablets at the prescribed time.
Initiation and execution of intention action	Patients may have forgotten what they wanted to do because of retrospective memory problems, executive dysfunction, or apathy. Even if execution was successfully started, patients may be interrupted and not be able to find their way back to the task.	Accidentally forgetting to put a piece of clothing on when you get dressed.
Evaluation of outcome	Postponing tasks may be necessary if they could not be executed in the recall situation. Other patients may not be able to extinguish the intention from memory even if it was successfully executed. In this case, they may start the task again later.	Checking whether or not you have already done something you planned to do.

measures of PM lack ecological validity and thus are of limited utility.

Behavioral Tasks. When experimental PM research was in its infancy, researchers (e.g., Hannon et al., 1995; Kinsella et al., 1996) often acquired and adapted simple experimental tasks (e.g., remembering to return a letter via post) from the aging literature to examine PM impairment after TBI. Experiments like these, however, had several methodological problems (e.g., lacked tight experimental control) and were quickly replaced with computerized behavioral tasks.

In one of the first studies to use a simple computerized task to assess PM impairment in a TBI population, Shum, Valentine, and Cutmore (1999) compared the performance of 12 individuals with severe TBI with that of 12 matched controls on time-, event-, and activity-based PM. The program was based on the influential dual task paradigm whereby the PM tasks are embedded in an ongoing activity; a general knowledge task. Results indicated that the performance of the TBI group was significantly impaired relative to that of the control group on all three types of PM. Furthermore, by keeping track of the time and frequency of clock checking, the researchers found that that

poorer performance on the time-based task was due to a non-strategic approach and a lower frequency of time monitoring. Another particularly germane finding was that PM forgetting could not be attributed to poor RM. This conclusion is based on the finding that TBI participants could recall the PM task instructions when questioned at the end of task. Shum et al.'s (1999) findings have been replicated by Matthias and Mansfield (2005) and Maujean, Shum, and McQueen (2003).

Behavioral tasks have gradually evolved past identifying between group differences on PM tasks to integrating dependent measures into experimental paradigms to allow for the systematic manipulation of factors relating to PM impairment. Innovative experiments that utilize such paradigms have been instrumental in identifying the cognitive processes which influence PM (e.g., working memory load of the ongoing task, local and focal PM cue, self- or experimenter-generated target, number of PM targets). One such experiment was conducted by Kliegel, Eschen, and Thöne-Otto (2004), who sought to investigate the role of executive functioning in prospective remembering. Participants included a group of patients with normal range RM, but with impaired executive functioning due to TBI ($n = 7$), 21 healthy older adults, and 19 healthy young adults. Results indicated that TBI patients obtained lower scores in the intention formation, intention re-instantiation, and intention execution phases, but not on the intention retention phase of PM. These findings offer preliminary evidence that executive functioning has a prominent role in prospective remembering.

Concurrently, Schmitter-Edgecombe and Wright (2004) examined the effect of cue salience on event-based prospective remembering using a computerized task. Participants included 24 individuals with severe TBI and 24 healthy controls. Results indicated that although controls responded to event-based PM cues more frequently than did participants with severe TBI, the groups did not differ on their performance on the ongoing working memory task. Contrary to expectation, the researchers found no difference between the ability of a cue to trigger prospective remembering when the cue was integrated with the ongoing memory task (focal cue) or peripheral to it. Consistent with evidence that frontal and medial temporal structures are involved in PM (e.g., Knight, Ethridge, Marsh, & Clementz, 2010; Simons, Scholvinck, Gilbert, Frith, & Burgess, 2006), the researchers found significant correlations with measures of attention/speeded processing and RM. In conclusion, Schmittter-Edgecombe, and Wright (2004) interpreted the TBI groups' fluctuating pattern of prospective remembering as momentary lapses of attention to task detail rather than prospective forgetting per se.

Another interesting study was that conducted by Henry et al. (2007) who, through manipulating the number of target events to be remembered in a PM task, investigated the specific effect of task complexity on prospective remembering. This manipulation was of interest because two competing models make different predictions about the effect of task complexity on controlled attentional processes. In the context of Smith and Bayen's (2004) preparatory attentional processes and memory processes (PAM) model, increasing the number of target events should increase requirements for controlled attentional processing. In contrast, McDaniel and Einstein's (2000) multiprocess framework assumes that distinct target events presented in focal awareness of the processing

activities required for the ongoing task are likely to depend on automatic processes. This latter model therefore leads to the prediction that increasing the number of target events should not increase demands upon controlled attentional processes. Consistent with McDaniel and Einstein's (2000) multiprocess framework, TBI patients were significantly and comparably impaired on the one- and the four-target-event conditions relative to controls. Further, by nature of the experimental procedure, the researchers were able to conclude that PM deficits in the TBI group could not be attributed to increased difficulty with the retrospective component of the prospective memory task.

A study by Carlesimo, Formisano, Bivona, Barba, and Caltagirone (2009/2010) sought to assess the sensitivity of patients who suffered a severe TBI to the manipulation of attentional resources and encoding instructions during the execution of time- and event-based PM tasks. This was achieved by manipulating the availability of attentional resources at the time of intention recall and encoding conditions at the time of giving instructions. Participants included 18 individuals with severe TBI and 18 healthy controls. Results indicated that simultaneous execution of a concurrent task was more detrimental to PM performance in the spontaneous recall of the prospective intention in the TBI group than in the control group. Moreover, the instruction to encode the PM task more elaborately by rehearsing aloud and mentally imaging the actions to be performed improved PM performance significantly more in the TBI group than in the control group. Utilizing these results, Carlesimo et al. concluded that prospective memory deficits in individuals with TBI is explained, in part, by the reduced availability of attentional resources and to poor encoding of actions to be performed.

Although computerized behavioral tasks have been commended for their ability to provide objective and reliable measures of PM post-TBI, they have two major limitations. First, tasks of this nature often lack verisimilitude (Chaytor & Schmitter-Edgecombe, 2003). That is the stimuli, materials, and procedures fail to capture the variety and level of difficulty demanded by naturalistic prospective remembering. Second, simple computerized behavioral tasks have been criticized for failing to demonstrate veridicality (Chaytor & Schmitter-Edgecombe, 2003). That is, none of the studies employing computerized behavioral tasks cited thus far provided evidence indicating that PM performance predicts social, occupational, and functional impairment. Ultimately, the absence of verisimilitude and veridicality reflects the widespread neglect for ecological validity that plagues memory assessment.

Psychometric Tests. As awareness and understanding of ecological validity has developed, a number of sensitive, valid, and standardized measures suitable for the assessment of PM deficits have manifested in the clinical sphere. One such measure is the Cambridge Prospective Memory Test (CAMPROMPT; Wilson et al., 2005). The CAMPROMPT comprises three time-based and three event-based PM tasks performed whilst engaged in number of filler activities. Utilizing an early version of this measure, Groot, Wilson, Evans, and Watson (2002) compared the PM performance of 36 individuals with TBI with that of 28 healthy controls. PM performance was found to be significantly poorer amongst the TBI group than amongst the control group. Furthermore, the PM performance of individuals with TBI as measured by the CAMPPROMPT significantly correlated with other neuropsychological processes (e.g., attention and executive function) considered to be mediated by the prefrontal cortex.

Another psychometric measure of time-and event-based PM is the Memory for Intentions Screening Test (MIST: Raskin, 2009). It is comprised of eight PM tasks (four time-based and four event-based) that require a two-minute or 15-minute delay and a verbal or action response. Tay, Ang, Lau, Meyyappan, and Collinson (2010) used the MIST to examine the PM of 38 individuals with mild TBI and 38 healthy controls within one month of injury and at three months post-injury. The performance of the TBI group was significantly more impaired than that of the control group within the first month following injury, indicating that PM impairment is part of the acute cognitive sequelae of mild TBI. Moreover, prospective forgetting persisted beyond three months post-injury. Taken

together, these results suggest that PM may be a sensitive indicator of cerebral compromise after TBI.

Psychometric tests have several advantages over other modes of PM assessment. For example, they focus on objective behavior, are of sound reliability and validity, and offer standardized instruction, and the norms which accompany psychometric measures permit inferences about the extent to which an individual with TBI varies from age-related peers allowing for calculation of reliable change indices. For these reasons, psychometric measures of PM are strongly supported within the extant PM literature, albeit not without criticism.

A commonly cited criticism of psychometric PM tests is that time- and event-based PM are rarely measured in a way that permits the respective difficulty of the two tasks to be directly compared (Shum et al., 2011). Moreover, the stimuli used and context within which the intention is realized are somewhat removed from routine daily life. Accordingly, results acquired using such measures may not generalize to environments outside the assessment context (Knight & Titov, 2009).

Virtual Reality Tasks. Virtual reality (VR) is a term used to describe computer-generated artificial environments with distinctive sensory properties that can be explored and interacted with in real time (Knight & Titov, 2009). The utility of virtual platforms in neuropsychological assessment and rehabilitation has only recently been recognized (Shum et al., 2011). This new development comes at a time when neuropsychologists have identified the limitations of many conventional tests of memory and are seeking new approaches to measure cognitive impairments. Despite their widespread endorsement, only a handful of studies have explored the validity and utility of VR PM tasks within TBI the population.

Knight, Harnett, and Titov (2005) developed one of the first computerized procedures for assessing the extent to which participants with severe TBI ($n = 25$) and healthy controls ($n = 20$) accurately predicted their PM performance. Participants completed a video-based PM test, a measure of RM, and tests of executive functioning. The context of the PM task was one in which the participant's car had been stolen and that they needed to complete a series of instructions when they reached the nearest city. Participants watched a video vignette that displayed the perspective of a person who was first driving though an unfamiliar city and then walking through a shopping precinct. Participants were instructed to recall 20 actions when their corresponding cue appeared (e.g., fix tire at a service station). Results indicated that event-based PM strongly correlated with measures of verbal fluency but not with measures of RM, suggesting that the task is sensitive to different levels of amnesic deficit. Furthermore, the TBI group's performance on the event-based PM task was significantly more impaired than that of the control group, albeit pre-test expectations of PM performance were similar amongst TBI and control participants.

Subsequently, Knight, Titov, and Crawford (2006) used a virtual reality PM task to assess the extent to which distraction affected PM performance following severe TBI. The researchers constructed a virtual shopping precinct which was divided into a low and high distraction zones. The latter zone contained increased visual and auditory noise. Twenty persons with severe TBI and 20 matched controls completed the task. The ongoing task required participants to imagine they were an inspector for the local council and to complete ten errands along the virtual street. Whilst engaged in this task participants were to remember to check whether or not food shops had a current licence and report the name of the shop in front of them if they heard a dog bark or saw a person carrying a box (i.e., event-based PM component). Knight et al., (2006) found that the TBI group performed significantly poorer than controls on both the ongoing and the PM component of the task. Additionally, the PM performance of the TBI patients was significantly poorer in the high- than low-distraction condition (see Table 5-3). Such results suggest that the TBI group was unable to distribute cognitive resources according to the demands of the PM task.

In one of the most recent studies of PM, Potvin, Rouleau, Audy, Charbonneau, and Giguere (2011) sought to evaluate the validity and sensitivity of the Test écologique de mémoire prospective (TEMP; i.e., Ecological Test of PM) for use with individuals with moderate and severe TBI ($n = 30$). The TEMP involves a 20-min movie that presents various areas of a city (i.e., commercial, residential and industrial) as if the participant were driving through its streets. Ten event-based tasks and five time-based tasks must be performed in order to prepare for a birthday dinner (version A) or a holiday (version B). The results show that TBI patients experienced more pronounced problems than matched controls ($n = 15$) in learning the content of delayed intentions (retrospective component) and retrieving

Table 5-3. Performance of TBI and Control Groups on the Ongoing and Prospective Components of the Study in the High and Low Distraction Zones

	TBI				Control			
	Low		High		Low		High	
	M	(SD)	M	(SD)	M	(SD)	M	(SD)
Ongoing errands								
P (cues)	.78	(.27)	.66	(.29)	.85	(.17)	.84	(.17)
P (task/cue)	.96	(.12)	.73	(.32)	.94	(.14)	.90	(.16)
Prospective tasks								
P (cues)	.43	(.30)	.19	(.23)	.68	(.27)	.50	(.36)
P (correct)	.29	(.26)	.15	(.20)	.59	(.31)	.43	(.35)
Checklist								
Times checked	7.85	(3.25)	6.10	(3.29)	7.55	(3.25)	6.70	(3.15)
Pages/check	15.75	(5.05)	22.90	(14.36)	22.70	(5.05)	24.87	(21,46)
Time/page (secs)	6.40	(2.10)	5.26	(2.06)	4.82	(.98)	3.99	(.90)

Note: P (cues) = Probability of correct detection cue: P (tasks/cue) = Probability of correct recall of a task given correct cue detection: P (correct) = Probability of correct completion of a prospective task.

these intentions in the right context (prospective component), especially in the time-based condition. Correlations revealed that the retrospective component was mainly supported by episodic RM processes, while the prospective component was supported by episodic RM processes, along with attention and executive function. Moreover, there was a significant correlation between performance on the TEMP and results on a questionnaire assessing PM functioning in daily living completed by participants' relatives. Such results indicate that the TEMP is a sensitive and ecologically valid measure of PM deficits for use with individuals with TBI.

Virtual reality has several advantages that have encouraged its widespread endorsement in the clinical and experimental literature. First, VR offers an ecologically valid medium through which to assess PM impairment (Lam, Man, Tam, & Weiss, 2006). Second, one of the primary goals of the neuropsychologist in administering tests of PM functioning is to determine whether patients have a normal capacity to remember a simple set of intentions and if not, identify the limits of their functional independence (Knight et al., 2005). Tests embedded in virtual environments (VEs) can help patients with disabilities to explore the limits of their competence in a non-threatening setting. Third, virtual PM tasks focus on behavioral responses rather than subjective data, thus providing a bridge between conventional neuropsychological tests, behavioral observation, and the logistical parameters of in-patient settings (Knight & Titov, 2009). Akin, VR maintains standardized procedure and tight control, thus is well placed to offer specificity and sensitivity. Lastly, virtual platforms are readily accepted by test-takers because of their inherent novelty and face validity (Knight & Titov, 2009).

Despite their many advantages of using simulated environments for PM assessment, there are a number of obstacles hindering their clinical application. First, current VR programs often fail to capture the full complexity of every-day prospective remembering (e.g., simultaneous demands of time-, event-, and activity-based tasks). Second, the added sensitivity and validity that VR programs supposedly offer has seldom been demonstrated. In parallel, few studies

have explored whether virtual PM performance is associated with social, occupational, and functional impairment and other neuropsychological functions.

Correlates of PM Performance in Individuals with TBI. Only a handful of studies have moved beyond identifying precedented group differences, to considering which TBI-related factors (e.g., injury severity, time since injury), as well as demographic variables and cognitive processes, predict PM performance (e.g., Kinch & McDonald, 2001; Martin, Kliegel, & McDaniel, 2003). One such study was that conducted by Fleming, Riley, Gill, Gullo, Strong, and Shum (2008). In this study, the researchers examined whether demographic factors, injury severity and site, executive function, and metacognitive factors predicted time- and event-based PM (as measured by the CAMPPROMPT) in adults with severe TBI ($n = 44$). Results indicated that both time- and event-based PM scores were predicted by measures of verbal fluency, length of PTA, and use of note-taking. The researchers concluded that patients with longer periods of PTA and greater executive dysfunction may be expected to display poorer PM.

Capitalizing on the understanding that successful prospective remembering requires the intact coordination of a number of neural processes, several researchers sought to map the relationship between PM and other frontal lobes processes such as attention (Mathias & Mansfield, 2005); executive function (EF) (Maujean, et al., 2003; Knight, et al., 2005), and RM (Schmitter-Edgecombe & Wright, 2004). The meta-analysis performed by Shum et al. (2011) described earlier also summarized those studies which have provided preliminary evidence of the association between PM performance of individuals with TBI and deficits in neuropsychological functioning. Results of the meta-analysis confirmed that PM (time- and event-based PM pooled) is significantly related to measures of attention, RM, and EF. This pattern of results corroborates imaging research that suggests PM relies on functional connectivity between the neural substrates responsible for the aforementioned cognitive processes (Knight, et al., 2010; Simons, et al., 2006). Knowledge of the factors which underpin PM processes has the potential to inform the development of rehabilitation programs designed to help individuals with TBI to obtain higher levels of functional independence.

Rehabilitation. Although the underlying nature and mechanisms of PM impairment in individuals with TBI have not been fully identified and clarified, researchers have already started to conduct studies to see if this problem can be treated or rehabilitated in this population. To date, most of these studies were based on either a remedial or a compensatory approach to improve PM performance in individuals with TBI. For example, in one of the earliest studies in this area, Sohlberg, White, Evans, and Mateer (1992) provided repetitive drill remediation (four to six hours per week and for 32 and 63 sessions) to one male (8 months post injury) and one female (72 months post injury) with severe TBI. Results of the study indicated that the two participants improved in their performance on PM tasks. In another study, Fleming, Shum, Strong, and Lightbody (2005) developed an eight-week compensatory plus self-awareness training (one to two hours per week) for three participants with TBI (two males and one female) on average six months after injury. They found improvements in the participants' scores on a psychometric PM test (viz., the MIST) and an increase in the number of diary entries for all the participants.

Potvin, Rouleau, Sénéchal & Giguère (2011) evaluated the efficacy of a PM rehabilitation program based on visual imagery techniques expected to strengthen the cue–action association. Ten moderate-to-severe TBI patients were taught to create a mental image representing the association between a prospective cue and an intended action within progressively more complex and naturalistic PM tasks. Serving as a control condition, 20 individuals with TBI received a short educational session. Contrary to expectation, increases in PM performance were observed in both conditions. Furthermore, evidence suggested that the techniques taught in the program generalized to patients' everyday lives. That is, TBI patients in the rehabilitation group and their relatives reported less everyday PM failures following the program. The researchers concluded that visual imagery

techniques appear to improve PM functioning by strengthening the memory trace of the intentions and inducing an automatic recall of the intentions.

Despite these promising results, it should be noted that most of these studies included a small number of participants and that they used inadequate designs (e.g., single case or pre/post assessment). The exception is a study by Shum, Fleming, Gill, Gullo, and Strong (2011) which conducted a randomized controlled trial to evaluate the effectiveness of compensatory PM training (6 weeks), preceded by self-awareness training (2 weeks) for 45 individuals with moderate-to-severe TBI living in the community. The individuals were randomly allocated into four intervention groups: self-awareness plus compensatory PM training; self-awareness plus active control; active control plus compensatory PM training; and active control only. Individuals in the four groups completed an eight-session (one session per week) individual intervention program (content of program depended on the group) with pre- and post-intervention assessment by a blind assessor on a standardized test of PM (i.e, the CAMPROMPT), relatives' ratings of PM failure, and assessments of psychosocial reintegration. Overall, larger changes in PM test scores and greater increases in strategy use were found in groups which were engaged in compensatory PM training. Taken together, the results of these studies constitute strong evidence that PM impairment in individuals with TBI can be improved with low intensity interventions.

Contextual and Autobiographical Memory

Contextual memory, otherwise known as source memory, is the conscious recall of the source or circumstances of a specific memory. A disruption of memory for source refers to the phenomenon whereby individuals have access to information learned during a prior experience but are impaired in their ability to report where or when that information was encountered (i.e., the context). Context can refer to the temporal frame (i.e., specific time), external surrounds (i.e., physical and situational) or internal states generated by (e.g., emotional or cognitive) the event in which a memory is formed (see Table 5-4 for examples of source memory). Simply, source memory refers to the background information of an item or event, such as its temporal order, spatial location, or modality of presentation. Memory for contextual information could be assessed explicitly and implicitly. For example, asking participants about the modality, font, or voice in which a word was originally presented would be considered as explicit measures of context, which is viewed as the equivalent of source memory. The facilitation due to correspondence of context (e.g., modality or font) of the words in learning and test would be considered as an implicit measure of context or context effect (see Vakil, Openheim, Falck, Aberbuch, & Groswasser, 1997).

A number of researchers have used facets of autobiographical memory to conceptualize and, in turn, assess source memory. *Autobiographical memory* is a complex, multifaceted concept which involves different kinds of knowledge pertaining to one's self—either episodic or semantic. The semantic component stores the general knowledge of one's past (e.g., date of birth). The episodic component, however, contains personal specific events situated in time and space (e.g., what one did for their 21st birthday). Intuitively, this latter aspect of autobiographical memory is strongly related to source memory.

The decline in the ability to access episodic or incidental aspects of experience has been described as the impairment of a specific memory system specialized with respect to spatiotemporal information. Shimamura and Squire (1987) suggest that frontal lobe dysfunction causes a disconnection between semantic memory and contextual memory, rather than causing amnesia for the context itself. Moscovitch (1992) links the concept of source memory deficits to the phenomenon of confabulation, which would not constitute a problem with a particular kind of memory per se, but as a problem with the strategic aspects of retrieval. Other researchers (e.g., Dywan, Segalowitz, Henderson, & Jacoby, 1993) have argued that source errors represent an attributional problem resulting from disordered attention. This is consistent with Mayes, MacDonald, Donlan, Pears and Meudel's (1992) definition of context as "information that falls on the periphery of attention" (p. 268).

While memory for source has been examined in a number of populations at risk of frontal brain damage, there is a paucity of research of this phenomenon in those who have suffered TBI. Neuropsychological studies which have assessed clinical patients (Kopelman, 1989, 2000, 2002; Piolino et al., 2003), together with functional imaging studies of normal subjects (Fink et al., 1996; Maguire, 2001; Piolino et al., 2004), have shown that autobiographical memory involves a widespread cerebral network, with particularly high recruitment from the anterior fronto-temporal region. As this region is the most frequent site of focal lesions after TBI resulting from severe TBI (Shum et al., 2011), it is perhaps unsurprising that this population frequently reports extensive autobiographical and source memory impairments.

Behavioral Studies and Correlates of Source Memory. Just as behavioral measures have been instrumental in developing our understanding of other areas of memory, such tasks are a common theme in the literature investigating the

Table 5-4. Examples of Source Memory

Content of Source Memory	Example
Example 1: Time and Place	You hear a song on the radio which sounds familiar. You recall that you first heard the song at your high school graduation in 2001.
Example 2: Place and Emotion	Somebody tells you a story and you realize that you have heard it before. You recall that you heard it on rainy afternoon from your grandmother several years ago and that, at the time, it made you feel very happy.
Example 3: Place	You know that your friend's daughter has moved to France. You recall that you learnt about this information from a family e-mail that she sent you a year ago.

integrity of source memory post-TBI population. In a series of studies, Vakil and colleagues have tested context memory in patients with TBI using explicit and implicit measures of memory. In accordance with the previously reported studies, individuals with TBI were consistently shown to be impaired relative to healthy controls on all the explicit memory tests of target information (e.g., word recall and recognition) and of context information (e.g., modality and temporal order judgment). However, when contextual information was tested implicitly, the patient and control groups did not differ significantly, that is, the groups showed the same magnitude of context effect (cf. Vakil, Blachstein, & Hoofien, 1991; re: temporal order judgment; cf. Vakil & Tweedy, 1994, re: frequency judgment; cf. Vakil, Golan, Grunbaum, Groswasser, & Aberbuch, 1996, re: perceptual context; cf. Vakil et al., 1997, re: modality of presentation).

In another study of source memory, Dywan et al. (1993) used a judgment task designed to distinguish TBI subjects' ability to recognize previously presented information from their ability to recognize the source of that information. The measure of source error in this paradigm differed from that derived from usual contextual memory paradigms in that source confusion occurred in a situation where monitoring the source of item familiarity was an implicit rather than an explicit task demand. As such, the paradigm was more closely related to the real world, in which "on-line" monitoring of task- or situation-based knowledge is a requirement in many tasks as well as in social encounters. Thirteen individuals with severe TBI and 24 healthy controls participated in the study. Relative to healthy controls, individuals with TBI were notably impaired on measures of verbal recall and recognition as well as source memory albeit, source memory was demonstrated to be independent of other indices of memory. Source memory was also found to be a sensitive index of coma duration (i.e., an injury severity index) in TBI participants. Furthermore, modest relationships were found between source memory and an index of executive functioning (i.e., The Wisconsin Card Sorting Test), and between source memory and participants' performance on a complex visual pattern matching task (i.e., Benton Facial Recognition). The researchers concluded that individuals with TBI are more likely to make source errors, because they experience more difficulty selectively ignoring salient aspects of their ongoing experience.

In a more recent investigation of source memory, Mangels, Craik, Levin, Schwartz, and Stuss (2002) examined the effects of TBI on memory for item and context under focused and divided attention. Participants included 13 patients with moderate-to-severe TBI and 10 healthy controls. Results indicated that TBI patients demonstrated intact performance on free recall, context-cued recall, and recognition memory tests when items were encoded under focused attention, but impaired performance when items were encoded under divided attention, suggesting that memory deficits were secondary to deficits in attentional resources. Additionally, a subset of patients with more severe TBI demonstrated a pattern of performance bias under divided attention suggestive of an additional deficit in the strategic control of attentional resources.

Subsequently, Knight and O'Hagan (2009) examined the ability of individuals with severe TBI, who were at least six years post-injury, to recall memories associated with famous names. Nineteen individuals with TBI and 19 healthy controls participated in the study. A list of 115 names of famous people was compiled, 25 of whom came to prominence in each decade from 1960 to 1999, and 15 in the period 2000 to 2005. Participants were first asked whether they recognized each name as being of a famous person and to state the reason for the individual's fame. For those names they correctly identified, they were asked to recall a memory associated with the person; each memory produced was categorized as a context-specific memory or a general memory. The ability to recognize and identify famous names was well preserved in the TBI group; however, they showed a consistent impairment in the ability to recall specific episodic memories acquired before and after the date of the TBI. This inability to generate personal and context-specific information is likely to have an impact on the ability of the person with TBI to participate in interpersonal interactions and problem solve in complex social situations.

In a study of autobiographical memory deficit after TBI, Piolino, Desgranges, Manning, North, Jokic, and Eustache (2007) recruited 25 TBI patients within one-year post injury to participate in a controlled autobiographical procedure specially designed to measure episodic autobiographical memories (i.e., unique, specific in time and space, and detailed). The ability to mentally travel back through time and re-experience the source of acquisition, (i.e. autonoetic consciousness), was assessed via the "Remember/Know" paradigm and a checking procedure of sense of remembering. Self-perspective in visual imagery, which is also critically involved in episodic recollection, was assessed by the "Field/Observer perspective" paradigm. In addition, the patients underwent a battery of standardized neuropsychological tests to assess episodic and semantic memory, orientation and executive functions. The results showed that the patients, compared to healthy controls, were significantly impaired in recalling episodic autobiographical memories (see Figure 5-4). This impairment was not related to the life period tested or the patients' ages nor intellectual impairment. Rather, deficits involved disturbances in sense of remembering and recollection of spatiotemporal details. Furthermore, a significant relationship was identified between the TBI patients' abnormal

sense of remembering and executive dysfunction. Although the aforementioned findings provide sound preliminary evidence of source memory deficits in the TBI population, our understanding of the neurocognitive and neuroanatomical correlates of this type of memory is greatly underdeveloped. Such conclusions are important because the deeper the understanding of the nature of impairments following TBI, the more likely appropriate interventions can be developed to the complex array of behavioral sequelae.

Future Directions and Conclusions

This review demonstrates the extensive research conducted to investigate the effect of moderate-to-severe TBI on a wide range of memory processes. In an attempt to characterize the profile of memory deficit following TBI, the findings were classified into theoretically driven memory categories. Namely, STM, LTM, working memory, prospective memory, and source memory. This review has drawn together information from a range of studies with unique emphases on behavioral tasks, functional imaging, neurocognitive assessments, and molecular genetics to provide a rounded synopsis of the literary database dedicated to memory impairments in the TBI population. The combination

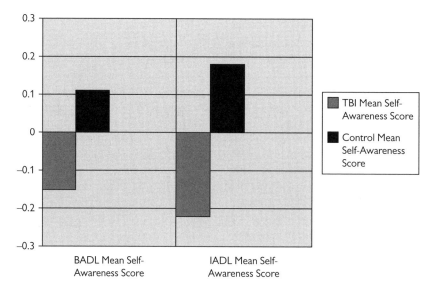

Figure 5-4. Mean self-awareness scores for the TBI and control groups on the BADL and IADL components of the CAPM.

of information concerning functional imaging, neurocognitive assessment, and molecular genetics can be applied to individuals with TBI to help explain the mechanisms that underlie deficits in memory and in turn, design treatment interventions based on this knowledge. A future challenge in the field of memory research will be to identify subgroups of patients with deficits in these areas of memory, either a priori according to a range of factors such as severity of injury, or a posteriori based on their specific memory deficit characteristics. Such a research approach has the potential of explaining much of the variability in findings reported in the literature on the effect of TBI on memory.

Furthermore, this review examined the evidence for these various approaches to memory rehabilitation, concluding that there remains a need for full scale randomized clinical trials, particularly for source memory, to determine their efficacy in improving memory functioning. One of the most crucial research questions may involve which methods most effectively lead to generalization and maintenance of gains, and evaluation of effective practical use of memory interventions during real-world activities. Other questions include: Which techniques are more effective in actually persuading individuals to implement the memory interventions in their daily life? How much influence do clients' personalities and interests have on their tendency to engage in rehabilitation? And to what extent do additional cognitive impairments (e.g., attention and executive functioning deficits) negatively affect the actual implementation of the memory interventions in day-to-day functioning outside of the hospital and therapeutic settings? Another key priority for future research concerning the rehabilitation of memory deficits in the TBI population is the need to investigate the psychosocial and functional outcomes of memory impairments and their targeted rehabilitation programs. Although there is strong evidence of memory deficit in this population, research exploring the extent to which such impairments predict quality of life has largely been neglected. Another challenge for researchers and clinicians alike is to bridge the gap between the theoretical and empirical models that have successfully explained memory processes in healthy adults and clinical populations and the functional interventions designed to help those with memory impairment.

In conclusion, TBI causes memory deficits expressed in a wide range of memory tasks. Memory impairment is one of the most debilitating cognitive consequences of TBI, mediated by impairments in a range of other cognitive domains such as attention, speed of processing, and executive functions. This chapter has important implications for the rehabilitation of memory problems after TBI, in that it highlights the need to tailor remediation programs to the unique characteristics of specific memory deficits (Sohlberg & Mateer, 2001).

Acknowledgments

Preparation of this book chapter was supported by the Project-Oriented Hundred Talents Programme (O7CX031003) and the Knowledge Innovation Project of the Chinese Academy of Sciences (KSCX2-EW-J-8), the Griffith University Allan Sewell Visiting Fellowship to Raymond Chan; an Australian Academy of Science, Scientific Visits to China Grant to David Shum, and a grant from the initiation fund of the CAS/SAFEA International Partnership Programme for Creative Research Teams (Y2CX131003) to Raymond Chan and David Shum.

References

Anderson, J., & Schmitter-Edgecombe, M. (2009). Predictions of episodic memory performance following moderate-to-severe traumatic brain injury during inpatient rehabilitation. *Journal of Clinical and Experimental Neuropsychology, 31,* 425–438.

Arnsten, A. T. (1998). Catecholamine modulation of prefrontal cortical cognitive function. *Trends in Cognitive Sciences, 2,* 436–447.

Atkinson, R., & Shiffrin, R. (1968). Human memory: A proposed system and its control processes. In K. W. Spence (Ed.), *The psychology of learning and motivation: Advances in research and theory* (pp. 89–195). New York: Academic Press.

Baddeley, A. (1987). *Working memory.* Oxford: Oxford University Press.

Baddeley, A. (2000). The episodic buffer: A new component of working memory. *Trends in Cognitive Science, 4,* 417–423.

Baddeley, A., Harris, J., Sunderland, A., Watts, K. P., & Wilson, B. A. (1987). Closed head injury and memory. In H. S. Levin, J. Grafman & H. M. Eisenberg (Eds.), *Neurobehavioral recovery from head injury* (pp. 295–317). New York: Oxford University Press.

Baddeley, A., & Hitch, G. (1974). Working Memory. In G. H. Bower (Ed.), *The psychology of learning and motivation: Advances in research and theory* (pp. 47–89). New York: Academic Press.

Baddeley, A., Kopelman, M., & Wilson, B. (2002). *The handbook of memory disorders* (2nd ed.). Chichester: Wiley.

Burgess, P. W., Scott, S. K., & Frith, C. D. (2003). The role of the rostral frontal cortex (area 10) in prospective memory: a lateral versus medial dissociation. *Neuropsychologia, 41*, 906–918.

Cabeza, R., & Nyberg, L. (2000). Imaging cognition II: An empirical review of 275 PET and fMRI studies. *Journal of Cognitive Neuroscience, 12*, 1–47.

Carlesimo, G., A., Formisano, R., Bivona, U., Barba, L., & Caltagirone, C. (2009/2010). Prospective memory in patients with severe closed-head injury: Role of concurrent activity and encoding instructions. *Behavioural Neurology, 22*, 101–110.

Chaytor, N., & Schmitter-Edgecombe, M. (2003). The ecological validity of neuropsychological tests. *Neuropsychology Review, 13*, 181–197.

Christodoulou, C., DeLuca, J., Ricker, J., Madigan, N., Bly, B., Lange, G....Ni, A. (2001). Functional magnetic resonance imaging of working memory impairment after traumatic brain injury. *Journal of Neurology, Neurosurgery & Psychiatry, 71*, 161–168.

Claparède, E. (1911). Recognition and me-ness. In D. Rapaport (Ed.), *The organization and pathology of thought: Selected sources* (pp. 58–75). New York: Columbia University Press. Craik, F. I. M., & Lockhart, R. S. (1972). Levels of processing: A framework for memory research. *Journal of Verbal Learning and Verbal Behavior, 11*, 671–684.

Crawford, F., Vanderploeg, R., Freeman, M., Singh, S., Waisman, M., Michaels, L. & Mullan, M. (2002). APOE genotype influences acquisition and recall following traumatic brain injury. *Neurology, 58*, 1115–1118.

Curtiss, G., Vanderploeg, R. D., Spencer, J., & Salazar, A. M. (2001). Patterns of verbal learning and memory in traumatic brain injury. *Journal of the International Neuropsychological Society, 7*, 574–585.

D'Esposito, M., Postle, B., & Rypma, B. (2000). Prefrontal cortical contributions to working memory: evidence from event-related fMRI studies. *Experimental Brain Research, 133*, 3–11.

Donders, K., Tulsky, D. S., & Zhu, J. (2001). Criterion validity of new WAIS-III subtest scores after traumatic brain injury. *Journal of the International Neuropsychological Society, 7*, 892–898.

Duval, J., Coyette, F., & Seron, X. (2008). Rehabilitation of the central executive component of working memory: a re-organisation approach applied to a single case. *Neuropsychological Rehabilitation, 18*, 460–460.

Dywan, J., Segalowitz, S., Henderson, D., & Jacoby, L. (1993). Memory for source after traumatic brain injury. *Brain and cognition, 21*, 20–43.

Einstein, G. O., & McDaniel, M. A. (1990). Normal aging and prospective memory. *Journal of Experimental Psychology: Learning, Memory, and Cognition, 16*, 717–726.

Ellis, J. (1996). Prospective memory of the realization of delayed intentions: A conceptual framework for research. In M. A., Brandimonte, G. O., Einstein, & M. A., McDaniel (Eds.), *Prospective memory: Theory and application* (pp. 1–22). New Jersey: Lawrence Erlbaum Associates.

Fink, G. R., Markowitsch, H. J., Reinkemeier, M., Bruckbauer, T., Kessler, J., & Heiss, W. D. (1996). Cerebral representation of one's own past: Neural networks involved in autobiographical memory. *Journal of Neuroscience, 16*, 4275–4282.

Fisher, D. C., Ledbetter, M. F., Cohen, N. J., Marmor, D., & Tulsky, D. S. (2000). WAIS-III and WMS-III profiles of mildly to severely brain-injured patients. *Applied Neuropsychology, 7*, 126–132.

Fleming, J. M., Riley, L., Gill, H., Gullo, M. J., Strong, J., & Shum, D. (2008). Predictors of prospective memory in adults with traumatic brain injury. *Journal of the International Neuropsychological Society, 14*, 823–831.

Fleming, J. M., Shum, D., Strong, J., and Lightbody, S. (2005). Prospective memory rehabilitation for adults with traumatic brain injury: a compensatory training programme. *Brain Injury, 19*, 1–10.

Goldstein, F. C., & Levin, H. S. (1995). Post-traumatic and anterograde amnesia following closed head injury. In A. D. Baddeley, B. A. Wilson & F. N. Watts (Eds.), *Handbook of memory disorders* (pp. 187–209). Chichester: John Wiley & Sons.

Graham, D., Gennarelli, T., McIntosh, T., & Luntus, P. (2002). Cellular and molecular consequences of TBI. In D. Graham & P. Lantos (Eds.), *Greenfield's neuropathology* (pp. 823–898). New York: Oxford University Press.

Groot, Y. C. T., Wilson, B. A., Evans, J., & Watson, P. (2002). Prospective memory functioning in people with and without brain injury. *Journal of the International Neuropsychological Society, 8*, 645–654.

Gualtieri, C. T. (1988). Pharmacotherapy and the neurobehavioural sequelae of traumatic brain injury. *Brain Injury, 2*, 101–129.

Hannon, R., Adams, P., Harrington, S., Fries-Dias, C., & Gipson, M. T. (1995). Effects of brain injury and age on prospective memory self-rating and performance. *Rehabilitation Psychology, 40,* 289–298.

Henry, J. D., Phillips, L. H., Crawford, J. R., Kliegel, M., Theodorou, G., & Summers, F. (2007). Traumatic brain injury and prospective memory: Influence of task complexity. *Journal of Clinical and Experimental Neuropsychology, 29,* 457–466.

James, W. (1890). *The Principles of Psychology.* New York: Henry Holt.

Kinch, J., & McDonald, S. (2001). Traumatic brain injury and prospective memory: An examination of the influences of the executive functioning and retrospective memory. *Brain Impairment, 2,* 119–130.

Kinsella, G., Murtagh, D., Landry, A., Homfray, K., Hammond, M., O'Beirne & Ponsford, J. (1996). Everyday memory following traumatic brain injury. *Brain Injury, 10,* 499–507.

Kliegel, M., Eschen A., & Thöne-Otto, A. I. T. (2004). Planning and realization of complex intentions in traumatic brain injury and normal aging. *Brain and Cognition, 56,* 43–54.

Kliegel, M., & Martin, M. (2003). Prospective memory research: Why is it relevant? *International journal of psychology, 38,* 193–194.

Kliegel, M., McDaniel, M. A., & Einstein, G. O. (2008). *Prospective memory: Cognitive, neuroscience, developmental, and applied perspective.* Mahwah: Erlbaum.

Klingberg, T., Forssberg, H., & Westerberg, H. (2002). Training of working memory in children with ADHD. *Journal of Clinical and Experimental Neuropsychology, 24,* 781–791.

Knight, J. B., Ethridge, L. E., Marsh, R. L., & Clementz, B. A. (2010). Neural correlates of attentional and mnemonic processing in event-based prospective memory. *Frontiers in Human Neuroscience, 4,* 5.

Knight, R. G., Harnett, M., & Titov, N. (2005). The effects of traumatic brain injury on the predicted and actual performance of a test of prospective remembering. *Brain Injury, 19,* 27–38.

Knight, R. G., & O'Hagan, K. (2009). Autobiographical memory in long-term survivors of severe traumatic brain injury. *Journal of Clinical and Experimental Neuropsychology, 31,* 575–583.

Knight, R. G., & Titov, N. (2009). Use of virtual reality tasks to assess prospective memory: Applicability and evidence. *Brain Impairment, 10,* 3–13.

Knight, R. G., Titov, N., & Crawford, M. (2006). The effects of distraction on prospective remembering following traumatic brain injury assessed in a simulated naturalistic environment. *Journal of the International Neuropsychological Society, 12,* 8–16.

Kopelman, M. D. (1989). Remote and autobiographical memory, temporal context memory and frontal atrophy in Korsakoff and Alzheimer patients. *Neuropsychologia, 27,* 437–460.

Kopelman, M. D. (2000). Focal retrograde amnesia and the attribution of causality: an exceptionally critical review. *Cognitive Neuropsychology, 17,* 585–621.

Kopelman, M. D. (2002). Disorders of memory. *Brain, 125,* 2152–2190.

Kvavilashvili, L. & Ellis, J. (1996). Varieties of intention: Some distinctions and classifications. In M. Brandimonte, G. O. Einstein & M. A. McDaniel (Eds.), *Prospective memory: Theory and applications* (pp. 23–52). New Jersey: Lawrence Erlbaum associates.

Lam, Y. S., Man, D. W. K., Tam, S. F., & Weiss, P. L. (2006). Virtual reality training for stroke rehabilitation: *NeuroRehabilitation, 21,* 245–253.

Langeluddecke, P. M., & Lucas, S. K. (2005). WMS-III findings in litigants following moderate to extremely severe brain injury. *Journal of Clinical and Experimental Neuropsychology, 27,* 536–590.

Leclercq, M., Couillet, J., Azouvi, P., Marlier, N., Martin, Y., Strypstein, E., & Rousseaux, M. (2000). Dual task performance after severe diffuse traumatic brain injury or vascular prefrontal damage. *Journal of Clinical and Experimental Neuropsychology, 22,* 339–350.

Levin, H. S. (1990). Memory deficit after closed head injury. *Journal of Clinical and Experimental Neuropsychology, 12,* 129–153.

Levin, H. S., Benton, A. L., & Grossman, R. G. (1982). *Neurobehavioral consequences of closed head injury.* New York: Oxford University Press.

Levin, H., & Hanten, G. (2002). Posttraumatic amnesia and residual memory deficit after closed head Injury. In A. D. Baddeley, M. D. Kopelman & B. A. Wilson (Eds.), *The handbook of memory disorders* (pp. 381–411). New York: Wiley.

Maguire, E. A. (2001). Neuroimaging studies of autobiographical memory. *Philosophical Transactions of the Royal Society of London, 29,* 1441–1451.

Mangels, J. A., Craik, F. I. M., Levine, B., Schwartz, M. L., & Stuss, D. T. (2002). Effects of divided attention on episodic memory in chronic traumatic brain injury: A function of severity and strategy. *Neuropsychologia, 40,* 2369–2385.

Martin, M., Kliegel, M., & McDaniel, M. A. (2003). The involvement of executive functions in prospective memory performance of adults. *International Journal of Psychology, 38,* 195–206.

Mateer, C. A., Sohlberg, M. M., & Crinean, J. (1987). Focus on clinical research: Perceptions of memory functions in individuals with closed head injury. *Journal of Head Trauma Rehabilitation, 2,* 74–84.

Mathias, J., & Mansfield, K. (2005). Prospective and declarative memory problems following moderate and severe traumatic brain injury. *Brain Injury, 19,* 271–282.

Maujean, A., Shum, D., & McQueen, R. (2003). Effect of cognitive demand on prospective memory in individuals with traumatic brain injury. *Brain Impairment, 4,* 135–145.

Mayes, A. R., MacDonald, C., Donlan, L., Pears, J., & Meudel, P. R. (1992). Amnesics have a disproportionately severe memory deficit for interactive context. *The Quarterly Journal of Experimental Psychology, 45,* 265–297.

McAllister, T., Flashman, L., McDonald, B., Ferrell, R., Tosteson, T.... Saykin, A. (2011). Dopaminergic Challenge With Bromocriptine One Month After Mild Traumatic Brain Injury: Altered Working Memory and BOLD Response. *Journal of Neuropsychiatry and Clinical Neuroscience, 23,* 277–286.

McDaniel, M. A., & Einstein, G. O. (2000). Strategic and automatic processes in prospective memory retrieval: A multiprocess framework. *Applied Cognitive Psychology, 14,* 127–144.

McDowell, S., Whyte, J., & D'Esposito, M. (1997). Working memory impairments in traumatic brain injury: Evidence from a dual-task paradigm. *Neuropsychologia, 35,* 1341–1353.

McWilliams, J., & Schmitter-Edgecombe, M. (2008). Semantic memory organization during the early stage of recovery from traumatic brain injury. *Brain Injury, 22,* 243–253.

Moscovitch, M. (1992). Memory and working with memory: A component process model based on modules and central systems. *Journal of Cognitive Neuroscience, 4,* 257–267.

Perlstein, W. M., Cole, M. A., Demery, J. A., Seignourel, P. J., Dixit, N. K. Larson, M. J., & Briggs, R. W. (2004). Parametric manipulation of working memory load in traumatic brain injury: Behavioural and neural correlates. *Journal of the International Neuropsychological Society, 10,* 724–741.

Piolino, P., Desgranges, B., Belliard, S., Matuszewski, V., Lalevee, C., De la Sayette, V., & Eustache, F. (2003). Autobiographical memory and autonoetic consciousness: Triple dissociation in neurodegenerative diseases. *Brain, 126,* 2203–2219.

Piolino, P., Desgranges, B., Manning, L., North, P., Jokic, C., & Eustache, F. (2007). Autobiographical memory, the sense of recollection and executive functions after severe traumatic brain injury. *Cortex, 43*: 176–195.

Piolino, P., Giffard-Quillon, G., Desgranges, B., Chetelat, G., Baron, J. C., & Eustache, F.(2004). Re-experiencing old memories via hippocampus: a PET study of autobiographical memory. *Neuroimage, 22,* 1371–1383.

Ponsford, J. L., Olver, J. H., & Curran, C. (1995). A profile of outcome: 2 years after traumatic brain injury. *Brain Injury, 9,* 1–10.

Potvin, M. J., Rouleau, I., Audy, J., Charbonneau, S., & Giguere, J. F. (2011). Ecological prospective memory assessment in patients with traumatic brain injury. *Brain Injury, 25,* 192–205.

Potvin, M. J., Rouleau, I., Senechal, G., & Giguere, J. F. (2011). Prospective memory rehabilitation based on visual imagery technique. *Neuropsychological Rehabilitation, 21,* 899–924.

Rabin, L., Burton, L., & Barr, W. (2007). Utilization rates of ecologically oriented instruments among clinical neuropsychologists. *The Clinical Neuropsychologist, 21,* 727–734.

Raskin, S. (2009). Memory for Intentions Screening Test: Psychometric properties and clinical evidence. *Brain Impairment, 10,* 23–33.

Reynolds, J. R., West, R., & Braver, T. S. (2009). Distinct neural circuits support transient and sustained processes in prospective memory and working memory. *Cerebral Cortex, 19,* 1208–1221.

Richardson, J. T. E. (2000). *Clinical and neuropsychological aspects of closed head injury* (2nd ed.). Psychology Press: Hove.

Roche, N., Fleming, J., & Shum, D. (2002). Self-awareness of prospective memory failure in adults with traumatic brain injury. *Brain Injury, 16*(11), 931–945.

Roche, N. L., Moody, A., Szabo, K., Fleming, J., & Shum, D. (2007). Prospective memory in adults with traumatic brain injury: An analysis of perceived reasons for remembering and forgetting. *Neuropsychological Rehabilitation, 17,* 314–334.

Roediger, H. L. (1990). Implicit memory: Retention without remembering. *American Psychologist, 45,* 1043–1056.

Ruff, R. M. (2003). A friendly critique of neuropsychology: Facing the challenge of the future. *Archives of Clinical Neuropsychology, 18,* 847–864.

Ryan, T., Sautter, S., Capps, C., Meneese, W., & Barth, J. (1992). Utilizing neuropsychological measures to predict vocational outcome in a head trauma population. *Brain Injury, 6,* 175–182.

Sanchez-Carrion, R., Fernandez,-Espejo, D., Junque, C., Falcon, C., Bargallo, N., Roig, T., et al. (2008). A longitudinal fMRI study of working memory in severe TBI patients with diffuse axonal injury. *Neuroimage, 43,* 421–429.

Schacter, D., & Crovitz, H. (1977). Memory function after closed head injury: A review of the quantitative research. *Cortex, 13,* 150–176.

Schmitter-Edgecombe, M., & Wright, M. (2004). Event-Based Prospective Memory Following Severe Closed-Head Injury. *Neuropsychology, 18,* 353–361.

Scheibel, R., Newsome, M., Steinberg, J., Pearson, D., Rauch, R., Mao, H.,…Levine, H. (2007). Altered brain activation during cognitive control in patients with moderate to severe traumatic brain injury. *Neurorehabilitation and Neural Repair, 21*, 36–45.

Serino, A., Ciaramelli, E., Di Santantonio, A., Malagu, S., Servadei, F., & Ladavas, E. (2006). Central executive system impairment in traumatic brain injury. *Brain Injury, 20*, 23–32.

Serino, A., Ciaramelli, E., Di Santantonio, A., Malagu, S., Servadei, F., & Ladavas, E. (2007). A pilot study for rehabilitation of central executive deficits after traumatic brain injury. *Brain Injury, 21*, 11–19.

Shimamura, A. P., & Squire, L. R. (1987). A neuropsychological study of fact memory and source amnesia. *Journal of Experimental Psychology: Learning, Memory, and Cognition, 13*, 464–473.

Shum, D., & Fleming, J. (2011). Prospective memory. In In J. Kreutzer, J. DeLuca, & B. Caplan, (Eds.) *Encyclopedia of Clinical Neuropsychology* (pp. 2056–2059). New York: Springer.

Shum, D., Fleming, J., Gill, H., Gullo, M., Strong, J. (2011). A randomized controlled trial of prospective memory rehabilitation in adults with traumatic brain injury. *Journal of Rehabilitation Medicine, 43*, 216–233.

Shum, D., Fleming, J., & Neulinger, K. (2002). Prospective memory and traumatic brain injury: A review. *Brain Impairment, 3*, 1–16.

Shum, D., Levin, H., & Chan, R. C. (2011). Prospective memory in patients with closed head injury: A review. *Neuropsychologia, 49*, 2156–2165.

Shum, D., McFarland, K., & Bain, J. (1990). Construct validity of eight tests of attention: Comparison of normal and closed head injured samples. *Clinical Neuropsychologist, 4*, 151–162.

Shum, D., Sweeper, S., & Murray, R. (1996). Performance on verbal implicit and explicit memory tasks following traumatic brain injury. *The Journal of Head Trauma Rehabilitation, 11*, 43–53.

Shum, D., Valentine, M., & Cutmore, T. (1999). Performance of individuals with severe long-term traumatic brain injury on time-, event-, and activity-based prospective memory tasks. *Journal of Clinical and Experimental Neuropsychology, 21*, 49–58.

Simons, J. S., Scholvinck, M. L., Gilbert, S. J., Frith, C. D., & Burgess, P. W. (2006). Differential components of prospective memory? Evidence from fMRI. *Neuropsychologia, 44*, 1388–1397.

Slovarp, L., Azuma, T., & LaPointe, L. (2012). The effect of traumatic brain injury on sustained attention and working memory. *Brain injury, 26*, 48–57.

Smith, R. E., & Bayen, U. J. (2004). A multinomial model of event based prospective memory. *Journal*

of Experimental Psychology: Learning, Memory, & Cognition, 30, 756–777.

Sohlberg, M. M., White, O., Evans, E., & Mateer, C. (1992). Background and initial case studies into the effects of prospective memory training. *Brain Injury, 6*, 129–138.

Sohlberg, M., & Mateer, C. (2001). *Cognitive rehabilitation: An integrative neuropsychological approach*. New York: The Guilford Press.

Squire, L. (1986). Mechanisms of memory. *Science, 232*, 1612–1619.

Tay, S., Ang, B., Lau, X., Meyyappan, A., & Collinson, S. (2010). Chronic impairment of prospective memory after mild traumatic brain injury. *Journal of Neurotrauma, 27*, 77–83.

Tulving, E. (1972). Episodic and semantic distinction. In E. Tulving,W. Donaldson & G. H. Bower (Eds.), *Organization of Memory* (pp. 381–403). New York: Academic Press.

Tulving, E. (2000). Concepts of memory. In E. Tulving & F. I. M. Craik (Eds), *The Oxford handbook of memory* (pp. 33–44). New York: Oxford University Press.

Tulving, E., & Craik, F. (2000). *The Oxford handbook of memory*. New York: Oxford University Press.

Uttl, B., & Kibreab, M. (2011). Self-report measures of prospective memory are reliable but not valid. *Canadian Journal of Experimental Psychology, 65*, 57–68.

Vakil, E. (2005). The effect of moderate to severe traumatic brain injury (TBI) on different aspects of memory: a selective review. *Journal of Clinical and Experimental Neuropsychology, 27*, 977–1021.

Vakil, E., Blachstein, H., & Hoofien, D. (1991). Automatic temporal order judgment: The effect of intentionality of retrieval on closed-head injured patients. *Journal of Clinical and Experimental Neuropsychology, 13*, 291–298.

Vakil, E., Golan, H., Grunbaum, E., Groswasser, Z., & Aberbuch, S. (1996). Direct and indirect measures of contextual information in brain-injured patients. *Neuropsychiatry, Neuropsychology, and Behavioural Neurology, 9*, 176–181.

Vakil, E., Openheim, M., Falck, D., Aberbuch, S., & Groswasser, Z. (1997). Indirect influence of modality on direct memory for words and their modality: Closed head injured and control participants. *Neuropsychology, 11*, 545–551.

Vakil, E., & Tweedy, J. (1994). Memory for temporal order and spatial position information: Tests of the automatic-effortful distinction. *Cognitive and Behavioral Neurology, 7*, 281.

Vallat, C., Azouvi, P., Hardisson, H., Meffert, R., Tessier, C., & Pradat-Diehl, P. (2005). Rehabilitaiton of verbal working memory after left hemisphere stroke. *Brain Injury, 19*, 1157–1164.

Vallat-Azouvi, C., Pradat-Diehl, P., & Azouvi, P. (2009). Rehabilitation of the central executive of working memory after severe traumatic brain injury: two single-case studies. *Brain Injury, 23*, 585–594.

Vallat-Azouvi, C., Weber, T., Legrand, L., & Azouvi, P. (2007). Working memory after severe traumatic brain injury. *Journal of the International Neuropsychological Society, 13*, 770–780.

Vanderploeg, R. D., Crowell, T. A., & Curtiss, G. (2001). Verbal learning and memory deficits in traumatic brain injury: Encoding, consolidation, and retrieval. *Journal of Clinical and Experimental Neuropsychology, 23*, 185–195.

Vanderploeg, R. D., Curtiss, G., & Belanger, H. G. (2005). Long-term neuropsychogocial outcomes following mild traumatic brain injury. *Journal of the International Neuropsychological Society, 11*, 228–236.

Watt, S., Shores, E. A., & Kinoshita, S. (1999). Effects of reducing attentional resources on implicit and explicit memory after severe traumatic brain injury. *Neuropsychology, 13*, 338–349.

West, L. K., Curtis, K. L., Greve, K. W., & Bianchini, K. J. (2011). Memory in traumatic brain injury: The effects of injury severity and effort on the Wechsler Memory Scale-III. *Journal of Neuropsychology, 5*, 114–125.

Williamson, D., Scott, J., & Adams, R. (1996). Traumatic brain injury. In R. L. Adams, O. A. Parsons, L. Culbertson & S. J. Nixon (Eds.), *Neuropsychology for clinical practice: Etiology, assessment and treatment of common neurological disorders*(pp. 9–64). Washington DC: American Psychological Press.

Wilson, B. A., Baddeley, A. D., Kapur, N. (1995). Dense amnesia in a professional musician following herpes simplex virus encephalitis. *Journal of Clinical and Experimental Neuropsychology, 17*, 668–681.

Wilson, B. A., Emslie, H., Foley, J., Shiel, A., Watson, P., Hawkins, K., & Groot, Y. (2005). *The Cambridge Prospective Memory Test*. Oxford: Harcourt Assessment.

6

Executive Function Impairments after Traumatic Brain Injury

Ya Wang, Raymond C. K. Chan, and David H. K. Shum

In this chapter we aim to review the latest findings in the area of executive function deficits and traumatic brain injury (TBI) and will concentrate on reviewing studies for the 10 years between 2000 and 2010. First we will provide a definition of executive function, and then we will identify three approaches in assessing executive function, then we will review the research progress during 2000 and 2010 in executive dysfunction studies in TBI, and finally we will provide our views on future research directions.

Definition of Executive Function and Componential Perspective

Executive function is an umbrella term for abilities such as planning, problem solving, working memory, impulse control, inhibition and shifting set, multitasking, the ability to deal with novelty, as well as initiation and monitoring of actions (Chan, Shum, Toulopoulou, & Chen, 2008; Stuss & Knight, 2002; Stuss, Shallice, Alexander, & Picton, 1995). Executive function can be divided into cool and hot components. While the former involve processes that are logically based, the latter involve processes of self-regulation, decision making, social cognition, and emotion (Bechara, Damasio, Damasio, & Lee, 1999; Chan et al., 2008).

Executive function generally refers to high-level cognitive abilities that are mainly mediated by the frontal lobes (Stuss & Knight, 2002). Neuroimaging evidence has revealed that the dorsolateral prefrontal cortex and orbitofrontal cortex are functionally related to cool and hot executive functions respectively (Bechara, Damasio, Damasio, & Anderson, 1994; Bush, Luu, & Posner, 2000). Executive function is crucial for goal-directed behavior (Jurado & Rosselli, 2007). However, there is no consensus on the number and nature of different components of executive function. Despite the lack of agreement, there is no argument regarding the importance of executive function in human adaptive behavior.

More and more evidence indicates that both cool and hot executive functions consist of multiple components, although cool executive function has been researched more extensively. In general, results from studies with both clinical and healthy samples suggest that executive function can be fractionated into six main components: initiation, sustained attention, online updating/working memory, switching and flexibility, disinhibition, attention allocation, and planning (Chan, Chen, Cheung, Chen, & Cheung, 2006; Chan, Chen, & Law, 2006). Initiation refers to the ability to start action and verbal responses. The ability to direct and focus cognitive activity on specific stimuli over a period of time is sustained attention. Online updating/working memory is the ability to monitor and code incoming information and keep track of the relevant information. The ability to shift attention from one source to another from the same modality or across modality is switching and flexibility. Disinhibition refers to the tendency of being unable to manage immediate impulsive

Table 6-1. Main Tests Included in the Review of This Chapter

Components	Measures	Brief description
Initiation	Trails Making Test (TMT) part A reaction time	Participants were asked to connect the circles numbered from 1 to 25 in sequential order as quickly as possible.
	Verbal fluency	Participants were asked to say as many words as possible from a category in one minute; the category can be semantic (e.g., fruits, animals) or phonemic (e.g., words begin with letter F, A, or S).
Sustained attention	Sustained Attention to Response Task (SART) Number of correct responses	In the SART, the computer presents single digits (1–9) at a rate of about one per second; participants were asked to press a button to every number except the number 3. All digits present at the same probability. The number of correct button press is an indicator of sustained attention.
	Number of correct responses on monotone counting test	To count series of auditory stimuli presented regularly at a fixed rate (1HZ).
Switching and flexibility	Part B of the TMT reaction time	To connect 25 consecutive circles, the circles are named by digits (1, 2, 3,…) or letters (A, B, C,…); the participants were asked to connect the circles alternately between numbers and letters (1, A, 2, B, etc.).
	Perseverative errors of the Wisconsin Card Sorting Test (WCST)	In WCST, four stimulus cards are presented to the participant first, the shapes on the cards are different in color, number, and figure. The participant is then given a stack of additional cards and asked to match each one to one of the stimulus cards, thereby forming separate piles of cards for each. The experimenter decides whether the cards are to be matched by color, number, or figure. The participant is not told the rules for matching cards; however, he or she is told whether a particular match is right or wrong. During the course of the test the matching rules are changed. Perseverative error means even if the participant is told that the rule he or she is applying is wrong, the participant still applies this wrong rule in sorting cards.
	Divided attention score from the Test of Everyday Attention child version (TEA-Ch)	Children complete two tasks at the same time. The first task asks children to count the number of target tones on an audiotape. The second task asks children to listen for an animal name during audio-taped news report which was played at the same time as the target tones. Children gain one point on trials in which both target tones and animal name were correctly reported.
Disinhibition	Stroop Color Word score	The name of color words were presented to participants printed in different colors, and the written color name differs from the color ink it is printed in; the participants need to name the ink color.
		The part B of HSCT consists of 15 sentences having the last word missing, and it requires subjects to complete sentences with nonsense ending words (and suppress sensible ones) giving measures of response suppression ability.
	Hayling Sentence Completion Test (HSCT) part B total errors	In the SART, the participants are presented with digits from 1 to 9, and asked to press a button to every digit except the digit 3, the commission error of SART means the false button press to digit "3;" it is a response inhibition measure.
	SART commission errors Go/No Go	There are two types of stimuli in the task; participants are asked to respond to one type of stimuli, and withhold response to the other type of stimuli. The performance in No Go condition reflects inhibition function.

	Stop signal task	Subjects are asked to respond as fast as they can to symbols presented on a computer screen. A certain portion of the trials will be accompanied by a stop signal (usually an auditory tone). This stop signal tells the participant that they are to withhold their response to the current symbol. The tone is unpredictable, and occurs at various latencies after the appearance of the symbol on the computer so that participants reached a rate of about 50% inhibition. The stop signal reaction time (SSRT) is an estimation of the time an individual needs to stop their usual behavior in response to the stop signal. It is a measure of inhibitory control.
Attention allocation and planning	WCST category	In WCST, when participants make six consecutive correct responses, they will get one score in WCST category, and the matching rule will change. The test finishes when participants get a category score of 6 or all cards have been sorted by participants.
	Symbol Digit Modality Test (SDMT)	Participants have 90 seconds to pair specific numbers with given geometric figures using a reference key; it usually has oral and written versions. The more they pair correctly the better the performance is.
	Paced Auditory Serial Addition Test (PASAT)	Participants are given a number every 2.4 seconds by audiotape and are asked to add the number they just heard with the number they heard before, and then tell the result to the experimenter. The original version presented the numbers every 2.4 seconds with 0.4 decrements for subsequent trials.
	TEAch sky search	Children were presented with an A3 sheet containing 128 pairs of spaceships; these spaceships are arranged in rows. Twenty target pairs containing identical spaceships were distributed among the 108 distracter pairs with mixed types of spaceships. Children were asked to circle all pairs with identical spaceships, and to mark a box when finished.
	Ruff 2 and 7 test	The test consists of 20 trials of a visual search and cancellation task. The participants need to detect and mark target digits: "2" and "7." In the 10 automatic detection trials, the target digits were embedded among letters which serve as distracters. In the 10 controlled search trials, the target digits were embedded among other digits which serve as distracters. Correct hits and errors are counted for each trial and serve as the basis for scoring the test.

Note: There are few standard tests on the hot component of executive function, so we do not provide measures on hot component here.

response to either internal automatic processes or external salient stimuli from the environment. Finally, the ability of being able to consistently mobilize and monitor the most appropriate schemata across different scenarios to obtain an optimal performance is attention allocation and planning.

Executive Function Assessment and Approaches

There are three main approaches to the assessment of executive function: psychometric, cognitive-experimental, and ecological. For the psychometric approach, the main goal is to develop tasks that are sensitive to brain damage. In addition, this approach emphasizes the importance of and evidence for psychometric properties such as reliability, validity, and norms. The cognitive-experimental approach is concerned with using well controlled tasks to measure and understand the underlying processes and the neural systems that mediate mental processes (Daniels, Toth, & Jacoby, 2006). However, in recent years the distinction between the two approaches is not as clear cut and sometimes similar tasks are used across the two approaches. Compared to the first two approaches, the ecological approach adopts tasks that use everyday materials as stimuli and require responding to tasks that are similar to those encountered in real-life. The main aim of this approach is to capture and reflect difficulties in everyday living in test takers.

The Hayling Sentence Completion Test (HSCT), Stroop Color Word Interference Test, Color Trails Test (CTT), Trails Making Test (TMT), Verbal Fluency Test, Wisconsin Card Sorting Test (WCST), Tower of Hanoi (TOH), and Delis-Kaplan Executive Function System (D-KEFS) are examples of executive function tests based on the psychometric approach. The Sustained Attention to Response Task (SART) and the Go/No Go task are examples of executive function tasks developed based on the cognitive-experimental approach. The Behavioral Assessment of the Dysexecutive Syndrome (BADS), Test of Everyday Attention (TEA), Dysexecutive questionnaire (DEX) are examples of tests/tasks developed based on the ecological approach.

Executive Function Deficits in TBI

The studies were identified by searching databases that included Elsevier, PsycARTICLE/PsycINFO, and ProQuest psychology journals, using the keywords of brain injury + executive function. For hot component of executive function, we identified three main areas of hot executive function according to Levin and Hanten's (2005) review: decision making, self regulation, and social cognition. Thus we also used the keywords brain injury + decision making/self regulation/social cognition from 2000 to December 31, 2010. In describing and discussing the results of our search, we group the psychometric and cognitive-experimental approaches together. Studies that used the ecological approach are presented separately.

Cool Components

For cool components, we organize our review based on the six executive functions (viz., initiation, sustained attention, online updating/working memory, switching and flexibility, disinhibition, attention allocation, and planning) we mentioned earlier. Because working memory will be reviewed in chapter 5 of this book, the topic is omitted in this section. See Table 6-1 for main measures reviewed in this chapter.

Initiation. The initiation component of executive function can be assessed using the TOH planning time, TMT part A, HSCT part A correct items, and Verbal Fluency Test number of correct items.

TMT part A was found to be slower after moderate to severe TBI at baseline assessment and six-months follow-up (Dreer, DeVivo, Novack, Krzywanski, & Marson, 2008); semantic fluency was found to be impaired in mild to moderate TBI patients within two months of injury (Rapoport et al., 2006), both at baseline and six-months follow-up (Dreer et al., 2008).

There were, nevertheless, some negative findings. Some studies (Cantin et al., 2007; Fortin, Godbout, & Braun, 2003) did not find patients with mild to severe TBI (one month since injury) to be slower than control in completing part A of TMT. Draper and Ponsford (2008) found moderate to severe TBI patients (on average 10 years post-injury) generated as many items as controls on a verbal fluency test.

Henry and Crawford (2004) conducted a meta-analysis in patients with TBI on verbal fluency performances, and found these patients to be impaired in phonemic ($r = 0.48$) and semantic ($r = 0.45$) fluency, with phonemic fluency significantly more sensitive to the presence of TBI than WCST. In sum, TBI patients show impairments in initiation to a moderate degree, with the severity of injury and time since injury probably influencing degree of impairment.

Sustained Attention. The sustained attention component of executive function is generally assessed using the SART measures, such as number of correct responses and the number of correct responses on the monotone counting test, and number of correct responses on the Continuous Performance Test (CPT). During our search period, few studies were conducted to examine the sustaining component of executive function in patients following TBI. One exception is a study conducted by Chan (2005) which found that patients with mild TBI showed deficits in SART and monotone counting performance.

Switching and Flexibility. Part B of the TMT and perseverative errors of the WCST are the two main measures of the switching and flexibility component of executive function.

Studies have found that patients with TBI are slower in completing part B of the TMT. These studies included patients with mild to severe TBI (mean time since injury = 12.5 months) (Perianez et al., 2007), with moderate to severe TBI at least 30 days since injury (Cantin et al., 2007), and at baseline and six months follow-up (Dreer et al., 2008). TMT completion time was found to differentiate groups with mild TBI from those with moderate to severe TBI. Derived indices (e.g., the ratio of reaction time of part B to part A, the difference of reaction time between part B and part A) were no better than the original scores (Lange, Iverson, Zakrzewski, Ethel-King, & Franzen, 2005).

Older adults with mild to moderate TBI one year after injury were found to make more perseverative errors on the WCST (Rapoport et al., 2006). Patients with severe TBI (on average seven years post injury) had fewer correct responses when switching categories on Verbal Fluency task than controls (Kennedy et al., 2009). With the divided attention score from the TEA-Ch (Test of Everyday Attention, child version) as the measure of cognitive flexibility and divided attention, patients with severe TBI five years after injury (on average) performed worse than a comparison group, suggesting impaired flexibility (Nadebaum, Anderson, & Catroppa, 2007). In an externally cued task-switching paradigm, participants with severe closed head injury (CHI) at least one year following injury exhibited slower response time and greater switch cost, but similar to controls, additional preparatory time reduced the switch cost (Schmitter-Edgecombe & Langill, 2006). However, some studies did not find impairments in this component of executive function. For example, nonsignificant between-group differences were reported for the Brixton Spatial Anticipation test and part B of the TMT (Draper & Ponsford, 2008; Fortin et al., 2003).

Overall, our review of the literature indicates that most TBI patients with a wide range of severity and time since injury show impairments in switching or flexibility.

Disinhibition. Measures that assess the disinhibition component of executive function include HSCT part B total errors, Stroop Color Word score, SART commission errors, CPT commission errors, TOH rule breaking, and the Six Element Test (SET) rule breaking.

Patients with TBI were found to show more interference effect on the Stroop (Cantin et al., 2007; Fortin et al., 2003). In a study by Seignourel et al. (2005), participants performed traditional card Stroop task and a single-trial Stroop task sensitive to context maintenance deficits. Moderate to severe CHI patients, with mean time since injury of 110 months, showed higher error rates but only on the single-trial Stroop task and only when task instructions had to be maintained over a long delay. Context maintenance could be a useful framework for characterizing cognitive control deficits in CHI. In another study, Draper and Ponsford (2008) reported semantic inhibition deficit in terms of

HSCT part B total errors in mild to severe TBI patients with mean time since injury of 10 years.

Patients with severe TBI injured on average seven years previously were found to be impaired on the Go/No Go task (Kennedy et al., 2009). In a study by Roche et al. (2004), TBI patients were found to be impaired on a Go/No Go task, and exhibited abnormal N2 and P3 event-related potential (ERP) waveforms to No Go stimuli (Roche et al., 2004). Patients with mild to severe TBI with mean time since injury of 10 years were found to make more commission errors on the SART, indicating response inhibition deficit (Draper & Ponsford, 2008).

Using another commonly used response inhibition task (viz., the stop signal task), patients with mild to severe TBI with eight weeks on average since injury were not found to perform worse in terms of inhibiting ongoing responses; none of the demographic and clinical variables were found to correlate significantly with inhibition time (Rieger & Gauggel, 2002). On a variant stop signal task, participants were asked to generate a saccade to a target appearing in peripheral vision, but to inhibit saccade execution if an auditory stop signal was presented. Results showed that saccadic reaction times and the stop signal reaction time were unexpectedly faster in the participants with mild TBI within two days of injury and they inaccurately inhibited saccades during 15% of the trials with no stop signals (DeHaan et al., 2007).

There are also some studies that did not find inhibition impairments in brain injury. For example, patients with severe TBI with average time since injury of 38 months were not found to be impaired on the Stroop task (Schroeter et al., 2007). Nevertheless, most studies found patients with TBI to have impairments in inhibition.

Attention Allocation and Planning. According to Chan, Chen, Cheung et al. (2006), the attention allocation and planning component of executive function can be measured by SET raw score, SET total profile, TOH profile, and WCST category.

Patients with mild to severe TBI with average time since injury of 20 months achieved less WCST category at baseline and marginally less at six-month follow-up (Fortin et al.,

2003). Performance speed on Ruff's 2 and 7 test was found to be impaired in TBI patients, suggesting deficient selective attention (Fortin et al., 2003). Moderate to severe TBI patients at least 30 days since injury were found to be impaired in divided attention measured by the Symbol Digit Modality Test (SDMT) (Cantin et al., 2007). Patients with TBI were impaired in an adjusting Paced Serial Addition Test. This test provided a threshold measure and offered a potentially more precise way of evaluating how TBI affects cognitive functioning than was achieved using the traditional Paced Auditory Serial Addition Test (PASAT). Severely injured patients were more impaired than mildly injured patients (Tombaugh, Stormer, Rees, Irving, & Francis, 2006). A study by Azouvi et al. (2004) found that the divided attention deficit of severe TBI patients (mean time since injury 9.6 months) was related to a reduction in available processing resources rather than an impairment of strategic processes responsible for attentional allocation and switching. Some studies found moderate to severe TBI patients at least 30 days since injury were not impaired in attention allocation and planning. For example, Cantin et al. (2007) did not find the performance of a test, which measures divided attention, to be impaired in TBI patients. Nadebaum et al. (2007) did not find attention control, as measured by sky search of the TEAch, to be impaired in mild to severe TBI patients with an average of five years since injury.

Results of a meta-analysis conducted by Mathias and Wheaton (2007) revealed that large and significant deficits were found in specific measures of attention span, focused/selective attention, sustained attention, and supervisory attentional control following severe TBI and post-injury interval showed a small correlation to attention impairment.

Hot Components

Decision Making. Decision making is an important function in daily living. The frontal cortex, particularly the orbitofrontal cortex (OFC), is thought to play a critical role in decision making processes (Bechara, Tranel, & Damasio, 2000; Body, 2007). Decision making is usually measured by gambling tasks such as the

Iowa Gambling Task, the Cambridge Gambling Task, and the Regret Gambling task. The Iowa Gambling Task (IGT) is a computerized task that simulates personal real-life decision making in the way that the test taker faces uncertainty of reward and punishment (Bechara et al., 1994). The aim of this task is to earn a maximum amount of money from an initial loan by selecting from four sets of cards. Two of these sets yield high gain and correspondingly high (intermittent and overall) loss; the other two sets yield relatively low (overall) gain with intermittent low loss. Typically, normal individuals learn to choose the safer decks over the more risky desks but patients with damage to the ventromedial prefrontal cortex consistently choose the high gain and high loss desks and eventually end up losing money. The other gambling tasks are variants that were developed from the IGT.

Sigurdardottir et al. (2010) found that mild to severe TBI patients failed to develop the advantageous strategy over time on the IGT at three-month follow-up. Schlund, Pace, and McGready (2001) studied decision-making and its related consequences by using different response-reinforcer contingencies. Results of their study suggested that patients with brain injury (TBI and other types of brain injury), at least two years post injury, had reduced sensitivity to contingencies, and this might function as one behavioral mechanism of maladaptive decision-making. In Hanten et al. (2006)'s study, they administered the modified IGT to a group of children with moderate to severe TBI and found that a subgroup of children with lesions in the amygdala were impaired on the task, but children with ventromedial lesions were not. These findings are inconsistent with those reported in previous studies and further studies are needed to examine the effects of TBI on decision making.

Self-Regulation. Self-regulation is defined as the capacity to manage one's own thoughts, feelings, and actions in adaptive and flexible ways across a variety of contexts (Ganesalingam, Sanson, Anderson, & Yeates, 2006). Self-regulation plays an important role in recovery and rehabilitation. Verbal self-regulation has been found by Arco, Cohen,

and Geddes (2004) to be effective in reducing impulsive behavior of young adults with severe frontal brain damage at least five years post injury, but it is unknown whether the positive changes are durable.

Researchers have developed a number of measures of self-regulation. Levine, Dawson, Boutet, Schwartz, and Stuss (2000) developed a real-life situation test in the laboratory on strategy application called the Revised Strategy Application Test. It has been found to be a valid and sensitive test of self-regulation. The Self-Regulation Skills Interview (SRSI) was designed by Ownsworth, McFarland, and Young (2000) to measure meta-cognitive skills such as planning, monitoring progress, and evaluating the outcome of treatment interventions. Results obtained indicate that the SRSI had good inter-rater and test-retest reliability and had three factors: awareness, readiness to change, and strategy behavior. Furthermore, these factors were found to relate significantly to neuropsychological performances, which supports the concurrent validity of the SRSI.

Cook, Chapman, and Levin (2008) compared a group of typically developing children and a group of children with severe TBI with one month to two years post injury on a naturalistic task. Children with TBI were found to exhibit significantly increased use of distracter objects in place of target objects and they were also found to demonstrate trends of increased rule breaking and failure to include necessary steps. These results suggest that patients are impaired in self-regulation, corresponding to a decreased ability to carry out goal-based top-down processing.

Studies found that self-regulation played an important part in social functioning. Children with moderate to severe TBI displayed deficits in self-regulation and social and behavioral functioning but the magnitude of deficit was not related to injury severity. Self-regulation accounted for significant variance in children's social and behavioral functioning (Ganesalingam et al., 2006). In another study, self-regulation (cognitive, emotional, and behavioral) and social and behavioral functioning were assessed in children (65 with TBI and 65 without TBI). Results showed that self-regulation accounted for individual variation in the outcomes and acted as a mediator of the effects of TBI on the outcomes (Ganesalingam, Sanson, Anderson, & Yeates, 2007).

Social Cognition. To be successful in social interactions, a person needs to perceive information, understand its stated and implied meaning, and respond in a way that is appropriate for the context. The set of skills required to achieve this has been referred to as social cognition (Turkstra, Williams, Tonks, & Frampton, 2008). Theory of mind (TOM) is one of the most important processes in social cognition. TOM refers to the ability to make inferences about others' mental states and use them to understand and predict others' behavior (Premack & Woodruff, 1978).

Havet-Thomassin, Allain, Etcharry-Bouyx, and Le Gall (2006) evaluated the performances of patients with severe TBI (average time after injury = 91 weeks) on two TOM tasks: "Reading the Mind in the Eyes' test" and "Character Intention Task." They found that patients were impaired on the two TOM tasks and executive function measures such as TMT and Stroop.

In their study, Muller et al. (2010) tested a group of patients with severe TBI with an average time since injury of 103 months with a battery of verbal and nonverbal TOM tasks that included the faux pas test, the first-order and second-order false belief task, the character intention task, and the Reading the Mind in the Eyes test. A number of non-TOM inference tasks and executive function tasks were also administered. The patients were found to perform significantly more poorly on all the TOM tasks except the first-order false belief task. And performances in TOM tasks were not correlated with empathy performances, thus Muller et al. (2010) suggested that TOM is probably distinct from other aspect of social cognition like empathy.

Stronach and Turktra (2008) used another method to measure social cognition. In their study, participants completed a three-minute conversation with a peer or research partner. Then conversations were analyzed to determine the cognitive state terms (such as *forget, pretend, understand*, and *wish*, etc.) relative to total words produced. Results showed that moderate to severe TBI adolescents (at least six months after injury) with low TOM ability expressed fewer cognitive state terms and significantly fewer self- versus-other-referenced terms than in the high TOM ability TBI group and controls, with the latter two groups not significantly different from each other. According to Stronach and Turktra (2008) these impairments were not caused by impoverished language ability and adolescents with TBI have domain-specific deficits in social cognition.

A number of studies have examined the stability of TOM impairments in patients with TBI. Milders, Ietswaart, Crawford, and Currie (2006) assessed TOM and executive functions in individuals with mild to severe injury shortly after injury and at one-year follow-up and found impairments in TOM and executive functions (digit symbol, alternating fluency) at both times. This finding indicates that TOM impairments are stable over time.

Adolescents with TBI are likely to have impairments in processes such as mental state attribution. These abilities and skills support both exchange of social knowledge and also the development and maintenance of personal relationships (Turkstra, 2008). Recently, a meta-analysis reviewed the performance of acquired brain injury patients on four widely-used TOM tasks: first-order false belief task, second-order false belief task, understanding indirect speech, and social faux pas. Results showed that patients had moderate to severe TOM impairment. For the faux pas task the effect size (ES) was 0.7 and for the understanding indirect speech task ES = 0.87. Moderate impairments were seen in second-order (ES = 0.6) and first-order (ES = 0.52) false belief tasks. The severity of TOM impairment was influenced by the ratio of patients with frontal lesions in the samples, ratio of right hemisphere injury, type of task, and the heterogeneity of etiology (Martin-Rodriguez & Leon-Carrion, 2010).

There are other aspects of social cognition in addition to TOM that have been studied, including sarcasm and social inference. A study by Channon, Pellijeff, and Rule (2005) explored the ability for comprehending sarcasm following severe CHI, with a mean time since injury of nine years. The ability was assessed for both sarcasm involving directly opposite meaning and sarcasm involving an indirect, non-literal but not directly opposite meaning. They found that patients made both literal interpretation and incorrect non-literal interpretation errors and showed a TOM deficit. TOM was correlated with sarcasm comprehension.

Adults with moderate to severe TBI at least two years since injury were also found to show social inference impairments. Turkstra (2008) designed the Video Social Inference Test (VSIT) to capture social inference processes that would be engaged in daily conversations and found that patients obtained lower scores than controls. Participants in both groups had lower scores when required to predict or explain future behaviors based on an initial social inference. Results suggested that story- and picture-based tasks might over-estimate social inference impairments in some individuals with TBI, as these tasks lack cues that can support social performance in everyday interactions.

Hanten et al. (2008) used the Interpersonal Negotiation Strategies (INS) task to assess social problem-solving and found that pediatric TBI patients with moderate to severe injury were impaired on this task. However, the rate of change in performance over one year did not differ from that of patients with orthopedic injury (OI), suggesting improvement in children with TBI was not due to recovery from injury. INS performance was found to relate to memory and language skills but weakly to emotion processing. Strong relationships were found between INS and increased apparent diffusion coefficient (ADC) measures indexing connectivity in the dorsolateral and cingulate regions in both TBI and OI groups.

Some studies have explored the neural correlates of social cognition in TBI patients. For example, in their study, Geraci, Surian, Ferraro, and Cantagallo (2010) administered two TOM tasks, namely, the Eyes Test and the Faux-Pas Test, to two groups of patients with TBI (ventromedial lesion group and dorsolateral lesion group). The two groups were found to perform equally poorly on the Eyes test, but only the ventromedial lesion group was impaired on the Faux-Pas test, suggesting that the ventromedial cortex plays an important role in inferential reasoning. In a study by Schroeter, Ettrich, Menz, and Zysset (2010), patients with severe TBI with

a mean time since injury of 31 months performed an evaluative judgments task contrasted with semantic memory retrieval and at the same time underwent event-related fMRI. They found that patients showed higher activations in frontomedian regions, temporal pole, superior temporal gyrus, and the inferior frontal gyrus. Healthy controls activated more ventral tegmental areas during evaluative judgments, suggesting that deficits in ventral tegmental area have to be compensated for by higher brain activations in frontomedian and anterior cingulate cortex in TBI patients. Finally, in a study by Newsome et al. (2010), adolescents who sustained moderate to severe TBI with average time since injury of 2.6 years underwent fMRI while performing a perspective taking task. Results showed that patients demonstrated greater activation in posterior brain regions, suggesting they recruited alternative neural pathways because their fronto-parietal networks mediating social cognition were disrupted.

Ecological Valid Approach Findings

Shallice and Burgess (1991) have pointed out that some brain injured patients perform well on traditional executive function tasks but show difficulties in everyday activity and perform worse than controls on tasks that are more ecologically based. In recent years, ecological validity is an issue that has attracted considerable attention and has become more important in neuropsychological assessment (Chan et al., 2008). In addition, some researchers have begun to develop tests that are based on real life scenarios or use realistic, everyday stimuli to assess EF abilities in patients with TBI.

Shallice and Burgess (1991) designed a test called the Multiple Errands Test and found it to be sensitive to damage to the prefrontal lobes. In this test, test takers are asked to undertake tasks in a shopping centre according to a set of rules. Patients with damage to the prefrontal area were found to complete fewer tasks and to break more rules.

Rochat, Ammann, Mayer, Annoni, and Van der Linden (2009) used the Behavioral Assessment of the Dysexecutive Syndrome (BADS) to measure executive functions and found that TBI patients displayed significantly lower executive performance than controls. In addition, they found that the Modified Six Elements Test from the BADS to be significantly related to behavioral changes, and more specifically to symptoms of externalizing disorders.

The Behavior Rating Inventory of Executive Function (BRIEF) was developed by Gioia and Isquith (2004) to capture the real world behavioral manifestations of executive dysfunction and provide an important bridge toward understanding the impact of component level deficits on children's everyday adaptive functioning. The BRIEF is a questionnaire completed by children's parents or teachers. A number of studies have found severe TBI groups to show more problems on the BRIEF than moderate TBI and control groups (Gioia, Isquith, Kenworthy, & Barton, 2002; Nadebaum et al., 2007; Proctor, Wilson, Sanchez, & Wesley, 2000). Chapman et al. (2010) found that children with severe TBI developed executive function problems measured by the BRIEF shortly after injury which persisted at 18-month follow-up. It is interesting to note that parental report on the BRIEF did not correlate with the results of traditional executive function test (e.g., WCST, TMT, Verbal Fluency) in moderate to severe TBI children on average 2.8 years post injury (Vriezen & Pigott, 2002).

Other ecological measures of executive function include the virtual reality assessment (Pugnetti, Mendozzi, Barbieri, & Motta, 1998), cognitive simulation assessment (Satish, Streufert, & Eslinger, 2008), and a meal preparation task (strategic planning and prospective memory) (Fortin, et al., 2003). A study found the Virtual Planning Test had good test-retest reliability over six to eight weeks in a group of TBI patients (O'Neil-Pirozzi, Goldstein, Strangman, Katz, & Glenn, 2010). A case study by Satish et al. (2008) used the cognitive simulation assessment with a TBI patient and found that the patient showed significant difficulties in response flexibility, effective decision-making and other functions despite normal neuropsychological test scores. After finishing an intervention program, the patient's performance on a parallel version of the cognitive simulation assessment improved significantly. The study supported the feasibility and validity of the cognitive simulation assessment. Fortin et al. (2003) found

that CHI patients performed relatively well on neuropsychological tests but showed marked abnormality on a simulated meal preparation task. The patients could not correctly execute large action sets, suggesting strategic planning and prospective memory deficits (Fortin et al., 2003). Milleville-Pennel, Pothier, Hoc, and Mathe (2010) used a simulated driving test and recorded participants' eye movements. They found that TBI patients showed a reduction in the variety of visual zones explored and a reduction in the distance of exploration. Despite these developments, there are still relatively few ecologically valid measures being used in research studies. Spooner and Pachana (2006) argued that ecological valid neuropsychological assessments, including those for executive functions, should be used more in future studies.

Relation between Hot and Cool Components of EF

Several studies have investigated the relationship between hot and cool components of EF and some have reported significant relationship between them. For example, a study found that social problem-solving measured by Interpersonal Negotiation Strategies Task (INS) was related to memory and language skills in moderate to severe TBI patients (Hanten, et al., 2008). Dennis et al. found that the executive functions of working memory and cognitive inhibition following TBI were significantly correlated with TOM (Dennis, Agostino, Roncadin, & Levin, 2009). Henry et al. found that TBI patients showed greater levels of alexithymia, in terms of difficulty identifying emotions and reduced introspection (Henry, Phillips, Crawford, Theodorou, & Summers, 2006). Difficulty in identifying emotions was associated with poorer quality of life and executive function deficits (Henry et al., 2006).

However, there are some studies that did not find relations between hot and cool components of EF. In one study, patients with severe TBI with average time since injury of 91 weeks were administered two TOM tasks, Reading the Mind in the Eyes test and the Character Intention Task. Patients were found to be impaired on both tasks and other EF measures such as TMT and Stroop. However, no significant relationships were found between the TOM task measures and the other EF measures, suggesting that executive functioning and social cognition were independent (Havet-Thomassin et al., 2006). A group of patients with severe TBI with average time since injury of 103 months were tested on verbal and nonverbal TOM tasks (the faux pas test, the first-order and second-order false belief task, the character intention task, and the Reading the Mind in the Eyes test) and on non-TOM inference tasks and EF tasks. Patients were found to perform significantly more poorly on most TOM tasks. However, the TOM and other EF tasks were not found to be related (Muller et al., 2010).

The inconsistency in results on the relationship between hot and cool EFs may arise from a number of reasons. The use of different hot and cool EF measures across studies, differences in etiology, severity of injury, age at injury, and time since injury may have individually or in combination influenced the performance of participants on the tasks.

Factors Affecting Executive Function Performances

From the above review it can be seen that although overall EF impairments have been found after TBI, results have not been wholly consistent. This is likely to be due to the many factors that could affect EF performances. In this section, we review some of the more important ones.

Injury Severity. It is well known that the performance of patients with TBI on neurocognitive measures is affected by severity of their injury. For example, Gioia and colleagues found that severe TBI patients reported more problems on the BRIEF than controls and patients with moderate TBI (Gioia et al., 2002). Draper and Ponsford (2008) found that greater injury severity was significantly correlated with poorer test performance across all neurocognitive domains, including EF measures. Proctor et al. (2000) found that severity of injury influenced test performance for both EF (profile of executive functioning) and WM (recognition memory test) measures.

Interestingly, injury severity has been found to affect executive function performance in the acute as well as the chronic stage. Gerrard-Morris et al. (2010) studied children with TBI in the acute phase and at 18-month follow-up, and found that severe TBI patients had generalized cognitive deficiencies and less severe TBI patients had impairments in visual memory and executive function. These deficits persisted to follow-up (Gerrard-Morris et al., 2010). In their five-year follow-up study, Nadebaum et al. (2007) showed that executive difficulties were still present in severe TBI children but were not in children with mild and moderate injury. Muscara and colleagues found that more severe TBI resulted in a larger degree of executive dysfunction in long term TBI (7-10 years post-injury) in specific domains such as cognitive flexibility, abstract reasoning, and goal setting (Muscara, Catroppa, & Anderson, 2008). This was true in adult TBI patients as well. Draper and Ponsford (2008) found that patients at 10 years following their injury were still impaired in processing speed, memory, executive function, and that greater injury severity was related to poorer test performance across all domains.

Age at Onset. Study indicated that age of onset was related to WM (digit span backward) impairments (Conklin, Salorio, & Slomine, 2008). Roncadin, Guger, Archibald, Barnes, and Dennis (2004) found age at injury predicted score on a Recognition Memory Test. Slomine et al. (2002) found younger age at injury leads to more EF impairments. Senathi-Raja, Ponsford, and Schonberger (2010) found poorer cognitive functioning was associated with older age at injury in patients aged 16 to 81 years at time of injury.

Time Since Injury. In their study, Roncadin et al. (2004) found that time since injury is a reliable predictor of score on the Recognition Memory Test in moderate TBI. Results of a meta-analysis (Belanger, Curtiss, Demery, Lebowitz, & Vanderploeg, 2005) showed that time since injury, patient characteristics, and sampling methods are all moderators in neuropsychological outcomes following TBI. In general, patients show less impairment with the passage of time.

Other Factors. In addition to those discussed, other factors have been found to be related to the extent of EF impairment. These include number of, location, and volume of lesions (Slomine et al., 2002); gender (Niemeier, Marwitz, Lesher, Walker, & Bushnik, 2007); and emotion (Rapoport, McCullagh, Shammi, & Feinstein, 2005). For example, female patients with TBI have been found to perform significantly better than their male counterparts on the WCST, and TBI patients with depression have been found to perform significantly poorer than those without depression on working memory, processing speed, and verbal memory.

Relation between Executive Function and Functional Outcome

Some studies have examined the relation between executive function and functional outcome in TBI patients. Yeates et al. found that long-term outcomes were in part accounted for by specific neurocognitive skills such as executive functions and pragmatic language in moderate to severe TBI patients at four year follow-up (Yeates et al., 2004). Work status following TBI was related to neurocognitive functions. For example, cognitive impairments are important in identifying those at risk for occupational impairment following mild TBI at 3 to15 months following injury (Drake, Gray, Yoder, Pramuka, & Llewellyn, 2000). Return to work was significantly correlated with global neuropsychological performance at five months post-injury in moderate to severe TBI and showed a trend toward significance at eight weeks. Logical memory performance significantly predicted return to productivity (Green et al., 2008). In the neuropsychological tests of executive functions, preserved flexibility was associated with full-time work status (Nybo, Sainio, & Muller, 2004). Wood and Rutterford (2006) found that impairment in working memory directly predicted employment status, community integration, and life satisfaction. Bottari et al. found that EF measures emerged as major determinants of instrumental activities of daily living (IADL) in moderate to severe TBI 14 months post injury (Bottari, Dassa, Rainville, & Dutil, 2009). To summarize, most findings found functional outcome were correlated with

executive function; however, functional outcome is also multifaceted and the relationship between specific executive function and functional outcome requires further exploration.

Rehabilitation of Executive Function Impairments after TBI

Many studies explored whether EF dysfunctions after TBI can be rehabilitated. In a case study, Satish et al. (2008) designed a two-stage intervention program for a man with TBI. EF was assessed using a cognitive simulation assessment that measured level of activity, initiative, information utilization, response flexibility, and effective decision making. They found improved executive function at post-cognitive training assessment. A cognitive orientation to occupational performance approach was used in three adults with TBI (Dawson et al., 2009). The intervention guided participants to use a meta-cognitive problem-solving strategy to perform daily tasks. Performance was improved after intervention and maintained at three-month follow-up. Cicerone et al. (2008) found that both comprehensive, holistic neuropsychological rehabilitation and standard, multidisciplinary rehabilitation for people with TBI could improve their neuropsychological functioning on the Trail Making Test, a verbal learning test, and a test of Verbal Fluency at post-intervention assessment and at six-month follow-up (Cicerone, et al., 2008). These studies suggest that executive functions can be improved through cognitive intervention and the improvement can be maintained for some time.

Future Research Directions

In terms of future studies in this area, there are a number of issues that need to be explored and resolved. First, compared to cool EFs, there is less consensus on the number and nature of aspects for hot EFs. Given that hot EFs are considered by some as more related to everyday functioning, it is important to provide an empirically based and agreed upon model with reliable and valid measures to progress research in this area. Second, compared to the psychometric and cognitive-experimental approaches, the ecological approach has been less commonly used to examine EF impairments in TBI. Because the ecological approach uses tasks that might be more relevant and predictive of everyday functioning, it is important for researchers to conduct more studies using this approach. Third, as discussed, EF performances have been found to be affected by a number of injury and non-injury related factors. To reliably ascertain the nature and extent of EF impairments in TBI patients, it is important that these factors are well controlled in future studies. Fourth, there is relatively little evidence to corroborate the relationship between EF impairments and outcome measures such as quality of life, everyday functioning, and vocational outcome, and more studies are needed to ascertain these relationships. Fifth, there is some evidence that EF can be improved through intervention. Whether, however, all aspects of EF can be rehabilitated through intervention and how long any improvement is maintained needs further study.

Summary

EF can be divided into cool and hot components and these two major components can be further subdivided. There are mainly three approaches to the assessment of EFs: psychometric, cognitive-experimental, and ecological. In this chapter we reviewed five aspects of cool EF: initiation, sustained attention, switching and flexibility, disinhibition, attention allocation, and planning. Results of the review suggest that a majority of studies have found impairment in all of these aspects, with the exception of a few studies that did not. In addition, we reviewed three aspects of hot EF: decision making, self-regulation, and social cognition. Our findings suggest that self-regulation is impaired and plays an important role in social dysfunction in TBI patients. Theory of mind and other aspects of social cognition are found to be impaired in TBI patients in most studies. Finally, TBI patients were also found to be impaired on EFs as measured using the ecological approach.

While some studies reported significant correlations between hot and cool components of EF, other studies did not. Thus, the relationships between hot and cool components of EF need clarification. Many factors such as injury severity, age at onset, and time since injury have been found to be related to EF performances in TBI patients.

Acknowledgments

Preparation of this book chapter was supported by the Project-Oriented Hundred Talents Programme (O7CX031003) and the Knowledge Innovation Project of the Chinese Academy of Sciences (KSCX2-EW-J-8), the Griffith University Allan Sewell Visiting Fellowship to Raymond Chan; an Australian Academy of Science, Scientific Visits to China Grant to David Shum, and a grant from the initiation fund of the CAS/SAFEA International Partnership Programme for Creative Research Teams (Y2CX131003) to Raymond Chan and David Shum.

References

Arco, L., Cohen, L., & Geddes, K. (2004). Verbal self-regulation of impulsive behavior of persons with frontal lobe brain injury. *Behavior Therapy, 35*(3), 605–619.

Azouvi, P., Couillet, J., Leclercq, M., Martin, Y., Asloun, S., & Rousseaux, M. (2004). Divided attention and mental effort after severe traumatic brain injury. *Neuropsychologia, 42*(9), 1260–1268.

Bechara, A., Damasio, A. R., Damasio, H., & Anderson, S. W. (1994). Insensitivity to future consequences following damage to human prefrontal cortex. *Cognition, 50*(1–3), 7–15.

Bechara, A., Damasio, H., Damasio, A. R., & Lee, G. P. (1999). Different contributions of the human amygdala and ventromedial prefrontal cortex to decision-making. *The Journal of Neuroscience, 19,* 5473–5481.

Bechara, A., Tranel, D., & Damasio, H. (2000). Characterization of the decision-making deficit of patients with ventromedial prefrontal cortex lesions. *Brain, 123*(11), 2189–2202.

Belanger, H. G., Curtiss, G., Demery, J. A., Lebowitz, B. K., & Vanderploeg, R. D. (2005). Factors moderating neuropsychological outcomes following mild traumatic brain injury: a meta-analysis. *Journal of International Neuropsychological Society, 11*(3), 215–227.

Body, R. (2007). Decision making and somatic markers in conversation after traumatic brain injury. *Aphasiology, 21*(3), 394–408.

Bottari, C., Dassa, C., Rainville, C., & Dutil, E. (2009). The criterion-related validity of the IADL

Profile with measures of executive functions, indices of trauma severity, and sociodemographic characteristics. *Brain injury, 23*(4), 322–335.

Bush, G., Luu, P., & Posner, M. I., (2000). Cognitive and emotional influences in anterior cingulated cortex. *Trends in Cognitive Sciences, 4,* 215–222.

Cantin, J. F., McFadyen, B. J., Doyon, J., Swaine, B., Dumas, D., & Vallee, M. (2007). Can measures of cognitive function predict locomotor behaviour in complex environments following a traumatic brain injury? *Brain injury, 21*(3), 327–334.

Chan, R. C. K. (2005). Sustained attention in patients with traumatic brain injury. *Clinical Rehabilitation, 19,* 188–193.

Chan, R. C. K., Chen, E. Y. H., Cheung, E. F. C., Chen, R. Y. L., & Cheung, H. K. (2006). The components of executive functioning in a cohort of patients with chronic schizophrenia: a multiple single-case study design. *Schizophrenia Research, 81*(2–3), 173–189.

Chan, R. C. K., Chen, E. Y. H., & Law, C. W. (2006). Specific executive dysfunction in patients with first-episode medication-naïve schizophrenia. *Schizophrenia Research, 82*(1), 51–64.

Chan, R. C. K., Shum, D., Toulopoulou, T., & Chen, E. Y. H. (2008). Assessment of executive functions: Review of instruments and identification of critical issues. *Archives of Clinical Neuropsychology, 23,* 201–216.

Channon, S., Pellijeff, A., & Rule, A. (2005). Social cognition after head injury: sarcasm and theory of mind. *Brain and Language, 93*(2), 123–134.

Chapman, L. A., Wade, S. L., Walz, N. C., Taylor, H. G., Stancin, T., & Yeates, K. O. (2010). Clinically significant behavior problems during the initial 18 months following early childhood traumatic brain injury. *Rehabilitation Psychology, 55*(1), 48–57.

Cicerone, K. D., Mott, T., Azulay, J., Sharlow-Galella, M. A., Ellmo, W. J., Paradise, S., et al. (2008). A randomized controlled trial of holistic neuropsychologic rehabilitation after traumatic brain injury. *Archives of physical medicine and rehabilitation, 89*(12), 2239–2249.

Conklin, H. M., Salorio, C. F., & Slomine, B. S. (2008). Working memory performance following paediatric traumatic brain injury. *Brain injury, 22*(11), 847–857.

Cook, L. G., Chapman, S. B., & Levin, H. S. (2008). Self-regulation abilities in children with severe traumatic brain injury: a preliminary investigation of naturalistic action. *NeuroRehabilitation, 23*(6), 467–475.

Daniels, K. A., Toth, J. P., & Jacoby, L. L. (2006). The Aging of Executive Functions. In E. Bialystok & F. I. M. Craik (Ed.), *Lifespan cognition: mechanisms of change* (pp. 96–111). New York: Oxford University Press.

Dawson, D. R., Anderson, N. D., Burgess, P., Cooper, E., Krpan, K. M., & Stuss, D. T. (2009). Further development of the Multiple Errands Test: standardized scoring, reliability, and ecological validity for the Baycrest version. *Archives of physical medicine and rehabilitation, 90*(11 Suppl), S41–51.

DeHaan, A., Halterman, C., Langan, J., Drew, A. S., Osternig, L. R., Chou, L. S., et al. (2007). Cancelling planned actions following mild traumatic brain injury. *Neuropsychologia, 45*(2), 406–411.

Dennis, M., Agostino, A., Roncadin, C., & Levin, H. (2009). Theory of mind depends on domain-general executive functions of working memory and cognitive inhibition in children with traumatic brain injury. *Journal of Clinical and Experimental Neuropsychology, 31*(7), 835–847.

Drake, A. I., Gray, N., Yoder, S., Pramuka, M., & Llewellyn, M. (2000). Factors predicting return to work following mild traumatic brain injury: a discriminant analysis. *Journal of Head Trauma Rehabilitation, 15*(5), 1103–1112.

Draper, K., & Ponsford, J. (2008). Cognitive functioning ten years following traumatic brain injury and rehabilitation. *Neuropsychology, 22*(5), 618–625.

Dreer, L. E., DeVivo, M. J., Novack, T. A., Krzywanski, S., & Marson, D. C. (2008). Cognitive Predictors of Medical Decision-Making Capacity in Traumatic Brain Injury *Rehabilitation Psychology, 53*(4), 486–497.

Fortin, S., Godbout, L., & Braun, C. M. J. (2003). Cognitive Structure of Executive Deficits in Frontally Lesioned Head Trauma Patients Performing Activities of Daily Living. *Cortex, 39*(2), 273–291.

Ganesalingam, K., Sanson, A., Anderson, V., & Yeates, K. O. (2006). Self-regulation and social and behavioral functioning following childhood traumatic brain injury. *Journal of International Neuropsychological Society, 12*(5), 609–621.

Ganesalingam, K., Sanson, A., Anderson, V., & Yeates, K. O. (2007). Self-regulation as a mediator of the effects of childhood traumatic brain injury on social and behavioral functioning. *Journal of International Neuropsychological Society, 13*(2), 298–311.

Geraci, A., Surian, L., Ferraro, M., & Cantagallo, A. (2010). Theory of Mind in patients with ventromedial or dorsolateral prefrontal lesions following traumatic brain injury. *Brain injury, 24*(7–8), 978–987.

Gerrard-Morris, A., Taylor, H. G., Yeates, K. O., Walz, N. C., Stancin, T., Minich, N., et al. (2010). Cognitive development after traumatic brain injury in young children. *Journal of International Neuropsychological Society, 16*(1), 157–168.

Gioia, G. A., & Isquith, P. K. (2004). Ecological assessment of executive function in traumatic brain injury. *Developmental Neuropsychology, 25*(1–2), 135–158.

Gioia, G. A., Isquith, P. K., Kenworthy, L., & Barton, R. M. (2002). Profiles of everyday executive function in acquired and developmental disorders. *Child Neuropsychology, 8*(2), 121–137.

Green, R. E., Colella, B., Hebert, D. A., Bayley, M., Kang, H. S., Till, C., et al. (2008). Prediction of return to productivity after severe traumatic brain injury: investigations of optimal neuropsychological tests and timing of assessment. *Archives of physical medicine and rehabilitation, 89*(12 Suppl), S51–60.

Hanten, G., Scheibel, R. S., Li, X., Oomer, I., Stallings-Roberson, G., Hunter, J. V., et al. (2006). Decision-making after traumatic brain injury in children: a preliminary study. *Neurocase, 12*(4), 247–251.

Hanten, G., Wilde, E. A., Menefee, D. S., Li, X., Lane, S., Vasquez, C., et al. (2008). Correlates of social problem solving during the first year after traumatic brain injury in children. *Neuropsychology, 22*(3), 357–370.

Havet-Thomassin, V., Allain, P., Etcharry-Bouyx, F., & Le Gall, D. (2006). What about theory of mind after severe brain injury? *Brain injury, 20*(1), 83–91.

Henry, J. D., & Crawford, J. R. (2004). A meta-analytic review of verbal fluency performance in patients with traumtic brain injury. *Neuropsychology, 18*, 621–628.

Henry, J. D., Phillips, L. H., Crawford, J. R., Theodorou, G., & Summers, F. (2006). Cognitive and psychosocial correlates of alexithymia following traumatic brain injury. *Neuropsychologia, 44*(1), 62–72.

Jurado, M. B., & Rosselli, M. (2007). The elusive nature of executive functions: a review of our current understanding. *Neuropsychology Review, 17*(3), 213–233.

Kennedy, M. R., Wozniak, J. R., Muetzel, R. L., Mueller, B. A., Chiou, H. H., Pantekoek, K., et al. (2009). White matter and neurocognitive changes in adults with chronic traumatic brain injury. *Journal of the International Neuropsychological Society, 15*(1), 130–136.

Lange, R. T., Iverson, G. L., Zakrzewski, M. J., Ethel-King, P. E., & Franzen, M. D. (2005). Interpreting the Trail Making Test Following Traumatic Brain Injury: Comparison of Traditional Time Scores and Derived Indices. *Journal of Clinical and Experimental Neuropsychology, 27*(7), 897–906

Levin, H. S., & Hanten, G. (2005). Executive functions after traumatic brain injury in children. *Pediatric Neurology, 33*, 79–93.

Levine, B., Dawson, D., Boutet, I., Schwartz, M. L., & Stuss, D. T. (2000). Assessment of strategic self-regulation in traumatic brain injury: its relationship to injury severity and psychosocial outcome. *Neuropsychology, 14*(4), 491–500.

Martin-Rodriguez, J. F., & Leon-Carrion, J. (2010). Theory of mind deficits in patients with acquired brain injury: a quantitative review. *Neuropsychologia, 48*(5), 1181–1191.

Mathias, J. L., & Wheaton, P. (2007). Changes in attention and information-processing speed following severe traumatic brain injury: a meta-analytic review. *Neuropsychology, 21*(2), 212–223.

Milders, M., Ietswaart, M., Crawford, J. R., & Currie, D. (2006). Impairments in theory of mind shortly after traumatic brain injury and at 1-year follow-up. *Neuropsychology, 20*(4), 400–408.

Milleville-Pennel, I., Pothier, J., Hoc, J. M., & Mathe, J. F. (2010). Consequences of cognitive impairments following traumatic brain injury: Pilot study on visual exploration while driving. *Brain injury, 24*(4), 678–691.

Muller, F., Simion, A., Reviriego, E., Galera, C., Mazaux, J. M., Barat, M., et al. (2010). Exploring theory of mind after severe traumatic brain injury. *Cortex, 46*, 1088–1099.

Muscara, F., Catroppa, C., & Anderson, V. (2008). The Impact of Injury Severity on Executive Function 7–10 Years Following Pediatric Traumatic Brain Injury *Developmental Neuropsychology, 33*(5), 623–636.

Nadebaum, C., Anderson, V., & Catroppa, C. (2007). Executive function outcomes following traumatic brain injury in young children: a five year follow-up. *Developmental Neuropsychology, 32*(2), 703–728.

Newsome, M. R., Scheibel, R. S., Chu, Z., Steinberg, J. L., Hunter, J. V., Lu, H., et al. (2010). Brain Activation While Thinking About the Self From Another Person's Perspective After Traumatic Brain Injury in Adolescents. *Neuropsychology, 24*(2), 139–147.

Niemeier, J. P., Marwitz, J. H., Lesher, K., Walker, W. C., & Bushnik, T. (2007). Gender differences in executive functions following traumatic brain injury. *Neuropsychological Rehabilitation, 17*(3), 293–313.

Nybo, T., Sainio, M., & Muller, K. (2004). Stability of vocational outcome in adulthood after moderate to severe preschool brain injury. *Journal of International Neuropsychological Society, 10*(5), 719–723.

O'Neil-Pirozzi, T. M., Goldstein, R., Strangman, G. E., Katz, D. I., & Glenn, M. B. (2010). Test-re-test reliability of the virtual planning test in individuals with traumatic brain injury. *Brain injury, 24*(3), 509–516.

Ownsworth, T. L., McFarland, K. M., & Young, R. M. (2000). Development and standardization of the Self-regulation Skills Interview (SRSI): a new clinical assessment tool for acquired brain injury. *The Clinical Neuropsychologist, 14*(1), 76–92.

Perianez, J. A., Rios-Lago, M., Rodriguez-Sanchez, J. M., Adrover-Roig, D., Sanchez-Cubillo, I., Crespo-Facorro, B., et al. (2007). Trail Making Test in traumatic brain injury, schizophrenia, and normal ageing: sample comparisons and normative data. *Archives of Clinical Neuropsychology, 22*(4), 433–447.

Premack, D., & Woodruff, G. (1978). Does the chimpanzee have a 'theory of mind?'. *Behavioural and Brain Sciences, 1*, 515–526.

Proctor, A., Wilson, B., Sanchez, C., & Wesley, E. (2000). Executive function and verbal working memory in adolescents with closed head injury (CHI). *Brain injury, 14*(7), 633–647.

Pugnetti, L., Mendozzi, L., Barbieri, E., & Motta, A. (1998). VR experience with neurological patients: basic cost/benefit issues. *Studies in Health Technology and Informatics, 58*, 243–248.

Rapoport, M. J., Herrmann, N., Shammi, P., Kiss, A., Phillips, A., & Feinstein, A. (2006). Outcome after traumatic brain injury sustained in older adulthood: a one-year longitudinal study. *American Journal of Geriatric Psychiatry, 14*(5), 456–465.

Rapoport, M. J., McCullagh, S., Shammi, P., & Feinstein, A. (2005). Cognitive impairment associated with major depression following mild and moderate traumatic brain injury. *Journal of Neuropsychiatry and Clinical Neuroscience, 17*(1), 61–65.

Rieger, M., & Gauggel, S. (2002). Inhibition of ongoing responses in patients with traumatic brain injury. *Neuropsychologia, 40*(1), 76–85.

Rochat, L., Ammann, J., Mayer, E., Annoni, J. M., & Van der Linden, M. (2009). Executive disorders and perceived socio-emotional changes after traumatic brain injury. *Journal of Neuropsychology, 3*(2), 213–227.

Roche, R. A., Dockree, P. M., Garavan, H., Foxe, J. J., Robertson, I. H., & O'Mara, S. M. (2004). EEG alpha power changes reflect response inhibition deficits after traumatic brain injury (TBI) in humans. *Neuroscience Letters, 362*(1), 1–5.

Roncadin, C., Guger, S., Archibald, J., Barnes, M., & Dennis, M. (2004). Working memory after mild, moderate, or severe childhood closed head injury. *Developmental neuropsychology, 25*(1–2), 21–36.

Satish, U., Streufert, S., & Eslinger, P. J. (2008). Simulation-based executive cognitive assessment and rehabilitation after traumatic frontal lobe injury: a case report. *Disability and Rehabilitation, 30*(6), 468–478.

Schlund, M. W., Pace, G. M., & McGready, J. (2001). Relations between decision-making deficits and discriminating contingencies following brain injury. *Brain Injury, 15*(12), 1061–1071.

Schmitter-Edgecombe, M., & Langill, M. (2006). Costs of a predictable switch between simple cognitive tasks following severe closed-head injury. *Neuropsychology, 20*(6), 675–684.

Schroeter, M. L., Ettrich, B., Menz, M., & Zysset, S. (2010). Traumatic brain injury affects the fronto-median cortex—an event-related fMRI study on evaluative judgments. *Neuropsychologia, 48*(1), 185–193.

Schroeter, M. L., Ettrich, B., Schwier, C., Scheid, R., Guthke, T., & von Cramon, D. Y. (2007). Diffuse axonal injury due to traumatic brain injury alters inhibition of imitative response tendencies. *Neuropsychologia, 45*(14), 3149–3156.

Seignourel, P. J., Robins, D. L., Larson, M. J., Demery, J. A., Cole, M., & Perlstein, W. M. (2005). Cognitive control in closed head injury: context maintenance dysfunction or prepotent response inhibition deficit? *Neuropsychology, 19*(5), 578–590.

Senathi-Raja, D., Ponsford, J., & Schonberger, M. (2010). Impact of age on long-term cognitive function after traumatic brain injury. *Neuropsychology, 24*(3), 336–344.

Shallice, T., & Burgess, P. W. (1991). Deficits in strategy application following frontal lobe damage in man. *Brain, 114*, 727–741.

Sigurdardottir, S., Jerstad, T., Andelic, N., Roe, C., & Schanke, A. K. (2010). Olfactory dysfunction, gambling task performance and intracranial lesions after traumatic brain injury. *Neuropsychology, 24*(4), 504–513.

Slomine, B. S., Gerring, J. P., Grados, M. A., Vasa, R., Brady, K. D., Christensen, J. R., et al. (2002). Performance on measures of executive function following pediatric traumatic brain injury. *Brain injury, 16*(9), 759–772.

Spooner, D. M., & Pachana, N. A. (2006). Ecological validity in neuropsychological assessment: a case for greater consideration in research with neurologically intact populations. *Archives of Clinical Neuropsychology, 21*(4), 327–337.

Stronach, S. T., & Turktra, L. S. (2008). Theory of mind and use of cognitive state terms by adolescents with traumatic brain injury. *Aphasiology, 22*(10), 1054–1070.

Stuss, D. T., & Knight, R. T. (Eds.). (2002). *Principles of Frontal Lobe Function.* New York: Oxford University Press.

Stuss, D. T., Shallice, T., Alexander, M. P., & Picton, T. W. (1995). A multidisciplinary approach to anterior attention functions. *Annals of the New York Academy of Sciences, 769,* 191–209.

Tombaugh, T. N., Stormer, P., Rees, L., Irving, S., & Francis, M. (2006). The effects of mild and severe traumatic brain injury on the auditory and visual versions of the Adjusting-Paced Serial Addition Test (Adjusting-PSAT). *Archives of Clinical Neuropsychology, 21*(7), 753–761.

Turkstra, L. S. (2008). Conversation-based assessment of social cognition in adults with traumatic brain injury. *Brain injury, 22*(5), 397–409.

Turkstra, L. S., Williams, W. H., Tonks, J., & Frampton, I. (2008). Measuring social cognition in adolescents: implications for students with TBI returning to school. *NeuroRehabilitation, 23*(6), 501–509.

Vriezen, E. R., & Pigott, S. E. (2002). The relationship between parental report on the BRIEF and performance-based measures of executive function in children with moderate to severe traumatic brain injury. *Child Neuropsychology, 8*(4), 296–303.

Wood, R. L., & Rutterford, N. A. (2006). Demographic and cognitive predictors of long-term psychosocial outcome following traumatic brain injury. *Journal of International Neuropsychological Society, 12*(3), 350–358.

Yeates, K. O., Swift, E., Taylor, H. G., Wade, S. L., Drotar, D., Stancin, T., et al. (2004). Short- and long-term social outcomes following pediatric traumatic brain injury. *Journal of International Neuropsychological Society, 10*(3), 412–426.

7

High-Level Language in Traumatic Brain Injury: Promising Metrics to Advance Brain Repair

Sandra B. Chapman and Lori G. Cook

Professionals involved in researching, diagnosing, and/or treating the long-term cognitive-linguistic impairments in individuals with traumatic brain injury (TBI) seek methodologies to advance long-term recovery. Exciting research advancements have found recently explicated discourse metrics to be both informative and sensitive to detecting the persistent impact of a TBI on cognitive-linguistic function (Chapman, Gamino, & Anand, 2012; Gamino, Chapman, & Cook, 2009; Vas, Chapman, & Cook, under review). Discourse metrics enhance the diagnostic sensitivity and usefulness for treatment planning as compared to that provided by basic measures of language function such as vocabulary and syntax (e.g., Chapman et al., 1997, 2001).

In the past, research interest in the linguistic sequelae associated with TBI has been subordinated to greater concerns about cognitive impairments, in general, and executive function deficits in particular. This attenuated focus on linguistic outcomes was largely due to the widely held, overly simplistic view in which language was defined primarily as the lexicon and syntax used for expression. Clearly, the majority of standardized language measures assess lower levels of language and fail to detect the complex cognitive-linguistic impairments that persist after TBI in children and adults (e.g., Coelho, Ylvisaker, & Turkstra, 2005; Ewing-Cobbs, Barnes, Fletcher, Levin, Swank, & Song, 2004; Ewing-Cobbs, Fletcher, Levin, Lovino, & Miner, 1998). In contrast, discourse (i.e., connected language) measures have demonstrated sensitivity to the long-term higher level cognitive deficits typically seen in TBI. Further, evidence points to a dynamic interdependence of performance on cognitive measures of executive control (described in chapter 6) and on high-level discourse metrics (Anand, Chapman, Rackley, Keebler, Zientz, & Hart, 2010; Brookshire, Chapman, Song, & Levin, 2000; Chapman et al., 2006, in press; Gamino, Chapman, & Cook, 2009; Vas et al., under review).

Although a number of discourse metrics have been studied, one promising metric focuses on the capacity to comprehend and convey generalized, core meaning(s) from the wealth of complex information to which one is exposed on a daily basis. Recent research reveals that impaired ability to abstract meaning, labeled as *gist reasoning,* is a lasting and debilitating consequence of sustaining a TBI, whether in childhood or adulthood (Chapman et al., in press; Gamino, Chapman, & Cook, 2009; Gamino, Chapman, Hull, & Lyon, 2010). Moreover, gist reasoning is impaired in the majority of individuals with TBI ranging from mild to severe and is linked to performance on cognitive control measures (Brookshire et al., 2000; Chapman et al., 2004, 2006; Gamino, Chapman, & Cook, 2009; Vas et al., under review; see also Cook, Chapman, & Gamino, 2007). The significance of this capacity to derive global meaning from the influx of massive amounts of information is that it is at the core of our human functionality (Gabrieli, 2004). That is, the human brain is constantly called upon to disregard/inhibit a majority of incoming data and to extract global meanings. We utilize this capacity over and over again throughout our day, whether it be attempting to extract meaning from a newspaper, research article, or Internet story; reviewing relevant information to engage in a series of job searches/interviews; identifying core advantages/disadvantages in insurance coverage choices; figuring out key steps when learning to use newly acquired technology such as cell phones; or seeking to understand the risks and benefits embedded in medical advice (Anand et al., 2010; Ulatowska & Chapman, 1994; Vas et al., under review).

In this chapter, we review research that motivates efforts to address deficits in high-level language skills after TBI. The main goal is to summarize the empirical evidence showing that high-level language/discourse skills are vulnerable to the long-term impact of TBI. A number of metrics of high-level language function, including constructs such as cohesion, coherence, and gist reasoning, have been developed, tested, and found sensitive to the persistent impact of TBI in both pediatric and adult populations. Second, we briefly discuss pivotal theories related to discourse-brain linkages to provide a theoretical basis for advancing the understanding and treatment of the complex cognitive-linguistic sequelae in TBI. Third, we will synthesize findings and offer implications for treatment to advance brain recovery in TBI. Additionally, we will discuss emerging directions in informing cognitive theory as discourse metrics are analyzed in relation to executive functions in TBI populations. The concluding section will offer promising directions for future research and clinical management based on the current state-of-the-art understanding of high-level language abilities in TBI populations, with the overarching emphasis that future directions need to point to longer-term monitoring and treatment.

Review of Recent Research on Language Function in TBI

Sustaining a TBI results in substantial long-term effects, including deficits in language, cognition, behavior, motor skills, psychosocial function, and learning (e.g., Chapman, Levin, Matejka, Harward, & Kufera, 1995; Chapman et al., 2001; Dennis & Barnes, 2001; Fletcher,

Miner, & Ewing-Cobbs, 1987). As summarized below, evidence indicates that many traditional language measures and achievement tests do not adequately detect post-injury deficits, particularly in the long term. Researchers suggest that this inadequacy may be due to an absence of specific measurement targeting high levels of language competency, such as the ability to convey ideas effectively. These metrics are not included in the majority of widely used language measures (Chapman, Levin, & Culhane, 1995; Chapman, Levin, Matejka, et al., 1995; Chapman et al., 1997).

Lower Levels of Language

Standardized language and aphasia batteries have been widely used to characterize language function after TBI. The performance patterns fail to reveal much, if any, residual cognitive-linguistic deficits after TBI in children or adults, largely because the commonly used language measurements focus predominately on discrete word- and sentence-level measures. The main focus of these traditional language measures is on the segmental aspects of language that measure basic understanding, use of, and ability to define vocabulary, and the ability to formulate grammatically correct, complete, and complex sentences. Indeed, basic linguistic skills such as semantics and syntax are infrequently impaired during everyday conversation or on structured tasks in individuals who have suffered a TBI, whether in adulthood or childhood (e.g., Chapman et al., 1997; Coelho, 2002; Cook et al., 2007; Mentis & Prutting, 1987).

Researchers propose that the majority of individuals with TBI regain the basic linguistic tools to codify their ideas. Individuals with moderate to severe TBI typically show rapid recovery of the formal aspects of language (i.e., phonology, syntax, and semantics) as early as three months post injury (Ewing-Cobbs et al., 1998, 2004). For example, most children and adults with TBI regain the ability to apply linguistic knowledge to use vocabulary appropriately and to formulate complex sentences (e.g., Chapman et al., 1997; Coelho, 2002; Hartley & Jensen, 1991). Furthermore, isolated measures of language function have demonstrated lack of correspondence with everyday functionality (e.g.,

Chapman, Levin, & Culhane, 1995; Chapman et al., 2001; Ulatowska & Chapman, 1994). Findings of relatively good recovery in lexical and sentential skills to within normal limits may explain why many of the communication deficits in TBI go undetected and therefore untreated. That is, the surface-level language abilities in individuals with TBI do not appear to provoke distress in the individual nor manifest obvious disruptions to the casual listener.

In addition, standardized measures of academic achievement are not sensitive to the cognitive-linguistic sequelae of TBI, as they tend to measure basic skills. For example, achievement tests administered in a school setting typically assess verbal abilities that are either over-learned or automatic, skills which are relatively spared following TBI or recover to within normal limits months after the injury (Ewing-Cobbs et al., 1998, 2004). Ewing-Cobbs and colleagues (1998) found that children who exhibited average scores on achievement testing two years after their brain injury nonetheless demonstrated incompetence in academic settings as evidenced by repeating a grade and/or requiring special education assistance.

In sum, basic linguistic skills typically recover to functional levels when evaluated on traditional measures of structured language function and academic achievement tests, particularly at chronic recovery stages, defined as longer than one year post injury (Chapman, 2006). This is not to say that all individuals with TBI fully recover age-appropriate or premorbid levels of skills in the domains of vocabulary and syntax. Indeed, a small percentage of individuals may continue to manifest deficits. Nonetheless, rehabilitation studies in TBI provide evidence that basic language re-training may improve performance on these segmental aspects of language, but the treatment often lacks a theoretical foundation to guide treatment development, lacks generalization to untrained domains, or fails to impact everyday life (Cannizzaro & Coehlo, 2002; Chen, Abrams, & D'Esposito, 2006; Chen & D'Esposito, 2010; Vas et al., under review). Thus, for the majority of patients with TBI, deficits in the isolated aspects of linguistic function will not likely be the dominant impairments that hinder long-term recovery and the capacity to return to high levels of functionality.

As an alternative to limited sensitivity in lower levels of language function, discourse, defined broadly as connected language typically representing complex information, may be particularly informative in individuals who have sustained a TBI, as it is crucial for academic success, job performance, social skill development, and functional independence (Biddle, McCabe, & Bliss, 1996; Chapman, Levin, Matejka, et al., 1995; Feagans & Applebaum, 1986; Gillam, McFadden, & van Kleek, 1995; Jacobs, 1988; Jordan & Murdoch, 1994; Klonoff, Clark, & Klonoff, 1993; Mazaux, Masson, Levin, Alaoui, Maurette, & Barat, 1997; Roth & Spekman, 1989; Westby, 1989). High-level language abilities, such as those represented at a discourse level, are rarely examined in standard clinical practice or in school or professional settings. As highlighted below, when discourse measures are administered, many individuals with TBI demonstrate marked difficulty conveying their ideas in connected language, even in the context of performing within normal limits on traditional standardized language measures (Chapman, 1997; Chapman, Levin, & Culhane, 1995; Chapman, Levin, Matejka, et al., 1995).

Discourse/High-Level Language

In contrast to relatively good recovery of lower language skills in TBI, significant impairments persist in high-level language abilities. Various high-order language deficits, associated with cognitive impairment, have been described extensively in the child and adult TBI literature (e.g., Chapman et al., 2001, 2004, 2006; Dennis & Barnes, 2001; Gamino, Chapman, & Cook, 2009; Hinchliffe, Murdoch, & Chenery, 1998; Jordan, Cremona-Meteyard, & King, 1996; Leblanc, De Guise, Feyz, & Lamoureux, 2006; Ylvisaker, 1992). The cognitive-linguistic sequelae associated with TBI in either childhood or adulthood typically include: (a) problems of a communicative nature (e.g., disorganized discourse, slow and inefficient word retrieval, impulsive communication style); (b) learning difficulties (e.g., problems with new learning for on-the-job training, concrete thinking, inefficient note-taking and study skills, disorganized writing); and (c) social/pragmatic struggles (e.g., impulsive and/or context-insensitive social interactions). For a more in-depth review of these areas of deficit after brain injury, see Ylvisaker and colleagues (2005). The impairment of these capacities affects the core of our human functionality.

We highlight recent research findings related to performance on discourse as a promising metric of higher-order language function that is commonly disrupted after TBI (Chapman et al., 2001, 2004, 2006; Chapman, Levin, & Lawyer, 1999; Chapman et al., 1998; Gamino, Chapman, & Cook, 2009; Snow, Douglas, & Ponsford, 1997, 1999; Yorkston, Jaffe, Liao, & Polissar, 1999; Yorkston, Jaffe, Polissar, Liao, & Fay, 1997; Wilson & Proctor, 2000, 2002). Discourse refers to connected language, or the "linguistic expression of ideas, wishes, and opinions in everyday life, typically conveyed as a sequence of sentences that has coherent organization and meaning" (Chapman & Sparks, 2003, p. 754). Evaluation of discourse is clinically informative because of its sensitivity to the higher level cognitive deficits typically seen in TBI and its relevance to daily life functions (Biddle et al., 1996; Brookshire et al., 2000; Reilly, Bates, & Marchman, 1998).

Two primary types of discourse are studied to categorize the forms that are central to everyday life communication functions, such as new learning and job training. These two types include monologues (i.e., procedural, descriptive, narrative, or expository) and conversational (i.e., interactive) discourse (e.g., Coelho, 2007), each of which have different cognitive and linguistic demands. Different tasks have been employed with individuals with TBI to elicit performance on these varying discourse genres. For example, a procedural discourse task may entail asking an individual to explain the steps involved in withdrawing money from a bank account (Snow et al., 1997), whereas a descriptive discourse task might involve asking someone to describe his or her family or what their home looks like (Hough & Barrow, 2003). Discourse has traditionally been assessed by means of eliciting either a straightforward retell (e.g., Chapman, 1997; Chapman et al., 2001) or a complex summarization of a story or text (e.g., Chapman et al., 2006; Gamino, Chapman, & Cook, 2009), either orally or in written form. A good retell conveys explicit content while

adhering to a standard discourse structure, which for a narrative includes a setting, an initiating event, character actions, and a conclusion (i.e., resolution). In contrast to a retell, a summary requires condensing and synthesizing information to form abstracted meanings, or gist-based concepts, with less focus on specific details.

Although discourse ability associated with TBI is heterogeneous, several common patterns of impairment have been identified. In general, discourse impairments in TBI are more commonly revealed by discourse metrics of content and organization of the information rather than by language measures that focus on amount of language and complexity of syntax (Chapman et al., 1997; Chapman, Levin, Matejka, et al., 1995). Discourse deficits are typically manifested on metrics of cohesion, coherence, and gist reasoning (defined as the ability to abstract meaning). Cohesion is defined as the ability to use linguistic devices such as pronoun reference or verb tense to sequentially link ideas so that the listener can readily follow the content. Coherence represents the overall core meaning around which the ideas are centered so that the flow of language does not seem tangential and incoherent. The discourse metrics of cohesion and coherence have been described in detail elsewhere (Coelho et al., 2005). Overall, there is ample evidence to indicate that the use of cohesive devices is disrupted after TBI, although these cohesive deficits appear to be influenced largely by the method of elicitation (e.g., story retell versus story generation; Coelho, Liles, & Duffy, 1991; Davis & Coelho, 2004; Hartley & Jensen, 1991; Liles, Coelho, Duffy, & Zalagens, 1989). Coherence has also been widely demonstrated to be sensitive to impairment in discourse performance after TBI (e.g., Chapman et al., 2006; Davis & Coelho, 2004; Gamino, Chapman, & Cook, 2009; Glosser & Deser, 1990; McDonald, 1993). Specifically, individuals with TBI have demonstrated impaired performance on metrics of information, where information metrics are defined by the number of key ideas conveyed, how well ideas are organized, and the ability to comprehend and convey the generalized message from a lesson or passage (Chapman et al., 1992, 1997, 2001, 2004, 2006; Chapman, Levin, Matejka, et al., 1995; Coelho et al., 2005; Davis & Coelho, 2004). For example, individuals with TBI may use many words, but say very little of importance or substance, and what they do say may not convey a coherent message (coherence) and may be poorly organized (cohesion), failing to sequentially link ideas in a logical manner.

In the subsequent sections of this chapter, we focus largely on the recently defined discourse metric of gist reasoning, which appears to be a promising domain to advance future research and treatment of the persistent sequelae of TBI in both children and adults. Gist reasoning, as elaborated below, refers to the ability to comprehend, construct, and convey abstracted meaning at a discourse/connected language level. Deficits in this capacity are widespread and have been documented in the majority of both children and adults with TBI, particularly when the injury was moderate to severe.

Discourse Metric of Gist Reasoning

Definition of Gist Reasoning

Recent findings point to gist reasoning as an informative metric to detect the persistent cognitive-linguistic deficiency in TBI, whether the brain injury occurs in childhood or in adulthood. Gist reasoning represents the dynamic cognitive-linguistic ability to combine details to form abstract meanings from complex information/connected language, whether the information is experienced through auditory, visual, or other sensory modalities (Chapman, Hart, Levin, Cook, & Gamino, under review; Gabrieli, 2004; Reyna, 2008; van Dijk, 1995). Daily, we are faced with the challenge to pay attention to only a small percentage of the massive amounts of incoming stimuli and to assimilate abstract meanings from the information we encounter at a high level of generalization. The same is true for information we encounter through a wide variety of forms such as texts (e.g., newspapers, Internet, books), audio (e.g., lectures, radio), or video (e.g., movies, television) as major content sources. This challenge is increased after one has suffered a TBI.

Gist reasoning has been linked to frontally mediated networks and operates as a top-down,

superordinate process that directs the capacity to encode and retrieve details and involves a complex interplay of cognitive, linguistic, and social skills (Anand et al., 2010; Brainerd & Reyna, 1995; Chapman et al., in press; Gabrieli, 2004; Gamino et al., 2010; Reyna, 2008). Developmentally, the ability to engage in gist reasoning begins to emerge in childhood at a relatively early age (approximately seven years of age), at least for familiar information. Gist reasoning abilities become increasingly more sophisticated in adolescence and young adulthood (e.g., Johnson, 1983), a period when the frontal brain networks are undergoing dramatic growth and remodeling (Gogtay et al., 2004).

In discourse, gist reasoning is manifest in the form of mini-texts such as titles, synopses, summaries, main concepts, and interpretative statements (Ulatowska & Chapman, 1994). Optimally, each minitext is constructed to express the abstracted gist meaning at a more global level than the component details that comprise the lengthier original information. This is to say that a gist-based text conveys the same central meaning as the original text but does so by means of a reduced and generalized version that omits the unimportant details. In contrast to rapid loss of specific, concrete details, abstracted gist meanings are posited to be more robustly stored and retrieved, making them more resilient to degradation (Brainerd & Reyna, 1995; Gabrieli, 2004; Reyna & Brainerd, 1995).

Gist Reasoning Impairment in TBI

The first efforts to elucidate the disruption to gist reasoning competence in TBI involved youth, with more recent investigations in adults emerging in the last few years (Chapman et al., 2001, 2004, 2006; Gamino, Chapman, & Cook, 2009; Vas et al., under review; Vas, Chapman, Krawczyk, Krishnan, & Keebler, 2010). In one of the first studies of gist reasoning, children who were ages 7 to 14 years when assessed two years after severe TBI showed impairments in combining details into gist-based meanings when compared to a typically developing control group (Chapman et al., 2004). Specifically, when asked to condense and synthesize meaning from a lengthy text of 540 words, the children/ adolescents with TBI used an immature, earlier developmental strategy of "copy and delete" (Brown & Day, 1983) to reduce information. In other words, they simply condensed (deleted) and retold (copied) the explicit detail information rather than reducing the volume of details through constructing higher-order, abstract meanings. In contrast, a group of typically developing children with comparable demographic characteristics was able to abstract gist-based meaning spontaneously in their summaries.

In a subsequent study, the capacity to construct gist meaning as well as the roles of both immediate and working memory in gist reasoning were examined in a group of pre-adolescent/ adolescents who had experienced a TBI (Chapman et al., 2006). In this study, 38 children with TBI were asked to summarize an expository text, where summarization had previously been shown to measure gist reasoning (Chapman et al., 2004). In addition, working memory was measured using an n-back working memory task (see Chapman et al., 2006, p. 181 for description), and immediate memory was measured using the first trial of the *California Verbal Learning Test (CVLT)-Children's Version* (Delis, Kramer, Kaplan, & Obler, 1986). Findings revealed that the children ages 8 to 14 years who had sustained either a mild or severe TBI (at least two years post injury) exhibited difficulty in abstracting gist compared to typically developing children. This study provides evidence that not only are children with severe brain injuries impaired on gist reasoning, but those who have suffered a mild TBI may also be vulnerable to lasting deficits when tested two or more years post-injury. Such a pattern informs future studies to further determine which individuals with mild TBI (i.e., Glasgow Coma Scale score of 13–15) have positive findings on brain imaging (i.e., CT or MRI scan) such that they should perhaps more appropriately be classified as "complicated mild" (Levin et al., 2008). This characterization coincides with a higher risk for exhibiting compromised long-term recovery, as in the moderate to severe injuries. In the Chapman and colleagues' (2006) study, it was not specified whether those with mild TBI were "complicated mild," which could help explain the persistent deficits observed on gist reasoning.

In contrast to the findings of impaired gist reasoning, group performance on the immediate memory measure (i.e., CVLT–first trial) was not found to be significantly different between the two groups. Interestingly, performance on the n-back measure of working memory was found to be related to gist reasoning ability. In contrast, no significant relation between immediate memory span and gist reasoning was identified.

Gist reasoning was further examined in a recent study of 20 adolescents with moderate to severe TBI one year post-injury as compared to a control group. Findings revealed a significant impairment in the ability to abstract gist meanings as compared to typically developing controls (Gamino, Chapman, & Cook, 2009). In contrast to a deficient pattern in gist reasoning, the adolescents with TBI exhibited relatively preserved ability to encode and recall details from the text when probed for brief answers. This finding builds upon the previous discourse studies discussed above which identified a disparity between relatively good recovery in ability to encode and retrieve explicit details versus poor recovery in ability to engage in gist reasoning to abstract meaning from the same text. Specifically, youth with TBI: (1) exhibited marked deficits in combining detail information into more generalized gist meanings (Chapman et al., 2004); (2) demonstrated predominant use of an immature strategy to reduce information by deletion (Chapman et al., 2006); and (3) condensed texts to the same degree as controls in production of summaries but tended to simply retell explicitly stated ideas without forming gist-based concepts (Chapman et al., 2006).

Several potential explanations have been explored to account for impaired gist reasoning after TBI in children. One possibility is that children with TBI tend to "over-select," in that they may not sufficiently inhibit irrelevant information to facilitate focus on important information to be learned (Hanten et al., 2004). Moreover, children with TBI may predominantly employ a "bottom-up" processing approach, due to disruption of prefrontal connections. as demonstrated by good recovery of straightforward information recall and poor recovery of higher-order functions, including marked deficiency in constructing abstract meaning from details (e.g., Chapman et al., 2004, 2006; Gamino, Chapman, & Cook, 2009; Hanten et al., 2004). As discussed below, the potential exists for associating an enhanced capacity to engage in gist reasoning by abstracting meaning with improvements in educational achievement and occupational outcomes.

Theoretical Framework for Discourse Metric: Gist Reasoning

Theoretical models of discourse-cognition-brain linkages have been derived from empirical evidence to motivate future research focused on the high-level cognitive-linguistic function of gist reasoning (Anand et al., 2010; Chapman et al., in press). As suggested above, gist reasoning is a sensitive behavioral marker to detect and perhaps guide remediation for this persistent and debilitating outcome of TBI. We focus on two aspects of a theoretical framework: one domain representing a cognitive-linguistic processing framework for encoding information at two levels; and a neurobiological domain, to support the potential explanatory power of elucidating gist reasoning skills.

Top-Down Information Modulation Aspect. The underlying framework for gist reasoning was adopted from the fuzzy trace model proposed by cognitive scientists, Brainerd and Reyna (Brainerd & Reyna, 1998; Reyna & Brainerd, 1995). In their information processing model, Reyna & Brainerd (1995, 2008) represented information as being encoded separately at two levels of meaning, i.e., verbatim and gist. Memory at a verbatim level is signified by encoding and recalling the component details/facts to which one is exposed. In contrast, gist memory represents the consolidation and interpretation of meaning at a generalized, abstract level. Regarding real-life performance, we can appreciate the distinction as one takes notes from a lecture or feedback session. At a rote, verbatim level, the individual will take down concrete facts as close as possible to those spoken. At a gist level, the individual will take notes by consolidating the details to construct abstract meanings (Lloyd & Reyna, 2009).

We propose that gist reasoning entails top-down modulation of information based on

empirical evidence. Researchers have shown that strong gist reasoning is more likely to enhance the capacity to retrieve specific facts, whereas memory for specific facts does not appear to elevate gist reasoning competence (Gamino et al., 2010). Thus, a top-down modulation bias for information at a gist level will improve verbatim memory, but no reverse benefit is observed. In contrast, a bottom-up approach represented by trying to learn as many details as possible is purportedly a less efficient and more transient form of learning as compared to gist reasoning.

Neurobiological Aspect. The utility of discourse metrics in TBI populations is motivated by a neurobiological framework representing two dimensions that distinguish brain-behavior relations proposed by Chen and colleagues (2006). Specifically, the two domains are labeled and defined as: (1) *functional specialization*— conceptualized as basic cognitive functions that are localized to specific cortical regions; and (2) *functional integration*—conceptualized as the dynamic interaction of complex networks across brain regions engaged during complex cognitive processing. With regard to language function, the domain of *functional specialization* would entail the capacity to use basic language functions such as semantics, syntax, and retrieval of simple, explicitly stated facts. From brain studies, specific brain lesions are associated with impaired semantics, typically areas in the left temporal region, whereas specific brain lesions in Broca's area are associated with impaired syntax. In contrast to these more localized functions, discourse functions of gist reasoning are shown to engage a complex brain network that is mediated by executive function processes, whereby the frontal cortex integrates neuronal activity from temporal and parietal cortices. That is, when one is engaging in gist reasoning by abstracting meaning, complex neuronal activation patterns are widely distributed across brain regions (Anand, 2008; Anand, Motes, Maguire, Moore, Chapman, & Hart, 2009; Nichelli, Grefman, Pietrini, Clark, Lee, & Miletich, 1995; Wong, Chapman, Cook, Anand, Gamino, & Devous, 2006).

In sum, the theoretical framework outlined above for elucidating cognitive-linguistic abilities in TBI populations is comprised of two aspects. One is related to the distinction between gist and detail level processing and implicates a superiority of a top-down modulation of information control to form a robust and longer lasting knowledge base than the one represented by encoding the isolated explicit details. The second aspect conceptualizes the complex neurobehavioral-biological interplay among cognitive-linguistic skills and cognitive functions of executive control, with a central role of frontal cortices in the integration of neuronal activity across multiple brain regions to achieve competency in deriving abstract meaning from complex information. This latter aspect, particularized by Chen and colleagues (2006), is also applicable to gist reasoning.

Discourse Gist Reasoning Approach to Intervention

Current research efforts focused on developing neurocognitive interventions that engage top-down cognitive-control processes seek to harness the brain's inherent use-dependent neuroplasticity to promote frontal lobe recovery at later stages post-injury (Chen et al., 2006; Chen & D'Esposito, 2010). In this section, we highlight evidence supporting the potential for discourse metrics to provide a framework for guiding development of promising top-down modulation treatment protocols, particularly at chronic stages post injury. With regard to gist reasoning, only recently has this theoretical construct been translated and applied to a more clinical domain to ask whether populations who show impaired gist reasoning are able to benefit from a systematic training protocol. As summarized below, the emerging data from populations including youth with attention deficit hyperactivity disorder (ADHD) (Gamino, Chapman, Hart, & Vanegas, 2009), youth from economically disadvantaged families (Gamino et al., 2010), cognitively healthy seniors (Anand et al., 2010), and young adults with TBI (Vas et al., under review) suggest that populations with potentially comprised/inefficient frontal lobe network functions may benefit from gist reasoning training in ways that not only impact the skill trained but also generalize to other cognitive functions of executive control (Chapman et al., in press).

Overall, intervention approaches which target pervasive discourse deficits after TBI have been few and far between, with the majority being reported via individual case studies rather than group-based investigations. In general, treatments targeting specific aspects of discourse (e.g., story grammar), have been demonstrated to yield some immediate treatment effects but limited maintenance and poor generalization (e.g., Cannizzaro & Coehlo, 2002). On the other hand, approaches which target higher-order language abilities, i.e., incorporating discourse skills within the context of other cognitive abilities, have shown more promise. One such treatment method is the Strategies of Observed Learning Outcomes (SOLO) approach of Biggs and Collis (1982). The SOLO training paradigm incorporates a five-level hierarchy designed to improve text comprehension by means of discourse texts deemed to be personally relevant for each participant. Each stage reflects an increase in level of abstraction, with participants being taught to answer questions of increasing complexity with each successive level, ranging from "prestructural" (e.g., no relation between question and answer) to "extended abstract" (e.g., elaboration and generalization to other situations). In a study by Penn and colleagues (1997), who employed the SOLO training with a young woman with TBI and an elderly woman post-stroke, improved text comprehension abilities were observed in both participants after 15 treatment sessions. Additionally, the participant with TBI demonstrated improvements in organization and integration of information as well as self-monitoring and self-cueing abilities.

Currently, clinical trial evidence is emerging from research that has employed a recently developed discourse-based neurocognitive intervention designed to target gist reasoning ability in both adolescents and adults. This training program is entitled *Strategic Memory and Reasoning Training* or SMART for short (Anand et al., 2010; Chapman et al., in press; Gamino et al., 2010; Vas et al., under review). The SMART program incorporates a wide range of core curriculum, predominantly text-based discourse materials to teach the gist reasoning strategies; however, the focus is neither content-specific nor situation-dependent, as the training is strategy-based rather than content-based. The individual is instructed to practice using the strategies as often as possible throughout their daily lives as they are faced with different forms of information they need to process. The training involves one month of intensive training of gist reasoning strategies, with the primary objective to improve the ability to abstract meaning, with number of sessions ranging from 8 to 12 depending on the clinical trial. Each stage builds upon previous strategies for transforming the concrete meaning to construct abstracted gist-based meanings. Throughout the training, responses that represent "absorbing the facts" or "getting the correct answer" are not accepted, both of which represent more of a bottom-up processing of information. Thus, the program almost "un-teaches" the strong bias and often-taught process to remember as much detail as close to verbatim as possible, putting a heavy workload on both immediate and working memory processes. This verbatim form of memory has been shown to be fragile in terms of long-term learning and memory (Brainerd & Reyna, 1998; Gabrieli, 2004; Radvansky, 1999).

Instead, the trained strategies require that the participants construct novel and appropriately derived meanings that combine the details to form abstracted ideas. Key components of the training program include: eliminating unimportant information; summarizing ideas at an abstract level of interpretation using one's own words; devising questions, answers, and supporting details; constructing multiple interpretations; synthesizing a "take-home" message; raising the information to a new level of understanding; and generalizing information to multiple situations. In essence, each successive stage puts greater challenges on the individual to employ top-down information-processing strategies of executive control to efficiently encode, store, and retrieve meaning at an abstract level. For example, when discussing a movie, the goal in the SMART program is not to give a straightforward listing of the events that took place, but rather to give the variety of life messages that the movie conveyed with justification.

Gamino and colleagues (2009) investigated the effectiveness of the SMART program with children/adolescents with ADHD in a randomized study as compared to an alternative training protocol focused on attention training. Results indicated significantly improved ability to abstract gist-based meaning after the SMART program on a separate measure (*The Test of Strategic Learning*; Chapman et al., under review). In contrast, there was no significant improvement in gist reasoning performance in children with ADHD who completed the alternate intervention focused on discrete functions of attention and inhibition. The results suggest that just focusing and paying greater attention to information will not translate to improved higher-order learning, per se.

Another randomized study that has implications for future clinical training trials in TBI populations was conducted to evaluate the effectiveness of the SMART program to advance gist reasoning within a classroom setting in a group of disadvantaged but otherwise typically developing middle-school students without prior diagnoses (Gamino et al., 2010). In this study, the SMART program was compared to two other control training groups, all of which involved the same number of sessions and a similarly structured manualized protocol. One control training group directly focused on improving memory for facts using the same content as the SMART program in a bottom-up fashion. The second control training group provided information about the teen brain, targeted to empower their belief that they could improve their brains' capacity to develop and learn based on brain science facts. Not only did the SMART group show improved gist reasoning on the *Test of Strategic Learning* (Chapman et al., under review), but the effects transferred to fact learning. Moreover, there was a positive relation between gist reasoning and the Critical Thinking subtest on school-district-wide standardized testing. The only significant gain that was identified in the control groups was in the memory-trained group, who showed improved memory for explicit facts, but no significant gains in ability to abstract meaning.

In terms of TBI, the benefits of chronic-stage SMART training were recently investigated in a group of 28 adults with TBI (ages 20–65) who were one year and longer post-injury (Vas et al., under review). For this investigation, the strategy-based SMART training was compared with an information-based program providing information on TBI. Overall, the group which underwent the SMART training demonstrated significantly improved gist reasoning ability. Additionally, benefits of the SMART training extended to untrained measures of immediate memory, executive functions of working memory, nonverbal reasoning, and cognitive switching, and improved performance in daily functional activities. Moreover, the benefits of the SMART training were evident both at short term (i.e., immediately post-training) and were maintained at six-months post-training. In contrast, no significant changes were evident in the information-based control training group. Transfer benefits of the SMART training to untrained measures of executive function have also been previously observed in a group of 26 cognitively healthy seniors (ages 64–85), who demonstrated improvements in gist reasoning as well as concept abstraction, cognitive switching, and verbal fluency (Anand et al., 2010).

Discourse Metrics Inform Cognitive Theory

In this section, we illustrate the promise of a conceptual framework that bridges findings between cognition and discourse performance to guide future research and clinical management in TBI. We focus predominately on the discourse metric of gist- reasoning, where deficits in TBI as well as other clinical populations have been associated with cognitive deficits, especially in top-down processes of executive control (Anand et al., 2010; Chapman et al., 2006; Vas et al., under review). Moreover, training the discourse metric of gist reasoning, as summarized above, has also been shown to not only improve the ability to abstract meaning from complex discourse information, but also to show a transfer benefit to performances on cognitive measures of executive control, such as working memory, inhibition, concept abstraction, cognitive switching, fluency, and nonverbal reasoning. Similarly to brain-behavior associations identified between frontal brain networks and cognitive measures of executive control, studies have shown that gist reasoning relies heavily on the integrity of frontal cortices and its extensive reciprocal connections

(e.g., Anand, 2008; Anand et al., 2009; Chapman et al., 2005; Wong et al., 2006).

Gist reasoning engages interactive top-down and bottom-up cognitive processes to derive gist-based meanings from incoming details (e.g., texts, verbal lectures, conversations). We set forth a framework that outlined three cognitive processes that we believe are foundational to the ability to engage in gist reasoning (Chapman et al., in press). The three core cognitive processes are comprised of *strategic attention, integrated reasoning*, and *elaborated reasoning*.

In brief, strategic attention is the process whereby the overload of the incoming information is reduced primarily by inhibiting less relevant information and then focusing and encoding the important (i.e., relevant) information. Integrated reasoning is the process whereby key stimuli are combined to construct higher-order abstracted meanings that are not explicitly depicted/stated in the stimuli/text. Integrated reasoning is achieved by integrating the explicit content in the context of one's own concepts to create novel ideas expressed in one's own words, combining these ideas with pre-existing knowledge to form more global, gist-based representation than originally conveyed. The third process, elaborated reasoning, draws on fluency and fluidity of thinking to derive multiple abstract interpretations and/or generalized applications beyond the explicit content to other contexts. For a schematic model and more elaborate explication of the model, see Chapman and colleagues (in press).

Another property of gist reasoning includes the integration of several higher-order cognitive processes with specific, goal-directed language behaviors. Although the specific cognitive mechanisms that contribute to processing of discourse gist are still under investigation, working memory has been shown to be one conceptual umbrella under which the processes that facilitate comprehension and production operate (e.g., Dennis & Barnes, 2001; Levin et al., 2002; Roncadin, Guger, Archibald, Barnes, & Dennis, 2004). More specifically, the working memory aspects of memory storage and executive function work concurrently to assist discourse processing and production (Chapman et al., 2006). Executive function subsystems, referred to by Baddley and Hitch (1974) as the central executive, are similar to pieces of a puzzle that fit together to create the basis of gist reasoning. The executive subsystems consist of various functions such as attention, inhibition, association, elaboration, and goal maintenance (Baddeley, 1992). Executive functions are regulated and coordinated by cognitive control. Cognitive control is the ability to willfully control thought processes in order to facilitate manipulation of information and goal maintenance. These subsystems work in serial and parallel sequence to facilitate efficient strategies for the achievement of desired goals.

In pediatric TBI, evidence suggests that deficits in gist reasoning are related to deficits in the working memory domain of executive functions (Chapman et al., 2006). Similarly, in typically developing children, there is evidence of a relation between working memory executive functions and reading comprehension ability (Swanson & Berninger, 1995; Yuill, Oakhill, & Parkin, 1989). Working memory storage systems facilitate the maintenance of information for short-term recall and manipulation of information online to perform high-order operations such as are required to abstract meaning. On the other hand, long-term memory serves to retain information for future needs. Both memory systems in conjunction with executive functions are important for comprehension and production.

In addition to manipulation and organization, cognitive control is proposed to play an important role in the ability to differentiate the important from the less important details during discourse gist processing (Chapman et al., in press). The strategies involved in discerning and selecting important information from a text are exemplified through selective learning. During gist reasoning, cognitive control allows for manipulation of information in memory storage. Manipulation refers to the ability to update meaning in short-term memory storage as conflicting or new incoming information is encountered. In addition, manipulation is used as a means to retrieve information from long-term memory storage to interpret and synthesize meaning in the context of the incoming new information.

During discourse production, cognitive control facilitates organization and manipulation

of the information necessary for deriving gist meanings. Thus, cognitive control allocates resources to achieve both logical semantic organization and global interpretation across the text (Singer & Ritchot, 1996). As an interesting hypothesis for future research, it would be informative to test how much the abstraction level of meaning that is held online in working memory matters and contributes to resource allocation efficiency. If details are held in a verbatim-like format in working memory, the capacity of working memory will be more quickly overloaded. If, on the other hand, details are combined into generalized abstracted meaning, the same units of information in working memory represent more information, perhaps analogous to a computer zipped file. Thus, based on preliminary evidence, we propose that individuals with TBI may show enhanced cognitive processing and elevated working memory spans when they are trained to encode information at more abstracted levels of meaning.

In addition to how meaning is encoded—either gist level or detail, another key cognitive ability associated with gist reasoning is what we referred to earlier as *strategic attention*. The ability to strategically select key information from among many facts is important for inferencing and recognizing the gist of a text, two major components of discourse comprehension and production. The term strategic attention refers to the ability to strategically select the most important information for learning while disregarding or suppressing less important information.

The ability to selectively learn is exemplified in summary production, whereby choosing the key information is a prerequisite to infer the gist of the discourse. In addition, the ability to prioritize information provides an organizational structure by which to recall important facts and facilitate production of a cohesive and coherent summary. More specifically, as Chapman and colleagues (2004, p. 51) noted, summarizing requires "comprehension of the isolated facts that make up the whole discourse text, sorting them according to importance, and appreciating the relation of the isolated facts to the central meaning of the whole discourse text." Hence, assessment of strategic attention of key information is a novel way to measure complex language comprehension skills. Selective learning ability is assessed by assigning differential values to information to be learned. Selective learning efficiency is demonstrated by the ability to determine and learn high-value information over low-value information. Consequently, information is prioritized for learning in relation to its value. In selective learning assessments, instructions provide the values of the information to be learned and an explanation of the objective to earn a substantial number of points by recalling information. Thus, in order to achieve the goal, high-value information must be strategically selected or prioritized over low-value information for learning and subsequent recall. However, a specific strategy for successfully achieving the goal must be inferred.

Selective learning has been assessed in children with TBI using word lists and expository discourse texts (Hanten et al., 2004; Hanten, Zhang, & Levin, 2002). Hanten and colleagues (2002, 2004) found that children with TBI manifested deficits in selective learning abilities when compared to age-matched typically developing peers. However, no significant differences in memory capacity were found between children with TBI and the control groups. These findings suggest that cognitive processes other than basic memory capacity have greater impact on the ability to selectively learn information. In particular, Hanten and colleagues postulated that selective learning requires cognitive control. Cognitive control, as discussed previously, would allow one to strategically select information for learning while suppressing or ignoring irrelevant information.

In sum, as information is gathered regarding the commonalities and disparities between the discourse metric of abstracting meaning and other measures of executive function, new directions in cognitive theory may emerge regarding whether these two domains are measuring related constructs or whether they share neural networks. Both appear to engage top-down modulation.

Future Directions

Emerging evidence indicates that we are at the cusp of filling the void in having access to informative cognitive-linguistic measures to advance research and clinical management of TBI. Specifically, newly developed discourse metrics address five key issues that are essential to systematically advancing methods for improving long-term recovery in TBI. The significance for discourse metrics, in general, and gist reasoning, in particular, to enhance long-term outcomes is suggested by five patterns that have been identified: (1) gist reasoning is diagnostically sensitive to the long-term cognitive-linguistic deficits in TBI; (2) gist reasoning has a testable theoretical basis from both a neurobiological perspective and a cognitive science perspective; (3) gist reasoning is ecologically salient, as it provides a performance index that encompasses the cognitive complexity required for personal functioning to achieve educational and occupational goals; (4) training of gist reasoning has been shown to benefit not only the skill trained, but also to show far-reaching impact on other cognitive controls functions; and (5) emerging evidence suggests that the neural processes that mediate gist reasoning versus those engaged during detail processing may provide a neuroscientific basis for development of brain biomarkers of either frontal lobe integrity and/or brain change in response to training (Anand et al., 2010; Chapman et al., 2004, 2006; Cook & Chapman, in press; Cook et al., 2007; Gamino, Chapman, & Cook, 2009; Gamino et al., 2010; Vas et al., under review).

At least five major challenges to advancing research and clinical management of cognitive-linguistic skills should be addressed in future studies. First, although there has been a paradigmatic shift away from focusing predominantly on lower levels of language function in TBI towards a growing momentum to adopt discourse metrics, discourse metrics still remain virtually inaccessible to the average practicing clinician. Efforts to publish experimental discourse measures that have validity and reliability should be a top priority so that both researchers and clinicians have access to practical discourse metrics that are efficient, easy to administer and score.

Second, future studies should address whether gist reasoning can be incorporated into daily life brain habits and determine whether training improves both abstracting meaning and recalling the supporting facts, and leads to improved educational achievement. Nonetheless, it would be informative to determine how actual school grades or, for adults with TBI, how work performance benefits as a result of gist reasoning training because new learning is the rule in everyday life, not the exception.

Third, greater efforts need to be expended on developing bio-markers that can serve as objective measures of the brain's response to cognitive training. Can we identify a marker of frontal lobe integrity that underlies gist processing versus detail-level processing? Preliminary evidence from brain activation studies using EEG and fMRI supports a potential to measure distinctions between functional specialization and functional integration of neural networks (Anand, 2008). In recent years, several functional brain imaging studies have examined the underlying neural differences in processing abstracted, gist-based information versus detail-based information. In particular, these studies have implicated the vital role of frontal brain regions in processing gist (Robertson et al., 2000). Comprehension of gist was associated with right inferior frontal activation, whereas comprehension of details was associated with left anterior temporal activation. Similar results of activation in the right prefrontal cortex were found in a PET study when abstracting gist-based meaning from discourse (Nichelli et al., 1995). In a SPECT study, Wong and colleagues (2006) found a positive correlation between perfusion in right frontal regions and more proficient gist abstraction abilities in children three years post-TBI. Chapman and colleagues (Chapman et al., 2005) found a similar relationship between gist scores and cerebral perfusion in the right frontal regions in a SPECT study involving individuals with frontotemporal lobar degeneration. Abstracting gist meaning appears to rely on frontal brain networks, the area of the brain that is the most vulnerable to disruption after sustaining a TBI and perhaps the most important neural system to repair and target with treatment. All of this evidence points to the potential to soon identify a brain pattern that could serve as a marker to implicate good prognosis for subsequent recovery of gist reasoning or a measure of brain change in response to targeted treatments.

Fourth, in the past there has been a major split between approaches that focus on the complexities of cognitive function (e.g. abstracting meaning from complex information) versus those taking more focused approaches on isolated sub-skills (e.g., attention, or recall of details). The elegance of the gist versus detail distinction in discourse processing is that it brings together these two extremes. Future studies should elucidate how both of these relate to cognitive control processes and to performance in real world settings.

Finally, perhaps one of the most important future directions for higher-order language research is to elucidate the long-term effects of TBI on cognitive-linguistic function. Knowing how an injury early in life (whether in childhood or early adulthood) detrimentally impacts cognitive-linguistic aging—even to the degree of increasing the risk of developing dementia—requires attention. Just as critical a need is to substantially extend research efforts to understand how delivering cognitive-linguistic interventions at chronic stages—even decades after injury—can have a significant beneficial impact on outcomes such as brain repair, improved cognitive performance, and, most relevant, higher functioning in real world contexts.

In closing, TBI has always been one of the major causes of death and disability, but now we are more keenly aware of the consequential impact of TBI on brain health that can worsen with increasing age. Public awareness of the devastating and lasting impact of TBI has greatly increased due to widely publicized combat-related injuries and concussions suffered during high-impact sports play, concomitantly associated with increased risk of dementia. Accumulating evidence reveals that top-down cognitive training of gist reasoning benefits the skill(s) trained. Moreover, training gains transfer to other untrained cognitive domains and even into real-life functionality, even when delivered at chronic stages post-TBI. Overall, clinical research initiatives need to establish follow-up assessment at regular intervals and short-term intensive treatment offerings. Such regular monitoring and timely cognitive training would serve to keep the cumulative effects of the TBI with aging in "remission," helping to stave off increasing rates of cognitive decline with advancing age to the greatest degree possible. Previously, TBI rehabilitation has not been designed to maximally harness the capacity for brain plasticity in response to top-down treatment approaches that remains at these neglected chronic phases post-injury. Now, rapidly advancing the field of brain repair in TBI by translating the breakthroughs of discourse metrics into clinical practice has never been more vital to the hundreds of thousands of individuals who suffer "invisible" but life altering injuries.

Acknowledgments

This work was supported by the National Institute of Neurological Disorders and Stroke (NINDS) Grant 2R01 NS 21889-16, the National Institute of Child Health and Human Development (NICHD) Grant R21-HD062835, as well the Horizon Foundation.

References

Anand, R. (2008). *Differences between gist and detail processing.* (Doctoral dissertation, University of Texas, 2008). Retrieved from ProQuest Dissertations and Theses database (UMI No. 3305835).

Anand, R., Chapman, S. B., Rackley, A., Keebler, M., Zientz, J., & Hart, J. (2010). Gist reasoning training in cognitively normal seniors. *International Journal of Geriatric Psychiatry, 26,* 961–968.

Anand, R., Motes, M. A., Maguire, M. J., Moore, P. S., Chapman, S. B., & Hart, J. (2009). *Neural basis of abstracted meaning.* Poster presented at Neurobiology of Language, Chicago, IL.

Baddeley, A. (1992). Working memory. *Science, 255,* 556–559.

Baddeley, A. D., & Hitch, G. (1974). Working memory. In G. A. Bower (Ed.), *The psychology of learning and motivation* (pp. 47–89). New York: Academic Press.

Biddle, K. R., McCabe, A., & Bliss, L. S. (1996). Narrative skills following traumatic brain injury in children and adults. *Journal of Communication Disorders, 29,* 447–468.

Biggs J. B., & Collis, K. F. (1982). *Evaluating the quality of learning: The SOLO taxonomy.* New York: Academic Press.

Brainerd, C. J., & Reyna, V. F. (1995). Mere memory testing creates false memories in children. *Developmental Psychology, 32,* 467–478.

Brainerd, C. J., & Reyna, V. F. (1998). Fuzzy-trace theory and children's false memories. *Journal of Experimental Child Psychology, 71,* 81–129.

Brookshire, B., Chapman, S. B., Song, J., & Levin, H. S. (2000). Cognitive and linguistic correlates of children's discourse after closed head injury: A three year follow-up. *Journal of the International Neuropsychological Society, 6,* 741–751.

Brown, A. L., & Day, J. D. (1983). Macrorules for summarizing texts: The development of expertise. *Journal of Verbal Learning and Verbal Behavior, 22,* 1–14.

Cannizzaro, M. S., & Coelho, C. A. (2002). Treatment of story grammar following traumatic brain injury: A pilot study. *Brain Injury, 16,* 1065–1073.

Chapman, S. B. (1997). Cognitive-communication abilities in children with closed head injury. *American Journal of Speech-Language Pathology, 6,* 50–58.

Chapman, S. B. (2006). Neurocognitive stall, a paradox in long term recovery from pediatric brain injury. *Brain Injury Professional, 3,* 10–13.

Chapman, S. B., Bonte, F. J., Wong, S. B., Zientz, J. N., Hynan, L. S., Harris, T. S, et al, (2005). Convergence of connected language and SPECT in variants of frontotemporal lobar degeneration. *Alzheimer Disease Association Disorder, 19,* 202–213.

Chapman, S. B., Culhane, K. A., Levin, H. S., Harward, H., Mendelsohn, D., Ewing-Cobbs, L., et al. (1992). Narrative discourse after closed head injury in children and adolescents. *Brain and Language, 43,* 42–65.

Chapman, S. B., Gamino, J. F., & Anand, R. (2012). Higher-order strategic gist reasoning in teens. In V. F. Reyna, S. B. Chapman, M. R. Dougherty, & J. Confrey (Eds.), *The adolescent brain: Learning, reasoning, and decision making* (pp. 123–151). Washington, DC: American Psychological Association.

Chapman, S. B., Gamino, J. F., Cook, L. G., Hanten, G., Li, X., & Levin, H. S. (2006). Impaired discourse gist and working memory in children after brain injury. *Brain and Language, 97,* 178–188.

Chapman, S. B., Hart, J., Levin, H. S., Cook, L. G., & Gamino, J. F. (under review). *The Test of Strategic Learning.*

Chapman, S. B., Levin, H. S., & Culhane, K. (1995). Language impairment in closed head injury. In H. Kirschner (Ed.), *Handbook of neurological speech and language disorders* (pp. 387–414). New York: Marcel-Dekker.

Chapman, S. B., Levin, H. S., & Lawyer, S. L. (1999). Communication problems resulting from brain injury in children: Special issues of assessment and management. In S. McDonald, L. Togher, & C. Code (Ed.), *Communication disorders following traumatic brain injury* (pp. 235–270). East Sussex, UK: Psychology Press.

Chapman, S. B., Levin, H. S., Matejka, J., Harward, H., & Kufera, J. A. (1995). Discourse ability in children with brain injury: Correlations with psychosocial, linguistic, and cognitive factors. *Journal of Head Trauma Rehabilitation, 10*, 36–54.

Chapman, S. B., Levin, H. S., Wanek, A., Weyrauch, J., & Kufera, J. (1998). Discourse after closed head injury in young children. *Brain and Language, 61*, 420–449.

Chapman, S. B., McKinnon, L., Levin, H. S., Song, J., Meier, M. C., & Chiu, S. (2001). Longitudinal outcome of verbal discourse in children with traumatic brain injury: Three-year follow-up. *Journal of Head Trauma Rehabilitation, 16*, 441–455.

Chapman, S. B., & Sparks, G. (2003). Language and discourse. In M. Aminoff & R. Daroff (Eds.), *Encyclopedia of the neurological sciences* (pp. 753–755). San Diego, CA: Academic Press.

Chapman, S. B., Sparks, G., Levin, H. S., Dennis, M., Roncadin, C., Zhang, L., et al. (2004). Discourse macrolevel processing after severe pediatric traumatic brain injury. *Developmental Neuropsychology, 25*, 37–61.

Chapman, S. B., Watkins, R., Gustafson, C., Moore, S., Levin, H. S., & Kufera, J. A. (1997). Narrative discourse in children with closed head injury, children with language impairment, and typically developing children. *American Journal of Speech-Language Pathology, 6*, 66–76.

Chen, A. J. W., & D'Esposito, M. (2010). Traumatic brain injury: From bench to bedside to society. *Neuron, 66*, 11–14.

Chen, A. J. W., Abrams, G. M., & D'Esposito, M. (2006). Functional reintegration of prefrontal neural networks for enhancing recovery after brain injury. *Journal of Head Trauma Rehabilitation, 21*, 107.

Coelho, C. A. (2002). Story narratives of adults with closed head injury and non-brain-injured adults: Influence of socioeconomic status, elicitation task, and executive functioning. *Journal of Speech, Language, and Hearing Research, 45*, 1232–1248.

Coelho, C. A. (2007). Management of discourse deficits following traumatic brain injury: Progress, caveats, and needs. *Seminars in Speech and Language, 28*, 122–135.

Coelho, C. A., Liles, B. Z., & Duffy, R. J. (1991). Discourse analyses with closed head injured adults: Evidence for differing patterns of deficits. *Archives of Physical Medicine and Rehabilitation, 72*, 465–468.

Coelho, C., Ylvisaker, M., Turkstra, L. S. (2005). Nonstandardized assessment approaches for individuals with traumatic brain injuries. *Seminars in Speech and Language, 26*, 223–41.

Cook, L. G., & Chapman, S. B. (in press). Neurocognitive stall in pediatric TBI: New directions for preventing later emerging deficits. *Journal of Medical Speech-Language Pathology.*

Cook, L. G., Chapman, S. B., & Gamino, J. F. (2007). Impaired discourse gist inpediatric brain injury: Missing the forest for the trees. In K. Cain and J. Oakhill (Eds.), *Children's comprehension problems in oral and written language: A cognitive perspective* (pp. 218–243). New York: Guilford Publications, Inc.

Davis, G. A., & Coelho, C. A. (2004). Referential cohesion and logical coherence of narration after closed head injury. *Brain and Language, 89*, 508–523.

Delis, D. C., Kramer, J. H., Kaplan, E., & Obler, B. A. (1986). *The California Verbal Learning Test: Research edition.* New York: The Psychological Corporation.

Dennis, M., & Barnes, M. A. (2001). Comparison of literal, inferential, and intentional text comprehension in children with mild or severe closed head injury. *Journal of Head Trauma Rehabilitation, 16*, 456–468.

Ewing-Cobbs, L., Barnes, M., Fletcher, J. M., Levin, H. S., Swank, P. R., & Song, J. (2004). Modeling of longitudinal academic achievement scores after pediatric traumatic brain injury. *Developmental Neuropsychology, 25*, 107–133.

Ewing-Cobbs, L., Fletcher, J. M., Levin, H. S., Iovino, I., & Miner, M. E. (1998). Academic achievement and academic placement following traumatic brain injury in children and adolescents: A two-year longitudinal study. *Journal of Clinical and Experimental Neuropsychology, 20*, 769–781.

Feagans, L., & Applebaum, M. L. (1986). Validation of language subtypes in learning disabled children. *Journal of Educational Psychology, 78*, 358–364.

Fletcher, J. M., Miner, M., & Ewing-Cobbs, L. (1987). Age and recovery from head injury in children: Developmental issues. In H. S. Levin, J. Graufman, & H. M. Eisenberg (Ed.), *Neurobehavioral recovery from head injury* (pp. 279–292). New York: Oxford University Press.

Gabrieli, J. D. E. (2004). Memory: Pandora's hippocampus? *Cerebrum, 6*, 39–48.

Gamino, J. F., Chapman, S. B., & Cook, L. G. (2009). Strategic learning in youth with traumatic brain injury: Evidence for stall in higher-order cognition. *Topics in Language Disorders, 29*, 224–235.

Gamino, J. F., Chapman, S. B., Hart, J., & Vanegas, S. (2009) *Improved reasoning in children with ADHD after strategic memory and reasoning* training: *A novel intervention for strategic learning impairment.* Abstract presented at: International Neuropsychological Society Annual Meeting, Atlanta, Georgia.

Gamino, J. F., Chapman, S. B., Hull, E. L., & Lyon, R. (2010). Effects of higher-order cognitive strategy training on gist reasoning and fact learning in adolescents. *Frontiers in Educational Psychology, 1,* 188.

Gillam, R., McFadden, T., & van Kleek, A. (1995). Improving narrative abilities: Whole language and language skills approaches. In M. Fey, J. Windsor, & S. Warren (Ed.), *Language intervention: Preschool through the elementary years* (pp. 145–182). Baltimore, MD: Paul H. Brookes Publishing Co.

Glosser, G., & Deser, T. (1990). Patterns of discourse production among neurologic patients with fluent language disorders. *Brain and Language, 40,* 67–88.

Gogtay, N., Giedd, J. N., Lusk, L., Hayashi, K. M., Greenstein, D., Vaituzis, A. C., et al. (2004). Dynamic mapping of human cortical development during childhood through early adulthood. *Proceedings of the National Academy of Science, 101,* 8174–8179.

Hanten, G., Chapman, S. B., Gamino, J. F., Zhang, L., Benton, S. B., Stallings-Roberson, G., et al. (2004). Verbal selective learning after traumatic brain injury in children. *Annals of Neurology, 56,* 847–853.

Hanten, G., Zhang, L., & Levin, H. S. (2002). Selective learning in children after traumatic brain injury: A preliminary study. *Child Neuropsychology, 8,* 107–120.

Hartley, L. L., & Jensen, P. J. (1991). Narrative and procedural discourse after closed head injury. *Brain Injury, 5,* 267–285.

Hinchliffe F. J, Murdoch B. E, & Chenery, H. J. (1998). Towards a conceptualization of language and cognitive impairment in closed-head injury: Use of clinical measures. *Brain Injury, 12,* 109–132.

Hough, M. S., & Barrow, I. (2003). Descriptive discourse abilities of traumatic brain-injured adults. *Aphasiology, 17,* 183–191.

Jacobs, H. E. (1988). The Los Angeles head injury survey: Procedures and initial findings. *The Archives of Physical Medicine and Rehabilitation, 69,* 425–431.

Johnson, N. S. (1983). What do you do if you can't tell the whole story? The development of summarization skills. In K. E. Nelson (Ed.), *Children's language* (pp. 314–383). New York: Gardner Press.

Jordan F. M., Cremona-Meteyard, S., & King, A. (1996). High-level linguistic disturbances subsequent to childhood closed head injury. *Brain Injury, 10,* 729–738.

Jordan, F. M., & Murdoch, B. E. (1994). Severe closed-head injury in childhood: Linguistic outcomes into adulthood. *Brain Injury, 8*(6), 501–508.

Klonoff, H., Clark, C., & Klonoff, P. S. (1993). Long-term outcome of head injuries: A 23 year follow up study of children with head injuries. *Journal of Neurology, Neurosurgery, and Psychiatry, 56,* 410–415.

Leblanc, J., De Guise, E., Feyz, M., & Lamoureux, J. (2006). Early prediction of language impairment following traumatic brain injury. *Brain Injury, 20,* 1391–1401.

Levin, H. S., Hanten, G., Chang, C., Zhang, L., Schachar, R., Ewing-Cobbs, L., et al. (2002). Working memory after traumatic brain injury in children. *Annals of Neurology, 52,* 82–88.

Levin, H. S., Hanten, G., Roberson, G., Li, X., Ewing-Cobbs, L., Dennis, M., et al. (2008). Prediction of cognitive sequelae based on abnormal computed tomography findings in children following mild traumatic brain injury. *Journal of Neurosurgery: Pediatrics, 1,* 461–470.

Liles, B. Z., Coelho, C. A., Duffy, R. J., & Zalagens, M. R. (1989). Effects of elicitation procedures on the narratives of normal and closed head-injured adults. *Journal of Speech and Hearing Disorders, 54,* 356–366.

Lloyd, F. J., & Reyna, V. F. (2009). Clinical gist and medical education: Connecting the dots. *The Journal of the American Medical Association, 302,* 1332–1333.

Mazaux, J. M., Masson, F., Levin, H. S., Alaoui, P., Maurette, P., & Barat, M. (1997). Long-term neuropsychological outcome and loss of social autonomy after traumatic brain injury. *Archives of Physical Medicine and Rehabilitation, 78,* 1316–1320.

McDonald, S. (1993). Pragmatic language loss following closed head injury: Inability to meet the informational needs of the listener. *Brain and Language, 44,* 28–46.

Mentis, M., & Prutting, C. A. (1987). Cohesion in the discourse of normal and head-injured adults. *Journal of Speech and Hearing Research, 30,* 583–595.

Nichelli, P., Grafman, J., Pietrini, P., Clark, K., Lee, K. Y., & Miletich, R. (1995). Where the brain appreciates the moral of a story. *Neuroreport, 6,* 2309–2313.

Penn, C., Jones, D., & Joffe, V. (1997). Hierarchical discourse therapy: A method for the mild patient. *Aphasiology, 11,* 601–632.

Radvansky, G. A. (1999). Memory retrieval and suppression: The inhibition of situation models. *Journal of Experimental Psychology: General, 128,* 563–579.

Reilly, J. S., Bates, E. A., & Marchman, V. A. (1998). Narrative discourse in children with early focal brain injury. *Brain and Language, 51,* 335–375.

Reyna, V. F. (2008). A theory of medical decision making and health: Fuzzy trace theory. *Medical Decision Making, 28*(6), 850–865.

Reyna, V. F., & Brainerd, C. J. (1995) Fuzzy trace theory: An interim synthesis. *Learning and Individual Differences, 7*(1), 1–75.

Robertson, D. A., Gernsbacher, M. A., Guidotti, S. J., Robertson, R. R. W, Irwin, W., Mock, B. J., et al. (2000). Functional neuroanatomy of the cognitive process of mapping during discourse comprehension. *Psychological Science, 11,* 255–260.

Roncadin, C., Guger, S., Archibald, J., Barnes, M., & Dennis, M. (2004). Working memory after mild, moderate, or severe childhood closed head injury. *Developmental Neuropsychology, 25,* 21–36.

Roth, F. P., & Spekman, N. J. (1989). Higher-order language processes and reading disabilities. In A. G. Kamhi & H. W. Catts (Ed.), *Reading disabilities: A developmental perspective* (pp. 159–198). Austin, TX: Pro-Ed.

Singer, M., & Ritchot, K. F. M. (1996). The role of working memory capacity and knowledge access in text inference processing. *Memory & Cognition, 24,* 733–743.

Snow, P., Douglas, J., & Ponsford, J. (1997). Procedural discourse following traumatic brain injury. *Aphasiology, 11,* 947–967.

Snow, P. C., Douglas, J. M., & Ponsford, J. L. (1999). Narrative discourse following severe traumatic brain injury: A longitudinal follow-up. *Aphasiology, 13,* 529–551.

Swanson, H. L., & Berninger, V. (1995). The role of working memory in skilled and less skilled readers' comprehension. *Intelligence, 21,* 83–108.

Ulatowska, H. K., & Chapman, S. B. (1994). Discourse macrostructure in aphasia. In R. L. Bloom, L. K. Obler, S. DeSanti, & J. S. Ehrlich (Ed.), *Discourse analysis and applications* (pp. 29–46). Hillsdale, NJ: Lawrence Erlbaum Associates.

van Dijk, T. A. (1995). On macrostructure mental models and other inventions: A brief personal history of the Kintsch-van Dijk Theory. In C. A. Weaver, S. Mannes, & C. R. Fletcher, (Ed.), *Discourse Comprehension* (pp. 383–410). Hillsdale, NJ: Lawrence Erlbaum Associates.

Vas, A. K., Chapman, S. B., & Cook, L. G. (under review). Higher-order reasoning training years post traumatic brain injury.

Vas, A., Chapman, S., Krawczyk, D., Krishnan, K., & Keebler, M. (2010). Executive control training to enhance frontal plasticity in traumatic brain injury. International Brain Injury Association's Eighth World Congress on Brain Injury, *Brain Injury, 24,* 115–463.

Westby, C. (1989). Assessing and remediating text comprehension problems. In A. Kamhi, & H. Catts (Ed.), *Reading disabilities: A developmental language perspective* (pp. 199–259). Boston: College Hill.

Wilson B. M., & Proctor, A. (2000). Oral and written discourse in adolescents with closed head injury. *Brain and Cognition, 43,* 425–429.

Wilson, B. M., & Proctor, A. (2002). Written discourse of adolescents with closed head injury. *Brain Injury, 16,* 1011–1025.

Wong, S. B. C., Chapman, S. B., Cook, L. G., Anand, R., Gamino, J. F., & Devous, M. D. (2006). A SPECT Study of language and brain reorganization three years after pediatric brain injury. In A. R. Moller (Ed.), *Reprogramming the brain: Progress in Brain Research* (pp. 173–185). Amsterdam: Elsevier.

Ylvisaker, M. (1992). Communication outcome following traumatic brain injury. *Seminars in Speech and Language, 13,* 239–250.

Ylvisaker, M., Adetson, P. D., Braga, L. W., Burnett, S. M., Glang, A., Feeney, T., et al. (2005). Rehabilitation and ongoing support after pediatric TBI: Twenty years of progress. *Journal of Head Trauma Rehabilitation, 20,* 95–109.

Yorkston, K. M., Jaffe, K. M., Liao, S., & Polissar N. L. (1999). Recovery of written language production in children with traumatic brain injury: Outcomes at one year. *Aphasiology, 13,* 691–700.

Yorkston, K. M., Jaffe, K. M., Polissar, N. L., Liao, S., & Fay, G. C. (1997). Written language production and neuropsychological function in children with traumatic brain injury. *The Archives of Physical Medicine and Rehabilitation, 78,* 1096–1102.

Yuill, N. M., Oakhill, J. V., & Parkin, A. J. (1989). Working memory, comprehension ability and the resolution of text anomaly. *British Journal of Psychology, 80,* 351–361.

8

Disorders of Emotion and Social Cognition Following Traumatic Brain Injury

Skye McDonald, Jacqueline Rushby, Michelle Kelly, and Arielle de Sousa

The nature of traumatic brain injury (TBI), resulting from acceleration-deceleration forces, often sustained in motor vehicle accidents, falls, and assault (Tate, McDonald, & Lulham, 1998), leads to heterogenous effects on the brain with a preponderance of multifocal damage to the lateral, anterior, and ventral surfaces of the frontal and temporal lobes (Courville, 1945; Gentry, Godersky, & Thompson, 1988) and diffuse axonal damage (Gentry, et al., 1988; Hadley et al., 1988).

People who experience severe TBI suffer both neurophysical and neuropsychological impairments in roughly equal proportions. But it is the neuropsychological changes to cognition, emotion, and behavior that are most strongly predictive of poor social outcome (Bond & Brooks, 1976; Tate & Broe, 1999) and relative stress (Brooks, Campsie, Symington, Beattie, & McKinlay, 1986; Kinsella, Packer, & Olver, 1991; Thomsen, 1984). Nearly 50% of patients suffering a severe TBI have limited or no social contacts and few leisure interests one year or more later (Tate, Lulham, Broe, Strettles, & Pfaff, 1989; Weddell, Oddy, & Jenkins, 1980), while between 64 and 68% rely more on their parents or spouse for emotional support than prior to the injury (Ponsford, Olver, & Curran, 1995) and have substantial difficulty forming new social relationships (Tate et al., 1989). The conundrum for researchers in this field has been to try to understand how neuropsychological deficits underpin such poor psychosocial function. Prediction of real-life functioning is strongest when the assessment measure relates directly to the kind of cognitive demands required in everyday tasks

(Kibby, Schmitter-Edgecombe, & Long, 1998). But there are few assessment measures that clearly translate to emotional and social functioning. Not surprisingly then, predictive relationships between standard neuropsychological measures and psychosocial function are typically poor (Burgess, Alderman, Evans, Emslie, & Wilson, 1998; Grattan & Eslinger, 1989; Saver & Damasio, 1991; Tate & Broe, 1999).

This has led to speculation that a different range of impairments than those assessed by standard neuropsychological tasks are responsible for personality and emotional changes following severe TBI. In this chapter we examine disorders of emotion, specifically emotion regulation, and also social cognition, i.e., the capacity to attend to, identify, and interpret social information including the emotional expressions and social behavior of others. Our focus is primarily on those who experience severe traumatic brain injury, as it is this sub-population that develops long-term disabilities in the psychosocial sphere.

Disorders of Emotion and Social Cognition: Definition and Significance

Emotional Regulation

Of all the problems that manifest following severe TBI, overt changes to emotional and social behavior are those that cause the most distress in family members as well as functional disability (Kinsella et al., 1991). Despite the heterogenous nature of TBI, two different groups of emotional-behavioral impairments are commonly observed clinically (Kinsella et al., 1991; Tate, 1999).

Disorders of Emotional Control

The first of these clusters of behavior reflects a decrease in self-monitoring and the control of emotions and behavior. This group of difficulties includes short temper, quarrelsomeness, aggression, emotional lability, self centeredness, and impulsivity (Kinsella et al., 1991). In addition, childishness and sexually disinhibited behavior are frequently reported (Brooks et al., 1986; Lezak, 1978; Thomsen, 1984). Disorders of control are very common following severe TBI. Prevalence rates of 34–67% are reported in the first year of injury (Brooks, Campsie, Symington, Beattie, & McKinlay, 1987; Kim, Manes, Kosier, Baruah, & Robinson, 1999) and maintain over time (Brooks et al., 1987; Oddy, Coughlan, Tyerman, & Jenkins, 1985). Indeed, irritability is one of the most common behavioral complaints made by people with TBI and their families (Demark & Gemeinhardt, 2002; Hanks, Temkin, Machamer, & Dikmen, 1999; McKinlay, Brooks, Bond, Martinage, & Marshall, 1981) with clinically significant levels of irritability and aggression continuing in approximately 12% of individuals with severe TBI at 18 months post-trauma (Tate et al., 2006). Problems with emotion regulation, i.e., mood swings, are also a significant predictor of relationship breakdown post-TBI (Wood, Liossi, & Wood, 2005).

Disorders of Emotional Arousal (Drive)

On the flip side of the coin, there may be a relative reduction of emotionality in people with severe TBI, reflecting a loss of motivation and arousal, i.e., drive. Thus, many individuals with TBI experience apathy, difficulties maintaining initiative and reductions in spontaneity and cognitive flexibility (Kinsella et al., 1991; Tate, 1999). Prevalence rates for apathy are 43–78% in those with severe TBI (Kant, Duffy, & Pivovarnik, 1998; Lane-Brown & Tate, 2009; Oddy et al., 1985) with clinically significant apathy occurring in 15% at 18 months post-trauma

(Tate et al., 2006). While depression can masquerade as apathy, the two disorders are independent (Lane-Brown & Tate, 2009; Levy et al., 1998), with apathy more strongly related to reduced cognitive function (Kant et al., 1998). While disorders of drive and control occur independently, they also occur together in roughly equal proportions (Tate, Fenelon, Manning, & Hunter, 1991).

Social Cognition

It is now well documented that a significant proportion of adults who experience severe TBI have difficulty in the processing of social information, including the ability to recognise basic emotional expressions in others (Milders, Fuchs, & Crawford, 2003), the ability to infer what another person is thinking (Bibby & McDonald, 2005), and also the ability to recognize inferred conversational meanings (Channon & Watts, 2003). They also have problems with empathy (Wood & Williams, 2008) and judging morality (Blair & Cipolotti, 2000). Social cognition is an umbrella term that encompasses the ability to attend to, process, and interpret these kinds of social meanings. Social cognition is considered an essential component of skilled social behavior (Boice, 1983; McFall, 1982). Failure to understand the feelings and intentions of others has immediate, deleterious impact on interpersonal behaviour, as has been demonstrated in both the normal population (Morrison & Bellack, 1981; Trower, 1980) and specifically, in people with TBI (McDonald, Flanagan, Martin, & Saunders, 2004).

Review of Latest Theories and Research

Emotional and social processes are attracting an increasing amount of attention in the neuroscience and clinical literature as their importance in explaining vital facets of human interactional behaviour is becoming more widely recognized. As relatively new targets for neuropsychological enquiry, research is exploratory. In the following section we shall review neural and functional models encompassing work from both focal lesion research and work focused primarily on traumatic brain injury.

Emotion Regulation

Neural models of emotion regulation are poorly specified but do suggest that there is differentiation of regulatory processes within the frontal lobes. The ventromedial surfaces, with close connections to the amygdala, insula, ventral striatum, and ventral anterior cingulate appear to mediate automatic emotion regulation (Phillips, 2003) and the control of inhibitions (Luria, 1973). The medial cortex is engaged in self-initiation and sustained behavior (Andrewes, 2001; Darby & Walsh, 2005; Eslinger, 2008; Luria, 1973; Stuss, Gow, & Hetherington, 1992) while the orbitobasal aspects are associated with the flexible control of excitation, inhibition, and emotional control of behavior (Walsh, 1985). Finally, a dorsal system that entails the hippocampus, dorsal aspects of the anterior cingulate gyrus, and dorsolateral prefrontal cortex (Phillips, Drevets, Rauch, & Lane, 2003) is involved in the effortful processing of emotional stimuli and the engagement of cognitive processes via connections to other cortical regions. The dorsal and ventromedial systems are intimately associated with many points of reciprocity and feedback. Further, the dorsal system regulates the ventromedial system in order to meet specific goals and tasks. For example, emotion processing that requires explicit, verbal mediation is associated with increased activation of dorsolateral prefrontal cortex and, concomitantly, reduced activation of the amygdala (Hariri, Bookheimer, & Mazziotta, 2000). Given the complex interplay of frontal systems that are both functionally intimate and in close proximity, it is not surprising that the blunt forces that result in TBI lead to variable and often overlapping constellations of deficits in emotional behavior as well as executive dysfunction (see also Chapter 7). The ventral, medial and orbitobasal frontal regions, regions specifically related to emotion regulation, are especially vulnerable. During acceleration-deceleration trauma the brain is mechanically abraded by the surfaces of the middle and cranial fossae leading to contusion along the ventral surface of the frontal and temporal lobes (Bigler, 2007). Recent behavioral and experimental work provides further insights into how these different processes of regulation are impaired following TBI.

Disorders of Control. Inhibitory control is an important function of the frontal executive system enabling deliberate suppression, interruption, or delay of an activated behavior or cognitive course of action (Aron, Robbins, & Poldrack, 2004; Starkstein, 1997). It is vital for adaptive, goal directed responding in line with changing requirements of our environment, providing a necessary delay in the cognitive system for successful regulation of behavior, including top-down regulation of emotional responses (Zelazo & Cunningham, 2007). Disinhibition across behavioral, cognitive and emotional domains is prevalent following severe TBI. For example, there may be inability to inhibit impulsive and habitual behavior and socially inappropriate responses such as inappropriate touching and verbal disinhibition (Rao & Lyketsos, 2000). Alternatively, when presented with cognitive tasks such as the Stroop test there may be an inability to respond effectively under competing response conditions (Seignourel et al., 2005).

Although there is evidence of common neural structures such as the right dorsolateral prefrontal and right inferior frontal cortices underlying inhibitory control measured in different experimental tasks (Rubia et al., 2001), the overwhelming evidence of dissociable patterns of impairment in clinical populations (Dimoska, McDonald, Kelly, Tate, & Johnstone, 2011; Johnstone, Barry, Markovska, Dimoska, & Clarke, 2008), as well as separate developmental trajectories. (van den Wildenberg & van der Molen, 2004), suggests inhibitory control is not a unitary construct (Nigg, 2000). Effortful inhibitory control encompasses a number of related sub-processes, including response inhibition and interference control. Response inhibition, referring to the overt suppression of an activated motor response (Nigg, 2000), has been found to be impaired following TBI. For example, adults with TBI commit a greater number of inhibition failures (i.e., failure to stop response when required) compared with controls, indicative of poor inhibitory control (Draper, Ponsford, & Schönberger, 2007; O'Keeffe, Dockree, & Robertson, 2004; Roche et al., 2004). Interference control refers to the ability to inhibit an automatic response in favor of the correct response such as commonly measured in the Stroop interference effect (Nigg, 2000) and deficits have also been reported in people with TBI (Bate, Mathias, & Crawford, 2001). Meta-analyses of studies examining overall inhibitory control deficits in people with TBI, ranging from mild to very severe, have revealed a small-to-moderate impairment (Dimoska et al., 2011; Mathias & Wheaton, 2007). However, the effect was larger for response inhibition, indicating a greater impairment in the complete cessation of a response, compared with resolving conflicts between competing responses.

Brain imaging of adults with TBI performing tasks requiring cognitive control support an inhibition deficit (Soeda et al., 2005) with reduced activation in prefrontal regions in patients with mild (McAllister et al., 1999; McAllister et al., 2001) and moderate-to-severe TBI (Christodoulou et al., 2001; Perlstein et al., 2004). However, it is unlikely that focal frontal lesions entirely underpin inhibitory deficits. Effective control relies on efficient transmission of inhibitory neural signals along prefrontal-subcortical thalamic circuits (Rubia et al., 2001). Therefore, reduced speed in information processing may also account for poor inhibitory control (Ponsford & Kinsella, 1992), whereby slow or delayed activation of the inhibition process is more likely to result in a failure to inhibit (Logan, 1994; Mathias & Wheaton, 2007). Slow information processing is prevalent following TBI (Frenchmen, Fox, & Mayberry, 2005; Mathias & Wheaton, 2007; Ponsford & Kinsella, 1992) and is likely due to diffuse axonal injury leading to a shearing of interconnections between networks (Felmingham et al., 2004). Studies examining information processing deficits following TBI through response speed (i.e., reaction time tasks) demonstrate an average moderate-to-large effect size (Dimoska et al., 2011).

Although effortful inhibitory control is important for the deliberate regulation of both cognition and socio-emotional behavior (Zelazo & Cunningham, 2007), it is not clear whether the same inhibitory processes are common to both. While poor inhibitory control should interfere with the successful completion of many complex neuropsychological tasks, we are again faced with the generally poor concordance between neuropsychological tests and reports of everyday behavior. This is improved if errors on standard tests are used as an index of poor inhibitory control. In such studies, errors have been found to predict relative reports of difficulties in emotional control (irritability, restlessness, aggression) (Tate, 1999; Tate & Broe, 1999) and social integration (Odhuba, van den Broek, & Johns, 2005). Further, in a direct manipulation of emotional reaction, we asked people with severe TBI to self-rate their emotions when watching film clips chosen to elicit feelings of anger (McDonald, Hunt, Henry, Dimoska, & Bornhofen, 2010). Those who demonstrated poorer inhibition in terms of a greater number of errors on tests were those who self-reported more angry responses to these provocative films. These few studies do suggest that problems of inhibitory control may affect both emotional behavior and more purely cognitive tasks, consistent with a common mechanism for both; however, whether sub-processes such as interference control and response inhibition are equally relevant to the control of emotional processes awaits further research.

Disorders of Drive. Disorders of drive appear to arise from medial and dorsal frontal pathology (Andrewes, 2001; Darby & Walsh, 2005; Eslinger, 2008; Luria, 1973; Stuss et al., 1992). However, as with control, it is unlikely that a single disordered process or neural system accounts for disorders of drive (Tate et al., 1991). In reviewing classical work by Luria and more recent conceptualizations of deficiencies following frontal lobe damage, Tate (1999) argued that lowered drive encompasses three concepts: (1) indifference, i.e., lower arousal and emotional responsivity to external and internal states, (2) aspontaneity, i.e., lowered regulation (especially up-regulation of arousal) in order to self-initiate activity in the absence of external stimulation, and (3) adynamia, i.e., lowered ability to engage/disengage cognition and behavior flexibly. Study into each of these facets of drive has occurred using a range of investigative techniques.

Indifference. Indifference refers to a failure to engage with and respond to emotionally salient information. Animal and human research studies suggest that the appraisal, identification, and initial response to emotionally significant stimuli engages the ventral neural system including the amygdala, ventral portions of the striatum, anterior cingulate, and insular and ventral and orbitofrontal cortex (Phillips, 2003). For example, work with rhesus monkeys suggests that focal amygdala damage results in greater placidity and less timidity (Emery et al., 2001; Machado et al., 2008), while human adults with amygdala lesions fail to respond to threatening stimuli normally (Adolphs, 2001; Adolphs, Tranel, & Damasio, 1998).

In our work using anger-inducing films (McDonald et al., 2010) we found that a minority (6/34) of our group of people with severe TBI (and 2/34 control participants) self-reported very little emotional reaction to the films. This does suggest that some participants had impairment in the initial appraisal and responsivity to external events. This concurs with other work with people with TBI which has documented a general impairment of emotional reactivity to materials designed to evoke negative emotions, including a muted startle response when viewing distressing images (Saunders, McDonald, & Richardson, 2006) and lack of differentiation of skin conductance response to unpleasant versus pleasant odors (Soussignan, Ehrle, Henry, Schaal, & Bakchine, 2005) or pictures of a negative versus positive nature (de Sousa et al., 2011; Hopkins, Dywan, & Segalowitz, 2002; Sánchez-Navarro, Martínez-Selva, & Román, 2005; Soussignan et al., 2005).

A change in level of arousal when faced with emotionally significant events has clear adaptive benefits in terms of readying for a "flight-or-fight" response. Absence or impairment of this mechanism will diminish the emotional experience of the individual and is also likely to impact upon social competence, although there has been little research to date examining this. In addition, there is increasing interest in the extent to which impaired emotional reactivity impacts upon cognition. This has been heralded by the work of Bechara et al. on the role of "somatic markers" in guiding decision making in cognitive domains (Bechara, Damasio, Damasio, & Anderson, 1994; Bechara, Damasio, & Damasio, 2000; Bechara, Damasio, Tranel, & Damasio, 1997; Damasio, Tranel, &

Damasio, 1991). This research arose following observations that patients with damage to the prefrontal cortex made inappropriate and risky decisions in their everyday lives, despite having an intact knowledge of social norms. E.V.R., an orbitofrontal lesion patient was famed for having an above-average intellect and memory, and scoring in the average range on a battery of neuropsychological tests, while displaying impaired social conduct. Damasio and colleagues argued that sociopathy associated with damage to the prefrontal cortex may be the consequence of impaired activation of the somatic states required to appreciate the implications of poor social decisions (Damasio, Tranel, & Damasio, 1990). Damasio and colleagues termed this autonomic activation, the somatic marker hypothesis (SMH), and for the most part supported their thesis with performance on the Iowa Gambling Task (IGT; Bechara et al., 1994).

Somatic Markers and the Iowa Gambling Task. The IGT requires participants to make 100 card selections from four decks with the aim of winning money. Two decks are disadvantageous as they yield large gains, but are associated with even larger losses and over time will yield a small profit. The two advantageous decks yield smaller gains, but also smaller losses, and, choosing from these two decks will lead to a larger profit in the long term. The SMH proposes that anticipation of complex response contingencies can be associated with somatic responses even prior to conscious awareness of those contingencies, that is, prior to conscious knowledge of the best decks (Bechara et al., 1997).

Healthy adults learn over trials to play the advantageous decks. E.V.R. and patients with ventromedial damage do not (Bechara et al., 1994; Bechara et al., 2000; Fellows & Farah, 2005). Both normal adults and those with ventromedial lesions display changes in their skin conductance when provided with feedback regarding their choices. However, importantly, normal adults start to exhibit changes in skin conductance in anticipation of their choice, even before they can verbalize the rules (see Maia & McClelland, 2004 for counter argument). People with ventromedial damage do not (Bechara et al., 1997; Bechara, Tranel, Damasio, & Damasio, 1996; Naccache et al., 2005).

Research on the SMH employing the IGT has largely been conducted with focal lesion patients. Patients with ventromedial damage confined to the right hemisphere were more likely to exhibit impairments in this task than were patients with left focal damage (Tranel, Bechara, & Denburg, 2002). Damage to the dorsomedial (Manes et al., 2002) and the dorsolateral (Fellows & Farah, 2005) (especially right) prefrontal cortex has also been implicated in poor IGT performance. Patients with bilateral focal amygdala damage perform similarly to the ventromedial patients, however, in these cases, there is no skin conductance change found at all, even on the advent of feedback (Bechara, Damasio, Damasio, & Lee, 1999). As a result of this work, it has been argued that somatic responses may be important to assist with decision making specifically. This may be especially the case in personal and social decision making situations, where a precise calculation of the outcome of any given course of action is not possible (Bechara, 2004).

Although the majority of research on the SMH has been conducted in patients with focal lesions, patients who have sustained a traumatic brain injury are also vulnerable to ventromedial frontal lesions. Consequently, similar problems may be anticipated. There are only a handful of studies examining performance on the IGT in TBIs. Levine et al. (2005) studied 25 mild, 26 moderate, and 20 severe TBI patients and found that the IGT was sensitive to TBI in general; however, contrary to predictions, performance was not correlated with TBI severity. Fujiwara, Schwartz, Gao, Black and Levine (2008) found that TBI patients started out in the task more conservatively than controls, however, took longer to identify the advantageous strategy. In contrast to the original claims of the authors of the IGT, evidence for the necessity of conscious knowledge of deck contingencies for better decisions was provided by Garcia-Molina et al. (2007), that is, those with greater reportable knowledge of the card game made better decisions. To date, there is no psychophysiological data to accompany the IGT behavioral data with TBI patients.

The Iowa Gambling Task has been heralded as a new, useful measure of poor decision making that may be more closely aligned to disorders of social conduct than conventional tests. It is important, however, to stress, that deficits on this task are not limited to those with frontal lesions (Levine et al., 2005) or even those with ventromedial frontal lesions (Fellows & Farah, 2005). Individuals with an eating disorder (Cavedini et al., 2004), substance abusers (Verdejo-Garcia, Perales, & Perez-Garcia, 2007), and those with gambling and alcohol addictions (Goudriaan, Oosterlaan, de Beurs, & van den Brink, 2005) also perform poorly on the task. Furthermore, although a relationship between apathy and poor IGT performance has been observed (Barrash, Tranel, & Anderson, 2000), alternative mechanisms such as working memory (Hinson et al., 2002) and reversal learning/inhibition (Fellows & Farah, 2005) may play a role in IGT performance (for review see Dunn, Dalgleish, & Lawrence, 2006). Self and observer reported everyday memory and emotion problems; working memory, cognitive flexibility and psychomotor speed all display moderate correlations with IGT performance in people with TBI (Bonatti et al., 2008; Levine et al., 2005). Futhermore, the IGT is not fool-proof. Namiki et al. (2008) reported a patient, H. N., who displays sociopathy and all the real-life decision making impairments as E.V.R., with clear lesions to the orbitofrontal cortex following a TBI, yet who performed within the normal range on the IGT. Finally, other concerns regarding the reliability and validity of the IGT have been raised (Buelow & Suhr, 2009), in addition to the question of whether the task is predictive of real-life social impairment. Indeed, the non-social nature of the IGT begs the question as to whether the task is actually socially relevant.

An alternative task for assessing social decision making has recently been developed. The Social Decision Making Task (SDMT; Kelly, McDonald, & Kellett, Submitted) is a pseudo online game of catch-and-throw that requires the participant to use social feedback to guide decisions that will increase the likelihood of future interactions in the game. Findings from the initial studies examining this novel task are promising. Adults with a severe TBI were shown to make poorer social decisions when compared with healthy control participants (Kelly, McDonald, & Kellett, submitted) even when given twice as many trials with which to learn (Kelly, McDonald, & Rushby, submitted). While much more work is needed, initial findings support the utility of this task, and highlight the importance of being able to use feedback from the social environment in order to guide pro-social behaviour.

Aspontaneity (Apathy). Disorders of drive may also be manifest in the failure to spontaneously regulate arousal in order to self-initiate behavior leading to a condition of apathy (Cummings, 1985) or pseudodepression (Blumer & Benson, 1975). The medial and dorsal frontal systems that mediate arousal and effortful regulation of emotional responses via extensive connectivity to the thalamus and mesencephalic reticular formation (Heilman, 2000; Phillips et al., 2003) may be specifically involved in this process. There has been very little experimental work published in English language journals that has examined deficits in self-initiation and maintenance of arousal. However, a number of Russian experimental studies in the 1960s examined basic processes of arousal using psychophysiological techniques and are reviewed in Luria (Luria, 1973). The extent to which apathy, (a failure in self-initiation and regulation of arousal) and indifference (a failure to respond to external stimuli) dissociate following TBI has been difficult to tease out as the two are functionally intertwined. Recent psychophysiological research in this area, based on the foundational work of the 1960s, holds promise to enable us to examine these in greater detail.

It has long been recognized that an individual's functional state moderates their response to a stimulus. A model of such responding in relation to cognitive/perceptual processing is the orienting reflex (OR). The concept of the OR was introduced by Pavlov (Pavlov, 1927) to describe the reflex that brings about an immediate response (both behavioral and physiological) to the slightest change in the environment. Sokolov (1960, 1963) proposed that a cortical representation (neuronal model) develops with repeated presentation of a given stimulus, and that new stimuli failing to match the model elicit an OR, the magnitude of which is proportional to the extent of the mismatch. Repeated presentations are reflected in extinction of the OR. Sokolov distinguished between ORs based on their duration: "phasic" refers to the rapid, short-lasting response, while "tonic" refers to the slower, longer-lasting state changes commonly associated with levels of arousal.

While Sokolov reported that a number of behavioral and autonomic measures co-varied in the extensive, organismic response (including interruption of ongoing behavior, increase in skin conductance response or SCR, respiratory arrest, peripheral vasoconstriction, cephalic vasodilation, and pupil dilation), a unidimensional concept of physiological arousal is not supported by current literature (Barry, Clarke, Johnstone, & Rushby, 2008; Critchley, 2009; Macefield, 2009). For example, the most commonly examined physiological components of the OR, the SCR and heart rate (HR) response show differential stimulus response outcomes. Specifically, SCRs have been shown to index new or novel stimuli, and are primarily reflected in habituation to repeated stimulus presentations (Connolly & Frith, 1978; Groves & Thompson, 1970; Rushby & Barry, 2007; Rushby & Barry, 2009; Webster, Dunlop, Simons, & Aitken, 1965) whereas, HR responses have been shown to reflect heightened sensory intake and increased attentional processing (Lacey & Lacey, 1978; Lacey & Lacey, 1980; Lacey, 1967). A different measure again is skin conductance level (SCL), which reflects the relatively slower, longer-lasting state changes commonly associated with levels of arousal and is emerging as the most widely accepted gold-standard for an objective measure of arousal in psychophysiological research (Barry, Clarke, McCarthy, Selikowitz, & Rushby, 2005; Critchley, Melmed, Featherstone, Mathias, & Dolan, 2001, 2002; Malmo, 1959; Raine, Lencz, Bihrle, LaCasse, & Colletti, 2000; Rushby & Barry, 2007; VaezMousavi, Barry, Rushby, & Clarke, 2007a, 2007b).

Physiological Responses to Emotionally Salient Events. These recent conceptualizations of physiological responsivity enable us to make a more refined analysis of problems with indifference and/or apathy in people with TBI when processing emotionally salient information. We examined the OR (indexed by the phasic SCR), attention (indexed by HR) and arousal (indexed by SCL) to repetitions of angry and happy emotional expressions in a group of 18 TBI participants and 18 healthy controls (McDonald, Rushby, et al., 2011). Each participant was presented with two blocks of eight angry and eight happy facial expressions. For block one participants passively viewed the faces, and for block two participants were required to identify the emotion expression after each slide. Consistent with previous research, control participants demonstrated enhanced ORs when passively viewing angry faces relative to happy. This was not the case for the participants with TBI, who showed attenuated responses that were similar in magnitude for both emotions. HR responses did not differ between emotion expressions for either group, but were attenuated for TBI participants compared with controls in both conditions suggesting that they experienced low sensory intake and attentional processing regardless of task demands. This is not surprising given the slow information processing speed and loss of cognitive efficiency seen as a result of TBI, and often attributed to diffuse axonal injury (Felmingham et al., 2004).

The lack of OR and attention to stimuli fits with the indifference, or absence of reactivity mentioned in the previous section. It suggests that emotional information does not automatically "grab" the attention of the people with TBI. Interestingly, for the attend task there were no differences apparent in SCR between groups, suggesting that instructions to attend normalized orientation in the TBI participants. This is consistent with prior research by Damasio and colleagues (1990) with patients with focal ventromedial frontal damage which demonstrated an absence of SCR when viewing distressing images passively; however, SCR normalized when they were asked to describe the pictures.

Marked differences were also observed between groups when looking at pre-stimulus arousal changes (SCL) across stimulus repetitions. Control participants exhibited marked decrement (habituation) to repetitions of happy expressions, but sensitization (an incremental increase in arousal) was shown to repetitions of angry facial expressions, whereas TBI participants appeared to habituate to both kinds of stimuli equally. It appears that these people with TBI failed to respond to negatively valenced emotional faces normally, including a failure to accord such signals privileged status as salient environmental events. Unlike measures of orientation, instructions to attend to the stimuli did not alter these arousal profiles in the TBI participants. Overall, these findings suggest that this group of people with severe TBI failed to orientate to environmental events (indifference) but that this was overcome by instructions to attend. On the other hand, they generally experienced low sensory intake and attentional processing regardless of task demands and also experienced lowered arousal that was not responsive to environmental contingencies, even when their attention is directed to the information. This is suggestive that self-initiated arousal was also impaired leading to increased apathy. These findings are consistent with Russian work from the 1960s. Homskaya et al. (as cited in Luria, 1973) used physiological measures to demonstrate that frontal (especially ventromedial) lesions lead to unstable intention and rapid habituation. She also reported that those with dorsolateral lesions were able to increase their attention temporarily given verbal instruction (cf: our "attend" condition, or the verbal description instruction in Damasio et al.1990) but this was poorly sustained.

Adynamia

Another dimension of drive/arousal is the ability to engage and disengage from cognitive tasks. Such flexibility requires, not only sufficient activation, but also inhibitory control in order to inhibit the prepotent response (Dimoska et al., 2011) so may well reflect the balance between arousal and control. It has been suggested that orbitobasal frontal systems mediate this flexible control (Walsh, 1985). In support of this Crowe (1992) found that while disinhibited errors on the Controlled Oral Word Associated Test (COWAT) were seen in patients with specific orbitofrontal lesions (surmised to mediate disinhibition), total word production was affected by lesions in the medial and dorsal cortex (thought to mediate apathy) as well as orbitofrontal lesions.

Adynamia is important, not only for cognitive tasks, but also emotional and social behavior. In her seminal paper, Lezak (1978) described some of the characterological changes seen following severe TBI as reflecting rigid, inflexible thinking, the tendency to be "black and white" in the appraisal of social information, and perseverative, rigid, and uncompromising when responding in social contexts. Such patients may also have difficulty perceiving the view point of others. The notion that there is a loss of empathy has been empirically supported by the finding that a group of TBI patients were incapable of filling out a personality questionnaire "as though they were someone else" (Spiers, Pouk, & Santoro, 1994), and also by low scores relative to healthy controls on self-reported empathy measures (de Sousa et al., 2010; Williams & Wood, 2010; Wood & Williams, 2007). The possibility that adynamia underpins low empathy is strengthened by the finding that loss of flexibility on neuropsychological tasks (indexed by perseverative errors and loss of generativity) is associated with measures of empathy (Eslinger & Grattan, 1993; Grattan & Eslinger, 1989) and more general estimates of social skill (Marsh & Knight, 1991). We will discuss empathy in greater detail in the following sections on social cognition.

Social Cognition

Although it has long been recognized that people with TBI have difficulties in social situations, and more specifically, that they are insensitive to others and do not pick up on social cues (e.g., Crosson, 1987; Prigatano, 1986) the accepted thinking regarding the reasons for this is changing. A widely held assumption that has held sway for decades is that failure to understand subtle social information following TBI reflects more general problems with executive function disrupting the ability to reason at a conceptual level. Difficulties with adynamia, as described in the previous section, leads to rigid, concrete thinking and does contribute to certain kinds of social processing tasks such as self-reported empathy (Grattan & Eslinger, 1989). Even so, there is growing argument that social information also requires specific, and in some cases unique, processes to be engaged that differ from those required for non-social information. By way of example, where most neuropsychological tests of conceptual reasoning rely upon static, logical, and categorical relationships, social cognition relies upon the ability to detect individual differences, dynamic, interactive contingencies, and inferences arising from complex and changing contextual cues (Corrigan & Toomey, 1995). It is perhaps unsurprising, then, that no relation has been found between conceptual reasoning and interpersonal functioning in traumatic brain injury (Tate & Broe, 1999).

Social neuroscience is a burgeoning new field of neuropsychological research, based upon the argument that social cognition has a privileged, if not unique, place in human information processing. As humans live in groups, their survival has relied upon the ability to negotiate social relationships so, social intelligence (i.e., the ability to interact with others in a complex and flexible manner) has long played an important role in natural selection (Adolphs, 2001). In addition, it is clear that social competence can be dissociated from intellectual (non-social) competence in developmental conditions. Adults with Aspergers Syndrome can excel at non-social problem solving but have seriously impaired social functioning. Conversely, Williams syndrome is associated with abnormally low intellectual skills but high levels of social competence (Karmiloff-Smith, Klima, Bellugi, Grant, & Baron-Cohen, 1995). This is also the case in adults with acquired brain injuries such as the celebrated case of E.V.R. with high intelligence, intact executive function, and poor social functioning (Saver & Damasio, 1991). Such dissociations are also consistent with the general observation that it is the orbitomedial aspects of the frontal lobes rather than the dorsolateral that are most relevant to personality and psychosocial function, whereas non-social problem solving tasks are more commonly associated with dorsolateral frontal functions. Current research into social cognition following TBI (as well as focal lesions and degenerative conditions) has addressed a number of facets of social processing including (1) emotion perception, (2) "theory of mind" (TOM), i.e., the ability to make inferences concerning another's beliefs and intentions and (3) empathy.

Emotion Perception. Clinicians working with people with severe TBI have probably long been aware that many such individuals had difficulty picking up emotional expression in others. However, there was virtually no published research regarding this prior to the 1980s, when two empirical studies emerged (Jackson & Moffat, 1987; Prigatano & Pribam, 1982). There are now numerous studies that attest to this. A significant proportion of adults with severe TBI have been demonstrated to have difficulty identifying emotional expressions in others in a variety of media including static facial expressions, dynamic visual portrayals, emotionally charged voices, and audiovisual displays (Croker & McDonald, 2005; Dimoska et al., 2010; Green, Turner, & Thompson, 2004; Hopkins et al., 2002; Ietswaart, Milders, Crawford, Currie, & Scott, 2008; McDonald & Flanagan, 2004; McDonald, Flanagan, Rollins, & Kinch, 2003; Milders et al., 2003; Spell & Frank, 2000; Watts & Douglas, 2006).

Brain-behavior relationships are difficult to document due to the diffuse and microscopic nature of pathology following TBI. However, there is a clear similarity between deficits in emotion perception in people with TBI and those with well-defined lesions to fronto-temporal structures including orbital and medial prefrontal cortex, amygdala, insular, anterior cingulate gyrus, and basal ganglia (e.g., Adolphs, 2002; Adolphs, Damasio, Tranel, & Damasio, 1996; Phillips, 2003). Thus, deficits in emotion perception following TBI are likely to arise from damage to similar structures.

In general, perception of negative emotions (anger, disgust, sadness, and fear) is affected more than perception of positive emotions (happiness and surprise), especially in the visual modality (Croker & McDonald, 2005; Green et al., 2004; Hopkins et al., 2002; Jackson & Moffat, 1987; McDonald et al., 2003). This is also consistent with focal lesion work that suggests separate neural systems underpinning different emotions (Adolphs & Tranel, 2004; Broks et al., 1998; Buchanan, Tranel, & Adolphs, 2004; Sprengelmeyer et al., 1996). For example, amygdala damage is associated with deficits in recognition of fear (Adolphs, 2002), anger (Adolphs, Russell, & Tranel, 1999), and sadness (Adolphs & Tranel, 2004). Furthermore, in normal adults, the orbitomedial prefrontal areas shows increased activity when viewing angry faces (Blair, Morris, Frith, Perrett, & Dolan, 1999) and, if temporarily disrupted using transcranial magnetic stimulation, processing of angry faces is slowed down significantly (Harmer, Thilo, Rothwell, & Goodwin, 2001).

Although people with TBI appear to have impairments with emotions expressed via a variety of media, this is not to suggest that impairment within any one individual is uniform across media. Although deficits in recognizing emotion in both voice and face commonly co-exist, they can also dissociate (Hornak, Rolls, & Wade, 1996; McDonald & Saunders, 2005), which indicates that the two media may rely upon separable, if overlapping neural systems (Adolphs, Damasio, & Tranel, 2002).

Facial Expressions. Tests of emotion identification typically use static photographs as stimuli. For example, the Ekman and Friesen series of posed black and white photographs (Ekman & Friesen, 1976) are widely used in research and also published tests (Young, Rowland, Calder, & Etcoff, 1997). However, such stimuli are unlike normal facial expressions because they do not provide the cues that arise from observation of faces that are moving in the natural evocation of an emotional state. Such cues provide important additional information, e.g., when viewers are restricted to seeing white dots on (blacked out) faces actively moving they are better than chance at recognizing emotions (Bassili, 1978). We have found that while adults with TBI are significantly impaired in the recognition of static facial expression, their performance was relatively closer to normal when they were asked to identify dynamic images (McDonald & Saunders, 2005). A similar pattern has been reported in people with focal frontotemporal lesions (Adolphs, Tranel, & Damasio, 2003). A converse finding, i.e., better performance on static than dynamic has been reported when the parietal cortices are compromised (Humphrey, Donnelly, & Riddoch, 1993). An explanation for this may be that dynamic facial movement is processed by the parietal and dorsolateral frontal cortices while static images may be processed by temporal-medial frontal systems (Adolphs et al., 2003). While both systems probably contribute to competent expression processing, this dissociation has implications for remediation following TBI, suggesting that if one mode of expression (still or dynamic) is particularly difficult to process, then the other may provide an easier set of cues to base discriminations upon.

Physiological Reactivity and Emotion Perception. An interesting question for facial affect recognition disorders is whether somatic feedback is involved in this process. It has been argued that there are parallel brain systems that process automatic and conscious components of emotion perception (Buck, 1993). Further, it appears that early automatic processing of emotional faces is associated with physiological changes. For example, work in the 1970–80s convincingly demonstrated faint facial mimicry as well as changes in skin conductance when viewing facial expressions even without conscious awareness (see McHugo & Smith, 1996). This fits with the neural model of emotion processing presented earlier in this chapter which entails a ventral neural circuit comprising the amygdala, insula, ventral striatum, and ventral regions of the anterior cingulate and prefrontal cortex that provides early orientation to and rapid appraisal of emotionally significant stimuli and affective responses even prior to conscious awareness (Phillips, 2003). In contrast, the dorsal system including the hippocampus, dorsal aspects of the anterior cingulate gyrus, and prefrontal cortex is involved in effortful, slower processing of emotional stimuli, including the engagement of other cognitive processes, such as language and memory, and the regulation of affective states.

There is increasing interest in the possibility that these early physiological responses to facial expressions aid interpretation, although this is not a new concept. As early as 1906, Lipps wrote "empathy is an innate, isomorphic response to another person's expression of emotion, whereby the observer automatically imitates the other with slight movements in facial expression ("motor mimicry")" (Hoffman, 1984, p. 107). His view was that such mimicry provides feedback, leading to a sharing of the affect and, consequently, recognition of the emotion being experienced. This facial feedback hypothesis has received some support in non-clinical research. Increased activity at the zygomaticus major (the muscle that lifts the lip to smile) and the corrugator supercilii (the muscle that

knits the brow) (Cacioppo, Petty, Losch, & Kim, 1986; Tassinary, Cacioppo, & Berntson, 2000) occurs during exposure to pictures of happy and angry faces respectively. Mimicry occurs rapidly, as early as 300 ms post-stimulus onset, compatible with the proposal that this is an automatic process (Dimberg & Thunberg, 1998; Dimberg, Thunberg, & Elmehed, 2000). Further, both observing and portraying particular facial expressions engenders congruent mood changes (Levenson, Ekman, & Friesen, 1990; Wild, Erb, & Bartels, 2001) and conversely, mimicry is influenced by the mood of the observer (Moody, McIntosh, Mann, & Weisser, 2007). This suggests an emotional contagion response to emotional expressions that may form the basis of an empathic response. We have examined facial mimicry in a group of adults with severe, chronic TBI and a group of matched controls when viewing happy versus angry facial expressions, both static and dynamically portrayed (McDonald, Li et al., 2011). The control participants showed the expected pattern of facial mimicry, i.e., enhanced brow activity when observing angry expressions and enhanced cheek activity when observing happy expressions. These changes were evident early, i.e., from 500–1000 ms post onset, consistent with an automatic process. The participants with TBI showed a similar pattern in response to happy expressions but no response to angry expressions, i.e., they failed to have a mimicry response to angry expressions suggesting this early automatic processing was absent or impaired. Other measures of arousal such as skin conductance changes and heart rate told a similar story (McDonald, Rushby et al., 2011).

The relationship between impaired emotional responsivity to facial expressions and accuracy in recognizing emotions is, however, less certain. Research to date has been inconsistent in demonstrating an association between emotional responsivity and emotion perception. For example, deliberate prevention of mimicry has been reported to impair emotion perception judgements (Niedenthal, Brauer, Halberstadt, & Innes-Ker, 2001) in normal adults or make the task seem more difficult (Blairy, Herrera, & Hess, 1999) but the relationship between mimicry and decoding accuracy is not always found (Hess & Blairy, 2001). Research in the

TBI population is similarly inconclusive. A relationship between subjective reports of altered emotional experience and accuracy in the recognition of emotions has been found in some studies (Croker & McDonald, 2005; Hornak et al., 1996) but not others (McDonald, Li et al., 2011; McDonald, Rushby et al., 2011).

Vocal Emotion. While the majority of research into emotion perception deficits has concentrated on facial emotion, deficits in perception of vocal emotion are also apparent in people with TBI (Dimoska et al., 2010; Marquardt, Rios-Brown, Richburg, Seibert, & Cannito, 2001; McDonald & Pearce, 1996; Milders et al., 2003; Spell & Frank, 2000) and may be even more severe (Spell & Frank, 2000) even when paired with visual emotional cues (McDonald & Saunders, 2005). They also improve less over time than facial emotion perception (Ietswaart et al., 2008). Yet relatively few studies have examined vocal affect deficits in TBI (Zupan, Neumann, Babbage, & Willer, 2009).

Focal lesion studies suggest that the right hemisphere mediates emotional prosody (Bowers, Coslett, Bauer, Speedie, & Heilman, 1987; Heilman, Bowers, Speedie, & Coslett, 1984; Heilman, Scholes, & Watson, 1975; Ross & Monnot, 2008) although this is not always found (Baum & Pell, 1999; Pell & Baum, 1997; for a review see Pell, 2006; Schlanger, Schlanger, & Gerstmann, 1976). Both emotional and grammatical prosody activate bilateral regions of the superior temporal gyrus, although evidence continues to favor right hemisphere specialization for emotion (for a review see Adolphs et al., 2002; Mitchell, Elliott, Barry, Cruttenden, & Woodruff, 2003). In addition, overlapping frontal-subcortical circuits become selectively activated depending on task demands.

To some extent, prosody judgments rely upon distinctiveness of prosodic elements including pitch, intonation, loudness, and tempo. Consequently some errors emerge due to similarity of prosodic parameters between emotions (Leinonen, Hiltunen, Linnankoski, & Laakso, 1997) making some emotions easier to identify that others. Anger is characterized by increased speech rate, wider range in pitch variations, and greater intensity, making it one of the most identifiable emotions in voice (Scherer,

Banse, Wallbott, & Goldbeck, 1991). Fear is also relatively easy to identify, while happiness is more difficult to recognize in vocal than facial expressions (Scherer et al., 1991; Zupan et al., 2009) and surprise is the most difficult to distinguish (Pell, 2006). In some studies TBI has been found to affect all emotions equally (Ietswaart et al., 2008; McDonald & Saunders, 2005) and conversely, to affect fear differentially more than anger (Dimoska et al., 2010) or happiness (Spell & Frank, 2000). These results do not accord with an explanation of deficit based solely upon acoustic discrimination and suggest other kinds of problems. One important aspect of emotional speech is that it conveys meaning via two channels, prosody and content. Although prosodic information is available and used early in comprehension (Kaganovich, Francis, & Melara, 2006; Steinhauer, Alter, & Friederici, 1999) there is a bias for processing semantic content over prosody (Lew, Chmiel, Jerger, Pomerantz, & Jerger, 1997). While directions to ignore prosody are easily complied with, semantic information is difficult to completely ignore when focusing on prosody (Besson, Magne, & Schön, 2002; Wambacq & Jerger, 2004). One possibility for the difficulties that people with TBI experience with emotional prosody could be, therefore, that they have trouble with the concurrent processing of both channels of emotional information, which could reflect cognitive impairments in working memory and information processing speed in this group. Many people with TBI show an overly literal interpretation of indirect conversational remarks such as sarcasm (McDonald & Flanagan, 2004) and this is frequently associated with deficits in information processing speed, working memory, and reasoning (Martin & McDonald, 2005; McDonald et al., 2006; McDonald & Pearce, 1996).

In order to examine this we conducted research in which we reduced the semantic content of emotional speech by either filtering the speech to make it unintelligible or using nonsense words (Dimoska et al., 2010). In both cases we found that people with TBI were reliant upon the semantic content and were worse off, relative to controls, when this was removed. This finding suggests poor identification of vocal emotion in TBI may be due to the perceptual processing of prosodic information per se, and is unrelated to the interference semantic processing may pose. However, findings also supported a role of working memory in the impairment of response-selection processes when semantically labelling emotions. Thus emotion perception problems following TBI likely reflect a number of deficiencies along the perceptual-cognitive processing trajectory.

Theory of Mind. Theory of mind (TOM) refers to the capacity to attribute mental states, such as thoughts, beliefs, desires, and intentions to others and is pivotal to the ability to make sense of social behavior and interpersonal communication. TOM has been thought to cause the social communication difficulties seen in autism. Many individuals with high functioning autism or Aspergers Syndrome and normal IQ have fluent and articulate speech but are, none-the-less, pedantic and over-literal (Happe et al., 1996), fail to interact normally in conversation, often talk at length on obscure or inappropriate topics (Ozonoff & Miller, 1996), have inappropriate non-verbal communication and poor adherence to social rules (Bowler, 1992). They also fail to appreciate how utterances are used to convey information in a socially appropriate manner (Surian, Baron-Cohen, & Van der Lely, 1996) and misinterpret both metaphor and irony (Happe, 1993).

Similar deficits in social reasoning and social communication as seen in autism have also been reported in adults with TBI who have been reported as egocentric, self-focused, lacking interest in other people, displaying inappropriate humor, frequently interrupting, having a blunt manner, making overly familiar and disinhibited remarks or advances and offering inappropriate levels of self-disclosure (Crosson, 1987; Flanagan, McDonald, & Togher, 1995; Levin, Grossman, Rose, & Teasdale, 1979; McDonald et al., 2004; McDonald & Pearce, 1998; McDonald & van Sommers, 1992). They have also been reported to find it difficult to identify the source of interpersonal conflict (Kendall, Shum, Halson, Bunning, & Teh, 1997) or otherwise interpret nonverbal interpersonal interactions (Bara, Cutica, & Tirassa, 2001; Cicerone & Tanenbaum, 1997). Deficits on explicit TOM tasks have also been found in people with TBI,

both adult and child (Bibby & McDonald, 2005; Dennis, Purvis, Barnes, Wilkinson, & Winner, 2001; Milders, et al., 2003; Milders, Ietswaart, Crawford, & Currie, 2006; Milders, Ietswaart, Crawford, & Currie, 2008; Santoro & Spiers, 1994; Stone, Baron-Cohen, & Knight, 1998; Turkstra, Dixon, & Baker, 2004). Tasks include complex stories requiring inferences about TOM, cartoon jokes (Bibby & McDonald, 2005; Milders et al., 2006; Milders et al., 2008), and judgements about mental states based upon the eye region of the face (Havet-Thomassin, Allain, Etcharry-Bouyx, & Le Gall, 2006; Henry, Phillips, Crawford, Ietswaart, & Summers, 2006). Furthermore, TOM performance has been linked to sarcasm comprehension. Specifically, those who experience difficulties understanding second order TOM inferences (i.e., what one person wants another person to believe) are also those most likely to experience problems understanding the meaning of sarcastic exchanges (Channon, Pellijeff, & Rule, 2005; McDonald & Flanagan, 2004).

The basis for TOM deficits in TBI (and other neurological conditions) remains controversial. Some have argued that TOM is a specialized, modular facet of social cognition representing a unique process (Havet-Thomassin et al., 2006; Rowe, Bullock, Polkey, & Morris, 2001). Such a stand is supported by evidence that there is no clear relation between measures of executive function and TOM performance in adults with focal frontal lesions (Rowe et al., 2001) or TBI (Spikman, Timmerman, Milders, Veenstra, & van der Naalt, 2012). Further, TOM deficits have been reported to be most severe following ventromedial lesions (Shamay-Tsoory, Tomer, & Aharon-Peretz, 2005) and not associated with dorsolateral frontal lesions, which commonly give rise to executive impairment. However, other work does suggest that problems with general inference-making secondary to executive deficits in TBI affect both non-social inferences and TOM (Martin & McDonald, 2005).

Working memory may also play a role. For example, a number of studies have shown that young children's performances on false belief tasks are influenced by working memory capacity (Davis & Pratt, 1995; Gordon & Olson, 1998; Hughes, 1998; Keenan, 1998), although the evidence suggests that it is not the sole contributing factor (Tager-Flusberg, Sullivan, & Boshart, 1997). In acquired brain injury, poor performance on tasks reliant upon working memory is associated with poor TOM performance (Bibby & McDonald, 2005; Havet-Thomassin et al., 2006; Henry et al., 2006; Stone et al., 1998) although such deficits do not totally explain the difficulties seen (Havet-Thomassin et al., 2006). Consequently, while there may be common processes required for social and non-social tasks; depending upon the medium and response requirements (spoken, written, etc.), there may also be unique requirements called into play when making TOM judgements. Whether TOM represents a modular function that is differentially impaired in TBI, or higher order ability reliant upon generic executive skills, it is clear that deficits in TOM have implications for interpersonal function. Despite this, efforts to link poor TOM and emotion perception to everyday social skills via self and parent report questionnaires have been unsuccessful (Milders et al., 2003; Milders et al., 2008) possibly because of the disparity in medium and

scope of the different instruments. On the other hand, in a study of people with severe TBI (McDonald et al., 2004), we found that failure to correctly interpret speaker intentions in video vignettes was significantly associated with poor social behaviour in a videoed social interaction.

Empathy. Empathy is a critical component necessary for successful interpersonal function that provides an individual with the ability to understand and respond to the emotional experiences of others (Decety & Jackson, 2004). Failure to empathize is considered to cause egocentrism, alienation, and conflict (Eslinger, 2002). It is widely documented that individuals who have sustained a severe TBI can be egocentric, self-centered, and insensitive to another person's needs (Elsass & Kinsella, 1987; Grattan & Eslinger, 1989; Newton & Johnson, 1985). This pattern has been attributed, at least in part, to a reduction in empathy. For example, preliminary evidence to date suggests that a large proportion of individuals with TBI report a loss of empathy, both emotional (Williams & Wood,

Table 8-1. Summary of Studies that Have Reported Empathy Deficits in Patients with Traumatic Brain Injury (TBI)

Study	Sample (n)	Type of empathy assessed	Empathy measure	Results
de Sousa et al. (2010)	TBI (21) Controls (22)	Emotional	BEES	66.7% (TBI) vs. 31.8% (Controls) reported low emotional empathy.
de Sousa et al. (Submitted, 2010)	TBI (20) Controls (22)	Emotional Cognitive	BEES (as above) IRI-EC subscale EQ-ER subscale IRI-PT subscale EQ-CE subscale	55% (TBI) vs. 22.6% (Controls) across all 3 measures reported low emotional empathy. 47.5% (TBI) vs. 18% (Controls) across all 2 measures reported low cognitive empathy.
Grattan & Eslinger (1989)	TBI (10) Stroke (27) Tumour (5) Aneurysm rupture + clipping (8) Controls (28)	Cognitive	EM	Overall, 56% of patients reported low cognitive empathy. Yet, % of TBI patients exhibiting low empathy unknown.
Wells, Dywan, & Dumas (2005)	TBI (72) Primary caregiver (72)	Cognitive	BAFQ empathy subscale	Impaired empathy reported in TBI group, which adversely affected caregivers' ratings of life satisfaction.
Williams & Wood (2009)	TBI (64) Controls (64)	Emotional	BEES	64.4% (TBI) vs. 34.4% (Controls) reported low emotional empathy.
Wood & Williams (2008)	TBI (89) Controls (84)	Emotional	BEES	60.7% (TBI) vs. 31% (Controls) reported low emotional empathy.

Note: BEES = the Balanced Emotional Empathy Scale; EM = the Empathy Scale; EQ = Empathy Questionnaire; BAFQ = the Brock Adaptive Functioning Questionnaire; EEQ = the Emotional Empathy Questionnaire.

2010; Wood & Williams, 2008) and cognitive (de Sousa, McDonald, & Rushby, 2012; de Sousa et al., 2010; Grattan & Eslinger, 1989; Wells, Dywan, & Dumas, 2005). For more details, please refer to Table 8-1.

Impairment in emotional and cognitive empathy is not surprising given that both are associated with brain structures susceptible to TBI, including the inferior frontal gyrus (emotional empathy: Nummenmaa, Hirvonen, Parkkola, & Hietanen, 2008; Schulte-Rüther, Markowitsch, Fink, & Piefke, 2007; Shamay-Tsoory, Aharon-Peretz, & Perry, 2009) and ventromedial prefrontal cortex (cognitive empathy: Nummenmaa et al., 2008; Shamay-Tsoory et al., 2009).

However, the reasons why adults with TBI lose the ability to empathize are not clear. A critical aspect of empathy is emotional responsivity to another person's feelings. From an early age, the normative response is to feel what another person is feeling; for example, happiness when someone is noticeably happy. Such heightened sensitivity to someone's display of emotion has been dubbed "emotional" empathy (Mehrabian & Epstein, 1972). A large proportion (in excess of 60%) of individuals with TBI self-report a loss of emotional empathy, i.e., a loss of affective reactions to the emotional displays of others (de Sousa et al., 2011; Williams & Wood, 2010), as measured by the Balanced Emotional Empathy Scale (BEES; (Mehrabian, 2000). A proportion of people with severe TBI also self-report blunting of emotional experience more generally post-injury (Croker & McDonald, 2005; Hornak et al., 1996). Further, as discussed above, responses to emotional presentations are affected, and include impaired facial mimicry (McDonald, Li et al., 2011) and skin conductance (Blair & Cipolotti, 2000; Hopkins et al., 2002; McDonald, Rushby et al., 2011), especially to angry facial expressions. Interestingly, low self-reported emotional empathy has been found to be significantly associated with such emotional response deficits to angry facial expressions in both people with TBI and normal adults (Sonnby-Borgström, Jönsson, & Svensson, 2003).

It has also been established via self-report that TBI produces a marked inability to adopt another person's point of view (i.e., cognitive empathy) (de Sousa et al., 2011; Grattan & Eslinger, 1989; Wells et al., 2005). While clearly related to emotional empathy, there is good evidence that the two kinds of empathy are dissociable and certainly different neural structures have been implicated (Nummenmaa et al., 2008; Shamay-Tsoory & Aharon-Peretz, 2007; Shamay-Tsoory et al., 2009). Conceptually, cognitive empathy is very similar to Theory of Mind (TOM), as it also involves the ability to infer information (i.e., events, situations, etc.) from another's perspective. Individuals with TBI are impaired on both measures of TOM (Bibby & McDonald, 2005) and cognitive empathy (de Sousa et al., 2010; Grattan & Eslinger, 1989; Wells et al., 2005). Disorders of both cognitive empathy and TOM have been associated with lesions to the ventromedial prefrontal cortex (Shamay-Tsoory, Tomer, Berger, & Aharon-Peretz, 2003). Finally, consistent with the view that different frontal systems mediate emotional and cognitive empathy (Shamay-Tsoory et al., 2009), self-reported cognitive versus emotional empathy deficits can dissociate after TBI (de Sousa et al., 2010; Eslinger, Satish, & Grattan, 1996).

Synthesis and Implications of Findings

As a relatively new field, social neuroscience holds great promise for understanding the kinds of interpersonal and social deficits experienced by many people with traumatic brain injuries. In the past, efforts to understand such deficits were restricted to either self and/or other report on questionnaires of everyday function, or extrapolation from laboratory and everyday tasks that are essentially non-social. This new focus allows us to orientate specifically to social information processing, applying ideas and methodologies from disparate fields ranging from psychophysiology to social psychology. And the implications of such research are not restricted to social cognitive processes. Psychophysiological research that enables us to measure arousal, attention, and information processing is far-reaching, providing new insights into how emotion regulation interacts with behavior, social and non-social cognitive processing, and decision making. The yield of this shift in orientation is rich, providing new insights into where and how people with TBI falter in social interactions. The ability to provide specific explanations for where impairments in social skills arise has major beneficial effects in terms of remediation.

Alongside the growth in social neurosciences, there has been an explosion of interest in rehabilitation of such deficits. Psychosocial intervention studies are being published at a rapid and exponential rate: e.g., 1970s ($n = 11$), 1980s ($n = 79$), 1990s ($n = 196$), and 2000s ($n = 361$) (www. PsycBITE.com). In parallel is fascinating new research concerning the capacity of the brain to reorganize and regenerate following injury (e.g., Cornelissen et al., 2003). This has lead to renewed optimism in neurological rehabilitation. The dominant view had been that brain injury is permanent and, therefore compensatory practice is the best that can be hoped for (Ogden, 2000). But emerging research has shown that skills can be re-established following brain-injury, provided the remediation targets are highly specific (see Robertson & Murre, 1999). The evidence favors an approach aimed at focusing attention on relevant stimuli or behavior and repeated practice of target processes. Critical, therefore, is a clear understanding of the processes that are impaired in order to identify target processes for remediation. For example, we have commenced remediation research to address specific deficits in emotion perception with some success (Bornhofen & McDonald, 2008a, 2008b).

New Developments and Directions for Research

The continued refinement of our understanding of specific deficits in emotion regulation and social cognition following TBI provides the opportunity to develop socially relevant assessment instruments and well circumscribed targets for remediation. Now that the windows into social neuroscience are opening, there are a plethora of phenomena that can be examined in people with TBI and a variety of methodologies borrowed from the social sciences and psychophysiology that enable us to do this. While there are many areas that can be developed further, three specific areas that can be identified within the existing literature are social knowledge, moral reasoning, and social communication.

Social Knowledge

While we have addressed several facets of social cognition in this chapter, there remain a range of phenomena that have had little systematic study within neuropsychology in general, and TBI in particular, but which are known to be critical to interpersonal behavior by social psychologists. For example, the capacity to learn implicitly, over time, relationships that have emotional significance has been argued to be a cornerstone of social intuition (Lieberman, 2000) and results in a store of implicit social knowledge that influences social behavior. Social neuroscience research has suggested that automatic social cognitions are mediated, once again, by the ventral frontal neural system and provide the basis for initial, habitual (stereotypical) responses to social phenomena that may or may not be subsequently regulated by more effortful executive control (Satpute & Lieberman, 2006). Functional neuroimaging work has associated ventral frontal systems with judgments concerning physical attractiveness (Kampe, Frith, Dolan, & Frith, 2001; O'Doherty et al., 2003) and sexual orientation (Ishai, 2007) while amygdala activation has been found when assessing "trustworthiness" based on facial characteristics (Winston, Strange, O'Doherty, & Dolan, 2002). Conversely, focal amygdala damage impairs judgments of trustworthiness (Adolphs et al., 1998) and frontal damage impairs judgments about personality characteristics (made from watching bodily movement) (Heberlein, Adolphs, Tranel, & Damasio, 2004).

There has been very little work that has examined these kinds of judgments in people with TBI, although some methods from social psychology may have utility in this regard. For example, a task that has (controversial) status in social psychology for measuring stereotypic beliefs is the Implicit Association Test (IAT). In this task, reaction time to items that are consistent with stereotypes are compared to reaction time to items that contradict stereotypes. Typically, in normal adults, people respond to the IAT in a manner that suggests they are influenced by social stereotypes (e.g., gender and race) although these same attitudes are not usually endorsed when the participants are asked explicitly about their attitudes on such issues (Greenwald, McGhee,

& Schwartz, 1998). Limited work with the IAT in neurological populations including TBI have produced ambiguous results. Consistent with the notion that the ventral frontal system mediates access to social stereotypes, people with ventro-medial lesions were reported to be less influenced by implicit stereotypes than normal control participants or those with dorsolateral frontal lesions (Milne & Grafman, 2001). On the other hand, work with specifically TBI participants has found that implicit affects were either intact (McDonald, Saad, & James, 2011) or indeed exaggerated (Barker, Andrade, & Romanowski, 2004) The latter findings suggest the influence of impaired executive control rather than implicit awareness on the expression of social attitudes. However, there is much work to be done to prop-erly examine these effects.

Moral Reasoning

One way in which the diminished social behaviors exhibited by people who have sus-tained severe TBI can be characterised is as a disturbance of moral behavior or the ability to follow ethical and accepted rules and norms (Blair & Cipolotti, 2000). Despite this, there has been virtually no research into moral rea-soning capacity following TBI. While failures of moral judgment may be the observed behav-ior, a number of different mechanisms could underpin this. For example, it could result from a loss of the knowledge of right or wrong. It could also result from an inability to rea-son through moral judgments. Alternatively, it could result from deficiencies in emotional responsiveness when confronted with moral dilemmas. According to a model advocated by Greene et al. (2001), people tend to have a salient, automatic emotional response to moral dilemmas that is amplified if they identify with any of the protagonists. In such a case, when moral standards are violated these elicit nega-tive emotional reactions. In humans, these initial emotional reactions can be overridden by subsequent impersonal moral reasoning and rational justifications (Greene, Nystrom, Engell, Darley, & Cohen, 2004). In a study of people with frontotemporal dementia, who share similar patterns of emotional and behav-ioral dysfunction to some people with TBI, it

was found that the clinical group did know moral right from wrong when presented with everyday scenarios, but were *less* reluctant than controls to take a "rational" solution to a moral dilemma (i.e., pushing one person on a railway track to save five people on a run-away trolley) (Mendez, Anderson, & Shapira, 2005). This suggests that they did not have a normal empathic response, in contrast to the control participants. Although there is no work to date with people with TBI, this work highlights the role of emotion in social reasoning tasks.

Communication

The topic of communication has been barely mentioned in this chapter despite the fact that communication is inherently social and that people with TBI present with a range of complex and disabling communication impairments. It is well documented that, following TBI, commu-nicative behavior is often poorly regulated, e.g., there occur frequent interruptions, disinhibited remarks, tangential conversations, egocentric conversational focus, or conversely inert, sparse, and fragmented output (Hartley & Jensen, 1992; McDonald, 1992a). Poor comprehension of con-versational inferences such as sarcasm (Bara, Tirassa, & Zettin, 1997; Channon et al., 2005; Channon & Watts, 2003; Dennis et al., 2001; McDonald, 1992b; McDonald & Flanagan, 2004; McDonald et al., 2003; McDonald & Pearce, 1996; Turkstra, McDonald, & Kaufmann, 1996) has been mentioned in prior sections although there has been virtually no work examining compre-hension of other kinds of conversational infer-ence in this population.

Poor emotion regulation and social cognition are very likely to have a role in communication difficulties but there has been very little work in this area. There has been some work exam-ining the relationship between social cognition and conversational inference, specifically, the role of TOM (Channon, et al., 2005; Martin & McDonald, 2005; McDonald & Flanagan, 2004) and emotion perception (McDonald & Flanagan, 2004; McDonald & Pearce, 1996). Both these aspects of social cognition, along with other non-social deficits such as working memory and information processing speed, do appear to play some role, but this does not appear to be the complete picture. Importantly, the potential contribution of emotional regulation (control and drive) in communication, both in the comprehension of socially inferred meanings (including sarcasm and other conversational inferences) and also communicative interaction has never been addressed. This represents a fascinating new avenue to pursue.

Conclusion

In conclusion, this chapter has overviewed recent advances in understanding how emotional and social processes break down following severe traumatic brain injury. The focus of this chapter has been on relating such deficits to neural structures that have been identified as mediating social and emotional processes in focal lesion and neuroimaging research. Given these same structures are commonly affected by TBI, the overlap is obvious. However, there are unique aspects of neuropathology underpinning TBI that also contribute to our understanding of how social and emotional information is mediated by brain processes. In particular, the role of diffuse axonal injury in delaying information processing and producing inefficiencies in the system needs to be considered.

People with TBI represent an enormously important neurological group for research into emotional and social processes. TBI is the most common cause of brain injury in the Western world and will surpass many diseases as the major cause of death and disability by the year 2020 (Hyder, 2007). There is an urgent need to better understand the neuropsychological underpinnings of the social dysfunction that characterises severe TBI so as to advance assessment and treatment of these disorders. The prevalence of TBI alongside the pressing need for better informed clinical practice also provides an impetus to advance neuropsychological models of social and emotional processes in the brain.

References

Adolphs, R. (2001). The neurobiology of social cognition. *Current Opinion in Neurobiology, 11*, 231–239.

Adolphs, R. (2002). Neural systems for recognizing emotion. *Current Opinion in Neurobiology, 12*(2), 169–177.

Adolphs, R., Damasio, H., & Tranel, D. (2002). Neural systems for recognition of emotional prosody: A 3-D lesion study. *Emotion, 2*(1), 23–51.

Adolphs, R., Damasio, H., Tranel, D., & Damasio, A. R. (1996). Cortical systems for the recognition of emotion in facial expressions. *Journal of Neuroscience, 16*(23), 7678–7687.

Adolphs, R., Russell, J. A., & Tranel, D. (1999). A role for the human amygdala in recognizing emotional arousal from unpleasant stimuli. *Psychological Science, 10*(2), 167–171.

Adolphs, R., & Tranel, D. (2004). Impaired Judgments of Sadness But Not Happiness Following Bilateral Amygdala Damage. *Journal of Cognitive Neuroscience, 16*(3), 453–462.

Adolphs, R., Tranel, D., & Damasio, A. R. (1998). The human amygdala in social judgement. *Nature, 393*, 470–474.

Adolphs, R., Tranel, D., & Damasio, A. R. (2003). Dissociable neural systems for recognizing emotions. *Brain & Cognition, 52*(1), 61–69.

Andrewes, D. (2001). *Neuropsychology: From theory to practice.* Hove and New York: Psychology Press.

Aron, A. R., Robbins, T. W., & Poldrack, R. A. (2004). Inhibition and the right inferior frontal cortex. *Trends in Cognitive Sciences, 8*(4), 170–177.

Bara, B. G., Cutica, I., & Tirassa, M. (2001). Neuropragmatics: Extralinguistic communication after closed head injury. *Brain and Language, 77*(1), 72–94.

Bara, B. G., Tirassa, M., & Zettin, M. (1997). Neuropsychological constraints on formal theories of dialogue. *Brain and Language, 59*, 7–49.

Barker, L. A., Andrade, J., & Romanowski, C. A. J. (2004). Impaired Implicit Cognition with Intact Executive Function After Extensive Bilateral Prefrontal Pathology: A Case Study. *Neurocase, 10*(3), 233–248.

Barrash, J., Tranel, D., & Anderson, S. (2000). Acquired personality distrubances associated with bilateral damage to the ventromedial prefrontal region. *Developmental Neuropsychology, 18*(3), 355–381.

Barry, R. J., Clarke, A. R., Johnstone, S. J., & Rushby, J. A. (2008). Timing of caffeine's impact on autonomic and central nervous system measures: clarification of arousal effects. *Biological Psychology, 77*(3), 304–346.

Barry, R. J., Clarke, A. R., McCarthy, R., Selikowitz, M., & Rushby, J. A. (2005). Arousal and Activation in a continuous performance task: an exploration of state effects in normal children. *Journal of Psychophysiology, 19*(2), 91–99.

Bassili, J. N. (1978). Facial motion in the perception of faces and of emotional expression. *Journal of Experimental Psychology: Human Perception and Performance, 4*, 373–379.

Bate, A. J., Mathias, J. L., & Crawford, J. R. (2001). Performance on the test of everyday attention and standard tests of attention following severe traumatic brain injury. *Clinical Neuropsychologist, 15*(3), 405–422.

Baum, S. R., & Pell, M. D. (1999). The neural bases of prosody: Insights from lesion studies and neuroimaging. *Aphasiology, 13*(8), 581–608.

Bechara, A. (2004). The role of emotion in decision-making: Evidence from neurological patients with orbitofrontal damage. *Brain & Cognition, 55*(1), 30–40.

Bechara, A., Damasio, A., Damasio, H., & Anderson, S. W. (1994). Insensitivity to future consequences following damage to human prefrontal cortex. *Cognition, 50*(1–3), 7–15.

Bechara, A., Damasio, H., & Damasio, A. R. (2000). Emotion, decision making and the orbitofrontal cortex. *Cerebral Cortex, 10*(3), 295–307.

Bechara, A., Damasio, H., Damasio, A. R., & Lee, G. P. (1999). Different contributions of the human amygdala and ventromedial prefrontal cortex to decision-making. *Journal of Neuroscience, 19*(13), 5473–5481.

Bechara, A., Damasio, H., Tranel, D., & Damasio, A. R. (1997). Deciding advantageously before knowing the advantageous strategy. *Science, 275*(5304), 1293–1294.

Bechara, A., Tranel, D., Damasio, H., & Damasio, A. (1996). Failure to Respond Autonomically to Anticipated Future Outcomes Following Damage to Prefrontal Cortex. *Cereb. Cortex, 6*(2), 215–225.

Besson, M., Magne, C., & Schön, D. (2002). Emotional prosody: sex differences in sensitivity to speech melody. *Trends in Cognitive Sciences, 6*(10), 405–407.

Bibby, H., & McDonald, S. (2005). Theory of mind after traumatic brain injury. *Neuropsychologia, 43*(1), 99–114.

Bigler, E. D. (2007). Anterior and middle cranial fossa in traumatic brain injury: relevant neuroanatomy and neuropathology in the study of neuropsychological outcome. *Neuropsychology, 21*(5), 515–531.

Blair, R. J. R., & Cipolotti, L. (2000). Impaired social response reversal: A case of "acquired sociopathy." *Brain, 123*, 1122–1141.

Blair, R. J. R., Morris, J. S., Frith, C. C., Perrett, D. I., & Dolan, R. J. (1999). Dissociable neural responses to facial expressions of sadness and anger. *Brain, 122*(5), 883–893.

Blairy, S., Herrera, P., & Hess, U. (1999). Mimicry and the judgment of emotional facial expressions. *Journal of Nonverbal Behavior, 23*(1), 5–41.

Blumer, D., & Benson, D. F. (1975). Personality changes with frontal and temporal lobe lesions. In D. F. Benson & D. Blumer (Eds.), *Psychiatric aspects of neurologic disease* (pp. 151–170). New York:: Grune & Stratton.

Boice, R. (1983). Observation skills. *Psychological Bulletin, 93*, 3–29.

Bonatti, E., Zamarian, L., Wagner, M., Benke, T., Hollosi, P., Strubreither, W., et al. (2008). Making decisions and advising decisions in traumatic brain injury. *Cognitive and behavioral neurology, 21*(3), 164–175.

Bond, M. R., & Brooks, D. N. (1976). Understanding the process of recovery as a basis for the investigation of rehabilitation for the brain injured. *Scandinavian Journal of Rehabilitation Medicine, 8*(3-4), 127–133.

Bornhofen, C., & McDonald, S. (2008a). Comparing strategies for treating emotion perception deficits in traumatic brain injury. *Journal of Head Trauma Rehabilitation, 23*, 103–115.

Bornhofen, C., & McDonald, S. (2008b). Treating Emotion Perception Deficits Following Traumatic Brain Injury. *Neuropsychological Rehabilitation, 18*, 22–24.

Bowers, D., Coslett, H. B., Bauer, R. M., Speedie, L. J., & Heilman, K. (1987). Comprehension of emotional prosody following unilateral hemispheric lesions: Processing defect versus distraction defect. *Neuropsychologia, 25*(2), 317–328.

Bowler, D. M. (1992). "Theory of mind" in Asperger's Syndrome. *Journal of Child Psychology and Psychiatry, 33*, 877–893.

Broks, P., Young, A. W., Maratos, E., Coffey, P. J., Calder, A. J., Isaac, C. L., et al. (1998). Face processing impairments after encephalitis: Amygdala damage and recognition of fear. *Neuropsychologia, 36*(1), 59–70.

Brooks, D. N., Campsie, L., Symington, C., Beattie, A., & McKinlay, W. (1986). The five year outcome of severe blunt head injury: A relative's view. *Journal of Neurology, Neurosurgery & Psychiatry, 49*(7), 764–770.

Brooks, D. N., Campsie, L., Symington, C., Beattie, A., & McKinlay, W. (1987). The effects of severe head injury on patient and relative within seven years of injury. *Journal of Head Trauma Rehabilitation, 2*(3), 1–13.

Buchanan, T. W., Tranel, D., & Adolphs, R. (2004). Anteromedial Temporal Lobe Damage Blocks Startle Modulation by Fear and Disgust. *Behavioral Neuroscience, 118*(2), 429–437.

Buck, R. (1993). What is this thing called subjective experience? Reflections on the neuropsychology of Qualia. *Neuropsychology, 7*, 490–499.

Buelow, M. T., & Suhr, J. A. (2009). Construct validity of the Iowa Gambling Task. *Neuropsychology Review, 19*(1), 102–114.

Burgess, P. W., Alderman, N., Evans, J., Emslie, H., & Wilson, B. A. (1998). The ecological validity of tests of executive function. *Journal of the International Neuropsychological Society, 4*(6), 547–558.

Cacioppo, J. T., Petty, R. E., Losch, M. E., & Kim, H. S. (1986). Electromyographic activity over facial muscle regions can differentiate the valence and intensity of affective reactions. *Journal of Personality and Social Psychology, 50*, 260–268.

Cavedini, P., Bassi, T., Ubbiali, A., Casolari, A., Giordani, S., & Zorzi, C. (2004). Neuropsychological investigation of decision-making in anorexia nervosa. *Neuropsychological Psychiatry Research, 127*, 259–266.

Channon, S., Pellijeff, A., & Rule, A. (2005). Social cognition after head injury: Sarcasm and theory of mind. *Brain and Language, 93*(2), 123–134.

Channon, S., & Watts, M. (2003). Pragmatic language interpretation after closed head injury: Relationship to executive functioning. *Cognitive Neuropsychiatry, 8*(4), 243–260.

Christodoulou, C., DeLuca, J., Ricker, J. H., Madigan, N. K., Bly, B. M., Lange, G., et al. (2001). Functional magnetic resonance imaging of working memory impairment after traumatic brain injury. *Journal Neurology Neurosurgery Psychiatry, 71*(2), 161–168.

Cicerone, K. D., & Tanenbaum, L. N. (1997). Disturbance of social cognition after traumatic orbitofrontal brain injury. *Archives of Clinical Neuropsychology, 12*, 173–188.

Connolly, J. F., & Frith, C. D. (1978). Effects of varying stimulus context on habituation and sensitisation of the OR. *Physiology and Behavior, 21*, 511–514.

Cornelissen, K., Laine, M., Tarkiainen, A., Jaervensivu, T., Martin, N., & Salmelin, R. (2003). Adult brain plasticity elicited by anomia treatment. *Journal of Cognitive Neuroscience, 15*(3), 444–461.

Corrigan, P. W., & Toomey, R. (1995). Interpersonal problem solving and information processing in schizophrenia. *Schizophrenia Bulletin, 21*(3), 395–403.

Courville, C. B. (1945). *Pathology of the nervous system (2nd Ed.)* Mountain View, CA California Pacific Press.

Critchley, H. D. (2009). Psychophysiology of neural, cognitive and affective integration: fMRI and autonomic indicants. *International Journal of Psychophysiology, 73*, 88–94.

Critchley, H. D., Melmed, R. N., Featherstone, E., Mathias, C. J., & Dolan, R. J. (2001). Brain activity during biofeedback relaxation. A functional neuroimaging investigation. *Brain, 124*, 1003–1012.

Critchley, H. D., Melmed, R. N., Featherstone, E., Mathias, C. J., & Dolan, R. J. (2002). Volitional control of autonomic arousal, A functional magnetic resonance study. *NeuroImage, 16*, 909–912.

Croker, V., & McDonald, S. (2005). Recognition of emotion from facial expression following traumatic brain injury. *Brain Injury, 19*, 787–789.

Crosson, B. (1987). Treatment of interpersonal deficits for head-trauma patients in inpatient rehabilitation settings. *The Clinical Neuropsychologist, 1*(4), 335–352 366.

Crowe, S. F. (1992). Dissociation of two frontal lobe syndromes by a test of verbal fluency. *Journal of Clinical and Experimental Neuropsychology, 14*(2), 327–339.

Cummings, J. L. (1985). *Clinical neuropsychiatry.* New York: Grune & Stratton.

Damasio, A. R., Tranel, D., & Damasio, H. (1990). Individuals with sociopathic behavior caused by frontal damage fail to respond autonomically to social stimuli. *Behavioural Brain Research, 41*(2), 81–94.

Damasio, A. R., Tranel, D., & Damasio, H. (1991). Somatic Markers and the Guidance of Behavior: Theory and Preliminary Testing. In H. S. Levin, H. M. Eisenberg & A. L. Benton (Eds.), *Frontal Lobe Function and Dysfunction* (pp. 217–229). New York: Oxford University Press, Inc.

Darby, D., & Walsh, K. W. (2005). *Walsh's Neuropsychology: A Clinical Approach* (5th ed.). Edinburgh: Elsevier.

Davis, H. L., & Pratt, C. (1995). The development of children's Theory of Mind: The working memory explanation. *Australian Journal of Psychology, 47*, 25–31.

de Sousa, A., McDonald, S., & Rushby, J. (2012). Changes in emotional empathy, affective responsivity and behaviour following severe traumatic brain injury *Journal of Clinical and Experimental Neuropsychology.*

de Sousa, A., McDonald, S., Rushby, J., Li, S., Dimoska, A., & James, C. (2010). Why don't you feel how I feel? Insight into the absence of empathy after severe Traumatic Brain Injury. *Neuropsychologia, 48*, 3585–3595.

de Sousa, A., McDonald, S., Rushby, J., Li, S., Dimoska, A., & James, C. (2011). Understanding deficits in empathy after traumatic brain injury: The role of affective responsivity. *Cortex, 47*(5), 526–535.

Decety, J., & Jackson, P. L. (2004). The functional architecture of human empathy. *Behavioral and Cognitive Neuroscience Reviews, 3*, 71–100.

Demark, J., & Gemeinhardt, M. (2002). Anger and it's management for survivors of acquired brain injury. *Brain Injury, 16*(2), 91–108.

Dennis, M., Purvis, K., Barnes, M. A., Wilkinson, M., & Winner, E. (2001). Understanding of literal truth, ironic criticism, and deceptive praise following childhood head injury. *Brain and Language, 78*, 1–16.

Dimberg, U., & Thunberg, M. (1998). Rapid facial reactions to emotional facial expressions. *Scandinavian Journal of Psychology, 39*, 39–45.

Dimberg, U., Thunberg, M., & Elmehed, K. (2000). Unconscious facial reactions to emotional facial reactions. *Psychological Science, 11*, 86–89.

Dimoska, A., McDonald, S., Kelly, M. A., Tate, R., & Johnstone, S. (2011). A meta-analysis of performance in inhibitory control paradigms in adults with traumatic brain injury (TBI). *Journal of Clinical and Experimental Neuropsychology, 33*, 471–485.

Dimoska, A., McDonald, S., Pell, M. C., Tate, R. L., & James, C. M. (2010). Recognising vocal expressions of emotion following traumatic brain injury: Is the 'what' more important than the 'how'?. *Journal of the International Neuropsychological Society, 16*, 369–382.

Draper, K., Ponsford, J., & Schönberger, M. (2007). Psychosocial and emotional outcomes 10 years following traumatic brain injury. *Journal of Head Trauma Rehabilitation, 22*(5), 278–287.

Dunn, B. D., Dalgleish, T., & Lawrence, A. D. (2006). The somatic marker hypothesis: A critical evaluation. *Neuroscience & Biobehavioral Reviews, 30*(2), 239–271.

Ekman, P., & Friesen, W. V. (1976). Pictures of Facial Affect.

Elsass, L., & Kinsella, G. (1987). Social interaction following severe closed head injury. *Psychological Medicine, 17*(1), 67–78.

Emery, N. J., Capitanio, J. P., Mason, W. A., Machado, C. J., Mendoza, S. P., & Amaral, D. G. (2001). The effects of bilateral lesions of the amygdala on dyadic social interactions in rhesus monkeys (Macaca mulatta). *Behavioral Neuroscience, 115*(3), 515–544.

Eslinger, P. J. (2002). *Neuropsychological Interventions: Clinical research and practice.* New York: The Guilford Press.

Eslinger, P. J. (2008). The frontal lobes: Executive, emotional and neurological functions. In P. Marien & J. Abutalebi (Eds.), *Neuropsychological research: A review* (pp. 379–408). New York: Psychology Press.

Eslinger, P. J., & Grattan, L. M. (1993). Frontal lobe and frontal-striatal substrates for different forms of human cognitive flexibility. *Neuropsychologia, 31*(1), 17–28.

Eslinger, P. J., Satish, U., & Grattan, L. M. (1996). Alterations in cognitive and affectively-based empathy after cerebral damage. *Journal of the International Neuropsychological Society, 2*, 15.

Fellows, L. K., & Farah, M. J. (2005). Different Underlying Impairments in Decision-making Following Ventromedial and Dorsolateral Frontal Lobe Damage in Humans. *Cerebral Cortex. Vol, 15*(1), 58–63.

Felmingham, K. L., Baguley, I. J., Green, A. M., Felmingham, K. L., Baguley, I. J., & Green, A. M. (2004). Effects of diffuse axonal injury on speed of information processing following severe traumatic brain injury. [Comparative Study]. *Neuropsychology, 18*(3), 564–571.

Flanagan, S., McDonald, S., & Togher, L. (1995). Evaluation of the BRISS as a measure of social skills in the traumatically brain injured. *Brain Injury, 9*, 321–338.

Frenchmen, K. A., Fox, A. M., & Mayberry, M. T. (2005). Neuropsychological studies of mild traumatic brain injury: A meta-analytic review of research since 1995. *Journal of Clinical and Experimental Neuropsychology, 27*, 334–351.

Fujiwara, E., Schwartz, M. L., Gao, F., Black, S. E., & Levine, B. (2008). Ventral frontal cortex functions and quantified MRI in traumatic brain injury. *Neuropsychologia, 46*(2), 461–474.

Garcia-Molina, A., Roig-Rovira, T., Ensenat-Cantallops, A., Sanchez-Carrion, R., Pico-Azanza, N., & Pena-Casanova, J. (2007). Examination of decision-making processes in patients with traumatic brain injury. *Neurologia, 22*(4), 206–212.

Gentry, L. R., Godersky, J. C., & Thompson, B. (1988). MR imaging of head trauma: review of the distribution and radiopathologic features of traumatic lesions *American Journal of Roentgenology, 150* 663–672.

Gordon, A. C. L., & Olson, D. R. (1998). The relation between theory of mind and capacity to hold in mind. *Journal of Experimental Child Psychology, 68*, 70–83.

Goudriaan, A. E., Oosterlaan, J., de Beurs, E., & van den Brink, W. (2005). Decision making in pathological gambling: a comparison between pathological gamblers, alcohol dependents, persons with Tourette syndrome, and normal controls. *Cognitive Brain Research, 23*, 137–151.

Grattan, L. M., & Eslinger, P. J. (1989). Higher cognition and social behavior: Changes in cognitive flexibility and empathy after cerebral lesions. *Neuropsychology, 3*(3), 175–185.

Green, R. E. A., Turner, G. R., & Thompson, W. F. (2004). Deficits in facial emotion perception in adults with recent traumatic brain injury. *Neuropsychologia, 42*, 133–141.

Greene, J. D., Nystrom, L. E., Engell, A. D., Darley, J. M., & Cohen, J. D. (2004). The neural bases of cognitive conflict and control in moral judgment. *Neuron, 44*, 389–400.

Greene, J. D., Sommerville, R. B., Nystrom, L. E., Darley, J. M., & Cohen, J. D. (2001). An fMRI investigation of emotional engagement in moral judgement. *Science, 293*, 2105–2107.

Greenwald, A. G., McGhee, D. E., & Schwartz, J. L. K. (1998). Measuring individual differences in implicit cognition: The implicit association test. *Journal of Personality & Social Psychology, 74,* 1464–1480.

Groves, P. M., & Thompson, R. F. (1970). Habituation: a dual process theory. *Psychological Review, 77,* 419–450.

Hadley, D. M., Teasdale, G. M., Jenkins, A., Condon, B., MacPherson, P., Patterson, J., et al. (1988). Magnetic resonance imaging in acute head injury. [Comparative Study Research Support, Non-U.S. Gov't]. *Clinical Radiology, 39*(2), 131–139.

Hanks, R. A., Temkin, N., Machamer, J., & Dikmen, S. S. (1999). Emotional and behavioural adjustment after traumatic brain injury. *Archives of Physical Medication and Rehabilitation, 80,* 991–997.

Happe, F. (1993). Communicative competence and theory of mind in autism: A test of relevance theory. *Cognition 48,* 101–119.

Happe, F., Ehlers, S., Fletcher, P., Frith, U., Johansson, M., Gillberg, C., et al. (1996). Theory of mind in the brain: Evidence from a PET scan study of Asperger Syndrome. *Neuroreport, 8,* 197–201.

Hariri, A. R., Bookheimer, S. Y., & Mazziotta, J. C. (2000). Modulating emotional responses: Effects of a neocortical network on the limbic system. *Neuroreport: For Rapid Communication of Neuroscience Research, 11*(1), 43–48.

Harmer, C. J., Thilo, K. V., Rothwell, J. C., & Goodwin, G. M. (2001). Transcranial magnetic stimulation of medial-frontal cortex impairs the processing of angry facial expressions. *Nature Neuroscience, 4,* 17–18.

Hartley, L. L., & Jensen, P. J. (1992). Three discourse profiles of closed-head-injury speakers: theoretical and clinical implications. *Brain Injury, 6,* 271–282.

Havet-Thomassin, V., Allain, P., Etcharry-Bouyx, F., & Le Gall, D. (2006). What about theory of mind after severe brain injury? *Brain Injury, 20*(1), 83–91.

Heberlein, A. S., Adolphs, R., Tranel, D., & Damasio, H. (2004). Cortical regions for judgments of emotions and personality traits from point-light walkers. *Journal of Cognitive Neuroscience, 16,* 1143–1158.

Heilman, K. M. (2000). Emotional experience: A neurological model. In R. D. Lane & L. Nadel (Eds.), *Cognitive Neuroscience of Emotions* (pp. 328–344). Oxford: Oxford University Press.

Heilman, K. M., Bowers, D., Speedie, L., & Coslett, H. B. (1984). Comprehension of affective and non-affective prosody. *Neurology, 34*(7), 917–921.

Heilman, K. M., Scholes, R., & Watson, R. (1975). Auditory affective agnosia: Disturbed comprehension of affective speech. *Journal of Neurology, Neurosurgery & Psychiatry, 38,* 69–72.

Henry, J. D., Phillips, L. H., Crawford, J. R., Ietswaart, M., & Summers, F. (2006). Theory of mind following traumatic brain injury: The role of emotion recognition and executive dysfunction. *Neuropsychologia, 44*(10), 1623–1628.

Hess, U., & Blairy, S. (2001). Facial mimicry and emotional contagion to dynamic emotional facial expressions and their influence on decoding accuracy. *International Journal of Psychophysiology, 40*(2), 129–141.

Hinson, J. M., Jameson, T. L., & Whitney, P. (2002). Somatic markers, working memory, and decision making. *Cognitive, Affective, & Behavioral Neuroscience, 2,* 341–353.

Hopkins, M. J., Dywan, J., & Segalowitz, S. J. (2002). Altered electrodermal response to facial expression after closed head injury. *Brain Injury, 16,* 245–257.

Hornak, J., Rolls, E., & Wade, D. (1996). Face and voice expression identification in patients with emotional and behavioural changes following ventral frontal lobe damage. *Neuropsychologia, 34*(4), 247–261.

Hughes, C. (1998). Executive function in preschoolers: Links with theory of mind and verbal ability. *British Journal of Developmental Psychology, 16,* 233–253.

Humphrey, G. W., Donnelly, N., & Riddoch, M. J. (1993). Expression is computed separately from facial identity and is computed separately for moving and static faces: Neuropsychological evidence. *Neuropsychologia, 31,* 173–181.

Hyder, A. A. (2007). The impact of traumatic brain injuries: A global perspective. *NeuroRehabilitation, 22,* 341–353.

Ietswaart, M., Milders, M., Crawford, J. R., Currie, D., & Scott, C. L. (2008). Longitudinal aspects of emotion recognition in patients with traumatic brain injury. *Neuropsychologia, 46*(1), 148–159.

Ishai, A. (2007). Sex, beauty and the orbitofrontal cortex. *International Journal of Psychophysiology, 63*(2), 181–185.

Jackson, H. F., & Moffat, N. J. (1987). Impaired emotional recognition following severe head injury. *Cortex, 23,* 293–300.

Johnstone, S. J., Barry, R. J., Markovska, V., Dimoska, A., & Clarke, A. R. (2008). ERPS and task performance during response inhibition and interference control in children with AD/HD. *International Journal of Psychophysiology, 69*(3), 195–195.

Kaganovich, N., Francis, A. L., & Melara, R. D. (2006). Electrophysiological evidence for early interaction between talker and linguistic information during speech perception. *Brain Research, 1114*(1), 161–172.

Kampe, K. K. W., Frith, C. D., Dolan, R. J., & Frith, U. (2001). Reward value of attractiveness and gaze. *Nature, 413,* 589.

Kant, R., Duffy, J. D., & Pivovarnik, A. (1998). Prevalence of apathy following head injury. *Brain Injury, 12*(1), 87–92.

Karmiloff-Smith, A., Klima, E., Bellugi, U., Grant, J., & et al. (1995). Is there a social module? Language, face processing, and theory of mind in individuals with Williams syndrome. *Journal of Cognitive Neuroscience, 7*(2), 196–208.

Keenan, T. (1998). Memory span as a predictor for false belief understanding. *New Zealand Journal of Psychology, 27,* 36–43.

Kelly, M., McDonald, S., & Kellett, D. (Submitted). Development of a Novel Task for Investigating Decision Making in a Social Context Following Traumatic Brain Injury

Kelly, M., McDonald, S., & Rushby, J. (Submitted). The Social Decision Making Task: Psychophysiological Indices of Social Learning Following Brain Injury.

Kendall, E., Shum, D., Halson, D., Bunning, S., & Teh, M. (1997). The assessment of social problem solving ability following traumatic brain injury. *Journal of Head Trauma Rehabilitation, 12,* 68–78.

Kibby, M. Y., Schmitter-Edgecombe, M., & Long, C. J. (1998). Ecological validity of neuropsychological tests: Focus on the California Verbal Learning Test and the Wisconsin Card Sorting Test. *Archives of Clinical Neuropsychology, 13*(6), 523–534.

Kim, S. H., Manes, F., Kosier, T., Baruah, S., & Robinson, R. G. (1999). Irritability following traumatic brain injury. *Journal of Nervous and Mental Disease, 187,* 327–335.

Kinsella, G., Packer, S., & Olver, J. (1991). Maternal reporting of behaviour following very severe blunt head injury. *Journal of Neurology, Neurosurgery & Psychiatry, 54*(5), 422–426.

Lacey, B. C., & Lacey, J. I. (1978). Two-way communication between the heart and the brain. Significance of time within the cardiac cycle. *American Psychologist, 33,* 99–113.

Lacey, B. C., & Lacey, J. I. (1980). Cognitive modulation of time-dependent primary bradycardia. *Psychophysiology, 17,* 209–221.

Lacey, J. I. (1967). Somatic response patterning and stress: some revisions of activation theory. In M. M. Apply & R. Trumbull (Eds.), *Psychological Stress: Issues in Research* (pp. 214–236). New York : Appleton-Century-Crofts.

Lane-Brown, A. T., & Tate, R. L. (2009). Measuring apathy after traumatic brain injury: Psychometric properties of the Apathy Evaluation Scale and the Frontal Systems Behavior Scale. *Brain Injury, 23,* 999–1007.

Leinonen, L., Hiltunen, T., Linnankoski, I., & Laakso, M. L. (1997). Expression of emotional–motivational connotations with a one-word utterance. *The Journal of the Acoustic Society of America, 102*(3), 1853–1863.

Levenson, R. W., Ekman, P., & Friesen, W. V. (1990). Voluntary facial action generates emotion-specific autonomic nervous system activity. *Psychophysiology, 27*(4), 363–384.

Levin, H. S., Grossman, R. G., Rose, J. E., & Teasdale, G. (1979). Long term neuropsychological outcome of closed head injury. *Journal of Neurosurgery, 50,* 412–422.

Levine, B., Black, S. E., Cheung, G., Campbell, A., O'Toole, C., & Schwartz, M. L. (2005). Gambling Task Performance in Traumatic Brain Injury: Relationships to Injury Severity, Atrophy, Lesion Location, and Cognitive and Psychosocial Outcome. *Cognitive and Behavioral Neurology. Vol, 18*(1), 45–54.

Levy, M. L., Cummings, J. L., Fairbanks, L. A., Masterman, D., Miller, B. L., Craig, A. H., et al. (1998). Apathy is not depression. *The Journal of Neuropsychiatry and Clinical Neurosciences, 10*(3), 314–319.

Lew, H., Chmiel, R., Jerger, J., Pomerantz, J., & Jerger, S. (1997). Electrophysiological indices of Stroop and Garner interference reveal linguistic influences on auditory and visual processing. *Journal of the American Academy of Audiology, 8,* 104–118.

Lezak, M. D. (1978). Living with the characterologically altered brain-injured patient. *Journal of Clinical Psychology, 39,* 592–598.

Lieberman, M. D. (2000). Intuition: A social cognitive neuroscience approach. *Psychology Bulletin, 126,* 109–137.

Logan, G. D. (1994). On the ability to inhibit thought and action: A users' guide to the stop signal paradigm. Inhibitory processes in attention, memory, and language. In D. Dagenbach & T. H. Carr (Eds.), *Inhibitory processes in attention, memory, and language* (pp. 189–239). San Diego, CA: Academic Press.

Luria, A. R. (1973). *The working brain.* London: Allen Lane: The Penguin Press.

Macefield, V. G. (2009). Developments in autonomic research: a review of the latest literature. *Clinical Autonomic Research, 19,* 133–136.

Machado, C. J., Emery, N. J., Capitanio, J. P., Mason, W. A., Mendoza, S. P., & Amaral, D. G. (2008). Bilateral neurotoxic amygdala lesions in rhesus monkeys (Macaca mulatta): Consistent pattern of behavior across different social contexts. *Behavioral Neuroscience, 122*(2), 251–266.

Maia, T. V., & McClelland, J. L. (2004). From the Cover: A reexamination of the evidence for the somatic marker hypothesis: What participants really know in the Iowa gambling task. *Proceedings of the National Academy of Sciences, 101*(45), 16075–16080.

Malmo, R. B. (1959). Activation: A neurophysiological dimension. *Psychology Review, 66,* 367–386.

Manes, F., Sahakian, B., Clark, L., Rogers, R., Antoun, N., Aitken, M., et al. (2002). Decision-making processes following damage to the prefrontal cortex. *Brain, 125*(3), 624–639.

Marquardt, T. P., Rios-Brown, M., Richburg, T., Seibert, L. K., & Cannito, M. P. (2001). Comprehension and expression of affective sentences in traumatic brain injury. *Aphasiology, 15*(10–11), 1091–1101.

Marsh, N. V., & Knight, R. G. (1991). Relationship between cognitive deficits and social skill after head injury. *Neuropsychology, 5*(2), 107–117.

Martin, I., & McDonald, S. (2005). Exploring the causes of pragmatic language deficits following traumatic brain injury. *Aphasiology, 19,* 712–730.

Mathias, J. L., & Wheaton, P. (2007). Changes in Attention and Information-Processing Speed Following Severe Traumatic Brain Injury: A Meta-Analytic Review. *Neuropsychology, 21,* 212–223.

McAllister, T. W., Saykin, A. J., Flashman, L. A., Sparling, M. B., Johnson, S. C., Guerin, S. J., et al. (1999). Brain activation during working memory one month after mild traumatic brain injury: A functional MRI study. *Neurology, 12,* 1300–1308.

McAllister, T. W., Sparling, M. B., Flashman, L. A., Guerin, S. J., Mamourian, A. C., & Saykin, A. J. (2001). Differential Working Memory Load Effects after Mild Traumatic Brain Injury. *NeuroImage, 14*(5), 1004–1012.

McDonald, S. (1992a). Communication disorders following closed head injury: New approaches to assessment and rehabilitation. *Brain Injury, 6,* 283–292.

McDonald, S. (1992b). Differential pragmatic language loss after closed head injury: Ability to comprehend conversational implicature. *Applied Psycholinguistics, 13*(3), 295–312.

McDonald, S., Bornhofen, C., Shum, D., Long, E., Saunders, C., & Neulinger, K. (2006). Reliability and validity of 'The Awareness of Social Inference Test' (TASIT): A clinical test of social perception. *Disability and Rehabilitation, 28,* 1529–1542.

McDonald, S., & Flanagan, S. (2004). Social Perception Deficits After Traumatic Brain Injury: Interaction Between Emotion Recognition, Mentalizing Ability, and Social Communication. *Neuropsychology, 18*(3), 572–579.

McDonald, S., Flanagan, S., Martin, I., & Saunders, C. (2004). The ecological validity of TASIT: A test of social perception. *Neuropsychological Rehabilitation, 14,* 285–302.

McDonald, S., Flanagan, S., Rollins, J., & Kinch, J. (2003). TASIT: A New Clinical Tool for Assessing Social Perception after traumatic brain injury. *Journal of Head Trauma Rehabilitation, 18,* 219–238.

McDonald, S., Hunt, C., Henry, J. D., Dimoska, A., & Bornhofen, C. (2010). Angry responses to emotional events: the role of impaired control and drive in people with severe traumatic brain injury. *Journal of Clinical and Experimental Neuropsychology, 32,* 855–864.

McDonald, S., Li, S., De Sousa, A., Rushby, J., Dimoska, A., James, C., et al. (2011). Impaired mimicry response to angry faces following severe traumatic brain injury. *Journal of Clinical and Experimental Neuropsychology, 33*(1), 17–29.

McDonald, S., & Pearce, S. (1996). Clinical insights into pragmatic theory: Frontal lobe deficits and sarcasm. *Brain and Language, 53*(1), 81–104.

McDonald, S., & Pearce, S. (1998). Requests that overcome listener reluctance: Impairment associated with executive dysfunction in brain injury. *Brain and Language, 61,* 88–104.

McDonald, S., Rushby, J., Li, S., de Sousa, A., Dimoska, A., James, C., et al. (2011). The influence of attention and arousal on emotion perception in adults with severe traumatic brain injury. *International Journal of Psychophysiology, 82*(1), 124–131.

McDonald, S., Saad, A., & James, C. (2011). Social dysdecorum following severe traumatic brain injury: Loss of implicit social knowledge or loss of control? *Journal of Clinical and Experimental Neuropsychology, 33*(6), 619–630.

McDonald, S., & Saunders, J. C. (2005). Differential impairment in recognition of emotion across different media in people with severe traumatic brain injury. *Journal of the International Neuropsychological Society, 11*(4), 392–399.

McDonald, S., & van Sommers, P. (1992). Differential pragmatic language loss following closed head injury: Ability to negotiate requests. *Cognitive Neuropsychology, 10,* 297–315.

McFall, R. M. (1982). A review and reformulation of the concept of social skills. *Behavioral Assessment, 4*(1), 1–33.

McHugo, G. J., & Smith, C. A. (1996). The power of faces: A review of John Lanzetta's research on facial expression and emotion. *Motivation and Emotion, 20,* 85–120.

McKinlay, W. W., Brooks, D. N., Bond, M. R., Martinage, D. P., & Marshall, M. M. (1981). The short-term outcome of severe blunt head injury as reported by relatives of the injured persons. *Journal of Neurology, Neurosurgery & Psychiatry, 44*(6), 527–533.

Mehrabian, A. (2000). *Manual for the Balanced Emotional Empathy Scale (BEES).*: Available from Albert Mehrabian, 1130 Alta Mesa Road, Monterey, CA 93040.

Mehrabian, A., & Epstein, N. (1972). A measure of emotional empathy. *Journal of Personality and Social Psychology, 40*(4), 525–543.

Mendez, M. F., Anderson, E., & Shapira, J. S. (2005). An investigation of moral judgement in frontotemporal dementia. *Cognitive and Behavioral Neurology, 18*, 193–197.

Milders, M., Fuchs, S., & Crawford, J. R. (2003). Neuropsychological impairments and changes in emotional and social behaviour following severe traumatic brain injury. *Journal of Clinical & Experimental Neuropsychology, 25*(2), 157–172.

Milders, M., Ietswaart, M., Crawford, J. R., & Currie, D. (2006). Impairments in Theory of Mind Shortly After Traumatic Brain Injury and at 1-Year Follow-Up. *Neuropsychology, 20*(4), 400–408.

Milders, M., Ietswaart, M., Crawford, J. R., & Currie, D. (2008). Social behavior following traumatic brain injury and its association with emotion recognition, understanding of intentions, and cognitive flexibility. *Journal of the International Neuropsychological Society, 14*(Print); (Electronic), 1469–7661.

Milne, E., & Grafman, J. (2001). Ventromedial prefrontal cortex lesions in humans eliminate implicit gender stereotyping. *Journal of Neuroscience, 21*(12), 1–6.

Mitchell, R. L. C., Elliott, R., Barry, M., Cruttenden, A., & Woodruff, P. W. R. (2003). The neural response to emotional prosody, as revealed by functional magnetic resonance imaging. *Neuropsychologia, 41*(10), 1410–1421.

Moody, E. J., McIntosh, D. N., Mann, L. J., & Weisser, K. R. (2007). More than mere mimicry? The influence of emotion on rapid facial reactions to faces. *Emotion, 7*(2), 447–457

Morrison, R. L., & Bellack, A. S. (1981). The role of social perception in social skill. *Behaviour Therapy, 12*, 69–79.

Naccache, L., Dehaene, S., Cohen, L., Habert, M. O., Guichart-Gomez, E., Galanaud, D., et al. (2005). Effortless control: Executive attention and conscious feeling of mental effort are dissociable. *Neuropsychologia. Vol, 43*(9), 1318–1328.

Namiki, C., Yamada, M., Yoshida, H., Hanakawa, T., Fukuyama, H., & Murai, T. (2008). Small orbitofrontal traumatic lesions detected by high resolution MRI in a patient with major behavioural changes. *Neurocase, 14*(6), 474–479.

Newton, A., & Johnson, D. A. (1985). Social adjustment and interaction after severe head injury. *British Journal of Clinical Psychology, 24*, 225–234.

Niedenthal, P. M., Brauer, M., Halberstadt, J. B., & Innes-Ker, Â. H. (2001). When did her smile drop? Facial mimicry and the influences of emotional state on the detection of change in emotional expression. *Cognition & Emotion, 15*, 853–864.

Nigg, J. T. (2000). On inhibition/disinhibition in developmental psychopathology: Views from cognitive and personality psychology and a working inhibition taxonomy. *Psychological Bulletin, 126*(2), 220–246.

Nummenmaa, L., Hirvonen, J., Parkkola, R., & Hietanen, J. K. (2008). Is emotional contagion special? An fMRI study on neural systems of affective cognitive empathy. *NeuroImage, 43*, 571–580.

O'Doherty, J., Winston, J., Critchley, H., Perrett, D., Burt, D., & Dolan, R. (2003). Beauty in a smile: The role of medial orbitofrontal cortex in facial attractiveness. *Neuropsychologia, 41*(2), 147–155.

O'Keeffe, F. M., Dockree, P. M., & Robertson, I. H. (2004). Poor insight in traumatic brain injury mediated by impaired error processing? Evidence from electrodermal activity. *Cognitive Brain Research, 22*(1), 101–112.

Oddy, M., Coughlan, T., Tyerman, A., & Jenkins, D. (1985). Social adjustment after closed head injury: a further follow-up seven years after injury. *Journal of Neurology, Neurosurgery & Psychiatry, 48*(6), 564–568.

Odhuba, R. A., van den Broek, M. D., & Johns, L. C. (2005). Ecological validity of measures of executive functioning. *British Journal of Clinical Psychology. Vol, 44*(2), 269–278.

Ogden, J. A. (2000). Neurorehabilitation in the third millenium: New roles for our environment, behaviors, and mind in brain damage and recovery? *Brain & Cognition, 42*(1), 110–112.

Ozonoff, S., & Miller, G. A. (1996). An explanation of right hemisphere contributions to the pragmatic impairments of autism. *Brain and Language, 52*(411–434).

Pavlov, I. P. (1927). *Conditioned Reflexes.* London: Oxford University Press.

Pell, M. D. (2006). Cerebral mechanisms for understanding emotional prosody in speech. *Brain and Language, 96*(2), 221–234.

Pell, M. D., & Baum, S. R. (1997). The ability to perceive and comprehend intonation in linguistic and affective contexts by brain-damaged adults. *Brain and Language, 57*, 80–99.

Perlstein, W. M., Cole, M. A., Demery, J. A., Seignourel, P. J., Dixit, N. K., Larson, M. J., et al.

(2004). Parametric manipulation of working memory load in traumatic brain injury: Behavioral and neural correlates. *Journal of the International Neuropsychological Society, 10*(05), 724–741.

Phillips, M. L. (2003). Understanding the neurobiology of emotion perception: Implications for psychiatry. *British Journal of Psychiatry, 182*(3), 190–192.

Phillips, M. L., Drevets, W. C., Rauch, S. L., & Lane, R. D. (2003). Neurobiology of emotion perception I: The neural basis of normal emotion perception. *Society of Biological Psychiatry, 54*, 504–514.

Ponsford, J., & Kinsella, G. (1992). Attentional deficits following close head injury. *Journal of Clinical and Experimental Neuropsychology, 14*(5), 822–838.

Ponsford, J., Olver, J. H., & Curran, C. (1995). A profile of outcome: 2 years after traumatic brain injury. *Brain Injury, 9*(1), 1–10.

Prigatano, G. P. (1986). Personality and psychosocial consequences of brain injury. In G. P. Prigatano, D. J. Fordyce, H. K. Zeiner, J. R. Roueche, M. Pepping & B. Casewood (Eds.), *Neuropsychological Rehabilitation after Brain Injury.* (pp. 29–50). Baltimore: John Hopkins University Press.

Prigatano, G. P., & Pribam, K. H. (1982). Perception and memory of facial affect following brain injury. *Perceptual and Motor Skills, 54*(3), 859–869.

Raine, A., Lencz, T., Bihrle, S., LaCasse, L., & Colletti, P. (2000). Reduced prefrontal gray matter volume and reduced autonomic activity in antisocial personality disorder. *Archives of General Psychiatry, 57*(2), 119–127.

Rao, V., & Lyketsos, C. (2000). Neuropsychiatric Sequelae of Traumatic Brain Injury. *Psychosomatics, 41*(2), 95–103.

Robertson, I. H., & Murre, J. M. J. (1999). Rehabilitation of brain damage: Brain plasticity and principles of guided recovery. *Psychological Bulletin, 125*(5), 544–575.

Roche, R. A., Dockree, P. M., Garavan, H., Foxe, J. J., Robertson, I. H., O'Mara, S. M., et al. (2004). EEG alpha power changes reflect response inhibition deficits after traumatic brain injury (TBI) in humans. [Comparative Study Research Support, Non-U.S. Gov't Research Support, U.S. Gov't, P.H.S.]. *Neuroscience Letters, 362*(1), 1–5.

Ross, E. D., & Monnot, M. (2008). Neurology of affective prosody and its functional-anatomic organization in the right hemisphere. *Brain and Language, 104*, 51–74.

Rowe, A. D., Bullock, P. R., Polkey, C. E., & Morris, R. G. (2001). 'Theory of mind' impairments and their relationship to executive functioning following frontal lobe excisions. *Brain, 124*(3), 600–616.

Rubia, K., Russell, T., Overmeyer, S., Brammer, M. J., Bullmore, E. T., Sharma, T., et al. (2001). Mapping motor inhibition: Conjunctive brain activations across different versions of go/no-go and stop tasks. *NeuroImage, 13*, 250–261.

Rushby, J. A., & Barry, R. J. (2007). Event-related potential correlates of phasic and tonic measures of the orienting reflex. *Biological Psychology, 75*(3), 248–259.

Rushby, J. A., & Barry, R. J. (2009). Single-trial event-related potentials to significant stimuli. *International Journal of Psychophysiology, 74*, 120–131.

Sánchez-Navarro, J. P., Martínez-Selva, J. M., & Román, F. (2005). Emotional response in patients with frontal brain damage: Effects of affective valence and information content. *Behavioural Neuroscience, 119*, 87–97.

Santoro, J., & Spiers, M. (1994). Social cognitive factors in brain injury associated with personality change. *Brain Injury, 8*(3), 265–276.

Satpute, A. B., & Lieberman, M. D. (2006). Integrating automatic and controlled processes into neurocognitive models of social cognition. *Brain Research, 1079*(1), 86–97.

Saunders, J. C., McDonald, S., & Richardson, R. (2006). Loss of Emotional Experience After Traumatic Brain Injury: Findings With the Startle Probe Procedure. *Neuropsychology, 20*(2), 224–231.

Saver, J. L., & Damasio, A. R. (1991). Preserved access and processing of social knowledge in a patient with acquired sociopathy due to ventromedial frontal damage. *Neuropsychologia, 29*, 1241–1249.

Scherer, K. R., Banse, R., Wallbott, H. G., & Goldbeck, T. (1991). Vocal cues in emotion encoding and decoding. *Motivation & Emotion, 15*(2), 123–148.

Schlanger, B., Schlanger, P., & Gerstmann, L. (1976). The perception of emotionally toned sentences by right hemisphere damaged and aphasic subjects. *Brain and Language, 3*, 396–403.

Schulte-Rüther, M., Markowitsch, H. J., Fink, G. R., & Piefke, M. (2007). Mirror neuron and theory of mind mechanisms involved in face-to-face interactions: a functional magnetic resonance imaging approach to empathy. *Journal of Cognitive Neuroscience, 19*, 1354–1372.

Seignourel, P. J., Robins, D. L., Larson, M. J., Demery, J. A., Cole, M., & Perlstein, W. M. (2005). Cognitive Control in Closed Head Injury: Context Maintenance Dysfunction or Prepotent Response Inhibition Deficit? *Neuropsychology, 19*(5), 578–590.

Shamay-Tsoory, S., & Aharon-Peretz, J. (2007). Dissociable prefrontal networks for cognitive and affective theory of mind: A lesion study. *Neuropsychologia, 45*, 3054–3067.

Shamay-Tsoory, S., Tomer, R., & Aharon-Peretz, J. (2005). The Neuroanatomical Basis of Understanding Sarcasm and Its Relationship to Social Cognition. *Neuropsychology, 19,* 288–300.

Shamay-Tsoory, S., Tomer, R., Berger, B. D., & Aharon-Peretz, J. (2003). Characterization of empathy deficits following prefrontal brain damage: The role of the right ventromedial prefrontal cortex. *Journal of Cognitive Neuroscience, 15,* 1–14.

Shamay-Tsoory, S. G., Aharon-Peretz, J., & Perry, D. (2009). Two systems for empathy: a double dissociation between emotional and cognitive empathy in inferior frontal gyrus versus ventromedial prefrontal lesions. *Brain, 132,* 617–627.

Soeda, A., Nakashima, T., Okumura, A., Kuwata, K., Shinoda, J., & Iwama, T. (2005). Cognitive impairment after traumatic brain injury: A functional magnetic resonance imaging study using the Stroop task. *Diagnostic Neuroradiology, 47,* 501–506.

Sokolov, E. N. (1960). Neuronal models and the orienting reflex. In M. A. Brazier (Ed.), *The Central Nervous System and Behavior* (pp. 187–276). New York: Josiah Macy, Jr. Foundation Publications.

Sokolov, E. N. (1963). *Perception and the Conditioned Reflex.* New York: Macmillan.

Sonnby-Borgström, M., Jönsson, P., & Svensson, O. (2003). Emotional Empathy as Related to Mimicry Reactions at Different Levels of Information Processing. *Journal of Nonverbal Behavior, 27*(1), 3–23.

Soussignan, R., Ehrle, N., Henry, A., Schaal, B., & Bakchine, S. (2005). Dissociation of emotional processes in response to visual and olfactory stimuli following frontotemporal damage. *Neurocase, 11,* 114–128.

Spell, L. A., & Frank, E. (2000). Recognition of nonverbal communication of affect following traumatic brain injury. *Journal of Nonverbal Behavior, 24*(4), 285–300.

Spiers, M. V., Pouk, J. A., & Santoro, J. M. (1994). Examining perspective-taking in the severely head injured. *Brain Injury, 8,* 463–473.

Spikman, J. M., Timmerman, M. E., Milders, M. V., Veenstra, W. S., & van der Naalt, J. (2012). Social cognition impairments in relation to general cognitive deficits, injury severity, and prefrontal lesions in traumatic brain injury patients. *Journal of Neurotrauma, 29*(1), 101–111.

Sprengelmeyer, R., Young, A. W., Calder, A. J., Karnat, A., & et al. (1996). Loss of disgust: Perception of faces and emotions in Huntington's disease. *Brain: A Journal of Neurology, 119*(5), 1647–1665.

Starkstein, S. E. (1997). Mechanism of Disinhibition After Brain Lesions. *Journal of Nervous & Mental Disease, 185*(2), 108–114.

Steinhauer, K., Alter, K., & Friederici, A. D. (1999). Brain potentials indicate immediate use of prosodic cues in natural speech processing. *Nature Neuroscience, 2,* 191–196.

Stone, V., Baron-Cohen, S., & Knight, R. T. (1998). Frontal lobe contributions to theory of mind. *Journal of Cognitive Neuroscience, 10*(5), 640–656.

Stuss, D. T., Gow, C. A., & Hetherington, C. (1992). "No longer gage": Frontal lobe dysfunction and emotional changes. *Journal of Consulting and Clinical Psychology, 60*(3), 349–359.

Surian, L., Baron-Cohen, S., & Van der Lely, H. (1996). Are children with autism deaf to Gricean maxims? *Cognitive Neuropsychiatry, 1*(1), 55–71.

Tager-Flusberg, H., Sullivan, K., & Boshart, J. (1997). Executive functions and performance on false belief tasks. *Developmental Neuropsychology. 13,* 487–493.

Tassinary, L. G., Cacioppo, J. T., & Berntson, G. G. (2000). The skeletomotor system: Surface electromyography *Handbook of psychophysiology* (*2nd ed.*). (pp. 163–199): Cambridge University Press: New York.

Tate, R. L. (1999). Executive dysfunction and characterological changes after traumatic brain injury: Two sides of the same coin? *Cortex, 35*(1), 39–55.

Tate, R. L., & Broe, G. A. (1999). Psychosocial adjustment after traumatic brain injury: What are the important variables? *Psychological Medicine, 29*(3), 713–725.

Tate, R. L., Fenelon, B., Manning, M., & Hunter, M. (1991). Patterns of neuropsychological impairment after severe blunt head injury. *Journal of Nervous and Mental Disease, 179*(3), 117–126.

Tate, R. L., Harris, R. D., Cameron, I. D., Myles, B. M., Winstanley, J. B., Hodgkinson, A. E., et al. (2006). Recovery of Impairments After Severe Traumatic Brain Injury: Findings From a Prospective, Multicentre Study. *Brain Impairment, 7*(1), 1–15.

Tate, R. L., Lulham, J., Broe, G. A., Strettles, B., & Pfaff, A. (1989). Psychosocial outcome for the survivors of severe blunt head injury: The results from a consecutive series of 100 patients. *Journal of Neurology, Neurosurgery and Psychiatry, 52,* 1128–1134.

Tate, R. L., McDonald, S., & Lulham, J. M. (1998). Incidence of hospital-treated traumatic brain injury in an Australian community. *Australian & New Zealand Journal of Public Health, 22*(4), 419–423.

Thomsen, I. V. (1984). Late outcome of very severe blunt head trauma: A 10-15 year second follow-up. *Journal of Neurology, Neurosurgery & Psychiatry, 47*(3), 260–268.

Tranel, D., Bechara, A., & Denburg, N. L. (2002). Asymmetric Functional Roles of Right and Left Ventromedial Prefrontal Cortices in Social

Conduct, Decision-Making, and Emotional Processing. *Cortex, 38*(4), 589–612.

Trower, P. (1980). Situational analysis of the components and processes of behaviour of socially skilled and unskilled patients. *Journal of Consulting and Clinical Psychology, 3*, 327–339.

Turkstra, L. S., Dixon, T. M., & Baker, K. K. (2004). Theory of Mind and social beliefs in adolescents with traumatic brain injury. *NeuroRehabilitation, 19*(3), 245–256.

Turkstra, L. S., McDonald, S., & Kaufmann, P. M. (1996). Assessment of pragmatic communication skills in adolescents after traumatic brain injury. *Brain Injury, 10*(5), 329–345.

VaezMousavi, S. M., Barry, R. J., Rushby, J. A., & Clarke, A. R. (2007a). Arousal and activation effects on physiological and behavioural responding during a continuous performance task. *Acta Neurobiologiae Experimentalis, 67*(4), 461–470.

VaezMousavi, S. M., Barry, R. J., Rushby, J. A., & Clarke, A. R. (2007b). Evidence for differentiation of arousal and activation in normal adults. *Acta Neurobiologiae Experimentalis, 67*(2), 179–186.

van den Wildenberg, W. P. M., & van der Molen, M. W. (2004). Developmental trends in simple and selective inhibition of compatible and incompatible responses. *Journal of Experimental Child Psychology, 87*(3), 201–220.

Verdejo-Garcia, A. J., Perales, J. C., & Perez-Garcia, M. (2007). Cognitive impulsivity in cocaine and heroin polysubstance abusers. *Addictive Behaviors, 32*(5), 950–966.

Walsh, K. W. (1985). *Understanding brain damage: A primer or neuropsychological evaluation.* Edinburgh: Churchill Livingstone.

Wambacq, I. J. A., & Jerger, J. F. (2004). Processing of affective prosody and lexical-semantics in spoken utterances as differentiated by event-related potentials. *Cognitive Brain Research, 20*(3), 427–437.

Watts, A. J., & Douglas, J. M. (2006). Interpreting facial expression and communication competence following severe traumatic brain injury. *Aphasiology, 20*(8), 707–722.

Webster, W. R., Dunlop, C. W., Simons, L. A., & Aitken, L. M. (1965). Auditory habituation: a test of a centrifugal and a peripheral theory. *Science, 148*(3670), 654–656.

Weddell, R., Oddy, M., & Jenkins, D. (1980). Social adjustment after rehabilitation: A two year follow-up of patients with severe head injury. *Psychological Medicine, 10*(2), 257–263.

Wells, R., Dywan, J., & Dumas, J. (2005). Life satisfaction and distress in family caregivers as related to specific behavioural changes after traumatic brain injury. *Brain Injury, 19*(13), 1105–1115.

Wild, B., Erb, M., & Bartels, M. (2001). Are emotions contagious? Evoked emotions while viewing emotionally expressive faces: quality, quantity, time course and gender differences. *Psychiatry Research, 102*, 109–124.

Williams, C., & Wood, R. L. (2010). Alexithymia and emotional empathy following traumatic brain injury. *Journal of Clinical and Experimental Neuropsychology, 32*(3), 259–267.

Winston, J. S., Strange, B. A., O'Doherty, J., & Dolan, R. J. (2002). Automatic and intentional brain responses during evaluation of trustworthiness of faces.[see comment]. *Nature Neuroscience, 5*(3), 277–283.

Wood, R. L., Liossi, C., & Wood, L. (2005). The impact of head injury neurobehavioural sequelae on personal relationships: preliminary findings. *Brain Injury, 19*(10), 845–851.

Wood, R. L., & Williams, C. (2007). Neuropsychological correlates of organic alexithymia. *Journal of the International Neuropsychological Society, 13*, 471–479.

Wood, R. L., & Williams, C. (2008). Inability to empathize following traumatic brain injury. *Journal of the International Neuropsychological Society, 14*, 289–296.

Young, A. W., Rowland, D., Calder, A. J., & Etcoff, N. L. (1997). Facial expression megamix: Tests of dimensional and category accounts of emotion recognition. *Cognition, 63*(3), 271–313.

Zelazo, P. D., & Cunningham, W. A. (2007). Executive function: Mechanisms underlying emotion regulation. In J. J. Gross (Ed.), *Handbook of emotion regulation* (pp. 135–158.). New York: Guilford.

Zupan, B., Neumann, D., Babbage, D. R., & Willer, B. (2009). The importance of vocal affect to bimodal processing of emotion: Implications for individuals with traumatic brain injury. *Journal of Communication Disorders, 42*, 1–17.

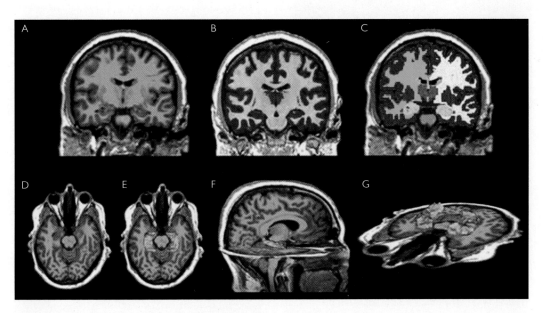

Figure 14-1. (A) T1-weighted coronal image in gray-scale format. (B) Segmentation of the gray scale image where red identifies gray matter, white as white matter and black as CSF. (C) Colorized classified image differentiating different brain regions by color. In this example, the yellow color identifies the hippocampus. (D) Axial view of the T1-weighted image showing the three-dimensional (3-D) identified hippocampus from a top-down view (E), lateral view (F) and left frontal oblique (G). *Summary of Literature to Date in TBI.*

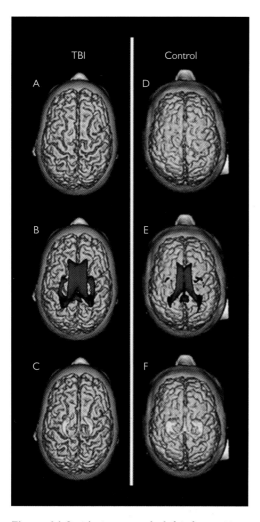

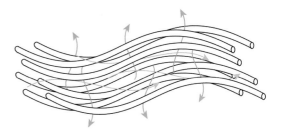

Figure 14-3. A model of diffusion of water molecules through axon bundles. Water molecules move preferentially along the direction of the axon (blue), representing more directional or anisotropic diffusion. However, molecules also move perpendicular to the axons (as indicated by green arrows).

Figure 14-2. The image on the left is from a 14-year old male child who sustained a severe TBI, compared to an age-matched healthy control on the right. A and D show a 3-D rendering of the brain from a top-down perspective where obvious prominence of the cerebral sulci is present, reflective of a more generalized atrophy. B and E show the ventricular dilation (ventricles depicted in blue) present in the child with TBI as compared to the uninjured child, also from a top-down view. The bottom two images (C and F) show a comparison between the two children of the hippocampus with a segment of the fornix (depicted in yellow) attached in the same view. Note the decreased volume in the hippocampus of the child with TBI.

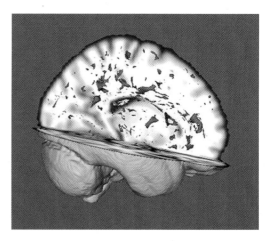

Figure 14-4. Results of a TBSS group analysis of veterans and service members with blast-related mild TBI versus "uninjured" military controls who had also been deployed during the wars in Iraq and Afghanistan. Regions indicated in blue are areas of significant FA decrease in the group with blast-related mild TBI rendered on a three-dimensional template.

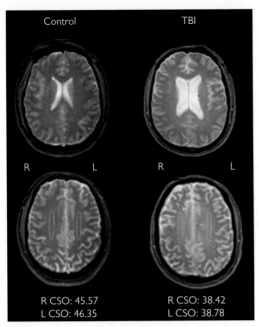

R CSO: 45.57   R CSO: 38.42
L CSO: 46.35   L CSO: 38.78

Figure 14-5. MTR measurement (ROI depicted in light blue) of the right and left hemishere cerebral white matter in the centrum semiovale in a patient with severe TBI (right bottom) as compared to an uninjured control subject of similar age and gender (left bottom). Note the dramatically decreased MTR bilaterally in the patient with TBI despite the absence of a great deal of visible pathology at the level of the centrum semiovale. The top images portray the brains of the same individuals at the level of the lateral ventricles, documenting volume loss.

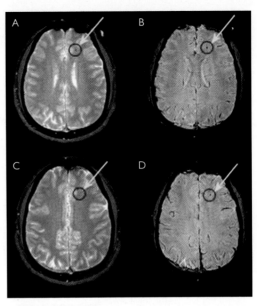

Figure 14-6. Gradient recalled echo (GRE; A) and SWI (B) in a patient with mild TBI (GCS=15; no findings on CT), demonstrating a small hemorrhagic foci (area of hypointensity) in the left frontal white matter (denoted by yellow arrows and red circle). This small bleed is apparent on both conventional GRE and SWI at one level (A), but is not as apparent on a higher slice on the GRE (C) as compared to SWI (D) identification at the same level, demonstrating the superiority of the SWI technique in this case.

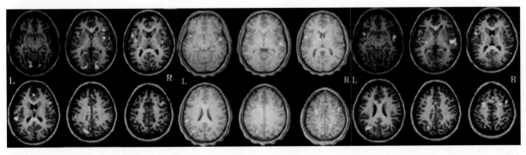

Figure 14-7. Between groups contrasts of working memory activation associated with performance of the Item Recognition Memory Test, which tested recognition memory of 1 item and 4 item sets. Groups included adolescents with moderate to severe TBI and a group of typically developing (TD) adolescents whose demographic background was similar to the TBI group. The brain activation conditions represented in the Figure include (a) Encoding Load 4 minus Load 1 (left panel), (b) Maintenance Load 4 minus Load 1 (center panel), and (c) Retrieval Load 4 minus Load 1 (right panel). The right hemisphere of the brain is displayed on the right side of the figure. Regions that showed significant clusters are displayed in black. The TBI group exhibited greater activation than the TD group under Encoding and Retrieval conditions, whereas the TD group had greater activation than the TBI patients under Maintenance, i.e. the delay period during which storage and rehearsal of the item information occurs. Consistent with the fMRI literature on this task, the TD group had maximum activation under Maintenance relative to Encoding and Retrieval, whereas the TBI group showed greater activation under Encoding and Retrieval as compared with Maintenance. Courtesy of Dr. Mary Newsome.

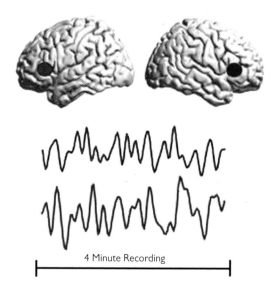

4 Minute Recording

Figure 14-8. A depiction of the general technique of functional connectivity fcMRI, which involves obtaining a BOLD time series from two regions in the brain (indicated here in red and blue) and finding the degree of correlation between the two time series as a measure of connectivity between these two regions. Figure courtesy of Jeff Anderson, MD, Ph.D.

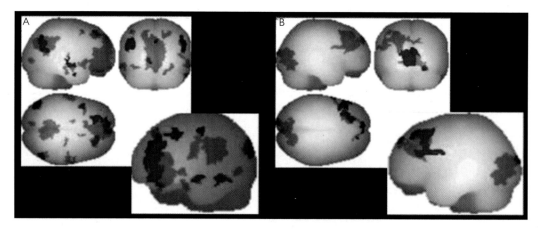

Figure 14-9. Brain regions in which functional connectivity with mesial prefrontal cortex was greater (as depicted in red color) in the group of veterans and service members who had sustained mild to moderate blast-related TBI as compared with the group of veterans who had no TBI or exposure to blast. Regions include areas outside of the default mode and cognitive control networks. Figure courtesy of Mary Newsome, Ph.D.

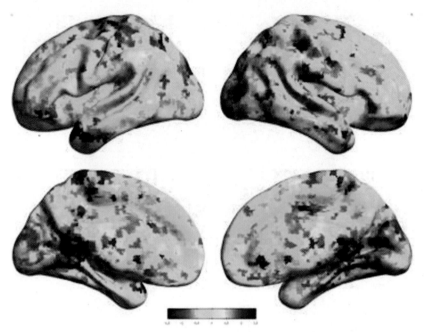

Figure 14-10. For each point in the brain, the degree of "connectedness" of that point to all other points in the brain is measured. Then a t-score is calculated for each connection between mTBI+PTSD and PTSD subjects. The average t-score is shown in color for all connections involving that point, with warmer colors indicating greater connectivity. Values are generally less than zero (cooler colors such as green and blue), meaning that global connectivity to the rest of the brain is lower throughout the brain in the subjects with mTBI (over and above PTSD, since all subjects have PTSD). Figure courtesy of Jeffrey Anderson, M.D., Ph.D.

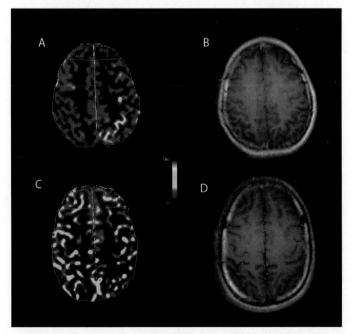

Figure 14-11. Part A demonstrates ASL-derived perfusion in a child with TBI as compared to the perfusion in an uninjured child (B). On the color scale, colors toward the warmer end reflect increased perfusion. Note the relative decreased perfusion in the child with TBI (C), even years post-injury and without obvious focal pathology evident on T1-weighted imaging (D).

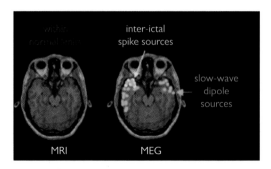

Figure 14-12. In the above image, the subject demonstrates significant slow-wave dipole sources (indicated in green) and interictal spike sources (indicated in yellow) in the temporal lobes as measured by MEG despite the absence of any visible abnormalities on a conventional T1-weighted MRI sequence. Figure adapted with permission from Lewine et al. (1999).

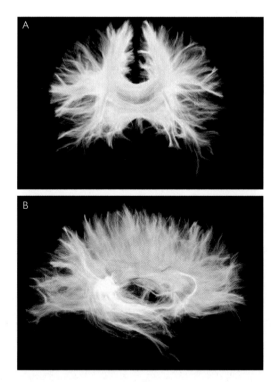

Figure 17-2. Diffusion tensor images of white matter fiber tracts commonly damaged in mTBI (a) coronal view and (b) sagittal view (Shenton et al., 2012). Reprinted from Shenton et al., 2012. Copyright 2012 by Springer Press. Reprinted with permission.

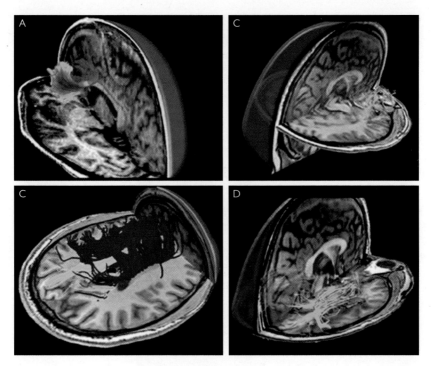

Figure 17-3. Detailed image of diffusion tensor images of white matter fiber tracts commonly damaged in mTBI including (a) the anterior corona and genu of the corpus callosum; (b) the uncinate fasciculus; (c) the cingulum bundle and the body of the corpus callosum and (d) the anterior fasciculus view (Shenton et al., 2012). Reprinted from Shenton et al., 2012. Copyright 2012 by Springer Press. Reprinted with permission.

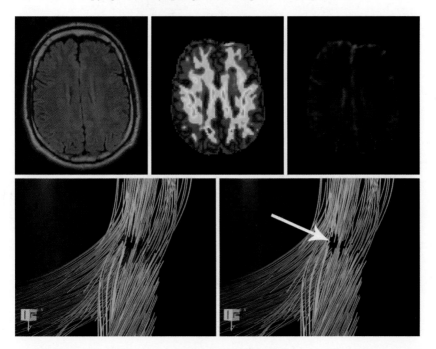

Figure 17-4. Imaging of disruption in white matter tracts within the frontal lobes for an individual with a mTBI 16 months post injury (Rutgers et al., 2008). Reprinted from Rutgers et al., 2008. Copyright 2008 by American Society of Neuroradiology. Reprinted with permission.

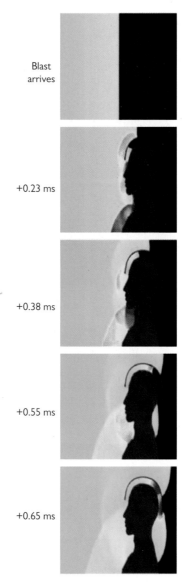

Figure 18-1. The physics of explosives and blast helmets. Pressure contours show the effect of a front-facing blast at various times after detonating 1.5 kg of C4 explosives from a distance of three meters. Black represents 1.0 atmosphere of pressure, and red indicates pressures over 3.5 atmospheres. NRL's Laboratory for Computational Physics and Fluid Dynamics; American Institute of Physics. Adapted from Mott D et al. (33); Accessed 6/22/12.

Part III

Outcomes and Rehabilitation

9

Measuring Outcomes Using the International Classification of Functioning, Disability and Health (ICF) Model, with Special Reference to Participation and Environmental Factors

Robyn L. Tate

Introduction

Bilbao and colleagues (2003) have observed that "professionals working with patients with brain injuries have an extremely complex task. Measuring physical, cognitive, and emotional capabilities; describing and comparing areas and patterns of dysfunction across time and subjects; and identifying, quantifying and initiating intervention are all essential aspects of their work in rehabilitation, consulting, forensic or research settings" (pp. 239-240). Add to this the overwhelming variety and number of available measuring instruments, along with the challenges of selecting the best instrument for the purpose at hand, and that task is a formidable one.

This chapter provides a review of pertinent research on outcome measures used in TBI, within the framework of the International Classification of Functioning, Disability and Health (ICF; WHO, 2001). A systematic review of electronic databases was conducted to identify the type of measures currently used in the research literature on TBI. More than 700 instruments were identified which were classified according to the ICF taxonomy and provide a representative sampling of relevant components and domains. By contrast, examination of published surveys of clinical practice identified gaps in measurement, particularly in the ICF components of participation and

environmental factors. The chapter thus also includes description of a selection of established and newly-developed instruments addressing participation and environmental factors.

What Is Outcome Measurement and Why Is It Important?

The term "outcome" implies a final endpoint that is fixed and immutable. But this is not necessarily the case: a person's outcome at rehabilitation discharge may differ radically from his or her outcome at five years post-trauma. In this sense, outcome is simply a point along the way. According to Dijkers, Whiteneck, and El-Jaroudi (2000, p. S64), "in health care, "outcomes" are those changes in the patients, their actions, behaviors or direct environment that are attributable to the care process, specifically "positive" changes that are the *intended* results of *planned* interventions." Although they indicate that outcome can also refer to "the final unfolding of a series of events," in their view, this is more likely to refer to the "natural history" of a health condition.

There are many practical and important reasons to measure outcome, at whatever point the patient occupies along the recovery continuum: to document improvement or deterioration, for differential diagnosis, to evaluate treatment effectiveness, to identify areas of need, plan treatments, help people make practical decisions, and educate people with TBI and their families and other professionals. Haigh et al. (2001) also highlight the importance of outcome measurement for quality assurance purposes and accountability for justifying expenses and resources. It is clear that no single measure can meet all needs (Wade, 2009) and it is thus necessary for the clinician and researcher to have access to a selection of high quality instruments that are appropriate for the various tasks at hand: "outcome assessment must produce reliable, valid, nonbiased data that reflect the key concerns of end users of the research findings" (Sherer, Roebuck-Spencer, & David, 2010, p. 92).

What Makes a Good Measure?

It would be a mistake to presume that the most frequently used measures in clinical practice and research are necessarily the best ones. Measures are selected for a variety of reasons that may have little to do with their calibre; short administration time and ease of administration and scoring are common reasons that a measure is selected. At a fundamental level, the essential elements of a good measure are the complementary features of reliability and validity. Unreliable measures produce inaccurate results; invalid measures do not assess the construct they purport to measure. Moreover, as Hall, Bushnik, Lakisic-Kazazic, Wright, and Cantagallo (2001, p. 368) have noted "using a measure at the wrong phase of recovery may.…jeopardize the validity of an otherwise valid scale." Scores may well be produced from unreliable or invalid instruments, but they are not useful—and indeed, such scores are misleading. In addition to reliability and validity, there are other features that make for a good measure, and this chapter draws on the framework described by Andresen (2000). The eleven characteristics identified by Andresen involve not only clinical considerations (administrative and respondent burdens, availability of alternate forms, cultural/language adaptations, normative/comparative data), but also conceptual underpinnings of the instrument and strength of its measurement properties (viz., conceptual characteristics, measurement model,

instrument bias, reliability, validity, responsiveness). Each characteristic can be ranked at one of three levels (A to C) which are operationally defined. These criteria are commonly used to provide the "gold standard" against which instruments can be evaluated and compared.

A Framework for Conceptualizing Outcome Measurement after Traumatic Brain Injury—In Other Words, What Areas of Functioning Should Be Measured?

The outcome measures that should be used for TBI are those that evaluate the areas of function that are likely to be compromised by TBI. Having knowledge of vulnerable areas of function is therefore the essential first step in making decisions about the measures that should be used. The ICF provides a framework to comprehensively describe health conditions and thence guidance on what to measure. Descriptions of the ICF and its applications are available from many sources (e.g., Australian Institute of Health and Welfare, 2003; Bruyère, van Looy, & Peterson, 2005; Cerniauskaite et al., 2011; Cieza et al., 2002; de Kleijn-deVrankrijker, 2003; Rauch, Cieza & Stucki, 2008; Stucki, Cieza & Melvin, 2007; Tate & Perdices, 2008; Üstün, Chatterji, Bickenbach, Kostanjsek, & Schneider, 2003; Wade & Halligan, 2003).

The ICF is essentially a taxonomy comprising a list of approximately 1,500 alphanumeric codes describing various aspects of functioning. In order to do this, it adopts a hierarchical, nested structure, described as stem-branch-leaf: There are two *parts* which are subdivided into five *components* (Body Functions, Body Structures, Activities/Participation, Environmental Factors, and Personal Factors). The components, in turn, contain a total of 30 *domains* which are further subdivided into *categories*. In an effort to facilitate a working knowledge of the very large number of ICF codes ($n = 1,424$ at the 3rd and 4th category levels), Tate and Perdices (2008) have graphically depicted the ICF structure of the parts, components, and domains, along with their corresponding codes, as an "ICF tree" to fit to a single page. The basic ICF tree is shown in Figure 9-1 below; ICF trees for the categories are also presented in the above reference.

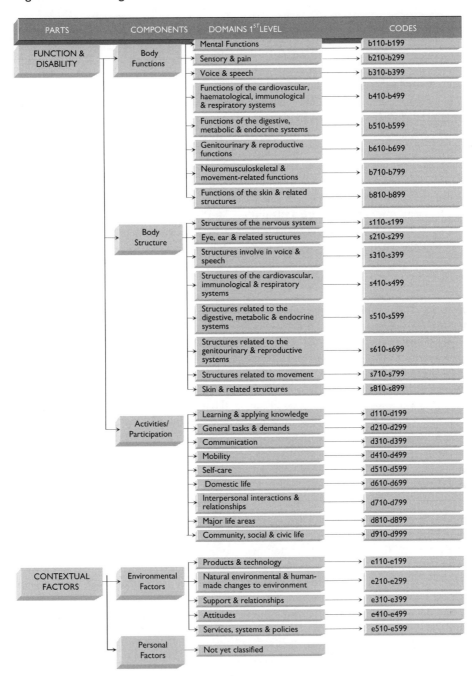

PARTS	COMPONENTS	DOMAINS 1ST LEVEL	CODES
FUNCTION & DISABILITY	Body Functions	Mental Functions	b110-b199
		Sensory & pain	b210-b299
		Voice & speech	b310-b399
		Functions of the cardiovascular, haematological, immunological & respiratory systems	b410-b499
		Functions of the digestive, metabolic & endocrine systems	b510-b599
		Genitourinary & reproductive functions	b610-b699
		Neuromusculoskeletal & movement-related functions	b710-b799
		Functions of the skin & related structures	b810-b899
	Body Structure	Structures of the nervous system	s110-s199
		Eye, ear & related structures	s210-s299
		Structures involve in voice & speech	s310-s399
		Structures of the cardiovascular, immunological & respiratory systems	s410-s499
		Structures related to the digestive, metabolic & endocrine systems	s510-s599
		Structures related to the genitourinary & reproductive systems	s610-s699
		Structures related to movement	s710-s799
		Skin & related structures	s810-s899
	Activities/ Participation	Learning & applying knowledge	d110-d199
		General tasks & demands	d210-d299
		Communication	d310-d399
		Mobility	d410-d499
		Self-care	d510-d599
		Domestic life	d610-d699
		Interpersonal interactions & relationships	d710-d799
		Major life areas	d810-d899
		Community, social & civic life	d910-d999
CONTEXTUAL FACTORS	Environmental Factors	Products & technology	e110-e199
		Natural environmental & human-made changes to environment	e210-e299
		Support & relationships	e310-e399
		Attitudes	e410-e499
		Services, systems & policies	e510-e599
	Personal Factors	Not yet classified	

Figure 9-1. Parts, components and domains of the International Classification of Functioning, Disability and Health, along with their corresponding codes. Adapted from Tate, R. L. & Perdices, M. (2008). Applying the International Classification of Functioning Disability and Health (ICF) to clinical practice and research in acquired brain impairment. *Brain Impairment, 9*(3), 282–292, Figure 2, p. 285, with permission of the authors.

The very large number of ICF categories makes it unwieldy for use in routine clinical practice and most research applications. One initiative to make the ICF more feasible, is the development of "core sets" which are codes that are identified for specific health conditions. They constitute the minimum number of codes that are necessary yet sufficient to describe a health condition, and hence provide a crucial guide for comprehensive outcome measurement. Core sets have been developed for selected neurological conditions, including stroke (Geyh et al., 2004), as well as in different settings, such as early post-acute rehabilitation (Stier-Jarmer et al., 2005). Development of a core set for TBI is currently in progress (Bernabeu et al., 2009; Laxe et al., 2013) and draws on the results of four preliminary studies: a systematic review of the literature, empirical study of the functioning of people with TBI using the extended ICF Checklist, focus groups of people with TBI, and an expert survey. A consensus conference was held in Barcelona, Spain, in March 2010 and using a Delphi procedure, ICF items identified from the four preliminary studies were voted on to produce a comprehensive core set, as well as a brief core set. The comprehensive core set for TBI contains 139 categories and the brief core set contains 23 codes.

At this stage items from the TBI core set are provisional and require validation in a broader study. When validated, the items will provide guidance as to the areas of functioning that should be assessed after TBI. In the interim, guidance on what to measure is available from a study conducted by Koskinen, Hokkinen, Sarajuuri, and Alaranta (2007) who used the ICF Checklist to document the most commonly occurring problems after TBI. A sample of 55 people with TBI representing the range of severity (mild: 35%, moderate: 11%, severe: 54%) was recruited from the Käpylä Rehabilitation Center, Helsinki, Finland. The participants were a subset of 305 patients admitted to the center over a three-year period from 2002 to 2004. Injuries had occurred between 3 months and 15 years previously (M = 2.7 years, SD = 2.6) and were most commonly traffic-related (64%). Median duration of post-traumatic amnesia was 20 days, and median score on the Functional Independence Measure (FIM) was 122 out of a possible score of 126. Patients scoring less than 3 on the extended Glasgow Outcome Scale (GOS-E) were excluded. The ICF Checklist is a summary form of the ICF classification, using 123 items for the ICF categories. Ratings are made on a five-point scale: 0 (not present), 1 (mild impairment/difficulty; present less than 25% of the time), 2 (moderate; 25–49%), 3

(severe; 50–95%), 4 (complete impairment/difficulty; 96-100%). Two clinicians independently completed the ICF Checklist based on information extracted from the written medical records of the patients, comprising documents from the neurologist (n = 55 reports), neuropsychologist (n = 55), nurse (n = 55), occupational therapist (n = 23), physiotherapist (n = 55), speech and language therapist (n = 53) and social worker (n = 54 reports).

The diverse set of problems that are encountered after TBI was confirmed in the Koskinen et al. (2007) study in that 100 of the 123 ICF Checklist categories were endorsed as present. Moreover, both raters documented 30 categories present in at least 30% of the sample and another 18 categories were endorsed by one of the raters for 30% or more. These categories are nested within three of the eight domains of the Body Function component, two of the eight domains of Body Structure, seven of the nine domains of Activities/Participation, and three of the five domains of Environmental Factors, as presented in Table 9-1, and were considered the most relevant problem areas for people with TBI. The remaining 75 of the 123 ICF Checklist categories endorsed by less than 30% of participants were considered less relevant.

In rank order of frequency, mental functions, with 100% endorsement, was the most commonly occurring domain within the Body Functions component, particularly the categories of memory and higher-level cognitive (viz., executive) functions (100% each); attention and emotional functions (96% each); energy and drive (86%); language (76%); sleep (73%); and perceptual (36%) functions. The sensory and pain domain of the Body Functions component ranked second (91%), with the categories of pain (69%), vestibular (including balance; 67%), and seeing (46%) functions agreed by both raters to be present in at least 30%. Impairments in the neuromusculoskeletal and movement related functions domain was present in 65%, with the category of muscle power present in 47%.

Within the Activities/Participation component, communication and major life areas (including work) were the most frequently endorsed domains (100% each), followed by the domestic life and interpersonal interactions and relationships domains (76% each),

Table 9-1. ICF Domains and Categories Rated as Present by Both Raters in 30% or More of the Sample (after Koskinen et al., 2007)

Component	Domain	Category
Body Functions	b1: mental functions: 100%	• memory: 100% • higher level cognitive (viz. executive) functions: 100% • attention: 96% • emotional functions: 96% • energy and drive functions: 86% • language functions: 76% • sleep: 73% • perceptual functions: 36%
	b2: sensory functions and pain: 91%	• pain: 69% • vestibular: 67% • seeing: 46%
	b7: neuro-musculoskeletal- and movement-related functions: 65%	• muscle power: 47%
Body Structures	s1: structure of the nervous system: 100%	• brain (% not specified in report, but >30%)
	s7: structures related to movement: 51%	
Activities/ Participation	d1: learning and applying knowledge: 64%	• solving problems: 60%
	d2: general tasks and demands: 58%	• undertaking multiple tasks: 58%
	d3: communication: 100%	• conversation: 89% • speaking: 82% • communication—receiving spoken messages: 40%
	d4: mobility: 73%	• fine hand use: 46% • driving: 35%
	d6: domestic life: 76%	• acquisition of goods and services: 58% • doing housework: 38%
	d7: interpersonal interactions and relationships: 76%	• complex interpersonal interactions: 69%
	d8: major life areas: 100%	• remunerative employment: 100%
Environmental Factors	e1: products and technology: 82%	• products and technology for personal consumption: 64% • products and technology for personal use in daily living: 49%
	e3: supports and relationships: 89%	• supports and relationships—health professionals: 96% • supports and relationships—immediate family: 82%
	e5: services, systems and policies: 100%	• health services, systems and policies: 100% • social security services, systems and policies: 73%

mobility (73%), general tasks and demands (58%), and learning and applying knowledge (64%). Three of the five domains of the Environmental Factors component were commonly endorsed: services, systems, and policies (100%), supports and relationships (89%) and products and technology (82%). The above 13 domains of functioning, endorsed by both raters for more than 30% of the sample thus constitute a benchmark regarding the areas of functioning at the behavioral level (i.e., excluding the two domains of Body Structures identified (viz. for nervous system and movement)) that should be measured after TBI.

Koskinen et al. (2007) commented on the surprising finding that in the Activities/Participation component, the domain of self-care occurred "rarely" in their sample, and they suggested that this may have been due to the selection criteria, in that the most severely disabled patients were excluded. They also considered that within the Activities/Participation component, the domain of community, social, and civic life was underrepresented, which they attributed to their procedure of collecting data via medical record documentation, that domain not being comprehensively addressed in the context of written documentation within hospital medical records. Nonetheless, the results of this study provide an empirical base on which to guide those areas which require assessment.

Outcome Measures used in TBI Research: A Systematic Review—in Other Words, What Instruments Should be Used to Measure Areas of Functioning?

In order to identify the type of outcome measures that are currently used in the research literature on TBI to assess the functional domains as described in the previous section of this chapter, a systematic search to locate relevant articles published in the last 13 years was conducted using two electronic databases (Medline and PsycINFO) last updated on September 6, 2012 (Tate, Godbee & Sigmundsdottir, 2013). The keywords "measurement" and "traumatic brain injury" were mapped to subject headings and combined with the keywords "tests" or "questionnaires." The following limits were used: articles published between 2000 and 2012, "human," "English language," and "adult." A total of 5,735 records were retrieved and the following exclusion criteria were applied: (i) studies addressing the experience of caregivers or families of people with TBI; (ii) nonbehavioral studies (e.g., neuroradiological, neurophysiological); (iii) reports on the topic of malingering/symptom validity; and (iv) articles that were not full-length publications in peer-reviewed journals.

After exclusions and deletion of duplicates, a final pool of 2,593 unique reports was subject to

further examination. The primary instrument/s used in the study was identified from the title or abstract, yielding 728 separate and unique instruments that met selection criteria. Each instrument was then classified within the ICF framework, using the five components. Multidimensional instruments that encompassed multiple ICF components (e.g., Body Functions and Activities/Participation) were considered separately, as were other measures that addressed concepts not covered by the ICF.

Half of the instruments ($n = 370/728$, 51%) addressed the mental functions domain of the ICF Body Functions component. Many of the objective, performance-based neuropsychological tests identified are described in Lezak, Howieson, Bigler and Tranel (2012), and the rating scales/questionnaires in Tate (2010). Together, they provide a representative evaluation of mental functions and the most frequently occurring ICF categories, as identified by Koskinen et al. (2007). A substantially smaller set of instruments was identified that evaluated specific motor-sensory and other body functions ($n = 64/728$), or were multi-domain across a number of body functions ($n = 32/728$). Almost half of the 109 instruments addressing activities/participation ($n = 48/109$) covered multiple domains, although scales exclusively focusing on communication ($n = 9$), mobility ($n = 27$), and other specific domains were also identified. A small number of instruments examined environmental ($n = 22$) and personal ($n = 36$) factors. An additional 60 instruments were multidimensional, covering multiple ICF components, as well as 35 instruments assessing concepts not covered in the ICF, including quality of life, and rehabilitation tools such as goal-attainment scaling.

Measuring Outcomes in Clinical Practice—In Other Words, What Instruments Are Currently Used in Clinical Practice?

Within the context of the foregoing sections of this chapter, there is evidence to suggest that results of research studies in the area of measuring outcomes after TBI as described in the foregoing have not effectively translated to clinical practice. A survey of 973 rehabilitation practitioners throughout the states of Australia, with 440 respondents (Douglas, Swanson, Gee, & Bellamy, 2005) identified, *inter alia*, the 10 most frequently used measures by 146 practitioners assessing patients with TBI. In rank order of frequency of practitioner usage, the instruments were as follows: Mini Mental State Examination (MMSE; $n = 79$ practitioners); FIM ($n = 74$); Westmead PTA Scale (WPTAS; $n = 65$); Glasgow Coma Scale (GCS; $n = 61$); Rivermead Behavioural Memory Test (RBMT; $n = 39$); Barthel Index—modified (BI-m; $n = 34$); Berg Balance Scale (BBS; $n = 25$); Modified Ashworth Scale (mAS; $n = 23$); Barthel Index—original (BI-o; $n = 12$); and Brisbane Perceptual Screening (BPS; $n = 11$). Eight of the ten instruments are reviewed in Tate (2010). The estimated maximum number of patients per annum assessed with a single measure was 4,701 with the FIM, followed by the MMSE ($n = 4,151$); the estimated minimum number of patients assessed per annum was $n = 13$ with the BI-o, followed by the mAS ($n = 17$).

The results for the TBI group were reported as being essentially the same as those previously found in a similar survey in Europe and the United Kingdom. In that study, Haigh et al. (2001) received responses from 418 out of 866 hospitals and rehabilitation centers surveyed. Within the TBI subset, an estimated 7,217 patients were assessed annually. The most commonly used instrument was the GCS (with 5,002 patients annually), followed by the FIM ($n = 4,214$) and MMSE ($n = 2,350$). The 10th ranking instrument was the Functional Assessment Measure (FAM, used with 1,076 patients annually). Instruments from these two studies are mapped to ICF components in Table 9-2.

Knowledge of the results of these surveys is important for at least two reasons: it informs us about the current state of play and how well the game is being played. As Table 9-2

Table 9-2. Practitioner Survey Results: Classification of the "Top 10" Instruments used in Practitioner Surveys

Body Functions		Activities/ Participation	Contextual factors
Mental functions	Motor-sensory functions		Environmental factors
Douglas et al. (2005)			
Consciousness/orientation: • Glasgow Coma Scale (GCS) • Westmead PTA Scale *Global screen of mental function:* • Mini Mental State Examination (MMSE) *Memory:* • Rivermead Behavioural Memory Test (RBMT) *Perception:* • Brisbane Perceptual Screening	*Motor:* • Modified Ashworth Scale *Sensory:* • Berg Balance Scale	*Activities:* • Barthel Index • Functional Independence Measure (FIM) *Participation:* nil	*Environmental:* nil
Haigh et al. (2001)			
Consciousness/orientation: • Glasgow Coma Scale (GCS) • Galveston Orientation and Amnesia Test (GOAT) *Global screen of mental function:* • Mini Mental State Examination (MMSE) *Memory:* • Rivermead Behavioural Memory Test (RBMT)	*Motor:* nil *Sensory:* nil	*Activities:* • Barthel Index • Functional Independence Measure (FIM) *Participation:* nil	*Environmental:* nil

Multidimensional scales of multiple ICF components: Chessington Occupational Therapy Neurological Assessment Battery, Glasgow Outcome Scale, and Functional Assessment Measure demonstrates, there appears to be a mismatch between, on the one hand, (a) areas identified as relevant to TBI in terms of the ICF (see Koskinen et al., 2007 reviewed above and Table 9-1), along with (b) the types of tests and measures used in the research literature as identified by systematic review (Tate et al., 2013), and on the other hand, the results of the Douglas et al. (2005) and Haigh et al. (2001) surveys of practitioner usage. Many instruments in their lists focus on motor-sensory (BBS, mAS) and functional (FIM, BI-m, BI-o) assessments. By contrast, in both studies cognitive assessment was limited to a brief screening test (MMSE), rating scale (FAM) and a few performance-based tests (RBMT, BPS, Chessington Occupational Therapy Neurological Assessment Battery). In terms of impairments of body (mental) functions, no specific instrument was included in the "top ten" that evaluated language, emotional or behavioral functioning; in terms of other pertinent domains, no measures of community participation or environmental factors were included. If results of these surveys reflect current rehabilitation practice in Australia, Europe, and the United Kingdom (and what is the state of play elsewhere?), then adequate assessment is not being provided regarding the characteristic impairments and common problems confronted by people with TBI, as overwhelmingly documented in the research literature (see also the chapter by Ponsford in this volume). This is a gravely concerning situation.

A number of studies have reported empirical data with a head-to-head comparison of measures. One such study is that of van Baalen, Odding, van Woensel, van Kessel, Roebroeck, and Stam (2006) who aimed to identify measures that would be suitable for use in a minimum data set. Inter-rater reliability and sensitivity to change were examined in a small sample of adult patients (aged 18–50 years) with moderate to severe TBI who were administered a set of measures on two occasions: at discharge from a neurosurgery ward and 12 months later. A set of nine rating scales sampling physical, cognitive, psychosocial and quality of life domains was administered at discharge to 25 patients, and 12 months later a broader selection of 19 measures was administered to 14 patients. The authors concluded that at hospital discharge the

FIM was the most appropriate measure to assess physical limitations, the FAM for the cognitive domain, and the Dartmouth Coop Functional Health Assessment Charts for quality of life. At later stages (viz., 12 months post-trauma in this study) the Neurobehavioral Rating Scale was also considered helpful in the cognitive domain, along with the Frenchay Activities Index for the psychosocial domain, and the Sickness Impact Profile for quality of life. One problem with the measures selected for examination in this study is that they are all rating scales and there were no objective, performance-based measures of cognitive or motor-sensory functioning included in the initial pool. Nor were measures of participation and environmental factors included.

Measuring Participation Outcomes and Environmental Factors

The final section of this chapter describes a selection of scales of participation and environmental factors, these being less well-known and used than the (mainly) functional, activity-based measures commonly employed to measure outcomes. Moreover, as highlighted by Whiteneck and Dijkers (2009, p. S22), "participation and environmental factors are two crucial constructs that have been placed centre stage by the ICF." Yet, they consider that "the measurement of both participation and the environment remains mired in conceptual and operational confusion" (p. S22). Participation is the term used in the ICF that replaces "handicap" which was used to refer to the comparable construct in the precursor to the ICF, the International Classification of Impairments, Disabilities, and Handicaps (ICIDH; WHO, 1980); it also encompasses such terms as psychosocial functioning and community integration. Participation is defined as "involvement in a life situation" and environmental factors as "the physical, social and attitudinal environment in which people live and conduct their lives" (WHO, 2001, p. 10). Community participation is important because the aim of health interventions is ultimately one of participation: that the patient obtains his or her "fullest physical, psychological, social, vocational, avocational, and educational potential" (DeLisa,

Currie, & Martin, 1998, p. 3). Environmental factors play a crucial role in either facilitating or causing barriers to participation. Noreau and Boschen (2010) and Mallinson and Hammel (2010) provide informative analysis of the complex interactions between participation and environmental factors.

Issues in Measuring Participation

It is well recognized that participation is a difficult construct to operationalize and measure (Sander, Clark, & Pappadis, 2010; Whiteneck & Dijkers, 2009; Dijkers, 2010). Over the past two decades an increasing number of scales of participation developed specifically for people with acquired brain impairment have appeared in the research literature (see Tate, 2010 for review). Although many of these instruments cover similar content areas, they differ markedly with respect to conceptual perspectives and scoring procedures. These differences must account for, at least in part, the curious finding of only modest correlation coefficients (in the order of $r = 0.3$-0.5) that sometimes have been reported between different scales of participation. This applies both to total scores, for example, $r = 0.34$ between the Community Integration Measure (CIM) and the Community Integration Questionnaire (CIQ; McColl, Davies, Carlson, Johnston, & Minnes, 2001; Reistetter, Spencer, Trujillo, & Abreu, 2005), and even between subscales sampling similar functional domains, for example, $r = 0.25$ between Social domains of the CIQ and Craig Handicap Assessment and Reporting Technique (CHART; Willer, Rosenthal, Kreutzer, Gordon, & Rempel, 1993); $r = 0.41$ between the respective Productive/Occupational domains of the CIQ and Sydney Psychosocial Reintegration Scale— Form A (SPRS; Kuipers, Kendall, Fleming, & Tate, 2004).

Whiteneck and Dijkers (2009) make a distinction among objective and subjective measures of participation, and quality of life, which they nonetheless argue "are empirically related" (p. S25). In this author's view, however, the descriptive labels of "objective" and "subjective" in the context of participation introduce confusion because the term "subjective" is used with multiple meanings and it is

entrenched in the quality of life literature (cf. subjective well-being). Whiteneck and Dijkers use the term "subjective" to refer to participation instruments that measure the experience and feelings of a person (these types of instruments have also been referred to in the past as client-centered or patient-centered measures). Yet the term "subjective" is also frequently used to refer to a measure in which a qualitative or value judgement is made, as well as a self-report response. In terms of the latter alternative, "objective" measures can be completed with a self-report response and indeed some "objective" scales such as the CIQ and CHART were intentionally designed to be completed as a self-report measure by the person with the injury. This does not make them "subjective" measures, however, in the sense of a client-centered measure. It is suggested that a sharper distinction among the types of participation scales can be gained by avoiding overlapping terminology. Figure 9-2 presents a possible taxonomy to classify scales of participation.

Using the nomenclature in Figure 9-2, the term "exteriorized" is considered a more specific descriptor than "objective" in that it emphasizes the perspective of the measure; the other main type of participation measure is referred to as "client-centered" in preference to "subjective." Although it has been argued that participation is essentially an ideographic construct which is captured by the client-centered perspective, there is also the case to be made that an exteriorized evaluation of participation provides an important complement, and the majority of participation scales are so constructed. Many exteriorized scales quantify participation using a frequency-type approach (e.g., number of hours of work, number of friends, as in the CHART or CIQ). An exclusive emphasis on frequency, however, provides an incomplete perspective of participation; quality is also an important consideration, particularly in the context of TBI where the nature and extent of compromised brain functioning can cause profound changes in the quality of the person's everyday competencies that may not be captured by a frequency count. It is argued that quality can be measured using an external frame of reference and some exteriorized scales attempt to do this

Type of measure

	Exteriorized		Client-centered
	Frequency	Quality	
Other rated (e.g., clinician, family member)	✓	✓	
Self-report	✓	✓	✓

(left vertical axis label: Respondent)

Figure 9-2. A taxonomy for scales of participation.

(e.g., standard of work performance, quality of relationships, as in the SPRS). Scales using such a "quality" perspective are not necessarily client-centered, however, and nor should they be confused with qualitative research methodology, where open-ended responses are coded according to grounded-theory or other model. The rating of "quality" can be done from an exteriorized, quantitative perspective (e.g., a Likert scale from "no change" to "extreme change"), although such evaluation involves a value judgement.

It is also recognized that different respondents can complete a measure, including informants (e.g., clinicians, family members) as well as the person with the brain injury. Self-report is a necessary but not sufficient condition of a client-centered measure. Although self-report with an exteriorized measure introduces a "subjective" component (and for people with major cognitive impairments in memory, judgment or insight may also raise validity issues), it does not make the scale a client-centered measure. To qualify as a client-centered measure, item content needs to address the "perspective of the disability insider, whose life it is" (Brown, Dijkers, Gordon, Ashman, Charatz, & Cheng, 2004, p. 460). Item content and response format of client-centered scales often include concepts such as satisfaction with participation, sense of autonomy, feeling of belongingness—in other words, the person's own feelings or experience

of participation, which by their very nature are qualitative estimations.

Within the group of scales that adopt an exteriorized perspective, the standard against which functioning is measured varies. Having a standard is essential to enable valid interpretation of the score. The standard for some participation scales is societal, using normative data often derived from convenience samples of healthy people living in the community (e.g., CHART, CIQ, SPRS—Form B). Thus, the obtained score is interpreted in terms of functioning compared with the average healthy person in the community. Other scales use comparison or reference data derived from groups of people with brain injury (e.g., Mayo-Portland Adaptability Inventory; MPAI), and for these types of instruments the score obtained is interpreted in terms of functioning compared with the average person with brain injury. Another method uses the person as his or her own control (e.g., SPRS—Form A), whereby the obtained score reflects quantitative and qualitative changes in the individual between pre-injury and post-injury functioning. In the course of selecting an instrument, the clinician or researcher needs to be aware of these different standards and the influence they will inevitably exert on score interpretation. No single standard is inherently better than another, but they do yield different types of information: does one want to know how the person with TBI compares with the average person without a brain injury, or with the average person who has a brain injury, or with their own pre-injury level of functioning?

Published Measures of Participation

An increasing number of instruments to evaluate participation and community integration are available. The scales fall into two classes: generic instruments developed to apply to a range of health conditions and those that are condition-specific. Magasi and Post (2010) provide a comparative review of eight generic scales of participation, along with their relationship to the ICF and six of these eight scales were also included in the systematic review of Noonan, Kopec, Noreau, Singer, and Dvorak (2009) who reviewed 10 participation instruments.

In terms of condition-specific scales used for TBI, Reistetter and Abreu (2005) conducted a systematic review of four electronic databases (PubMed, CINAHL, Sociological Abstracts, Cochrane Library) from 1990 to January 2004. Both generic terms (community integration, community re-integration, community re-entry, participation, and brain injuries) as well as terms pertinent to three participation scales (CIQ, CHART, CIM) were used. They identified 145 articles, of which 72 met eligibility criteria. Six participation measures were identified and in rank order of frequency, they were as follows: CIQ (used in 52 studies), CHART (11 studies), CIM (2 studies), Reintegration to Normal Living Index (RNL; 2 studies), SPRS (2 studies), and Brain Injury Rehabilitation Outcomes (BICRO; 1 study).

Reistetter and Abreu (2005) concluded their review recommending use of the CIQ (and additional return to work information) as outcome measures for evaluating community integration; "moderate evidence" was provided for the CHART in this respect, but "little evidence" for the remaining measures. They pointed to the importance of using both "objective" (cf. exteriorized) as well as "subjective" (cf. client-centered) measures in evaluating community participation, along with the need for further development and validation of measures for community integration. In the eight years since their publication, the latter area has been addressed for some of their measures

and in particular there is now a substantial literature attesting to the very good psychometric properties of the CHART and SPRS. A search of Medline on March 1 2013 using keyword "brain injuries" mapped to subject headings combined with the titles of the above six scales as keywords identified the increasing use of some measures in the literature, although the rank order remains similar. The CIQ (used in 87 studies) remains the most common, followed by CHART (25 studies) and SPRS (24 studies), CIM (11 studies), RNL (3 studies), and BICRO (2 studies). The salient characteristics and psychometric properties of the four more commonly used instruments are summarized in Table 9-3.

Additional scales of participation used with people with TBI are available that were not identified in the Reistetter and Abreu (2005) review. Some of these assess participation in the context of other areas of functioning, for example, Glasgow Outcome Scale-Extended (GOS-E), Functional State Examination (FSE), and MPAI, or alternatively, are client-centered scales, such as the Impact on Participation and Autonomy Questionnaire (IPA) and Participation Objective: Participation Subjective (POPS). The descriptive features and psychometric properties of these scales are also summarized in Table 9-3. Other instruments have been developed within the ICF construct of Activities/Participation (e.g., Assessment of Life Habits; LIFE-H; ICF Measure of Participation and ACTivities; IMPACT-S; World Health Organization Disability Assessment Schedule II; WHODAS 2). These generic instruments are described in detail below.

Assessment of Life Habits (LIFE-H). The LIFE-H is a generic, self-report instrument developed by a Canadian group (Fougeyrollas, Noreau, Bergeron, Cloutier, Dion, & St Michel, 1998) based on their conceptual model of handicap (i.e., the interaction between the person's characteristics, viz., impairments and disabilities, and the environment). Their model addressed shortcomings of the ICIDH: the "serious omission in the [ICIDH] model [was] not to include the environment of an individual as a factor explaining the extent of social consequences following disease or trauma" (p. 129), which was rectified in the revision of the

Table 9-3. Descriptive Featurs of Established Participation Scales Used in TBI

Scale	Item description	Administration time, response format and scoring	Psychometric properties
Community Integration Measure (McColl et al., 2001)	10 items; 4 areas (Assimilation, Social Support, Occupation, Independent Living)	Administration time: 3–5 mins Response format: Likert rating scale, 5-point rating scale: 1 (always agree) to 5 (always disagree) Scoring: Score range 10–50; higher scores = better integration	Internal consistency: alpha coefficient 0.87 Temporal stability: no information Patient-proxy agreement: no information Validity: (i) Factor analysis resulted in a two-factor solution (Belonging; Independent participation) (ii) Concurrent with standard handicap measures is low (CIQ r = 0.34), but higher and statistically significant for more socially focused measures (ISEL r = 0.48) (iii) Discriminant: significant group differences between TBI and two nonbrain-damaged groups (iv) Convergent/divergent: evidence of hypothesized associations with similar and dissimilar constructs of the CIQ Responsiveness: may be subject to ceiling effects; at least 2/10 items had more than 50% obtaining maximum score
Community Integration Questionnaire (Willer et al., 1993)	15 items; 3 subscales (Home Integration, Social Integration, Productive Activities). Revised 13 item version (Sander, Fuchs, High, Hall, Kreutzer, & Rosenthal, 1999)	Administration time: <15 mins Response format: Open-ended responses converted to 3-point rating scale for most items. Scoring: Score range for total 0-29; higher scores = better integration. 13-item version score range 0–25.	Internal consistency: alpha coefficients range 0.35–0.84; 1/3 domains > 0.8 Temporal stability: (7-10 days) 0.83-0.93 for domains Patient-proxy agreement: 0.74–0.96 for all domains Validity: (i) Factor analysis: 3 factors (Home, Social, Productive) (Sander et al., 1999); (ii) Concurrent with DRS (Sander et al. 1999) (e.g., Employability/Productive—r = 0.58; Level of Functioning/ Home Competency—r = 0.46) (iii) Discriminant: significant group differences between TBI and nonbrain damaged groups, and for TBI subgroups with different levels of residential independence (iv) Convergent/divergent: evidence of hypothesized associations with similar and dissimilar constructs of the CHART Responsiveness: significant improvement in treatment group, with large effect size d = 1.18 (Cicerone, Mott, Azulay, & Friel, 2004)

Measure	Items/Dimensions	Administration & Scoring	Psychometric Properties
Craig Handicap and Reporting Technique (Whiteneck, Charlifue, Gerhart, Overholser, & Richardson, 1992)	32 items; 6 dimensions (Physical Independence, Cognitive Independence, Mobility, Occupational, Social Integration, Economic Self-sufficiency)	Administration time: ~15 mins. Response format: interview; open-ended responses. Scoring: responses weighted. Score range 0–100 for each dimension; higher scores = greater independence (percent independence)	Internal consistency: Rasch analysis indicates a well calibrated linear scale. Temporal stability: (1 week): 0.93 for total; > 0.80 for all domains. Patient-proxy agreement: > 0.75 for 3/5 domains; Cognitive domain in TBI sample 0.82. Validity: (i) Concurrent with FIM: r = 0.41 (Segal & Schall, 1995). (ii) Discriminant: significant group differences on 4/5 domains for those rated by clinicians having high vs low handicap. (iii) Convergent/divergent: evidence of hypothesized associations with similar and dissimilar constructs of the FIM (Segal & Schall, 1995). Responsiveness: no information available
Functional Status Examination (Dikmen, Machamer, Miller, Doctor, & Temkin 2001)	10 categories covering 3 broad domains: Physical (Personal care, Ambulation, Travel), Social (Work/School, Home Management, Leisure and Recreation, Social Integration, Financial Independence, Standard of Living), Psychological (Cognitive/Behavioral Competencies)	Administration time: ~ 15 mins. Response format: interview. Scoring: 4-point rating scale: 0 (no change from pre-injury) to 3 (completely dependent on others/does not perform the activity at all). Score range 0–30; higher scores = poorer functioning	Internal consistency: no information available. Temporal stability: (2-3 weeks): rs = 0. 80. Inter-rater reliability: temporal stability was established using different examiners and hence the temporal stability coefficient (r = 0.80) provides an estimate of inter-rater reliability. Validity: (i) Concurrent with GOS: rs = -0.75. (ii) Discriminant: significant group differences among mild, moderate and severe injuries (Hudak et al., 2005). (iii) Convergent/divergent: evidence of hypothesized associations with similar and dissimilar constructs of the SF-36. Responsiveness: significant improvement between 1 and 6 months post-trauma, with large effect size: d = 1.33
Glasgow Outcome Scale (Pettigrew, Wilson & Teasdale, 1998; Teasdale, Pettigrew, Wilson, et al., 1998)	19 items addressing 7 areas (Consciousness, Independence in the Home, Independence outside the Home, Work, Social and Leisure, Family and Friends, Return to Normal Life) + 3 additional "related factors" (e.g., epilepsy)	*Administration time:* no information, but administration is straightforward. *Response format:* Mostly dichotomous (*yes/no*). *Scoring:* Responses to specific items are used to determine GOS category. Category range: 1–8; higher category = better outcome	*Internal consistency:* NA. *Temporal stability:* (6 days) $k_w=0.84$; (16 days) $k_w=0.85$. *Inter-rater reliability:* $k_w=0.85$. *Validity:* (i) concurrent validity with DRS: r=-0.89; Barthel Index: r=0.46; SF-36 subscales: r=0.47-0.71. *Responsiveness:* no information available

(*continued*)

Table 9-3. (continued)

Scale	Item description	Administration time, response format and scoring	Psychometric properties
Impact on Participation and Autonomy Questionnaire (Cardol, de Haan, de Jong, van den Bos, & de Groot, 2001)	39 items, with 31 items assessing "perceived participation" in 5 domains (Autonomy Indoors, Family Role, Autonomy Outdoors, Social Relations, Work/ Educational Opportunities) and 8 items addressing "perceived problems"	Administration time: ~30 mins Response format: Perceived participation: 5-point rating scale: 1 (very good) to 5 (very poor); Perceived problems: 3-point scale: 0 (no problem) to 2 (severe problem) Scoring: Scores summed separately for each domain; higher scores = greater restrictions	Internal consistency: alpha coefficients range 0.81-0.91 for domains Temporal stability: (15 days) ICC = 0.83-0.91 for domains Patient-proxy agreement: no information available Validity: (i) Factor analysis: 4 factors: Autonomy Indoors, Family Role, Autonomy outdoors, Social Relations (ii) Concurrent with SF-36 Physical: range r = -0.26 to -0.51; SF-36 Mental: range r = 0.43-0.50 (iii) Convergent/divergent: evidence of hypothesized associations with similar and dissimilar constructs of the London Handicap Scale Responsiveness: small effect size over 3 months for some domains: ~d = 0.1
Mayo-Portland Adaptability Inventory (Malec & Lezak, 2003/2008)	35 items, with 29 core items in 3 scales: Ability, Adjustment and Participation; the 6 "non-core" items are not scored	Response format: 5-point rating scale, with response descriptors tailored to individual items: 0 (equivalent of no problem) to 4 (equivalent of severe problem) Scoring: Summed raw scores for each scale and total score can be converted to T-scores, for comparison with other brain injury groups; higher scores = greater problems	Internal consistency: alpha coefficients 0.89; Rasch analysis indicated a well calibrated scaleTemporal stability: no information available Patient-proxy agreement: at item level range 27% to 70% Validity: (i) Factor analysis: 7 components—not labeled (ii) Concurrent with Disability Rating Scale r = 0.81 (iii) Discriminant: significant group differences between Levels 7 and 8 of the Rancho Levels of Cognitive Functioning scale (iv) Convergent/divergent: evidence of hypothesized associations with similar and dissimilar constructs from cognitive tests Responsiveness: significant differences between pre-treatment and discharge scores, with large effect size: d = 1.21
Participation Objective Participation Subjective (Brown, Dijkers, Gordon, Ashman, Charatz & Cheng, 2004; Brown, 2010)	26 items; 2 components (Participation Objective (PO), Participation Subjective (PS)), 5 subscales for each component (Domestic Life; Interpersonal Interactions and Relationships; Major Life Areas; Transportation; Community, Recreation and Civic Life).	Administration time: reported as 10-20 mins Response format: PO component: rating scale of factual/ frequency data which varies for each subscale; PS component: 2 rating scales: 5-point "importance" scale and 3-point "desire to change" scale	Internal consistency: subscale-total correlations: PO r = 0.35-0.63; PS r = 0.60-0.73Temporal stability: 1-3 weeks: total scores—PO ICC = 0.75; PS ICC = 0.80 Patient-proxy/interrater agreement: no information Validity: (i) concurrent validity PO with BDI r = -0.21 (mild TBI); -0.19 (moderate/severe TBI); PS with BDI r = -0.43 (mild TBI); -0.39 (moderate/severe TBI)

		(ii) discriminant validity: PS mild TBI M = -0.40 vs moderate/severe TBI M = 0.1; but no differences on PO component Responsiveness: no information available

Scoring: PO component uses a statistical program (SPSS); higher scores = better functioning.

PS component multiplies importance score for each item (range 0–4) by the change score (-1 or +1); using the mean of the 26 items total PS score ranges from-4 to +4; higher scores = higher subjective satisfaction

---

Sydney Psychosocial Reintegration Scale (Tate, et al., 1999; 2011)

12 items; 3 domains (Occupational Activity, Interpersonal Relationships, Independent Living Skills)

Originally 7-point rating scale ("no change" to "extreme change"). Score range for total 0-72. Higher scores = better reintegration; Revised to 5-point scale (SPRS-2); Tate et al., 2011); score range for total 0-48.

Internal consistency: alpha coefficients range 0.70 to 0.89; > 0.8 for 1/3 domains; Rasch analysis on SPRS-2 showed good fit to the modelStability: (1 month) ICC = 0.90
Interrater agreement: ICC = 0.95 scharge scores
Validity:
(i) factor analysis: 2 dimensions: productivity/personal life and independent/dependent
(ii) concurrent validity with GOS r = -0.77, LHS r = -0.85, SIP r = -0.76;
(iii) Discriminant: significant group differences among GOS subgroups;
(iv) Convergent/divergent: convergent validity with similar domains on SIP (e.g., Psychosocial/Relationships -0.76), and discriminant validity with dissimilar domains (e.g., Physical/Relationships -0.23)
Responsiveness:
significant group differences between admission and discharge scores, with large effect size d = 2.15 (Tate et al., 1999); significant improvement after intervention, with large effect size d = 0.81 (Simpson et al., 2004)

ICIDH, resulting in the ICF. The authors developed a comprehensive set of categories covering "life habits," defined as "daily activities and social roles that ensure the survival and development of a person in society throughout his or her life" (p. 130). The scale was initially constructed and tested in French and the authors subsequently translated it to English. A Dutch version has also been validated (Lemmens, van Engelen, Beurskens, Wolters, & de Witte, 2007). Following examination of its content validity with 12 rehabilitation experts (Fougeyrollas et al., 1998), item content underwent slight revision.

The LIFE-H was initially described as having short (58 items) and long (248 items) forms (Fougeyrollas et al., 1998). Item content of the short form, however, appears not yet to be finally established: version 3.0 is described in Noreau, Desrosiers, Robichaud, Fougeyrollas, Rocjette, and Viscogliosi (2004), and contains 69 items; Poulin and Desrosiers (2009) describe version 3.1 with 77 items. The short form of the LIFE-H currently contains 12 categories that form two subscales: the Daily Activities subscale (containing the categories of Nutrition with 4 items, Fitness 4 items, Personal care 8 items, Communication 8 items, Housing 8 items and Mobility 5 items) and the Social Roles subscale (containing the categories of Responsibility with 8 items, Interpersonal Relationships 7 items, Community Life 8 items, Education 3 items, Employment 7 items, and Recreation 7 items). Leemons et al. (2007) found that administration time for the short form in samples of stroke and healthy older people was on average 25 mins, but the range was large (15–90 mins).

Each item is rated on a 10-point scale that integrates level of difficulty and type of assistance required from 0 (not performed) to 9 (performed with no difficulty and no assistance). Examples of intermediate ratings are 8 (performed with no difficulty but technical aid/adaptation used); 2 (performed with difficulty with technical aid/adaption and human assistance). The mean score is used for each of the 12 categories, two subscales and total score (range 0–9, with higher scores indicating better functioning), which overcomes the issue of the categories having a variable number of items.

Psychometric properties of the LIFE-H have been published with samples of both adults and children with a range of health conditions, including spinal cord injury and stroke. Current evidence is promising. In terms of reliability, the summary scores show excellent two-week temporal stability in adults (intraclass correlation coefficient (ICC) = 0.83), although, using the short form, coefficients were lower for children (ICC = 0.67; Fougeyrollas et al., 1998); for respective scores for total, daily activities, and social roles Noreau et al. (2004) reported test-retest ICCs = 0.95, 0.96, 0.76; Lemmons et al. (2007) reported ICCs = 0.80, 0.78, 0.78. Inter-rater reliability of the respective summary scores was also excellent (ICCs = 0.89, 0.91, 0.64; Noreau et al., 2004). In all reliability studies, however, some of the categories had low coefficients. Summary scores show strong evidence of concurrent validity with the IPA (r = 0.82, 0.82, 0.80 respectively) and discriminant validity with group differences between chronically ill and healthy older people (Lemmons et al., 2007). Content validity was established in an initial investigation (Fougeyrollas et al., 1998). No information is currently available on the responsiveness of the LIFE-H.

ICF Measure of Participation and ACTivities (IMPACT-S).

The IMPACT-S (Post, de Witte, Reichrath, Verdonschot, Wijhuizen, & Perenboom, 2008) was developed from the ICF itself rather than an item pool. It is a generic, self-report instrument that has two levels: Level 1 is a 33-item[1] "screener" and Level 2 is a longer version, which is still in the developmental stages and will contain a series of modules. Post and colleagues recognized that the ICF makes no recommendation in partitioning the Activities/Participation component, and so they adopted the approach of no overlap. The initial version of the IMPACT-S was pilot tested in two small samples: 11 people injured in road traffic crashes and 18 rehabilitation professionals. Results were used to refine item content.

---

[1] Van der Zee et al. (2010) describe the IMPACT-S as a 32-item scale. In the final version of the IMPACT-S the two items on economic transactions were merged (personal communication, M. Post, 8 March, 2013).

The 32 items of the final version of the Level 1 screener are grouped into the nine domains of the ICF Activities/Participation component. The Activities section of the IMPACT-S contains five subscales: Learning and Applying Knowledge (3 items), General Tasks and Demands (2 items), Communication (3 items), Mobility (7 items), and Self-Care (3 items). The Participation section contains four subscales: Domestic Life (4 items), Interpersonal Interactions and Relationships (4 items), Major Life areas (2 items), and Community, Social and Civic (4 items). Items are rated on a 3-point scale[2] : no limitation, minor limitation, major limitation. Summary scores use the mean of the item scores for relevant subscales, which are then converted to a 0-100 point scale, with higher scores indicating better functioning.

Psychometric properties of the IMPACT-S are reported in Post et al. (2008) who studied a sample of 275 people injured in road traffic crashes, 37% of whom also sustained TBI. Current evidence is promising. Internal consistency was excellent, both for the total score and the Activities and Participation sections (Cronbach alpha coefficients of 0.96, 0.92, and 0.92 respectively). Temporal stability was examined in a subset of the sample (n = 197) who completed the IMPACT-S four weeks later, again with excellent results (ICCs = 0.94, 0.93, and 0.90 respectively). Principal components analysis extracted two components, although the factor loadings did not reflect the Activities/Participation split of the subscale structure. There was strong evidence of concurrent validity with comparable domains of the WHODAS II, ranging from r = 0.61 (IMPACT-S Major life Areas versus WHODAS II Life Activities subscales) to r = 0.79 (IMPACT-S Mobility versus WHODAS II Getting Around). Correlation between the total scores of the two scales was r = 0.88. No information is yet available on the responsiveness of the IMPACT-S.

World Health Organization Disability Assessment Schedule 2 (WHODAS 2).

The WHODAS 2 (WHO, 2000/2011), like the LIFE-H and IMPACT-S, is a generic, self-report instrument, suitable for use with a variety of health conditions. It is a revision of the WHO Disability Assessment Schedule (WHODAS), which aimed to evaluate social adjustment and behavioral disturbances in people with mental disorders. The WHODAS 2 is a (slight) refinement of the WHODAS II (WHO, 2000), which "represents a complete revision" of the original WHODAS, incorporating the different conceptual underpinnings of the ICF Activities/Participation component, aiming to assess functioning in everyday activities. It was not designed solely for people with mental disorders, or necessarily for it to be clinician-rated. A series of field trials was conducted in order to develop and refine item content.

The WHODAS 2 is an important instrument, in that it is the disability measure both developed and endorsed by the World Health Organization. It is a 36-item scale (32 items for respondents who do not work) that covers six activity domains, as well as overall disability. The six domains and their items directly map to the ICF Activities/Participation component: Cognition (six items, which also includes the cognitive areas of concentration, learning, memory and problem solving), Mobility (five items), Self-Care (four items), Getting Along with Other People (five items), Life Activities (which address domestic areas, four items, as well as school/employment areas, four items), and Participation in Society (8 items). A short 12-item form is also available, with self, informant, and interviewer-administered versions. The scale is available from the WHO website (http://www.who.int/icidh/whodas/index.html) and also includes reference to a manual. Administration time for the 36-item version is 20 minutes, and the 12-item version takes five minutes.

Responses are made in terms of difficulties experienced in the past 30 days. A five-point scale is used: 1 (equivalent of no difficulties) to 5 (extreme/cannot do). For the 36-item version, scores are available for each of the six domains and an overall score. The WHODAS 2 website describes two scoring methods: The "simple scoring method" uses the sum of the items, without regard to weighting. An alternative method of scoring applies weights to items to take into account different levels of difficulty of

---

[2] Van der Zee et al. (2010) use a fourth response category (*cannot do at all*)

the items. A computer program for this purpose is available from the WHO website. Using the computer program, the final score ranges from 0 to 100, with higher scores indicating greater difficulty.

Psychometric studies available for the WHODAS II with brain-injured populations are limited, but available evidence shows areas of strength. The sample of 904 rehabilitation patients studied by Pösel, Cieza, and Stucki (2007) included 116 patients with stroke. Internal consistency of the scale with this group was excellent (Cronbach alpha coefficients for the domains ranged from 0.84–0.97); there was evidence of concurrent validity with the Medical Outcomes Study Health Survey Short Form-36 (SF-36) with moderate magnitude coefficients (Physical: $r = 0.62$; Mental: $r = 0.50$) and evidence of convergent/divergent validity with hypothesized similar and dissimilar constructs of the SF-36. Effect sizes following a rehabilitation intervention were, however, small, providing limited evidence of its responsiveness in this sample. In the study of Chisholm, Abrams, McArdle, Wilson, and Doyle (2005), who examined 380 older adults with hearing loss on two occasions with a two-week interval, temporal stability was excellent (ICC = 0.93 for total score; ICC = 0.81–0.91 for domains).

Published Measures of Enviromental Factors

Environmental Factors are defined in the ICF as encompassing five disparate domains: products and technology; natural environmental and human-made changes to the environment; support and relationships; attitudes; and services, systems and policies. It is a new construct within the ICF and no instruments were previously available that provided a comprehensive overview of Environmental Factors as defined. Two recently developed instruments are available that were constructed according to the ICF model and provide an overview of Environmental Factors: Craig Hospital Inventory of Environmental Factors (CHIEF) and Measure of Quality of the Environment (MQE). In the domain of supports and relationships, two types of measures are pertinent: those addressing functional social supports (candidate measures being Social Support Survey, SSS, and Interpersonal Support and Evaluation List, ISEL) and those assessing more practical supports (such as the Care and Needs Scale, CANS, and the Northwick Park Care Needs Assessment, NPCNA). These six instruments are described below.

(i) Overview measures of environmental factors

Craig Hospital Inventory of Environmental Factors (CHIEF). The CHIEF (Whiteneck, Harrison-Felix, Mellick, Brooks, Charlifue, & Gerhart, 2004) is a generic, self-report scale that measures perceived negative environmental influences or barriers to functioning. It was carefully developed, using results from a series of two-day meetings of a group of 32 people with expertise in disabilities (including consumers, family members, and advocacy groups, clinicians, governmental agencies), as well as pilot testing. The CHIEF contains 25 items in five subscales: (i) Physical and Structural (six items); (ii) Attitudes and Support (five items); (iii) Services and Assistance (seven items); (iv) Policy (four items); and (v) Work and School (three items). Administration time is 10 to 15 mins. A 12-item short form is also available, comprising two to three items from each of the subscales.

Items are rated on a five-point scale for frequency of occurrence: 0 (never); 1 (less than monthly); 2 (monthly); 3 (weekly); 4 (daily); and those items with a score of 1 or higher are also rated in terms of the magnitude of the problem (1 = a little problem; 2 = a big problem). The total and subscale scores use the mean score of endorsed items (range 0–8), with higher scores representing greater perceived environmental barriers. Normative data are available in Whiteneck, Harrison-Felix, et al., 2004) for a large sample ($n = 1,788$).

Psychometric properties of the CHIEF have been examined in multiple samples with good results. Principal components analysis of data from a population-based telephone survey of 2,269 people extracted five components which formed the five subscales. A clinical sample of 409 people, including 120 with TBI, was used to examine internal consistency (Cronbach alpha coefficients of 0.93 for total score; and 0.76–0.81 for subscales) and two-week temporal stability in a subset (n = 103) which was excellent (ICC = 0.93 for total score, 0.77–0.89 for subscales). The report of Whiteneck, Gerhart, and Cuisick (2004) used a clinical sample of 73 people with TBI to examine concurrent and convergent/divergent validity. The CHIEF showed a statistically significant although low correlation with the CHART (r = -0.38) and there was support for hypothesized relationships with the CHART subscales. No information is available on responsiveness of the CHIEF.

Measure of Quality of the Environment (MQE). The MQE (Fougeyrollas, Noreau, & St-Michel, 1997), like the CHIEF, is a generic, self-report instrument, designed to assess the perceived influence of physical and social environmental factors (both positive and negative) on participation. An important strength of the MQE is the inclusion of facilitators as well as barriers. It was initially developed in French, within the same conceptual framework developed by the authors that was used in the construction of the LIFE-H, described earlier in this chapter. Their group, the Québec Committee (QC) of the ICIDH was formed to improve an understanding of the disablement process, and had proposed that a new concept, environmental factors, be introduced to the ICIDH (Fougeyrollas, 1995). In constructing the MQE, a list of 84 situations and factors covering most environmental categories of their model was generated and grouped into six themes which formed the categories of the scale. Content validity was formally examined with a group of clinicians and researchers.

Version 2.0 of the MQE comprises 109 items in six categories: Support and Attitudes of Family and Friends (14 items); Income, Job and Income Security (15 items); Governmental and Public Services (27 items); Equal Opportunity and Political Orientation (10 items); Physical Environment and Accessibility (38 items); and Technology (5 items). The first four categories are described as encompassing the social environment and the last two categories relate to the physical environment. Only those items that apply to the individual's circumstances are rated, which reduces administration time of this lengthy instrument.

Responses are made on a seven-point rating scale, ranging from -3 to +3 and including zero. Negative responses indicate barriers (from -3 = *major barrier* to -1 = *minor barrier*), and conversely, positive responses indicate facilitators (from +1= *minor facilitator* to +3 = *major facilitator*). The zero response is made when an item (environmental factor) does not influence social participation for the respondent. Scores are summed separately for barriers and facilitators. A higher absolute numerical value indicates greater facilitators if the score is positive, or greater barriers if the score is negative.

Limited information is available in English about the psychometric properties of the MQE. In a stroke sample (n = 51 without aphasia or cognitive impairment, six months after discharge from rehabilitation) Rochette, Desrosiers, and Noreau (2001) found evidence for concurrent validity with the LIFE-H for barriers (r = 0.42), but not facilitators (r = -0.08); convergent and divergent validity was supported with hypothesized similar and dissimilar constructs of the MQE and LIFE-H. Temporal stability over a two-week period with the initial 84 item version was good for 44% of the items (n = 37/84 with k > 0.6; Boschen, Noreau, & Fougeyrollas, 1998). Information on the responsiveness of the MQE is not available.

(ii) Measures of social support

Interpersonal Support and Evaluation List (ISEL). The ISEL (Cohen, Mermelstein, Karmack, & Hoberman, 1985) measures perceived social supports. It was developed within the context of the literature on stress, appraisal, and coping, and specifically the protective role of social supports against stress. Social supports were defined as the resources that are provided by other people, and four categories were suggested: tangible support (i.e., material aid); appraisal support (someone to talk to about one's problems); self-esteem support (availability of a positive comparison in relation to others); and belonging support (people available with whom to do things). Cohen et al. (1985, p. 89) consider that "the most important contribution of the scale is the ability to indicate the type of resources that operate to improve health and well-being in any particular situation."

The general population version of the ISEL, available from the following website (http://www.psy.cmu.edu/~scohen/ISEL.html), contains 40 items which are grouped into four dimensions, each with 10 items: Tangible support, Appraisal support, Self-Esteem support, and Belonging support. Responses are made using a four-point scale: definitely true, probably true, probably false, definitely false. The scale is designed for self-report and is easily completed. Half of the items require reverse scoring. The score range is 0 to 120, with higher scores indicating greater perceived social support.

Psychometric studies of the ISEL in neurological populations are limited. McColl et al. (2001) used an adapted version of the ISEL in a TBI sample and found evidence of concurrent validity with the CIM ($r = 0.43$) and CIQ ($r = 0.34$). Discriminant validity in distinguishing between groups with high versus low stress ($p < 0.02$) was reported by Cohen and Hoberman (1983). Six-week temporal stability was studied in a sample of 64 people attending a smoking cessation program (Mermelstein, Cohen, and Lichtenstein (1983; cited in Cohen et al., 1985) with adequate results (type of reliability coefficient not specified: 0.70 for total; dimension range 0.63–0.69). Responsiveness has not been reported.

Social Support Survey (SSS). The SSS (Sherbourne & Stewart, 1991) is a self-rating scale, designed to measure the perceived availability of functional supports in patients with "chronic conditions." They distinguished between functional and structural approaches to measuring social support. Structural social support refers to the social network—"the existence and quantity of social relationships" (Sherbourne & Stewart, 1991, p. 705), whereas functional social support has a qualitative component in that it refers to "the degree to which interpersonal relationships serve particular functions." The SSS was developed using judges to allocate an initial pool of 50 items to categories. Item content was then piloted and refined.

The 19 items represent five dimensions of functional social support: (i) Emotional support (4 items, e.g., empathic understanding from other people); (ii) Informational support (4 items, e.g., offering of advice); (iii) Tangible supports (4 items, e.g., provision of material aid);

(iv) Affectionate support (3 items, e.g., expression of love); and (v) Positive social interactions (4 items, e.g., availability of other people for recreation). An additional two items (marital status and number of people in whom the person can confide) provide contextual background, but are not scored. The SSS is an easily completed, self-administered scale. Responses for the 19 functional items are made on a five-point scale: 1 (none of the time), 2 (a little of the time), 3 (some of the time), 4 (most of the time), 5 (all of the time). Mean scores are generally used, thereby anchoring the score back to the five response categories, resulting in an easily interpreted metric.

Psychometric properties of the SSS are not currently available for TBI or other neurological groups, but in patients with other health conditions they are sound. Sherbourne and Stewart (1991) examined the measurement characteristics of the SSS in a large sample ($n = 2,987$) drawn from the U.S. population Medical Outcomes Study. Internal consistency was excellent (Cronbach alpha 0.97; dimension range 0.91–0.96). Concurrent validity was demonstrated with a range of variables, such as loneliness ($r = -0.67$) and family functioning ($r = 0.53$). Convergent and divergent validity was established with hypothesized similar and dissimilar constructs. Confirmatory factor analysis produced four factors: a combined Emotional/Informational support factor and three factors comparable to the remaining three SSS dimensions. Yu, Lee, and Woo (2004) used a Chinese version of the SSS in a sample of 110 cardiac patients and found moderate correlation with the Hospital Anxiety and Depression Scale ($r = -0.58$; dimension range $r = -0.53$ to -0.60). Two-week temporal stability in that sample was excellent (ICC = 0.84). No information on responsiveness has been reported.

(iii) Measures of practical supports

Care and Needs Scale (CANS). The CANS (Tate, 2004) is a condition-specific scale that was specifically developed for adults with TBI; a children's version is also available (Soo, Tate, Williams, Waddington, & Waugh, 2008). It is a summary document, intended to be clinician-completed, that can be administered in face-to-face interview, clinician-completed based on knowledge of the patient/client, and also has the facility of being able to be completed based on information obtained from multiple sources to document those support needs that are required to engage in everyday functional activities and community living. The CANS (adult version) contains two sections: (i) the Needs Checklist comprises 24 items that match eight of the nine ICF Activities/Participation domains and assess the *type* of support need (ranging in intensity, e.g., from tracheostomy management through to informational supports); (ii) the Support Levels comprise an eight-level classificatory scale that relates to three of the five ICF Environmental Factors: (e1: products and technology, e3: supports and relationships, and e5: services, systems and policies). The Support Levels are hierarchically arranged from 0 (equivalent of does not need contact for support) to 7 (cannot be left alone). A distinctive feature of the CANS is that it has three intermediate response categories between full independence (Level 0) and needing support for part of each day (Level 4), thereby enabling it to capture support requirements of people whose needs are less than daily.

Each of the 24 items from the Needs Checklist is endorsed by the clinician if the person has a need in that area, irrespective of its nature or extent. This information is then used to classify the needs into one of the eight Support Levels, using prepared conversion procedures. Some degree of clinical judgment is used in synthesizing the information from the Needs Checklist and converting it to a Support Level, and also taking account of current contextual factors in the individual's life that may have bearing on the level of support required. Training in this decision-making process is covered in a two-hour training workshop and general principles are described in the manual. Administration time when based on the clinician's knowledge of the patient is very brief, a matter of minutes; alternatively, the CANS can be completed interview-style with a knowledgeable informant in which case it takes 10 to 15 mins.

The psychometric properties of the CANS have been examined in independent TBI samples with very good results. It shows excellent inter-rater reliability with three clinicians (ICC = 0.93-0.96) and 1-week temporal stability (ICC = 0.98) in a sample of 30 people with TBI who were living in the community (Soo et al., 2007). A sample of 40 people with TBI receiving inpatient rehabilitation was used to examine criterion validity, both concurrent and six-month predictive with the Supervision Rating Scale ($r = 0.68$ and 0.43 respectively), FIM ($r = -0.59$ and -0.41), SPRS ($r = -0.54$ and -0.47) and Disability Rating Scale (DRS; $r = 0.64$ and 0.42), yet there was evidence of divergent validity with a measure of personality (NEO-Five Factor Inventory; subscale range $r = 0.07–0.16$; Soo et al., 2010). The CANS also showed discriminant validity when the sample was stratified on injury severity (duration of post-traumatic amnesia), FIM and DRS scores. That sample was also used to examine responsiveness between rehabilitation discharge and six-month follow-up and a large effect size ($d = 0.98$) was found.

Northwick Park Care Needs Assessment (NPCNA). The NPCNA (Turner-Stokes, Nyein, & Halliwell, 1999) is a clinician rating scale, used in conjunction with the Northwick Park Dependency Score (NPDS) developed by the same research group (Turner-Stokes, Tonge, Nyein, Hunter, Nielson, & Robinson, 1998). It was specifically designed for people with acquired brain impairment living in the community and was developed to provide a direct measure of the patient's needs, operationalized as the amount of time taken and number of staff required to attend to a patient. The NPCNA provides a directly-costable care package tailored to the patient's needs.

Items from the NPDS ($n = 12$, but some items contain sub-items, making 16 in total) and NPCNA ($n = 5$) focus on self-care, mobility, communication, and behavior. Ratings are made using a variable format, with the total score ranging from 0 to 100. A simple computer program, available from the author (lynne.turner-stokes@dial.pipex.com), provides automatic calculation of NPCNA output: an estimate of the number of hours of care, the configuration, and the cost. Fourteen care packages are described, ranging from domestic assistance to two live-in caregivers. Completion time for the NPCNA is very quick, approximately five minutes for the ratings and another five minutes for the calculation of the care package.

Psychometric properties of the NPDS on which the NPCNA is based are very good. The NPDS shows excellent inter-rater reliability for the total score ($r = 0.90$; although there is some variability at the item level, with $r < 0.6$ for 4/16 items) and two-day temporal stability ($r = 0.93$). The NPDS also shows very high correlation with the Barthel Index ($r = -0.91$). Post, Visser-Meily, and Gispen (2002) reported on responsiveness finding moderate to large effect sizes ($d = 0.58/1.3$ for four-week/admission-discharge ratings respectively). In terms of psychometric properties of the NPCNA, Turner-Stokes et al. (1999) found very high correlation ($r = 0.90$) between the NPCNA and the usual 40 to 60 minute detailed structured interview. Nyein, Turner-Stokes, and Robinson (1999) examined responsiveness of the NPCNA in 39 patients comparing admission and discharge scores during inpatient neurorehabilitation ($p < 0.001$). Strong correlation coefficients were also found between the NPCNA and FIM ($r = -0.77$ admission; $r = -0.84$ discharge).

Concluding Remarks

Systematic review of the literature described in this chapter reveals the availability of more than three hundred instruments to measure mental functions alone in people with TBI, as well as more than 100 measures of activities/participation (Tate et al., 2013). By contrast, other areas of body functioning and contextual factors rely on far fewer instruments. Whether this is because the small number of available instruments already adequately assesses these components and domains, or that additional instruments need to be developed, or that such components are less frequently addressed in the research literature is unclear and will require further examination. Within the mental functions and activities/participation areas, however, new instruments which have been developed to improve measurement of these complex constructs continually appear in the literature. With respect to measures of participation and environmental factors, Whiteneck and Dijkers (2009, p. S22) hold an extreme view that "despite decades of work and publication

of scores of instruments, there is no commonly accepted, metrically sound tool to measure either of these constructs." Their group's work in developing the Participation Assessment with Recombined Tools—Objective (PART-O; Whiteneck et al., 2011), in which the best items from multiple scales were selected to produce a single "recombined tool," is offered as a solution to this problem and may also serve the purpose of reducing instrument redundancy.

Although Wade (2003) lamented the limited development of scales of participation and their rare appearance in clinical trials, and notwithstanding the complexities of measuring the participation construct (Whiteneck & Dijkers, 2009), the field is presently at an exciting point in time. Some good scales, as reviewed in this chapter, are available, which have been subject to a careful developmental process and have sound psychometric properties. In terms of client-centered measures, instruments yielding both detail (IPA, POPS) and overview (CIM, RNL) provide an essential perspective that is not captured by the more commonly-used exteriorized and quantitative scales. Newly-developed generic measures drawing on the ICF Activities/Participation component, such as the LIFE-H, IMPACT-S and WHODAS 2, as well as those adopting both an exteriorized and client-centered perspective (e.g., Utrecht Scale for Examining Rehabilitation—Participations; USER-P; Post et al., 2012) show promise, but have yet to be validated with TBI populations. The older condition-specific scales of participation developed for or validated with people with TBI, (such as the, CHART, CIQ, FSE, MPAI and SPRS), still have a place in that they capture the specificity of consequences of TBI in a way that generic measures find difficult to match. They also address the essential elements of the construct of participation (viz., occupation, relationships, and community living), are psychometrically sound, and have accumulated a substantial body of data from multiple research studies and clinical service sites.

Recognition of the role of environmental factors in the ICF model has opened up a previously neglected area of research activity and clinical practice. Because it is a newly identified area warranting evaluation, it is anticipated that the current dearth of appropriate measuring instruments will be gradually rectified. All rehabilitation professionals use environmental factors to a greater or lesser extent, and some domains are addressed better than others. Rehabilitation is often seen as synonymous with provision of aids and technology (cf, ICF e1), along education of families, employers, educators, and others who will come into contact with the person with TBI (cf. ICF e4, attitudes); by contrast, with some notable exceptions, many services have a long way to go in terms of including and empowering families in the rehabilitation process, in relation to supports and relationships (cf. ICF e3). The current challenge is to develop a range of instruments suitable to evaluate the variety of environmental factors that apply to people with TBI.

In the context of the above comments, the field is not yet in a position to authoritatively recommend a minimum core set of instruments that provide a necessary yet sufficient evaluation of functioning after TBI. Efforts made to date are generally based on an ad hoc selection of some 10 to 20 instruments that are heavily biased to functional activities (see Tate et al., 2013). Clearly, development of a representative core set of instruments is an important challenge in measuring outcomes after TBI. The systematic work conducted by Bernabeu and colleagues (2009) and Laxe et al. (2013) in the development of an ICF core set for TBI is a critical initial step in this direction. Thereafter it will be important that adequate instruments are available which are representative of the functions that need evaluation after TBI.

Acknowledgments

I thank my colleagues, Drs. Michael Perdices, Grahame Simpson and Cheryl Soo, for helpful discussions on the conceptual structure and measurement of participation.

References

Andresen, E. M. (2000). Criteria for assessing the tools of disability outcomes research. *Archives of Physical Medicine and Rehabilitation, 81*(Suppl. 2), S15–S20.

Australian Institute of Health and Welfare. (2003). *ICF Australian user guide. Version 1.0.* Canberra: Australian Institute of Health and Welfare.

Bernabeu, M., Laxe, S., Lopez, R., Stucki, G., Ward, A., Barnes, M., et al. (2009). Developing core sets for persons with traumatic brain injury based on the International Classification of Functioning, Disability and Health. *Neurorehabilitation and Neural Repair, 23*(5), 464–467.

Bilbao, A., Kennedy, C., Chatterji, S., Üstün, B., Barquero, J. L. V., & Barth, J. T. (2003). The ICF: applications of the WHO model of functioning, disability and health to brain injury rehabilitation. *NeuroRehabilitation, 18*, 239–250.

Boschen, K. A., Noreau, L., & Fougeyrollas, P. (1998). Reliability studies of the Measure of the Quality of the Environment (MQE). *Canadian Journal of Rehabilitation, 11*(4), 184–185.

Brown, M. (2010). Participation: the insider's perspective. *Archives of Physical Medicine and Rehabilitation, 91*(Suppl.1), S34–S37.

Brown, M., Dijkers, M. P. J. M., Gordon, W. A., Ashman, T., Charatz, H., & Cheng, Z. (2004). Participation Objective, Participation Subjective: A measure of participation combining outside and insider perspectives. *Journal of Head Trauma Rehabilitation, 19*(6), 459–481.

Bruyère, S. M., Van Looy, S. A., & Peterson, D. B. (2005). The International Classification of Functioning, Disability and Health: Contemporary literature overview. *Rehabilitation Psychology, 50*(2), 113–121.

Cardol, M., de Haan, R. J., de Jong, B. A., van den Bos, G. A., & de Groot, I. J. M. (2001). Psychometric properties of the Impact on Participation and Autonomy Questionnaire. *Archives of Physical Medicine and Rehabilitation, 82*(2), 210–216.

Cerniauskaite, M., Quintas, R., Boldt, C., Raggi, A., Cieza, A., Bickenbach, J. E., & Leonardi, M. (2011). Systematic literature review on ICF from 2001 to 2009: its use, implementation and operationalization. *Disability and Rehabilitation, 33*(4), 281–309.

Cicerone, K. D., Mott, T., Azulay, J., & Friel, J. C. (2004). Community integration and satisfaction with functioning after intensive cognitive rehabilitation for traumatic brain injury. *Archives of Physical medicine and Rehabilitation, 85*, 943–950.

Chisholm, T. H., Abrams, H. B., McArdle, R., Wilson, R. H., & Doyle, P. J. (2005). The WHO-DAS II: Psychometric properties in the measurement of functional health status in adults with acquired hearing loss. *Trends in Amplification, 9*(3), 111–126.

Cieza, A., Brockow, T., Ewert, T., Amman, E., Kollerits, B., Chatterji, S., et al. (2002). Linking health-status measurements to the International Classification of Functioning, Disability and Health. *Journal of Rehabilitation Medicine, 34*(5), 205–210.

Cohen, S., & Hoberman, H. M. (1983). Positive events and social supports as buffers of life change stress. *Journal of Applied Social Psychology, 13*(2), 99–125.

Cohen, S., Mermelstein, R., Karmack, T., & Hoberman, H. M. (1985). Measuring the functional components of social support. In: I. G. Sarason & B. R. Sarason (Eds.), *Social support: Theory, research and application* (pp. 73–94). Dordrecht: Martinus Nijhoff.

DeLisa, J. A., Currie, D. M., & Martin, G. M. (1998). Rehabilitation Medicine. Past, present and future. In: J. A. DeLisa, & B. M. Gans (Eds). *Rehabilitation medicine. Principles and practice.* (3rd ed.) (pp. 3–32). Philadelphia, USA: Lippincott-Raven.

de Kleijn-deVrankrijker, M. W. (2003). The long way from the International Classification of Impairments, Disabilities and Handicaps (ICIDH) to the International Classification of Functioning, Disability and Health (ICF). *Disability and Rehabilitation, 25*(11–12), 561–564.

Dikmen, S., Machamer, J., Miller, B, Doctor, J., & Temkin, N. (2001). Functional Status Examination: A new instrument for assessing outcome in traumatic brain injury. *Journal of Neurotrauma, 18*(2), 127–140.

Dijkers, M. P. (2010). Issues in the conceptualization and measurement of participation: an overview. *Archives of Physical Medicine and Rehabilitation, 91*(Suppl.1), S5–S16.

Dijkers, M. P., Whiteneck, G., & El-Jaroudi, R. (2000). Measures of social outcomes in disability research. *Archives of Physical Medicine and Rehabilitation, 81*(Suppl. 2), S63–S80.

Douglas, H., Swanson, C., Gee, T., & Bellamy, N. (2005). Outcome measurement in Australian rehabilitation environments. *Journal of Rehabilitation Medicine, 37*, 325–329.

Fougeyrollas, P. (1995). Documenting environmental factors for preventing the handicap creation process: Québec contributions relating to ICIDH and social participation of people with functional differences. *Disability and Rehabilitation, 17*(3/4), 145–153.

Fougeyrollas, P., Noreau, L., Bergeron, H., Cloutier, R., Dion, S-A., & St-Michel, G. (1998). Social consequences of long term impairments and disabilities: Conceptual approach and assessment of handicap. *International Journal of Rehabilitation Research, 21*, 127–141.

Fougeyrollas, P., Noreau, L., & St-Michel, G. (1997). The Measure of the Quality of Environment. *ICIDH and Environmental Factors International Network, 9*, 32–39.

Geyh, S., Cieza, A., Schouten, J., Dickson, H., Frommelt, P., Omar, Z., et al. (2004). ICF Core sets for stroke. *Journal of Rehabilitation Medicine, 44*, 134–141.

Haigh, R., Tennant, A., Biering-Sorensen, F., Grimby, G., Marinček, Č., Phillips, S., et al. (2001). The use of outcome measures in physical rehabilitation within Europe. *Journal of Rehabilitation Medicine, 33*, 273–278.

Hall, K. M., Bushnik, T., Lakisic-Kazazic, B., Wright, J., & Cantagallo, A. (2001). Assessing traumatic brain injury outcome measures for long-term follow-up of community-based individuals. *Archives of Physical Medicine and Rehabilitation, 82*(3), 367–374.

Hudak, A. M., Caesar, R. R., Frol., A. B., Krueger, K., Harper, C. R., Temkin, N. R., et al. (2005). Functional outcome scales in traumatic brain injury: A comparison of the Glasgow Outcome Scale (Extended) and the Functional Status Examination. *Journal of Neurotrauma, 22*(11), 1319–1326.

Koskinen, S., Hokkinen, E-M., Sarajuuri, J., & Alaranta, H. (2007). Applicability of the ICF Checklist to traumatically brain-injured patients in post-acute rehabilitation settings. *Journal of Rehabilitation Medicine, 39*, 467–472.

Kuipers, P., Kendall, M., Fleming, J., & Tate, R. (2004). Comparison of the Sydney Psychosocial Reintegration Scale (SPRS) with the Community Integration Questionnaire (CIQ): Administration and psychometric properties of two outcome measures. *Brain Injury, 18*(2), 161–177.

Laxe, S., Zasler, N., Selb, M., Tate, R., Tormos, J. M., & Bernabeu, M. (2013). Development of the International Classification of Functioning, Disability and Health Core Sets for traumatic brain injury: an international consensus process. *Brain Injury, 27*(4), 379–387.

Lemmens, J., van Engelen, E. I. S. M., Post, M. W. M., Beurskens, A. J. H. M., Wolters, P. M. J. C., & de Witte, P. (2007). Reproducibility and validity of the Dutch Life Habits Questionnaire (LIFE-H 3.0) in older adults. *Clinical Rehabilitation, 21*, 853–862.

Lezak, M. D., Howieson, D. B., Bigler, E. D., & Tranel, D. (2012). *Neuropsychological assessment.* (5th ed.). Oxford: Oxford University Press.

Magasi, S., & Post, M. W. (2010). A comparative review of contemporary participation measures' psychometric properties and content coverage. *Archives of Physical Medicine and Rehabilitation, 91*(Suppl.1), S17–S28.

Malec, J. F. & Lezak, M. D. (2003/2008). *Manual for the Mayo-Portland Adaptability Inventory (MPAI-4).* Revised. Retrieved March 8, 2013, from http://www.tbims.org/combi/mpai

Mallinson, T., & Hammel, J. (2010). Measurement of participation: intersecting person, task, and environment. *Archives of Physical Medicine and Rehabilitation, 91*(Suppl. 1), S29–S33.

McColl, M. A., Davies, D., Carlson, P., Johnston, J., & Minnes, P. (2001). The Community Integration Measure: Development and preliminary validation. *Archives of Physical Medicine and Rehabilitation*, 82(4), 429–434.

Noonan, V. K., Kopec, J. A., Noreau, L., Singer, J., & Dvorak, M. F. (2009). A review of participation instruments based on the International Classification of Functioning, Disability and Health. *Disability and Rehabilitation*, 31(23), 1883–1901.

Noreau, L., & Boschen, K. (2010). Intersection of participation and environmental factors: a complex interactive process. *Archives of Physical Medicine and Rehabilitation*, 91(Suppl. 1), S44–S53.

Noreau, L., Desrosiers, J., Robichaud, L., Fougeyrollas, P., Rochette, A., & Viscogliosi C. (2004). Measuring social participation: reliability of the LIFE-H in older adults with disabilities. *Disability and Rehabilitation*, 26(6), 346–352.

Nyein, K., Turner-Stokes, L., & Robinson, I. (1999). The Northwick Park Care Needs Assessment (NPCNA): A measure of community care needs: sensitivity to change during rehabilitation. *Clinical Rehabilitation*, 13(6), 482–491.

Pösel, M., Cieza, A., & Stucki, G. (2007). Psychometric properties of the WHODAS II in rehabilitation patients. *Quality of Life Research*, 16, 1521–1531.

Post, M. W. M., de Witte, L. P., Reichrath, E., Verdonschot, M. M., Wijhuizen, G. J., & Perenboom, R. J. M. (2008). Development and validation of IMPACT-S, an ICF-based questionnaire to measure activities and participation. *Journal of Rehabilitation Medicine*, 40, 620–627.

Post, M. W. M., van der Zee, C. H., Henninks, J., Schafrat, C. G., Visser-Meily, J. M. A., & van Berlekom, S. B, (2012). Validity of the Utrecht Scale for Evaluation of Rehabilitation-Participation. *Disability and Rehabilitation*, 34(6), 478–485.

Post, M. W. M., Visser-Meily, J. M. A., & Gispen, L. S. F. (2002). Measuring nursing needs of stroke patients in clinical rehabilitation: A comparison of validity and sensitivity to change between the Northwick Park Dependency Score and the Barthel Index. *Clinical Rehabilitation*, 16(2), 182–189.

Poulin, V., & Desrosiers, J. (2009). Reliability of the LIFE-H satisfaction scale and relationship between participation and satisfaction of older adults with disabilities. *Disability and Rehabilitation*, 31(16), 1311–1317.

Rauch, A., Cieza, A., & Stucki, G. (2008). How to apply the International Classification of Functioning, Disability and Health (ICF) for rehabilitation management in clinical practice. *European Journal of Physical and Rehabilitation Medicine*, 44, 329–342.

Reistetter, T. A., Spencer, J. C., Trujillo, L., & Abreu, B. C. (2005). Examining the Community Integration Measure (CIM): A replication study with life satisfaction. *NeuroRehabilitation*, 20(2), 139–148.

Reistetter, T. A., & Abreu, B. C. (2005). Appraising evidence on community integration following brain injury: a systematic review. *Occupational Therapy International*, 12(4), 196–217.

Rochette, A., Desrosiers, J., & Noreau, L. (2001). Association between personal and environmental factors and the occurrence of handicap situations following a stroke. *Disability and Rehabilitation*, 23(13), 559–569.

Sander, A. M., Clark, A., & Pappadis, M. R. (2010). What is community integration anyway? Defining meaning following traumatic brain injury. *Journal of Head Trauma Rehabilitation*, 25(2), 121–127.

Sander, A. M., Fuchs, K. L., High, W. M., Hall, K. M., Kreutzer, J. S., & Rosenthal, M. (1999). The Community Integration Questionnaire revisited: An assessment of factor structure and validity. *Archives of Physical Medicine and Rehabilitation*, 80, 1303–1308.

Segal, M. E., & Schall, R. R. (1995). Assessing handicap of stroke survivors. A validation study of the Craig Handicap Assessment and Reporting Technique. *American Journal of Physical Medicine and Rehabilitation*, 74(4), 276–286.

Sherbourne, C. D., & Stewart, A. L. (1991). The MOS Social Support Survey. *Social Science in Medicine*, 32(6), 705–714.

Sherer, M., Roebuck-Spencer, T., & David, L. C. (2010). Outcome assessment in traumatic brain injury clinical trials and prognostic studies. *Journal of Head Trauma Rehabilitation*, 25(2), 92–98.

Simpson, G., Secheny, T., Lane-Brown, A., Strettles, B., Ferry, K., & Phillips, J. (2004). Post-acute rehabilitation for people with traumatic brain injury: A model description and evaluation of the Liverpool Hospital Transitional Living Program. *Brain Impairment*, 5(1), 67–80.

Soo, C., Tate, R., Aird, V., Allaous, J., Browne, S., Carr, B., et al. (2010). Validity and responsiveness of the Care and Needs Scale (CANS) for assessing support needs following traumatic brain injury. *Archives of Physical Medicine and Rehabilitation*, 91(6), 905–912.

Soo, C., Tate, R., Hopman, K., Forman, M., Secheny, T., Aird, V.,...Coulston, C. (2007). Reliability of the Care and Needs Scale for assessing support needs after traumatic brain injury. *Journal of Head Trauma Rehabilitation*, 22(5), 288–295.

Soo, C., Tate, R. L., Williams, L., Waddingham, S., & Waugh, M-C. (2008) Development and validation of the Paediatric Care and Needs Scale (PCANS) for assessing support needs of children and young people with acquired brain injury. *Developmental Neurorehabilitation, 11*(3), 204–214.

Stier-Jarner, M., Grill, E., Ewert, T., Bartholomeyczik, S., Finger, M., Mokrusch, T., et al. (2005). ICF Core Set for patients with neurological conditions in early post-acute rehabilitation facilities. *Disability and Rehabilitation, 27*(7/8), 389–395.

Stucki, G., Cieza, A., & Melvin, J. (2007). The International Classification of Functioning, Disability and Health: A unifying model for the conceptual description of the rehabilitation strategy. *Journal of Rehabilitation Medicine, 39,* 279–285.

Tate, R. L. (2004). Assessing support needs for people with traumatic brain injury: the Care and Needs Scale (CANS). *Brain Injury, 18*(5), 445–460.

Tate, R. L. (2010). *A compendium of tests, scales and questionnaires: the practitioner's guide to measuring outcomes after acquired brain impairment.* Hove, UK: Psychology Press.

Tate, R. L., Godbee, K, & Sigmundsdottir (2013). A systematic review of assessment tools for adults used in traumatic brain injury research and their relationship to the ICF. *Neurorehabilitation, 32,* 729–750.

Tate, R. L, Hodgkinson, A., Veerabangsa, A, & Maggiotto, S. (1999). Measuring psychosocial recovery after traumatic brain injury: psychometric properties of a new scale. *Journal of Head Trauma Rehabilitation, 14*(6), 543–557.

Tate, R. L., Perdices, M. (2008). Applying the International Classification of Functioning Disability and Health (ICF) to clinical practice and research in acquired brain impairment. *Brain Impairment, 9*(3), 282–292.

Tate, R. L., Simpson, G, K., Soo, C., A., & Lane-Brown, A. T. (2011). Participation after acquired brain injury: clinical and psychometric considerations of the Sydney Psychosocial Reintegration Scale (SPRS). *Journal of Rehabilitation Medicine, 43,* 609–618.

Teasdale, G. M., Pettigrew, L. E. L., Wilson, J. T., Murray, G., & Jennett, B. (1998). Analysing outcome of treatment of severe head injury: a review and update on advancing the use of the Glasgow Outcome Scale. *Journal of Neurotrauma, 15*(8), 587–597.

Turner-Stokes, L., Nyein, K., & Halliwell, D. (1999). The Northwick Park Care Needs Assessment (NPCNA): A directly costable outcome measure in rehabilitation. *Clinical Rehabilitation, 13*(3), 253–267.

Turner-Stokes, L., Tonge, P., Nyein, K., Hunter, M., Nielson, S., & Robinson, I. (1998). The Northwick Park Dependency Score (NPDS): A measure of nursing dependency in rehabilitation. *Clinical Rehabilitation, 12*(4), 304–318.

Üstün, T. B., Chatterji, S., Bickenbach, J., Kostanjsek, N., & Schneider, M. (2003). The International Classification of Functioning, Disability and Health: A new tool for understanding disability and health. *Disability and Rehabilitation, 25*(11-12), 565–571.

Van Baalen, B., Odding, E., van Woensel, M. P. C., van Kessel, M. A., Roebroeck, M. E., & Stam, H. J. (2006). Reliability and sensitivity to change of measurement instruments used in a traumatic brain injury population. *Clinical Rehabilitation, 20,* 686–700.

van der Zee, C. H., Priesterbach, A. R., van der Dussen, L., Kap, A., Schepers, V. P. M., Visser-Meily, J. M. A., & Post, M. W. M. (2010). Reproducibility of three self-report participation measures: The ICF Measure of Participation and Activities Screener, the Participation Scale, and the Utrecht Scale for Evaluation of Rehabilitation—Participation. *Journal of Rehabilitation Medicine, 42,* 752–757.

Wade, D. T. (2003). Outcome measures for clinical rehabilitation trials: Impairment, function, quality of life or value. *American Journal of Physical Medicine & Rehabilitation, 82*(10), S26–S31.

Wade, D. T., & Halligan, P. (2003). New wine in old bottles: The WHO ICF as an explanatory model of human behaviour. *Clinical Rehabilitation, 17*(4), 349–354.

Wade, D. (2009). Generic or global outcome measures in rehabilitation: are they appropriate for measuring (and improving) service quality? *Clinical Rehabilitation, 23,* 867–872.

Whiteneck, G. G., Dijkers, M. P., Heinemann, A. W., et al. (2011). Development of the Participation Assessment with Recombined Tools—Objective for use after traumatic brain injury. *Archives of Physical Medicine and Rehabilitation, 92,* 542–551.

Whiteneck, G., & Dijkers, M. P. (2009). Difficult to measure constructs: Conceptual and methodological issues concerning participation and environmental factors. *Archives of Physical Medicine and Rehabilitation, 90*(1), S22–S35.

Whiteneck, G. G., Gerhardt, K. A., & Cusick, C. P. (2004). Identifying environmental factors that influence the outcomes of people with traumatic brain injury. *Journal of Head Trauma Rehabilitation, 19*(3), 191–204.

Whiteneck, G. G., Harrison-Felix, C. L., Mellick, D. C., Brooks, C. A., Charlifue, S. B., & Gerhart, K. A. (2004). Quantifying environmental factors: A measure of physical, attitudinal, service, productivity, and policy barriers. *Archives of Physical Medicine and Rehabilitation, 85,* 1324–1335.

Whiteneck, G. G., Charlifue, S. W., Gerhart, K. A., Overholser, J. D., & Richardson, G. N. (1992). Quantifying Handicap: A new measure of long-term rehabilitation outcomes. *Archives of Physical Medicine and Rehabilitation, 73*(6), 519–526.

Willer, B., Rosenthal, M., Kreutzer, J. S., Gordon, W. A., & Rempel, R. (1993). Assessment of community integration following rehabilitation for traumatic brain injury. *Journal of Head Trauma Rehabilitation, 8*(2), 75–87.

Wilson, J. T. L., Pettigrew, L. E. L., & Teasdale, G. M. (1998). Structured interviews for the Glasgow Outcome Scale and the Extended Glasgow Outcome Scale: guidelines for their use. *Journal of Neurotrauma, 15*(8), 573–585.

World Health Organization. (2001). *International classification of functioning, disability and health.* Geneva: World Health Organization.

World Health Organization. (1980). *International classification of impairments, disabilities, and handicaps.* Geneva: World Health Organization.

World Health Organization. (2000/2011). *Disability Assessment Schedule. WHODAS 2.* Retrieved March 8, 2013 from at http://www.who.int/icidh/whodas/index.html.

Yu, D. S. F., Lee, D. T. F., & Woo, J. (2004). Psychometric testing of the Chinese version of the Medical Outcomes Study Social Support Survey (MOS-SSS-C). *Research in Nursing and Health, 27,* 135–143.

10

Short and Long-Term Outcomes in Survivors of Traumatic Brain Injury

Jennie Ponsford

Introduction

Traumatic brain injury (TBI) causes a broad range of sensori-motor and neurobehavioral changes, as outlined in previous chapters. These changes have a major impact on the lives of those affected and their families. This chapter aims to explore the effects of these changes on short-and long-term outcome following TBI. The term "outcome" has been frequently used in the literature on TBI, but it is rarely explicitly defined. In its everyday use "outcome" is defined as "the result or consequence" (Heinemann Australian Dictionary, 1989, p. 741). TBI has many consequences. According to findings from a study involving 8,927 patients from 46 countries from the corticosteroid randomization after significant head injury (CRASH) trial (De Silva et al., 2009), approximately one quarter of individuals admitted to hospital with TBI die within six months of injury. The majority of people who are rendered comatose by TBI regain consciousness within two weeks. Most will then experience post-traumatic amnesia (PTA), and will go on to display varying patterns and levels of severity of ongoing disability in the longer term. Between 1 and 7% will enter either a vegetative or minimally conscious state. In the study by De Silva and colleagues, one third of patients had moderate to severe disability, and just under half experienced a "Good recovery," according to the Glasgow Outcome Scale. This chapter will explore the specific nature of these outcomes.

As discussed by Tate in chapter 9, the ICF framework, incorporating Body Functions, Body Structures, Activities/Participation,

Environmental Factors, and Personal Factors provides a useful taxonomy for describing the effects of TBI. Whilst the "core set" of ICF factors pertinent to TBI is still in the process of being established, the study of Koskinen, Hokkinen, Sarajuuri and Alaranta (2007), discussed in Tate's chapter, provides some preliminary findings. Using the ICF checklist, Koskinen et al. found that the most common Body Functions endorsed in a sample of rehabilitation patients with TBI were mental functions, including memory and higher level cognitive (executive) functions, attention and emotional functions, energy and drive, language and sleep (endorsed in more than 70% of cases), followed by pain, vestibular and seeing functions from the sensory and pain domain, and neuromusculoskeletal and movement related functions. The most affected Activities/Participation domains were Communication and major life areas (including work), domestic life, interpersonal interactions and relationships domains, mobility, general tasks and demands, and learning and applying knowledge. The most important Environmental Factors components were services, systems and policies, supports and relationships, and products and technology. These domains reflect pertinent aspects of outcome which require examination.

The aim of this chapter, which focuses on adults who survive moderate to severe TBI is, therefore, to discuss the consequences of TBI for the injured survivors in the domains of impairment, activity limitations, and restrictions on participation in community life and "psychosocial adjustment." Factors associated with or predictive of these outcomes will also be explored. Willer, Rosenthal, Kreutzer, Gordon, and Rempel (1993) define community integration as "effective role performance in community settings," including home integration (operation of the home), social integration (participation in activities outside the home and interpersonal relationships), and productive activities, including employment, study, or voluntary activities. A comprehensive understanding of outcome measured from all these perspectives and of predictive factors is important to create greater understanding of the problems faced by individuals with TBI and their families as a basis for allocation of resources, and planning of services to meet their needs.

At what point should one optimally measure outcome following moderate to severe TBI? This depends on the context of the assessment and may range from the time of discharge from the acute hospital, from rehabilitation or at some longer term point three, six months, or one, two, five, ten or even 20–30 years post-injury. As Tate has stated in chapter 9, "outcome is simply a point along the way" (p. 163). The majority of studies have focused on periods of six months, one, two, or five years post-injury. However, in recent years some studies have examined outcome at periods of 10 years or more post-injury.

An understanding of long-term outcome is important given the young age at which the majority of individuals sustain TBI, their prospect of a normal lifespan, and the associated developmental factors. Whilst TBI can occur in people of any gender, age, or socio-economic class, it is most frequently sustained by adolescent and young adult males (Kraus & McArthur, 1999; O'Rance & Fortune, 2007). These young people are generally in the process of becoming independent of their parents, in practical, financial, and emotional terms. They are also in the process of developing an identity, and studying or training towards a vocation. Forming social and intimate relationships are a priority during this life stage. The attainment of these "life goals" is disrupted by the TBI, which causes functional, cognitive, social, and emotional disabilities that prevent many individuals with TBI from resolving age-relevant issues. This can in itself cause reduced self-esteem and long-term

emotional adjustment problems (Fryer, 1989). There is another peak incidence of TBI in the elderly, who bring numerous pre-existing vulnerabilities which may also impact on outcome.

A significant proportion of people who sustain TBI come from a lower socioeconomic group, have low educational attainment, unstable employment, drug or alcohol abuse, other psychiatric disorders, previous head injury, or learning difficulties (Kraus & McArthur, 1999; Robinson & Jorge, 2002), factors shown to impact negatively on post-injury outcome (MacMillan, Hart, Martelli, & Zasler, 2002). The outcomes for the individual who has sustained moderate or severe TBI therefore result from a complex interplay of physical, cognitive, behavioral, and emotional changes resulting directly from the brain injury, as well as personal and social factors (Cooper-Evans, Alderman, Knight, & Oddy, 2008).

This raises the need to separate the effects of TBI from those which might be present in individuals of similar demographic background from the general population or those who have experienced some form of trauma not involving the head. Relatively few outcome studies have included such comparison groups, which make it possible to isolate factors unique to TBI. Many studies have been flawed by poor definition of inclusion criteria, by selection bias such as those when patients are recruited on presentation to clinics, and by significant drop-out rates. This review will endeavor to place emphasis on findings from controlled prospective studies.

Another important consideration is the perspective from which outcomes should be assessed. Outcomes have been measured in terms of cognitive test results and in terms of self-report by the patient, close others, or by therapists. Most studies have documented these changes using subjective reports obtained via scales or semi-structured interviews with injured patients and/or close others. However, some authors have questioned the extent to which reports of TBI patients' and close others' reliably reflect their daily functioning, raising questions as to the conclusions which may be drawn from these studies. Some individuals with TBI lack awareness of their limitations as a consequence of frontal lobe injury, which can affect feedback mechanisms allowing them to see that their skills or behaviors are not meeting the demands of the environment. On the other hand, relatives' reports may be influenced by their level of exposure to the behaviors in question, and by their personality and level of emotional adjustment to the effects of the injury. It is therefore important to consider the perspectives of each of these parties.

Agreement between reports by individuals with TBI and their close others has been found to differ according to the function being reported (Hart, Seignourel, & Sherer, 2009; Hart, Sherer, Whyte, Polansky, & Novack, 2004). Comparisons of subjective reports by patients with TBI and close others two to five years post-injury have revealed good agreement in reporting of sensory and physical impairments, but poorer agreement for cognitive impairment, and the poorest agreement for behavioral and emotional problems, with TBI participants being less likely to report these problems than close others (Cusick, Gerhart, & Mellick, 2000; Hart, et al., 2009; Hart et al., 2003; Port, Willmott, & Charlton, 2002). Agreement may increase over time post-injury, however. A study comparing reported changes by TBI individuals and their close others at 10 years post-injury showed generally good agreement (greater than 70%) on the frequency and severity of reported problems on the Neurobehavioral Functioning Inventory in all areas of functioning (Draper & Ponsford, 2007). Agreement was higher in the domain of motor problems and lower in the domains of emotion and cognition, in keeping with previous studies. However, where there was disagreement about cognitive and behavioral changes the TBI person was more likely to report a change.

The psychological state of the individual with TBI and their relatives may also influence their reporting of TBI sequelae. A number of studies conducted between six months and ten years post-injury have found that TBI patients' subjective reports of problems are inflated by the presence of emotional distress, such as anxiety and depression, so that there is commonly poor agreement between subjectively reported and objectively measured cognitive impairments (Chamelian & Feinstein, 2006; Dikmen, Machamer, Powell, & Temkin, 2003; Draper & Ponsford, 2007; Hoofien, Gilboa, Vakil, &

Barak, 2004; Wallace & Bogner, 2000). These factors need to be considered when examining the results of outcome studies.

A further consideration is the nature of the sampling procedures for follow-up studies. A number of studies have focused on samples including individuals with extremely severe injuries, for example (Koskinen, 1998; Tate, Broe, Cameron, Hodgkinson, & Soo, 2005; Thomsen, 1984; Thomsen, 1992). These studies have been important in highlighting the devastating consequences for this group. However, their outcomes are not representative of the broader population of individuals with moderate to severe TBI. In this chapter, reference will be made to the characteristics of samples as outcomes are discussed.

In a study of the longitudinal course of health-related quality of life from one month to three to five years after TBI, relative to patients with general trauma, Pagulayan, Temkin, Machamer, Dikmen (2006) found that TBI was associated with significant early limitations in most aspects of everyday life. Considerable improvement was noted over the first six months post-injury, especially in physical domains. Some aspects of psychosocial functioning also improved, although reported limitations in communication, cognitive, and emotional domains remained constant over time. The studies below provide further detail to better understand these problems, documented in terms of self-reported symptoms, cognitive impairments, global disability, integration into home, occupational and social activities, and psychological outcome, and their predictive factors.

Impairment Outcome Measured in Terms of Symptom Reporting

A study by Dikmen and colleagues (Dikmen, Machamer, Fann, & Temkin, 2010) examined rates of reporting of new or worse post-traumatic symptoms on a checklist documenting experience of headaches, fatigue, dizziness, blurred vision, difficulty concentrating, bothered by noise, bothered by light, irritability, temper, memory problems, anxiety, trouble with sleep in 732 patients across the spectrum of injury severity assessed at both one month and one year post-TBI, relative to that for 120 non-brain-injured trauma controls. More symptoms were reported by TBI participants at one month than at one year post-injury, but at both time-points the TBI group reported more symptoms overall and was significantly more likely to report problems with memory, concentrating, fatigue, dizziness, headaches, blurred vision, and being bothered by light. They were more likely to be bothered by noise at one month than at one year post-injury and more likely to report irritability, temper problems, and anxiety at one year but not at one month post-injury. Fifty-three percent of participants with TBI and 24% of trauma controls reported three or more continuing symptoms at one year post-injury.

In a more severely injured group followed up at one month, one and two years post-injury, and compared with a control group of their friends, Dikmen, Machamer and Temkin (1993) found that whilst fatigue, headache, and dizziness were prominent symptoms at one month post-injury, their reported frequency decreased to 20–30% by two years after injury. On the other hand, the frequency of reported concentration and memory difficulties and irritability remained high (40–60%) and increased over time. Blurred vision, being bothered by noise, insomnia, and anxiety were reported by 20–30% of participants at each time-point. In a further follow-up study at 3–5 years post-injury, Dikmen et al. (Dikmen, et al., 2003) found that 60% of the cohort were reporting ongoing cognitive difficulties in daily activities or required assistance from others because of their cognitive difficulties.

The nature of symptoms reported in these studies is limited by the symptoms included on the questionnaires used. The questionnaire used in the Dikmen et al. (2010) study did not ask about executive problems. Another longitudinal study by our own research group, extending an earlier published study by Olver, Ponsford & Curran (1996), has documented a somewhat more comprehensive range of symptoms in a cohort of patients referred for rehabilitation following predominantly moderate to very severe injuries. The rates of reported symptoms, documented relative to pre-injury functioning, were compared with those reported by a demographically similar uninjured control group assessed at a single time-point and asked to reflect on whether the symptoms had been experienced by them more in the last two years. The subgroup followed up at one, two and five years comprised 291 individuals with TBI, 69.5% male, with mean age at injury of 34.3 years (range = 13–79), mean education 11.07 years (range = 5–18), mean GCS of 7.17 (range = 3–15), and a mean PTA duration of 30.36 days (range =. 01–270). Control participants comprised 215 non-head injured individuals, matched for age, years of education, and gender. The most frequent neurological complaint was physical fatigue, reported by 66% of individuals at one year post-injury and 63% at five years. Balance problems were also common, reported by over 43% of patients at one, two, and five years post-injury. Epilepsy occurred in approximately 5% of the sample over five years post-injury. Rates of sensory disturbance affecting vision (37.4% at one year, 29% at five years), smell (24.8% at one year, 26.9% at five years), and to a lesser extent, hearing (14.4% at one year, 14.7% at five years), as well as dizziness (22.2% at one year, 23.5% at five years), remained fairly constant. Memory problems were the most frequent cognitive complaint, reported by 63% of patients at one year and 75% at five years, with slowed thinking, concentration difficulties, mental fatigue, word-finding difficulty, and irritability reported by more than 55% of the sample, and showing no reduction in reported frequency over time. Executive behaviors were also documented, with reported planning difficulties increasing from 40% at one year to 46% at five years post-injury, and reduced initiative, reported by 40%, impulsivity by 31% and more self-centeredness by 26% of patients five years post-injury. Increased anxiety and/or depression relative to pre-injury were reported by more than 40% of the sample at each time-point, with reports of social isolation increasing with time post-injury to 33.5% at five years post-injury. All changes were significantly more common in TBI patients than controls. A similar cohort comprising 309 patients from the same center followed up at 10 years post-injury, with mean age of 31.03 years at time of injury and mean PTA duration of 37.64 days (range =. 1-270), revealed little overall change in the rates of reported problems.

Of other studies documenting symptoms over longer periods after injury, O'Connor and colleagues (O'Connor, Colantonio, & Polatajko, 2005) used the Head Injury Symptom Checklist (McLean, Dikmen, Temkin, Wyler, & Gale, 1984) to investigate symptoms following mild to severe TBI in 57 participants at 10 years post-injury. Irritability was the most frequently reported problem, followed by "loses temper easily," "anxiety", and "tires easily." These findings confirm the results of earlier studies documenting persisting cognitive, behavioral, and emotional changes associated with TBI from the perspectives of people with TBI and/or their relatives. It would appear that these changes do not dissipate over long periods of time after injury for many of those injured.

Cognitive Impairments

In support of the subjectively reported symptoms, a number of studies have also documented cognitive difficulties in controlled studies using neuropsychological tests of specific functions, with impairments most commonly found on tests of memory, attention, and speed of information processing (Boake et al., 2001; Dikmen, et al., 2003; Dikmen, Machamer, Winn, & Temkin, 1995a; Green et al., 2008; Lehtonen et al., 2005; Millis, Rosenthal, Novack, Sherer, Nick, Kreutzer, et al., 2001; Novack, Bush, Meythaler, & Canupp, 2001; Satz et al., 1998; Spitz, Ponsford, Rudzki, & Maller, 2012; Tate & Broe, 1999). For example Dikmen et al. (2003) found impaired performances relative to trauma controls on tests of memory (California Verbal Learning Test) and attention and information processing speed (Paced Auditory Serial Addition Task, or PASAT).

Fewer follow-up studies have included tests of executive function when investigating cognitive impairment following TBI. Tate and Broe (1999) reported that in comparison with a group of 30 demographically matched control participants the TBI group (n = 60) demonstrated significantly poorer levels of performance on the Thurstone Word Fluency, Design Fluency, and Wisconsin Card Sorting tests. It was concluded that the TBI group had impaired self-regulatory abilities (Tate & Broe, 1999). More recently Spitz et al. (G Spitz, et al., 2012) showed impaired

performances on several executive tests (the Trail Making Test—Part B, Zoo Map and Controlled Word Association tests), in addition to tests of memory (the Rey Auditory-Verbal Learning Test) and processing speed (Symbol Digit Modalities Test), in individuals with TBI tested at three and six months post-injury in comparison with controls. Multilevel modeling revealed that impaired performances on executive tests were most strongly predictive of poorer functional outcomes.

In a study focused on patients with moderate to severe TBI (mean PTA 26 days) and demographically matched controls, Draper and Ponsford (2008) documented cognitive performance at an average of 10.6 years post-injury (range = 10–12 years). The TBI group demonstrated significant cognitive impairment on measures of processing speed (Symbol Digit Modalities Test (SDMT), Digit Symbol Coding), memory (Rey AVLT, Doors and People tests) and executive function (Hayling C and SART errors) relative to controls. Logistic regression analyses showed that the SDMT, Rey AVLT and Hayling C, and SART errors most strongly differentiated the groups in the domains of attention/processing speed, memory and executive function respectively. This study confirmed and extended findings from other studies examining individuals with TBI between 5 and 30 years post-injury, which have documented persisting impairments on various WAIS subtests assessing verbal and visuo-motor skills, and specifically on tests of processing speed, learning and memory, and executive functions, where these were assessed (Colantonio et al., 2004; Himanen et al., 2006; Hoofien, Gilboa, Vakil, & Donovick, 2001; Wood & Rutterford, 2006b). In examining patterns of recovery of cognitive function, Millis et al. (2001), found no set pattern, with impairment still evident five years after injury.

In recent years there has been greater focus on the effects of blast–related TBI or penetrating TBI on cognitive and psychological functions. In a review of studies to date Dikmen and colleagues (2009) concluded that both moderate and severe penetrating TBI result in cognitive impairments six months post-injury, whereas there was insufficient evidence to conclude that a single mild TBI was associated with persisting cognitive deficits six months post-injury. Another recent paper reviewing studies comparing cognitive outcomes of blast-related versus other mechanisms of TBI by Belanger, Kretzmer, Yoasgh-Gantz, Pickett and Tupler (2009) concluded that there were no significant differences in the cognitive sequelae associated with TBI due to blast injuries and those associated with other mechanisms.

Global Functional Outcomes

A number of studies have used global outcome scales to measure functional outcome. One of the most widely used measures of outcome after TBI is the Glasgow Outcome Scale (GOS). The major categories are death, persistent vegetative state, severe disability (conscious but disabled, requiring assistance in activities of daily living, ADL), moderate disability (disabled but independent in ADL), and good recovery (returned to previous activities, but may have some symptoms) (Jennett & Bond, 1975). The Extended Glasgow Outcome Scale or GOSE (Wilson, Pettigrew, & Teasdale, 1998) includes additional categories to improve the scale's ability to discriminate levels of disability and base ratings on an objective set of questions. Information about consciousness, independence in the home and community, employment, social and leisure activities, family and friendships, and return to normal life is obtained via structured interview and used to rate outcome in the following categories: upper good recovery, lower good recovery, upper moderate disability, lower moderate disability, upper severe disability, lower severe disability, vegetative state, or dead.

Studies using the GOS to document outcome following TBI at periods of one to five years post-injury have reported variable outcome ratings depending on injury severity of samples, with higher rates of good recovery in samples including mild injuries (Dikmen, Machamer, Powell, & Temkin, 2003). Walker et al. (2010) found that, of a rehabilitation cohort from the U.S. Model Systems database, proportionally more patients had Good Recovery (44% versus 39%) and less Severe Disability (19% versus 23%) at year two than at year one on the GOS. Sigurdottir, Andelic, Roe, and Schanke (2009) reported that 64% of a rehabilitation cohort

showed good recovery on the GOSE at one year post-injury and 36% moderate recovery.

In a study focused on patients with moderate to severe TBI (means PTA 26 days) and demographically matched controls, Ponsford and colleagues (Ponsford, Draper, & Schönberger, 2008) documented functional outcome on the GOSE at an average of 10.6 years post-injury (range = 10–12 years). Of this group 32% and 20% scored in the upper and lower good recovery categories respectively, 32% and 11% in the upper and lower moderate disability categories, and 3% and 2% in the upper and lower severe disability categories.

However, the global scores on these scales say little about the individual's capacity for independent living, work, study, leisure, and relationships. Studies examining outcome in the three domains of independent living skills, occupation, and social and leisure functions/relationships will be reviewed separately in the following sections.

Home Integration/Independent Living Skills

In general, studies have found relatively high levels of independence in mobility, personal, and domestic activities of daily living (ADL) at all time-points from one to more than 24 years post-injury as compared with instrumental ADL (Colantonio, et al., 2004; Dikmen, et al., 2003). In a prospective study of outcome three to five years post-injury in a group of 210 patients with moderate to severe TBI, Dikmen and colleagues (Dikmen, et al., 2003) showed that personal care and standard of living were least affected overall, with around 30% of participants reporting some difficulty, but only 12% needing help with personal care. While few needed help with ambulation, 47% reported some difficulty and 40% had some difficulty with travel. More than 30% required some assistance with financial management. Whereas none were living in a restricted environment pre-injury, 8% were living in a nursing home or group home after injury. In a detailed examination of home management activities one year after moderate to severe TBI, Powell, Temkin, Machamer and Dikmen (2007) found that 59% of the sample reported greater difficulty or need for assistance in home management activities one year post-injury. This need was associated with poorer cognitive function as well as older age.

Our own outcome figures for the cohort of 291 people with moderate to severe TBI studied at one, two and five years post-injury, as described earlier, and compared with a control group, show a similar pattern, with more than 64% of the group able to walk, run, or jump independently, more than 96% independent in personal ADL, and 85% in light domestic ADL at one, two and five years post-injury. A slightly lower proportion (> 72%) were independent in heavy domestic activities, and in shopping (79% at one year, 83% at five years), financial management (81% at both one and five years), and public transport (75% at one year, 85% at five years). It would appear that cognitive impairments interfere with independence in these more complex instrumental activities. A high proportion of this sample also returned to driving over time, with 51.6 % driving at one year and 8% with restrictions, 62% at two years and 5% with restrictions, and 71% at five years, with a further 8% driving with restrictions. In terms of accommodation, 34% were living independently alone or with friends and 58% with family (including a spouse) at one year, 35% alone or with friends and 52% with family (including a spouse) at two years, and 46% were living alone or with friends and 48% with family (including a spouse) at five years post-injury.

Similar patterns are evident in longer term follow-up studies. In a cohort of 306 people with moderate to severe TBI followed up between 7and 24 years post-injury (mean = 14.2 years), Colantonio et al. (2004) found that at least 88% could bathe, dress, eat, transfer, use the toilet, and telephone independently. Greater limitations were evident in instrumental ADLs, with 22–30% requiring some assistance with housework, shopping, managing money, and going to places out of walking distance respectively. Of this sample, 40.2% were living with a spouse at follow-up, 23.5% were living alone, and 17% with family. Only 9.2 were living in institutional settings. Hoofien et al. (2001) also used a combination of subjective reports and objective tests to assess outcome in 76 participants who had sustained a severe TBI between five and 25 years previously and found that the majority

of TBI participants were independent in ADL, although problems with employment, social functioning, and relationships remained significant. Similarly Wood and Rutterford (2006c) found that 72% of a sample of 80 people with TBI (mean PTA duration = 19.30 days) assessed 10–32 years post-injury were independent in ADL. Overall it is apparent that while most people with TBI become physically independent in ADL, a proportion requires ongoing supervision or assistance with more complex activities such as shopping and financial management due to their cognitive impairments.

Occupational Integration/ Outcome

TBI also causes significant disruption to occupational or other productive activities. Many studies have used employment or return to study as an indicator of outcome following TBI. Although the reported productivity rates vary widely due to differing study methods and injury severity (from 17.8% to 71%), findings generally indicate that less than half of those who sustain moderate to severe TBI return to employment (Kreutzer et al., 2003; Machamer, Temkin, Fraser, Doctor, & Dikmen, 2005; Ownsworth & McKenna, 2008; Ponsford, Olver, Curran, & Ng, 1995; Possl, Jurgensmeyer, Karlbauer, Wenz, & Goldenberg, 2001; Shames, Treger, Ring, & Giaquinto, 2007; Sherer, Novack, et al., 2002; Sherer, Sander, et al., 2002). Temkin et al., (2009) concluded that TBI decreases the probability of employment after injury in those who were workers before their injury, lengthens the timing of their return if they do return to work, and decreases the likelihood that they will return to the same position. In a study of people working pre-injury, Doctor and colleagues (2005) found that the risk of unemployment one year after TBI was 42% as compared to a 9% expected relative risk of unemployment for the sample under a validated risk-adjusted econometric model of employment in the U.S. population.

Furthermore, many injured individuals cannot maintain employment over time (Kreutzer, et al., 2003; Machamer, et al., 2005; Possl, et al., 2001; Shames, et al., 2007). Of participants in the Dikmen et al. (2003) study of outcome in a sample of whom 60% had mild TBI, 20%

moderate, and 20% severe injuries, approximately 40% were not performing their major life role activity three to five years post-injury. Fewer than a third of pre-injury workers were employed three to five years post-injury, a further 10% reported a significant change to their job responsibilities, and 20% were experiencing difficulty performing their responsibilities (e.g., taking longer to do things, having conflict with co-workers). Of our sample of 291 followed up at one, two, and five years post-injury, 63% of those employed prior to injury were working at one year and this diminished to 56% at five years. Of the 111 individuals employed at one year post-injury, 84% were employed at two years, and 76% were employed at five years post-injury. Of the 103 individuals unemployed at one year post-injury, 16% were employed at two years, and 23% were employed at five years. While at one year only 32% of individuals with TBI were obtaining their income from employment, this increased to 47% at five years. When asked about the quality of their experience at work, about a quarter of the sample reported making more mistakes than prior to injury and approximately 30% had greater difficulty keeping up. Fatigue was a significant problem for about half of the sample. There was increasing awareness of difficulty getting on with people at work over time.

A number of factors have been shown to be significantly associated with short- and long-term employment outcome. These include the injured person's age, with those over the age of 40 years being less likely to return to work; their education; previous employment status, type, and income; severity of injury; degree of resultant cognitive and behavioral impairment, particularly executive impairment; disability in performing activities of daily living; self-awareness; pre-and post-injury emotional or psychiatric status; the presence of multiple trauma, particularly spinal and limb injuries; and access to transportation (Machamer, et al., 2005; Ownsworth & McKenna, 2008; Ponsford, et al., 1995; Schönberger, Ponsford, Olver, Ponsford, & Wirtz, 2011; Shames, et al., 2007; Sherer, Sander, et al., 2002). Walker, Marwitz, Kreutzer, Hart and Novack (2006) found that the rate of successful return to work was greatest for professional/managerial (56%), lower

for skilled (40%), and lowest for manual labour (32%), yielding an odds ratio of 2.959 between the highest and lowest groups. Of those with successful return to work, most did so within the same occupational category grouping. Ponsford et al. (1995) and Possl and colleagues (2001) noted a range of other factors which influenced individual employment outcomes in people with severe TBI. Positive factors included employer support and benefits, and the presence of determination and adaptability on the part of the injured individual. Negative influences were the lack of employer support, presence of continuing problems with fatigue, difficulty learning new information, keeping up with the job due to attentional and memory difficulties, presence of psychiatric illness, substance abuse or other adjustment problems, behavioral and interpersonal difficulties resulting from the injury, and availability of other means of financial support, such as support from a spouse or disability support income. Kendall (2003) found a significant association of vocational adjustment (though not actual employment status) with family and social support and self-esteem.

There have been relatively few studies focusing on return to study following moderate to severe TBI. In the cohort followed up at one, two, and five years post-injury, there were 40 individuals who were studying at secondary or tertiary levels prior to injury. Of these, 57.5% were studying at one year, 34.2% at two years, and 23.1% at five years. Of those studying prior to injury, 16%, 40%, and 46% had moved into employment at one, two, and five year post-injury, respectively. Many students moved from full-time study to part-time study and had required tutoring support following their injury. Approximately 40% reported that they were having moderate difficulty keeping up with the workload, learning new information, and getting fatigued, thus needing to put more effort into their studies in order to pass their course, relative to pre-injury. Other studies have reported that tertiary or college students reported a need for increased effort and use of compensatory strategies in their studies, a decline in grades, changes in their educational or vocational goals, a decline in their social and peer group interactions, and a tendency to feel anxious and overwhelmed, with a sense that others do not understand their difficulties (Kennedy,

Krause, & Turkstra, 2008; Todis & Glang, 2008). Todis and Glang (2008) found that students who did not receive support were less likely to complete post-secondary education.

Social Integration (Leisure and Recreation, Social Interaction, Interpersonal Relationships)

Social integration, including functioning in areas such as leisure and recreation, social activities, and in making and maintaining relationships has been shown to be significantly impacted in many individuals with TBI relative to pre-injury, often resulting in social isolation (Tate et al., 2005; Winkler, Unsworth, & Sloan, 2006).

Of the participants in the Dikmen et al. (2003) study of outcome three to five years post-injury in the social domain, while 55% reported no problems, 10% had more difficulty relating to others, 25% had lost friends, had trouble making new friends, or had less contact with friends, and 10% were completely isolated, with total reliance on family or care staff for social contact. Our own follow-up study of 291 people with moderate to severe TBI at one, two, and five years post-injury revealed a significantly greater proportion than the control group who reported having lost friends or become more socially isolated since the injury (27% at one year, 34% at five years). Approximately 23% reported having more difficulties in relationships and 20% reported more difficulty making friends. A significant proportion (55% at one year and 40% at five years) could not pursue previous leisure activities.

Two other studies found that more than 80% of their TBI participants experienced disruption of leisure participation due to factors including physical disabilities, problems with transportation, limited finance, impairment of cognition, behavior, and social skills, lack of initiative or self-confidence, poor family or social support, or simply a lack of networking (Bier, Dutil, & Couture, 2009; Wise et al., 2010). Participants in the study by Wise et al. (2010) reported the greatest decline in activities such as partying, drug and alcohol use, and various sports, whereas watching television was the most frequent "new" activity after injury. Sixty percent of those who did not return to pre-injury levels of leisure activity were moderately to severely bothered by the changes. Moreover, the problems with social participation, leisure activities, and relationships have been shown to persist at longer periods of time after injury (Draper, Ponsford, & Schönberger, 2007; Engberg & Teasdale, 2004; Hoofien et al., 2001; Winkler, et al., 2006; Wood & Rutterford, 2006c).

Early studies focusing on very severely injured groups reported high rates of marital breakdown more than five years following severe TBI, ranging from 78% in samples with very severe disabilities (Thomsen, 1984) to 42% in those with "good" outcomes (Tate, Lulham, Broe, Strettles, & Pfaff, 1989; Wood & Yurdakul, 1997). However studies recruiting consecutive series of patients with a wider range of injury severity, have painted a different picture. Of the TBI individuals in our sample of 291 moderate to severe TBI patients who were married or de facto prior to injury, 6.8% were separated, divorced, or widowed at one year post-injury, 8.3% at two years and 15.9% at five years. Of those single prior to injury, 11% were married or de facto one year post-injury, 12.8% at two years, and 20.3% at five years post-injury, there being a small net increase in the proportion of the sample married. Of another sub-group from the same rehabilitation cohort followed up at 10 years post-injury only 17.3% were separated, divorced, or widowed, while 33% had married. Similar findings have come from two U.S. studies. Kreutzer and colleagues (2007) found that only 25%, of a group of 120 individuals with mild-severe TBI who had been married pre-injury had separated or divorced at 30–96 month follow-up and Arango-Lasprilla et al. (2008) found that only 15% of a group of 977 people with moderate to severe TBI had separated or divorced two years after injury. Factors associated with marital stability in these studies included being married longer before injury, older age, less severe injury, being female, and non-violent injury.

There is, however, substantial evidence that for many the quality of relationships may decline following TBI. Bracy and Douglas (2002) found that wives of TBI husbands reported greater marital dissatisfaction and poorer communication with their partner than spouses of orthopedically injured controls, and used avoidance coping to deal with recurring marital problems. Burridge and colleagues (2007) noted that greater reduction in relationship satisfaction evident in couples in which one partner had TBI was associated with poorer socio-emotional functioning, especially empathetic skill.

It is clear that moderate to severe TBI may have a significant impact on the family. As a consequence of their reduced social networks and relationship difficulties, individuals with TBI may come to rely more on their families for social contact (Dianne Winkler, Unsworth, & Sloan, 2005; Winkler, et al., 2006). Studies examining the effects of TBI on family life have revealed that it can create significant stress, which tends to increase, rather than decrease, over time (Ponsford & Schönberger, 2010). These studies have found that it is the changes in behavior and personality, rather than physical disabilities, which are most stressful for families (Anderson, Parmenter, & Mok, 2002; Ergh, Rapport, Coleman, & Hanks, 2002; Ponsford & Schönberger, 2010; Ponsford, Olver, Ponsford, & Nelms, 2003; Testa, Malec, Moessner, & Brown, 2006; Winstanley, Simpson, Tate, & Myles, 2006). The picture is not always negative, however, or may not remain so. As Perlesz et al. (1999; 2000) have cogently pointed out, the fact that many families cope well and the majority do not exhibit clinically significant anxiety or depression needs to be highlighted more strongly. A number of authors have observed that some families appear to cope surprisingly well, and may actually become stronger and more resilient in the face of the chronic challenges presented by TBI (Perlesz, 1999; Perlesz, Kinsella, & Crowe, 1999). The adjustment process may take place over many years, however. There is therefore a need to take a very long-term view in terms of availability of support and assistance. Finally, it must be noted that not all changes in personality following TBI are necessarily negative. Occasionally families report that their injured relative has become more even-tempered or compliant, or has a more positive outlook on life after having survived and recovered from such trauma.

Psychological Outcome

Given the many changes experienced by individuals with TBI, affecting their home, work and social integration, and often interfering with the attainment of major life goals to have a job, friendship group, and get married, it is not surprising that many experience psychological adjustment problems. Reduced self-esteem, depression, and anxiety are evident in a significant proportion of cases (Cooper-Evans, et al., 2008; Goodinson, Ponsford, Johnston, & Grant, 2009; Gouick & Gentleman, 2004). Prevalence rates for anxiety and depression vary widely according to sampling and measurement methods, but recent studies have found that between 42 and 53% of individuals with complicated mild to severe TBI experience a depressive disorder in the first 12 months post- injury, most commonly Major Depressive Disorder (MDD; Bombardier et al., 2010; Gould, Ponsford, Johnston, & Schönberger, 2011c; Whelan-Goodinson, Ponsford, Johnston, & Grant, 2009). Onset increases over the first two to three years post-injury, and plateaus thereafter (Ashman et al., 2004; Whelan-Goodinson, et al., 2009), although high rates of depression are still reported between 10 and 30 years post-injury (Draper, et al., 2007; Hoofien, et al., 2001; Koponen et al., 2002). Depression is comorbid with anxiety in more than 70% of cases (Gould, et al., 2011c; Jorge et al., 2004; Whelan-Goodinson, et al., 2009).

The only prospective study of anxiety disorders found that these occurred in 44.1% of cases in the first year after injury (Gould et al., 2011c), with the most common disorders being Generalised Anxiety Disorder (GAD), PTSD, Specific Phobia, Panic Disorder (PD) and Social Phobia, and low rates of Obsessive Compulsive Disorder and Agoraphobia (Gould et al., 2011c; Whelan-Goodinson et al., 2009). Retrospective studies in samples with mild-severe TBI reported that anxiety disorders were present in 38% of cases up to five years post-injury (Whelan-Goodinson et al., 2009), 57% up to eight years post-injury (Hibbard, Uysal, Kepler, Bogdany, & Silver, 1998) and 17.4% up to 30 years post-injury (Koponen et al., 2002). The presence of these disorders has been shown to be associated with poorer functional outcomes (Gould, Ponsford, Johnston, & Schönberger, 2011a; Whelan-Goodinson, Ponsford, & Schönberger, 2008). Pagulayan et al. (2008) and Schönberger and colleagues (Michael Schönberger, Ponsford,

Gould, & Johnston, 2011) concluded that anxiety and depression follow the experience of poorer functional outcome, and thus appear to be a consequence rather than a cause of these poor outcomes.

Factors Influencing Outcome Following TBI

Despite the common features of outcome discussed in the sections above, there is considerable variability in outcome across individuals in each of the reported domains. This has led to a significant body of research examining factors associated with outcome. A range of injury-related, personal, and social factors have been shown to influence survival, coma depth and duration, and PTA, as well as cognitive, functional and employment outcome.

Acute Injury-Related Factors

Various biomarkers have been associated with early response to injury. Of these, S100β levels early after injury have been associated with intracranial hypertension, cerebral hypoperfusion in the early stages after injury (Stein et al., 2011), with longer PTA duration, and more severe neuropsychological deficits after emergence from PTA (Watt, Shores, Baguley, Dorsch, & Fearnside, 2006), and with poorer functional outcome on the GOS at six months post-injury (Wiesmann et al., 2010).

Maas et al. (2007) examined the association between acute CT findings and outcome at six months post-injury measured on the GOS in a cohort of over 5,000 patients from the IMPACT database. The CT classification was strongly related to outcome, with worst outcome for patients with diffuse injuries in CT class III (swelling; OR 2.50; CI 2.09–3.0) or CT class IV (shift; OR 3.03; CI 2.12–4.35). The prognosis in patients with mass lesions was better for patients with an epidural hematoma (OR 0.64; CI 0.56–0.72) and poorer for an acute subdural hematoma (OR 2.14; CI 1.87–2.45). Partial obliteration of the basal cisterns (OR 2.45; CI 1.88–3.20), tSAH (OR 2.64; CI 2.42–2.89), or midline shift (15 mm-OR 1.36; CI 1.09–1.68); >5 mm-OR 2.20; CI 1.64–2.96) were strongly related to poorer outcome. Maas Hukkelhoven, Marshall,

and Steyerberg (2005) concluded that it is preferable to use combinations of individual CT predictors rather than the Marshall CT classification for prognostic purposes in TBI, including at least the following parameters: status of basal cisterns, shift, traumatic subarachnoid or intraventricular hemorrhage, and presence of different types of mass lesions. Tasaki et al. (2009) found that a predictive model based on age, absence of pupillary light reflex, presence of extensive subarachnoid hemorrhage, intracranial pressure, and midline shift was shown to have high predictive value.

Magnetic resonance imaging and diffusion tensor imaging have been shown to be more sensitive to some of the pathology associated with TBI. Sidaros et al. (2008) found that indices of diffusion tensor imaging were predictive of outcome 12 months post-injury. Specifically, lambda (parallel) and lambda (perpendicular) in the cerebral peduncle and in corpus callosum, both increased during the 8-week to 12-month post-injury scan interval and fractional anisotropy remained depressed in patients with unfavorable outcome, whereas it increased in patients with favorable outcomes.

Sherer and colleagues (2008) found that age, year of injury, GCS, pupillary responsiveness, and CT pathology were predictive of loss of consciousness (LOC). Age, years of education, year of injury, GCS, LOC, pupillary responsiveness, and intracranial operations were predictive of duration of post-traumatic amnesia (PTA). Age, years of education, year of injury, GCS, LOC, and pupillary responsiveness were predictive of PTA-LOC. GCS and LOC effects were influenced by age.

GCS and PTA

Researchers have found both Glasgow Coma scores (GCS) and duration of post-traumatic amnesia (PTA) to be predictive of functional outcomes following TBI, particularly in the acute stages post-injury. Studies conducted up to five years post-injury have found significant associations between both lower GCS and longer PTA duration and poorer outcome on global outcome measures, such as the GOS and GOSE (de Guise, LeBlanc, Feyz, & Lamoureux, 2006; Dikmen et al., 2010; Rapoport, 2000;

Sigurdardottir et al., 2009), employment outcome (Avesani, Salvi, Rigoli, & Gambini, 2005; Brown et al., 2005; Doctor et al., 2005; Machamer et al., 2005; Ponsford et al., 1995; Schönberger et al., 2011), and cognitive outcome (Green et al., 2008).

However, more recent studies have found that whilst GCS is more widely used internationally, and is a strong indicator of the likelihood of survival following severe TBI, it does not do as well as PTA in predicting longer term functional outcome in its survivors (Brown et al., 2005; Sherer et al., 2008) or brain injury lesion size (Schönberger, Ponsford, Reutens, Beare, & O'Sullivan, 2009). A number of studies conducted 10 years or more post-injury have also documented a strong association of PTA with functional outcome in the areas of self-care, living skills, relationships, and employment (Draper et al., 2007; Nakase-Richardson et al., 2011; Ponsford et al., 2008; Tate et al., 2005). On the other hand, Hoofien et al. (2002) found socioeconomic variables, rather than injury severity, to be stronger predictors of outcome more than 10 years post-injury. Nakase-Richardson et al. (2009) found that most individuals with PTA fewer than 14 days had favorable one-year outcome (68% productive), whereas worse outcomes were associated with PTA more than 28 days (18% productive). Walker et al. (2010) found that longer PTA resulted in an incremental decline in probability of Good Recovery and a corresponding increase in probability of Severe Disability. When PTA ended within four weeks, Severe Disability was unlikely (<15% chance) at year one, and Good Recovery was the most likely GOS at year two. When PTA lasted beyond eight weeks, Good Recovery was highly unlikely (<10% chance) at year one, and Severe Disability was equal to or more likely than Moderate Disability at year two.

Multivariate models combining PTA with age, pre-injury occupational status, and physical, cognitive and behavioral disability have accounted for 60% or more of the variance in employment outcome at one and six years post-injury, and over much longer periods (Brown et al., 2005; Nakase-Richardson, et al., 2011; Schönberger, et al., 2011; Spitz, et al., in press; Tate, et al., 2005; Winkler, et al., 2006). This suggests that a number of factors, in combination, may influence outcome. Bush and colleagues (2003) and Schönberger et al. (2011) concluded that injury severity indirectly influences outcome through its effects on cognitive and functional status.

Other System Injuries

Dacey and colleagues (1991) have noted the contribution of other system injuries to psychosocial outcome following TBI. Using a structural equation modeling approach to predicting employment outcome in a group of 949 patients with moderate to severe injuries, Schönberger et al. (2011) found that presence of limb injuries, along with age, education, pre-injury employment, and injury severity was a significant predictor of return to employment one year post-injury, having both a direct influence and an influence via their effect on mood. Schönberger and colleagues found that limb injuries had less influence on outcome five years post-injury, however. The structural equation model representing the factors influencing employment outcome and their interrelationships is shown in Figure 10.1.

Personal Factors

Age. Of demographic factors, age has emerged as by far the strongest and most consistent predictor of outcome following TBI. Numerous studies conducted up to five years post-injury have demonstrated that older age is associated with poorer outcome following moderate to severe TBI (Brown, et al., 2005; Dikmen, et al., 2010; Green, et al., 2008; Hukkelhoven et al., 2003; Keyser-Marcus et al., 2002; LeBlanc, de Guise, Gosselin, & Feyz, 2006; Livingston et al., 2005; Mushkudiani et al., 2007; Nakase-Richardson et al., 2011; Ponsford et al., 1995; Schönberger et al., 2011). For patients aged over 50 years, outcome rated by the GOS has been found to be significantly worse, the incidence of disability higher, community integration poorer (LeBlanc et al., 2006), and unemployment higher (Ponsford et al., 1995; M. Schönberger et al., 2011), although this has not always been the case (Formisano et al., 2004). Age combined with other variables, including education, injury severity and post-injury impairment has

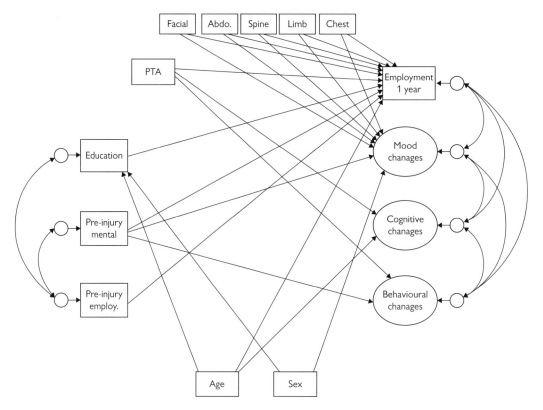

Figure 10-1. Structural equation model predicting functional and employment outcome one year after traumatic brain injury. Reprinted with permission from Schönberger, M., Ponsford, J., Olver, J., Ponsford, M. Wirtz, M. (2011). Prediction of functional and employment outcome one year after Traumatic Brain Injury: A Structural Equation Modelling approach. *Journal of Neurology, Neursurgery and Psychiatry,* 82, 936-941.

been found to account for larger percentages of the variance in outcome (Brown et al., 2005; Nakase-Richardson et al., 2011; Ponsford et al., 1995; Schönberger et al., 2011; Spitz et al., 2012; Winkler et al., 2006).

Studies conducted at 10 years or more post-injury have reported conflicting findings regarding the impact of age on outcome following TBI. Wood and Rutterford (2006a) found an association between age and long-term employment. Himanen et al. (2006) found that older age at injury was significantly associated with poorer cognitive function following TBI. On the other hand, studies by Draper et al. (2008; 2007), Hoofien et al. (2002), and Tate et al. (2005) have found no significant association between age and any of the outcome variables investigated, which included the GOSE, mobility, ADL independence, psychiatric symptoms, independent living status, employment status,

relationships, life satisfaction, and community integration.

This may in part be explained by the findings of Senathi-Raja and colleagues, who conducted a follow-up study of patients 5–20 years post-injury, comparing them with demographically matched controls. Whilst Senathi-Raja, Ponsford, & Schönberger (2009; 2010b) found significantly greater cognitive impairment and poorer functional outcomes on the GOSE and lower rates of return to employment in people with moderate to severe TBI of increasing age, there was no such association evident for emotional adjustment (Senathi-Raja, Ponsford, & Schönberger, 2010a). Consistent with a finding by Deb and Burns (2007), who found that 18–65 year old patients were likely to be at a greater risk of psychiatric morbidity following TBI, Senathi –Raja et al. (2010a) found that those who were older showed better long-term emotional adjustment than those who were younger, perhaps reflecting the fact that they had achieved their life goals and had stronger relationships prior to injury. The findings of this study are important, because relatively few follow-up studies have employed age-matched controls, which is clearly important in order to separate the effects of TBI from the general decline in cognition and functional status which may occur with increasing age.

In their cross-sectional studies, both Senathi-Raja et al. (2010b) and Ashman et al. (2008) have not found a disproportionate decline with increasing time post-injury in older patients with TBI. Furthermore they did not find evidence of an association of greater cognitive decline with presence of the apolipoprotein E (ApoE) e4 allele or of a higher rate of onset of Alzheimer's Disease than that in the general population. Whilst it has been argued that TBI increases the risk of Alzheimer's disease (Mehta et al., 1999; Plassman et al., 2000), particularly in individuals possessing the ApoE e4 allele, more recent studies have not supported this (Fleminger, Oliver, Lovestone, Rabe-Hesketh, & Giora, 2003; Rapoport, 2000; Raymont et al., 2008). Following from Corkin and colleagues' (1989) finding of deteriorating cognitive function with advancing age in war veterans who had sustained missile wounds to the brain, and Himanen's (2006) finding of greater cognitive deterioration with advancing age, Raymont et al. (2008) examined factors associated with long-term cognitive decline in a group of Vietnam veterans with predominantly penetrating head injury (PHI) suffered more than 30 years ago. They found that those with PHI demonstrated a greater degree of cognitive decline overall during the 36–39 years following recovery from injury compared with a control group of uninjured Vietnam veterans, which became increasingly significant later in life. However, dementia, and specifically Alzheimers disease, were not apparent, with only 4.9% of the group scoring <24 on the MMSE. Pre-injury intelligence and to a lesser extent education were the most consistent predictors of cognitive outcome across all phases of potential recovery and decline after such injuries. While laterality of lesion was not a factor, some associations were found between atrophy and specific regions of tissue loss and long-term cognitive functioning. There was no evidence of an association between level of cognitive decline following PHI and the presence of the ApoE or catechol-o-methyltransferase (COMT) genotype, but cognitive decline was associated with possession of the genetic marker GRIN, a glutamate receptor which acts as a marker of neuronal death.

Gender

As far as gender differences are concerned, results of animal studies have suggested that acute response to injury may be influenced by hormonal factors, creating an advantage for women (Stein, 2001). Progesterone appears to afford protection in the immediate post-injury period due to its anti-inflammatory properties. Estrogen is also thought to act as a neuroprotectant. However, this finding has not been so evident in humans. Studies have shown either no gender differences in outcome (Davis et al., 2006) or show poorer survival rates or functional outcomes for women overall (Farace & Alves, 2000), or those in either younger (Czosnyka et al., 2008) or in older age-groups (Kirkness, Burr, Mitchell, & Newell, 2004; Kraus, Peek-Asa, & McArthur, 2000; Ponsford et al., 2008).

Following the return of consciousness the influence of gender on long-term functional outcome in survivors of TBI appears to be relatively limited. The majority of studies have found no gender differences in motor and cognitive functioning or employment outcomes at rehabilitation discharge and up to six years post-injury (Brown, et al., 2005; Moore, Ashman, Cantor, Krinick, & Spielman, 2010; Mushkudiani, et al., 2007; Ponsford, Olver,Curran, & Ng, 1995; Schönberger, et al., 2011; Slewa-Younan et al., 2008). In keeping with the findings of these short-term studies, studies conducted at 10 years or more post-injury have found that gender alone has a very limited influence on outcome (Kristy Draper & Jennie Ponsford, 2008; Draper, et al., 2007). One study by Steadman-Pare et al. (2001) found that females rated their quality of life more highly than males when interviewed 9–24 years post-injury. On the other hand, Colantonio and colleagues (Colantonio, Harris, Ratcliff, Chase, & Ellis,

2010) found some other gender differences in the same sample, in that significantly more men reported difficulty setting realistic goals and restlessness and reported sensitivity to noise and sleep disturbances as significantly more problematic than women, whereas significantly more women reported headaches, dizziness, and loss of confidence and found lack of initiative and needing supervision were significantly more problematic in daily functioning.

As with age, it has been found in one study that when gender is combined with other variables, including injury severity, demographic factors and post-injury impairment a total of 14% to 26% of the variance in physical independence, employment, and social integration outcomes can be accounted for (Dawson & Chipman, 1995). These findings suggest that the impact of age and gender on long-term outcomes may be limited when these factors are considered alone. However when combined with other factors, such as injury severity, education, and residual impairment, age and gender may contribute to the variability in outcome.

Pre-Injury Intelligence, Education, and Employment Status. As noted earlier, Raymont and colleagues (2008) found that higher pre-injury intelligence was associated with better long-term cognitive outcome in Vietnam veterans who had sustained penetrating head injuries. This was also the finding of Green and colleagues (2008) in a general TBI sample. Several studies conducted up to five years post-injury have found that higher pre-injury education and/or pre-injury employment status are associated with better educational or employment outcomes following TBI (Franulic, Carbonell, Pinto, & Sepulveda, 2004; Keyser-Marcus et al., 2002; Mushkudiani et al., 2007; Novack et al., 2001; M. Schönberger et al., 2011; Sherer, Sander, et al., 2002; Sigurdardottir et al., 2009). As with other variables, combining factors, such as pre-injury education, PTA, and post-injury disability, with pre-injury employment accounts for a much larger percentage of the variance in productivity status (Schönberger et al., 2011; Sherer, Sander, et al., 2002; Willemse-van Son, Ribbers, Verhagen, & Stam, 2007).

Studies conducted 10 years or more post-injury have also found that higher pre-injury education

is associated with better outcome in the areas of cognition, employment, social functioning, and community integration (Draper & J. Ponsford, 2008; Draper, et al., 2007; Hoofien, et al., 2002; Raymont, et al., 2008; Wood & Rutterford, 2006a). Pre-injury education alone has been found to account for 12% and 7% of the variance in social functioning and home ADL, respectively (Hoofien, et al., 2002). Multivariate studies have also found that pre-injury education is a significant contributor to outcomes in physical independence, community integration, and employment when combined with other variables including injury severity, age, gender and post-injury physical and cognitive disability (Hoofien, et al., 2002; Tate, et al., 2005; Wood & Rutterford, 2006a). Pre-injury employment has received limited investigation as a predictor in follow-up studies 10 years or more post-injury, although Tate et al.(2005) found that more highly skilled pre-injury employment was associated with better outcome in the domains of living skills, relationships, and employment.

Genetic Status. Whilst a number of genes have been implicated as influencing the outcome following TBI, the most extensively studied has been the ApoE gene. ApoE genotype has been shown to influence coma duration, rate, and degree of functional outcome, cognitive and behavioral impairments, and risk of post-traumatic seizures, as well as cognitive and behavioral functions following TBI, with possession of the e4 allele said to have a negative influence (Alexander et al., 2007; Jordan, 2007; Ponsford et al., 2011). Pathologically, presence of the ApoE e4 allele has been associated with increased amyloid deposition, amyloid angiopathy, larger intracranial hematomas, and more severe contusional injury. The proposed mechanism by which ApoE affects the clinicopathological consequences of TBI has not been clearly established, but is most likely multifactorial, including the influence of this gene on oxidative stress, neuroprotection, central nervous system plasticity in response to injury, amyloid deposition, disruption of cytoskeletal stability, and cholinergic dysfunction.

A number of other genes which potentially impact on other pathophysiological processes following TBI have been studied less extensively.

The catechol-o-methyltransferase or COMT and DRD2 genes may influence cognitive processes such as executive/frontal lobe functions via their impact on dopamine. The inflammatory response to TBI is mediated by the interleukin genes. Apoptosis may be modulated by polymorphisms of the p53 gene. The ACE gene may affect mechanisms of cerebral blood flow. The CACNA1A gene may influence calcium channels and hence the development of cerebral edema (Jordan, 2007). Much further investigation is needed. However, given the many and variable factors and genetic influences operating simultaneously following TBI, it is going to be difficult to isolate a significant impact of individual genes on outcome.

Social Factors

Family and Social Support

Kendall and Terry (2009) found that family support was the most significant direct predictor of long-term emotional well-being following TBI. How well the family was functioning prior to injury influences the family's adaptation to TBI, in both adults and children, and this, in turn influences outcome (Curtiss, Klemz, & Vanderploeg, 2000; Sander et al., 2002; Yeates et al., 2004). For many families, particularly those with pre-existing problems, TBI increases their vulnerability, making them weaker and more dysfunctional. However, other families may actually become stronger and more resilient in the face of the chronic challenges presented by TBI (Perlesz, 1999).

Social support and other social factors may also be influential on outcome. In a study of 7,612 people hospitalized for TBI in the United States (McCarthy et al., 2006), 29% of participants reported poor psychosocial health. Inadequate or moderate social support, along with Medicaid coverage, lack of health insurance, and comorbidities such as pre-injury substance abuse, younger age, being female, cognitive complaints, and limitation in ADL were associated with poor psychosocial well-being.

Neighborhood characteristics, such as the economic, educational, and employment status of neighbors and proportion with disability in the local community, have been shown

to make a unique contribution to outcome (Corrigan & Bogner, 2008). In a study of social support-seeking, Farmer, Clark and Sherman (2003) found that living in a rural area was associated with more openness in seeking social supports, which was in turn associated with better quality of life outcomes. This finding possibly explains the fact that, while living in rural areas is potentially problematic due to limitations in services and employment opportunities, this has not always translated into poorer outcomes (Ponsford, Olver, Ponsford, & Schönberger, 2010).

Cultural Background

In the study by De Silva et al. (2009) involving patients from 46 countries, outcomes six months after TBI were compared between high- and lower-income countries. Patients from lower income countries were more than twice as likely to die following severe TBI, but were half as likely to be disabled following mild and moderate TBI.

Mushkudiani et al. (2007) found that outcome in black patients was poorer than that in whites in a combined cohort from the IMPACT study, although it was noted that there was a need for further examination of mediating factors. In a study involving 151 persons with mild to severe TBI (38% black; 38% Hispanic; 24% white) recruited from consecutive admissions to the neurosurgery service of a county level I trauma center, Sander et al. (2009) showed that after accounting for injury severity, age, education, and income, race/ethnicity contributed significantly to the variance in CIQ total score, Home Integration Scale, and Productive Activity Scale, with blacks scoring lower than white and Hispanic participants on the CIQ Home Integration and Productive Activity Scales. These differences were still evident after accounting for income, although as income was more predictive than race/ethnicity for certain aspects of community integration, it should be accounted for in all studies investigating racial/ethnic differences in outcomes. Hart and colleagues (Hart, Whyte, Polansky, Kersey-Matusiak, & Fidler-Sheppard, 2005) also found that at one year post-TBI, African Americans with TBI reported significantly lower social integration subscale scores and had lost more income than whites. All other outcome measures were comparable between groups.

In an Australian study comparing participants from culturally and linguistically diverse (CALD) backgrounds with moderate to severe TBI, with those from English-speaking backgrounds, Saltapidas and Ponsford (2007; 2008) found that despite the groups having similar levels of participation in rehabilitation, CALD participants showed poorer outcomes in several domains including post-injury employment, cognitive independence, mobility, and social integration on the Craig Handicap Assessment and Reporting Technique (CHART). CALD participants also experienced greater negative emotions, showed higher levels of distress about changes to certain life roles and were less likely to have internal locus of control causal beliefs than English-speaking background participants. Regression analyses indicated that cultural value system, level of understanding about the injury, and emotional response to injury, as well as years of education, were significant predictors of outcome on the CHART. It would appear that beliefs, attitudes, and coping styles in the context of injury are important variables in influencing outcome.

Pre-Injury Psychiatric History and Coping Style

Whilst some outcome studies have excluded people with pre-injury psychiatric disturbance, recent findings have suggested pre-injury psychiatric history has a significant influence on outcome, through its influence on post-injury psychological adjustment (Schönberger, et al., 2011). Whelan-Goodinson et al. (2008), Bombardier et al. (2010) and Gould, Ponsford, Johnston and Schönberger (2011b) and have all found that presence of pre-injury history of psychiatric disorder was a significant risk factor for post-injury psychiatric disorder and that post-injury psychiatric disorders were in turn associated with poorer functional outcome and/or quality of life. Dikmen et al. (2010) found that pre-injury alcohol use and pre-injury psychiatric history were associated with greater symptom reporting at one year post-injury. Jorge

et al. (2005) found that both Alcohol Abuse/Dependence (AA/D) and mood disorders following TBI were associated with a poor vocational outcome. In a systematic review of 35 articles reporting on 14 cohorts, Willemse-van Son et al. (2007) found that pre-injury substance abuse was a significant predictor of both long-term disability and productivity status, in combination with other factors.

Coping style is another variable which has recently emerged as a significant predictor of psychosocial and emotional adjustment after TBI. Coping strategies are commonly defined as either problem-focused or emotion-focused (Lazarus & Folkman, 1984). Problem-focused coping strategies attempt to deal with the problem, for example by seeking information, planning, or seeking social support. Emotion-focused coping attempts to modulate the emotional reaction to the stressful event. Recent studies have shown that the use of non-productive emotion-focused or avoidant coping strategies such as worry, wishful thinking, self-blame, and substance use has been associated with poorer psychosocial outcomes following TBI (Anson & Ponsford, 2006; Curran, Ponsford, & Crowe, 2000; Spitz, Ponsford, & Schönberger, in press; Tomberg, Toomela, Ennok, & Tikk, 2007; Wolters, Stapert, Brands, & Van Heugten, 2010).

Conclusions

TBI results in significant changes in mobility, cognition, behavior, and emotional state. While many physical problems resolve in the first six months after injury, cognitive and behavioral changes are reportedly more persistent, along with more subtle problems with balance, which affect mobility. There are high rates of return to independence in personal activities of daily living, but a greater number require assistance in community-based activities and financial management due to cognitive impairments. More than half of those with moderate to severe TBI are not able to return to employment or other productive activities. Difficulties with social and leisure activities and relationships are also common for about a third of those injured, resulting in social isolation and increased dependence on family support. Many families suffer ongoing stress as a result of the burden of caring for their injured loved ones and the quality of marital relationships may decline. Outcomes are ultimately determined by a complex interaction between biological factors relating to the severity of injury (PTA, GCS, imaging findings), as well as a range of personal factors, including age, gender, genetic status, education, pre-injury employment status, pre-injury psychiatric status, and coping style, as well as social factors, including family and social support and cultural background. An understanding of these factors and their interactions is vital to maximize the efficiency of resource allocation and the effectiveness of rehabilitative interventions to enhance outcomes following TBI.

References

Alexander, S., Kerr, M., Kim, Y., Kamboh, M., Beers, S., & Conley, Y. (2007). Apolipoprotein E4 allele presence and functional outcome after severe traumatic brain injury. *Journal of Neurotrauma*, 24(5), 790–797.

Anderson, M. I., Parmenter, T. R., & Mok, M. (2002). The relationship between neurobehavioural problems of severe traumatic brain injury (TBI), family functioning and the psychological well-being of the spouse/caregiver: path model analysis. *Brain Injury*, 16(9), 743–757.

Anson, K., & Ponsford, J. (2006). Coping style and emotional adjustment following traumatic brain injury. *Journal of Head Trauma Rehabilitation*, 21(3), 248–259.

Arango-Lasprilla, J. C., Ketchum, J. M., Dezfulian, T., Kreutzer, J. S., O'Neil-Pirozzi, T. M., Hammond, F., et al. (2008). Predictors of marital stability 2 years following traumatic brain injury. *Brain Injury*, 22(7-8), 564–574.

Ashman, T. A., Cantor, J. B., Gordon, W. A., Sacks, A., Spielman, L., Egan, M., et al. (2008). A comparison of cognitive functioning in older adults with and without traumatic brain injury. *Journal of Head Trauma Rehabilitation*, 23(3 May-Jun), 139–148.

Ashman, T. A., Spielman, L. A., Hibbard, M. R., Silver, J. M., Chandna, T., & Gordon, W. A. (2004). Psychiatric challenges in the first 6 years after traumatic brain injury: cross-sequential analyses of Axis I disorders. *Archives of Physical Medicine and Rehabilitation*, 85, 36–42.

Avesani, R., Salvi, L., Rigoli, G., & Gambini, M. G. (2005). Reintegration after severe brain injury: a retrospective study. *Brain Injury*, 19(11 Oct), 933–939.

Belanger, H. G., Kretzmer, T., Yoash-Gantz, R., Pickett, T., & Tupler, L. A. (2009). Cognitive

sequelae of blast-related versus other mechanisms of brain trauma. *Journal of the International Neuropsychological Society*, 15(1), 1–8.

Bier, N., Dutil, E., & Couture, M. (2009). Factors affecting leisure participation after a traumatic brain injury: an exploratory study. *Journal of Head Trauma Rehabilitation*, 24(3), 187–194.

Boake, C., Millis, S. R., High, W. M., Delmonico, R. L., Kreutzer, J. S., Rosenthal, M., et al. (2001). Using early neuropsychological testing to predict long-term productivity outcome from traumatic brain injury. *Archives of Physical Medicine and Rehabilitation*, 82, 761–768.

Bombardier, C. H., Fann, J. R., Temkin, N. R., Esselman, P. C., Barber, J., & Dikmen, S. S. (2010). Rates of major depressive disorder and clinical outcomes following traumatic brain injury. *JAMA*, 303, 1938–1945.

Bracy, C. A., & Douglas, J. M. (2002). Comparison of a group of long-term TBI marital dyads with a control group of orthopaedic marital dyads, on measures of marital satisfaction, marital coping, and perception of husbands' communication skills. *Brain Impairment*, 3(1), 71.

Brown, A. W., Malec, J. F., McClelland, R. L., Diehl, N. N., Englander, J., & Cifu, D. (2005). Clinical elements that predict outcome after traumatic brain injury: A prospective multicenter Recursive Partitioning (Decision-Tree) Analysis. *Journal of Neurotrauma*, 22(10), 1040–1051.

Brown, A. W., Malec, J. F., McClelland, R. L., Diehl, N. N., Englander, J., & Cifu, D. X. (2005). Clinical elements that predict outcome after traumatic brain injury: A prospective multicentre recursive partitioning (decision-tree) analysis. *Journal of Neurotrauma*, 22, 1040–1051.

Burridge, A. C., Williams, W. H., Yates, P. J., Harris, A., & Ward, C. D. (2007). Spousal relationship satisfaction following acquired brain injury: The role of insight and socio-emotional skill. *Neuropsychological Rehabilitation*, 17(1), 95–105.

Bush, B. A., Novack, T. A., Malec, J. F., Stringer, A. Y., Millis, S. R., & Madan, A. (2003). Validation of a model for evaluating outcome after traumatic brain injury. *Archives of Physical Medicine and Rehabilitation*, 84(12 Dec), 1803–1807.

Chamelian, L., & Feinstein, A. (2006). The effect of major depression on subjective and objective cognitive deficits in mild to moderate traumatic brain injury. *Journal of Neuropsychiatry and Clinical Neuroscience*, 18(1), 33–38.

Colantonio, A., Harris, J. E., Ratcliff, G., Chase, S., & Ellis, K. (2010). Gender differences in self reported long term outcomes following moderate to severe traumatic brain injury. *BMC Neurology*, 10, 102.

Colantonio, A., Ratcliff, G., Chase, S., Kelsey, S., Escobar, M., & Vernich, L. (2004). Long term outcomes after moderate to severe traumatic brain injury. *Disability and Rehabilitation, 26*(5), 253–261.

Cooper-Evans, S., Alderman, N., Knight, C., & Oddy, M. (2008). Self-esteem as a predictor of psychological distress after severe acquired brain injury: An exploratory study. *Neuropsychological Rehabilitation, 18*(5-6), 607–626.

Corkin, S., Rosen, T. J., Sullivan, E. V., & Clegg, R. A. (1989). Penetrating head injury in young adulthood exacerbates cognitive decline in later years. *Journal of Neuroscience, 9*(11 Nov), 3876–3883.

Corrigan, J. D., & Bogner, J. A. (2008). Neighbourhood characteristics and outcomes after traumatic brain injury. *Archives of Physical Medicine and Rehabilitation, 89*, 912–921.

Curran, C. A., Ponsford, J. L., & Crowe, S. (2000). Coping strategies and emotional outcome following traumatic brain injury: A comparison with orthopaedic patients. *Journal of Head Trauma Rehabilitation, 15*(6), 1256–1274.

Curtiss, G., Klemz, S., & Vanderploeg, R. D. (2000). Acute impact of severe traumatic brain injury on family structure and coping responses. *Journal of Head Trauma Rehabilitation, 15*, 1113–1122.

Cusick, C., Gerhart, K. A., & Mellick, D. (2000). Participant-proxy reliability in traumatic brain injury outcome research. *Journal of Head Trauma Rehabilitation, 15*, 739–749.

Czosnyka, M., Radolovich, D., Balestreri, M., Lavinio, A., Hutchinson, P., Timofeev, I., et al. (2008). Gender-related differences in intracranial hypertension and outcome after traumatic brain injury. *Acta Neurochirurgica Supplement, 102*, 25–28.

Dacey, R., Dikmen, S., Temkin, N., McLean, A., Armsden, G., & Winn, H. R. (1991). Relative effects of brain and non-brain injuries on neuropsychological and psychosocial outcome. *Journal of Trauma-Injury Infection & Critical Care., 31*(2 Feb), 217–222.

Davis, D. P., Douglas, D. J., Smith, W., Sise, M. J., Vilke, G. M., Holbrook, T. L., et al. (2006). Traumatic brain injury outcomes in pre- and post-menopausal females versus age-matched males. *Journal of Neurotrauma, 23*(2 Feb), 140–148.

Dawson, D. R., & Chipman, M. (1995). The Disablement Experienced by Traumatically Brain-Injured Adults Living in the Community. *Brain Injury, 9*(4), 339–353. doi:10.3109/02699059509005774

de Guise, E., LeBlanc, J., Feyz, M., & Lamoureux, J. (2006). Prediction of outcome at discharge from acute care following traumatic brain injury. *Journal of Head Trauma Rehabilitation, 21*(6 Nov-Dec), 527–536.

De Silva, M. J., Roberts, I., Perel, P., Edwards, P., Kenward, M. G., Fernandes, J., et al. (2009). Patient outcome after traumatic brain injury in high-, middle- and low-income countries: analysis of data on 8927 patients in 46 countries. *International Journal of Epidemiology, 38*(2), 452–458.

Deb, S., & Burns, J. (2007). Neuropsychiatric consequences of traumatic brain injury: a comparison between two age groups. *Brain Injury, 21*(3 Mar), 301–307.

Dikmen, S., Machamer, J., Fann, J. R., & Temkin, N. R. (2010). Rates of symptom reporting following traumatic brain injury. *Journal of the International Neuropsychological Society 16*, 401–411.

Dikmen, S. S., Corrigan, J. D., Levin, H. S., Machamer, J., Stiers, W., & Weisskopf, M. G. (2009). Cognitive outcome following traumatic brain injury. *Journal of Head Trauma Rehabilitation, 24*(6(Nov-Dec)), 430–438.

Dikmen, S. S., Machamer, J., & Temkin, N. (1993). Psychological outcome in patients with moderate to severe brain injury. *Brain Injury, 15*, 747–762.

Dikmen, S. S., Machamer, J. E., Powell, J. M., & Temkin, N. R. (2003). Outcome three to five years after moderate to severe traumatic brain injury. *Archives of Physical Medicine and Rehabilitation, 84*(10), 1449–1457.

Dikmen, S. S., Machamer, J. E., Winn, R., & Temkin, N. R. (1995a). Neuropsychological outcome at one-year post head injury. *Neuropsychology, 9*, 80–90.

Doctor, J. N., Castro, J., Temkin, N. R., Fraser, R. T., Machamer, J. E., & Dikmen, S. S. (2005). Workers' risk of unemployment after traumatic brain injury: a normed comparison. *Journal of the International Neuropsychological Society, 11*(6 Oct), 747–752.

Draper, K., & Ponsford, J. (2007). Long-term outcome following traumatic brain injury: How should this be measured? *Neuropsychological Rehabilitation, 19*(5), 645–661.

Draper, K., & Ponsford, J. (2008). Cognitive functioning ten years following traumatic brain injury and rehabilitation. *Neuropsychology, 22*(5), 618–625.

Draper, K., Ponsford, J., & Schönberger, M. (2007). Psychosocial and emotional outcome following traumatic brain injury. *Journal of Head Trauma Rehabilitation, 22*(5), 278–287.

Engberg, A. W., & Teasdale, T. W. (2004). Psychosocial outcome following traumatic brain injury in adults: A long-term population-based follow-up. *Brain Injury, 18*(6), 533–545.

Ergh, T. C., Rapport, L. J., Coleman, R. D., & Hanks, R. A. (2002). Predictors of caregiver and family functioning following traumatic brain injury. *Journal of Head Trauma Rehabilitation, 17*(2), 155–174.

Farace, E., & Alves, W. M. (2000). Do women fare worse: A metaanalysis of gender differences in traumatic brain injury outcome. *Journal of Neurosurgery, 93*, 539–545.

Farmer, J. E., Clark, M. J., & Sherman, A. K. (2003). Rural Versus Urban Social Support Seeking as a Moderating Variable in Traumatic Brain Injury Outcome. *The Journal of Head Trauma Rehabilitation, 18*(2), 116–127.

Fleminger, S., Oliver, D. L., Lovestone, S., Rabe-Hesketh, S., & Giora, A. (2003). Head injury as a risk factor for Alzheimers Disease: the evidence 10 years on; a partial replication. *Journal of Neurology Neurosurgery and Psychiatry, 74*, 857–862.

Formisano, R., Carlesimo, G. A., Sabbadini, M., Loassess, A., Penta, F., Vinicola, V., et al. (2004). Clinical predictors and neuropsychological outcome in severe traumatic brain injury patients. *Acta Neurochirurgica, 146*, 457–462.

Franulic, A., Carbonell, C. G., Pinto, P., & Sepulveda, I. (2004). Psychosocial adjustment and employment outcome 2, 5 and 10 years after TBI. *Brain Injury, 18*, 119–129.

Fryer, J. (1989). Adolescent community integration. In P. Bach-y-Rita (Ed.), *Traumatic Brain Injury* (pp. 255–286). New York: Demos Publications.

Goodinson, R., Ponsford, J., Johnston, L., & Grant, F. (2009). Psychiatric disorders following traumatic brain injury: Their nature and frequency. *Journal of Head Trauma Rehabilitation, 24*(5), 324–332.

Gouick, J., & Gentleman, D. (2004). The emotional and behavioural consequences of traumatic brain injury. *Trauma, 5*, 285–292.

Gould, K. R., Ponsford, J., Johnston, L., & Schönberger, M. (2011a). The relationship between psychiatric disorders and one-year psychosocial outcome. *Journal of Head Trauma Rehabilitation, 26*(1), 79–89.

Gould, K. R., Ponsford, J. L., Johnston, J., & Schönberger, M. (2011b). Predictive and associated factors of psychiatric disorders after traumatic brain injury: A prospective study. *Journal of Neurotrauma, 28*(7), 1149–1154.

Gould, K. R., Ponsford, J. L., Johnston, L., & Schönberger, M. (2011c). The nature, frequency and course of psychiatric disorders in the first year after traumatic brain injury, a prospective study. *Psychological Medicine, 41*(10), 2099–2109.

Green, R. E., Colella, B., Christensen, B., Johns, K., Frasca, D., Bayley, M., et al. (2008). Examining moderators of cognitive recovery trajectories after moderate to severe traumatic brain injury. *Archives of Physical Medicine and Rehabilitation, 89*(12 Suppl Dec), S 16–24.

Hart, T., Seignourel, P. J., & Sherer, M. (2009). A longitudinal study of awareness of deficit after moderate to severe traumatic brain injury. *Neuropsychological Rehabilitation, 19*(2), 161–176.

Hart, T., Sherer, M., Whyte, J., Polansky, M., & Novack, T. A. (2004). Awareness of behavioural, cognitive, and physical deficits in acute traumatic brain injury. *Archives of Physical Medicine and Rehabilitation, 85*, 1450–1456.

Hart, T., Whyte, J., Polansky, M., Kersey-Matusiak, G., & Fidler-Sheppard, R. (2005). Community outcomes following traumatic brain injury: impact of race and preinjury status. *Journal of Head Trauma Rehabilitation., 20*(2 Mar-Apr), 158–172.

Hart, T., Whyte, J., Polansky, M., Millis, S., Hammond, F., Sherer, M., et al. (2003). Concordance of patient and family report of neurobehavioural symptoms at one year after traumatic brain injury. *Archives of Physical Medicine and Rehabilitation, 84*, 204–213.

Hibbard, M. R., Uysal, S., Kepler, K., Bogdany, J., & Silver, J. (1998). Axis I psychopathology in individuals with traumatic brain injury. *The Journal of Head Trauma Rehabilitation, 13*, 24–39.

Himanen, L., Portin, R., Isoniemi, H., Helenius, H., Kurkj, T., & Tenovuo, O. (2006). Longitudinal cognitive changes in traumatic brain injury: A 30-year follow-up study. *Neurology, 66*, 187–192.

Hoofien, D., Gilboa, A., Vakil, E., & Barak, O. (2004). Unawareness of cognitive deficits and daily functioning among persons with traumatic brain injuries. *Journal of Clinical and Experimental Neuropsychology, 26*, 278–290.

Hoofien, D., Gilboa, A., Vakil, E., & Donovick, P. J. (2001). Traumatic brain injury 10-20 years later: A comprehensive outcome study of psychiatric symptomatology, cognitive abilities, and psychosocial functioning. *Brain Injury, 15*, 189–209.

Hoofien, D., Vakil, E., Gilboa, A., Donovick, P. J., & Barak, O. (2002). Comparison of the predictive power of socio-economic variables, severity of injury and age on long-term outcome of traumatic brain injury: Sample-specific variables versus factors as predictors. *Brain Injury, 16*, 9–27.

Hukkelhoven, C. W., Steyerberg, E. W., Rampen, A. J., Farace, E., Habbema, J. D., Marshall, L. F., et al. (2003). Patient age and outcome following severe traumatic brain injury: an analysis of 5600 patients. *Journal of Neurosurgery, 99*(4), 666–673. doi:10.3171/jns.2003.99.4.0666

Jennett, B., & Bond, M. (1975). Assessment of outcome after severe brain damage: A practical scale. *The Lancet, 305*(7905), 480–484.

Jordan, B. D. (2007). Genetic influences on outcome following traumatic brain injury. *Neurochemical Research, 32*(4-5 Apr-May), 905–915.

Jorge, R. E., Robinson, R. G., Moser, D., Tateno, A., Crespo-Facorro, B., & Arndt, S. V. (2004). Major depression following traumatic brain injury. *Archives of General Psychiatry, 61*, 42–50.

Jorge, R. E., Starkstein, S. E., Arndt, S., Moser, D., Crespo-Facorro, B., & Robinson, R. G. (2005). Alcohol misuse and mood disorders following traumatic brain injury. *Archives of General Psychiatry, 62*(7 Jul), 742–749.

Kendall, E. (2003). Predicting vocational adjustment following traumatic brain injury: A test of a psychosocial theory. *Journal of Vocational Rehabilitation, 19*, 31–45.

Kendall, E., & Terry, D. (2009). Predicting emotional well-being following traumatic brain injury: a test of mediated and moderated models. *Social Science & Medicine., 69*(6 Sep), 947–954.

Kennedy, M., Krause, M., & Turkstra, L. (2008). An electronic survey about college experiences after traumatic brain injury. *NeuroRehabilitation, 23*, 219–231.

Keyser-Marcus, L. A., Bricout, J. C., Wehman, P., Campbell, L. R., Cifu, D. X., Englander, J., et al. (2002). Acute predictors of return to employment after traumatic brain injury: A longitudinal follow-up. *Archives of Physical Medicine and Rehabilitation, 83*, 635–641.

Kirkness, C. J., Burr, R. L., Mitchell, P. H., & Newell, D. W. (2004). Is there a sex difference in the course following traumatic brain injury? *Biological Research for Nursing, 5*(4 Apr), 299–310.

Koponen, S., Taiminen, T., Portin, R., Himanen, L., Isoniemi, H., Heinonen, H., et al. (2002). Axis I and II Psychiatric disorders after traumatic brain injury: A 30-year follow-up study. *American Journal of Psychiatry, 159*, 1315–1321.

Koskinen, S. (1998). Quality of life 10 years after a very severe traumatic brain injury: The perspective of the injured and the closest relative. *Brain Injury, 12*, 631–648.

Koskinen, S., Hokkinen, E.-M., Sarajuuri, J., & Alaranta, H. (2007). Applicability of the ICF Checklist to traumatically brain-injured patients in post-acute rehabilitation settings. *Journal of Rehabilitation Medicine, 39*, 467–472.

Kraus, J. F., & McArthur, D. L. (1999). Incidence and prevalence of and costs associated with traumatic brain injury. In M. Rosenthal, E. R. Griffith, J. S. Kreutzer & B. Pentland (Eds.), *Rehabilitation of the adult and child with traumatic brain injury* (pp. 3–17). Philadelphia: FA Davis.

Kraus, J. F., Peek-Asa, C., & McArthur, D. (2000). The independent effect of gender on outcomes following traumatic brain injury: a preliminary investigation. *Neurosurgical Focus, 8*(1 Jan 15), e5.

Kreutzer, J. S., Marwitz, J. H., Hsu, N., Williams, K., & Riddick, A. (2007). Marital stability after brain injury: An investigation and analysis. *NeuroRehabilitation, 22*(1), 53–59.

Kreutzer, J. S., Marwitz, J. H., Walker, W., Sander, A., Sherer, M., Bogner, J. A., et al. (2003). Moderating factors in return to work and job stability after traumatic brain injury. *Journal of Head Trauma Rehabilitation, 18*(2), 128–138.

Lazarus, R., & Folkman, S. (1984). *Stress, appraisal and coping.* New York: Springer Publishing Company.

LeBlanc, J., de Guise, E., Gosselin, N., & Feyz, M. (2006). Comparison of functional outcome following acute care in young, middle-aged and elderly patients with traumatic brain injury. *Brain Injury 20*(8 Jul), 779–790.

Lehtonen, S., Stringer, A. Y., Millis, S., Boake, C., Englander, J., Hart, T., et al. (2005). Neuropsychological outcome and community reintegration following traumatic brain injury: The impact of frontal and non-frontal lesions. *Brain Injury, 19*, 239–256.

Livingston, D. H., Lavery, R. F., Mosenthal, A. C., Knudson, M. M., Lee, S., Morabito, D., et al. (2005). Recovery at one year following isolated traumatic brain injury: a Western Trauma Association prospective multicenter trial. *Journal of Trauma, 59*(6 Dec), 1298–1304.

Maas, A. I., Hukkelhoven, C. W., Marshall, L. F., & Steyerberg, E. W. (2005). Prediction of outcome in traumatic brain injury with computed tomographic characteristics: a comparison between the computed tomographic classification and combinations of computed tomographic predictors. *Neurosurgery, 57*(6 Dec), 1173–1182.

Maas, A. I., Steyerberg, E. W., Butcher, I., Dammers, R., Lu, J., Marmarou, A., et al. (2007). Prognostic value of computerized tomography scan characteristics in traumatic brain injury: results from the IMPACT study. *Journal of Neurotrauma, 24*(2 Feb), 303–314.

Machamer, J., Temkin, N., Fraser, R., Doctor, J., & Dikmen, S. (2005). Stability of employment after traumatic brain injury. *Journal of the International Neuropsychological Society, 11*, 807–816.

MacMillan, P. J., Hart, R. P., Martelli, M. F., & Zasler, N. D. (2002). Pre-injury status and adaptation following traumatic brain injury. *Brain Injury, 16*(1), 41–49.

McCarthy, M. L., Dikmen, S. S., Langlois, J. A., Selassie, A. W., Gu, J. K., & Horner, M. D. (2006). Self-reported psychosocial health among adults with traumatic brain injury. *Archives of Physical Medicine & Rehabilitation, 87*(7 Jul), 953–961.

McLean, A., Dikmen, S., Temkin, N., Wyler, A. R., & Gale, J. L. (1984). Psychosocial functioning one month after head injury. *Neurosurgery, 14*, 393–399.

Mehta, K., Ott, A., Kalmijn, S., Slooter, A., van Duijn, C., Hofman, A., et al. (1999). Head trauma and risk of dementia and Alzheimer's disease: The Rotterdam study. *Neurology, 53*(9), 1959–1962.

Millis, S. R., Rosenthal, M., Novack, T. A., Sherer, M., Nick, T. G., Kreutzer, J. S., et al. (2001). Long-term neuropsychological outcome after traumatic brain injury. *Journal of Head Trauma Rehabilitation, 16*(4), 343–355.

Moore, D. W., Ashman, T. A., Cantor, J. B., Krinick, R. J., & Spielman, L. A. (2010). Does gender influence cognitive outcome after traumatic brain injury? *Neuropsychological Rehabilitation, 20*(3 Jun), 340–354.

Mushkudiani, N. A., Engel, D. C., Steyerberg, E. W., Butcher, I., Lu, J., Marmarou, A., et al. (2007). Prognostic value of demographic characteristics in traumatic brain injury: results from the IMPACT study. *Journal of Neurotrauma, 24*(2 Feb), 259–269.

Nakase-Richardson, R., Sepehri, A., Sherer, M., Yablon, S. A., Evans, C., & Tanja, M. (2009). Classification Schema pf Posttraumatic Amnesia Duration-Based Injury Severity Relative to 1-Year Outcome: Analysis of Individuals with Moderate to Severe Traumatic Brain Injury. *Archives of Physical Medicine and Rehabilitation, 90*(January), 17–19.

Nakase-Richardson, R., Sherer, M., Seel, R. T., Hart, T., Hanks, R., Arango-Lasprilla, J. C., et al. (2011). Utility of post-traumatic amnesia in predicting 1-year productivity following traumatic brain injury: comparison of the Russell and Mississippi PTA classification intervals. *Journal of Neurology, Neurosurgery and Psychiatry, 82*(5), 494–499.

Novack, T. A., Bush, B. A., Meythaler, J. M., & Canupp, K. (2001). Outcome after traumatic brain injury: Pathway analysis of contributions from premorbid, injury severity and recovery variables. *Archives of Physical Medicine and Rehabilitation, 82*, 300–305.

O'Rance, L., & Fortune, N. (2007). *Disability in Australia: acquired brain injury.* Canberra: Australian Government.

O'Connor, C., Colantonio, A., & Polatajko, H. (2005). Long-term symptoms and limitations of activity of people with traumatic brain injury: A ten-year follow-up. *Psychological Reports, 97*, 169–179.

Olver, J. H., Ponsford, J. L., & Curran, C. (1996). Outcome following traumatic brain injury: A comparison between 2 and 5 years after injury. *Brain Injury, 10*, 841–848.

Ownsworth, T., & McKenna, K. (2008). Investigation of factors related to employment outcome following traumatic brain injury: a critical review and conceptual model. *Disability and Rehabilitation, 26*(13), 765–783.

Pagulayan, K. F., Hoffman, J. M., Temkin, N. R., Machamer, J. E., & Dikmen, S. S. (2008). Functional limitations and depression after traumatic brain injury: examination of the temporal relationship. *Archives of Physical Medicine & Rehabilitation, 89*(10, October), 1887–1892.

Pagulayan, K. F., Temkin, N. R., Machamer, J., & Dikmen, S. S. (2006). A longitudinal study of health-related quality of life after traumatic brain injury. *Archives of Physical Medicine & Rehabilitation., 87*(5 May), 611–618.

Perlesz, A. (1999). Complex responses to trauma: Challenges in bearing witness. *Australian and New Zealand Journal of Family Therapy, 20*(1), 11–19.

Perlesz, A., Kinsella, G., & Crowe, S. (1999). Impact of traumatic brain injury on the family: A critical review. *Rehabilitation Psychology, 44*, 6–35.

Perlesz, A., Kinsella, G., & Crowe, S. (2000). Psychological distress and family satisfaction following traumatic brain injury: injured individuals and their primary, secondary, and tertiary caregivers. *Journal of Head Trauma Rehabilitation, 15*(3), 909–929.

Plassman, B. L., Havlik, R. J., Steffens, D. C., Helms, M. J., Newman, T. N., Drosdick, D., et al. (2000). Documented head injury in early adulthood and risk of Alzheimers Disease and other dementias. *Neurology, 55*, 1158–1166.

Ponsford, J., Draper, K., & Schönberger, M. (2008). Functional outcome 10 years after traumatic brain injury: Its relationship with demographic, injury severity, and cognitive and emotional status. *Journal of the International Neuropsychological Society, 14*, 233–242.

Ponsford, J., McLaren, A., Schönberger, M., Burke, R., Rudzki, D., Olver, J. H., et al. (2011). The Association between Apolipoprotein E and Traumatic Brain Injury Severity and Functional Outcome in a Rehabilitation Sample. *Journal of Neurotrauma, 28*(9), 1683–1692.

Ponsford, J., Olver, J., Ponsford, M., & Schönberger, M. (2010). A comparison of outcomes in city versus regional dwelling patients with traumatic brain injury. *Brain Impairment, 11*, 253–261.

Ponsford, J., & Schönberger, M. (2010). Long-term family functioning following traumatic brain injury. *Journal of the International Neuropsychological Society, 16*, 1–12.

Ponsford, J. L., Myles, P. S., Cooper, D. J., Mcdermott, F. T., Murray, L. J., Laidlaw, J., et al. (2008). Gender differences in outcome in patients with hypotension and severe traumatic brain injury. *Injury, 39*(1 Jan), 67–76.

Ponsford, J. L., Olver, J. H., Curran, C., & Ng, K. (1995). Prediction of employment status 2 years after traumatic brain injury. *Brain Injury, 9*, 11–20.

Ponsford, J. L., Olver, J. H., Curran, C., & Ng, K. (1995). Prediction of employment status two years after traumatic brain injury. *Brain Injury, 9*, 11–20.

Ponsford, J. L., Olver, J. H., Ponsford, M., & Nelms, R. (2003). Long-term adjustment of families following traumatic brain injury where comprehensive rehabilitation has been provided. *Brain Injury, 17*(6), 453–468.

Port, A., Willmott, C., & Charlton, J. (2002). Self-awareness following traumatic brain injury and implications for rehabilitation. *Brain Injury, 16*(4), 277–289.

Possl, J., Jurgensmeyer, S., Karlbauer, F., Wenz, C., & Goldenberg, G. (2001). Stability of employment after brain injury: A 7-year follow-up study. *Brain Injury, 15*(1), 15–27.

Powell, J. M., Temkin, N. R., Machamer, J. E., & Dikmen, S. S. (2007). Gaining insight into patients' perspectives on participation in home management activities after traumatic brain injury. *American Journal of Occupational Therapy, 61*(3 May-Jun), 269–279.

Rapoport, M. J., Feinstein, A. (2000). Outcome following traumatic brain injury in the elderly: a critical review. *Brain Injury, 14*, 749–761.

Raymont, V., Greathouse, A., Reding, K., Lipsky, R., Salazar, A., & Grafman, J. (2008). Demographic, structural and genetic predictors of late cognitive decline after penetrating head injury. *Brain 131*(Pt 2 Feb), 543–558.

Robinson, R. G., & Jorge, R. E. (2002). Longitudinal course of mood disorders following traumatic brain injury. *Archives of General Psychiatry, 59*(1), 23–24.

Saltapidas, H., & Ponsford, J. (2007). The Influence of Cultural Background on Motivation for and Participation in Rehabilitation and Outcome Following Traumatic Brain Injury. *Journal of Head Trauma Rehabilitation, 22*(2), 132–139.

Saltapidas, H., & Ponsford, J. (2008). The influence of cultural background on experiences and beliefs following traumatic brain injury and their association with outcome. *Brain Impairment, 9*(1), 1–13.

Sander, A. M., Caroselli, J. S., High, W. M., Becker, C., Neese, L., & Scheibel, R. (2002). Relationship of family functioning to progress in a post-acute rehabilitation programme following traumatic brain injury. *Brain Injury, 16*(8), 649–657.

Satz, P., Zaucha, K., Forney, D. L., McCleary, C., Asarnow, R. F., Light, R., et al. (1998). Neuropsychological, psychosocial and vocational correlates of the Glasgow Outcome Scale at six months post-injury: A study of moderate to severe traumatic brain injury patients. *Brain Injury, 12*, 555–567.

Schönberger, M., Ponsford, J., Olver, J., Ponsford, M., & Wirtz, M. (2011). Prediction of functional and employment outcome one year after Traumatic Brain Injury: A Structural Equation Modelling approach. *Journal of Neurology, Neurosurgery and Psychiatry, 82*, 936–941

Schönberger, M., Ponsford, J., Reutens, D., Beare, R., & O'Sullivan, R. (2009). The relationship between age, injury severity and MRI findings following traumatic brain injury. *Journal of Neurotrauma, 26*, 2157–2167.

Schönberger, M., Ponsford, J. L., Gould, K. R., & Johnston, L. (2011). The temporal relationship between depression, anxiety and functional status after traumatic brain injury: A cross-lagged analysis. *Journal of the International Neuropsychological Society, 17* 1–7.

Senathi-Raja, D., Ponsford, J., & Schonberger, M. (2009). Association of age with long-term psychosocial outcome following traumatic brain injury. *Journal of Rehabilitation Medicine, 41*(8), 666–673.

Senathi-Raja, D., Ponsford, J., & Schönberger, M. (2010a). The association of age and time post-injury with long-term emotional outcome following TBI. *Journal of Head Trauma Rehabilitation, 25*(5), 330–338.

Senathi-Raja, D., Ponsford, J., & Schönberger, M. (2010b). Impact of age and time post-injury on long-term cognitive function after traumatic brain injury. *Neuropsychology, 24*(3), 336–344.

Shames, J., Treger, I., Ring, H., & Giaquinto, S. (2007). Return to work following traumatic brain injury: Trends and challenges. *Disability and Rehabilitation, 29*(7), 1387–1395.

Sherer, M., Novack, T. A., Sander, A. M., Struchen, M. A., Alderson, A., & Nakase Thompson, R. (2002). Neuropsychological assessment and employment outcome after traumatic brain injury: A review. *The Clinical Neuropsychologist, 16*(2), 157–178.

Sherer, M., Sander, A. M., Nick, T. G., High, W. M., Malec, J. F., & Rosenthal, M. (2002). Early cognitive status and productivity outcome after traumatic brain injury: Findings from the TBI Model Systems. *Archives of Physical Medicine and Rehabilitation 83*, 183–192.

Sherer, M., Struchen, M. A., Yablon, S. A., Wang, Y., & Nick, T. G. (2008). Comparison of indices of traumatic brain injury severity: Glasgow Coma Scale, length of coma and post-traumatic amnesia. *Journal of Neurology, Neurosurgery & Psychiatry, 79*(Oct 10), 678–685. doi:10.1136/jnnp.2006.111187

Sidaros, A., Engberg, A. W., Sidaros, K., Liptrot, M. G., Herning, M., Petersen, P., et al. (2008). Diffusion tensor imaging during recovery from severe traumatic brain injury and relation to clinical outcome: a longitudinal study. *Brain, 131*(Feb (Pt 2)), 559–572.

Sigurdardottir, S., Andelic, N., Roe, C., & Schanke, A. K. (2009). Cognitive recovery and predictors of functional outcome 1 year after traumatic brain injury. *Journal of the Internaitional Neuropsychological Society, 15*(5), 740–750.

Slewa-Younan, S., Baguley, I. J., Heriseanu, R., Cameron, I. D., Pitsiavas, V., Mudaliar, Y., et al. (2008). Do men and women differ in their course following traumatic brain injury? A preliminary prospective investigation of early outcome. *Brain Injury, 22*(2), 183–191. doi:10.1080/02699050801888808

Spitz, G., Ponsford, J., Rudzki, D., & Maller, J. (2012). The Association between Cognitive Performance and Functional Outcome Following Traumatic Brain Injury: A Longitudinal Multilevel Examination. *Neuropsychology, 26*(5), 604–612.

Spitz, G., Ponsford, J., & Schönberger, M. (in press). The relationship between cognitive impairment, coping style, and emotional adjustment following traumatic brain injury. *Journal of Head Trauma Rehabilitation* doi:10.1097/HTR.0b013e3182452f4f

Steadman-Pare, D., Colantonio, A., Ratcliff, G., Chase, S., & Vernich, L. (2001). Factors associated with perceived quality of life many years after traumatic brain injury. *Journal of Head Trauma Rehabilitation, 16*(4 Aug), 330–342.

Stein, D. G. (2001). Brain damage, sex hormones and recovery: a new role for progesterone and estrogen? *Trends in Neuroscience, 24*, 386–391.

Stein, D. M., Kufera, J. A., Lindell, A., Murdock, K. R., Menaker, J., Bochicchio, G. V., et al. (2011). Association of CSF biomarkers and secondary insults following severe traumatic brain injury. *Neurocritical Care., 14*(2 Apr), 200–207.

Tasaki, O., Shiozaki, T., Hamasaki, T., Kajino, K., Nakae, H., Tanaka, H., et al. (2009). Prognostic indicators and outcome prediction model for severe traumatic brain injury. *Journal of Trauma, 66*(2 Feb), 304–308.

Tate, R. L., & Broe, G. A. (1999). Psychosocial adjustment after traumatic brain injury: what are the important variables? *Psychological Medicine, 29*(3 May), 713–725.

Tate, R. L., Broe, G. A., Cameron, I. D., Hodgkinson, A. E., & Soo, C. A. (2005). Pre-injury, injury and early post-injury predictors of long-term functional and psychosocial recovery after severe traumatic brain injury. *Brain Impairment, 6*, 75–89.

Tate, R. L., Lulham, J. M., Broe, G. A., Strettles, B., & Pfaff, A. (1989). Psychosocial outcome for the survivors of severe blunt head injury: The results from a consecutive series of 100 patients. *Journal*

of Neurology, Neurosurgery, and Psychiatry, 52, 1128–1134.

Temkin, N. R., Corrigan, J. D., Dikmen, S. S., & Machamer, J. (2009). Social Functioning After Traumatic Brain Injury. *The Journal of Head Trauma Rehabilitation, 24*(6), 460–467

Testa, J. A., Malec, J. F., Moessner, A. M., & Brown, A. W. (2006). Predicting family functioning after TBI: impact of neurobehavioral factors. *Journal of Head Trauma Rehabilitation, 21*(3), 236–247.

Thomsen, I. V. (1984). Late outcome of very severe blunt head injury: a ten to fifteen year second follow-up. *Journal of Neurology, Neurosurgery, and Psychiatry, 47*, 260–268.

Thomsen, I. V. (1992). Late psychosocial outcome in severe traumatic brain injury. *Scandinavian Journal of Rehabilitation Medicine, 26*(Suppl.), 142–152.

Todis, B., & Glang, A. (2008). Redefining success: results of a qualitative study of postsecondary transition outcomes for youth with traumatic brain injury. *Journal of Head Trauma Rehabilitation 23*(4), 252–263.

Tomberg, T., Toomela, A., Ennok, M., & Tikk, A. (2007). Changes in coping strategies, social support, optimism and health-related quality of life following traumatic brain injury: A longitudinal study. *Brain Injury, 21*, 479–488.

Walker, W. C., Ketchum, J. M., Marwitz, J. H., Chen, T., Hammond, F., & Sherer, M., et al. (2010). A multicentre study on the clinical utility of post-traumatic amnesia duration in predicting global outcome after moderate-severe traumatic brain injury. *Journal of Neurology, Neurosurgery & Psychiatry, 81*(1), 87–89.

Walker, W. C., Marwitz, J. H., Kreutzer, J. S., Hart, T., & Novack, T. A. (2006). Occupational categories and return to work after traumatic brain injury: a multicenter study. *Archives of Physical Medicine & Rehabilitation., 87*(12 Dec), 1576–1582.

Wallace, C. A., & Bogner, J. (2000). Awareness of deficits: Emotional implications for persons with brain injury and their significant others. *Brain Injury, 14*(6), 549–562.

Watt, S. E., Shores, E. A., Baguley, I. J., Dorsch, N., & Fearnside, M. R. (2006). Protein S-100 and neuropsychological functioning following severe traumatic brain injury. *Brain Injury 20*(10 Sep), 1007–1017.

Whelan-Goodinson, R., Ponsford, J., Johnston, L., & Grant, F. (2009). Psychiatric disorders following traumatic brain injury: Their nature and frequency. *Journal of Head Trauma Rehabilitation, 24*, 324–332.

Whelan-Goodinson, R., Ponsford, J., & Schönberger, M. (2008). The association between psychiatric state and outcome following traumatic brain injury. *Journal of Rehabilitation Medicine, 40*(10), 850–857.

Wiesmann, M., Steinmeier, E., Magerkurth, O., Linn, J., Gottmann, D., & Missler, U. (2010). Outcome prediction in traumatic brain injury: comparison of neurological status, CT findings, and blood levels of S100B and GFAP. *Acta Neurologica Scandinavica, 121*(3 Mar), 178–185.

Willemse-van Son, A. H., Ribbers, G. M., Verhagen, A. P., & Stam, H. J. (2007). Prognostic factors of long-term functioning and productivity after traumatic brain injury: a systematic review of prospective cohort studies. *Clinical Rehabilitation 21*(11), 1024–1037.

Willer, B., Rosenthal, M., Kreutzer, J. S., Gordon, W. A., & Rempel, R. (1993). Assessment of community integration following rehabilitation for traumatic brain injury. *Journal of Head Trauma Rehabilitation, 8*, 75–87.

Wilson, J. T. L., Pettigrew, L. E. L., & Teasdale, G. M. (1998). Structured interviews for the Glasgow Outcome Scale and the Extended Glasgow Outcome Scale: Guidelines for their use. *Journal of Neurotrauma, 15*, 573–585.

Winkler, D., Unsworth, C., & Sloan, S. (2005). Time use following a severe traumatic brain injury. *Journal of Occupational Science, 12*(2), 69–81.

Winkler, D., Unsworth, C., & Sloan, S. (2006). Factors that lead to successful community integration following severe traumatic brain injury. *Journal of Head Trauma Rehabilitation 21*, 8–21.

Winstanley, J., Simpson, G., Tate, R., & Myles, B. (2006). Early indicators and contributors to psychological distress in relatives during rehabilitation following severe TBI: Findings from Brain Injury Outcomes Study. *Journal of Head Trauma Rehabilitation, 21*(6), 453–456.

Wise, E. K., Mathews-Dalton, C., Dikmen, S., Temkin, N., Machamer, J., Bell, K., et al. (2010). Impact of traumatic brain injury on participation in leisure activities. *Archives of Physical Medicine and Rehabilitation, 91*(9), 1357–1362.

Wolters, G., Stapert, S., Brands, I., & Van Heugten, C. (2010). Coping styles in relation to cognitive rehabilitation and quality of life after brain injury. *Neuropsychological Rehabilitation, 20*, 587–600.

Wood, R. L., & Rutterford, N. A. (2006a). Demographic and cognitive predictors of long-term psychosocial outcome following traumatic brain injury. *Journal of the International Neuropsychological Society, 12*, 350–358.

Wood, R. L., & Rutterford, N. A. (2006b). The long term effect of head trauma on intellectual abilities: A 16 year outcome study. *Journal of Neurology, Neurosurgery and Psychiatry, 77*(10), 1180–1184.

Wood, R. L., & Rutterford, N. A. (2006c). Psychosocial adjustment 17 years after severe brain injury. *Journal of Neurology, Neurosurgery and Psychiatry, 77*, 71–73.

Wood, R. L., & Yurdakul, L. K. (1997). Change in relationship status following traumatic brain injury. *Brain Injury, 11*(7), 491–502.

Yeates, K. O., Swift, E., Taylor, H. G., Wade, S. L., Drotar, D., Stancin, T., et al. (2004). Short- and long-term social outcomes following pediatric traumatic brain injury. *Journal of the International Neuropsychological Society, 10*(3), 412–426.

11

Cognitive Rehabilitation Following Traumatic Brain Injury

Tom Manly, Jonathan J. Evans, Jessica E. Fish, Fergus Gracey, and Andrew Bateman

Introduction: What Is Cognitive Rehabilitation?

Wilson (1996) characterized cognitive rehabilitation as applying to "any intervention strategy or technique which intends to enable patients and their families to live with, manage, bypass, reduce, or come to terms with cognitive deficits." For many people who implicitly or explicitly view rehabilitation as being primarily concerned with the reduction of impairment, the ordering of the terms within this definition may come as a surprise. Wilson makes the point that improvements in underlying cognitive abilities, if possible, are but one means of achieving rehabilitation goals and that important clinical gains can be made without any such underlying recovery. Rehabilitation is primarily about the attainment of functional goals in patients' day-to-day lives (mobility, self-care, independence, occupation, mood, fun, etc.) and not about cognitive constructs (working memory, attention, face-processing, etc.). It is important to keep this in mind when reading this chapter for a number of reasons. Most important, the view that rehabilitation is primarily about the restoration of lost abilities can lead to disillusionment and disengagement for patients and therapists. Secondly, for ease of exposition, we have largely structured this chapter around cognitive/emotional domains rather than the attainment of functional goals—the former being common across individuals, the latter being more esoteric. At the end of the chapter we will, however, outline a goal-based approach,

the broad principles of which can be applied regardless of cognitive difficulty or the specifics of the goals, and that represents perhaps the most powerful tool that we can bring to the rehabilitation process.

Rehabilitation of Memory Impairments

Problems with memory are very commonly reported following traumatic brain injury (Cicerone, 2000). However "memory" covers a diversity of functions. These include: *working memory* (retention and manipulation of items in conscious awareness); *priming* (nonconscious facilitation of task performance on the basis of prior exposure to relevant stimuli); *episodic/autobiographical memory* (remembering events or experiences throughout one's life, from things that happened yesterday to childhood); *semantic memory* (our store of acquired knowledge or facts, such as knowing that the capital of Kyrgystan is Bishkek or what a fork is for); *procedural memory* (skills such as riding a bike or driving a car); and *prospective memory* (remembering to do something in the future). Further distinctions can be made based on the type of information in question (verbal, nonverbal), the timescale (remote, recent), and whether you are asked to freely recall the information or simply to recognize it. Brain injury can lead to problems in one or more of these areas and the relative degree of impairment in each can have quite different functional implications for everyday life. Assessment and interview that can disentangle these types of memory is an important prerequisite for effective intervention.

Another important distinction in relation to TBI is between learning new information since the injury (anterograde memory) and recalling information learned before the injury (retrograde memory). When considering TBI the three most common memory complaints are in learning new information and procedures, remembering events and experiences that have occurred since the injury, and in remembering to do things in the future. We now turn to strategies that have value in each of these areas.

Learning New Information and Procedures

We need to learn new information all the time: the names of new colleagues, family news, new routes, how to operate new appliances, the details of when and where to meet with friends, and so on. None of us do this perfectly and there are a range of techniques that increase our likelihood of success. Only rarely will TBI cause such severe amnesia that no new learning is possible and, although acquisition is often slowed and more error prone, these same techniques can have value.

Berg, Koning-Haanstra, and Deelman (1991), for example, emphasized the importance of paying keen attention during learning, taking more time to allow information to sink in, and of repeating information. One of the most robust findings in memory research is that recall is enhanced by encoding information more "deeply" (i.e., in a more meaningful way, linking new information with already existing knowledge; Baddeley, Eysenck, and Anderson, 2009). To psychologists, it is sometimes surprising how little this is known in the general population and it can be easily demonstrated to clients by, for example, asking them to remember one word list using deep encoding (e.g., by thinking of a synonym for each word or creating an image involving all the words) and contrasting recall performance with simple passive listening. Many memory strategies are based on this principle, including Mind Maps,

or PQRST[1], which can be effective following TBI (Wilson, 2009). Deeper encoding of material is generally more effortful. For clients with insight into their memory problems and a sense of what constitutes important information (i.e., when this effort is most useful), it can improve confidence and performance.

One of the most widely studied learning strategies is "errorless learning." Under normal circumstances, if a person was not sure of the answer to the question "What was the name of that new teacher?" we might encourage her to guess; perhaps the real answer is there somewhere. A problem for people with memory impairments is that an incorrect guess may become associated with the teacher, whilst the fact that it was an error may be forgotten. Repeated production of the wrong name will make the correct one increasingly difficult to learn. The main principle of errorless learning is to avoid that interference by reducing the probability of error. For example, in the case of the teacher, we could first say, "The teacher's name is James.... what is the teacher's name?" An error under these circumstances is very unlikely and the individual has her first experience with the correct response. Subsequently, we might ask "This teacher's name begins with a J, A, M and E—what is this teacher's name?" By progressively reducing cues whilst maintaining a high probability of accuracy the learner only ever experiences the correct response in relation to that teacher, each episode strengthening the trace.

This technique, pioneered in work with people with learning disabilities (Jones & Earys, 1992), has more recently been applied to teaching people with acquired neurological impairment, with Baddeley and Wilson (1994) first demonstrating superior learning, compared with trial and error, in people with amnesia. Since then, several single case and small group studies have shown benefits including, crucially, in practical everyday information and procedures (Clare, Wilson, Breen, & Hodges,

---

[1] The PQRST acronym reflects better understanding/learning of text by first *Previewing* (skimming through the text to get the gist), setting *Questions* (what do you hope to get from reading it?), then *Reading* it, *Stating* the main points back to yourself and finally *Testing* your understanding against the text (Robinson, 1970).

1999; Hunkin, Squires, Aldrich, & Parkin, 1998; Lloyd, Riley, & Powell, 2009; Squires, Hunkin, and Parkin, 1996; Wilson, Baddeley, Evans, & Shiel, 1994). Errorless learning is a principle rather than a single technique. Our teacher example used Vanishing Cues (Glisky, Schacter, & Tulving, 1986b; Haslam, Moss, & Hodder, 2010) and Retrieval Practice (Sumowski, Wood, Chiaravalloti, Wylie, Lengenfelder, & DeLuca, 2010). Clearly these techniques can require considerable effort from patients, family members, and therapists and may not be necessary for everyone. In a critical review, Clare and Jones (2008), suggested that errorless learning methods were most appropriate in the context of severe memory impairment.

Remembering Events and Experiences

The ability to remember events, episodes, and experiences is important to our sense of self and relationships with others (Fivush, 2011). Shared experiences, and shared recollection of experiences, shape relationships. Memories of past situations may help us to tackle new problems that have similar features.

One strategy widely used by head injured and non-head injured people is to keep and refer to a diary. However, for some people with memory impairment it can be difficult to retain events long enough to be later written down (the use of a voice recorder during the day for later transcription is an interesting strategy to overcome this; see Wilson, Wilson, & Hughes, 1997). Another issue is that in the general population, a diary entry may be sufficient to reactivate an "intact" memory of the events, with rich elaboration and ephemeral details jogged from memory helping people to "re-experience" the moment. If these traces are more fragile, written details may allow a person to know broadly what happened but not permit such subjective time-travel. If a "picture paints a thousand words" a new and only recently possible innovation holds some promise in this respect. The SenseCam is a digital camera, developed by Microsoft Research, worn around the neck that captures an image every 15–30 seconds or when it senses changes in lighting, temperature, or movement that may indicate a new relevant

episode. This allows entire days to be subsequently reviewed in fast-forward from the first person perspective. Berry et al. (2007) showed that use of SenseCam improved recollection of autobiographical experiences (days out) in a woman with amnesia following limbic encephalitis, compared with a written diary. This result has been replicated in a case of TBI (Brindley, Bateman, & Gracey, 2010). Issues relating to the acceptability of wearing a currently somewhat obvious aid, others' privacy, and so on will need careful thought. It seems clear, however, that the various ways now available to digitally capture and store aspects of our daily experiences may well have a significant impact on the accessibility of our pasts.

Remembering to Do Things

The aids most commonly used by memory impaired people are "to do" lists, calendars, and appointment diaries (Evans, Wilson, Needham, & Brentnall, 2003), methods primarily for remembering to do things in the future rather than recalling the past. This emphasizes the importance of prospective memory to everyday function: If we forget to pay bills, forget to pick up the children from school, forget to take medication, or forget to attend appointments, the consequences can be severe. Successful prospective remembering requires memory, but also executive and attention functioning. Even something simple such as posting a letter requires some planning (deciding where and when to post the letter), memory (forming an intention to post the letter at a particular postbox on the way to work in the morning and remembering the intention until the opportunity arises), and attention (noticing the postbox; attending to the intention in order to maintain the attention in an active state).

One of the limitations of standard written to-do aids is that they do not prompt recollection at the relevant time. The NeuroPage system sought to overcome this by sending specific reminders to users at the appropriate moment via a standard belt worn pager (Wilson, Emslie, Quirk, & Evans, 2001). The reminders (e.g., "take your medication," "water the plants") are determined by the users, caregivers, and therapists and entered into a computer that interacts automatically with the paging company's transmitters. Whilst this limits the flexibility of the system it has the major advantage that users, who may have severe problems in learning new procedures, have only to look at the message having been prompted by the buzzer. A further speculative advantage of the pager, at least for some users, may be the perception that the message comes from someone else. Fish, Manly, and Wilson (2008), for example, describe the case of a lady who showed significant functional gains from a NeuroPage but not from a self-programmed personal organizer that ostensibly served the same purpose.

The NeuroPage system has now been evaluated in clinical trials and single case studies, and shown to be very effective in increasing functional performance and independence in people with TBI (Fish et al., 2008; Wilson et al., 2001). As a result, recent major systematic reviews of cognitive rehabilitation have recommended that electronic memory aids should used in clinical practice (Cappa, 2005; Cicerone, 2000).

For some people with TBI, the main problem with remembering to do things lies not in the remembering *what* has to be done, but remembering to do it at the right time. As is discussed further below, a recent series of studies have demonstrated that "content-free cues," that do not provide specific information but rather orient the individual to review his or her own intentions, can improve prospective remembering in people with a brain injury (Fish et al., 2007; Manly, Hawkins, Evans, Woldt, & Robertson, 2002).

Memory Rehabilitation in Clinical Practice

The techniques, strategies, and aids discussed can be thought of as items in a memory rehabilitation toolbox. Some are tools that are given to the person with memory impairment to use independently, whilst others are more usually applied by a rehabilitation therapist to facilitate learning of specific information. Whether or not the memory impaired person will be able to learn to use strategies/aids independently will depend on a wide variety of factors including severity of impairment, insight and awareness, current demands, and pre-morbid experience of

using aids (Evans et al., 2003). All of the tools are best employed in the context of individualized rehabilitation goals (see below). As part of a goal-focused neuropsychological rehabilitation program, memory rehabilitation can be undertaken in a group format, something that offers a powerful opportunity for people with memory impairment to learn from each other what helps and what does not (Wilson, 2009)

Rehabilitation of Attention

Impairments in attention are commonly reported consequences of brain injury; in a recent study of 363 patients who attended the Oliver Zangwill Center for Neuropsychological Rehabilitation, for example, the most commonly self-reported problem was "distractibility" (Simblett & Bateman, 2011). Because attention is required to successfully complete almost all tasks, problems in this area are likely to manifest themselves across many domains of individuals' lives. In this section we first outline strategies for managing and compensating for poor attention and then turn to attempts to systematically retrain attention. Finally we address a particular and striking form of attention deficit, unilateral spatial neglect, and discuss a variety of techniques that have been used to correct this bias.

Practical Management of Attention

Human attention is capacity limited; we can only attend to so many events for so long. Many of us take steps to manage our environment and ourselves to optimize performance on tasks that we consider important. We might listen to radio whilst washing-up without cost but turn it off to prevent interference when reading or writing. If we know that we have a particularly challenging task tomorrow we might ensure that we have a good night's sleep and not schedule other demanding activities around it. We might take short breaks during activity to maintain a high level of performance or stop before boredom kicks in and mistakes start to happen.

People differ in their attention capacities and styles. Some people's performance may improve with relatively high stimulation whilst another person might find similar conditions overly distracting. A problem for people who have sustained a brain injury is that a life-time of habits developed to suit one capacity/style may no longer be ideal. There may also be difficulties in adjusting to these new conditions due to poor insight, reduced error detection, inefficient problem-solving, and behavioral inflexibility. It is therefore important that clinicians actively assess rather than assume that people will appropriately adjust their habits and environment to maximize post-injury ability.

Terms like "concentration" and "focus" are rather abstract. It is useful to discuss the particular *tasks* with which an individual struggles. Important questions include at what time of day the task is attempted and the environment and context in which it is performed (noisy or quiet, under time-pressure during a hectic day or open ended?). It is also important to ask about sleep patterns, fatigue, and motivation to do the task, as well as the possible influence of any psychoactive substances, prescribed or otherwise, on performance. Once the picture is clearer it is then possible to think with the patient about behavioral experiments in which the influence of different factors can be judged. For example, if it turns out that the task is typically attempted whilst listening to the radio, what happens if it is tried without? What happens if a rest break is scheduled every 10 minutes? Is it different if the task is attempted during the morning rather than late at night? Working collaboratively with clients on such experiments is useful in terms of identifying factors that might maximize function. It can also be useful in increasing peoples' sense of personal control and giving them problem-solving tools that might be applied across many situations. Thinking in terms of tasks also helps to consider other variables that strongly interact with attention. A good example is when people undertake a new course of study. Initially the materials may be "difficult" and not make a great deal of sense and, as a result, attention easily wanders from the lesson, lecture, or page. However, as the themes begin to link up and there is interest how the current information relates to the growing knowledge base, the task often becomes more engaging. Whether or not there are generalized improvements in attention, such changes to the motivational context

can make attending easier. Helping patients and families to see how motivation, reward, and attention interact may yield useful strategies.

Can Attention Be Retrained?

If we practice physical or cognitive tasks, our brains, bodies, and strategies change and we almost invariably get better at them. While memory training (e.g., practice at learning lists) has generally proved disappointing in its generalization (Glisky, Schacter, & Tulving, 1986a) it does not follow that all cognitive functions will be so resistant. Wilson and Robertson (1992) worked with a man who had relatively well-preserved intellectual and memory abilities following a traumatic brain injury. He found, however, that he now had great difficulty in keeping his mind on an accountancy text book that he needed to digest for an exam. To establish a baseline, he was asked to read a novel and to move a counter from one pile to another every time he felt that his attention had wandered. To progressively shape his performance, he was then asked to read only for very brief periods during which a slip was unlikely to occur. If he was successful, the duration was increased by 10% for the next trial. If not, the duration was shortened. In this manner, over 160 sessions spread over 40 days his ability to read without lapse progressively increased until he reliably reached his target of five minutes of reading without slip. Importantly, these gains generalized to the arguably less engaging accountancy text. The factors that contributed to these gains are not entirely clear. It is possible, for example, that improved confidence through his experience of slip-free reading played a role. As we discuss in the section on goal-setting, in function-directed rehabilitation the factors leading to improvement are of interest but not crucial. The results are certainly consistent with attention on a particular task being amenable to progressive training.

Intensive one-to-one professional rehabilitation is expensive. In contrast, personal computers can provide training opportunities over long durations now at minimal cost. This can occur at convenient times in people's own homes. Tasks can be automatically titrated to an individual's initial level of abilities and progress in difficulty as performance improves. Computer training may also have engaging game-like qualities and provide positive feedback on performance. It is not surprising, therefore, that there is intensive interest in whether such training produces functional benefits for brain-injured and other people.

In an early study of computerized attention training, Gray, Robertson, Pentland, and Anderson (1992) developed a battery broadly derived from neuropsychological measures (e.g., reaction time task, a digit-symbol translation task, color-word Stroop). Using a randomized controlled design (RCT) a group of patients given 15 hours of the training showed immediate post-training benefits on two neuropsychological measures. At six-month follow up, the attention training group showed more generalized gains on tests. However, generalization to everyday activities was not assessed.

Sturm, Willmes, Orgass, and Hartje (1997) evaluated the efficacy of the AIXTENT attention training program in a group of patients with acquired brain injury, principally through stroke. The package had separate modules designed to target different forms of attention (alertness, sustained attention, selective attention, and divided attention). Thirty-eight patients were randomly allocated to receive the modules in different orders. The results of approximately 56 hours of training were consistent with benefits on untrained computer tasks that were rather specific to the modules, reaction time improving more following reaction time training, for example, than with dual-task training. Comparable results were obtained in a further study of effects of the AIXTENT training in people with multiple sclerosis (Plohmann et al., 1998).

Perhaps the most striking claims regarding computerized cognitive training in recent years have come from studies using progressive computerized working memory exercises. Working memory refers to the short term retention and sometimes manipulation of verbal or spatial information (Baddeley, 1983). Although working memory is often characterized as, say, "the capacity to hold in mind a phone number between reading and dialing," the scope of the model is much more profound and may be best considered as the capacity of current conscious thought. Whether it is considered

primarily mnemonic, attentional, or executive is largely a matter of terminological preference or emphasis.

Various working memory training packages have been evaluated. Some require users to retain and reproduce sequences of increasing length (e.g., letters, digits, or spatial locations indicated on a grid) whilst others require judgment about whether the current stimulus in a series is the same as that presented 1, 2 or n trials previously (hence "n-back tasks"). In both cases the tasks are set to increase in difficulty as users improve (or become easier if users struggle), with training generally being undertaken over four to six weeks, in 20 to 40 minute daily sessions. Populations studied have included those with TBI (Serino, Ciaramelli, Santantonio, Malagu, Servadei, & Ladavas, 2007); stroke (Westerberg et al., 2007); children with Attention Deficit Hyperactivity Disorder (ADHD; Klingberg et al., 2005); and poor working memory (Holmes, Gathercole, & Dunning, 2009), as well as neurologically healthy participants (Dahlin, Neely, Larsson, Backman, & Nyberg, 2008; Jaeggi, Buschkuehlm, Jonides & Perrig, 2008). Invariably, the participants become more adept at the tasks that they practice. In addition, improvements on untrained working memory measures have generally been observed. There have been reports of generalization to other executive measures and even to tests of fluid intelligence. These gains in fluid IQ have been identified in RCTs with neurologically-healthy controls (Jaeggi et al., 2008), and in children with ADHD (Klingberg et al., 2005), although they were not detectable in older adults or adults who had experienced a stroke (Dahlin et al., 2008; Westerberg et al., 2007). Benefits were also reported in parent ratings of attention, inhibition, and hyperactivity in children with ADHD (Klingberg et al, 2005) and on the Cognitive Failures Questionnaire in stroke patients (Westerberg et al., 2007). While we do not yet know whether the changes reflect the development of (generalizable) strategy or increased capacity, these results clearly indicate potential for rehabilitative gains.

It is important to add, however, that not all studies have returned positive findings (e.g., Owen et al., 2010) and more work is required in understanding what works for whom.

The Rehabilitation of Unilateral Spatial Neglect

Unilateral spatial neglect refers to a marked difficulty in attending to and acting on information on one side of space that cannot be readily explained by sensory or motor loss. Although primarily associated with stroke, it can occur following focal brain injury, in progressive neurological conditions, and after traumatic brain injury (McKenna, Cooke, Fleming, Jefferson, & Ogden, 2006). For many patients, marked neglect resolves relatively quickly (although the proportion showing residual mild biases is difficult to gauge). Persistent spatial neglect is overwhelmingly associated with damage to the right hemisphere of the brain and a tendency to ignore information from the left (Stone, Halligan, & Greenwood, 1993).

If you close one eye and move around a black dot on a white page until it magically disappears, you have located your blind spot. Even if you have done this many times before and "know" that it is there, it is impossible to be *aware* of it under normal circumstances—the brain makes the world look complete. Similarly, patients with neglect may "know" that they have problems in noticing things on the left because they have been told this or had it demonstrated (although some will vehemently deny even the possibility of a problem). However, because the world appears complete there is no impetus to look into neglected space; it is not a black area, it simply is not there.[2] Given that many patients can make leftward eye or head moments, or be aware of an object on the left if cued to do so (Riddoch & Humphreys, 1983), an obvious rehabilitative strategy is to overcome the lack of spontaneous impetus to look to the left by training and reinforcing this behavior. This has been tried in many ways, often to good effect. Lawson (1962), for example, worked with a person with neglect who missed words from the left side of the page as she was reading. She followed the strategy of placing a red bookmark to the left of the page and ensuring that she visually located the bookmark before reading each line. The number of

omitted words accordingly dropped. In this and other reports, however, there was extraordinary little generalization of the gains beyond the trained context, even to a different book. While there is nothing wrong, therefore, in engaging patients in, for example, a spatial game in which they are cued to notice things on the left, it is important not to assume that gains made on the task will be apparent in other aspects of the patient's life. Generally, it will be more productive to direct such training towards a functionally useful or enjoyable activity. Pizzamiglio and colleagues (1992) and Antonucci et al. (1995) have demonstrated, however, that scanning training can produce generalized benefits if it is sufficiently systematic, varied, and prolonged. Here, over approximately 40 hours of training. patients were initially given highly salient cues to attend to the left and reinforced for even small leftward scans. As the training progressed the range of tasks was expanded as were the spatial scales involved (e.g., tracking lights moving on a distant wall). Benefits were seen on untrained and functionally relevant activities.

Scanning training can be seen as trying to build a behavioral habit (i.e., something that the patients will not need to remember or necessarily intend to do) that will help overcome a lack of spontaneous leftward exploration. Researchers have investigated a range of other techniques that may also induce involuntary leftward orienting. We have only space to summarize these here and refer readers to more detailed texts.

Hemifield Patching

In hemifield patching, patients are asked to wear spectacles that have the right side of *each* lens masked off, thus obliging them to scan left to see anything. Positive effects were observed following a three-month trial in which the glasses were worn for 12 hours a day during normal activity (Beis, Andre, Baumgarten, & Challier, 1989). Two recent RCTs, however, have reported more disappointing results (Fong et al., 2007; Tsang, Sze, & Fong, 2009).

Caloric Vestibular Stimulation

A temperature difference across the vestibular system (e.g., induced by pouring cold water

---

[2] It is important to point out that the blind spot, while useful in thinking about the strange phenomenology of spatial neglect is, strictly speaking, more equivalent to a visual field loss (e.g., hemianopia).

into one ear) can induce involuntary compensatory eye movements. These have been reported to increase patients' visual awareness of the left (Adair, Na, Schwartz, & Heilman, 2003; Cappa, Stezi, Vallar, & Bisiach, 1987; Rubens, 1985). Interestingly, some patients also show improved motor function, tactile sensitivity, and an increased sense of ownership of left limbs with this technique (Bottini et al., 2005; Rode, Charles, Perenin, Vighetto, Trillet, & Aimard, 1992). Such effects, which extend beyond the targeted modality, have been observed with a number of techniques discussed here and are consistent with neglect reflecting a rather central distortion to spatial representation. Whilst the beneficial effects of this technique appear to persist after both stimulation and involuntary eye movements have ceased, its long-term impact, if any, is less clear.

Neck Muscle Vibration

Just as the brain may be "fooled" into compensating for illusory rotation induced by vestibular input, distortions to the proprioceptive system (coding the relative location of the head, trunk, and limbs) can produce similar effects. Schindler and colleagues (2002) randomly allocated patients to either 15 daily sessions (each of 40 minutes) of performing spatial tasks while exposed to 80 Hz mechanical vibration of the neck muscles or to 15 sessions involving just the spatial tasks. Muscle vibration was associated with significantly greater improvements on spatial tests and everyday activities. Spatial practice on its own, as we would suspect from many previous studies, had little effect. The gains were maintained at two-month follow-up.

Limb Activation

A useful way to think about the primary function of our representation of space is that it guides *action*. Might there be an effect of the location of our actions on our awareness of space? Halligan, Manning, and Marshall (1990) observed that a patient with left neglect showed less leftward inattention when using his left rather than right hand. Robertson and colleagues went on to demonstrate that these benefits to visual awareness occurred in a good number of patients and did not depend on the patients being able to see their actions (i.e., it was not purely a visual cueing effect). Crucially, however, it did appear to depend on where the action was made. Actions of the left hand to the left side of the body produced increased awareness. Actions of the same hand placed to the right of the body midline did not. Simultaneous movements of both hands also appeared to cancel the effect and movements of the right hand to the left of body midline did not produce significant gains (Robertson & North, 1993, 1994; Robertson, North, & Geggie, 1992). Observing that some neglect patients with adequate function in the left hand nevertheless tended to underuse or ignore that limb, Robertson and colleagues developed a simple cueing device, a switch held in the left hand. If no button pushes were detected in a given interval, a buzzer would sound reminding the user to keep moving. A number of studies have demonstrated that such training can produce significant gains across a range of functions which, in some cases, appear to be lasting (Maddicks, Marzillier, & Parker, 2003; Robertson, Hogg, & McMillan, 1998a; Robertson, McMillan, MacLeod, Edgeworth, & Brock, 2002).

Unfortunately many patients with neglect cannot move their left hand due to paralysis on one side of the body (hemiplegia). An interesting new technique may prove very useful in this context. In Functional Electrical Stimulation (FES) a small and painless electrical impulse is used to create contraction and relaxation of arm muscles without the need for self-generated motor commands. A double-blind, placebo-controlled RCT compared the effects of a four-week, 20-session program of Visual Scanning Training either combined with FES to the forearm or with sham FES (the same apparatus delivering no current). Benefits attributable to FES were found on measures of spatial performance (Polanowska, Seniow, Paprot, Lesniak, & Czlonkowska, 2009). Harding and Riddoch (2009) found that, of four patients they studied, three showed significant benefits of three weeks of left arm FES on spatial measures and measures of everyday coping—gains that were maintained over a long follow-up period.

Increasing Alertness

Patients with persistent left neglect often appear rather drowsy, indeed it has been suggested that abnormally low levels of alertness may be an important factor that allows neglect to persist (Husain & Rorden, 2003; Posner, 1993; Robertson & Manly, 1999). In line with this, a number of experimental studies have shown reductions in neglect with increased alertness from auditory, cognitive, or pharmacological stimulation (George, Mercer, Walker, & Manly, 2008; Malhotra. Parton, Greenwood, & Husain, 2006; Robertson, Mattingley, Rorden, & Rorden, 1998b). Roberston and colleagues (1995) reported reduced spatial bias in patients following training in a self-alerting technique, although the long term maintenance of these gains was not assessed. Sturm also reported reductions in neglect following computerized alertness training (Sturm et al., 2004), although unfortunately these were not well maintained. Whilst the efficacy of alertness interventions is yet to be established, the likely broader benefits to patients of a more responsive, engaged state make this an avenue worth exploring.

Prism Lens Adaptation

Glasses fitted with prism lenses can be used to produce a coherent spatial displacement, for example, shifting the visual scene 10 degrees to the right. When first trying to reach towards an object under these conditions, people will typically overshoot to where the object appears to be. However, the error is visible and people adjust their reaches to regain accuracy. When, after making a number of reaches, the glasses are removed, errors often occur in the opposite direction for a short time. This after-effect indicates that there has been a significant, involuntary recalibration of the spatial-action system. Rossetti et al. (1998) investigated whether this recalibration might assist patients with left neglect to explore further into left space. They demonstrated that after removing the glasses following just five minutes of reaching practice with rightward deviating prisms, patients indeed performed better on spatial tasks. Remarkably, the effects were, if anything, greater two hours after this brief prism exposure

(i.e., long after the standard after-effect would have dissipated). Subsequent studies have produced results consistent with this effect and indicated that, as with some other interventions for neglect, the benefits extend beyond the ostensible target (in this case, visually guided action), for example, improving access to imagery, tactile exploration, and reading. Frassinetti, Angeli, Meneghello, Avanzi, & Ladavas (2002) reported that benefits of a two-week prism-adaptation training (20 minutes per day) were apparent five weeks after the end of training in comparison with an untreated control group. Some randomized control trials have produced less positive results. Nys and colleagues (2008)found that initial gains on two of the four spatial outcome measures were not maintained at one-month follow-up. An RCT with 37 patients found no consistent improvements on tests or functional outcome from 10 sessions of prism adaptation training conducted over two weeks (Turton, O'Leary, Gabb, Woodward, & Gilchrist, 2009). More work is required in understanding what works for whom (in terms of the presentation of neglect, time since injury, etc.). However, as with limb activation and some of the other techniques that we have discussed, their efficacy can be explored on a single-case basis. In addition to these interventions, there is preliminary evidence that using transcranial magnetic stimulation or direct current stimulation to reduce excitability in the contralesional hemisphere and increase activity in the lesioned hemisphere can benefit neglect. It will be interesting to see how these techniques develop (Brighina et al., 2003; Sparing, Thimm, Hesse, Kust, Karbe, & Fink, 2009).

The Rehabilitation of Executive Function

"Executive function" is a broad term that can refer to a rather disparate range of capacities. From the perspective of rehabilitation, one rather unfortunate way to consider executive function would be to draw up a list of characteristics an individual would ideally *have* to make the best recovery from a brain injury. These might include good error detection and realistic evaluation of capacities; the ability to think creatively about new strategies and the behavioral flexibility to act upon them; the ability to suppress old habits that are no longer useful and, in general, coordinate behavior in a goal-directed fashion. Put this way, it is easy to see why problems in executive functions present such difficulties for patients and their families and are associated with poor outcome. It is also obvious why rehabilitation for executive impairments is inherently challenging—the very functions that would facilitate change are compromised. The fact that these impairments can undermine the *useful* expression of many abilities that may be relatively intact also indicates that, if we are able to make gains, the benefit to patients may be considerable.

An early example of an executive training program was provided by von Cramon, Matthes-von Cramon, and Mai (1991). They alternately allocated 37 people who had problem-solving difficulties following stroke or TBI to either a problem-solving therapy group or a control "memory training" condition. It has been suggested that neuropsychological tests, even those putatively of frontal lobe function, often fail to quite capture the disruption experienced by patients in everyday life (Burgess, Alderman, Evans, Emslie, & Wilson, 1998) and an interesting aspect of this study lay in the use of trained therapist ratings based on observation of the participants attempting novel tasks. For example, the therapists rated features such as a lack of heuristics (e.g., a participant would just see what happens rather than having an obvious strategy), failure to weigh up the pros and cons of an action, ignoring task rules, problems in flexibly changing strategy in light of poor results, and so on. Over 25, hour-long sessions, the problem-solving group participants completed a range of tasks such as composing newspaper adverts (where brevity and relevance are key), planning complex journeys using a variety of time-tables and constraints, and assembling the relevant clues from detective stories. As they worked on these problems they were encouraged to be very systematic, first in defining the problem (e.g., reading and then summarizing instructions and working out what information was relevant to the problem). Patients were asked to generate as many alternative solutions as possible and to consciously weigh up the pros and cons of each. Once they had decided on and begun to act on

a strategy, they were then encouraged to check whether or not it was working. Compared with the memory training control group, the problem-solving group showed significantly greater pre- post-training gains on two sequencing and logical tasks. When therapists again observed the participants tackling novel problems, their (blind) ratings also showed a trend for more of the problem-solving group to have improved in terms of the number of goal-directed ideas generated and general problem-solving skill—in other words, elements of the training were demonstrated without being directly cued.

Effective behavior can be viewed as moving an individual from a current state to one in which a goal has been achieved. Goals can be immediate and solved by instinctive or well-learned routine behaviors or long term, and likely to solved by the completion of myriad sub-goals (e.g., "I want to progress in my career"). Some have argued that the decomposition of goals into tractable sub-goals and the effective maintenance of these representations to drive useful, sequential action is the hallmark of intelligent behavior and is highly dependent on lateral prefrontal function (Duncan et al., 2000). Certainly aspects of the disorganization shown by patients with frontal lesions fits well with a failure to coordinate activity in this way (Luria, 1966). Goal Management Training (GMT) was developed as a structured, interactive manual-based rehabilitation protocol designed to help patients to think about errors that they may be making and develop strategies to reduce this likelihood. In an evaluation of this approach, Levine et al. (2000) worked with 30 patients with a range of TBI severity seen three to four years after sustaining their injuries. The participants were randomly assigned to GMT or a motor training control. In both cases the training was extremely brief with the key outcome measures being administered immediately after training. The training focused on different phases in problem-solving: (1) stopping to think rather than pushing on with a possibly ill-thought through plan; (2) defining the main goal; (3) breaking the goal down into sensible subgoals; (4) encoding these subgoals to increase the likelihood of remembering what comes next in the sequence; (5) monitoring activity in terms of the plan and the subgoal (e.g., noticing if one is about to be derailed by a different activity). This brief session of GMT was associated with significantly greater gains on a series of pen and paper tasks (e.g., planning seating arrangements for a wedding meal) than the motor training control. The results of a study in the healthy aging population (n = 49), in which a four-session version of GMT was compared with a wait-list control, produced consistent results—with outcome again being assessed on paper and pencil "life-like" tasks (Levine et al., 2007). Significant improvements on sustained attention and Tower of London style problem-solving tests were reported in a subsequent study comparing GMT with an active control in 19 patients with brain injury of mixed etiology, although no improvement in self-reported problems on questionnaires was noted (Levine et al., 2011).

Miotto, Evans, de Lucia, and Scaff (2009) evaluated an intervention based on the Attention and Problem-solving Group model developed in the United Kingdom's Oliver Zangwill Center for Neuropsychological Rehabilitation (see below), itself influenced by von Cramon et al.'s work and Goal Management Training. Thirty participants, including people with focal frontal injuries and TBI, took part and were allocated to three groups: Attention and Problem-solving Group (APS), a similar duration of receiving information and education on brain injury, or treatment as usual. Initial assessment included a modification of Shallice and Burgess' (1991) Multiple Errands Task. This task was developed to try and capture aspects of patients' difficulties in complex, unconstrained daily life situations that may be missed with conventional neuropsychological assessments. In essence, the task gives participants a series of goals that need to be completed within a particular time, and according to certain rules, in a shopping center. Raters record which of the tasks were achieved, the efficiency of the strategy and instances of rule breaks.

APS groups were run in a weekly 90 minute session for 10 weeks. The program was designed to increase awareness of attention and executive problems that can arise from brain injury, to allow participants to think about and experiment with strategies for the management of attention (e.g., taking breaks, managing fatigue)

and to apply a systematic framework to solving complex life problems. The framework involved defining the problem and the particular goal or subgoal that needed to be achieved. As with von Cramon et al.'s approach, there followed a solution generation phase, an evaluation of pros and cons, and the construction of a plan. During plan execution, participants were encouraged to reflect on its efficacy and, if necessary, change strategy. This framework was applied to various tasks, for example, organizing a trip for the group (e.g., taking into account transport options, time-tables, opening hours, availability, etc.). The results indicated that most standard neuropsychological measures, even those putatively of executive function such as the Wisconsin Card Sorting Test, showed little change other than that attributable to practice. In contrast, participants who received the APS showed significantly greater improvements on the Multiple Errands measure and a decline in reported difficulty compared with the control groups. In a nice feature of the design, both control groups were then crossed-over into receiving APS and broadly showed similar gains, strengthening the attribution of the improvement specifically to APS. No significant further improvements were observed at six-months follow-up but the gains relative to baseline were well maintained.

There is evidence, therefore, that structured training in developing a systematic approach to problem-solving can lead to improvements on untrained tasks. A limitation of early studies in this area is that assessment was generally conducted immediately after training and arguably on somewhat artificial measures. The Miotto et al. (2009) study is therefore particularly encouraging in showing that effects can transfer to a (near) real-life shopping task *and* be maintained at six-month follow-up. Generalization is an important issue and there may be particular barriers to it in patients with executive difficulties that may include, for example, problems extracting from the particular training instance to the more general. Von Cramon et al. (von Cramon & Matthes-von Cramon, 1994), for example, present the case report of a doctor who, following frontal brain damage, became impulsive in his diagnostic practices as well as other aspects of his life. They showed that systematic training in step-by-step diagnostic procedures did indeed improve his performance in the clinic but did not generalize beyond it.

Recent work has examined whether automated cueing can help patients to think about strategies developed in training as they go about their daily lives. As indentified by Luria and many others, patients with executive problems can show a pronounced tendency to fail to act on their stated intentions, despite often being perfectly able to say what these were. An example of this frequently occurs on Shallice and Burgess' (1991) 6-Elements test. Here, participants are told about six simple tasks that they should attempt within a fixed period of time and informed that they cannot possibly complete all of the items in the time available. The emphasis is therefore on switching between the activities to comply with the main goal of attempting all of the tasks. Despite stating that this is their intention before starting the test and that it was their intention when asked after the test, patients may completely ignore this during performance, beginning and completing one task before moving on. Manly et al. (2002) considered what would happen if such patients received a tone at random intervals during performance, having previously been instructed "if you hear a tone, just try to think about what you are doing in the task." They found that TBI patients, who were significantly impaired on the task under normal circumstances, showed performance that was indistinguishable from that of IQ-matched healthy control participants when the tones were present. The finding suggests that interrupting performance can help people to act on their stored, but currently neglected, intentions.

Fish et al. (2007) examined whether this technique could be used amid the hustle and bustle of patients' real-lives. Participants with everyday organizational problems (predominantly following TBI) were asked to perform the ecologically relevant task of making phone calls at particular times of the day. The times were learned using an errorless technique to ensure that any failure to make the calls was likely to reflect oversight rather than forgetting the relevant times. Participants were then given a brief version of GMT in which the processing

of stopping activity to review one's intentions was linked with a cue phrase: "Stop!." Over the subsequent test period, "Stop!" cue SMS messages were sent at random intervals to the participants' cell phones. To separate the effects of cueing from the effects of GMT, the SMS messages were only sent on half of the study days, determined at random for each participant. Despite the SMS messages being at least half an hour away from a scheduled call time, cued days saw a highly significant increase in patients' ability to perform this delayed intention task, an improvement that persisted over the two weeks of the study. Although it is likely that making the phone calls was particularly primed by the cues (in both being related to the study and both involving the phone) the results suggest that interruption to current activity combined with reviewing one's intentions does make subsequent execution of those intentions more likely. Further work is underway in evaluating how well this can apply to patients' own spontaneous goals.

Emotional Support Following Traumatic Brain Injury

So far we have addressed interventions designed to manage, reduce, or compensate for the major cognitive problems reported by people following TBI: memory, attention, and executive functions. Many epidemiological studies now also highlight the significant negative social and emotional consequences of acquired brain injury, notably increased incidence and prevalence of emotional disorders (Rose & Johnson, 1996), increased risk of suicide (Teasdale & Engberg, 2001), and criminal justice system contact (Slaughter, Fann, & Ehde, 2003). While for theoretical investigations it can be useful to treat these as a separate domains of function, for any given individual, mood, social, and cognitive functions are closely interwoven. It is widely acknowledged, for example, that low mood, rumination, and anxiety can exert a strong influence over cognitive function, reducing mental flexibility, motivation, and diverting attention away from the task at hand. Cognitive impairments in memory, attention, problem-solving, and cognitive control can reduce an individual's defenses to mood disturbance, for example, by weakening resistance to ruminative thoughts, failing to pick up on or remember cues from others that may be important to the maintenance of a relationship, finding it difficult to spot early signs of where anger may be a problem, and so on (Krpan, Levine, Stuss, & Dawson, 2006). In addition, of course, people with acquired brain injury have had a relatively recent highly traumatic event that may have spiraling consequences for their cognitive and physical abilities, pre-existing lifestyle, and aspirations as to what their future will be like.

Cognitive Behavioral Therapy (CBT) has been a success across a range of mental health issues in the non-brain-injured population, including unipolar depression, generalized anxiety disorder, panic disorder, social phobia, post-traumatic stress disorder, and childhood depressive and anxiety disorders (Butler, Chapman, Forman, & Beck, 2006). Not surprisingly, therefore, this has probably been the primary model adopted as an adjunct to cognitive rehabilitation (although see Prigatano, 1999 for a more psychodynamic perspective) and a growing series of reports and single-case studies suggest that it can bring benefits (Anson & Ponsford, 2006; Bradbury, Christensen, Lau, Ruttan, Arundine, & Green, 2008; Dewar & Gracey, 2007; Gracey, Oldham, & Kritzinger, 2007; Tiersky et al., 2005; Williams, Evans, & Fleminger, 2003).

Gracey, Brentnall, and Megoran (2009), for example, describe a CBT approach with a 31-year-old woman who sustained a severe head injury a year and a half before to the intervention. She had memory difficulties and a range of executive problems, including in mental flexibility. Since the accident she had lost her job, rarely ventured outside of her apartment, and had little contact with friends. Further discussion indicated that the client was very fearful of making mistakes that might be observed by others and that she had a strong rule of "no room for error" because she wanted to prevent the injury from dominating her life. Her anxiety responses were formulated within a CBT model, namely that her retreat to "safe" situations reinforced avoidant behavior and prevented exposure to disconfirmatory evidence. The increases in autonomic arousal that accompanied this anxiety were in turn interpreted by her as signs

of imminent loss of control, further reinforcing the underlying belief and the social withdrawal. In addition, she was troubled by self-critical ruminations about the situation.

Gracey et al. outline how, through discussion, the client was able to entertain the idea that her attempts to prevent the injury dominating her life may paradoxically have the reverse effect. This in turn motivated a series of behavioral experiments. In one example, the client's fear that unless she rushed in and out of a shop she would begin to panic, lose control, and behave inappropriately was tested against an alternative account: that this rushing and concern itself fostered the sense of panic. Accordingly, she set herself the goal of trying to shop deliberately and slowly to establish which if either of these predictions (more versus less panic) was correct. In fact, she did find herself less panicked and "fighting with herself" with the slower approach and reflected on focusing on the task at hand rather than imagining catastrophic possibilities. In this manner, the client achieved a series of goals over the program, including thinking differently about situations that previously triggered anxiety.

Goal Setting in Rehabilitation

As clinicians working in the area of brain injury it is very easy to become daunted by the scale of difficulties that some patients face in relation to our knowledge and tools to assist them. How billions of neurons interact to produce thought and behavior is, to say the least, a complex problem. Even were our understanding very much more advanced, it is not obvious that this would always help in rehabilitation; we might, for example, have an excellent model of how the brain does speech production and yet be clueless in helping someone to speak who has sustained severe damage to the relevant networks. How can we help to effect positive change when we do not fully understand the problem?

One method, a method so simple, obvious, and general that we may not even think of it as a method, is goal setting. When done well, the process of setting iterative, achievable goals is probably our most powerful tool for helping people to move from a given starting point to somewhere better. Goal setting is a means, for the patient, their family, and the therapist, to carve what may appear an overwhelming and insurmountable set of problems into a discrete and evolving set of targets.

There are various formulae as to what makes effective goals but the SMART heuristic is a useful starting place. SMART is the acronym for *Specific, Measurable, Agreed, Realistic* and *Time-limited*.[3] Effective goals tend to be specific. "I will walk 10 steps" is specific, "I will walk better" is not. One's success in walking 10 steps is easily observable (i.e. *Measurable*), while there may be a range of views on what constitutes "walking better." *Agreed* means that the people involved in setting the goal (e.g., a patient and her therapist) both genuinely think that it would be desirable. What is *Realistic* will clearly vary with context; a useful place to start is the smallest possible step from the current situation. If, for example, I am currently able to walk 9 steps, setting the goal of walking 10 steps seems very achievable; planning to walk 100 steps may not. The view here is that *achieving* goals is useful, not just for the goal in itself, but in the boosting confidence, mastery, and engagement in the goal-setting process. Overly ambitious goals may have the reverse effect. *Time-limited* means setting a deadline at which the attainment of the measurable goal will be judged. Setting and reviewing goals at regular intervals helps to develop a momentum and allows goals that turn out to be unrealistic to be changed (Scobbie, Dixon, & Wyke, 2011; Scobbie, Wyke, & Dixon, 2009).

With this in mind, it is possible to consider goals in various domains of people's lives: social integration, reinforcing activities, self-care, financial independence, cognitive function, and so on. Let us take a couple of examples from the beginning and end of our list. Firstly, social isolation is a problem for children and adults who have sustained a brain injury and it is a difficult area in which to set goals because the behavior and attitudes of other people are relevant to the problem. Having the goal of "having more friends" may be a general aim but it breaks the SMART rules and needs to be broken down to something specific, measurable, agreed,

realistic and time-limited. Patient and therapist may agree that the chance of making more friends is more likely if there is more contact with others and they may do some work identifying local social opportunities. Barriers such as social anxiety can be examined and an agreed, achievable goal arrived at, for example, visiting a youth club for five minutes with a caregiver or contacting a voluntary organization to see what contributions the people there need. Success in achieving these goals will then be examined at the agreed interval and the next goals set.

To take a cognitive example, a patient may complain of poor attention. This could lead to the SMART goal of achieving a certain amount of practice on a working memory training program (see above). Sometimes it might be more useful to ask, what task does the person find it difficult to achieve because of poor attention? Then, as we have discussed, it is possible to agree discrete behavioral goals like taking a break every five minutes, trying the task in the morning rather than the evening, etc. These goals can be achieved and feed information into the goal setting process.

Clearly, setting and reviewing goals can be quite labor intensive. A hope is, however, that this very structured experience is useful not simply in terms of the goals that are achieved but the *process* that people and families may begin to integrate into their own problem-solving styles. Where possible, this shift in perspective from multiple, insurmountable problems to discrete, achievable steps may have more profound benefits on mood, confidence and self-efficacy.

Putting It All Together: The Oliver Zagwill Center for Neuropsychological Rehabilitation—A Comprehensive Approach

So far we have considered specific components of rehabilitation directed towards ameliorating the effects of memory, attention, and executive function and improving mood management. The manner in which rehabilitation is best delivered will vary depending on the severity of an individual's injury and the context. In this final section of the chapter we briefly outline a model of cognitive rehabilitation instantiated

---

[3] There are various versions of this acronym but the key points are generally similar.

in the Oliver Zangwill Center, (OZC) in the county of Cambridgeshire, United Kingdom.

The OZC was founded by clinical neuropsychologist Barbara Wilson in 1996, with joint funding from the National Health Service and the Medical Research Council. It was designed as a research active, comprehensive rehabilitation center helping clients in the post-acute phase following brain injury and their families to minimize, compensate for, and adjust to cognitive impairments resulting from brain injury. Access to the center follows an assessment of cognitive, emotional, and functional status and a discussion of the kind of goals clients may wish to pursue. People whose impairments are so great that they are unlikely to benefit from this particular program or those with severe behavioral problems, likely to disrupt the program for other clients, are not admitted. Up to 12 clients can be in the program at any one time.

Clients meet with a key worker to discuss goals in more detail and to convert general aspirations into SMART goals as outlined above. With the goals in place, clients work with clinical psychologists, occupational therapists, and speech and language therapists as appropriate to work on specific targets. Clients contribute to psycho-educational groups examining the effects of brain injury: memory management, attention, and executive strategies, communication, and mood—these groups incorporating many of the techniques highlighted in this chapter. A six-week intensive phase in which clients attend the center during working hours is followed by a 12-week integration phase in which clients divide their time between the center and their own community. This provides an opportunity to work with families, caregivers, and employers to facilitate generalization of strategies to the home/work setting and/or adjust goals and strategies in light of the experience.

Through continuous examination of goal attainment, the center's daily activities also become its prime outcome measure. In an evaluation, Bateman (2006) reported that clients achieved or partially achieved between 90 and 99% of goals set, with complete achievement varying between 39 and 63% (goal attainment was divided by problem severity as measured by the European Brain Injury Questionnaire (EBIQ; Teasdale et al. (1997), with people with

greater difficulties generally achieving fewer goals). This suggests that the goal setting process at the OZC, in line with SMART principles, is generally realistic with the partial-attainment rate at least suggesting that the goals are not overly trivial to achieve. Other evidence on efficacy comes from significant improvements in clients' ratings of difficulties on the EBIQ before and after attendance (Bateman, 2006). Client anecdotes about their experiences at the Centre, which of course are likely to have a positive bias but also provide more vivid detail about the program, can be found at http://www.ozc.nhs.uk. A more detailed account of the ethos behind and day-to-day running of the centre can be found in Wilson et al. (2009).

Summary

In this chapter we have emphasized that cognitive rehabilitation is not simply about improvement in cognitive capacity but rather a range of techniques that can help clients and families to adapt to, compensate for, and reduce the functional impact of impairment. We discussed how memory function can be supported by encoding strategies such as errorless learning and automated aids such as NeuroPage. We emphasized the importance of thinking about simple strategies that can maximize attention function, such as protecting the environment from distraction and taking scheduled breaks in activities. We also discussed evidence on computerized retraining of attention and the promise suggested by recent studies on working memory training as well as a raft of techniques that have been applied to the management of unilateral spatial neglect. Turning to executive function, we highlighted positive results from studies attempting to train a more executive stance to activities and from the use of cueing in clients' everyday lives to increase the likelihood of generalization. Although the research base is not yet well developed, we discussed the likely importance of incorporating interventions that help clients to manage mood as part of cognitive rehabilitation programs. In the final section we discussed a general principle of goal-setting that has application across many therapeutic domains and the work of the Oliver Zangwill Center, a program that employs SMART goal-setting and many of the other techniques outlined here to maximize outcome following brain injury.

References

Adair, J. C., Na, D. L., Schwartz, R. L., & Heilman, K. M. (2003). Caloric stimulation in neglect: Evaluation of response as a function of neglect type. *Journal of the International Neuropsychological Society*, *9*(7), 983–988.

Anson, K., & Ponsford, J. (2006). Evaluation of a coping skills group following traumatic brain injury. *Brain Injury*, *20*, 167–178.

Antonucci, G., Guariglia, C., Judica, A., Magnotti, L., Paolucci, S., Pizzamiglio, L., et al. (1995). Effectiveness of neglect rehabilitation in a randomized group study. *Journal of Clinical and Experimental Neuropsychology*, *17*, 383–389.

Baddeley, A., & Wilson, B. A. (1994). When implicit learning fails: amnesia and the problem of error elimination. *Neuropsychologia*, *32*, 53–68.

Baddeley, A. D. (1983). Working memory. *Philosophical Transactions of the Royal Society, London*, *302*, 311–324.

Baddeley, A. D., Eysenck, M., & Anderson, M. C. (2009). *Memory*. Hove: Psychology Press.

Bateman, A. (2006). *Oliver Zangwill Centre Outcomes*. Paper presented at the Oliver Zangwill 10th Anniversary Conference, Cambridge.

Beis, J. M., Andre, J. M., Baumgarten, A., & Challier, B. (1989). Eye patching in unilateral spatial neglect: Efficacy of two methods. *Archives of Physical Medicine and Rehabilitation*, *80*, 71–76.

Berg, I. J., Koning-Haanstra, M., & Deelman, B. G. (1991). Long term effects of memory rehabilitation: A controlled study. *Neuropsychological Rehabilitation*, *1*, 91–111.

Berry, E., Kapur, N., Williams, L., Hodges, J., Watson, P., Smyth, G., et al. (2007). The use of a wearable camera, SenseCam, as a pictorial diary to improve autobiographical memory in a patient with limbic encephalitis. *Neuropsychological Rehabilitation*, *17*(4/5), 582–681.

Bottini, G., Paulesu, E., Gandola, M., Loffredo, S., Scarpa, P., Sterzi, R., et al. (2005). Left caloric vestibular stimulation ameliorates right hemianesthesia. *Neurology*, *65*, 1278–1283.

Bradbury, C. L., Christensen, B. K., Lau, M. A., Ruttan, L. A., Arundine, A. L., & Green. R. E. (2008). The efficacy of cognitive behaviour therapy in the treatment of emotional distress after acquired brain injury. *Archives of Physical Medicine and Rehabilitation*, *89*(Suppl 2), S61–68.

Brighina, F., Bisiach, E., Oliveri, M., Piazza, A., La Bua, V., Daniele, O., et al. (2003). 1 Hz repetitive transcranial magnetic stimulation of the unaffected hemisphere ameliorates contralesional visuospatial neglect in humans. *Neuroscience Letters*, *336*(2), 131–133.

Brindley, R., Bateman, A., & Gracey, F. (2010). Exploration of use of SenseCam to support autobiographical memory retrieval within a cognitive-behavioural therapeutic intervention following acquired brain injury. *Memory*, *15*, 1–13.

Burgess, P. W., Alderman, N., Evans, J., Emslie, H., & Wilson, B. A. (1998). The ecological validity of tests of executive function. *Journal of the International Neuropsychological Society*, *4*, 547–558.

Butler, A. C., Chapman, J. E., Forman, E. M., & Beck, A. T. (2006). The empirical status of cognitive-behavioral therapy: a review of meta-analyses. *Clinical Psychology Review*, *26*(1), 17–31.

Cappa, S. F. (2005). EFNS guidelines on cognitive rehabilitation: report of an EFNS task force. *European Journal of Neurology*, *12*, 665–680.

Cappa, S. F., Sterzi, R., Vallar, G., & Bisiach, E. (1987). Remission of hemineglect and anosognosia during vestibular stimulation. *Neuropsychologia*, *25*, 775–782.

Cicerone, K. D. (2000). Evidence based cognitive rehabilitation: recommendations for clinical practice. *Archives of Physical Medicine and Rehabilitation*, *81*, 1596–16145.

Clare, L., & Jones, R. S. P. (2008). Errorless learning in the rehabilitation of memory: a critical review. *Neuropsychology Reviews*, *18*, 1–23.

Clare, L., Wilson, B. A., Breen, K., & Hodges, J. R. (1999). Errorless learning of face-name associations in early Alzheimer's disease. *Neurocase*, *5*, 37–46.

Dahlin, E., Neely, A. S., Larsson, A., Bäckman, L., & Nyberg, L. (2008). Transfer of learning after updating training mediated by the striatum. *Science*, *320*(5882), 1510–1512.

Dewar, B. K., & Gracey, F. (2007). "Am not was": Cognitive-behavioural therapy for adjustment and identity change following herpes simplex encephalitis. *Neuropsychological Rehabilitation*, *17*(4), 602–620.

Duncan, J., Seitz, R. J., Kolodny, J., Bor, D., Herzog, H., Ahmed, A., Newell, F. N., & Emslie, H. (2000). A Neural Basis for General Intelligence. *Science*, *289*, 457–460.

Evans, J. J., Wilson, B. A., Needham, P., & Brentnall, S. (2003). Who makes good use of memory aids? Results of a survey of people with acquired brain injury. *Journal of the International Neuropsychological Society*, *9*, 925–935.

Fish, J., Evans, J. J., Nimmo, M., Martin, E., Kersel, D., Bateman, A., et al. (2007). Rehabilitation of executive dysfunction following brain injury: "Content-free cueing" improves everyday prospective memory performance. *Neuropsychologia*, *45*(6), 1318–1330.

Fish, J., Manly, T., & Wilson, B. A. (2008). Long-Term Compensatory Treatment Of Organizational Deficits In A Patient With Bilateral Frontal Lobe Damage. *Journal of the International Neuropsychological Society*, *14*(1), 154–163.

Fivush, R. (2011). The development of autobiographical memory. *Annual Review of Psychology*, *62*, 559–582.

Fong, K. N., Chan, M. K., Ng, P. P., Tsang, M. H., Chow, K. K., Lau, C. W., et al. (2007). The effect of voluntary trunk rotation and half-field eye-patching for patients with unilateral neglect in stroke: a randomized controlled trial. *Clinical Rehabilitation*, *21*(8), 729–741.

Frassinetti, F., Angeli, V., Meneghello, F., Avanzi, S., & Ladavas, E. (2002). Long-lasting amelioration of visuospatial neglect by prism adaptation. *Brain*, *125*, 608–623.

George, M. S., Mercer, J. S., Walker, R., & Manly, T. (2008). A demonstration of endogenous modulation of unilateral spatial neglect: The impact of apparent time-pressure on spatial bias. *Journal of the International Neuropsychological Society*, *14*(1), 33–41.

Glisky, E. L., Schacter, D. L., & Tulving, E. (1986a). Computer learning by memory-impaired patients: acquisition and retention of complex knowledge. *Neuropsychologia*, *24*, 313–328.

Glisky, E. L., Schacter, D. L., & Tulving, E. (1986b). Learning and retention of computer-related vocabulary in memory-impaired patients: method of vanishing cues. *Journal of Clinical and Experimental Neuropsychology*, *8*, 292–312.

Gracey, F., Brentnall, S., & Megoran, R. (2009). Judith: learning to do things 'at the drop of a hat': behavioural experiments to explore and change the 'meaning' in meaningful functional activity. In B. A. Wilson, F. Gracey, J. J. Evans & A. Bateman (Eds.), *Neuropsychological Rehabilitation Theory, Models, Therapy and Outcome* (pp. 256–271). Cambridge: Cambridge University Press.

Gracey, F., Oldham, P., & Kritzinger, R. (2007). Finding out if "The 'me' will shut down": Successful cognitive-behavioural therapy of seizure-related panic symptoms following subarachnoid haemorrhage: A single case report. *Neuropsychological Rehabilitation*, *17*(1), 106–119.

Gray, J. M., Robertson, I. H., Pentland, B., & Anderson, S. I. (1992). Microcomputer based cognitive rehabilitation for brain damage: a randomised group controlled trial. *Neuropsychological Rehabilitation*, *2*, 97–116.

Halligan, P. W., Manning, L., & Marshall, J. (1990). Hemispheric activation vs spatio-motor cueing in visual neglect: A case study. *Neuropsychologia*, *29*(2), 165–176.

Harding, P., & Riddoch, M. J. (2009). Functional electrical stimulation (FES) of the upper limb alleviates unilateral neglect: a case series analysis. *Neuropsychological Rehabilitation*, *19*(1), 41–63.

Haslam, C., Moss, Z., & Hodder, K. (2010). Are two methods better than one? Evaluating the effectiveness of combining errorless learning with vanishing cues. *Journal of Clinical and Experimental Neuropsychology*, *32*(9), 973–985.

Holmes, J., Gathercole, S. E., & Dunning, D. L. (2009). Adaptive training leads to sustained enhancement of poor working memory in children. *Developmental Science*, *12*, F9–15.

Hunkin, N. M., Squires, E. J., Aldrich, F. K., & Parkin, A. J. (1998). Errorless learning and the acquisition of work processing skills. *Neuropsychological Rehabilitation*, *8*, 433–449.

Husain, M., & Rorden, C. (2003). Non-Spatially lateralized mechanisms in hemispatial neglect. *Nature Reviews Neuroscience*, *4*, 26–36.

Jaeggi, S. M., Buschkuehlm, M., Jonides, J., & Perrig, W. J. (2008). Improving fluid intelligence with training on working memory. *Proceedings of the National Academy of Sciences*, *105*, 6829–6833.

Jones, R. S., & Earys, C. B. (1992). The use of errorless learning procedures in teaching people with a learning disability: a critical review. *Mental Handicap Research*, *5*, 204–212.

Klingberg, T., Fernell, E., Olesen, P. J., Johnson, M., Gustafsson, P., Dahlstro, M. K., et al. (2005). Computerized training of working memory in children with ADHD—A randomized, controlled trial. *Journal of the American Academy of Child and Adolescent Psychiatry*, *44*(2), 177–186.

Krpan, K. N., Levine, B., Stuss, D. T., & Dawson, D. R. (2006). Executive function and coping at one-year post traumatic brain injury. *Journal of Clinical and Experimental Neuropsychology*, *29*(1), 36–46.

Lawson, I. R. (1962). Visual-spatial neglect in lesions of the right cerebral hemisphere: A study in recovery. *Neurology*, *12*, 23–33.

Levine, B., Robertson, I. H., Clare, L., Carter, G., Hong, J., Wilson, B. A., et al. (2000). Rehabilitation of executive functioning: An experimental-clinical validation of Goal Management Training. *Journal of the International Neuropsychological Society*, *6*, 299–312.

Levine, B., Schweizer, T. A., O'Connor, C., Turner, G., Gillingham, S., Stuss, D. T., et al. (2011). Rehabilitation of executive functioning in patients with frontal lobe brain damage with goal management training. *Frontiers in Human Neuroscience*, 5, 1–9.

Levine, B., Stuss, D. T., Winocur, G., Binns, M. A., Fahy, L., Mandic, M., et al. (2007). Cognitive rehabilitation in the elderly: Effects on strategic behavior in relation to goal management. *Journal of the International Neuropsychological Society*, 13(1), 143–152.

Lloyd, J., Riley, G. A., & Powell, T. E. (2009). Errorless learning of novel routes through a virtual town in people with acquired brain injury. *Neuropsychological Rehabilitation*, 19(1), 98–109.

Luria, A. R. (1966). *Higher cortical functions in man.* London: Tavistock.

Maddicks, R., Marzillier, S. L., & Parker, G. (2003). Rehabilitation of unilateral neglect in the acute recovery stage: The efficacy of limb activation therapy. *Neuropsychological Rehabilitation*, 13(3), 391–408.

Malhotra, P. A., Parton, A. D., Greenwood, R., & Husain, M. (2006). Noradrenergic modulation of space exploration in visual neglect. *Annals of Neurology*, 59(1), 186–190.

Manly, T., Hawkins, J., Evans, J. J., Woldt, K., & Robertson, I. H. (2002). Rehabilitation of Executive Function: Facilitation of effective goal management on complex tasks using periodic auditory alerts. *Neuropsychologia*, 40(3), 271–281.

McKenna, K., Cooke, D. M., Fleming, J., Jefferson, A., & Ogden, S. (2006). The incidence of visual perceptual impairment in patients with severe traumatic brain injury. *Brain Injury*, 20(5), 507–518.

Miotto, E. C., Evans, J. J., de Lucia, M. C., & Scaff, M. (2009). Rehabilitation of executive dysfunction: a controlled trial of an attention and problem solving treatment group. *Neuropsychological Rehabilitation*, 19(4), 517–540.

Nys, G. M., de Haan, E. H., Kunneman, A., de Kort, P. L., & Dijkerman, H. C. (2008). Acute neglect rehabilitation using repetitive prism adaptation: A randomised placebo-controlled trial. *Restorative Neurology and Neuroscience*, 26, 1–12.

Owen, A. M., Hampshire, A., Grahn, J. A., Stenton, R., Dajani, S., Burns, A. S., et al. (2010). Putting brain training to the test. *Nature*, 465(7299), 775–778.

Pizzamiglio, L., Antonucci, G., Judica, A., Montenero, P., Prazzano, C., & Zoccolotti, P. (1992). Cognitive rehabilitation of the hemineglect disorder in chronic-patients with unilateral right brain-damage. *Journal of Clinical and Experimental Neuropsychology*, 14(6), 901–923.

Plohmann, A. M., Kappos, L., Ammann, W., Thordai, A., Wittwer, A., Huber, S., et al. (1998). Computer assisted retraining of attentional impairments in patients with multiple sclerosis. *Journal of Neurology, Neurosurgery, and Psychiatry*, 64, 455–462.

Polanowska, K., Seniów, J., Paprot, E., Leśniak, M., & Członkowska, A. (2009). Left-hand somatosensory stimulation combined with visual scanning training in rehabilitation for post-stroke hemineglect: a randomised, double-blind study. *Neuropsychological Rehabilitation*, 19(3), 364–382.

Posner, M. (1993). Interaction of arousal and selection in the posterior attention network. In A. Baddeley & L. Weiskrantz (Eds.), *Attention: Selection, Awareness and Control.* (pp. 390–405). Oxford: Clarendon Press.

Prigatano, G. P. (1999). *Principles of Neuropsychological Rehabilitation.* New York: Oxford University Press.

Riddoch, M. J., & Humphreys, G. W. (1983). The effect of cueing on unilateral neglect. *Neuropsychologia*, 21, 589–599.

Robertson, I. H., Hogg, K., & McMillan, T. M. (1998a). Rehabilitation of Unilateral Neglect: Improving Function by Contralesional Limb Activation. *Neuropsychological Rehabilitation*, 8(1), 19–29.

Robertson, I. H., & Manly, T. (1999). Sustained Attention Deficits in Time and Space. In G. W. Humphreys, J. Duncan & A. M. Treisman (Eds.), *Attention, space, and action: Studies in cognitive neuroscience* (pp. 297–310). Oxford: Oxford University Press.

Robertson, I. H., Mattingley, J., Rorden, C., & Rorden, J. (1998b). Phasic alerting of neglect patients overcomes their spatial deficit in visual awareness. *Nature*, 395, 169–172.

Robertson, I. H., McMillan, T. M., MacLeod, E., Edgeworth, J., & Brock, D. (2002). Rehabilitation by limb activation training reduces left-sided motor impairment in unilateral neglect patients: A single-blind randomised control trial. *Neuropsychological Rehabilitation*, 12(5), 439–454.

Robertson, I. H., & North, N. (1993). Active and passive activation of left limbs: influence on visual and sensory neglect. *Neuropsychologia*, 31, 293–300.

Robertson, I. H., & North, N. (1994). One hand is better than two: motor extinction of left hand advantage in unilateral neglect. *Neuropsychologia*, 32, 1–11.

Robertson, I. H., North, N., & Geggie, C. (1992). Spatio-motor cueing in unilateral neglect: three single case studies of its therapeutic effectiveness. *Journal of Neurology, Neurosurgery and Psychiatry*, 55, 799–805.

Robertson, I. H., Tegnér, R., Tham, K., Lo, A., & Nimmo-Smith, I. (1995). Sustained attention training for unilateral neglect: Theoretical and rehabilitation implications. *Journal of Clinical and Experimental Neuropsychology*, 17, 416–430.

Robinson, F. P. (1970). *Effective Study*. New York: Harper and Row.

Rode, G., Charles, N., Perenin, M.-T., Vighetto, A., Trillet, M., & Aimard, G. (1992). Partial remission of hemiplegia and somatoparaphrenia through vestibular stimulation in a case of unilateral neglect. *Cortex, 28*, 203–208.

Rose, F. D., & Johnson, D. A. (1996). *Brain Injury and After: Towards Improved Outcome*. Chichester: John Wiley and Sons.

Rossetti, Y., Rode, G., Pisella, L., Farne, A., Li, L., Boisson, D., et al. (1998). Prism adaptation to a rightward optical deviation rehabilitates left hemispatial neglect. *Nature, 395*, 166–169.

Rubens, A. B. (1985). Caloric stimulation and unilateral visual neglect. *Neurology, 35*, 1019–1024.

Schindler, I., Kerkhoff, G., Karnath, H. O., Keller, I., & Goldenberg, G. (2002). Neck muscle vibration induces lasting recovery in spatial neglect. *Journal of Neurology Neurosurgery and Psychiatry, 73*, 412–419.

Scobbie L., Dixon D., & Wyke, S. (2011). Goal setting and action planning in the rehabilitation setting: development of a theoretically informed practice framework. *Clinical Rehabilitation, 25*(5), 468–482.

Scobbie, L., Wyke, S., & Dixon, D. (2009). Identifying and applying psychological theory to setting and achieving rehabilitation goals. *Clinical Rehabilitation, 23*(4), 321–333.

Serino, A., Ciaramelli, E., & Santantonio, A. D., Malagù, S., Servadei, F., Làdavas, E. (2007). A pilot study for rehabilitation of central executive deficits after traumatic brain injury. *Brain Injury, 21*(1), 11–19.

Shallice, T., & Burgess, P. (1991). Deficit in strategy application following frontal lobe damage in man. *Brain, 114*, 727–741.

Simblett, S. K., & Bateman, A. (2011). Dimensions of the Dysexecutive Questionnaire (DEX) examined using Rasch analysis. *Neuropsychological Rehabilitation, 21*(1), 1–25.

Slaughter, B., Fann, J. R., & Ehde, D. (2003). Traumatic brain injury in a county jail population: prevalence, neuropsychological functioning and psychiatric disorders. *Brain Injury, 17*(9), 731–741.

Sparing, R., Thimm, M., Hesse, M. D., Küst, J., Karbe, H., & Fink, G. R. (2009). Bidirectional alterations of interhemispheric parietal balance by non-invasive cortical stimulation. *Brain, 132*(11), 3011–3020.

Squires, E., Hunkin, N. M., & Parkin, A. J. (1996). Memory notebook training in a case of severe amnesia: Generalising from paired associate learning to real life. *Neuropsychological Rehabilitation, 6*, 55–65.

Stone, S. P., Halligan, P. W., & Greenwood, R. J. (1993). The incidence of neglect phenomena and related disorders in patients with an acute right or left-hemisphere stroke. *Age and Ageing, 22*(1), 46–52.

Sturm, W., Longoni, F., Weis, S., Specht, K., Herzog, H., Vohn, R., et al. (2004). Functional reorganisation in patients with right hemisphere stroke after training of alertness: a longitudinal PET and fMRI study in eight cases. *Neuropsychologia, 42*(4), 434–450.

Sturm, W., Willmes, K., Orgass, B., & Hartje, W. (1997). Do specific attention deficits need specific training? *Neuropsychological Rehabilitation, 7*(2), 81–103.

Sumowski, J. F., Wood, H. G., Chiaravalloti, N., Wylie, G. R., Lengenfelder, J., & Deluca, J. (2010). Retrieval practice A simple strategy for improving memory after traumatic brain injury. *Journal of the International Neuropsychological Society, 16*(6), 1147–1150.

Teasdale, T. W., Christensen, A., Willmes, K., Deloche, G., Braga, L., Stachowiak, F., et al. (1997). Subjective experience in brain-injured patients and their close relatives: a european brain injury questionnaire study. *Brain Injury, 11*(8), 543–563.

Teasdale, T. W., & Engberg, A. W. (2001). Suicide after traumatic brain injury: a population study. *Journal of Neurosurgery and Psychiatry, 71*(4), 436–440.

Tiersky, L. A., Anselmi, V., Johnston, M. V., Kurtyka, J., Roosen, E., Schwartz, T., et al. (2005). A trial of neuropsychological rehabilitation in mild-spectrum traumatic brain injury. *Archives of Physical Medicine and Rehabilitation, 86*, 1565–1574.

Tsang, M. H., Sze, K. H., & Fong, K. N. (2009). Occupational therapy treatment with right half-field eye-patching for patients with subacute stroke and unilateral neglect: a randomised controlled trial. *Disability and Rehabilitation, 31*(8), 630–637.

Turton, A. J., O'Leary, K., Gabb, J., Woodward, R., & Gilchrist, I. D. (2009). A single blinded randomised controlled pilot trial of prism adaptation for improving self-care in stroke patients with neglect. *Neuropsychological Rehabilitation, 21*, 1–17.

von Cramon, D., & Matthes-von Cramon, G. (1994). Back to work with a chronic dysexecutive syndrome. *Neuropsychological Rehabilitation, 4*, 399–417.

Von Cramon, D., Matthes-von Cramon, G., & Mai, N. (1991). Problem-solving deficits in brain-injured patients: a therapeutic approach. *Neuropsychological Rehabilitation, 1*, 45–64.

Westerberg, H., Jacobaeus, H., Hirvikoski, T., Clevberger, P., Ostensson, M. L., Bartfai, A., et al.

(2007). Computerized working memory training after stroke—A pilot study. *Brain Injury*, *21*(1), 21–29.

Williams, W. H., Evans, J. J., & Fleminger, S. (2003). Neurorehabilitation and cognitive behaviour therapy of anxiety disorders: An overview and a case illustration of obsessive-compulsive disorder. *Neuropsychological Rehabilitation*, *13*, 133–148.

Wilson, B. A. (1996). Cognitive rehabilitation: How it is and how it might be. *Journal of the International Neuropsychological Society*, *3*, 487–496.

Wilson, B. A. (2009). *Memory Rehabilitation: Integrating Theory and Practice*. New York: The Guilford Press.

Wilson, B. A., Baddeley, A., Evans, J., & Shiel, A. (1994). Errorless learning in the rehabilitation of memory impaired people. *Neuropsychological Rehabilitation*, *4*, 307–326.

Wilson, B. A., Emslie, H. C., Quirk, K., & Evans, J. J. (2001). Reducing everyday memory and planning problems by means of a paging system: a randomised control crossover study. *Journal of Neurology Neurosurgery and Psychiatry*, *70*(4), 477–482.

Wilson, B. A., Gracey, F., Evans, J. J., & Bateman, A. (2009). *Neuropsychological Rehabilitation Theory, Models, Therapy and Outcome*. Cambridge: Cambridge University Press.

Wilson, B. A., Wilson, J. C., & Hughes, E. (1997). Coping with amnesia: The natural history of a compensatory memory system. *Neuropsychological Rehabilitation*, *7*, 43–56.

Wilson, C., & Robertson, I. H. (1992). A home-based intervention for attentional slips during reading following head injury: a single case study. *Neuropsychological Rehabilitation*, *2*, 193–205.

12

Community Adjustment and Re-engagement

Tamara Ownsworth and Jennifer Fleming

Introduction

Individuals with traumatic brain injury (TBI) commonly face many challenges in reintegrating into the community following their hospitalization. The transition from hospital to home is a particularly significant adjustment period in which individuals often first experience the effects of their injury in everyday activities within a familiar environment (Fleming, Winnington, McGillivray, Boyana, & Ownsworth, 2006). As individuals attempt to re-engage in former activities and social roles they typically begin to better appreciate the extent and implications of their injury-related impairments. Feelings of frustration, anxiety and depression commonly arise in reaction to changes in personal abilities, lifestyle, and sense of self (Gracey, Malley & Evans, 2009; Ownsworth & Oei, 1998). As outcomes are covered in chapters 10 and 11, this chapter aims to examine empirical findings in the TBI literature relating to the processes involved in community adjustment and re-engagement, which, for the purpose of the following review, will be defined as the first 12 months post-discharge. A considerable body of research has investigated factors influencing adjustment during this period, including pre-injury functioning, the nature and severity of TBI, psychological characteristics, and social and environmental factors (Kendall & Terry, 2009; Tate & Broe, 1999). The following review focuses on key findings and methodological issues in the literature relating to community adjustment and re-engagement processes, particularly the significance of awareness of deficits and emotional reactions, resuming activities and social roles, and the impact of environmental factors (including the type of post-acute rehabilitation) during early community reintegration.

Hospital Discharge Processes and Outcomes

Rehabilitation facilities aim to prepare inpatients with brain injury for their return home using various discharge planning processes. These may include home visits to determine the need for home modifications to ensure access and safety in activities of daily living, family meetings to discuss post-discharge support and care arrangements, as well as any activity restrictions, and day visits or weekend leave to spend extended time with family before discharge. Pathways of care and discharge planning processes vary for those who are discharged directly from acute care into the community or are discharged to a long term care facility rather than home (Mellick, Gerhart, & Whiteneck, 2003). Some individuals are referred to outpatient or community-based rehabilitation services following discharge, although this is not a certainty with two-thirds of people with TBI in one study ($n = 1059$) not receiving any post-discharge services (Mellick et al., 2003), and reports of difficulties accessing and negotiating appropriate support and rehabilitation services following discharge in other studies (Nalder, Fleming, Foster, Cornwell, & Khan, 2012a; Turner et al., 2007; Turner, Fleming, Ownsworth, & Cornwell, 2011).

For many individuals with TBI, discharge home is a long-awaited milestone accompanied by much anticipation and high expectations

235

about returning to "normal." In contrast, family members report feeling apprehensive about their ability to cope and concerned about the uncertainties associated with the future (Turner et al., 2007). Furthermore, a number of individuals will experience a change in living situation on discharge back into community due to the need for additional support or financial reasons. Often this involves adult children returning to live with their parents after living independently with friends or in shared accommodation. In a study of transition from hospital to home (Nalder et al., 2012a), approximately 16% of individuals with TBI had experienced a change to a more restrictive living situation at one-month post-discharge, and this change in living situation was related to a more successful transition experience from the perspective of the individual with TBI. Interestingly though, it was also significantly related to a less successful transition experience from the perspective of the family caregiver involved. This suggests that while family support is undoubtedly a resource for enhancing community integration, it may come at a cost to those providing the support, and may justify the pre-discharge apprehensions of family members. We have recently conducted a series of qualitative and quantitative studies investigating the processes of community re-engagement during the transition from hospital to home after brain injury, and in this chapter we draw on this research and other work on the development of self-awareness, emotional adjustment, and environmental factors which influence the success of the transition phase. Like all aspects of brain injury rehabilitation, community adjustment and re-engagement is not a simple process and the wide variation in outcomes is influenced by multiple individual and contextual factors (Fleming, Kuipers, Foster, Smith, & Doig, 2009).

Adjustment to Life at Home

Most individuals with moderate to severe TBI spend many months in hospital receiving acute care and inpatient rehabilitation. Although they may have had community outings and visits home prior to discharge, the process of leaving the hospital and returning to their previous home or a new home in the community represents a major transition. Research suggests that in the first month post-discharge individuals usually experience various positive emotional reactions such as excitement and relief about their perceived new found freedom and ability to engage in certain pre-injury activities (Turner, Ownsworth, Cornwell & Fleming, 2009). However, over the first few months post-discharge these positive feelings may be replaced by frustration, anxiety and despair as expectations of life at home are not fulfilled. In particular, many individuals become more aware of their persisting physical, cognitive, and behavioral impairments as they attempt to engage in familiar activities (Fleming & Strong, 1999; Hart, Seignourel, & Sherer, 2009). Difficulties may be evident from their own perceptions or feedback from others regarding their slowness, errors, and fatigue, or the inability to complete an activity successfully (Turner et al., 2009). Further, there is often a mismatch between the occupational activities individuals wish to resume (e.g., driving and work) and the activities they can actually perform (e.g., self-care and home duties). Individuals with TBI commonly experience restrictions in their daily routine; hobbies and habits (e.g., playing sport and consuming alcohol) might not be possible or at least ill advised due to motor deficits and interaction with medications. There may also be reduced independence and increased supervision (Turner et al., 2009).

Despite these challenges, individuals typically perceive that returning home facilitates functional gains, in part due to the familiarity of the environment as well as their participation in real life and meaningful activities. McColl and Karlovits (1998) conducted repeated interviews across the first 12 months post-discharge and observed a tendency for individuals to more positively assess their community reintegration over time. Individuals defined their sense of community reintegration along four dimensions, including general integration (e.g., fitting in, feeling accepted, and being familiar with their local community); social support (e.g., people in their close social network as well as the general public); occupation (e.g., involvement in regular leisure and productive activities); and independent living (e.g., self-determining one's own actions and living arrangements).

In a longitudinal investigation of quality of life during the first year after discharge, Conneeley (2003) found that learning to manage uncertainty about the future as well as establishing personal autonomy was central to individuals' subjective well-being. The ability to develop and pursue modified goals for life after TBI can be greatly undermined by awareness deficits.

The Significance of Awareness Deficits

Many individuals with TBI are observed to lack insight into their post-injury changes, particularly during the first few months after their injury. Impaired awareness is a concern clinically because inaccurate self-appraisal may compromise safety during activities, increase support needs, reduce motivation for therapy and strategy use, and lead to unrealistic expectations of the future (Fleming, Strong, & Ashton, 1996; Ownsworth & Clare, 2006). Although the phenomenon of awareness deficits in the context of neurological injury is well established in the literature (see seminal review by McGlynn & Schacter, 1989), there are conflicting opinions concerning the presence and magnitude of awareness deficits, as well as the origin or aetiology of awareness deficits. Further, the relationship between awareness deficits and rehabilitation outcome is unclear.

Presence and Magnitude of Awareness Deficits

Prevalence rates of impaired awareness following TBI vary considerably. A review by Flashman and McAllister (2002) identified that up to 45% of individuals with moderate to severe TBI exhibit awareness deficits. However, research by Sherer et al. (1998) found that approximately 76 to 97% of individuals with TBI displayed some level of impaired awareness during the post-acute phase of recovery. Various methodological issues appear to contribute to these discrepant findings, including the timing of assessment, measurement approaches, and criteria applied for determining the presence of awareness deficits. Awareness of deficits is a complex phenomenon for which clinical inferences are made about subjective experiences based on a specific approach

to measurement (see Ownsworth, Clare & Morris, 2006). Measurement approaches include standardized questionnaires that involve comparing self-ratings of functional skills with significant others' ratings (or occasionally test performance), semi-structured interviews to elicit individuals' verbal description of their impairments, and behavioral observation of verbal and non-verbal indicators of awareness during task performance (see review by Fleming et al., 1996). The most common method in research involves examining the level of agreement or concordance between self-ratings and significant others' ratings of functional status on the same questionnaire.

Despite using a questionnaire-based approach, studies report conflicting findings concerning the presence and magnitude of awareness deficits during early community re-integration. Research by Pagulayan, Temkin, Machamer, and Dikmen (2007) investigated awareness of deficits during the acute and post-acute phases of recovery (i.e., 1 and 12 months post-injury) by comparing self-reports and significant other (SO) reports of the patients' functioning ($n = 120$) on the original version of the Sickness Impact Profile (SIP). Pagulayan et al. distinguished between "reduced awareness" (underestimation of impairment) and "hyperawareness" (overestimation of impairment) as forms of awareness dysfunction using cut-off points. Interestingly, Pagulayan et al. (2007) found that self-reported problems on the SIP domains did not differ significantly from SO reports at either 1 month or 12 months post-injury. Further, in some cases, individuals with TBI reported greater problems than their SO. Such findings challenge the widely held belief that awareness deficits are prevalent during the acute and phase of recovery after TBI.

These findings contrast with outcomes reported by Hart and colleagues (2009) who employed a similar 12-month longitudinal design ($n = 123$) to examine changes in self-awareness between the subacute stage (approximately 45 days after injury) and one-year follow-up. Unlike Pagulayan et al. (2007), Hart et al. assessed awareness of deficits using self- and SO ratings on the Awareness Questionnaire (AQ) and Patient Competency Rating Scale (PCRS). Significant discrepancies were evident on both measures at the subacute stage, thus reflecting patients' overestimation of their functional status, whilst smaller discrepancy scores and stronger correlations between participant and family ratings were evident at follow-up. Patients demonstrated relatively accurate self-appraisal of sensory/motor impairments at both time points, while awareness of impairments on the behavioral/affective domain improved at follow-up. Nevertheless, patients were still found to overestimate their functional status at the one-year follow-up compared to their SO.

It is important to note that the SIP is generic measure of health-related quality of life which, unlike the AQ and PCRS, was not specifically developed to assess awareness of TBI impairments. The AQ and PCRS consist of items that reflect common TBI-related impairments for which awareness may be compromised, and both are well validated measures of awareness deficits (Sherer, Hart, & Nick, 2003). It could be argued that the PCRS and AQ are more sensitive to the presence and degree of awareness deficits following TBI than the SIP, thus accounting for the different findings between these studies. Nonetheless, the study by Pagulayan et al. (2007) highlights the need for a more uniform approach to both the assessment and classification of self-awareness, including cut-off points to characterize the magnitude of both reduced awareness and hyperawareness.

Overall, most recent studies in the field suggest that a significant proportion of individuals with TBI display some level of awareness deficits in the more acute phase of recovery (e.g., Hart et al., 2009; Malec, Testa, Rush, Brown, & Moessner, 2007). Further, awareness of deficits is typically found to significantly improve over the first 12 months post-injury (Fleming & Strong, 1999; Hart et al., 2009; Lanham, Weissenberger, Schwab, & Rosner, 2000). Use of particular approaches may yield different findings concerning the frequency and magnitude of the issue (Pagulayan et al., 2007), which highlights that awareness of deficits is, in part, socially constructed phenomena (Ownsworth et al., 2006). This point was aptly demonstrated by Sherer et al. (1998) who found that specific questions about individuals' injury-related impairments yielded responses that were more consistent with relatives' reports than their responses to global questions. Therefore, the approach to measurement is

likely to influence individuals' capacity to demonstrate their awareness of deficits and hence clinical opinions formed.

Origin or Etiology of Awareness Deficits

The origin or etiology of awareness deficits has been of longstanding interest in the field (McGlynn & Schacter, 1989; Weinstein & Kahn, 1955). In general, there is acknowledgment of the likely role of both neurological and psychological mechanisms of unawareness. However, this conceptualization has been extended in more recent years to incorporate biopsychosocial levels of explanation (Ownsworth, Clare & Morris, 2006). In terms of biological or neurological factors, lesion studies support the involvement of the right frontal lobe in self-reflective capacity (Stuss & Anderson, 2004). Function-specific awareness deficits (e.g., for sensory and motor functions) are most prevalent when lesions encompass both frontal and parietal regions (Pia Neppi-Modona, Ricci, & Berti, 2004). More global awareness deficits that extend across functional domains are most consistently associated with impaired executive function (Ownsworth & Fleming, 2005) and a higher number, but not specific location, of brain lesions (Sherer, Hart, Whyte, Nick, & Yablon, 2005). Cognitive neuropsychological accounts propose that accurate self-appraisal of post-injury impairments relies upon higher-order cognitive processes to monitor, compare, and evaluate experiences of relative success and failure on tasks in everyday living with premorbid levels in order to update one's store of self-knowledge and beliefs about personal abilities (McGlynn & Schacter, 1989; Stuss, Picton, & Alexander, 2001). While cognitive neuropsychological models have intuitive appeal as well as empirical support (see review by Ownsworth, Clare et al., 2006), such accounts fail to address psychosocial factors that likely influence individuals' self-perceptions of impairment and how they represent these in a social context.

The deficits arising from TBI can be emotionally threatening and difficult to understand, and thus individuals with "partial awareness" may strive to make sense of their difficulties by employing different coping strategies. According to Prigatano (1999), individuals may employ "defensive" coping strategies such as denial or avoidance to protect against emotional distress. Ownsworth, McFarland, and Young (2002) further identified that highly defensive individuals may perceive their impairments on some conscious level, but elect not to disclose their difficulties to others. Alternatively, an individual who senses that something is amiss, but has difficulty making sense of these changes may continue to behave as though everything is normal (i.e., reacting as he or she would before the injury). This coping style represents "non-defensive" coping (Prigatano, 1999). Either coping style is likely to contribute to reduced symptom reporting during assessment, although individuals with the latter coping style are typically more amenable to learning alternative coping strategies (see Ownsworth, Fleming, Desbois, Kuipers, & Strong, 2006).

Awareness deficits are also, in part, a product of an individual's social environment (Ownsworth, Clare et al., 2006; Prigatano & Weinstein, 1996). Accuracy of self-appraisal is influenced by access to information about one's abilities and meaningful opportunities to learn about post-injury impairments. Excessive levels of support provided by family or professionals can ensure that individuals largely avoid failure on tasks, which may not provide the opportunity to learn and adjust to post-injury changes (Ylvisaker, Szekeres, & Feeney, 1998). Consistent with this view, effective awareness interventions typically involve providing individuals with personalized psychoeducation, feedback on strengths and difficulties, and creating supportive opportunities for learning about post-injury changes on functional tasks in individual and/or group therapy settings (Fleming & Ownsworth, 2006).

Many researchers have highlighted that although the tendency to overestimate abilities can be problematic, the issue of underestimating one's competency following TBI can be just as concerning. Malec, Brown, Moessner, Stump, and Monahan (2010) usefully distinguish between two dimensions of impaired awareness which differ in cognitive style. The first, as discussed so far in the chapter, reflects difficulty identifying or interpreting changes in one's abilities after TBI. A second dimension is the tendency to excessively focus attention on post-injury deficits "to the exclusion of context,

temporal, or other mitigating factors" (Malec et al., 2010, p. 1089). This cognitive style leads to over reporting of problems relative to the assessment of others. The latter type of awareness dysfunction is found to be related to emotional distress and social environmental factors such as medico-legal status (Ownsworth, Fleming, & Hardwick, 2006). Either dimension of impaired awareness can potentially impede adjustment during early community reintegration through motivational difficulties (e.g., lack of motivation to pursue goals or participate in rehabilitation) and maladaptive coping efforts.

Awareness Deficits and Rehabilitation Outcome

A further issue stimulating debate in the awareness literature concerns whether accurate self-appraisal is a prerequisite for favorable community reintegration outcomes and, related to this issue, whether there is a need to specifically target awareness deficits through an intervention. Many authors argue that accurate self-appraisal improves active participation and the capacity to benefit from rehabilitation (e.g., Robertson & Murre, 1999; Sherer et al., 1998). Other researchers have demonstrated that behavioral and functional gains can be achieved through other mechanisms, including behavioral modification, task-specific learning and habit formation (Sohlberg, Mateer, Penkman, Glang, & Todis, 1998).

Ownsworth and Clare (2006) conducted a systematic review of empirical studies investigating the relationship between awareness of deficits at the beginning of a rehabilitation program and post-rehabilitation outcomes. This review incorporated other causes of brain injury because only three of the eligible 12 studies focused solely on TBI, with other studies employing mixed ABI or stroke-specific samples. Overall, the review found that four studies supported the perspective that greater awareness of deficits is associated with more favorable rehabilitation outcome. For example, in a TBI sample ($n = 123$), Sherer et al. (2003) found that level of awareness on the AQ at admission to inpatient rehabilitation significantly predicted staff ratings of employability at program discharge. Six studies provided partial support, whereby the relationship between awareness and rehabilitation outcome was evident for only selected functional outcomes or a particular awareness index. For example, a TBI study by Anson and Ponsford (2006) found that greater awareness of deficits on the PCRS prior to a 10-session coping skills intervention was associated with better emotional adjustment at post-intervention. However, pre-intervention level of awareness on the Self-Awareness of Deficits Interview (Fleming et al., 1996) was not significantly related to any therapeutic changes. It should be noted that the sample size for this study was quite small ($n = 33$), and thus the analysis may have lacked statistical power.

There were two studies that failed to support the hypothesized positive relationship between awareness of deficits and rehabilitation outcome (Malec, Buffington, Moessner, & Degiorgio, 2000; Noe et al., 2005). Interestingly, the study by Noe et al. (2005) found a trend for the opposite effect. Specifically, although individuals classified at pre-intervention as either "low" or "high" self-awareness on the PCRS improved on most measures after the six-month intensive multi-disciplinary program, the low self-awareness group typically improved to a greater extent than the high self-awareness group on measures of neuropsychological and functional skills. However, interpretation of these findings is impeded by the small and heterogeneous mixed ABI sample ($n = 36$) and failure to control for pre-intervention levels of functioning. The second study by Malec et al. (2000) examined vocational outcomes of a mixed ABI sample ($n = 114$) of varied chronicity and found that awareness of deficits at service admission did not significantly predict level of vocational independence at initial placement or at one year follow-up. Malec et al. concluded that although awareness deficits may serve as a barrier to a return to work, this issue may be overcome by matching individuals to supportive work environments and providing task-specific training.

The review by Ownsworth and Clare (2006) provided clinical guidelines to support decision making about the need to target awareness deficits in treatment. Awareness deficits may warrant the focus of treatment during community reintegration when: a) such deficits represent a likely obstacle to the client achieving their own personally valued goals; b) there is a safety concern that cannot otherwise be managed effectively through behavioral approaches, or environmental modification; c) the possible emotional effects of increasing awareness are considered less detrimental than persisting awareness deficits; and d) there is sufficient scope in the rehabilitation setting to employ theory-driven approaches (i.e., based on a biopsychosocial conceptualization of the factors likely to underpin awareness deficits) and support is available to buffer the psychological impact of increased self-awareness. The systematic application of these guidelines has been illustrated in single-case experimental research (Ownsworth, Fleming, Desbois, et al., 2006).

Although various studies have highlighted that awareness of deficits is positively associated with emotional distress in the early community reintegration phase (e.g., Fleming et al., 2006; Fleming, Strong & Ashton, 1998), individuals who lack insight into their post-injury changes are potentially at greater risk of emotional distress in the long-term if their expectations of recovery are not met. Although awareness deficits may initially protect against emotional distress, in the long-term it is generally more adaptive for people to be aware of their post-injury difficulties in order for them to develop appropriate compensatory strategies and to maximize their independence (Ownsworth & Clare, 2006; Ownsworth, 2005). A review of awareness interventions and outcomes in the literature is beyond the scope of this chapter, however, the evidence base for the effectiveness of awareness interventions is mounting for holistic rehabilitation, group therapy approaches, psychoeducation and feedback, and interventions that train awareness and strategy use on functional tasks in real-life environments (see review by Fleming & Ownsworth, 2006).

Emotional Adjustment during Early Community Reintegration

Emotional distress is frequently observed clinically during the early community reintegration phase following TBI. A large body of empirical research has investigated the prevalence and etiology of emotional dysfunction during this period (e.g., Jorge, Robinson, Moser, Tateno, Crespo-Facorro, & Arndt, 2004; Malec et al.,

2010). A key issue in clinical practice relates to the impact of early emotional distress on functional outcomes of TBI. In particular, the early onset of depression is believed to contribute to poorer social outcomes in the long term and is often viewed as a secondary source of disability. However, the nature and direction of the relationship between emotional dysfunction and functional outcome is not well understood. In this section a review of the prevalence and etiology of emotional dysfunction is presented followed by discussion on the relationship between emotional dysfunction and community reintegration outcomes.

Prevalence of Emotional Disorders Early Post-TBI

Reported prevalence rates of depression and anxiety during the first 12 months post-discharge differ in the literature. For example, rates of depression during the first 12 months post-discharge range between 27% (Ownsworth et al., 2011) and 53% (Bombardier, Fann, Temkin, Esselman, Barber, & Dikmen, 2010). Rates for anxiety are typically lower than depression during early community reintegration, although this varies for different diagnostic subtypes. For example, the reported rate for Obsessive Compulsive Disorder is approximately 2% (Deb, Lyons, Koutzoukis, Ali & McCarthy, 1999), 11% for Generalized Anxiety Disorder (Jorge, Robinson, Starkstein, and Arndt, 1993), 9% for Panic Disorder (Deb et al., 1999) and 13–24% for Post-traumatic Stress Disorder (Bryant & Harvey, 1998; Levin et al., 2001). Rates also differ according to the approach to measurement and classification. In particular, some researchers have reported level or degree of emotional distress on standardized questionnaires and used cut-off points to differentiate between individuals in the non-clinical and clinical range (e.g., Malec et al., 2007; Malec et al., 2010; Ownsworth et al., 2011). Other researchers employed clinical interview schedules and diagnostic criteria (e.g., DSM-IV or ICD-10 criteria) to classify the absence or presence of different psychological disorders. It is noteworthy that prevalence rates differ even using a similar interview approach and diagnostic criteria (e.g., Bombardier et al., 2010; Whelan, Ponsford & Schonenberger, 2009).

The high degree of comorbidity between anxiety and depression (73–77%) (Jorge et al., 2004; Whelan et al., 2009) is a further issue likely to affect prevalence rates whereby common symptoms (e.g., low mood, rumination, irritability, concentration difficulties) complicate the distinction between these emotional disorders. Some researchers view depression and anxiety as part of a broader emotional disturbance following TBI rather than distinct disorders (Williams & Evans, 2003). Irrespective of the approach to assessment and classification, various somatic, cognitive, and behavioral sequelae of TBI overlap with mood symptomatology, which can lead to either overestimation or underestimation of the emotional effects of TBI (Ownsworth, Little, Turner, Hawkes, & Shum, 2008).

A multitude of factors have been implicated in the development of emotional distress following TBI. These factors broadly include the exacerbation of a pre-morbid psychological disorder or vulnerability (Ownsworth & Oei, 1998), neurologically mediated changes in emotional regulation from damage to cortico-limbic pathways (Jorge et al., 2004), and reactive mood disturbance in relation to changes in personal identity and loss of social roles (Ownsworth et al., 2011). There is empirical support for each explanation of depression during early community reintegration, as well as the relationship between emotional dysfunction and various functional outcomes.

A prospective cohort study by Bombardier and colleagues (2010) found that 297 of 559 TBI patients (53%) met the criteria for Major Depressive Disorder (MDD) at some point during the first 12 months post-injury. The best predictors in a multivariate model included the presence of MDD either prior to or at the time of injury, age ($\geq$60 versus 18–29 years), and lifetime alcohol dependence. After controlling for these predictors, the presence of MDD was significantly related to poorer quality of life at 12 months post-TBI.

In a similar prospective cohort study, Jorge et al. (2004) found that a comparable rate of 52% of their TBI sample ($n = 91$) met the diagnostic criteria for a mood disorder (note: this was mainly MDD) during the first 12 months post-injury. Those with a mood disorder were more likely to report a personal history of psychological disorder. In contrast to Bombardier et al. (2010), however, Jorge et al. (2004) did not find a significant association between post-TBI depression and history of substance use. Jorge et al. found that post-TBI depression was significantly related to impairments in executive function, but not severity of TBI. Further, volumetric analyses of TBI individuals with MDD and a matched subgroup of TBI individuals without MDD revealed that those with MDD had significantly decreased frontal gray matter volumes (mainly due to left lateral and inferior region differences). Although individuals with MDD did not differ on global measures of functional independence, those with depression had significantly poorer social outcomes at the six-month and 12 month follow-ups.

Malec et al. (2007) examined the influence of pre-injury factors, the presence and severity of TBI, self-perceived impairment and social support on depression at discharge, and "late" depression at 1–2 years post-injury ($n = 84$). Their findings indicated that depression levels did not differ according to severity of TBI or between the TBI and orthopedic control samples. Pre-injury factors accounted for a modest amount of variance (pre-injury psychiatric history and education = 12.5%) in depression. The best predictor of depression at both assessment periods was self-reported impairment at discharge (72% of variance explained), with social support contributing an extra 2% of variance in the model. In a subsequent study that employed structural equation modeling ($n = 158$), Malec and colleagues (2010) again found a moderately strong relationship between self-perceived impairment and depression, and further confirmed the lack of direct association between injury severity and depression. Functional outcome (role participation) at 12 months post-injury was significantly related to both depression and TBI severity. The findings of these studies highlight that self-appraisal of impairment contributes to the development of depression. Malec et al. (2010) referred to this relationship as "mutually enhancing and therefore bidirectional" (p. 1089), whereby increased self-perceived impairment contributes to emotional distress which, in turn, serves to heightens one's focus on personal short-comings.

In a further study investigating a psychosocial account of emotional dysfunction, Kendall and Terry (2009) tested mediation and moderation models for predicting emotional well-being during short-term (one-month post-discharge) and longer-term adjustment (nine-months post-discharge) after TBI ($n = 90$). In the mediation model the role of self-appraisal (perceived threat/self-efficacy) and coping strategies was examined while the moderation model examined the stress buffering effects of resources (self-esteem, social support, financial security, and life events) on emotional status. The findings indicated a mediating effect of perceived threat and a buffering effect of self-esteem on short-term emotional well-being. A recursive model identified that the majority of variables influenced longer-term emotional adjustment through their effect on short-term emotional well-being. Further, although a stress buffering effect was not evident for longer term emotional well-being; family support had a significant direct effect on emotional adjustment during this period. Kendall and Terry's study is the first prospective longitudinal study of its kind that provides rigorous support for the role of psychosocial variables in the development of emotional dysfunction. However, the potential influence of premorbid psychological adjustment, neurocognitive status, and functional independence on the predictor and outcome variables was not examined.

Overall, it is apparent that no single model or explanation can adequately account for the development of depression post-TBI. Despite general consensus in the literature regarding the probable interplay between neurological, psychological, and social factors (Williams & Evans, 2003), research is yet to systematically investigate the multiple etiological pathways and how these may interact to influence the development and maintenance of depression (Ownsworth & Oei, 1998). Such research would optimally be guided by a comprehensive biopsychosocial framework. Research has, nonetheless, consistently demonstrated an association between emotional status and functional outcomes during community reintegration.

The development of depression during the first few months after TBI has been found to predict poorer employment outcomes at one to two years post-injury (Felmingham, Baguley, & Crooks, 2001; Ruff et al., 1993). Depression has also been found to affect individuals' ability to maintain close relationships during the first year post-injury (Gomez-Hernandex, Max, Kosier, Paradiso, & Robinson, 1997), which may partly account for the association commonly found between depression and poor long-term social outcomes (Ownsworth & Fleming, 2005). Although depression has been viewed as a predictor of poor long-term functional outcomes, it is unclear whether depression is an *antecedent* for poor psychosocial outcomes, or an *outcome* of the functional consequences of TBI (e.g., inability to drive, work, or live independently) which threaten sense of self and social identity (Ownsworth & McKenna, 2004).

Our own recent research has begun to shed new light on the nature of this relationship. In a prospective cohort study ($n = 96$), Ownsworth et al. (2011) found that poorer progress in resuming pre-morbid lifestyle between discharge and three-months post-discharge was significantly related to the development of depressive symptoms at three-months post-discharge through an association with change in perceived functional consequences of TBI. Specifically, individuals who made less progress in resuming their independence and social roles during hospital transition perceived less improvement (or even a decline) in their abilities since discharge and, subsequently, reported more depressive symptoms at three-months follow-up. Because level of depression at discharge was controlled for in the analysis, and was not significantly related to progress in resuming premorbid lifestyle (e.g., return to work, driving, and independence), the findings support a model of reactive depression. Thus, extending the findings of Malec et al. (2007), the ability to re-engage in valued activities and roles was found to influence self-appraisal of post-injury functioning which, in turn, contributed to level of depression during early community reintegration. Ultimately, however, it is likely that depression can operate as either a risk factor for poor community adjustment, or develop in reaction to difficulties in resuming pre-injury activities and lifestyle.

Engagement in Meaningful Activity

The role of engagement in meaningful activity has received relatively minimal attention in brain injury rehabilitation research. A small number of qualitative studies with this population have reported themes surrounding the importance of meaningful activity for adjustment during the transition from hospital to home (Gage, Cook, & Fryday-Field, 1997; Turner et al., 2007; 2009). In a qualitative study of 27 people with TBI, Gage et al. (1997) identified themes relating to the importance of "doing," its role in facilitating recognition of abilities and limitations, and the association with loss of independence and control. In another qualitative study of re-engagement in meaningful occupations conducted with 20 individuals with acquired brain injury and their caregivers, Turner et al. (2009) found that there was a discrepancy between desired and actual occupations during the first three months following discharge, with returning to driving and returning to work being the desired occupations of many participants. The desire of individuals to regain these valued roles in the face of medical restrictions and persisting impairments was described as "a struggle for independence" in which individuals expressed high levels of frustration at not being able to engage in these activities. Further highlighting the importance of engaging in meaningful activities is the fact that a major issue facing individuals with brain injury in the early stages after returning home from hospital appears to be boredom—having "something to do" in the major part of the day has been associated with a more successful transition back into the community (Turner et al., 2007). Achieving structure and balance in time use is difficult in the adjustment phase following discharge from hospital, and accounts from individuals suggest that a large proportion of time is taken up with passive leisure activities such as watching television, playing computer games, or listening to music, with comparatively few productive activities or activities which involve actively socializing with other people. This theme is exemplified by the following quote from a patient in the Turner et al. (2009) study when asked what a typical day is like for him:

Get out of bed, watch TV, get up have breakfast, sit back down and watch TV. Go out and get the mail at half past 11. Go back in, watch TV, get up and have lunch at half past 12, quarter to one, watch TV until four or five or six o'clock and get up and have tea with the family. That's me basic day (p. 616).

For many individuals the main structure to their week during the transition phase is provided by attendance at outpatient therapy appointments, although there is commonly a perception that the amount of therapy provided is insufficient (Turner et al., 2007). It is reasonable to conclude, therefore, that while access to more rehabilitation services in the community is desirable, there may be other less costly ways in which individuals with brain injury could meaningfully and productively spend their time during this phase of recovery. There has been little to no research investigating the use of daily and weekly routines and structured meaningful activities in promoting adjustment, relief of boredom, and re-engagement for people with acquired brain injury. Given the prevalence and extent of executive dysfunction after traumatic brain injury, it is likely that planning and implementing structured routines may be challenging tasks for which many individuals require support or assistance. This could be a fruitful area of future research and advancement of rehabilitation strategies during the community reintegration phase.

Engagement in meaningful activity also has implications for the development of self-awareness. A qualitative study with three people with acquired brain injury found that the development of self-awareness was a slow process that involved the person comparing their current performance with their pre-morbid performance (Dirette, 2002). This finding was supported in a subsequent longitudinal study with 18 adults with TBI conducted over the first year post-injury (Dirette, Plaisier, & Jones, 2008). Participants with TBI described the primary antecedents to the development of self-awareness as being comparison of their current and pre-morbid ability to perform occupations. This emerging research suggests that re-engagement in meaningful occupations plays a pivotal role in well-being and the development of self-awareness after brain injury.

Other studies have attempted to demonstrate a link between interventions using engagement in real-life occupations and gains in self-awareness (Fleming, Lucas, & Lightbody, 2006; Ownsworth et al., 2006), however these have used case studies and single case experimental design approaches. An occupation-based individual intervention used with 10 individuals as part of a larger randomized controlled trial led to significant gains in goal achievement and psychosocial well-being, although this study did not specifically examine changes in self-awareness (Ownsworth, Fleming, Shum, Kuipers, & Strong, 2008). Goverover, Johnston, Toglia, & Deluca, (2007) conducted a randomized controlled trial investigating the use of an occupation-based intervention encompassing self-awareness and self-regulation strategies compared to a control condition of therapeutic practice of the same tasks. They found selective gains in self-awareness and functional performance for the intervention group; however, the focus of this study was on the use of self-awareness training strategies, not on the effect of engagement in occupation as such.

Often it is not until an individual has returned home from hospital and attempts to perform familiar activities associated with their valued life roles that the full extent of the impact of persisting impairments begins to become apparent. The structured and supported environment of the hospital ward, coupled with the lack of real-life opportunities to engage in personally relevant activities, may mask the presence of limitations in performing activities that place demands on executive functions (Fleming, Doig, & Katz, 2000). Consequently, it is in the initial weeks and months after returning to the community that individuals are exposed for the first time to repeated experiences of difficulty performing activities that pre-morbidly were within their abilities. Ironically, this exposure to repeated difficulties or failure experiences comes at the same time that involvement in intensive rehabilitation services is ceasing and access to ongoing support can be problematic. This highlights the need for ongoing access to rehabilitation and support services to ensure that gains in self-awareness are channeled into the adoption of strategies to enhance functional outcomes, rather than compromising individuals' emotional well-being (Ownsworth et al., 2011). In order to provide structured and supported re-engagement in meaningful activities, an understanding of individual client goals is an important component of rehabilitation. While goals can be highly individualized, there are common goals which are often seen during the transition phase and beyond.

Key Goals during Community Reintegration

Although some individuals with TBI express what are considered unrealistic goals with respect to the severity of their ongoing disability, many goals reflect a desire to return to their pre-morbid lifestyle. In a study that examined the self-identified goals of 60 people with acquired brain injury (including 40 with TBI), goals were classified into six main categories (Turner, Ownsworth, Turpin, Fleming, & Griffin, 2008). These were: work and education ($n = 47$); daily life management ($n = 37$) which included driving, injury/rehabilitation ($n = 32$); health and leisure ($n = 30$); relationships ($n = 24$); and general life/personal goals ($n = 19$). There were no significant differences between a post-acute subgroup (approximately one year post-injury) and a long-term subgroup (approximately five years post-injury) in the number of goals in each category, except for one subcategory in "injury/rehabilitation" goals. This subcategory was labeled "improve function/rehabilitation" and, not surprisingly, the post-acute subgroup identified more goals relating to it than the long-term group. The goal taxonomy developed by Turner et al. (2007) highlights the way in which personal goals after TBI are grounded in re-engagement in meaningful life roles and occupations. In particular, individuals have self-identified goals which involve return to work or study, return to driving, relationships with friends and family, engaging in leisure and fitness pursuits, and improving or maintaining their current living situation. In contrast to the foregoing taxonomy developed by Turner et al. (2007) regarding personal goals, a taxonomy developed from documented rehabilitation goals of clients in community-based brain injury rehabilitation was in the domains of "me and my body," "looking after myself," addressing psychosocial issues," "relating to others," and "services and information" (Kuipers, Foster, Carlson, & Moy, 2003). While there were some commonalities with the personal goal taxonomy, the rehabilitation goals had less focus

on meaningful occupations. However, both studies found that the number of goals relating to improving physical function decreased over time, suggesting that as self-awareness and the ability to set more realistic goals develops, goals may change from an impairment focus to reflect more general life goals (Turner et al., 2007).

Our current research on the transition from hospital to home gives insight into the rate and success of re-engagement in meaningful life roles by individuals with moderate and severe acquired brain injury (ABI) during the first six months post-discharge from acute care or rehabilitation (Nalder et al., 2012b). One of the first areas of goal achievement is the return to independence in the home and community. In a sample of 90 participants with ABI (64% TBI) discharged home from hospital, 89% reported that they had regained independence in the home and were able to be left at home alone for a substantial period of time (e.g., four hours) within the first six months post-discharge, with most individuals achieving this milestone soon after discharge. This was closely followed by regaining independence in accessing the community and using public transport with 78% of participants achieving this goal in the first six months of community reintegration (Nalder et al., 2012b). Given that activities of daily living are a primary focus in hospital-based rehabilitation, it is to be expected that basic independence in the home and community will be achieved soon after discharge by all but those with the severest brain injuries.

Goals which depend on more high level cognitive functioning are slower and less likely to be achieved in the first six months post-discharge. These include the commonly identified goals of return to work or study, and return to driving. In the Nalder et al. (2012b) study, return to work or study in some capacity was reported by 62% of participants with ABI in the first six months post-discharge. This is higher than reported in longer-term outcome studies where the rates of returning to work sit around 40–50% of people with TBI (Kreutzer et al., 2003). A range of variables impacts upon the ability to return to work after brain injury as highlighted in a systematic review by Ownsworth and McKenna (2004). However this review highlighted a need for further research to investigate the role played by modifiable factors such as metacognitive, emotional, and social environmental factors in determining employment outcomes. As discussed above, the transition period is a time when metacognitive skills such as self-awareness may be developing, and the process of attempting to return to pre-morbid work positions or study may highlight subtle or less observable problems in cognitive functions such as attention, memory, and executive functions as well as physical problems with fatigue and endurance. Failure experiences, such as being unable to return to work or unable to maintain employment, may be associated with emotional distress and loss of motivation, further impacting on the adjustment and re-engagement process.

Returning to driving has been identified as the most important goal for many people with TBI, above any other functional limitations (Rapport et al., 2006). Given that gaining a driver's license represents a rite of passage into adulthood, driving is considered highly relevant to the independence and self-identity particularly of young males with TBI. Unfortunately for people with severe TBI, driving demands the integration of high level physical, sensory, cognitive, and executive function skills within a complex, changing environment. Poor driving performance can endanger the lives of others, and therefore driving is regulated by law, unlike other forms of transport or community activity (Brooks & Hawley, 2005). Consequently, obtaining medical clearance to resume driving following TBI is often a vexing issue with strict guidelines as to when restrictions can be lifted, and although legislation varies from country to country, some form of formal driving assessment is recommended for most individuals with severe TBI (Brooks & Hawley, 2005). Nalder et al. (2012b) found that almost half (47%) of individuals with ABI returned to driving in the first six months after hospital discharge, with the majority receiving medical clearance to drive in the first three months. Research on driving after TBI has concentrated on identifying predictors of driving performance by correlating off-road screening tests of neuropsychological and neurological variables with the outcomes of simulated or on-road driving tests (Brooks & Hawley, 2005). There has been very little research on understanding the impact of driving cessation,

or having a lengthy wait for medical clearance to drive, on adjustment and community integration after brain injury. While knowing the factors related to safe driving performance is important for clinical decision making, it is also important to understand the processes involved for those who are temporarily or permanently unable to drive. Further research is required to examine this important occupational role, and to guide the development of intervention guidelines to assist individuals to adjust to this loss, both in practical and emotional terms.

Re-engagement in pre-morbid leisure and social activities, or the development of alternative forms of recreation post-injury, is another goal for many individuals with TBI. Long term outcome studies have found that leisure participation decreases following ABI (Brown, Gordon, & Spielman, 2003; Eriksson, Tham, & Borg, 2006) and this lack of participation is apparent in the early post-discharge phase, and while some gains are made over time, the majority do not return to pre-morbid levels. Wade, King, Wenden, Crawford, & Caldwell (1998) reported that 61% of participants with severe brain injury continued to experience social disabilities, including problems with leisure activities, at six-months post-injury. Kersel, Marsh, Havill, & Sleigh (2001) found that adults with moderate-to-severe brain injury were engaged in significantly fewer leisure activities at six-month and one-year post-injury follow-ups compared to pre-injury, although leisure participation was observed to increase between the six-month and one-year follow-up periods. Reasons for this lack of engagement in leisure and social pursuits are varied; undoubtedly, physical impairments such as fatigue and poor coordination play a role in limiting return to some sporting or other physical activities, and communication impairments contribute to engagement in social activities. However, qualitative accounts of the community integration experience suggest that formal restrictions also play a major role in limiting re-engagement in some activities (Turner et al., 2009). For example, engagement in contact sports such as football or high-risk activities such as motor bike racing is often contra-indicated in the immediate post-injury period to minimize the risk of a second brain injury. Coupled with restrictions to driving and medical advice not to consume alcohol during this recovery phase, leisure and social opportunities may be severely restricted (Turner et al., 2007; 2009), particularly for many young men for whom sport, social activities involving alcohol, and driving are culturally relevant. While these limitations are imposed to maximize the individual's safety and optimize neurological recovery, they appear to contribute to the lack of meaningful activity described above.

The impact of restrictions and lack of meaningful activity on social relationships is also recognized (Turner et al., 2009). In particular, friendship networks are known to shrink following TBI with increasing reliance upon close family members as the primary source of social support for individuals with brain injury (Turner et al., 2007). It is usually the responsibility of family members to enforce activity restrictions following discharge, and this can lead to enhanced frustration for the individual with TBI, particularly in cases where self-awareness is still developing, and there is ongoing conflict within family relationships. This burden can manifest as increased levels of stress and strain amongst family caregivers with the associated risk of relationship breakdown (Turner et al., 2007). In the Nalder et al. (2012b) study, the rate of relationship breakdown amongst family members or with a partner was 18% in the first six months post-discharge. This figure has been found to increase to approximately 49% (separation or divorce from partner) by five to eight years post-TBI (Wood & Yurdakul, 1997).

As a consequence, it is important that rehabilitation and community integration services address not only vocational pursuits but alternative leisure and social activities to maximize community re-engagement. Both family members and individuals with TBI need to be aware of the potential impact of formal and informal restrictions, and be assisted to select strategies to minimize their impact. Researchers are beginning to address the complex interplay of emotional, psychosocial, and functional issues that contribute to successful re-engagement in meaningful activities and social relationships after TBI. Integrating these findings into early post-discharge rehabilitation programs to minimize the impact of TBI and facilitate adjustment to ongoing disability, and systematically

evaluating their success is another aspect yet to be addressed.

Facilitators and Barriers to Re-engagement

The International Classification of Functioning, Disability and Health (World Health Organization, 2001) is a framework which describes the contribution of personal and environmental factors, as well as a person's health condition, to participation in life roles and the community. Thus far in this chapter we have addressed a number of injury-related consequences which act as barriers or facilitators to community re-engagement after TBI, such as self-awareness and emotional responses. According to the ICF, participation outcomes are also influenced by dynamic interactions with personal and environmental factors. Personal factors include variables such as age, socio-economic status, and educational level which are generally fixed for the individual and unlikely to be able to be manipulated to improve the person's outcome. The ICF defines environmental factors as the physical, social, and attitudinal environment in which people conduct their lives (World Health Organization, 2001). Environmental factors are increasingly being recognized as determinants of health outcomes, and these can be targeted to improve participation levels both at the individual and societal level. Community reintegration after TBI may be affected by a person's environmental context including physical and structural, policy, work and school, attitude and support, and services and assistance barriers (Whiteneck, Gerhart, & Cusick, 2004).

In a study conducted at one-year post injury, Whiteneck et al. (2004) found the availability of transportation, aspects of surroundings, government policies, other people's attitudes at home, and the natural environment to be the most important environmental barriers identified by people with TBI. Other research involving consensus workshops with health practitioners in an outpatient brain injury rehabilitation setting, as well as interviews with their patients and caregivers, found the most important environmental considerations for rehabilitation to be: psychosocial support and relationships; access to information and communication during transition to outpatient rehabilitation; and subsequent connection with community, vocational and support services (Kuipers, Foster, Smith, & Fleming, 2009). These findings were then used to design a group intervention program for outpatients with TBI and their significant others (Fleming et al., 2009). The six week program named "Personal Environments Enhancing Rehabilitation," or the PEER group, aimed to assist group members to understand the significance of environmental factors and to provide them with strategies for minimizing environmental barriers (such as lack of information and community access) and maximizing facilitators (such as social support networks and communication with rehabilitation staff). The PEER group was trialed with 18 participants with ABI (n =12 TBI) and their significant others, and compared to a historical non-intervention group, the participants showed greater gains in self-reported psychosocial integration and a reduction in depressive symptoms over the intervention time period, and the gains in psychosocial integration were maintained over a one-month follow-up period (Fleming et al., 2009). The PEER group provides an example of how the ICF Environment dimension can be operationalized in an intervention for people with brain injury.

Current debate on the role of the environment in brain injury rehabilitation relates to the context for the delivery of rehabilitation services. There has been a recent trend towards shifting rehabilitation from hospital settings to community based settings such as the individual's home environment in the form of both early supported discharge and community based rehabilitation services (Doig, Fleming, Kuipers, & Cornell., 2011a). Consistent with the ICF model, providing rehabilitation in real-life home and community settings is likely to lead to better generalization of skills and strategies, and improved functional outcomes for individuals with cognitive impairment after TBI, compared to interventions conducted using simulated environments in clinical settings (Doig et al., 2011a). In addition to enhanced performances, therapy programs conducted in real-life contexts have also been associated with better relationships and collaboration between patient and therapist (Koch, Wottrich, & Holmqvist, 1998); higher patient satisfaction (Doig,

Fleming, Cornwell, Kuipers, & Khan, 2011b); and greater access to and involvement of family members in the goal setting and rehabilitation process (Seigert & Taylor, 2004). However, there is a lack of research evidence concluding that home or community based contexts lead to better rehabilitation outcomes. The findings of a systematic review of studies comparing the two environments were that the outcomes of rehabilitation delivered in home or community contexts for individuals with ABI were at least equivalent to those delivered in a hospital or outpatient setting (Doig et al., 2011a). However 14 out of the 16 studies identified by the review were on people with stroke primarily over the age of 65, with little evidence available concerning the use of community-based rehabilitation for younger people with TBI, indicating a need for further research. Another issue requiring investigation is a comparison of the costs involved in providing rehabilitation in community contexts compared to traditional hospital or center-based services. Ultimately, both the clinical and cost-effectiveness of such approaches need to be evaluated with respect to the social and economic burden of TBI (e.g., the cost of care, caregiver burden, and health care resources). Understanding the role of environmental factors in both the rehabilitation and community integration of people with TBI is emerging as an important area of brain injury research which may change the way services are provided in the future.

Overview of Intervention Approaches for Improving Community Adjustment

There is considerable diversity in programs designed to improve the community integration of individuals with TBI (Powell, Heslin, & Greenwood, 2002). Malec and Basford (1996) described five different types of comprehensive brain injury rehabilitation programs, namely: (1) neurobehavioral programs, (2) residential community reintegration programs, (3) holistic day treatment programs, 4) outpatient community re-entry programs, 5) community-based services. While all programs types aim to facilitate community integration, the programs vary considerably in the amount and intensity of therapy, the service setting (residential, outpatient or community-based), the proportion of group to individual therapies versus case management services, and the focus of the intervention (i.e., behavioral, vocational, social focus). More recently, McColl (2007) described three models of service delivery for community integration programs, which were client-centered rehabilitation, community-based rehabilitation, and independent living programs. However, it could be argued that these models may overlap and there are some programs that aim to incorporate two or even three of these components (e.g., Doig et al., 2011b). This heterogeneity in program characteristics makes it difficult to compare the effectiveness of programs and to identify the active ingredients contributing to successful program outcomes (Powell et al., 2002). In addition, the amount and quality of current research evidence supporting the use of community integration interventions following TBI is insufficient (McCabe, Lippert, Weier, Hilditch, Hartridge, & Villamere, 2007; Turner, Fleming, Cornwell, & Ownsworth, 2008).

In a review of the literature on the transition from hospital to home after brain injury, Turner et al. (2008) identified 17 articles published since 1986 on post-discharge services. The majority of these papers (11 of the 17) however were not designed for people with TBI, but were services for people with stroke, typically older than 65 years. Of the research relating to TBI samples, the results of the review suggest that post-discharge support is perceived as inadequate or ceased too early by many people with TBI (e.g., Rusconi & Turner-Stokes, 2003). Research has demonstrated that injury severity is related to rehabilitation access with those with more mild to moderate injuries being less likely to receive services (Barnes, Frank, Montgomery, & Nichols, 2005; Mellick et al., 2003). Other factors influencing rehabilitation pathways include whether the individual has access to private medical insurance or compensation (Barnes et al., 2005; Horn, Yoels, & Bartolucci, 2000).

The review by Turner et al. (2008) also identified a number of studies relating to transitional living programs or services, which are services specifically designed to bridge the gap between inpatient rehabilitation and community living with a focus on developing independent living skills. Generally, transitional living programs are residential in nature and operate in a home-like environment located in the community with input from a multidisciplinary team (Turner et al., 2008). Three empirical articles were identified that used prospective longitudinal studies to investigate outcomes from transitional living programs, and while none used a randomized controlled design, all reported promising results (Harrick, Krefting, Johnston, Carlson, & Minnes, 1994; Olver & Harrington, 1996; Simpson, Secheny, Lane-Brown, Strettles, Ferry, & Phillips, 2004). In a Canadian study, Harrick et al. (1994) found that transitional living care led to improvements in functional status, productive activity, place of residence, and level of supervision in 21 individuals with acquired brain injury. In transitional living programs in Australia, Olver and Harrington (1996) reported significant gains in independence in instrumental activities of daily living, independent living, community access, and supervision needs in 95 people with TBI, and Simpson et al. (2004) reported improvements in independent living skills, psychosocial outcomes, and global functioning in 50 people with TBI.

Another form of post-discharge services which has shown potential for improving community re-engagement and adjustment is telephone support programs (Bell et al., 2005). In a randomized controlled trial, Bell et al. (2005) demonstrated that regular telephone contact for one-year post-discharge resulted in higher functional status and better quality of life in 171 patients with TBI compared to a control group who received standard outpatient follow-up only. The telephone support program included motivational interviewing, provision of education and counseling, and facilitation of referrals and assistance and/or support where necessary. This study highlights the need for further research to look at the effectiveness of various components of interventions (e.g., individual/group/telephone contact) and their relative cost-efficiency in delivering improved outcomes during the period of reintegration into the community following TBI.

Conclusion and Future Research Directions

This chapter has examined the period of community adjustment and re-engagement which occurs in the first year after discharge from hospitalization for individuals with TBI. This phase of the rehabilitation continuum is typically associated with rapid functional gains and the return of independence in the home and community, as well as being a time in which individuals often become more aware of their post-injury impairments through feedback, task difficulty, and failure. For many, such experiences can elicit emotional distress and highlight the need to adjust expectations and goals for the future. While our understanding of the inter-relationships between these processes has developed considerably over the past two decades, there remain a number of unanswered questions and relatively little empirical evidence to guide the development of post-discharge services for people with TBI. The following points represent a list of future research directions arising from the above review:

- Further research is required to understand the extent to which impaired self-awareness impacts on community integration, and hence, the extent to which awareness deficits should be targeted in rehabilitation.
- The ongoing debate regarding the etiology of awareness deficits following TBI suggests a need for further research on the contribution of neurological, psychological, and socio-environmental factors to reduced self-awareness, and in particular, appropriate intervention approaches to use depending on the basis of unawareness.
- In addition to classifying awareness deficits on the basis of underlying factors, there is a need for a more uniform approach to the assessment and categorization of impaired self-awareness and hyperawareness.
- Further controlled intervention studies examining the various approaches to facilitating the development of self-awareness (such as group therapy approaches, psycho-education and feedback, and training awareness and strategy use on everyday functional tasks) are needed to expand the limited evidence currently available.
- Although the link between emotional status and functional outcome has been demonstrated, systematic investigation of the neurological, psychological and social factors

associated with the development and maintenance of depression after TBI is required to guide intervention studies.
- The role of engagement in meaningful occupations, client-centered goal-setting, and the structured use of time and routines are potential areas of future research, which may assist with the development of self-awareness as well as adjustment and re-engagement during the early post-discharge period.
- The development and evaluation of education and support programs to assist individuals and their families to adjust to the loss of occupational roles such as work, driving, leisure, and social activities is recommended, including strategies for coping with formal restrictions placed on the individual during reintegration.
- Further research is needed on the contribution of environmental factors to community integration outcomes after TBI, including the development and evaluation of interventions to minimize environmental barriers both for individuals with TBI and their families, and at a broader societal level.
- Examination of the importance of context in rehabilitation service provision is another emerging area of research, for example, comparing therapy processes and outcomes in clinic versus real-life environments.
- There is very limited systematic empirical research investigating the effectiveness of different intervention models in the community adjustment phase. The use of randomized controlled trials with this population is usually not possible due to ethical concerns about withholding timely intervention from a control group, as well as the heterogeneity of the TBI population. Hence, there is a need for more creative methodologies (e.g., single case designs) to determine the effectiveness of interventions, preferably with approaches that enable identification of the active ingredients of programs and some economic evaluation to determine the costs associated with the benefits of different programs.
- Research is needed that examines interventions to promote community integration across the spectrum of TBI, including identification of those with mild to moderate injury at risk of ongoing problems, as well as those

with more severe injuries who have primarily been the focus of services and research interventions to date.

References

Anson, K., & Ponsford, J. (2006). Who benefits? Outcome following a coping skills group intervention for traumatically brain injured individuals. *Brain Injury, 20*, 1–13.

Barnes, E., Frank, E., Montgomery, A., & Nichols, M. (2005). Factors predicting rehabilitative service provision in adults with traumatic brain injury. *Journal of Speech-Language Pathology, 13*(1), 69–84.

Bell, K., Temkin, N., Esselman, P., Doctor, J., Bombardier, C., Fraser, R., et al. (2005). The effect of a scheduled telephone intervention on outcome after moderate to severe traumatic brain injury: a randomized trial. *Archives of Physical Medicine Rehabilitation, 86*, 851–856.

Bombardier, C. H., Fann, J. R., Temkin, N. R., Esselman, P. C. Barber J. & Dikmen S. S. (2010). Rates of major depressive disorder and clinical outcomes following traumatic brain injury. *Journal of the American Medical Association, 303*, 1938–45.

Brown, M., Gordon, W., & Speilman, L. (2003). Participation in social and recreational activity in the community by individuals with traumatic brain injury. *Rehabilitation Psychology, 48*, 266–74.

Bryant, R. A., & Harvey, A. G. (1998). Relationship between acute stress disorder and posttraumatic stress disorder following mild traumatic brain injury. *The American Journal of Psychiatry, 155*, 625–629.

Conneeley, A. L. (2003). Quality of life and traumatic brain injury: A one-year longitudinal study. *British Journal of Occupational Therapy, 66*, 440–446.

Deb, S., Lyons, I., Koutzoukis, C., Ali, I., & McCarthy, G. (1999). Rate of psychiatric illness 1 year after traumatic brain injury. *The American Journal of Psychiatry, 156*, 374–378.

Dirette, D. (2002). The development of awareness and the use of compensatory strategies for cognitive deficits. *Brain Injury, 16*(10), 861–871.

Dirette, D., Plaisier, B. R., & Jones, S. J. (2008). Patterns and antecedents of the development of self-awareness following traumatic brain injury: the importance of occupation. *British Journal of Occupational Therapy, 71*(2), 44–51.

Doig, E. J., Fleming J., Cornwell, P., & Kuipers, P., Khan, A. (2011b). A goal-directed outpatient rehabilitation for adults with traumatic brain injury: programme effectiveness and comparison of outcomes in home and day hospital settings. *Brain Injury, 25*(2), 1114–1125.

Doig, E., Fleming, J., Kuipers, P., & Cornwell, P. (2011a). Comparison of rehabilitation outcomes in day hospital and home settings for people with acquired brain injury—a systematic review. *Disability and Rehabilitation, 33*, 1203–1214.

Eriksson, G., Tham, K., & Borg, J. (2006). Occupational gaps in everyday life 1-4 years after acquired brain injury. *Journal of Rehabilitation Medicine, 38*, 159–165.

Felmingham, K., Baguley, I., & Crooks, J. (2001). A comparison of acute and post-discharge predictors of employment 2 years after traumatic brain injury. *Archives of Physical and Medical Rehabilitation, 82*, 435–439.

Flashman, L. A., & McAllister, T. W. (2002). Lack of awareness and its impact in traumatic brain injury. *Neurorehabilitation, 17*, 285–296.

Fleming, J. M., Doig, E., & Katz, N. (2000). Beyond dressing and driving: The use of occupation in neurorehabilitation. *Brain Impairment, 1*(2), 141–150.

Fleming, J. M., Kuipers, P., Foster, M., Smith, S., & Doig, E. (2009). Evaluation of an outpatient, peer group intervention for people with acquired brain injury based on the ICF 'environment' dimension. *Disability and Rehabilitation, 31*, 1666–1675.

Fleming, J., Lucas, S., & Lightbody, S. (2006). Using occupation to facilitate self-awareness after acquired brain injury. *Canadian Journal of Occupational Therapy, 73*(1), 44–55.

Fleming, J & Ownsworth, T. (2006). A review of awareness interventions in brain injury rehabilitation. *Neuropsychological Rehabilitation, 16*, 474–500.

Fleming, J. M. & Strong, J. (1999). A longitudinal study of self-awareness: Functional deficits underestimated by persons with brain injury. *The Occupational Therapy Journal of Research, 19*, 3–17.

Fleming, J. M., Strong, J., & Ashton, R. (1996). Self-awareness of deficits in adults with traumatic brain injury: How best to measure? *Brain Injury, 10*, 1–15.

Fleming, J. M., Strong, J., & Ashton, R. (1998). Cluster analysis of self-awareness levels in adults with traumatic brain injury and relationship to outcome. *Journal of Head Trauma Rehabilitation, 13*, 39–51.

Fleming, J. M., Winnington, H. T., McGillivray, A. J., Boyana, A. T., & Ownsworth, T. (2006). The development of self-awareness and emotional distress during early community re-integration after traumatic brain injury. *Brain Impairment, 7*, 83–94.

Gage, M., Cook, J., & Fryday-Field, K. (1997). Understanding the transition to community living after discharge from an acute care hospital: an exploratory study. *American Journal of Occupational Therapy, 51*(2), 96–103.

Gomez-Hernandez, R., Max, J. E., Kosier, T., Paradiso, S., Robinson, R. G. (1997). Social impairment and depression after traumatic brain injury. *Archives of Physical Medicine Rehabilitation, 78,* 1321–1326.

Goverover, Y., Johnston, M. V., Toglia, J., & Deluca, J. (2007). Treatment to improve self-awareness in persons with acquired brain injury. *Brain Injury, 21*(9), 913–923.

Gracey, F., Evans, J. J., & Malley, D. (2009). "Capturing process and outcome in complex rehabilitation interventions: A "Y-shaped" model." *Neuropsychological Rehabilitation, 19,* 867–890.

Harrick, L., Krefting, L., Johnston, M., Carlson, P., & Minnes, P. (1994). Stability of functional outcomes following transitional living programme participation: 3 year follow-up. *Brain Injury, 8*(5), 439–447.

Hart, T., Seignourel, P. J., & Sherer, M. (2009). A longitudinal study of awareness of deficit after moderate to severe traumatic brain injury. *Neuropsychological Rehabilitation, 19,* 161–176.

Horn, W., Yoels, W., & Bartolucci, A. (2000). Factors associated with patients' participation in rehabilitation services: a comparative injury analysis 12 months post-discharge. *Disability and Rehabilitation, 22*(8), 358–362.

Jorge, R. E., Robinson, R. G., Moser, D., Tateno, A., Crespo-Facorro, B., & Arndt, S. (2004). Major depression following traumatic brain injury. *Archives of General Psychiatry, 61,* 42–50.

Jorge, R. E., Robinson, R. G., Starkstein, S. E., & Arndt, S. V. (1993). Depression and anxiety following traumatic brain injury. *The Journal of Neuropsychiatry and Clinical Neurosciences, 5,* 369–374.

Kendall, E. & Terry, D. (2009). Understanding the adjustment following traumatic brain injury: is the goodness of fit coping hypothesis useful? *Social Science and Medicine, 67,* 1217–1224.

Kersel, D., Marsh, N., Havill, J., & Sleigh, J. (2001). Psychosocial functioning during the year following severe brain injury. *Brain Injury, 15,* 683–96.

Koch, L. V., Wottrich, A. W., & Holmqvist, W. L. (1998). Rehabilitation in the home versus the hospital: the importance of context. *Disability and Rehabilitation, 20*(10), 367–372.

Kreutzer, J. S., Marwitz, J. H., Walker, W., Sander, A., Sherer, M., Bogner, J., et al. (2003). Moderating factors in return to work and job stability after traumatic brain injury. *Journal of Head Trauma Rehabilitation, 18,* 128–138.

Kuipers, P., Foster, M., Carlson, G., & Moy, J. (2003). Classifying client goals in community-based ABI rehabilitation: A taxonomy for profiling service delivery and conceptualizing outcomes. *Disability and Rehabilitation, 25,* 154–162.

Kuipers, P., Foster, M., Smith, S., & Fleming J. (2009). Using ICF-Environment factors to enhance the continuum of outpatient ABI rehabilitation: An exploratory study. *Disability and Rehabilitation, 31,* 144–151.

Lanham, R. A. Jr, Weissenburger, J. E., Schwab, K. A., & Rosner, M. M. (2000). A longitudinal investigation of the concordance between individuals with traumatic brain injury and family or friend ratings on the Katz adjustment scale. *Journal of Head Trauma Rehabilitation, 15,* 1123–1138.

Levin, H. S., Brown, S. A., Song, J. X., McCauley, S. R., Boake, C., Constant, C. F., et al. (2001). Depression and posttraumatic stress disorder at three months after mild to moderate traumatic brain injury. *Journal of Clinical and Experimental Neuropsychology, 23,* 754–769.

Malec, J. F. & Basford, J. S. (1996). Post-acute brain injury rehabilitation. *Archives of Physical Medicine and Rehabilitation, 77*(2), 198–207.

Malec, J. F., Brown, A. W., Moessner, A. M., Stump, T. E., & Monahan, P. (2010). A Preliminary Model for Posttraumatic Brain Injury Depression. *Archives of Physical Medicine and Rehabilitation, 91,* 1087–1097.

Malec, J., Buffington, A., Moessner, A., & Degiorgio, L. (2000). A medical/vocational case coordination system for persons with brain injury: An evaluation of employment outcomes. *Archives of Physical and Medical Rehabilitation, 81,* 1007–1015.

Malec, J. F., Testa, J. A., Rush, B. K., Brown, A. W., & Moessner, A. M. (2007). Self-assessment of impairment, impaired self-awareness, and depression after traumatic brain injury. *Journal of Head Trauma Rehabilitation, 22,* 156–166.

McCabe, P., Lippert, C., Weiser, M., Hilditch, M., Hartridge, C., & Villamere, J. (2007). Community reintegration following acquired brain injury. *Brain Injury, 21*(2), 231–257.

McColl, M. A. (2007). Postacute programming for community integration: A scoping review. *Brain Impairment, 8*(3), 238–250.

McColl, M. A., Carlson, P., Johnston, J., Minnes, P., Shue, K., Davies, D., et al. (1998). The definition of community integration: Perspectives of people with brain injuries. *Brain Injury, 12,* 15–30.

McGlynn, S. M. & Schacter, D. L. (1989). Unawareness of deficits in neuropsychological syndromes. *Journal Clinical Experimental Neuropsychology, 11,* 143–205.

Mellick, D., Gerhart, K. A., & Whiteneck, G. (2003). Understanding outcomes based on the post-acute hospitalization pathways followed by persons with traumatic brain injury. *Brain Injury, 17,* 55–71.

Nalder, E., Fleming, J., Foster, M., Cornwell, P., & Khan, A. (2012a). Identifying factors associated with perceived success in the transition from hospital to home following brain injury. *Journal of Head Trauma Rehabilitation, 27*, 143–153.

Nalder, E., Fleming, J., Cornwell, P, Foster, M., Ownsworth, T., Shields, C., & Haines, T. (2012b). Recording sentinel events in the life course of individuals with acquired brain injury. *Brain Injury, 26*, 1381–1396.

Noé, E., Ferri, J., Caballero, M. C., Villodre, R., Sanchez, A., & Chirivella, J. (2005). Self-awareness after acquired brain injury: Predictors and rehabilitation. *Journal of Neurology, 252*, 168–175.

Olver, J., & Harrington, H. (1996). Functional outcomes after a transitional living programme for adults with traumatic brain injury. In J. Ponsford, V. A. Anderson, & P. Snow (Eds.). *International Perspectives in Traumatic Brain Injury Conference Proceedings* (pp. 359–361). Queensland: Australian Academic Press.

Ownsworth, T. (2005). The impact of defensive denial upon adjustment following traumatic brain injury. *Neuro-Psychoanalysis, 7*, 83–94.

Ownsworth, T., & Clare, L. (2006). The association between awareness deficits and rehabilitation outcome following acquired brain injury. *Clinical Psychology Review, 26*, 783–795.

Ownsworth, T., Clare, L., & Morris, R. (2006). An integrated biopsychosocial approach for understanding awareness disorder in Alzheimer's disease and brain injury. *Neuropsychological Rehabilitation, 16*, 415–438.

Ownsworth, T., & Fleming, J. (2005). The relative importance of metacognitive skills, emotional status and executive functioning in psychosocial adjustment following acquired brain injury. *Journal of Head Trauma Rehabilitation, 20*, 315–332.

Ownsworth, T., Fleming, J., Desbois, J., Strong, J., & Kuipers, P. (2006). A metacognitive contextual intervention to enhance error awareness and functional performance following traumatic brain injury: A single case experimental design. *Journal of the International Neuropsychological Society, 12*, 54–63.

Ownsworth., T, Fleming, J., Haines, T., Cornwell, P., Kendall M., Nalder, E. & Gordon, G. (2011). Development of depressive symptoms during early community reintegration after traumatic brain injury. *Journal of the International Neuropsychological Society, 17*, 112–119.

Ownsworth, T., Fleming, J., Shum, D., Kuipers, P., & Strong, J. (2008). Comparison of individual, group and combined intervention formats in a randomized controlled trial for facilitating goal attainment and improving psychosocial function following acquired brain injury. *Journal of Rehabilitation Medicine, 40*, 81–88.

Ownsworth, T. L., Little, T., Turner, B., Hawkes, A., & Shum, D. (2008). Assessing emotional status following acquired brain injury: The clinical potential of the Depression, Anxiety and Stress Scales, *Brain Injury, 22*, 858–869.

Ownsworth, T. L., McFarland, K., & Young, R. McD. (2002). Investigation of factors underlying deficits in self-awareness and self-regulation. *Brain Injury, 16*, 291–309.

Ownsworth, T. & McKenna, K. (2004). Investigation of factors related to employment outcome following traumatic brain injury: a critical review and conceptual model. *Disability and Rehabilitation, 26*, 765–784.

Ownsworth, T., & Oei, T. P. S. (1998). Depression after traumatic brain injury: Conceptualisation and treatment considerations. *Brain Injury, 12*, 735–751.

Pagulayan, K. F., Temkin, N. R., Machamer, J. E., & Diman, S. S. (2007). The measurement and magnitude of awareness difficulties after traumatic brain injury: A longitudinal study. *Journal of the International Neuropsychological Society, 13*, 561–570.

Pia, L., Neppi-Modona, M., Ricci, R., & Berti, A. (2004). The anatomy of anosognosia for hemiplegia:Ameta-analysis. *Cortex, 40*, 367–377.

Powell, J., Heslin, J., & Greenwood, R. (2002). Community based rehabilitation after severe traumatic brain injury: A randomised controlled trial. *Journal of Neurology, Neurosurgery and Psychiatry, 69*(2), 193–202.

Prigatano, G. P. (1999). *Principles of neuropsychological rehabilitation*. New York: Oxford University Press.

Prigatano, G. P., & Weinstein, E. A. (1996). Edwin A. Weinstein's contributions to neuropsychological rehabilitation. *Neuropsychological Rehabilitation, 6*, 305–326.

Robertson, I. H., & Murre, J. M. J. (1999). Rehabilitation of brain damage: Brain plasticity and principles of guided recovery. *Psychological Bulletin, 125*, 544–575.

Ruff, R., Marshall, L., Crouch, M., Klauber, M., Levin, S., Barth, J., et al. (1993). Predictors of outcome following severe head trauma: Follow up data from the Traumatic Coma Data Bank. *Brain Injury, 7*, 101–111.

Rusconi, S., & Turner-Stokes, L. (2003). An evaluation of aftercare following discharge from a specialist in-patient rehabilitation service. *Disability and Rehabilitation, 25*, 1281–1288.

Seigert, R. J., & Taylor, W. J. (2004). Theoretical aspects of goal-setting and motivation in rehabilitation. *Disability and Rehabilitation, 26*(1), 1–8.

Sherer, M., Bergloff, P., Levin, E., High, W. M., Oden, K. E., & Nick, T. G. (1998). Impaired awareness and employment outcome after traumatic brain injury. *Journal of Head Trauma Rehabilitation*, 13(5), 52–61.

Sherer, M., Boake, C., Levin, E., Silver, B. V., Ringholz, G., & High, W. M. (1998). Characteristics of impaired awareness after traumatic brain injury. *Journal of the International Neuropsychological Society*, 4, 380–387.

Sherer, M., Hart, T., & Nick, T. G. (2003). Measurement of impaired self-awareness after traumatic brain injury: A comparison of the patient competency rating scale and the awareness questionnaire. *Brain Injury*, 17, 25–37.

Sherer, M., Hart, T., Nick, T. G., Whyte, J., Thompson, R. N., & Yablon, S. A. (2003). Early impaired self-awareness after traumatic brain injury. *Archives of Physical Medicine Rehabilitation*, 84, 168–176.

Sherer, M., Hart, T., Whyte, J., Nick, T. G., & Yablon, S. A. (2005). Neuroanatomical basis of impaired self-awareness after traumatic brain injury: Findings from early computed tomography. *Journal of Head Trauma Rehabilitation*, 20, 287–300.

Simpson, G., Secheny, T., Lane-Brown, A., Strettles, B., Ferry, K., & Phillips, J. (2004). Post-acute rehabilitation for people with traumatic brain injury: a model description and evaluation of the Liverpool Hospital Transitional Living Program. *Brain Impairment*, 5, 67–80.

Stuss, D. T. & Anderson, V. (2004). The frontal lobes and theory of mind: Developmental concepts from adult focal lesion research. *Brain and Cognition*, 55, 69–83.

Stuss, D. T., Picton, T. W., & Alexander, M. P. (2001). Consciousness, self-awareness and the frontal lobes. In S. Salloway, P. Malloy, & J. Duffy (Ed.), *The frontal lobes and neuropsychiatric illness* (pp. 101–109). Washington DC: American Psychiatric Press, Inc.

Tate, R. L. & Broe, G. A. (1999). Psychosocial adjustment after traumatic brain injury: What are the important variables? *Psychological Medicine*, 29, 713–725.

Turner, B., Fleming, J., Cornwell, P., Ownsworth, T. (2008). The transition from hospital to home for individuals with acquired brain injury: a literature review and research recommendations. *Disability and Rehabilitation*, 30, 1153–1176.

Turner, B., Fleming, J., Ownsworth, T., & Cornwell, P. (2011). Perceptions of recovery during the early transition phase from hospital to home following

acquired brain injury: a journey of discovery. *Neuropsychological* Rehabilitation, 21, 64–91.

Turner, B., Fleming, J., Worrall, L., Cornwell, P., Haines, T., Ownsworth, T., et al. (2007). A qualitative study of the transition from hospital to home for individuals with acquired brain injury and their family caregivers. *Brain Injury*, 21, 1119–1130.

Turner, B., Ownsworth, T., Cornwell, P., & Fleming, J. (2009). Re-engagement in meaningful occupations during the transition from hospital to home for individuals with acquired brain injury and their family caregivers. *American Journal of Occupational Therapy*, 62(5), 609–620.

Turner, B., Ownsworth, T., Turpin, M., Fleming, J., & Griffin, J. (2008). Self-identified goals and the ability to set realistic goals following acquired brain injury: A classification framework. *Australian Journal of Occupational Therapy*, 55, 96–107.

Wade, D., King, N., Wenden, F., Crawford, S., & Caldwell, F. (1998). Routine follow-up after head injury: a second randomised control trial. *Journal of Neurology, Neurosurgery and Psychiatry*, 65, 177–183.

Weinstein, E. A., & Kahn, R. L. (1955). *Denial of illness: Symbolic and physiological aspects.* Springfield, Ill: Charles C Thomas.

Whelan-Goodinson, R., Ponsford, J., Johnston, L., & Grant, F. (2009). Psychiatric disorders following traumatic brain injury: Their nature and frequency. *Journal of Head Trauma Rehabilitation*, 24, 324–332.

Whiteneck, G. G., Gerhart, K. A., & Cusick, C. P. (2004). Identifying environmental factors that influence the outcomes of people with traumatic brain injury. *Journal of Head Trauma Rehabilitation*, 19(3), 191–204.

Williams, W. H., & Evans, J. J. (2003). Brain injury and emotions: An overview to a special issue on biopsychosocial approaches in neurorehabilitation. *Neuropsychological Rehabilitation*, 13(1/2), 1–11.

Wood, R. L., & Yurdakul, L. K. (1997). Change in relationship status following traumatic brain injury. *Brain Injury*, 11, 491–501.

World Health Organization (2001). *International Classification of Functioning, Disability, and Health: (ICF).* Geneva, Switzerland: World Health Organization.

Ylvisaker, M., Szekeres, S., & Feeney, T. (1998). Cognitive rehabilitation: executive functions. In: M. Ylvisaker (Ed.). *Traumatic brain injury rehabilitation: children and adolescents* (pp. 221–269). Boston: Butterworth-Heinemann.

13

The Neurobiological Basis of Pharmacological Approaches for Patients with Traumatic Brain Injury

Rashed Harun and Amy K. Wagner

Introduction

Cognitive dysfunction is the most common complaint cited by caregivers and individuals with traumatic brain injury (TBI) that extends years after injury (Oddy, Coughlan, Tyerman, & Jenkins, 1985; van Zomeren & van den Burg, 1985). Multiple neuropsychological domains of cognition are often impaired following TBI, which include attention, arousal, memory, and executive control. Cognitive deficits mirror the severity of injury as indicated by the extent of diffuse axonal injury (DAI), generalized atrophy, as well as the location and extent of focal injuries (Katz & Alexander, 1994; Wilson, Hadley, & Wiedmann, 1995; Kwentus, Hart, Peck, & Kornstein, 1985). Age, preexisting conditions, substance abuse, and major systemic insults like hypoxia and hypotension can also affect the level and nature of cognitive deficits after injury.

The neuropharmacological approaches to treating cognitive deficits following brain trauma are largely drawn from the literature and practice of treating other disorders associated with persistent cognitive deficits such as attention deficit hyperactivity disorder (ADHD), Parkinson's disease, narcolepsy, and Alzheimer's dementia. However, the patho-mechanisms of cognitive deficits after TBI are not wholly similar to these other diseases, and mechanisms also vary between individuals with TBI. However, the concentration of contusions in frontal-orbital and temporal regions and generalized diffuse axonal injury

produces a degree of consistency in the neuropsychiatric and behavioral sequelae associated with TBI.

The sequela of cognitive deficits follows a pattern that can be divided into four phases of recovery, which vary greatly according to the gradation of injury (Levin, 1987; Cripe, 1987; Rao & Lyketsos, 2000; Povlishock, & Katz, 2005). The acute phase of mild and moderate injury often includes a period of loss of consciousness (LOC), with a period of coma common in more severe injuries. In the sub-acute phase, patients with more significant injuries emerge from unconsciousness and display marked confusion and anterograde memory impairments, and thus this period is referred to as post-traumatic amnesia (PTA). Furthermore, patients in the subacute phase have a variety of cognitive and behavioral abnormalities stemming from dysfunctional states of arousal, disorientation, confusion, and agitation. In the third phase, the patient emerges from the confusional state. Then ensues a period of recovery and restoration of function, until a plateau is reached in the chronic phase after TBI. The recovery process greatly varies in duration and nature for patients with differing levels of injury. Many patients with mild TBI may not experience a loss of consciousness, and can pass through the different phases very rapidly. On the other hand, patients with moderate to severe injuries almost invariably experience loss of consciousness or coma. The extent of DAI is correlated to the duration in post-traumatic amnesia, which is a predictor of the duration of other recovery phases and eventual outcome (Katz & Alexander, 1994).

Neurobiological Basis of Cognitive Changes after TBI—Brief Overview

Arousal is a fundamental cognitive function that enables one to react to stimuli and process information. It is primarily governed by reticulo-thalamic, thalamo-cortical, and reticulo-cortical circuits. Monoaminergic projections arising from the brainstem and reticular formation have diffuse projections to the cortex to influence arousal, with norepinephrine playing a central role. General levels of arousal create a basal interplay between sleep and wakefulness that can be described by terms such as alertness, somnolence, lethargy, or stupor. Impaired arousal is a ubiquitous and significant problem associated with brain injury. In the acute phase, patients often lose consciousness, which is thought to result from the presence of DAI. Disruptions of the reticular activating system, or their cortical innervation targets, can precipitate a period of coma, which is almost universal after severe TBI. In the subacute phase, patients exhibit sleep disturbances, which further contributes to hypoarousal states.

Attention is a cognitive process that is facilitated by arousal. Attention uniquely requires the ability to selectively devote cognitive resources to a stimulus and ignore others, a function that is distinct from the generalized increase in responsivity that characterizes arousal. Attention can be operationalized into several constructs that include pre-attentive, selective, divided, and sustained attentional components. The neural networks responsible for attention are widely distributed and vary according to the attentional construct. Sensory gating is a pre-attentive process that filters incoming cognitive and sensory stimuli in order to limit information into attention processing networks. Sensory gating requires thalamic, hippocampal, and prefrontal functions to gate distracting cognitive and sensory stimuli and direct attention toward appropriate stimuli (Aciniegas & Beresford, 2001). Cortico-striato-thalamic pathways are important for selective attention and

divided attention, and it is generally accepted that dopamine (DA) plays a significant motivational role in attention (Wise, Murray, & Gerfen, 1996; Brennan & Arnsten, 2008). Concentration, or sustained attention, is a prerequisite for learning (formation of new memories). The circuitry responsible for sustained attention requires intact interactions between the circuitry responsible for arousal and fronto-striato-thalamic pathways, medial temporal lobes, and the right parietal lobe. Damage to any of these areas, or the connections between them, could precipitate deficits in sustained attention. Deficits in sustained attention and divided attention are common after injury, and often patients find themselves easily distracted, unable to focus on more than one task at a time, and mentally fatigued rapidly, requiring frequent breaks in activity.

Memory includes processes that can be encoded, stored, and retrieved. Memory is broadly classified into declarative memory, the memory of facts and events that can be consciously discussed, and procedural memory, e.g., the memory of motor patterns that enables one to perform a task. Memory can also be divided into temporal domains of short-term memory and long-term memory. The storage, consolidation, and retrieval of declarative and procedural memory require different circuits. The hippocampus is involved with the encoding of spatial and temporal memories, but storage is widely distributed throughout the brain (Buckley, 2005). Declarative memories are an associative process, in that, any areas involved with consolidation of memories can be tapped for retrieval. In contrast, procedural memory is a hippocampus-independent process, and is retrieved by tapping into processes only involved in learning the task. Because of the key role of the hippocampus in memory formation, and its vulnerability to injury, hippocampal damage is fundamental to memory deficits following brain injury. Disruption of cholinergic systems projecting to the hippocampus is also implicated in memory disturbances after TBI. Furthermore, dopaminergic signaling in the prefrontal cortex and striatum are implicated in memory formation (Budding, 2009; Goldman-Rakic, 1995). Memory formation is not an isolated phenomenon; rather, arousal, attention, and sleep all contribute to memory formation.

Among TBI survivors, acute and persisting memory deficits are quite common (Thomsen, 1984; van Zomeren, & van den Burg, 1985). In the subacute phase, a period of PTA is common in which the patients have difficulty encoding and retrieving new information. Normally, PTA clears over time with persisting deficits in memory. In large part, procedural memory remains intact following TBI (Ewert, Levin, Watson, & Kalisky, 1989; Brayer et al. 2013).

Executive functions (EF) are loosely defined brain processes involving the prefrontal cortex (PFC) that control other aspects of cognition. These processes include organizational components such as decision-making, planning, sequencing, problem-solving, and also regulatory components such as initiation and inhibition of action, self-monitoring, and task switching. Working memory (WM) is also considered an executive function in that it involves the prefrontal cortex to perform on-line manipulations of short term memory and to remember bits of information over a transient time interval. Dopaminergic projections to the prefrontal cortex (PFC) and PFC-striatal loops are important for executive functioning. Damage to the PFC is common after injury, and thus deficits in EF are common after TBI. Because EF controls other brain processes, EF deficits precipitate a constellation of other cognitive, behavioral, and emotional deficits. After TBI, deficits can cause socially inappropriate behaviors, impulsivity, slowed information processing, poor working memory, difficulty planning and initiating tasks, and difficulties in abstract reasoning.

Neurobiology Based Pharmacological Strategies for Treating Cognitive Dysfunction after TBI

Several guiding principles should be used in the treatment of patients with TBI. This patient population is often highly medicated, and it is important to periodically check the whole medication regimen and discontinue the usage of any unnecessary medications as continued use only further complicates treatment. Most times, psychotropic medications have effects in more than one cognitive domain. Treating with medications that have possible efficacy in treating deficits observed in multiple domains is preferable.

The literature suggests people with TBI may be particularly sensitive to several types of pharmacological agents. Thus, benzodiazepines, antipsychotics, and agents that have anti-cholinergic or pro-convulsant properties should be used with particular caution. When appropriate medication is selected, it is important to start at low doses and titrate to higher doses slowly, augmenting any beneficial effects with complementary pharmacological strategies. Various neuropsychiatric and behavioral scales can aid in determining appropriate dosages by objectively monitoring drug-induced changes in functioning. The injured brain is often vulnerable to the side effects and adverse effects of psychotropic agents. Furthermore, the complex biochemical alterations that occur following injury can vary greatly between patients and influence the drug and dose responses observed after injury.

Many of the current therapeutic treatments for the neuropsychiatric and behavioral sequelae of TBI act on acetylcholine, dopamine, and norepinephrine neurotransmitter systems. As discussed below, there is evidence from clinical studies and animal models of TBI that suggests these transmitter systems are disrupted following TBI and/or that TBI patients benefit from augmentation of specific transmitter systems.

Cholinergic Dysfunction in TBI

Cholinergic systems play a role in attention, arousal, and other cognitive domains, especially memory. The primary therapeutic target of cholinergic agents in the TBI population is the hippocampus. Animal models of TBI have consistently demonstrated memory impairments, with memory impairment associated with loss of hippocampal neurons in some studies (Gorman, Shook, & Becker, 1993; Kotapka, Gennarelli, Adams, Thubault, Ross, & Ford, 1991; Hicks, Smith, Lowenstein, Saint Marie, & McIntosh, 1993). However, even in the absence of any overt damage to the hippocampus or its connections, memory impairments can be observed. This suggests neuronal susceptiblity to some degree of dysfunction rather than overt damage (Lyeth et al., 1990).

In multiple animal models of TBI, structural and functional cholinergic disruptions have consistently been identified in cholinergic nuclei and cholinergic target areas. Immediately following the fluid percussion injury (FPI) model of TBI, there is a rapid increase in the release of ACh (Gorman, Fu, Hovda, Becker, & Katayama, 1989; Saija, Hayes, Lyeth, Dixon, Yamamoto, & Robinson, 1988), which is followed by a chronic hypofunctional cholinergic state (Dixon, Bao, Johnson, Yang, Whitson, & Clifton, 1995). The acute surge in ACh release mediates some of the degenerative processes of TBI. In fact, treating rats 15 minutes prior to FPI or 30 seconds post-FPI with the muscarinic M1 receptor antagonist scopolamine prevented the surge in ACh typically observed (Saija et al., 1988). Furthermore, this treatment attenuated the weight loss, transient behavioral suppression, and some of the motor and cognitive deficits often observed following injury (Robinson, et al., 1990; Lyeth, et al., 1988; Hamm, O'Dell, Pike, & Lyeth, 1993).

The chronic cholinergic hypofunctional state may be, in part, caused by the observed deficits in uptake of choline into fibers, which could be due to decreased cholinergic innervation and/ or impaired uptake (Dixon, Bao, Begmann, & Johnson, 1994). Cholinergic innervation to the hippocampus through the septo-hippocampal pathway is susceptible to degeneration over the course of 10 days post-experimental TBI, with concomitant loss of cholinergic neurons in the septal area (Leonard, Grady, Lee, Paz, & Westrum, 1997; Schmidt & Grady, 1995).

The synthetic enzyme of ACh, choline acetyltransferase (ChAT), shows decreased activity 1hr post-FPI, in the hippocampus (25%), frontal cortex (32%), and temporal cortex (23%). However, five days after FPI, there is an (18%) increase ChAT activity in the septal area compared to control animals (Gorman, Fu, Hovda, Murray, & Traystman, 1996). This pattern of activity is consistent with transient lower levels of ChAT immunoreactivity (Dixon, Flinn, Yang, Whitson, & Hayes, 1995). ChAT activity levels after injury appear to be responding in an effort to maintain homeostasis by initially attenuating

a hypercholinergic state and later by augmenting a hypofunctioning cholinergic state.

Chronic changes in cholinergic receptor expression patterns and affinities have also been noted after animal models of TBI, (Lyeth, Jiang, Delahunty, Phillips, & Hamm, 1994; DeAngelis, Hayes, & Lyeth, 1994; Ciallella, et al., 1998) with one study showing an upregulation of muscarinic receptors observed in the hippocampus and neocortex 15 days post FPI (Jiang, Lyeth, Delahunty, Phillips, & Hamm, 1994).

Chronic disruption in cholinergic system physiology has also been observed in animal models of TBI. Scolopolamine, an M1 auto-receptor antagonist, evokes the release of acetylcholine. Injured animals have attenuated scopolamine-evoked release of ACh in the hippocampus and neocortex 14 days after controlled cortical impact (CCI) model of TBI, suggesting impaired cholinergic function despite normal levels of measured ACh (Dixon, Ma, & Marion, 1997; Dixon, Bao, Johnson, Yang, Whitson, & Clifton, 1995).

In addition to identifying molecular, histological, and functional changes in cholinergic neurotransmission, animal models of TBI have been used to elucidate subtle differences in cholinergic function after TBI. Even after rats appear to have recovered from injury, as assessed by Morris Water Maze (MWM) spatial learning and memory tasks (no overt deficits), they still continue to have subtle cholinergic deficits as evidenced by increased sensitivity to the anti-cholinergic agents like scopolamine (Dixon, Hamm, Taft, & Hayes, 1994; Dixon, et al., 1995). Interestingly, enhancing cholinergic neurotransmission with chronic administration of cytidine 5'-diphosphocholine (CDP-choline) can attenuate both clear and more subtle cholinergic deficits following CCI. Even a single injection CDP-choline (100mg/ kg) significantly improves performance on the MWM task in the first day post-injury (Dixon, Ma, & Marion, 1997).

Animal models seem to mirror many of the reported changes associated with the cholinergic system after human TBI. Individuals with TBI exhibit an acute rise in ACh levels in cerebrospinal fluid (CSF) (Grossman, Beyer, Kelly, & Haber, 1975). These individuals also show damage to cerebral cholinergic nuclei (Murdoch,

Nicoll, Graham, & Dewar, 2002), widespread cholinergic deafferentation with the preservation of postsynaptic nicotinic and muscarinic receptors (Dewar & Graham, 1996; Murdoch, Perry, Court, Graham, & Dewar, 1998), and dysfunction in acetylcholine dependent circuitries located in the hippocampus, thalamus, and frontal cortex (Arciniegas, Adler, Topkoff, & al., 1999; Arciniegas, Olincy, Topkoff, & al., 2000). Furthermore, because of this general hypofunctional cholinergic state, TBI patients show less tolerance to drugs with anti-cholinergic properties when compared to the healthy population (Stanislav, 1997; Sandel, Olive, & Rader, 1993; Muller, Murai, Bauer-Wittmund, & von Cramon, 1999).

An excellent electrophysiological measure of cholinergic function (or dysfunction) is the assessment of electrophysiological markers of auditory sensory gating. Individuals with TBI who have complaints of impaired attention have markedly impaired sensory gating as assessed by auditory electrophysiological studies (Arciniegas et al., 2000). Also, improvements in sensory gating can be achieved with a six-week donepezil treatment, with 5 mg per day being more efficacious than 10 mg per day (Arciniegas D. B., Topkoff, Anderson, Filley, & Adler, 2002).

Cholinergic Agents in TBI Recovery

The psychiatric consequences of the cholinergic dysfunction following TBI resembles many of the cognitive deficits observed in Alzheimer's disease (AD) and that are thought to result from cholinergic deficits. As such, cholinergic agents clinically indicated for AD have been used in TBI (Griffin, van Reekum, & Masanic, 2003). Due to the disruptions in cholinergeric systems observed after TBI, medications with anticholinergic properties (such as typical antipsychotics, monoamine oxidase inhibitors, and tricyclic antidepressants) should be used with caution (Arciniegas, Topkoff, & Silver, 2000; Stanislav, 1997).

A review of clinical trials that implement cholinesterase inhibitors and other cholinergic agents in cases of TBI has been published recently by Poole and Agrawal (Poole & Agrawal, 2008). A few highlights from these studies are discussed below.

Physostigmine is a reversible cholinesterase inhibitor that has shown improvements in cognition in several clinical reports. Two case studies provide anecdotal evidence of improvements in orientation, attention, memory, language abilities, and the ability to participate in activities of daily living (Earnes & Sutton, 1995; Weinberg, Auerbach, & Moore, 1987). In these cases, drug-induced improvements deteriorated upon drug withdrawal. In a double-blind, placebo-controlled, crossover investigation of physostigmine treatment (4 mg, thrice daily for 8 days), improvements in long-term memory, divided attention, and information processing tasks were observed in 16 of 36 patients with a history of severe TBI (Cardenas, Mclean, Farrell-Roberts, et al., 1994).

Physostigmine in combination with the choline precursor lecithin showed greater efficacy than physostigmine alone in improving memory storage and retrieval in AD patients (Peters & Levin, 1979). Thus, the combination therapy was tested in cases of TBI. In a double-blind placebo crossover case study of a 36-year-old man two years after severe TBI, there were significant improvements in memory during the treatment phases. However, only mild additive effects of a combination therapy were demonstrated in a double-blind, placebo-controlled investigation on 16 moderate to severely injured patients (Levin et al., 1986). Furthermore, its poor oral bioavailability and its risk of systemic cholinergic toxicity make use of this agent impractical. More recent interest has thus been focused on other cholineseterase inhibitors such as galantamine, rivastigmine, donepezil. Donepezil, a more selective and longer acting reversible inhibitor of CNS acetylcholinesterase, has received the most attention in the TBI literature.

In a retrospective study assessing the use of the cholinesterase inhibitors donepezil, galantamine, and rivastigmine for treating fatigue, poor memory, or inattention following TBI, over half of the patients reported subjective improvements in concentration and initiation, with the most robust effects on vigilance. All three agents appeared to be similarly efficacious, with a possible trend towards galantamine and rivastigmine having greater efficacy than donepezil. All three agents also have a similar adverse effects profile despite slightly different mechanisms of action. In a multi-center randomized placebo controlled, double-blind crossover trial on chronic (>12 months) TBI patients, Silver et al. (2006) failed to show significant improvements with rivastigmine (3–6 mg per day for 12 weeks) in the primary analysis. However, in a subgroup of patients that showed baseline impairments in learning, there were significantly more responders to rivastigmine. Treatment with acetylcholinesterase inhibitors is thus considered more efficacious in patients with moderate to severe memory deficits (Silver et al., 2006).

Donepezil was effective in improving short-term memory and sustained attention in a small double-blind placebo controlled cross-over investigation with TBI patients in the post-acute phase. Importantly, the group receiving donepezil first had carryover effects through the end of the 10-week placebo trial, indicating that recovery may be facilitated by the donepezil (Zhang, Plotkin, Wang, Sandel, & Lee, 2004). In a case series of 10 chronic TBI patients with cognitive deficits, eight patients saw benefit in at least one cognitive domain with donepezil, with the most marked improvements found in tests of information processing, learning, and divided attention. Most reported better functioning in daily activities as well (Khateb, Ammann, Annoni, & Diserens, 2005). Interestingly, daily treatment with donepezil results in cortical increases in metabolism, and magnitude of metabolic change is associated with degree of clinical treatment response (Kim, Kim, Shin, Park, & Lee, 2009). Donepezil has also shown some beneficial effects in treating disorientation in the sub-acute phase of TBI (Nakamura, Ikegami, Yoshimoto, & Ozaki, 2002).

The acetylcholine precursor CDP-choline has shown some therapeutic efficacy on TBI populations. CDP-choline is a key intermediate in the biosynthesis of phosphatidylcholine, which is important for the integrity and repair of neural plasma membranes. Furthermore, it enhances brain metabolism and enhances the activity of acetylcholine as well as dopamine and norepinephrine (Secades, 2995; Dixon, Ma, & Marion, 1997; Ross, Mamalias, Moszczynska, Rajput, & Kish, 2001). Because of the pleiotropic effects of CDP-choline, it was hypothesized that the compound could attenuate neurodegeneration as well as improve cognitive functioning. In preclinical studies, treatment with CDP-choline attenuated edema, contusion volume, neural loss, blood-brain barrier disruption, and cognitive deficits following TBI in rats (Dempsey & Rao, 2003; Dixon, Ma, & Marion, 1997). In stroke, CDP-choline resulted in neurologic, functional, and cognitive improvements in stroke patients when administered within 24 hours after stroke and continued for six weeks (Clark, Warach, Pettigrew, Gammans, & Sabounjian, 1997). CDP-choline administration after stroke improved recovery of concsiousness in an RCT following acute, moderate to severe cerebral infarctions (Tazaki et al., 1988).

Several smaller clinical studies have shown the efficacy of CDP-choline on human TBI. A single-blind RCT of moderate to severly injured patients placed on a three-month treatment with CDP-choline were more likely to end up in the "good recovery group" for the GOS, with trends showing greater improvements in cognitive and psychiatric measures (Calatayud-Maldonado, Calatayud-Perez, & Aso-Escario, 1991). CDP-choline administration in mild to moderately injured TBI patients resulted in improvements of postconcussional symptoms, with very limited effects on neuropsychiatric tests of cognition (Levin, 1991). In another investigation that examined the effects of a neuropsychological memory rehabilitation program in conjunction with CDP-choline or placebo, the group that had undergone the rehabilitation program alone showed no improvements in measured neuropsychological functions; however, the group treated with CDP-choline in conjunction with rehabilitation showed improvements in word memory and verbal fluency, suggesting the importance of combinatorial approaches in treating cognitive deficits following TBI (Leon-Carrion, Dominguez-Roldan, Murillo-Cabezas, del Rosario Dominguez-Morales, & Munoz-Sanchez, 2000). However, a large multisite clinical study evaluating 90 days of CDP-choline administration did not result in improved outcomes for patients with complicated mild to severe TBI (Zafonte et al., 2012).

The small clinical trials and case studies summarized here suggest that there are positive effects of cholinergic drugs, particularly

CDP-choline and donepezil on memory, especially in conjunction with other therapies. CDP-choline largely lacks major side-effects at clinically relevant doses, and its pleiotropic effects make it a particularly attractive therapy that may attenuate secondary injury as well if used early enough. However, a large multisite trial failed to show significant improvements in a heterogeneous population with TBI.

Catecholaminergic Dysfunction after TBI

Following brain injury, cognitive deficits such as impaired sustained attention, information processing speed, and working memory are common. Phamacological treatment with psychostimulants and other catecholaminergic agents can have positive effects in improving some of these symptoms, which is initially what implicated catecholaminergic dysfunction following injury. Among the catecholamines, dopaminergic deficits have received the most attention.

Dopaminergic systems have been shown in a number of studies to be dysfunctional. Regiospecific alterations in tissue dopamine (DA) content have been observed following various experimental injury models. Following moderate severity fluid percussion injury (FPI), increased striatal and hypothalamic dopamine content were observed at early time points (<1 day), while cortical deficits in tissue DA content were observed acutely and persisted over the course of the two weeks examined (McIntosh, Yu, & Gennarelli, 1994). This work contrasts with observations from a CCI model which showed increased DA content in the frontal cortex acutely that returned back to baseline, with similar findings in the striatum (Massucci, Kline, Ma, Zafonte, & Dixon, 2004). Both of these studies contrast with findings from a more recent CCI study that asserts that at two weeks post-CCI there is increased tissue DA content in the infralimbic and prelimbic corticies, critical to working memory function (Kobori, Clifton, & Dash, 2006). All of these studies use different injury paradigms and examine different regions of interest, thus making the results difficult to integrate. Thus, it is unclear whether cortical DA content is persistently decreased, unchanged, or

increased following injury. Most likely, alterations in the dopaminergic system are regio-specific and dependent on the injury-type, severity, and time since injury. Tissue levels of DA may, for the most part, return to preinjury levels, however it also may be the case that preinjury levels of DA are insufficient in the injured brain (Bales, Wagner, Kline, & Dixon, 2009). Moreover, tissue and basal DA levels are only an indicator of dopaminergic dysfunction when they differ from the norm. However, even when tissue and basal DA levels are "normal" as it has been shown in the striatum two weeks after various injury models (Massucci, Kline, Ma, Zafonte, & Dixon, 2004; McIntosh, Yu, & Gennarelli, 1994) electrically evoked DA levels in the striatum continue to show deficits in CCI rats compared to naïve (Wagner, et al., 2005b; Wagner, et al., 2009a).

Dopaminergic dysfunction is likely due to altered autoregulatory mechanisms through alterations in DA signaling and through the D2 autoreceptors or proteins involved in the biosynthesis and synaptic transmission of DA. Several DA system proteins undergo dynamic changes after experimental injury. Tyrosine hydroxylase (TH) is the rate limiting enzyme for the synthesis of catecholamines, and several studies showed a delayed increase in its expression and activity in the frontal cortex after injury (Kobori, Clifton, & Dash, 2006; Yan, Kline, Ma, Hooghe-Peters, Marion, & Dixon, 2001). A similar delayed increase in TH expression has also been observed in the striatum (Yan, Ma, Chen, Li, Shao, & Dixon, 2007). Aside from TH expression, changes in TH phosphorylation state occur (Kobori, Clifton, & Dash, 2006). Indeed, TH activity has been shown to decrease one-week following moderate CCI which may in part be accounted for by the concomitant reduction of pSER40-TH levels expression (Shin, Brayer, Zhang, & Dixon, 2011). Modulation by the negative and positive modulatory proteins α-synuclein and 14-3-3, respectively, may also affect TH function (Perez, Waymire, Lin, Liu, Guo, & Zigmond, 2002; Ichimura, et al., 1988).

The dopamine transporter (DAT) is the primary means of DA clearance in the striatum, and it is the main site of action of psychostimulants like methylphenidate and amphetamine. Total tissue DAT expression in cortex and striatum has been shown consistently to decrease following injury in male rats (Wagner, Chen, Kline, Li, Zafonte, & Dixon, 2005a; Wagner et al., 2009a; Wilson et al., 2005; Yan, Kline, Ma, Li, & Dixon, 2002). Interestingly DAT expression decreases to a lesser extent in female rats following CCI (Wagner, Chen, Kline, Li, Zafonte, & Dixon, 2005a). Decreased DAT expression following injury are consistent with diminished DA clearance rates following electrically evoked DA release in the striatum (Wagner et al., 2009a). Furthermore, these animal injury models are consistent with diminished DAT binding in a human SPECT imaging study on 10 patients with mostly severe brain injury and relative preservation of the striatum (Donnemiller et al., 2000). Furthermore, the DAT genotype that promotes higher DAT expression has been correlated with higher cerebrospinal fluid (CSF) DA levels in humans acutely after TBI, an effect that was especially pronounced in women (Wagner et al., 2007).

It is debatable whether decreases in DAT expression are beneficial. The decreases in DAT expression may be a compensatory mechanism for attenuating dopaminergic deficits, presumably by increasing the half-life of DA in the extracellular space. Environmental enrichment (EE), a paradigm shown to improve place learning after experimental models of TBI (Hicks, Li, Zhang, Dhillon, Prasad, & Seroogy, 1999; Hamm, Temple, O'Dell, Pike, & Lyeth, 1996; Passineau, Green, & Dietrich, 2001; Wagner, Kline, Sokoloski, Zafonte, Capulong, & Dixon, 2002) tends to decrease DAT expression further after injury (Wagner, Chen, Kline, Li, Zafonte, & Dixon, 2005a). Also, striatal DAT decreases are not as pronounced in females after EE (Wagner, Chen, Kline, Li, Zafonte, & Dixon, 2005a). These studies suggest that decreased DAT expression after injury may be regulated by sex perhaps through gondal hormones like estrogen, which can regulate TH expression and morphology of nigrostriatal dopaminergic neurons (Kuppers, Ivanova, Karolczak, & Beyer, 2000), among other things.

Psychostimulants in TBI Recovery

Psychostimulants like D-amphetamine (AMPH) and methylphenidate (MPH) augment DA and norepinephrine neurotransmission by acting primarily on their cognate transporters. MPH is a transporter blocker, while amphetamine is a transporter substrate that is internalized after binding to DAT and promotes the efflux of neurotransmitters into the extracellular space through a reverse transport mechanism. In addition, AMPH inhibits degradation of monoamines by inhibiting monoamine oxidase (MAO) and depleting vesicular neurotransmitter content (Fleckenstein, Volz, Riddle, Gibb, & Hanson, 2007). Though the two have different mechanisms of action on the same neurotransmitter systems, they have similar effects, and thus, are used almost interchangeably for disorders like narcolepsy and ADHD. Some of the psychiatric similarities between TBI and ADHD and narcolepsy in terms of fatigue, mental slowing, and distractibility have led to the off-label use of psychostimulants in the treatment of TBI. The success of psychostimulants in treating cognitive deficits following TBI is what initially led to the clinical impression that DA systems are altered after TBI (McAllister, Flashman, Sparling, & Saykin, 2004).

Animal models of TBI have been used to demonstrate various aspects of dopaminergic deficits following TBI (see above) and how psychostimulants work in the injured brain. Chronic daily MPH treatment for two weeks after CCI can restore some of the observed deficits in DA neurotransmission following injury when using an electrically evoked DA release paradigm and fast-scan cyclic voltammetry (FSCV) (Wagner et al., 2009a). Furthermore, two weeks after CCI, striatal monitoring using FSCV shows that injured rats are less able to augment striatal dopaminergic outflow in response to an acute MPH challenge compared to naïve animals. However, daily chronic MPH treatment after injury restores the responsiveness to an acute MPH challenge (Wagner, et al., 2009b). Behaviorally, chronic MPH treatment improves spatial learning following CCI in male rats (Kline, Yan, Bao, Marion, & Dixon, 2000); however, the same effect was not observed in injured females given the same dosing of MPH. Consistent with other literatuture on gender differences in dopaminergic drugs of abuse, females were more sensitive to daily MPH therapy and had increased locomotor activity in an open field chamber as well as increased swimming speeds with this dose of MPH treatment (Wagner, et al., 2007b.) These studies suggest that chronic treatment with MPH is beneficial recovery after injury. However, the role of gender with MPH pharmacotherapy sensitivity and efficacy needs to be examined further to evaluate if dosing needs to be titrated in a gender specific manner after TBI (Bales, Wagner, Kline, & Dixon, 2009).

Clinically, psychostimulants have been used to enhance emergence from coma, vegetative states, or minimally conscious states. However, meta-analysis of single-subject studies on MPH effects suggests that there is no conclusive evidence to support its use for this purpose (Martin & Whyte, 2007). However, acute use of MPH (0.3mg/kg twice daily) when begun within the second day after injury tended to decrease ICU stays in cases of moderate TBI and ICU and hospital stays in cases of severe TBI (Moein, Khalili, & Keramatian, 2006). Furthermore, two studies suggest that MPH leads to faster recovery based on disability rating scale (DRS) score (Kaelin, Cifu, & Matthies, 1996; Plenger, Dixon, Castillo, Frankowski, Yablon, & Levin, 1996).

In the post-acute phase, MPH has beneficial effects on cognitive functioning, especially in the domain of attention. In a study involving individuals with TBI and attentional complaints, MPH treatment increased information processing speed and attentiveness, while decreasing off-task behavior in individual work tasks. However, these positive findings may be attributable to very stringent inclusion criteria in this study (Whyte, et al., 2004). In another double-blind, placebo-controlled crossover investigation on 12 chronic TBI patients, MPH showed no significant effects on tests of attention, but trends towards improvement in reaction time, divided attention, memory, and mental speed tasks (Speech, Rao, Osmon, & Sperry, 1993).

MPH is recommended in treating deficits in attention like slowed mental processing speed and sustained attention after TBI (Warden, et al., 2006). In contrast, there is mostly negative evidence that would suggest its efficacy in treating memory deficits (Gualtieri & Evans, Stimulant treatment or for the neurobehvioral sequale of associated with TBI, 1988; Speech,

Rao, Osmon, & Sperry, 1993; Mooney & Haas, 1993; Tiberti, Sabe, Jason, et al., 1998). However, MPH also can have positive effects on mood, which indirectly may improve cognition.

The efficacy of AMPH is less characterized than MPH in the TBI population. However, their similar molecular targets of action and similar effects in other populations suggest that AMPH would act similarly in TBI patients. In a retrospective study of patients with severe TBI and attentional deficits that hindered their participation in rehabilitation, about half the patients had positive effects of AMPH (5–30mg/day) that helped facilitate their participation in rehabilitation (Hornstein, Lennihan, Seliger, Lichtman, & Schroeder, 1996). In a case study of an individual with TBI with concentration problems five years after mild injury, a 5-mg dose of D-amphetamine improved consistency of performance on tasks of attention and working memory when compared to placebo (Bleiberg, Garmoe, Cederquist, Reeves, & Lux, 1993).

MPH is sometimes given cautiously to TBI patients because of the listed contraindication of seizures cited in the *Physicians' Desk Reference*. However, some evidence suggests that MPH may be safe to use in TBI patients at risk for post-traumatic seizures (PTS). In a retrospective study of 30 patients that had an active history of seizures following brain injury, seizure frequency was decreased in the MPH treatment group. Three of the four patients that had increased seizure frequencies while on MPH, were also on tricyclic antidepressants (TCA). Thus, the combination TCAs with MPH may be detrimental (Wroblewski, Leary, Phelan, Whyte, & Manning, 1992). In a non-TBI population, the relationship to seizures and MPH seems to be small. In a study of 119 ADHD children with epilepsy or EEG abnormalities and without a history of seizures, MPH treatment did not change seizure frequency in the epileptic population, nor did it precipitate seizures in the population with abnormal EEGs (Gucuyener, Erdemoglu, Senol, Serdaroglu, Soysal, & Kockar, 2003). Furthermore, MPH does not affect GABA, glutamate, or aspartate neurotransmitter systems, nor does MPH have any known effects on sodium or calcium channel activities, each of which are linked to the pathophysiology of epilepsy, diminishing the idea that MPH is a pro-convulsant (Tan & Appleton, 2005).

DA Agonists in TBI Recovery: Amantadine

Amantadine (AMH) is a DA enhancing drug that may improve cognitive function and arousal after brain injury (Sawyer, Mauro, & Ohlinger, 2008). AMH was originally introduced as an anti-viral agent for Type A influenza, which unexpectedly was noted to have beneficial effects on treating Parkinsonian symptoms. Specifically, AMH enhances the efficacy of levodopa while reducing its dyskinetic side-effects in Parkinson's disease and neuroleptic-induced Parkinsonism (Metman, Dotto, LePoole, Konitsiotis, Fang, & Chase, 1999; Fann & Lake, 1976). The mechanism of AMH action is loosely characterized. It can increase extracellular DA levels, which possibly occurs through NMDA antagonism and reuptake inhibition through the DAT (Mizoguchi, Yokoo, Yoshida, Tanaka, & Tanaka, 1994; Takahashi, Yamashita, Zhang, & Nakamura, 1996; Heikkila & Cohen, 1972). Conversely, chronic AMH treatment reportedly also can increase DAT activity (Page, Peeters, Maloteaux, & Hermans, 2000). AMH may also alter the dopaminergic system by increasing DA receptor expression as well as altering receptor conformation states (Gianutsos, Chute, & Dunn, 1985; Allen, 1983; Rogoz, Dlaboga, & Dziedzicka-Wasylewska, 2003; Moresco et al., 2002).

AMH has beneficial effects on fatigue associated with multiple sclerosis and can control agitation, anxiety, and mood alterations associated with cocaine withdrawal (Pike, 1989; Cohen & Fisher, 1989). Its clinical relevance in the context of TBI is similar to psychostimulants, however, classic stimulant-like effects of AMPH and MPH are lacking with AMH, making AMH useful as a cognitive enhancer, especially for hyperkinetic, agitated, or restless patients (Van Reekum et al., 1995).

Clinical case reports have shown that AMH may be effective in the sub-acute phase of injury to hasten emergence from coma and hypoarousal states. In a case study, AMH treatment improved responsivity and awareness on the coma/near coma (CNC) scale in a severely injured patient in a persistent minimally conscious state. CNC scores worsened when AMH dosage was titrated down and improved when titrated up again (Zafonte, Watanabe, & Mann, 1998; Wu & Garmel, 2005). These case studies lack placebo controls, making it difficult to attribute progression out of coma to AMH versus natural recovery. However, in a longitudinal observational study, TBI patients in a vegetative state (VS) or minimally conscious state (MCS) between 4 to 16 weeks after TBI showed significant improvements on the DRS after AMH treatment initiation and DRS scores 16 weeks TBI (Whyte, et al., 2005). Further, a randomized, double-blind, crossover investigation of AMH use in the sub-acute phase after injury showed that treatment tended to expedite the rate of recovery compared to placebo in several outcome domains such as the Mini-Mental Status Examination (MMSE), Disability Rating Scale (DRS), Glasgow Outcome Scale (GOS), and Functional Independence Measure-Cognitive Scale (FIM-cog) (Meythaler, Brunner, Johnson, & Novack, 2002). These studies were further bolstered by a recent large randomized clinical trial which showed that AMH has some benefits on speed of recovery for persons with severe TBI who were in either a vegetative or minimally conscious state and in the sub-acute stages of recovery, further supporting the use of this drug, particularly for very severely injured populations (Giacino et al., 2012).

The early use of AMH is also supported by another retrospective pilot study, which showed that AMH treatment begun within three days after severe brain injury was associated with significantly larger improvements in the GCS upon discharge from the ICU, and treatment also resulted in significantly lower fatality rates than an untreated group (Saniova, Drobny, Kneslova, & Minarik, 2004). The highly positive findings in this study should be viewed with caution as the authors do not report the AMH regimen, patient demographics, or the length of ICU stay in the untreated or active treatment groups. In contrast, another retrospective study failed to establish a relationship between AMH treatment and emergence from coma, but the authors identify a strong selection bias for treating a group with a poorer diagnosis that was likely to affect their results (Hughes

S., Colantonio, Santaguida, & Paton, 2005). The use of AMH to promote emergence from coma until recently has been limited, but due to some of the evidence suggesting its positive effects, its relative safety, its inexpensive cost, and lack of other alternatives, AMH is a rational therapy to improve early recovery from TBI (Hughes S., Colantonio, Santaguida, & Paton, 2005).

Positive benefits of AMH on cognition and behavior have been observed in both the sub-acute and chronic stages of TBI. AMH may be beneficial for the treatment of a range of frontal lobe dysfunction common to TBI, such as problem solving, working memory, and initiation (Kraus & Maki, 1997a; Kraus & Maki, 1997b). Interestingly, a 12-week daily AMH regimen (400 mg) in chronic TBI patients improved neuropsychiatric measures of executive function, which was positively correlated with the left PFC glucose utilization (Kraus et al., 2005). In several studies, AMH has been effective in attenuating a broad range of cognitive and behavioral deficits that are commonly observed after TBI. AMH has been noted to improve arousal, concentration, information processing speed, and motivation among many other domains (Nickels, Schneider, Dombovy, & Wong, 1994). The broad range of improvements associated with AMH may in large part be attributed to the positive effects of AMH on arousal, which is essential for many of the other cognitive, behavioral, and emotional functions.

Despite the favorable side effect profile of AMH, it should be used with caution in TBI patients that are at risk for seizures, as seizures occurred in 2 of 12 patients with a history of seizures while on AMH (Nickels, Schneider, Dombovy, & Wong, 1994). In a small study of 10 non-TBI subjects, AMH worsened symptoms of sufferers of tonic-clonic seizures (Drake, Pakalnis, Denio, & Phillips, 1991). On the other hand, AMH has reported effects in managing other types of seizures (Shahar & Brand, 1992; Drake, Pakalnis, Denio, & Phillips, 1991) Furthermore, the combined use of psychostimulants with AMH may cause unstable increases in blood pressure and increase the occurrence of irritability, insomnia, nervousness, and seizures. It has been shown that NMDA antagonism acts synergistically to potentiate the response of AMPH in rodents

(Miller & Abercrombie, 1996). Thus combined treatment with the weak NMDA receptor antagonist AMH and other psychostimulants can create a higher dopaminergic tone than might be expected, which could have desirable or detrimental effects.

DA Agonists in TBI Recovery: Bromocriptine

Bromocriptine (BRO) is a dopaminergic drug, which may be beneficial in treating hypoarousal states, executive, and motor dysfunction. BRO is a D2 DA receptor agonist with antioxidant properties that may also be clinically relevant. D2 receptors are located pre- and post-synaptically throughout in the cortex, striatum, and other regions that receive dopaminergic innervation. Two isoforms of the D2 receptor, the short from (D2S) and the long form (D2L) exist. D2S is theorized to mediate presynaptic autoinhibitory functions, and D2L mediates postsynaptic signaling cascades that facilitate neuroleptic effects of antipsychotics (Lindgren, et al., 2003). Agonism of postsynaptic D2 receptors with BRO may promote arousal, which contrasts with the sedating effects of high doses of antipsychotics, most of which are D2 antagonists. Consistent with D2 mediated autoinhibition, high doses of BRO (10 or 20mg/kg) in rats can inhibit DA release and metabolism (Pagliari, Peyrin, & Crambes, 1995), while lower doses (2.5mg/kg and 5mg/kg) paradoxically increased extracellular DA concentration. This paradoxical effect suggests that regulation of DA levels by BRO cannot simply be explained by D2S mediated autoinhibition which would be expected to decrease DA release alone, suggesting a more complex mechanism for low dose BRO. However, at later time points there were decreased DA metabolite levels following all doses of BRO tested, consistent with D2S mediated inhibition of TH activity by BRO (Brannan, Martínez-Tica, Di Rocco, & Yahr, 1993). In other dopaminergic therapies like psychostimulants and AMH, DA levels are augmented; however, DA levels with BRO are decreased with a concomitant increase in D2 mediated signaling. Because some functions like working memory are thought to largely be modulated by D1 signaling, it is unclear whether the decrease in DA levels caused by BRO would be detrimental to some D1-modulated functions.

D2 agonists like bromocriptine (BRO) and ropinirole may attenuate oxidative stress. In a study on mice, ropinirole treatment increased glutathione, catalase, and superoxide dismutase (SOD) activities in the striatum and protected against 6-hydroxydopamine toxicity. These effects were blocked by D2 antagonism, strongly suggesting D2 receptor activation with neuroprotective antioxidant properties (Iida, Miyazaki, Tanaka, Kabuto, Iwata-Ichikawa, & Ogawa, 1999). Administration of BRO 15 minutes prior to controlled cortical impact has been shown to attenuate lipid peroxidation in the striatum and substantia nigra and reduce hippocampal CA3 cell loss, which was correlated with improvements in spatial learning in a water maze task (Kline, Massucci, Ma, Zafonte, & Dixon, 2004). This work suggests that BRO can attenuate oxidative stress associated with the initial cerebrovascular or traumatic event; however, the beneficial effects included of these studies required pre-treating animals before their insults in order to confer behavioral and neuroprotective effects. Daily BRO after CCI similarly showed benefits in spatial learning, working memory, and attenuated injury-induced cell death in hippocampal CA3 neurons, which suggests that BRO affords some neuroprotection against secondary injury and improves cognitive function in the post-acute phase (Kline, Massucci, Marion, & Dixon, 2002).

In clinical cases of TBI, BRO may aid in the recovery from minimally conscious and vegetative states following TBI (Passler & Riggs, 2001). BRO also has beneficial effects on dysautonomia or hyperadrenergia likely by acting on dopamine receptors in the hypothalamus in addition to the striatum (Russo & O'Flaherty, 2000). In a case series, BRO was effective in treating motivational deficits that follow injury, with improvements observed in responsivity to reward, attention, verbal fluency, and participation in rehabilitation. In general, these improvements were sustained after BRO withdrawal (Powell, al-Adawi, Morgan, & Greenwood, 1996). As a selective D2 agonist, BRO acts more specifically than other dopaminergic agents that bring about generalized increases in

dopaminergic tone. Working memory is a prefrontal function that is mostly modulated by D1 receptors and has been shown to be unaffected by D2 agonism by BRO (Müller, von Cramon, & Pollmann, 1998). Consistent with this idea, BRO showed improvements in some prefrontal cortex functions, but not others like working memory in a small double-blind placebo-controlled crossover investigation (McDowell, Whyte, & D'Esposito, 1998).

DA Substrate Enhancement in TBI Recovery

Dopaminergic therapies have been helpful in treating cognitive deficits and enhancing recovery following TBI, and thus substrate enhancement of DA with L-DOPA/carbidopa and Monoamine Oxidase Inhibitors (MAOis) could be hypothesized to have similar clinical utility. Only a handful of studies in the literature have reported on the DA substrate enhancers in the context of TBI.

L-DOPA/carbidopa therapy has been suggested to have beneficial effects on recovery of consciousness following TBI with a favorable adverse effects profile. In a case study on a 24-year-old man in a persistent vegetative state following TBI, L-DOPA/carbidopa enhanced the recovery of the patient, where he became responsive and conversant within days of therapy (Haig & Ruess, 1990). Likewise, L-DOPA/carbidopa and/or physostigmine therapy resulted in clinical improvements in 29 out of 45 patients in persistent vegetative states following severe head injuries (van Woerkom, Minderhoud, Gottschal, & Nicolai, 1982). Restoration of responsivity and consciousness following TBI was observed to occur within a short time frame of pharmacological intervention with a dose-dependent relationship, suggesting that L-DOPA/carbidopa therapy can have a strong role in the recovery process (Krimchansky, Keren, Sazbon, & Groswasser, 2004).

In the chronic and rehabilitation phase, dopamine substrate enhancement can have positive effects on cognition and behavior. In a case study on a 50-year-old woman with persistent frontal lobe dysfunction following TBI, improvements in impulsivity and perseveration were observed with AMH treatment. Further improvements in mental flexibility and divided attention were observed upon adjunctive treatment with L-DOPA/carbidopa (Kraus & Maki, 1997a). Similarly, L-DOPA/carbidopa therapy improved cognition and behavior in all 12 patients that reached a plateau in their rehabilitation programs following severe TBI (Lal, Merbitz, & Grip, 1988). Blocking the degradation of monoamines with the monoamine oxidase inhibitor L-deprenyl has been implicated in being able to treat amotivation symptoms that can develop post TBI, with the mechanism of action involving both serotonergic and dopaminergic systems (Newburn & Newburn, 2005; Moutaouakil, El Otmani, Fadel, & Slassi, 2009).

Neuropharmacological Strategies for Treating Behavioral Changes after TBI

Clinical and Neurobiological Basis of Fatigue

Fatigue and sleep disturbances are two interrelated problems that commonly occur following all severities of TBI. These issues disrupt patients' participation in rehabilitation and daily activities. Despite the common occurrence of these issues, there is limited objective data analyzing the prevalence of these problems, the efficacy of treatments, and their pathophysiology.

There is no consensus on the definition of fatigue, but in general, fatigue is a lack of mental and/or physical energy that is needed to carry out activities. Mental fatigue is the inability to initiate or sustain attention on cognitively demanding tasks, which often leads to complaints of inability to focus or sustain attention.

The neural substrates of fatigue are not well understood and may include the subjective experience of generalized dysfunction in neural processing in a variety of circuitries. It is likely that the neural correlates are widespread and involve circuitries that mediate arousal and attention. The inability to maintain a level of arousal and attention to carry out activities leads to the subjective experience of fatigue. Pro-inflammatory cytokines and their effects on neural metabolism can also cause fatigue. This may be a major determinant of fatigue in

the acute and sub-acute phases of TBI, when initial trauma and secondary inflammation cascades lead to elevations in pro-inflammatory cytokines. In fact recent data suggests elevated serum cytokines for several weeks/months after severe TBI (Boles, Wagner & Goyal, 2013). Furthermore, disruptions of the HPA axis, which commonly occur after TBI, lead to neuroendocrine dysfunction like hypothyroidism and hypogonadism, complications commonly associated with fatigue (Bondanelli, Ambrosio, Zatelli, DeMarinis, & Uberti, 2005) (Wagner et al., 2012).

Normally, fatigue is a physiological response to extensive physical, emotional, mental stress, or lack of sleep. Pathologically, fatigue can be a sign of some underlying physical dysfunction or psychological disturbances such as anxiety or depression. Fatigue can be peripheral, in which muscles are exhausted of glycogen stores, lactic acid build-up, or strain; however, fatigue associated with TBI is generally associated with central fatigue in which subjects lack the mental energy required to carry out tasks.

Clinically, fatigue has a strong subjective component, and thus, the incidence reports of post-traumatic fatigue are often based on a person's self-report rather than physiological or psychometric testing. One study evaluated fatigue in normal subjects and those with TBI (average 44.3 months post-injury) using three subjective self-report scales and an objective measurement of physical fatigue. The TBI groups showed increased subjective ratings of cognitive, physical, and social fatigue (LaChapelle & Finlayson, 1998). Another study showed no differences in quadriceps strength or endurance in normal subjects versus individuals with TBI with or without complaints of fatigue, consistent with the idea that TBI results primarily in fatigue that is central in nature (Walker, Cardenas, Guthrie, McLean, & Brooke, 1991).

Because of differences in patient populations and methods for analyzing fatigue, the prevalence of post-traumatic fatigue greatly vary (Middleboe, Andersen, Birket-Smith, & Friis, 2009; Olver, Ponsford, & Curran, 1996). Fatigue has been examined in the chronic phase after TBI across a range of severities in 231 adults, which showed an association between injury severity and the prevalence of subjective complaints of fatigue (35.1% of mild, 32.4% of moderate, and 57.7% severe injuries) (Masson, et al., 1996). Also, several studies suggest post-traumatic fatigue is more common and severe in women (Cantor, et al., 2008; Englander, Bushnik, Oggins, & Katznelson, 2010). Fatigue can often be secondary to sleep disturbances or other psychological problems that frequently occur after TBI (Kruetzer, Seel, & Gourley, 2001). In patients that reported having sleep disturbances, 80% also reported of having problems with fatigue (Clinchot, Bogner, Mysiw, Fugate, & Corrigan, 1998).

Often, TBI sufferers view fatigue as their most difficult symptom (LaChapelle & Finlayson, 1998). The injured brain is inefficient and has to work harder to meet the same goals needed for normal performance, which may underlie cognitive impairments in working memory, information processing speed, divided attention, and other cognitive functions that induce fatigue (van Zomeren, Brouwer, & Deelman, 1984). More recently, fMRI studies confirm the need for additional cerebral resources for cognitive processes by showing larger areas of brain activation during cognitive tasks in subjects with TBI compared to controls (Russell, Arenth, Scanlon, Kessler, & Ricker, 2011; Arenth, Russell, Scanlon, Kessler, & Ricker, 2012).

Treatment of Post-Traumatic Fatigue

Pharmacological treatment of post-traumatic fatigue requires the evaluation of the cause of fatigue. Patients with TBI are often on many medications, several of which have sedating properties. This is especially common with anticonvulsants, benzodiazepines, and pain medications. When possible, medications that have less sedative properties should be used. When fatigue occurs secondary to depression, sleep disturbances, or neuroendocrine dysfunction, treating the primary causes can resolve the associated fatigue.

In the chronic and recovery phases of TBI, fatigue may be tightly linked with commonly reported cognitive deficits in sustained attention and vigilance. Several studies have characterized the beneficial effects of catecholaminergic agents like AMPH, MPH, AMH, and BRO on sustained attention in TBI patients.

Though there are no studies that specifically evaluate the pharmacological treatment of post-traumatic fatigue, MPH is effective in treating fatigue associated with Parkinson disease, HIV, and cancer (Mendonca, Menezes, & Jog, 2007; Sarhill, Walsh, Nelson, Hornsi, LeGrand, & Davis, 2001; Breitbart, Rosenfeld, Kaim, & Funesti-Esch, 2001). Similarly, BRO has been shown to be effective in treating post-polio fatigue and AMH in the treatment of MS-associated fatigue (Bruno, Zimmerman, Creange, Lewis, Molzen, & Frick, 1996; Krupp et al., 1995).

Modafinil in Fatigue. Modafinil (MOD) is a newer agent that has shown efficacy in treating MS-associated fatigue (Zifko, Rupp, Schwarz, Zipko, & Maida, 2002). Compared to AMPH and MPH, modafinil treatment in felines resulted in less activation of various cortical areas and subcortical areas, but greater activation in the anterior hypothalamus (Lin, Hou, & Jouvet, 1996). MOD has been shown to increase glutamate while decreasing GABA levels in the medial preoptic nucleus and the posterior hypothalamus in rats (Ferraro et al., 1999), and it has been shown to increase glutamate transmission in the ventrolateral and ventromedial thalamus (Ferraro, Antonelli, O'Connor, Tanganelli, Rambert, & Fuxe, 1997). MOD-mediated increases in glutamate neurotransmission in all of these areas are associated with behavioral arousal or wakeful state (Azuma, Kodama, Honda, & Inoue, 1996). As the anterior hypothalamus seems ideally located in an area that controls sleep-wake cycles, it has been postulated the MOD acts more selectively on sleep pathways than psychostimulants (Lin, Hou, & Jouvet, 1996).

The clinical use of MOD in 10 patients with closed head injury seemed to be well tolerated and result in subjective improvements in wakefulness, cognitive functions, and well-being in most patients (Tietelman, 2001). To date, the use of MOD has only been studied in one randomized, double-blind, placebo controlled cross-over trial in 53 patients with TBI requiring inpatient rehabilitation at least one year post-TBI. This study found sporadic statistically significant evidence of improvements in fatigue, but concluded that there were no clear persistent benefits of MOD observed with the Fatigue Severity Scale (FSS) or Epworth Sleepiness Scale (ESS) (Jha et al., 2008).

Substrates and Etiology of Sleep Disturbances after TBI

Sleep disturbances are common after TBI, with one study showing a prevalence of 46% in a TBI population of heterogeneous severities greater than three months post-injury (Castriotta, Wilde, Lai, Atanasov, Masel, & Kuna, 2007). However, the literature on sleep disturbances specific to TBI and its management is largely lacking. Evidence suggests that following acute brain injury, various neurological factors disrupt sleep patterns. As these processes normalize, sleep architecture can be expected to normalize as well in most patients, though the presence of brain stem lesions can prolong sleep abnormalities (Ron, Algom, & Cohen, 1980; Markand & Dyken, 1976). Sleep disturbances are very common in the sub-acute and chronic stages following TBI, but psychosocial factors rather than neurological factors often play a larger role in these later stages. Sleep disturbances are not always a result of the TBI, but they could be a preexisting condition since sleep disorders occur in approximately 30% of adults in non-injured populations (Rosekind, 1992).

Three general types of sleep disorders are frequently encountered in the TBI population: hypersomnia, insomnia, and circadian rhythm sleep disorders (CRSDs) (Harada, Minami, Hattori, Nakamura, & Kabashima, 1976). Hypersomnia is characterized by excessive daytime drowsiness that is independent of interrupted nighttime sleep. Insomnia refers to the difficulty in initiating or maintaining sleep, which leads to a significant reduction in deep sleep and often results in daytime fatigue and somnolence. With CRSDs, subjects have irregular sleep-wake patterns that lack a 24-hour periodicity or have a delayed sleep phase syndrome (DSPS) that prevents subjects from sleeping at desired clock times.

In a mixed injury severity population one year after TBI, 50% had sleep complaints, of which 25% described sleeping more than usual, and 45% and 64% described problems falling asleep or waking up too early, respectively

(Clinchot, Bogner, Mysiw, Fugate, & Corrigan, 1998). Cohen et al. have shown temporal associations with the incidence and types of sleep disturbances following TBI. Sleep complaints were common in both hospitalized TBI patients in the rehabilitation unit and also patients discharged at two or three year follow-ups post-TBI (72.7% versus 51.9%, respectively). The nature of sleep disorders at the two time points after injury was noted to be different, with the majority of hospitalized patients exhibiting difficulties initiating and maintaining sleep, while patients in the recovery phase were more likely to have problems with excessive somnolence (Cohen, Oksenberg, Snir, Stern, & Groswasser, 1992). However, studies assessing sleep in hospitalized non-TBI patients show that the noise and atmosphere of the hospital setting contributes to sleep fragmentation and decreases the amount of stage 3, 4, and REM sleep, suggesting that the hospital settings and not the TBI itself, may be contributing to the difficulty sleeping in hospitalized TBI patients in the study conducted by Cohen et al. (1992) (Freedman, Kotzer, & Schwab, 1999; Aaron, Carlisle, Carskadon, Meyer, Hill, & Millman, 1996; Broughton & Baron, 1978; Cohen, Oksenberg, Snir, Stern, & Groswasser, 1992).

Hypersomnia can produce deficits in physical, cognitive, and social functioning and can hinder participation in rehabilitation. In the TBI population, hypersomnia is often due to sleep disorders like sleep apnea or periodic limb movement disorders (Masel, Scheibel, Kimbark, & Kuna, 2001; Castriotta & Lai, 2001). In fact, the severity of injury shows a strong correlation to daytime drowsiness at one month post-injury, which largely subsides by one year post injury (Watson, Dikmen, Machamer, Doherty, & Temkin, 2007). Hypersomnia in TBI patients may often be a pre-existing condition, as somnolence is a major cause of motor vehicle accidents (Leger, 1994). Excessive daytime drowsiness should be examined, along with insomnia or nighttime sleep disturbances, to determine the etiology of somnolence during the day; however, this is rarely done in studies evaluating hypersomnia in the TBI population.

The reported prevalence of insomnia after TBI greatly varies across studies, which show a range between of 36% to 70% (Mclean, Dikmen,

Temkin, Wyler, & Gale, 1984; Keshavan, Channabasavanna, & Reddy, 1981). Several studies also have shown a correlation between pain and insomnia (Ouellet, Beaulieau-Bonneau, & Morin, 2006; Beetar, Guilmette, & Sparadeo, 1996). Insomnia is also correlated with depression after TBI (Fitchtenberg, Millis, Mann, Zafonte, & Milllard, 2000). This is not surprising as insomnia is associated with depression in the general population as well (Riemann, Berger, & Voderholzer, 2001; Ford & Kamerow, 1989). In several studies, insomnia was more prevalent in patients with mild TBI (Clinchot, Bogner, Mysiw, Fugate, & Corrigan, 1998; Beetar, Guilmette, & Sparadeo, 1996; Fitchtenberg, Millis, Mann, Zafonte, & Milllard, 2000). This finding may be an artifact of study design in which more severely injured TBI patients underreport their deficits (Clinchot, Bogner, Mysiw, Fugate, & Corrigan, 1998), or it may be due to psychosocial factors, where head injured patients with minor deficits are more aware of their impairments, leading to anxiety/depression and secondary insomnia (Fitchtenberg, Millis, Mann, Zafonte, & Milllard, 2000). Consistent with this notion, a study with 54 patients in the sub-acute phase (<3 months since injury) showed that the prevalence of sleep disturbances most strongly correlated to anxiety that developed following injury (Rao, et al., 2008). The nature of the relationship between severity of TBI, depression, and sleep disturbances remains to be elucidated. In the more acute phases of injury, insomnia may reflect neurological deficits caused by trauma more than psychosocial factors, as it has been shown that longer coma durations correlate to less time spent in REM sleep, more time spent in a wakeful state, and more awakenings throughout a night in adolescents with TBI at one month post-recovery of consciousness (George, Landau-Ferey, Benoit, Dondey, & Cophignon, 1981).

CRSD can often manifest itself similar to insomnia, and patients with TBI are often misdiagnosed with insomnia when, in actuality, they have CRSDs (Ayalon, Borodkin, Dishon, Kanety, & Dagan, 2007). TBI can cause DSPS in which the body temperature fluctuations and sleep architecture follows a 24-hour cycle but is offset from the timing observed in the general population. It is often thought that mild TBI can cause DSPS as a result of an inability to phase shift circadian rhythms (Ayalon, Borodkin, Dishon, Kanety, & Dagan, 2007). Irregular sleep wake patterns (ISWPs) can also emerge as a consequence of TBI in which patients have irregularities in sleep patterns and attenuated temperature fluctuation amplitudes. Interestingly TBI subjects with ISWPs may exhibit a normal 24-hour periodicity of melatonin level fluctuations or they may completely lack circadian melatonin rhythms (Ayalon, Borodkin, Dishon, Kanety, & Dagan, 2007).

Sleep complaints in patients with chronic TBI have been significantly correlated to neurobehavioral impairments and occupational outcome, emphasizing the importance of managing sleep disorders in this population early during their recovery (Cohen, Oksenberg, Snir, Stern, & Groswasser, 1992). Studies examining the efficacy of pharmacological agents that manage sleep disturbances are lacking in a TBI population, thus the clinical utility of many agents are drawn from the efficacy they have in the general population.

Benzodiazepine Sedative-Hypnotics. Benzodiazepines (BZ) are a group of sedative-hypnotic agents that can improve subjective and objective measures of sleep quality and quantity (Chokroverty, 2000). Benzodiazepines allosterically activate $GABA_A$ receptors, thereby increasing GABAergic tone. By augmenting the tone of the main inhibitory neurotransmitter in the CNS, these drugs have their broad ranging sedative, anxiolytic, anticonvulsant, and muscle relaxant effects. In addition, BZs cause the accumulation of the hypnogenic factor adenosine in the extracellular space by inhibiting adenosine transporters (Narimatsu, Niiya, Kawamata, & Namiki, 2006). In the general population, BZ use impairs various cognitive functions acutely such as memory consolidation and attention, and causes psychomotor slowing (Buffett-Jerrott, Stewart, Bird, & Teehan, 1998). However, long-term use of BZs may lead to persistent cognitive deficits that may not be reversed upon drug discontinuation (Steward, 2005). Furthermore, chronic BZ use is associated with a high likelihood of dependence, which has been estimated to occur in approximately

10–30% of chronic users. Approximately 50% of all users suffer from withdrawal symptoms (Quick reference guide: zaleplon, zolpidem and zopiclone for the short-term management of insomnia, 2004) Specific to TBI, an animal study has shown that three weeks of treatment with diazepam following injury resulted in prolonged functional deficits that did not recover over the examined 12-week period, while delaying this treatment regimen to start three weeks post-injury resulted in only minor transient deficits (Schallert, Hernandez, & Barth, 1986). In contrast, O'Dell et al. showed that BZ administration 15 minutes prior to or following FPI can greatly decrease mortality and improve outcome in rats, while pre-injury administration of the $GABA_A$ receptor antagonist bicuculline worsens outcome (O'Dell, Gibson, Wilson, DeFord, & Hamm, 2000). These studies suggest that GABA signaling and augmentation have a neuroprotective function in the acute phase; however, it may impair functional recovery when used chronically in the subacute and chronic phases of TBI. Based on this experimental literature, benzodiazepines may have a limited role for short-term use acutely after a significant TBI in which sleep or other behavioral disorders are problematic. However, at this time, the literature does not support uniform BZ use simply as a neuroprotectant in the acute phases of injury.

Non-Benzodiazepine Sedative-Hypnotics. Non-benzodiazepine sedative-hypnotics are a newer generation of drugs that act more selectively on the α1-containing $GABA_A$ receptor sub-units that are preferentially expressed in brain regions involved with sedation (Wamsley & Hunt, 1991). Non-benzodiazepines include zolpidem, zopiclone, and zaleplon, termed the "z-drugs," and they all have relatively short half-lives ranging from one hour for zaleplon to four to six hours for zopiclone. Zolpidem and zaleplon act more selectively than BZs on the α_1-$GABA_A$ receptor subunit that mediates sedation (Rudolph & Möhler, 2004), while zopiclone has been shown to cause less receptor desensitization, which would be expected to result in less tolerance and withdrawal symptoms (Doble, Martin, & Nutt, 2003). Several studies show that these properties may produce significant

clinical benefits or decrease adverse effects associated with short-acting BZs (Hajak, Muller, Wittchen, Pittrow, & Kirch, 2003; Leufkens, Lund, & Vermeeren, 2009; Verster, Veldhuijzen, & Volkerts, 2004; Allain, Bentué-Ferrer, Polard, Akwa, & Patat, 2005). In non-TBI subjects, bedtime administration with recommended doses of the z-drugs has less residual cognitive and psychomotor (driving) impairing effects than benzodiazepines in the following morning, with the shorter half-life agents, zaleplon and zolpidem, showing minimal impairments (Leufkens, Lund, & Vermeeren, 2009; Verster, Veldhuijzen, & Volkerts, 2004). Though cognitive and motor impairments are common to benzodiazepine hypnotics, and also z-drugs among elderly subjects, impairments caused by z-drugs are generally less problematic (Allain, Bentué-Ferrer, Polard, Akwa, & Patat, 2005). In the context of TBI, the efficacy and side-effects profile of z-drugs have not been demonstrated.

Interestingly, there are several small clinical and case studies in which zolpidem appears to enhance recovery from vegetative or minimally conscious states in some brain injured patients, a seemingly paradoxical effect for a hypnotic agent. However, this effect may be related to the propensity of zolpidem to cause parasomnias like sleepwalking. Clauss and Nel (2006) reported on three patients in permanent vegetative states as a result of moving vehicle accidents (MVAs) (n=2) or near drowning accidents (n=1) who responded favorably to zolpidem treatment with significant improvements in GCS and Ranchos Los Amigos Cognitive scores acutely after drug administration. Chronic treatment with zolpidem did not decrease efficacy or result in long-term side-effects, suggesting that a subset of patients with disorders of consciousness could benefit from zolpidem treatment (Clauss & Nel, 2006). The arousing effects of zolpidem correlate with evidence of increases in cerebral metabolism observed in postrolandic and frontal cortices following acute zolpidem treatment (Brefel-Courbon, et al., 2007). Though the effects of zolpidem on TBI recovery can be highly significant, reports of these effects are rare, as one prospective study found only 1 of 15 minimally conscious or vegetative patients responded positively to zolpidem treatment. With the limited data, it is unknown what factors determine responders from non-responders (Whyte & Myers, 2009). A recent functional imaging study in conjunction with zolpidem treatment suggests increased peri-injury regional blood flow, particularly for those without brainstem lesions as soon as one hour after administration. Changes in blood flow with daily treatment did not different from the acute response associated with the first dose, indicating a static "on-off" effect rather than gradual improvement (Du, Shan, Zhang, Zhong, Chen, & Cai, 2013).

Melatonin. Melatonin is a hormone that is secreted by the pineal gland to facilitate sleep and facilitate sleep/wake cycles. As such, melatonin supplements are commonly taken to treat sleep cycle alterations caused by shift work and jet lag. Melatonin is also a powerful antioxidant in itself and increases the activity and/or expression of several other antioxidants including glutathione peroxidase, and superoxide dismutase (Kotler, Rodriguez, Sainz, Antolin, & Menendez, 1998; Barlow-Walden, et al., 1995). In vitro and in vivo experiments have shown that melatonin protects against oxidative damage and neurological deficits in several models of oxidative stress including 6-OHDA, D-galactose, and beta-amyloid peptide 25–35 toxicity (Mayo, Sainz, Uria, Antolin, Esteban, & Rodriguez, 2007; Shen, Xu, Wei, Sun, Yang, & Dong, 2002; Shen, et al., 2002). Furthermore, melatonin reportedly can attenuate infarct volume, apoptosis, oxidative damage, and neurological deficits in several models of stroke (Reiter, Sainz, Lopez-Burillo, Mayo, Manchester, & Tan, 2003). In a mouse model of TBI, one study has shown that acute melatonin administration reduced neurological deficits (Mesenge, Margail, Verrecchia, Allix, Boulu, & Plotkine, 1998).

The secretion of melatonin is regulated by activity of pacemaker cells in the suprachiasmatic nucleus (SCN) of the hypothalamus. Ambient light highly influences the SCN pacemaker activity and thereby indirectly melatonin secretion (Klien & Weller, 1972; Lewy, Wehr, Goodwin, Newsome, & Markey, 1980). In addition, the stress hormone cortisol and certain pharmacological agents like beta-blockers, alcohol, benzodiazepines, and ibuprofen

attenuate melatonin secretion (Zisapel, 1999; Yuwiler, 1989).

As mentioned earlier, hospitalized patients, including critically ill patients, commonly experience sleep disturbances. Though a variety of factors contribute to altered sleeping patterns in this population, the desynchronization and reduction of normal melatonin secretion that is commonly found in ICU patients may contribute to these sleep disturbances as well (Shilo et al., 2000; Olofsson, Alling, Lundberg, & Malmros, 2004). A few small studies in the ICU population show sleep quality and duration can improve with the use of melatonin (Bourne, Mills, & Minelli, 2008; Shilo et al., 2000).

In the general population, melatonin levels are altered in subjects with abnormal circadian rhythms such as those that have offset sleep schedules as in DSPS (Shibui, Uchiyama, & Okawa, 1999; Rodenbeck, Huether, Rüther, & Hajak, 2007). In non-TBI subjects with DSPS, melatonin can have efficacy in reaching desired sleep times (Nagtegaal, Kerkhof, Smits, & Van Der Meer, 1998). Furthermore, nocturnal melatonin levels are often decreased in elderly non-TBI populations, and this phenomenon is thought to play a role in precipitating insomnia that often occurs with age (Wurtman, 2000). This type of insomnia has also been shown to be effectively treated with melatonin, with physiological doses (0.3mg) having greater sleep restorative effects than hypo- or supra-physiological doses (0.1 or 3.0mg, respectively) (Zhdanova, Wurtman, Regan, Taylor, Shi, & Leclair, 2001).

The literature on the use of melatonin in the TBI population to treat sleep disturbances is largely lacking. However, altered melatonin rhythms have been reported in a few studies in the TBI population, primarily in subjects that had sleep disturbances (Nagtegaal, Kerkhof, Smits, Swart, & van der Meer, 1997; Shekleton, Parcell, Redman, Ponsford, & Rajaratnam, 2010; Boivin, James, Santo, Caliyurt, & Chalk, 2003). Small studies conducted on the general TBI population have shown decreases in melatonin levels compared to healthy controls. However, melatonin levels are primarily reduced in the subset of TBI patients that also have documented sleep disturbances (Shekleton, Parcell, Redman, Ponsford, & Rajaratnam, 2010; Steele, Rajaratnam, Redman, & Ponsford, 2005). A few studies have shown that melatonin can be effective for the management of DSPS following TBI, with benefits in decreasing sleep latency and subjective reports of feeling more refreshed in the morning (Nagtegaal, Kerkhof, Smits, Swart, & van der Meer, 1997; Nagtegaal, Kerkhof, Smits, & Van Der Meer, 1998).

Valerian. Herbal remedies such as valerian, chamomile, melatonin, and lavender are sometimes used to promote sleep. These herbal supplements have mostly mild effects, with limited scientific evidence for the treatment of insomnia even in the general population. Valerian treatment for insomnia goes back thousands of years, and its use been described by ancient Greek and Roman physicians Hippocrates and Galen. The root of *Valeriana officinalis* contains active hypnotic and anxiolytic compounds. The basic scientific study of its mechanism of action has focused on its effects on the GABAergic system. Valerian may act to inhibit GABA uptake and promote the release of GABA (Oritz, Nieves-Natal, & Chavez, 1999). Two constituents of valerian extract, valernic acid and valerenol, bind to GABA$_A$ receptors and enhance GABA signaling similar to benzodiazepines (Benke, et al., 2009; Khom, et al., 2007). Unlike benzodiazepines, however, valerian has been shown to preserve cognitive and psychomotor performance, and it is non-addictive with minimal side-effects or withdrawal effects (Hallam, Olver, McGrath, & Norman, 2003; Kuhlmann, Berger, Podzuweit, & Schmidt, 1999). No standard dosing for valerian exists, but 300 mg to 900 mg of valerian extract taken from 30 minutes to two hours before bedtime is within the normal range of use. Valerian may not be particularly useful in alleviating acute insomnia, as it has been shown that it may take several days or longer to see a significant effect on improving sleep (Donath, Quispe, Diefenbach, Maurer, Fietze, & Roots, 2000). Since benzodiazepines can impair plasticity, valerian may be an alternative in the TBI population in managing insomnia. However, specific research has not addressed how valerian may impact recovery and cognition.

Trazodone. Trazodone is a sedating antidepressant that primarily acts as a 5-HT$_{2A}$ receptor antagonist with lower affinity antagonism on the serotonin transporter (SERT) and the 5-HT$_{2C}$ receptor, and partial agonism on the 5-HT$_{1A}$ receptor. Trazodone also inhibits α-adrenergic receptors without effects on the norepinephrine transporter. Compared to other tricyclic antidepressants (TCAs), trazodone has significantly less anticholinergic effects, making it a particularly attractive treatment for adjunct treatment for depression in the TBI population, especially when accompanied by insomnia or anxiety. Insomnia is often optimally treated with trazodone doses between 50 and 100 mg/day in non-TBI populations, which is less than the 150 mg/day dose recommended for its antidepressant effects (Mashiko, et al., 1999). However, studies suggest that higher doses (150-600 mg/day) also improve sleep efficiency, sleep time, and decrease intra-sleep awakenings (Scharf & Sachais, 1990; Mouret, Lemoine, Minuit, Benkelfat, & Renardet, 1988). Because trazodone is a phenylpiperazine compound with a slightly different mechanism of action from SSRIs that act mainly on SERT, it can be used effectively to augment the action of other antidepressants, to alleviate depression and promote sleep (Mendelson, 2005).

Self-Medication. Alcohol, over-the-counter sleep medications, and other remedies are often used to induce sleep. Many of these self-medication procedures may have unfavorable consequences in the TBI population. Over-the-counter sleep-aids often contain diphenhydramine or doxylamine, both of which are antihistamines with anticholinergic properties that may have negative effects on patients with TBI who have compromised cholinergic function. Alcohol abuse is common in the TBI population that both predates and/or occurs after the injury. Alcohol abuse can impair rehabilitation participation, cognitive functioning, and also has many adverse interactions with many drugs commonly prescribed for TBI relevant problems. Alcohol is often used as a sleep aid. Though it may increase sleep time at low doses, higher doses can have a detrimental effect or no effect on sleep (Stone, 1980). Alcohol may also promote wakefulness in the second half of the night when the majority of REM sleep normally occurs (Roth, Roehrs, Zorick, & Conway, 1985). Furthermore, long-term alcohol use as a sleep aid leads to tolerance, addiction, and worsening of insomnia by decreasing deep sleep. As such, practitioners should actively engage and educate their population with TBI regarding alcohol utilization and its effects on sleep and recovery from the injury.

Neurobiology and Clinical Course of Agitation and Aggression

Agitation is an irritable and hyper-aroused state of consciousness that often manifests itself in excessive and extraneous verbal and motor behavior. Agitation can escalate to aggression depending on a number of factors including personal disposition, confusion, poor impulse control, substance abuse, drug interactions, hallucinations, and delusions. Agitation is a normal phase of behavior after moderate to severe TBI encountered as patients progress through different stages of recovery outlined in the Ranchos Los Amigos Scale (Hagan, Malkmus, & Durham, 1979; Denny-Brown, 1945). Restoration of cognitive functions following emergence from coma often precedes improvements in agitation, in line with the idea that the post-traumatic confusional state contributes to agitation (Rakier, Guilburd, Soustiel, Zaaroor, & Feinsod, 1995). Agitation warranting pharmacological intervention has been estimated to occur in up to 30% of severe TBI survivors, with a recent study estimating that agitation in general occurs in 70% of rehabilitation inpatients with varying severities of TBI (Mysiw, Jackson, & Corrigan, 1988; Nott, Chapparo, & Baguley, 2006).

The neural circuitry for agitation and aggression involves various neurotransmitter systems and brain regions, with many of these regions lying in the ventral anterior and medial temporal regions of the brain that are prone to damage from TBI. The orbitofrontal cortex participates in decision making and processing the emotional value of actions, with damage to this region leading to disinhibited and socially unacceptable behaviors including aggression (Kringelbach, 2005). Structures in the medial aspects of the temporal lobe such as the amygdala form part of the limbic circuitry, which also plays a strong role in aggression (Decoster, Herbert, Meyerhoff, & Potegal, 1996).

The prevalence of aggressive behaviors can be as high as 33.7% within the first six months after injury (Tateno, Jorge, & Robinson, 2003). In the subacute phase following TBI, aggression may occur during the confused/agitated phase (Kaydan, Mysiw, Bogner, Corrigan, Fugate, & Clinchot, 2004), in which patients are unaware of their behavior from moment to moment and may have clear psychiatric disturbances. Causes of aggression in the early phases following TBI include the injury itself, substance abuse, pre-morbid psychiatric disturbances, personality, or drug-induced side-effects. In this stage, pharmacotherapy usually follows unsuccessful attempts at reducing the behavior through environmental means, and medications are mainly directed at aborting aggressive behaviors with short-acting benzodiazepines or neuroleptics.

Unlike the acute/subacute phase, aggression in the chronic phase is more likely to occur in a normal state of consciousness, which can be particularly distressing to caregivers and detrimental to social reintegration. However, aggression in the chronic phase is often impulsive rather than planned and premeditated, suggesting there may be problems associated with behavioral suppression (Brooks, Campsie, Symington, Beattie, & McKinlay, 1987). Chronic aggression after severe TBI is strongly correlated with pre-morbid aggressive behavior, leading to the hypothesis that injury may expose a pre-existing attribute (Greve, Sherwin, Stanford, Mathias, Love, & Ramzinski, 2001). However, aggression can also be caused by the injury itself, as damage to the prefrontal cortex, hypothalamus, and paralimbic temporal lobe regions are linked to aggression (Brower & Price, 2001; Anderson & Silver, 1998; Tonkonogy, 1991).

Premeditated aggression that occurs in a clear state of mind may not be particularly amenable to pharmacological intervention. However, aggression that occurs in a psychotic episode and impulsive aggression may be managed with behavioral and pharmacological interventions. Aggression involves the interplay of NE, DA, GABA, and 5-HT systems, and pharmacological means of controlling aggression are often aimed at these systems.

Dopaminergic Mechanisms and Therapies. The mesolimbic dopaminergic system participates in motivated behaviors that play a permissive role in aggression. Dopamine signaling through post-synaptic D2 receptors modulates arousal and stress responses, thus D2 antagonists like haloperidol and risperidone are commonly used to treat agitation or aggression acutely or of psychotic origin. As such, haloperidol is the most commonly used (or misused) agent to treat post-traumatic agitation, particularly in the acute phase (Vincent, Zimmerman, & van Haren, 1986). Unfortunately, these drugs are often used for their sedative rather than antipsychotic properties. Tolerance to these agents often develops, requiring larger doses that are associated with higher prevalence of side-effects such as akathisia, which is commonly mistaken as agitation and tardive dyskinesia. Based on these side-effects, haloperidol use for the agitation or aggression management is not recommended.

However, all antipsychotics should be used with caution in the TBI population as antipsychotics interfere with cognition and may delay the recovery process. Clinically, TBI patients administered haloperidol to control agitation after injury can have significantly longer durations of PTA (Rao, Jellinek, & Woolston, 1985). Similarly, haloperidol and risperidone, both of which have high affinity for the D2 receptor, impairs spatial learning in rodent models of TBI (Kline, Hoffman, Cheng, Zafonte, & Massucci, 2008; Kline, Massucci, Zafonte, Dixon, DeFeo, & Rogers, 2007; Wilson, Gibson, & Hamm, 2003). It is unclear whether the newer generation of antipsychotics poses great advantages over typical antipsychotics in this population. However, because some atypical antipsychotics have significantly less D2 antagonism and have mechanisms that involve other neurotransmitter systems, these newer atypical antipsychotics may have greater efficacy with less adverse effects in the TBI population (Elovic, Jasey, & Eisenberg, 2008). As an example, the atypical antipsychotic quetiapine has lesser effects on the D2 receptor and improves cognitive functions while reducing aggression scores in a small clinical study (Kim & Bijlani, 2006).

GABAergic Mechanisms and Anticonvulsant Treatments. In addition to their use with sleep disorders, benzodiazepines (BZs) are sometimes used to manage acute agitation and aggression. In rare cases, BZs can paradoxically cause increased hostility and agitation. Allosteric activation of $GABA_A$ receptor with BZ exhibits an inverted U-shaped dose response curve as it relates to aggression, with low and high doses decreasing aggression and moderate doses evoking aggression (Miczek, Fish, de Bold, & de Almeida, 2002).

Benzodiazepine usage in injured populations should be used cautiously. Preclinical studies have shown that chronic diazepam administration can impede functional recovery permanently (Schallert, Hernandez, & Barth, 1986). Brain injury may increase the susceptibility to the motoric side-effects of BZs such as incoordination in humans (Silver, Yudofsky, & Anderson, Aggressive disorders, 2005). Due to the detrimental effects on cognition, paradoxical effects of increasing agitation and aggression in some, and possible hindrance of neurological recovery, BZ treatment is not ideal, except perhaps during the very early stages following injury where it has been shown to minimize functional deficits and histological damage in animal models of TBI by presumably mitigating excitotoxicity associated with the initial insult (O'Dell, Gibson, Wilson, DeFord, & Hamm, 2000). Since BZ only control agitation and aggression and not treat it, other means of treating underlying psychiatric causes should be sought and treated.

Some anticonvulsant medications, like valproic acid and carbamazepine, can have efficacy in treating pathological aggression in TBI patients with and without epileptic disorders. Both drugs act to inhibit voltage-gated sodium channels and to augment GABA neurotransmission. Carbamazepine may be particularly useful in the TBI population as a double-blind pilot study on assaultive behavior in frontal lobe-damaged subjects and controls demonstrated a preferential improvement in cognitive, affective, and behavioral measures in the injured subjects (Foster, Hillbrand, & Chi, 1989). In another small case series of 10 patients with agitation and outbursts following severe TBI, 8 of the 10 patients showed behavioral improvements in an eight-week trial of carbamazepine (Azouvi, Jokic, Attal, Denys, Markabi, & Bussel, 1999). Though valproic acid is primarily an anticonvulsant, it also has broad ranging effects on behaviors associated with other affective disorders, including cases where these behaviors were resistant to other agents including carbamazepine (Geracioti, 1994; Mazure, Druss, & Cellar, 1992; Wroblewski, Joseph, Kupfer, & Kalliel, 1997). Also, drugs like valproic acid may confer some effects on behavior/mood due to their ability to modify epigenetic markings regulating gene transcription (Costa et al., 2009; Machado-Vieira, Ibrahim & Zarate, 2011).

Early use of anticonvulsants to manage agitation and aggression may also be beneficial in preventing seizures as well. Supportive evidence for the prolonged seizure prophylactic use of any anticonvulsants is limited. In fact, preclinical evidence suggests that chronic phenytoin administration following experimental TBI decreases hippocampal cell survival and impedes cognitive and motor recovery (Darrah, et al., 2010) Clinically, prolonged use of phenytoin has also been associated poorer cognitive and motor performance (Dikmen, Temkin, Miller, Machamer, & Winn, 1991; Pullianen & Jokelainen, 1995). Interestingly, valproate use is also linked clinically to worse cognition after TBI (Massagli, 1991). Levetiracetam is a newer anticonvulsant gaining popularity in seizure prophylaxis and treatment after TBI. Unlike phenytoin, long term treatment with Levetiracetam confers multiple behavioral and histological benefits in preclinical models, which may be mediated by beneficial effects on chronic neuroinflammation and normalization of glutamatergic systems (Zou, Brayer, Hurwitz, Fowler, & Wagner, 2013). Further, preliminary evidence suggests that in both epilepsy and also aging populations, Levetiracetam may have beneficial effects on cognition (Zhou, Zhang, Tian, Xiao, Stefan, & Zhou, 2008; Cumbo & Ligori, 2010), while conferring some benefits on mood and other behavioral symptoms (Mazza, Martini, Scoppetta, & Mazza, 2007; Farooq, Bhatt, Majid, Gupta, Khasnis, & Kassab, 2009). However more work is needed to fully assess any potential benefit of Levitiracetam with behavioral management after TBI.

Serotonergic Mechanisms and Treatments

The role of the serotonergic system has been most studied, and it has the strongest link to aggression. Serotonin neurotransmission in the PFC activates this brain region to inhibit brain circuitries mediating aggressive behavior (Tobin & Logue, 1994). Consistent with this idea, 5-HT levels in the PFC increase when rodents display aggressive behaviors (van Erp & Miczek, 2000). In humans, reduced activation of the PFC and low CSF levels of the 5-HT metabolite, 5-hydroxyindoleacetic acid (5-HIAA) are correlated to aggressive behavior, while daily treatment with the SSRI fluoxetine was shown to increase metabolism in the PFC and reduce aggression (Coccaro & Kavoussi, 1997; New, et al., 2004; Brown, Goodwin, Ballenger, & Goyer, 1979).

There is some sparse evidence for trazodone in treating aggression associated with organic brain syndromes, including for some cases in which aggression was resistant to neuroleptics (Simpson & Foster, 1986; Pinner & Rich, 1988). Buspirone is a $5-HT_{1A}$ partial receptor agonist that is primarily implicated for managing anxiety, but also can reduce outbursts and aggression in patients with organic-related psychiatric diagnoses and brain injury (Stainslav, Fabre, Crimson, & Childs, 1994; Gualtieri, 1991). Several preclinical studies suggest that $5-HT_{1A}$ receptor agonism administered acutely after injury has neuroprotective effects and improves cognitive recovery following brain injury (Kline, Yu, Massucci, Zafonte, & Dixon, 2002; Kline, Yu, Horváth, Marion, & Dixon, 2001). However, studies in non-injured rats suggest that $5-HT_{1A}$ receptor agonism impairs spatial navigation and affective memory (Liang, Tsui, Tyan, & Chiang, 1998; Carli & Samanin, 1992). Serotonergic agents like the SSRI fluoxetine and sertraline improve anger, irritability, or impulsive aggression in cases of personality disorders (Coccaro & Kavoussi, 1997; Salzman, et al., 1995; Markovitz, Calabrese, Schulz, & Meltzer, 1991; Cornelius, Soloff, Perel, & Ulrich, 1990). Furthermore, chronic fluoxetine treatment resulted in improvements on cognitive tests of attention and working memory in a small pilot study on a heterogeneous group of head-injured subjects with no or moderate depression (Horsfield, Rosse, Tomasino, Schwartz, Mastropaolo, & Deutsch, 2002). However, these improvements were only observed in a subset of cognitive measures, and preclinical study on rats failed to show improvements in cognitive or motor recovery following TBI with chronic fluoxetine treatment (Wilson & Hamm, 2002). Though SSRIs may have limited beneficial effects on cognition and behavior, these effects may be limited or are secondary to their possible effects on mood.

The Etiology and Presentation of Post-Traumatic Depression

TBI can damage neural circuitries that increase susceptibility to depression, like the paralimbic regions of the prefrontal cortex, an area which can be hypo-metabolic in patients with primary depression (Mayberg, Lewis, Regenold, & Wagner, 1994). Depression after TBI is associated with decreased gray matter volumes in the dorsolateral and ventrolateral prefrontal cortex (Jorge, Robinson, Moser, Tateno, Crespo-Facorro, & Arndt, 2004; Hudak, Warner, Marquez de la Plata, Moore, Harper, & Diaz-Arrastia, 2011). Disruptions of these monoaminergic systems, particularly 5-HT, may underlie the neural basis of many cases of depression. The frontal lobe, which serves as a conduit for many of these monoaminergic innervations to the cortex, is susceptible to damage from TBI (Rosenthal, Christensen, & Ross, 1998). Following moderate to severe TBI, these neurotransmitter systems undergo an acute surge in activity, and evidence suggests that some of these systems are chronically dysfunctional (Busto, Dietrich, Globus, Alonso, & Ginsberg, 1997; Wagner, et al., 2005b; Bales, Wagner, Kline, & Dixon, 2009); however, the chronic state of the serotonergic system after injury has not been thoroughly investigated. Evaluating and interpreting available data is complex in that serotonin regulates NE and DA neurotransmission, where depressive symptoms overlap with cognitive dysfunction in domains like attention and arousal, or reward and motivation.

In addition to TBI mediated pathology, other biological, psychological, and social factors can cause and exacerbate depression. In the diathesis-stress model, there are both genetic and biological factors that predispose one to depression, which can be triggered by stressors and environmental factors. There is strong support for this model in depression as it has been shown that genetics influence susceptibility to depression; a strong correlation between a polymorphism in the promoter region of the 5-HT transporter gene that decreases its expression has been associated with developing depressive symptoms following stressful life experiences (Kendler, et al., 1995; Caspi, et al., 2003). However, a study examining depression following TBI failed to show a similar association in the 5-HT transporter polymorphism (Chan, et al., 2008). Interestingly, recent work suggests that homozygosity for the long-allele (higher transporter expression) is associated with higher risk of depression in moderate to severe TBI patients with no history of mood disorders at six months post-injury (Failla et al., 2013). Similarly, variable associations between the 5-HT transporter polymorphisms and depression in Parkinson's and Alzhemier's disease patients have been observed (Assal, Alarcon, Solomon, Masterman, Geschwind, & Cummings, 2004; Micheli, et al., 2006; Burn, Tiangyou, Allcock, Davison, & Chinnery, 2006; Mossner et al., 2001). Thus, genetic factors that predict depression in a general population may lose association in psychiatrically complex TBI populations as other factors could play larger roles. There is growing interest in determining biological factors that could predict drug responses in individuals. A recent study has shown that single nuclear polymorphisms in the brain derived neurotrophic factor (BDNF) and methylene tetrahydrofolate reductase (MTHFR) genes were able to predict greater responses to citalopram in the treatment of PTD, whereas polymorphisms in the 5-HT transporter-linked promoter region was able to predict adverse events (Lanctôt et al., 2010).

Aside from genetically mediated associations with PTD, it is no surprise that the stressors associated with TBI can cause depression. The adjustment to TBI can be immensely psychologically taxing. Substance abuse, unemployment, and impoverishment can further contribute to PTD (Seel, Kreutzer, Rosenthal, Hammond, Corrigan, & Black, 2003). The relationship between injury severity and depression is unclear, with one study suggesting that individuals with mild TBI and persistent neurologic symptoms are more likely to have depression than people with severe TBI (Alexander, 1992). Within the first year of injury, an estimated 33–51% of subjects with TBI experience major depressive disorder compared to a rate of 6.7% in the general population (Jorge, Robinson, Moser, Tateno, Crespo-Facorro, & Arndt, 2004; Bombardier, Fann, Temkin, Esselman, Barber, & Dikmen, 2010; Kessler, Chiu, Demler, Merikangas, & Walters, 2005). In chronic stages of TBI, when awareness of deficits typically improves and social support systems may wane, depression can be exacerbated, with a cumulative prevalence of major depression estimated to be 61% in the chronic phase (Hibbard, Uysal, Kepler, Bogdany, & Silver, 1998; Holsinger, et al., 2002; Fordyce, Roueche, & Prigatano, 1983). Anxiety, aggression, fatigue, poor concentration and impaired social functioning are commonly observed in depressed TBI subjects, with feelings of hopelessness, worthlessness, and difficulty enjoying activities being factors most differentiating TBI patients with clinical depression from those without (Jorge, Robinson, Moser, Tateno, Crespo-Facorro, & Arndt, 2004; Kreutzer, Seel, & Gourley, 2001; Seel, Kreutzer, Rosenthal, Hammond, Corrigan, & Black, 2003).

Treatment of Post-Traumatic Depression

Treatment of post-traumatic depression (PTD) has not been systematically evaluated across all of the available options, especially with the newer classes of selective serotonin reuptake inhibitors (SSRIs) and serotonin agonist/reuptake inhibitors (SARIs). Currently, treatment approaches for PTD are largely derived from knowledge of treating depressive symptoms in the general and stroke populations. Previously, depression treatments relied primarily on tricyclic antidepressants (TCAs), but these drugs have largely been replaced by the newer generation of selective serotonin reuptake inhibitors (SSRIs) and serotonin-norepinephrine reuptake inhibitors (SNRI), among other medications. Many TCAs increase the risk of seizures, and their strong anticholinergic muscarinic effects can impair attention and memory (Wroblewski, McColgan, Smith, Whyte, & Singer, 1990). Despite the possibilities for depression treatment post-TBI, large scale clinical trials and comparative effectiveness studies are lacking to provide clear guidance on how to treat individuals with post-traumatic depression (Barker-Collo, Starkey, & Theadom, 2013; Warden et al., 2006).

Sertraline is an SSRI with weak inhibitory effects on the dopamine transporter, and it has been shown to not only treat depression, but also improve cognitive efficiency and verbal and visual memory (Fann, Uomoto, & Katon, 2001; Bolden-Watson & Richelson, 1993). However, in 11 severely injured patients, sertraline (100mg/day for 2 weeks) did not improve arousal or attentional impairments when treatment was initiated within two weeks following injury (Meythaler, Depalma, Devivo, Guin-Renfroe, & Novack, 2001). In an open-label trial involving 17 adult patients with brain injuries of various etiologies including TBI, sertraline treatment improved depressive symptoms in all patients. Of significance, 11 of the 17 patients failed to show a response to a different SSRI treatment (Turner-Stokes, Hassan, Pierce, & Clegg, 2002). In mild TBI patients suffering from major depression between 3 and 24 months following injury, treatment responses were observed in 13 of 15 subjects, with 10 subjects achieving remission scores on the Hamilton Rating Scale for Depression (Fann, Uomoto, & Katon, 2000). Sertraline can also reduce irritability and aggression after TBI (Kant, Smith-Seemiller, & Zeiler, 1998). Fluoxetine has also had some beneficial effects in several small open label studies, including one where benefits were noted with attention, psychomotor speed, and working memory (Cassidy, 1989; Horsfield, Rosse, Tomasino, Schwartz, Mastropaolo, & Deutsch, 2002). Citalopram is a newer SSRI that has similar response and remission rates in treating depression in TBI and non-TBI populations (Rapoport, Chan, Lanctot, Herrmann, McCullagh, & Feinstein, 2008). Effectiveness of other new SSRIs are largely lacking for the treatment of depression following TBI, thus use of newer agents like venlafaxine, mirtazapine, or bupropion must be used without clinical studies available for guidance of risks and benefits of treatment. Exercise has been cited as a potent intervention for MDD treatment, with similar or slightly greater effectiveness compared to SSRI treatment (Hoffman et al., 2011). However, exercise RCT studies in PTD are rather sparse, and those that have been conducted have met with limited success (Hoffman et al., 2010; Bateman, Culpan, Pickering, Powell, Scott, & Greenwood, 2001).

Psychostimulants have been advocated for use in treating fatigue that may or may not be associated with depression following TBI (Challman & Lipsky, 2000). Furthermore, there is some evidence for the use of MPH for elevating mood following TBI (Gualtieri & Evans, Stimulant treatment for the neurobehavioral sequalae of traumatic brain injury, 1988). Also, apathy is a disturbance of motivation that can be secondary to depression or other conditions. Treating apathy as something distinct from depression may be pharmacologically advantageous, as antidepressants may resolve depression but have minimal effects on decreased motivation. On the other hand, psychostimulants may affect apathy but have limited effects on depression (Watanabe, Martin, DeLeon, Gaviria, Pavel, & Trepashko, 1995). Treating disorders of diminished motivation may maximize participation in rehabilitation. However, the use of psychostimulants and concomitant TCAs may increase the risk of seizures and thus should be used with caution (Wroblewski, Leary, Phelan, Whyte, & Manning, 1992). The successful combination of MPH with SSRIs without major side-effects have been reported in several studies; however, two case studies in children have suggested that the combination can cause seizures in a few patients (Lavretsky, Park, Siddarth, Kumar, & Reynolds, 2006; Findling, 1996; Stoll, Pillay, Diamond, Workum, & Cole, 1996; Kafka & Hennen, 2000; Feeney & Klykylo, 1997; Schertz & Steinberg, 2008).

Emotional Lability

Emotional lability is a chronic disturbance of emotional states rather than disturbances of mood as in depression. Often subjects with emotional lability may exhibit exaggerated emotional reactions to even minor sentimental stimuli without any persistent change in mood. Following TBI, the presence of emotional lability has been estimated to be around 21% in the year following injury (Jorge and Robinson 2003). A similar disturbance is pathological crying and/or laughing (PLC), a disturbance in emotional expression in which uncontrollable crying and laughing episodes may occur many times throughout the day without changes in affective states. PLC following TBI is infrequently encountered, with an estimated prevalence of 5.3% (Zeilig et al 1996). The neural circuitries in the control of mood and affect are similar, and thus, many of the medications used to treat emotional lability and PLC are similar to those used to treat depression (Arciniegas, Topkoff, & Silver, 2000). As with depression, SSRIs are preferred over TCAs. SSRIs like fluoxetine, sertraline, and paroxetine are used to treat emotional lability that develops following stroke or TBI (Nahas, Arlinghaus, Kotrla, Clearman, & George, 1998; Sloan, Brown, & Pentland, 1992). Lower doses than typically used for depression may often be used to treat emotional lability effectively, and treatment response is often observed in less than one week (Sloan, Brown, & Pentland, 1992).

Noradrenergic and dopaminergic agents may also have some effects on emotional lability. Early treatment of PLC (<1 year after onset) may prevent it from becoming a chronic condition that requires continual treatment (Müller, Murai, Bauer-Wittmund, & von Cramon, 1999). One case study on a subject in the chronic phase of TBI showed improvements in memory, attention, and emotional stability following either MPH or AMPH treatment (Evans, Gualtieri, & Patterson, 1987). Thus, if emotional lability is compounded with diminished motivation and cognitive impairments, psychostimulants like MPH potentially may be effective in treating both sets of symptoms.

Anxiety Disorders

Anxiety commonly occurs following TBI. Anxiety may develop as a consequence of the brain injury itself, the psychological reaction to deficits following injury, or the presence of other social and environmental factors. Generalized anxiety disorders are often co-morbid with depression in individuals with TBI (Jorge, Robinson, Starkstein, & Arndt, 1993). Lesions in the right hemisphere are associated with anxious depression, whereas non-anxious depressive subjects often have left anterior lesions. Furthermore, anxious depression tends to have a longer median duration than non-anxious depression (7.5 mo. vs. 1.5 mo. respectively). Although often presenting together, dissociation of the two may represent distinct disorders that are sensitive to different pharmacological treatments (Jorge, Robinson, Starkstein, & Arndt, 1993).

In order to control anxiety acutely, short-half-life benzodiazepine drugs like lorazepam may be helpful. In TBI, benzodiazepine usage should be kept limited because of psychomotor-impairing effects and the propensity for physical dependence. The anxiolytic effects of benzodiazepine are primarily mediated by α_2-GABA$_A$ receptors as opposed to the sedative effects which are mediated through α_1-GABA$_A$ receptors (Löw, et al., 2000). However, current conventional benzodiazepines are nonselective for α_1 and α_2-GABA$_A$ receptors. Interestingly, the α_2-GABA$_A$ receptors are also expressed in the dorsal horn and motor neurons in the spinal cord, consistent with the muscle relaxant effects mediated through the α_2-GABA$_A$ receptor in animal models (Bohlhalter, Weinmann, Möhler, & Fritschy, 1996; Crestani, Löw, Keist, Mandelli, Möhler, & Rudolph, 2001). As such, benzodiazepines can be used to manage muscle spasticity that can develop following TBI. However, due to adverse effects of benzodiazepines, other agents like dantrolene, which inhibits muscle calcium release, or baclofen, which acts on GABA$_B$ receptors, are recommended.

Treatment of chronic anxiety disorders heavily relies upon SSRIs, though no controlled clinical trials have evaluated the efficacy of these agents in the case of anxiety disorders caused by TBI. Busiprone is an agent that is moderately effective in treating generalized anxiety disorder. The anxiolytic effects of buspirone have a long latency of onset of about two or three weeks, which contrasts its own rapid actions on post-traumatic agitation (Gualtieri, 1991). Buspirone is used as an adjunct to SSRIs to treat anxiety disorders that follow TBI.

References

Aaron, J., Carlisle, C., Carskadon, M., Meyer, T., Hill, N., & Millman, R. (1996). Environmental noise as a cause of sleep disruption in an intermediate respiratory care unit. *Sleep, 19,* 707–710.

Aaron, J., Carlisle, C., Carskadon, M., Meyer, T., Hill, N., & Millman, R. (2001). Basic Cognition. In D. B. Aciniegas, & T. P. Beresford, *Neuropsychiatry: An Introductory approach* (pp. 32–51). Cambridge, UK: Cambridge University Press.

Alexander, M. P. (1992). Neuropsychiatric correlates of persistent postconcussive syndrome. *Journal of Head Trauma Rehabilitation, 7*(2), 60–69.

Allain, H., Bentué-Ferrer, D., Polard, E., Akwa, Y., & Patat, A. (2005). Postural instability and consequent falls and hip fractures associated with use of hypnotics in the elderly: A comparative review. *Drugs & Aging, 22*(9), 749–765.

Allen, R. M. (1983). Role of amantadine in the management of neuroleptic-induced extrapyramidal syndromes: Overview and pharmacology. *Clinical Neuropharmacology, 6,* S64–73.

Allman, P. (1992). Drug treatment of emotionalism following brain damage. *Journal of the Royal Society of Medicine, 85*(7), 423–424.

Anderson, K., & Silver, J. M. (1998). Modulation of Anger and Aggression. *Seminars in Clinical Neuropsychiatry, 3*(3), 232–242.

Arciniegas, D. B. (2003). The cholinergic hypothesis of cognitive impairment caused by traumatic brain injury. *Current Psychology Reports, 5,* 391–399.

Arciniegas, D. B., Topkoff, J. L., Anderson, C. A., Filley, C. M., & Adler, L. E. (2002). Low-dose donepezil normalizes P50 physiology in traumatic brain injury patients. *Journal of Neuropsychiatry and Clinical Neurosciences, 14,* 115.

Arciniegas, D. B., Topkoff, J., & Silver, J. M. (2000). Neuropsychiatric aspects of traumatic brain injury. *Current Treatment Options in Neurology, 2,* 167–186.

Arciniegas, D., Adler, L., Topkoff, J., et al. (1999). Attention and memory dysfucntion after traumatic brain injury: Cholinergic mechanisms, sensory gating, and a hypothesis for further investigation. *Brain Injury, 13,* 1–13.

Arciniegas, D., Olincy, A., Topkoff, J., et al. (2000). Impaired auditory gating and P50 nonsuppression following traumatic brain injury. *Journal of Neuropsychiatry and Clinical Neurosciences, 12,* 77–85.

Arciniegas, D., Olincy, A., Topkoff, J., McRae, K., Cawthra, E., Filley, C. M., et al. (2000). Impaired auditory gaiting and P50 nonsupression following traumatic brain injury. *Journal of Neuropsychiatry and Clinical Neurosciences, 12*(1), 77–85.

Arenth, P. M., Russell, K. C., Scanlon, J. M., Kessler, L. J., & Ricker, J. H. (2012). Encoding and recognition after traumatic brain injury: Neuropsychological and functional magnetic resonance imaging findings. *Journal of Clinical and Experimental Neuropsychology, 34*(4), 333–344.

Assal, F., Alarcon, M., Solomon, E. C., Masterman, D., Geschwind, D. H., & Cummings, J. L. (2004). Association of the serotonin transporter and receptor gene polymorphisms in neuropsychiatric symptoms in Alzheimer disease. *Archives of Neurology, 61*, 1249–1253.

Ayalon, L., Borodkin, M. A., Dishon, M. A., Kanety, H., & Dagan, Y. (2007). Circadian rhythm sleep disorders following mild traumatic brain injury. *Neurology, 68*, 1136–1140.

Azouvi, P., Jokic, C., Attal, N., Denys, P., Markabi, S., & Bussel, B. (1999). Carbamazepine in agitation and aggressive behaviour following severe closed-head injury: Results of an open trial. *Brain Injury, 13*(10), 797–804.

Azuma, S., Kodama, T., Honda, K., & Inoue, S. (1996). State-dependent changes of extracellular glutamate in medial preoptic area in freely behaving rats. *Neuroscience Letters, 214*(2-3), 179–182.

Bales, J. W., Wagner, A. K., Kline, A. E., & Dixon, C. E. (2009). Persistent cognitive dysfunction after traumatic brain injury: A dopamine hypothesis. *Neuroscience and Behavioral Reviews, 33*, 981–1003.

Barker, M. J., Greenwood, K. M., Jackson, M., & Crowe, S. F. (2004). Persistence of cognitive effects after withdrawal from long-term benzodiazepine use: A meta-analysis. *Archives of Clinical Neuropsychology, 19*(3), 437–453.

Barker-Collo, S., Starkey, N., & Theadom, A. (2013). Treatment for depression following mild traumatic brain injury in adults: A meta-analysis. *Brain Injury, 27*(10), 1124–1133.

Barlow-Walden, L. R., Reiter, R. J., Abe, M., Pablos, A., Menendez-Pelaez, L., Chen, D., et al. (1995). Melatonin stimulates brain glutathione peroxidase activity. *Neurochemistry International, 26*(5), 497–502.

Barron, J., & Sandman, C. A. (1985). Paradoxical excitement to sedative-hypnotics in mentally retarded clients. *American Journal of Mental Deficiency, 90*(2), 124–129.

Bateman, A., Culpan, F. J., Pickering, A. D., Powell, J. H., Scott, O. M., & Greenwood, R. J. (2001). The effect of aerobic training on rehabilitation outcomes after recent severe brain injury: A randomized controlled evaluation. *Archives of Physical Medicine and Rehabilitation, 82*(2), 174–182.

Beetar, J. D., Guilmette, T. J., & Sparadeo, F. R. (1996). Sleep and pain complaints in symptomatic traumatic brain injury and neurologic populations. *Archives of Physical Medicine and Rehabilitation, 77*(4), 1298–1302.

Benke, D., Barberis, A., Kopp, S., Altmann, K. H., Schubiger, M., Vogt, K. E., et al. (2009). GABA A receptors as in vivo substrate for the anxiolytic action of valerenic acid, a major constituent of valerian root extracts. *Neuropharmacology, 56*(1), 174–181.

Bleiberg, J., Garmoe, W., Cederquist, J., Reeves, D., & Lux, W. (1993). Effects of dexedrine on performance consistency following brain injury: A double-blind placebo crossover case study. *Neuropsychology and Behavioral Neurology, 6*(4), 245–248.

Bohlhalter, S., Weinmann, O., Möhler, H., & Fritschy, J. M. (1996). Laminar compartmentalization of GABAA-receptor subtypes in the spinal cord: An immunohistochemical study. *Journal of Neuroscience, 16*, 283–297.

Boivin, D. B., James, F. O., Santo, B. A., Caliyurt, O., & Chalk, C. (2003). Non-24-hour sleep–wake syndrome following a car accident. *Neurology, 60*, 1841–1843.

Bolden-Watson, C., & Richelson, E. (1993). Blockade by newly-developed antidepressants of biogenic amine uptake into rat brain synaptosomes. *Life Sciences, 52*(12), 1023–1029.

Boles, J. A., Wagner, A. K., & Goyal, A. (2013). Chronic inflammation after severe traumatic brain injury: Characterization and associations with outcome. *Journal of Neurotrauma, 30*(8), OC–C05.

Bombardier, C. H., Fann, J. R., Temkin, N. R., Esselman, P. C., Barber, J., & Dikmen, S. S. (2010). Rates of major depressive disorder and clinical outcomes following traumatic brain injury. *Journal of the American Medical Association, 303*(19), 1938–1945.

Bondanelli, M., Ambrosio, M. R., Zatelli, M. C., DeMarinis, L., & Uberti, E. C. (2005). Hypopituitarism after traumatic brain injury. *European Journal of Endocrinology, 152*(5), 679–691.

Bourne, R. S., Mills, G. H., & Minelli, C. (2008). Melatonin therapy to improve nocturnal sleep in critically ill patients: Encouraging results from a small randomised controlled trial. *Critical Care, 12* (2:R52).

Brannan, T., Martínez-Tica, J., Di Rocco, A., & Yahr, M. D. (1993). Low and high dose bromocriptine have different effects on striatal dopamine release: An in vivo study. *Journal of Neural Transmission: Parkinson's Disease and Dementia Section, 6*(2), 81–87.

Brayer, S. W., Kumar, K., Henderson, C., Ketcham, S., Fuletra, J., Zou, H., et al. (2013). Developing a clinically relevant model of cognitive rehabilitative therapy after traumatic brain injury. *Journal of Neurotrauma, 30*(8), 160.

Brefel-Courbon, C., Payoux, P., Ory, F., Sommet, A., Slaoui, T., Raboyeau, G., et al. (2007). Clinical and imaging evidence of zolpidem effect in hypoxic encephalopathy. *Annals of Neurology, 62*(1), 102–105.

Breitbart, W., Rosenfeld, B., Kaim, M., & Funesti-Esch, J. (2001). A randomized, double-blind, placebo-controlled trial of psychostimulants for the treatment of fatigue in ambulatory patients with Human Immunodeficiency Virus Disease. *Archives of Internal Medicine, 161*(3), 411–420.

Brennan, A. R., & Arnsten, A. F. (2008). Neuronal mechanisms underlying attention deficit hyperactivity disorder: The influence of arousal on prefrontal cortical function. *Annals of the New York Academy of Sciences, 1129*, 236–245.

Brett, C. A., McCullough, E. H., Niyonkuru, C., Loucks, T., Dixon, C. E., Ricker, J. H., et al. (2012). Persistent hypogonadism influences estradiol synthesis, cognition and outcome in males after severe TBI. *Brain Injury, 26*(10), 1226–1242.

Brooke, M. M., Questad, K. A., Patterson, D. R., & Bashak, K. J. (1992). Agitation and restlessness after closed head injury: A prospective study of 100 consecutive admissions. *Archives of Physical Medicine and Rehabilitation, 73*(4), 320–323.

Brooks, N., Campsie, L., Symington, C., Beattie, A., & McKinlay, W. (1987). The effects of severe head injury on patient and relative within seven years of injury. *The Journal of Head Trauma Rehabilitation, 2*(3), 1–13.

Broughton, R., & Baron, R. (1978). Sleep patterns in the intensive care unit and on the ward after acute myocardial infarction. *Electroencephalography and Clinical Neurophysiology, 45*(3), 348–360.

Brower, M. C., & Price, B. H. (2001). Neuropsychiatry of frontal lobe dysfunction in violent and criminal behaviour: A critical review. *Journal of Neurology, Neurosurgery, and Psychiatry, 71*, 720–726.

Brown, G. L., Goodwin, F. K., Ballenger, J. C., & Goyer, P. F. (1979). Aggression in humans correlates with cerebrospinal fluid amine metabolites. *Psychiatry Research, 1*, 131–139.

Bruno, R. L., Zimmerman, J. R., Creange, S. J., Lewis, T., Molzen, T., & Frick, N. M. (1996). Bromocriptine in the treatment of post-polio fatigue: A pilot study with implications for the pathophysiology of fatigue. *American Journal of Physical Medicine and Rehabilitation, 75*(5), 340–347.

Bryant, R. A., Marosszeky, J. E., Crooks, J., & Gurka, J. A. (2000). Posttraumatic stress disorder after traumatic brain injury. *The American Journal of Psychiatry, 157*, 629–631.

Bryant, R. A., Moulds, M., Guthrie, R., & Nixon, R. D. (2003). Treating acute stress disorder following mild traumatic brain injury. *The American Journal of Psychiatry, 160*, 585–587.

Bryant, R. A., Salmon, K., Sinclair, E., & Davidson, P. (2007). The relationship between acute stress disorder and posttraumatic stress disorder in injured children. *Journal of Traumatic Stress, 20*(6), 1075–1079.

Buckley, M. J. (2005). The role of the perirhinal cortex and hippocampus in learning, memory, and perception. *The Quarterly Journal of Experimental Psychology, 58*(3–4), 246–268.

Budding, D. E. (2009). *Subcortical Structures and Cognition: Implications for Neuropsychological Assessment.* New York, NY: Springer.

Buffett-Jerrott, S. E., Stewart, S. H., Bird, S., & Teehan, M. D. (1998). An examination of differences in the time course of oxazepam's effects on implicit vs explicit memory. *Journal of Psychopharmacology, 12*(4), 338–347.

Burn, D. J., Tiangyou, W., Allcock, L. M., Davison, J., & Chinnery, P. F. (2006). Allelic variation of a functional polymorphism in the serotonin transporter gene and depression in Parkinson's disease. *Parkinsonism and Related Disorders, 12*, 139–141.

Busto, R., Dietrich, W. D., Globus, M. Y., Alonso, O., & Ginsberg, M. D. (1997). Extracellular Release of Serotonin following Fluid-Percussion Brain Injury in Rats. *Journal of Neurotrauma, 14*(1), 35–42.

Calatayud-Maldonado, V., Calatayud-Perez, J. B., & Aso-Escario, J. (1991). Effects of CDP-choline on the recovery of patients with head injury. *Journal of Neurological Sciences, 103*, S15–18.

Cantor, J. B., Ashman, T., Gordon, W., Ginsberg, A., Engmann, C., Egan, M., et al. (2008). Fatigue after traumatic brain injury and its impact on participation and quality of life. *Journal of Head Trauma Rehabilitation, 23*(1), 41–51.

Cardenas, D. D., Mclean, A., Farrell-Roberts, L., et al. (1994). Oral physostigmine and impaired memory in adults with brain injury. *Brain Injury, 8*, 579–587.

Carli, M., & Samanin, R. (1992). 8-Hydroxy-2-(di-n-propylamino)tetralin impairs spatial learning in a water maze: Role of postsynaptic 5-HT1A receptors. *British Journal of Pharmacology, 105*(3), 720–726.

Caspi, A., Sugden, K., Moffitt, T. E., Taylor, A., Craig, I. W., Harrington, H., et al. (2003). Influence of life stress on depression: Moderation by a polymorphism in the 5-HTT gene. *Science, 301*(5631), 386–389.

Cassidy, J. W. (1989). Fluoxetine: A new serotonergically active antidepressant. *Journal of Head Trauma Rehabilitation, 4*(2), 67–69.

Castriotta, R. J., & Lai, J. M. (2001). Sleep disorders associated with traumatic brain injury. *Archives of Physical Medicine and Rehabilitation, 82*(10), 1403–1406.

Castriotta, R. J., Wilde, M. C., Lai, J. M., Atanasov, S., Masel, B. E., & Kuna, S. T. (2007). Prevalence and consequences of sleep disorders in traumatic brain injury. *Journal of Clinical Sleep Medicine*, 3(4), 349–356.

Challman, T. D., & Lipsky, J. J. (2000). Methylphenidate: Its pharmacology and uses. *Mayo Clinic Proceedings*, 75(7), 711–721.

Chan, F., Lanctôt, K. L., Feinstein, A., Hermann, N., Strauss, J., Sicard, T., et al. (2008). The serotonin transporter polymorphisms and major depression following traumatic brain injury. *Brain Injury, 22*, 471–479.

Chokroverty, S. (2000). Diagnosis and treatment of sleep disorders caused by co-morbid disease. *Neurology, 54*(5 Suppl 1), S8–15.

Ciallella, J. R., Yan, H., Ma, X., Wolfson, B. M., Marion, D. W., DeKosky, S. T., et al. (1998). Chronic Effects of Traumatic Brain Injury on Hippocampal Vesicular Acetylcholine Transporter and M2Muscarinic Receptor Protein in Rats. *Experimental Neurology, 152*(1), 11–19.

Clark, W. M., Warach, S. J., Pettigrew, L. C., Gammans, R. E., & Sabounjian, L. A. (1997). A randomized dose-response trial of citicoline in acute ischemic stroke patients. Citicoline Stroke Study Group. *Neurology, 49*(3), 671–678.

Clauss, R., & Nel, W. (2006). Drug-induced arousal from the permanent vegetative state. *NeuroRehabilitation, 21*(1), 23–28.

Clinchot, D. M., Bogner, J., Mysiw, W. J., Fugate, L., & Corrigan, J. (1998). Defining sleep disturbance after brain injury. *American Journal of Physical Medicine and Rehabilitation, 77*(4), 291–295.

Coccaro, E. F., & Kavoussi, R. J. (1997). Fluoxetine and impulsive aggressive behavior in personality disordered subjects. *Archives of General Psychiatry, 54*(12), 1081–1088.

Cohen, M., Oksenberg, A., Snir, D., Stern, M. J., & Groswasser, Z. (1992). Temporally related changes of sleep complaints in traumatic brain injured patients. *Journal of Neurology, Neurosurgery, and Psychiatry, 55*(4), 313–315.

Cohen, R. A., & Fisher, M. (1989). Amantadine treatment of fatigue associated with multiple sclerosis. *Archives of Neurology, 46*(6), 676–680.

Cornelius, J. R., Soloff, P. H., Perel, J. M., & Ulrich, R. F. (1990). Fluoxetine trial in borderline personality disorder. *Psychopharmacology Bulletin, 26*(1), 151–154.

Costa, E., Chen, Y., Dong, E., Grayson, D. R., Kundakovic, M., Maloku, E., et al. (2009). GABAergic promoter hypermethylation as a model to study the neurochemistry of schizophrenia vulnerability. *Expert Review of Neurotherapeutics, 9*(1), 87–98.

Crestani, F., Löw, K., Keist, R., Mandelli, M., Möhler, H., & Rudolph, U. (2001). Molecular targets for the myorelaxant action of diazepam. *Molecular Pharmacology, 59*, 442–445.

Cripe, L. I. (1987). The neuropsychological assessment and management of closed heard injury: General guidelines. *Cognitive Rehabilitation, 5*, 18–22.

Cumbo, E., & Ligori, L. D. (2010). Levetiracitam, lamotrigine, and phenobarbital in patients with epileptic seizures and alzheimer's disease. *Epilepsy & Behavior, 17*(4), 464–466.

Darrah, S. D., Chuang, J., Mohler, L., Chen, X., Cummings, E., Burnett, T., et al. (2010). Dilantin Therapy in an Experimental Model of Traumatic Brain Injury: Effects of Limited versus Daily Treatment on Neurological and Behavioral Recovery. *Journal of Neurotrauma*, [Epub ahead of print].

DeAngelis, M. M., Hayes, R. L., & Lyeth, B. G. (1994). Traumatic brain injury causes a decrease in M2 muscarinic cholinergic receptor binding in the rat brain. *Brain Research, 653*(1–2), 39–44.

Decoster, M., Herbert, M., Meyerhoff, J. L., & Potegal, M. (1996). Brief, high-frequency stimulation of the corticomedial amygdala induces a delayed and prolonged increase of aggressiveness in male Syrian Golden Hamsters. *Behavioral Neuroscience, 110*, 401–412.

Dempsey, R. J., & Rao, V. L. (2003). Cytidinediphosphocholine treatment to decrease traumatic brain injury-induced hippocampal neuronal death, cortical contusion volume, and neurological dysfunction in rats. *Journal of Neurosurgery, 98*(4), 867–873.

Denny-Brown, D. (1945). Disability arising from closed head injury. *JAMA, 127*, 429–436.

Dewar, D., & Graham, D. I. (1996). Depletion of choline acetyltransferase but preservation of M1 and M2 muscarinic receptor binding sites in temporal cortex following head injury: A preliminary human postmortem study. *Journal of Neurotrama, 13*, 181–187.

Dikmen, S., Temkin, N., Miller, B., Machamer, J., & Winn, H. (1991). Neurobehavioral effects of phenytoin prophylaxis of posttraumatic seizures. *JAMA, 265*, 1271–1277.

Dinan, T. G., & Mobayed, M. (1992). Treatment resistance of depression after head injury: A preliminary study of amitriptyline response. *Acta Psychiatrica Scandinavica, 85*(4), 292–294.

Dixon, C. E., Bao, J., Begmann, J. S., & Johnson, K. M. (1994). Traumatic brain injury reduces hippocampal high-affinity [3H]choline uptake but not extracellular choline levels in rats. *Neuroscience letters, 180*(2), 127–130.

Dixon, C. E., Bao, J., Johnson, K. M., Yang, K., Whitson, J., & Clifton, G. L. (1995). Basal and scopolamine evoked release of hippocampal acetylcholine following traumatic brain injury in rats. *Neuroscience Letters, 198,* 111–114.

Dixon, C. E., Flinn, P., Yang, K., Whitson, J. S., & Hayes, R. L. (1995). Traumatic brain injury (TBI) produces a transient loss of choline acetyltransferase immunoreactivity: An immunohistochemical study in rats. *Journal of Neurotrauma, 12,* 491.

Dixon, C. E., Hamm, R. J., Taft, W. C., & Hayes, R. L. (1994). Increased anticholinergic sensitivity following closed skull impact and controlled cortical traumatic brain injury in the rat. *Journal of Neurotrauma, 11*(3), 275–287.

Dixon, C. E., Kraus, M. F., Kline, A. E., Ma, X., Yan, H. Q., Griffith, R. G., et al. (1999). Amantadine improves water maze performance without affecting motor behavior following traumatic brain injury in rats. *Restorative Neurology and Neuroscience, 14*(4), 285–294.

Dixon, C. E., Liu, S., Jenkins, L. W., Bhattachargee, M., Whitson, J. S., Yang, K., et al. (1995). Time course of increased vulnerability of cholinergic neurotransmission following traumatic brain injury in the rat. *Behavioural Brain Research, 70,* 125–131.

Dixon, C. E., Ma, X., & Marion, D. W. (1997). Effects of CDP-choline treatment on neurobehavioral deficits after TBI and on hippocampal and neocortical acetylcholine release. *Journal of Neurotrauma, 14*(3), 161–169.

Dixon, C. E., Ma, X., & Marion, D. W. (1997). Reduced evoked release of acetylcholine in the rodent neocortex following traumatic brain injury. *Brain Research, 749,* 127–130.

Doble, A., Martin, I., & Nutt, D. (2003). *Calming the Brain.* London: Martin Dunitz.

Donath, F., Quispe, S., Diefenbach, K., Maurer, A., Fietze, I., & Roots, I. (2000). Critical Evaluation of the Effect of Valerian Extract on Sleep Structure and Sleep Quality. *Pharmacopsychiatry, 33*(2), 47–53.

Donnemiller, E., Brenneis, C., Wissel, J., Scherfler, C., Poewe, W., Riccabona, G., et al. (2000). Impaired dopaminergic neurotransmission in patients with traumatic brain injury: A SPECT study using 123I-beta-CIT and 123I-IBZM. *European Journal of Nuclear Medicine, 27*(9), 1410–1414.

Drake, M. E., Pakalnis, A., Denio, L. S., & Phillips, B. (1991). Amantadine hydrochloride for refractory generalized epilepsy in adults. *Acta Neurologica Belgica, 91*(3), 159–164.

Du, B., Shan, A., Zhang, Y., Zhong, X., Chen, D., & Cai, K. Zolpidem arouses patients in vegetative state after brain injury: Quantitative evaluation and indications. *The American Journal of the Medical Sciences,* [Epub ahead of print].

Dyer, K. F., Bell, R., McCann, J., & Rauch, R. (2006). Aggression after traumatic brain injury: Analysing socially desirable responses and the nature of aggressive traits. *Brain Injury, 20*(11), 1163–1173.

Earnes, P., & Sutton, A. (1995). Protracted posttraumatic confusional state treated with physostigmine. *Brain Injury, 9,* 729–734.

Elovic, E. P., Jasey, N. N., & Eisenberg, M. E. (2008). The use of atypical antipsychotics after traumatic brain injury. *Journal of Head Trauma Rehabilitation, 23*(2), 132–135.

Englander, J., Bushnik, T., Oggins, J., & Katznelson, L. (2010). Fatigue after traumatic brain injury: Association with neuroendocrine, sleep, depression and other factors. *Brain Injury, 24*(12), 1379–1388.

Evans, R. W., Gualtieri, C. T., & Patterson, D. (1987). Treatment of chronic closed head injury with psychostimulant drugs: A controlled case study and an appropriate evaluation procedure. *Journal of Nervous and Mental Disease, 175*(2), 106–110.

Ewert, J., Levin, H. S., Watson, M. G., & Kalisky, Z. (1989). Procedural memory during posttraumatic amnesia in survivors of severe closed head injury. Implications for rehabilitation. *Archives of Neurology, 46*(8), 911–916.

Failla, M. D., Burkhardt, J. N., Miller, M. A., Scanlong, J. M., Conley, Y. P., Ferrell, R. E., et al. (2013). Variants of the slc6a4 gene in depression risk following severe tbi. *Brain Injury, 27*(6), 696–706.

Fann, J. R., Uomoto, J. M., & Katon, W. J. (2001). Cognitive improvement with treatment of depression following mild traumatic brain injury. *Psychosomatics, 42*(1), 48–54.

Fann, J. R., Uomoto, J. M., & Katon, W. J. (2000). Sertraline in the treatment of major depression following mild traumatic brain injury. *Journal of Neuropsychiatry and Clinical Neurosciences, 12*(2), 226–232.

Fann, W. E., & Lake, C. R. (1976). Amantadine versus trihexyphenidyl in the treatment of neuroleptic-induced parkinsonism. *American Journal of Psychiatry, 133,* 940–943.

Farooq, M. U., Bhatt, A., Majid, A., Gupta, R., Khasnis, A., & Kassab, M. Y. (2009). Levetiracetam for managing neurologic and psychiatric disorders. *American Journal of Health-System Pharmacy, 66*(16), 541–561.

Feeney, D. J., & Klykylo, W. M. (1997). Medication-induced seizures. *Journal of the American Academy of Child and Adolescent Psychiatry, 36*(8), 1018–1019.

Ferraro, L., Antonelli, T., O'Connor, W. T., Tanganelli, S., Rambert, F. A., & Fuxe, K. (1997). The antinarcoleptic drug modafinil increases glutamate release in thalamic areas and hippocampus. *Neuroreport, 8,* 2883–2887.

Ferraro, L., Antonelli, T., Tanganelli, S., O'Conner, W. T., de la Mora, M. P., Mendez-Franco, J., et al. (1999). The vigilance promoting drug modafinil increases extracellular glutamate levels in the medial preoptic area and the posterior hypothalamus of the conscious rat: Prevention by local GABAa receptor blockade. *Neuropsychopharmacology, 20*(4), 346–356.

Fichtenberg, N. L., Zafonte, R. D., Putnam, S., Mann, N. R., & Millard, A. E. (2002). Insomnia in a post-acute brain injury sample. *Brain Injury, 16*(3), 197–206.

Findling, R. L. (1996). Open-label treatment of comorbid depression and attentional disorders with co-administration of serotonin reuptake inhibitors and psychostimulants in children, adolescents, and adults: A case series. *Journal of Child and Adolescent Psychopharmacology, 6*(3), 165–175.

Fitchtenberg, N. L., Millis, S. R., Mann, N. R., Zafonte, R. D., & Milllard, A. E. (2000). Factors associated with insomnia among post-acute traumatic brain injury survivors. *Brain Injury, 14*(7), 659–667.

Fleckenstein, A. E., Volz, T. J., Riddle, E. L., Gibb, J. W., & Hanson, G. R. (2007). New insights into the mechanism of action of amphetamines. *Annual Review of Pharmacology and Toxicology, 47*, 681–698.

Ford, D. E., & Kamerow, D. B. (1989). Epidemiologic study of sleep disturbances and psychiatric disorders: An opportunity for prevention? *JAMA, 262*, 1479–1484.

Fordyce, D. J., Roueche, J. R., & Prigatano, G. P. (1983). Enhanced emotional reactions in chronic head trauma patients. *Journal of Neurology, Neurosurgery, and Psychiatry, 46*, 620–624.

Foster, H. G., Hillbrand, M., & Chi, C. C. (1989). Efficacy of carbamazepine in assaultive patients with forntal lobe dysfunction. *Progress in Neuro-Psychopharmacology and Biological Psychiatry, 13*(6), 865–874.

Freedman, N. S., Kotzer, N., & Schwab, R. J. (1999). Patient perception of sleep quality and etiology of sleep disruption in the intensive care unit. *American Journal of Respiratory and Critical Care Medicine, 159*, 1155–1162.

George, B., Landau-Ferey, J., Benoit, O., Dondey, M., & Cophignon, J. (1981). Night sleep disorders during recovery of severe head injuries. *Neuro-Chirurgie, 27*(1), 35–38.

Geracioti, T. D. (1994). Valproic acid treatment of episodic explosiveness related to brain injury. *Journal of Clinical Psychiatry, 55*(9), 416–417.

Giacino, J. T., Whyte, J., Bagiella, E., Kalmar, K., Childs, N., Khademi, A., et al. (2012). Placebo-controlled trial of amantadine for severe traumatic brain injury. *New England Journal of Medicine, 366*(9), 819–826.

Gianutsos, G., Chute, S., & Dunn, J. P. (1985). Pharmacological changes in dopaminergic systems induced by long-term administration of amantadine. *European Journal of Pharmacology, 110*, 357–361.

Gingrich, J. A., & Hen, R. (2001). Dissecting the role of the serotonin system in neuropsychiatric disorders using knockout mice. *Psychopharmacology, 155*(1), 1–10.

Glötzner, F. L., Haubitz, I., Miltner, F., Kapp, G., & Pflughaupt, K. W. (1983). Seizure prevention using carbamazepine following severe brain injuries. *Neurochirurgia, 26*(3), 66–79.

Goldman-Rakic, P. S. (1995). Cellular basis of working memory. *Neuron, 14*, 477–485.

Gorman, L. K., Fu, K., Hovda, D. A., Becker, D. P., & Katayama, Y. (1989). Analysis of acetylcholine release following concussive brain injury in the rat. *Journal of Neurotrauma*, 203.

Gorman, L. K., Fu, K., Hovda, D. A., Murray, M., & Traystman, R. J. (1996). Effects of traumatic brain injury on the cholinergic system in the rat. *Journal of Neurotruama, 13*, 457–463.

Gorman, L. K., Shook, B. L., & Becker, D. P. (1993). Traumatic brain injury produces impairments in long-term and recent memory. *Brain Research, 614*, 29–36.

Greve, K. W., Sherwin, E., Stanford, M. S., Mathias, C., Love, J., & Ramzinski, P. (2001). Personality and neurocognitive correlates of impulsive aggression in long-term survivors of severe traumatic brain injury. *Brain Injury, 15*(3), 255–262.

Griffin, L. S., van Reekum, R., & Masanic, C. (2003). A review of cholinergic agents in the treatment of neurobehavioral deficits following traumatic brain injury. *Journal of Neuropsychiatry and Clinical Neurosciences, 15*, 17–26.

Griffiths, R. R., & Johnson, M. W. (2005). Relative abuse liability of hypnotic drugs: A conceptual framework and algorithm for differentiating among compounds. *Journal of Clinical Psychiatry, 66*(Suppl. 9), 31–41.

Grossman, R., Beyer, C., Kelly, P., & Haber, B. (1975). Acetylcholine and related enzymes in human ventricular and subarachnoid fluids following brain injury. *76*(3), 506.

Gualtieri, C. T. (1991). Buspirone for the behavior problems of patients with organic brain disorders. *Journal of Clinical Psychopharmacology, 11*(4), 280–281.

Gualtieri, C. T. (1991). Buspirone: Neuropsychiatric effects. *Journal of Head Trauma Rehabilitation, 6*(1), 90–92.

Gualtieri, C. T., & Evans, R. W. (1988). Stimulant treatment for the neurobehavioral sequale of traumatic brain injury. *Brain Injury, 2*(4), 273–290.

Gucuyener, K., Erdemoglu, A. K., Senol, S., Serdaroglu, A., Soysal, S., & Kockar, I. (2003). Use of methylphenidate for Attention-Deficit Hyperactivity Disorder in patients with epilepsy or electroencephalographic abnormalities. *Journal of Child Neurology, 18*(2), 109–112.

Hagan, C., Malkmus, D., & Durham, P. (1979). Levels of Cognitive Functioning. In *Rehabilitation of the head injured adult: Comprehensive cognitive management.* Downey, CA: Professional Staff Association of Ranchos Los Amigos Hospital, Inc.

Haig, A. J., & Ruess, J. M. (1990). Recovery from vegetative state of six months' duration associated with Sinemet (levodopa/carbidopa). *Archives of Physical Medicine and Rehabilitation, 71*(13), 1081–1083.

Hajak, G., Muller, W. E., Wittchen, H. U., Pittrow, D., & Kirch, W. (2003). Abuse and dependence potential for non-benzodiazepine hypnotics zolpidem and zopiclone: A review of case reports and epidemiological data. *Addiction, 98,* 1371–1378.

Hallam, K. T., Olver, J. S., McGrath, C., & Norman, T. R. (2003). Comparative cognitive and psychomotor effects of single doses of Valeriana officianalis and triazolam in healthy volunteers. *Human Psychopharmacology, 18*(8), 619–625.

Hamm, R. J., O'Dell, D. M., Pike, B. R., & Lyeth, B. R. (1993). Cognitive impairment following traumatic brain injury: The effect of pre- and post-injury administration of scopolamine and MK-801. *Cognitive Brain Research, 1,* 223–226.

Hamm, R. J., Temple, M. D., O'Dell, D. M., Pike, B. R., & Lyeth, B. G. (1996). Exposure to environmental complexity promotes recovery of cognitive function after traumatic brain injury. *Journal of Neurotrauma, 13,* 41–47.

Harada, M., Minami, R., Hattori, E., Nakamura, K., & Kabashima, K. (1976). Sleep in brain-damaged patients. An all night sleep study of 105 cases. *Kumamoto Medical Journal, 29*(3), 110–127.

Harvey, A. G., & Bryant, R. A. (1998). The relationship between acute stress disorder and posttraumatic stress disorder: A prospective evaluation of motor vehicle accident survivors. *Journal of Consulting and Clinical Psychology, 66*(3), 507–512.

Harvey, A. G., & Bryant, R. A. (2000). Two-year prospective evaluation of the relationship between acute stress disorder and posttraumatic stress disorder following mild traumatic brain injury. *The American Journal of Psychiatry, 157,* 626–628.

Heikkila, R. E., & Cohen, G. (1972). Evaluation of amantadine as a releasing agent or uptake blocker for H3-dopamine in rat brain sliced. *European Journal of Pharmacology, 20*(2), 156–160.

Henry, J. M., Talukder, N. K., Lee, A. B., & Walker, M. L. (1997). Cerebral trauma-induced changes in corpus striatal dopamine receptor subtypes. *Journal of Investigative Surgery, 10*(5), 281–286.

Hibbard, M. R., Uysal, S., Kepler, K., Bogdany, J., & Silver, J. (1998). Axis I psychopathology in individuals with traumatic brain injury. *Journal of Head Trauma Rehabilitation, 13*(4), 24–39.

Hicks, R. R., Li, C., Zhang, L., Dhillon, H. S., Prasad, M. R., & Seroogy, K. B. (1999). Alterations in BDNF and trkB mRNA levels in the cerebral cortex following experimental brain trauma in rats. *Journal of Neurotrauma, 16*(6), 501–510.

Hicks, R. R., Smith, D. H., Lowenstein, R., Saint Marie, R., & McIntosh, T. K. (1993). Mild Experimental Brain Injury in the Rat Induces Cognitive Deficits Associated with Regional Neuronal Loss in the Hippocampus. *Journal of Neurotrauma, 10*(4), 405–414.

Hoffman, A. N., Cheng, J. P., Zafonte, R. D., & Kline, A. E. (2008). Administration of haloperidol and risperidone after neurobehavioral testing hinders the recovery of traumatic brain injury-induced deficits. *Life Sciences, 83*(17–18), 602–607.

Hoffman, B. M., Babyak M. A., Craighead, W. E., Sherwood, A., Doraiswamy, P. M., Coons, M. J., et al. (2011). Exercise and pharmacotherapy in patients with major depression: One-year follow-up of the smile study. *Psychosomatic Medicine, 73*(2), 127–133.

Hoffman, J., Bell, K. R., Powell, J. M., Behr, J., Dunn, E. C., Dikmen, S., et al. (2010). A randomized controlled trial of exercise to improve mood after traumatic brain injury. *PM&R: The Journal of Injury, Function, and Rehabilitation, 2*(10), 911–919.

Holbrook, A. M., Crowther, R., Lotter, A., Cheng, C., & King, D. (2000). Meta-analysis of benzodiazepine use in the treatment of insomnia. *Synthèse, 162*(2), 225–233.

Holsinger, T., Steffens, D. C., Phillips, C., Helms, M. J., Havlik, R. J., Breitner, J. C., et al. (2002). Head injury in early adulthood and the lifetime risk of depression. *Archives of General Psychiatry, 59*(1), 17–22.

Hornstein, A., Lennihan, L., Seliger, G., Lichtman, S., & Schroeder, K. (1996). Amphetamine in recovery from brain injury. *Brain Injury, 10*(2), 145–148.

Horsfield, S. A., Rosse, R. B., Tomasino, V., Schwartz, B. L., Mastropaolo, J., & Deutsch, S. I. (2002). Fluoxetine's effects on cognitive performance in patients with traumatic brain injury. *International Journal of Psychiatry in Medicine, 32*(4), 337–344.

Hudak, A., Warner, M., Marquez de la Plata, C., Moore, C., Harper, C., & Diaz-Arrastia, R. (2011).

Brain morphometry changes and depressive symptoms after traumatic brain injury. *Psychiatry Research, 191*(3), 160–165.

Hughes, A., Colantonio, A., Santaguida, P. L., & Paton, T. (2005). Amantadine to enhance readiness for rehabilitation following severe traumatic brain injury. *Brain Injury, 19*(14), 1197–1206.

Ichimura, T., Isobe, T., Okuyama, T., Takahashi, N., Araki, K., Kuwano, R., et al. (1988). Molecular cloning of cDNA coding for brain-specific 14-3-3 protein, a protein kinase-dependent activator of tyrosine and tryptophan hydroxylases. *Proceedings of the National Academy of Sciences, 85*(19), 7084–7088.

Iida, M., Miyazaki, I., Tanaka, K., Kabuto, H., Iwata-Ichikawa, E., & Ogawa, N. (1999). Dopamine D2 receptor-mediated antioxidant and neuroprotective effects of ropinirole, a dopamine agonist. *Brain Research, 838*(1–2), 51–59.

Jha, A., Weintraub, A., Allshouse, A., Morey, C., Cusick, C., Kittelson, J., et al. (2008). A randomized trial of modafinil for the treatment of fatigue and excessive daytime sleepiness in individuals with chronic traumatic brain injury. *The Journal of Head Trauma Rehabilitation, 23*(1), 52–63.

Jiang, J. Y., Lyeth, B. G., Delahunty, T. M., Phillips, L. L., & Hamm, R. J. (1994). Muscarinic cholinergic receptor binding in rat brain at 15 days following traumatic brain injury. *Brain Research, 651*(1–2), 123–128.

Jorge, R. E., Robinson, R. G., Moser, D., Tateno, A., Crespo-Facorro, B., & Arndt, S. (2004). Major depression following traumatic brain injury. *Archives of General Psychiatry, 61*(1), 42–50.

Jorge, R. E., Robinson, R. G., Starkstein, S. E., & Arndt, S. V. (1993). Depression and anxiety following traumatic brain injury. *Journal of Neuropsychiatry and Clinical Neurosciences, 5*, 369–374.

Kaelin, D. L., Cifu, D. X., & Matthies, B. (1996). Methylphenidate effect on attention deficit in the acutely brain-injured adult. *Archives of Physical Medicine & Rehabilitation, 77*, 6–9.

Kafka, M. P., & Hennen, J. (2000). Psychostimulant augmentation during treatment with selective serotonin reuptake inhibitors in men with paraphilias and paraphilia-related disorders: A case series. *Journal of Clinical Psychiatry, 61*, 664–670.

Kant, R., Smith-Seemiller, L., & Zeiler, D. (1998). Treatment of aggression and irritability after head injury. *Brain Injury, 12*(8), 661–666.

Katz, D. I., & Alexander, M. P. (1994). Traumatic brain injury: Predicting course of recovery and outcome for patients admitted to rehabilitation. *Archives of Neurology, 51*, 661–670.

Kaydan, V., Mysiw, J. W., Bogner, J. A., Corrigan, J. D., Fugate, L. P., & Clinchot, D. M. (2004). Gender differences in agitation after traumatic brain injury. *American Journal of Physical Medicine & Rehabilitation, 83*(10), 747–752.

Kendler, K. S., Kessler, R. C., Walters, E. E., MacLean, C., Neale, M. C., Heath, A. C., et al. (1995). Stressful life events, genetic liability, and onset of an episode of major depression in women. *American Journal of Psychiatry, 152*, 833–842.

Keshavan, M. S., Channabasavanna, S. M., & Reddy, G. N. (1981). Post-traumatic psychiatric disturbances: Patterns and predictors of outcome. *The British Journal of Psychiatry, 138*, 157–160.

Kessler, R. C., Chiu, W. T., Demler, O., Merikangas, K. R., & Walters, E. E. (2005). Prevalence, severity, and comorbidity of 12-month DSM-IV disorders in the National Comorbidity Survey Replication. *Archives of General Psychiatry, 62*(6), 617–627.

Khateb, A., Ammann, J., Annoni, J. M., & Diserens, K. (2005). Cognition enhancing effects of donepezil in traumatic brain injury. *European Neurology, 54*, 39–45.

Khom, S., Baburin, I., Timin, E., Hohaus, A., Trauner, G., Kopp, B., et al. (2007). Valerenic acid potentiates and inhibits GABA(A) receptors: Molecular mechanism and subunit specificity. *Neuropharmacology, 53*(1), 178–187.

Kim, E., & Bijlani, M. (2006). A pilot study of quetiapine treatment of aggression due to traumatic brain injury. *Journal of Neuropsychiatry and Clinical Neurosciences, 18*(4), 547–549.

Kim, Y. W., Kim, D. Y., Shin, J. C., Park, C. I., & Lee, J. D. (2009). The changes of cortical metabolism associated with the clinical response to donepezil therapy in traumatic brain injury. *Clinical Neuropharmacology, 32*(2), 63–68.

Klien, D. C., & Weller, J. L. (1972). Rapid light-induced decrease in pineal serotonin N-acetyltransferase activity. *Science, 177*, 532–533.

Kline, A. E., Hoffman, A. N., Cheng, J. P., Zafonte, R. D., & Massucci, J. L. (2008). Chronic administration of antipsychotics impede behavioral recovery after experimental traumatic brain injury. *Neuroscience Letters, 448*(3), 263–267.

Kline, A. E., Massucci, J. L., Ma, X., Zafonte, R. D., & Dixon, C. E. (2004). Bromocriptine reduces lipid peroxidation and enhances spatial learning and hippocampal neuron survival in a rodent model of focal brain trauma. *Journal of Neurotrauma, 21*(12), 1712–1722.

Kline, A. E., Massucci, J. L., Marion, D. W., & Dixon, C. E. (2002). Attenuation of working memory and spatial acquisition deficits after a delayed and chronic bromocriptine treatment regimen in rats subjected to traumatic brain injury by contolled cortical impact. *Journal of Neurotrauma, 19*(4), 415–425.

Kline, A. E., Massucci, J. L., Zafonte, R. D., Dixon, C. E., DeFeo, J. R., & Rogers, E. H. (2007). Differential effects of single versus multiple administrations of haloperidol and risperidone on functional outcome after experimental brain trauma. *Critical Care Medicine, 35*(3), 919–924.

Kline, A. E., Yan, H. Q., Bao, J., Marion, D. W., & Dixon, C. E. (2000). Chronic methylphenidate treatment enhances water maze performance following traumatic brain injury in rats. *Neuroscience Letters, 280*(3), 163–166.

Kline, A. E., Yu, J., Horváth, E., Marion, D. W., & Dixon, C. E. (2001). The selective 5-HT(1A) receptor agonist repinotan HCl attenuates histopathology and spatial learning deficits following traumatic brain injury in rats. *Neuroscience, 106*(3), 547–555.

Kline, A. E., Yu, J., Massucci, J. L., Zafonte, R. D., & Dixon, C. E. (2002). Protective effects of the 5-HT1A receptor agonist 8-hydroxy-2-(di-n-propylamino) tetralin against traumatic brain injury-induced cognitive deficits and neuropathology in adult male rats. *Neuroscience Letters, 333*(3), 179–182.

Kobori, N., Clifton, G. L., & Dash, P. K. (2006). Enhanced Catecholamine Synthesis in the Prefrontal Cortex after Traumatic Brain Injury: Implications for Prefrontal Dysfunction. *Journal of Neurotrauma, 23*(7), 1094–1102.

Kotapka, M. J., Gennarelli, T. A., Adams, J. H., Thibault, L. E., Ross, D. T., & Ford, I. (1991). Selective vulnerability of hippocampal neurons in acceleration-induced experimental head injury. *Journal of Neurotrauma, 8,* 247–258.

Kotler, M., Rodriguez, C., Sainz, R. M., Antolin, I., & Menendez, P. A. (1998). Melatonin increases gene expression for antioxidant enzymes in the rat brain cortex. *Journal of Pineal Research, 24,* 83–89.

Kraus, M. F., & Maki, P. M. (1997b). Effect of amantadine hydrochloride on symptoms of frontal lobe dysfunction in brain injury: Case studies and review. *Journal of Neuropsychiatry, 9*(2), 222–230.

Kraus, M. F., & Maki, P. (1997a). The combined use of amantadine and l-dopa/carbidopa in the treatment of chronic brain injury. *Brain Injury, 11*(6), 455–460.

Kraus, M. F., Smith, G. S., Butters, M., Donnell, A. J., Dixon, C. E., Yilong, C., et al. (2005). Effects of the dopaminergic agent and NMDA receptor antagonist amantadine on cognitive function, cerebral glucose metabolism and D2 receptor availability in chronic traumatic brain injury: A study using positron emission tomography (PET). *Brain Injury, 7*(47), 1–9.

Kreutzer, J. S., Seel, R. T., & Gourley, E. (2001). The prevalence and symptom rates of depression after traumatic brain injury: A comprehensive examination. *Brain Injury, 15*(7), 563–576.

Krimchansky, B. Z., Keren, O., Sazbon, L., & Groswasser, Z. (2004). Differential time and related appearance of signs, indicating improvement in the state of consciousness in vegetative state traumatic brain injury (VS-TBI) patients after initiation of dopamine treatment. *Brain Injury, 18*(11), 1099–1105.

Kringelbach, M. L. (2005). The orbitofrontal cortex: Linking reward to hedonic experience. *Nature Reviews Neuroscience, 6,* 691–702.

Kruetzer, J. S., Seel, R. T., & Gourley, E. (2001). The prevalance and symptom rates of depression after traumatic brain injury: A comprehensive examination. *Brain Injury, 15*(7), 563–576.

Krupp, L. B., Coyle, P. K., Doscher, C., Miller, A., Cross, A. H., Jandorf, L., et al. (1995). Fatigue therapy in multiple sclerosis. *Neurology, 45,* 1956–1961.

Kuhlmann, J., Berger, W., Podzuweit, H., & Schmidt, U. (1999). The influence of valerian on "reaction time, alertness and concentration" in volunteers. *Pharmacopsychiatry, 32,* 235–241.

Kuppers, E., Ivanova, T., Karolczak, M., & Beyer, C. (2000). Estrogen: A multifunctional messenger to nigrostriatal dopaminergic neurons. *Journal of Neurocytology, 29,* 375–385.

Kwentus, J. A., Hart, R. P., Peck, E. T., & Kornstein, S. (1985). Psychiatric complications of closed head trauma. *Psychosomatics, 26*(1), 8–17.

Löw, K., Crestani, F., Keist, R., Benke, D., Brünig, I., Benson, J. A., et al. (2000). Molecular and neuronal substrate for the selective attenuation of anxiety. *Science, 290*(5489), 131–134.

LaChapelle, D. L., & Finlayson, M. A. (1998). An evaluation of subjective and objective measures of fatigue in patients with brain injury and healthy controls. *Brain Injury, 12*(8), 649–659.

LaChapelle, D. L., & Finlayson, M. A. (1998). An evaluation of subjective and objective measures of fatigue in patients with brain injury and healthy controls. *Brain Injury, 12,* 649–659.

Lal, S., Merbitz, C. P., & Grip, J. C. (1988). Modification of function in head-injured patients with Sinemet. *Brain Injury, 2*(3), 225–233.

Lanctôt, K. L., Rapaport, M. J., Chan, F., Rajaram, R. D., Strauss, J., Sicard, T., et al. (2010). Genetic predictors of response to treatment with citalopram in depression secondary to traumatic brain injury. *Brain Injury, 24*(7–8), 959–969.

Lavretsky, H., Park, S., Siddarth, P., Kumar, A., & Reynolds, C. F. (2006). Methylphenidate-enhanced antidepressant response to citalopram in the elderly: A double-blind, placebo-controlled pilot trial. *American Journal of Geriatric Psychiatry, 14,* 181–185.

Leger, D. (1994). The cost of sleep-related accidents: A report for the National Commission on Sleep Disorders Research. *Sleep, 17,* 84–93.

Leonard, J. R., Grady, M. S., Lee, M. E., Paz, J. C., & Westrum, L. E. (1997). Fluid Percussion Injury Causes Disruption of the Septohippocampal Pathway in the Rat. *Experimental Neurology, 143*, 177–187.

Leon-Carrion, J., Dominguez-Roldan, J. M., Murillo-Cabezas, F., del Rosario Dominguez-Morales, M., & Munoz-Sanchez, M. A. (2000). The role of citicholine in neuropsychological training after traumatic brain injury. *NeuroRehabilitation, 14*(1), 33–40.

Leufkens, T. R., Lund, J. S., & Vermeeren, A. (2009). Highway driving performance and cognitive functioning the morning after bedtime and middle-of-the-night use of gaboxadol, zopiclone and zolpidem. *Journal of Sleep Research, 18*(4), 387–396.

Levin, H. S. (1987). Neurobehavioral sequelae of head injury. In P. R. Cooper (Ed.), *Head Injury*. Baltimore, MD: Williams and Wilkins.

Levin, H. S. (1991). Treatment of postconcussional symptoms with CDP-choline. *Journal of Neurological Sciences, 103*, S39–42.

Levin, H. S., Peters, B. H., Kalisky, Z., High Jr., W. M., von Laufen, A., Eisenberg, H. M., et al. (1986). Effects of oral physostigmine and lecithin on memory and attention in closed head-injured patients. *Central Nervous System, 3*, 333–342.

Levy, M. L., Cummings, J. L., Fairbanks, L. A., Masterman, D., Miller, B. L., Craig, A. H., et al. (1998). Apathy is not depression. *Journal of Neuropsychiatry and Clinical Neurosciences, 10*(3), 314–319.

Lewy, A. J., Wehr, T. A., Goodwin, F. K., Newsome, D. A., & Markey, S. P. (1980). Light suppresses melatonin secretion in humans. *Science, 210*, 1267–1269.

Liang, K. C., Tsui, K. Y., Tyan, Y. M., & Chiang, T. C. (1998). Buspirone impaired acquisition and retention in avoidance tasks: Involvement of the hippocampus. *Chinese Journal of Physiology, 41*(1), 33–44.

Lin, J. S., Roussel, B., Akaoka, H., Fort, P., Debilly, G., & Jouvet, M. (1992). Role of catecholamines in the modafinil and amphetamine induced wakefulness, a comparative pharmacological study in the cat. *Brain Research, 591*(2), 319–326.

Lin, J., Hou, Y., & Jouvet, M. (1996). Potential brain neuronal targets for amphetamine-, methylphenidate-, and modafinil-induced wakefulness, evidenced by c-fos immunocytochemistry in the cat. *Proceedings of the National Academy of Sciences of the United States of America, 93*(24), 14128–14133.

Lindgren, N., Usiello, A., Goiny, M., Haycock, J., Erbs, E., Greengard, P., et al. (2003). Distinct roles of dopamine D2L and D2S receptor isoforms in the regulation of protein phosphorylation at presynaptic and postsynaptic sites. *Proceedings of the National Academy of Sciences, 100*(7), 4305–4309.

Lyeth, B. G., Dixon, C. E., Jenkins, L. W., Hamm, R. J., Alberico, A., Young, H. F., et al. (1988). Effects of scopolamine treatment on long-term behavioral deficits following concussive brain injury in the rat. *Brain Research, 452*, 39–48.

Lyeth, B. G., Jenkins, L. W., Hamm, R. J., Dixon, C. E., Phillips, L. L., Clifton, G. L., et al. (1990). Prolonged memory impairment in the absence of hippocampal cell death following traumatic brain injury in the rat. *Brain Research, 526*, 249–258.

Lyeth, B. G., Jiang, J. Y., Delahunty, T. M., Phillips, L. L., & Hamm, R. J. (1994). Muscarinic cholinergic receptor binding in rat brain following traumatic brain injury. *Brain Research, 640*(1–2), 240–245.

Müller, U., Murai, T., Bauer-Wittmund, T., & von Cramon, D. Y. (1999). Paroxetine versus citalopram treatment of pathological crying after brain injury. *Brain Injury, 13*(10), 805–811.

Müller, U., von Cramon, D. Y., & Pollmann, S. (1998). D1- versus D2-receptor modulation of visuospatial working memory in humans. *Journal of Neuroscience, 18*(7), 2720–2728.

Machado-Vieira, R., Ibrahim, L., & Zarate, C. A. Jr. (2011). Histone deacetylases and mood disorders: Epigenetic programming in gene-environment interactions. *CNS Neuroscience & Therapeutics, 17*(6), 699–704.

Madigan, N. K., DeLuca, J., Diamond, B. J., Tramontano, G., & Averill, A. (2000). Speed of information processing in traumatic brain injury: Modality-specific factors. *Journal of Head Trauma Rehabilitation, 15*(3), 943–956.

Markand, O. N., & Dyken, M. L. (1976). Sleep abnormalities in patients with brain stem lesions. *Neurology, 26*(8), 769–776.

Markovitz, P. J., Calabrese, J. R., Schulz, S. C., & Meltzer, H. Y. (1991). Fluoxetine in the treatment of borderline and schiotypal personality disorders. *American Jouranl of Psychiatry, 148*(8), 1064–1067.

Martin, R. T., & Whyte, J. (2007). The effects of methylphenidate on command following and yes/no communication in persons with severe disorders of consciousness: A meta-analysis of n-of-1 studies. *American Journal of Physical Medicine & Rehabilitation/ Association of Academic Physiatrists, 86*(8), 613–620.

Masel, B. E., Scheibel, R. S., Kimbark, T., & Kuna, S. T. (2001). Excessive daytime sleepiness in adults with brain injuries. *Archives of Physical Medicine and Rehabilitation, 82*(11), 1526–1532.

Mashiko, H., Niwa, S., Kumashiro, H., Kaneko, Y., Suzuki, S., Numata, Y., et al. (1999). Effect of trazodone in a single dose before bedtime for sleep disorders accompanied by a depressive state: Dose-finding study with no concomitant use of hypnotic agent. *Psychiatry and Clinical Neurosciences, 53*(2), 193–194.

Massagli, T. L. (1991). Neurobehavioral effects of phenytoin, carbamazepine, and valproic acid: Implications for use in traumatic brain injury. *Archives of Physical Medicine and Rehabilitation, 72*(3), 219–226.

Masson, F., Maurette, P., Salmi, L. R., Dartigues, J., Vecsey, J., Destaillats, J., et al. (1996). Prevalance of impairments 5 years after a head injury, and their relationship with diabilities and outcome. *Brain Injury, 10*(7), 487–497.

Massucci, J. L., Kline, A. E., Ma, X., Zafonte, R. D., & Dixon, C. E. (2004). Time dependent alterations in dopamine tissue levels and metabolism after experimental traumatic brain injury in rats. *Neuroscience Letters, 373*, 127–131.

Mayberg, H. S., Lewis, P. J., Regenold, W., & Wagner, H. N. (1994). Paralimbic hypoperfusion in unipolar depression. *The Journal of Nuclear Medicine, 35*(6), 929–934.

Mayo, J. C., Sainz, R. M., Uria, H., Antolin, I., Esteban, M. M., & Rodriguez, C. (2007). Melatonin prevents apoptosis induced by 6-hydroxydopamine in neuronal cells: Implications for Parkinson's disease. *Journal of Pineal Research, 24*(3), 179–192.

Mazure, C. M., Druss, B. G., & Cellar, J. S. (1992). Valproate treatment of older psychotic patients with organic mental syndromes and behavioral dyscontrol. *Journal of the American Geriatrics Society, 40*(9), 914–916.

Mazza, M., Martini, A., Scoppetta, M., & Mazza, S. (2008). Effect of levetiracetam on depression and anxiety in adult epileptic patients. *Progress in Neuro-Phychopharmacology & Biological Psychiatry, 32*(2), 539–543.

McAllister, T. W., Flashman, L. A., Sparling, M. B., & Saykin, A. J. (2004). Working memory deficits after traumatic brain injury: Catecholaminergic mechanisms and prospects for treatment- a review. *Brain Injury, 18*(4), 331–350.

McDowell, S., Whyte, J., & D'Esposito, M. (1998). Differential Effect of a Dopaminergic Agonist on Prefrontal Function in Traumatic Brain Injury. *Brain: A Journal of Neurology, 121*(6), 1155–1164.

McIntosh, T. K., Yu, T., & Gennarelli, T. A. (1994). Alterations in Regional Brain Catecholamine Concentrations After Experimental Brain Injury in the Rat. *Journal of Neurochemistry, 63*(4), 1426–1433.

Mclean, A., Dikmen, S., Temkin, N., Wyler, A., & Gale, J. (1984). Psychosocial functioning at 1 month after head injury. *Neurosurgery, 14*(4), 393–399.

Mendelson, W. B. (2005). A review of the evidence for the efficacy and safety of trazodone in insomnia. *Journal of Clinical Psychiatry, 66*(4), 469–476.

Mendonca, D. A., Menezes, K., & Jog, M. S. (2007). Methylphenidate improves fatigue scores in Parkinson disease: A randomized controlled trial. *Movement Disorders, 22*(14), 2070–2076.

Mesenge, C., Margail, I., Verrecchia, C., Allix, M., Boulu, G., & Plotkine, M. (1998). Protective effect of melatonin in a model of traumatic brain injury in mice. *Journal of Pineal Research, 25*(1), 41–46.

Metman, L. V., Dotto, P. D., LePoole, K., Konitsiotis, S., Fang, J., & Chase, T. (1999). Amantadine for levodopa-induced dyskinesias: A 1-year follow up study. *Archives of Neurology, 56*, 1383–1386.

Meythaler, J. M., Brunner, R. C., Johnson, A., & Novack, T. A. (2002). Amantadine to Improve Neurorecovery in Traumatic Brain Injury–Associated Diffuse Axonal Injury: A Pilot Double-blind Randomized Trial. *Journal of Heard Trauma Rehabilitation, 14*(4), 300–313.

Meythaler, J. M., Depalma, L., Devivo, M. J., Guin-Renfroe, S., & Novack, T. A. (2001). Sertraline to improve arousal and alertness in severe traumatic brain injury secondary to motor vehicle crashes. *Brain Injury, 15*(4), 321–331.

Micheli, D., Bonvicini, C., Rocchi, A., Ceravolo, R., Mancuso, M., Tognoni, G., et al. (2006). No evidence for allelic association of serotonin 2a receptor and transporter gene polymorphisms with depression in alzheimer disease. *Journal of Alzheimers Disease, 10*, 371–378.

Miczek, K. A., Fish, E. W., de Bold, J. F., & de Almeida, R. M. (2002). Social and neural determinants of aggressive behavior: Pharmacotherapeutic targets at serotonin, dopamine and gamma-aminobutyric acid systems. *Psychopharmacology, 163*, 434–458.

Middleboe, T., Andersen, H. S., Birket-Smith, M., & Friis, M. L. (2009). Minor head injury: Impact on general health after 1 year. A prospective follow-up study. *Acta Neurologica Scandinavica, 85*(1), 5–9.

Miller, D. W., & Abercrombie, E. D. (1996). Effects of MK-801 on spontaneous and amphetamine-stimulated dopamine release in striatum measured with in vivo microdialysis in awake rats. *Brain Research Bulletin, 40*(1), 57–62.

Mizoguchi, K., Yokoo, H., Yoshida, M., Tanaka, T., & Tanaka, M. (1994). Amantadine increases the extracellular dopamine levels in the striatum by re-uptake inhibition and by N-methyl-D-aspartate antagonism. *Brain Research, 662*(1–2), 255–258.

Moein, H., Khalili, H. A., & Keramatian, K. (2006). Effect of methylphenidate on ICU and hospital length of stay in patients with severe and moderate traumatic brain injury. *Clinical Neurology and Neurosurgery, 108*(6), 539–542.

Mooney, G. F., & Haas, L. J. (1993). Effect of methyl-phenidate on brain-injury related anger. *Archives of Physical Medicine and Rehabilitation, 74*, 153–160.

Moresco, R. M., Volonte, M. A., Messa, C., Gobbo, C., Galli, L., Carpinelli, A., et al. (2002). New perspectives on neurochemical effects of amantadine in the brain of parkinsonian patients: A PET—[11C] raclopride study. *Journal of Neural Transmission, 109*(10), 1265–1274.

Mort, J. R., & Aparasu, R. R. (2002). Prescribing of psychotropics in the elderly: Why is it so often inappropriate? *CNS Drugs, 16*, 99–109.

Mossner, R., Henneberg, A., Schmitt, A., Syagailo, Y. V., Grassle, M., Hennig, T., et al. (2001). Allelic variation of serotonin transporter expression is associated with depression in Parkinson's disease. *Molecular Psychiatry, 6*, 350–352.

Mouret, J., Lemoine, P., Minuit, M. P., Benkelfat, C., & Renardet, M. (1988). Effects of trazodone on the sleep of depressed subjects—a polygraphic study. *Psychopharmacology, 95*, S37–43.

Moutaouakil, F., El Otmani, H., Fadel, H., & Slassi, I. (2009). Severe apathy following head injury: Improvement with Selegiline treatment. *Neuro-Chirurgie, 55*(6), 551–554.

Muller, U., Murai, T., Bauer-Wittmund, T., & von Cramon, D. Y. (1999). Paroxetine versus citalopram treatment of pathological crying after brain injury. *Brain Injury, 10*, 805–811.

Murdoch, I., Nicoll, J. A., Graham, D. I., & Dewar, D. (2002). Nucleus basalis of Meynert pathology in the human brain after fatal head injury. *Journal of Neurotrauma, 19*, 279–284.

Murdoch, I., Perry, E. K., Court, J. A., Graham, D. I., & Dewar, D. (1998). Cortical cholinergic dysfunction after human head injury. *Journal of Neurotrauma, 15*, 295–305.

Murray, T. J. (1985). Amantadine therapy for fatigue in multiple sclerosis. *Canadian Journal of Neurological Science, 12*, 251–254.

Mysiw, W. J., Jackson, R. D., & Corrigan, J. D. (1988). Amitriptyline for post-traumatic agitation. *American Journal of Physical Medicine and Rehabilitation, 67*(1), 29–33.

Nagtegaal, J. E., Kerkhof, G. A., Smits, M. G., & Van Der Meer, Y. G. (1998). Delayed sleep phase syndrome: A placebo-controlled cross-over study on the effects of melatonin administered 5 hours before dim light melatonin onset. *Journal of Sleep Research, 7*(2), 135–143.

Nagtegaal, J. E., Kerkhof, G. A., Smits, M. G., Swart, A. C., & van der Meer, Y. G. (1997). Traumatic brain injury-associated delayed sleep phase syndrome. *Functional Neurology, 12*(6), 345–348.

Nahas, Z., Arlinghaus, K. A., Kotrla, K. J., Clearman, R. R., & George, M. S. (1998). Rapid response of emotional incontinence to selective serotonin reuptake inhibitors. *Journal of Neuropsychiatry and Clinical Neurosciences, 10*(4), 453–455.

Nakamura, T., Ikegami, K., Yoshimoto, K., & Ozaki, R. (2002). Marked improvement in disorientation in response to treatment with donepezil in patients with subacute and chronic traumatic brain injury. *International Journal of Neuropsychopharmacology, 5*, S193–S194.

Narimatsu, E., Niiya, T., Kawamata, M., & Namiki, A. (2006). The mechanisms of depression by benzodiazepines, barbiturates and propofol of excitatory synaptic transmissions mediated by adenosine modulation. *Masui, 55*(6), 684–691.

New, A. S., Buchsbaum, M. S., Hazlett, E. A., Goodman, M., Koenigsberg, H. W., Lo, J., et al. (2004). Fluoxetine increases relative metabolic rate in prefrontal cortex in impulsive aggression. *Psychopharmacology, 176*(3–4), 451–458.

Newburn, G., & Newburn, D. (2005). Selegiline in the management of apathy following traumatic brain injury. *Brain Injury, 19*(2), 149–154.

Nickels, J. L., Schneider, W. N., Dombovy, M. L., & Wong, T. M. (1994). Clinical use of amantadine in brain injury rehabilitation. *Brain Injury, 8*(8), 709–718.

Nott, M. T., Chapparo, C., & Baguley, I. J. (2006). Agitation following traumatic brain injury: An Australian sample. *Brain Injury, 20*(11), 1175–1182.

Oddy, M., Coughlan, T., Tyerman, A., & Jenkins, D. (1985). Social adjustment after closed heard injury: A further follow-up seven years after injury. *Journal of Neurology, Neurosurgery, and Psychiatry, 48*, 564–568.

O'Dell, D. M., Gibson, C. J., Wilson, M. S., DeFord, S. M., & Hamm, R. J. (2000). Positive and negative modulation of the GABA(A) receptor and outcome after traumatic brain injury in rats. *Brain Research, 861*(2), 325–332.

Olofsson, K., Alling, C., Lundberg, D., & Malmros, C. (2004). Abolished circadian rhythm of melatonin secretion in sedated and artificially ventilated intensive care patients. *Acta Anaesthesiologica Scandinavica, 48*(6), 679–684.

Olver, J. H., Ponsford, J. L., & Curran, C. A. (1996). Outcome following traumatic brain injury: A comparison between 2 and 5 years after injury. *Brain Injury, 10*(11), 841–848.

Oritz, J. G., Nieves-Natal, J., & Chavez, P. (1999). Effects of Valeriana officinalis extracts on [3H] flunitrazepam binding, synaptosomal [3H]GABA uptake, and hippocampal [3H]GABA release. *Neurochemical Research, 24*(11), 1373–1378.

Ouellet, M. C., Beaulieu-Bonneau, S., & Morin, C. M. (2006). Insomnia in patients with traumatic brain injury: Frequency, characteristics, and risk factors. *Journal of Head Trauma Rehabilitation, 21*(3), 199–212.

Page, G., Peeters, M., Maloteaux, J., & Hermans, E. (2000). Increased dopamine uptake in striatal synaptosomes after treatment with amantadine. *European Journal of Pharmacology, 403*, 75–80.

Pagliari, R., Peyrin, L., & Crambes, O. (1995). Differential regional and kinetics effects of piribedil and bromocriptine on dopamine metabolites: A brain microdialysis study in freely moving rats. *Journal of Neural Transmission: General Section, 101*(1–3), 13–26.

Parkes, J. D., Curzon, G., Knott, P. J., Tattersall, R., Baxter, R. C., Knill-Jones, R. P., et al. (1971). Treatment of Parkinson's Disease with amantadine and levodopa. *The Lancet, 297*(7709), 1083–1087.

Parsey, R. V., Oquendo, M. A., Simpson, N. R., Ogden, R. T., van Heertum, R., Arango, V., et al. (2002). Effects of sex, age, and aggressive traits in man on brain serotonin 5-HT1A receptor binding potential measured by PET using [C–11]WAY-100635. *Brain Research, 954*(2), 173–182.

Passineau, M. J., Green, E. J., & Dietrich, W. D. (2001). Therapeutic effects of environmental enrichment on cognitive function and tissue integrity following severe traumatic brain injury in rats. *Experimental Neurology, 168*, 373–384.

Passler, M. A., & Riggs, R. V. (2001). Positive outcomes in traumatic brain injury-vegetative state: Patients treated with bromocriptine. *Archives of Physical Medicine and Rehabilitation, 82*(3), 311–315.

Perez, R. G., Waymire, J. C., Lin, E., Liu, J. J., Guo, F., & Zigmond, M. J. (2002). A role for alpha-synuclein in the regulation of dopamine biosynthesis. *Journal of Neuroscience, 22*(8), 3090–3099.

Peters, B. H., & Levin, H. S. (1979). Effects of physostigmine and Lecithin on memory in Alzheimer Disease. *Annals of Neurology, 6*(3), 219–221.

Pike, R. F. (1989). Cocaine withdrawal. *Postgraduate Medicine, 85*, 115–121.

Pinner, E., & Rich, C. L. (1988). Effects of trazodone on aggressive behavior in seven patients with organic mental disorders. *American Journal of Psychiatry, 145*(10), 1295–1296.

Plenger, P. M., Dixon, C. E., Castillo, R. M., Frankowski, R. F., Yablon, S. A., & Levin, H. S. (1996). Subacute methylphenidate treatment for moderate to moderately severe traumatic brain injury: A preliminary double-blind placebo-controlled study. *Archives of Physical Medicine & Rehabilitation, 7*, 536–540.

Poole, N. A., & Agrawal, N. (2008). Cholinomimetic agents and neurocognitive impairment following

head injury: A systematic review. *Brain Injury, 22*(7–8), 519–534.

Povlishock, J. T., & Katz, D. I. (2005). Update of neuropathology and neurological recovery after traumatic brain injury. *Journal of Head Trauma, 20*(1), 76–94.

Powell, J. H., al-Adawi, S., Morgan, J., & Greenwood, R. J. (1996). Motivational deficits after brain injury: Effects of bromocriptine in 11 patients. *Journal of Neurology, Neurosurgery, and Psychiatry, 60*(4), 416–421.

Pullianen, V., & Jokelainen, M. (1995). Comparing the cognitive effects of phenytoin and carbamazepine in long term monotherapy: A 2 year follow-up. *Epilepsia, 36*, 1195–1202.

Quick reference guide: zaleplon, zolpidem and zopiclone for the short-term management of insomnia. (2004). Retrieved August 13, 2010, from http://www.nice.org.uk/nicemedia/live/11530/32845/ 32845.pdf

Rakier, A., Guilburd, J. N., Soustiel, J. F., Zaaroor, M., & Feinsod, M. (1995). Head injuries in the elderly. *Brain Injury, 9*(2), 187–194.

Ramakrishnan, K., & Schied, D. C. (2007). Treatment options for insomnia. *American Family Physician, 76*(4), 517–526.

Rao, N., Jellinek, H. M., & Woolston, D. C. (1985). Agitation in closed head injury: Haloperidol effects on rehabilitation outcome. *Archives of Physical Medicine and Rehabilitation, 66*(1), 30–34.

Rao, V., & Lyketsos, C. (2000). Neuropsychiatric sequelae of traumatic brain injury. *Psychosomantics, 41*(2), 95–103.

Rao, V., & Rollings, P. (2002). Sleep disturbances following traumatic brain injury. *Current Treatment Options in Neurology, 4*, 77–87.

Rao, V., Spiro, J., Vaishnavi, S., Rastogi, P., Mielke, M., Noll, K., et al. (2008). Prevalence and types of sleep disturbances acutely after traumatic brain injury. *Brain Injury, 22*(5), 381–386.

Rapoport, M. J., Chan, F., Lanctot, K., Herrmann, N., McCullagh, S., & Feinstein, A. (2008). An open-label study of citalopram for major depression following traumatic brain injury. *Journal of Psychopharmacology, 22*(8), 860–864.

Reiter, R. J., Sainz, R. M., Lopez-Burillo, S., Mayo, J. C., Manchester, L. C., & Tan, D. X. (2003). Melatonin ameliorates neurologic damage and neurophysiologic deficits in experimental models of stroke. *Annals of The New York Academy of Sciences, 993*(Neuroprotective Agents: Sixth International Conference), 35–47.

Riegel, A. C., & Kalivas, P. W. (2010). Role of Zolpidem in the Management of Insomnia. *Nature, 463*(7282), 743–744.

Riemann, D. D., Berger, M., & Voderholzer, U. (2001). Sleep and depression- Results from psychobiological studies: An overview. *Biological Psychology, 57*(1-3), 67–103.

Robinson, S. E., Foxx, S. D., Posner, M. G., Martin, R. M., Davis, T. R., Guo, H., et al. (1990). The effect of M1 muscarinic blockade on behavior and physiologic responses following traumatic brain injury in the rat. *Brain Research, 511*, 141–148.

Rodenbeck, A., Huether, G., Rüther, E., & Hajak, G. (2007). Altered circadian melatonin secretion patterns in relation to sleep in patients with chronic sleep-wake rhythm disorders. *Journal of Pineal Research, 25*, 201–210.

Rodriguiz, R. M., Chu, R., Caron, M. G., & Wetsel, W. C. (2004). Aberrant responses in social interaction of dopamine transporter knockout mice. *Behavioural Brain Research, 148*(1-2), 185–198.

Rogoz, Z., Dlaboga, D., & Dziedzicka-Wasylewska, M. (2003). Effect of combined treatment with imipramine and amantadine on the central dopamine D2 and D3 receptors in rats. *Journal of Physiology and Pharmacology, 54*(2), 257–270.

Ron, S., Algom, D., & Cohen, M. (1980). Time-related changes in the distribution of sleep stages in brain injured patients. *Electroencephalography and Clinical Neurophysiology, 48*(4), 432–441.

Rosekind, M. R. (1992). The epidemiology and occurrence of insomnia. *Journal of Clinical Psychiatry, 53*(Suppl), 4–6.

Rosenthal, M., Christensen, B. K., & Ross, T. P. (1998). Depression following traumatic brain injury. *Archives of Physical Medicine and Rehabilitation, 79*(1), 90–103.

Ross, B. M., Mamalias, N., Moszczynska, A., Rajput, A. H., & Kish, S. J. (2001). Elevated activity of phospholipid biosynthetic enzymes in substantia nigra of patients with Parkinson's disease. *Neuroscience, 102*, 899–904.

Roth, T., Roehrs, T., Zorick, F., & Conway, W. (1985). Pharmacological effects of sedative-hypnotics, narcotic analgesics, and alcohol during sleep. *The Medical Clinics of North America, 69*(6), 1281–1288.

Rudolph, U., & Möhler, H. (2004). Analysis of GABAA receptor function and dissection of the pharmacology of benzodiazepines and general anesthetics through mouse genetics. *Annual Review of Pharmacology and Toxicology, 44*, 475–498.

Rudolph, U., & Möhler, H. (2006). GABA-based therapeutic approaches: GABAA receptor subtype functions. *Current Opinion in Pharmacology, 6*(1), 18–23.

Russell, K. C., Arenth, P. M., Scanlon, J. M., Kessler, L. J., & Ricker, J. H. (2011). A functional magnetic resonance imaging investigation of episodic memory after traumatic brain injury. *Journal of Clinical and Experimental Neuropsychology, 33*(5), 538–547.

Russo, R. N., & O'Flaherty, S. (2000). Bromocriptine for the management of autonomic dysfunction after severe traumatic brain injury. *Journal of Paediatrics and Child Health, 36*(3), 283–285.

Saija, A., Hayes, R. L., Lyeth, B. G., Dixon, C. E., Yamamoto, T., & Robinson, S. E. (1988). The effect of concussive head injury on central cholinergic neurons. *Brain Research, 452*(1-2), 303–311.

Saija, A., Robinson, S. E., Lyeth, B. G., Dixon, C. E., Yamamoto, T., Clifton, G. L., et al. (1988). The effects of scopolamine and traumatic brain injury on central cholinergic neurons. *Journal of Neurotrauma, 5*(2), 161–170.

Salzman, C., Wolfson, A. N., Schatzberg, A., Looper, J., Henke, R., Albanese, M., et al. (1995). Effect of fluoxetine on anger in symptomatic volunteers with borderline personality disorder. *Journal of Clinical Psychopharmacology, 15*(1), 23–29.

Samel, A., Wegmann, H. M., Vejvoda, M., Maass, H., Gundel, A., & Schütz, M. (1991). Influence of melatonin treatment on human circadian rhythmicity before and after a simulated 9-hr time shift. *Journal of Biological Rhythms, 6*(3), 235–248.

Sandel, M. E., Olive, D. A., & Rader, M. A. (1993). Chlorpromazine-induced psychosis after brain injury. *Brain Injury, 7*(1), 77–83.

Saniova, B., Drobny, M., Kneslova, L., & Minarik, M. (2004). The outcome of patients with severe head injuries treated with amantadine sulphate. *Journal of Neural Transmission, 111*, 511–514.

Saran, A. S. (1985). Depression after minor closed head injury: Role of dexamethasone suppression test and antidepressants. *Journal of Clinical Psychiatry, 46*(8), 335–338.

Sarhill, N., Walsh, D., Nelson, K. A., Hornsi, J., LeGrand, S., & Davis, M. P. (2001). Methylphenidate for fatigue in advanced cancer: A prospective open-label pilot study. *American Journal of Hospice & Palliative Medicine, 18*(3), 187–192.

Sawyer, E., Mauro, L. S., & Ohlinger, M. J. (2008). Amantadine enhancement of arousal and cognition after traumatic brain injury. *Annals of Pharmacotherapy, 42*, 247–252.

Schallert, T., Hernandez, T. D., & Barth, T. M. (1986). Recovery of function after brain damage: Severe and chronic disruption by diazepam. *Brain Research, 379*(1), 104–111.

Schallert, T., Hernandez, T. D., & Barth, T. M. (1986). Recovery of function after brain damage: Severe and chronic disruption by diazepam. *Brain Research, 379*(1), 104–111.

Scharf, M. B., & Sachais, B. A. (1990). Sleep laboratory evaluation of the effects and efficacy of trazodone in depressed insomniac patients. *Journal of Clinical Psychiatry, 51*, 13–17.

Schertz, M., & Steinberg, T. (2008). Seizures induced by the combination treatment of methylphenidate and sertraline. *Journal of Child and Adolescent Psychopharmacology, 18*(3), 301–303.

Schmidt, R. H., & Grady, S. (1995). Loss of forebrain cholinergic neurons following fluid-percussion injury: Implications for cognitive impairment in closed head injury. *Journal of Neurosurgery, 83*, 496–502.

Secades, J. J. (2995). Citicholine: Pharmacological and clinical review, 2006 updated. *Methods & Findings in Experimental & Clinical Pharmacology, 17*, S1–54.

Seel, R. T., Kreutzer, J. S., Rosenthal, M., Hammond, F. M., Corrigan, J. D., & Black, K. (2003). Depression after traumatic brain injury: A National Institute on Disability and Rehabilitation Research Model Systems multicenter investigation. *Archives of Physical Medicine and Rehabilitation, 84*(2), 177–184.

Shahar, E. M., & Brand, N. (1992). Effect of add-on amantadine therapy for refractory absence epilepsy. *Journal of Pediatrics, 121*(5), 819–821.

Shankle, W. R., Nielson, K. A., & Cotman, C. W. (1995). Low-dose propranolol reduces aggression and agitation resembling that associated with orbitofrontal dysfunction in elderly demented patients. *Alzheimer Disease & Associated Disorders, 9*(4), 233–237.

Shekleton, J. A., Parcell, D. L., Redman, J. R., Ponsford, J. L., & Rajaratnam, S. M. (2010). Sleep disturbance and melatonin levels following traumatic brain injury. *Neurology, 74*(21), 1732–1738.

Shen, Y. X., Xu, S. Y., Wei, W., Sun, X. X., Liu, L. H., Yang, J., et al. (2002). The protective effects of melatonin from oxidative damage induced by amyloid beta-peptide 25–35 in middle-aged rats. *Journal of Pineal Research, 32*(2), 85–89.

Shen, Y. X., Xu, S. Y., Wei, W., Sun, X. X., Yang, J., & Dong, C. (2002). Melatonin reduces memory changes and neural oxidative damage in mice treated with D-galactose. *Journal of Pineal Research, 32*(3), 173–178.

Shibui, K., Uchiyama, M., & Okawa, M. (1999). Melatonin Rhythms in Delayed Sleep Phase Syndrome. *Journal of Biological Rhythms, 14*(72), 72–76.

Shilo, L., Dagan, Y., Smorjik, Y., Weinberg, U., Dolev, S., Komptel, B., et al. (2000). Effect of melatonin on sleep quality of COPD intensive care patients: A pilot study. *Chronobiology International, 17*(1), 71–76.

Silver, J. M., Koumaras, B., Chen, M., Mirski, D., Potkin, S. G., Reyes, P., et al. (2006). Effects of rivastigmine on cognitive function in patients with traumatic brain injury. *Neurology, 67*(5), 748–755.

Silver, J. M., Yudofsky, S. C., & Anderson, K. E. (2005). Aggressive disorders. In J. M. Silver, T. W. McAllister, & S. C. Yudofsky, *Textbook of Traumatic Brain Injury* (pp. 259–277). Washington D.C.: American Psychiatric Publishing, Inc.

Simpson, D. M., & Foster, D. (1986). Improvement in organically disturbed behavior with trazodone treatment. *Journal of Clinical Psychiatry, 47*(4), 191–193.

Sloan, R. L., Brown, K. W., & Pentland, B. (1992). Fluoxetine as a treatment for emotional lability after brain injury. *Brain Injury, 6*(4), 315–319.

Speech, T. J., Rao, S. M., Osmon, D. C., & Sperry, L. T. (1993). A double-blind controlled study of methylphenidate treatment in closed head injury. *Brain Injury, 7*(4), 333–338.

Stainslav, S. W., Fabre, T., Crimson, M. L., & Childs, A. (1994). Buspirone's efficacy in organic-induced aggression. *Journal of Clinical Psychopharmacology, 14*(2), 126–130.

Stanislav, S. W. (1997). Cognitive effects of antipsychotic agents in persons with traumatic brain injury. *Brain Injury, 11*(5), 335–341.

Steele, D. L., Rajaratnam, S. M., Redman, J. R., & Ponsford, J. L. (2005). The Effect of Traumatic Brain Injury on the Timing of Sleep. *Chronobiology International, 22*(1), 89–105.

Steward, S. A. (2005). The effects of benzodiazepines on cognition. *Journal of Clinical Psychiatry, 66*(2), S9–13.

Stoll, A. L., Pillay, S. S., Diamond, L., Workum, S. B., & Cole, J. O. (1996). Methylphenidate augmentation of serotonin selective reuptake inhibitors: A case series. *Journal of Clinical Psychiatry, 57*, 72–76.

Stone, B. M. (1980). Sleep and low doses of Alcohol. *Electroencephalography and Clinical Neurophysiology, 48*, 706–709.

Takahashi, T., Yamashita, H., Zhang, Y., & Nakamura, S. (1996). Inhibitory effect of MK-801 on amantadine-induced dopamine release in the rat striatum. *Brain Research Bulletin, 41*(6), 363–367.

Tan, M., & Appleton, R. (2005). Attention deficit and hyperactivity disorder, methylphenidate, and epilepsy. *Archives of Disease in Childhood, 90*, 57–59.

Tateno, A., Jorge, R. E., & Robinson, R. G. (2003). Clinical correlates of aggressive behavior after traumatic brain injury. *Journal of Neuropsychiatry & Clinical Neuroscience, 15*, 155–160.

Temkin, N. R., Dikmen, S. S., Anderson, G. D., Wilensky, A. J., Holmes, M. D., Cohen, W., et al. (1999). Valproate therapy for prevention of posttraumatic seizures: A randomized trial. *Journal of Neurosurgery, 91*(4), 593–600.

Temkin, N. R., Dikmen, S. S., Wilensky, A. J., Keihm, J., Chabal, S., & Winn, H. R. (1990). A randomized, double-blind study of phenytoin for the prevention of post-traumatic seizures. *New England Journal of Medicine, 323*(8), 497–502.

Tenovuo, O. (2005). Central acetylcholinesterase inhibitors in the treatment of chronic traumatic brain injury-clinical experience in 111 patients. *Progress in Neuropsychopharmacology, Biology and Psychiatry, 29*, 61–67.

Thomsen, I. V. (1984). Late outcome of very severe blunt head trauma: A 10-15 year second follow-up. *Journal of Neurology, Neurosurgery & Psychiatry, 47*, 260–268.

Tiberti, C., Sabe, L., Jason, L., & al., e. (1998). A randomized, double-blind placebo-controlled study of methylphenidate in patients with organic amnesia. *European Journal of Neurology, 5*(3), 297–299.

Tietelman, E. (2001). Off-label uses of modafinil. *The American Journal of Psychiatry, 158*(6), 970–971.

Tobin, H., & Logue, A. W. (1994). Self-control across species (Columba livia, Homo sapiens, and Rattus norvegicus). *Journal of Comparative Psychology, 108*(2), 126–133.

Tonkonogy, J. M. (1991). Violence and temporal lobe lesion: Head CT and MRI data. *Journal of Neuropsychiatry & Clinical Neurosciences, 3*, 189–196.

Turner-Stokes, L., Hassan, N., Pierce, K., & Clegg, F. (2002). Managing depression in brain injury rehabilitation: The use of an integrated care pathway and preliminary report of response to sertraline. *Clinical Rehabilitation, 16*(3), 261–268.

van Erp, A. M., & Miczek, K. A. (2000). Aggressive behavior, increased accumbal dopamine and decreased cortical serotonin in rats. *Journal of Neuroscience, 15*, 9320–9325.

Van Reekum, R., Bayley, M., Garner, S., Burke, I. M., Fawcett, S., Hart, A., et al. (1995). N of 1 Study: Amantadine for the amotivational syndrome in a patient with traumatic brain injury. *Brain Injury, 9*(1), 49–53.

van Woerkom, T. C., Minderhoud, J. M., Gottschal, T., & Nicolai, G. (1982). Neurotransmitters in the treatment of patients with severe head injuries. *European Neurology, 21*(4), 227–234.

van Zomeren, A. H., & van den Burg, W. (1985). Residual complaints of patients two years after severe head injury. *Journal of Neurology, Neurosurgery & Psychiatry, 48*, 21–28.

van Zomeren, A. H., Brouwer, W. H., & Deelman, B. G. (1984). Attentional deficits: The riddles of selectivity, speed, and alertness. In D. Brooks (Ed.), *Closed Head Injury: Psychological, Social, and Family Consequences* (pp. 74–107). New York: Oxford University Press.

Verster, J. C., Veldhuijzen, D. S., & Volkerts, E. R. (2004). Residual effects of sleep medication on driving ability. *Sleep Medicine Reviews, 8*(4), 309–325.

Vincent, F. M., Zimmerman, J. E., & van Haren, J. (1986). Neuroleptic malignant syndrome complicating closed head injury. *Neurosurgery, 18*(2), 190–193.

Wagner, A. K., Drewencki, L. L., Chen, C., Santos, R. F., Khan, A. S., Harun, R., et al. (2009a). Chronic methylphenidate treatment enhances striatal dopamine neurotransmission after experimental traumatic brain injury. *Journal of Neurochemistry, 108*, 986–997.

Wagner, A. K., Kline, A. E., Ren, D., Willard, L. A., Wenger, M. K., Zafonte, R. D., et al. (2007b). Gender associations with chronic methylphenidate treatment and behavioral performance following experimental traumatic brain injury. *Behavioural Brain Research, 181*, 200–209.

Wagner, A. K., Ren, D., Conley, Y. P., Ma, X., Kerr, M. E., Zafonte, R. D., et al. (2007). Sex and genetic associations with cerebrospinal fluid dopamine and metabolite production after severe traumatic brain injury. *Journal of Neurosurgery, 106*, 538–547.

Wagner, A. K., Sokoloski, J. E., Chen, X., Harun, R., Clossin, D. P., Khan, A. S., et al. (2009b). Controlled cortical impact injury influences methylphenidate-induced changes in striatal dopamine neurotransmission. *Journal of Neurochemistry, 110*, 801–810.

Wagner, A. K., Sokoloski, J. E., Ren, D., Chen, X., Khan, A. S., Zafonte, R. D., et al. (2005b). Controlled cortical impact injury affects dopaminergic transmission in the rat striatum. *Journal of Neurochemistry, 95*(2), 457–467.

Walker, G. C., Cardenas, D. D., Guthrie, M. R., McLean, A., & Brooke, M. M. (1991). Fatigue and depression in brain-injured patients correlated with quadriceps strength and endurance. *Archives of Physical Medicine and Rehabilitation, 72*(7), 469–472.

Wamsley, J. K., & Hunt, M. A. (1991). Relative affinity of quazepam for type-1 benzodiazepine receptors in brain. *Journal of Clinical Psychiatry, 52*(Suppl 9), S15–20.

Warden, D. L., Gordon, B., McAllister, T. W., Silver, J. M., Barth, J. T., Bruns, J., et al. (2006). Guidelines for the pharmacologic treatment of neurobehavioral sequelae of traumatic brain injury. *Journal of Neurotrauma, 23*(10), 1468–1501.

Watanabe, M. D., Martin, E. M., DeLeon, O. A., Gaviria, M., Pavel, D. G., & Trepashko, D. W. (1995). Successful methylphenidate treatment of apathy after subcortical infarcts. *Journal of Neuropsychiatry and Clinical Neurosciences, 7*, 502–504.

Watson, N. F., Dikmen, S., Machamer, J., Doherty, M., & Temkin, N. (2007). Hypersomnia following traumatic brain injury. *Journal of Clinical Sleep Medicine, 3*(4), 363–368.

Weinberg, R. M., Auerbach, S. H., & Moore, S. (1987). Pharmacological treatment of cognitive deficits: A case study. *Brain Injury, 1,* 57–59.

Whyte, J., & Myers, R. (2009). Incidence of clinically significant responses to zolpidem among patients with disorders of consciousness: A preliminary placebo controlled trial. *American Journal of Physical Medicine & Rehabilitation, 88*(5), 410–418.

Whyte, J., Hart, T., Vaccaro, M., Grieb-Neff, P., Risser, A., Polansky, M., et al. (2004). Effects of methylphenidate on attention deficits after traumatic brain injury: A multidimensional, randomized, controlled trial. *American Journal of Physical Medicine & Rehabilitation, 83,* 401–420.

Whyte, J., Katz, D., Long, D., DiPasquale, M. C., Polansky, M., Kalmar, K., et al. (2005). Predictors of outcome in prolonged posttraumatic disorders of consciousness and assessment of medication effects: A multicenter study. *Archives of Physical Medicine and Rehabilitation, 86*(3), 453–462.

Wilson, J. T., Hadley, D. M., & Wiedmann, K. D. (1995). Neuropsychological consequences of two patterns of brain damage shown by MRI in survivors of severe head injury. *Journal of Neurological Psychiatry, 59,* 328–331.

Wilson, M. S., & Hamm, R. J. (2002). Effects of fluoxetine on the 5-HT1A receptor and recovery of cognitive function after traumatic brain injury in rats. *American Journal of Physical Medicine & Rehabilitation, 81*(5), 364–372.

Wilson, M. S., Chen, X., Ma, X., Ren, D., Wagner, A. K., Reynolds, I. J., et al. (2005). Synaptosomal dopamine uptake in rat striatum following controlled cortical impact. *Journal of Neuroscience Research, 80*(1), 85–91.

Wilson, M. S., Gibson, C. J., & Hamm, R. J. (2003). Haloperidol, but not olanzapine, impairs cognitive performance after traumatic brain injury in rats. *American Journal of Physical Medicine & Rehabilitation, 82*(11), 871–879.

Wise, S. P., Murray, E. A., & Gerfen, C. R. (1996). The frontal cortex-basal ganglia system in primates. *Critical Reviews in Neurobiology, 10*(3–4), 317–356.

Wroblewski, B. A., Joseph, A. B., & Cornblatt, R. R. (1996). Antidepressant pharmacotherapy and the treatment of depression in patients with severe traumatic brain injury: A controlled, prospective study. *Journal of Clinical Psychiatry, 57*(12), 582–587.

Wroblewski, B. A., Joseph, A. B., Kupfer, J., & Kalliel, K. (1997). Effectiveness of valproic acid on destructive and aggressive behaviours in patients with acquired brain injury. *Brain Injury, 11*(1), 37–47.

Wroblewski, B. A., Leary, J. M., Phelan, A. M., Whyte, J., & Manning, K. (1992). Methylphenidate and seizure frequency in brain injured patients with seizure disorders. *Journal of Clinical Psychiatry, 53*(3), 86–89.

Wroblewski, B. A., McColgan, K., Smith, K., Whyte, J., & Singer, W. D. (1990). The incidence of seizures during tricyclic antidepressant drug treatment in a brain-injured population. *Journal of Clinical Psychopharmacology, 10*(2), 124–128.

Wu, T. S., & Garmel, G. M. (2005). Improved neurological function after Amantadine treatment in two patients with brain injury. *Journal of Emergency Medicine, 28*(3), 289–292.

Wurtman, R. J. (2000). Age-related decreases in melatonin secretion—clinical consequences. *The Journal of Clinical Endocrinology & Metabolism, 85*(6), 2135–2136.

Yan, H. Q., Kline, A. E., Ma, X., Hooghe-Peters, E. L., Marion, D. W., & Dixon, C. E. (2001). Tyrosine hydroxylase, but not dopamine beta-hydroxylase, is increased in rat frontal cortex after traumatic brain injury. *Neuroreport, 12*(11), 2323–2327.

Yan, H. Q., Kline, A. E., Ma, X., Li, Y., & Dixon, C. E. (2002). Traumatic brain injury reduces dopamine transporter protein expression in the rat frontal cortex. *NeuroReport, 13*(15), 1899–1901.

Yan, H. Q., Ma, X., Chen, X., Li, Y., Shao, L., & Dixon, C. E. (2007). Delayed increase of tyrosine hydroxylase expression in rat nigrostriatal system after traumatic brain injury. *Brain Research, 1134,* 171–179.

Yuwiler, A. (1989). Effects of steroids on serotonin-N-acetyltransferase activity of pineals in organ culture. *Journal of Neurochemistry, 52,* 46–53.

Zafonte, R. D., Bagiella, E., Ansel, B. M., Novack, T. A., Friedewald, W. T., Hesdorffer, D. C., et al. (2012). Effect of citicoline on functional and cognitive status among patients with traumatic brain injury: Citicoline brain injury treatment trial (cobrit). *Journal of the American Medical Association, 308*(19), 1993–2000.

Zafonte, R. D., Watanabe, T., & Mann, N. R. (1998). Amantadine: A potential treatment for the minimally conscious state. *Brain Injury, 12*(7), 617–621.

Zafonte, R., Friedewald, W. T., Lee, S. M., Levin, B., Diaz-Arrastia, R., Ansel, B., et al. (2009). The Citicoline Brain Injury Treatment (COBRIT) Trial: Design and Methods. *Journal of Neurotrama, 26*(12), 2207–2216.

Zhang, L., Plotkin, R. C., Wang, G., Sandel, E., & Lee, S. (2004). Cholinergic augmentation with donepezil enhances recovery in short-term memory and sustained attention after traumatic brain injury. *Archives of Physical Medicine and Rehabilitation, 85,* 1050–1055.

Zhdanova, I. V., Wurtman, R. J., Regan, M. M., Taylor, J. A., Shi, J. P., & Leclair, O. U. (2001). Melatonin treatment for age-related insomnia. *The*

Journal of Clinical Endocrinology & Metabolism, 86(10), 4727–4730.

Zhou, B., Zhang, Q., Tian, L., Xiao, J., Stefan, H., & Zhou, D. (2008). Effects of levetirecitam as an add-on therapy on cognitive function and quality of life in patients with refractory partial seizures. *Epilepsy & Behavior, 12*(2), 305–310.

Ziegler, G., Ploch, M., Miettinen-Baumann, A., & Collet, W. (2002). Efficacy and tolerability of valerian extract LI 156 compared with oxazepam in the treatment of non-organic insomnia-a randomized, double-blind, comparative clinical study. *European Journal of Medical Research, 7*(11), 480–486.

Zifko, U. A., Rupp, M., Schwarz, S., Zipko, H. T., & Maida, E. M. (2002). Modafinil in treatment of fatigue in multiple sclerosis: Results of an open-label study. *Journal of Neurology, 249,* 983–987.

Zisapel, N. (1999). The use of melatonin for the treatment of insomnia. *Biological Signals and Receptors, 8,* 84–89.

Zou, H., Brayer, S., Hurwitz, M., Fowler, L., & Wagner, A. K. (2013). Neuroprotective, neuroplastic, and neurobehavioral effects of daily treatment with levetiracetam in experimental TBI. *Neurorehabilitation and Neural Repair, 27*(9), 878–888.

Part IV

Methodological and Technological Advances

14

Advanced Neuroimaging in Traumatic Brain Injury

Elisabeth A. Wilde, Kareem W. Ayoub, Erin D. Bigler, Jill V. Hunter, and Harvey S. Levin

Neuroimaging has begun to play an increasingly important role in the clinical diagnosis and management of traumatic brain injury (TBI). Computed tomography (CT) is routinely used in the acute setting to assess the presence of pathology, particularly forms of pathology that may require surgical intervention. Description of findings on conventional magnetic resonance imaging (MRI) sequences, including T1-weighted, T2-weighted, and fluid attenuated inversion recovery (FLAIR) sequences, have also been used clinically to examine the presence of or change in chronic forms of TBI-related pathology. However, in addition to more conventional sequences, advanced quantitative applications of MRI and other imaging modalities have opened new possibilities for the role of neuroimaging in TBI clinical diagnosis and management as well as in research application. For example, several recently-developed MRI sequences have shown significant promise in the detection of more subtle structural pathology or tissue alteration as well as functional change. Recent imaging studies have also enhanced our perspective of short- and long-term TBI-related changes and their interactions with normal development. Additionally, various brain imaging modalities have provided greater insight into the complexities of focal and diffuse injury and the manner in which these affect the cognitive and functional outcomes following TBI. In this chapter, we offer a brief introduction to the history of quantification in CT and MRI, and then present several promising advanced and

quantitative imaging modalities, providing a brief explanation of the sequence or modality, a review of its application in TBI, and some notes regarding special considerations and limitations of the technique.

History of Quantification in Neuroimaging

Prior to the advent of modern neuroimaging techniques, there were few non-invasive methods to visually inspect the brain in patients with TBI. This changed with the advent of CT in the early 1970's, where an immediate utility was demonstrated in evaluating TBI (French & Dublin, 1977). Brain CT imaging is based on a density coefficient reflecting differences in brain parenchyma from skull and cerebrospinal fluid (CSF), but the images in the 1970's were crude, and their interpretation strictly clinical, as image quantification techniques were not initially used. However, it soon became evident that quantification may provide an advantage, and limited application of quantification was attempted. Some of the first attempts at image quantification predate CT and were derived using pneumoencephalography (PEG), a neuroimaging technique which was based on replacing CSF with air to provide a silhouette of the ventricle from a standard skull film or fluoroscopy. The established quantitative metric developed for PEG studies was based on the linear distance of the width of the lateral ventricle, typically with respect to the frontal view where the side-to-side distance of the lateral ventricle was compared to linear distance in the same plane of the inner table of the skull. This metric was termed the ventricle-to-brain ratio or VBR (Booker, Matthews, & Whitehurst, 1969). An established post-mortem neuropathological finding in TBI was ventricular enlargement as a reflection of generalized cerebral atrophy (Strich, 1956), and increased VBR as defined in PEG studies of TBI was considered an indicator of the degree of cerebral atrophy (Isherwood, Mawdsley, & Ferguson, 1966). While CT was a distinct improvement over PEG, there were neither established methods nor computer-based techniques to measure trauma-induced atrophic changes, so VBR measurement adapted from PEG was applied to CT imaging, with manual measurement of the same type of linear distances. Thus, VBR was the first quantitative measurement applied to CT imaging in assessing the effects of TBI on neurological and neuropsychological outcome (Cullum & Bigler, 1986; Levin, Meyers, Grossman, & Sarwar, 1981; Meyers, Levin, Eisenberg, & Guinto, 1983). These simple linear measurements, in addition to clinical radiological judgment, remained the primary method of documenting atrophic brain changes following brain injury, well into the 1980's.

Improvements in computer technology in the 1980's facilitated development of a variety of image analysis software programs that allowed investigators to trace the entire brain (Turkheimer, Cullum, Hubler, Paver, Yeo, & Bigler, 1984). Additionally, the advent of MRI, which provided enhanced image resolution and the ability to image in planes other than the axial plane, facilitated the measurement of additional regions of interest (ROI) such as the hippocampus on MRI (Bigler et al., 1997). Although there are continuing attempts to use quantification of CT in improving prediction of outcome in patients with TBI (Yuh, Cooper, Ferguson, & Manley, 2012), many methods of advanced imaging quantification utilize MRI in one form or another. In current clinical practice, CT (standard clinical reading) remains the preferred imaging modality for initial screening and diagnosis because it can be acquired rapidly and allows excellent visualization of pathology that may require immediate intervention,

although there are now new concerns regarding radiation dosage, especially in children (Alliance for Radiation Safety in Pediatric Imaging, 2012). MRI has been increasingly used clinically to characterize anatomical features of the brain and to identify expanding lesions or brain swelling that require urgent treatment (Chanraud, Zahr, Sullivan, Pfefferbaum, 2010; Pagani, Bizzi, Di Salle, De Stefano, & Filippi, 2008). While many of the quantitative imaging techniques described below are not currently routinely utilized in clinical decision making, there has been increasing interest in the possibility of adding quantitative imaging measurement to address questions of diagnosis, prognosis, and decisions related to clinical intervention and patient management.

Advanced Neuroimaging Techniques

Advanced MRI modalities, including those specific to diffusion, blood flow, perfusion, magnetization transfer effect, metabolic alteration, and local field inhomogeneities, have yielded higher sensitivity in uncovering more subtle abnormalities which are less detectable on conventional imaging techniques and which appear to correlate with outcome of TBI (Ashwal, Wycliffe & Holshouser, 2010; Bigler et al., 2010; Pagani et al., 2008; Tong et al., 2003; Van Boven et al., 2009; Xu et al. 2010). Other technological advances have improved image resolution by optimized data acquisition and improved filling of k-space, which is the temporary image space in which raw data from digitized MR signals are stored during data acquisition and mathematically processed to reconstruct a final image. In addition, more efficient post-processing of imaging data has elucidated several important causes of TBI-related pathology. Some of the more commonly used imaging techniques that have evolved from basic MRI principles include: 1) detailed volumetric analysis, 2) diffusion tensor imaging (DTI), 3) magnetization transfer imaging (MTI), 4) susceptibility-weighted imaging (SWI), 5) functional MRI (fMRI), including resting state connectivity analysis (fcMRI), 6) arterial spin labeling (ASL), 7) magnetic resonance spectroscopy (MRS), and 8) magnetic source imaging (MSI)/magnetoencephalography (MEG), and these will be the focus of this chapter. These advanced sequences may serve as imaging-based biomarkers that allow us to improve diagnosis and the detection of additional TBI-related pathology, particularly in regard to mild TBI where focal pathology may not be evident on conventional imaging. Additionally, these imaging techniques may allow a better understanding of the time course of TBI-related changes during recovery, and also perhaps inform prognostic decision-making and intervention

Volumetrics

Summary of Technique and Uses

Since MRI is the current method of choice for detailed image quantification, MRI classification will be used as an example of the manner in which differences in tissue type can be examined and quantified. For the purposes of this discussion, methods for volumetric analysis will highlight the hippocampus as an example, but the reader should be aware that similar methods of quantification can now be applied to any ROI. In this case, the hippocampus was selected because of its strategic importance for episodic memory and other neuropsychiatric sequelae associated with hippocampal damage (Geuze, Vermetten & Bremner, 2005). Also, the hippocampus represents one of the most vulnerable structures affected by TBI (Wilde et al., 2007).

Figure 14-1 shows the MRI output of an uninjured adult at the level of the hippocampus on the T1-weighted gray scale image. From standard neuroanatomy texts (Duvernoy 1998), the boundaries of the hippocampus are well defined in gray scale. However, to better define and differentiate the hippocampus for image quantification, the tissue can be *segmented* into the basic contrast between white matter, gray matter and CSF as shown in Figure 14-1. This is done because each tissue type named above has a somewhat distinct *classification* designated by a range of MRI-derived gray scale values defined by the spin-lattice relaxation times of different tissue types in the body. Computer software that assesses the similarity of pixel classification immediately around any given pixel typically

aids the classification process. For example, white matter pixels should have similar values, which in turn reflect classification of white matter, which can be differentiated from distinctly different tissues like gray matter or CSF in the myelinated brain. On the border between gray and white matter or between brain parenchyma and CSF, a pixel may be of varying values, and so algorithms that assess the likelihood of a particular pixel most likely belonging to one tissue type help define the borders between different tissue types.

In contemporary image quantification, the first step is to classify and segment the MRI-derived pixels into gray matter, white matter or CSF and, where necessary, strip the image of the skull and other tissues, so that just brain parenchyma and CSF are present. As can be seen in the illustration shown in Figure 14-1, even though the hippocampus contains both white and gray matter, it has more gray than white matter, and is therefore classified as a predominantly gray matter structure in the segmented image. For each slice that contains classified hippocampal tissue, the surface area is calculated. Next, if the slice thickness of the MRI image and the gap distance between slices are known, the hippocampal volume for each slice can be calculated, and by summing these measurements, an estimate of total hippocampal volume is computed. Repeating this basic process for any ROI will yield the volume of the brain structure under examination.

It is well established that one of the long-term consequences of TBI is cerebral atrophy. The time course for progression of atrophy, the brain regions most affected, and the pattern and magnitude of changes in their volumes have been the object of some research (Ariza et al., 2006; Bigler, Anderson, & Blatter, 2002; Gale, Johnson, Bigler, & Blatter, 1995; MacKenzie et al., 2002). Measurement of brain region volumes based on conventional MRI has improved because of significant leaps in image quantification by standardization through automated methods of image analysis (Jovicich et al., 2009) and the development of large normative databases for image comparison (Brewer, Magda, Airriess, & Smith, 2009). The "gold-standard" of image quantification has traditionally been manual tracing, but as shown by Bigler and colleagues

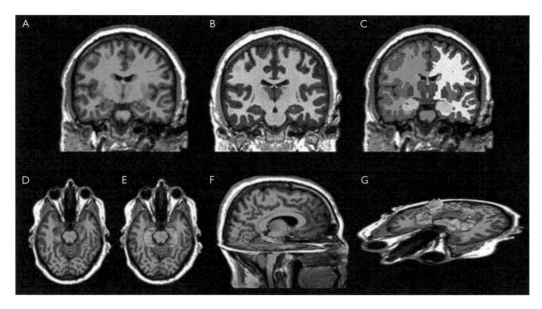

Figure 14-1. (A) T1-weighted coronal image in gray-scale format. (B) Segmentation of the gray scale image where red identifies gray matter, white as white matter and black as CSF. (C) Colorized classified image differentiating different brain regions by color. In this example, the yellow color identifies the hippocampus. (D) Axial view of the T1-weighted image showing the three-dimensional (3-D) identified hippocampus from a top-down view (E), lateral view (F) and left frontal oblique (G). *Summary of Literature to Date in TBI.* See color insert.

(Bigler et al., 2010), as well as other researchers (Irimia et al., 2011), automated methods approach the robustness of operator-controlled methods and provide a very reliable and fast method for volumetric determination. Also, these techniques provide computational methods for calculating various metrics associated with volume measurement and cortical thickness estimates for all Brodmann areas (Merkley, Bigler, Wilde, McCauley, Hunter, & Levin, 2008; Palacios et al., 2012). In the above example using the hippocampus, manual, operator-controlled methods take hours of tracing to quantify a single hippocampal volume. If other structures are also measured, image quantification for a single subject can take days. In contrast, automated methods can be achieved with minimal operator time and are highly reproducible; therefore, these represent the current standard in the field of image quantification in TBI (Warner et al., 2010).

Recent studies have concluded that volumetric imaging does not reveal uniform differences in brain region volumes between TBI and control groups, but atrophic changes that do occur have been reported to be most prominent in the frontal white matter, the thalamus, cingulum bundle, hippocampus, corpus callosum, and parts of the cerebellum following moderate to severe TBI (Bendlin et al., 2008; Wilde et al., 2007; Wu et al., 2010). Atrophic changes measured on imaging have been reported up to well over a year post-injury as several regions continue to exhibit decreases in volume (Bendlin et al., 2008; Farbota et al., 2012; Wu et al., 2010). Further longitudinal studies are needed to examine the extent of these changes and determine whether they plateau or continue long-term, particularly at older age ranges. Investigators have attributed reduction in brain region volume primarily to Wallerian degeneration where the torn axons exhibit die-back and die-forward effects as they are separated from the neuron cell body. However, other longitudinal studies in children have postulated that in addition to tissue loss that results in decreased volume, TBI sustained in childhood may alter the trajectory of developmental cortical thinning in certain regions (Wilde, Merkley, et al., 2012).

Figure 14.2 readily demonstrates how volumetrics and three-dimensional (3-D) imaging

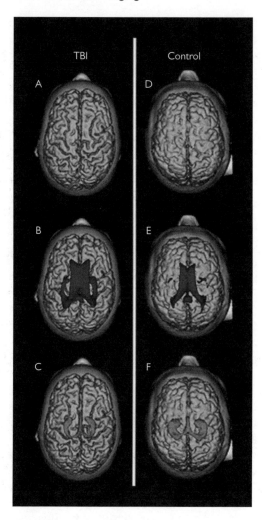

Figure 14-2. The image on the left is from a 14-year old male child who sustained a severe TBI, compared to an age-matched healthy control on the right. A and D show a 3-D rendering of the brain from a top-down perspective where obvious prominence of the cerebral sulci is present, reflective of a more generalized atrophy. B and E show the ventricular dilation (ventricles depicted in blue) present in the child with TBI as compared to the uninjured child, also from a top-down view. The bottom two images (C and F) show a comparison between the two children of the hippocampus with a segment of the fornix (depicted in yellow) attached in the same view. Note the decreased volume in the hippocampus of the child with TBI. See color insert.

from the same subject using the segmented and classified imaging data. Data from any particular patient can be rendered and visually compared to a control image to illustrate differences between the injured and non-injured brain as depicted in Figure 14-2. In this figure, the 3-D rendering of an atrophic hippocampus in the child with TBI is presented side-by-side with an age-matched control child to readily demonstrate a 40% reduction in hippocampal volume.

Limitations and Special Considerations

While the acquisition of data commonly utilized for volumetric analysis (e.g., 3-D T1-weighted imaging) is relatively straightforward, several important considerations related to volumetric measurement and analysis deserve mention. First, automated programs for volumetric measurement may have accuracy limitations in brain regions that are difficult to model (e.g., medial temporal areas) or that contain large focal lesions or extreme distortion of the cortical surface. Moreover, many of the more automated methods of volumetric analysis utilize only T1-weighted imaging, so smaller lesions or certain kinds of pathology that are not as distinguishable on T1-weighted imaging (e.g., appear isointense on T1-weighted imaging), such as gliosis, will be easily missed. Finally, determination of TBI-related cortical change requires an appropriate normative comparison given the dynamic changes that occur over time, especially in children and adolescents, and with neurodegeneration and atrophy in the elderly. Several manual and semi-automated techniques produce inaccuracies in segmentation of white and gray matter in very young children because of the different water content of the infant brain and consequent reduction in contrast.

Interpretation may also be complicated by several factors. TBI-related volumetric changes can evolve over an extended period of time (Farbota, Sodhi et al., 2012; Sidaros et al., 2009; Trivedi et al., 2007; Wu et al., 2010) and may be evident later than changes seen on other advanced imaging techniques like DTI (Bendlin et al. 2008; Groen, Buitelaar, van der Gaag, & Zwiers, 2010; Hutchinson et al., 2010; Wu et al., 2010). The relation between brain tissue integrity as measured by volumetry

can be applied. Volumetric analyses permit not only a reliable calculation of volume, but also a graphical display of an ROI as a 3-D image and functional outcome may be complex and dynamic, particularly in the earlier phases of recovery as trajectories of rapid cognitive recovery and progressive degenerative tissue change may be divergent in direction and magnitude. This relation becomes even more complex in infants, children, adolescents and the elderly where TBI-related parenchymal and cognitive changes are occurring within a context of known developmental (e.g., linear increases/decreases in white matter with myelination, regional reductions in regional cortical thickness and volume related to programmed apoptosis) or degenerative brain changes. Variations in severity of injury, nature and location of brain insult, mechanism of injury, and other co-morbidities present additional challenges for group level volumetric analysis in TBI. Clearly, much still needs to be understood in order for these techniques to be widely utilized as predictive tools in a clinical setting at an individual level. Although several studies have found relationships between cognitive measures in TBI and volumetric changes (Bergeson et al., 2004; Himanen, Portin, Isoniemi, Helenius, Kurti, & Tenovio, 2005; Serra-Grabulosa, Junque, Verger, Salgado-Pineda, Maneru, & Mercader, 2005; Sherer et al., 2006; Palacios et al., 2012), many studies have found no correlation between the two (Anderson, Bigler & Blatter, 1995; Sherer et al., 2006; Yount et al., 2002). As seen in the DTI section below, it is plausible that disruption of connectivity of brain circuitry involved in cognitive operations such as frontal-parietal and frontal-hippocampal connections subserving episodic memory may be more strongly related to cognitive performance after TBI than atrophic changes in the participating regions (Palacios et al., 2012).

Diffusion Tensor Imaging

Summary of Technique and Uses

DTI is a noninvasive *in vivo* interrogation of the brain's architecture via the use of water diffusion properties. Specifically, diffusion imaging sequences utilize water diffusion properties in tissue over a given time interval based on random molecular (Brownian) motion. In the process of diffusion, the interaction of the water molecules with the surrounding environment provides information about the degree and direction of water motion, and allows inference regarding structural information. If the water molecules encounter regularly-ordered barriers that restrict the direction of motion of the water along one direction relative to another direction during the same amount of time, the diffusion is considered to be anisotropic. In contrast, isotropic diffusion refers to the phenomenon of equal diffusion in all directions, such as that which occurs when there are no barriers to diffusion or when the barriers are randomly oriented. These fundamental concepts serve as the basis for DTI. Essentially, greater or lesser diffusion of the water molecules in the tissue convey information about its microstructural properties, including the medium viscosity and morphology that might present barriers to diffusion (Figure 14-3) (Chanraud, Zahr et al. 2010). DTI thus provides a refined characterization of the complex network of fibers in the brain in addition to potential information related to the structural connection of the fibers.

Fractional anisotropy (FA) measures the directional variance in diffusion in the direction of the axon. This is a fraction between 0 and 1, with 0 being completely isotropic (random and unconstrained) diffusion and 1 being completely anisotropic diffusion. The diffusion in the two axes perpendicular to the axon is diminished because the cell membrane effectively acts as a barrier to diffusion. This gives rise to the radial diffusivity (RD) metric, which

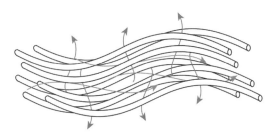

Figure 14-3. A model of diffusion of water molecules through axon bundles. Water molecules move preferentially along the direction of the axon (blue), representing more directional or anisotropic diffusion. However, molecules also move perpendicular to the axons (as indicated by green arrows). See color insert.

is the average of diffusion measured in the axes perpendicular to the primary eigenvector, or primary direction of diffusion. The overall magnitude of diffusion of water molecules in the brain is determined by a measure of its apparent diffusion coefficient (ADC). Mean diffusivity (MD) can also be derived as the average of the three eigenvalues. These and other DTI metrics have been used to quantify several of the pathologies associated with a traumatic insult to the brain.

Some researchers have suggested that DTI may be useful in measurement and characterization of TBI-induced diffuse axonal injury and demyelination in white matter. TBI has been associated with disruption of myelin integrity, at least in the early post-injury stages (Levin, 2003; Mac Donald, Dikranian, Song, Bayly, Holtzman, & Brody, 2007; Wilde et al., 2008; Chanraud et al., 2010). DTI studies have also generally reported decreased FA at sites of diffuse axonal injury. These mechanisms of injury, along with retrograde or anterograde Wallerian degeneration, effectively increase interstitial space by altering physical barriers (axons) that would otherwise restrict diffusion (Saxena & Caroni, 2007). Thus, the result is alteration in one or more DTI metrics, such as decrease in FA and increased RD and MD due to an increase in overall diffusion (Ge, Law, & Grossman, 2005). Additionally, DTI may be useful in examination of other forms of acute TBI-related pathology, such as cytotoxic edema (Bazarian, Zhong, Blyth, Zhu, Kavcic, & Peterson, 2007; Mayer et al., 2010; Wilde, McCauley, Hunter et al., 2008).

There are several methods of DTI analysis, but three that have been most frequently used in recent studies will be highlighted here. The first method, the ROI approach, specifies brain regions to measure a priori, and DTI metrics for these regions are calculated. This approach is useful when a specific region is hypothesized to be affected. The second method, fiber tractography, allows for a reconstruction of the fiber tracts of the brain based on a collection of the diffusion of water molecules around those tracts. This enables visual inspection of the changes in patients with TBI and the DTI metrics of those streamline-generated "fiber tracts." This analytic method is useful when

performing a cross-modality approach with a technique like volumetric analysis and the user must specify the fiber tract. A third analytic technique using DTI is voxel-based analysis (VBA), or whole brain analysis, such as is performed with tract-based spatial statistics (TBSS). VBA and whole brain analysis allow a holistic approach to analyzing changes in the DTI metrics of the brain without designating a specific region. VBA is useful for comparing DTI findings in two groups when there is no specific region hypothesized to differentiate the groups. Figure 14-4 below demonstrates results from an analysis performed using whole brain analysis (i.e., TBSS) in a group of veterans and service members with blast-related mild TBI versus uninjured military (previously deployed) controls. All of these analytical techniques have provided great insights into the changes in TBI post-injury as summarized below. The reader is cautioned that DTI analysis is an evolving technology so the following sections should be interpreted as a status report.

Summary of Literature to Date in TBI

Significant differences in the FA, ADC or MD or other DTI-derived diffusivity metrics have been demonstrated in studies of TBI in both adults (Betz, Zhuo, Roy, Shanmuganathan, & Gullapalli, 2012; Kraus, Susmaras, Caughlin, Walker, Sweeney, & Little, 2007; Lipton et al. 2008; McCauley et al., 2010; Palacios et al., 2012; Perlbarg, Puybasset, Tollard, Lehericy, Benali, & Galanaud, 2009; Warner et al., 2010) and children (Ewing-Cobbs et al., 2008; Kurowski et al., 2009; Levin, 2008; McCauley et al., 2011; Wilde et al., 2006; Wilde et al., 2010; Wu et al., 2010; Wozniak et al., 2007; Yuan et al., 2007), with decreases in FA and increases in measures of diffusivity often found in chronic post-injury intervals. More importantly, changes in DTI-derived measures have shown correlation with injury severity (Arfanakis, Haughton, Carew, Rogers, Dempsey, & Meyerand, 2002; Benson et al., 2007; Betz et al., 2012; Wilde et al., 2010; Yuan et al., 2007), functional outcome (Huisman, Schwamm et al., 2004; Levin et al., 2008; Salmond et al., 2006; Wozniak et al., 2007), neurologic functioning (Caeyenberghs et al., 2010; Caeyenberghs et al., 2010) and

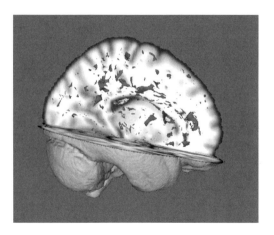

Figure 14-4. Results of a TBSS group analysis of veterans and service members with blast-related mild TBI versus "uninjured" military controls who had also been deployed during the wars in Iraq and Afghanistan. Regions indicated in blue are areas of significant FA decrease in the group with blast-related mild TBI rendered on a three-dimensional template. See color insert.

cognitive ability (Ewing-Cobbs et al.; 2008; Kraus et al., 2007; Kumar, Husain et al., 2009; Levin et al., 2008; McCauley, Wilde et al. 2010; McCauley, Wilde et al., 2011; Niogi et al., 2008; Palacios et al., 2012; Salmond et al., 2006; Warner et al., 2010; Wilde, Ramos et al. 2010). Longitudinal studies have also indicated that DTI may reveal tissue changes during recovery from TBI (Bendlin et al., 2008; Farbota, Bendlin, Alexander, Rowley, Dempsey, & Johnson, 2012; Sidaros et al., 2008; Wilde, Ayoub et al., 2012; Wilde, McCauley et al., 2012; Wu, Wilde et al., 2010).

DTI studies examining the time course of injury have suggested that structural changes following TBI in damaged structures such as the corpus callosum continue well into 18 months post-injury (Wu, Wilde et al., 2010), though incomplete recovery as manifested by continued low FA and increased MD (or ADC) is evident in longitudinal studies of both children and adults with TBI as compared to uninjured controls (Sidaros et al., 2008; Wu, Wilde et al., 2010). In fact, Sidaros and colleagues (2008) showed that some white matter regions demonstrate continued neurodegenerative change (i.e., decreased FA) over time following severe TBI.

In addition to the chronic changes that occur over time, the pattern of DTI-related changes in acute and sub-acute periods is also incompletely understood, and the presence, significance, degree, direction of change, and the presumed underlying mechanism(s) of change, remain points of controversy. Wilde and colleagues recently suggested that semi-acute change in DTI parameters such as FA was present in some patients imaged serially over the first week post-injury in uncomplicated mild TBI, but that the nature and degree of change was not consistent across all subjects (Wilde, McCauley et al., 2012). Clearly, more work is required in understanding the nature and degree of post-injury changes as assessed by DTI, but this modality may provide an important tool in examining such changes as well as the relation of these changes to brain functioning and any underlying pathology.

In summary, DTI remains a promising tool in the field of TBI for 1) assisting in clinical diagnosis (particularly in mild TBI), where focal pathology may not be evident or may not explain symptoms (Bazarian et al., 2007; Mayer et al., 2010; Miles, Grossman, Johnson, Babb, Biller, & Inglese, 2008; Wilde et al., 2008; Zappala, Thiebaut de Schotten, & Eslinger, 2012) and prognosis (Betz et al., 2012; Newcombe et al., 2007; Perlbarg et al., 2009), 2) understanding the nature, pattern and temporal course of degenerative brain changes *in vivo* (Wilde et al., 2012), 3) uncovering potential evidence for neuroplastic changes (e.g., reorganization or recovery), and 4) evaluating therapeutic interventions and the effects of rehabilitation (Farbota et al., 2012; Wilde et al., 2012).

Limitations and Special Considerations

Although advances have been made in the field of DTI research as applied to TBI, there are a few limitations that must be noted. Further studies are necessary to validate and more completely understand the neuropathological bases that underlie differences in DTI-derived metrics and how these are related to different forms of pathology in human subjects (Adams, Jennett, Murray, Teasdale, Gennarelli, & Graham, 2011), particularly given the complexity of TBI-induced tissue changes. Additionally, particular challenges surround the potential for the use of DTI in multi-site or longitudinal studies given the difficulty in establishing comparability in quantitative measures derived from data that utilize different scanner hardware or software, acquisition parameters, or methods of analysis. DTI data can also be quite vulnerable to distortion and artifacts (e.g., artifacts induced by metal, eddy current, motion, and susceptibility). At present, there is no consensus on which specific DTI metric is best used in TBI-related studies because each may be sensitive to different forms of pathology co-occurring in TBI. Indeed, studies utilizing multiple metrics examining the relation of DTI to outcome have often found disparate results between the metrics (Wilde et al., 2012). Certain forms of analysis, such as a single-slice ROI approach are challenging to reliably employ in longitudinal studies due to the difficulty in replicating the precise ROI across time points due to differences in slice placement because of altered head placement. Additionally, large focal lesions may also create challenges in many forms of DTI analysis, given field susceptibility from hemosiderin deposition, gliosis and encephalomalacia, which may skew diffusion parameters. The time course of DTI-related changes remains unknown and may vary with injury severity, mechanism of injury, and age of the participants; therefore, these factors require careful consideration. Finally, as with many advanced techniques, appropriate normative data are necessary because age-related differences can be substantial, particularly at the extreme ranges of the age spectrum. Given the sensitivity of DTI data to changes in just about any acquisition parameter (e.g., echo time, number of gradient directions, etc.), such normative data is ideally acquired using the same protocol and on the same scanner.

Techniques such as ROI or fiber tracking rely on a limited number of user-specified regions to investigate change, a requirement that could bias studies. Although VBA allows a whole-brain approach to looking for changes, it is constrained by the need for spatial registration (stretching and warping) of each individual brain from different patients to a single subject template or representative brain for the purpose of placing all brains in the same standard space. Variability in DTI results may reflect demographic and clinical features of the specific sample of patients scanned, the DTI sequence performed, scanner characteristics, time since injury, and the analytical approach to be taken (Van Boven et al., 2009). Because of the dependence on these factors, DTI analysis must be well controlled to be compared against other studies and results from different groups.

Magnetization Transfer Imaging

Summary of Technique and Uses

Unlike conventional MRI which is based on the contrast differences in T1-weighted, T2-weighted, and proton density sequences (which depend on free water protons), magnetization transfer imaging (MTI) examines the interaction between free water protons and macromolecular protons to provide a form of imaging that assesses the presence or absence of macromolecules such as those inherent in neural membranes. Particularly in cerebral white matter, the major macromolecules are proteins and phospholipids that coat the axonal membranes and myelin sheaths (Duckworth & Stevens, 2010). Through measurement of the magnitude of the magnetization interaction between molecules, MTI provides greater sensitivity in detecting changes in brain (or other neural tissue) microstructure that conventional MRI cannot detect (Duckworth & Stevens, 2010).

The imaging technique is achieved through magnetization interaction based on dipolar and/or chemical exchange. In order to do this, an off resonance radio frequency (RF) pulse is applied to macromolecular protons and some of their excited magnetization is transferred to free water protons. Through application of this pulse, the resulting signal is attenuated according to the magnitude of magnetization transfer between the macromolecules initially pulsed and the bulk water. The presence or absence of macromolecules can be inferred depending on the degree of attenuation of the signal.

MT ratio (MTR) is the quantifiable MTI parameter, which is the calculated percent variation of the saturated RF pulse image sequence with the unsaturated RF pulse image sequence (Pagani et al., 2008). The equation is as follows, where M_0 is the sequence without the RF pulse and M_s is the signal intensity with the RF pulse.

$$MTR = (M_0 - M_s)/M_0 \times 100\%$$

The MTR has proven to be sensitive as a clinical marker of pathologic change in numerous neurological diseases, and, generally, decreased MTR is thought to reflect pathological change in both white and gray matter.

Summary of Literature to Date in TBI

Across populations, MTI has generally been applied in three important areas: 1) assessment of microstructural changes in otherwise normal-appearing brain tissue, 2) development as a contrast agent to improve detection of certain pathologic processes, and 3) use as a measure to grade severity of pathology. Specific to TBI, studies have demonstrated decreased MTR in white matter regions of patients with TBI (Bagley et al., 2000; Kourtidou et al., 2012; McGowan et al., 2000) even in the absence of any observable pathology on conventional imaging (Duckworth & Stevens, 2010; Kimura et al., 1996; Mamere, Saraiva, Matos, Carneiro, & Santos, 2009; Sinson et al., 2001). MTI has proven sensitive in detecting even subtle changes, such as those that may occur in patients with mild head injury (McGowan et al., 2000). It has been postulated that decreased MTR in TBI may reflect an increase in the concentration of microglia, amyloid, phagocytic vacuoles and/ or other injury products within both the gray and white matter. MTI is thought to be particularly sensitive to white matter demyelination and Wallerian degeneration because the myelin sheath surrounding axons holds a substantial number of tethered proteins that transfer magnetization (Symms, Jager, Schmierer, & Yousry, 2004). Decreased MTR has been correlated with worse overall outcome in TBI (Sinson et al., 2001) and also with specific neuropsychological deficits (McGowan et al., 2000) including processing speed (Kourtidou et al., 2012).

Figure 14-5 below demonstrates MTR values in a patient with severe TBI in various white matter regions. MTR decrease is most dramatic near regions of obvious white matter change, but is also evident in regions that appear normal on conventional imaging.

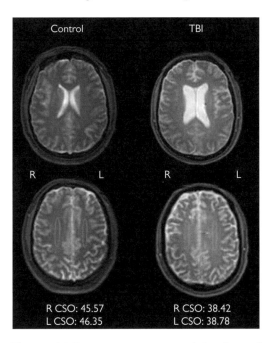

Figure 14-5. MTR measurement (ROI depicted in light blue) of the right and left hemishere cerebral white matter in the centrum semiovale in a patient with severe TBI (right bottom) as compared to an uninjured control subject of similar age and gender (left bottom). Note the dramatically decreased MTR bilaterally in the patient with TBI despite the absence of a great deal of visible pathology at the level of the centrum semiovale. The top images portray the brains of the same individuals at the level of the lateral ventricles, documenting volume loss. See color insert.

Limitations and Special Considerations

As with all imaging modalities, there are special considerations related to the acquisition, analysis and interpretation of MTI data (Hunter, Wilde, Tong, & Holshouser, 2012). First, MTI sequences can be lengthy, rendering them vulnerable to motion artifact in some patients, and motion artifact can influence MTR values substantially. Second, quantitative results obtained with different acquisition parameters or scanners may not be directly comparable across sites and may be somewhat difficult to apply in multi-site studies (Pagani et al., 2008) or clinical practice. Third, as with DTI indices, although MTR may be considered a sensitive measure in revealing microstructural alteration, its specificity in detecting specific forms of pathology (e.g., inflammation, edema, Wallerian degeneration, demyelination) is yet undetermined, particularly in TBI where multiple forms of pathology may co-present and since different forms of pathology may reduce the MTR. Fourth, inter- and intra-rater reliability of the measurements should be established when manual region of interest approaches are utilized. Because of the inherent tissue differences in white matter, gray matter and CSF, great care should be taken to ensure samples include only the tissue type of interest since inclusion of other types (especially CSF) may distort values. This is particularly true for measurement of cortical gray matter given the relative thickness of the cortical mantle and sulci and difficulty in defining the gray-white matter junction. Finally, not all studies have found MTR abnormalities associated with functional outcome (Bagley et al., 2000; Sinson et al., 2001), and additional research in this area is warranted. However, because of its relative sensitivity compared with conventional imaging, MTI has proven capable of demonstrating more subtle white and gray matter changes in otherwise normal-appearing tissue following TBI and could advance understanding of transient or persistent microstructural alteration following TBI (McGowan, Yang et al. 2000; Sinson, Bagley et al. 2001; Kumar, Gupta et al. 2003).

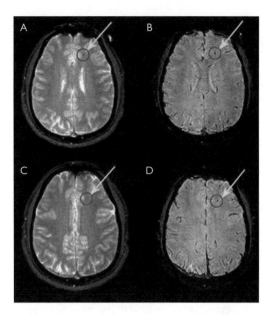

Figure 14-6. Gradient recalled echo (GRE; A) and SWI (B) in a patient with mild TBI (GCS=15; no findings on CT), demonstrating a small hemorrhagic foci (area of hypointensity) in the left frontal white matter (denoted by yellow arrows and red circle). This small bleed is apparent on both conventional GRE and SWI at one level (A), but is not as apparent on a higher slice on the GRE (C) as compared to SWI (D) identification at the same level, demonstrating the superiority of the SWI technique in this case. See color insert.

Susceptibility Weighted Imaging

Summary of Technique and Uses

Susceptibility weighted imaging (SWI) is a high-resolution 3D gradient recalled-echo (GRE) MRI technique that utilizes the magnetic properties of blood products (including deoxyhemoglobin, intracellular methemoglobin and hemisiderin), to detect small amounts of altered blood (Haacke, Xu, Cheng, & Reichenbach, 2004; Reichenbach, Venkatesan, Schillinger, Kido, & Haacke, 1997; Sehgal et al., 2005) on imaging. These findings appear as areas of signal loss on post-processed images, where the phase information is incorporated into the magnitude information to enhance the contrast in the imaging. Figure 14-6 below demonstrates the appearance of small areas of hemorrhage using SWI, which are not as apparent in other more conventional forms of imaging. Newer techniques are being developed for quantification of iron based upon the phase imaging from SWI (Haacke et al., 2009).

SWI has been considered useful primarily in the identification of hemorrhagic axonal injury, as it may allow visualization of smaller hemorrhages that are not visible on CT or conventional MRI sequences (Ashwal, Holshouser, & Tong, 2006) and in detecting areas of hypoxia-ischemia induced secondary injury. This technique may be helpful in the early detection of these "micro hemorrhages" (e.g., early acute and subacute phases of injury), where SWI-related effects are primarily related to deoxyhemoglobin and intracellular methemoglobin.

More recently, SWI has also been used in the identification of subarachnoid hemorrhage. Although CT is usually considered the initial choice for detection of acute hemorrhage because of its wide availability, low cost, and sensitivity to TBI-related injuries involving blood, the sensitivity of CT can be limited, particularly with longer post-injury scanning intervals, or smaller degrees of hemorrhagic injury. Conventional MR imaging sequences may also be insensitive to acute subarachnoid hemorrhage, and SWI may provide information incremental to CT in detecting small amounts of subarachnoid hemorrhage and intraventricular hemorrhage (Wu, Li, Lei, An, & Haacke, 2010).

In experimental rodent studies, SWI has also been utilized as a means to monitor functional blood oxygenation changes and to quantify cerebral blood flow (CBF) changes in animals after trauma. The authors concluded that SWI might be useful in quantifying changes in CBF and venous vasculature thereby elucidating the hemodynamics of TBI. It may represent a noninvasive, safe, and dynamic method of monitoring cerebral blood flow changes, which may be useful in evaluating the effect of experimental pharmacological agents or differences in clinical management (e.g., hyperventilation management of patients with increased intracranial pressure) (Shen, Kou, Kreipke, Petrov, Hu, & Haacke, 2007).

Summary of Literature to Date in TBI

In a preliminary study of 7 children with TBI in the early subacute phase of injury (5 ± 3 days), Tong et al. demonstrated that the number of hemorrhagic DAI lesions seen on SWI was 6 times greater than that visualized on conventional T2*-weighted 2D GRE imaging and that the hemorrhage volume was nearly twice as large (Tong et al., 2003). These findings were extended in a subsequent study also involving 40 children with TBI, which demonstrated that the extent of the hemorrhage correlated with injury severity as measured by Glasgow Coma Scale score, coma duration and long-term outcome measured by the Pediatric Cerebral Performance Category Scale (PCPCS) score at 6-12 months post-injury (Trainor, Fitts, Grolimund, Bargar, & Brown, 1999). This study also described the pattern of distribution of lesions in these children, with SWI-revealed lesions being most prominent in frontal white matter or parieto-temporal-occipital gray or white matter. Tong and colleagues have also demonstrated a correlation between the

number and volume of SWI-detected hemorrhagic lesions and both 1) general intelligence quotient (IQ) and a composite neuropsychological index score comprised of domains of cognitive function frequently disrupted in TBI including attention, executive functioning, verbal and nonverbal memory, language, visual perceptual abilities and academic achievement (Babikian et al., 2005). In a more recent study of children with TBI, Beauchamp and colleagues (2011) also demonstrated greater sensitivity of SWI in detecting traumatic lesions than CT or MRI (Beauchamp et al., 2011), and subsequently showed that the number and volume of SWI lesions were significantly correlated with clinical outcome variables including GCS, surgical intervention, length of hospital stay and length of intubation, as well as with intellectual functioning (Beauchamp et al., 2013).

In a study of 38 adult patients who were scanned an average of 5.6 days post-injury, Chastain et al. demonstrated the sensitivity of SWI in detecting a larger number of lesions and in defining smaller areas of damage in comparison to CT, T2-weighted imaging, and fluid-attenuated inversion recovery (FLAIR) imaging. However, in this study SWI was not superior to T2-weighted imaging or FLAIR in discriminating between good and poor outcomes by median total lesion volume, median volume per lesion and median number of lesions (Chastain et al., 2009). A recent study comparing inter-rater-reliability, lesion detection and clinical relevance of T2-weighted imaging, FLAIR, T2*-gradient recalled echo and SWI found that T2*-GRE and SWI were more sensitive in detecting traumatic, hemorrhagic punctuate lesions than more conventionally applied T2 weighted imaging and FLAIR. Furthermore, the authors reported a correlation between number of punctuate lesions on T2*-GRE/SWI and GCS (Geurts, Andriessen, Gorai, & Vos, 2012).

In TBI-related secondary injuries, SWI may also be used to demonstrate increased oxygen extraction in areas of tissue infarction or hypoxemia. Increased deep medullary veins can be observed surrounding an area of infarction, which may reflect impaired cerebral blood flow in the area around an infarct. In this area, lower levels of oxygenated red blood cells, and therefore higher levels of deoxygenated red blood cells, may account for increased visibility of veins. The evolution of injury after severe hypoxia-ischemia includes a period of time when increased oxygen extraction occurs as cerebral blood flow dramatically decreases because of increasing cerebral edema and increased ICP (Hunter et al., 2012).

Limitations and Special Considerations

Challenges in utilizing SWI include its susceptibility to artifacts in regions of air-tissue interface, including the orbitofrontal and temporal areas, regions of distinct vulnerability to insult in TBI. Adequate training and familiarity with the technique are needed to differentiate veins and other normal anatomy from small hemorrhages. Quantification using this technique has primarily been applied as lesion area/volume or number of lesions, but quantification can become complex in irregularly shaped-lesions that extend through multiple slices. In regards to the use of SWI in the detection of hemorrhage, SWI may not be as sensitive to subarachnoid hemorrhage in cisterns where bone structures are in close proximity (Wu et al., 2010). It is currently unknown whether SWI can be used to differentiate normal, subarachnoid, or subdural hemorrhage in the tentorium (Wu et al., 2010). As with many of these advanced forms of imaging, further validation *in vitro* or in experimental studies need to be performed to validate the actual presence of blood where SWI findings occur.

Functional MRI, Including Functional Connectivity Analysis

Summary of Technique and Uses

fMRI measures the blood oxygen level dependent (BOLD) signal with the assumption that increased arterial blood is diverted to regions of increased neural activity. This results in an overabundance of oxygenated blood in the venous effluent from this brain region. The resulting ratio of oxy- to deoxy-hemoglobin changes the paramagnetic/diamagnetic properties of the tissue, which can be recorded using a $T2^*$ acquisition.

A specific stimulus may be applied, with appropriate alternating periods of rest and stimulation or alternation of control and experimental task conditions. The activation related to the stimulation (or experimental task) is estimated by subtracting the activation during the control periods from the stimulation or activation condition, thereby removing background noise. The acquired results of a series of repeated stimuli are summed and subtracted to increase the robustness of the data and statistical parametric maps are derived which can then be rendered upon high-spatial resolution T1-weighted imaging. In block design fMRI, the task condition is alternated with control condition to provide robust activation data over relatively few trials, facilitating data collection over a relatively brief duration. However, block design fMRI may be limited because it generally combines activation data on trials in which the subject responded incorrectly with data acquired on trials on which the subject responded correctly. In contrast, event-related fMRI can analyze brain activation specifically for trials in which the subject responds correctly. The disadvantage is that event-related fMRI may entail more trials and a longer acquisition time, which imposes greater demand on the subject to control their movement.

Summary of Literature to Date in TBI

FMRI has been used to examine functional activation patterns in patients with TBI at all levels of severity in both adults (Cazalis, Feydy, Valabreque, Peleqrini-Issac, Pierot, & Azouvi, 2006; Christodoulou et al., 2001; McAllister et al., 1999; Maruishi, Miyatani, Nakao, & Muranaka, 2007; McAllister, Sparling, Flashman, Guerin, Mamourian, & Saykin, 2001; Newsome et al., 2007; Perlstein et al., 2004; Rasmussen et al., 2008; Scheibel et al., 2003; Scheibel et al., 2007; Schmitz, Rowley, Kawahara, & Johnson, 2006; Soeda, Nakashima, Okumura, Kuwata, Shinoda, & Iwama, 2005;) and children (Lovell et al., 2007; Scheibel et al., 2003; Scheibel et al., 2007). In a study of working memory using the Sternberg Item Recognition Task, Newsome, Steinberg, Scheibel et al. (2008) used event-related fMRI to show that adolescents who had sustained moderate to severe TBI exhibited increased activation during encoding and retrieval of letters but not during the maintenance phase (Newsome

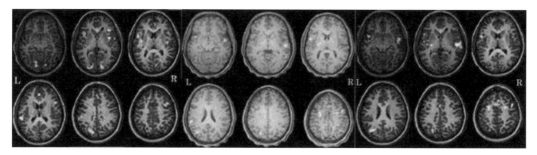

Figure 14-7. Between groups contrasts of working memory activation associated with performance of the Item Recognition Memory Test, which tested recognition memory of 1 item and 4 item sets. Groups included adolescents with moderate to severe TBI and a group of typically developing (TD) adolescents whose demographic background was similar to the TBI group. The brain activation conditions represented in the Figure include (a) Encoding Load 4 minus Load 1 (left panel), (b) Maintenance Load 4 minus Load 1 (center panel), and (c) Retrieval Load 4 minus Load 1 (right panel). The right hemisphere of the brain is displayed on the right side of the figure. Regions that showed significant clusters are displayed in black. The TBI group exhibited greater activation than the TD group under Encoding and Retrieval conditions, whereas the TD group had greater activation than the TBI patients under Maintenance, i.e. the delay period during which storage and rehearsal of the item information occurs. Consistent with the fMRI literature on this task, the TD group had maximum activation under Maintenance relative to Encoding and Retrieval, whereas the TBI group showed greater activation under Encoding and Retrieval as compared with Maintenance. Courtesy of Dr. Mary Newsome. See color insert.

et al., 2010). In contrast, the comparison group of adolescents without TBI exhibited a pattern previously reported on this task in healthy college students, i.e., increased activation during maintenance relative to encoding and retrieval (Figure 14-7). Here fMRI demonstrated a dissociation between TBI and comparison groups in their allocation of cortical resources to the encoding, maintenance, and retrieval phases of working memory on the Sternberg task. Longitudinal extension of this study could examine whether this dissociation diminishes as a result of cognitive rehabilitation or recovery processes.

Integration of fMRI with DTI is informative because this approach can analyze the relation of task-related activation to white matter tracts that connect the participating brain regions. Palacios et al. (2012) used an N-back working memory task for faces in a study of adults who had sustained severe diffuse TBI consistent with presumed diffuse axonal injury. Lower integrity of associative white matter tracts (e.g., cingulum, superior longitudinal fasciculus) implicated in the frontal parietal circuitry for working memory was associated with reduced working memory-related activation (Palacios,

Sala-Llonch et al., 2012). TBI patients who had better working memory performance also showed more deactivation of the default mode network during the task, suggesting that their cognitive resources were focused on the demands of the task rather than task-irrelevant events. This integrative approach to multimodality brain imaging is likely to increase in research designed to identify the neural mechanisms of recovery and the effects of rehabilitation.

FMRI may also be important in understanding recovery from mild TBI (Chen, Johnston, Collie, McCrory, & Ptito, 2007; Chen, Johnston, Frey, Petrides, Worsley, & Ptito, 2004; Chen, Johnston, Petrides, & Ptito, 2008; Jantzen, Anderson, Steinberg, & Kelso, 2004; Lovell, 2007) or the effects of rehabilitation in more severe TBI (Kim, Yoo, Ko, Park, Kim, & Na, 2009; Laatsch, Little et al. 2004; Laatsch, Thulborn et al. 2004; Strangman, O'Neil-Pirozzi et al. 2005; Strangman, O'Neil-Pirozzi et al. 2008; Kim, Yoo et al. 2009). On tasks such as working memory, patients undergoing fMRI at one month post-mTBI have shown a pattern of task-related activation that differs from healthy control subjects. Although the level of performance was similar in the mTBI and control groups, the relation of task difficulty to extent of activation differed. McAllister et al. suggested that alteration of neurotransmitters may explain this difference in modulation of brain activation after mTBI (McAllister et al., 2012). More recently, alteration of task-related activation has been confirmed in collegiate athletes who had sustained a concussion several months prior to imaging. Chen et al. found that athletes who had been concussed and were depressed exhibited reduced dorsolateral pre-frontal-striatal activation on a working memory task as compared with the control athletes and athletes who were not depressed following their concussion (Chen et al., 2008). The depressed subgroup of concussed athletes also showed diminished deactivation of anterior and poste-rior cingulate, medial orbitofrontal cortex, and the parahippocampal region, a pattern which was inversely related to prefrontal activation. Chen et al. (2008) interpreted the reduction in deactivation as evidence for compromised inhi-bition of task-irrelevant regions while perform-ing the working memory task and noted that a similar pattern has been reported in patients with primary major depression.

In contrast to the effects of mTBI on task-related brain activation during fMRI, the findings in severe TBI patients have generally shown more extensive activation as compared with uninjured control subjects. This recruit-ment of brain regions that are not typically acti-vated in healthy subjects during performance of tasks such as working memory or response conflict has been interpreted as compensatory for diminished neural resources. However, the sparse longitudinal fMRI data in patients with severe TBI has mitigated against a rigorous test of this explanatory mechanism. Similarly, there is a dearth of fMRI data obtained before and after rehabilitation in patients with severe TBI. A challenge in designing appropriate cog-nitive tasks for administration during fMRI to patients with severe TBI is the requirement that performance exceed chance level, prefer-ably reaching a level comparable to a compari-son group without TBI. Activation associated with responding by a patient who does not clearly understand the task or is otherwise per-forming at a chance level is uninformative for

elucidating the brain regions engaged by the task. Undue fatigue and motion artifact are also potential threats to the validity of fMRI data in patients with severe TBI. These caveats apply to acquiring fMRI in brain injured children in whom developmental and TBI-related limita-tions potentially complicate acquisition of good quality data. As a result, there are few published fMRI studies in pre-adolescent aged children with moderate to severe TBI.

Resting State fMRI

More recently there has been increasing inter-est in the concept of what the brain does at rest, and data have been collected with a subject in the scanner using the BOLD techniques but without any stimulus. This resting state fMRI (rfMRI) data has been analyzed to look for neu-ral networks or areas of connectivity (fcMRI) within the brain. There are currently two pub-lished ways in which this has been performed (1) by identifying clusters of voxels with high "activation" using a priori knowledge of 8 pre-designated nodes (James et al., 2009) and (2) by

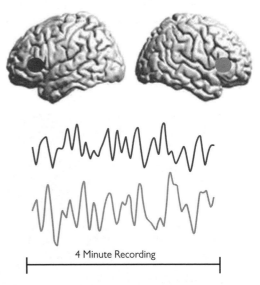

4 Minute Recording

Figure 14-8. A depiction of the general technique of functional connectivity fcMRI, which involves obtaining a BOLD time series from two regions in the brain (indicated here in red and blue) and find-ing the degree of correlation between the two time series as a measure of connectivity between these two regions. Figure courtesy of Jeff Anderson, MD, Ph.D. See color insert.

applying independent components analysis (Calhoun, Adali, Pearlson, van Zijl, & Pekar, 2002) (ICA) to look for connectivity within different areas of the brain. Functional connectivity has been recently applied in both mild TBI (Mayer, Mannell, Ling, Gasparovic & Yeo, 2011) and more severe TBI (Marquez de la Plata et al., 2011) and understanding the coherence of functional networks may provide important insights into recovery and therapeutic interventions. Graph theory has also now been applied to this area of research. Of interest is a recent study on thalamic resting state networks purporting to demonstrate disruption in patients with mild TBI (Tang et al., 2011).

In an ongoing study using rfMRI in veterans of the wars in Iraq or Afghanistan who had sustained one or more mild TBIs, Newsome and colleagues found an altered pattern of activation as compared with veterans who had not been exposed to blast and did not sustain TBI during deployment. Figure 14-9 shows the brain regions wherein the TBI group exhibited greater functional connectivity between the medial prefrontal region and other regions.

An additional study by Wilde and colleagues has also demonstrated functional changes in another cohort of veterans and service members of the wars in Iraq or Afghanistan, comparing the activation patterns in a group with mTBI+PTSD versus PTSD alone, indicating generally decreased activation in the group with mTBI in numerous regions.

Limitations and Special Considerations

While there does appear to be some commonality in patterns of brain activation when data are acquired using the BOLD technique in the resting state, it remains unclear which, if either, of the current techniques described above is optimal in demonstrating connectivity and displaying neural networks. All of the previously stated concerns regarding vulnerability to motion and other artifact apply, including the particular problem of T2* artifact generated at air/bone/fluid/soft tissue interfaces as well as the T2* artifact inherent in blood and calcium which may be present in patients who have sustained recent or prior trauma.

Arterial Spin Labeling

Summary of Technique and Uses

Arterial spin tag labeling (ASL) perfusion MRI is a technique for measuring cerebral perfusion that utilizes arterial blood water as an endogenous contrast agent. In ASL, the protons in arterial blood water are electromagnetically labeled proximal to the tissue of interest, and the effects

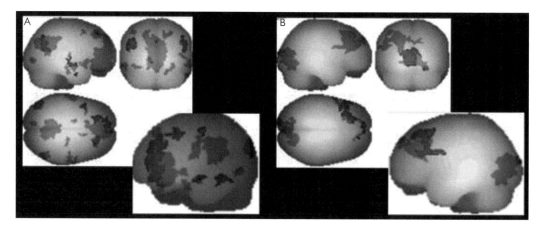

Figure 14-9. Brain regions in which functional connectivity with mesial prefrontal cortex was greater (as depicted in red color) in the group of veterans and service members who had sustained mild to moderate blast-related TBI as compared with the group of veterans who had no TBI or exposure to blast. Regions include areas outside of the default mode and cognitive control networks. Figure courtesy of Mary Newsome, Ph.D. See color insert.

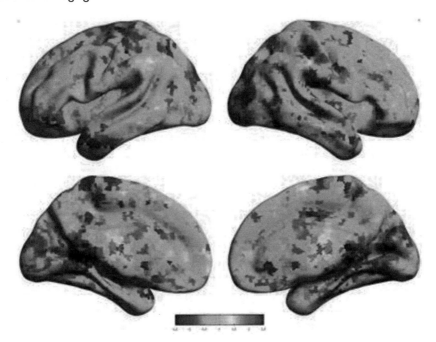

Figure 14-10. For each point in the brain, the degree of "connectedness" of that point to all other points in the brain is measured. Then a t-score is calculated for each connection between mTBI+PTSD and PTSD subjects. The average t-score is shown in color for all connections involving that point, with warmer colors indicating greater connectivity. Values are generally less than zero (cooler colors such as green and blue), meaning that global connectivity to the rest of the brain is lower throughout the brain in the subjects with mTBI (over and above PTSD, since all subjects have PTSD). Figure courtesy of Jeffrey Anderson, M.D., Ph.D. See color insert.

of labeling are determined by comparison with images acquired using control labeling. The rate of signal decay from a known band proximal to the ROI can be used qualitatively and quantitatively to compare perfusion of different brain areas on the same slice as well as calculate cerebral blood flow using known parameters of protons in the blood based on numerical values abstracted from the literature (Buxton, 2005). There are now at least four different variations on ASL including continuous ASL (CASL) (Detre & Alsop, 1999), pulsed ASL (PASL), continuous PASL (cPASL) and velocity selected ASL (VSASL) (Wong, Cronin, Wu, Inglis, Frank, & Liu, 2006).

Summary of Literature to Date in TBI

ASL has been applied in rodent models of TBI (Forbes, Hendrich, Kochanek et al., 1997; Forbes, Hendrich, Schiding et al., 1997; Hendrich, Kochanek, Williams, Schiding, Marion, & Ho, 1999; Kochanek et al., 2005; Kochanek, Hendrich, Dixon, Schiding, Williams, & Ho, 2002; Robertson et al., 2000), and has more recently also been used in patient studies involving both adults and children (Kim et al., 2010; Kim et al., 2012; Newsome et al., 2012). Several promising applications for ASL have been proposed in the context of TBI, including characterization of regional brain function in more severe TBI where task-evoked responses are difficult to obtain, determination of the relation between changes in regional cerebral blood flow (CBF) and cognitive deficits to identify potential targets for pharmacological therapy or other intervention, and utilization as a biomarker for pharmaceutical trials (van Boven et al., 2009). Perfusion parameters that can be developed from ASL include quantitative CBF and oxygen extraction fraction. ASL may be of interest both in acute mild TBI as well as during the subacute and later phases of recovery from more moderate to severe TBI to chronicle both transient and persistent TBI-related changes in cerebral perfusion. It has also been used to better understand perfusion changes which may underlie fMRI activation changes ascribed to TBI (Newsome et al., 2012). However, the literature utilizing this technique in patient studies remains limited and further study is warranted.

Figure 14-11 below demonstrates differences evident on ASL in a child with TBI as compared to a control child. In this case, changes in perfusion appear to exist even at a chronic interval.

Limitations and Special Considerations

The acquisition of ASL sequence data may require specialized parameters not routinely available. Additionally, care must be used to obtain a uniform positioning of the slices at acquisition because CBF may vary by region and is measured on a limited number of slices. Challenges for the interpretation of ASL include a lack of normative data, which may be quite important particularly in children where higher

intrinsic brain water, faster inherent blood flow rate, smaller head size, and typical absence of stenoses or atherosclerosis, may all contribute to an increased duration and intensity of the tracer signal (Hunter et al., 2012).

Magnetic Resonance Spectroscopy

Summary of Technique and Uses

MRS uses the magnetic properties of certain nuclei to determine physical and chemical properties of the molecules which contain them. It provides a sensitive, noninvasive assessment of post-injury biochemical or neurometabolite alteration through providing information about the structure, dynamics, reaction state and chemical environment of molecules. MRS uses a continuous band of radio wave frequencies to excite atoms in a variety of chemical compounds other than water. These compounds absorb and emit radio energy at characteristic frequencies, or spectra, which can be used to

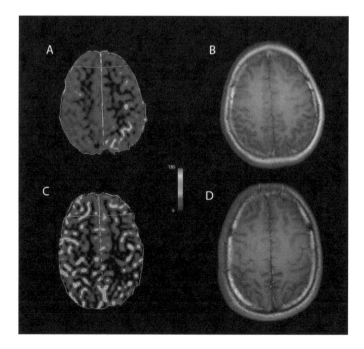

Figure 14-11. Part A demonstrates ASL-derived perfusion in a child with TBI as compared to the perfusion in an uninjured child (B). On the color scale, colors toward the warmer end reflect increased perfusion. Note the relative decreased perfusion in the child with TBI (C), even years post-injury and without obvious focal pathology evident on T1-weighted imaging (D). See color insert.

identify them. MRS can therefore be used to quantify metabolic indices of neuronal/axonal integrity (N-acetyl aspartate or NAA), energetic metabolism (creatine or Cre), and membrane breakdown and/or inflammation (choline or Cho), as well as other indicators of cellular function and dysfunction.

Summary of Literature to Date in TBI

There has been great interest in utilizing MRS to determine the presence of metabolite alteration following TBI, particularly in tissue with no or little visible injury on conventional imaging (Gasparovic et al., 2009; Garnett, Blamire, Corkill, Cadoux-Hudson, Rajagopalan, & Style, 2000; Holshouser, Tong, & Ashwal, 2005). MRS has also shown potential for providing early prognostic information regarding clinical outcome in patients with accidental and non-accidental TBI (Aaen et al., 2010; Ashwal et al., 2000; Babikian, Freier, Ashwal, Riggs, Burley, & Holshouser, 2006; Holshouser et al., 1997; Brenner, Freier, Holshouser, Burley, & Ashwal, 2003; Holshouser et al., 2005; Hunter et al., 2005; Makoroff, Cecil, Care, & Ball, 2005; Yeo, Phillips, Jung, Brown, Campbell, & Brooks, 2006). A number of metabolites have been investigated in studies of TBI, but the most common include N-acetylaspartate (NAA), choline (Cho), total creatine (Cr), lactate (Lac), glutamate and glutamine (Glx), and myoinsotol. Briefly, reductions in NAA are typically associated with neuronal loss or dysfunction or neuronal mitochondrial dysfunction, and several studies have shown a direct correlation of reduced NAA and impaired long-term neuropsychologic function or general poor outcome in children (Brenner et al., 2003; Hunter et al., 2005; Yeo et al., 2006) and adults (Friedman et al., 1999; Tollard et al., 2009). Elevated Cho has been associated with shearing of myelin and cellular membranes (diffuse axonal injury) and/or repair. Cr is assumed to be fairly constant; however, recent studies have shown that Cr changes in various disease states including TBI (Gasparovic et al., 2009). Lac accumulates as a result of anaerobic glycolysis and may be a response to release of glutamate in TBI (Alessandri et al., 2000) and may be related to hypoxia. Studies have shown that the presence of lactate is more common in

children after non-accidental TBI compared to accidental TBI (Aaen et al., 2010; Holshouser et al., 1997) but is strongly correlated with poor outcome in both groups. Glutamate and subsequently formed glutamine (Glx) are excitatory amino acid neurotransmitters released to the extracellular space after injury that play a major role in neuronal death (Ashwal et al., 2004; Babikian et al., 2005; Bullock et al., 1998; Gasparovic et al., 2009). In studies using ^{1}H-MRS, elevation in the sum of the glutamate and glutamine signals (Glx) and Cho was related to poorer outcome on the Glasgow Outcome Scale from 6 months to 1 year later in severely injured adults (Shutter, Tong, & Holshouser, 2004). ^{1}H-MRS Glx has also been demonstrated to be elevated in moderate to severe pediatric TBI (Ashwal et al., 2004), and Glx levels measured within semi acute (2–10 days of TBI) post-injury intervals have been negatively correlated with cognitive function in children 1–4 years after injury (Babikian et al., 2006). Myoinositol (Ins), an organic osmolyte located in astrocytes, increases as a result of glial proliferation and has been correlated with poor outcome after TBI (Ashwal et al., 2004; Garnett et al., 2001); the presence of Lac implicates membrane breakdown and/or inflammation. Lipids and macromolecules produce broad peaks at the lower end of the spectrum and may increase as a result of severe brain injury due to a breakdown of cell membrane and release of fatty acids (Panigrahy, Nelson, & Bluml, 2010). Spectral processing identifies metabolites according to their chemical shift resonance and measures the area under each peak proportional to their concentration. The findings are often reported as peak area metabolite ratios such as NAA/Cr or Cho/Cr, etc.

A recent experimental study examining changes using high field serial imaging in rodents in vivo disclosed alteration of 19 different metabolites using MRS suggestive of edema, excitotoxicity, oxidative stress, neuronal and glial integrity, cell membrane turnover and inflammation, and bioenegetics, suggesting the potential utility of using MRS as a biomarker of the complex and dynamic response of the brain to injury (Harris et al., 2012). Other studies have recently been utilized to examine the time course of MRS-detectable alterations, and how these may be used to determine a therapeutic window for intervention (Lescot et al., 2010; Pascual et al., 2007; Xu et al., 2011). More limited attempts have been made to examine the time course of changes in humans (Babikian et al., 2010), and such studies are critical to the potential use of MRS as a biomarker.

Limitations and Special Considerations

Scanner manufacturers now provide spectroscopy packages with standard sequences such as PRESS (point resolved spectroscopy) and STEAM (stimulated echo acquisition mode). These may be used with techniques such as single voxel spectroscopy (SVS), which allows acquisition of a single spectrum from one volume element (voxel), and two or three-dimensional magnetic resonance spectroscopic imaging (2D-MRSI/3D-MRSI), also called chemical shift imaging (CSI), which allows simultaneous acquisition of multiple spectra in a defined region of interest (ROI) through multiple slabs in the brain. CSI provides more information than SVS, but also typically requires longer acquisition times.

The field strength (e.g., 1.5T, 3T), type of sequence, and sequence parameters (e.g., repetition time, echo time, etc.) determine the metabolites that can be detected and the appearance of the spectrum. In order to compare findings between imaging sites, strict protocols must be used not only for spectral acquisition, but also for the post-processing, as this can substantially influence the information obtained. Other considerations for interpretation of MRS data include the dependence of metabolite levels on anatomic region (Frahm, Bruhn, Gyngell, Merboldt, Hanicke, & Sauter, 1989) and rapid change in these levels as the brain develops (Kreis, Ernst, & Ross, 1993) requiring the use of normal age-matched reference data for interpreting MR spectra from children. Although normal age related metabolite levels and ratios have been published (Holshouser et al., 1997; Huppi, Posse, Lazeyras, Burri, Bossi, & Herschkowitz, 1991; Pouwels et al., 1999), most institutions still must establish their own "control" values for comparison in patient studies since values may vary with specific scanners, field strengths and protocols. Similar to other advanced imaging modalities, the post-processing and analysis of MRS may require specialized expertise. However, proton MRS software packages that require minimal training to use with standard sequences and fully automated shimming, water suppression and reference scanning are available by some manufacturers. In addition, commercially available packages (e.g., LCModel (Provencher, 1993)) for automated spectral fitting and post-processing are available and widely used.

Magnetic Source Imaging/ Magnetoencephalography

Summary of Technique and Uses

Magnetoencephalography (MEG) is a method of recording magnetic flux on the surface of the head which is associated with intracranial electrical currents produced between synapses or within the axons or dendrites of neurons. Similar to electroencephalogram (EEG) and evoked potential (EPs) recordings, MEG can be used to detect abnormalities in spontaneous brain activity (resting-state MEG recording procedures), which may be ideal for use in some patients with TBI because they are independent of performance and effort. However, task-related MEG paradigms can also be used for localization and estimation of the order and time course for these signals and allow construction of images of brain activity, a process often referred to as magnetic source imaging (MSI).

Summary of Literature to Date in TBI

Because of its high degree of both spatial and temporal resolution, MSI has been considered a potentially useful tool in TBI-related research (Bigler, 1999), particularly for diagnosis of mild TBI where MR findings may be unrevealing (Huang et al., 2009; Lewine et al., 2007; Lewine, Davis, Sloan, Kodituwakku, & Orrison, 1999). Initial studies have demonstrated sensitivity to abnormal neuronal signals resulting from axonal injury signified by focal or multi-focal low-frequency neuronal magnetic signal (delta-band 1–4 Hz, or theta-band 5–7 Hz) that can be directly measured and localized using MEG. A recent study utilizing MEG detected low frequency signal in patients both with and without blast-related mild TBI, and the number of cortical regions that generated abnormal slow-waves correlated significantly with the total post-concussive symptom scores in symptomatic TBI patients (Huang et al., 2012). However, there remain limited published studies regarding the use of MEG in TBI.

Limitations and Special Considerations

A few challenges and special considerations remain in the use of MEG/MSI as either a clinical or research tool. First, in terms of acquisition, few medical centers have access to magnetometers or gradiometers, and data analysis also requires specialized expertise. Second, although the temporal resolution of MEG is excellent, variations in signaling can be introduced through a number of sources (e.g., external stimulation, movement, unrelated mental activity, etc.), so challenges exist related to its use in acute or more severe TBI because drowsiness, a suboptimal level of cooperation by the subject, and states of altered consciousness may limit the robustness of findings. MSI is best used for measurement of surface cortical activity; therefore, brain regions such as the basal temporal or subcortical areas may be substantially more difficult to accurately measure depending on the modeling used. Finally, although Huang et al. (2012) have recently proposed a standardized

solution for MEG analysis, MEG slow-wave detection and localization have traditionally been performed manually, which necessarily introduces some reliance upon the rater, rendering it difficult to compare results across different operators and MEG centers (Huang et al., 2012). Certain medications, including some sedative neuroleptics and hypnotics, are known to increase delta-wave power), and the influence of medication use should be considered in data interpretation. Finally, little is known regarding the long-term persistence or time course of MEG-related changes.

Conclusion

The early success of these imaging modalities in detecting various TBI-related changes, as discussed above, has led to many research efforts geared towards the development and further evolution of these techniques. The hope is that in conjunction with each other and advanced post-processing techniques, these sequences might help to diagnose TBI, especially mild TBI, wherein an imaging biomarker such as DTI might differentiate insult to the brain from general trauma or intoxication. Brain imaging may have the potential to elucidate the mechanisms mediating post-injury recovery in patients with TBI and ultimately be a prognostic tool used in patient management and for the evaluation of therapeutic interventions. Imaging metrics may be useful as surrogate outcome measures, indicating the effects of an intervention on neurologic recovery.

Abbreviations

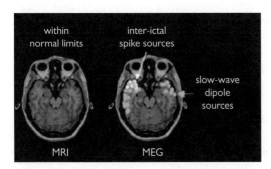

Figure 14-12. In the above image, the subject demonstrates significant slow-wave dipole sources (indicated in green) and interictal spike sources (indicated in yellow) in the temporal lobes as measured by MEG despite the absence of any visible abnormalities on a conventional T1-weighted MRI sequence. Figure adapted with permission from Lewine et al. (1999). See color insert.

D-MRSI	two-dimensional magnetic resonance spectroscopic imaging
3D-MRSI	three-dimensional magnetic resonance spectroscopic imaging
ASL	arterial spin labeling
CASL	continuous ASL
CBF	cerebral blood flow
cPASL	continuous PASL
CSF	cerebrospinal fluid
CSI	chemical shift imaging
CT	computed tomography
DTI	diffusion tensor imaging

EEG	electroencephalogram
EP	evoked potential
fcMRI	functional connectivity magnetic resonance imaging
FLAIR	fluid attenuated inversion recovery
fMRI	functional magnetic resonance imaging
GCS	Glasgow Coma Scale
GRE	gradient recalled echo
MEG	magnetoencephalography
MRI	magnetic resonance imaging
MRS	magnetic resonance spectroscopy
MSI	magnetic source imaging
MTI	magnetization transfer imaging
PASL	pulsed ASL
PRESS	point resolved spectroscopy
STEAM	stimulated echo acquisition mode
SVS	single voxel spectroscopy (SVS)
SWI	susceptibility-weighted imaging
TBI	traumatic brain injury
VSASL	velocity selected ASL

Acknowledgments

The authors wish to acknowledge funding sources including NIH/NINDS NS56202-04, DAMD W81XWH-08-2-0133, VA Merit Review B4596R, VA Center of Excellence for Traumatic Brain Injury HFP90020, NIH/NICHD R01 NS021889-28, NIH/NINDS R03 NS069943-02. We also wish to express our gratitude to the Poelman Foundation for their donation to the Brain Imaging and Behavior Laboratory at Brigham Young University. We express our sincere gratitude for the contributions of Tracy Abildskov, Jeff Anderson, M.D., Ph.D., Mary Newsome, Ph.D., and Ragini Yallampalli, M.S., in preparation of figures. We also thank Danielle MacDonald for assistance in manuscript preparation.

References

Aaen, G. S., Holshouser, B. A., Sheridan, C., Colbert, C., McKenney, M., Kido, D., et al. (2010). Magnetic resonance spectroscopy predicts outcomes for children with nonaccidental trauma. *Pediatrics*, *125*(2), 295–303.

Adams, J. H., Jennett, B., Murray, L. S., Teasdale, G. M., Gennarelli, T. A., & Graham, D. I. (2011). Neuropathological findings in disabled survivors of a head injury. *Journal of Neurotrauma*, *28*(5), 701–709.

Alessandri, B., Basciani, R., Langemann, H., Lyrer, P., Pluess, D., Landolt, H., et al. (2000). Chronic effects of an aminosteroid on microdialytically measured parameters after experimental middle cerebral artery occlusion in the rat. *Journal of Clinical Neuroscience*, *7*(1), 47–51.

Alliance for Radiation Safety in Pediatric Imaging. (2012). *Image Gently Impact Campaign*. Retrieved October 22, 2012, from http://www.pedrad.org/associations/5364/ig.

Anderson, C. V., Bigler, E. D., & Blatter, D. D. (1995). Frontal lobe lesions, diffuse damage, and neuropsychological functioning in traumatic brain-injured patients. *Journal of Clinical and Experimental Neuropsychology*, *17*(6), 900–908.

Arfanakis, K., Haughton, V. M., Carew, J. D., Rogers, B. P., Dempsey, R. J., & Meyerand, M. E. (2002). Diffusion tensor MR imaging in diffuse axonal injury. *American Journal of Neuroradiology*, *23*(5), 794–802.

Ariza, M., Serra-Grabulosa, J. M., Junque, C., Ramire, B., Mataro, M., Poca, A., et al. (2006). Hippocampal head atrophy after traumatic brain injury. *Neuropsychologia 44*(10), 1956–1961.

Ashwal, S., Holshouser, B., Tong, K., Serma, T., Osterdock, R., Gross, M., et al. (2004). Proton MR spectroscopy detected glutamate/glutamine is increased in children with traumatic brain injury. *Journal of Neurotrauma*, *21*(11), 1539–1552.

Ashwal, S., Holshouser, B., Tong, K., Serma, T., Osterdock, R., Gross, M., et al. (2004). Proton spectroscopy detected myoinositol in children with traumatic brain injury. *Pediatric Research*, *56*(4), 630–638.

Ashwal, S., Holshouser, B. A., Shu, S. K., Simmons, P. L., Perkin, R. M., Tomasi, L. G., et al. (2000). Predictive value of proton magnetic resonance spectroscopy in pediatric closed head injury. *Pediatric Neurology*, *23*(2), 114–125.

Ashwal, S., Holshouser, B. A., & Tong, K. A. (2006). Use of advanced neuroimaging techniques in the evaluation of pediatric traumatic brain injury. *Developmental Neuroscience*, *28*(4-5), 309–326.

Ashwal, S., Wycliffe, N. D., & Holshouser, B. A. (2010). Advanced neuroimaging in children with nonaccidental trauma. *Developmental Neuroscience 32*(5-6), 343–360.

Babikian, T., Freier, M. C., Ashwal, S., Riggs, M. L., Burley, T., & Holshouser, B. A. (2006). MR spectroscopy: predicting long-term neuropsychological outcome following pediatric TBI. *Journal of Magnetic Resonance Imaging*, *24*(4), 801–811.

Babikian, T., Freier, M. C., Tong, K. A., Nickerson, J. P., Wall, C. J. Holhouser, B. A., et al. (2005). Susceptibility weighted imaging:

neuropsychologic outcome and pediatric head injury. *Pediatric Neurology*, 33(3), 184–194.

Babikian, T., Marion, S. D., Copeland, S., Alger, J. R., O'Neill, J., Cazalis, F., et al. (2010). Metabolic levels in the corpus callosum and their structural and behavioral correlates after moderate to severe pediatric TBI. *Journal of Neurotrauma*, 27(3), 473–481.

Bagley, L. J., McGowan, J. C., Grossman, R. I., Sinson, G., Kotapka, M., Lexa, F. J., et al. (2000). Magnetization transfer imaging of traumatic brain injury. *Journal of Magnetic Resonance Imaging*, 11(1), 1–8.

Bazarian, J. J., Zhong, J., Blyth, B., Zhu, T., Kavcic, V., & Peterson, D. (2007). Diffusion tensor imaging detects clinically important axonal damage after mild traumatic brain injury: a pilot study. *Journal of Neurotrauma*, 24(9), 1447–1459.

Beauchamp, M. H., Beare, R., Ditchfield, M., Coleman, L., Babl, F. E., Kean, M., et al. (2013). Susceptibility weighted imaging and its relationship to outcome after pediatric traumatic brain injury. *Cortex*, 49(2), 591–598. doi:10.1016/j.cortex.2012.08.015. Epub 2012 Sep 3.

Beauchamp, M. H., Ditchfield, M., Babl, F. E., Kean, M., Catroppa, C., Yeates, K. O., et al. (2011). Detecting traumatic brain lesions in children: CT versus MRI versus susceptibility weighted imaging (SWI). *Journal of Neurotrauma*, 28(6), 915–927.

Bendlin, B. B., Ries, M. L., Lazar, M., Alexander, A. L., Dempsey, R. J., Rowley, H. A., et al. (2008). Longitudinal changes in patients with traumatic brain injury assessed with diffusion-tensor and volumetric imaging. *Neuroimage*, 42(2), 503–514.

Benson, R. R., Meda, S. A., Vasudevan, S., Kou, Z., Govindarajan, K. A., Hanks, R. A., et al. (2007). Global white matter analysis of diffusion tensor images is predictive of injury severity in traumatic brain injury. *Journal of Neurotrauma*, 24(3), 446–459.

Bergeson, A. G., Lundin, R., Parkinson, R. B., Tate, D. F., Victoroff, J., Hopkins, R. O., et al. (2004). Clinical rating of cortical atrophy and cognitive correlates following traumatic brain injury. *Archives of Clinical Neuropsychology*, 18(4), 509–520.

Betz, J., Zhuo, J., Roy, A., Shanmuganathan, K., Gullapalli, R. P. (2012). Prognostic value of diffusion tensor imaging parameters in severe traumatic brain injury. *Journal of Neurotrauma*, 29(7), 1292–1305.

Bigler, E. D. (1999). Neuroimaging in pediatric traumatic head injury: diagnostic considerations and relationships to neurobehavioral outcome. *Journal of Head Trauma Rehabilitation*, 14(4), 406–423.

Bigler, E. D., Abildskov, T. J., Wilde, E. A., McCauley, S. R., Li, X., Merkley, T. L., et al. (2010). Diffuse damage in pediatric traumatic brain injury: a comparison of automated versus operator-controlled quantification methods. *Neuroimage* 50(3), 1017–1026.

Bigler, E. D., Anderson, C. V., & Blatter, D. D. (2002). Temporal lobe morphology in normal aging and traumatic brain injury. *American Journal of Neuroradiology*, 23(2), 255–266.

Bigler, E. D., Blatter, D. D., Anderson, C. V., Johnson, S. C., Gale, S. D., Hopkins, R. O., et al. (1997). Hippocampal volume in normal aging and traumatic brain injury. *American Journal of Neuroradiology*, 18(1), 11–23.

Booker, H. E., Matthews, C. G., & Whitehurst, W. R. (1969). Pneumoencephalographic planimetry in neurological disease. *Journal of Neurology Neurosurgery & Psychiatry*, 32(3), 241–248.

Brenner, T., Freier, M. C., Holshouser, B. A., Burley, T., & Ashwal, S.(2003). Predicting neuropsychologic outcome after traumatic brain injury in children. *Pediatric Neurology*, 28(2), 104–114.

Brewer, J. B., Magda, S., Airriess, C., & Smith, M. E. (2009). Fully-automated quantification of regional brain volumes for improved detection of focal atrophy in Alzheimer disease. *American Journal of Neuroradiology*, 30(3), 578–580.

Bullock, R., Zauner, A., Woodward, J. J., Myseros, J., Choi, S. C., Ward, J. D., et al. (1998). Factors affecting excitatory amino acid release following severe human head injury. *Journal of Neurosurgery*, 89(4), 507–518.

Buxton, R. B. (2005). "Quantifying CBF with arterial spin labeling." *Journal of Magnetic Resonance Imaging*, 22(6), 723–726.

Caeyenberghs, K., Leemans, A., Geurts, M., Taymans, T., Linden, C. V., Smits-Engelsman, B. C., et al. (2010). Brain-behavior relationships in young traumatic brain injury patients: DTI metrics are highly correlated with postural control. *Human Brain Mapping*, 31(7), 992–1002.

Caeyenberghs, K., Leemans, A., Geurts, M., Taymans, T., van der Linden, C., Smits-Engelsman, B. C., et al. (2010). Brain-behavior relationships in young traumatic brain injury patients: fractional anisotropy measures are highly correlated with dynamic visuomotor tracking performance. *Neuropsychologia*, 48(5), 1472–1482.

Calhoun, V. D., Adali, T., Pearlson, G. D., van Zijl, P. C., & Pekar, J. J. (2002). Independent component analysis of fMRI data in the complex domain. *Magnetic Resonance in Medicine*, 48(1), 180–192.

Cazalis, F., Feydy, A., Valabreque, R., Peleqrini-Issac, M., Pierot, L., & Azouvi, P. (2006). fMRI study of problem-solving after severe traumatic brain injury. *Brain Injury*, *20*(10), 1019–1028.

Chanraud, S., Zahr, N., Sullivan, E. V., Pfefferbaum, A. (2010). MR diffusion tensor imaging: a window into white matter integrity of the working brain. *Neuropsychological Review*, *20*(2), 209–225.

Chastain, C. A., Oyoyo, U. E., Zipperman, M., Joo, E., Ashwal, S., Shutter, L. A., et al. (2009). Predicting outcomes of traumatic brain injury by imaging modality and injury distribution. *Journal of Neurotrauma*, *26*(8), 1183–1196.

Chen, J. K., Johnston, K. M., Collie, A., McCrory, P., & Ptito, A. (2007). A validation of the post concussion symptom scale in the assessment of complex concussion using cognitive testing and functional MRI. *Journal of Neurology, Neurosurgery, and Psychiatry*, *78*(11), 1231–1238.

Chen, J. K., Johnston, K. M., Frey, S., Petrides, M., Worsley, K., & Ptito, A. (2004). Functional abnormalities in symptomatic concussed athletes: an fMRI study. *Neuroimage*, *22*(1), 68–82., J. K., Johnston, K. M., Petrides, M., & Ptito, A. (2008). Neural substrates of symptoms of depression following concussion in male athletes with persisting postconcussion symptoms. *Archives of General Psychiatry*, *65*(1), 81–89.

Christodoulou, C., DeLuca, J., Ricker, J. H., Madigan, N. K., Bly, B. M., Lange, G., et al. (2001). Functional magnetic resonance imaging of working memory impairment after traumatic brain injury. *Journal of Neurology, Neurosurgery, and Psychiatry 71*(2), 161–168.

Cullum, C. M., & Bigler, E. D. (1986). Ventricle size, cortical atrophy and the relationship with neuropsychological status in closed head injury: a quantitative analysis. *Journal of Clinical Experimental Neuropsychology*, *8*(4), 437–452.

Detre, J. A., & Alsop, D. C. (1999). Perfusion magnetic resonance imaging with continuous arterial spin labeling: methods and clinical applications in the central nervous system. *European Journal of Radiology*, *30*(2), 115–124.

Duckworth, J. L., & Stevens, R. D. (2010). Imaging brain trauma. *Current Opinion in Critical Care*, *16*, 92–97. Duvernoy, H. M. (1998). *The Human Hippocampus*. Berlin, Springer.

Ewing-Cobbs, L., Prasad, M. R., Swank, P., Kramer, L., Cox, C. S. Jr., Fletcher, J. M., et al. (2008). Arrested development and disrupted callosal microstructure following pediatric traumatic brain injury: relation to neurobehavioral outcomes. *Neuroimage 42*(4), 1305–1315.

Farbota, K. D., Bendlin, B. B., Alexander, A. L., Rowley, H. A., Dempsey, R. J., & Johnson, S. C. (2012). Longitudinal diffusion tensor imaging and neuropsychological correlates in traumatic brain

injury patients. *Frontiers in Human Neuroscience*, *6*, 160.

Farbota, K. D., Sodhi, A., Bendlin, B. B., McLaren, D. G., Xu, G., Rowley, H. A., et al. (2012). Longitudinal Volumetric Changes following Traumatic Brain Injury: A Tensor-Based Morphometry Study. *Journal of the International Neuropsychologial Society*, *18*(6), 1006–1018.

Forbes, M. L., Hendrich, K. S., Kochanek, P. M., Williams, D. S., Schiding, J. K., Wisniewski, S. R., et al. (1997). Assessment of cerebral blood flow and CO_2 reactivity after controlled cortical impact by perfusion magnetic resonance imaging using arterial spin-labeling in rats. *Journal of Cerebral Blood Flow & Metabolism*, *17*(8), 865–874.

Forbes, M. L., Hendrich, K. S., Schiding, J. K., Williams, D. S., Ho, C., DeKosky, S. T. (1997). Perfusion MRI assessment of cerebral blood flow and CO_2 reactivity after controlled cortical impact in rats. *Advances in Experimental Medicine and Biology*, *411*, 7–12.

Frahm, J., Bruhn, H., Gyngell, M. L., Merboldt, K. D., Hanicke, W., & Sauter, R. (1989). Localized proton NMR spectroscopy in different regions of the human brain in vivo. Relaxation times and concentrations of cerebral metabolites. *Magnetic Resonance in Medicine*, *11*(1), 47–63.

French, B. N., & Dublin, A. B. (1977). The value of computerized tomography in the management of 1000 consecutive head injuries. *Surgical Neurology*, *7*(4), 171–183.

Friedman, S. D., Brooks, W. M., Jung, R. E., Chiulli, S. J., Sloan, J. H., Montoya, B. T., et al. (1999). Quantitative proton MRS predicts outcome after traumatic brain injury. *Neurology*, *52*(7), 1384–1391.

Gale, S. D., Johnson, S. C., Bigler, E. D., & Blatter, D. D. (1995). Nonspecific white matter degeneration following traumatic brain injury. *Journal of the International Neuropsychological Society*, *1*(1), 17–28.

Garnett, M. R., Blamire, A. M., Corkill, P. G., Cadoux-Hudson, T. A., Rajagopalan, B., & Styles, P. (2000). Early proton magnetic resonance spectroscopy in normal-appearing brain correlates with outcome in patients following traumatic brain injury. *Brain*, *123*(10), 2046–2054.

Garnett, M. R., Corkill, R. G., Blamire, A. M., Rajagopalan, B., Manners, D. N., Young, J. D., et al. (2001). Altered cellular metabolism following traumatic brain injury: a magnetic resonance spectroscopy study. *Journal of Neurotrauma*, *18*(3), 231–240.

Gasparovic, C., Yeo, R., Mannell, M., Ling, J., Elgie, R., Phillips, J., et al. (2009). Neurometabolite concentrations in gray and white matter in mild traumatic brain injury: an 1H-magnetic resonance spectroscopy study. *Journal of Neurotrauma,* *26*(10), 1635–1643.

Ge, Y., Law, M., & Grossman, R. I. (2005). Applications of diffusion tensor MR imaging in multiple sclerosis. *Annals of the New York Academy of Sciences,* *106*(4), 202–219.

Geurts, B. H., Andriessen, T. M., Gorai, B. M., & Vos, P. E. (2012). The reliability of magnetic resonance imaging in traumatic brain injury lesion detection. *Brain Injury, 26*(12), 1439–1450.

Geuze, E., Vermetten E., & Bremner, J. D. (2005). MR-based in vivo hippocampal volumetrics: 2. Findings in neuropsychiatric disorders. *Molecular Psychiatry, 10*(2), 160–184.

Groen, W. B., Buitelaar, J. K., van der Gaag, R. J., & Zwiers, M. P. (2010). Pervasive microstructural abnormalities in autism: a DTI study. *Journal of Psychiatry and Neuroscience, 36*(1), 32–40.

Haacke, E. M., Makki, M., Ge, Y., Maheshwari, M., Sehgal, V., Hu, J., Selvan, M., et al. (2009). Characterizing iron deposition in multiple sclerosis lesions using susceptibility weighted imaging. *Journal of Magnetic Resonance Imaging, 29*(3), 537–544.

Haacke, E. M., Xu, Y., Cheng, Y. C., & Reichenbach, J. R. (2004). Susceptibility weighted imaging (SWI). *Magnetic Resonance in Medicine, 52*(3), 612–618.

Harris, J. L., Yeh, H. W., Choi, I. Y., Lee, P., Berman, N. E., Swerdlow, R. H., et al. (2012). Altered neurochemical profile after traumatic brain injury: (1) H-MRS biomarkers of pathological mechanisms. *Journal of Cerebral Blood Flow & Metabolism, 32*(12), 2122–2134.

Hendrich, K. S., Kochanek, P. M., Williams, D. S., Schiding, J. K., Marion, D. W., & Ho, C. (1999). "Early perfusion after controlled cortical impact in rats: quantification by arterial spin-labeled MRI and the influence of spin-lattice relaxation time heterogeneity." *Magnetic Resonance in Medicine, 42*(4), 673–681.

Himanen, L., Portin, R., Isoniemi, H., Helenius, H., Kurki, T., & Tenovuo, O. (2005). Cognitive functions in relation to MRI findings 30 years after traumatic brain injury." *Brain Injury, 19*(2), 93–100.

Holshouser, B. A., Ashwal, S., Luh, S., Kahlon, S., Auld, K. L., Tomasi, L. G., et al. (1997). Proton MR spectroscopy after acute central nervous system injury: outcome prediction in neonates, infants, and children. *Radiology, 202*(2), 487–496.

Holshouser, B. A., Tong, K. A., & Ashwal, S.(2005). Proton MR spectroscopic imaging depicts diffuse axonal injury in children with traumatic brain injury. *American Journal of Neuroradiology, 26*(5), 1276–1285.

Huang, M. X., Nichols, S., Robb, A., Angeles, A., Drake, A., Holland, M., Asmussen, S., et al. (2012).

An automatic MEG low-frequency source imaging approach for detecting injuries in mild and moderate TBI patients with blast and non-blast causes. *Neuroimage, 61*(4), 1067–1082.

Huang, M. X., Theilmann, R. J., Robb, A., Angeles, A., Nichols, S., Drake, A., et al. (2009). Integrated imaging approach with MEG and DTI to detect mild traumatic brain injury in military and civilian patients. *Journal of Neurotrauma, 26*(8), 1213–1226.

Huisman, T. A., Schwamm, L. H., Schaefer, P. W., Koroshetz, W. J., Shetty-Alva, Osunar, Y., et al. (2004). Diffusion tensor imaging as potential biomarker of white matter injury in diffuse axonal injury. *American Journal of Neuroradiology, 25*(3), 370–376.

Hunter, J. V., Thornton, R. J., Wang, Z. J., Levin, H. S., Roberson, G., Brooks, W. M., et al. (2005). Late proton MR spectroscopy in children after traumatic brain injury: correlation with cognitive outcomes. *American Journal of Neuroradiology, 26*(3), 482–488.

Hunter, J. V., Wilde, E. A., Tong, K. A., & Holshouser, B. A. (2012). Emerging imaging tools for use with traumatic brain injury research. *Journal of Neurotrauma, 29*(4), 654–671.

Huppi, P. S., Posse, S., Lazeyras, F., Burri, R., Bossi, E., & Herschkowit, N. (1991). Magnetic resonance in preterm and term newborns: 1H-spectroscopy in developing human brain. *Pediatric Research, 30*(6), 574–578.

Hutchinson, E., Pulsipher, D., Dabbs, K., Myers y Gutierrez, A., Sheth, R., Jones, J., et al. (2010). Children with new-onset epilepsy exhibit diffusion abnormalities in cerebral white matter in the absence of volumetric differences. *Epilepsy Research, 88*(2-3), 208–214.

Irimia, A., Chambers, M. C., Alger, J. R., Filippou, M., Prstawa, M. W., Wang, B., et al. (2011). Comparison of acute and chronic traumatic brain injury using semi-automatic multimodal segmentation of MR volumes. *Journal of Neurotrauma, 28*(11), 2287–2306.

Isherwood, I., Mawdsley, C., & Ferguson, F. R. (1966). Pneumoencephalographic changes in boxers. *Acta Radiologica: Diagnosis (Stockh) 5,* 654–661.

James, G. A., Kelley, M. E., Craddock, R. C., Holtzheimer, P. E., & Dunlop, B. W, et al. (2009). Exploratory structural equation modeling of resting-state fMRI: applicability of group models to individual subjects. *Neuroimage, 45*(3), 778–787.

Jantzen, K. J., Anderson, B., Steinberg, F. L., & Kelso, J. A. (2004). A prospective functional MR imaging study of mild traumatic brain injury in college football players. *American Journal of Neuroradiology, 25*(5), 738–745.

Jovicich, J., Czanner, S., Han, X., Salat, D., van der Kouwe, A., Quinn, B., et al. (2009). MRI-derived measurements of human subcortical, ventricular and intracranial brain volumes: Reliability effects of scan sessions, acquisition sequences, data analyses, scanner upgrade, scanner vendors and field strengths. *Neuroimage, 46*(1), 177–192.

Kim, J., Whyte, J., Patel, S., Avants, B., Europa, E., Wang, J., et al. (2010). Resting cerebral blood flow alterations in chronic traumatic brain injury: an arterial spin labeling perfusion FMRI study. *Journal of Neurotrauma, 27*(8), 1399–1411.

Kim, J., Whyte, J., Patel, S., Europa, E., Slattery, J., Coslett, H. B., et al. (2012). A perfusion FMRI study of the neural correlates of sustained-attention and working-memory deficits in chronic traumatic brain injury. *Neurorehabilitation and Neural Repair, 26*(7), 870–880.

Kim, Y. H., Yoo, W. K., Ko, M. H., Park, C. H., Kim, S. T., & Na, D. L. (2009). Plasticity of the attentional network after brain injury and cognitive rehabilitation. *Neurorehabilitation and Neural Repair, 23*(5), 468–477.

Kimura, H., Meaney, D. F.; McGowan, J. C., Grossman, R. I., Lenkinski, R. E., Ross, D. T., et al. (1996). Magnetization transfer imaging of diffuse axonal injury following experimental brain injury in the pig: characterization by magnetization transfer ratio with histopathologic correlation. *Journal of Computer Assisted Tomography, 20*(4), 540–546.

Kochanek, P. M., Hendrich, K. S., Dixon, C. E., Schiding, J. K., Williams, D. S., & Ho, C. (2002). Cerebral blood flow at one year after controlled cortical impact in rats: assessment by magnetic resonance imaging. *Journal of Neurotrauma, 19*(9), 1029–1037.

Kochanek, P. M., Hendrich, K. S., Jackson, E. K., Wisniewski, S. R., Melick, J. A., Shore, P. M., et al. (2005). Characterization of the effects of adenosine receptor agonists on cerebral blood flow in uninjured and traumatically injured rat brain using continuous arterial spin-labeled magnetic resonance imaging. *Journal of Cerebral Blood Flow & Metabolism, 25*(12), 1596–1612.

Kourtidou, P., McCauley, S. R., Bigler, E. D., Traipe, E., Wu, T. C., Chu, Z. D., et al. (2012). Centrum Semiovale and Corpus Callosum Integrity in Relation to Information Processing Speed in Patients With Severe Traumatic Brain Injury. *The Journal of Head Trauma Rehabilitation.*

Kraus, M. F., Susmaras, T., Caughlin, B. P., Walker, C. J., Sweeney, J. A., & Little, D. M. (2007). White matter integrity and cognition in chronic traumatic brain injury: a diffusion tensor imaging study. *Brain, 130*(Pt 10), 2508–2519.

Kreis, R., Ernst, T., & Ross, B. D. (1993). Development of the human brain: in vivo quantification of metabolite and water content with proton magnetic resonance spectroscopy. *Magnetic Resonance in Medicine, 30*(4): 424–437.

Kumar, R., Gupta, R. K., Rao, S. B., Chawla, S., Husain, M., & Rathore, R. K. (2003). Magnetization transfer and T2 quantitation in normal appearing cortical gray matter and white matter adjacent to focal abnormality in patients with traumatic brain injury. *Magnetic Resonance Imaging, 21*(8), 893–899.

Kumar, R., Husain, M., Gupta, R. K., Hasan, K. M., Haris, M., Agarwal, A. K., et al. (2009). Serial changes in the white matter diffusion tensor imaging metrics in moderate traumatic brain injury and correlation with neuro-cognitive function. *Journal of Neurotrauma, 26*(4), 481–495.

Kurowski, B., Wade, S. L., Cecil, K. M., Wal, N. C., Yuan, W., Rajagopal, A., et al. (2009). Correlation of diffusion tensor imaging with executive function measures after early childhood traumatic brain injury. *Journal of Pediatric Rehabilitation Medicine, 2*(4), 273–283.

Laatsch, L., D. Little, & Thulborn, K. (2004). Changes in fMRI following cognitive rehabilitation in severe traumatic brain injury: A case study. *Rehabilitation Psychology 49*(3): 262–267.

Laatsch, L. K., Thulborn, K. R., Krisky, C. M., Shobat, D. M., & Sweeney, J. A. (2004). Investigating the neurobiological basis of cognitive rehabilitation therapy with fMRI. *Brain Injury, 18*(10), 957–974.

Lescot, T., Fulla-Oller, L., Po, C., Chen, X. R., Puybasst, L., Gillet, B., et al. (2010). Temporal and regional changes after focal traumatic brain injury. *Journal of Neurotrauma, 27*(1), 85–94.

Levin, H. S. (2003). Neuroplasticity following nonpenetrating traumatic brain injury. *Brain Injury, 17*(8), 665–674.

Levin, H. S., Meyers, C. A., Grossman, R. G., & Sarwar, M. (1981). Ventricular enlargement after closed head injury. *Archives of Neurology, 38*(10), 623–629.

Levin, H. S., Wilde, E. A., Chu, Z., Yallampalli, R., Hanten, G. R., Li, X., et al. (2008). Diffusion tensor imaging in relation to cognitive and functional outcome of traumatic brain injury in children. *Journal of Head Trauma Rehabilitation, 23*(4) 197–208.

Lewine, J. D., Davis, J. T., Bigler, E. D., Thoma, R., Hill, D., Funke, M., et al. (2007). Objective documentation of traumatic brain injury subsequent to mild head trauma: multimodal brain imaging with MEG, SPECT, and MRI. *Journal of Head Trauma Rehabilitation, 22*(3), 141–155.

Lewine, J. D., Davis, J. T., Sloan, J. H., Kodituwakku, P. W., & Orrison, W. W. (1999). Neuromagnetic assessment of pathophysiologic brain activity induced by minor head trauma. *American Journal of Neuroradiology, 20*(5), 857–866.

Lipton, M. L., Gellella, E., Lo, C., Gold, T., Ardekani, B. A., Shifiteh, K., et al. (2008). Multifocal white matter ultrastructural abnormalities in mild traumatic brain injury with cognitive disability: a voxel-wise analysis of diffusion tensor imaging. *Journal of Neurotrauma, 25*(11), 1335–1342.

Lovell, M. R., Pardini, J. E., Welling, J., Collins, M. W., Bakal, J., Lazar, N., et al. (2007). Functional brain abnormalities are related to clinical recovery and time to return-to-play in athletes. *Neurosurgery, 61*(2), 352–359.

Mac Donald, C. L., Dikranian, K., Song, S. K., Bayly, P. V., Holtzman, D. M., & Brody, D. L. (2007). Detection of traumatic axonal injury with diffusion tensor imaging in a mouse model of traumatic brain injury. *Experimental Neurology, 205*(1), 116–131.

MacKenzie, J. D., Siddiqi, F., Babb, J. S., Bagley, L. J., Mannon, L. J., Sinson, G. P., et al. (2002). Brain atrophy in mild or moderate traumatic brain injury: a longitudinal quantitative analysis. *American Journal of Neuroradiology, 23*(9), 1509–1515.

Makoroff, K. L., Cecil, K. M., Care, M. & Ball, W. S. Jr (2005). Elevated lactate as an early marker of brain injury in inflicted traumatic brain injury. *Pediatric Radiology, 35*(7), 668–676.

Mamere, A. E., Saraiva, L. A., Matos, A. L., Carneiro, A. A., & Santos, A. C.(2009). Evaluation of delayed neuronal and axonal damage secondary to moderate and severe traumatic brain injury using quantitative MR imaging techniques. *American Journal of Neuroradiology, 30*(5), 947–952.

Marquez de la Plata, C. D., Garces, J., Shokri Kojori, E., Grinnan, J., Krishnan, K., Pidikiti, R., et al. (2011). Deficits in functional connectivity of hippocampal and frontal lobe circuits after traumatic axonal injury. *Archives of Neurology, 68*(1), 74–84.

Maruishi, M., Miyatani, M., Nakao, T., & Muranaka, H. (2007). Compensatory cortical activation during performance of an attention task by patients with diffuse axonal injury: a functional magnetic resonance imaging study. *Journal of Neurology, Neurosurgery, and Psychiatry, 78*(2), 168–173.

Mayer, A. R., Ling, J., Mannell, M. V., Gasparovic, C., Phillips, J. P., Doezema, D., et al. (2010). A prospective diffusion tensor imaging study in mild traumatic brain injury. *Neurology, 74*(8), 643–650.

Mayer, A. R., Mannell, M. V., Ling, J., Gasparovic, C., & Yeo, R. A. (2011). Functional connectivity in mild traumatic brain injury. *Human Brain Mapping, 32*(11), 1825–1835.

McAllister, T. W., Flashman, L. A., Maerlender, A., Greenwald, R. M., Beckwith, J. G., Tosteson, T.

D., et al. (2012). Cognitive effects of one season of head impacts in a cohort of collegiate contact sport athletes. *Neurology, 78*(22), 1777–1784.

McAllister, T. W., Saykin, A. J., Flashman, L. A., Sparkling, M. B., Johnson, S. C., Guerin, S. J., et al. (1999). Brain activation during working memory 1 month after mild traumatic brain injury: a functional MRI study. *Neurology, 53*(6), 1300–1308.

McAllister, T. W., Sparling, M. B., Flashman, L. A., Guerin, S. J., Mamourian, A. C., & Saykin, A. J. (2001). Differential working memory load effects after mild traumatic brain injury. *Neuroimage, 14*(5), 1004–1012.

McCauley, S. R., Wilde, E. A., Bigler, E. D., Chu, Z., Yallampalli, R., Oni, M. B., et al. (2011). Diffusion Tensor Imaging of Incentive Effects in Prospective Memory after Pediatric Traumatic Brain Injury. *Journal of Neurotrauma, 28*(4), 503–516.

McCauley, S. R., Wilde, E. A., Merkley, T. L., Schnelle, K. P., Bigler, E. D., Hunter, J. V., et al. (2010). Patterns of cortical thinning in relation to event-based prospective memory performance three months after moderate to severe traumatic brain injury in children. *Developmental Neuropsychology, 35*(3), 318–332.

McGowan, J. C., Yang, J. H., Plotkin, R. C., Grossmn, R. I., Umile, E. M., Cecil, K. M., et al. (2000). Magnetization transfer imaging in the detection of injury associated with mild head trauma. *American Journal of Neuroradiology, 21*(5), 875–880.

Merkley, T. L., Bigler, E. D., Wilde, E. A., McCauley, S. R., Hunter, J. V., & Levin, H. S. (2008). Diffuse changes in cortical thickness in pediatric moderate-to-severe traumatic brain injury. *Journal of Neurotrauma, 25*(11), 1343–1345.

Meyers, C. A., Levin, H. S., Eisenberg, H. M., & Guinto, F. C. (1983). Early versus late lateral ventricular enlargement following closed head injury. *Journal of Neurology, Neurosurgery, & Psychiatry 46*(12), 1092–1097.

Miles, L., Grossman, R. I., Johnson, G., Babb, J. S., Diller, L., & Inglese, M. (2008). Short-term DTI predictors of cognitive dysfunction in mild traumatic brain injury. *Brain Injury, 22*(2), 115–122.

Newcombe, V. F., Williams, G. B., Nortie, J., Bradley, P. G., Harding, S. G., Smielewski, P., et al. (2007). Analysis of acute traumatic axonal injury using diffusion tensor imaging. *British Journal of Neurosurgery, 21*(4), 340–348.

Newsome, M. R., Scheibel, R. S., Chu, Z., Hunter, J. V., Li, X., Wilde, E. A., et al. (2012). The relationship of resting cerebral blood flow and brain activation during a social cognition task in adolescents with chronic moderate to severe traumatic brain injury: a preliminary investigation. *International*

Journal of Developmental Neuroscience, *30*(3), 255–266.

Newsome, M. R., Scheibel, R. S., Hanten, G., Chu, Z., Steinberg, J. L., Hunter, J. V., et al. (2010). Brain activation while thinking about the self from another person's perspective after traumatic brain injury in adolescents. *Neuropsychology*, *24*(2), 139–147.

Newsome, M. R., Scheibel, R. S., Steinberg, J. L., Troyanskaya, M., Sharma, R. G., Rauch, R. A., et al. (2007). Working memory brain activation following severe traumatic brain injury. *Cortex*, *43*(1), 95–111.

Niogi, S. N., Mukherjee, P., Ghajar, J., Johnson, C., Kolster, S. A., Sarkar, R., et al. (2008). Extent of microstructural white matter injury in postconcussive syndrome correlates with impaired cognitive reaction time: a 3T diffusion tensor imaging study of mild traumatic brain injury. *American Journal of Neuroradiology*, *29*(5), 967–973.

Pagani, E., Bizzi, A., Di Salle, F., De Stefano, N., Filippi, M. (2008). Basic concepts of advanced MRI techniques. *Neurological Science*, 29 (3) 290–295.

Palacios, E. M., Sala-Llonch, R., Junque, C., Fernandez-Espejo, D., Roig, T., Tormos, J. M., et al. (2012). Long-term declarative memory deficits in diffuse TBI: Correlations with cortical thickness, white matter integrity and hippocampal volume. *Cortex*, 49(3), 646-657.

Palacios, E. M., Sala-Llonch, R., Junque, C., Roig, T., Tormos, J. M., Bargallo, N., et al. (2012). White matter integrity related to functional working memory networks in traumatic brain injury. *Neurology*, 78(12), 852–860.

Panigrahy, A., Nelson, M. D. Jr., & Bluml, S (2010). Magnetic resonance spectroscopy in pediatric neuroradiology: clinical and research applications. *Pediatric Radiology*, 40(1), 3–30.

Pascual, J. M., Solivera, J., Prieto, R., Barrios, L., Lopez-Larrubia, P., Cerdan, S., et al. (2007). Time course of early metabolic changes following diffuse traumatic brain injury in rats as detected by (1)H NMR spectroscopy. *Journal of Neurotrauma*, 24(6), 944–959.

Perlbarg, V., Puybasset, L., Tollard, E., Lehericy, S., Benali, H., & Galanaud, D. (2009). Relation between brain lesion location and clinical outcome in patients with severe traumatic brain injury: a diffusion tensor imaging study using voxel-based approaches. *Human Brain Mapping*, 30(12), 3924–3933.

Perlstein, W. M., Cole, M. A., Demery, J. A., Seignourel, P. J., Dixit, N. K., Larson, M. J., et al. (2004). Parametric manipulation of working memory load in traumatic brain injury: behavioral and neural correlates. *Journal of the International Neuropsychological Society*, 10(5), 724–741.

Pouwels, P. J., Brockmann, K., Kruse, B., Wilken, B., Wick, M., Hanefeld, F., et al. (1999). Regional age dependence of human brain metabolites from infancy to adulthood as detected by quantitative localized proton MRS. *Pediatric Research*, *46*(4), 474–485.

Provencher, S. W. (1993). Estimation of metabolite concentrations from localized in vivo proton NMR spectra. *Magnetic Resonance in Medicine*, *30*(6), 672–679.

Rasmussen, I. A., Xu, J., Antonsen, I. K., Brunner, J., Skandsen, T., Axelson, D. E., et al. (2008). Simple dual tasking recruits prefrontal cortices in chronic severe traumatic brain injury patients, but not in controls. *Journal of Neurotrauma*, 25(9), 1057–1070.

Reichenbach, J. R., Venkatesan, R., Schillinger, D. J., Kido, D. K., & Haacke, E. M. (1997). Small vessels in the human brain: MR venography with deoxyhemoglobin as an intrinsic contrast agent. *Radiology*, *204*(1), 272–277.

Robertson, C. L., Hendrich, K. S., Kochanek, P. M., Jackson, E. K., Melick, J. A., Graham, S. H., et al. (2000). Assessment of 2-chloroadenosine treatment after experimental traumatic brain injury in the rat using arterial spin-labeled MRI: a preliminary report. *Acta Neurochirurgica Supplement*, *76*, 187–189.

Salmond, C. H., Menon, D. K., Chatfield, D. A., Williams, G. B., Pena, A., Sahakian, B. J., et al. (2006). Diffusion tensor imaging in chronic head injury survivors: correlations with learning and memory indices. *Neuroimage*, *29*(1), 117–124.

Saxena, S. & P. Caroni (2007). Mechanisms of axon degeneration: from development to disease. *Progress in Neurobiology*, *83*(3G), 174–191.

Scheibel, R. S., Newsome, M. R., Steinberg, J. L., Pearson, D. A., Rauch, R. A., Mao, H., et al. (2007). Altered brain activation during cognitive control in patients with moderate to severe traumatic brain injury. *Neurorehabilitation and Neural Repair*, *21*(1), 36–45.

Scheibel, R. S., Pearson, D. A., Faria, L. P., Kotrla, K. J., Aylward, E., Bachevalier, J., et al. (2003). An fMRI study of executive functioning after severe diffuse TBI. *Brain Injury*, *17*(11), 919–930.

Schmitz, T. W., Rowley, H. A., Kawahara, T. N., & Johnson, S. C. (2006). Neural correlates of self-evaluative accuracy after traumatic brain injury. *Neuropsychologia*, *44*(5), 762–773.

Sehgal, V., Delproposto, Z., Haacke, E. M., Tong, K. A., Wycliffe, N., Kido, D. K., et al. (2005). Clinical applications of neuroimaging with susceptibility-weighted imaging. *Journal of Magnetic Resonance Imaging*, *22*(4), 439–450.

Serra-Grabulosa, J. M., Junque, C., Verer, K., Salgado-Pineda, P., Maneru, C., & Mercader, J. M.

(2005). Cerebral correlates of declarative memory dysfunctions in early traumatic brain injury. *Journal of Neurology, Neurosurgery, & Psychiatry* 76(1), 129–131.

Shen, Y., Kou, Z., Kreipke, C. W., Petrov, T., Hu, J., & Haacke, E. M. (2007). In vivo measurement of tissue damage, oxygen saturation changes and blood flow changes after experimental traumatic brain injury in rats using susceptibility weighted imaging. *Journal of Magnetic Resonance Imaging*, 25(2), 219–227.

Sherer, M., Stouter, J., Hart, T., Nakase-Richardson, R., Oliver, J., Manning, E., et al. (2006). Computed tomography findings and early cognitive outcome after traumatic brain injury. *Brain Injury*, 20(10), 997–1005.

Shutter, L., Tong, K. A., & Holshouser, B. A. (2004). Proton MRS in acute traumatic brain injury: role for glutamate/glutamine and choline for outcome prediction. *Journal of Neurotrauma*, 21(12), 1693–1705.

Sidaros, A., Engberg, A. W., Sidaros, K., Liptrot, M. G., Herning, M., Petersen, P., et al. (2008). Diffusion tensor imaging during recovery from severe traumatic brain injury and relation to clinical outcome: a longitudinal study. *Brain*, 131(Pt 2): 559–572.

Sidaros, A., Skimminge, A., Liptrot, M. G., Sidaros, K., Engberg A. W., Herning, M., et al. (2009). Long-term global and regional brain volume changes following severe traumatic brain injury: a longitudinal study with clinical correlates. *Neuroimage*, 44(1), 1–8.

Sinson, G., Bagley, L. J., Cecil, K. M., Torchia, M., McGowan, J. C., Lenkinski, R. E., et al. (2001). Magnetization transfer imaging and proton MR spectroscopy in the evaluation of axonal injury: correlation with clinical outcome after traumatic brain injury. *American Journal of Neuroradiology*, 22(1), 143–151.

Soeda, A., Nakashima, T., Okumura, A., Kuwata, K., Shinoda, J., & Iwama, T. (2005). Cognitive impairment after traumatic brain injury: a functional magnetic resonance imaging study using the Stroop task. *Neuroradiology*, 47(7), 501–506.

Strangman, G. E., O'Neil-Pirozzi, T. M., Goldstein, R., Kelkar, K., Katz, D. I., Burke, D., et al. (2008). Prediction of memory rehabilitation outcomes in traumatic brain injury by using functional magnetic resonance imaging. *Archives of Physical Medicine and Rehabilitation*, 89(5), 974–981.

Strangman, G. M., O'Neil-Pirozzi, T. M., Burke, D., Cristina, D., Goldstein, R., Rauch, S. L, et al. (2005). Functional neuroimaging and cognitive rehabilitation for people with traumatic brain injury. *American Journal of Physical Medicine & Rehabilitation*, 84(1), 62–75.

Strich, S. J. (1956). Diffuse degeneration of the cerebral white matter in severe dementia following head injury. *Journal of Neurology, Neurosurgery, & Psychiatry* 19(3), 163–185.

Symms, M., Jager, H., Schmierer, K., & Yousry, T. (2004). A review of structural magnetic resonance neuroimaging. *Journal of Neurology, Neurosurgery, & Psychiatry*, 75(9), 1235–1244.

Tang, L., Ge, Y., Sodickson, D. K., Miles, L., Zhou, Y., Reaume, J., et al. (2011). Thalamic Resting-State Functional Networks: Disruption in Patients with Mild Traumatic Brain Injury. *Radiology*, 260(3), 831–840.

Tollard, E., Galanaud, D., Perlbarg, V., Sanchez-Pena, P., Le Fur, Y., Abdennour, L., et al. (2009). Experience of diffusion tensor imaging and 1H spectroscopy for outcome prediction in severe traumatic brain injury: Preliminary results. *Critical Care Medicine*, 37(4), 1448–1455.

Tong, K. A., Ashwal, S., Holshouser, B. A., Shutter, L. A., Herigault, G., Haacke, E. M., et al. (2003). Hemorrhagic shearing lesions in children and adolescents with posttraumatic diffuse axonal injury: improved detection and initial results. *Radiology* 227(2), 332–339.

Trainor, T. P., Fitts, J. P., Grolimund, D., Bargar, J. R., & Brown, G. E. Jr.(1999). Grazing-incidence XAFS studies of aqueous Zn(II) on sapphire single crystals. *Journal of Synchrotron Radiation*, 6(Pt 3), 618–620.

Trivedi, M. A., Ward, M. A., Hess, T. M., Gale, S. D., Dempsey, R. J., Rowley, H. A., et al. (2007). Longitudinal changes in global brain volume between 79 and 409 days after traumatic brain injury: relationship with duration of coma. *Journal of Neurotrauma*, 24(5), 766–771.

Turkheimer, E., Cullum, C. M., Hubler, D. W., Paver, S. W., Yeo, R. A., & Bigler, E. D. (1984). Quantifying cortical atrophy. *Journal of Neurology, Neurosurgery, & Psychiatry*, 47(12), 1314–1318.

van Boven, R., Harrington, G. S., Hackney, D. B., Ebel, A., Gauger, G., Bremner, J. D., et al. (2009). Advances in neuroimaging of traumatic brain injury and posttraumatic stress disorder. *Journal of Rehabilitation Research and Development*, 46(6), 717–757.

Warner, M. A., Marquez de la Plata, C., Spence, J., Wang, J. Y., Harper, C., Moore, C., et al. (2010). Assessing spatial relationships between axonal integrity, regional brain volumes, and neuropsychological outcomes after traumatic axonal injury. *Journal of Neurotrauma* 27(12), 2121–2130.

Wilde, E. A., Ayoub, K. W., Bigler, E. D., Chu, E. D., Hunter, J. V., Wu, T. C., et al. (2012). Diffusion tensor imaging in moderate-to-severe pediatric traumatic brain injury: changes within an 18 month post-injury interval. *Brain Imaging Behavior*, 6(3), 404–416.

Wilde, E. A., Bigler, E. D., Hunter, J. V., Fearing, M. A., Scheibel, R. S., Newsome, M. R., et al. (2007). Hippocampus, amygdala, and basal ganglia morphometrics in children after moderate-to-severe traumatic brain injury. *Development Medicine & Child Neurology*, 49(4), 294–299.

Wilde, E. A., Chu, Z., Bigler, E. D., Hunter, J. V., Fearing, M. A., Hanten, G., et al. (2006). Diffusion tensor imaging in the corpus callosum in children after moderate to severe traumatic brain injury. *Journal of Neurotrauma*, 23(10), 1412–1426.

Wilde, E. A., S. R. McCauley et al. (2012). Serial measurement of memory and diffusion tensor imaging changes within the first week following uncomplicated mild traumatic brain injury. *Brain Imaging Behavior*, 6(2), 319–328.

Wilde, E. A., McCauley, S. R., Hunter, J. V., Bigler, E. D., Chu, Z., Wang, Z. J., et al. (2008). Diffusion tensor imaging of acute mild traumatic brain injury in adolescents. *Neurology*, 70(12), 948–955.

Wilde, E. A., Merkley, T. L., Bigler, E. D., Max, J. E., Schmidt, A. T., Ayoub, K. W., et al. (2012). Longitudinal changes in cortical thickness in children after traumatic brain injury and their relation to behavioral regulation and emotional control. *International Journal of Developmental Neuroscience*, 30(3), 267–276.

Wilde, E. A., Ramos, M. A., Yallampalli, R., Bigler, E. D., McCauley, S. R., Chu, Z., et al. (2010). Diffusion tensor imaging of the cingulum bundle in children after traumatic brain injury. *Developmental Neuropsychology*, 35(3), 333–351.

Wong, E. C., Cronin, M., Wu, W. C., Inglis, B., Frank, L. R., & Liu, T. T. (2006). Velocity-selective arterial spin labeling. *Magnetic Resonance in Medicine*, 55(6), 1334–1341.

Wozniak, J. R., Krach, L., Ward, E., Mueller, B. A., Muetzel, R., Schnoebelen, S., et al. (2007). Neurocognitive and neuroimaging correlates of pediatric traumatic brain injury: a diffusion tensor imaging (DTI) study. *Archives of Clincal Neuropsychology*, 22(5), 555–568.

Wu, T. C., Wilde, E. A., Bigler, E. D., Li, X., Merkley, T. L., Yallampalli, R., et al. (2010). Longitudinal

Changes in the Corpus Callosum following Pediatric Traumatic Brain Injury. *Developmental Neuroscience*. 32(5–6), 361–373.

Wu, Z., Li, S., Lei, J., An, D., & Haacke, E. M. (2010). Evaluation of traumatic subarachnoid hemorrhage using susceptibility-weighted imaging. *American Journal of Neuroradiology*, 31(7), 1302–1310.

Xu, Q., Zhou, Y., Li, Y. S., Cao, W. W., Lin, Y., Pan, Y. M., et al. (2010). Diffusion tensor imaging changes correlate with cognition better than conventional MRI findings in patients with subcortical ischemic vascular disease. *Dementia and Geriatric Cognitive Disorders*, 30(4), 317–326.

Xu, S., Zhuo, J., Racz, J., Shi, D., Roys, S., Fiskum, G., et al. (2011). Early microstructural and metabolic changes following controlled cortical impact injury in rat: a magnetic resonance imaging and spectroscopy study. Journal of Neurotrauma, 28(10), 2091–2102.

Yeo, R. A., Phillips, J. P., Jung, R. E., Brown, A. J., Campbell, R. C., & Brooks, W. M. (2006). Magnetic resonance spectroscopy detects brain injury and predicts cognitive functioning in children with brain injuries. *Journal of Neurotrauma*, 23(10), 1427–1435.

Yount, R., Raschke, K. A., Biru, M., Tate, D. F., Miller, M. J., Abildskov, T., et al. (2002). Traumatic brain injury and atrophy of the cingulate gyrus. *The Journal of Neuropsychiatry and Clinical Neurosciences*, 14 (4), 416–423.

Yuan, W., Holland, S. K., Schmithorst, V. J., Walz, N. C., Cecil, K. M., Jones, B. V., et al. (2007). Diffusion tensor MR imaging reveals persistent white matter alteration after traumatic brain injury experienced during early childhood. *American Journal of Neuroradiology*, 28(10), 1919–1925.

Yuh, E. L., Cooper, S. R., Ferguson, A. R., & Manley, G. T. (2012). Quantitative CT improves outcome prediction in acute traumatic brain injury. *Journal of Neurotrauma* 29(5), 735–746.

Zappala, G., Thiebaut de Schotten, M., & Eslinger, P. J. (2012). Traumatic brain injury and the frontal lobes: what can we gain with diffusion tensor imaging? *Cortex*, 48(2), 156–165.

Part V

Special Populations

15

Children and Adolescents

Vicki Anderson and Keith Owen Yeates

Traumatic Brain Injury: A Review of the Research and Future Directions

Childhood traumatic brain injury (TBI) is the most frequent cause of interruption to normal development and results in significant impairments in many survivors. Predicting outcome is difficult, and the long-term consequences depend on a complex interaction of a number of factors including premorbid abilities, injury characteristics, environmental context, developmental stage, and access to rehabilitation, as well as factors yet to be identified. While injury severity is the best established index of poor outcome, ongoing impairment has also been linked to premorbid learning or behavior problems, reduced access to intervention and support services, and environmental factors such as social disadvantage and family stress. Age or developmental level at the time of injury is a further critical factor in the recovery from childhood TBI. Though some have argued that younger children recover better than adolescents and adults because their brains are more adaptable (or "plastic"), studies now show that the developing brain may be particularly vulnerable to early injury because of the potential for brain damage to disrupt critical stages of neural and cognitive maturation. The goal of the present chapter is to provide an overview of the current state of knowledge regarding pediatric TBI, to critique the existing research and to suggest potentially fruitful directions for future investigation.

Epidemiology

Accurate statistics regarding the incidence and prevalence of TBI are difficult to obtain, with epidemiological studies varying widely in terms of injury definition, sources of data, data collection techniques, case descriptions and ages of target populations. Population estimates of child TBI presentations range between 250 and 799 per 100,000 per year, with variations across age groups and gender (Crowe, Babl, Anderson & Catroppa, 2010; Kraus, 1995; Langlois, Rutland-Brown & Thomas, 2006; Tate, McDonald, & Lulham, 1998). Of these, approximately 80% will be mild injuries (Kraus, Fife, Cox, Ranstein, & Conroy, 1986; Leschoihier & DiScala, 1993), half will not seek any medical care, between 5 and 10 percent will experience temporary and/or permanent neuropsychological sequelae, and 5 to 10 percent will receive fatal injuries (Goldstein & Levin, 1987). One in every 30 newborn children will sustain a TBI before age 16 (Annegers, 1983). Examination of data relating specifically to children admitted to hospital with a severe TBI shows that the mortality rate is approximately one third, with another third of child victims making a good recovery, and the last third exhibiting residual disability (Michaud, Rivara, Grady, & Reay, 1992). Such incidence levels establish childhood TBI as a significant community problem.

Cause of Injury

Data regarding the cause of TBI can provide important information about the mechanism of brain injuries. The most common causes of TBI are transportation-related accidents and falls, which, together account for more than 50% of all pediatric TBI (Crowe et al., 2010; Langlois et al.,

2006). Infants and toddlers are especially likely to sustain TBI through falls, as well as via inflicted injuries secondary to child abuse (Holloway, Bye & Moran, 1994; Keenan & Bratton, 2006). Young children are most likely to be injured through falls and motor vehicle collisions, either as occupants or pedestrians. In older children, sports and recreational accidents, and pedestrian or bicycle collisions with motor vehicles account for an increasing proportion of TBI. Adolescents are especially likely to be injured in motor vehicle collisions, with assaults also common.

Demographic Characteristics

There is evidence that patient fatality rates increase as age decreases. Michaud and colleagues (Michaud et al., 1992) report that, in their study of serious TBI, 14% of children injured over the age of 14 years died from their injury, while the fatality rate for children under two years was 50%. In addition, they found better recovery with increasing age. Death was the most common outcome for the under 2 age group, while the majority of children injured over 14 years were classified as showing good recovery. These data are consistent with the causes of injury across childhood, with inflicted injuries being most common in infancy and more likely to result in poor outcome, while sporting injuries are more common in older children and teenagers, which are usually linked to milder insults and better recovery.

As is commonly reported, boys and girls are not equally at risk of sustaining TBI. A comparison of gender ratios shows that, in children under age 2, the male to female ratio is approximately equal (Crowe et al., 2010). In contrast, school-aged males are more than twice as likely as age-matched females to suffer TBI (Kraus, 1995). Further, Kraus and colleagues (1986) noted that the incidence of TBI increases in males through childhood and adolescence, with a relative decline for females through childhood.

Epidemiological research demonstrates that childhood TBI occurs most frequently on weekends, holidays, and afternoons, when children are more likely to be involved in leisure activities (Crowe et al., 2010). Such trends have been interpreted as an indication that many such injuries result from reckless behaviors in poorly supervised environments (Chadwick, Rutter, Brown, Shaffer, & Traub, 1981; Dalby & Obrzut, 1991). Further, it is often stated that TBI is more common in families where parents are socially disadvantaged, unemployed, or emotionally disturbed (Anderson et al., 1997; Brown, Chadwick, Shaffer, Rutter, & Traub, 1981; Parslow, Morris, Tasker, Forsyth, & Hawley, 2005; Rivara et al., 1993; Taylor et al., 1995), where parental neglect and poor supervision are evident (Moyes, 1980), and in children with pre-existing learning and behavioral deficits (Asarnow et al., 1995; Brown et al., 1981; Ponsford et al., 1999).

Neuropathology and Pathophysiology

Closed head injury accounts for the majority of instances of child TBI. In closed head injury, the skull is not penetrated, but rather the brain is shaken around within the skull cavity, resulting in multiple injury sites, as well as diffuse axonal damage. The most common cause of such injuries is motor vehicle accidents, associated with high velocity deceleration forces. Damage results from compression and deformation of the skull at the point of impact, and the primary pathology includes contusion, or bruising, at point of impact of the blow and at other cerebral sites. Research suggests that there are specific areas of the brain which are particularly vulnerable to such injury-related contusions, including basal frontal regions and temporal lobes, where severe surface damage may occur to blood vessels and cortical tissue (Bigler, 2007; Courville, 1945; Wilde et al., 2005). Additionally, in response to the impact, the brain is shaken backwards and forwards and rotated, with the extent of this process dependent on the force of the blow. The associated injuries caused by this shaking include damage to cerebral areas opposite the site of damage and shearing injuries to white matter, as these nerve tracts are bent and torn (Amacher, 1988).

The pathophysiology of TBI begins at the time of impact, but continues over a period of days or weeks and perhaps even longer. Indeed, recent research indicates that the brain damage resulting from TBI involves more complex, prolonged, and interwoven processes than was previously recognized (Farkas & Povlishock, 2007;

Giza & Hovda, 2001; Povlishock & Katz, 2005). The consequences of child TBI may be different from that observed in adults, as the immature brain responds differently to trauma than the mature brain (Giza, Mink, & Madikians, 2007). Research has found that children are more likely to suffer from post-traumatic brain swelling, hypoxic-ischemic insult, and diffuse, rather than focal, injuries, but less likely to present with intracranial hematomas. Compared to adults, children have a greater head-to-body ratio, less myelination, and greater relative proportion of water content and cerebral blood volume. Once children reach adolescence, TBI-related pathology begins to more closely resemble that seen in adults.

The typical pathophysiology of TBI may be classified based on the relationship to the initial insult: (i) *primary impact injuries* occur as a direct result of the application of force to the brain and include fractures, contusions and lacerations, and diffuse axonal damage. Such injuries are generally permanent, and show little response to early treatment; (ii) *secondary injuries* occur as a consequence of the primary injury. Raised intracranial pressure and brain swelling are two major secondary complications which are particularly common in children (Kochanek, 2006). Hypoxia, and infection, as well as metabolic changes including hypothermia, electrolyte imbalance, and respiratory difficulties may also occur (Begali, 1992; North, 1984; Pang, 1985). Secondary injuries have been found to be predictive of poor outcome (Quattrocchi, Prasad, Willits, & Wagner, 1991), but are also more responsive to appropriate and timely medical interventions.

While less common in children than adults, mass effects, often related to vascular interruptions, lead to increased cerebral volume, and raised intracranial pressure. If not treated quickly, usually via surgical evacuation, these secondary complications may cause cerebral herniation and ultimately death. The major types of hematoma include: epidural, subdural, and intracerebral, with the labels defining the site of the blood collection. Epidural and subdural hematomas are situated within the meningeal coverings of the brain. *Epidural hematomas*, refer to bleeds above the dura, just below the surface of the skull, and not directly involving brain tissue. They are usually related to a skull fracture, where vessels in the meninges have been damaged. *Subdural hematomas* present as a collection between the dura and the arachnoid mater, resulting from injury to the blood vessels in the cortex, or to the venous sinuses. These are more common and serious than epidural collections, mostly occurring as a consequence of massive cortical disruption and lacerations to blood vessels within the brain where the underlying damaged brain may undergo rapid edema formation leading to mass effect, and requiring surgical evacuation. *Intracerebral hematomas* occur within the brain parenchyma, and often follow the same spatial distribution as contusions. They may result from shear injuries to brain tissue. When treated promptly, outcome from these complications is good (Michaud et al., 1992). If left untreated, increasing blood mass may cause cerebral shift and herniation.

While relatively uncommon following closed head injury, a number of delayed medical complications may also develop in the sub-acute stages post-injury. Communicating hydrocephalus may occur when there is an obstruction of the flow of cerebrospinal fluid, due to vascular disruption. Cerebral infections may arise in association with skull fractures. These infections usually take the form of meningitis or cerebral abscess. Each of these complications may be detected on the basis of increased intracranial pressure, and associated late deterioration in function. Following closed head injury patients also have increased risk of epilepsy. Early seizures occur quite frequently post-injury, but later post-traumatic epilepsy is less common, with risk factors including more severe injury, presence of focal pathology, and younger age at insult (Jennett & Bond 1975; Pang, 1985; Raimondi & Hirschauer, 1984).

Neurochemical and Neurometabolic Mechanisms

Recent research has suggested that further secondary damage may be due to neurochemical processes, mediated by a cascade of biochemical and metabolic reactions that take place following a TBI (Farkas & Povlishock, 2007; Novack, Dillon, & Jackson, 1996). TBI can result in a variety of neurochemical events, including the production of free radicals and excitatory amino acids and the disruption of normal calcium homeostasis, as well as changes in glucose metabolism and cerebral blood flow (Giza & Hovda, 2001). These events act in concert to exacerbate the hypoxic-ischemic insult that commonly occurs following TBI. Animal research suggests that pharmacological interventions may be successful in reducing brain injury due to such mechanisms (Novack et al., 1996), although the results of human trials have been disappointing.

Late Effects

TBI can be associated with a variety of late effects. Neuroimaging studies have indicated that severe TBI often results in a gradual and prolonged process of white matter degeneration and cortical thinning, with associated cerebral atrophy and ventricular enlargement (Ghosh et al., 2009; Merkley, 2008). In some cases, ventricular dilatation results from an actual disturbance in the circulation of cerebrospinal fluid and is associated with hydrocephalus. Post-traumatic hydrocephalus, as opposed to cerebral atrophy and associated ventricular enlargement, is relatively uncommon, and typically develops only after severe injuries associated with certain predisposing factors, such as subarachnoid hemorrhage (McLean et al., 1995).

Early post-traumatic seizures, defined as occurring within the first week after TBI, occur in many children, and can involve focal status epilepticus (Statler, 2006). Very young children seem especially vulnerable to such seizures. The occurrence of seizures soon after injury does not necessarily place children at risk for later epilepsy, which occurs in about 10-20% of children with severe TBI. Post-traumatic epilepsy is more common in children with penetrating injuries, inflicted injuries, or depressed skull fracture, all of which are indicative of focal pathology. Most post-traumatic seizures occur within the first 2 years post-injury, and have been linked to poor outcome (Anderson et al., 2009a).

Neurobehavioral Consequences

An exhaustive review of the literature addressing the consequences of child TBI is beyond the scope of this chapter. To summarize, research indicates that serious TBI can cause impairments in alertness and orientation, intellectual functioning, language and communication skills, nonverbal skills, attention, memory, and executive functions, motor skills, academic achievement, social and behavioral function and adaptive abilities. Following is an overview of current literature.

Early Behavioral Consequences— Post-Traumatic Amnesia

Post-traumatic amnesia (PTA), characterized by disturbances of orientation and alertness are often observed following TBI, particularly during acute recovery. Most children with TBI, especially those that are moderate or severe, experience a period of fluctuating arousal, disorientation, confusion, and memory loss immediately post-injury. Length of PTA, which has been argued to reflect disruption to the attentional system, has been identified as a strong predictor of chronic outcome. Various measures are available to assess the presence and duration of PTA in children using standardized methods, such as the Children's Orientation and Amnesia Test (COAT; Ewing-Cobbs, Levin, Fletcher, Miner & Eisenberg, 1990), the Westmead Posttraumatic Amnesia Scale— child version (Marosszeky et al., 1993), and the Starship PTA Scale for preschoolers (Fernando, Eaton, Faulkner, Moodley, & Setchell, 2002). Unfortunately, few have adequate psychometric properties or are appropriate for preschoolers or pre-lingual children.

Intellectual Functioning

Most studies employ IQ either as an outcome measure or as a sample descriptor (Anderson & Moore, 1995; Chadwick et al., 1981; Ewing-Cobbs et al., 1997; Prior, Kinsella, Sawyer, Bryan, & Anderson, 1994; Todd, Anderson, & Lawrence, 1996). Intellectual impairment following child TBI was originally documented in the early 1980s when Chadwick et al. (1981) identified reduced intellectual function in school-aged children acutely after TBI, with these problems persisting for at least 2 years post-injury. Since then, intellectual deficits have been consistently reported, with the magnitude of these deficits related to injury severity. Early research, which focused on school-aged children, suggested that nonverbal domains were particularly vulnerable, due to the involvement of fluid problem-solving skills and speeded motor output. The verbal domain was thought to be more resilient, being more dependent on previously acquired knowledge. In contrast, more recent studies have found deficits in both nonverbal and verbal aspects of intellectual functioning (Anderson, Catroppa, Morse, Haritou, & Rosenfeld, 2005b; Anderson. Morse, Catroppa, Haritou, & Rosenfeld, 2004; Taylor et al., 1999).

Prospective, longitudinal studies indicate that children who sustain serious TBI demonstrate significant recovery in intellectual functioning following TBI, most dramatic in the acute recovery period and the early years post-insult. IQ scores tend to increase over the first 2-3 years following TBI, with the largest increases occurring among children with more severe injuries (Anderson et al, 2005a; Yeates, 2002). Recent research shows a plateau in intellectual development 3-5 years after injury (Anderson et al, 2009b). However, despite substantial recovery, IQ scores often continue to be depressed relative to premorbid levels following moderate to severe TBI. Persistent deficits in IQ appear to be especially likely among children with severe TBI and those injured early in life (Anderson et al., 2004, 2005a). In contrast to these poor outcomes, mild TBI results in few, if any, intellectual consequences (Anderson et al, 2005b; 2009b).

Language and Communication Skills

Expressive and receptive language deficits are sometimes observed immediately after TBI (Levin et al., 1983), but overt aphasic disorders are rare, even acutely post-injury. In contrast, more subtle language difficulties are common and often persist, again most often following moderate to severe injuries. These may include problems with slowed speech, language dysfluency, poor logical sequencing of ideas, word finding difficulties and complex comprehension (Ewing-Cobbs & Barnes, 2002). Language deficits typically improve over time, with the

most improvement seen following severe TBI (Catroppa & Anderson, 2004).

Children with TBI are also at risk of difficulties with the pragmatic aspects of language (Chapman, 1995; Dennis & Barnes, 1990). These skills develop late in childhood through early adolescence, and so may only become evident as the injured child reaches these developmental stages. Deficits have been demonstrated in a variety of skills, such as interpreting ambiguous sentences, making inferences, understanding humor, formulating sentences from individual words, and explaining figurative expressions. For example, Chapman and colleagues (Chapman et al., 2004; Chapman, 1995) have shown that, on a task of narrative discourse, children with severe TBI produce stories with fewer words and sentences, that contain less information, are not as well organized, and are less complete than those produced by children with milder injuries or by normal controls. This pattern of impoverished output has been replicated in children with insults during the preschool period (Catroppa & Anderson, 2004; Didus, Anderson, & Catroppa, 1999). Deficits in such skills reflect a general impairment in discourse, which has the potential to impact on the child's capacity to communicate effectively within their environment and possibly contribute to the academic and social difficulties that children with TBI often experience.

Nonverbal and Motor Skills

Non-verbal skills encompass both perceptual/spatial and constructional abilities, and residual deficits in these skills are common after child TBI. Deficits have been reported on a variety of constructional tasks, including block and puzzle tasks and drawing and copying (Thompson et al., 1994; Yeates, Patterson, Waber, & Bernstein, 2003). Some of these difficulties may be underpinned by fine motor incoordination and reduced motor control and motor planning, which are also commonly reported after child TBI. Further, these problems are particularly marked where responses involve time constraints (Bawden, Knights, & Winogron, 1985; Winogren, Knights, & Bawden, 1984). Less research has focused on perceptual or spatial skills which do not involve motor output, but available data do suggest that children with TBI also experience deficits in these domains (Lehnung et al., 2001; Verger et al., 2000).

Attention

Deficits in attention and information processing skills may impede learning and accumulation of new knowledge, potentially resulting in the global cognitive dysfunction commonly reported in the long term following childhood TBI (Anderson & Moore, 1995; Dennis, Wilkinson, Koski, & Humphreys, 1995). Within the adult literature, research findings suggest quite specific attention problems, with sustained and focused attention largely intact, and psychomotor slowness underpinning many observed "attention" deficits (Shum, McFarland, Bain, & Humphreys, 1990; Stuss et al., 1989).

Early studies generally focused on continuous performance test paradigms (Anderson & Pentland, 1998; Ewing-Cobbs et al., 1998b; Kaufmann, Fletcher, Levin, Miner, & Ewing-Cobbs, 1993) and consistently reported that younger, severely injured children exhibited greatest difficulties. Murray, Shum, and McFarland (1992), using a task which enabled identification of specific stages of information processing, found that children with TBI exhibited difficulty with rate of motor execution and response selection, and with other aspects of processing intact, suggesting a wider range of deficits than has been identified following adult TBI (Shum et al., 1990; Stuss et al., 1989). More recent studies have shown deficits in sustained, selective, shifting, and divided attention, particularly on more complex and timed measures (Anderson, Fenwick, Manly, & Robertson, 1998; Catroppa & Anderson, 2005; Catroppa, Anderson, Morse, Haritou, & Rosenfeld, 2007; Ewing-Cobbs et al., 1998b). The deficits show some recovery, but can persist across time, especially in more severely injured children (Catroppa, Anderson, & Stargatt, 1999).

Memory

The implications of memory impairment in the child are substantial, given that the day-to-day tasks of childhood largely revolve around acquiring knowledge and learning and perfecting new skills. Memory problems may interfere with this process, resulting in a failure to develop at an age-appropriate rate. Childhood TBI frequently results in complaints of memory deficits (Ward, Shum, Dick, McKinlay, & Baker-Tweney, 2004). Deficits have been reported in a variety of memory components, including storage, retention, and retrieval (Roman et al., 1998; Yeates, Blumenstein, Patterson, & Delis, 1995a), with the magnitude of the impairment depending on injury severity (Catroppa & Anderson, 2002, 2007; Levin et al., 1988; Yeates et al., 1995a, 2003).

Guided by advances in the developmental neurosciences, research has begun to examine types of memory, with a critical distinction drawn between explicit and implicit memory. Explicit memory involves the conscious recollection of past events or experiences and is typically measured through recall or recognition, whereas implicit memory involves demonstrations of learning or facilitation of performance in the absence of conscious recollection. Several studies have indicated that children with TBI are less likely to show deficits in implicit memory than in explicit memory, using measures of both procedural learning and perceptual and conceptual priming (Shum, Jamieson, Bahr, Wallace, 1999; Ward, Shum, Wallace, & Boon, 2002; Yeates & Enrile, 2005). A number of studies have also investigated working memory skills in children with TBI. Mandalis and colleagues (Mandalis, Kinsella, Ong, & Anderson, 2007) examined a group of children with moderate-severe TBI and found impaired function in both the phonological loop and central executive components of working memory, which they linked to poor encoding and acquisition of new information as well as reductions in retrieval and recognition memory.

Prospective memory is another form of recall that has received recent attention. Prospective memory involves remembering to perform an intended action at some time in the future. Children and adolescents with moderate to severe TBI display deficits in prospective memory when compared to children with orthopedic injuries (McCauley & Levin, 2004; McCauley, McDaniel, Pedroza, Chapman, Levin, 2009) or to typically developing children (Ward, Shum, McKinlay, Baker, Wallace, 2007). Like other high-level cognitive abilities, these skills develop later in childhood and may only become apparent when environmental demands increase, and deficits may underpin the school-based difficulties described for adolescents with TBI, for example, forgetting homework tasks.

Executive Functions

Deficits in executive function are frequently reported in children who have suffered TBI, in keeping with the vulnerability of the pre-frontal regions as a result of head trauma (Anderson, Levin, & Jacobs, 2002; Courville, 1945). Over the past decade, research on executive function in TBI has broadened from an emphasis on "cold" or cognitive aspects of executive skills (e.g., planning, mental flexibility) to include "hot" executive functions, such as emotional and behavioral regulation. Levin and his colleagues have studied executive functions extensively, using standardized clinical tests, and reporting deficits in planning and inhibitory control (Levin et al., 1996; Levin & Hanten, 2005), which have also been identified on everyday tasks of executive skills (Mangeot, Armstrong, Colvin, Yeates, & Taylor, 2002; Sesma, Slomine, Ding, & McCarthy 2008). The magnitude of deficits on executive function tasks has been shown to correlate with injury severity. Garth, Anderson, and Wrennall (1997) described poor planning and problem solving, reduced capacity for abstract thought, and slowed speed of response in children with moderate and severe TBI. Similarly, Pentland, Todd and Anderson (1998) asked adolescents with and without TBI to construct a plan for hosting a party, including details such as when to send out invitations or pick up party food, as well as delegating tasks to family members, and fitting these tasks within a specified time frame. They found that severely injured adolescents were more impulsive, made more errors and used less efficient strategies, and provided ineffective or unworkable planning strategies as a result. For mild injuries outcomes were less clear, with some evidence that this group does not entirely escape executive function sequelae (Todd et al., 1996).

A number of factors, in addition to injury severity, have been found to contribute to executive dysfunction in children with TBI.

Levin and colleagues have shown a relationship between executive skills and volume of lesions in the frontal lobes, but not with extrafrontal lesion volume (Levin et al., 1994; 1997). Age at injury also appears relevant, with young children with severe injuries particularly vulnerable to executive deficits (Anderson & Catroppa, 2005; Ewing-Cobbs et al., 2004b). Moreover, these deficits have been linked to broader difficulties with social and behavioral adjustment (Ganesalingam, Sanson, Anderson, Yeates, 2006, 2007; Muscara, Catroppa, & Anderson, 2008a; Muscara, Eren, Catroppa, & Anderson, 2008) and longitudinal research has found that these deficits can persist for years after injury (Muscara, Catroppa, & Anderson, 2008b; Nadebaum, Anderson, & Catroppa, 2007).

Academic Performance

Academic difficulties demonstrated post-TBI may reflect the secondary effects of the many cognitive consequences of TBI described above. Research has documented declines in academic performance post-TBI (Ewing-Cobbs et al., 2004a; Taylor et al., 2002), with an increased risk of grade retention, placement in special education, and other indicators of academic difficulties (Ewing-Cobbs et al., 1998; Kinsella et al., 1995; Taylor et al., 2003). However, the reported academic difficulties do not necessarily translate into deficits on formal achievement testing. Deficits in academic achievement following TBI are most likely to be apparent in children injured at a young age (Ewing-Cobbs et al., 2004a, 2006), even when injuries are quite mild (Gronwall, Wrightson, & McGinn, 1997). Children injured at a later age do not necessarily display deficits on standardized achievement tests (Kinsella et al., 1995; Taylor et al., 2002), likely reflecting that some educational skills (e.g., word reading, spelling) are well established by late childhood and thus more resistant to the effects of TBI.

The academic difficulties demonstrated by children with TBI are predicted by a variety of different factors, including the child's premorbid academic functioning (Catroppa & Anderson, 2007) and post-injury neuropsychological functioning (Kinsella et al., 1997; Miller & Donders, 2003; Stallings, Ewing-Cobbs,

Francis, & Fletcher, 1996), as well as the child's post-injury behavioral adjustment (Yeates & Taylor, 2006). Family environment may also moderate academic performance, such that a more supportive and functional home lessens the impact of TBI (Taylor et al., 2002), possibly in association with higher quality education of intervention facilities.

Social Functioning

Childhood TBI often results in problems with social functioning, with children often rating this domain as of most concern (Bohnert, Parker, & Warschausky, 1997). A growing literature indicates that children with TBI, regardless of injury severity, are rated as less socially competent and lonelier than healthy children or children with injuries not involving the brain. These poor social outcomes have been found to persist over time (Andrews, Rose, & Johnson, 1998; Bohner et al., 1997; Dennis, Purvis, Barnes, Wilkinson, & Winner, 2001; Rosema, Crowe, & Anderson, in press; Yeates et al., 2004). The relationship between TBI and social outcomes appears to be moderated more by environmental variables than injury factors (Yeates et al. 2004). In particular, poor social outcome following TBI can be exacerbated by poor family functioning, lower socioeconomic status, and lack of family resources.

The poor social outcomes displayed by children with TBI may be mediated by deficit cognitive skills, including language, attention, executive function and social information processing. Following TBI, children display deficits in the understanding of emotion (Dennis et al., 1998) and mental states (Dennis, Wilkinson, Koski, & Humphreys, 2001b), as well as in social problem solving (Hanten et al., 2008; Janusz, Kirkwood, Yeates, Taylor, 2002; Warschausky, Cohen, Parker, Levendosky, & Okun, 1997). Collectively, deficits in executive functions, language pragmatics, and social problem solving account for significant variance in social outcomes among children with TBI (Yeates et al., 2004).

To date, much of the research addressing social deficits post-TBI has been based on "broad-band" measures of social function, which have been mostly parent- or teacher-rated. Recent advances in the social neurosciences suggests that the social deficits shown by children with TBI may be linked specifically to damage to the neural network underpinning social function, including anterior brain regions. Children with frontal lobe injury in association with TBI are more likely to have problems with social discourse (Dennis et al. 2001a) and social problem solving (Hanten et al., 2008), as well as more generally with social functioning (Levin et al., 2004).

Behavioral and Psychiatric Disorders

Over the years there has been considerable debate regarding the etiology of behavioral and adaptive problems following TBI. As previously noted, some authors argue that these problems reflect premorbid behavioral and family problems, while others support an important impact of brain injury (Farmer & Eakman, 1996; Max, Castillo et al., 1997; Max, Smith et al. 1997; Prior et al., 1994; Wade et al., 1996). These inconsistent interpretations may be due to the methodological problems inherent in measuring behavior. The absence of objective pre-injury measures, the use of subjective or generic tools, such as parent report, and the lack of appropriate or sensitive objective measures, all hinder our understanding in this area.

Numerous studies have documented that moderate to severe TBI in children increases the risk for a wide range of emotional and behavioral problems (Asarnow et al., 1995; Bohnert et al., 1997; Brink, Imbus, & Woo-Sam, 1980; Brown et al., 1981; Fletcher, Ewing-Cobbs, Miner, Levin, & Eisenberg, 1990; Klonoff, Clark, Klonoff, 1995; Schwartz et al., 2003; Taylor et al., 2002). For example, Schwartz and colleagues (2003) found that at 4 years post-injury, 36% of a severe TBI group displayed significant behavioral problems, compared with 22% of a moderate TBI group and 10% of an orthopedic injury comparison group. Max and colleagues (1997a, 1997b, 1997c, & 1998d) conducted a series of studies following the development of new psychiatric disorders in a cohort of children with TBI at 3, 6, 12, and 24 months post-injury. They found 46 percent of the participants met criteria for a new psychiatric disorder at 3 months,

24 percent at 6 months, 37 percent at 12 months, and 35 percent at 24 months post-injury.

A number of studies report increased incidence of psychiatric disturbance post-TBI (Brink et al., 1980; Brown et al., 1981; Cattelani, Lombardi, Brianti, & Mazzucchi, 1998; Perrot, Taylor, & Montes, 1991). This pattern may be due to the direct effects of TBI, e.g., increased impulsivity, hyperactivity associated with frontal damage, or may be related to depression or other adjustment factors, coming to terms with disabilities and long term implications of injury. Bohnert and colleagues (Bohnert et al., 1997) comment on the negative consequences of these behavioral problems in the context of social interactions and peer relationships. They report that children sustaining TBI are less socially competent and have difficulty developing intimacy in their friendships, with these problems more debilitating for children with a history of severe injury.

The most common psychiatric diagnoses identified following childhood TBI are oppositional defiant disorder (ODD; Max et al., 1998a), attention-deficit/hyperactivity disorder (ADHD; Gerring et al., 1998; Levin et al., 2007; Massagli et al., 2004; Max et al., 2005b; Yeates & Taylor, 2005), and organic personality syndrome (now termed personality change due to TBI; Max et al., 2000, 2001, 2005a). Internalizing disorders, while less frequent, have also been documented following pediatric TBI, including obsessive-compulsive symptoms, generalized anxiety, separation anxiety, and depression (Grados et al., 2008; Luis & Mittenberg 2002; Vasa et al., 2002). Symptoms of post-traumatic stress disorder (PTSD) are also elevated following childhood TBI, although relatively few children meet full diagnostic criteria for PTSD (Gerring et al., 2002; Iselin, Le Brocque, Kenardy, Anderson, & McKinlay, 2010; Levi, Drotar, Yeates, & Taylor, 1999; Max et al., 1998b).

Following mild TBI, a variety of somatic, cognitive, and behavioral complaints, which are commonly referred to as post-concussive symptoms, are often reported by children and parents. Post-concussion syndrome is a controversial diagnosis for which research criteria were included in the fourth edition of the Diagnostic and Statistical Manual of Mental Disorders (DSM-IV; American Psychiatric Association, 2004). Several studies have shown that children with mild TBI show more post-concussional symptoms than children with injuries not involving the brain (Mittenberg, Wittner, & Miller, 1997; Ponsford et al., 1999; Yeates et al., 1999). Yeates and colleagues (2009) recently examined longitudinal trajectories of post-concussional symptoms in children with mild TBI as compared to children with orthopedic injuries. They found that children with mild TBI, particularly those that were more severely injured, were more likely to demonstrate trajectories showing high acute levels of symptoms, as well as persistent increases in post-concussional symptoms, in the first year post-injury.

Behavioral functioning following childhood TBI does not appear to be closely related to cognitive outcomes. For instance, Fletcher and colleagues (Fletcher et al., 1990) found small and generally non-significant correlations between neuropsychological measures and measures of adaptive functioning and behavioral adjustment. Thus, cognitive and behavioral outcomes might be somewhat independent following TBI, and their determinants might differ considerably. For instance, cognitive outcomes appear to be more closely associated with injury-related variables, whereas behavioral outcomes are related more strongly to measures of pre-injury family functioning (Catroppa, Anderson, Morse, Haritou, & Rosenfeld, 2009; Yeates et al., 1997).

Moderate or severe TBI is also associated with persistent adaptive behavior deficits (e.g., poorer communication, socialization, and daily living skills) and functional limitations (Fay et al., in press; Max et al., 1998c; Taylor et al., 1999). Deficits in adaptive behavior appear to be especially likely in the presence of family dysfunction (Taylor et al., 1999). More generally, children with TBI demonstrate significant declines in their overall quality of life, although the differences are more pronounced from the perspective of parents than when based on children's self-reports (McCarthy et al., 2006; Stancin et al., 2002).

Predictors of Outcome

While group-based research in child TBI has now established a set of characteristic cognitive and behavioral consequences of injury, these findings do not translate readily to the individual case level, and prognoses for individual children remain difficult to predict. The substantial variations observed in individual outcomes are likely to reflect the interplay among injury characteristics, non-injury related influences, and developmental factors. To add to this complexity, it may be that different variables are predictive of impairment at different developmental stages as well as time post-injury. For example, while injury severity is a crucial predictor of function in the acute stages of recovery, it may become less important as other factors, such as premorbid skills, interventions, and family function and parent mental health come into play (Anderson et al., 2005b; 2006; Rivara et al., 1993; Yeates et al., 1997). Further, the interactions among some of these factors (e.g., severity, age at injury, environment) may not be simply additive, but may impact differently in different contexts. Gaining a better understanding of the relationships between these influences may have important clinical implications, potentially enhancing our capacity to accurately target children and families who are most in need of treatment and support. To this end, recent research has advanced from simple group comparison designs, to include examination of factors which may assist in identifying children at greatest risk of poor recovery.

Injury Characteristics

Injury severity is now a well-established predictor of outcome from TBI, with more severe injuries associated with poorer outcomes. Severity has generally been assessed in a global manner, using a variety of fairly gross clinical metrics, including level of consciousness, duration of impaired consciousness, and length of post-traumatic amnesia. Unfortunately, these measures are often not reliable for younger children and infants. More recent research has begun to take a more detailed approach, using quantitative neuroimaging methods, as well as considering clinical biomarkers that might shed some light on variations in outcomes. Regardless of the tools employed, there is consensus that moderate to severe TBI results in substantial and persistent morbidity, whereas mild TBI has been considered more benign (Anderson

et al., 2005a; Yeates et al., 2009). Of interest, some recent work, which has divided mild TBI (defined as GCS of 13-15) into "complicated" and "uncomplicated" injuries, with the distinction between the two being persisting symptoms and/or abnormalities on brain imaging, suggests that at least some cases of mild TBI are also associated with persistent cognitive deficits (Bigler, 2008; Kirkwood et al., 2008; McCrory, Collie, Anderson, & Davis, 2004; Yeates et al., 2009). Moving away from the problems associated with clinical/observational ratings of severity, structural and functional brain imaging studies report disappointingly inconsistent findings. Some authors report relationships similar to those seen in adult samples, for example, poor social outcome (Levin et al., 2004), and reduced working memory (Newsome et al., 2008) linked to frontal pathology. Others argue that adult models are not necessarily applicable after child injury. For instance, frontal lesion volume is not a consistent predictor of attention or executive function (Power, Catroppa, Coleman Ditchfield, & Anderson, 2007; Slomine et al., 2002). Further, lesions within the frontotemporal regions have not been found to be predictors of memory function (Catroppa et al., 2008; Salorio et al., 2005), but diffuse axonal injury appears more critical (Catroppa et al., 2008).

Additional potential indices of injury severity include serum biomarkers, such as S100B and neuron-specific enolase, that may be tied to the neurochemical cascade that occurs following TBI (Berger, Adelson, Richichi, & Kochanek, 2006; Shore et al., 2007). Serum concentrations of glial fibrillary acidic protein have also been found to correlate with outcome at six months post-injury. While requiring the drawing of blood, the use of biomarkers may be particularly important for diagnosis of TBI in young children, for whom conventional indices such as the Glasgow Coma Scale are often invalid, and for children who suffer inflicted TBI, who may suffer head trauma which may not be disclosed voluntarily (Berger, Ta'Asan, Rand, Lokshin & Kochanek, 2009).

Developmental Factors: Age at Injury

The persisting effects of brain damage in infancy and early childhood have been reported recently, with evidence that young children sustaining generalized brain insult are at great risk for long-term cognitive deficits (Anderson, Bond et al., 1997; Anderson, Smibert, Ekert & Godber, 1994; Cousens, Ungerer, Crawford & Stevens, 1991; Taylor & Alden, 1997), perhaps due to the vulnerability of the immature brain and the lack of established skills and knowledge in the young child at time of insult. Interestingly, the areas of function commonly documented as deficient following TBI, such as information processing, memory and executive function, implicate involvement of neural substrates particularly vulnerable to the impact of TBI. Further, these regions and associated neural networks are in a rapid state of development in early childhood. Deficiencies in these skills are particularly significant for children, as they reduce the ability to interact with and learn from the surrounding environment, potentially affecting not only cognitive ability but also social and emotional development (Anderson, 1988).

A handful of studies have addressed the relationship between age at injury and neuropsychological performance, including very young children in their samples. While several have detected no relationship between age at injury and neurobehavioral outcome in older children (Chadwick et al., 1981a; Klonoff et al., 1977; Tompkins et al, 1990), a number have identified differences between children sustaining TBI during the preschool years and those injured in later childhood (Kriel, Krach, & Panser, 1989; Lange-Cosack, Wider, Schlesner, Grumme & Kubicki, 1979). Studies conducted in one of the authors' laboratories (Anderson & Moore, 1995; Anderson et al., 2005a), found that while children injured after age 7 years showed recovery profiles similar to those seen in adults, children injured prior to age 7 demonstrated less recovery. In contrast to the generally reported trends for IQ, younger age at injury was related to deterioration in Verbal IQ scores over time, perhaps indicating a failure to acquire verbal knowledge from the environment. For Performance IQ, a small increase in scores was evident for both age groups, but this was greater for children injured after age 7, suggesting "recovery" of performance skills is not so evident for younger injuries.

Other researchers have reported a shorter period of potential recovery for children injured

in the preschool years (Ewing-Cobbs et al., 1997), with recovery curves plateauing as early as six months post-injury, rather than within the second year post-injury, as has been documented for adults.

Non-injury Related Influences

Traditionally studies of recovery following childhood TBI have emphasized injury-related variables, even though injury severity fails to account for most of the variance in post-injury outcomes (Fletcher et al., 1995). Recently, research has begun to focus on non-injury related factors, for example, children's premorbid functioning. Yeates and colleagues showed that premorbid attention problems increased the risk of post-injury attention problems among children with moderate to severe TBI (Yeates et al., 2005). Such findings are consistent with theories of cognitive and brain reserve capacity, which suggests that children's vulnerability to neurological insults varies as a function of their pre-injury cognitive abilities and brain integrity (Dennis, 2000; Dennis, Yeates, Taylor, & Fletcher, 2007).

Environmental influences may help to explain variations in post-TBI recovery. Indices of socioeconomic status and family demographics are consistently associated with outcomes, as are measures of family function and family burden (Anderson et al., 2005b; 2006; Taylor et al., 1999, 2002; Yeates et al., 1997, 2004). One critical issue addressed by studies of environmental factors as determinants of recovery is whether the environment affects the functioning of children with TBI in the same way that it does children without such injuries. In a prospective, longitudinal study addressing the contribution of the family and social environment to recovery, the effects of severe TBI relative to orthopedic injuries were more pronounced for children from dysfunctional families than for those from more functional families (Taylor et al., 1999, 2002; Yeates et al., 1997, 2004).

Intervention

Neuropsychological outcomes following childhood TBI have been comprehensively investigated.

By contrast, research regarding treatments for the psychosocial and cognitive sequelae is limited, and the studies that exist tend to be hindered by small sample size and lack of inclusion of ecologically informative outcome measures. The majority of intervention studies are limited to single case study design or non-randomized group studies, perhaps due to the ethical considerations in withholding treatments during critical periods, and the need for age-specific interventions (Anderson & Catroppa, 2006).

Medical Intervention and Acute Rehabilitation

Acute medical care, rehabilitation and education also need to be considered. Guidelines exist for the acute medical management of childhood TBI, but by and large are not based on rigorous evaluation through randomized controlled trials (Adelson et al., 2003; Jankowitz & Adelson, 2006; McLean et al., 1995). Comprehensive reviews of the inpatient and outpatient rehabilitation of children with TBI also highlight the relative paucity of empirical evidence in this domain (Anderson & Catroppa, 2006; Beaulieu, 2002; Ylvisaker et al., 2005a).

Pharmacology

Few studies have systematically evaluated the efficacy of medication to address the range of psychiatric changes that can occur following TBI. In a review of studies using methylphenidate for secondary ADHD post-TBI, the effects of medication were found to be modest (Jin & Schachar, 2004). Medication was more likely to reduce the hyperactive, impulsive symptoms than improve concentration skills and reduce cognitive fatigue. The authors concluded that the introduction of stimulant medication within months of the injury was most effective, and did not carry adverse effects.

Cognitive Intervention

Cognitive remediation programs have been developed for pediatric TBI, but few have been the focus of empirical validation (Butler, 2007; Van't Hooft, 2010). Laatsch and colleagues (2007) conducted an evidence-based review of cognitive and behavioral treatment studies of pediatric TBI and determined that cognitive remediation for attention skills is supported by the literature, as is the involvement of family members as active members of the treatment team. Catroppa and Anderson (2006) have also reviewed studies of executive skills interventions following childhood TBI and found few methodologically sound examples and limited support for any specific cognitive interventions.

Van't Hooft et al. (2007), however, is worthy of note. These authors conducted a study that targeted cognitive and behavioral training, and involved parents or educators in conjunction with weekly feedback from a psychologist or teacher. They found significant improvement in selective attention and verbal working memory in children with ABI (mean of two years post-injury), with improvements maintained at six months post-treatment. While these results are promising, the implications of these cognitive gains for functional outcomes (academic, social, behavioral) are yet to be determined.

Behavioral Intervention

Some empirical support exists for treatments of behavioral and social problems following pediatric TBI (Ylvisaker et al., 2005b, 2007), For instance, operant conditioning has been found to be effective in decreasing aggressive behavior. Additionally, case-based positive behavioral intervention and support (PBIS) has been employed successfully by some authors (Feeney & Ylivasaker, 2008; Ylivasaker et al., 2005b; 2007) to reduce disruptive and challenging behaviors post-TBI, which impact in both home and school settings. PBIS uses positive antecedent-focused procedures, and teaches children, parents and teachers strategies for effective behaviors. School-based social interventions also have some empirical support (Warschausky, Kewman, & Kay 1999). In contrast, few studies have focused on treatments for internalizing problems (i.e., depression and anxiety) following TBI.

Family Intervention

The inclusion of family members in the rehabilitation of children with TBI has been supported by many studies (Braga, Da Paz, & Ylvisaker, 2005; Wade, in press), as has the integration of home and school services following discharge from inpatient rehabilitation (Ylvisaker et al., 2005a). With increasing knowledge of the importance of family variables for outcome, many intervention studies are now focusing on enhancing the skills of the family to improve outcomes in the child with TBI.

At the clinical level, families are involved with therapists to identify meaningful goals for rehabilitation. Braga and colleagues (2005) demonstrated, using a RCT design, that children who received home-based cognitive, behavioral and physical intervention from their parents for a period of 12 months had significantly improved outcomes compared to children who received routine hospital-based rehabilitation. The socio-economic background of the family did not contribute to outcomes. Using e-therapy techniques, Wade (Wade, Carey, & Wolfe, 2006; Wade et al., 2006) demonstrated the effectiveness of on-line cognitive behavioral intervention provided to families. The Family Problem Solving (FPS) program, delivered via the Internet in this study, focuses on appropriate social skills and problem solving skills in children, and educates families about strategies for managing challenging behaviors. Findings indicated that children in families receiving FPS showed improved self-regulatory skills, while parents reported reductions in anxiety and depressive symptoms and distress. The children who showed greatest improvement were from families of low socio-economic backgrounds, suggesting there is potential to enhance outcome in this disadvantaged group. In addition, web-based programs allow families who live in remote communities to access interventions.

Implications of Findings

Clinical

Children with severe injury, children injured earlier in life, the presence of premorbid dysfunction, and those from disadvantaged socio-economic backgrounds are most vulnerable to poor outcomes following TBI. Consideration of these factors as a component of initial history taking will help to identify children and families at greatest risk of dysfunction following TBI. Severe injury is frequently associated with chronic cognitive and behavioral impairment, thus the allocation of intensive resources for the long term is likely to be required. Research highlights the importance of monitoring children over time as their needs may change, particularly as the gap between the child with TBI and their peers widens. With this in mind, rehabilitation services need to intervene throughout childhood and adolescence, irrespective of the age at which the child is injured. Given the strong influence of family and environmental factors, interventions involving the family are also essential for any change to take effect in the child.

Methodological

Sampling. Many previous studies on TBI suffer from shortcomings in the selection and recruitment of research participants, which means they may become unrepresentative of the general TBI population because of sampling bias or selective attrition over time. The selection of comparison groups in research on TBI also has been problematic. Much early research failed to include adequate comparison samples. While more recent studies include control groups more frequently, there remains controversy about the optimal control group. In general the aim has been to control for confounding variables including socio-demographic factors or pre-injury behavior, which characterize children sustaining TBI. Common techniques for achieving this include use of non-injured children matched for age, gender, and other demographic variables; children who have sustained injuries not involving the head; or exclusion of children with pre-injury diagnoses. As cause of TBI differs across childhood, according to either social context (e.g., parent neglect: in infants and toddlers) or child behaviors (e.g., impulsivity: in older children), different approaches may be required depending on the age group under study.

Measurement. Although traditional measures of injury severity (Glasgow Coma Scale, duration of loss of consciousness, post-traumatic amnesia) are usually correlated, differences in how and when severity is assessed increase the variability in results across studies. Future studies will likely need to incorporate multidimensional approaches to classifying severity that include clinical indicators, neuroimaging, and possibly biomarkers. Detailed and accurate measurement of non-injury factors, such as distal and proximal measures of psychosocial context, have also been problematic. Future research will need to pay greater attention to measures of children's environments to determine the mechanisms by which the environments influence outcomes of childhood TBI, and should increasingly include measures of children's premorbid status, including genetic differences that are likely to moderate the effects of TBI.

Outcome measures are also limited. Early research focused on standard intellectual assessment, which is now recognized as insufficient to characterize the full range of impairment associated with child TBI. Tests designed to assess specific aspects of skill deficits or that employ experimental manipulations of task demands yield more precise information about the nature and brain basis of cognitive sequelae of TBI (Taylor, 2010). Less attention has been paid to emotional and social functioning (Yeates et al., 2007), or quality of life (McCarthy et al., 2006).

Study Design. Most previous studies of childhood TBI have employed a cross-sectional design, which precludes investigation of the process of post-injury recovery of function. Longitudinal studies are needed to examine recovery over time and to determine the relative importance of age at injury and time since injury as predictors of outcomes (Taylor & Alden, 1997).

Developmental Variations. The developmental context creates its own challenges and pediatric researchers cannot assume that all children are at the same level of development, or that the same injury will have an equal impact across childhood. In fact, increasing evidence indicates that age and skill attainment at the time of injury are important considerations in assessing likely recovery. The child's need to acquire new skills and knowledge and meet educational demands, in the context of

increased risk of physical, cognitive and behavioral impairment, generates unique challenges for rehabilitation and reintegration following pediatric TBI.

Future Directions & Conclusions

To this point, we have been reasonably successful in describing the consequences of pediatric TBI. The natural history of pediatric TBI has been examined extensively, and we have a working understanding of the acute and long-term effects of injury for the child. At a group level, research has demonstrated that children with milder injuries are likely to recover well, with few residual problems. With increasing severity, recovery is less complete, and we know that those with severe injury are at risk for ongoing difficulties across a range of physical, cognitive, and socio-emotional domains, and that these difficulties may persist through childhood and into adulthood (Hessen et al., 2007; Jaffe, Polissar, Fay, & Liao, 1995; Yeates et al., 2004). In contrast, at the individual level, outcomes are highly variable, leading to uncertainty with respect to prognosis and key predictive factors. More precise information is critical to determining which children are at high risk and to effectively allocating limited resources for management and treatment. Research has been only modestly successful in providing guidance with respect to which factors contribute most to recovery and outcome, and an evidence base for effective treatment, at both acute and more chronic stages of recovery post-TBI, is largely lacking.

References

Adelson, P. D., Bratton, S. L., Carney, N. A., Chesnut, R. M., du Coudray, H. E., Goldstein, B. et al. (2003). Guidelines for the acute medical management of severe traumatic brain injury in infants, children, and adolescents. Chapter 1: Introduction. *Pediatric Critical Care Medicine, 4* (3):2–4.

Amacher, A. L. (1988). *Pediatric head injuries.* St Louis, Missouri: Warren H. Green Inc.

Anderson, V. (1988). Recovery of function in children: The myth of cerebral plasticity. In M. Matheson & H. Newman (Ed.), *Proceedings from the Thirteenth Annual Brain Impairment Conference* (pp. 223–247), Sydney: Academic Press.

Anderson, V., Bond, L., Catroppa, C., Grimwood, K., Keir, E., & Nolan, T. (1997). Childhood bacterial meningitis: Impact of age at illness and medical complications on long term outcome. *Journal of the International Neuropsychological Society, 3,* 147–158.

Anderson, V., & Catroppa, C. (2005). Recovery of executive skills following paediatric traumatic brain injury (TBI): A 2 year follow-up. *Brain Injury, 19,* 459–470.

Anderson, V.,& Catroppa, C. (2006). Advances in postacute rehabilitation after childhood acquired brain injury: A focus on cognitive, behavioural, and social domains. *American Journal of Physical Medicine and Rehabilitation, 85,* 767–778.

Anderson, V., Catroppa, C., Dudgeon, P., Morse, S., Haritou, F. & Rosenfeld, J. (2006). Understanding predictors of functional recovery and outcome thirty-months following early childhood head injury. *Neuropsychology, 20,* 42–57.

Anderson, V. A., Catroppa, C., Morse, S., Haritou, F., & Rosenfeld, J. (2005a). Functional plasticity or vulnerability after early brain injury? *Pediatrics, 116,* 1374–1382.

Anderson, V., Catroppa, C., Morse, S., Haritou, F. & Rosenfeld, J. (2005b). Identifying factors contributing to child and family outcome at 30 months following traumatic brain injury in children. *Journal of Neurology, Neurosurgery & Psychiatry, 76,* 401–408.

Anderson, V., Catroppa, C., Morse, S., Haritou, F., & Rosenfeld, J. (2009a). Intellectual Outcome from Preschool Traumatic Brain Injury: A 5-year prospective, longitudinal study. *Pediatrics, 124*(6),1064–1071.

Anderson, V., Fenwick, T., Manly, T., & Robertson, I. (1998). Attentional skills following traumatic brain injury in childhood: A componential analysis. *Brain Injury, 12,* 937–949.

Anderson, V., Levin, H. & Jacobs, R. (2002). Executive Functions after Frontal Lobe Injury: A Developmental Perspectivve.In D. Stuss & R. Knight (Ed). *Principles of frontal lobe function* (pp. 504–527). New York: Oxford University Press..

Anderson, V. & Moore, C. (1995). Age at injury as a predictor of outcome following pediatric head injury. *Child Neuropsychology, 1,* 187–202.

Anderson, V. A., Morse, S., Catroppa, C., Haritou, F., & Rosenfeld, J. (2004). Thirty month outcome from early childhood head injury: a prospective analysis of neurobehavioural recovery. *Brain, 127,* 2608–2620.

Anderson, V. A., Morse, S. A., Klug, G., Catroppa, C., Haritou, F., Rosenfeld, J. V. et al. (1997). Predicting recovery from head injury in young children: A prospective analysis. *Journal of the International Neuropsychological Society, 3,* 568–580.

Anderson, V., & Pentland, L. (1998). Residual attention deficits following childhood head injury. *Neuropsychological Rehabilitation, 8,* 283–300.

Anderson, V., Smibert,.E, Ekert, H., & Godber, T. (1994). Intellectual, educational and behavioral sequelae following cranial irradiation and chemotherapy. *Archives of Disease in Childhood, 70,* 476–483.

Anderson, V. Spencer–Smith, M., Leventer, R., Coleman, L., Anderson, P., Williams, J. et al. (2009b). Childhood brain insult: Can age at insult help us predict outcome? *Brain, 132,* 45–56.

Anderson, V. A., & Yeates, K. O. (Eds.). (2010). New directions in pediatric traumatic brain injury: Multidisciplinary and translational perspectives. New York: Oxford University Press.

Andrews, T. K., Rose, F. D., & Johnson, D. A. (1998). Social and behavioural effects of traumatic brain injury in children. *Brain Injury, 12,* 133–138.

Annegers, J. F. (1983). The epidemiology of head trauma in children. In K. Shapiro (Ed.), Pediatric Head Trauma (pp. 1–10). Mount Kisco, NY: Futura.

Asarnow, R. F., Satz, P., Light, R., Zaucha, K., Lewis, R., & McCleary, C. (1995). The UCLA study of mild closed head injuries in children and adolescents. In S. H. Broman & M. E. Michel (Ed.), Traumatic Head Injury in Children (pp. 117–146). New York: Oxford University Press.

Bawden, H. N., Knights, R. M., & Winogron, H. W. (1985). Speeded performance following head injury in children. *Journal of Clinical Neuropsychology, 7,* 39–54.

Beaulieu, C. L. (2002). Rehabilitation and outcome following pediatric traumatic brain injury. *Surgical Clinics of North America, 82,* 393–408.

Begali, V. (1992). *Head injury in children and adolescents. 2nd Edition.* Brandon, VT: Clinical Psychology Publishing Company Inc.

Berger, R. P., Adelson, P. D., Richichi, R., & Kochanek, P. M. (2006). Serum biomarkers after traumatic and hypoxemic brain injuries: Insights into the biochemical response of the pediatric brain to inflicted brain injury. *Developmental Neuroscience, 28,* 327–335.

Berger, R. P., Ta'Asan, S., Rand, R., Lokshin, A., & Kochanek, P. (2009). Multiplex assessment of serum biomarker concentrations in well-appearing children with inflicted brain injury. *Pediatric Research, 65,* 97–102.

Bigler, E. D. (2007). Anterior and middle cranial fossa in traumatic brain injury: Relevant neuroanatomy and neuropathology in the study of neuropsychological outcome. *Neuropsychology, 21,* 515–31.

Bohnert, A. M., Parker, J. G., & Warschausky, S. A. (1997). Friendship and social adjustment of children following a traumatic brain injury: An exploratory investigation. *Developmental Neuropsychology, 13*, 477–486.

Braga, L. W., Da Paz Júnior, A. C., & Ylvisaker, M. (2005). Direct clinician-delivered versus indirect family-supported rehabilitation of children with traumatic brain injury: A randomized controlled trial. *Brain Injury, 19*, 819–831.

Brink, J., Imbus, C., & Woo-Sam, J. (1980). Physical recovery after closed head trauma in children and adolescents. *The Journal of Pediatrics, 97*, 721–727.

Brown, G., Chadwick, O., Shaffer, D., Rutter, M. & Traub, M. (1981). A prospective study of children with head injuries: II. Psychiatric sequelae. *Psychological Medicine, 11*(1), 49–62.

Butler, R. W. (2007). Cognitive rehabilitation. In S. J. Hunter & J. Donders (Ed.), *Pediatric Neuropsychological Intervention* (pp. 444–464). New York, Cambridge University Press.

Catroppa, C., & Anderson, V. (2002). Recovery in memory function in the first year following TBI in children. *Brain Injury, 16*, 369–384.

Catroppa, C., & Anderson, V. (2004). Recovery and predictors of language skills two years following pediatric traumatic brain injury. *Brain and Language, 88*, 68–78.

Catroppa, C., & Anderson, V. (2005). A prospective study of the recovery of attention from acute to 2 years post pediatric traumatic brain injury. *Journal of the International Neuropsychological Society, 11*, 84–98.

Catroppa, C., & Anderson, V. (2007) Recovery in memory function, and its relationship to academic success, at 24 months following pediatric TBI. *Child Neuropsychology, 13*, 240–61.

Catroppa, C., Anderson, V. A., Morse, S. A., Haritou, F., & Rosenfeld, J. V. (2007). Children's attentional skills 5 years post-TBI. *Journal of Pediatric Psychology, 32*, 354–369.

Catroppa, C., Anderson, V. A., Morse, S. A., Haritou, F., & Rosenfeld, J. V. (2008). Outcome and predictors of functional recovery 5 years following pediatric traumatic brain injury. *Journal of Pediatric Psychology, 33*, 707–718.

Catroppa, C., Anderson. V., & Stargatt, R. (1999). A prospective analysis of the recovery of attention following pediatric head injury. *Journal of the International Neuropsychological Society, 5*, 48–57.

Cattelani, R., Lombardi, F., Brianti, R., & Mazzucchi, A. (1998). Traumatic brain injury in childhood: intellectual, behavioural and social outcome into adulthood. *Brain Injury, 12*, 283–296.

Chadwick, O., Rutter, M., Brown, G., Shaffer, D., & Traub, M. (1981). A prospective study of children with head injuries: II. Cognitive sequelae. *Psychological Medicine, 11*, 49–61.

Chapman, S. B. (1995). Discourse as an outcome measure in pediatric head-injured populations. In S. H. Broman & M. E. Michel (Ed.), *Traumatic Head Injury in Children* (pp. 95–116). New York: Oxford University Press.

Chapman, S. B., Sparks, G., Levin, H. S., Dennis, M., Roncadin, C., Zhang, L. et al. (2004). Discourse macrolevel processing after severe pediatric traumatic brain injury. *Developmental Neuropsychology, 25*, 37–60.

Courville, C. B. (1945). *Pathology and the Nervous System.* Mountain View CA: Pacific Press.

Cousens, P., Ungerer, J. A., Crawford, J. A., & Stevens, M. M. (1991). Cognitive effects of childhood leukemia therapy: A case for four specific deficits. *Journal of Pediatric Psychology, 16*, 475–488.

Crowe, L., Anderson, V., Catroppa, C., & Babl, F. (2010). Head injuries related to sports and recreation activities in school-age children and adolescents: Data from a referral centre in Victoria, Australia. *Emergency Medicine Australasia, 22*(1), 56–61.

Dalby, P. R. & Obrzut, J. E. (1991). Epidemiologic characteristics and sequelae of closed head-injured children and adolescents: A review. *Developmental Neuropsychology, 7*, 35–68.

Dennis, M. (2000). Childhood medical disorders and cognitive impairment: Biological risk, time, development, and reserve. In K. O. Yeates, M. D. Ris, & H. G. Taylor (Ed.), *Pediatric Neuropsychology: Research, Theory, and Practice* (pp. 3–22). New York: Guilford Press.

Dennis, M., & Barnes, M. A. (1990). Knowing the meaning, getting the point, bridging the gap, and carrying the message: Aspects of discourse following closed head injury in childhood and adolescence. *Brain and Language, 39*, 428–446.

Dennis, M., Purvis, K., Barnes, M. A., Wilkinson, M., & Winner, E. (2001b). Understanding of literal truth, ironic criticism, and deceptive praise following childhood head injury. *Brain and Language, 78*, 1–16.

Dennis, M., Wilkinson, M., Koski, L., & Humphreys, R. P. (1995). Attention deficits in the long term after childhood head injury. In S. H. Broman & M. E. Michel (Ed.), *Traumatic Head Injury in Children* (pp. 165–187). New York: Oxford University Press.

Dennis, M., Yeates, K. O., Taylor, H. G., & Fletcher, J. M. (2007). Brain reserve capacity, cognitive reserve capacity, and age-based functional plasticity after congenital and acquired brain injury in children. In Y. Stern (Ed.), *Cognitive Reserve* (pp. 53–83). New York: Taylor & Francis.

Didus, E., Anderson, V. & Catroppa, C. (1999). The development of pragmatic communication skills in head-injured children. *Pediatric Rehabilitation*, 3, 177–186.

Ewing-Cobbs, L., & Barnes, M. (2002). Linguistic outcomes following traumatic brain injury in children. *Seminars in Pediatric Neurology, 9*, 209–217.

Ewing-Cobbs, L., Barnes, M., Fletcher, J. M., Levin, H. S., Swank, P. R., & Song, J. (2004a). Modeling of longitudinal academic achievement scores after pediatric traumatic brain injury. *Developmental Neuropsychology, 25*, 107–133.

Ewing-Cobbs, L., Fletcher, J. M., Levin, H. S., Francis, D. J., Davidson, K., & Miner, M. E. (1997). Longitudinal neuropsychological outcome in infants and preschoolers with TBI. *Journal of the International Neuropsychological Society, 3*, 581–591.

Ewing-Cobbs, L., Fletcher, J.M., Levin, H.S., Iovino, I., & Miner, M.E. (1998a). Academic achievement and academic placement following traumatic brain injury in children and adolescents: A two-year longitudinal study. *Journal of Clinical and Experimental Neuropsychology, 20*, 769–781.

Ewing-Cobbs, L., Levin, H. S., Fletcher, J. M., Miner, M. E., & Eisenberg, H. M. (1990). The Children's Orientation and Amnesia Test: Relationship to severity of acute head injury and to recovery of memory. *Neurosurgery, 27*, 683–691.

Ewing-Cobbs, L., Prasad, M., Fletcher, J. M., Levin, H. S., Miner, M. E., & Eisenberg, H. M. (1998b). Attention after pediatric traumatic brain injury: A multidimensional assessment. *Child Neuropsychology, 4*, 35–48.

Ewing-Cobbs, L., Prasad, M. R., Kramer, L., Cox, C. S., Jr., Baumgartner, J., Fletcher, S. et al. (2006). Late intellectual and academic outcomes following traumatic brain injury sustained during early childhood. *Journal of Neurosurgery, 105*, 2887–2896.

Ewing-Cobbs, L., Prasad, M. R., Landry, S. H., Kramer, L., & DeLeon, R. (2004). Executive functions following traumatic brain injury in young children: A preliminary analysis. *Developmental Neuropsychology, 26*, 487–512.

Farkas, O., & Povlishock, J. T. (2007). Cellular and subcellular change evoked by diffuse traumatic brain injury: A complex web of change extending far beyond focal damage. *Progress in Brain Research, 161*, 43–59.

Farmer, J. E., & Eakman, A. M. (1996). The relationship between neuropsychological functioning and instrumental activities of daily living following acquired brain injury. *Applied Neuropsychology, 2*, 107–115.

Fay, T. B., Yeates, K. O., Wade, S. L., Drotar, D., Stancin, T., & Taylor, H. G. (in press). Predicting longitudinal patterns of functional deficits in children with traumatic brain injury. *Neuropsychology*.

Feeney T., & Ylvisaker M. (2008). Context-sensitive behavioral supports for young children with TBI: A second replication study. *Journal of Positive Behavior Interventions,10*(2): 115–128.

Fernando, K., Eaton, L., Faulkner, M., Moodley, Y., & Setchell, R. (2002). Development and piloting of the Starship Post-traumatic Amnesia Scale for children aged between four and six years. *Brain Impairment, 3*, 34–41.

Fletcher, J. M., Ewing-Cobbs, L., Francis, D. J., & Levin, H. S. (1995). Variability in outcomes after traumatic brain injury in children: A developmental perspective. In S. H. Broman & M. E. Michel (Ed.), *Traumatic Head Injury in Children* (pp. 3–21). New York: Oxford University Press.

Fletcher, J. M., Ewing-Cobbs, L., Miner, M. E., Levin, H. S., & Eisenberg, H. M. (1990). Behavioural changes after closed head injury in children. *Journal of Consulting and Clinical Psychology, 58*, 93–98.

Ganesalingam, K., Sanson, A., Anderson, V., & Yeates, K. O. (2006). Self-regulation and social and behavioural functioning following childhood traumatic brain injury. *Journal of the International Neuropsychological Society, 12*, 609–621.

Ganesalingam, K., Sanson, A., Anderson, V., & Yeates, K. O. (2007). Self-regulation as a mediator of the effects of childhood traumatic brain injury on social and behavioural functioning. *Journal of the International Neuropsychological Society, 13*, 298–311.

Garth, J., Anderson, V.A., & Wrennall, J. (1997). Executive functions following moderate to severe frontal lobe injury: Impact of injury and age at injury. *Pediatric Rehabilitation, 1*, 99–108.

Gerring, J. P., Brady, K. D., Chen, A., Vasa, R., Grados, M., Bandeen-Roche, K. et al. (1998). Premorbid prevalence of ADHD and development of secondary ADHD after closed head injury. *Journal of the American Academy of Child and Adolescent Psychiatry, 37*, 647–654.

Gerring, J. P., Slomine, B., Vasa, R. A., Grados, M. Chen, A., Rising, W. et al. (2002). Clinical predictors of posttraumatic stress disorder after closed head injury in children. *Journal of the American Academy of Child and Adolescent Psychiatry, 41*, 157–165.

Ghosh, A., Wilde, E. A., Hunter, J. V., Bigler, E. D., Chu, Z., Li, X. et al. (2009). The relation between Glasgow Coma Scale score and later cerebral atrophy in pediatric traumatic brain injury. *Brain Injury, 23*, 228–233.

Giza, C. C., & Hovda, D. (2001). The neurometabolic cascade of concussion. *Journal of Athletic Training, 36*, 228–235.

Giza, C. C., Mink, R. B., & Madikians, A. (2007) Pediatric traumatic brain injury: Not just little adults. *Current Opinions in Critical Care*, *13*, 143–52.

Giza, C. C., & Prins, M. L. (2006). Is being plastic fantastic? Mechanisms of altered plasticity after developmental traumatic brain injury. *Developmental Neuroscience*, *28*, 364–379.

Goldstein, F. C. & Levin, H. S. (1987). Epidemiology of pediatric closed head injury: Incidence, clinical characteristics and risk factors. *Journal of Learning Disabilities*, *20*, 518–525.

Grados, M. A., Vasa, R. A., Riddle, M. A., Slomine, B. S., Salorio, C., Christensen, J. et al. (2008). New onset obsessive-compulsive symptoms in children and adolescents with severe traumatic brain injury. *Depression and Anxiety*, *25*, 398–407.

Gronwall, D., Wrightson, P., & McGinn, V. (1997). Effect of mild head injury during the preschool years. *Journal of the International Neuropsychological Society*, *3*, 592–597.

Hanten, G., Wilde, E. A., Menefee, D. S., Li, X., Lane, S., Vasquez, C. et al. (2008) Correlates of social problem solving during the first year after traumatic brain injury in children. *Neuropsychology*, *22*, 357–370.

Holloway, M., Bye, A., & Moran, K. (1994). Non-accidental head injury in children. *The Medical Journal of Australia*, *160*, 786–789.

Iselin, G., Le Brocque, R., Kenardy, J., Anderson, V., & McKinlay, L. (2010) Which method of posttraumatic stress disorder classification best predicts psychosocial function inchildren with traumatic brain injury? *Journal of Anxiety Disorders*, *24*, 774–779.

Jaffe, K. M., Polissar, N. L., Fay, G. C., & Liao, S. (1995). Recovery trends over three years following pediatric traumatic brain injury. *Archives of Physical Medicine and Rehabilitation*, *76*, 17–26.

Jankowitz, B. T., & Adelson, P. D. (2006). Pediatric traumatic brain injury: Past, present, and future. *Developmental Neuroscience*, *28*, 264–275.

Janusz, J. A., Kirkwood, M. W., Yeates, K. O. & Taylor, H. G. (2002). Social problem-solving skills in children with traumatic brain injury: Long-term outcomes and prediction of social competence. *Child Neuropsychology*, *8*, 179–194.

Jennett, B., & Bond, M. (1975). Assessment of outcome after severe brain damage: A practical scale. *Lancet*, *1*, 480–484.

Jin, C. & Schachar, R. (2004) Methylphenidate treatment of attention-deficit/hyperactivity disorder secondary to traumatic brain injury: A critical appraisal of treatment studies. *CNS Spectrum*, *9*, 217–226.

Jonsson, C. A., Horneman, G., & Emanuelson, I. (2004). Neuropsychological progress during 14 years after severe traumatic brain injury in childhood and adolescence. *Brain Injury*, *18*, 921–934.

Katz-Leurer, M., Rotem, H., Lewitus, H., Keren, O., & Meyer, S. (2008). Relationship between balance abilities and gait characteristics in children with post-traumatic brain injury. *Brain Injury*, *22*, 153–159.

Kaufmann, P., Fletcher, J., Levin, H., Miner, M., & Ewing-Cobbs, L. (1993). Attention disturbance after pediatric closed head injury. *Journal of Child Neurology*, *8*, 348–353.

Keenan, H. T., & Bratton, S. L. (2006). Epidemiology and outcomes of pediatric traumatic brain injury. *Developmental Neuroscience*, *28*, 256–263.

Kinsella, G., Prior, M., Sawyer, M., Murtagh, D., Eisenmajer, R., Anderson, V. et al. (1995). Neuropsychological deficit and academic performance in children and adolescents following TBI. *Journal of Pediatric Psychology*, *20*, 753–767.

Kinsella, G., Prior, M., Sawyer, M., Ong, B., Murtagh, D., Eisenmajer, R. et al. (1997). Predictors and indicators of academic outcome in children 2 years following traumatic brain injury. *Journal of the International Neuropsychological Society*, *3*, 608–616.

Kirkwood, M. W., Yeates, K. O., Taylor, H. G., Randolph, C., McCrea, M., & Anderson, V. A. (2008). Management of pediatric mild traumatic brain injury: A neuropsychological review from injury through recovery. *The Clinical Neuropsychologist*, *22*, 769–800.

Klonoff, H., Clark, C., & Klonoff, P. S. (1995). Outcomes of head injuries from childhood to adulthood: A twenty-three year follow-up study. In S. H. Broman & M. E. Michel (Ed.), *Traumatic Head Injury in Children* (pp. 219–234). New York: Oxford University Press.

Kraus, J. F. (1995). Epidemiological features of brain injury in children: Occurrence, children at risk, causes and manner of injury, severity, and outcomes. In S. H. Broman & M. E. Michel (Ed.), *Traumatic Head Injury in Children* (pp. 22–39). New York: Oxford University Press.

Kraus, J. F., Fife, D., Cox, P., Ramstein, K., & Conroy, C. (1986). Incidence, severity, and external causes of pediatric brain injury. *American Journal of Epidemiology*, *119*, 186–201.

Kriel, R. L., Krach, L. E., & Panser, L. A. (1989). Closed head injury: Comparisons of children younger and older than six years of age. *Pediatric Neurology*, *5*, 296–300.

Laatsch, L., Harrington, D., Hotz, G, Marcantuono, J., Mozzoni, M. P., Walsh, V. et al. (2007). An evidence-based review of cognitive and behavioural rehabilitation treatment studies in children with acquired brain injury. *Journal of Head Trauma Rehabilitation, 22*, 248–256.

Lange-Cosack, H., Wider, B., Schlesner, H. J., Grumme, T. & Kubicki, S. (1979). Prognosis of brain injuries in young children (one until five years of age). *Neuropaediatrie, 10*, 105–127.

Langlois, J. A., Rutland-Brown, W., & Thomas, K. E. (2005). The incidence of traumatic brain injury among children in the United States: Differences by race. *Journal of Head Trauma Rehabilitation, 20*, 229–238.

Langlois, J. A., Rutland-Brown, W., & Thomas, K. E. (2006). *Traumatic brain injury in the United States: Emergency Department Visits, Hospitalizations, and Deaths.* Atlanta, GA: Centers for Disease Control and Prevention, National Center for Injury Prevention and Control.

Lehnung, M., Leplow, B., Herzog, A., Benz, B., Ritz, A., Stolze, H. et al. (2001). Children's spatial behaviour is differentially affected after traumatic brain injury. *Child Neuropsychology, 7*, 59–71.

Lescohier, I., & DiScala, C. (1993). Blunt trauma in children: causes and outcomes of head versus extracranial injury. *Pediatrics, 91*, 721–725.

Levi, R. B., Drotar, D., Yeates, K. O., & Taylor, H. G. (1999). Posttraumatic stress symptoms in children following orthopedic or traumatic brain injury. *Journal of Clinical Child Psychology, 28*, 232–243.

Levin, H. S., Fletcher, J. M., Kufera, J. A., Howard, H., Lilly, M. A., Mendelsohn, D. et al. (1996). Dimensions of cognition measured by the Tower of London and other cognitive tasks in head-injured children and adolescents. *Developmental Neuropsychology, 12*, 17–34.

Levin, H. S., & Hanten, G. (2005). Executive functions after traumatic brain injury in children. *Pediatric Neurology, 33*, 79–93.

Levin, H., Hanten, G., Max, J, Li, X., Swank, P., Ewing-Cobbs, L. et al. (2007) Symptoms of attention-deficit/hyperactivity disorder following traumatic brain injury in children. *Journal of Developmental & Behavioural Pediatrics, 28*, 108–118.

Levin, H. S., High, W. M., Ewing-Cobbs, L., Fletcher, J. M., Eisenberg, H. M., Miner, M. E. et al. (1988). Memory functioning during the first year after closed head injury in children and adolescents. *Neurosurgery, 22*, 1043–1052.

Levin, H. S., Zhang, L., Dennis, M., Ewing-Cobbs, L., Schachar, R., Max, J. et al. (2004). Psychosocial outcome of TBI in children with unilateral frontal lesions. *Journal of the International Neuropsychological Society, 10*, 305–316.

Luis, C.A., & Mittenberg, W. (2002). Mood and anxiety disorders following pediatric traumatic brain injury: A prospective study. *Journal of Clinical and Experimental Neuropsychology, 24*, 270–279.

Mandalis, A., Kinsella, G., Ong, B., & Anderson, V. (2007). Working memory and its relationship to new learning following pediatric traumatic brain injury. *Developmental Neuropsychology, 32*(2), 683–701.

Mangeot, S., Armstrong, K., Colvin, A. N., Yeates, K. O., & Taylor, H. G. (2002). Long-term executive function deficits in children with traumatic brain injuries: Assessment using the Behaviour Rating Inventory of Executive Function (BRIEF). *Child Neuropsychology, 8*, 271–284.

Marosszeky, N. E., Batchelor, J., Shores, E. A., Marosszeky, J. E., & Boonschate, M. (1993). The performance of hospitalised, non-head injured children on the Westmead PTA Scale. *The Clinical Neuropsychologist, 7*, 85–95.

Massagli, T. L., Fann, J. R., Burington, B. E., Jaffe, K. M., Katon, W. J., & Thompson, R. S. (2004). Psychiatric illness after mild traumatic brain injury in children. *Archives of Physical Medicine and Rehabilitation, 85*, 1428–1434.

Max, J. E., Castillo, C. S., Bokura, H., Robin, D. A., Lindgren, S. D., Smith, W. L. et al. (1998a). Oppositional defiant disorder symptomatology after traumatic brain injury: A prospective study. *Journal of Nervous and Mental Disease, 186*, 325–332.

Max, J. E., Castillo, C. S., Robin, D. A., Lindqren, S. D., Smith, W. L. Jr., Sato, Y. et al. (1998b). Posttraumatic stress symptomatology after childhood traumatic brain injury. *Journal of Nervous & Mental Disorders, 186*, 589–596.

Max, J. E., Koele, S. L., Castillo, C. C., Lindgren, S. D., Arndt, S., Bokura, H. et al. (2000). Personality change disorder in children and adolescents following traumatic brain injury. *Journal of the International Neuropsychological Society, 6*, 279–289.

Max, J. E., Koele, S. L., Lindgren, S. D., Robin, D. A., Smith, W. L., Jr., Sato, Y. et al. (1998c). Adaptive functioning following traumatic brain injury and orthopedic injury: A controlled study. *Archives of Physical Medicine and Rehabilitation, 79*, 893–899.

Max, J. E., Levin, H. S., Landis, J., Schachar, R., Saunders, A., Ewing-Cobbs, L. et al. (2005a). Predictors of personality change due to traumatic brain injury in children and adolescents in the first six months after injury. *Journal of the American Academy of Child & Adolescent Psychiatry, 44*, 434–442.

Max, J. E., Lindgren, S. D., Robin, D. A., Smith, W. L., Sato, Y., Mattheis, P. J. et al. (1997a). TBI in children and adolescents: Psychiatric disorders in the second three months. *Journal of Nervous and Mental Disease, 185*, 394–401.

Max, J. E., Robertson, B. A., & Lansing, A. E. (2001). The phenomenology of personality change due to traumatic brain injury in children and adolescents. *Journal of Neuropsychiatry and Clinical Neuroscience, 13*, 161–170.

Max, J. E., Robin, D. A., Lindgren, S. D., Smith, W. L., Sato, Y., Mattheis, P. J. et al.(1997b). TBI in children and adolescents: Psychiatric disorders at two years. *Journal of the American Academy of Child and Adolescent Psychiatry, 36*, 1278–1285.

Max, J. E., Robin, D. A., Lindgren, S. D., Smith, W. L., Jr., Sato, Y., Mattheis, P.J. et al.(1997c). Traumatic brain injury in children and adolescents: Psychiatric disorders at two years. *Journal of the American Academy of Child and Adolescent Psychiatry, 36*, 1278–1285.

Max, J. E., Robin, D. A., Lindgren, S. D., Smith, W. L., Sato, Y., Mattheis, P. J. et al. (1998d). Traumatic brain injury in children and adolescents: Psychiatric disorders at one year. *Journal of Neuropsychiatry and Clinical Neuroscience, 10*, 290–297.

Max, J. E., Schachar, R. J., Levin, H. S., Ewing-Cobbs, L., Chapman, S. B., Dennis, M. et al. (2005b). Predictors of secondary attention-deficit/hyperactivity disorder in children and adolescents 6 to 24 months after traumatic brain injury. *Journal of the American Academy of Child & Adolescent Psychiatry, 44*, 1041–1049.

McCarthy, M. L., MacKenzie, E. J., Durbin, D. R,, Aitken, M. E., Jaffe, K. M., Paidas, C. N. et al. (2006). Health-related quality of life during the first year after traumatic brain injury. *Archives of Pediatric and Adolescent Medicine, 160*, 252–60.

McCauley, S. R., & Levin, H. S. (2004). Prospective memory in pediatric traumatic brain injury: A preliminary study. *Developmental Neuropsychology, 25*, 5–20.

McCauley, S. R., McDaniel, M. A., Pedroza, C., Chapman, S. B., & Levin, H. S. (2009). Incentive effects on event-based prospective memory performance in children and adolescents with traumatic brain injury. *Neuropsychology, 23*, 201–209.

McCrory, P., Collie, A., Anderson, V, & Davis, G (2004). Can we manage sport-related concussion in children the same as in adults? *British Journal of Sports Medicine, 38*, 5126–5519.

McLean, D. E., Kaitz, E. S., Kennan, C. J., Dabney, K., Cawley, M. F., & Alexander, M. A. (1995). Medical and surgical complications of pediatric brain injury. *Journal of Head Trauma Rehabilitation, 10*, 1–12.

Merkley, T. L., Bigler, E. D., Wilde, E. A., McCauley, S. R., Hunter, J. V., & Levin, H. S. (2008). Diffuse changes in cortical thickness in pediatric moderate-to-severe traumatic brain injury. *Journal of Neurotrauma, 25*, 1343–1345.

Michaud, L. J., Rivara, F. P., Grady, M. S., & Reay, D. T. (1992). Predictors of survival and severe disability after severe brain injury in children. *Neurosurgery, 31*, 254–264.

Miller, L. M., & Donders, J. (2003). Prediction of educational outcome after pediatric traumatic brain injury. *Rehabilitation Psychology, 48*, 237–241.

Mittenberg, W., Wittner, M. S., & Miller, L. J. (1997). Postconcussion syndrome occurs in children. *Neuropsychology, 11*, 447–452.

Moyes, C. (1980). Epidemiology of serious head injuries in childhood. *Child Care, Health, and Development, 6*, 1–9.

Muscara, F., Catroppa, C., & Anderson, V. (2008a). Social problem solving skills as a mediator between executive function and long-term social outcome following pediatric traumatic brain injury. *Journal of Neuropsychology, 2*, 445–462.

Muscara, F., Catroppa, C. & Anderson, V. (2008b). The impact of injury severity on executive function 7-10 years following pediatric traumatic brain injury. *Developmental Neuropsychology, 5*, 623–636.

Muscara, F., Catroppa, C., Eren, S., & Anderson, V. (2009). The impact of injury severity on long-term social outcome following pediatric traumatic brain injury (TBI). *Neuropsychological Rehabilitation, 19*(4), 541–561.

Nadebaum, C., Anderson, V., & Catroppa, C. (2007). Executive function outcomes following traumatic brain injury in young children: A five year follow-up. *Developmental Neuropsychology, 32*, 703–728.

Newsome, M. R., Steinberg, J. L., Scheibel, R. S., Troyanskaya, M., Chu, Z., Hanten, G. et al. (2008). Effects of traumatic brain injury on working memory-related brain activation in adolescents. *Neuropsychology, 22*, 419–425.

North, B. (1984). *Jamieson's first notebook of head injury. (3rd Eds.).* London: Butterworths.

Novack, T. A., Dillon, M. C., & Jackson, W. T. (1996). Neurochemical mechanisms in brain injury and treatment: A review. *Journal of Clinical and Experimental Neuropsychology, 18*, 685–706.

Pang, D. (1985). Pathophysiologic correlates of neurobehavioral syndromes following closed head injury. In M. Ylvisaker (Ed.), *Head injury rehabilitation: Children and adolescents.* (pp. 3–70). London: Taylor & Francis.

Parslow, R. C., Morris, K. P., Tasker, R. C., Forsyth, R. J., & Hawley, C. A. (2005). Epidemiology of traumatic brain injury in children receiving intensive care in the UK. *Archives of Disease in Childhood, 90*, 1182–1187.

Pentland, L., Todd, J. A., & Anderson, V. (1998). The impact of head injury severity on planning ability in adolescence: A functional analysis. *Neuropsychological Rehabilitation*, 8, 301–317.

Perrott, S. B., Taylor, H. G., & Montes, J. L. (1991). Neuropsychological sequelae, familial stress, and environmental adaptation following pediatric head injury. *Developmental Neuropsychology*, 7, 69–86.

Ponsford, J., Willmott, C., Rothwell, A., Cameron, P., Ayton, G., Nelms, R. et al. (1999). Cognitive and behavioural outcomes following mild traumatic head injury in children. *Journal of Head Trauma Rehabilitation*, 14, 360–372.

Povlishock, J. T., & Katz, D. I. (2005). Update of neuropathology and neurological recovery after traumatic brain injury. *Journal of Head Trauma Rehabilitation*, 20, 76–94.

Power, T., Catroppa, C., Coleman, L., Ditchfield, M., & Anderson, V. (2007). Do lesion site and severity predict deficits in attentional control after preschool traumatic brain injury (TBI)? *Brain Injury*, 21, 279–292.

Prior, M., Kinsella, G., Sawyer, M., Bryan, D., & Anderson, V. (1994). Cognitive and psychosocial outcomes after head injury in childhood. *Australian Psychologist*, 29, 116–123.

Quattrocchi, K., Prasad, P., Willits, N., & Wagner, F. (1991). Quantification of midline shift as a predictor of poor outcome following head injury. *Surgical Neurology*, 35, 183–188.

Raimondi, A. & Hirschauer, J. (1984). Head injury in the infant and toddler. *Child's Brain*, 11, 12–35.

Rivara, J. B., Jaffe, K. M., Fay, G. C., Polissar, N. L., Martin, K. M., Shurtleff, H. A. et al. (1993). Family functioning and injury severity as predictors of child functioning one year following traumatic brain injury. *Archives of Physical Medicine and Rehabilitation*, 74, 1047–1055.

Roman, M. J., Delis, D. C., Willerman, L., Magulac, M., Demadura, T. L., de la Peña, J. L. et al. (1998). Impact of pediatric TBI on components of verbal memory. *Journal of Clinical and Experimental Neuropsychology*, 20, 245–258.

Salorio, C. F., Slomine, B. S., Grados M, A., Vasa, R. A., Christensen, J. R., & Gerring, J. P. (2005). Neuroanatomic correlates of CVLT-C performance following pediatric traumatic brain injury. *Journal of the International Neuropsychological Society*, 11, 686–696.

Schwartz, L., Taylor, H. G., Drotar, D., Yeates, K. O., Wade, S. L. & Stancin, T. (2003). Long-term behaviour problems following pediatric traumatic brain injury: Prevalence, predictors, and correlates. *Journal of Pediatric Psychology*, 28, 251–263.

Sesma, H. W., Slomine, B. S., Ding, R., & McCarthy, M. L. (2008) Executive functioning in the first year after pediatric traumatic brain injury. *Pediatrics*, 121, 1686–1695.

Shore, P. M., Berger, R. P., Varma, S., Janesko, K. L., Wisniewski, S. R., Clark, R. S. et al. (2007). Cerebrospinal fluid biomarkers versus glasgow coma scale and glasgow outcome scale in pediatric traumatic brain injury: the role of young age and inflicted injury. *Journal of Neurotrauma*, 24, 75–86.

Shum, D., Jamieson, E., Bahr, M., & Wallace, G. (1999). Implicit and explicit memory in children with traumatic brain injury. *Journal of Clinical and Experimental Neuropsychology*, 21, 149–158.

Shum, D. K., McFarland, K. A., Bain, J. D. & Humphreys, M. S. (1990). The effects of closed head injury upon attentional processes: An information processing stage analysis. *Journal of Clinical and Experimental Neuropsychology*, 12, 247–264.

Slomine, B. S., Gerring, J. P., Grados, M. A., Vasa, R., Brady, K. D., Christensen, J. R. et al. (2002). Performance on measures of executive function following pediatric traumatic brain injury. *Brain Injury*, 16, 759–772.

Stancin, T., Drotar, D., Taylor, H. G., Yeates, K. O., Wade, S. L., & Minich, N. M. (2002). Health-related quality of life of children and adolescents after traumatic brain injury. *Pediatrics*, 109, 34..

Stallings, G. A., Ewing-Cobbs, L., Francis, D. J., & Fletcher, J. M. (1996). Prediction of academic placement after pediatric head injury using neurological, demographic, and neuropsychological variables. *Journal of the International Neuropsychological Society*, 2, 39.

Statler K. D. (2006). Pediatric posttraumatic seizures: Epidemiology, putative mechanisms of epileptogenesis and promising investigational progress. *Developmental Neuroscience*, 28, 354–363.

Stuss, D. T., Stethem, L. L, Hugenholtz, H., Picton, T., Pivik, J., & Richard, M. T. (1989). Reaction time after head injury: Fatigue, divided and focused attention, and consistency of performance. *Journal of Neurology, Neurosurgery, and Psychiatry*, 52, 742–748.

Tate, R. L., McDonald, S., & Lulham, J. M. (1998) Incidence of hospital-treated traumatic brain injury in an Australian community. *Australian and New Zealand Journal of Public Health*, 22, 419–423.

Taylor, H. G. (2010). Neurobehavioural outcomes of pediatric traumatic brain injury. In V. A. Anderson & K. O. Yeates (Ed.), *New directions in pediatric traumatic brain injury: Multidisciplinary and translational perspectives* (pp. 36–53). New York: Oxford University Press.

Taylor, H. G., & Alden, J. (1997). Age-related differences in outcome following childhood brain injury: An introduction and overview. *Journal of the International Neuropsychological Society*, *3*, 555–567.

Taylor, H. G., Drotar, D., Wade, S., Yeates, K. O., Stancin, T., & Klein, S. (1995). Recovery from TBI in children: The importance of the family. In S. H. Broman & M. E. Michel (Ed.), *Traumatic Head Injury in Children* (pp. 188–218). New York: Oxford University Press.

Taylor, H. G., Yeates, K. O., Wade, S. L., Drotar, D., Klein, S. K., & Stancin, T. (1999). Influences on first-year recovery from traumatic brain injury in children. *Neuropsychology*, *13*, 76–89.

Taylor, H. G., Yeates, K. O., Wade, S. L., Drotar, D., Stancin, T., & Minich, N. (2002). A prospective study of long- and short-term outcomes after traumatic brain injury in children: Behaviour and achievement. *Neuropsychology*, *16*, 15–27.

Taylor, H. G., Yeates, K. O., Wade, S L., Drotar, D., Stancin, T., & Montpetite, M. (2003). Long-term educational interventions after traumatic brain injury in children. *Rehabilitation Psychology*, *48*, 227–236.

Tenovuo, O. (2006). Pharmacological enhancement of cognitive and behavioural deficits after traumatic brain injury. *Current Opinion In Neurology*, *19*, 528–533.

Thompson, N. M., Francis, D. J., Stuebing, K. K., Fletcher, J. M., Ewing-Cobbs, L., Miner, M. E. et al. (1994). Motor, visual-spatial, and somatosensory skills after TBI in children and adolescents: A study of change. *Neuropsychology*, *8*, 333–342.

Todd, J. A., Anderson, V. A., & Lawrence, J. A. (1996). Planning skills in head injured adolescents and their peers. *Neuropsychological Rehabilitation*, *6*, 81–99.

Tompkins, C. A., Holland, A. L., Ratcliff, G., Costello, A., Leahy, L., & Cowell, V. (1990). Predicting cognitive recovery from closed head injury in children and adolescents. *Brain and Cognition*, *13*, 86–97.

Van't Hooft, I., Andersson, K., Bergman, B., Sejersen, T., von Wendt, L., & Bartfai, A. (2007). A randomized controlled trial on children with acquired brain injuries reveals sustained favorable effects of cognitive training. *Neurorehabilitation*, *22*, 109–116.

Vasa, R. A., Gerring, J. P., Grados, M., Slomine, B., Christensen, J. R., Rising, W. et al. (2002). Anxiety after severe pediatric closed head injury. *Journal of the American Academy of Child and Adolescent Psychiatry*, *41*,148–156.

Verger, K., Junque, C., Jurado, M. A., Tresserras, P., Bartumeus, F., Noques, P. et al. (2000). Age effects on long-term neuropsychological outcome in paediatric traumatic brain injury. *Brain Injury*, *14*, 495–503.

Wade, S. L. (2010). Psychosocial treatments for pediatric traumatic brain injury. In V. A. Anderson & K. O. Yeates (Ed.). *New directions in pediatric traumatic brain injury: Multidisciplinary and translational perspectives* (pp. 179–191). New York: Oxford University Press.

Wade, S. L., Carey, J., & Wolfe, C. R. (2006). An online family intervention to reduce parental distress following pediatric brain injury. *Journal of Consulting and Clinical Psychology*, *74*, 445–454.

Wade, S. L., Taylor, H. G., Walz, N. C., Salisbury, S., Stancin, T., Bernard, L. A. et a. (2008). Parent-child interactions during the initial weeks following brain injury in young children. *Rehabilitation Psychology*, *53*, 180–190.

Wade, S. L., Taylor, H. G., Yeates, K. O., Drotar, D., Stancin, T., Minich, N. M. et al. (2006). Long-term parental and family adaptation following pediatric brain injury. *Journal of Pediatric Psychology*, *31*, 1072–1083.

Ward, H., Shum, D., Dick, B., McKinlay, L., & Baker-Tweney, S. (2004). Interview study of the effects of paediatric traumatic brain injury on memory. *Brain Injury*, *18*, 471–495.

Ward, H., Shum, D., McKinlay, L., Baker, S., & Wallace, G. (2007). Prospective memory and pediatric traumatic brain injury: Effects of cognitive demand. *Child Neuropsychology*, *13*, 219–239.

Ward, H., Shum, D., Wallace, G., & Boon, J. (2002). Pediatric traumatic brain injury and procedural memory. *Journal of Clinical and Experimental Neuropsychology*, *24*, 458–470.

Warschausky, S., Cohen, E. H., Parker, J. G., Levendosky, A. A., & Okun, A. (1997). Social problem-solving skills of children with traumatic brain injury. *Pediatric Rehabilitation*, *1*, 77–81.

Warschausky, S., Kewman, D., & Kay, J. (1999). Empirically supported psychological and behavioural therapies in pediatric rehabilitation of TBI. *Journal of Head Trauma Rehabilitation*, *14*, 373–383.

Wilde, E. A., Hunter, J. V., Newsome, M. R., Scheibel, R. S., Bigler, E. D., Johnson, J. L. et al. (2005). Frontal and temporal morphometric findings on MRI in children after moderate to severe traumatic brain injury. *Journal of Neurotrauma*, *22*, 333–344.

Winogron, H. W., Knights, R. M., & Bawden, H. N. (1984). Neuropsychological deficits following head injury in children. *Journal of Clinical Neuropsychology*, *6*, 269–286.

Yeates, K. O. (2000). Closed-head injury. In K. O. Yeates, M. D. Ris, & H. G. Taylor (Ed.), *Pediatric neuropsychology: Research, theory, and practice* (pp. 92–116). New York: Guilford.

Yeates, K. O., Armstrong, K., Janusz, J., Taylor, H. G., Wade, S., Stancin, T. et al. (2005). Long-term attention problems in children with traumatic brain injury. *Journal of the American Academy of Child and Adolescent Psychiatry, 44*, 574–584.

Yeates, K. O., Bigler, E. D., Dennis, M., Gerhardt, C. A., Rubin, K. H., Stancin, T. et al. (2007). Social outcomes in childhood brain disorder: A heuristic integration of social neuroscience and developmental psychology. *Psychological Bulletin, 133*, 535–556.

Yeates, K. O., Blumenstein, E., Patterson, C. M., & Delis, D. C. (1995a). Verbal learning and memory following pediatric TBI. *Journal of the International Neuropsychological Society, 1*, 78–87.

Yeates, K. O., & Enrile, B. G. (2005). Implicit and explicit memory in children with congenital and acquired brain disorder. *Neuropsychology, 19*, 618–628.

Yeates, K. O., Luria, J., Bartkowski, H., Rusin, J., Martin, L., & Bigler, E. D. (1999). Post-concussive symptoms in children with mild closed-head injuries. *Journal of Head Trauma Rehabilitation, 14*, 337–350.

Yeates, K. O., Patterson, C. M., Waber, D. P., & Bernstein, J. H. (2003). Constructional and figural memory skills following pediatric closed-head injury: Evaluation using the ROCF. In J. A. Knight & E. Kaplan (Ed.), *The handbook of Rey-Osterrieth Complex Figure usage: Clinical and research applications* (pp. 83–93). Odessa, FL: Psychological Assessment Resources.

Yeates, K. O., Swift, E., Taylor, H. G., Wade, S. L., Drotar, D., Stancin, T. et al. (2004). Short- and long-term social outcomes following pediatric traumatic brain injury. *Journal of the International Neuropsychological Society, 10*, 412–426.

Yeates, K. O., & Taylor, H. G. (2005). Neurobehavioural outcomes of mild head injury in children and adolescents. *Pediatric Rehabilitation, 8*, 5–16.

Yeates, K. O., & Taylor, H. G. (2006). Behaviour problems in school and their educational correlates among children with traumatic brain injury. *Exceptionality, 14*, 141–154.

Yeates, K. O., Taylor, H. G., Barry, C. T., Drotar, D., Wade, S. L., & Stancin, T. (2001). Neurobehavioural symptoms in childhood closed-head injuries: Changes in prevalence and correlates during the first year post-injury. *Journal of Pediatric Psychology, 26*, 79–91.

Yeates, K. O., Taylor, H. G., Rusin, J., Bangert, B., Dietrich, A., Nuss, K. et al. (2009). Longitudinal trajectories of post-concussive symptoms in children with mild traumatic brain injuries and their relationship to acute clinical status. *Pediatrics, 123*, 735–743.

Ylvisaker, M., Adelson, D., Braga, L.W., Burnett, S.M., Glang, A., Feeney, T. et al. (2005a). Rehabilitation and ongoing support after pediatric TBI: Twenty years of progress. *Journal of Head Trauma Rehabilitation, 20*, 90–104.

Ylvisaker, M., Turkstra, L. S., & Coelho, C. (2005b). Behavioural and social interventions for individuals with traumatic brain injury: A summary of the research with clinical implications. *Seminars in Speech and Language, 26*, 256–267.

Ylvisaker, M., Turkstra, L., Coehlo, C., Yorkston, K., Kennedy, M., Sohlberg, M. M. et al. (2007). Behavioural interventions for children and adults with behaviour disorders after TBI: A systematic review of the evidence. *Brain Injury, 21*, 769–805.

16

Traumatic Brain Injury in Older Adults: Does Age Matter?

Glynda J. Kinsella, John Olver, Ben Ong, Eleanor Hammersley, and Bethan Plowright

Over the next 40 years, developed countries throughout the world are expected to experience a dramatic increase in the number of people aged over 60, with predictions that by the year 2050, older adults will constitute nearly one third of the population (United Nations, 2012). Furthermore, although positive health trends in aging have led to a healthier and more mobile older population, older adults remain at risk of sustaining traumatic brain injury (TBI) through falls or road traffic accidents, and frequently require hospitalization as a result of these injuries (Bradley, 2013; Coronado, Thomas, Sattin, & Johnson 2005; Faul, Xu, Wald, & Coronado 2010; Helps, Henley, & Harrison, 2008).

However, in contrast to the increasingly well documented outcome literature on younger adults with TBI (for example, Dikmen, Machamer, Fann & Temkin, 2010; McCrae, 2008; Ponsford, Draper, & Schonberger, 2008), comparatively few studies have focused on detailing the functional outcomes for older adults further than documenting the high mortality rates. The need for an increased priority of investigating TBI outcome in older adults was raised in 2004 by the WHO Collaborating Center for Neurotrauma Task Force (Carroll, Cassidy, Holm, Kraus, & Coronado, 2004) but progress has been slow. Due to our aging populations, TBI in older adults represents a growing public health concern worldwide; however, very little is known about outcome as it impacts quality of life and costs to health services. As a preliminary step in addressing this issue, the following chapter will focus on reviewing the characteristics and predictors of outcome following TBI in older adults.

Incidence and Characteristics of Older Adults Who Experience TBI

Although TBI is most common in young adults involved in motor vehicle incidents (Helps et al., 2008; Kraus & Chu, 2005; O'Connor, 2002), another important age group presenting to emergency departments and trauma services are older adults (65 years +), who have experienced either falls or road trauma. Thompson, McCormick, and Kagan (2006) report that in the United States it has been estimated that 80,000 adults aged over 65 years are treated for TBI in hospital emergency departments each year and at least 75% of these presentations result in hospitalization. The age-adjusted rate of hospitalization for nonfatal TBI in the general population is 60.6 per 100,000 population; however, for adults aged 65 years or older, this rate more than doubles to 155.9; and increasing age in the older population increases the risk of mortality (Coronado et al., 2005; Thompson, McCormick, & Kagan, 2006).

In younger TBI populations, males are reported to be at a much higher risk of sustaining a TBI than females, particularly during adolescence, and Kraus and Chu (2005) report the male/female rate ratio as varying across studies from approximately 1.6 to 2.8. However, in older samples, although TBI hospitalization rates as a

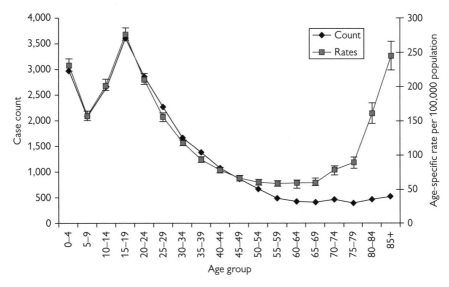

Figure 16-1. Incidence of TBI by age group (counts and age-specific rates), hospital separations; Australia 1997–98 (based on estimated incident cases). Source: Australian Institute of Health and Welfare

result of road trauma are still higher for males (Helps et al., 2008; Fig 2.7), interestingly, there are reports that there is little difference between males and females when the mechanism of injury is a fall. Thomas, Stevens, Sarmiento, and Wald (2008) reported that U.S. hospitalizations for nonfatal fall-related TBI among people aged over 65 years were similar among men and women (146.3 per 100,000 and 158.3 per 100,000, respectively).

In contrast to younger patients with TBI who mainly present following road traffic accidents, the cause of injury for older adults is most frequently related to falls (Helps et al., 2008; Kraus & Chu, 2005). 6,800 Australians over 65 years of age were hospitalized due to falls in 2005–6 and head injuries constituted 17% of these cases, the second most common falls-related diagnosis following hip and lower limb injuries (Bradley, 2013). Thompson et al. (2006) also report that a single fall is a risk factor for a subsequent fall, thereby increasing the risk of additive effects from serial injuries. This is important within the context of an aging community: older adult populations worldwide are predicted to increase from 672 million in 2005 to nearly 1.9 billion by 2050 (United Nations, 2012). In 2000 in the United States, direct medical costs for fall injuries in persons > 65 years was $0.2 billion United States dollars for fatal injuries and $19 billion for

nonfatal injuries (Stevens, Corso, Finkelstein, & Miller, 2006). Similarly, using data from 2003–4, falls in the older adult Australian population cost the health care system up to $571 million U.S. dollars (Bradley & Harrison, 2007). The combination of these statistics highlights the potential for rapidly escalating costs in health care systems associated with services provided for TBI in older people.

Why Should TBI in Older Adults Be Considered "Special"?

The presentation of traumatic brain injury in an older population raises a number of issues as distinct from those for a younger population. Further to the difference in the mechanism of injury as described above, older adults have been reported to sustain more secondary intracranial injuries potentially related to both the mechanism of injury (falls) and pre-existing cerebral deterioration associated with normal aging or age-related cerebral fragility (Rathlev et al., 2006), which places them at risk of more complicated and poorer outcome. TBI in older adults is associated with an increased risk of intracranial hemorrhage and subdural hematomas (Goleburn & Golden, 2001; Rathlev et al., 2006). Goleburn and Golden have argued that this may occur as a consequence of age-related

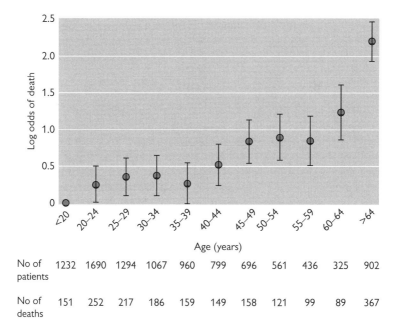

Figure 16-2. Relation between age and mortality at 14 days. Reproduced from "Predicting outcome after traumatic brain injury: practical prognostic models based on large cohort of international patients" by MRC CRASH Trial Collaborators, vol. 336, copyright 2008 with permission from BJM Publishing Group Ltd.

changes in the pathophysiological structures of the older brain including the more common presence of cerebral atrophy and vascular rigidity, leading to a cascade of secondary effects; for example, stretching of the parasagittal bridging veins leading to greater vulnerability to tear after trauma, thus resulting in subdural hematoma. Furthermore, it has been found that both increasing age and the use of oral anticoagulation increase the risk of mortality after TBI (Franko, Kish, O'Connell, Subramanian, & Yuschak, 2006). The increased risk of age-related cerebrovascular disease and/or hypertension and associated medication will challenge capacity for vascular response and recovery following cerebral injury in the older population (Thompson et al., 2006).

A further issue is that independent of the injury, the process of aging can lead to cognitive changes (Grady, 2012); loss of cerebral white matter integrity (Madden, Bennett, & Song, 2009); and a reduction in cognitive reserve (Whalley, Deary, Appleton, & Starr, 2004); and, with any additional cognitive effects of TBI superimposed, it has been suggested that older adults are more at risk of demonstrating

significant ongoing cognitive deficits following even mild TBI (Kinsella, 2010). A further challenge is that the presence of pre-existing cognitive impairment related to the pre-clinical stage of a dementia disorder will provide an additional risk of poor cognitive recovery following TBI in older adults. This is especially problematic as it is now recognized that many degenerative disorders, such as Alzheimer's disease, have a long pre-clinical phase (termed mild cognitive impairment) before formal diagnosis (Petersen, 2004); and, the interaction of mild cognitive impairment with mild TBI involving similar neural circuitry, has potential to provide interactive impairments resulting in significant cognitive disability. Future research needs to investigate the extent of this risk in older TBI populations.

Aging populations face additional problems of the presence of pre-existing chronic co-morbid conditions (for example, arthritis or diabetes) which can lead to limited functional ability or significant ill-health and increase risk of poor outcome post-trauma (Camilloni, Farchi, Giorgi Rossi, Chini, & Borgi 2008; Coronado et al., 2005), although this has not consistently been found (Utomo, Gabbe, Simpson, & Cameron, 2009). In a population-based study, Ventura et al. (2010) investigated mortality after discharge from hospitalization following TBI (n = 18,918). The median time of follow-up for each patient was 4.4 years (range 1–8 years). Ventura et al. reported that risk factors for mortality in adults aged over 20 years included severity of injury, increasing age, and poorer health at time of injury (> 3 co-morbid health conditions). Unexpectedly, although still significant, the size of the co-morbidity effect actually reduced in the older age groups. Ventura et al. suggested that this finding was due to the generally higher prevalence of co-morbidities in the older age groups, and, as the co-morbid health variable was based on a simple count of the number of co-morbidities present without reference to the seriousness of the condition, this would have attenuated any specific association of this variable with mortality in these older age groups. If correct, this suggests that further research into the specificity of the co-morbid condition and its impact on TBI recovery is needed to inform prediction of outcome for older people following trauma.

Finally, it has also been suggested that emotional problems are likely to affect older adults' recovery following TBI (Goldstein, Levin, Goldman, Clark, & Altonen, 2001; Rapoport, Herrmann, Shammi, Kiss, Phillips, & Feinstein, 2006); although whether older adults are especially vulnerable following an isolated TBI, as distinct from effects following multisystem trauma, has yet to be demonstrated. Taken together these various issues indicate a need for scrutiny of outcome following TBI in older adults as a distinct process to that of review of younger populations.

Mortality, Morbidity, and General Functional Outcome

Much of the research to date investigating TBI in older adults has primarily focused on mortality and morbidity or measures of gross functional outcome and has been highlighting the particular risk associated with incurring a TBI at an older age (Hukkelhoven et al., 2003; McIntyre et al., 2013; Mosenthal et al., 2004; Thomas et al., 2008). For example, in a very large multi-site trauma study (MRC CRASH Trial Collaborators, 2008) involving 10,008 patients, increasing age was identified as one of the predictors of unfavorable outcome (death or severe disability) as measured by the Glasgow Outcome Scale (GOS).

In a recent Australian study investigating mortality and functional outcome in 428 older adults with moderate to severe TBI, Utomo et al. (2009) reported that 27.6% of patients died in the hospital, and for patients aged over 75 years the odds were three times higher than for patients aged 65–74 years. They also reported poorer functional outcome in older adults, particularly in older adults aged over 75 years who had a 60% lower chance of achieving independent living (GOS-E > 5 or above) at six months post-injury than older adults aged 65–74 years. No patients with a GCS < 9 had a good six month outcome, and most died. A study by Gerber, Ni, Härtl, and Ghajar (2009) focusing on fall-related injuries, found that even without accounting for people who died at the scene or in emergency departments, mortality in older adults who sustained a severe TBI as a result of falls from heights less than three meters was 42% and this proportion increased to 48% following falls from greater heights.

Although high mortality rates may be expected in severe TBI populations, this trend has also been demonstrated in older adults who have a mild or moderate TBI. Mosenthal et al. (2002) compared mortality rates in younger (< 65 years) and older (> 65 years) adults who had sustained an isolated TBI (i.e., no extracranial injuries) and found that despite less than 5% mortality in younger adults with a mild-moderate TBI, in older adults the rate of mortality was over 40% following a moderate TBI, and 10% following a mild TBI. Similarly, Susman et al. (2002) also reported this trend in a sample of 11,727 patients with head injury, with older patients demonstrating nearly twice the relative risk of mortality (24%) than their younger counterparts (12.8%) and noted that even older patients with a mild TBI (GCS score 13-15) had an odds ratio of dying of 7.8 as compared with younger adults of similar TBI severity.

Having noted that the majority of the literature concludes that older age is a predictor of

poor outcome, Mosenthal et al. (2002) acknowledge that the reason for this is largely unknown,
although probably multi-factorial. In their study
of 155 patients aged > 65 years, they found no
relationship between increased mortality and
significant secondary blood loss, overt hypotension or less intensive therapy, which are all
factors that have been proposed as risks in older
populations. They also reported that patients
who survived hospitalization had a poorer
short-term outcome as indexed by discharge
GOS score. It can be speculated that older age
may simply be a proxy variable for multiple vulnerabilities, including the presence of significant co-morbidities such as hypertension which
could impact the cerebrovascular response to
injury (Thompson et al., 2006). Although intuitively persuasive, strong evidence for this view
is yet to emerge in the literature.

In regards to general functional outcome, an
early study by Cifu and colleagues (1996) investigated functional outcomes in older adults
(> 54 years) as compared to younger adults
(18–54 years) in acute care and rehabilitation
facilities. They reported that older adults spent
nearly twice as long in rehabilitation facilities,
and at time of discharge older adults demonstrated greater levels of disability. Importantly,
they found that the groups were not differentiated so much in terms of physical disability,
but in behavior and cognition, with older adults
faring worse. Nevertheless, the researchers
emphasized that the vast majority of patients,
regardless of age, were discharged to community settings, including their own homes. In a
later study, Frankel and colleagues (2006) found
that although there was no significant difference between older adults and younger adults
in their length of stay in acute care, older adults
spent significantly more time in rehabilitation
than younger adults and a significantly smaller
percentage of older adults were discharged
back into the community than younger adults
(80.8% and 94.3% respectively). Nevertheless,
the researchers in this study again emphasized
that the vast majority of older adults were able
to return to their own homes following rehabilitation, which was encouraging.

Although many studies have focused on relatively short-term functional outcome following
traumatic brain injury, a study conducted in

Singapore by Gan, Lim, and Ng (2004) used the
Glasgow Outcome Scale (GOS) at six months
post-injury with older and younger adults who
had incurred a moderate-severe traumatic brain
injury. They found that only 23% of older adults
had a "favorable" outcome as compared to nearly
65% of younger adults. Similarly, Testa et al.,
(2005) reported that older age patients post-TBI
were more likely than younger age patients with
TBI to have changes in employment at one to
two years after injury. Furthermore, a study
conducted by Rothweiler, Temkin, and Dikmen
(1998) investigated gross functional outcome,
living situation, and employment status at one
year post injury. They found that 80% of their
participants aged over 60 were at least moderately disabled at the 12-month follow up.

In contrast to these pessimistic findings,
Mosenthal et al. (2004) encouragingly reported
a generally favorable outcome for older adults
at six months post-injury as indexed by the
GOS. They suggested that their more positive
findings were attributable to the study investigating patients with isolated TBI of predominantly mild severity. They argued that when
multisystem trauma is controlled for, older and
younger patients have fairly similar outcomes at
six months post injury. Mosenthal et al. (2004)
acknowledged that when multisystem trauma
accompanies TBI, this context may be more
problematic for recovery by older adults due to
the possible physiological interaction of brain
and trauma injuries. This is important as multisystem trauma is not uncommon in older populations. A further limitation that Mosenthal
et al. acknowledged was that the study did not
evaluate cognitive or emotional outcome which
may not demonstrate similar levels of good
recovery post-trauma.

Cognitive Functioning Following TBI in Older Adults

Change in cognitive function can be the most
difficult post-injury challenge facing people
who have sustained a TBI (Sherer, Sander, Nick,
High, Malec, & Rosenthal, 2002). Impairments
in memory, speed of information processing,
attention, and executive functioning have been
well documented in the general TBI literature
(Dikmen, Machamer, Powell, & Tempkin,

2003; Ponsford et al., 2008; Sherer et al., 2002; Sigurdardottir, Andelic, Roe, Jerstad, & Schanke, 2009). The nature of cognitive functioning in older adults following TBI, however, is not so well understood, with very few studies specifically investigating cognitive outcome.

In a retrospective analysis of 112 people who experienced TBI, Senathi-Raja, Ponsford, and Schonberger (2010) reported that older age was associated with poorer cognitive functioning at the time of injury and increased time post-injury. However, in an earlier study Rapoport and Feinstein (2000) reviewed the findings of a number of studies that had specifically investigated cognitive outcome in older adults following TBI. From this review, Rapoport and Feinstein (2000) concluded that it was premature to argue from the existing published research pre-2000 that older adults had uniformly a poor cognitive and functional outcome post-TBI. Included in their review was a study by Aharon-Peretz and colleagues (1997) which examined cognitive functioning six weeks post injury and found that older adults (aged over 60 years) with mild-moderate TBI demonstrated impaired verbal fluency, memory (verbal and visual), and abstract reasoning as compared to healthy controls. However, importantly, the TBI group did not significantly differ from an orthopedic control group. These findings led Aharon-Peretz et al. (1997) to speculate that cognitive decline may predate injury and might have increased risk of exposure to an injury for participants in both the TBI and orthopedic control group. Although Rapoport and Feinstein (2000) cautioned that the study had not controlled for between-group education differences and the sample size of the assessed groups was small (18 TBI, 10 healthy and 10 orthopedic controls), the question raised remains important. As later argued by Mosenthal et al. (2004), the impact of multi-system traumatic injury needs to be carefully controlled for when attempting to isolate the specific legacy of TBI in the functional outcome of older adults.

As the chance of survival from severe injury is poor, the focus for evaluating cognitive outcome is on those older adults who experience mild-moderate TBI. This is especially relevant as the majority of research studies and recent meta-analyses with younger populations have reported that neuropsychological recovery is expected following uncomplicated mild TBI, with no indication of persistent deficit by three months post-injury (Frencham, Fox, & Murray, 2005; Iverson, 2006; McCrae, 2008). Whether older adults can achieve a similar positive neuropsychological outcome from uncomplicated mild TBI is yet to be consistently replicated; although emerging research is encouraging.

Goldstein et al. (2001) reported that two months post injury, older adults with moderate TBI demonstrated impaired attention, speed of information processing, memory, language, and executive functioning compared to those with mild TBI and a healthy control group. Importantly, this study found no difference between those with mild TBI and a healthy control group on any of the domains, apart from producing fewer words on a verbal fluency task. More recently, Rapoport et al. (2006) investigated cognitive outcome one year post mild-moderate TBI in older adults. They found that even after this considerable time period, when controlling for age, education, and medical co-morbidities among those participants, older adults with moderate TBI were demonstrating impairments in processing speed, verbal memory, language (confrontation naming), and executive functioning. However, these difficulties were not evident in the mild TBI group as compared to an age-matched control group.

These studies provide support for the view that a relatively good outcome can be achieved by older adults following an uncomplicated mild TBI, although complicated mild TBI, i.e., when acute intra-cranial abnormalities are detected on imaging, has yet to be specifically evaluated. These findings are in contrast to previous pessimistic views of recovery in older adults following TBI. As severity of TBI increases, so does the likelihood of cognitive impairment; both studies demonstrated that moderate TBI typically results in impairment in the expected TBI-sensitive domains of processing speed, memory, and executive function. However, both research groups note that their studies focused on previously healthy older adults and the high incidence of pre-injury risk factors, such as presence of co-morbidities or early dementia, etc., will be problematic in

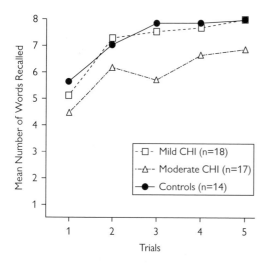

Figure 16-3. Mean number of words recalled on each of the five trials of the CVLT for mild and moderate TBI patients and controls. Courtesy of Felicia C. Goldstein.

general clinical samples. In addition, Goldstein et al. (2001) comment that neuropsychological measures that challenge domains of cognition known to be vulnerable to cognitive aging, such as complex cognitive speed (Salthouse, 2010), may have highlighted vulnerabilities in the mild TBI groups. This maybe especially relevant to an older population exposed to a potential interaction of sub-clinical deficits from cognitive aging and TBI.

Depression and Psychosocial Issues

Research into the development of emotional problems and their impact on cognitive or functional outcome following TBI in older adults is limited, which prevents definitive statements about psychiatric outcome for older adult's post-TBI.

Goldstein et al. (2001) provided one of the few studies focusing on depression in older adults. By using self-report measures, the Geriatric Depression Scale, and the Neurobehavioral Rating Scale, the researchers found that one in three in a sample of 35 older adults with mild or moderate TBI experienced significant symptoms of depression, anxiety, and somatic concerns at two months post-injury as compared to

an age-matched community control group. This incidence in symptoms of depression is consistent with similar reports from younger age TBI samples. The estimated prevalence of depression has been varied in younger TBI patient groups, but by using structured interview and the *DSM-IV* criteria, Seel and colleagues (2003) reported a 27% prevalence of major depression in a sample of 666 outpatients who had moderate to severe head injuries and were assessed 10 to 126 months after injury. Similarly, Jorge and colleagues (2004) reported that major depressive disorder, also assessed by structured clinical interview and *DSM-IV* criteria, was observed in 33% of 91 patients during the first year after sustaining a TBI of varying severity. However, the Goldstein et al. (2001) study with older adults relied on self-report rating scales to determine symptoms of depression, and as noted by Levin et al. (2001), estimating depression through rating scales as opposed to using *DSM* diagnostic criteria may provide elevated scores because of an overlap between post-concussion symptoms and depressive symptoms. This raises the question whether older adults following mild to moderate TBI will display similar vulnerability to major depression as found in younger populations following more severe TBI if assessed through structured interview and *DSM* diagnostic criteria.

Considering these issues, Rapoport et al. (2006) evaluated the presence of major depression in a clinical sample of 69 adults over the age of 50 years (mean age 67 years) within two months of sustaining a mild to moderate TBI and compared to 77 age-matched community controls, and followed them prospectively for one year. Using the Structured Clinical Interview for *DSM-IV* Axis I disorders (SCID; First, Spitzer, Gibbon, & Williams, 1996) they found 15.9% of the patients had developed major depression at baseline and at one year post-injury 12.2% of the TBI patients, but only 1.5% of the control group, met criteria for a major depressive episode. Five of the 11 patients with TBI and major depression at baseline also met criteria at one year follow-up. However, as noted by the researchers, the rate of depression in this older sample, although significantly higher than a community control comparison group, is substantially lower than the levels of depression reported in younger samples (Jorge et al., 2004; Seel et al., 2003). This finding has to be considered in the context that the severity of TBI is significantly milder than in the studies with younger samples. It may be that biological explanations for depression, including presence of frontal subdural lesions leading to significant compromise of fronto-striatal-thalamic circuits (Jorge et al., 2004; Rao et al., 2010), may not be as pertinent in this older sample with milder injuries. Further support for the position that older adults post-mild TBI may unexpectedly be less at risk of developing major depression, was provided by Rapoport, McCullagh, Streiner and Feinstein (2003) who compared older and younger patients following a mild TBI for the presence of depression. They found that older patients (> 60 years) had lower rates of major depression (6.3%) than younger patients (21.2%).

Nevertheless, although at a reduced level to that found in younger samples, both Rapoport et al. (2006) and Goldstein et al. (2001) did identify that major depression and depressive symptoms are significantly more frequent following mild-moderate TBI in older adults than in age-matched healthy comparison groups. It should be noted, however, that neither study included comparison groups with only extra-cranial traumatic injury to control for general trauma impact; and, as argued by Mosenthal et al. (2004) the impact of multisystem injuries on functional outcome and quality of life is significant, thereby increasing the risk of depressive symptoms as a function of trauma per se rather than specifically related to brain injury. In this respect, Goldstein et al. (2001) note that although the mild TBI participants in their study made a good recovery, they continued to demonstrate depressive symptoms equivalent to the moderate TBI participants. This was important, as although their study demonstrated a dose-response relationship between severity of injury and cognitive functioning, affective disturbances did not follow this pattern. Goldstein et al. (2001) suggest that this dissociation between cognitive and emotional recovery is indicative of factors other than brain injury effects which contribute to emotional distress post-TBI in older adults.

Additional risk factors which have been identified through studies with younger TBI samples (Jorge et al., 2004), and include being unemployed at the time of injury, presenting with a history of mood disorder, and being socially isolated, all of which might suggest that older patients will be more rather than less at risk of post-injury disorder. Furthermore, it should also be noted that there are contradictory reports in the research literature of the view that older adults are less vulnerable to post-TBI depression as some research groups have found increasing age to be predictive of major depression post-TBI (Levin et al., 2005; Rao et al., 2010). In this respect, an important consideration is that the mechanism of injury differs between older and younger cohorts. As previously noted the most common cause of TBI in older adults is falls, and it has been found that following a fall, many older adults experience ongoing "fear of falling" or "post-fall syndrome" (Murphy & Isaacs, 1982) which has capacity to provide a pervasive negative impact on everyday activities (Tinetti, Richman, & Powell, 1990). For example, a study by Cumming, Salkeld, Thomas, and Szonyi (2000) found that fear of falling was associated with reduced ability to perform activities of daily living.

However, the factors that are associated with the incidence and maintenance of emotional and psychological responses to traumatic brain injury are not thoroughly understood with regard to older adults, and, until there is available more consistent assessment of large cohorts of older adults with varying levels of severity of TBI, the psychiatric outcome of TBI in older adults remains debatable.

The Relationship between TBI and Dementia

TBI has been identified as a risk factor for Alzheimer's disease (AD) (Fleminger, Oliver, Lovestone, Rabe-Hesketh, & Giora, 2003); fronto-temporal dementia (McMurtray, Clark, Christine, & Mendez, 2006); or dementia more generally (Goleburn & Golden, 2001). For example, Plassman et al. (2000) investigated a population of 7000 veterans in the United States, 548 with brain injury and 1,228 without brain injury. He reported that any history of brain injury more than doubled the risk of developing Alzheimer's disease and non-Alzheimer's dementia, even after adjustment for the effects of age. However, these views have been contentious with several early studies failing to find TBI as a significant risk factor for dementia (for example, Nemetz et al., 1999). A limiting factor in evaluating the research evidence has been that many studies have been flawed by having small sample sizes, which is particularly problematic when studying this research question as differences between groups in their rates of conversion to Alzheimer's dementia are prone to subtlety. However, with the use of more powerful analyses such as meta-analysis, the evidence of a connection between a history of TBI and risk of dementia is starting to mount and potential theoretical explanations are being evaluated.

In an early meta-analysis of seven case-control studies, Mortimer et al. (1991) found that for a history of TBI with loss of consciousness there was a relative risk of developing AD of 1.82, 95% confidence interval (CI) 1.26 to 2.67. This finding remained significant when adjusting for family history of dementing illness, education, and alcohol consumption but only for males (2.67, 95% CI 1.64 TO 4.41) and not for females (0.85, 95% CI 0.41 to 1.70). A more recent meta-analysis, Fleminger et al. (2003) extended these findings by evaluating a further seven case-control studies but could not replicate Mortimer et al.'s initial findings. However, when they analyzed the total fifteen studies they did find a significant relative risk of AD for a history of TBI (odds ratio 1.58, 95% CI 1.21 to 2.06). Interestingly, the finding of TBI as a risk factor for AD was again only found in males (odds ratio 2.29, 95% CI 1.47 to 2.06) and not for females (odds ratio 0.91, 95% CI 0.56 to 1.47).

Fleminger et al. proposed that the gender differences in the relationship between TBI and dementia can be evaluated by considering the role of female hormones—estrogen and progesterone. They suggest that females with TBI are protected from developing AD by citing evidence that animal models of response to trauma have found a neuroprotective and neuroregenerative effect from female hormones (Bramlett & Dietrich, 2001); in addition, estrogen has been proposed as providing a protective factor to the development of AD (Pike, Carroll, Rosario, & Barron, 2009). A further explanation

is provided by Rapoport, Verhoeff and van Reekum (2004) who raise the possibility of the gender differences in risk ratios being related to primary gender differences in the cause of the trauma which resulted in TBI. This will be especially interesting to pursue in older adults as the primary cause of injury are falls for which there is not the male predominance as found for road traffic accidents (Kraus & Chu, 2005; Thomas et al., 2008).

The specificity of the relationship between TBI and dementia has been extended by several researchers examining the risk to specific forms of dementia. Jellinger, Paulus, Wrocklage, and Litvan (2001) reviewed 58 consecutive autopsies on patients who had experienced severe TBI. Alzheimer's pathology was evident in 22.4% of the series as compared to 14% expected in an age-matched general population. However, the evidence is not so convincing in relation to the potential of an interaction between TBI and ApoE $_{\epsilon4}$, the genetic risk factor for Alzheimer's disease (Millar, Nicoll, Thornhill, Murray, & Teasdale 2003). One recent study failed to support the relationship between AD and TBI; Rapoport et al. (2008) found no significant difference between older adults who had sustained a TBI in later life and a cognitively healthy age-matched control group in the rate of diagnoses of mild cognitive impairment and conversion to Alzheimer's disease. Nor did they find any moderating interaction between ApoE $_{\epsilon4}$ and cognitive functioning. However, the sample size was small and the follow-up period was limited to two years, suggesting the need for ongoing longitudinal study of large prospective samples of older adults following TBI.

In findings from a cohort study of 1,283 adults who had suffered TBI, Nemetz et al. (1999) highlight that the risk exerted by TBI may not be in terms of absolute frequency of AD but in terms of earlier onset of AD (median 10 years from TBI as opposed to 18 years for population-based age specific incidence rates). In confirmation, McMurtray et al. (2006) reported that in a sample of 278 patients with younger onset dementia (age < 65 years), history of TBI was significantly more frequent that in late onset dementia. This raises another issue that the proportion of AD in younger onset dementia is only about 30%, and frontotemporal dementia is more prevalent than in late onset dementia. In this respect, Jawaid, Rademakers, Kass, Kalkonde and Schulz (2009) comment that TBI remains the only established environmental risk factor of frontotemporal dementia and also that frontotemporal lobar degeneration associated with loss of function of the progranulin gene is the most common pathological subtype. Jawaid et al. (2009) propose that TBI can moderate progranulin processing and expression which may be one factor in its association as a causative agent in this condition; although, Jawaid et al. also caution that the role of TBI in the pathogenesis of frontotemporal dementia is likely to be multifactorial with complex pathways of increasing risk.

In a review of TBI as a risk factor for Alzheimer's disease, Lye and Shores (2000) discuss additional theoretical postulates of how TBI may lead to dementia. Specifically, they discuss a theory developed by Satz (1993), who suggests a potentially crucial mediating factor of "brain reserve capacity" in neural circuitry which will differ between individuals, thus placing some people at a higher vulnerability than others. This theory suggests that there is individual difference between people in regards to neural circuitry capacity and the threshold level to withstand neurological insult without clinical symptoms. According to Lye and Shores, Satz (1993) suggests that those with lower brain reserve capacity have a lower threshold and are thus more vulnerable to clinical manifestations of neurological impairment. Specifically, when a person incurs a TBI, their brain capacity reserve is lowered and thus they become more vulnerable to degenerative disease processes. In contrast, those individuals who have a higher brain reserve capacity can incur neuronal loss (such as a TBI) and still maintain enough brain reserve capacity to withstand further neuropathological changes associated with aging or neurodegenerative processes, such as Alzheimer's disease.

Nevertheless, these theoretical explanations remain to be comprehensively tested through prospective longitudinal studies; which, if we accept that TBI provides a probable risk factor for emergent dementia, will allow us to reliably predict which individuals with TBI are more likely to develop dementia.

What We Need to Know about TBI in Older Adults: Needs and Directions for Future Research

Our societies are aging worldwide and TBI in older adults is a rapidly growing health concern as a reflection that older age is a strong risk factor for both falls and road traffic accidents (Binder, 2002; Harvey & Close, 2012). Nevertheless, older age TBI remains a poorly charted issue in health services and there is an urgency to develop appropriate and useful measures of outcome as a basis for strategic approaches to intervention.

As described in this chapter, there is a significant gap in knowledge about post-TBI outcome for older adults and the research that does exist has primarily focused on mortality as the primary outcome index. If the injury is severe, outcome following TBI in older age is generally reported as poor with high rates of mortality and significant disability (for example, Hukkelhoven et al., 2003; McIntyre et al., 2013; Utomo et al., 2009; Ventura et al., 2010). Although this provides important information for acute-based care it does not address the more long-term needs following mild-moderate injury, whether in relation to rehabilitation or managed care. This is relevant as emerging research is suggesting that when the injury is mild and uncomplicated the potential for recovery from TBI in older age can be as positive as for a younger sample (Goldstein et al., 2001; Mosenthal et al., 2004). Nevertheless, due to pre-existing age-related cerebral changes the risk of secondary cerebral complications (including subdural haematomas) is greater following TBI in older age and the specific outcome of this group of patients with complicated mild TBI has yet to be investigated. This is important as the primary mechanism of injury in older age is an incident of a fall which may also contribute to a greater risk of secondary cerebral complications. More broadly, the differential outcome of fall-related injury versus road traffic related injury requires further attention in an older age sample.

Methodological issues that have been identified in earlier research (Goleburn & Golden, 2001) continue to be problematic as many studies have small sample sizes, use variable follow-up assessment intervals, and vary in the age at which patients are to be considered "older." While most studies use healthy age-matched groups to control for the effect of normal aging on performance, very few studies use an additional cognitively normal trauma group to control for the confounding effects of trauma per se on functioning. This is an important consideration in an older population that often will have suffered multisystem trauma, and the psychological and physiological effects of this trauma need to be separated from the specific effects of TBI (Mosenthal et al., 2004).

Outcome needs to be defined differently for older adults. Measurement of cognitive outcome is liable to error as clinicians struggle with neuropsychological tests that have not been designed for patients over the age of 65 years, who are often presenting with additional sensory impairments or increased fatigue levels. In addition, many cognitive tests have inadequate norms for patients in their 70s, 80s and 90s +, thereby imposing constraints on the viability and accuracy of extended neuropsychological assessment. Common approaches to measurement of functional outcome in younger samples have included assessing academic achievement or rates of return to employment, but these outcomes are not as relevant to older people. An alternative approach for older people can be to focus on competence in everyday skills. For example, many everyday activities rely on prospective memory, defined as the ability to perform an intended action sometime in the future without an explicit request to remember (e.g., remembering to take medication, going to the post office during a shopping trip, etc.); the importance of prospective memory is that it has been found to be sensitive to TBI deficits in younger samples (Fleming, Riley, Gill, Gullo, Strong, & Shum, 2008; Shum, Levin, & Chan, 2011) and also linked to maintenance of an independent lifestyle (Shum, Fleming, & Neulinger, 2002). Consequently, assessment of prospective memory is an example of a useful approach to measurement of everyday cognitive competence following TBI in older age, potentially providing a more valid estimate of cognition in the real world than performance on single domain, traditional neuropsychological tests.

A major feature emerging out of analysis of TBI in older adulthood is that prevention of injury for this population demographic requires a different focus to that required for younger samples. In younger ages, public health programs have appropriately focused on prevention of injury from road traffic accidents (wearing of seat belts and helmets, for example). In older people, the focus needs to shift to the implementation of fall prevention strategies, thereby significantly reducing the health care costs associated with injury in older age (Dellinger & Stevens, 2006; Thomas et al., 2008).

To answer the question posed by this chapter—does age matter?—yes; we would argue that TBI in older age results from different mechanisms of injury, and is contextualized with different additional risk factors and co-morbidities, and thereby, demands different approaches to management, intervention, and assessment of outcome. All of these areas of research need significant research effort in the coming decade as our communities continue to age.

References

Aharon-Peretz, J., Kilot, D., Amyel-Zvi, E., Tomer, R., Rakier, A., & Feinsod, M. (1997). Neurobehavioural consequences of closed head injury in the elderly. *Brain Injury, 11*, 871–875.

Binder, S. (2002). Injuries among older adults: the challenge of optimizing safety and minimizing unintended consequences. *Injury Prevention, 8*, 2–4.

Bradley, C., & Harrison, J. (2007). *Hospitalisations due to falls by older people, Australia 2003-04*. Canberra: Australian Institute of Health and Welfare.

Bradley C. (2013). *Hospitalisations due to falls by older people, Australia 2009–10*. Injury research and statistics series no. 70. Cat. no. INJCAT 146; Canberra: AIHW.

Bramlett, H. M., & Dietrich, W. D. (2001). Neuropathological protection after traumatic brain injury in intact female rats versus males or ovariectomized females. *Journal of Neurotrauma, 18*, 891–900.

Camilloni, L., Frachi, S., Giorgi Rossi, P., Chini, F., & Borgi, F. (2008). Mortality in elderly injured patients: the role of comorbidities. *International Journal of Injury Control and Safety Promotion, 15*, 25–31.

Carroll, L. J., Cassidy, J. D., Holm, L., Kraus, J., Coronado, V. G. (2004). Methodological issues and research recommendations for mild traumatic brain injury: The WHO collaborating centre task force on mild traumatic brain injury. *Journal of Rehabilitation Medicine, 43,* 113–125.

Cifu, D. X., Kreutzer, J. S., Marwitz, J. H., Rosenthal, M., Englander, J., & High, W. (1996). Functional outcomes of older adults with traumatic brain injury: A prospective multicentre analysis. *Archives of Physical Medicine and Rehabiliation, 77,* 883–888.

Coronado, V. G., Thomas, K. E., Sattin, R. W., & Johnson, R. L. (2005). The CDC traumatic brain injury surveillance system: Characteristics of persons aged 65 years and older hospitalized with a TBI. *Journal of Head Trauma Rehabilitation, 20,* 215–228.

Cumming, R. G., Salkeld, G., Thomas, M., & Szonyi, G. (2000). Prospective study of the impact of fear of falling on activities of daily living, SF-36 scores, and nursing home admission. *The Journals of Gerontology, 55,* 299–305.

Dellinger, A. M., & Stevens, J. A. (2006). The injury problem among older adults: Mortality, morbidity and costs. *Journal of Safety Research, 37,* 519–522.

Dikmen, S. S., Machamer, J. E., Powell, J. M., & Tempkin, N. R. (2003). Outcome 3 to 5 years after moderate to severe traumatic brain injury. *Archives of Physical Medicine and Rehabilitation, 84,* 1449–1457.

Faul, M., Xu, L., Wald, M. M., & Coronado, V. G. (2010). *Traumatic brain injury in the United States: Emergency department visits, hospitalizations and deaths 2002-2006.* Atlanta: Centers for Disease Control and Prevention.

First, M. B., Spitzer, R. L., Gibbon, M., & Williams, J. (1996). *Structured Clinical Interview for DSM-IV Axis I disorders—Patient Edition (SCID-I/P, Version 2.0).* New York: Biometrics Research Department, New York State Psychiatric Institute.

Fleming, J., Riley, L., Gill, H., Gullo, M. J., Strong, J., & Shum, D. (2008). Predictors of prospective memory in adults with traumatic brain injury. *Journal of the International Neuropsychological Society, 14,* 823–831.

Fleminger, S., Oliver, D. L., Lovestone, S., Rabe-Hesketh, S., & Giora, A. (2003). Head Injury as a risk factor for Alzheimer's disease: the evidence 10 years on; a partial replication. *Journal of Neurology, Neurosurgery and Psychiatry, 4,* 857–862.

Frankel, J. E., Marwitz, J. H., Cifu, D. X., Kreutzer, J. S., Englander, J., & Rosenthal, M. (2004). A follow up study of older adults with traumatic brain injury: Taking into account decreasing length of stay. *Archives of Physical Medicine and Rehabilitation, 87,* 57–62.

Franko, J., Kish, K. J., O'Connell, B. G., Subramanian, S., & Yuschak, J. V. (2006). Advanced age and preinjury Warfarin anticoagulation increase the risk of mortality after head trauma. *The Journal of Trauma, Injury, Infection and Critical Care, 61,* 107–110.

Frencham, K. A. R., Fox, A. M., & Murray, M. T. (2005). Neuropsychological Studies of Mild Traumatic Brain Injury: A Meta-Analytic Review of Research since 1995. *Journal of Clinical and Experimental Neuropsychology, 27,* 334–351.

Gan, P. K., Lim, J. H. G., & Ng, I. H. B. (2004). Outcome of moderate and severe traumatic brain injury amongst the elderly in Singapore. *Annals Academy of Medicine, 33,* 63–67.

Gerber, L. M., Ni, Q., Härtl, R., & Ghajar, J. (2009). Impact of falls on early mortality from severe traumatic brain injury. *Journal of Trauma Management and Outcomes, 3,* 9.

Goldstein, F. C., Levin, H. S., Goldman, W. P., Clark, A. N., & Altonen, T. K. (2001). Cognitive and neurobehavioural functioning after mild versus moderate traumatic brain injury in older adults. *Journal of International Neuropsychological Society, 7,* 373–383.

Goleburn, C. R., & Golden, C. J. (2001). Traumatic brain injury outcome in older adults: A critical review of the literature. *Journal of Clinical Geropsychology, 7,* 161–187.

Grady, C. (2012). The cognitive neuroscience of ageing. *Nature Reviews Neuroscience, 13,* 491–505.

Harvey, L. A., & Close, J. C. T. (2012). Traumatic brain injury in older adults: characteristics, causes and consequences. *Injury, 43,* 1821–1826.

Helps, Y., Henley, G., & Harrison, J. (2008). *Hospital Separations due to Traumatic Brain Injury, Australia 2004-05.* Canberra: Australian Institute of Health and Welfare.

Hukkelhoven, C. W. P. M., Steyerberg, E. W., Rampen, A. J. J., Farace, E., Habbema, J. D. F., Marshall, L. F., Murray, G. D., & Maas, A. I. R. (2003). Patient age and outcome following severe traumatic brain injury: an analysis of 5600 patients. *Journal of Neurosurgery, 99,* 666–673.

Iverson, G. (2006). Complicated vs. uncomplicated mild traumatic brain injury: Acute neuropsychological outcome. *Brain Injury, 20,* 1335–1344.

Jawaid, A., Rademakers, R., Kass, J. S., Kalkonde, Y., & Schulz, P. E. (2009). Traumatic brain injury may increase the risk for Frontotemporal dementia through reduced Progranulin. *Neurodegenerative Diseases, 6,* 219–220.

Jellinger, K. A., Paulus, W., Wrocklage, C., & Litvan, I. (2001). Effects of closed head injury and genetic factors on the development of Alzheimer's disease. *European Journal of Neurology, 8,* 707–710.

Jorge, R. E., Robinson, R. G., Moser, D., Tateno, A., Crespo-Facorro, B., & Arndt, S. (2004). Major depression following traumatic brain injury. *Archives of General Psychiatry, 61*, 42–50.

Kinsella, G. (2010). Everyday memory for everyday tasks: Prospective memory as an outcome measure following TBI in older adults. *Brain Impairment, 11*, 37–41.

Kraus, J. F., & Chu, L. D. (2005). Epidemiology. In: J. M. Silver, T. W. McAllister, S. C. Yudofsky (Ed.),*Textbook of Traumatic Brain Injury.* Washington DC: American Psychiatric Publishing, Inc.

Levin, H. S., Brown, S. A., Song, J. X., McCauley, S. R., Boake, C., Contant, C. F., et al. (2001). Depression and posttraumatic stress disorder at three months after mild to moderate traumatic brain injury. *Journal of Clinical and Experimental Neuropsychology, 23*, 754–769.

Levin, H. S., McCauley, S. R., Josic, C. P., Boake, C., Brown, S. A., Goodman, H. S., et al. (2005). Predicting depression following mild traumatic brain injury. *Archives of General Psychiatry, 62*, 523–528.

Lye, T. C., & Shores, A. E. (2000). Traumatic brain injury as a risk factor for Alzheimer's disease: A review. *Neuropsychological Review, 10*, 115–129.

Madden, D. J., Bennett, I. J., & Song, A. W. (2009). Cerebral white matter integrity and cognitive aging: Contributions from diffusion tensor imaging. *Neuropsychological Review, 19*, 415–435.

McCrae, M. A. (2008). *Mild Traumatic Brain Injury and Postconcussion Syndrome.* New York:Oxford University Press.

McIntryre, A., Mehta, S., Aubut, J., Dijkers, M., & Teasell, R. W. (2013). Mortality among older adults after a traumatic brain injury: A meta-analysis. *Brain Injury, 27*, 31–40.

McMurtray, A., Clark, D. G., Christine, D., & Mendez, M. (2006). Early-onset dementia: frequency and causes compared to Late-onset dementia. *Dementia and Geriatric Cognitive Disorders, 21*, 59–64.

Millar, K., Nicoll, J. R., Thornhill, S., Murray, G. D., & Teasdale, G. M. (2003). Long term neuropsychological outcome after head injury: relation to APOE genotype. *Journal of Neurology, Neurosurgery and Psychiatry, 74*, 1047–1052.

MRC CRASH Trial Collaborators (2008). Predicting outcome after traumatic brain injury: practical prognostic models based on large cohort of international patients. *British Medical Journal, 336*, 425.

Mortimer, J. A., van Duijn, C. M., Chandra, V., Fratiglioni, L., Graves, A. B., Heyman, A., et al. (1991). Head trauma as a risk factor for Alzheimer's disease: A collaborative re-analysis of case-control studies. *International Journal of Epidemiology, 20*, 28–35.

Mosenthal, A. C., Lavery, R. F., Addis, M., Kaul, S., Ross, S., Marburger, R., et al. (2002). Isolated traumatic brain injury: Age is an independent predictor of mortality and early outcome. *The Journal of Trauma, Injury, Infection and Critical Care, 52*, 907–911.

Mosenthal, A. C., Livingston, D. H., Lavery, R. F., Knudson, M., Lee, S., Morabito, D., et al. (2004). The effect of age on functional outcome in mild traumatic brain injury: 6-month report of a prospective multicentre trial. *The Journal of Trauma, Injury, Infection and Critical Care, 56*, 1042–1048.

Murphy, J., & Isaacs, B. (1982). The post fall syndrome. A study of 36 elderly patients. *Gerontology, 28*, 265–270.

Nemetz, P. N., Leibsen, C., Naessens, J. M., Beard, M., Kokmen, E., Annegers, J. F., et al. (1999). Traumatic brain injury and time to onset of Alzheimer disease: a population based study. *American Journal of Epidemiology, 149*, 32–40.

O'Connor, P. (2002). *Hospitalisation due to traumatic brain injury (TBI), Australia 1997- 98. Injury Research and Statistics Series.* Adelaide: Australian Institute of Health and Welfare.

Petersen, R. C. (2004). Mild cognitive impairment as a diagnostic entity. *Journal of Internal Medicine, 256*, 183–194.

Plassman, B. L., Havlik, R. J., Steffens, D. C., Helms, M. J., Newman, T. N., Drosdick, D., et al.(2000). Documented head injury in early adulthood and risk of Alzheimer's disease and other dementias. *Neurology, 55*, 1158–66.

Pike, C. J., Carroll, J. C., Rosario, E. R., & Barron, A. M. (2009). Protective actions of sex steroid hormones in Alzheimer's disease. *Frontiers Neuroendocrinology, 30*, 239–258.

Ponsford, J., Draper, K. & Schönberger, M. (2008). Functional outcome 10 years after traumatic brain injury: Its relationship with demographic, injury severity, cognitive and emotional status. *Journal of the International Neuropsychological Society, 14*, 233–242.

Rao, V., Bertrand, M., Rosenberg, P., Makley, M., Schretlen, D. J., Brandt, J., et al. (2010). Predictors of new-onset depression after mild traumatic brain injury. *The Journal of Neuropsychiatry and Clinical Neurosciences, 22*, 100–104.

Rapoport, M., & Feinstein, A. (2000). Outcome following traumatic brain injury in the elderly: a critical review. *Brain Injury, 14*, 749–761.

Rapoport, M., Herrmann, N., Shammi, P., Kiss, A., Phillips, A., & Feinstein A. (2006). Outcome after traumatic brain injury sustained in older adulthood: A one year longitudinal study. *The American Journal of Geriatric Psychiatry, 14*, 456–465.

Rapoport, M., McCullagh, S., Streiner, D., & Feinstein A. (2003). Age and major depression after mild traumatic brain injury. *The American Journal of Geriatric Psychiatry, 11*, 365–369.

Rapoport, M., Verhoeff, P. L. G., & van Reekum, R. (2004). Traumatic brain injury and dementia. *The Canadian Alzheimer Disease Review, September*, 4–8.

Rapoport, M., Wolf, U., Herrmann, N., Kiss, A., Shammi, P., Reis, M., et al. (2008). Traumatic brain injury, Apolipoprotein E-Є4, and cognition in older adults: A two year longitudinal study. *Journal of Neuropsychiatry and Clinical Neurosciences, 20*, 68–73.

Rathlev, N. K., Medzon, R., Lowery, D., Pollack, C., Bracken, M., Barest, G., et al. (2006). Intracranial pathology in elders with blunt head trauma. *Academic Emergency Medicine, 13*, 302–307.

Rothweiler, B., Tempkin, N. R., & Dikmen, S. S (1998). Aging effect on psychosocial outcome in traumatic brain injury. *Archives of Physical Medicine and Rehabilitation, 79*, 881–887.

Salthouse, T. A. (2010). Selective review of cognitive aging. *Journal of the International Neuropsychological Society, 16*, 754–760.

Satz., P. (1993). Brain reserve capacity on symptom onset after brain injury: A formulation and review of evidence for threshold theory. *Neuropsychology, 7*, 273–295

Seel, R. T., Kruetzer, J. S., Rosenthal, M., Hammond, F. M., Corrigan, J. D., & Black, K. (2003). Depression after traumatic brain injury: A national institute on disability and rehabilitation research model systems multicentre investigation. *Archives of Physical Medicine and Rehabilitation, 84*, 177–184.,

Senathi-Raja, D., Ponsford, J., & Schonberger, M. (2010). Impact of Age on Long-Term Cognitive Function After Traumatic Brain Injury. *Neuropsychology, 24*, 336–344.

Sherer, M., Sander, A. M., Nick, T. G., High, W. M., Malec, J. F., & Rosenthal, M. (2002). Early cognitive status and productivity outcome after traumatic brain injury: Findings from the TBI model systems. *Archives of Physical Medicine and Rehabilitation, 83*, 183–192.

Shum, D., Fleming, J., & Neulinger, K. (2002). Prospective memory and traumatic brain injury: A review. *Brain Impairment, 3*, 1–16.

Shum, D., Levin, H., & Chan, R. C. K. (2011). Prospective memory in patients with closed head injury: A review. *Neuropsychologia, 49*, 2156–2165.

Sigurdardottir, S., Andelic, N., Roe, C., Jerstad, T., & Schanke, A. K. (2009). Cognitive recovery and predictors of functional outcome 1 year after traumatic brain injury. *Journal of the International Neuropsychological Society, 15*, 740–750.

Stevens, J. A., Corso, P. S., Finkelstein, E. A., & Miller, T. R. (2006). The cost of fatal and non fatal falls among older adults. *Injury Prevention, 12*, 290–295.

Susman, M., DiRusso, S. M., Sulllivan, T., Risucci, D., Nealon, P., Cuff, S., et al. (2002). Traumatic brain injury in the elderly: Increased mortality and worse functional outcome at discharge despite lower injury severity. *The Journal of Trauma, Injury,Infection and Critical Care, 53*, 219–224.

Testa, J. A., Malec, J. F., Moessner, A. M., & Brown, A. W. (2005). Outcome After Traumatic Brain Injury: Effects of Aging on Recovery. *Archives of Physical Medicine and Rehabilitation, 86*, 1815–1823.

Thomas., K. E., Stevens, J. A., Sarmiento, K., & Wald, M. M. (2008). Fall related traumatic brain injury deaths and hospitalizations among older adults United States, 2005. *Journal of Safety Research, 39*, 269–272.

Thompson, H. J., McCormick, W. C., & Kagan, S. H. (2006). Traumatic brain injury in older adults: Epidemiology, outcomes and future implications. *Journal of the American Geriatric Society, 54*, 1590–1595.

Tinetti, M. E., Richman, D., & Powell, L. (1990). Fall efficacy as a measure of a fear of falling. *Journal of Gerontology, 45*, 239–243.

United Nations. (2012). *Ageing in the Twenty-First Century: A Celebration and a Challenge*. New York: United Nations Fund for Population Ageing (UNFPA).

Utomo, W. K., Gabbe, B. J., Simpson, P. M., & Cameron, P. A. (2009). Predictors of in hospital mortality and 6 month functional outcomes in older adults after moderate to severe traumatic brain injury. *Injury, International Journal for the Care of the Injured, 40*, 973–977.

Ventura, T., Harrison-Felix, C., Carlson, N., DiGuiseppi, C., Gabella, B., Brown, A., et al. (2010). Mortality after discharge from acute care hospitalization with traumatic brain injury: A population based study. *Archives of Physical Medicine and Rehabilitation, 91*, 20–29.

Whalley, L. J., Deary, I. J., Appleton, C. L., & Starr, J. M. (2004). Cognitive reserve and the neurobiology of cognitive aging. *Aging Research Reviews, 3*, 369–382.

17

Mild Traumatic Brain Injury

Sarah A. Raskin, David W. Lovejoy, Michael C. Stevens, Marta Zamroziewicz, and Howard J. Oakes

Introduction

The research and clinical literature addressing the topic of mild traumatic brain injury (mTBI) has grown exponentially over the past the decade. Areas related to diagnosis and classification of mTBI, identification and evaluation of sports concussion, neuroimaging of cellular/axonal damage and its functional correlates, postconcussion sympoms and conceptualizations of outcome in mTBI have all been represented in the literature, over the past decade. As a result, our understanding of this fairly common and often times complex diagnosis has grown significantly. With that said, the field of mTBI continues to be characterized by scholarly debate, especially with regard to the topic of unfavorable outcomes in mTBI. The research and conceptual literature related to mTBI can be daunting for the clinician struggling to understand and treat the n = 1 case.

What has become clearer is that mTBI is characterized by significant diversity. mTBI has come to be seen as a multifactorial condition that has eluded and extended beyond simple cause and effect explanations. Differences in how mTBI is diagnosed, differences in the histories and psychological makeups of those who have come to be injured, differences in the physics and injury characteristics of mTBIs, differences in how microstructural damage manifests from individual to individual, differences in symptom presentation, differences in how individuals cope with their injury, differences in resiliency to psychiatric distress after injury and differences in individual outcomes are all characteristic of the diagnosis. This chapter seeks to summarize and discuss some of the foundational information and newer developments related to mTBI, as they apply to classification, pathophysiology, trends in neuroimaging, conceptualization of outcome, recovery of functionality and basic clinical management of mTBI.

A Word about Terminology

With regard to mTBI terminology, it is important to recognize that in much of the research and clinical literature, the terms mTBI, concussion and mild/minor head injury have been used synonymously. The interested reader will note that within this chapter, efforts are made to separate the terms mTBI and concussion whenever possible, although some degree of overlap cannot be avoided. The term concussion is often used in the literature to denote the mildest end of the severity continuum for mTBI and it is often used to describe injuries sustained on the sports field. In this context, sports concussions have been associated with a growing literature that is quite specific to this form of injury, in terms of injury dynamics, diagnostic criteria, populations studied, research methodologies employed to study these populations, pathophysiology and functional outcomes. Some of the overlap and conceptual confusion may also relate to the intermingling of the often comorbid diagnosis of postconcussion syndrome (PCS), for both mTBI and concussion populations. Confusion may also result from attempts in the literature to separate these terms and populations, without clear definitional criteria as to where concussion begins and where it ends, within the larger spectrum of mTBI. There have been emerging efforts within the literature to distinguish between these two terms and cautions not to be overly liberal in generalizing research findings from one population to the other. In this chapter, it is acknowledged that the conceptual separation of the terms concussion and mTBI is imperfect at present, but nonetheless important. The terms "mild head injury" and "minor head injury" are not used in this chapter as they may also be used to describe a head injury in the absence of brain/cerebral insult.

The Importance of Research Methodology & Sampling

Investigators have made meaningful comments over the years on the importance of appropriate research designs and statistical analyses in studying aspects of mTBI (Bigler, 2008; Iverson, 2005; Larabee, 2012; McCrae, 2008; Pertab, Ruff, 2009; Satz, Alfano, Light, Morgenstern, Zaucha, Arsanow & Newton, 1999). Research designs have essentially served to shape the current corpus of knowledge related to mTBI. Some of the broader research themes that resurface both in the literature and in this chapter include:

- Problems with differing definitions of mTBI
- Problems with differing definitions of postconcussive syndrome and posttraumatic concussive disorder
- The importance of prospective and longitudinal research designs
- The importance of examining consecutive referrals
- The importance of control groups including medical control groups that have not sustained a brain injury

- The importance of identifying and studying symptomatic versus asymptomatic subgroups within the larger mTBI population
- The importance of examining how various factors might moderate clinical outcome in mTBI populations
- Cautions related to collapsing research across sports concussion and mTBI populations

With regard to the final point above, there are emerging opinions that sports concussions are both qualitatively and quantitatively different in terms of injury dynamics from mTBIs sustained as a result of other mechanisms of injury such as motor vehicle accidents. It should also be noted that sports concussion populations and the mTBI populations typically seen through a hospital ED or a trauma department differ substantially in terms of demographics, premorbid histories and active comorbidities. 17-1 presents patient data from 230 consecutive patients who met diagnostic criteria (ACRM, 1993) for mTBI admitted to the Trauma Service at Hartford Hospital (a Level I trauma facility). This sample excludes children as this population is seen through the trauma service at an affiliated children's medical center. The vast majority of these patients sustained injuries as occupants in automobile accidents (66%), followed by motorcycle accidents (15%), being struck by automobiles (8%), sustaining falls (7%) and being assaulted/other (4%).

The mTBI population described in Table 17-1 differs significantly from research samples described in the sports concussion literature. In comparison to sports concussion samples, mTBI samples collected from hospital populations (excluding children's hospitals) are typically characterized by older age ranges, differing mechanisms of injury,

Table 17-1. mTBI Patient Characteristics at Hartford Hospital

Male:	71%	Positive Cranial CT:	17%
Caucasian:	76%	Reported Substance Abuse Hx	36%
African American:	12%	Reported Psychiatric Hx	27%
Hispanic:	10%	(depression/Anxiety)	
Other:	2%	Comorbid Ortho Injury	45%
Average Age:	34 (18-83)	Reported Medical History	51%
Average Education:	12.5 (2-21)	(diabetes, HTN, cardiac, seizure,	
Modal GCS:	14 (13-15)	pulmonary, etc.)	
Average PTA:	56 mins		
Average LOC	5.7 mins		

greater possibilities for comorbid orthopedic or other organ injuries and more complex past medical, psychiatric and substance use histories. These differences are indicative of a more heterogeneous and vulnerable population, in relation to emotional/psychiatric, physical and central nervous system resiliencies. Investigators have long cautioned about making generalizations from the sports concussion literature to the patient who has suffered a mTBI, acknowledging that sports concussion subjects are younger, healthier, and more likely to minimize complaints post injury (Bailey, 2006, 2009; Echemedia, 2006; Ruff, 2009). The research methodology used to study sports concussion, in addition to having the advantage of a "purer population" also often has the advantage of pre-injury baseline testing to clearly identify declines from premorbid cognitive abilities and serial cognitive testing to track cognitive recovery (e.g., McCrea, 2008).

As discussed later in this chapter, there is a myriad of confounding factors when attempting to understand outcome (whether it is neuropathologic outcome, symptom outcome, vocational outcome, etc.) in mTBI and concussion populations. There are also basic differences in research designs that have been employed for concussion populations vs. mTBI populations. As noted earlier, sports concussion research has had the benefit of examining concussion-related injuries in highly controlled environments, so much so that actual concussions are sometimes available for video review. This sports concussion research model was pioneered in the 1980s at the University of Virginia and became known as the Sports as a Laboratory Assessment Model (SLAM) (Barth, Freeman, Broshek & Varney, 2001). McCrea (2008) notes that the advantages of the sports concussion research model include among other advantages: being able to prospectively identify large samples of athletes at risk for concussion; having a sample that is "clean" in terms of other confounds such as legal involvement, poor motivation, complicated histories; the ability to easily access a non-head-injured control sample; the ability to obtain preinjury baseline testing for the sample; the ability to witness and document injury dynamics and injury severity variables; the ability to evaluate athletes within minutes of an injury; and the ability to

perform serial evaluations to track recoveries. Research studies utilizing the advantages of this assessment model have helped us to understand injury characteristics, symptom presentation and outcome in the purest populations (i.e., sports concussion populations).

As described in Table 17-1, medically based and/or treated mTBI populations are far more heterogeneous and are characterized by multiple comorbidities and injury-related variables that create more complex research challenges. As will be discussed later in this chapter, there are a number of moderator variables beyond the injury itself that have been shown to impact the expression and long-term course of symptoms following a mTBI. These variables include depression, learning disabilities, litigation status, orthopedic injuries, other CNS insults, stress, poor motivation, somatization, psychological expectations about symptom presentation, etc. For some research questions it is important to control for potential moderator variables. For instance, if the question relates to how mTBI impacts white matter integrity then it will be important to control for variables that may also present with abnormalities in white matter integrity such as ADHD, other CNS insults, depression, etc. (Iverson, Hakulinen, Waljas, Dastidar, Lange, et al., 2012). When examining behavioral or other symptom outcomes in mTBI, it becomes difficult to identify and control for all possible moderator variables in a single research study. It is also sometimes advantageous to retain moderator variables to examine how they interact with an injury over time. For instance Norrie, Heitger, Leathem, Anderson, Jones and Flett (2010) examined long-term symptoms of pathological fatigue following mTBI. The authors found that depression was an important moderator for some individuals, in association with long-term complaints of fatigue post mTBI.

With regard to sampling in the mTBI research literature, the most typical paradigms include studying consecutive acute admissions or referrals to hospitals, studying consecutive referrals to post-acute clinics or studying samples of symptomatic patients from clinics or other referral sources. Satz et al. (1999) proposed a research methodology for mTBI that would help to clarify the drivers of symptom presentation. In that paper, the authors described the importance of using control samples for mTBI investigations. Designs that yoke a non-brain injured injury control sample (e.g., an orthopedic injury group) as well as a healthy uninjured control sample to the mTBI group are emphasized. This method was designed to help clarify the degree to which reported symptoms are unique to mTBI or whether symptom reports post-mTBI represent more of a generalized injury effect. mTBI research studies that have incorporated medical non-brain injured control groups are discussed in later sections of this chapter, with regard to outcomes in mTBI.

It is worth spending a moment to discuss some of the general strengths and weaknesses associated with the two primary research designs encountered in relation to mTBI populations. The research in relation to mTBI samples has largely consisted of either cross-sectional research or longitudinal research designs. Longitudinal designs typically follow mTBI patients from the point of injury forward. These designs have the advantage of characterizing the natural history of mTBI symptom presentations, as they mitigate selection bias by prospective recruitment of all comers to an injury who meet the eligibility criteria for the study. Consecutive referrals are emphasized in many of the longitudinal research studies to ensure the representativeness of a population. In this fashion, unbiased estimates of symptom presentation and recovery curves can be generated for time intervals of interest. For instance, a research design may focus on the presence of postconcussive complaints over a one-year time frame. Incidence of persistent postconcussive complaints can be tabulated for multiple time points. Depending upon the variables identified during the study (e.g., psychiatric history, injury severity variables, emergence of depression, etc.) analyses can also help to gain an understanding of the factors that serve to predict persistent complaints or a favorable recovery. As described, longitudinal designs have numerous strengths; however, such studies have been subjected to criticism for their relative inability to identify and characterize important subgroups. Concerns have also been raised about longitudinal studies that have high attrition rates or fail to capture a representative population from the study's initiation.

Cross-sectional studies are the other primary design encountered in relation to mTBI research. These designs often focus on a subgroup of interest, such as a symptomatic population. These designs have the advantage of being able to study and characterize aspects of symptomatic subgroups. However, these studies are unable to generate an accurate picture of how symptoms and variables of interest manifest over time. They are sometimes criticized for their over-estimation of symptom base rates and a reliance on more biased samples.

Although both of the research designs described above (especially with the inclusion of multiple control groups for comparison) have offered useful information on mTBI populations in relation to natural history of symptom presentations and characterization of relevant subgroups, investigators have suggested that large scale prospective studies that are designed to tease apart and analyze subgroups of interest (e.g., those with poor outcomes from those with from those with good outcomes) may also be of great benefit to the field (Pertab et al., 2009).

Epidemiology and Incidence of mTBI

From an epidemiologic standpoint, mTBIs are a relatively common event, accounting for approximately eighty-five percent of all brain injuries (Centers for Disease Control and Prevention, 2007), with a reported incidence in the United States that exceeds one million injuries per year (Bazarian, McClung, Shah, Cheng, Flesher & Krauss, J., 2005; National Center for Injury Prevention and Control, 2003). There have been long-standing concerns that the true incidence of mTBI is much higher, as many individuals who have suffered an mTBI are not hospitalized or do not present to a hospital emergency department for evaluation (Bazarian et al., 2005; Ryu, Feinstein, Colantonio, Streiner, & Dawson, 2009). It is estimated that approximately 70% of all TBI cases seen through the emergency department represent mTBI cases (Udekwu et al., 2004). Powell, Ferrarro, Dikmen, Temkin, and Bell (2008) raised concerns about the accurate identification of mTBI in medical settings, reporting high false negative rates for accurate mTBI diagnoses in the emergency department

(ED). Investigators have also noted that difficulties with accurately determining the incidence rates for mTBI may relate to the disparities in multiple definitional criteria and methodological rigor employed across studies (Caroll, Cassidy, Holm, Kraus & Coronado, 2004). The concerns that surround the incidence of mTBI and its associated economic and societal impact in the United States were amplified in a 2003 Centers for Disease Control and Prevention (CDC) report to Congress that characterized mTBI as a "silent epidemic." (National Center for Injury Prevention and Control, 2003).

Definitional & Diagnostic Criteria for mTBI

At present, there is no single set of generally endorsed or utilized diagnostic criteria for mTBI. This represents one of the most significant challenges in both mTBI research and clinical work. Within the overall field of Traumatic Brain Injury (TBI), multiple classification systems have been developed, over the years, in attempts to classify TBI injury severity, from mild through severe (Stein, 1996). Most, if not all, classification systems were developed with a focus on injury-severity variables that are present at the time of injury, rather than upon the quality of functional outcome from the injury. Such acute injury characteristics might include Glasgow Coma Scale Score (GCS), loss of consciousness (LOC), posttraumatic amnesia (PTA), as well as indicators of the presence of an alteration in mental status when basic consciousness has not been altered. Onset of postconcussion symptoms (e.g., headache, dizziness) immediately or shortly after injury may also support the diagnosis of mTBI. Mittenberg and Strausman (2000) note that the differences in classification systems used to define mTBI have created conceptual challenges in the research literature when attempting to compare and generalize results across studies.

In this section, multiple definitional and diagnostic criteria are referenced for the identification of mTBI. The interested reader will observe that mTBI can be conceptualized as falling along a spectrum of severity, from mild sports-related concussions that may be identified by the emergence of a single postconcussive symptom, through more significant mTBIs that may involve more lengthy losses of consciousness, posttraumatic amnesia, and focal neurologic signs. Research involving the pathophysiology of mTBI and outcomes for mTBI also support the concept of a continuum of severity within the definitional paramaters of mTBI. These topics will be covered in more detail in later sections of this chapter.

Clinical practitioners and researchers associated with medical centers that treat the spectrum of TBI patients are likely more familiar with three grading systems applicable to mTBI. These include: 1) the use of GCS score alone or in combination with other injury severity variables (Teasdale & Jennett, 1974; Jennett & Teasdale, 1981; Stein, 1996); 2) the criteria put forth by the American Congress of Rehabilitation Medicine (ACRM) Mild Traumatic Brain Injury Committee of the Head Injury Interdisciplinary Special Interest Group (ACRM, 1993) and 3) the criteria put forth by the World Health Organization (Carroll et al., 2004).

The Glasgow Coma Scale (GCS), Loss of Consciousness & Posttraumatic Amnesia as Indicators of Injury Severity

The GCS is one of the most familiar tools in the acute care medical setting for grading the severity of a TBI. The GCS was developed to evaluate level of consciousness for patients who have suffered a TBI (Teasdale & Jennett, 1974) and the GCS yields total scores from 3 to 15, with lower scores indicating greater impairment of consciousness. The three components include eye opening (maximum of 4 points), motor response (maximum of 6 points), and verbal response (maximum of 5 points). Within the GCS classification system, scores of 13-15 represent a "Mild" injury, scores of 9-12 represent a "Moderate" injury and scores from 3-8 represent a "Severe" injury. In acute care medical centers, GCS scores are often coded on multiple occasions, beginning with initial emergency medical contact at the scene of an injury, through ED evaluation and intensive care unit (ICU) or trauma floor admission.

When used in isolation, the GCS remains a fairly blunt instrument for evaluation of mTBI. Its use is clearly more applicable for neurologic insults that cause serious alterations in consciousness. McCrea (2008) noted that the majority of patients discharged from EDs have a GCS score of 15, indicating a ceiling effect for this measure when it is applied to a more mild spectrum of injuries. Moreover, McCrea (2008) observed that the GCS is not sensitive to the defining characteristics or symptoms of mTBI. For many symptomatic patients, these defining characteristics include symptoms such as headaches, dizziness, nausea, phonophobia, photophobia, fatigue, difficulties with learning and memory, information processing speed, attention and concentration. As a result, it would be an error to infer that a normal GCS score reflects a normal TBI-related neurologic status. In fact, Teasdale and Jennett did not advocate that the GCS score alone was sufficient for diagnosis of TBI or to determine acute or chronic outcome post TBI.

Loss of Consciousness & Posttraumatic Amnesia in Combination with GCS

A recommended approach to classification of injury severity involves integration of multiple acute injury characteristics. Stein (1996) proposed a classification system for grading TBI severity that combined GCS scores with duration of LOC and PTA. In this classification system, mTBI is defined in accordance with acute injury severity variables as follows: 1) a GCS score between 13 and 15; 2) less than 20 minutes of LOC and 3) less than 24 hours of PTA. In this classification schema, a GCS score < 13, a LOC of > 20 minutes or PTA > 24 hours moves a patient into a classification for moderate TBI. This approach should also include observation over time as it is possible for delayed deterioration, especially in cases that involve positive neuroimaging. Classification schemas, such as this, that employ multiple injury severity variables formed the foundation for newer mTBI diagnostic classification systems.

ACRM, WHO & CDC Definitions and Diagnostic Criteria for mTBI

The Mild Traumatic Brain Injury Committee of the Head Injury Interdisciplinary Special Interest Group of the American Congress of Rehabilitation Medicine (ACRM, 1993) the World Health Organization (Carroll et al.,

2004) and the Center for Disease Control and Injury Prevention (National Center for Disease Control and Injury Prevention, 2003) have each put forth definitions of mTBI, as well as sets of diagnostic criteria for mTBI. Together, these definitions are probably the most commonly cited mTBI criteria in both research and clinical practice, involving medical/trauma populations. This is in contrast to the research and clinical literature that emphasizes sports concussion (definitional criteria related to this area will be addressed in the following section). The mTBI definitions and criteria offered by the ACRM, WHO and CDC overlap a great deal, but also have differences. They are presented together for purposes of comparison and are outlined in Tables 17-2, 17-3 and 17-4.

As noted earlier, these three sets of criteria share some degree of overlap. For instance, all three sets of criteria use some combination of acute injury severity variables to differentiate mTBI from moderate TBI to severe TBI (e.g., GCS score of 13-15, LOC < 30 minutes and PTA < 24 hours). It is important to note that all three sets of criteria are also inclusive of injuries that involve acceleration-deceleration forces acting on the brain, without evidence for a blow to the head (i.e., whiplash-type injuries). All three sets of criteria also allow for the presence of what is commonly termed a "complicated" mTBI. Complicated mTBIs are injuries that meet the

Table 17-2. ACRM criteria for mTBI

mTBI is a traumatically induced physiologic disruption of brain function, as manifested by at least one of the following:

1. Any period of loss of consciousness
2. Any loss of memory for events immediately before or after the injury
3. Any alteration in mental state at the time of the -injury (e.g., feeling dazed, disoriented, confused)
4. Focal neurological deficit(s) that may or may not be transient

But where the severity of the injury does not exceed the following:

Loss of consciousness (LOC) of 30 minutes
After 30 minutes an initial Glasgow Coma Scale (GCS) score of 13-15
Posttraumatic amnesia (PTA) not greater than 24 hours.

Table 17-3. WHO criteria for mTBI

mTBI is an acute brain injury resulting from mechanical energy to the head from external forces. Operational criteria for clinical identification include:

a. One or more of the following:
    i. Confusion or disorientation
    ii. Loss of consciousness for 30 minutes or less
    iii. Posttraumatic amnesia for less than 24 hours
    iv. Other transient neurological abnormalities such as focal signs, seizure, intracranial lesion not requiring surgery
b. Glasgow Coma Scale score of 13-15 after 30 minutes post injury or later on presentation for health care
c. These manifestations of mTBI must not be:
    i. Due to drugs alcohol or medication
    ii. Caused by other injuries or treatment for other injuries (e.g., systemic injuries, facial injuries, or intubation)
    iii. Caused by other problems (e.g., psychological trauma, language barrier, or coexisting medical conditions)
    iv. Caused by penetrating craniocerebral injury

Table 17-4. CDC Criteria for mTBI

mTBI is an occurrence of injury to the head resulting from blunt trauma or acceleration or deceleration forces with one or more of the following conditions attributable to the head injury during the surveillance period.

Any period of observed or self-reported transient confusion, disorientation or impaired consciousness

Any period of observed or self-reported dysfunction of memory (amnesia) around the time of the injury

Observed signs of other neurological or psychological dysfunction, such as:

Seizures acutely following head injury

Among infants and very young children: irritability, lethargy or vomiting following head injury

Symptoms among older children and adults such as headache, dizziness, irritability, fatigue, or poor concentration, when identified soon after injury, can be used to support the diagnosis of mTBI, but can not be used to make the diagnosis in the absence of loss of consciousness. Further research may provide additional guidance in this area.

Any period of observed or self-reported loss of consciousness lasting 30 minutes or less

More severe brain injuries were excluded from the definition of mTBI and include one or more of the following conditions attributable to the injury.

Loss of consciousness lasting longer than 30 minutes

Posttraumatic amnesia lasting longer than 24 hours

Penetrating craniocerebral injury

criteria for a mTBI, but are also accompanied by positive cerebral radiologic findings (e.g., traumatically induced brain contusions, hemorrhages, etc.). There is evidence to indicate that patients who have suffered a complicated mTBI have outcomes more similar to patients that have suffered a moderate TBI (Iverson, 2012). Other investigators have suggested that these "complicated" injuries should actually be classified as moderate TBIs (Williams, Levin & Eisenberg, 1990).

Finally, all three sets of criteria incorporate more subtle forms of an alteration in mental status as indicating the presence of a mTBI. For instance, all three sets of criteria allow for a diagnosis of mTBI, with evidence (sometimes self-reported) for having been disoriented or confused. The ACRM guidelines also include the term "dazed" as evidence for a subtle alteration in mental status at the time of injury. It is important to recognize that these sets of definitional criteria can result in a somewhat extreme range of injuries being diagnosed as mTBI. For instance, an individual who suffers a whiplash-type injury in a car accident and reported feeling dazed or disoriented at the scene of the accident, with no evidence of LOC, PTA and a GCS score of 15 in the emergency department would meet criteria for a mTBI.

Conversely, an individual who fell from a height of eight feet striking his head, with 20 minutes of observed LOC, 20 hours of PTA and bilateral frontal contusions observed on a cranial CT scan would also meet inclusion criteria for a mTBI. Simply put, there are likely gradations of severity within the parameters of the mTBI inclusion criteria described above. The concept of meaningful gradations of severity within the diagnostic parameters of mTBI has been supported empirically, within the acute recovery phase from an mTBI. For instance, McCrea (2008) has illustrated differences in the acute recovery from sports-related concussion for athletes that sustained LOC or PTA and a concussion with no LOC or PTA.

Definitional criteria were also offered in association with the Third International Conference

Table 17-5. ICCS Criteria for Concussion in Sports

A concussion is a complex pathophysiological process affecting the brain, induced by traumatic biochemical forces.

Common features that incorporate constructs that may be utilized in defining the nature of a concussive head injury include:

Concussion may be caused either by a direct blow to the head, face, or neck or a blow elsewhere on the body with an "impulsive" force transmitted to the head.

Concussion typically results in the rapid onset of short-lived impairment of neurologic function that resolves spontaneously.

Concussion may result in neuropathological changes, but the acute clinical symptoms largely reflect a functional disturbance rather than a structural injury.

Concussion results in a graded set of clinical symptoms that may or may not involve loss of consciousness. Resolution of the clinical and cognitive symptoms typically follows a sequential course. In a small percentage of cases, however, postconcussive symptoms may be prolonged.

No abnormality on standard structural neuroimaging studies is seen in concussion.

on Concussion in Sports (ICCS) (McCrory, Meeuwisse, et al., 2009; Table 17-5).

It is important to note that these definitional criteria were developed particularly for the care of athletes who have suffered sports-related concussion. For diagnosis, the ICCS document includes a range of postconcussive symptoms associated with the Sports Concussion Assessment Tool (SCAT2) that aid in establishing the presence of a concussion. These postconcussion symptoms fall in the domains of physical symptoms, cognitive symptoms, emotional symptoms and sleep symptoms (Halstead and Walter, 2010). Examples of these postconcussive complaints are as follows: 1) physical (e.g., headache, nausea, vomiting, dizziness, seizure, neck pain, sensitivity to light or sound, balance problems, blurred vision, fatigue, low energy, feeling stunned or dazed); 2) cognitive (e.g., feeling like "in a fog," difficulty concentrating, difficulty remembering, feeling slowed down, forgetful of recent events, confusion, repeating questions, answering slowly, amnesia); 3) emotional (e.g., irritability, not feeling "right," sadness, nervousness or anxiousness, being more emotional or feeling a pressure in the head") and 4) sleep-related (e.g., sleeping

more than usual, sleeping less than usual, having trouble falling asleep).

The criteria indicate that a concussion should be suspected in the presence of any one or more of the above symptoms, following some form of head injury. The document limits the definitional and diagnostic criteria to the "majority of (80%–90%) of concussions that resolve in a short (7 to 10-day) period, although the time frame may be longer in children and adolescents" (p. 757). Again, it is important to note that these criteria were developed for evaluation in a sports concussion setting. It is noted that the criteria were not meant for application and identification of mTBI in an ED or hospital setting, because the mechanism and dynamics of mTBI, outside of a sports concussion setting, may be different. Although the term concussion and mTBI are often used interchangeably, the ICCS document and associated criteria emphasize the need to distinguish concussion and mTBI as separate conditions and/or entities, with different mechanisms and dynamics of injury and potentially different outcomes. With regard to mechanism of injury, impacts that occur from motor vehicle accidents, falls and assaults, particularly when the head is not protected by a helmet, likely result in greater impact and/or kinetic forces acting on the body and/or head than in sports concussions (McCrory, Johnston, et al., 2005).

Efforts to perhaps characterize what would currently be seen as the mildest form of mTBI as a concussion and to separate the terms concussion and mTBI based upon the setting in which the injury occurs (sports vs. other) and the individual who suffers the neurologic insult (the athlete vs. other) may be a difficult endeavor. Complexities involve areas of overlap in diagnostic criteria for concussion and mTBI, the possibility that some sports-related injuries will occur in the absence of a helmet and may also involve greater impact force or injury (e.g., contusion or hemorrhage), as well as the current wide-spread use of the terms (concussion and mTBI) in an interchangeable fashion. On the other hand, some of the conceptual and empirical underpinnings behind the movement to separate "concussion" from "mTBI" are understandable and important to consider. Indeed, the collapsing of these conceptual conditions (i.e., concussion as described in the ICCS criteria and mTBI) do cause some degree of confusion, with regard to clinical presentation, outcome research, and understanding of pathophysiology. Understanding the many differences between sports concussion and hospital-based/other mTBIs can be important for how we understand the range of outcomes and consequences associated with these populations and injuries.

Postconcussion Syndrome (PCS)

PCS relates to a constellation of symptoms that can be experienced after a brain injury. These symptoms include cognitive complaints (e.g., attention and concentration problems, decreased information processing speed, decreased memory, feeling cognitively foggy, etc.), physical complaints (e.g., headaches, fatigue, sleep disturbance, phonophobia, photophobia, dizziness, vertigo, visual changes, nausea, tinnitus, etc.), and/ or emotional complaints (e.g., increased irritability, feelings of depression, feelings of anxiety, apathy, etc.).

Two sets of definitional criteria are commonly utilized in practice and within the research literature and include criteria from the WHO (ICD-10; World Health Organization, 1992) and the American Psychiatric Association (DSM-IV; American Psychiatric Association, 1994). These criteria are presented in tables 17-6 and 17-7.

There are important differences between these sets of criteria. These differences include the following:

- The ICD-10 criteria emphasize that a loss of consciousness should be present in association with a head injury, whereas DSM-IV indicates that a history of head trauma that causes significant cerebral concussion should be present.
- ICD-10 requires symptoms to be present for more than a month, whereas DSM-IV requires symptoms to be present for three months.
- The DSM-IV emphasizes the presence of cognitive impairments and requires quantitative evidence from neuropsychological testing or cognitive assessment of impairment, whereas ICD-10 does not require the presence of

Table 17-6. ICD-10 Criteria for Postconcussional Syndrome:

A. History of head trauma with loss of consciousness precedes symptom onset by a maximum of four weeks.
B. Symptoms in three or more of the following symptom categories:
- Headache, dizziness, malaise, fatigue, noise intolerance
- Irritability, depression, anxiety, emotional lability
- Subjective concentration, memory, or intellectual difficulties without neuropsychological evidence of marked impairment
- Insomnia
- Reduced alcohol tolerance
- Preoccupation with above symptoms and fear of brain damage with hypochondriacal concern and adoption of sick role

cognitive impairment or require quantitative evaluation strategies.
- The DSM-IV acknowledges that the symptom presentation may reflect an exacerbation of premorbid symptoms, whereas the ICD-10 is quiet on this matter.
- DSM-IV requires evidence that the symptoms result in impairments in occupational or social functioning, whereas ICD-10 does not require evidence of a negative functional impact.

The multiple differences between these two PCS definitions and entry criteria result in differences related to diagnostic sensitivity and specificity. These two sets of criteria do not mesh well with the various diagnostic criteria for mTBI and concussion presented in the previous section of this chapter or research focusing on symptom presentation in mTBI or concussion. For instance, the ICD-10 emphasis on a loss of consciousness as an entry criteria for PCS conflicts with current mTBI and concussion diagnostic and definitional statements that allow for inclusion, without a loss of consciousness. Indeed, the majority of sports concussions and mTBIs treated through medical centers lack evidence for a loss of consciousness (MrCrea, 2008). Also, the DSM-IV emphasis on objectively measured cognitive decline is at odds with the growing body of research indicating that postconcussive symptom presentations may include lasting symptoms that do not reflect

Table 17-7. DSM-IV Research Criteria for Postconcussional Disorder

A. A history of head trauma that causes significant cerebral concussion. Note: The manifestations of concussion include loss of consciousness, posttraumatic amnesia, and, less commonly, posttraumatic onset of seizures. The specific method of defining this criterion needs to be established by further research.
B. Evidence from neuropsychological testing or quantified cognitive assessment of difficulty in attention (concentrating, shifting focus of attention, performing simultaneous cognitive tasks) or memory (learning or recall of information).
C. Three (or more) of the following occur shortly after the trauma and last at least three months:
    Becoming fatigued easily
    Disordered Sleep
    Headache
    Vertigo or dizziness
    Irritability or aggression
    Anxiety, depression, or affective instability
    Changes in personality (e.g., social or sexual inappropriateness)
    Apathy or lack of spontaneity
The symptoms in criteria B and C have their onset following head trauma or else represent a substantial worsening of pre-existing symptoms.
D. The disturbance causes significant impairment in social or occupational functioning and represents a significant decline from a previous level of functioning. In school-age children, the impairment may be manifested by a significant worsening in school or academic performance dating from the trauma.
E. The symptoms do not meet criteria for Dementia Due to Head Trauma and are not better accounted for by another mental disorder (e.g., Amnestic Disorder Due to Head Trauma, Personality Change Due to Head Trauma.

cognitive complaints, such as fatigue (Norrie et al., 2010) and that subjective cognitive complaints may not correspond for many patients to easily measureable and/or quantifiable neuropsychological impairments. This last point is exemplified in studies that have observed high rates of persistent postconcussion symptoms and little to no indication in the same sample of quantifiable cognitive impairments on tests of neuropsychological functioning (Dikmen, Machamer, Winn & Temkin, 1995; Dikmen, Machamer, Fann, and Temkin, 2010; Mayer, 2011). This observed discrepancy may be due to a number of interrelated issues addressed in later sections of this chapter including: the incidence of persisting complaints and impairments in sports concussion vs. mTBI populations (Bigler, 2008); issues related to the types of tests and measures used to evaluate cognitive impairment in mTBI populations (Ozen & Fernandes, 2012; Ruff, 2009, Pertab et al., 2009), issues related to the group statistics used to analyze outcomes (Iverson, 2010) and issues related to whether these cognitive complaints even reflect a condition or an experience to which neuropsychological tests are reliably sensitive.

Problems with the diagnosis of PCS extend well beyond the technical structure of the criteria themselves. For instance, there is now clear recognition that the cognitive, emotional and physical symptoms associated with PCS are nonspecific in nature. That is, these symptoms are displayed in numerous populations including psychiatric populations, various medical populations, pain populations, litigating populations and "normal" populations (Iverson, 2012). This nonspecificity with regard to these symptoms has caused investigators to use the terms "postconcussion-like symptoms" or "posttraumatic symptoms."

Problems with the current definitional conceptualizations of PCS have resulted in concerns and doubts about whether the constellation of symptoms associated with PCS serve to create valid and reliable diagnostic criteria (Ettenhofer & Barry, 2012; Larabee, 2012). The evidence mentioned earlier related to the non-specificity of postconcussive symptoms raises obvious concerns about false positive error rates when applying these criteria. The perhaps overly stringent ICD-10 emphasis on loss of consciousness and the DSM-IV emphasis on measured cognitive impairment also raise concerns about false negative errors. These observations also highlight why diagnoses of mTBI and/or concussion rely upon injury severity variables and not on the nature or severity of postconcussion symptoms alone (Ruff, Iverson, Barth, Bush & Broshek, 2009).

Neuropathophysiology of mTBI

There are a number of extensive and excellent reviews associated with the topic of mTBI-related neuropathophysiology (e.g., Barkhoudarian, Hovda and Giza, 2011; Bigler & Maxwell, 2012; Greve, & Zinc, 2009; Saatam, Serbst and Berkhardt, 2009). As noted previously, mTBI can be conceptualized as a continuum of injury severity, with very mild sports concussions anchoring one end of the continuum and more significant mTBIs defined by more lengthy losses of consciousness, post-traumatic amnesia and focal neurologic signs anchoring the other end of the continuum.

mTBI begins with an event that exerts enough force to the brain to result in a rapid mechanical deformation of brain tissue. Such forces result from an impact and/or rapid acceleration/deceleration of the brain. It is important to recognize that multiple forces acting upon brain parenchyma may be present at the time of injury. Lezak (2012) reported that these biomechanical forces involve translational acceleration wherein the head moves in a straight line in accordance with the brain's center of gravity. Inertial forces are also present and include rotational acceleration, as the brain rotates around its center of gravity and central axis (i.e., the upper brain stem). As the head and neck are in motion during impact, angular acceleration can also result in a combination of both translational as well as rotational acceleration. In that the brain is exposed to the rapid onset of multiple forces, the result is that brain parenchyma must endure not just a single episode of mechanical strain, but a series of axonal strains, in multiple directions, over time, until movement of the brain is complete following acceleration/deceleration (Bigler & Maxwell, 2012). These mechanical events occur within milliseconds. Figure 17-1 provides a depiction of the types of forces (including rotational, linear and tensile) that can result in injury to the brain.

Axons are vulnerable to injury and damage with the rapid onset of mechanical forces.

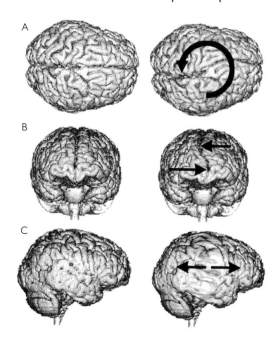

Figure 17-1. Forces acting on the brain that can result in injury (A) rotational; (B) linear; (C) tensile (Bigler, 2001). Reprinted from Bigler 2001. Copyright 2012 by Springer Press. Reprinted with permission.

Neural networks that rely upon a complex scaffolding of long white matter tracts and matrices that serve to interconnect regions in the frontal lobes, temporal lobes and limbic system are uniquely vulnerable to injury associated with the strain of biomechanical forces, as are areas such as the upper brainstem, thalamus, fornix, corpus callosum, cingulate gyrus and frontal lobe (Bigler & Maxwell, 2012). Injury to white matter tracts adversely impacts the brain's interconnectivity, in turn, impacting the regulation of functional abilities (emotional, behavioral, & cognitive) that rely on the coordinated intercommunication associated with intact white matter pathways and matrices. In short, injury to white matter pathways causes functional problems that reflect full or partial disconnections, depending upon injury severity. Figure 17-2 provides coronal and sagittal view of white matter fiber tracts as visualized with diffusion tensor imaging. Figure 17-3 provides more specific diffusion tensor images of white matter fiber tracts commonly damaged in mTBI including: a) the anterior corona and genu of the corpus callosum, b) the uncinate fasciculus,

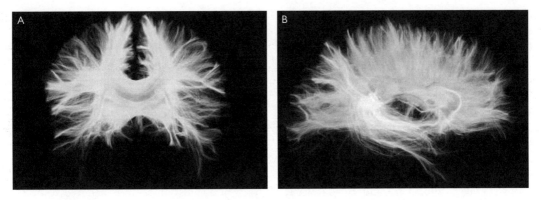

Figure 17-2. Diffusion tensor images of white matter fiber tracts commonly damaged in mTBI (A) coronal view and (B) sagittal view (Shenton et al., 2012). Reprinted from Shenton et al., 2012. Copyright 2012 by Springer Press. Reprinted with permission. See color insert.

c) the cingulum bundle and the body of the corpus callosum and d) the anterior fasciculus.

At a basic level, it is the relative intensity of these biomechanical forces that result in differences in severity of traumatic brain injury (TBI) and associated traumatic axonal injury (TAI). In more severe forms of traumatic brain injury, TAI may result in an actual shearing or a mechanical tearing of axons, often referred to in the TBI literature as diffuse axonal injury (DAI). However, in mTBI, damage is believed to result more from a trauma induced stretching or deformation of axons. This, in turn, can result in an ongoing neuropathological process that

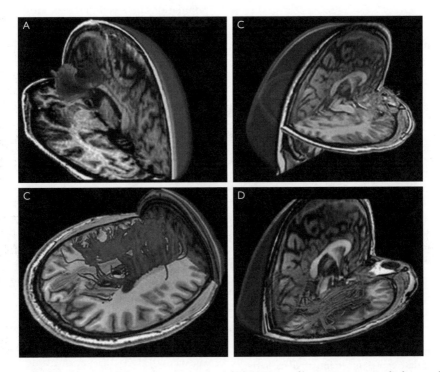

Figure 17-3. Detailed image of diffusion tensor images of white matter fiber tracts commonly damaged in mTBI including (A) the anterior corona and genu of the corpus callosum; (B) the uncinate fasciculus; (C) the cingulum bundle and the body of the corpus callosum and (D) the anterior fasciculus view (Shenton et al., 2012). Reprinted from Shenton et al., 2012. Copyright 2012 by Springer Press. Reprinted with permission. See color insert.

causes damage to the underlying cytoskeletal structure, resulting in cellular damage or death (Lezak, 2012). Bigler (2012) notes that TBIs fall on a continuum of trauma induced injury severity and that the primary factor associated with injury severity is how transient or permanent the degree of cellular damage or TAI.

In the mildest cases of concussions or mTBIs where individuals rapidly return to an asymptomatic baseline, neuroimaging may not demonstrate permanent microstructural damage to axons (Lezak p. 202). Giza and Hovda, 2001; Barkhoudarian, Hovda and Giza (2011) have proposed a model that outlines a neurometabolic cascade that begins with the deformation of cellular structures. The neurometabolic cascade posits a transient group of adverse cellular events that are believed to underlie those mTBIs and sports concussions that return to asymptomatic baseline and experience good functional recoveries (i.e., the majority of such injuries). The events surrounding this "neurometabolic cascade" are summarized in Table 17-8.

Table 17-8. The Neurometabolic Cascade

1. The neurometabolic cascade begins with the application of translational and/or rotational forces to the brain that result in a concussion or mTBI.
2. Within minutes of the injury, the release of excitatory neurotransmitters including glutamate contribute to wide spread neuronal depolarization, with an efflux of potassium and an influx of calcium.
3. This wide-spread ionic shift results in straining of sodium-potassium pumps to return neuronal membranes to normal potentials. This strain results in greater demand for energy/adenosine triphosphate (ATP), causing a glucose-related hypermetabolism, in the context of disrupted cerebral homeostasis and decreased cerebral blood flow.
4. This state of glucotic hypermetabolism in conjunction with diminished blood flow creates a state of increased cellular energy demands and decreased cellular energy supply, in turn, leading to a state of depressed cerebral metabolism with decreased production of ATP and increased lactate accumulation.
5. Heightened ongoing levels of calcium that may persist for days contribute to impaired oxidative metabolism and damage to cellular structures (microtubules & neurofilaments). These events, in turn, can lead to axonal swelling/edema, secondary axotomy and perhaps apoptosis.

In more severe TBIs, there is an abrupt shearing of axons with a rapid and irreversible set of biologic events that leads to destruction of the cell's cytoskeleton (primary axotomy). Again, in mTBI, axons are not believed to undergo a "shearing." Instead, the injury-associated mechanical loading damages the axon and sets in motion the neurometabolic events described above. If there is no cellular recovery from this cascade of events, fragmentation of the axon occurs (secondary axotomy). In the mildest form of concussion there is believed to be no structural injury to the axon (Lezak, 2012).

As is discussed in the following section, a fairly robust research literature has developed, over the better part of the past decade related to study of TAI and its functional correlates. Investigators have now shown that individuals who have sustained a mTBI can demonstrate white matter abnormalities both acutely and chronically. From an acute standpoint, these abnormalities are believed to reflect abnormalities associated with axonal swelling/edema, with chronic abnormalities observed in mTBI populations believed to reflect more permanent microstructural white matter damage (Bigler & Maxwell, 2012). Figure 17-4 demonstrates neuroimaging evidence for disruption in white matter tracts within the frontal lobe for an individual who suffered a mTBI. These images were generated 16 months post injury from mTBI (Rutgers et al., 2008).

Chronic Traumatic Encephalopathy (CTE)

Chronic traumatic encephalopathy (CTE) is a progressive neurodegenerative disorder that has been suggested to occur after repeated mTBI events (Saulle & Greenwald, 2012). It is most often reported in athletes in high contact sports such as professional wrestling, hockey and football and has also been reported in returning war veterans (Kelly, Amerson & Barth, 2012). It has been diagnosed in relatively young athletes who committed suicide (Gavett, Stern & McKee, 2011). At the present time, there is no clear consensus on the number of events or severity of each trauma that is required to cause CTE, although some authors suggest it can occur after a single TBI.

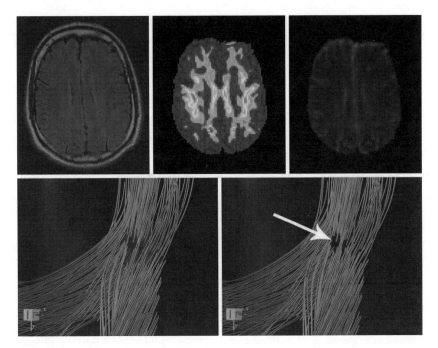

Figure 17-4. Imaging of disruption in white matter tracts within the frontal lobes for an individual with a mTBI 16 months post injury (Rutgers et al., 2008). Reprinted from Rutgers et al., 2008. Copyright 2008 by American Society of Neuroradiology. Reprinted with permission. See color insert.

The mechanism is unknown but may involve an ongoing metabolic and immunologic cascade called immunoexcitotoxicity (Blaylock & Maroon, 2011). This refers to an interaction between immune receptors within the central nervous system and excitatory glutamate receptors that triggers a series of events, such as extensive reactive oxygen species/reactive nitrogen species generation, accumulation of lipid peroxidation products, and prostaglandin activation. These events, in turn, lead to dendritic retractions, synaptic injury, damage to microtubules, and mitochondrial suppression.

The diagnosis of CTE is made neuropathologically. The neuropathology includes atrophy of the cerebral hemispheres, as well as the medial temporal lobe, thalamus, mammillary bodies and brainstem along with ventricular dilatation. It is histologically identified by the presence of tau-immunoreactive neurofibrillary tangles, astrocytic tangles, and spindle-shaped and threadlike neurites throughout the brain, with some cases having a TDP-43 proteinopathy or beta-amyloid plaques (McKee et al., 2009). Because CTE shares some neuropathological changes with Alzheimer's disease (AD) it has

also been suggested that there may be a common pathogenesis. Further, mTBI may interact additively with AD to produce greater clinical impact. And individuals who possess ApoE3 or ApoE4 appear to be at higher risk for developing CTE (Saulle & Greenwald, 2012).

There are no clear diagnostic criteria for a clinical diagnosis. Clinical presentation includes memory disturbance, behavioral and emotional changes and can progress to Parkinsonism, speech and gait abnormalities (McKee et al., 2009). The onset of CTE symptoms typically starts at an older age and frequently after the person is no longer a competitive athlete. In 30% of reported cases, mood disturbances were the initial symptom. The course of symptom progression seems to follow a somewhat continuous path beginning with cognitive and emotional decline leading to eventual motor deterioration, like Parkinsonism, ataxia, gait disturbance, and dysarthric speech.

The initial symptoms are typically poor concentration, attention, and memory along with disorientation, dizziness, and headaches. Symptoms then have been reported to progress to irritability, outbursts of violent or aggressive behavior, confusion, and speech abnormalities. As the disease continues to progress in severity, there is a greater involvement of motor functioning. It has been difficult to document the full progression, since some individuals with CTE have committed suicide, overdosed on drugs, or died from accidents (McKee et al., 2009).

Magnetic Resonance Imaging in mTBI

One of the difficulties involved in diagnosis and treatment of mTBI is the lack of objective biomarkers associated with a clinically meaningful injury profile (Tate, Shenton & Bigler, 2012), particularly any marker that might reliably predict adverse recovery in terms of more persistent postconcussive complaints, enduring cognitive impairment or psychiatric distress. Over the past two decades, researchers have used structural and functional neuroimaging methods in attempts to describe specific types of neurobiological injury in mTBI, with inconsistent results (see review Bigler, William, Maxwell, 2012). As reviewed more fully in chapter 14, nneuroradiological techniques like CT or conventional MRI assessment of structure (e.g., T1-weighted images) are often used during the acute phase of TBI clinical evaluation, with MRI typically used in sub-acute phases to confirm and extend baseline neuroimaging or to track the evolution of identified lesions (Gean, 1984; Orrison, 2000; Atlas, 2001; Bigler, 2005). CT/MRI are important indicators of macroscopic vascular compromise and structural damage including intracranial hematomas, contusions, and large hemorrhages (Jenkins, Teasdale, et al., 1986; Levin, Amparo, et al., 1987; Eisenberg and Levin, 1989). These vascular-based injuries usually are prognostic of a more adverse functional outcome (Bigler, 2001; Vasa, Grados, et al., 2004). Most mTBI research makes an effort to differentiate between "complicated" TBI (in which cases have small petechial hematomas, contusions, large hemorrhages, etc.) from "uncomplicated" TBI (i.e., radiologically unremarkable). However, although there are indications that the complicated versus uncomplicated distinction is related to functional outcome (Yuh et al., 2013), it has not proven reliable in predicting rapid resolution of symptoms or

persistence of neurocognitive impairment in mTBI (e.g., Weight, 1998; Lange, 2009) and falls short of usefulness in making medical recommendations. Furthermore, CT/MRI in general has not proven specifically informative about likelihood or type of persistent cognitive or emotional impairments (Dikmen, Machamer, et al., 2001; Temkin, Machamer, et al., 2003). For example, negative CT/MRI findings occur in up to 68% of mild TBI patients (Hofman, Stapert, et al., 2001; Hughes, Jackson, et al., 2004) and do not rule out long-term complaints and functional declines in those who have sustained a mTBI (Gean, 1984; Orrison, 2000; Atlas, 2001; Dikmen, Machamer, et al., 2001; Temkin, Machamer, et al., 2003; Bigler, 2005). Other MRI-based indices also have been examined in not yet successful attempts to explain why some patients experience persistent symptoms. For instance, MRI-measured volume loss in the months and years following TBI is a consistent feature of head injury. However, many published studies have not differentiated between mild and moderate/severe TBI patients in their sampling (Shenton, Hamoda et al., 2012). As a result, the nature and specificity of any link between global or regional volume abnormalities and patient neurocognitive function is not clear. Overall, reliable indicators have yet to be found that accurately predict which mTBI patients will have objectively measured cognitive problems or postconcussive complaints, despite a belief that some presumably measureable pathophysiological change must cause such difficulties.

Over the past decade, there has been increased interest in employing experimental MRI techniques to detect microscopic damage to brain tissue and to link patient brain structure and function to objectively measured or subjectively reported complaints, following brain injury. One such technique is diffusion tensor imaging (DTI) (see chapter 14), which has shown sensitivity to the microstructural white matter damage that defines TAI/DAI. DTI is a relatively new MRI technique that measures the diffusion of water molecules in the brain. The sensitivity of DTI to white matter capitalizes on the preferential orientation (or anisotropy) of magnetically polar water molecules repelled by highly myelinated white matter tracts. The most commonly employed DTI measurement in TBI research is fractional anisotropy (FA), which quantifies the degree of anisotropy in any given voxel of an image. Reduced FA values indicate less white matter coherence in a given region (i.e., greater diffusivity). In TBI, reduced FA likely reflects numerous structural changes known to occur in TAI/DAI including: misalignment of axonal membranes, changes in shape due to lobulation during sub-acute and chronic recovery, and membrane degeneration following axonal disconnection (Arfanakis, Haughton, et al., 2002).

With regard to TBI, it has been confirmed with histological staining in animals that sustained controlled impact injuries that FA actually measures TAI/DAI (MacDonald, Dikranian et al., 2007; Bennett, MacDonald, 2012). To date, numerous studies of children (Wilde, Chu et al., 2006) and adults (Arfanakis, Haughton et al., 2002; Huisman, Sorensen et al., 2003; Huisman, Schwamm et al., 2004; Inglese, Makani et al., 2005; Chappell, Ulug et al., 2006; Nakayama, Okumura et al., 2006; Salmond, Menon et al., 2006; Benson, Meda et al., 2007) show that DTI identifies white matter abnormalities that are not seen and/or detected on conventional MRI scans. These studies most consistently show reduced regional FA intensities in the white matter of TBI patients, particularly in the corpus callosum, brainstem and internal capsule (see reviews Shenton, Hamoda & Schneiderman et al., 2012; Niogi Mukherjee, 2010). Injuries to white matter in the temporal and frontal lobes also have been reported (Chappell, Ulug, et al., 2006; Salmond, Menon, et al., 2006). Although research has indicated that there are areas of the brain that are preferentially vulnerable to white matter injury, investigators have also reported that there is a high degree of interindividual difference in location of white matter injuries from patient to patient (Lipton, Kim, Park, Hulkower, Gardin, et al., 2012).

In a recent review of 31 published DTI investigations addressing mTBI, over 25 different brain regions of interest were identified as being vulnerable to microstructural damage in mTBI populations (Shenton, Hamoda, Schneiderman, Bouix, Pasternak, et al., 2012). Although literature reviews as well as recent meta-analytic findings support that certain brain areas are more vulnerable to microstructural damage during mTBI (Aoki et al., 2012), not all investigations have been successful in replicating findings of microstructural damage in particular regions of interest (ROIs) (Lange, Iverson, Brubacher, Madler, et al., 2012). Even studies with presumably more homogenous sports concussion samples find considerable variability in location of specific DTI-measured injury (Gardner, Kay-Lambkin, Stanwell, et al., *Journal of Neurotrauma*, 2012). Lipton et al. (2012) have emphasized that the microstructural damage in mTBI manifests with a large degree of interindividual heterogeneity with regard to location. These investigators have shown that DTI studies that emphasize an *a priori* ROI or a group comparison approach in looking for microstructural damage, may limit their sensitivity and ability to capture the true individual variability that defines patterns of white matter damage in mTBI. It is yet to be determined what research approach (i.e., ROI vs consideration of overall injury profile through the use of summary statistics) might best have clinical, prognostic significance. Regardless, when the dozens of published DTI TBI studies are taken together, they do provide strong evidence that DTI-measured abnormalities are present to varying degrees across (i.e., a likely dose/response relationship) different levels of injury severity (i.e., mild, moderate, or severe TBI classification) (Arfanakis, Haughton, et al., 2002; Inglese, Makani, et al., 2005; Aoki, Inokuchi, Gunshin, Yahagi & Suwa, 2012). There also is emerging evidence that type of DTI-measured abnormality is related to phase of injury-related recovery (subacute vs. chronic) (Arfanakis, Haughton, et al., 2002; Inglese, Makani, et al., 2005; Nakayama, Okumura, et al., 2006; Salmond, Menon, et al., 2006), which also might ultimately prove to be clinically meaningful. A recent and comprehensive review of DTI research in mTBI populations concluded that this imaging method definitely supports the presence of "small and subtle brain injuries in mTBI" (Shenton, Hamoda, Schneiderman, Bouix, Pasternak, et al., 2012, p. 181).

Importantly, recent studies also have begun to link DTI-measured regional white matter abnormalities with functional impairments such as subjective postconcussive complaints and quantitatively measured cognitive dysfunction.

For example, Niogi et al. (Mukherjee, Ghajar, 2008) showed relationships between specific white matter tracts and attentional performance. More recently, Geary et al. (2010) have linked verbal learning deficits to reduced FA in the uncinate and superior longitudinal fasciculi, while Wu et al. (2010) (Wilde, Chu, Bigler et al., 2006)) found a relationship between the integrity of the cingulum bundles and memory function in adolescents who sustained a mTBI. These are just a few examples of emerging evidence for specific links between mTBI-related white matter injury and abnormal neurocognitive function. Much more research is needed; however, if studies ultimately can reliably link even a handful of specific DTI-measured regional white matter injury to either cognitive dysfunction or PCS-related symptomatology, a significant advance in understanding the causes of mTBI symptoms will be made.

To complicate understanding of the relationship between DTI-measured abnormalities and clinical impairment, some studies do not report DTI-measured deficits in mTBI. Instead, there is evidence that mTBI patients show relative increases of FA measurements within the first few days following TBI, during the acute to sub-acute recovery period. For example, Bazarian et al. (2007) imaged mild TBI patients 72 hours after TBI and again 1 month later. They reported increased FA values in posterior corpus callosum that correlated with post-concussive symptom checklist scores at both DTI assessments. Since then, several other studies have reported similar patterns of increased FA in mTBI (e.g., Bazarian et al., 2011; Henry et al., 2011; Mayer et al., 2010; Hartikainen et al., 2010), often in conjunction with reduced regional mean diffusivity (MD) indices. MD measurements are simply calculated from the DTI scan differently than FA, where MD represents a scalar value of the total amount of diffusion found in any given voxel. In at least one of these studies (Hartikainen et al., 2010), the degree of FA increase was more prominent in symptomatic patients, leading some to suggest that TBI-induced increases in FA and reduced MD bear further examination as a potential outcome predictor (Shenton, Hamoda, Schneiderman, et al., 2012). The significance of such FA increases is not yet entirely

clear. In some cases, greater FA can be ascribed to reductions of one of several indices that comprise the global FA score (e.g., reduced radial diffusivity as found in Mayer et al., 2010). However, physiological interpretations related to possible compensatory neural processes such as inflammation, in the face of neuronal damage, cannot be ruled out.

At present, there is a paucity of longitudinal outcome studies of mTBI patients focusing on whether increases or decreases in FA can predict outcome or how and whether these injuries resolve over time. In one early DTI TBI study, evidence was reported for FA-measured abnormalities improving over time, suggesting a restorative or regenerative process at work (Arfanakis, Haughton, et al., 2002). A recent study showed DTI-measured structural integrity was disrupted within the first 3 weeks post mTBI, but a 6-month follow-up showed partial resolution (Messe et al., 2012). Moreover, the severity of white matter injury was linked to the presence of clinically meaningful postconcussion symptoms. Another recent study of mTBI patients at 2 weeks, 3 months, and 6 months found evidence for reduced FA in numerous deep and subcortical white matter regions (Lipton et al., 2012). Importantly, nearly every patient also had evidence for increased FA in the chronic recovery period, a finding not reported in the vast majority of previous studies of comparable patients. Thus, the individualized approach to identifying and quantifying FA abnormality employed by Lipton et al. (2012) appeared better able to identify and quantify the large degree of spatial variability in white matter injury unique to each patient in their sample than an approach that only considered group differences at the mean level. Emerging evidence suggests that the inclusion of regional and global DTI indices are more sensitive markers of injury in more severe TBI and improve short-term prognosis accuracy (Betz, Zho, Roy, et al., 2012), but it remains to be seen if such a relationship holds for mTBI. Although more work is needed, the available prospective studies have shed some insight into how DTI-identified white matter abnormalities recover.

Another experimental technique employed in the search for predictive biomarkers in mild TBI is functional magnetic resonance imaging (fMRI). Although a considerable number of fMRI studies have examined TBI populations (see reviews Hunter, Wilde Tong, 2012; Duckwork & Stevens, 2010; Belander, Vanderploeg Curtiss, et al., 2007), relatively fewer have specifically examined mTBI (see McDonald, Saykin, McAllister, 2012). Moreover, existing studies generally are limited by their small sample sizes, use of diverse and complex cognitive tasks during brain activity assessment, and incomplete reporting on potential complicating factors, such as structural and vascular abnormalities. This heterogeneity prevents clear conclusions about the nature of brain dysfunction, as measured by more standard fMRI methods in mTBI. The extant fMRI literature has focused on working memory ability, and several reports describe prefrontal cortex activation abnormalities in mTBI (McAllister, 1999; 2001), particularly the failure to more greatly engage the neural substrates of working memory when the size of the "load" on working memory is increased (Perlstein, Cole, 2004). Such a finding has been interpreted as a failure to allocate processing resources effectively (McDonald, Saykin, McAllister, 2012). Interestingly, fMRI-measured brain activation deficits persisted as long as 1 year post-injury (McAllister, 2002; 2006), even when post-concussion symptoms had waned. mTBI patients have shown brain function deficits in other cognitive contexts as well. For instance, Witt, Lovejoy et al. (2010) used a simple auditory attention task to demonstrate that mTBI patients showed decreased left dorsolateral prefrontal cortex activation, despite a lack of impairment on objective measures of accuracy or reaction time when compared to non-TBI controls. mTBI deficits have been shown on tasks measuring auditory orienting (Mayer, 2009), response inhibition (Matthews, Strigo, 2011) cognitive control (Scheibel, 2012; Larson, Farrer & Clayson, 2011), and episodic memory (McAllister, 2001; 2006).

Variability in profiles of regional brain activation, across the body of TBI fMRI studies have led researchers to ask whether TBI results in fundamental changes in how large-scale, distributed brain networks engage to mediate performance on cognitive tasks. Animal and human research indicates that when the brain is at rest, (i.e., in the absence of cognitive or behavioral demands) it is characterized by spontaneous neuronal fluctuations that synchronously occur over identifiable and distinct large-scale networks (Raichle, Macleod, Snyder, et al., 2001; Raichle & Mintum, 2006; Smith, Fox, Miller, et al., 2009). Research associated with these strongly correlated patterns of synchronous brain activity among distant brain regions (i.e., "functional connectivity") (Friston, 2002) indicates that these regions communicate via well-described and distinct excitatory neurotransmission pathways, in ways that fMRI research has begun to model effectively (Deco, Jirsa et al., 2010; Deco and Corbetta, 2011). In humans, functional connectivity is measured as inter-regional correlations among spontaneous fluctuations of hemodynamic activity during a "resting state," while participants lie passively in the MRI machine, but no active cognitive or behavioral demands are imposed (Raichle et al., 2001; Shulman, Fiez, Corbetta, et al., 1997).

Studies of fMRI-measured resting state data have reliably identified numerous discrete neural networks (Calhoun et al., 2008; Damoiseaux, Rombouts, Barkhof, et al., 2006; De Luca, Beckman, DeStefano, et al., 2006; Beckman, DeLuca, Devlin & Smith, 2005a,b). These neural networks include well-described motor, sensory, language, and visual networks (Cordes, Haughton, Arfanakis, et al., 2000), and others that comprise brain regions characteristically engaged for various higher-order cognitive operations often found to be impaired in TBI, including frontoparietal, cingulo-opercular networks, and frontostriatal networks (Beckmann et al., 2005a,b; Fransson, 2005; Dosenbach, Fair, Miezen, et al., 2007; Seeley, Menon, Schatzberg, et al., 2007). It is estimated that the resting brain expends the vast majority (up to 80%) of its resources to maintain a homeostasis among resting state neural networks (Raichle & Mintum, 2006), suggesting that resting state networks (RSN) may be excellent indicators of disruptions in neural function and communication in coordinated brain regions following brain injury. Researchers have shown particular interest in the "default mode" network, which is a group of interconnected midline cortical regions that show high activity in the absence of externally-imposed cognitive processing. This well-defined network includes the rostral anterior cingulate gyrus, posterior cingulate gyrus, superior temporal/supramarginal gyrus, and ventromedial prefrontal cortex, with the cingulate structures serving as a central hub. Reduced connectivity in this network is believed to be associated with problems with higher-level cognitive abilities, such as the mediation of aspects of attention and executive functions, the sense that one's mind wanders, distractibility, etc. (Buckner, Andrews-Hanna, & Schacter, 2008; Eichele, Debener, Calhoun, et al., 2008; Kelley, Macrae, Wyland, et al., 2002; Mason, Norton, Van Horn, et al., 2007; McAllister, Flashman, McDonald, & Saykin, 2006, Raichle et al., 2001; Weissman, Roberts, Visscher, et al., 2006).

Although functional neuroimaging studies have reported distributed neural network functional disconnections in moderate-to-severe TBI samples using magnetoencephalography (Castellanos, Paul, et al., 2010) and fMRI (Nakamura, Hillary, et al., 2009; Kasahara, Menon, et al., 2010; Hillary, Slocomb, et al., 2011; Kasahara, Menon, et al., 2011), at present, only a small handful of studies have focused on mTBI. Johnson et al. (*Neuroimage*, 2012) examined concussed student athletes and found reduced connections between posterior default mode network brain regions (posterior cingulate and parietal cortex), but increased connections for medial prefrontal cortex. Slobuounov Gay et al. (2011) reported similar disconnection across the brains in patients with sports-related concussion who were otherwise asymptomatic and neuropsychologically normal. In another study, Mayer, Mannell, Ling, Gasparovic and Yeo (2011) examined radiologically-confirmed uncomplicated mTBI patients using fMRI resting state, diffusion tensor imaging (DTI) of white matter microstructure, and neuropsychological assessment within 3 weeks of injury, and a sub-sample at 3-5 month follow-up. These investigators reported decreased default mode connectivity. Moreover, abnormalities in functional connectivity were associated with the persistence of subjective cognitive/postconcussive complaints but not with impairment on formal measures of neuropsychological tests. The investigators reported a high degree of sensitivity and specificity associated with measures of functional connectivity, with an overall

classification accuracy rate of 84.3%. Stevens, Lovejoy, Kim, Oakes et al. (2012) examined multiple distributed neural networks identified during resting state using independent component analysis functional connectivity methods in data collected from a sample of consecutively referred mTBI patients from an ED and a concussion follow-up clinic. This study found evidence for disconnection or "over-connection" in every single neural network examined. Moreover, the severity of post-concussion complaints was significantly linked to both regional disconnection (especially the anterior cingulate, and brain regions associated with cognitive control, action monitoring, and attention), as well as to microstructural white matter damage, as measured by DTI.

These mild TBI functional connectivity studies are perhaps the clearest evidence to date that radiologically-normal mild TBI patients have compromised integration of distributed neural networks, and that this profile differs from profiles found in more severe TBI. Both under- and over-connectivity have been shown, which could reflect TBI-related damage and compensatory processes respectively, though additional research is needed to confirm this speculation. Moreover, these studies have begun to link TBI and mTBI-related postconcussive consequences to both brain function and brain structure, suggesting that ultimate understanding of these complex relationships is likely to require multi-modal neuroimaging methods. Of note, these fMRI studies are also supported by research using EEG techniques to examine neuroelectric activity in mild TBI patients. Two EEG studies have reported abnormal coherence or phase synchrony across scalp recording sites in mTBI during resting state EEG assessment (Kumar, Rao, et al., 2009; Sponheim, McGuire, et al., 2010), working memory (Kumar, Rao, et al., 2009), and episodic memory (Tsirka, Simos, Vakis, 2011).

Although empirical relationships have been established between white matter structural abnormalities and disruption of distributed neural networks and the presence of functional problems, it is not yet clear whether DTI identified abnormalities or measures of functional connectivity will be able to help in reliably predicting symptom course and outcome in mTBI populations. Given the myriad of physiologic, psychiatric, psychological, social and environmental variables known to impact postconcussive trajectories, it may be that DTI-identified white matter abnormalities will be shown to work in concert with other factors in predicting functional outcome for some. The differences between mTBI and more severely injured patients, at a minimum, should urge caution in assuming that the relationships between changes in brain structure and functional outcome will be the same across TBI severity-defined groups. Moreover, caution is needed to assume that findings that can be confirmed on the group level will apply to any specific individual who sustains an MTBI. Although much progress has been made in this area, additional longitudinal studies are needed to more fully understand the course and clinical significance of DTI-identified microstructural white matter damage. Estimates of sensitivity and specificity for the imaging techniques discussed above are beginning to emerge from the literature when mTBI groups are compared with normal control samples. The use of normal control groups and the exclusion of comorbid conditions are important in demonstrating pure associations between radiologic findings and microstructural damage in mTBI, however, research efforts will also have to address the issue of differential sensitivity as mTBI patients may present with comorbidities that have also been shown to present with white matter abnormalities (Iverson, 2011). That microscopic damage and neuronal dysfunction occurs as a consequence of mTBI is not in question. However, questions related to how often damage occurs, who is most vulnerable to damage and dysfunction, how damage and dysfunction manifests over time for different groups and how to best classify and quantify damage and dysfunction in the n=1 case are lofty questions that lie before the mTBI research and clinical communities.

The Presence of Persistent Postconcussive Complaints & Impairments

What is clear from the research literature is that a subgroup of individuals who have sustained a mTBI go on to experience persistent postconcussive-like symptom complaints that cause personal distress for the patient as well as clinical concerns for treaters. It has been observed that within the realm of disability, the possibility for both distress and functional impairment exists whether symptom complaints occur as a diagnosable constellation of postconcussive symptoms (i.e., a syndrome) or as a sub-syndromal group of symptoms. Within this context, the overarching question shifts from a concern about diagnostic criteria and whether a postconcussive syndrome is diagnosable to a different perspective where the driving concern is whether symptom complaints cause impairments regardless of cause and contributors (Lovejoy & Oakes, 2012).

Vocational impairment has frequently been used as a marker for functional impairments associated with mTBI. It is important to recognize that this relationship is often complicated, as disability can be a multifactorial phenomenon with contributions associated with economic times, job market, job dissatisfaction, etc. Vocational impairment associated with mTBI has been comprehensively reviewed (Iverson & Lange, 2012, Iverson, Lange, Gaetz, & Zasler, 2007). These investigators reported that across studies that focus on mTBI, return to work rates range from 38% to 83% at six to nine months post-injury, 47% to 83% at one to two years post-injury, and 62% to 88% at three or more years post-injury. At their most conservative end, these ranges suggest that a significant subgroup of individuals experience long-term social consequences following mTBI. The research does suggest that both mTBI as well as postconcussive complaints correlate with reports of vocational impairment. However, as Iverson et al. (2007) note, given the methodological differences between studies in terms of inclusion and exclusion criteria, how work impairment is defined, etc., it is difficult to clearly identify how mTBI results in work-related impairments.

As noted earlier, it is widely recognized that the majority of individuals who have sustained a single uncomplicated mTBI or sports concussion may experience a range of initial postconcussive difficulties, but return to their functional baselines within hours, days or weeks (Williams, Potter and Ryland, 2010). For

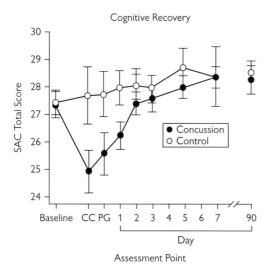

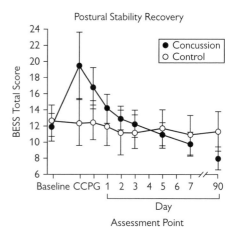

Figure 17-5. Recovery curve of cognitive functions following concussion on the Standardized Assessment of Concussion (SAC) (McCrae, 2008). Reprinted from McCrae, 2008. Copyright 2008 by Oxford University Press. Reprinted with permission.

Figure 17-6. Recovery curve of postural stability following concussion on the Balance Error Scoring System (BESS) (McCrae, 2008). Reprinted from McCrae, 2008. Copyright 2008 by Oxford University Press. Reprinted with permission.

individuals who have sustained a sports-related concussion, cognitive, emotional and physical postconcussion symptoms typically reach an apex at 72 hours after injury, and then resolve progressively over the course of 2 to 30 days. This point was illustrated by McCrae (2008) in relation to overall symptomatic recovery, measured cognitive recovery and recovery of balance. These data are presented in Figures 17-5, 17-6 and 17-7. The recovery curves presented here also map fairly well onto the time frames for proposed normalization of neurometabolic functioning outlined by Giza and Hovda (2001), and highlight biophysiologic mechanisms that, for most, result in temporary functional problems, with a good recovery to baseline functionality.

The presence of persistent postconcussive complaints (> 3, 6, and 12 months), particularly in adult mTBI samples, has been a source of debate, in terms of both incidence and etiology (McCrae, 2008; Greiffenstein, 2008; Larabee, 2012; Ruff, 2009). Iverson (2012, p. 45) notes that "most experienced clinicians and researchers agree that there is a subgroup of people who report ongoing symptoms and problems long after a mTBI. The confusion, disagreement, and lack of consensus relates to what is causing

and maintaining the symptoms and problems." Ruff (1996) coined the term "miserable minority" to describe the 10%-20% of mTBI patients that appeared to present with persistent postconcussive symptoms. Studies using retrospective self-reported mTBI data have indicated that these impairments may last for years after mTBI

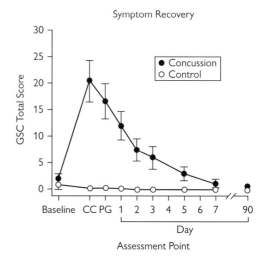

Figure 17-7. Recovery curve of symptoms on the Graded Symptom Checklist (GSC) following concussion (McCrae, 2008). Reprinted from McCrae, 2008. Copyright 2008 by Oxford University Press. Reprinted with permission.

(Klein et al., 1996; Berstein et al., 1996; Carlsson et al., 1987; King & Kirwilliam, 2011).

Some investigators have suggested that true incidence rates for persistent PCS fall well below the miserable minority base rate estimates of 10%-20% (Greiffenstein, 2008, Iverson, 2005, Larabee, 2012, McCrae, 2008). Criticisms related to research that has identified base rates of 10-20% have included small sample sizes, a lack of control groups, the mTBI inclusion criteria utilized in studies, the impact of attrition rates in longitudinal studies, the failure to capture all individuals with mTBIs, how persistent postconcussive complaints are defined and the potential inclusion of symptom exaggerators in samples.

In discussing the methodological issues associated with estimation of persistent PCS, McCrae (2008, pp. 165-166) indicated that estimates of 15-20% of MTBI patients having persistent PCS is severely inflated and is more a reflection of clinical lore than empirical evidence. McCrae offered a revised base rate estimate for PCS of between 1% and 5%. The following observations were offered to support this argument:

1) "An estimated 25% of individuals who have suffered mTBI never seek medical treatment after injury and therefore are never accounted for in the PCS incidence denominator."

2) "Most mTBI patients have neither LOC (perhaps as many as 90% of all injuries) nor lengthy posttraumatic amnesia (30-50%) associated with their injury, which technically precludes them from the diagnosis of PCS based on DSM-IV and ICD-10 criteria."

3) "Research studies on PCS also often only accrue only those patients referred to clinics because of persistent complaints, which we know are highly nonspecific."

4) McCrae (2008) citing Iverson, Zasler and Lange (2006) indicated that at one year post-injury, some studies consider patients to have had persistent problems if they endorsed only a single symptom, whereas endorsement of multiple symptoms that would qualify for a disorder or syndrome at one year is far less frequent (< 5% of subjects).

Despite these observations, research that has addressed many of the above noted concerns has continued to identify high base rates of persistent postconcussive complaints in mTBI populations (Dikmen, Machamer, Fann, and Temkin, 2010; Kashluba, Paniac & Casey, 2008; Ettenhofer, & Barry, 2012; Kraus, Schaffer, Ayers, Stenehjem, Shen, & Afifi, 2005; Lannsjo, Geijerstam, Johansson, Bring, & Borg, 2009; Lundin, De Boussard, Edman, & Borg, 2006; Ponsford, Cameron, Fitzgerald, Grant, Antonina, Mikoska-Walus, 2010). For instance, Dikmen et al. (2010) reported on the presence of postconcussive complaints for a group of TBI patients that were consecutively referred, longitudinally followed, and yoked to a control sample of matched orthopedically injured patients. These investigators reported very low attrition rates for follow-up evaluations. A dose response relationship was observed in association with TBI severity, with more severely injured patients reporting higher rates of postconcussion symptoms, at three- and 12-month time intervals post injury. However, whereas mTBI patients as a group appeared very similar to trauma controls on performance-based neuropsychological tests at a 12-month interval (Dikmen et al., 1995), an impressive proportion (44%) of mTBI patients reported persistent postconcussive complaints ($\geq$ to 3 symptoms) at the 12-month interval, in contrast to the lower rates observed for the matched trauma controls (24%). The authors reported that the symptom reports were likely the result of a blending of direct and indirect consequences of brain injury, as well as non-TBI factors that contributed to or exacerbated the ongoing symptom presentation. In this study, variables such as age, gender, pre-injury alcohol abuse and psychiatric history were identified as moderator variables associated with symptom presentation.

In another recent study, Ponsford, et al. (2010) prospectively followed a group of 123 trauma patients and 100 matched trauma controls evaluated through a hospital ED. These investigators reported that the mTBI group reported a greater burden of postconcussive complaints at three months post injury than did the trauma controls and indicated that a significant proportion of the mTBI patients (20%-30%) were reporting reduced concentration and memory difficulties that affected their daily activities. The authors indicated that litigation did not appear to be a significant contributing factor to persistent complaints.

Multiple well-designed longitudinal, cross-sectional as well as population-based epidemiologic studies indicate base rates for persistent postconcussive symptoms consistent with or above the rates initially used to characterize the "miserable minority." Certainly one of the primary reasons for higher base rates in many studies relates to whether postconcussive complaints were defined by individual symptoms or DSM-IV/ICD-10 PCS criteria that require a higher volume of symptoms. A study requirement that persistent symptoms meet formal criteria for a disorder or syndrome would certainly lower the base rates of those being classified as experiencing persistent symptoms. Individuals struggling with concerning subsyndromal presentations would be missed (false negatives) in such studies. This problem was recently demonstrated and discussed by Ponsford et al. (2010).

Given the research cited earlier, the question does not relate to whether or not there is a subgroup of mTBI patients that manifests persistent complaints—the more relevant question relates to why these symptoms persist. Variables that are associated with more persistent postconcussive complaints will be discussed in greater depth in later sections of this chapter. Broadly speaking, outcome related to mTBI depends on the mTBI or concussion population that was studied and the methodology used for studying the population. Base rates of postconcussive complaints will differ depending upon whether one is standing in an emergency room, on a trauma floor, in a subacute mTBI or sports concussion clinic that follows consecutively referred patients or in a clinic that treats only symptomatic patients.

The Presence and Problems with Documenting Measurable Cognitive Impairments

There has been great interest in studying the presence of persistent and measurable cognitive impairments in mTBI populations. This has been seen as particularly important given that the DSM-IV PCS criteria require evidence of quantifiable cognitive impairments. However, this has proven to be a difficult task, with variability of findings reported in the research literature and disagreement among investigators as to the presence of persisting cognitive problems in mTBI populations.

Studies employing statistical meta-analysis (a method of combining and analyzing multiple published data sets) have focused on measured cognitive outcome, as identified by neuropsychological testing, following mTBI (Belanger & Vanderploeg, 2005; Binder, Rholing & Larabee, 1997; Frenchman, K. Fox, A., & Maybery, M., 2005; Schretlin & Shapiro, 2003; Zakzanis, Leach & Kaplan, 1999). As a group, these meta-analytic studies have been interpreted by some to indicate that neuropsychological deficits may last for up to three months, but the "norm" is complete recovery (Larabee, 2012). These studies are also viewed as consistent with the findings of other large-scale prospective studies focusing on measured cognitive outcome following mTBI. For instance, Dikmen, Machamer, Winn and Temkin (1995) conducted one of the most stringently designed studies focusing on measured cognitive outcome across the spectrum of severity for TBI. This study was prospective in nature and included a trauma control group that had no evidence of brain injury. Recall that injury control groups are viewed as an important addition to research designs for cognitive and postconcussive outcome in mTBI, as it has been well established that factors outside of mTBI alone such as pain and general injury effects have been shown to impact postconcussive presentations (Iverson, 2012). The study results (Dikmen et al., 1995) indicated a dose response relationship for injury severity, as it related to level and duration of cognitive impairment. For the identified mTBI group, it was reported that, at one year post injury, the mTBI group was statistically indistinguishable from the trauma control group, on a large battery of cognitive/neuropsychological tests.

In recent years, investigators have offered cautions about the interpretation of large-scale group and meta-analytic studies as indicating that that there are no lasting measurable cognitive effects associated with a single uncomplicated mTBI (Belanger & Vanderploeg, 2005, Bigler, 2012; Dikmen, 1995; Pertab, James, & Bigler, 2009; Iverson, 2010; Ruff, 2009). For instance, Iverson (2010) indicated that in meta-analytic studies subsamples of mTBI patients with different cognitive outcomes are combined to derive an overall effect. This process may obfuscate important subgroup differences with regard to cognitive functioning. This point was acknowledged by Frenchman et al. (2005), who indicated "it is possible that a sub-sample in the studies summarized did have more severe cognitive deficits, and that the effect of their results has been lost (in terms of statistical significance) by the pooling of data (p. 347)." Dikmen et al. (1995) echoed this observation, indicating that given their group data they could not rule out that a subsample of patients may have experienced more significant impairments.

Belanger and Vanderploeg (2005) reported that an analysis of moderator variables was important when examining cognitive outcomes in their meta-analytic study. That is, their analysis found evidence for moderate to large neuropsychological effect sizes for litigating and clinic samples in post-acute (> 90 days) periods. They also reported that the litigating sample tended to worsen with regard to cognitive functioning over time. The authors noted that the effects for litigation did not appear to be attributable to cognitive symptom exaggeration or malingering, as the cognitive effects were similar for samples screened and analyzed with and without symptom validity tests. The authors indicated that potential reasons for the persisting neuropsychological effects for the litigating and clinic samples were unclear and that further investigation would be important to identify the relative contributions of lasting brain dysfunction or potential psychological effects.

Pertab et al. (2009) engaged in a meta-analytic re-analysis of the studies used in the Binder et al. (1997) meta-analysis and its extension (Frencham et al., 2005). The investigators reported that they employed inclusion and exclusion criteria that emphasized whether studies used consecutive referrals and control groups. Studies that did not include standardized neuropsychological tests were also excluded, as were studies in which effect sizes could not be calculated. The meta-analytic results supported the presence of persistent neuropsychological impairments on a subset of cognitive measures for those who had suffered

an mTBI. Belanger, Speigel and Vanderploeg (2010) conducted a meta-analysis of the sports concussion literature focusing on the effects of multiple concussions. Although there was little effect found for two or more concussions, small but significant effect sizes were noted for subtest domains emphasizing executive functions and delayed memory.

The meta-analytic studies completed by Belanger et al. (2005) and Pertab et al. (2009) indicate the presence of persistent and measurable cognitive changes following mTBI. This point is amplified by recent longitudinal and cross-sectional studies that have also demonstrated group differences on measures of cognitive abilities suggestive of persistent cognitive changes (Ponsford et al., 2010; Vanderploeg, Curtiss & Belanger, 2005). Larabee (2012) appropriately notes that there is often a lack of correlation in the research literature between cognitive complaints and documented impairments on neuropsychological tests. Larabee (2012) indicates that in populations with more severe neurologic insult (e.g., moderate to severe TBI, stroke or Alzheimer's Disease, etc.) that a neurologically-mediated decline in self-awareness or anosognosia may contribute to this lack of correlation. In these instances, cognitive impairment may be evident on neuropsychological tests or through family observations, with a relative lack of cognitive complaints noted by the patient. Investigators have reported that those with mTBI can present with a greater intensity of cognitive complaints than do more severely brain-injured populations (Green & Allen, 2000) The research literature also holds examples of studies that failed to find evidence for cognitive dysfunction on neuropsychological tests, in the context of ongoing postconcussive and cognitive symptom complaints (Brooks, Mckay, Mrazik, & Barlow, in press; Mayer, et al., 2011; Dikmen, Machamer, Winn & Temkin, 1995; Dikmen, Machamer, Fann, & Temkin, 2010).

Larabee (2012) recently suggested that the lack of correlation between cognitive complaints and impairment on neuropsychological tests in mTBI populations may be more indicative of many other factors, some of which are discussed in the following sections of this chapter, including: emotional distress, somatization and symptom exaggeration. Alternatively, investigators have also raised separate concerns that conventional neuropsychological tests may lack the sensitivity to reliably evaluate the subtle cognitive difficulties experienced by some, in the more chronic phases of mTBI recovery (Cicerone, 1997, Raskin et al., 1998, Pertab, 2009; Lezak, 2012; Vanderploeg, 2005). Problems with test sensitivity are not unknown to the field of neuropsychology, especially in relation to populations that may experience variability in functioning across time, particularly related to issues associated with cognitive load, cognitive stamina and premorbid intelligence (Lovejoy, Ball, Keats, Stutts, Spain, Janda, & Janusz, 1999; Woods, Lovejoy, Stutts, Ball, & Fals-Stewart, 2002). Investigators (Iverson & Brooks, 2011; Oakes, Lovejoy Tartar, & Holdnack, in press) have also pointed out that cognitive impairment that is subtle in nature and that occurs at lower base rates within a population can be exceptionally difficult to differentiate from normal test variability. In many instances, conventional neurospsychological tests may be viewed as blunt instruments that lack the reliable precision to detect the mild cognitive changes experienced by some, in more chronic stages of mTBI recovery. This observation is supported by studies of mTBI populations that have shown relationships between postconcussive/cognitive complaints and neuropsysiologic abnormalities (Bazarian, Zhong, Blyth, Zhu, Kavcic, & Peterson, 2007; Fitzgerald & Crosson, 2011; Lipton, 2008; Messe, Caplan, Pelegrini-Isaac, Blancho, Montrenil, et al., 2012; Messé, Caplain, Paradot, Garrigue, Mineo, Soto Ares, et al., 2010; Smits, Houston, Dippel, Wielopolski, Vernooij, Koudstaal, et al., 2011; Stevens et al., 2012), studies that have shown relationships between postconcussive complaints and neurophysiologic abnormalities but not with conventional neuropsychological tests, and studies that have demonstrated the presence of subtle cognitive impairments using non-conventional neuropsychological tests or testing paradigms (Heitger, Jones, Macleod, et al., 2009; Mayer et al., 2011; Pontifex, O'Connor, Broglio, & Hillman, 2009).

This is not to say that all cognitive complaints following mTBI are pure reflections of neurophysiologic dysfunction or that neuropsychological evaluation is not useful in helping to more comprehensively understand a patient's presentation following mTBI. It is only to indicate that many conventional neuropsychological tests may lack the sensitivity to identify the subtle cognitive problems experienced in populations with more mild neurologic abnormalities. Iverson, Brooks and Holdnack (2012) describe a continuum of neuropsychological impairment, noting that at the milder end of the impairment spectrum that cognitive changes may be noticed by the individual, but that neuropsychological testing may not be sensitive enough to reliably characterize such cognitive changes.

Factors That Can be Associated with Persistent Symptom Presentations and Poor Functional Outcomes

Research has indicated that a number of variables can contribute to persistent postconcussive symptom presentations in mTBI. Some of these variables relate to the actual injury, while others relate to premorbid characteristics or the later development of psychiatric distress. Understanding how any single factor or a combination of factors contribute to ongoing postconcussive problems in the n = 1 case is an exceedingly difficult task. It is often the case that an individual's functioning changes following an mTBI. As noted earlier, research has indicated that individuals can experience acute problems in relation to cognitive functioning as well as other postconcussive symptoms following a concussion or a mTBI. There is debate in the field as to the presence and drivers of persistent symptoms and functional impairments after about three months. Iverson (2012) advocates for a biopsychosocial approach in understanding and conceptualizing poor outcomes following mTBI. The proposed model includes over 20 variables that may interact in the wake of an mTBI to produce persistent postconcussion-like symptoms and functional problems. This model includes acute injury variables such as microstructural injury and altered neurotransmitter systems as well as multiple other injury-related, personality, psychosocial, and psychiatric contributors to poor outcome. The various potential combinations of these factors in contributing to persistent problems following an mTBI is literally overwhelming.

At present, there is no one research study that has clearly defined how injury and non-injury factors interact to produce a poor outcome in any one mTBI or concussion patient. This task still rests with the clinical judgment and evaluative skills of the individual clinician. Rosenbaum and Lipton (2012) point out that the great diversity in clinical features associated with mTBI should be expected, given the heterogeneity in underlying pathology and the myriad of premorbid inter-individual differences. The authors note that the stark contrast between the majority of individuals that recover from mTBI without complication and the approximately 30% of individuals who suffer from poor outcomes exemplifies the inter-individual differences in this population. The following sections discuss some of the factors that have been shown to influence symptom and functional outcomes following mTBI.

Premorbid Factors

The research literature has indicated that some individuals come to an injury with qualities or conditions that create vulnerabilities for the development of persistent postconcussive symptoms. From this perspective, mTBIs should be conceptualized as occurring against a backdrop of moderating factors that characterize an individual.

For instance, the concept of cognitive reserve or brain reserve has been put forth to account for observations that there are interindividual differences in the degree to which brain damage or brain pathology impacts functional abilities (Stern, 2003). Brain reserve capacity is believed to be genetically/biologically rooted. Reflections of brain reserve capacity might include synapse count (i.e., richness of brain connectivity/networks) and brain size. The cognitive reserve model suggests that the brain attempts to cope with damage or insult through compensatory processes. Individuals with greater cognitive reserve would be more successful in compensating for cerebral insult. The model assumes that the same amount of brain injury or pathology will have differing effects from individual to individual. The concept of

cognitive reserve provides a potential explanation as to why research, across neurologic populations, demonstrates that higher levels of intelligence and educational attainment are good predictors as to which individuals can tolerate higher levels of cerebral insult, before manifesting functional impairment. Simply put, this model posits that those with more cognitive reserve are better able to neurologically cope with brain injury. Research has demonstrated that lower levels of cognitive reserve (as indicated by IQ or educational attainment) are associated with a propensity for development of persistent postconcussive complaints in both adults and children (Fay, Yeates, Taylor, Bangert, Dietrich, Nuss, 2010; Meares, Shores, Taylor, Batchelor, Bryant, et al., 2008; Vickery, Sherer, Nick, Nakase-Richardson, Corrigan, Hammond, et al., 2008). The concepts of brain reserve and cognitive reserve also provide frameworks for understanding how premorbid brain insults or conditions (e.g., cerebrovascular disease, previous concussion, cardiovascular disease, substance use, age, psychiatric disturbance etc.) serve to create individual biologic vulnerabilities for the expression of functional impairments and postconcussive symptoms following mTBI.

Age at the time of injury has been shown to be a moderating factor for persistent complaints, with younger individuals and older individuals displaying unique injury-related vulnerabilities, more lengthy recovery times and a greater chance for development of postconcussion symptom persistence (Blinman, Houseknecht, Snyder, Wiebe, & Nance, 2009; Field, Collins, Lovell, & Maroon, 2003; Grady, 2010; Mosenthal, Livingston, Lavery, Knudson, et al., 2004; Stapert, Houx, de Kruijk, Ponds & Jolles, 2006). Women have also been shown to be more vulnerable for heightened levels of postconcussion symptoms, in both the acute and chronic phases of mTBI recovery (Dischinger, Ryb, Kufera, & Auman, 2009; Grady, 2010; Meares et al., 2008).

Preexisting emotional or psychiatric disturbance (particularly depression and anxiety) also create a vulnerability for the development of persistent postconcussive complaints (Dikmen et al., 2010; Dischinger et al., 2009; Meares, 2008; Ponsford et al., 2001; Ponsford et al.,

2010). Research has not yet yielded answers as to whether premorbid psychiatric difficulties account for postconcussive complaints alone or whether they serve as a catalyst, in combination with mTBI, for a heightened expression of postconcussive complaints. Psychiatric and emotional disturbances may also be accompanied by deficits in coping abilities that can adversely impact how an individual negotiates or perceives postconcussive changes.

Personality disorders can play a role in the persistence of postconcussive complaints. Patients with obsessive compulsive personality traits tend to be disciplined and are characterized by a certain level of perfectionism, thus making the mTBI healing process difficult, due to its uncontrollable nature. For these patients, prolonged recovery may be viewed as a personal failure. Patients with a histrionic personality style may seek support and recognition from others and because post-concussive symptoms often elicit attention from family, friends, and physicians, the coping response may involve an overly dramatic presentation of symptoms. Finally, while narcissistic patients are typically overconfident, grandiose, and at times manipulative, they may be ill-equipped to cope with challenges after mTBI, as a result of their high expectations and previous avoidance of personal weakness (Evered et al., 2003). Individuals with personality factors such as over-achievement, dependence, insecurity, grandiosity, and borderline personality characteristics have been found to be particularly vulnerable to more persistent deficits following a brain injury (Kay et al., 1992).

Alcohol intoxication is very common among those acutely hospitalized for brain injury and premorbid alcohol abuse has also been identified as a comorbidity associated with potential poor recovery from mTBI (Corrigan, 1995; Lange, Iverson & Franzen, 2007). Contributors to poor outcome in this population may include a host of demographic factors (Corrigan, 1995) as well as neurophysiologic factors (Allen, Goldstein, Caponigro, & Donahue, 2009).

Variables Associated with the Injury Itself

Every mTBI begins with brain parenchyma responding to external mechanical forces.

Researchers (Vanderploeg, Curtiss, Duchnik & Luis, 2003; Vanderploeg, Curtiss, Luis, & Salazar, 2007) have found that the mTBI itself increased the likelihood of persistent postconcussive complaints and serves to moderate the influence of an individual's pre-injury characteristics in relation to functional outcomes such as work and marital status. Findings such as these indicate that mTBI, as an injury or perhaps as an event can be pivotal for some individuals who experience persistent symptom presentations.

For some, the resulting microstructural white matter damage has now been shown to be associated with postconcussive complaints, in both the acute and chronic phases of recovery from mTBI (Shenton, Hamoda & Schneiderman, et al., 2012). Injury severity variables such as LOC and PTA are also associated with poor outcome in mTBI. This is primarily true for complicated mTBIs that involve positive neuroimaging findings. Reviews of this literature (Larrabee, 2012; Iverson, 2012) indicate that those who have sustained a complicated mTBI can have postconcussive and functional outcomes that are more similar to outcomes associated with moderate TBI. However, these investigators report that the research is somewhat mixed, as to this conclusion, and some studies do not show differences in outcome between those who have sustained complicated or uncomplicated mTBIs, again emphasizing the role of individual differences in this population. King, Crawford, Wenden et al. (1999) reported that injury severity factors such as length of PTA became less useful in predicting persistent postconcussive complaints after approximately six months, with psychosocial variables showing stronger predictive relationships at that time.

Investigators have identified factors that are present within hours or days after injury that serve as predictors for the development of persistent symptom complaints and poor outcomes. Although severity measures such as LOC, GCS and PTA have not proven to be consistent predictors of persistent postconcussive complaints in uncomplicated mTBI (Rosenbaum & Lipton, 2012), researchers (Faux, Sheedy, Delaney, Riopelle, 2011; Sheedy, Geffen, Donelly, Faux & Shores, 2006; Sheedy, Harvey, Faux, Geffen & Shores, 2009) have prospectively demonstrated with cross-validation, that predictive models emphasizing memory declines and pain (particularly headaches) soon after injury are able to predict for the development of a persistent postconcussive presentation, at three months post injury. The authors note that the identification of headache pain as an independent predictor for poor outcome suggests that persisting symptoms may not be exclusively related to head trauma, especially since cervical injuries can be prevalent in this population and can also contribute to headache-related pain. Similarly, other investigators have reported that higher rates of postconcussive symptoms in general, in the acute wake of an mTBI, are predictive of the development of a persistent postconcussion symptom presentation at three months (Lundin et al., 2006; Stulemeijer, van der Werf, Borm & Vos, 2008).

Variables that Emerge in the Acute and Chronic Phases of Recovery

Just as the pre-injury presence of emotional/psychiatric distress has been shown to be a moderator variable for persistent postconcussive complaints in those who have sustained a mTBI, the development of emotional/psychiatric distress after the injury has also been shown to be a moderating factor for persistent postconcussive complaints.

While depression is the most frequently reported single psychological symptom associated with mTBI, with 28% experiencing major depression and almost 90% reporting symptoms of depression, anxiety disorders are also quite prevalent, with comorbid estimates in civilian populations of approximately 24% (Moore, Terryberry-Spohr & Hope, 2006). Posttraumatic Stress Disorder is reported in approximately 13% of civilian patients (Alexander, 1992; Levin et al., 2001), but estimates of PTSD and mTBI comorbidity in military populations may be has high as 44% for those who sustained an LOC and approximately 27% for those who sustained only an alteration in mental status (Hoge, McGurk, Thomas, Cox, Engel & Castro, 2008). Overall, psychiatric problems resulting in moderate disability are reported in 50% of patients, illustrating the importance of this aspect of recovery after mTBI (Levin et al., 2001).

The persistence of psychiatric co-morbidities, such as depression and post-traumatic stress disorder, can not only impact quality of life in an emotional sense, but can also influence neuropsychological outcomes. Severe depression has been associated with widespread cognitive deficits, as indicated by poor performance on a variety of neuropsychological tests, and more mild forms of depression have been associated with lower levels of cognition in older adults, as portrayed through poor performance on the Dementia Rating Scale and Logical Memory tests (Naismith et al., 2003; Lichtenbery et al., 1995). Furthermore, depression has been linked to worse neuropsychological performance in TBI patients (Paul et al., 1998).

Impaired neuropsychological scores have also been found in individuals with PTSD, as poor attention and memory performance have been reported in this patient population (Leskin & White, 2007; Moradi et al., 1999; Vasterling & Brailey, 2005). It has been hypothesized that PTSD and mTBI overlap in relation to neuropathology and neurophysiology, helping to explain similarities in both cognitive and postconcussion symptom presentations post injury (Verfaellie, Amick, & Vasterling, 2012).

One model of post-concussive syndrome characterizes the disorder as one of biogenic origin with psychogenic long-term sequelae (Fenton & McClelland, 1993). In fact, studies have indicated that between 12% to 44% of mTBI patients are diagnosed with a psychiatric condition (primarily depression and anxiety) within the first three months of injury (Iverson, 2012). Investigators have reported that nearly half of mTBI patients diagnosed with a psychiatric condition following injury showed no improvement in psychiatric outcomes at four years post injury (Fenton & McClelland, 1993; Merskey & Woodforde, 1972). Consideration of psychiatric disturbances in mTBI patients are also especially important when determining quality of life outcomes (Petchprapai & Winkelman, 2007). Relatedly, level of social support has also been shown to be a moderating factor in symptom presentation post mTBI, in both adults and children (Kashluba et al., 2008; McCauley et al., 2001; Yeates, 2010).

Somatization, or the psychological process through which individuals convert or express emotional distress as somatic or physically-based symptoms, has been associated with persistent postconcussive complaints (Putnam & Millis, 1994). Theories that focus on aspects of somatization in mTBI largely emphasize the emergence of a selective bias in attention, with an over-focus on common internal states, stresses, feelings of arousal and bodily sensations. Mittenberg et al. (1992) found that when non-injured individuals were asked to imagine that they suffered an mTBI, the non-injured individuals endorsed an array of postconcussive symptoms similar to those endorsed by actual mTBI groups. This effect became known as "expectation as etiology," referring to the naïve anticipation that a head injury will result in postconcussive symptoms, thereby contributing to a potential ongoing misattribution of normal everyday symptoms to an mTBI. This line of research has heightened awareness as to the relevance of suggestibility, in relation to postconcussive symptom presentations, or the notion that the belief that one has sustained a brain injury can, in and of itself, lead to self-reports of symptoms consistent with brain injury. Relatedly, investigators have also reported that individuals who have suffered a mTBI as well as other injuries are vulnerable to overestimating the ways in which an injury has negatively impacted them (Davis, 2002; Gunstad & Suhr, 2001). Suhr and Gunstad (2002 & 2005) further observed that individuals who were told that neuropsychological testing was being conducted to identify the effects of mTBIs performed more poorly on such tests than groups tested without such a leading message. This psychological process/expectation bias has become known as "diagnosis threat" and raises real concerns about the potential for iatrogenically-caused symptoms in mTBI. Finally, Delis and Wetter (2007) proposed criteria for Cogniform Disorder and Cogniform condition. These criteria essentially describe a cognitive somatoform disorder and are characterized by excessive or atypical cognitive symptom reports, in the absence of a documented neurologic problem or malingering. Larrabee (2012) notes that many of the psychological processes and conditions described above are considered to be unintentional and thus fall outside of the realm of "conscious control." (p. 248).

Studies also have pointed out the importance of litigation and secondary gain in relation to symptom presentation following mTBI (Binder et al., 1993; Flaro, Green, Robertson, 2007). However, other studies have failed to find relationships between litigation and persistent symptoms (Bohnen et al., 1994; McCauley et al., 2001; Stulemeijer et al., 2007) or differences in the presentation and performance of non-litigating and litigating samples (Belanger et al., 2005; Evered et al., 2003; Ponsford et al., 2000; Ponsford et al., 2010). It is interesting to note that persistent postconcussive symptoms are also present in countries that do not incorporate a social structure for injury-related litigation (Ruff & Jamora, 2009). In a recent review related to the impact of litigation on postconcussive symptoms, McAllister (2005) indicated that compensation factors alone could not singularly account for persistent postconcussive symptom presentations (p. 288).

An associated topic involves the presence of symptom exaggeration as a moderator factor for persistent postconcussive complaints. For instance, patients who fail the Test of Memory Malingering (TOMM), a measure of effort, not only performed more poorly on tests of memory, attention, and executive functioning, but also reported more post-concussive symptoms as well as cognitive complaints (Lange et al., 2010). Gervais, Ben-Porath, Wygant and Green (2008) also found that when subjects in their sample failed symptom validity testing that any association between memory complaints and deficits noted on a memory test (California Verbal Learning Test) disappeared. Because of such research, assessing symptom report and task engagement with measures of symptom validity and performance validity, respectively, has become standard of practice for neuropsychological evaluations (Bush, Ruff, Troster, Barth, Koffler, Pliskin, Reynolds, & Silver, 2005). With that said, some degree of caution is recommended with regard to the interpretation of these measures in mTBI populations. For instance, somatization was described earlier as a potential moderating factor for symptom presentation. Investigators have cautioned that somatization may adversely impact symptom validity measures (Boone & Lu, 1999; Peck, Schroeder, Heinrichs, VonDran, Brockman,

Webster, & Baade, in press; Williamson, Holsman, Chaytor, Miller, & Drane, 2012; Silver, 2012). Moreover, recent research has indicated that other conditions such as medication effects (Loring, Marino, Drane, Farfitt, Finney, Meador, 2011), manifestations of subclinical seizures (Drane, Williamson, Stroup, Holmes, Jung, Koerner, Chaytor, Wilenski & Miller, 2006) and psychological distress or personality style (Stulemeijer, Andriessen, Brauer, Vos & van der Werf, 2007) can also adversely impact symptom validity testing. Donders and Boonstra (2007) observed that premorbid psychosocial factors and/or psychiatric history were associated with a four-fold increase in failure on symptom validity testing, especially in relation to mTBI. For a review of many of these complicated contributing factors see Silver (2012).

Management

The natural course of recovery after mild traumatic brain injury (mTBI) for those with persistent symptoms is a nonlinear and heterogeneous process involving a complex of interacting symptoms. Although research has yielded considerable data regarding the involvement and progression of specific symptoms, there are a number of factors whose influence on recovery after mTBI has yet to be definitively identified. Recovery from mTBI involves the resolution of any physical symptoms (dizziness, fatigue, sleep difficulty, nausea, headache, blurred vision, and sensitivity to intense light and sound), cognitive symptoms (difficulty concentrating, memory problems, and impaired problem solving), as well as behavioral symptoms (irritability, anger outbursts, depression, anxiety, and poor social functioning) (Bernstein, 1999; McCrea et al., 2009). McHugh (2006) outlined a general timeline of recovery. At one week post-injury, physical symptoms and pain are reported, along with findings of cognitive deficits, such as reduced verbal abilities. At seven months post-injury, only cognitive symptoms such as verbal fluency and working memory impairment remain (McHugh, 2006; Raskin & Rearick, 1996).

Ruff (2011) has suggested that post-concussive syndrome might be divided into four subtypes, all of which entail a different mechanism of recovery. Post concussive syndrome with neuropathological features is characterized by neuroimaging that shows brain damage consistent with TBI and a three-month post-injury neuropsychological profile that indicates cognitive dysfunction caused by brain dysfunction. Post concussive syndrome with neurocognitive features is associated with negative imaging findings and cognitive symptoms specifically due to injury-induced brain dysfunction. Post concussive syndrome with psychopathological features is also characterized by negative imagining findings, but includes psychological problems, such as irritability, anxiety, depression, affective lability, apathy, and changes in personality. Finally, post concussive syndrome with mixed features is a mixedsymptom complex encompassing symptoms from two or more subtypes (Ruff, 2011).

Although the majority of individuals with mTBI recover from their injury within the acute post-injury period, the small proportion that continues to report deficits may require some kind of management. The debate in the literature over the nature of these reported deficits has led to a somewhat complex conceptualization of the type of management that is best suited to these individuals. In this chapter we will take the approach eloquently summarized by Ruff (2011) that the question of brain-based versus not brain-based is moot in the realm of treatment, given that all emotional disorders are also, in reality, brain-based. Rather, we will take a patient-centered approach of trying to summarize which approaches to management seem to lead to the greatest recovery of functioning in daily life. Within a biopsychosocial model, all of these symptoms interact. Thus, cognitive deficits can lead to difficulty paying attention and therefore ability to perform in occupational or social settings and this inability can lead to increased isolation, negative mood and feelings of worthlessness as well as stress related exacerbation of physical symptoms such as pain, which can then cause further cognitive decrements (Ruff, 2011).

Immediately following the injury, most guidelines include both physical and cognitive rest (Meehan, 2011). A gradual return to usual activities is then attempted with reduction in activities if any symptoms return or are exacerbated. Specific interventions for mTBI can be subdivided into four broad categories, including pharmacotherapy, cognitive rehabilitation, psychotherapy and patient education (Comper et al., 2005). Treatment can focus on individual symptoms or be multidisciplinary.

Several forms of pharmacotherapy may be utilized in the treatment of specific somatic, cognitive, psychiatric, and psychological symptoms (Comper et al., 2005). Anti-depressant medications have been used widely both to treat depression and to treat headache (Fann et al., 2001; Meehan, 2011). Additionally, a migraine abortive preparation by the name of dihydro-ergotamine was shown to improve headaches, decrease memory dysfunction, and reduce sleep disturbance and dizziness (McBeath & Nanda, 1994). Amantadine has been used to treat fatigue related headaches as well (Meehan, 2011). Employment of the anti-diuretic DDAVP (Demopressin Acetate) was associated with minor improvement in information processing speed as well as immediate recall. Despite the partial successes of some medications, no one specific drug treatment has been proven effective for one or more symptoms (Comper et al., 2005). For more comprehensive reviews of pharmacotherapy for mTBI please see Silver, McAllister, and Arciniegas (2006) or Meehan (2011).

A variety of manual, physical, biofeedback and chiropractic treatments have also been used to treat somatic symptoms such as headache (Meehan, 2011). Jensen and colleagues employed manual therapy in an attempt to ameliorate post-traumatic headaches. Manual therapy involved twelve weeks of either manual mobilization of hyper-mobile spinal segments or application of a cold pack to the neck and shoulders. The study revealed that manual manipulation in fact reduced pain associated with post-mTBI headaches. Follow-up work on such therapy is lacking, and thus the efficacy of this intervention requires further support (Jensen et al., 1990).

Cognitive rehabilitation is also a commonly employed intervention, and specifically targets the cognitive symptoms of mTBI, which in turn may have an effect on psychiatric and psychological symptoms (Raskin & Mateer, 2000). The purpose of cognitive rehabilitation is to target attention and information processing skills, memory functioning, and problem solving skills (Snell et al., 2008). Such treatment has shown success in some patients, and those with the greatest improvements on neuropsychological measures of cognition and on post concussive syndrome factors display the best functional outcomes (Cicerone et al., 1996). The success in cognitive rehabilitation lies in the individual tailoring of rehabilitation for a patient's cognitive symptoms (Snell et al., 2008). Unfortunately, the literature on treatment for mTBI is still quite sparse. In a systematic review, Comper et al. (2005) reviewed 1,055 published studies and identified 163 that were not merely case studies or case series designs and that did not utilize individuals over five years post injury. From these 163 studies, only 20 met their criteria for validity, selection bias, withdrawals and dropouts, intervention and integrity and analyses.

One of the most widely targeted deficits for cognitive rehabilitation is attention. Attention is, of course, multifaceted and can include basic alertness, sustained attention, divided attention or alternation attention (Sohlberg et al., 1996). One of the most widely documented approaches to attention training is attention process training (Sohlberg et al., 2002). This approach involves a set of standardized auditory and visual procedures made increasingly challenging through a structured hierarchy of task complexity and increased distraction. The Attention Process Training (APT)-II program, utilizes a hierarchal construction to specifically target cognitive symptoms of mTBI (Sohlberg et al., 1996). This intervention builds upon the retained attentional skills after mTBI in an attempt to re-establish a pre-injury level of cognition. The program consists of auditory components as well as visual exercises. The auditory portion includes sixteen cassette tapes with four exercises for sustained, selective, alternating, and divided attention. Each exercise is five minutes long, and includes both a slow and fast version as well as an easy and hard version of each application. The activities require the mental manipulation of words, numbers, and letters. In the hierarchal process, patients are only allowed to proceed to a more difficult exercise after having successfully completed the exercise at hand, with a maximum of one missed target on two consecutive trials. The success in the APT-II program, as with other cognitive rehabilitation, lies in the tailoring of the program to each individual patient in order to address his or her area of deficit and its severity (Sohlberg, McLaughlin & Pavese, 2002). This intervention has been shown to restore attention to some degree of its pre-injury state in patients under certain conditions, and has done so in a stable and persistent manner (Palmese & Raskin, 2000). Despite such success, limitations of the APT-II program lie in the question of whether these improvements are treatment specific (Palmese & Raskin, 2000).

Another approach to attention deficits, working memory rehabilitation, utilizes a strategy-training model in order to encourage compensation for residual deficits as well as the adoption of strategies for more effective allocation of retained attentional resources. In particular, time pressure management aims to ameliorate the consequences of slowed information processing. This form of working memory rehabilitation encourages the development of steps to reduce the pressure of time when completing tasks (Fasotti et al., 2000). Working memory rehabilitation has been shown to yield improvements on speeded stimulus processing, possibly as a result of an increased awareness and management of temporal demands by the patient. Moreover, individuals were able to resume their pre-injury vocational and social roles after treatment, suggesting that generalization of cognitive gains is associated with this form of rehabilitation (Cicerone, 2002).

Management of memory deficits after mTBI includes both strategy training and the training in the use of external aids. Memory strategy training using visual imagery has been shown to be effective for individuals with mTBI (Kaschel, Della Sala, Cantagallo, et al., 2002) and, in fact, was more effective than in individuals with more severe injuries. After 30 sessions over 10 weeks, significant improvement of delayed recall in everyday memory was demonstrated.

Memory prosthetics, such as notebooks, iPhone apps, pagers, etc. have been used with success (Thickpenny-Davis & Barker-Collow, 2007). In all cases the greatest success is found when the use of the aid is embedded in a systematic training program, such as focusing on how the use of a notebook could help to solve problems in daily activities (Ownsworth & McFarland, 1999).

Metacognitive strategies appear to be a particularly useful approach in this population. Strategies include the use of multiple steps, problem-solving training and goal setting. Goal Management Training involves identifying a goal, breaking it down into steps and monitoring performance (Levine & Robertson, 2000). In a study with higher-level individuals with brain injury, Rath, Simon, Langenbahn, Sherr, and Diller (2003) used a problem-solving strategy that was aimed at both emotional self-regulation and logical thinking and reasoning. Outcome was measured with standard neuropsychological measures, measures of self-appraisal, and independent observer's measures of videotaped role-playing sessions.

Psychotherapy

Treatment of emotional issues typically involves a combination of medication and psychotherapy. The most commonly used form of psychotherapy is Cognitive Behavioral Therapy (CBT). CBT techniques have been used to treat various symptoms including both somatic and emotional difficulties. CBT is a brief, structured, goal-oriented treatment. It involves helping individuals recognize maladaptive thoughts and beliefs and introducing more adaptive thoughts while slowly reintroducing the individual into enjoyable and productive activities. It is often paired with some form of relaxation training. In cases of headache and chronic pain CBT has been used to help individuals regain control over the pain and change maladaptive thoughts and behaviors that maintain and exacerbate the experience of pain (Otis, McGlinchey, Vasterling, & Kerns, 2011).

CBT has been used successfully in cases of depression, anxiety and anger following mTBI (Anson & Ponsford, 2006; Silver, McAllister & Arciniegas, 2009). Multidisciplinary treatments that included CBT and CR have perhaps proven to be the most useful approach in individuals who experience depression after mTBI (Raskin & Stein, 2000). This is because decreases in cognitive functioning can lead to feelings of depression while symptoms of depression can lead to decreased cognitive functioning (Ghaffer, McCullagh, Ouchteriony, & Feinstein, 2006). Multidisciplinary treatments have been demonstrated to decrease depression, anxiety and anger and to improve problem-solving skills, self-esteem and psychosocial functioning (Sohlberg, 2000).

Although the existence of post-traumatic stress disorder (PTSD) following TBI remains somewhat controversial in cases of post-traumatic amnesia, in veterans with mTBI it is common to report symptoms of PTSD if not the full syndrome (Lippa, Pastorek, Benge, & Thornton, 2010) and it has been reported in nonveterans as well (McCauley et al., 2012). CBT has been reported to be effective in reducing the development of PTSD (Bryant, Moulds, Guthrie, & Nixon, 2003) and in treating the symptoms (Otis et al., 2011). Otis, Keane, Kerns, Monson and Scioli (2009) reported on an integrated interdisciplinary treatment approach that included Cognitive Processing Therapy (CPT) for PTSD and CBT for chronic pain management. This included relaxation training, activity goal setting, cognitive restructuring, and introduction of return to pleasurable activities.

Chard et al. (2010) also used a CPT based treatment which they modified for use with individuals who have mTBI. CPT is a common treatment technique for PTSD that involves having the individuals write about the traumatic event, read it to the therapist and then re-read it daily in the context of cognitive restructuring to challenge false beliefs (e.g., Resick & Schnicke, 1993). In the study by Chard et al. (2010), the modifications included taping the treatment sessions for review, adding booster sessions and modifying the treatment materials.

In a pilot study, Cicerone et al. (2012) used a mindfulness-based stress reduction program with a group of 22 individuals with mTBI. The program had been specifically tailored for individuals with mTBI. After 10 weeks of training they noted significant improvement on measures of quality of life and self-efficacy with smaller improvements on measures of working memory and management of attention.

One of the most effective approaches to management has been patient education. Ponsford, Wilmott, Rothwell, Cameron, Kelly, Nelms and Curran (2002) demonstrated that just giving an information booklet at one week post injury led to fewer reported symptoms at three months compared to a control group that did not receive an information booklet. Typically, patient education provides mTBI patients with educational information, reassurance regarding expected recovery, as well as guidance about symptom management and return to pre-injury lifestyle (Snell et al., 2008). Routine follow-up soon after injury, including a printed and oral review of symptom management with a therapist, has been shown to be more effective than usual hospital services for not only symptom improvement, but also social and functional disability (Mittenberg et al., 2001; Wade et al., 1997).

Patient education approaches can be brief, with minimal involvement, or more long-term and intensive. Some of the intensive models have included cognitive behavioral therapy, such as education and progressive muscle relaxation therapy, alongside education-based supportive counseling in order to prevent the development of PTSD (Bryant et al, 2003). Paniak et al., reported that when applied within three weeks post injury, brief education and reassurance-oriented intervention is equally effective as more intensive and expensive educational models (Paniak et al., 1998; Paniak et al., 2000). Thus, simple education through supportive patient-centered interactions and the provision of symptom-related information by a physician is an effective option for mTBI intervention (Comper et al., 2005).

Implementation of psychosocial therapy as a treatment for mTBI has been limited, but has shown some promising results. The "Outward Bound Course—Three Days of Outdoor Challenge Experience" was developed by Lemmon and colleagues as a psychosocial approach. The program involved group sessions and activities to address creativity, communication, problem solving strategies, and issues related to brain injury rehabilitation. The intervention was successful in providing positive psychosocial effects, as indicated by patient reports of increases in self-esteem and problem-solving abilities (Lemmon et al., 1996).

A consensus is yet to emerge on the best practices for treatment of individuals with mTBI. A recent report by the Institute of Medicine (Koehler, Wilhelm, & Shoulson, 2011) concluded that cognitive rehabilitation remains promising but that the evidence for its therapeutic value continues to be limited due to the heterogeneity of TBI, the lack of operational definitions of different forms of treatment, small sample sizes in most studies and the variable impact of premorbid and comorbid conditions. This committee made several important suggestions to improve the quality of evidence. This includes mining clinical practice data, standardized techniques within each cognitive domain across sites, and a more rigorous review of adverse effects of treatment. Overall, there is a great need for further research into the best practices for management of mTBI. In a series of articles, Cicerone and his colleagues (Cicerone, Azulay & Trott, 2009; Cicerone et al., 2005) have reviewed current research for evidence-based practice and made recommendations of best practices. They suggest that future research should move beyond demonstrating whether cognitive rehabilitation is effective, and examine specific aspects of therapy and patient characteristics that optimize the clinical outcomes of cognitive rehabilitation. At this time, however, it seems clear that individuals who are unable to return to work or social activities may require some intervention, regardless of whether the etiology of the symptoms is easily determined or multiply determined. It should not come as a surprise that emotional, social, and metacognitive functions may be simultaneously involved and may also require some form of management. Some attempts to construct a straightforward guide to referral and treatment have been made (Helmick et al., 2010) and represent a considerable move in the direction of comprehensive care of those currently experiencing post-concussive symptoms.

References

Alexander, M. P. (1992). Neuropsychiatric correlates of persistent postconcussive syndrome. Journal of *Head Trauma Rehabilitation, 7*, 60–69.

Alexander, M. P. (1995). Mild traumatic brain injury: pathophysiology, natural history, and clinical management. *Neurology, 45*, 1253–1260.

Allen, D. N., Goldstein, G., Caponigro, J. M., & Donahue, B. (2009). The effects of alcoholism comorbidity on neurocognitive function following traumatic brain injury. *Applied Neuropsychology, 16*, 186–192.

American Congress of Rehabilitation Medicine. (1993). Definition of mild traumatic brain injury. *Journal of Head Trauma & Rehabilitation, 8*, 86–87.

American Psychiatric Association (1994). Diagnostic and statistical manual of mental disorders (4th ed.). Washington, DC: Author.

Anson, K., & Ponsford, J. (2006). Coping and emotional adjustment following traumatic brain injury. *Journal of Head Trauma Rehabilitation, 21*(3), 248–259.

Aoki, Y., Inokuchi, R., Gunshin, M., Yahagi, N., & Suwa, H. (2012). Diffusion tensor imaging studies of mild traumatic brain injury: a meta-analysis. *Journal of Neurology, Neurosurgery & Psychiatry, 10*, 1–7.

Arfanakis, K., Haughton, V. M., et al. (2002). Diffusion tensor MR imaging in diffuse axonal injury. *American Journal of Neuroradiology, 23*(5), 794–802.

Atlas, S. (2001). *Imaging of the Brain and Spine*. Hagerstown, MD, Lippincott Williams & Williams.

Bailey, C. M., Barth, J., & Bender, S. (2009). SLAM on the stand: How sports-related concussion literature can inform the expert witness. *Journal of Head Trauma Rehabilitation, 24*, 123–130.

Bailey, C. M., Echemendia, R. J., & Arnett, P. A. (2006). The impact of motivation on neuropsychological performance in sports-related mild traumatic brain injury. *Journal of the International Neuropsychological Society, 12*, 475–484.

Barkhoudarian, G., Hovda, D. A., & Giza, C. C. (2011). The molecular pathophysiology of concussive brain injury. *Clinics in Sports Medicine, 30*, 33–48.

Barth, J. T., Freeman, J. R., Broshek, D. K., & Varney, R. N. (2001). Acceleration-deceleration sport-related concussion: The gravity of it all. *Journal of Athletic Training, 36*, 253–256.

Bazarian, J. J., McClung, J., Shah, M. N., Cheng, Y. T., Flesher, W., & Krauss, J. (2005). Mild traumatic brain injury in the United States, 1998-2000. *Brain Injury, 19*, 85–91.

Bazarian, J., Zhong, J., Blyth, B., Zhu, T., Kavcic, V., & Peterson, D. (2007). Diffusion tensor imaging detects clinically important axonal damage after mild traumatic brain injury: A pilot study. *Journal of Neurotrauma, 24*, 1447–1459.

Bazarian, J. J., Blyth, B., & Cimpello, L. (2006). Bench to bedside: Evidence for brain injury after concussion—looking beyond the computed tomography scan. *Academic Emergency Medicine, 13*(2), 199–214.

Beckmann, C. F., DeLuca, M., Devlin, J. T., & Smith, S. M. (2005a). Investigations into resting-state connectivity using independent component analysis *Philosophical Transactions of the Royal Society of London, Series B: Biological Sciences; 360*(1457), 1001–1013.

Belanger, H. G., Curtiss, G., Demery, J. A., Lebowitz, B. K., & Vanderploeg, R. D. (2005). Factors moderating neuropsychological outcomes following mild traumatic brain injury: a meta-analysis. *Journal of the International Neuropsychological Society, 11*, 215–227.

Belanger, H. G., Spiegel, E., & Vanderploeg, R. D. (2010). Neuropsychological performance following a history of multiple self-reported concussions: A meta-analysis. *Journal of the International Neuropsychological Society, 16*, 262–267.

Benson, R. R., Meda, S. A., et al. (2007). Global white matter analysis of diffusion tensor images is predictive of injury severity in traumatic brain injury. *J Neurotrauma 24*(3), 446–459.

Bernstein, D. M. (1999). Recovery from mild head injury. Brain injury, *13*, 151–172.

Bigler (2008). Neuropsychology and clinical neuroscience of persistent postconcussive syndrome. *Journal of the International Neuropsychological Society, 14*, 1–22.

Bigler, E. D. (2001). Quantitative magnetic resonance imaging in traumatic brain injury. *Journal of Head Trauma Rehabilitation, 16*(2), 117–134.

Bigler, E. G. (2001). The lesion(s) in traumatic brain injury: implications for clinical neuropsychology. *Archives of Clinical Neuropsychology, 16*(2), 95–131.

Bigler, E. D. (2005). *Structural Imaging*. Textbook of Traumatic Brain Injury. J. M. Silver, T. W. McAllister and S. C. Yudofsky. Washington, DC, American Psychiatric Press.

Bigler, E. D., & Maxwell, W. L. (2012). Neuropathology of mild traumatic brain injury: Relationship to neuroimaging findings. *Brain Imaging and Behavior, mTBI* Special Issue.

Binder, L. M. (1997). A review of mild head trauma. Part II: clinical implications. *Journal of Clinical and Experimental Neuropsychology, 19*, 5–20.

Binder, L. M., Rohling, M., & Larrabee, G. (1997). A review of mild head trauma. I. Meta-analytic review of neuropsychological studies. *Journal of Clinical and Experimental Neuropsychology, 19*, 421–437.

Blaylock, R., & Maroon, J. (2011). Immuno-excitotoxity as a central mechanism in chronic traumatic encephalopathy—A unifying hypothesis. *Surgical Neurology International, 2*, 107.

Blinman, T. A., Houseknecht, E., Snyder, C., Wiebe, D. J., & Nance, M. L. (2009). Postconcussive symptoms in hospitalized pediatric patients after mild traumatic brain injury. *Journal of Pediatric Surgery, 44*, 1223–1228.

Boone, K. B., & Lu, P. H. (1999). Impact of somatoform symptomatology on credibility of cognitive performance. *The Clinical Neuropsychologist, 13*, 414–419

Brooks, B. L., Mckay, C., Mrazik, M., & Barlow, K. M. (2013). Subjective, but not objective, lingering effects of multiple past concussions in adolescents. *Journal of Neurotrauma, 30*, 1469–1475.

Bryant, R., Moulds, A., Guthrie, R., et al. (2003). Treating acute stress disorder following mild traumatic brain injury. *American Journal of Psychiatry, 160*, 585–587.

Buckner, R. L., Andrews-Hanna, J., & Schacter, D. (2008): The brain's default network: Anatomy, function and relevance to disease. *Annals of the New York Academy of Sciences, 1124*, 1–38.

Bush, S. S., Ruff, R. M., Troster, A. I., Barth, J. T., Koffler, S. P., Pliskin, N. H., Reynolds, C. R., & Silver, C. H. (2005). Symptom validity assessment: Practice issues and medical necessity: NAN Policy & Planning Committee. *Archives of Clinical Neuropsychology, 20*, 419–426.

Calhoun, V. D., Kiehl, K. A., & Pearlson, G. D. (2008). Modulation of temporally coherent brain networks estimated using ICA at rest and during cognitive tasks. *Human Brain Mapping, 29*(7), 828–838.

Carlsson, G. S., Svardsudd, K., & Welin, L. (1987). Long-term effects of head injuries sustained during life in three mail populations. *Journal of Neurosurgery, 67*, 197–205.

Caroll, L. J., Cassidy, J. D., Holm, L., Kraus, J., & Coronado, V. J. (2004). Methodological issues and research recommendations for mild traumatic brain injury. *Journal of Rehabilitation Medicine, 43*, 28–60.

Caroll, L. J., Cassidy, J. D., Holm, L., Kraus, J., & Coronado, V. J. (2004). Methodological issues and research recommendations for mild traumatic brain injury: The WHO collaborating centre task force on mild traumatic brain injury. *Journal of Rehabilitation Medicine*, Suppl. *43*, 84–105.

Castellanos, N. P., Paul, N., et al. (2010). Reorganization of functional connectivity as a correlate of cognitive recovery in acquired brain injury. *Brain, 133*(Pt 8), 2365–2381.

Chappell, M. H., Ulug, A. M., et al. (2006). Distribution of microstructural damage in the brains of professional boxers: a diffusion MRI study. *Journal of Magnetic Resonance Imaging, 24*(3), 537–542.

Chard, K. M., Schumm, J. A., Owens, G. P., & Cottingham, S. M. (2010). A comparison of OEF and OIF veterans and Vietnam veterans receiving cognitive processing therapy. *Journal of Traumatic Stress, 23*(1), 25–32.

Cicerone, K. D. (2002). Remediation of 'working attention' in mild traumatic brain injury. *Brain Injury, 16*, 185–195.

Cicerone, K. D. (2012). Facts, theories, values: Shaping the course of neurorehabilitation. The 60th John Stanley Coulter Memorial Lecture. *Archives of Physical Medicine and Rehabilitation, 93*(2), 188–191.

Cicerone, K. D., Azulay, J., & Trott, C. (2009). Methodological quality of research on cognitive rehabilitation after traumatic brain injury. *Archives of Physical Medicine and Rehabilitation, 90*, 52–59.

Cicerone, K. D., Mott, T., Azulay, J., & Friel, J. C. (2004). Community integration and satisfaction with functioning after intensive cognitive rehabilitation for traumatic brain injury. *Archives of Physical Medicine and Rehabilitation, 85*(6), 943–950.

Cicerone, K. D., Smith, L. C., Ellmo, W., et al. (1996). Neuropsychological rehabilitation of mild traumatic brain injury. *Brain Injury, 10*, 277–286.

Comper, P. Bisschop, S. M., Carnide, N., & Tricco, A. (2005). A systematic review of treatments for mild traumatic brain injury. *Brain Injury, 19*, 863–880.

Cordes, D., Haughton, V. M., Arfanakis, K., Wendt, G. J., Turski, P. A., Moritz, C. H., et al. (2000). Mapping functionally related regions of brain with functional connectivity MR Imaging. *American Journal of Neuroradiology, 21*, 1636–1664.

Corrigan, J. D. (1995). Substance abuse as a mediating factor in outcome from Traumatic Brain Injury. *Archives of Physical Medicine & Rehabilitation, 76*, 302–309.

Damoiseaux, J. S., Rombouts, S. A., Barkhof, F., Scheltens, P., Stam, C. J., Smith, S. M., et al. (2006). Consistent resting-state networks across healthy subjects. *Proceedings of the National Academy of Sciences of the United States of America, 103*(37), 13848–13853.

Davis, C. H. (2002). Self-perception in mild traumatic brain injury. *American Journal of Physical Medicine & Rehabilitation, 81*, 609–621.

De Luca, M., Beckmann, C. F., De Stefano, N., Matthews, P. M., & Smith, S. M. (2006). fMRI resting state networks define distinct modes of long-distance interactions in the human brain. *Neuroimage, 29*(4), 1359–1367.

Deco, G., & Corbetta M. (2011). The dynamical balance of the brain at rest. *Neuroscientist, 17*(1), 107–123.

Deco, G., Jirsa, V. K., et al. (2010). Emerging concepts for the dynamical organization of resting-state activity in the brain. *Nature Reviews Neuroscience, 12*(1), 43–56.

Delis, D. C. & Wetter, S. R. (2007). Cogniform disorder and cogniform condition: Proposed diagnoses for excessive cognitive symptoms. *Archives of Clinical Neuropsychology, 22*, 683–687.

Dikmen, S., Machamer, J., et al. (2010). Rates of symptom reporting following traumatic brain injury. *Journal of the International Neuropsychological Society, 16*(3), 401–411.

Dikmen, S. S., Ross, B. L., et al. (1995). One year psychosocial outcome in head injury. *Journal of the International Neuropsychological Society, 1*(1), 67–77.

Dikmen, S., Machamer, J., et al. (2001). Functional status examination: a new instrument for assessing outcome in traumatic brain injury. *Journal of Neurotrauma, 18*(2), 127–140.

Dikmen, S., Machamer, J., et al. (2001). Mild head injury: facts and artifacts. *Journal of Clinical and Experimental Neuropsychology, 23*(6), 729–738.

Dischinger, P. C., Ryb, G. E., Kufera, J. A., & Auman, K. M. (2009). Early predictors of postconcussive syndrome in a population of trauma patients with mild traumatic brain injury. *The Journal of Trauma, 66*, 289–296.

Donders, J., & Boonstra, T. (2007). Correlates of invalid neuropsychological test performance after traumatic brain injury. *Brain Injury, 21*, 319–326.

Dosenbach, N. U., Fair, D. A., Miezin, F. M., Cohen, A. L., Wenger, K. K., Dosenbach, R. A., et al. (2007a). Distinct brain networks for adaptive and stable task control in humans. *Proceedings of the National Academy of Sciences of the United States of America, 104*(26), 11073–11078.

Drane, D. L., Williamson, D. J., Stroup, E., Holmes, M. D., Jung, M., Koerner, E., Chaytor, N., Wilenski, A. J., & Miller, J. W. (2006). Cognitive impairment is not equal in patients with epileptic and psychogenic non-epileptic seizures. *Epilepsia, 47*, 1879–1886.

Eichele, T., Debener, S., Calhoun, V. D., Specht, K., Engel, A. K., Hudgahl, K., von Cramon, D. Y., & Ullsperger, M. (2008). Prediction of human errors by maladaptive changes in event-related brain networks. *Proceedings of the National Academy of Sciences, 105*, 6173–6178.

Eisenberg, H. M., & Levin, H. S. (1989). *Computed tomography and magnetic resonance imaging in mild to moderate head injury.* Mild Head Injury. H. S. Levin, H. M. Eisenberg and A. Benton. New York, Oxford University Press, 133–141.

Ettenhofer, M. L., & Barry, D. M. (2012). A comparison of long-term postconcussive symptoms between university students with and without a history of mild traumatic brain injury or orthopedic injury. *Journal of the International Neuropsychological Society, 18*, 451–460.

Evered, L., Ruff, R., Baldo, J., & Isomura, A. (2003). Emotional risk factors and postconcussional disorder. *Assessment, 10*, 420–427.

Fann, F. R., Uomoto, J. M., & Katon, W. J. (2001). Cognitive improvement with treatment of depression following mild traumatic brain injury. *Psychosomatics, 42*, 48–54.

Fasotti, L., Jovacs, F., Eling, P. A. T. M., et al. (2000). Time pressure management as a compensatory training strategy after close head injury. *Neuropsychological Rehabilitation, 10*, 47–65.

Faux, S., Sheedy, J. O., Delaney, R. & Riopelle, R. (2010). Emergency department prediction of post-concussive syndrome following mild traumatic brain injury—an international cross validation study. *Brain Injury, 25*, 14–22.

Fay, T. B., Yeates, K. O., Taylor, H. G., Bangert, B., Dietrich, A., & Nuss, K. E., et al. (2010). Cognitive reserve as a moderator of postconcussive symptoms in children with complicated and uncomplicated mild traumatic brain injury. *Journal of the International Neuropsychological Society, 16*, 94–105.

Fenton, G., & McClelland, R. (1993). The postconcussional syndrome: social antecedents and psychological sequelae. *British Journal of Psychiatry, 162*, 493–497.

Field, M., Collins, M. W., Lovell, M. R., & Maroon, J. (2003). Does age play a role in recovery from sports-related concussion? A comparison of high school and collegiate athletes. *Journal of Pediatrics, 142*, 546–553.

Fitzgerald, D. B., & Crosson, B. A. (2011). Diffusion weighted imaging and neuropsychological correlates in adults with mild traumatic brain injury. *International Journal of Psychophysiology, 82*, 79–85.

Fransson, P. (2005). Spontaneous low-frequency BOLD signal fluctuations: an fMRI investigation of the resting-state default mode of brain function. *Human Brain Mapping, 26*, 15–29.

Frencham, K. A. R., Fox, A. M., & Maybery, M. T. (2005). Neuropsychological studies of mild traumatic brain injury: a meta-analytic review of research since 1995. *Journal of Clinical and Experimental Neuropsychology, 27*, 334–351.

Frencham, K. A. R., Fox, A. M., & Maybery, M. T. (2005). Neuropsychological studies of mild traumatic brain injury: a meta-analytic review of research since 1995. *Journal of Clinical and Experimental Neuropsychology, 27*, 334–351.

Friston, K. (2002). Functional integration and inference in the brain. *Progress in Neurobiology, 68*(2), 113–143.

Gavett, B., Stern, R., & McKee, A. (2011). Chronic traumatic encephalopathy: a potential late effect of sport-related concussive and subconcussive head trauma. *Clinical Sports Medicine, 30*, 179–88.

Gean, A. D. (1984). *Imaging of Head Trauma.* New York, Raven Press.

Gervais, R. O., Ben-Porath, Y. S., Wygant, D. B., & Green, P. (2008). Differential sensitivity of the Response Bias Scale (RBS) and MMIP-2 validity scales to memory complaints. *The Clinical Neuropsychologist, 22*, 1061–1079.

Giza, C. C. & Hovda, D. A. (2001). The neurometabolic cascade of concussion. *Journal of Athletic Training, 36*, 228–235.

Grady, M. F. (2010). Concussion in the adolescent athlete. *Current Problems in Pediatric and Adolescent Health Care, 40*, 154–169.

Greiffenstein, M. (2008). Clinical myths of forensic neuropsychology. *The Clinical Neuropsychologist, 22*, 1–11.

Green, P., & Allen, L. M. (2000). Pattern of memory complaints in 577 consecutive patients passing or failing symptom validity tests. *Archives of Clinical Neuropsychology, 15*, 844–845.

Greve, M. W., & Zinc, B. J. (2009). Pathophysiology of traumatic brain injury. *Mount Sinai Journal of Medicine, 76*, 97–104.

Gunstad, J., & Suhr, J. A. (2001). Expectation as etiology versus the good old days: Postconcussion syndrome symptom reporting in athletes, headache sufferers, and depressed individuals. *Journal of the International Neuropsychological Society, 7*, 323–333.

Halstead, M. E., & Walter, K. D. (2010). American Academy of Pediatrics Clinical Report: Sports-related concussion in children and adolescents. *Pediatrics, 126*, 597–615.

Heitger, M. H., Jones, R. D., Macleod, A. D., et al. (2009). Impaired eye movements in postconcussive-syndrome indicate suboptimal brain function beyond the influence of depression, malingering or intellectual ability. *Brain, 132*, 2850–2870.

Helmick, K. and members of Concensus Conference (2010). Cognitive rehabilitation for military personnel with mild traumatic brain injury and chronic post-concussional disorder: Results of the April 2009 conference. *Neurorehabilitation, 26*, 2399–255.

Hillary, F. G., Slocomb, J., et al. (2011). Changes in resting connectivity during recovery from severe traumatic brain injury. *International Journal of Psychophysiology, 82*, 115–123.

Hofman, P. A., Stapert, S. Z., et al. (2001). MR imaging, single-photon emission CT, and neurocognitive performance after mild traumatic brain injury. *American Journal of Neuroradiology, 22*(3), 441–449.

Hoge, C. W., McGurk, D., Thomas, J. L., Cox, A. L., Engel, C. C. & Castro, C. A. (2008). Mild traumatic brain injury in U.S. soldiers returning from Iraq. *The New England Journal of Medicine, 358*, 453–463.

Hughes, D. G., Jackson, A., et al. (2004). Abnormalities on magnetic resonance imaging seen acutely following mild traumatic brain injury: correlation with neuropsychological tests and delayed recovery. *Neuroradiology, 46*(7), 550–558.

Huisman, T. A., Sorensen, A. G., et al. (2003). Diffusion-weighted imaging for the evaluation of diffuse axonal injury in closed head injury. *Journal of Computer Assisted Tomography, 27*(1), 5–11.

Huisman, T. A., Schwamm, L. H., et al. (2004). Diffusion tensor imaging as potential biomarker of white matter injury in diffuse axonal injury. *American Journal of Neuroradiology, 25*(3), 370–376.

Inglese, M., Makani, S., et al. (2005). Diffuse axonal injury in mild traumatic brain injury: a diffusion tensor imaging study. *Journal of Neurosurgery, 103*(2), 298–303.

Iverson, G. L., & Lange, R. T. (2012). Traumatic brain injury in the work place. In S. S. Bush and G. L. Iverson (Eds.), *Neuropsychological Assessment of Work-Related Injuries* (pp. 9–67). New York: Guilford.

Iverson, G. L. (2005). Outcome from mild traumatic brain injury. *Current Opinion in Psychiatry, 18*, 301–307.

Iverson, G. L. (2010). Mild traumatic brain injury meta-analyses can obscure individual differences. *Brain Injury, 24*, 1246–1255.

Iverson, G. L. (2012). A biopsychosocial conceptualization of poor outcome from mild traumatic brain injury. In J. V. Vasterling, R. A.,Bryant, & T. M. Keane, (Eds.), *PTSD and Mild Traumatic Brain Injury* (pp. 37–60). New York: The Guilford Press.

Iverson, G. L., Lange, R. T., Gaetz, M., & Zasler, N. D. (2006). Mild TBI. In N. D. Zasler, H. T. Katz & R. D. Zafonte (Eds.), *Brain Injury Medicine: Principles and Practice* (pp. 333–371). New York: Demos.

Iverson, G. L., Zasler, N. D., & Lange, R. T. (2006). Post-concussive disorder. In N. D. Zasler, H. T. Katz & R. D. Zafonte (Eds.), *Brain Injury Medicine: Principles and Practice* (pp. 373–405). New York: Demos.

Iverson, G. L., Lovell, M. R., Smith, S., & Franzen, M. D. (2000). Prevalence of abnormal CT scans following mild head injury. *Brain Injury, 14*, 1057–1061.

Jennett, B., & Teasdale, G. (1981). *Management of Head Injuries*. Philadelphia, PA: FA Davis.

Jenkins, A., Teasdale, G., et al. (1986). Brain lesions detected by magnetic resonance imaging in mild and severe head injuries. *Lancet, 2*(8504), 445–446.

Jensen, O. K., Nielson, F. F., & Vosmar, L. (1990). An open study comparing manual therapy with the use of cold packs in the treatment of post-traumatic headache. *Cephalalgia, 10*, 241–250.

Kasahara, M., Menon, D. K., et al. (2010). Altered functional connectivity in the motor network after traumatic brain injury. *Neurology, 75*(2), 168–176.

Kasahara, M., Menon, D. K., et al. (2011). Traumatic brain injury alters the functional brain network mediating working memory. *Brain Injury, 25*(12), 1170–1187.

Kaschel, R., Della Sala, S., Cantagallo, A., Fahlbock, A., Laaksonen, R., & Kazen, M. (2002). Imagery mnemonics for the rehabilitation of memory: A randomized group controlled trial. *Neuropsychological Rehabilitation: An International Journal, 12*(2), 127–153.

Kashluba, S., Paniac, C., & Casey, J. E. (2008). Persistent symptoms associated with factors identified by the WHO task force on mild traumatic brain injury. *Clinical Neuropsychology, 22*, 195–208.

Kay, T., Newman, B., Cavallo, M., Ezrachi, O., & Resnick, M. (1992). Toward an neuropsychological model of functional disability after mild traumatic brain injury. *Neuropsychology, 6*, 371–384.

Kelley, W. M., Macrae, C. N., Wyland, C. L., Caglar, S., Inati, S., & Heatherton, T. F. (2002). Finding the self? An event-related fMRI study. *Journal of Cognitive Neuroscience, 14*, 785–794.

Kelly, J., Amerson, E., & Barth, J. (2012). Mild traumatic brain injury: Lessons learned from clinical, sports and combat concussions. *Rehabilitation Research and Practice*, Article ID *371970*, 5 pages.

King, N. S., Crawford, S., Wenden, F. J., et al. (1999). Early prediction of persisting post-concussion symptoms following mild and moderate head injuries. *British Journal of Clinical Psychology, 38*, 15–25.

Klein, M., Houx, P. J., & Jolles, J. (1996). Long-term persisting cognitive sequelae of traumatic brain injury and the effect of age. *Journal of Nervous and Mental Disease, 184*, 459–467.

Kraus, J., Schaffer, K. Ayers, K., Stenehjem, J., Shen, H., & Afifi, A. (2005). Physical complaints, medical service use, and social and employment service changes following mild traumatic brain injury: A 6-month longitudinal study. *Journal of Head Trauma and Rehabilitation, 20*, 239–256.

Kumar, S., Rao, S. L., et al. (2009). Reduction of functional brain connectivity in mild traumatic brain injury during working memory. *Journal of Neurotrauma, 26*(5), 665–675.

Lange, R. T., Iverson, G. L., & Franzen, M. D. (2007). Short-term neuropsychological outcome following uncomplicated mild TBI: Effects of day-of-injury intoxication and pre-injury alcohol abuse. *Neuropsychology, 21*, 590–598.

Lange, R. T., Iverson, G. L., Brubacher, J. R., Madler, B., & Heran, M. K. (2012). Diffusion tensor imaging findings are not strongly associated with post-concussional disorder two months following mild traumatic brain injury. *Journal of Head Trauma and Rehabilitation, 27*, 188–198.

Lange, R. T., Iverson, G. L., Brookes, B. L., & Rennison, V. L. A. (2010). Influence of poor effort on self-reported symptoms and neurocognitive test performance following mild traumatic brain injury. *Journal of Clinical and Experimental Neuropsychology, 32*, 961–972.

Lannsjo, M., Geijerstam, J. L., Johansson, U., Bring, J., & Borg, J. (2009). Prevalence and structure of symptoms at 3 months after mild traumatic brain injury in a national cohort. *Brain Injury, 23*, 213–219.

Larrabee, G. J. (2012). Mild Traumatic Brain Injury. In G. J. Larrabee (Ed.), *Forensic Neuropsychology: A Scientific Approach*, 2nd edition. New York: Oxford.

Lemmon, J., Latourrette, D., & Hauver, S. (1996). One year outcome study of outward bound experience on the psychosocial functioning of women with mild traumatic brain injury. *Journal of Cognitive Rehabilitation, 14*, 18–23.

Leskin, L., & White, P. (2007). Attentional networks reveal executive function deficits in posttraumatic stress disorder. *Neuropsychology, 21*, 275–284.

Levin, H. S., Amparo, E., et al. (1987). Magnetic resonance imaging and computerized tomography in relation to the neurobehavioral sequelae of mild and moderate head injuries. *Journal of Neurosurgery, 66*(5), 706–713.

Levin, H. S., Brown, S. A., Song, J. X., McCauley, S. R., Boake, C., Contant, C. F., et al. (2001). Depression and posttraumatic stress disorder at three months after mild to moderate traumatic brain injury. *Journal of Clinical and Experimental Neuropsychology, 23*, 754–769.

Levine, B., Robertson, I. H., Clare, L., Hong, J., Wilson, B. A., Duncan, J., & Stuss, D. T. (2000). Rehabilitation of executive functioning: an experimental-clinical validation of goal management training. *Journal of the International Neuropsychological Society, 6*(3), 299–312.

Lichteberg, P. A., Kimbarow, M. L., MacKinnon, D, Morris, P. A., & Bush, J. V. (1995). An interdisciplinary behavioural treatment program for depressed geriatric rehabilitation inpatients. *Gerontologist, 35*(5), 688–690.

Lippa, S. M., Pastorek, N. J., Benge, J. F., & Thornton, G. M. (2010). Postconcussive symptoms after blast and nonblast-related mild traumatic brain injuries in Afghanistan and Iraq war veterans. *Journal of the International Neuropsychological Society, 16*(5), 856–866.

Lipton, M. L., Kim, N., Park, Y. K., Hulkower, M., Tova, G. M., Shifteh, K., Kim, M., Zimmerman, M. E., Lipton, R. B., & Branch, C. A. (2012). Robust detection of traumatic axonal injury in individual mild traumatic brain injury patients: Intersubject variation, change over time and bidirectional changes in anisotropy. *Brain Imaging and Behavior, 6*, 329–342.

Loring, D. W., Marino, S. E., Drane, D. L., Farfitt, D. D., Finney, G. R., & Meador, K. J. (2011). Lorazepam effects on Word Memory Test performance: a randomized, double-blind, placebo-controlled, crossover trial. *The Clinical Neuropsychologist, 25*, 799–811.

Lovejoy, D. W., & Oakes, H. J. (2012). The behavioral health provider as a participant in the disability determination process: Evaluations, terminology and systems. In S. S. Bush and G. L. Iverson (Eds.), *Neuropsychological Assessment of Work-Related Injuries* (pp. 321–343). New York: Guilford.

Lovejoy, D. W., Ball, J. D., Keats, M., Stutts, M., Spain, E. H., Janda, L. & Janusz, J. (1999). Neuropsychological performance of adults with attention deficit hyperactivity disorder (ADHD): Diagnostic classification estimates for measures of frontal lobe/executive functioning. *Journal of the International Neuropsychological Society, 5*, 222–233.

Lundin, A., De Boussard, C., Edman, G., & Borg, J. (2006), Symptoms and disability until 3 months after mild TBI. *Brain Injury, 20*, 799–806.

Mac Donald, C. L., Dikranian, K., et al. (2007). Detection of traumatic axonal injury with diffusion tensor imaging in a mouse model of traumatic brain injury. *Experimental Neurology, 205*(1), 116–131.

Mason, M. F., Norton, M. I., Van Horn, J. D., Wegner, D. M., Grafton, S. T., & McCrae, C. N. (2007). Wandering minds: The default network and stimulus-independent thought. *Psychobiology, 315*, 393–395.

Mayer, A. R., Mannell, V., Ling, J., Gasparovic, C., & Yeo, R. A. (2011). Functional connectivity in mild traumatic brain injury. *Human Brain Mapping, 32*, 1825–1835.

McAllister, T. W. (2005). Mild brain injury and the postconcussion syndrome. In J. M. Silver et al. (Eds.), *Textbook of Traumatic Brain Injury*. Washington D. C.: American Psychiatric Press, 239–264.

McAllister, T. W., Flashman, L. A., McDonald, B. C. & Saykin, A. J. (2006). Mechanisms of working memory dysfunction after mild and moderate TBI: Evidence from functional MRI and neurogenetics. *Journal of Neurotrauma, 23*, 1450–1467.

McBeath, J. G., & Nanda, A. (1994). Use of dihydroergotamine in patients with postconcussion syndrome. *Headache, 34*, 148–151.

McCrea, M. A. (2008). *Mild traumatic brain injury and postconcussion syndrome. The new evidence base for diagnosis and treatment.* New York: Oxford University Press.

McCrea, M., Iverson, G. L., McAllister, T. W., Hammeke, T. A., Powell, M. R., Barr, W. B., & Kelly, J. P. (2009). An integrated review of recovery after mild traumatic brain injury (mTBI): implications for clinical management. *Clinical Neuropsychologist, 23*, 1368–1390.

McCrory, P., Johnston, K., Meeuwisse, W., et al. (2005). Summary and agreement statement of the 2nd International Conference on Concussion in Sports, Prague 2004. *British Journal of Sports Medicine, 39*, 196–204.

McCrory, P., Meeuwisse, W., Johnston, K., et al. (2009). Consensus statement on concussion in sport: The 3rd International Conference on Concussion in Sport: held in Zurich, November 2008. *British Journal of Sports Medicine, 43*(Suppl. 1), i76–i90.

McKee, A., Cantu, R., Nowinski, C., Hedley-Whyte, T., Gavett, B., Budson, A., Santini, V., Loo, H-S, Kubilis, C. & Stern, R. (2009). Chronic Traumatic Encephalopathy in Athletes: Progressive Tauopathy following repetitive head injury. *Journal of Neuropathology and Experimental Neurology, 68*(7), 709–735.

Meares, S., Shores, E. A., Taylor, A. J., Batchelor, J. Bryant, R. A., Baguley, I. J., et al. (2008). Mild traumatic brain injury does not predict acute postconcussion syndrome. *Journal of Neurology, Neurosurgery & Psychiatry, 79*, 300–306.

Merskey, H., & Woodforde, J. M. (1972). Psychiatric sequelae of mild head injury. Brain, *95*, 321–328.

Messé, A., Caplain, S., Paradot, G., Garrigue, D., Mineo, J. F., Soto Ares, G., et al. (2010). Diffusion tensor imaging and white matter lesions at the subacute stage in mild traumatic brain injury with persistent neurobehavioral impairment. *Human Brain Mapping, 32*, 999–1011.

Messé, A., Caplain, S., Pelegrini-Isaac, M., Blancho, S., & Montreuil, M. (2012). Structural integrity & postconcussion syndrome in mild traumatic brain injury patients. *Brain Imaging & Behavior*, 283–292.

Mittenberg, W., & Strausman, S. (2000). Diagnosis of mild head injury and the post-concussion syndrome. *Journal of Head Trauma Rehabilitation, 15*, 783–791.

Mittenberg, W., Canyock, E., Condit, D., et al. (2001). Treatment of post-concussion syndrome following mild head injury. *Journal of Neurology, Neurosurgery, and Psychiatry, 23*, 829–836.

Mittenberg, W., DiGiulio, D. V., Perrin, S., & Bass, A. E. (1992). Symptoms following mild head injury: Expectation as aetiology. *Journal of Neurology, Neurosurgery & Psychiatry, 55*, 200–204.

Moore, E. L., Terryberry-Spohr, L., & Hope, D. A. (2006). Mild traumatic brain injury and anxiety sequelae: A review of the literature. *Brain Injury, 20*, 117–132.

Mosenthal, A. C., Livingston, D. H., Lavery, R. F., Knudson, M. M., Lee, S., Morabito, D., et al. (2004). The effect of age on functional outcome in mild traumatic brain injury: 6-month report of a prospective multicenter trial. *The Journal of Trauma, 56*, 1042–1048.

Naismith, S. L. Hickie. I. B., Turner, K., Little, C. L., Winter, V., Ward, P. B., Wilhelm, K., Mitchell, P., & Parker, G. (2003). Neuropsychological performance in patients with depression is associated with clinical, etiological, and genetic risk factors. *Journal of Clinical and Experimental Neuropsychology, 25*, 866–877.

Nakamura, T., Hillary, F. G., et al. (2009). Resting network plasticity following brain injury. *PLoS One, 4*(12), e8220.

Nakayama, N., Okumura, A., et al. (2006). Evidence for white matter disruption in traumatic brain injury without macroscopic lesions. *Journal of Neurology, Neurosurgery, & Psychiatry, 77*(7), 850–855.

National Center for Injury Prevention & Control, Centers for Disease Control and Injury Prevention (2003). *Report to Congress on mild traumatic brain injury in the United States: Steps to prevent a serious public health problem.* Atlanta, GA.

Norrie, J., Heitger, M., Leathem, J., Anderson, T., Jones, R., & Flett, R. (2010). Mild traumatic brain injury and fatigue: A prospective longitudinal study. *Brain Injury, 24*, 1528–1538.

Oakes, H., Lovejoy, D., Tartar, S., & Holdnack, J. A. (2013). Understanding Index and Subtest Scatter in Healthy Adults. In J. Holdnack & G. Iverson (Eds.), *WAIS-IV, WMS-IV, and ACS* (pp. 191–257). New York: Elsevier, 103–169.

Orrison, W. W. (2000). *Neuroimaging*. Philadelphia, PA, WB Saunders.

Otis, J. D., Keane, T. M., Kerns, R. D., Monson, C., & Scioli, E. (2009). The development of an integrated treatment for veterans with comorbid chronic pain and posttraumatic stress disorder. *Pain Medication, 10*(7), 1300–1311.

Otis, J. D., McGlinchey, R., Vasterling, J. J., & Kerns, R. D. (2011). Complicating factors associated with mild traumatic brain injury: impact on pain and posttraumatic stress disorder treatment. *Journal of Clinical Psychology in Medical Settings, 18*(2), 145–154.

Ownsworth, T. L., & Mcfarland, K. (1999). Memory remediation in long-term acquired brain injury: two approaches in diary training. *Brain Injury, 13*(8), 605–626.

Ozen, L. J., & Fernandes, M. A. (2012). Slowing down after mild traumatic brain injury: A strategy to improve cognitive task performance. *Archives of Clinical Neuropsychology, 27*, 85–100.

Palmese, C. A., & Raskin, S. A. (2000). The rehabilitation of attention in individuals with mild traumatic brain injury, using the APT-II programme. *Brain Injury, 14*, 535–548.

Paniak, C., Toller-Lobe, G., Durand, A., et al. (1998). A randomized trial of two treatments for mild traumatic brain injury. *Brain Injury, 12*, 1011–1023.

Paniak, C., Toller-Lobe, G., Reynolds, S., Melnyk, A., & Nagy, J. (2000). A randomized trial of two treatments for mild traumatic brain injury: 1 year follow-up. *Brain Injury, 14*, 219–226.

Paul, S., Forney, D. L., Asarnow, R. R., Light, R., Mccleary, C., Levin, H., Kelly, D., Bergsneider, M.,

Hovda, D., Martin, N., Namerow, N., & Becker, D. (1998). Depression, cognition, and functional correlates of recovery outcomes after traumatic brain injury. *Brain Injury*, *12*(7), 537–553.

Peck, C. P., Schroeder, R. W., Heinrichs, R. J., VonDran, E. J., Brockman, C. J., Webster, B. K., & Baade, L. E. (2013). Differences in MMPI-2 FBS and RBS scores in brain injury, probable malingering, and conversion disorder groups: A preliminary study. *The Clinical Neuropsychologist, 27*, 693–707.

Pertab, J. L., James, K. M., & Bigler, E. D. (2009). Limitations of mild traumatic brain injury meta-analyses. *Brain Injury*, *23*, 498–508.

Petchprapai, N., & Winkelman, C. (2007). Mild traumatic brain injury: determinants and subsequent quality of life. A review of the literature. *Journal of Neuroscience Nursing*, *39*, 260–272.

Ponsford, J., Willmott, C., et al. (2000). Factors influencing outcome following mild traumatic brain injury in adults. *Journal of the International Neuropsychological Society, 6*(5), 568–579.

Ponsford, J., & Schonberger, M. (2010). Family functioning and emotional state two and five years after traumatic brain injury. *Journal of the International Neuropsychological Society, 16*(2), 306–317.

Ponsford, J., Willmott, C., Rothwell, A., Cameron, P., Kelly, A. M., Nelms, R., & Curran, C. (2002). Impact of early intervention on outcome following mild head injury in adults. *Journal of Neurology, Neurosurgery, & Psychiatry, 73*(3), 330–332.

Pontifex, M. B., O'Connor, P. M., Broglio, S. P., & Hillman, C. H. (2009). The association between mild traumatic brain injury history and cognitive control. *Neuropsychologia*, *47*, 3210–3216.

Powell, J. M., Ferraro, J. T., Dikmen, S. S. Temkin, N. R., & Bell, K. R. (2008). Accuracy of mild traumatic brain injury diagnosis. *Archives of Physical Medicine & Rehabilitation*, *89*, 1550–1555.

Putnam, S. H., & Millis, S. R. (1994). Psychosocial factors in the development and maintenance of chronic somatic and functional symptoms following mild traumatic brain injury. *Advances in Medical Psychotherapy*, *7*, 1–22.

Raichle, M. E., & Mintum, M. A. (2006). Brain work and brain imaging. *Annual Review of Neurosciences*, *29*, 449–476.

Raichle, M. E., MacLeod, A. M., Snyder, A. Z., Powers, W. J., Gusnard, D. A., & Shulman, G. L. (2001). A default mode of brain function. *Proceedings of the National Academy of Sciences*, *98*, 676–682.

Raskin, S. A., & Mateer, C. A. (2000). *Neuropsychological management of mild traumatic brain injury*. New York, NY: Oxford University Press.

Raskin, S. A., & Rearick, E. (1996). Verbal fluency in individuals with mild traumatic brain injury. *Neuropsychology*, *10*(3), 416–422.

Raskin, S. A., Mateer, C. A., & Tweeten, R. (1998). Neuropsychological assessment of individuals with mild traumatic brain injury. *The Clinical Neuropsychologist*, *12*(1), 21–30.

Raskin, S. A., & Stein, P. N. (2000). Depression. In: Raskin, S. A. and Mateer, C. (Eds.), *Neuropsychological management of mild traumatic brain injury*, pp. 157–170. Oxford University Press, New York.

Rath, J. F., Simon, D., Langenbahn, D. N., Sherr, R. L., & Diller, L. (2003). Group treatment of problem solving deficits in outpatients with traumatic brain injury: A randomized outcome study. *Neuropsychological Rehabilitation*, *13*, 461–488.

Resick, P. A., & Schnicke, M. K. (1992). Cognitive processing therapy for sexual assault victims. *Journal of Consulting and Clinical Psychology*, *60*(5), 748–756.

Rosenbaum, S. B., & Lipton, M. L. (2012). Embracing the chaos: The scope and importance of clinical and pathological heterogeneity in mTBI. *Brain Imaging and Behavior*, *6*, 255–282.

Ruff, R. M., & Jamora, C. W. (2009). Myths and mild traumatic brain injury. *Psychological Injury and the Law*, *2*, 34–42.

Ruff, R. M. (2005). Two decades of advances in understanding of mild traumatic brain injury. *The Journal of Head Trauma and Rehabilitation*, *20*, 5–18.

Ruff, R. M., Camenzuli, L., & Mueller, J. (1996). Miserable minority: emotional risk factors that influence the outcome of a mild traumatic brain injury. *Brain Injury*, *10*, 551–565.

Ruff, R. M., Iverson, G. L., Barth, J. T., Bush, S. S., & Broshek, D. K. (2009). Recommendations for diagnosing a mild traumatic brain injury: A National Academy of Neuropsychology education paper. *Archives of Clinical Neuropsychology*, *24*, 3–10.

Ruff, R. M. (2011). Mild traumatic brain injury and neural recovery: rethinking the debate. *Neurorehabilitation*, *28*, 167–180.

Rutgers, D. R., Toulgoat, F., Cazejust, J., Fillard, P., Lasjaunais, P., & Ducreux, D. (2008). White matter abnormalities in mTBI: A diffusion tensor imaging study. *American Journal of Neuroradiology, 29*, 514–519.

Ryu, W. H., Feinstein, A., Colantonio, A., Streiner, D. L., & Dawson, D. R. (2009). Early identification and incidence of mild TBI in Ontario. *Canadian Journal of Neurological Sciences*, *36*, 429–435.

Salmond, C. H., Menon, D. K., et al. (2006). Diffusion tensor imaging in chronic head injury survivors: correlations with learning and memory indices. *Neuroimage 29*(1), 117–124.

Satz, P., Alfano, M. S., Light, R., Morgenstern, H., Zaucha, K. Asarnow, R. F., & Newton, F. (1999). Persistent postconcussion syndrome: A proposed methodology and literature review to determine the effects, if any, of mild head and other bodily injury. *Journal of Clinical and Experimental Neuropsychology, 21*, 620–628.

Saulle, M., & Greenwald, B. (2012). Chronic traumatic encephalopathy: A review. *Rehabilitation Research Practice*, Article ID *816069*, 9 pages.

Schretlen, D., & Shapiro, A., (2003). A quantitative review of the effects of traumatic brain injury on cognitive functioning. *International Review of Psychiatry, 15*, 341–349.

Sheedy, J. Harvey, E., Faux, S., Geffen, G., & Shores, E. A. (2009). Emergency department assessment of mild traumatic brain injury and prediction of postconcussion symptoms: A three-month prospective study. *Journal of Head Trauma and Rehabilitation, 24*, 333–343.

Sheedy, J., Geffen, G., Donnelly, J., Faux, S., & Shores, A. (2006). Emergency department assessment of mild traumatic brain injury and prediction of postconcussion symptoms. *Journal of Clinical and Experimental Neuropsychology, 28*, 755–772.

Shenton, M. E., Hamoda, H., Schneiderman, J., Bouix, S., Pasternack, O., Rathi, Y., Vu, M-A., Purohit, M., Helmer, K., Koerte, I., Lin, A., Westin, C. F., Kikinis, R., Kubicki, M., Stern, R., & Zafonte, R. (2012). A Review of Magnetic Resonance Imaging and Diffusion Tensor Imaging Findings in Mild Traumatic Brain Injury. *Brain Imaging and Behavior, 6*, 137–192.

Shulman, G. L., Fiez, J. A., Corbetta, M., Buckner, R. L., Miezin, F. M., Raichle, M. E., et al. (1997). Common blood flow changes across visual tasks: I. Increases in subcortical structures and cerebellum, but not in non-visual cortex. *Journal of Cognitive Neuroscience, 9*, 648–663.

Sigurdardottir, S., Andelic, N., Roe, C., Jerstad, T., & Schanke (2009). Postconcussion symptoms after traumatic brain injury at 3 and 12 months post injury: A prospective study. *Brain Injury, 23*, 489–497.

Silver, J. M. (2012). Effort, exaggeration and malingering after concussion. *Journal of Neurology, Neurosurgery and Psychiatry, 83*, 836–841.

Silver, J. M., McAllister, T. W., & Arciniegas, D. B. (2009). Depression and cognitive complaints following mild traumatic brain injury, *American Journal of Psychiatry, 166*(6), 653–661.

Smits, M., Houston, G. C., Dippel, D. W., Wielopolski, P. A., Vernooij, M. W., Koudstaal, P. J., et al. (2011). Microstructural brain injury in post-concussion syndrome after minor head injury. *Neuroradiology, 53*, 553–563.

Snell, D. L., Surgenor, L. J., Hay-Smith, J. C., & Siegert, R. J. (2008). A systematic review of psychological treatments for mild traumatic brain injury: an update on the evidence. *Journal of Clinical and Experimental Neuropsychology, 31*, 20–38.

Sohlberg, M., Johnson, L., Paule, L., Raskin,S., & Mateer, C.(1996). *Attention process training*, San Antonio, TX: Pearson Assessment Company.

Sohlberg, M. M. (2000). Assessing and managing unawareness of self. *Seminars in speech and language, 21*(2), 135–150.

Sohlberg, M. M., McLaughlin, K. A., Pavese, A., Heidrich, A., & Posner, M. I. (2000). Evaluation of attention process training and brain injury education in persons with acquired brain injury. *Journal of Clinical and Experimental Neuropsychology, 22*(5), 656–676.

Sponheim, S. R., McGuire, K. A., et al. (2010). Evidence of disrupted functional connectivity in the brain after combat-related blast injury. *Neuroimage, 54*(Suppl 1), S21–29.

Stapert, S., Houx, P., de Kruijk, J., Ponds, R., & Jolles, J. (2006). Neurocognitive fitness in the sub-acute stage after mild TBI: The effect of age. *Brain Injury, 20*, 161–165.

Stein, S. C. (1996). Classification of head injury. In Narayan, R. K., Povlishock, J. T., Wilberger, J. E. (Eds.), *Neurotrauma*. New York: McGraw-Hill.

Stern, Y. (2006). Cognitive reserve and Alzheimer's Disease. *Alzheimer's Disease and Associated Disorders, 20*, 112–117.

Stern, Y. (2003). The concept of cognitive reserve: A catalyst for research. *Journal of Clinical and Experimental Neuropsychology, 25*, 589–593.

Stevens, M. C., Lovejoy, D., Kim, J., Oakes, H. Kureshi, I., & Witt, S. T. (2012). Resting state network functional connectivity abnormalities in mild traumatic brain injury. *Brain Imaging & Behavior, 6*, 293–318.

Stulemeijer, M., Andriessen, T. M. J. C., Brauer, J. M. P., Vos, P. E., & van der Werf, S. P. (2007). Cognitive performance after mild traumatic brain injury: the impact of poor effort on test results and its relation to distress, personality, and litigation. *Brain Injury, 21*, 309–318.

Suhr, J. A., & Gunstad, J. (2002). Diagnosis threat: The effect of negative expectations on cognitive performance in head injury. *Journal of Clinical and Experimental Neuropsychology, 24*, 448–457.

Suhr, J. A., & Gunstad, J. (2005). Further exploration of the effect of "diagnosis threat" on cognitive performance of individuals with mild head injury. *Journal of the International Neuropsychological Society, 11*, 23–29.

Teasdale, G., & Jennett, B. (1974). Assessment of coma and impaired consciousness; A practical scale. *Lancet, 2*, 81–84.

Temkin, N. R., Machamer, J. E., et al. (2003). Correlates of functional status 3-5 years after traumatic brain injury with CT abnormalities. *Journal of Neurotrauma, 20*(3), 229–241.

Thickpenny-Davis, K. L., & Barker-Collo, S. L. (2007). Evaluation of a structure group format memory rehabilitation program for adults following brain injury. *Journal of Head Trauma Rehabilitation, 22*(5), 303–313.

Udekwu, P., Kromhout-Schiro, S., Vaslef, S., Baker, C., & Oller, D. (2004). Glasgow coma scale score, mortality and functional outcome in head-injured patients. *Journal of Trauma, 56*, 1084–1089.

Vanderploeg, R. D., Curtiss, G., Duchnick, J. J., & Luis, C. A. (2003). Demographic, medical, and psychiatric factors in work and marital status after mild head injury. *Journal of Head Trauma and Rehabilitation, 18*, 148–163.

Vanderploeg, R. D., Curtiss, G., Luis, C. A., & Salazar, A. M. (2007). Long-term morbidities following self-reported mild traumatic brain injury. *Journal of Clinical and Experimental Neuropsychology, 29*, 585–598.

Vanderploeg, R. D., Curtiss, G., & Belanger, H. G. (2005). Long-term neuropsychological outcomes following mild traumatic brain injury. *Journal of the International Neuropsychological Society, 11*, 228–236.

Vasa, R. A., Grados, M., et al. (2004). Neuroimaging correlates of anxiety after pediatric traumatic brain injury. *Biological Psychiatry, 55*(3), 208–216.

Vasterling, J. J., & Brailey, K. (2005). Neuropsychological findings in adults with PTSD. In J. Vasterling & C. R. Brewin (Eds.), *Neuropsychology of PTSD: Biological, Cognitive, and Clinical Perspectives* (pp. 178–207). New York: The Guilford Press.

Verfaellie, M., Amick, M. M., & Vasterling, J. J. (2012). Effects of traumatic brain injury-associated neurocognitive alterations on posttraumatic stress disorder. In J. V. Vasterling, R. A. Bryant, & T. M. Keane, (Eds.), *PTSD and Mild Traumatic Brain Injury* (pp. 37–60). New York: The Guilford Press.

Vickery, C. D., Sherer, M., Nick, T. G., Nakase-Richardson, R., Corrigan, J. D., Hammond, F., et al. (2008). Relationship among premorbid alcohol use, acute intoxication, and early functional status after traumatic brain injury. *Archives of Physical Medicine and Rehabilitation, 89*, 48–55.

Wade, D. T., Crawford, S., Wenden, F. J., et al. (1997). Does routine follow up after head injury help?

A randomized controlled trial. *Journal of Neurology, Neurosurgery, & Psychiatry, 62*, 478–484.

Weissman, D. H., Roberts, K. C., Visscher, K. M., & Woldorff, M. G. (2006). The neural bases of momentary lapses in attention. *Nature Neuroscience, 9*, 971–978.

Wilde, E. A., Chu, Z., et al. (2006). Diffusion tensor imaging in the corpus callosum in children after moderate to severe traumatic brain injury. *Journal of Neurotrauma 23*(10), 1412–1426.

Williams, D. H., Levin, H. S., & Eisenberg, H. M. (1990). Mild head injury classification. *Neurosurgery*, 422–427.

Williams, W. H., Potter, S., & Ryland, H. (2010). Mild traumatic brain injury and postconcussion syndrome: A neuropsychological perspective. *Journal of Neurology, Neurosurgery, and Psychiatry, 81*, 1116–1122.

Williamson, D. J, Holsman, M., Chaytor, N., Miller, J. W., & Drane, D. L. (2012). Abuse, not financial incentive, predicts non-credible cognitive performance in patients with psychogenic non-epileptic seizures. *The Clinical Neuropsychologist, 26*, 588–598.

Woods, S. P., Lovejoy, D. W., Stutts, M. L., Ball, J. D., & Fals-Stewart, W. (2002). Comparative efficiency of a discrepancy analysis for the classification of Attention Deficit Hyperactivity Disorder (ADHD) in adults. *Archives of Clinical Neuropsychology, 17*, 351–369.

World Health Organization. (1992). *International statistical classification of disease and related health problems—10th edition*. Geneva, Switzerland: Author.

Yehuda, R., Keefer, R. S. E., Harvey, P. D., Levengood, R. A., Gerber, D. K., GEni, J., & Siever, L. J. (1995). Learning and memory in combat veterans with post-traumatic stress disorder. *American Journal of Psychiatry, 152*, 137–139.

Yuh, E. L., Mukherjee, P., et al. (2013). Magnetic resonance imaging improves 3-month outcome prediction in mild traumatic brain injury. *Annals of Neurology, 73*(2), 224–235.

Ziejewski, M. (in Press). *Biomechanics of head injury, head trauma cases: Law and medicine* (2nd ed.). New York.

Zielinski, J. J. (1994). Malingering and defensiveness in the neuropsychological assessment of mild traumatic brain injury. *Clinical Psychology: Science and Practice, 1*, 169–184.

18

Blast-Related Traumatic Brain Injury: Pathophysiology, Comorbidities, and Neurobehavioral Outcomes

Ralph G. De Palma, Gerald M. Cross, Clifford J. Buckley, James M. Ecklund, and William Gunnar

Blast related traumatic brain injury (BTBI), called a "signature" injury of current military conflicts (Desmoulin & Dionne, 2009; Elder & Cristian, 2009; Snell & Halter, 2010), is also a threat for civilian populations subject to terrorist attacks. BTBI are heterogeneous injuries (Ling, Bandak, Armonda, Grant, & Ecklund, 2009) which cause or are associated with varying immediate and long term neurobehavioral deficits. During the military actions in Afghanistan, Operation Enduring Freedom (OEF), and in Iraq, Operation Iraqi Freedom (OIF), improvised explosive devices (IEDs) became weapons of choice for insurgents, while terrorists; so far, have used conventional high explosive devices to injure civilian populations. With increasing use of explosive weapons, blast related brain injury, in the absence of direct skull trauma or penetration, is reported with increasing frequency. Depending upon intensity of exposure, BTBI causes immediate symptoms and signs, followed by an intermediate period of evolving neuropathologic effects, and later chronic functional disabilities. Traumatic brain injury variants caused by direct skull impacts and rotational forces have been well described (Gennerlli & Graham, 2005) particularly as modeled to reduce TBI in automobile accidents (Nirula, Kaufman, & Tencer, 2003). Recently new insights have been gained into the effects of repetitive blunt sport injuries causing diffuse TBI (Mckee et al., 2009).

In contrast, the pathophysiology of primary blast induced neurotrauma (BINT; Cernak & Noble-Haeusslein, 2010), closed blast related brain injury (cBTBI) (Moore et al., 2008), or primary blast concussive injury remains incompletely understood. For lexicographic consistency, this chapter considers Cernak's term (Cernak & Noble-Haeusslein, 2010), blast induced neurotrauma, BINT, and cBTBI as synonyms and refers to mild trauma induced brain injury as mTBI. Abbreviations used in the text are summarized in Table 18-1. The mTBI injury is common, most often closed and the term is widely used in the literature. However explosions also cause severe degrees of direct, penetrating, and rotational TBI, some of which, including closed head injuries, require surgical interventions.

While these named categories overlap, their use provides a framework for considering *blast-related traumatic brain injury*, particularly the type designated as mTBI. Mild traumatic brain injury has been estimated to occur in 10 to 20% (Elder & Cristian, 2009) of returning veterans. A 2005 report stated that 59% of blast-injured patients from OEF/OIF admitted to Walter Reed Army Medical Center had mild TBI (Okie, 2005). These estimates require qualification. The Veterans Health Administration (VHA) encourages reporting data as numbers of combatants who "have incurred mTBI" or are "diagnosed with having incurred mTBI."

Table 18-1. Abbreviations and Definitions

BINT	Blast-induced neurotrauma
BTBI	Blast-related traumatic brain injury
cBTBI	Closed-blast induced brain injury
CCATT	Critical-Case Aeromedical Transport Team
CT	Computerized tomography
cTBI	Closed-traumatic brain injury
DARPA	Defense Advanced Research Projects Agency
DAI	Diffuse axonal injury
DSM-IV	Diagnostic and Statistical Manual of Mental Disorders-Fourth Ed
DTI	Diffusion tensor imaging
ECG	Electrocardiogram
EEG	Electroencephalogram
GCS	Glasgow Coma Scale
HUMVEE	High mobility multipurpose wheeled vehicle
IED	Improvised explosive device
MRI	Magnetic resonance imaging
mTBI	Mild traumatic brain injury
OEF/OIF	Operation Enduring Freedom/ Operation Iraqi Freedom
PTSD	Post traumatic stress disorder
TBI	Traumatic brain injury
VHA	Veterans Health Administration

Reporting individuals "*with* mTBI" infers that all individuals so affected continue to suffer from the condition, while many recover, improve without medical intervention, and do not appear to require ongoing care. While 18.5–20% of veterans *screen* positive due to the high sensitivity and low specificity of screening questions, approximately 8 % of all OEF/OIF veterans screened are diagnosed on specialty examinations of having incurred a TBI. These data are presented in the section on neurobehavioral outcomes.

The coexistence of mTBI and post-traumatic stress disorder (PTSD; Hoge et al., 2008; Jaffee & Meyer, 2009; McCrea et al., 2008; Rosenfeld & Ford, 2010; Warden, 2006) further complicates distinctions between these two conditions. Controversy persists concerning the pathophysiology of mTBI and its relationship to PTSD. This chapter outlines current literature to describe the pathophysiology of cBTBI, its associated comorbidities, and challenges in assessing neurobehavioral outcomes as these evolve over time.

Pathophysiology

Overview of Blast Characteristics

Understanding blast wave characteristics is a first step for delineating injury mechanisms. In its simplest iteration, explosion of a conventional high explosive bomb generates a blast wave that spreads out from a point source. The resulting blast wave consists of two parts — a *shock wave* of high pressure, followed closely by a *blast wind*, or air in motion. While theoretically depicted as a spherical explosive expansion, the blast waves are actually nonlinear, chaotic, and complex. Blast wave characteristics vary between nuclear explosions, single point conventional explosive devices, and enhanced explosive munitions. Piston compression devices are often used experimentally to mimic explosions Moore et al., 2008. Detailed monographs (Batsanov, 1994; Sachdev, 2004) describe the complex physics of the shock wave in relation to its following zone of overpressure, along with heat, molecular and electromagnetic energy transfers occurring at the interface between the shock wave and following barometric over and under pressure waves commonly depicted. In the case of brain injury, occurring within the closed confines of the skull, shock wave characteristics requires further consideration. Damage produced by explosions in the open decreases exponentially with distance from a blast point source. Within closed spaces, however, secondary shock waves summate leading to injuries seemingly unrelated to the point source of the explosion. This phenomenon, described in the terrorist bombing of a public house in Birmingham, England during the 1970s was cited in an earlier review of primary blast injuries (Cooper, Maynard, Cross, & Hill, 1983). Similar injury patterns were later described with blasts occurring in closed vehicles (DePalma, Burris, Champion, & Hodgson, 2005; Phillips & Richmond, 1991)).

Blast effects fall into four categories that cause injury. These are primary (direct effects of shock waves and pressure); secondary (effects due to projectiles and debris causing penetrating wounds); tertiary (effects or blunt injuries due to wind translating the body); and quaternary (burns, hypoxia, and exposure to toxins, toxic inhalants and other effects) (Arnold, Halperin, Tsai, & Smithline, 2004; Cullis, 2001; DePalma,

Burris, Champion, & Hodgson, 2005; Philips & Richmond, 1991; Gans & Kennedy, 1996; Miller & Chang, 2003)). Specific considerations of primary cBTBI focus upon the blast shock wave and blast overpressure as these forces encounter the skull. Blast traumatic brain injury can also relate to vascular surge from the thorax through the neck vessels, air embolism, and possibly, piezoelectric currents (Johnson et al., 2011) generated between skull and the shock wave. Based on modeling, viscoelastic dynamic rippling of the skull itself has been postulated (Moss, King, & Blackman, 2009). Interactions between the advancing shock wave and blast overpressure, the configuration of the skull, and the brain, including its meninges and cerebrospinal fluid, are likely as complex as the blast wave itself. The end results are heterogeneous injury patterns (Ling et al., 2009) including delayed cerebral vasospasm (Armonda et al., 2006) observed by surgeons treating these injuries in the field.

Explosive blasts are capable of damaging the grey and white matter of brain tissue and raising cerebrospinal fluid pressure at the moment of impact. However the precise vulnerabilities during primary blast exposures continue to be controversial (Taber, Warden, & Hurley, 2006). The dimensions of blast severity from point explosions or piston devices are measured in milliseconds (msec), fractions of milliseconds, and pounds per square inch (psi) of barometric overpressure. To a degree, the magnitude and duration of overpressure determines tissue damage and lethality of blast exposures particularly in air-containing organs such as the lung and intestines (Phillips & Richmond, 1991; Guy, Glover & Cripps, 1998). Dynamic pressure changes at tissue-density (e.g., air–fluid) interfaces due to the interactions of a high-frequency stress wave and a lower frequency shear wave are the classically accepted mechanisms of organ damage. In the brain, housed within its closed skull compartment, shears at interfaces between grey and white matter and cerebrospinal fluid, and spallation or cavitation associated with rotational movements (Stuhmiller, 2008; Zhang, Yang, & King, 2004) might be potential mechanisms of cBTBI injury. Effects of passage of the shock front may also condition brain injury as contrasted with barotraumatic effects in air containing organs such as the lungs and intestines.

Tympanic membrane perforation is a common and sensitive physical sign of blast injury. Rupture can occur with as little as five psi over baseline atmospheric pressure of 14.7 psi. In contrast, overpressures of 56 to 76 psi (3.8 to 5.6 atm), depending on pulse duration, usually damage other organs, particularly the lungs and hollow viscera (Philips & Richmond, 1991). Another dimension in assessing blast wave effect, according to Stuhmiller (2008), is the "incident" or "side on" pressure measured as loading to the body or body part on the side facing the blast. A blast wave traveling at 340 m/second in air may exert acceleration effects as it encounters the skull. At maximum peak survival pressures, simulations show the head might be accelerated with forces up to 300 G (Stuhmiller, 2008). These forces are of sufficient magnitude to produce brain tissue stresses, possibly cavitation, in subjects who survive.

On the other hand, damage to brain structures within the closed confines of the skull may result from more than conventionally measured blast overpressures. The unique characteristics of an advancing shock wave front caused by explosions have been elaborated by Sachdev (2004):

A shock is a surface of discontinuity across which the flow variables pressure, particle velocity, density and entropy suffer a jump. Only the front surface of discontinuity is termed a shock, while the entire disturbed flow of gas and overpressure is called the shock wave.... Explosion forces most of the air within the shock front into a thin shell just inside the front.

Batsanov (1994) describes the dimensions and time relationship of the shock front as: "....a narrow region of the order of the free path length of molecules of a free compressed substance (e.g air or water RDP) propagating in space with supersonic speed. The time of increase in pressure from zero to maximum value varies from 10^{-12} to 10^{-10} s (seconds), the time of exposure to high pressure varies about 10^{-6}, and pressure drop (unloading) varies from 10^{-6} to 10^{-5} s.

The dimensions of time and magnitude for the shock front are remarkably small as compared to the overall time frame in milliseconds of blast wave overpressure. Closed brain injuries produced by blasts and explosions may be conditioned by the energetics of the shock front itself, an important notion for modeling cBTBI. Xydackis and colleagues (Xydakis et al., 2007) suggested that rupture of the tympanic membrane signifies TBI blast injury probably including mTBI in the absence of other organ damage. In recommending the observation of tympanic rupture as a marker for observation in otherwise asymptomatic patients, DePalma at el (2005) noted that lethal pulmonary blast injury was sometimes seen in the absence of tympanic membrane rupture. This disconnect occurred in a series of blast victims injured in a closed environment in Israel (Katz, Ofek, Adler, Abramowitz, & Krausz, 1989) and during the Madrid train bombing (Gutierrez de Ceballos et al., 2005). Observations of blast injury patterns denote the importance of location of the subject, position of the body and head relative to the direction of the blast front, and shock wave as well as amplification of shock and blast waves within structures.

While blast injury severity varies according to intensity, duration of overpressure, blast wave propagation related to media density, and inversely from the distance from the explosive source, explosions also generate toxic gases, electromagnetic waves, and heat. Improvised explosive devices (IEDs), commonly used tactical weapons in OEF/OIF, range in explosive force according to materials they contain, and the position of the subject with reference to the advancing shock wave: facing it directly, lateral to its axis, or away from the blast front. Standing, supine, and prone positions also influence blast injury. Blast waves, as previously mentioned, are nonlinear, chaotic phenomena often causing casualties in non-intuitive ways, particularly within structures or vehicles. Subject location in a corner as opposed to standing near a flat wall also exposes individuals to more severe blast waves and increasingly severe injuries. Blast wave coupling and potential enhancements between a helmet and the skull are of particular interest in BTBI. Possible coupling of and enhancement of blast waves beneath helmets have been modeled by Mott et al. (2008) for a *frontal blast* using manikins as shown in figure 18-1. Models and testing strategies with known nonlethal blasts are important developmental tools to best design protection for military personnel.

Operational definitions of blast exposure for military personnel include subject exposures

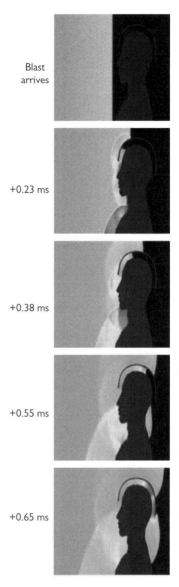

Figure 18-1. The physics of explosives and blast helmets. Pressure contours show the effect of a front-facing blast at various times after detonating 1.5 kg of C4 explosives from a distance of three meters. Black represents 1.0 atmosphere of pressure, and red indicates pressures over 3.5 atmospheres. NRL's Laboratory for Computational Physics and Fluid Dynamics; American Institute of Physics. Adapted from Mott D et al. (33); Accessed 6/22/12. See color insert.

within fifty meters of an open air blast and any blast exposure within closed structures or vehicles. Frequently, a clinical history suggesting mTBI is defined by the event itself and self-reporting of symptoms. A working definition of mTBI history comprises any post-event exposure, alteration of mental state at the time of injury, development of post-concussive symptoms, or alternatively GCS 13 to 15. These definitions have yet to meet needs for accurate pathophysiologic quantification of brain injury. Current research and screening aims to sharpen the definition of graded heterogeneous injuries, particularly mTBI and PTSD (Brenner, Vanderploeg, & Terrio, 2009). To assess long term neurobehavioral effects, the Department of Veterans Affairs recently implemented a directive for post-deployment screening measures (Veterans Health Administration, 2010).

While blast dynamics are complex and some of the mechanisms resulting in injuries are unclear, the challenges involved in cBTBI analyses ought not to be viewed as obstacles for prevention and mitigation of blast injury. Blast forces can be quantified using static blast measurement devices placed in the open or within structures. These recordings proved useful for modeling lung injury and for development of protective body armor (Stuhmiller et al., 1996). Although as yet incomplete, clinical and experimental observations and novel imaging advances now offer important information about the pathophysiology of cBTBI and its relationships to long term neurobehavioral changes.

Clinical and Historical Observations. Recent reviews (Moore et al., 2008; Jones, Fear, & Wessely, 2007; Kocsis & Tessler, 2009) provide detailed insights into cBTBI. Experience with "shell shock" during World Wars I and II suggest that labeling primary traumatic brain blast injury as a "signature injury" of current conflicts may be an overstatement. Jones et al. (2007) point out the pitfalls of labels which might affect prognosis in that subjects who believe that their symptoms have lasting effects will experience more long lasting disorders. The aura attached to "shell shock" was such that in 1922 a report of the British War Office by Lord Southborough (1922) eliminated the use of this term to describe a clinical disorder. Thus, blast injury disorder became controversial such that, at the onset of World War II, the term "shell shock" was proscribed. Brain blast injuries suffered in the past were similar to those seen today,

but were diagnosed less frequently and not as carefully investigated in the past as is mTBI now combined with what we now recognize as PTSD (Moore et al., 2008; Warden, 2006; Hoge et al., 2008; Jaffee & Meyer, 2009; Rosenfeld & Ford, 2010; Brenner et al., 2010). Additionally, many more combatants survive TBI associated with other severe injuries because of remarkable improvement in triage, treatment, and resuscitation by military surgeons.

To gain better insight into blast brain injury mechanisms, robust examples of cBTBI would be those associated with death in the absence of other injuries confirmed by autopsy findings. Clinical observations, apart from those derived from experimental models, are relatively sparse, though past examples appear and are instructive. *Lancet* ("BLAST IN 1812," 1943) provides an account by Naval Surgeon Mr. William McTernan of brain death thought to be due to barotrauma, "Case of Death from Wind of a Shot." During the action of HMS Northumberland in May 1812 a marine died on deck after a near miss from a cannon shot. Mr. McTernan described the findings as follows:

"I returned to search for the cause of his death,--neither from his mouth, nose, or ears, or eyes was there the slightest exudation. I had him stripped completely and neither fracture nor lividity of the slightest description could be detected. His continence was serene and tranquil." He went on to conclude, with reservations, that the" Wind of the Shot" accounted for his death. This case has been cited and considered to be due to BTBI ("BLAST IN 1812," 1943; Moore et al., 2008). However, as is usual in combat, brain autopsy observations were unavailable.

In 1916, Mott autopsied cases of "aerial compression" due to exposure to high explosives, documenting post mortem punctate hemorrhages and chromatolyis. Denny-Brown (1945) contested these findings as being due to carbon monoxidemia. During World War II, Fulton (1942) provided morphologic descriptions of brain damage due to "blast and concussion." Moore et al. (2008) focused attention upon the OEF/OIF era, emphasizing the challenges and difficulties in parsing out factors responsible for cBTBI underscoring the similarities to "post concussion" syndrome noted by earlier authors

(Denny-Brown, 1945; Fulton, 1942). These were comprehensively summarized by Varney and Roberts in a 1999 monograph, *The Evaluation and Treatment of Mild Traumatic Brain Injury*.

Pathologic and Neurophysiologic Findings in BTBI

The classic pathologic changes associated with TBI in general have been described by Gennarelli (2005). Mechanisms of injury include direct impacts, skull fracture, and rotational forces with resulting bleeding, direct tissue damage, and diffuse axonal injury (DAI). Clearly, during a blast exposure, rotational and direct traumatic injuries can occur with secondary projectile or penetrating injuries, tertiary closed injuries and quaternary blast effects. Koscis (2009) documented intracerebral and leptomenigeal bleeding in autopsied human subjects exposed to blast. Morphologic findings included multifocal hemorrhage in white matter, important in documenting DAI, but qualified because white matter hemorrhages may be caused by other mechanisms such as carbon monoxidemia, and air or fat emboli.

Recently, with availability of CT scanning near front lines, cases of cBTBI with subdural and epidural hematomas, contracoup contusions, and lacerations of frontal and temporal lobes have been seen. Ideally, autopsy studies performed on individuals succumbing to cBTBI would reveal the morphology of brain injury leading to death. The chaos surrounding blast events, whether combat or civilian, compromises accurate analysis of the mechanisms of injury whether impact or non-impact related. Experimental models serve as inferential surrogates and provide important insights into possible mechanisms of human injury.

A wealth of experimental data, spanning two decades, obtained from animals subjected to blast-induced neurotrauma, has been presented by Cernak and Noble-Haeusslein (2010). Animal models include mice and rats, rabbits, sheep, pigs, and non human primates. In contrast to direct impact injury models, the small mammal studies use compressed air or gas or blast tubes with a fixed explosive charge to generate measured blast waves. Integral to these experiments are devices to fix the animal in place to prevent injury from tertiary effects while restraining the skull, thus avoiding rotational forces. Blast wave devices usually replicate "ideal blasts" or those that occur in the open air modeled (Axelson, Hjelmquist, Medin, Pearson, & Suneson, 2000; Cernak & Noble-Haeusslein, 2010) in a variety of circumstances. The magnitude of blast overpressures in these published experiments range from 7.54-49.31 psi (Cernak & Noble-Haeusslein, 2010).

A study (Bauman et al., 2009) using pigs subjected to a blast in a HUMMVEE surrogate and four sided unroofed structures is of interest. This combat casualty model (Bauman et al., 2009) developed in response to in theatre clinical observations (Armonda et al., 2006) of brain edema, hemorrhage, and vasospasm as salient pathophysiolgic findings in cBTBI. This research program is part of the DARPA (Defense Advanced Research Projects Agency) PREVENT (Preventing Violent Explosive Neurotrauma) blast research program. Closed blast injuries in recent combat have been recognized as unique, with rapidly progressing edema, accompanied by hemorrhage and vasospasm associated with non penetrating head injuries.

The DARPA experiments aimed to gain insight into these injuries. The apparatus employs non-encased explosives producing open pressure waves in duration of 315 to 345 msec maximum overpressure of 24 psi and a negative impulse of about -3.0 to -6.0 at about 335 to 343 msec. Protected leads in the forebrain, thalamus, and hindbrain of swine, fitted with armor protecting the chest and upper abdomen, were placed to measure pressure transients in brain tissue. To detect "vascular surge," pressure monitors were implanted in the external jugular vein, descending aorta, vena cava, and the common carotid artery. Major carotid artery pressure peaks corresponded to intraparencymal pressure peaks at the same millisecond intervals after blast exposure. Pre-blast and post-blast angiography showed post-blast vasospasm, probably similar to that observed clinically. Pre-blast and post-blast EEG and ECG showed loss of EEG signals and transient cardiac arrhythmias lasting about one minute after blast exposure.

White matter degeneration and astrocytosis were seen two weeks after injury including dead axons and dendrites in white matter. Additional studies showed elevated brain and serum inflammatory biomarkers after exposure in the HUMMVEE surrogate. Observation and recording of motor movements such as cyclic-foot-up, foot-down coordinated motion remained disrupted post-blast presumably up to the time of autopsy studies two weeks later. The authors endorse the use of an open blast tube model and discuss limitations in skull shape and rigidity in the murine and swine animal models as these affect pressure transmission of blast injury into the skull.

Cernak's summary of evidence supports the reality of primary closed blast injury, BINT or cBTBI (Cernak & Noble-Haeusslein, 2009), importantly describing blast-induced neurotrauma as a complex series of events related to interacting cerebral, local, and systemic responses. These are initiated at the time of blast exposure and are accompanied by autonomic nervous system activation. The immune system then contributes to molecular and inflammatory changes resulting in a cascading brain injury which goes on for some time after blast exposure. The summation of temporal sequences revealed by these animal experimental data suggest that time based strategies have the potential to diminish immediate cBTBI injury, to modulate intermediate responses, and to test diagnostic accuracy and treatment efficacy. As recently as 2008, controversy continued concerning possible singular effects of the blast overpressure as causing neuronal damage in a report published by the Office of the Surgeon General in U.S. Army Medical Department (Traumatic Brain Injury Task Force Report, 2008).

Imaging Techniques

Recent advances in imaging techniques (Provenzale, 2010; Van Boven et al., 2009) have proven crucial in providing new insights into the pathophsiology of cBTBI. Techniques evolving far beyond conventional computerized tomographic (CT) scanning can now identify anatomic and physiologic and biochemical changes after injury. General neuroimaging techniques (Ashwal, Holshouser & Tong, 2006) include: (1) Susceptibility Weighted three dimensional magnetic resonance Imaging (SWI) to detect hemorrhagic lesions in associated DAI; (2) Magnetic Resonance Spectroscopy to define metabolic information reflecting neuronal integrity and function; (3) Diffusion Weighted Imaging, based on differential brain water diffusion, also can detect early ischemic injury; (4) Diffusion Tensor Imaging (DTI), a form of diffusion weighted imaging, detects white matter injury. DTI delineates white matter fiber tracts utilizing anisotropic effects of water diffusion and is sensitive for detecting DAI.

Conventional CT imaging, widely available in emergency rooms and in the field, identifies gross abnormalities predicting the need for surgical intervention in individuals with TBI. However, CT is an imperfect predictor for occurrence of later mTBI. Jacobs et al. (2010) observed TBI patients presenting with Glasgow Coma Scale grades 13–15, scores consistent with mTBI. Perfusion CT performed during the acute phase of TBI in patients with negative initial CT scans demonstrated disturbed cerebral perfusion. Metting et al. (2009) showed that TBI victims with lower GCS scores had decreased cerebral flow and blood volume which predicted worse outcomes measured by later extended GCS evaluations. While CT imaging is the procedure of choice for initial evaluation, MRI is recommended in TBI when the CT fails to account for neurological findings and for evaluation and monitoring of sub-acute and chronic TBI (Le & Gean, 2009). Susceptibility weighted MRI can detect cerebral microbleeds not otherwise found in mTBI by CT scanning (Park, Park, Kang, Nam, Min, & Hwang, 2009).

DTI has been used in mTBI to detect white matter injury; to follow the time sequences of DAI, and to attempt to relate white matter damage to functional results. Cytotoxic edema with disruption of ionic homeostasis in the white matter structures begins after injury. Mayer et al. (2010) documented white matter abnormalities in the sub-acute stage of mTBI after a mean of 12 days post-injury. Relating these changes to functional test results remains a challenge.

Levin et al. (2010) studied 37 veterans with mild to moderate TBI to relate white matter injury to the Neurobehavioral Symptom Inventory, PTSD Civilian Check List, and Brief Symptom Inventory for depression which were worse in the TBI group. No group differences in DTI fractional anisotropy and apparent diffusion coefficients were detected. A group from Leuven (Caeyenberghs et al., 2010) related eye-hand coordination deficits to white matter lesions in young civilians with TBI, likely more severe and not blast related, to performing dynamic tracking tasks. More recent studies using DTI have detected blast-related TBI injury in combat injured veterans (MacDonald et al., 2011) as well as studying PTSD severity in the context of blast exposure causing mTBI (Bazarian, Donnelly, Peterson, Warner, Zhu, & Zhong, 2012). Recently, the effects of chronic mTBI on white matter integrity in OEF/OIF veterans were assessed using high angular resolution diffusion imaging (Morey et al., 2012). Distributed loss of white matter integrity correlated with post-injury loss of consciousness duration or feeling of being dazed or confused, but not with the diagnosis of PTSD. Additionally, application of electroencephalogram phase synchronization combined with DTI also yielded findings suggesting diminished interhemispheric coordination of brain activity in the frontal areas after blast exposure possibly related to damaged anterior white matter tracts (Sponheim, 2011).

Whole brain proton MR spectroscopic images capture brain metabolites N-Acetyl aspartate (NAA), total choline (Cho), and total creatine (Cre). Govind et al. (2010) observed 29 subjects with GCS scores ranging from 10–15, finding widespread decrease of NAA, and NAA/Cre within all lobes of the TBI subjects with the greatest changes in white matter. Though not without controversy, white matter damage, DAI, challenging to quantify, appears to be an increasing recognized aspect of brain blast injury. This correlation is important in choosing optimal functional tests to assess subtle aspects neurobehavioral dysfunction. It is acknowledged that reliable methods to diagnose mTBI remain highly challenging. Changes in activity of biomolecules or biomarkers possibly reflect the severity of injury or disease responses to treatment. These evolving techniques (Dash, Zhao, Hergenroeder, & Moore, 2010), combined with imaging, offer promise of better objective assessment of mTBI.

Comorbidities

Polytrauma

About 75% of combat injuries in OEF/OIF are reported to result from blasts and explosions (Owens, Kragh, Wenke, Macaitis, Wade, & Holcomb, 2008). These cause complex and multiple injuries, in the past called "multiple injury extreme"; now termed "poly" (many) "trauma" (injuries). VHA has developed a system of care, a Polytrauma Network, to manage these injuries long term, including TBI (Agarwal, 2010). Associated injuries include traumatic amputation, diffuse muscular loss and fractures, compartment syndromes, abdominal visceral and thoracic injury, vascular disruption, eye, ear, maxillofacial, and spinal cord injury. Hemorrhagic shock inevitably accompanies polytrauma and, in addition to surgical damage control, requires fluid resuscitation that can, in turn, affect the brain to cause swelling. During the present conflicts, protective body armor and skillful surgical front line resuscitation and treatment have greatly reduced the case fatality rate of severely wounded combatants as compared to other conflicts (Kelly et al., 2008). While blasts and explosions account for more injuries, more TBI patients now survive.

Overenthusiastic crystalloid or dextran resuscitation predisposes to brain swelling in TBI. Experimental studies suggest that resuscitation with blood (Timmons, 2006) or hypertonic saline in canine brain injury models offer distinct advantages in preventing brain swelling (Gunnar, Jonasson, Merliottii, Stone, & Barrett, 1988; Gunnar, Kane, & Barrett, 1989; Pinto, Capone-Neto, Prist, e Silva, & Poli-de-Figueiredo, 2006,). Burris et al. (1999) recommended fluid replacement sufficient to reduce pulse rate to about 80 while maintaining a blood pressure sufficient to support warm perfusion. A rat model subjected to blast overpressure while protected by armor exhibits reduced tolerance to subsequent hemorrhagic shock, likely related to the impact of brain injury on homeostatic mechanisms (Long, Bentley, Wessner, Cerone, Sweeney, & Bauman, 2009).

In spite of cautious resuscitation, some patients with cBTBI experience rapidly progressive edema requiring craniectomy for relief (Ling et al., 2009). Emergency decompressive craniectomy has been used to treat rapidly progressing brain swelling due to cBTBI. Two randomized trials are underway to assess the efficacy of this procedure for TBI; however they pose challenges due to the heterogeneity of injuries (Aarabi & Simard, 2009; Winter, Adamides, & Rosenfeld, 2005). Complications of craniectomy include increased edema, infection, venous infarction, and derangement of the cerebrospinal fluid circulation with hydrocephalus or hygroma development, paradoxical herniation following lumbar puncture, or further neurobehavioral derangements called syndrome of the trephined (Akins & Guppy, 2008; Stiver, 2009).

Special Senses

Exposure to the shock wave and blast overpressure causes eye injuries including rupture of the globe, serous retinitis, and hyphema (Abbotts, Harrison, & Cooper, 2007; Blanch & Scott, 2008). Isolated orbital fractures are signaled by enophthalmos and diplopia even in the absence of globe damage. Implosion and "mini re-explosion" due to blast injury of the nasal, orbital, ethmoidal, and maxillary sinuses have been described in a series of injuries suffered by Iraqis (Shuker, 2010) in instances of civilians injuring civilians.

In addition to hearing loss, tinnitus, and perforated ear drums, vestibular injury signaled by vertigo, gaze instability, and motion intolerance occurs in cBTBI (Scherer & Schubert, 2009). Dizziness, vertigo, and osscilopsia (illusory visual motion) have been described in the days and weeks following the injury and may persist for months. Shupak et al. (1993) described vestibular injury in Israeli soldiers occurring even in the absence of tympanic membrane perforation.

Anosmia; Impaired Olfaction

Anosmia has been described after TBI occurring in about 12% of cases, though not necessarily due to blast; 11% additionally complain of decreased sense of smell (Haxel, Grant, & Mackay-Sim, 2008). Mechanisms leading to post traumatic anosmia include sinus injury, olfactory nerve damage, and damage of cerebral olfactory centers (Collet, Grulois, Bertrand, Rombaux, 2009). Anosmia has been cited previously as a useful finding to support an objective diagnosis of post-concussive mTBI (Varney & Roberts, 1999). Ruff et al. (2012), in a case controlled study, recently showed that impaired olfaction was the most frequently occurring neurologic disorder occurring in 65 of 126 combat veterans sustaining mTBI.

Aeromedical Evacuation and Traumatic Brain Injury

Polytrauma casualties due to blast injury often require air evacuation which may affect (TBI) as it progresses from its primary stages to secondary damage from the systemic effects of hypoxia, hypotension, and inflammation. These processes are coupled with the local effects of brain tissue hypoxia, cerebral edema, blood brain barrier degradation, and neuronal inflammation (Goodman et al., 2010). After cBTBI, a neuronal inflammatory response begins as early as one hour post injury and extends through several days or longer depending upon the injury severity (Morganti-Kossmann, Satgunaseelan, Bye, & Kossmann, 2007; Schmidt, Heyde, Ertel, & Stahel, 2005). The neural inflammatory response is reflected by the release of cytokines and chemokines, interleukins 1, 6, 8, 10, and 18. Tumor necrosis factor- alpha and transforming growth factor-beta are also representative of inflammatory biomarkers (Morganti-Kossmann et al, 2007). Reduction in detectable levels of selected biomarkers in serum and cerebrospinal fluid possibly reflect an improving neuroinflammatory state. Accurate measurement and quantification of these biomarker trends might play a future role in consideration of air evacuation of individuals with TBI.

Commercial airline flights produce moderate exposure to altitude change with cabin pressures equivalent to 5,000–8,000 feet. At these levels, passengers with no significant medical problems regularly experience peripheral oxygen saturation levels of 89% (Morganti-Kossmann et al., 2007). Military aeromedical evacuation aircraft are routinely pressurized from 4,500–8,800 feet during long distance flights. Patients with poor perfusion experience oxygen saturation levels in the dangerous range of the hemoglobin oxygen saturation curve. Additional risk factors for poor oxygen saturation include concomitant respiratory tract infection, dehydration, and age greater than 50 years (Basnyat & Murdoch, 2003). Acute exposure to altitude above 6,500 feet can produce altitude or mountain sickness syndrome. Further exposure to higher altitude hypobaric pressures cause high altitude pulmonary edema and high altitude cerebral edema. The pathogenesis of these syndromes is currently unknown, but they may result, directly or indirectly, from the effects of hypobaric hypoxia (Carlton & Jenkins, 2008).

Patients experiencing closed head injury develop levels of neural inflammation and cerebral edema which may vary directly with the injury severity. Exposure to the hypobaric effects of altitude superimposed on this acute inflammatory process potentially produces a "dual injury" model of critical illness. The closed head injury, the initial insult, is followed by a continuing cerebral inflammatory process. A second insult may relate to the altitude-induced inflammatory changes from hypobaric hypoxia encountered during aeromedical evacuation. In this situation, severity of injury, morbidity, and mortality from the traumatic brain injury might worsen (Goodman et al., 2010).

Synchronized aeromedical evacuation is the mainstay for current military casualty management and is associated with the lowest mortality from battlefield wounds in the history of American wars (Gawande, 2004). Overall improved casualty survival rates have been attributed to the expeditious transport of casualties from the combat environment to tertiary care medical facilities. Unfortunately, because of the effects of hypobaric hypoxia, aeromedical evacuation might exert deleterious effects in patients with TBI. Not only do these patients develop lower arterial oxygen saturation, but they also experience the effects of increased gas expansion in body cavities and organ systems. A solution to the adverse pressure and relative hypoxemic effects of aeromedical evacuation could be increase in cabin pressurization. This, however, reduces fuel efficiency, increases flight

duration, reduces energy available to operate other aircraft systems, limits the operational lifetime of aluminum airframes, and necessitates increased structural aircraft weight, all of which are counterproductive to military flight operations (Muhm et al., 2007).

It is imperative that every attempt be made to prevent secondary brain injury while rapidly transporting patients with traumatic brain injury to definitive care facilities. Tissue hypoxemia superimposed on traumatic brain injury has been associated with worse neurological outcome and increased mortality in casualties with moderate to severe TBI (Grissom, Weaver, Clemmer, & Morris, 2006). Aeromedical evacuation, using current cabin pressurization levels, exposes the casualty to lower partial pressure of oxygen at altitude and increases the risk for additional tissue hypoxia especially in the inflamed or edematous brain.

Systemic inflammation, producing multisystem organ failure, is a frequent cause of late death in severely traumatized casualties. Systemic and cerebral inflammatory responses to traumatic brain injury increase the casualties' susceptibility to hypobaric hypoxemia related to altitude exposure possibly enhancing inflammatory responses. This second level of injury may also render traumatic brain injury patients at greater risk from multiorgan dysfunction. Goodman et al. (Goodman et al., 2010) theorize that serial assessments of head injured casualties serum inflammatory cytokine profiles could define an optimal time when the brain is "fit to fly" by minimizing "altitude-induced" exacerbation of the posttraumatic brain injury neuroinflammatory response. Identifying the "time to fly" might reduce the potential for secondary injury during aeromedical evacuation exposure to hypobaric hypoxemia to improve outcomes for polytrauma casualties with concomitant TBI.

When aeromedical evacuation is considered essential because of critical injuries in addition to TBI, the Air Force Critical Care Aeromedical Transport Team (CCATT) has been used. The majority of these patients are transported intubated and mechanically ventilated and more than a third have had intracranial pressure monitors in place throughout the transport (CCATT Data Base, Dec 2008). These additional measures help combat the effects of hypobaric hypoxemia related to required long-distance aeromedical evacuation.

Post-Traumatic Stress Disorder (PTSD)

PTSD emerges as an important comorbidity of mTBI. Psychological investment in the symptoms and the association of mTBI and PTSD present perplexing clinical problems as pointed out by Berlanger et al. (2009). Howe's review (2009), stresses the importance on not erring in either extreme in assessing PTSD in relation to blast injury. PSTD is defined in DSM-IV as follows:

The essential feature of Posttraumatic Stress Disorder is the development of characteristic symptoms following exposure to an extreme traumatic stressor involving direct personal experience of an event that involves actual or threatened death or serious injury, or other threat to one's physical integrity; or witnessing an event that involves death, injury, or a threat to the physical integrity of another person; or learning about unexpected or violent death, serious harm, or threat of death or injury experienced by a family member or other close associate (Criterion A1). The person's response to the event must involve intense fear, helplessness, or horror (or in children, the response must involve disorganized or agitated behavior) (Criterion A2). The characteristic symptoms resulting from the exposure to the extreme trauma include persistent reexperiencing of the traumatic event (Criterion B), persistent avoidance of stimuli associated with the trauma and numbing of general responsiveness (Criterion C), and persistent symptoms of increased arousal (Criterion D). The full symptom picture must be present for more than 1 month (Criterion E), and the disturbance must cause clinically significant distress or impairment in social, occupational, or other important areas of functioning (Criterion F). The condition may be further specified as acute i.e. <3 months duration; chronic> than 3 months duration; or delayed, i.e., occurring 6 months after the event.

The Pubmed National Institutes of Health database, at the time of this review, references over 20,430 citations for the search term PTSD extending back to 1962. The term, *post-traumatic syndrome*, first appears in a clinical report of an automobile accident victim in 1968 (Landy, 1968). Previous titles include thematic variations on post-traumatic neuroses and reports focusing on separating out head injuries from other causes or from compensation based claims. Rutherford (1977) working in Belfast in the 1970's analyzed 145 patients with concussion due to minor head injuries and concluded that a significant correlation existed between positive neurologic signs and symptoms at 24 hours and a high rate of symptoms persisting at six weeks. He suggested that both organic and "neurotic" factors are involved in the pathogenesis of symptoms at this time. PTSD as a diagnosis first appeared in DSM-III in 1980.

DSM- IV core criteria for self reported PTSD diagnosis include association with specific trauma characteristics, re-experiencing the event, avoidance, hyperarousal, duration of symptoms, and level of impairment. Boals and Hathaway (2010) suggested that an Impact of Events Scale may produce misleading results in making emotional reactions to obviously non-traumatic events appear to be PTSD. While acute PTSD symptoms often accompany mTBI, amnesia after injury (Klein, Caspi, & Gil, 2003), along with actual organic brain injury, has been described as reducing PTSD frequency. Dimensions of trauma-specific symptoms reported by soldiers in combat zones include exposure to blast, arousal, and irritability. Accurate recording of clinical findings immediately after blast exposure may later help to separate functional from organic disorders due to PTSD and mTBI along with combinations of both conditions. As an illustration of the difficulties of assessing mTBI or "concussion" during combat, Wilk et al. (2010) report a lack of association of blast mechanisms with persistent post-concussive symptoms. The most important limitation of current outcome assessment appears to be reliance upon self-reported disorders.

Neurobehavioral Outcomes of BTBI

Under contract with the Department of Veterans Affairs, a committee of the Institute of Medicine (Ishibe, Wlordaaczyk, & Fidco, 2009) examined the long-term consequences of TBI using a comprehensive search of 14, 302 citations between 1960 and 2008, identifying 152 primary and secondary publications meeting inclusion criteria to provide the basis for their conclusions based upon sufficient evidence of a *causal relationship; sufficient evidence for an association; limited/suggestive evidence of an association; inadequate evidence to determine whether or not an association exists; limited/suggestive evidence of no association.* The committee cited evidence of *causal* relationships between penetrating TBI and subsequent seizures and premature mortality. Sufficient evidence of an *association* included penetrating trauma and decline in neurocognitive function with the area of brain involvement and long-term unemployment. Severe TBI was *associated* with neurocognitive deficits; moderate or severe TBI was *associated* with dementia, Parkinsonism, hormonal (hypituitary) disorders, adverse social functioning, more disability, and premature death.

Mild TBI received determinations of *limited/suggestive associations* with conditions such a loss of consciousness, amnesia, deteriorating or loss of vision, dementia, and associated PTSD with mTBI in Gulf War Veterans. *Insufficient evidence* for determination of *an association* was noted in mTBI for neurocognitive deficits, dementia, and long-term adverse social functioning. In contrast to findings in the military population, *no association* between mTBI and PTSD was noted in civilian populations. The committee did not provide evidence of *no association* for any of these conditions while underscoring variability in assessing mild, moderate and severe TBI based on Glasgow Coma Score and duration of post-traumatic amnesia. TBI can also be assessed as mild, moderate, or severe based upon the changes between early indicators of severity and outcomes at an (arbitrary) six month interval. It is important to note that these conclusions relate to First Gulf War Veterans rather than OEF/OIF combatants.

Belanger et al. (2009) examined blast and non-blast related TBIs to determine whether or not cognitive sequelae differed from one another. They conclude that BTBI versus non-blast TBI participants do not differ significantly with respect to cognitive measures based upon

a battery of neuropsychological tests in subjects exposed to blast with cBTBI and subjects with non-blast TBI. In this study, however, the participants with blast injury more frequently evidenced PTSD in comparison to non-blast TBI participants. The authors suggest that hyperarousal occurs during combat missions where IEDs most commonly cause the blast injury. These conditions are associated with pre-blast and post-blast multisensory inputs and perceptions of horror. These experiences differ from motor vehicle accidents and even civilian blast injury where victims are taken by surprise. Hoge et al. (2008, 2009), combining individuals with loss of consciousness and alteration of consciousness after blast, estimated that 32.6 % of combatants may have PTSD.

Evaluation of long term neurobehavioral disorders in combatants continues to be jointly assessed by the Department of Defense and the Veterans Administration (2009) including multiple dimensions of impairment with attention to visual disorders since visual defects are more often associated with blast than with non-blast events (Brahm, Wilgenburg, Kirby, Ingalla, Chang, & Goodrich, 2009). Since TBI screening was initiated in DVA from April 2007 through April 2012, 613,887 OEF/OIF veterans reported and were screened for possible mTBI; 121,751 (19.8%) screened positive and were offered referral for follow-up comprehensive evaluation. Among 86,596 completing comprehensive evaluations, 48,197 (7.8–7.9%) of those reporting and completing screening) received a diagnosis of a having incurred mTBI. Additionally, those who screened positive and were not diagnosed with having incurred mTBI were referred to specialty teams for further follow-up of reported symptoms.

The assessment of neurobehavioral disorders after blast-traumatic brain injury, as can be seen, remains challenging due to the heterogeneity of blast brain injuries and the variability of neurobehavioral outcomes. Military exposures have received considerable attention while less is reported about civilian injuries. BTBI from initial exposure to intermediate inflammatory processes to resolution or stabilization requires better characterization. TBI has been recognized as one of the foremost medical problems of the actions in Iraq and Afghanistan, in sharp contrast to the dismissiveness of blast injury or "shell shock" following World War I which continued into the 21st century (DePalma, Cross, Beck, & Chandler, 2011). This recognition has stimulated comprehensive research support by the Veterans Affairs Office of Research and Development, National Institutes of Health, and Department of Defense for diagnosis, understanding of short- and long-term TBI effects, evaluation of existing treatments, and development of new approaches for rehabilitation and community reintegration (Kupersmith, Lew, Ommaya, Jaffee, & Koroshetz, 2009). Robust and focused methods of physical protection might be based upon better understanding of the physics of the blast shock wave as it encounters the skull and underlying brain, in contrast to barotrauma injuring the lung and visceral organs. Treatment based on evidence can be derived from blast injury animal models providing better characterization of ongoing changes from the time of initial insult to ongoing inflammatory processes. Better understanding of the brain anatomy and neurophysiologic responses in humans exposed to blasts in the future will likely be more objectively based upon imaging, biomarker measurements, and functional testing not previously available.

Acknowledgments

The authors acknowledge the invaluable assistance of the VA Central Office Library, Ms Caryl Kazen, Director and Ms Vivian Stahl, Reference Librarian for literature search and David W Chandler, Ph.D., Deputy Chief and Lucille B Beck, Ph.D., Chief Consultant, Rehabilitation Services Department of Veterans Affairs for their assistance and Colonel David G Burris M.D., MCUSA for his insights into resuscitation. Members of the DoD Brain Injury Computational Modeling Expert Panel chaired by Michael Leggieri Col U.S.A. (ret) and Raj Gupta Col U.S.A/ (ret) provided important guidance in considering potential mechanisms of brain blast injury. The opinions expressed herein are those of the authors and not necessarily those of the Department of Veterans Affairs or the United States Government.

References

Aarabi, B., & Simard, J. M. (2009). Traumatic brain injury. *Current Opinion in Critical Care, 15*(6), 548–553.

Abbotts, R., Harrison, S. E., & Cooper, G. L. (2007). Primary blast injuries to the eye: A review of the evidence. *Journal of the Royal Army Medical Corps, 153*(2), 119–123.

Agarwal, M. (2010). *Transitioning Heroes: New Era, Same Problems?: Hearing Before the Subcommittee on Oversight and Investigations of the Committee on Veterans' Affairs, US House of Representatives, One Hundred Eleventh Congress, Second Session, January 21, 2010*: Government Printing Office.

Akins, P. T., & Guppy, K. H. (2008). Sinking skin flaps, paradoxical herniation, and external brain tamponade: A review of decompressive craniectomy management. *Neurocritical Care, 9*(2), 269–276.

Armonda, R. A., Bell, R. S., Vo, A. H., Ling, G., DeGraba, T. J., Crandall, B., et al. (2006). Wartime traumatic cerebral vasospasm: Recent review of combat casualties. *Neurosurgery, 59*(6), 1215–1225.

Arnold, J. L., Halpern, P., Tsai, M., & Smithline, H. (2004). Mass casualty terrorist bombings: a comparison of outcomes by bombing type. *Annals of Emergency Medicine, 43*(2), 263–273.

Ashwal, S., Holshouser, B. A., & Tong, K. A. (2006). Use of advanced neuroimaging techniques in the evaluation of pediatric traumatic brain injury. *Developmental Neuroscience, 28*(4–5), 309–326.

Axelsson, H., Hjelmqvist, H., Medin, A., Persson, J. K. E., Anders, & Suneson. (2000). Physiological changes in pigs exposed to a blast wave from a detonating high-explosive charge. *Military Medicine, 165*(2), 119–126.

Basnyat, B., & Murdoch, D. R. (2003). High-altitude illness. *The Lancet, 361*(9373), 1967–1974.

Batsanov, S. S. (1994). *Effects of explosions on materials: modification and synthesis under high-pressure shock compression*: Springer: Moscow.

Bauman, R. A., Ling, G., Tong, L., Januszkiewicz, A., Agoston, D., Delanerolle, N., et al. (2009). An introductory characterization of a combat-casualty-care relevant swine model of closed head injury resulting from exposure to explosive blast. *Journal of Neurotrauma, 26*(6), 841–860.

Bazarian, J., Donnelly, K., Peterson, D., Warner, G., Tong, Z., & Zhong, J. (2012). The Relation Between Posttraumatic Stress Disorder and Mild Traumatic Brain Injury Acquired During Operations Enduring Freedom and Iraqi Freedom. *Journal of Head Trauma Rehabilitation, 28*(1), 1–12.

Belanger, H. G., Kretzmer, T., Yoash-Gantz, R., Pickett, T., & Tupler, L. A. (2009). Cognitive sequelae of blast-related versus other mechanisms of brain trauma. *Journal of the International Neuropsychological Society*, *15*(1), 1–8.

Blanch, R. J., & Scott, R. A. (2008). Primary blast injury of the eye. *Journal of the Royal Army Medical Corps*, *154*(1), 76.

Boals, A., & Hathaway, L. M. (2010). The importance of the DSM-IV E and F criteria in self-report assessments of PTSD. *Journal of Anxiety Disorders*, *24*(1), 161–166.

Boven, R. W. Van, Harrington, G. S., Hackney, D. B., Ebel, A., Gauger, G., Bremner, J. D., et al. (2009). Advances in neuroimaging of traumatic brain injury and posttraumatic stress disorder. *Journal of Rehabilitation Research and Development*, *46*(6), 717–757.

Brahm, K. D., Wilgenburg, H. M., Kirby, J., Ingalla, S., Chang, C., & Goodrich, G. L. (2009). Visual impairment and dysfunction in combat-injured service members with traumatic brain injury. *Optometry and Vision Science*, *86*(7), 817–825.

Brenner, L. A., Ivins, B. J., Schwab, K., Warden, D., Nelson, L. A., Jaffee, M., & Terrio, H. (2010). Traumatic brain injury, posttraumatic stress disorder, and postconcussive symptom reporting among troops returning from Iraq. *The Journal of Head Trauma Rehabilitation*, *25*(5), 307–312.

Brenner, L. A., Vanderploeg, R. D., & Terrio, H. (2009). Assessment and diagnosis of mild traumatic brain injury, posttraumatic stress disorder, and other polytrauma conditions: Burden of adversity hypothesis. *Rehabilitation Psychology*, *54*(3), 239.

Burris, D., Rhee, P., Kaufmann, C., Pikoulis, E., Austin, B., Eror, A., et al. (1999). Controlled resuscitation for uncontrolled hemorrhagic shock. *The Journal of Trauma and Acute Care Surgery*, *46*(2), 216–223.

Caeyenberghs, K., Leemans, A., Geurts, M., Taymans, T., Linden, C. V., Smits-Engelsman, B. C. M., et al. (2010). Brain-behavior relationships in young traumatic brain injury patients: fractional anisotropy measures are highly correlated with dynamic visuomotor tracking performance. *Neuropsychologia*, *48*(5), 1472–1482.

Carlton, P. K., & Jenkins, D. H. (2008). The mobile patient. *Critical Care Medicine*, *36*(7), 255–257.

Cernak, I., & Noble-Haeusslein, L. J. (2010). Traumatic brain injury: An overview of pathobiology with emphasis on military populations. *Journal of Cerebral Blood Flow and Metabolism*, *30*(2), 255–266.

Collet, S., Grulois, V., Bertrand, B., & Rombaux, P. (2009). Post-traumatic olfactory dysfunction: A cohort study and update. *B-ENT*, *5*, 97–107.

Cooper, G. J., Maynard, R. L., Cross, N. L., & Hill, J. F. (1983). Casualties from terrorist bombings. *The Journal of Trauma and Acute Care Surgery*, *23*(11), 955–967.

Cottrell, J. J., Lebovitz, B. L., Fennell, R. G., & Kohn, G. M. (1995). Inflight arterial saturation: continuous monitoring by pulse oximetry. *Aviation, Space, and Environmental Medicine*, *66*(2), 126–130.

Cullis, I. G. (2001). Blast waves and how they interact with structures. *Journal of the Royal Army Medical Corps*, *147*(1), 16–26.

Dash, P. K., Zhao, J., Hergenroeder, G., & Moore, A. N. (2010). Biomarkers for the diagnosis, prognosis, and evaluation of treatment efficacy for traumatic brain injury. *Neurotherapeutics*, *7*(1), 100–114.

Denny-Brown, D. (1945). Cerebral concussion. *Physiological Reviews*, *25*(2), 296–325.

DePalma, R. G., Burris, D. G., Champion, H. R., & Hodgson, M. J. (2005). Current Concepts: Blast injuries. *New England Journal of Medicine*, *352*(13), 1335–1342.

DePalma, R. G., Cross, G. M., Beck, L. B., & Chandler, D. W. (2011). *Epidemiology of mTBI due to blast: History, DOD/VA data bases: Challenges and opportunities.* Proc NATO RTO-MP-HFM-207 Symposium on a Survey of Blast Injury across the Full Landscape of Military Science.

Department of Veterans Affairs, Department of Defense. (2009). VA/DoD clinical practice guideline for management of concussion/mild traumatic brain injury. *Journal of Rehabilitation Research and Development*, *46*(6), 1–68.

Desmoulin, G. T., & Dionne, J. (2009). Blast-induced neurotrauma: Surrogate use, loading mechanisms, and cellular responses. *The Journal of Trauma and Acute Care Surgery*, *67*(5), 1113–1122.

Dickson, D. (1943). Blast in 1812. *Lancet*, *1*, 385.

Elder, G. A., & Cristian, A. (2009). Blast-related mild traumatic brain injury: mechanisms of injury and impact on clinical care. *Mount Sinai Journal of Medicine: A Journal of Translational and Personalized Medicine*, *76*(2), 111–118.

Fulton, J. F. (1942). Blast and concussion in the present war. *New England Journal of Medicine*, *226*(1), 1–8.

Gans, L., & Kennedy, T. (1996). Management of unique clinical entities in disaster medicine. *Emergency medicine clinics of North America*, *14*(2), 301–326.

Gawande, A. (2004). Casualties of war—military care for the wounded from Iraq and Afghanistan. *New England Journal of Medicine*, *351*(24), 2471–2475.

Gennerelli, T. A., & Graham, D. I. (2005). Chapter 2 Neuropathology. In J. M. Silver, T. W.

McAllister & S. C. Yudofski (Eds.), *Textbook of Traumatic Brain Injury* (pp. 27–50). Washington, London: American Psychiatric Publishing Inc.

Goodman, M. D., Makley, A. T., Lentsch, A. B., Barnes, S. L., Dorlac, G. R., Dorlac, W. C., et al. (2010). Traumatic brain injury and aeromedical evacuation: When is the brain fit to fly? *Journal of Surgical Research, 164*(2), 286–293.

Govind, V., Gold, S., Kaliannan, K., Saigal, G., Falcone, S., Arheart, K., et al. (2010). Whole-brain proton MR spectroscopic imaging of mild-to-moderate traumatic brain injury and correlation with neuropsychological deficits. *Journal of neurotrauma, 27*(3), 483–496.

Grissom, C. K., Weaver, L. K., Clemmer, T. P., & Morris, A. H. (2006). Theoretical advantage of oxygen treatment for combat casualties during medical evacuation at high altitude. *The Journal of Trauma and Acute Care Surgery, 61*(2), 461–467.

Gunnar, W., Jonasson, O., Merlotti, G., Stone, J., & Barrett, J. (1988). Head injury and hemorrhagic shock: studies of the blood brain barrier and intracranial pressure after resuscitation with normal saline solution, 3% saline solution, and dextran-40. *Surgery, 103*(4), 398–407.

Gunnar, W., Kane, J., & Barrett, J. (1989). Cerebral blood flow following hypertonic saline resuscitation in an experimental model of hemorrhagic shock and head injury. *Brazillian Journal of Medical and Biological Research, 22*(2), 287–289.

Gutierrez de Ceballos, J. P., Fuentes, F. T., Diaz, D. P., Sanchez, M. S., Llorente, C. M., & Sanz, J. R. G. (2005). Casualties treated at the closest hospital in the Madrid, March 11, terrorist bombings. *Critical Care Medicine, 33*(1), 107–112.

Guy, R. J., Glover, M. A., & Cripps, N. P. (1998). The pathophysiology of primary blast injury and its implications for treatment. Part I: The thorax. *Journal of the Royal Naval Medical Service, 84*(2), 79–86.

Haxel, B. R., Grant, L., & Mackay-Sim, A. (2008). Olfactory dysfunction after head injury. *The Journal of Head Trauma Rehabilitation, 23*(6), 407–413.

Hoge, C. W., Goldberg, H. M., & Castro, C. A. (2009). Care of war veterans with mild traumatic brain injury-flawed perspectives. *New England Journal of Medicine, 16*(360), 1588–1591.

Hoge, C. W., McGurk, D., Thomas, J. L., Cox, A. L., Engel, C. C., & Castro, C. A. (2008). Mild traumatic brain injury in US soldiers returning from Iraq. *New England Journal of Medicine, 358*(5), 453–463.

Howe, L. S. (2009). Giving context to post-deployment post-concussive-like symptoms: blast-related potential mild traumatic brain injury and comorbidities. *The Clinical Neuropsychologist, 23*(8), 1315–1337.

Ishibe, N., Wlordarczyk, R. C., & Fulco, C. (2009). Overview of the institute of medicine's committee search strategy and review process for gulf war and health: Long-term consequences of traumatic brain injury. *The Journal of Head Trauma Rehabilitation, 24*(6), 424–429.

Jacobs, B., Beems, T., Stulemeijer, M., A. B. van Vugt, T. M. van der Vliet, Borm, G. F., & Vos, P. E. (2010). Outcome prediction in mild traumatic brain injury: Age and clinical variables are stronger predictors than CT abnormalities. *Journal of Neurotrauma, 27*(4), 655–668.

Jaffee, C. M., & Meyer, K. S. (2009). A brief overview of traumatic brain injury (TBI) and post-traumatic stress disorder (PTSD) within the Department of Defense. *The Clinical Neuropsychologist, 23*(8), 1291–1298.

Johnson, S. G., Lee, K. Y. K., Nyein, M. K., Moore, D. F., Joannopoulos, J. D., Socrate, S., et al. (2011). Blast-induced electromagnetic fields in the brain from bone piezoelectricity. *Neuroimage, 54*, 30–36.

Jones, E., Fear, N., & Wessely, S. (2007). Shell shock and mild traumatic brain injury: a historical review. *American Journal of Psychiatry, 164*(11), 1641–1645.

Katz, E., Ofek, B., Adler, J., Abramowitz, H. B., & Krausz, M. M. (1989). Primary blast injury after a bomb explosion in a civilian bus. *Annals of surgery, 209*(4), 484–488.

Kelly, J. F., Ritenour, A. E., McLaughlin, D. F., Bagg, K. A., Apodaca, A. N., Mallak, C. T., et al. (2008). Injury severity and causes of death from Operation Iraqi Freedom and Operation Enduring Freedom: 2003–2004 versus 2006. *The Journal of Trauma and Acute Care Surgery, 64*(2), 21–27.

Klein, E., Caspi, Y., & Gil, S. (2003). The relation between memory of the traumatic event and PTSD: Evidence from studies of traumatic brain injury. *Canadian Journal of Psychiatry, 48*(1), 28–33.

Kocsis, J. D., & Tessler, A. (2009). Pathology of blast-related brain injury. *Journal of Rehabilitation Research and Development, 46*(6), 667–672.

Kupersmith, J., Lew, H. L., Ommaya, A. K., Jaffee, M. S., & Koroshetz, W. J. (2009). Traumatic brain injury research opportunities: Results of Department of Veterans Affairs Consensus Conference. *Journal of Rehabilitation Research and Development, 46*(6), 7–17.

Landy, P. J. (1968). The post-traumatic syndrome in closed head injury accident neurosis. *Proceedings of the Australian Association of Neurologists Journal 5*, 4463–4466.

Le, T. H., & Gean, A. D. (2009). Neuroimaging of traumatic brain injury. *Mount Sinai Journal of Medicine: A Journal of Translational and Personalized Medicine, 76*(2), 145–162.

Levin, H. S., Wilde, E., Troyanskaya, M., Petersen, N. J., Scheibel, R., Newsome, M., et al. (2010). Diffusion tensor imaging of mild to moderate blast-related traumatic brain injury and its sequelae. *Journal of Neurotrauma, 27*(4), 683–694.

Ling, G., Bandak, F., Armonda, R., Grant, G., & Ecklund, J. (2009). Explosive blast neurotrauma. *Journal of Neurotrauma, 26*(6), 815–825.

Long, J. B., Bentley, T. L., Wessner, K. A., Cerone, C., Sweeney, S., & Bauman, R. A. (2009). Blast overpressure in rats: recreating a battlefield injury in the laboratory. *Journal of Neurotrauma, 26*(6), 827–840.

MacDonald, C. L., Johnson, A. M., Cooper, D., Nelson, E. C., Werner, N. J., Shimony, J. S., et al. (2011). Detection of blast-related traumatic brain injury in US military personnel. *New England Journal of Medicine, 364*(22), 2091–2100.

Mayer, A. R., Ling, J., Mannell, M. V., Gasparovic, C., Phillips, J. P., Doezema, D., et al. (2010). A prospective diffusion tensor imaging study in mild traumatic brain injury. *Neurology, 74*(8), 643–650.

McCrea, M., Pliskin, N., Barth, J., Cox, D., Fink, J., French, L., et al. (2008). Official Position of the Military TBI Task Force on the Role of Neuropsychology and Rehabilitation Psychology in the Evaluation, Management, and Research of Military Veterans with Traumatic Brain Injury. *The Clinical Neuropsychologist, 22*(1), 10–26.

McKee, A. C., Cantu, R. C., Nowinski, C. J., Hedley-Whyte, E. T., Gavett, B. E., Budson, A. E., et al. (2009). Chronic traumatic encephalopathy in athletes: progressive tauopathy following repetitive head injury. *Journal of Neuropathology and Experimental Neurology, 68*(7), 709–735.

Metting, Z., Rödiger, L. A., Stewart, R. E., Oudkerk, M., Keyser, J. De, & J. van der Naalt. (2009). Perfusion computed tomography in the acute phase of mild head injury: regional dysfunction and prognostic value. *Annals of Neurology, 66*(6), 809–816.

Miller, K., & Chang, A. (2003). Acute inhalation injury. *Emergency Medicine Clinics of North America, 21*(2), 533–557.

Moore, D. F., Radovitzky, R. A., Shupenko, L., Klinoff, A., Jaffee, M. S., & Rosen, J. M. (2008). Blast physics and central nervous system injury. *Future Neurology, 3*(3), 243–250.

Morey, R. A., Haswell, C. C., Selgrade, E. S., Massoglia, D., Liu, C., Weiner, J., et al. (2012). Effects of chronic mild traumatic brain injury on white matter integrity in Iraq and Afghanistan war veterans. *Human Brain Mapping, 34*(11), 2986–2999.

Morganti-Kossmann, M. A., Satgunaseelan, L., Bye, N., & Kossmann, T. (2007). Modulation of immune response by head injury. *Injury, 38*(12), 1392–1400.

Moss, W. C., King, M. J., & Blackman, E. G. (2009). Skull flexure from blast waves: a mechanism for brain injury with implications for helmet design. *Journal of the Acoustical Society of America, 125*(4), 2650–2650.

Mott, D., Schwer, D., Young, T., Levine, J., Dionne, J., Makris, A., & Hubler, G. (2008). Blast-induced pressure fields beneath a military helmet for non-lethal threats. *Bulletin of the American Physical Society, 53*.

Mott, F. W. (1916). The effects of high explosives upon the central nervous system. *Lancet, 1*(12), 331–338.

Muhm, J. M., Rock, P. B., McMullin, D. L., Jones, S. P., Lu, I., Eilers, K. D., et al. (2007). Effect of aircraft-cabin altitude on passenger discomfort. *New England Journal of Medicine, 357*(1), 18–27.

Nirula, R., Kaufman, R., & Tencer, A. (2003). Traumatic brain injury and automotive design: making motor vehicles safer. *The Journal of Trauma and Acute Care Surgery, 55*(5), 844–848.

Okie, S. (2005). Traumatic brain injury in the war zone. *New England Journal of Medicine, 352*(20), 2043–2047.

Owens, B. D., Jr, J. F. Kragh, Wenke, J. C., Macaitis, J., Wade, C. E., & Holcomb, J. B. (2008). Combat wounds in operation Iraqi Freedom and operation Enduring Freedom. *The Journal of Trauma and Acute Care Surgery, 64*(2), 295–299.

Park, J., Park, S., Kang, S., Nam, T., Min, B., & Hwang, S. (2009). Detection of Traumatic Cerebral Microbleeds by Susceptibility-Weighted Image of MRI. *Journal of Korean Neurosurgical Society, 46*(4), 365–369.

Phillips, Y. Y., & Richmond, D. R. (1991). Chapter 6 Conventional Warfare: Ballistic, Blast and Burn Injuries. *Conventional Blast Injury and Basic Research.* Washington DC: Department of the Army, Borden Institute, Office of the Surgeon General.

Pinto, F., Capone-Neto, A., R. Prist, Ricardo, M. R. e Silva, & Poli-de-Figueiredo, L. F. (2006). Volume replacement with lactated Ringer's or 3% hypertonic saline solution during combined experimental hemorrhagic shock and traumatic brain injury. *The Journal of Trauma and Acute Care Surgery, 60*(4), 758–764.

Provenzale, J. M. (2010). Imaging of traumatic brain injury: Q review of the recent medical literature. *American Journal of Roentgenology, 194*(1), 16–19.

Rosenfeld, J. V., & Ford, N. L. (2010). Bomb blast, mild traumatic brain injury and psychiatric morbidity: a review. *Injury, 41*(5), 437–443.

Ruff, R. L., Riechers, R. G., Wang, X., Piero, T., & Ruff, S. S. (2012). A case–control study examining whether neurological deficits and PTSD in combat veterans are related to episodes of mild TBI. *British Medical Journal, 2*(2), 1–12.

Rutherford, W. H., Merrett, J. D., & Mcdonali, J. R. (1977). Sequelae of concussion caused by minor head injuries. *The Lancet, 309*(8001), 1–4.

Sachdev, P. L. (2004). *Shock Waves and Explosions*: CRC Press: London.

Scherer, M. R., & Schubert, M. C. (2009). Traumatic brain injury and vestibular pathology as a comorbidity after blast exposure. *Physical Therapy, 89*(9), 980–992.

Schmidt, O. I., Heyde, C. E., Ertel, W., & Stahel, P. F. (2005). Closed head injury—an inflammatory disease? *Brain Research Reviews, 48*(2), 388–399.

Shuker, S. T. (2010). Maxillofacial air-containing cavities, blast implosion injuries, and management. *Journal of Oral and Maxillofacial Surgery, 68*(1), 93–100.

Shupak, A., Doweck, I., Nachtigal, D., Spitzer, O., & Gordon, C. R. (1993). Vestibular and audiometric consequences of blast injury to the ear. *Archives of Otolaryngology—Head and Neck Surgery, 119*(12), 1362.

Snell, F. I., & Halter, M. J. (2010). A signature wound of war: mild traumatic brain injury. *Journal of Psychosocial Nursing and Mental Health Services, 48*(2), 22–28.

Southborough, L. (1922). *Report of the War Office Committee of Enquiry Into "Shell-Shock."*. London, His Majesty's Stationery Office.

Sponheim, S. R., McGuire, K. A., Kang, S. S., Davenport, N. D., Aviyente, S., Bernat, E. M., & Lim, K. O. (2011). Evidence of disrupted functional connectivity in the brain after combat-related blast injury. *Neuroimage, 54*(1), 21–29.

Stiver, S. I. (2009). Complications of decompressive craniectomy for traumatic brain injury. *Neurosurgical Focus, 26*(6), 1–16.

Stuhmiller, J. H. (2008). *Blast Injury: Translating Research into Operational Medicine*. Washington DC: Office of the Surgeon General.

Stuhmiller, J. H., Ho, K. H., Vorst, M. J. Vander, Dodd, K. T., Fitzpatrick, T., & Mayorga, M. (1996). A model of blast overpressure injury to the lung. *Journal of Biomechanics, 29*(2), 227–234.

Taber, K., Warden, D., & Hurley, R. (2006). Blast-related traumatic brain injury: What is known? *The Journal of Neuropsychiatry and Clinical Neurosciences, 18*(2), 141–145.

Timmons, S. D. (2006). The life-saving properties of blood mitigating cerebral insult after traumatic brain injury. *Neurocritical Care, 5*(1), 1–3.

Traumatic Brain Injury Task Force Report. (2008). Traumatic Brain Injury Task Force Report. Retrieved August, 2012, from http://www.army-medicine.armymil/prr/tbifr.html

Varney, Nils R, & Roberts, Richard J. (1999). The Evaluation and Treatment of Mild Traumatic Brain Injury. New Jersey: Laurence Erlbaum Associates.

Veterans, Department of Defence and the Veterans Administration. (2009). Screening and Evaluation of possible traumatic brain injury in operations enduring freedom (OEF) and Operation Iraqi Freedom (OIF) Veterans. *VHA Directive 2010–2012*.

Warden, D. (2006). Military TBI during the Iraq and Afghanistan wars. *The Journal of Head Trauma Rehabilitation, 21*(5), 398–402.

Wilk, J. E., Thomas, J. L., McGurk, D. M., Riviere, L. A., Castro, C. A., & Hoge, C. W. (2010). Mild traumatic brain injury (concussion) during combat: lack of association of blast mechanism with persistent postconcussive symptoms. *The Journal of Head Trauma Rehabilitation, 25*(1), 9–14.

Winter, C. D., Adamides, A., & Rosenfeld, J. V. (2005). The role of decompressive craniectomy in the managment of traumatic brain injury: A critical review. *Journal of Clinical Neuroscience, 12*(6), 619–623.

Xydakis, M. S., Bebarta, V. S., Harrison, C. D., Conner, J. S., Grant, G. A., & Robbins, A. S. (2007). Tympanic-membrane perforation as a marker of concussive brain injury in Iraq. *New England Journal of Medicine, 357*(8), 830–831.

Zhang, L., Yang, K. H., & King, A. I. (2004). A proposed injury threshold for mild traumatic brain injury. *Journal of Biomechanical Engineering, 126*(2), 226–236.

Part VI

Future Opportunities and Challenges

19

Future Challenges

Harvey S. Levin, David H. K. Shum, and Raymond C. K. Chan

Discussion of future research and clinical practice in the TBI population involves a degree of speculation. Our discussion of the future challenges associated with TBI is organized into three sections. The first section explores assessment techniques that have the potential to lead to a reduction in TBI-related morbidity and improved outcomes. These include emerging assessment instruments and techniques in areas of chemical/cellular biomarkers, brain imaging, and ecologically valid neuropsychological assessment. The second section of this concluding chapter focuses on efforts to reduce the secondary effects of TBI, and advances in the realm of cognitive rehabilitation, particularly the innovative use of electronic technologies including assistive devices and virtual reality. The third section is dedicated to exploring advances in social cognitive research, the status of randomized controlled trial (RCTs) in the TBI population, and international collaborative efforts devoted to improving research and clinical care in the TBI population. Furthermore, this chapter will highlight important questions for consideration and explore the various obstacles hindering future developments in the field.

Assessment

Biomarkers of Injury Severity

The need to identify methods that objectively measure severity of TBI on the battlefield or the football field, at the scene of an accident or in the emergency room cannot be overstated. The paucity of clinically validated diagnostic biomakers as an internal indicator of tissue damage at the cellular, biochemical, and molecular levels has been identified as a major limiting factor to diagnostic and therapeutic development for brain injury (Pelsers, Hermens, & Glatz, 2005). As such, a burgeoning field of neurological research has focused on identifying biomarkers of injury severity that overcome the limitations of existing standardized tools.

The Glasgow Coma Scale (GCS) is a neurological scale used to assess level of consciousness after a TBI. It is based on three component scores (ocular, motor, and verbal response) that are summed to obtain a total score which is used to divide patients into broad categories: mild, moderate, and severe injury. The GCS is widely relied upon to provide an independent indication of acute injury in a range of clinical and medical settings. This is contrary to the early recommendations of the tool's developers, Teasdale and Jennett (1974), who emphasized concurrent examination of pupils and other neurological signs to supplement the GCS. Notwithstanding, the GCS has established utility in the clinical management and prognosis of severe TBI patients at the time of evaluation and during intensive care. However, it provides limited information about the pathophysiological mechanisms responsible for a patient's neurological deficits. Similarly, although the GCS is useful for differentiating coma from impaired consciousness, it is less sensitive to mild, transient alterations of consciousness as often seen in some TBI subpopulations such as mild TBI. This relative insensitivity to gradations of severity within the mild TBI range is problematic because this subgroup represents about 80% of all TBI cases among persons sustaining closed head trauma (Faul, Xu, Wald, &

433

Coronado, 2010). An additional limitation of the GCS relates to the verbal component of the assessment, which can be threatened by the effects of acute intoxication (e.g., exasperate confusion and memory deficits) and relies on patients' cooperation and comprehension of the language spoken by the examiner. These limitations highlight the need for sensitive and specific biochemical markers of TBI with diagnostic and prognostic capabilities that will allow clinicians to evaluate acute, mild cerebral dysfunction and potentially detect intracranial pathology independently of the GCS and the patient's capability to respond to commands. Such developments have the potential to improve clinical assessment, patient management, and can facilitate therapeutic evaluations.

For a comprehensive review of recent advances in neuroproteomics, particularly in the area of candidate biomarkers with demonstrated preclinical potential, refer to chapter 13 by Harum and Wagner in this book. An additional interesting avenue of research in this field is the predictive value of serum concentrations after severe TBI. Neuron specific enolase (NSE) and S-100B in serum and cerebrospinal fluid have been reported to be potential markers of cell damage in the human central nervous system, particularly severity of traumatically induced axonal damage (Bohmer et al., 2011; Thornhill, Teasdale, Murray, Roy, & Penny, 2000). NSE is an isoenzyme of enolase and is located mainly in neurons but also in smooth muscle fibers and adipose tissue (Bohmer et al., 2011). S-100 is an acidic calcium binding protein found in the brain as the isoforms S-100B (95%) and S-100A (5%). S-100B is found in high concentrations in glial cells and Schwann cells and is highly specific for lesions of the central nervous system (Bohmer et al., 2011). Serum S-100B and NSE concentration peaks have been measured within 48 hours following TBI and these indices have been found to reflect the severity of the mechanical disruption of the brain tissue in adults (Kruijk, Leffers, Menheere, Meerhoff, Rutten, & Twijnstra, 2002; Stein et al., 2012) and children (Chiaretti et al., 2009; for conflicting results see Geyer, Ulrich, Grafe, Stach, & Till, 2009).

A major challenge for researchers in this field is that a majority of potential biomarkers exist in blood or CSF at extremely low levels, often at or beyond the detection capabilities of conventional technology (Bandyopadhyay, Hennes, Gorelick, Wells, & Walsh-Kelly, 2005). This ultimate challenge may necessitate the use of advanced technology (e.g., nanotechnology) to increase their detection sensitivity as well as their specificity. The ultimate objective, following the successful development of such methods, is to translate them into a user-friendly, hand-held point-of-care device capable of monitoring a panel of biomarkers in the body fluids such as blood or urine with minimally invasive procedures.

Overall, the future of biomarker driven assays to diagnose and guide therapeutic development and treatment of TBI is promising. As studies continually expand our knowledge of the internal workings of the brain under various pathological conditions and, as we develop a more advanced understanding of the proteins that constitute the brain, the closer we come to finding a means to diagnose and treat TBI. The technical, financial, legal and regulatory hurdles that need to be overcome before commercial biomarker products will be available are substantial but not insurmountable. By improving clinicians' diagnostic and treatment capabilities, we have the potential to greatly enhance the outcomes of future patients who sustain TBI.

Behavioral Markers of Post-Traumatic Complaints in Severe TBI

There is a growing need to identify parameters at first presentation after severe TBI that are predictive of the severity of long-term post-traumatic symptoms (PTS; e.g., headaches, nausea, irritability, balancing problems) after six months (Kruijk et al., 2002). It is believed that these symptoms are caused by a combination of brain injury and psychological, emotional, and motivational factors. The severity of PTS often declines during the first three months after severe TBI but the prevalence of having multiple complaints six months after the trauma is still estimated to be 20–80% (Kruijk et al., 2002). Educating outpatients shortly after TBI about the expected prognosis of possible complications may help to reduce the severity and long-term impact of PTS. Furthermore, because many mild TBI patients do not experience persistent PTS, reducing needless follow up would result in long-term economic savings as the financial and medicinal burden of treating healthy individuals would be avoided (Kruijk et al., 2002).

There has been a recent trend in the literature to use mild TBI patients to help identify prognostic indicators of PTS (i.e., otherwise referred to as post-concussive symptoms in mild TBI). Such research has found that female gender, more advanced age, and prior mild TBI are associated with poor outcome (Thornhill et al., 2000). Further, Krujik et al. (2002) found that the presence of headache, dizziness, or nausea in the ER after mild TBI was strongly associated with the severity of most PTS after six months. Interestingly, the absence of these symptoms in combination with normal serum marker concentrations (S-100B) within six hours after the trauma seems highly predictive of full recovery after six months. Future research should go beyond identifying established associations between neuropsychological dysfunction and early increased S-100B and NSE concentrations in serum, to identifying the relation between these biomarkers and PTS. Research such as this has the potential to greatly enhance long-term outcomes of patients who sustain TBI.

Neuroimaging Biomarkers

Diffuse axonal injury (DAI) is identified as a leading cause of mortality and severe disability in patients with TBI (Huisman et al., 2004). A quantification of neural injury in the acute phase is essential for making treatment decisions, for developing and monitoring new treatments, and for providing appropriate counseling to patients concerning their long-term prognosis. Currently, few imaging techniques offer reliable information that correlates with outcome in TBI. One technique which has showed promise in this area is diffusion weighted imaging (DWI). This technique involves the use of diffusion-weighted images to calculate the apparent diffusion coefficient (i.e., ADC). This method can be used to show lesions with decreased ADC in patients with DAI, in both the acute and subacute periods after TBI. Furthermore, DWI has been shown to be valuable in evaluating DAI because it can

depict additional shearing injuries not visible on conventional T2/FLAIR or T2* MR images (Huisman, Sorensen, Hergan, Gonzalez, & Schaefer, 2003).

Another relatively recent modality involves the use of diffusion tensor imaging (DTI), which is a more complex form of DWI. DTI takes advantage of the directionality of water diffusion in the human brain and allows analysis of the white matter tracts (Mori, Crain, Chacko, & van Zijl, 1999). Water diffusion is considered isotropic when motion is free and equal in all directions. In the normal brain tissue, there are physical boundaries that restrict water diffusion in the white matter tracts, with greater water mobility parallel to the axons and restriction of mobility perpendicular to the axons. This diffusion restriction is termed fractional anisotropy (FA) or the ratio of anisotropy to isotropy (Klingberg, Vaidya, Gabrieli, Moseley, & Hedehus, 1999). FA ranges from 0 to 1, where values closer to 0 represent isotropy or increased diffusion, for example, as a result of injury. In contrast, values closer to 1 represent water diffusion more parallel to the white matter tracts in normal brain tissue. Water diffusion by isotropy is also measured by ADC (Sundgren, Dong, Gómez-Hassan, Mukherji, Maly, & Welsh, 2004). Although the association between FA and ADC in the white matter tracts are very complex and incompletely understood, FA has been found to be inversely related to ADC. That is, higher FA and lower ADC values are associated with intact white matter tracts. The degree of anisotropic diffusion is related to the degree of directionality and the integrity of white matter fiber tracts within the brain. Densely packed white matter tracts show a high degree of anisotropic diffusion, whereas gray matter has a low degree of anisotropic diffusion. White matter tracts are typically disrupted in DAI. Consequently, by measuring white matter anisotropy, DTI is a promising diagnostic tool to quantify the degree of tissue injury (Sundgren et al., 2004).

A burgeoning field of research that has explored the association between functional connectivity and neurocognitive performance suggests that resting state fMRI may have promise as an imaging biomarker for outcome after mTBI. For example, a recent study by Mayer, Mannell, Ling, Gasparovic and Yeo (2011) examined whether resting state fMRI provides objective markers of injury and predicts cognitive, emotional and somatic complaints in mTBI patients semi-acutely (< 3 weeks post-injury) and in late recovery (3–5 month) phases. Twenty-seven mTBI patients and 26 gender, age, and education matched controls were involved in the study. Results indicated that the TBI group reported significantly worse cognitive, emotional, and somatic complaints (all $p <$ .05), despite normal clinical imaging and neuropsychological testing results. Mild TBI patients demonstrated decreased functional connectivity within the rostral anterior cingulate gyrus, posterior cingulate gyrus, superior temporal/supramarginal gyrus, and ventromedial prefrontal cortex (i.e., the default-mode network, DMN) and hyper-connectivity between the DMN and lateral prefrontal cortex. Measures of functional connectivity exhibited high levels of sensitivity and specificity for patient classification and predicted cognitive complaints in the semi-acute injury stage. However, no changes in functional connectivity were observed across a four month recovery period. The authors concluded that abnormal connectivity between the DMN and frontal cortex may provide objective biomarkers of mTBI and underlie cognitive impairment.

Although further research is needed to determine whether these advanced imaging modalities will allow early and reliable recognition of reversible secondary brain insults, it would be exceptionally valuable if parallel research considered the extent to which these new modalities can inform treatment strategies. Assessments of this kind have remarkable value, as conventional imaging tools (e.g., MRI and CT) are often criticized as having low sensitivity and specificity for diffuse or mild brain injuries. For a comprehensive description of the use of neuroimaging in TBI and recent advances in this area, refer to chapter 14 by Wilde, Ayoub, Bigler, Hunter, and Levin in this book.

Ecologically Valid Neuropsychological Assessment

Neuropsychology has begun to shift from a primary focus on diagnostic evaluations designed to identify neuropathological impairments in specific cognitive domains to greater emphasis on the consideration of the functional implications of neuropsychological test results and their relationship to an individual's performance of everyday tasks (Rabin, Burton, & Barr, 2007; Standen & Brown, 2005). A significant limitation of current neuropsychological assessment is that traditional neuropsychological tests designed to diagnose neuropathology are currently being used to make predictions about real world functioning, despite the absence of research confirming their ecological validity (Rabin et al 2007; Standen & Brown, 2005). As such, there has been a heightened emphasis within the literature on developing "ecologically valid" measures of neuropsychological functioning.

Chaytor and Schmitter-Edgecombe (2003) developed a two-tier definition of ecological validity: verisimilitude and veridicality. Verisimilitude refers to the extent to which stimuli, materials, and procedures capture the variety and level of difficulty demanded by naturalistic tasks. Veridicality, on the other hand, refers to the extent to which a measure predicts social, occupational, and functional impairment. Measures which adopt these properties have been shown to be more effective than traditional neuropsychological tests in determining the extent to which an intervention improves an individual's performance on everyday cognitive tasks.

Over the last decade, several neuropsychological measures have been designed with ecological validity as a primary consideration. They include the Test of Everyday Attention (TEA; Ward & Ridgeway, 1994), the Behavioural Assessment of the Dysexecutive Syndrome (BADS; Wilson, Alderman, Burgess, Emslie, & Evans, 1996), the Rivermead Behavioural Memory Test (RBMT; Wilson, Cockburn, & Baddeley, 1985), the Cambridge Test of Prospective Memory (CAMPROMPT, Barbara et al., 2004), and the Multiple Errands Test (MET; Alderman, Burgess, Knight, & Henman, 2003; Burgess et al., 2006; Knight, Alderman, & Burgess, 2002; Shallice & Burgess, 1991). They differ from traditional neuropsychological measures by focusing on identifying limitations in functional abilities rather than discriminating brain injured from healthy people or determining the etiology of brain dysfunction (Chaytor & Schmitter-Edgecombe, 2003). However, there is tremendous variability in the everyday demands facing individuals with TBI and they may require very different skill sets. For example, the cognitive skills required of a teacher differ from those of a carpenter. Therefore, most of these tests, particularly in the domain of executive functioning, lack specificity, even when they are sensitive to dysfunction (Cicerone, Levin, Malec, Stuss, & Whyte, 2006).

Despite the many advantages of using ecologically valid assessment platforms for neuropsychological assessment (see chapter 5 of this book), there are a number of obstacles hindering their widespread application. First, current measures often struggle to achieve verisimilitude (e.g., measuring multiple processes in parallel) which in turn can limit the content validity of the measures. Second, the added sensitivity and validity that ecological measures supposedly offer has seldom been demonstrated. The sensitivity of a new measure needs to be compared with that of conventional tasks. In parallel, few studies have explored whether ecological measures accurately predict functional status. Despite these challenges, the heightened emphasis on ecological validity in neuropsychological evaluation has several important implications. For example, ecologically valid measures will help clinicians design treatment protocols to the individual needs of the patient and can inform patients about the degree of recovery that can reasonably be expected. Although conventional measures are more widely used than ecological platforms, this balance may change as researchers and clinicians become more aware of the value in predicting real-world outcomes.

Uniform Outcome Measures

There is a growing need for the use of uniform outcome measures across different TBI studies (Thurmond et al., 2010). A group of TBI experts who participated in the NIH Common Data Elements TBI Outcomes Workshop (Wilde et al., 2010) reviewed the relevant literature and considered costs in selecting key domains and their corresponding measures for inclusion of assessment of TBI patients for observational research

and clinical trials. Nine well-established "core measures" were identified that would be applicable to most TBI studies. For studies with a focus on certain populations or specific functions, the workshop also recommended "supplemental measures." Finally, a set of new but potentially influential measures are identified as "emerging measures." The use of these uniform outcome measures by researchers and clinicians has the potential to produce reliable and robust research findings that can be directly compared across studies and to improve clinical practice based on these findings.

Rehabilitation

Although considerable strides have been made in decreasing overall TBI-related mortality through advances in early intervention by first responders, emergency medicine centers, and neurointensive care, many individuals develop chronic impairments, often resulting in life-long disability. New treatment approaches will need to be tailored to the heterogeneous needs of TBI populations, taking account of heterogeneity in injury, age, genotype, and complications of injury.

Preventing Secondary Effects of TBI

The last decade of pathophysiological research has been characterized by identifying methods in which to reduce or prevent secondary effects of TBI such as inflammation. Inflammation is generally accompanied by gliosis and apoptosis in brain areas proximal and distal to the locus of injury (Saatman, Feeko, Pape, & Raghupathi, 2006). The insult triggers an invasion of macrophages and neutrophils into the impact area, producing much of the inflammation and swelling associated with CNS damage. These potentially cytotoxic events can directly affect patient outcome after TBI, which can be further worsened by uncontrolled, increased intracranial pressure (ICP) caused by a rise in brain water content (cerebral edema). Uncontrolled ICP can produce greater secondary injury through ischemia and an increase in mortality caused by herniation of the brain. Other than mannitol, which has limited effects on edema, there are few therapeutic agents which have been shown to effectively, rapidly, and safely reduce both marked swelling and inflammation after brain injury (Saatman et al., 2006).

Therapeutic interventions utilizing progesterone are currently being evaluated in phase three clinical trials. In their phase two randomized clinical trial, Wright and colleagues (2007) found that intravenous progesterone did not cause more adverse events than placebo and it reduced the probability of death within 30 days post-injury. Those with moderate TBI were more likely to obtain good outcomes if they received progesterone. Because the safety of administering progesterone following TBI has been demonstrated, a phase three trial is in progress. Progesterone and its metabolite allopregnanolone (5α-pregnan-3β-ol-20-one) have been shown to reduce the expression of inflammatory cytokines in the acute stages of brain injury. However, the processes underlying the effect of progesterone are poorly understood. VanLandingham et al. (2007) demonstrated that both progesterone and allopregnanolone treatments enhance the production of CD55 following contusion injuries of the cerebral cortex in rats. CD55, a single-chain type 1 cell surface protein, is a potent inhibitor of the complement convertases which are activators of the inflammatory cascade. The increased expression of CD55 could be an important mechanism by which steroids help to reduce the cerebral damage caused by inflammation (VanLandingham et al., 2007). Future research that dissects the chain of injury-induced inflammation at the point of amplification has the potential to help explain how neurosteroids reduce the neuropathology related to inflammation such as blood brain barrier dysfunction, cerebral edema, and apoptosis associated with TBI.

Assistive Devices and Virtual Reality

Rapid advances in computer technology have led to the creation of multiple virtual reality (VR) applications which allow the user to interact with, and become immersed in, a computer-generated environment that simulates a real world environment (Chute, 2002; Rizzo, Buckwalter, & Neumann, 1997). VR techniques can be used as a means to bridge the gap between diagnostic measurement tools and

ability to function in natural environments by using computer-based interactive instruments to assess level of functioning in real life simulations, thereby creating more ecologically valid and dynamic assessment and training. They also have the capacity to provide a consistent environment with the potential for infinite repetitions of the same assessment or training task while maintaining the flexibility to alter sensory presentations, task complexity, response requirements, and the nature and pattern of feedback in order to adapt to a user's unique impairments. Thus VR offers the potential to develop both neuropsychological assessment tools and treatment environments that can accurately determine cognitive and functional performance by precisely controlling complex stimulus presentation (Schultheis, Himelstein, & Rizzo, 2002).

VR is a relatively new approach in rehabilitation medicine, yet it offers considerable potential to achieve significant successes in assessment, treatment, and improved outcome (Johnson, Rose, Rushton, Pentland, & Attree, 1998; Rose, Brooks, & Rizzo, 2005). The technology is rapidly becoming more available and affordable for rehabilitation research and the clinical application allows flexibility for investigators and clinicians to tailor the system to particular interests or needs (Baumann et al., 2003). The simulation of real world activities can facilitate the evaluation of an individual's cognitive capacity and performance ability for tasks in their own natural environment. Additionally, VR tasks can provide a safe setting to assess skills that might be too risky in the real world (e.g., driving). The individual's own fear of the reaction of others to faulty attempts in a natural environment are minimized, and limited resources that often make trips to a real environment difficult are easily addressed. VR technology can also be used for interventions, particularly when sensory, motor, and cognitive consequences of brain injury combine to make environmental interaction difficult or dangerous. Interventions have been evaluated in the areas of exercise, yielding improvements in reaction times (Grealy, Johnson & Rushton, 1999; Thornton, Marshall, McComas, Finestone, McCormick, & Sveistrup, 2005) and balance (Morganti, Gaggioli, Strambi, Rusconi,

& Giuseppe, 2007; Sveistrup et al., 2003). In cases where the actual activity is too complex for an individual to perform, the VR world can be manipulated to break down the activity into multiple and progressively more difficult tasks, so that the person can learn in a safe realm. VR has been used in the area of rehabilitation to increase skills for independent living, enhance cognitive performance, and improve social skills. Although virtual technology is less developed as a rehabilitative intervention than as a method of assessment (Standen & Brown, 2005), recent intervention studies are promising.

Social Cognition

As alluded to in chapter 8, the field of social cognitive neuroscience is in its infancy. As such, more sophisticated paradigms are needed that allow for a separate, and ideally parametric, assessment of social cognitive constructs such as theory of mind, empathy, their sub-processes, and their neuronal correlates. In real life social cognitive processes unfold over time and cognitive and emotional empathic/mentalizing processes will mix and affect each other (Dziobek, 2012). In fact, it is in complex everyday-life settings that problems with mentalizing and empathizing are most pronounced in individuals with autism, whereas they often remain unremarkable in laboratory settings that focus on isolated subprocesses. To fully understand the subprocesses of social cognition, and their interactions, a promising direction for future research will be to increase ecological validity in cognitive neuroscience studies by (a) making use of audiovisual stimuli that more closely approximate real-life settings and; (b) including "online" social interaction paradigms whereby participants actively engage with other avatars. While psychological research has traditionally been individual-centered, online settings through Internet-based platforms provide for true interactions between test-takers rather than relying on contexts in which participants are requested to passively observe others. Furthermore, identifications of the neuronal underpinnings of interactions between social cognitive subprocesses will greatly benefit from the development of new imaging techniques such as hyperscan fMRI, whereby participants

are scanned simultaneously while interacting over the Internet (Dziobek, 2012).

Online tasks, which utilize economic game paradigms, are still the exception in social cognitive neuroscience studies. Although such interactive paradigms have been applied in social decision-making and cognitive theory of mind contexts (Sanfey, 2007), they have not been applied in the context of theory of mind and empathy. Moreover, they do not involve naturalistic stimuli or allow for performance scores. A paradigm from social psychology that would involve those features is the empathic accuracy paradigm (Ickes, Stinson, Bissonnette, & Garcia, 1990). In this paradigm, people make inferences about the naturalistically occurring feelings of stimulus persons that they have interacted with, and these inferences are scored for accuracy against the stimulus persons' self-reported feelings. As such, it involves real interactions and provides performance scores of cognitive empathy, and its implementation in a neuroimaging context could thus be a fruitful endeavor. In summary, in an effort to better understand the complex nature of social cognition, future efforts should be dedicated to developing ecologically valid online social paradigms.

Status of Randomized Control Trials (RCTs) in TBI

Clinical trials in acute TBI have shown limited success in providing an evidence base for the introduction of successful new therapies into clinical practice. In addition to the problems that are common to all such studies in critical illness, trials in acute TBI are complicated by the extremely short temporal window for intervention, failure of many candidate drugs to cross the blood-brain barrier, ethical and regulatory obstacles associated with research in subjects who cannot provide consent, and difficulty in subject recruitment. The shortcomings of translating interventions supported by experimental animal models into clinical trials may reflect the heterogeneity of human TBI, complications of TBI in humans, and differences across centers in clinical management despite evidenced-based guidelines (Menon, 2009).

Although there is wide recognition that the clinical trial process has failed in TBI for a variety of reasons, several recent developments provide a basis for optimism. These include improved trial logistics, a more rational regulatory regimen, the use of appropriately large sample sizes to account for patient heterogeneity, a recognition of the importance of high-quality critical care, the use of experimental medicine approaches (including positron emission tomography microdosing) to screen candidate targets and interventions, and better trial design. Other encouraging developments in the area of RCTs in TBI include the increasing use of human experimental medicine strategies to assess blood-brain barrier penetration and dose ranging, and provide proof of concept and proof of mechanism. Novel approaches to trial design, such as sliding dichotomy, coupled with robust outcome prediction models, have the potential to increase statistical power and improve trial design (Menon, 2009). The Institute of Medicine (2011) carried out a comprehensive review on the efficacy and effectiveness of cognitive rehabilitation therapy (CRT) in treating patients with TBI. It was concluded that there is some support for the use of CRT. However, more large scale and standardized research is needed across different cognitive domains and patient subgroups in order to inform practice and benefit individual patients.

International Collaboration

International collaborative projects are a key medium through which to improve the future of TBI research and clinical care. Two such programs are described below.

International Mission for Prognosis and Analysis of Clinical Trials in TBI. The IMPACT project was initiated in 2003 and is a collaborative venture between the University Hospital Antwerp, the Erasmus University Medical Center, Rotterdam, The Netherlands, the University of Edinburgh, United Kingdom, and the Virginia Commonwealth University, Richmond, United States. The global aim of IMPACT was to optimize clinical trial methodology in the field of TBI to maximize the chance of demonstrating benefit of effective new therapies. The project critically examined the methodological challenges posed by TBI trials, and

investigated the application of conventional and innovative methods for design and analysis of trials in TBI. Data sets from completed randomized controlled trials (RCTs) and observational studies were used as "culture media" in which to develop and test these methods. The insight obtained from these investigations led to informed recommendations for future clinical trials in TBI.

The International Initiative for Traumatic Brain Injury Research (InTBIR). InTBIR is a collaborative effort of the European Commission (EC), the Canadian Institutes of Health Research (CIHR) and the National Institutes of Health (NIH), set up in October 2011, to advance clinical TBI research, treatment and care. Essentially, InTBIR is a global effort to coordinate and harmonize clinical research activities across the full spectrum of TBI injuries with the long-term goal of improving outcomes and lessening the global burden of TBI by 2020. Key objectives of InTBIR include establishing and promoting the use of international standards for TBI clinical data collection, creating a TBI patient registry by building common databases and linking them through an accessible, user-friendly interface for both entry and data search, and developing and applying sophisticated analytical tools to enable Comparative Effectiveness Research (CER) for TBI and identify best practices in early diagnosis and treatment. In order for such a long-awaited initiative to achieve its goals in enhancing patients' outcomes and alleviating disease burden, all those related, including the researchers, pharmaceutical industry, policy makers, and funding agencies from around the world should participate and together support high-quality research (*Lancet Neurology*, 2012).

Overall, international collaborative programs such as those described above have the potential to facilitate the development of RCTs that explore and validate surrogate markers of injury and recovery and a patho-anatomical and biomarker-based patient classification system. Furthermore, such efforts will help determine the benefits of current and new treatments and improve the quality of management across the continuum of care. Lastly, unified approaches to improving TBI-related research and clinical practice demonstrate the widespread hope of alleviating the debilitating burdens faced by this population.

Future Challenges and Research

As explained throughout this book, there are many issues waiting to be addressed in future studies on TBI. Currently, it is difficult to compare different epidemiological studies because of methodological variations and cultural differences (chapter 2). The exact mechanisms and nature by which TBI leads to other long-term problems such as those in other organs still need to be explained (chapter 3). As covered in chapter 4, there remains a need for further understanding of the associations between various cognitive deficits and well-designed and carefully controlled evaluations should be done for both behavioral and pharmacological interventions in elevating attention deficits post-TBI. The current variability of findings from memory research should be explored in future research by identifying patient subgroups (chapter 5). Also, the relationship between memory impairments and quality of life should be explored and the effectiveness of memory interventions in improving the patient's daily life needs to be tested in randomized clinical trials (chapter 5). As explained in chapter 6, hot executive functions, the relationship between hot and cool executive functions, and their influence on outcome measures remain to be understood in well controlled studies, possibly with an ecological approach. Five key issues are discussed in chapter 7 for higher-order language research, including the need for the development of bio-markers that can indicate response to treatments. Future of research in the area of emotion and social cognition after TBI is likely to take three main directions: social knowledge, moral reasoning, and communication (chapter 8). As reviewed in chapter 9, there are a limited number of measures available for body functioning and contextual factors and little consensus on the use of measure of participation and environmental factors in TBI research. Covered in chapter 10, the complex relationships between biological, personal and social factors following TBI need to be understood in more depth for successful rehabilitation interventions. Recommendations for cognitive rehabilitation

and pharmacological approaches can be found in chapters 11 and 13, respectively. Chapter 12 talks about rehabilitation after discharge from hospitalization and suggests many topics for further studies, including the assessment and intervention for self-awareness. Advanced neuroimaging techniques in studying TBI are evaluated in chapter 14 and studies that have used these techniques are reviewed. There is currently a lack of identified factors in successfully predicting recovery and outcome for pediatric TBI (chapter 15). There is also a research gap in the understanding and assessment of outcomes for older adults following TBI and many methodological issues need to be addressed in studies involving older adults (chapter 16). Further research is also needed for mild TBI (chapter 17) to find out specific intervention and patient characteristics that would be useful for optimizing rehabilitation outcome. Finally, as reviewed in chapter 18, blast-related TBI needs to be examined and researched more.

Conclusions

TBI is a common and devastating cause of disability and can cause a wide spectrum of secondary deficits. Despite the enormity of the problem, there is insufficient understanding of both normal and impaired cerebral development and function and the factors that impact outcomes post-TBI. This has had a direct impact on the development of assessment and rehabilitation techniques that address real world functional status. Advances in understanding cerebral physiology and function and assessment tools, in addition to the development of innovative research designs, will provide the necessary framework to better develop treatments that are specific to individuals with unique injury characteristics. It is almost a certainty that any single future intervention will be insufficient to address the multitude of physical, behavioral, and cognitive problems caused by TBI. Therefore, as new technologies and treatments evolve, it will likely become evident that various treatment "cocktails" will emerge that combine approaches to assessments and treatment that will result in improved recovery by tailoring approaches to the specific and unique needs of individuals with TBI.

References

Alderman, N., Burgess, P. W., Knight, C., & Henman, C. (2003). Ecological validity of a simplified version of the multiple errands shopping test. *Journal of the International Neuropsychological Society, 9,* 31–44.

Bandyopadhyay, S., Hennes, H., Gorelick, M. H., Wells, R. G., & Walsh-Kelly, C. M. (2005). Serum neuron-specific enolase as a predictor of short-term outcome in children with closed traumatic brain injury. *Academic Emergency Medicine, 12,* 732–738.

Baumann, S., Neff, C., Fetzick, S., Stangl, G., Basler, L., Vereneck, R., et al. (2003). A virtual reality system for neurobehavioral and functional MRI studies. *Cyberpsychology & Behaviour, 6,* 259–66.

Bohmer, A. E., Oses, J. P., Schmidt, A. P., Peron, C. S., Krebs, C. L., Oppitz, P. P., et al. (2011). Neuron-specific enolase, S100B, and glial fibrillary acidic protein levels as outcome predictors in patients with severe traumatic brain injury. *Neurosurgery, 68*(6), 1624–1630.

Burgess, P. W., Alderman, N., Forbes, C., Costello, A., Coates, L., Dawson, D. R., et al. (2006). The case for the development and use of ecologically valid measures of executive function in experimental and clinical neuropsychology. *Journal of the International Neuropsychological Society, 12,* 194–209.

Burgess, J. A., Lescuyer, P., Hainard, A., Burkhard, P. R., Turck, N., Michel, P., et al. (2006). Identification of brain cell death associated proteins in human post-mortem cerebrospinal fluid. *Journal of Proteome Research, 5,* 1674–1681.

Faul, M., Xu, L., Wald, M., & Coronado, V. (2010). *Traumatic Brain Injury in the United States: Emergence Department Visits, Hospitalizations and Deaths 2002–2006.* U.S. Department of Health and Human Services: Centre for Disease Control.

Chaytor, N., & Schmitter-Edgecombe, M. (2003). The ecological validity of neuropsychological tests. *Neuropsychology Review, 13,* 181–197.

Chiaretti, A., Barone, G., Riccardi, R., Antonelli, A., Pezzotti, P., Genovese, O., et al. (2009). NGF, DCX, and NSE upregulation correlates with severity and outcome of head trauma in children. *Neurology, 72,* 609–616,

Chute, D. L. (2002). Neuropsychological technologies in rehabilitation. *Journal of Head Trauma Rehabilitation, 17,* 369–377.

Cicerone, K., Levin, H., Malec, J., Stuss, D., & Whyte, J. (2006). Cognitive rehabilitation interventions for executive function: Moving from bench to bedside in patients with traumatic brain injury. *Journal of Cognitive Neuroscience, 18,* 1212–1222.

Dziobek, I. (2012). Comment: Towards a more ecologically valid assessment of empathy. *Emotion Review, 4,* 18–19.

Grealy, M. A., Johnson, D. A., & Rushton, S. K. (1999). Improving cognitive function after brain injury: The use of exercise and virtual reality. *Archives of Physical Medicine and Rehabilitation, 80,* 661–667.

Geyer, C., Ulrich, A., Grafe, G., Stach, B., & Till, H. (2009). Diagnostic value of S100B and neuron-specific enolase in mild pediatric traumatic brain injury. *Journal of Neurosurgery: Pediatrics. 4,* 339–344.

Huisman, L. H., Schwamm, L. H., Schaefer, P. W., Koroshetz, W. J., Shetty-Alva N et al. (2004). Diffusion tensor imaging as potential biomarker of white matter injury in diffuse axonal injury. *American Journal Neuroradiology, 25,* 370–376.

Huisman, T., Sorensen, A., Hergan, K, Gonzalez, R., & Schaefer, P. (2003). Diffusion-weighted imaging for the evaluation of diffuse axonal injury in closed head injury. *Journal of Computerised Assisted Tomography, 27,* 5–11.

Ickes, W., Stinson, L., Bissonnette, V., & Garcia, S. (1990). Naturalistic social cognition: Empathic accuracy in mixed-sex dyads. *Journal of Personality and Social Psychology, 59,* 730–742.

Institute of Medicine. (2011). *Cognitive rehabilitation therapy for traumatic brain injury: Evaluating the evidence.* Washington, DC: The National Academies Press.

Johnson, D. A., Rose, F. D., Rushton, S. K., Pentland, B., & Attree, E. A. (1998). Virtual reality: A new prosthesis for brain injury rehabilitation. *Scottish Medical Journal, 43,* 81–83.

Klingberg, T., Vaidya, C. J., Gabrieli, J. D., Moseley, M. E., & Hedehus, M. (1999). Myelination and organization of the frontal white matter in children: a diffusion tensor MRI study. *NeuroReport, 10*(13), 2817–2821.

Knight, C., Alderman, N., & Burgess, P. W. (2002). Development of a simplified version of the multiple errands test for use in hospital settings. *Neuropsychological Rehabilitation, 12,* 231.

Kruijk, J., Leffers, P., Menheere, P., Meerhoff, S., Rutten, J., & Twijnstra, A. (2002). Prediction of post-traumatic complaints after mild traumatic brain injury: early symptoms and biochemical markers. *Journal of Neurology, Neurosurgery & Psychiatry, 73,* 727–732.

Mayer, A. R., Mannell, M. V., Ling, J., Gasparovic, C., & Yeo, R. A. (2011). Functional connectivity in mild traumatic brain injury. *Human Brain Mapping, 32*(11), 1825–1835.

Menon, D. (2009). Unique challenges in clinical trials in traumatic brain injury. *Critical Care Medicine, 37*(1), 12–135.

Morganti, F., Gaggioli, A., Strambi, L., Rusconi, M., & Giuseppe, R. (2007). A virtual reality extended neuropsychological assessment for topographical disorientation: A feasibility study. *Journal of Neuroengineering Rehabilitation, 4,* 26.

Mori, S., Crain, B. J., Chacko, V. P., & van Zijl, P. C. (1994). Three-dimensional tracking of axonal projections in the brain by magnetic resonance imaging. *Annals of Neurology, 45*(2), 265–269.

Pelsers, M. M., Hermens, W. T., & Glatz, J. F. (2005). Fatty acid-binding proteins as plasma markers of tissue injury. *Clinica Chimica Acta, 352,* 15–35.

Rabin, L. A., Burton, L. A., & Barr, W. B. (2007). Utilization rates of ecologically oriented instruments among clinical neuropsychologists. *Clinical Neuropsychology, 21,* 727–743.

Rizzo, A. A., Buckwalter, J. G., & Neumann, U. (1997). Virtual reality and cognitive rehabilitation: A brief review of the future. *Journal of Head Trauma Rehabilitation, 12,* 1–15.

Rose, F. D., Brooks, B. M., & Rizzo, A. A. (2005). Virtual reality in brain damage rehabilitation: review. *Cyberpsychology & Behaviour, 8,* 241–262.

Saatman, K. E., Feeko, K. J., Pape, R. L., & Raghupathi, R. (2006). Differential behavioural and histopathological responses to graded cortical impact injury in mice. *Journal of Neurotrauma, 23,* 1241–1253.

Sanfey, A. G. (2007). Social decision-making: Insights from game theory and neuroscience. *Science, 318,* 598–602.

Schultheis, M. T., Himelstein, J., & Rizzo, A. A. (2002). Virtual reality and neuropsychology: Upgrading the current tools. *Journal of Head Trauma Rehabilitation, 17,* 378–394.

Shallice, T. & Burgess, P. W. (1991). Deficits in strategy application following frontal lobe damage in man. *Brain, 114,* 727–741.

Sundgren, P. C., Dong, Q., Gómez-Hassan, D., Mukherji, S. K., Maly, P., & Welsh, R. (2004). Diffusion tensor imaging of the brain: Review of clinical applications. *Neuroradiology, 46*(5), 339–350.

Standen, P. J., & Brown, D. J. (005). Virtual reality in the rehabilitation of people with intellectual disabilities: Review. *Cyberpsychology & Behaviour, 8,* 272–282.

Stein, D., Lindell, A., Murdock, K., Kufera, J., Menaker, J., Bochicchio, A., et al. (2012). Use of serum biomarkers to predict cerebral hypoxia after severe traumatic brain injury. *Journal of Neurotrauma, 29*(6), 1140–1149.

Sveistrup, H., McComas, J., Thornton, M., Marshall, S., Finestone, H., McCormick, A., et al. (2003). Experimental studies of virtual reality-delivered compared to conventional exercise programs for rehabilitation. *Cyberpsychology & Behaviour, 6,* 245–249.

The Lancet Neurology. (2012). The changing landscape of traumatic brain injury research. *The Lancet Neurology, 11,* 651.

Teasdale, G. & Jennett, B. (1974). Assessment of coma and impaired consciousness. A practical scale. *The Lancet, 2*(7872), 81–84.

Thornhill, S., Teasdale, G., Murray, G., Roy, C., & Penny, K. (2000). Disability in young people and adults one year after head injury: prospective cohort study. *British Medical Journal, 320,* 1631–1635.

Thornton, M., Marshall, S., McComas, J, Finestone, H., McCormick, A., & Sveistrup, H. (2005). Benefits of activity and virtual reality based balance exercise programmes for adults with traumatic brain injury: Perceptions of participants and their caregivers. *Brain Injury, 19,* 989–1000.

Thurmond, V. A., Hicks, R., Gleason, T., Miller, A. C., Szuflita, N., Orman, J., et al. (2010). Advancing integrated research in psychological health and traumatic brain injury: Common data elements. *Archives of Physical Medicine and Rehabilitation, 91,* 1633–1636.

VanLandingham, J. W., Cutler, S. M., Virmani, S., Hoffman, S. W., Covey, D. F., Krishnan, K. (2006). The enantiomer of progesterone acts as a molecular neuroprotectant after traumatic brain injury. *Neuropharmacology, 51,* 1078–1085.

Ward, T. & Ridgeway, V. (1994). *The test of everyday attention manual.* England: Thames Valley Test Company.

Wilde, E. A., Whiteneck, G. G., Bogner, J., Bushnik, T., Cifu, D. X., Dikmen, S., et al. (2010). Recommendations for the use of common outcome measures in traumatic brain injury research. *Archives of Physical Medicine and Rehabilitation, 91,* 1650–1660.

Wilson, B., Alderman, N., & Burgess, P., Emslie, H., & Evans, J. (1996). *Behavioural assessment of the dysexecutive syndrome.* England: Thames Valley Test Company.

Wilson, B. A., Cockburn, J., & Baddeley, A. D. (1985). *The Rivermead Behavioural Memory Test Manual.* Suffolk: Thames Valley Test Company.

Barbara, A., Wilson, B. A., Emslie, H., Foley, J., Shiel, A., Watson, K., et al. (2004). *Cambridge Test of Prospective Memory.* England: Thames Valley Test Company.

Wright, D. W., Kellermann, A. L., Hertzberg, V. S., Clark, P. L., Frankel, M., Goldstein, F. C., et al. (2007). ProTECT: A randomized clinical trial of progesterone for acute traumatic brain injury. *Annals of Emergency Medicine, 49*(4), 391–402.

INDEX

Abernathy, J., 15–16
Abrams, H. B., 180
Abreu, B. C., 173
academic performance deficits,
    339–340
acetylcholine (ACh), 258–259
ACRM (American Congress of
    Rehabilitation Medicine),
    375–376, 375t
activities of daily living (ADLs),
    195–196
activity-based tasks, 82
Adams, P., 82
ADC (apparent diffusion
    coefficient), 307, 435
ADLs (activities of daily living),
    195–196
adolescents. See pediatric TBI
adynamia, 140–141
aeromedical evacuations, 421–423
age
    as predictor of outcome, 109,
        201–203, 342–343
    TBI distribution based on,
        19–21, 19–21f, 21–22t
    See also elderly TBI populations
    See also pediatric TBI
aggression and agitation, etiology
        and treatments for, 274–277
Agrawal, N., 259
Aharon-Peretz, J., 361
Aimaretti, G., 36
AIXTENT attention training
        program, 220
Alaranta, H., 166, 190
Albucasis, 13
alertness training, 223

Allen, D. N., 59
Alzheimer's dementia, 31–32, 37,
    203, 358, 363–365
amantadine, 65, 264–265, 267,
    268, 400
American Congress of
    Rehabilitation Medicine
    (ACRM), 375–376, 375t
amino acid abnormalities, 39–40
Ammann, J., 107–108
amnesia, 200–201, 255–257, 275,
    336, 375
amphetamines, 262, 263, 265,
    268, 279
amyloid precursor proteins
    (APPs), 32
ancient world, TBI in, 8–12,
    9–10f, 12f
Andelic, N., 195
Anderson, C. V., 41
Anderson, J., 76
Anderson, S. I., 220
Anderson, T., 372
Anderson, V. A., 339, 344
Andresen, E. M., 164
Ang, B., 86
Angeli, V., 223
animal-related injuries, 9–10, 18n3
anisotropic diffusion, 306
Annoni, J. M., 107–108
anosmia, 421
Anson, K., 240
anticonvulsant agents, 275–276
antidepressant agents, 263,
    273, 400
antipsychotic agents, 275
Antonucci, G., 221

anxiety disorders
    comorbidity with depression,
        241, 279–280
    insomnia and, 270
    pharmacological treatments for,
        279–280
    prevalence of, 199–200, 241
apathy, 139, 140
apolipoprotein D (ApoD), 32
apoptosis, 41–43, 42t
apparent diffusion coefficient
    (ADC), 307, 435
APPs (amyloid precursor
    proteins), 32
APT (Attention Process Training),
    66, 400
AQ (Awareness Questionnaire),
    237–238, 239
Aquiliani, R., 39
Arango-Lasprilla, J. C., 198
Archibald, J., 109
Arco, L., 105
arousal deficits, 256, 257–258, 264,
    265, 266
    See also emotional arousal
    disorders
arterial spin tag labeling (ASL),
    316–318
Asclepius (god of medicine), 12
Ashman, T. A., 203
ASL (arterial spin tag labeling),
    316–318
Asloun, S., 62–63
Aspergers Syndrome, 141, 145
aspontaneity, 139, 140
assessment, future challenges for,
    433–437